Volume 1

LITERARY PERSPECTIVES

An Anthology of Multicultural Currents in Western and Nonwestern Literature

Second Edition

Edited by Don L. Powell
South Carolina State University

KENDALL/HUNT PUBLISHING COMPANY
4050 Westmark Drive   Dubuque, Iowa 52002

IN MEMORIAM

This revision is dedicated to the loving memory of my
son, Don Lance Powell, Jr., whose untimely death has
brought immense grief to our family and to the countless
friends who also miss him dearly, but whose life was a
shining example for all to see.

Artwork Sources

Cover: Artwork by Leo F. Twiggs.

pages 261
and 262:   From *Temne Stories* by Abdul Karim Turay. Reprinted by permission of Rudiger Koppe Verlag, West
                Germany.

page 282:   Reprinted from *Maoshi pinwu tukao (An Illustrated Study of Objects and Creatures in the* Book of Songs*)*,
                compiled by Oka Gempo of Osaka (1724, reprint Shanghai: Saoye Shanfang, 1924). 4.la.

page 574:   From *The Divine Comedy of Dante Alighieri*, translated by Charles Eliot Norton, 1952.

page 715:   Donald Keene, ed. *Twenty Plays of the Nō Theatre*. New York: Columbia University Press, 1970.

page 947:   Gibbons in a Pine Tree. Contemporary painting in traditional Chinese free-style. Water color on
                mulberry paper. Artist: Janet Kozachek.

Contents

UNIT TWO

Cultural Currents from the 4th Century A.D. to the 14th Century A.D.

UNIT THREE

Multicultural Currents of the Early
Modern Period: Tradition and
Innovation 1350–1650 A.D.

Contributors

Nearly all of the introductions in Volume I of *Literary Perspectives* were written by the following individuals, who (unless otherwise indicated) are current faculty members in the English Department at South Carolina State University. The contributor's initials are given at the end of each author or period introduction.

EUB   Eloise U. Belcher, Professor Emerita

TJC   Thomas J. Cassidy, Ph.D. (State University of New York at Binghamton), Assistant Professor

AHF   Allen H. Fleming, M.Ed. (South Carolina State University), Assistant Professor

GRG   Ghussan R. Greene, Ph.D. (University of South Carolina), Associate Professor

CGH   Celia G. Hezekiah, M.Ed. (South Carolina State University), Assistant Professor

CDH   Calvin D. Hutson, Ph.D. (University of South Carolina), Professor

BJJ   Beverly J. Jamison, M.Ed. (South Carolina State University), Assistant Professor

ACJ   Alex C. Johnson, Ph.D. (University of Ibadan), Professor

JK   Janet Kozachek, Certificate in Chinese Painting (Beijing Central Art Academy) and M.F.A. (Parsons), Artist

EEN   Evenly E. Nettles, Ph.D. (University of Tennessee), Professor

DLP   Don L. Powell, Ph.D. (University of Illinois), Professor and Chairman

NW   Nathaniel Wallace, Ph.D. (Rutgers University), Assistant Professor

Preface

This revision of *Literary Perspectives*, Volume 1, represents the commitment of World Literature instructors to give voice to the diversity of the literary experience in various cultures. The original objective of exposing students to the rich tapestry of this literature has therefore been preserved and made more expansive in the present edition, and the thematic linkages clearly established. The revised title (*Literary Perspectives; An Anthology of Multicultural Currents in Western and Nonwestern Literature*) reflects the unifying focus or "currents" of the three units comprising the text. Unit one of the first edition, for example, was largely Eurocentric; focusing on such standard works of the ancient period as Homer's *Iliad* and *Oyssey*, Aeschylus' *Agamemnon*, and Euripides' *Medea*. While these and other important works representative of the traditional literary canon are still found in this section, it now includes Chapter 6 of *Awakening Osiris: A New Translation of the Egyptian Book of the Dead*. The ethnic and cultural importance of the Egyptians is thus underscored. An effort has also been made to diversify selections dealing with African Myth and folklore, as well as fables. Unit one also now contains excerpts from Plato's *Symposium* and Aristotle's *Poetics* ("On the Art of Poetry "). The *Phormio*, a play by the Roman poet, Terence, is also found in the first unit. The section on Confucius (Asian Cultures: China) has been extended, particularly in terms of selections from *The Book of Songs*, Notes on Chinese names and terms have also been added for the benefit of students and instructors. Indian Literature finds notable expression in the selections included from Valmiki's *Ramayana*, a work that was not included in the first edition of *Literary Perspectives*. The Greek female poet, Sappho, has been retained in unit one.

Unit two of this edition also reflects important changes. For example, the *Sundiata*, an African epic of Old Mali, is now more detailed. A map tracing the various journeys of this epic hero has been added, also. Excerpts from *The Hermit and the Love-Thief*, by the Indian writer, Bhartrihari, is included for the first time, and the treatment of Chinese male and women poets is now more inclusive. In fact, this is the initial inclusion of the latter. This is also the case with the Japanese selection from *Man'yōshū* (or "Collection of Ten Thousand Leaves"). Various sections from *Beowulf* have been added, also, along with new tales from Chaucer's *The Canterbury Tales*.

Unit three of the present edition, which deals with multicultural "currents" or themes of the early modern period, also has new selections. These include from Petrarch's *Travel*, "The Ascent of Mount Ventoux," and excerpts from Boccacio's *The Decameron*. The *Birds of Sorrow*, by the Japanese writer Seami Motokiyo, is also represented for the first time. Cervante's *Don Quixote* has also been expanded, and an excerpt from *The Enchantments of Love* by Maria de Zayas, believed to be Spain's first female novelist, has been added, as well. Finally, there is also inclusion of Oral poetry from Africa, and selections from the Indian woman poet, Mirabai.

For the current edition, a bibliography has been added at the end of each author introduction. Questions for Consideration by students, followed by critical thinking questions, appear at the end of each selection. These serve as evaluation measures for instructors, but are not meant to substitute for thorough in-class examinations. A more detailed index has also been compiled to reflect the scope of writers and works included.

Don L. Powell, Ph.D.
Chairman, Department of English
South Carolina State University

Acknowledgments

The revision of the present Volume I of *Literary Perspectives: An Anthology of Multicultural Currents in Western and Nonwestern Literature* required the sustained efforts of a number of individuals, most notably those faculty members who comprise the Editorial Board in the capacity of Associate Editors. These persons are also primary contributors to this edition: Dr. Calvin D. Hutson, Professor of English; and Dr. Nathaniel O. Wallace, Assistant Professor of English. These individuals were also quite instrumental—and successful—in identifying important literary works that are now in the public domain. In addition, the identified faculty members, along with Dr. Ghussan R. Greene, Associate Professor of English, Ms. Beverly J. Jamison, Assistant Professor of English, and Mrs. Celia G. Hezekiah, Assistant Professor of English, supplied essays, study questions, and critical thinking exercises that have been incorporated into this revised volume. For their diligence and exemplary contributions, I am immensely grateful.

These persons made constructive contributions to the current edition, as well:

Janet Kozachek	Artist, Orangeburg, SC. Introduction for the Chinese *Book of Songs*
Janet A. Walker	Department of Comparative Literature, Rutgers University. Advice on Japanese literature.
Steven F. Walker	Department of Comparative Literature, Rutgers University. Advice on Indian literature.
Robert E. Hegel	Department of Asian & Near Eastern Languages & Literatures, Washington University. Advice on Chinese literature and on graphic art to accompany Chinese selections.
Tan Ye	Department of Asian and Germanic Languages, University of South Carolina. Advice on Chinese poetry.
Eustace Palmer	Department of English, Georgia College and State University. Advice on various literary works.

Bringing this revision to fruition also required other kinds of assistance. There was, for example, the need to seek permission from various publishers to reprint literary works and/or selections in which there was an interest, an undertaking that is very time consuming and, occasionally, frustrating as well. For her usual patience and thoroughness in word processing and collating needed materials, I wish to express thanks to my Administrative Specialist, Ms. Mary A. Jenkins. The help of Ms. Corley Smith, reference librarian, is also noted in acquiring many literary works for me via interlibrary loan. Special thanks also goes to Mrs. Eloise U. Belcher, Associate Professor of English (Retired), who made various literary contributions. I would also like to acknowledge the important contributions of Dr. Leo F. Twiggs, a friend and colleague who chairs the department of Art. Dr. Twiggs, a nationally known artist, is responsible for the unique cover design that is featured on this volume of *Literary Perspectives.* Finally, I would like to thank my devoted wife, Bessie, whose unequivocal support has always been a source of inspiration to me in my various endeavors. The individual and combined contributions of all persons mentioned herein made my task as editor much easier and, hopefully, the product one that will serve the cultural and intellectual need envisioned.

Cultural Currents of the Ancient World

UNIT ONE

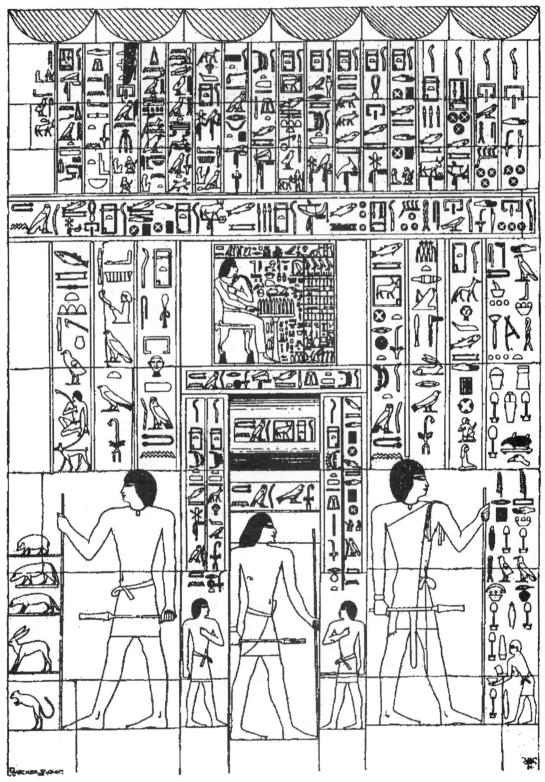

The career of Amten as Shown on a
Funeral Monument

Introduction

Awakening Osiris:
A New Translation of the Egyptian Book of the Dead

Most historians agree that Egypt, located in North Africa, is one of the first true civilizations. If civilization is the advanced stage of human life where people have writing with which to communicate, a calendar to keep track of time, and a government to rule, Egypt is the model birthplace of civilization. Therefore, history really begins in this northern section of the continent of Africa and its importance as an ancient civilization is considerable. First, it is the oldest civilization, with known developments of institutions going back 6000 years; second, more evidences of the way of life and the civilization have been retained and discovered here than in any other land; and third, later civilizations, including those of the West, have often been based on Egyptian ideas from which they have developed (Burns, Ralph, Learner, and Meacham 36, 38). Through Egypt's artifacts, its monuments and its hieroglyphic writing on papyrus, historians have been able to put together in reasonably accurate and authentic fashion a picture of this great civilization.

Writing was of great importance to the Egyptians. The basis of education among them was learning to write through the copying of hieroglyphic figures, and later the learning of sounds. Writing rather than reading was the most important element of the scholar's training. In the area of writing, the Egyptians made great progress and were, in fact, the first people to write with facility. The development of this skill was encouraged owing to the importance of public records and the availability of paper papyrus (Mertz, 13, 14).

Until the discovery of the Rosetta Stone in 1799, scholars found it impossible to decipher the writings of ancient Egypt. Captain Boussard, an engineering officer on Napoleon's expedition to Egypt, found this monument, carved in 196 B.C. to honor Ptolemy V Epiphanes, near the village of Rosetta about twenty miles east of Alexandria. The Egyptian inscriptions were picture writing now known as hieroglyphics. They had been noticed in abundance on obelisks and ruins of temples, but their meaning had remained a mystery (Lepre, 297). Lepre gives the following description of the monument:

"The Rosetta Stone is a black granite slab 3 feet 9 inches high, 2 feet 4 inches wide, and 11 inches thick, which contains three registers of inscriptions. The bottom register is made up of Greek capital letters, the middle is written in demonic script (the common cursive Egyptian writing), while the broken top part is hieroglyphs. By translating the Greek and inferring (correctly) that the Egyptian parts of the monument told the same story, several Europeans identified personal names in the upper registers. With the lead, Jean Champollion, a young French scholar, successfully deciphered the Egyptian hieroglyph. His discoveries were announced in 1822, and proved to be the clue that solved the riddle of ancient Egyptian writing" (Lepre).

As a result of this discovery, scholars have made accessible to those interested in antiquity, the extensive remains of Egyptian literature which have been brought to light by the labors of Egyptologists. This literature deserves to be known not only because it is the oldest literature, but because it affords us insight into an active, intellectual life which is just as important as the achievements of the Egyptians in the artistic and technical spheres. Thus the peak of the Egyptian art of writing, as far as technique and beauty are concerned, is found in the best copies of the *Book of the Dead*. This book consists of series of spells which, when recited, generated magical power which was believed to make life easier for the dead. These books were frequently beautifully illustrated with pictures of the deceased with his wife and family in the underworld. This ancient Egyptian literature covers a wide variety of subjects: wisdom, meditation, poetry, hymns, magic, stories, travel, letters, business and legal records, science and astronomy (Larue, 157). In this connection, the term *"Book of the Dead"* is misleading for it is not sufficiently inclusive to describe the miscellaneous compilation mentioned above. The ancient Egyptian title is more accurately translated as the *Coming Forth by Day*. This title emphasizes the longing and the hope to return by day from wherever the hereafter might be centered—within the earth or traversing the sky—to see again at will the familiar scenes of earth (Larue, 157).

The *Book of the Dead*, as gathered and reconstructed from various tombs and mummies, consists of 166 chapters. No one period or section of ancient Egypt had the entire text; one city knew certain portions, other cities possessed other chapters or versions. Nevertheless, a homogeneous theme pervades the heterogeneous mass: guidance for departed souls on their journey to the Land of the Dead (Larue, 158). To the Egyptian, oblivion was the worst of all fates! Their religious doctrines were, therefore, centered in an intense longing for, and belief in, a resurrection of the dead. They were convinced of the literal resurrection of the physical body and continuation of their old lives, rather than reincarnation in new forms. Life is brief, the real life is after death. The Egyptians made ready for the life beyond. Chief among the documents of importance to the Egyptians in the next life was the *Book of the Dead* (Rosenberg, 170). Without some knowledge of its contents, the soul could not hope for happiness after death.

The predominant religions of modern times—Judaism, Christianity, Islam, Buddhism, Confucianism, Hinduism—owe little to the mythologies and superstitions of Greece and Rome. From the *Book of the Dead* comes an advanced code for ethical conduct in its essentials later embodied in the principal religions of the west. Among the entirely negative declarations recited from the *Book of the Dead* by the righteous soul are these:

> . . . I have not done iniquity.
> . . . I have not robbed with violence.
> . . . I have not done violence to any man.
> . . . I have not committed theft.
> . . . I have not slain man or woman.
> . . . I have not made light the bushel.
> . . . I have not acted deceitfully.
> . . . I have not purloined the things which belong unto God.
> . . . I have not uttered falsehood.
> . . . I have not carried away food.
> . . . I have not uttered evil words.
> . . . I have attacked no man.
> . . . I have not killed the beasts, which are the property of God.
> . . . I have not laid waste the lands which have been plowed.
> . . . I have never pried into matters to make mischief.
> . . . I have not set my mouth in motion against any man.
> . . . I have not given way to wrath concerning myself without cause.
> . . . I have not defiled the wife of a man.
> . . . I have not committed any sin against purity.
> . . . I have not struck fear into any man.
> . . . I have not encroached upon sacred times and seasons.

. . . I have not been a man of anger.

. . . I have not made myself deaf to the words of right and truth.

. . . I have not stirred up strife.

. . . I have made no man to weep.

. . . I have not committed acts of impurity . . .

. . . I have not eaten my heart.

. . . I have abused no man.

. . . I have not acted with violence.

. . . I have not judged hastily.

. . . I have not taken vengeance upon the god.

. . . I have not multiplied my speech overmuch.

. . . I have not acted with deceit, and I have not worked wickedness.

. . . I have not uttered curses on the King.

. . . I have not fouled water.

. . . I have not made haughty my voice.

. . . I have not cursed the god.

. . . I have not sought for distinctions.

. . . I have not increased my wealth, except with such things as are justly mine own possessions.

. . . I have not thought scorn of the god who is in my city.

(From E. A. Wallis Budge, *The Book of the Dead: The Chapters of Coming Forth by Day*.)

As in most ancient societies, religion saturated Egyptian life and influenced every aspect of her culture. "The Kings of Egypt were gods; its pyramids were an 'act of faith'; its art was rooted in religious decoration of tombs, temples, and pyramids; its science centered in the temple; its gods were conceived to be in intimate touch with men and alive as men; a vast part of its wealth and energy was spent in the effort to secure the continuance of the physical life after death" (Mortz 81, 84, 85).

Two systems of theology were current among the ancient Egyptians. One, probably the older, was dominated by the worship of the sun-god, Re or Ra, represented on tombs and other inscriptions by the lion, cat, and falcon, and usually wearing the solar disk. The worship of Re was essentially a royal cult, in which even the nobles played a subsidiary role and the common people had no part. According to mythology, the Pharaoh was Re's son and after death joined the god in his daily voyage across his realm, the eastern sky.

In the second theological scheme, the god Osiris was preeminent. The generally accepted mythological version held that Osiris as a king on earth had been slain by his brother Set, the god of evil. After various misadventures, his body had been found and embalmed by his wife and sister Isis. Thereafter, Osiris lived again as king of the underworld. The story of this god represents the oldest literature in the world. It is one of the oldest to come down to us, written two thousand years before Homer wrote down the tales of the Trojan War. The story of Isis and Osiris was the great myth of Ancient Egypt for over three thousand years. There was a strong ethical element in the worship of Osiris, who promised resurrection and immortality to all his followers who had led virtuous lives on earth. Gradually the religion of the whole Egyptian people came to be founded on the story of Osiris—subordinating the worship of the solar deity Re. Salvation was now open to all, a dogma that of course increased the popularity of the *Book of the Dead* (Rosenberg, 168, 169). (CDH)

BIBLIOGRAPHY

Andrews, Carol. *The Ancient Egyptian Book of the* Dead. Trans. Raymond Faulkner. New York: Macmillan Publishing Company, 1985.

___. *The British Museum Book of the Rosetta Stone*. London: Sheldon Press, 1988.

Brendan, Nagle D. *The Ancient World: A Social and Cultural History*. Englewood Cliffs, New Jersey: Prentice Hall, Inc., 1989.

Budge, E.A. Wallis. *The Literature of the Ancient Egyptians*. London: J.M. Dent and Sons, 1914.

___. *The Egyptian Book of the Dead (The Papyrus of Ani) Egyptian Text Transliteration and Translation*. New York: Dover Publications, Inc., 1895.

Ceram, C.W. *Gods, Graves and Scholars: The Story of Archaeology*. New York: Bantam Books, 1972.

Larue, Gerald A. *Ancient Myth and Modern Man*. Englewood Cliffs, New Jersey: Prentice-Hall, Inc., 1975.

Lepre, J.P. *The Egyptian Pyramids: A Comprehensive, Illustrated Reference, 1990*. London: McFarland and Company, 1990.

Lichtheim, Miriam. *Ancient Egyptian Literature: A Book of Reading*. Berkeley: University of California Press, 1980.

Macquitty, William. *The Wisdom of the Ancient Egyptians*. London: Sheldon Press, 1988.

Poole, Gray, and Lynn Gray. *Men Who Dig Up History*. New York: Dodd Mead & Company, 1988.

Smith, Page. *The Historian and History*. New York: Alfred A. Knopf, 1964.

Osiris in the Hall of Truth with Isis and Nephthys Behind Him (Circa 1310 B.C.)

from Awakening Osiris:
A New Translation of the Egyptian
Book of the Dead

Translated by Normandi Ellis

Normandi Ellis discusses the following in the Introduction to her book *Awakening Osiris: The Egyptian Book of the Dead:*

What has survived of Egyptian literature is primarily texts of religious rites, hymns, love songs and work songs. (Some notable exceptions include The Tale of Two Brothers and a wonderful dialogue between a man weary of life and his soul, which was beautifully translated by Bika Reed as *The Rebel in the Soul.*) Little poetry or fiction as we tend to think of it has survived. Although rhyme was not a consideration, certain poetic elements appear such as repetition, alliteration, assonance, allusion, imagery and parallel structure. These were enhanced by a strong meter and rhythm in th work. The Egyptians loved puns of all and even their religious texts are full Many times they intertwined s fane images. It is interestin uses of the anagram expressing a part spelled backw idea. For exam while akh indicate

Language as of sence it cast a type of s felt that if words coul proper sequence and those words could produ Fourth Gospel begins: "In Word." In like manner the the Creation of the Gods and with the words of Temu:

I am he who came into being, being what I created—
the creator of the creations . . .
After I created my own becoming,
I created many things
that came forth from my mouth.

(Nuk pu kheper em Kheperå
kheper-nå kheper kheper
kheper kheperu
neb em-khet kh
em per em

I

being! bea
man may s
river while w
the cities and t
in white linen l
of heaven.
I am the priest
other worlds. I am
mother's belly, a tre

I cross an open field of stones s
hearts and say to the rocks: th
break, and this hold the rain, and this o
and this other crumble and its grains
shall mark my passage. Beat. Beat. Be
power of my Self is moving. My heart. M
My coming into existence. My passions. My

incorporated into the greater gods and goddesses. Still, there seems to have been a time early in the development of the religion where the gods were one. The text often refers to one god—sometimes Temu, sometimes Ptah, sometimes Ra, depending on the interpretations of the priests that have been passed down to us. This one god was the creator of himself and all things therein. His name is secret and hidden. All the other gods and goddesses issue forth from him. One might think, then, of the other multitudes as aspects of the one god.

The Egyptian word which we have translated as "god" is neter, as in the "neterworld." But the word god, though common to us, seems imprecise when applied to Egyptian religion. Neter refers primarily to a spiritual essence, or principle. Our word "nature" may derive from it through the Latin. The multitudes of neters, then, represent the multitudinous natures of supreme being. As John West pointed out in his book, *Serpent in the Sky*, the various religious centers of

Heliopolis, Memphis, Hermopolis and Thebes, for example, were not advocating different gods. They were advocating differing aspects of god.

From the mouth of one supreme god came what is known as the Great Ennead, or the nine gods (neters) of the one. In Heliopolis these were: Temu, Shu, Tefnut, Geb, Nut, Osiris, Isis, Set and Nephthys. In Memphis, Ptah and Hathor play major roles. In Hermopolis, Thoth is elevated. Ra, as a principle of light, eternity, power and rebirth, attained prominence nearly everywhere.

Temu and Ptah are aspects of one neter. Temu may be thought of as the primordial act, the first creation, pure essence and spirit. Ptah is Temu come to earth: the same principle of spirit, but in this instance he is the manifestation of the act of creating matter. The remaining neters of the great ennead are paired male and female. They are unified dual natures. Shu and Tefnut are the twin children of Ra, the breath of light one might say. He personifies the dry air and she the mist. Geb, the father, is earth; Nut, the mother, is sky.

34
Awakening Osiris

r and each are my horizons. What lies
tween is what I am. Oh, infinite form of
st and stone and vegetable—the way a
tand in his garden or dance by the
akes of small boats rock the reeds,
e people in them, gods who walk
ke women under the blue stone

in a hidden house, guide to
the idea of myself in my
mbling star in the bright

memory of morning, a grain of sand blown east. I am the husband of Isis: woman, widow and witch. On her lips are the charms of ripening wheat; from her arms fly flocks of birds. With a word she drives the snakes from the river and the boats sail far to its mouth.

Air is what I breathe and earth is where I stand. I have given myself to Amentet. It is white with heat. The world is bright as metal. Dead men rise to breathe air and stare into my face, already a yellow disk on the eastern horizon.

4
The Speeches

aped all like
s one shall
ne be still,
of sand
t. The
birth.
in-

difference. The sun within warms me; the heart enlightens the intellect. I am my Self coming forth, a creature bearing light.

May I stand amazed in the presence of god. May the rhythm of my heart stir music that enslaves darkness. May my heart witness what my hands create, the words I utter, the worlds I think. May my flesh be a sail propelled by the breath of dream. May I ride in calm waters toward destiny. May life flow through me as the seed from the phallus flows, with a shout of joy, life begetting life.

May I stand in the midst of celestial fire until my heart is molten gold. May twelve goddesses dance every day about me, a circle of flesh aflame. May I spin among them, my face flushed with heat. May I walk on earth radiant, everywhere complete. May the omniscient eye observe my deeds and know the law my heart knows, the zodiac of men and beasts alive, the call of angels, the word. May my body bend toward the will of the heart. May I not think and act diversely. May truth rest on me light as a tail feather dropped from a falcon in cloudless sky.

Thou spirit within, you are my Self, my power, my ka, the fire of god. May I create words of beauty, houses of wonder. May the labor of my hands be mirrors unto god. May I dance in the gyre and draw down heaven's blessing. May I be given a god's duty, a burden that matters. May I make of my days a thing wholly. May I know myself in every pore of skin. May the god's fire burn in my belly and heart. May I be stronger than these bones and bits of flesh. May my health be the wholeness of divinity.

On earth I walk daily before the gods, but in the house of heaven my feet are still. There is no need for haste. My heart is a lyre that hums. My lungs fill with the breath of fire. A cool breeze encircles me. I rest in god's bosom here, while on earth my hands are busy. And when work is done, I return to the heart afire, center of the universe, peace, unto god.

I remember the names of my ancestors. I speak the names of those I love. I speak their names and they live again. May I be so well-loved and remembered. In truth, may the gods hear my name. May I do work with my hands worth remembering.

I am an old man travelling amid strange cities and faces. I've prayed in temples from the plains to the delta. In Hermopolis, beneath the crumbling feet of a statue, I found this heart of stone, encircled in bronze, ringed all in silver, made of lapis lazuli. It was inscribed in iron by the god in the god's own hand before the dawn of history, and it was this book wherein lay the law that is. It was the secret name of god. And I lay the stone heart upon my own that I might memorize it, that its words might be etched into my being. Great is the nothingness, the all that is. I am a being of light.

Thoth speaks:

The ibis and the ink pot—these are blessed. For as the ibis pecks along the bank for a bit of food, so the scribe searches among his thoughts for some truth to tell. All the work is his to speak, its secrets writ down in his heart from the beginning of time, the gods' words rising upward through his dark belly, seeking light at the edge of his throat. We are made of god stuff, the explosion of stars, particles of light, molded in the presence of gods. The gods are with us. Their secrets writ only in the scrolls of men's hearts, the law of creation, death and change inscribed in the blood and seed of man's love. In the beginning and at the end, the book is opened and we see what in life we are asked to remember.

Hear, then, my words, the ringing of my speech, as the heart and the scroll of this life fall open. Truth is the harvest scythe. What is sown—love or anger or bitterness—that shall be your bread. The corn is no better than its seed, then let what you plant be good. Let your touch on earth be light so that when earth covers you, the clods of dirt fall lightly. The soul of a man forgets nothing. It stands amazed at its own being. The heart beats the rhythm of its life. The lungs breathe the ions of its own vibration. The mind recalls its thoughts. The glands respond to its emotions. The body is a soul's record. And when a man's life ends, his body is given back to gods and the gods shall see what use their laws have been. They shall see the deeds its hands have made, the sparks of light its heart set in the world. They shall see whether or not their love, their powers have been wasted, whether the plants it has grown were nourishing or poison. And like the ibis, the gods shall circle about him, hunting for seeds that remain uncultivated, for ideas that lie dormant, thoughts left unexpressed. They shall find new seeds from the plants he has tended. And these shall be planted again in the clay of a new man and he shall be sent back to the world until all the gods have seen fit to create in man is cultivated, and then, in final death, he shall be welcomed home as one of them.

The gods speak:

Let the great wheel turn. We sit at the hub of the universe and the stars spin around. A man's fortunes rise and decline. He makes plans and his plans are changed. When the moon is full, it shall grow thin. Some days it's easier to commune with gods than others. Bless the wheel where all things spin. This is the story of a life. A man learns nature is not always kind. Nature acts according to nature. Crocodiles eat fish and no one can be blamed. A man takes his fortunes in stride. Swaying first to his left foot and then the right, he learns to walk and hold his balance. He sees that gods surround him, but most days he walks his path alone. With one foot always forward, a man reaches heaven.

The oar is in the water and the boat glides along. The seeds are planted, the ideas, the inspiration; the words rise like wheat from his mouth. Let one's speech be thoughtful so that small things said unthinkingly shall not fall as bad seed and sprout vines that surround him. A man reaps what he sows. What he dreams of shall come to pass. Before the world formed it was the Great One's idea, and so a man is careful about what he wishes. He knows his death is but another harvest. His life is spent nourishing his people. He saves seeds for the future. He offers up life and gives the gods their due. We've not seen the last of him. He is not greedy and so has all he needs—all the love, the joy, the days. When he hungers, there is bread. When he thirsts, the water is cool. He gives himself and the Self is given to him. He comes and goes in the presence of gods. He is given a field to tend and he tends it, therefore, his harvest is plentiful. As he cares for his children, so is he cared for in his old age. What goes around comes around, and so the great wheel turns.

Horus speaks:

I am life rushing on, born from the egg of the world, from the belly of a magic woman, born of my father's dreams. I am the screech of wind, the rush of falcon wings, talons sharp as knives. I came after you. I stand before you. I am with you always. I am the power that dispels darkness. Look upon the dark face of my father, Osiris. He is nothing. Embrace him. Even nothing can not last. The seed laid into the void must grow. The candle's only purpose is to shine in the darkness. Bread is meant to be ground to pulp in the teeth. The function of life is to have something to offer death. Ah, but the spirit lies always between, coming and going in and out of heaven, filling and leaving the houses of earth. A man forgets, but his heart remembers—the love and the terror, the weeping, the beating of wings.

I am an Osiris, a man waking in the night, listening to the varied voices of stars. The gods speak through me and I am one of them. Yet, at times, they seem to shine so far away from me. Some days I push the plow, gather corn, make bread for the children, dig wells and wait for them to fill; and nothing of my life seems holy. It is only labor, sweat drying on sun-burnt skin. I go on believing in miracles. I bend my back and lift heavy stones, legs trembling, and I strive to believe it when I say, "I do the work of gods. The fields will be cleared The temples will be built." If I were an animal perhaps I could be happy, untortured by bitterness, unconfused by what I think. I am learning to master thought, to do as I say I do, to say I feel what I feel. I am not angry when I speak gentle words. I do not beat the donkey and call myself beloved of gods. Truly, I strive to carry the load without noticing the burden, to be on this hot earth a cool jug of water, to stand in the wind like sturdy sycamore branches, a place where birds rest, where cattle gather, where sap rises, wherein earth and sky are home.

5
Coming Forth By Day

The forepaw of a lion, the forearm of a man, the primal ray of sun. I wake in the dark to the stirring of birds, a murmur in the trees, a flutter of wings. It is the morning of my birth, the first of many. The past lies knotted in its sheets asleep. Winds blow, flags above the temple ripple. Out of darkness the earth spins toward light. I feel a change coming. My thoughts flicker, glow a moment and catch fire. I come forth by day singing.

Blessed are the cattle asleep in the fields. They shake their horns, tearing the dream. Blessed are the bulls waking, their first thoughts of creation. This day I make myself anew. I create life; my flesh coils about me foot to head. My breath rushes through and my blood. The mind sparkles, dances, the world whirls beneath the sun. I am given to know things I knew not yesterday. I burn like a god aflame, sail my boat upstream at dawn, pushing on quietly among the reeds, softly.

For you I light a fire in the sky. My love dispels darkness. I place the pot over the fire, add water, flour and meat. We shall nourish each other with words and bread. Born of stars, of pale moonlight skimming mountaintops, we are men and women exchanging glances at the crossroads. I am born of sky, filled with light. I darken. I am various as weather. I am predictable as sunrise, moonset, the winds that blow, breathtaking as Sirius rising. I am for you. I am the utterer of your name. Speak of me often and we shall live.

I am a thought that came to pass. Long believed, I live forever. I am words repeated often. I am a happy man. I am a blessed man. I am a perfecting man. I am love and shall endure forever. I am a thankful man, a man of peace, poetry, dream. I am a well-fed man. I am a dancing man beloved of gods. I am an old man who has lived long. I am heading home.

I am an old tree by the Nile banks. A thousand birds nested in my branches and beneath, women cooled themselves from the sun. Years passed. I grew slowly and with grace. This earth I love, the water, the sky. Tomorrow I fall and, at last, the women with baskets on their heads shall make a passage across the river. They will speak for the first time in years to the women on the opposite bank. They will clasp hands and hold their voices to whispers. They shall marvel at each other's faces. And that will be as good a death as any for me, with women weeping, lotus blooming, and cool breezes blowing. That will be a victory. And so on, through the ages, have I been useful and loved.

I come forth by day. I go out burning. To the end, I burn white with heat. On the day of unwrapping the mummy cloths, on the day of opening the storehouse, on the day of washing the body, on the day of speaking secrets, I am with you, my love, as gods are. I stand beside you at the lotus pool watching that pink bud ready to flower. It is I, Osiris. I am joyful as a stone. It is not the joy of men I feel; it is the joy of matter. I am a presence. I am of the world. I am magic. I went the circuitous path of the unseen, from nothing but thought into becoming. I am anointed in oil. The power shivers from my heart down into my arms. Self-sacrifice is only learning to make one's self holy, to be the sum of a man, more than his parts. These breaths I release to the wind, make me one with the wind. This blood flows back to the river like water. This flesh dries, it cracks and scatters, dust again. When the light in my eyes flickers out, the spark flies back to the flaming heart of gods. It is only flesh and breath, blood, bones and hair. I come and go out of the fire unchanged.

I am air and flame, water and dust. I am a wick burning in a blue bowl of oil, a fiery sun rising in a tranquil sky. I am the phoenix. I am light. I come forth by day. I am heat burning up mist. I am power, an ancient river overflowing. I am love and memory and sorrow that drift away.

My time is a reflection on the surface of water. A leaf falls and the dream shatters, breaks to pieces; the leaf drifts off. Slowly the waters calm and draw themselves together. And the leaf's life, like a thought, passes from me on the ripple of its own vibration. It enters the world. I am a holy man, not because I am so wise, but because I am a temple of god. I am a priest of the heart. I know what is mine to feel. I let the rain from heaven fill me. I give love away as easily as water.

I am changeable, yes. It is like this. A hummingbird's wings beat so fast he seems to fly standing still. Atoms in the rock whirl about, yet the rock holds together. Lions roar in the temple and the earth trembles. It is only yesterday and tomorrow keeping watch over today. The solid earth like a baby is lifted up to be kissed, to be blessed and set down again. I see things other men don't see. Secret words repeated in mirrors, bits of legend fallen from the lips of slave girls. I gather the greater seed as they thresh their wheat. I am an old priest dancing the mad dance, whirling, whirling, whirling.

I have studied the manifestations of gods and men, and I've seen the dead conversing in thin, reedy voices amid the air. I have read books of magic and made offerings of moly. I have longed to be free, to rise up as smoke from earth into air. I am a priest of change.

I am a priest of love, a courtier enchanted by the slender ankles of women, by bells and incense, dances and gauze. Beneath the moon my boat rocks gently. I scoop up fish by the fistful and feed the ibis outside the temple. I remember to weave my garlands of onions and flowers on feast days. I plant my seeds and carry god in my hands through the fields to bless them. I drag the large stones to higher ground and write prayers to last forever, songs to gods and creations, women and kings. I have turned the spade and smelled the black moist secret smell of earth and I knead the clods gently in my hand. They are supple and innocent as woman. In the right season, I plant my seeds.

Oh spirits that guide a man through the dark halls at death, guide me safely in life past sorrow and depression, steer me from fear and anger and hopelessness. Let me always know the reason for my becoming. Let me hear what gods hear, see what gods see. When the sun is blotted from the sky, let even a small light shine to steer a man's feet. Let me stand in light, bathe in light, clothe myself in light. Let me sit in the lap of gods and hear words of comfort. Oh offerers of cake and bearers of beer, let me not also starve for love, thirst for wisdom. Let my spirit be stronger today than it was yesterday, my heart more peaceful, my mind more fertile, my hands more gentle. Let gods touch my face. Let me go forth shining. Let my feet know the way. Let me walk and pass through fire. Let wild beasts and thieves by the roadside go on sleeping pleasant dreams. Let me pass undeterred into heaven.

For I have made a reckoning of myself, of the things I have done and said and of my intentions; and I long for nothing but to live as a light within, to enter god's heart singing a song so stirring that even slaves at the mill and asses in the field might raise their heads and answer.

6
The History Of Creation

In the land beneath I come and go and the earth bends over, wraps its legs around darkness. In black waters boats glide ferrying dead men, gods. It is quiet here, full of stars and boats that slice the water, slick river dripping from every oar. Men whisper, women . . . or are they only my selves? Is the world at ease? Do I dream it? I've come somehow through this veil of mist. This skin I wear is imagination. I take the shapes of light.

In the great hall, stone lotus pillars rise, light slants in through clerestory windows and incense curls through my beard. I sit alone playing senet, contemplating my path, slow to move one token across the board. I go forth by chance and design, Uplifted by faith, beaten down by worry until I make an end to my passage.

I am a hawk with the heart and soul of a man. I fly through the smoke of incensers. I graze the bald heads of priests with lustral wings. I spin above a maelstrom of dancers. I fly up through sunlight. I've the handsome face of a man with black hair, a dark beard. I am a teller of tales, a divinity, a power, a presence.

At first a voice cried against the darkness, and the voice grew loud enough to stir black waters. It was Temu rising up—his head the thousand-petaled lotus. He uttered the word and one petal drifted from him, taking form on the water. He was the will to live. Out of nothing he created himself, the light. The hand that parted the waters, uplifted the sun and stirred the air. He was the first, the beginning, then all else followed, like petals drifting into the pool.

And I can tell you that story.

It was in a world out of time, for there was neither sun nor moon and nothing to mark the night from day until Temu reached down into the abyss and uplifted Ra. The sun shone on Temu's bright face, day began and Ra lived with him from the beginning of time. That was the first day of the world. In gratitude, the sun raised itself and marked the days' flow.

But on that first day, when Temu held the sun, a spark flew out from him. The globe he held caught and reflected first light. The light flew back and he saw the light was himself, he saw that he was god and only after Temu created Ra was he visible even to himself.

In the beginning the earth languished with the sky, nothing lay between them, neither height nor depth, and they were not separate. Each encompassed the other like a lover, and the power of life pulsed between. At a word, Temu parted them and they became heaven and earth so that the sun might move between, that it might ride over and under the bodies of two worlds giving both its light. There was space above and below and between and on all four sides so that all of the things Temu thought might take shape—beast and stone and season.

Yet because they had lain so long together, heaven and earth were still part of each other. Spirit manifested in matter and matter was infused with spirit. Between them ran three pillars of air, earth and water, and these were named thought, form and desire. The spark of his fire pulsed in all of them and this Temu called life. He created himself and his body burned, writhing with dark shapes. Out of himself he created everything else—in a word: the skies, the oceans, the mountains, the plants, the gods and men, and he named them. Of his fire, made of fire, each held fire of its own; therefore, they created and perpetuated life, a cycle of being without end. Man he gave the power to create himself, to name himself and his destiny and to be in it, living eternally in the company of gods. And Temu is with him.

Of fire returning to fire, he can not be turned away, unless a man extinguishes his light himself, unless he casts out god. If he casts out god, he shall die. He shall be nothing, will be nothing, and will have been nothing. He shall have never existed.

But there is more to this story than the world's creation. There is its destruction.

From fire, out of fire and into fire, Temu takes back what is given. One day he'll destroy what he has created—from nothing returning to nothing. Time shall swallow itself, the lesser days and the eons. How can one remember what never existed?

But today, on this river bank the palm fronds are stirring, Temu lives in light, Ra rises up. There is time for wisdom, deed and possibility. There is yesterday, today and tomorrow. Though we pass quickly, the earth and heaven remain. Let us make something useful with our hands. Though time forgets us, let it not forget our passing. Grant that today we may do work that matters.

I know the future for us all and it is death. As we live we fight sluggishness. We gather our seeds. We put our hearts into the labor of our hands. We make children to live and remember us. We spend our lives preparing for death, for the moment when we offer up our days and labor, our sayings and doings, the sum of ourselves, and beg the gods to call it good.

Like the sun at day's end, we pass west through the gap in the mountains. We go quickly or slowly toward Amentet, the stony plateau. It is only the darkness before light, the hidden place, the house of transformation. It is the slaughterhouse where matter is sliced from spirit, the place where gods are made, the place of fire, of bones, sinew, blood and meat. It is death, the struggle. It is nothing. It is Amentet that makes Ra stand and fight, the last blast of fire we call sunset. It is darkness that makes a man shine brightest. It is the destiny of things in the land of Osiris.

Do you know magic? Can you utter the name of your soul and bring yourself back to light? Can you speak your destiny, create life for yourself from yourself as Temu created Ra? From the light of your works do you know who you are?

I am a phoenix, a soul sparking, a tongue of fire burning up flesh. I consume myself and rise. I am light of the Light, keeper of the book of my becomings: what was, what is, what will be. I am Osiris, a god and the ashes of man. I am the skin he takes on and sheds. I am the cord that binds him from this world to the next. I am his excrement. I am his forms. I am Osiris forever, forever changing, eternal as day, everlasting as night. Can it be said more plainly? Life and death are one. Osiris and Ra.

I am the lightning bolt, the erection, the resurrection and the power of regeneration. I am Amsu, a hare nibbling lettuce. I am a man in love. I am Min, the enumeration of one in the nature of things. I am a child, the rememberer of my father. I am what lives on after the man.

Do you know the story of your birth, how it is like the story of Horus, how Isis wept over the corpse of her husband and her tears were magic and stirred the god's member to rise? They mated and the child was conceived. He was life born out of death, carrier of his father's wisdom. He was the living emblem of love. He was light triumphing over darkness, the first man, the miracle of nature. His was the power of a man to live again not only in deed, but in the world. He was the healing of the wound. He travelled forth in the world telling the story of his birth, the glory of his father, the goodness of his death. And he was followed by magic. A pair of hawks circled above him. They were his mother Isis and her sister Nephthys. They dropped two plumes which he placed on his forehead, two gifts that fell from the sky—intuition and love, gifts from the goddesses—that he might walk toward heaven and his father and never lose his way.

We are like Horus. We are children of Osiris. We are light defying darkness. He was twice-born—once of sky, once of his mother; that is, once of spirit and once of matter. Having fought cunning and deceit, he came at last to the house of Osiris and was uplifted to heaven. The sun and moon became his eyes. He was light giving light, reflecting light.

That is one story.

Rise up, Osiris. You are an inundation, you are living water, the oar that guides the boat, the delta created by flood. You are the parts of yourself come together. Your child Horus has made an end to your exile. Rise up like corn and nourish the people in a land made fruitful by the word of Temu.

I am an Osiris, too, an old man ready for judgement. I left the city and crossed the plains. Entering the dark house, I cast off doubts and feebleness, I burned up fear, I lit candles and incense. I stand bold before gods, lusting neither for blood nor life nor flesh. I quit the petty concerns of day. It is the hour of our birth, my transformation, my coming into becoming. I anoint myself and rise from the lotus pool. I am changed—a new man, a lapwing among stars. My name is prayer. My spirit hawk flees the egg, leaves its shell. I am fresh as a fledgling in its mother's nest. This life is my offering, what common men give gods.

I am like Ra, born of two worlds in endless space and time. I ride between water and air. I am a word escaped between two lips, desire and thought crystallized into form. I rise from two pools of natron and niter. I rise from the Neter-world. I am the purpose of god, infinite one, multiplicity of his forms. I rise from a green sea of Being; being infinite, I live a millon years. I am the action of god's action. I am many things lasting forever. Like Ra himself, I am a child of Temu.

I walked the road toward truth, toward the island between the two worlds. I know its beginnings, how it was made, how the land built itself up one grain of sand at a time, how a man's deed becomes his fate. And I've seen truth piled up like the thin, worn-out husks of men, skins cast off at the door of the tomb. These burn up and their ashes become god's truth. Blown by wind, the ashes fall and are carried into the stream of unknowing. They form a silt in the river that grows the food that feeds men. So a man's life ended nourishes another; and, depending on his deeds, the food dead men proffer may be poison or nectar.

Some things Temu spoke remain always true: life and death, boundlessness and restraint, intuition and magic, nature and nurture, the earth and sky. His children last forever. The sun rolls ever onward. The doors of heaven open. They open. Light returns to light. The great knowing descends—genius and genesis. His lips part, breath blows over his teeth; the air moves over the stones. He tells the story of being and it comes to be. This was the world in the beginning. The fire of god dances on two legs. A beetle rolled its ball over the dark sky. What Temu spoke is holy.

"When I became," said he, "the becoming became. I have become the becoming. I am one seeing myself, divided. I am two and four and eight. I am the universe in diversity. I am my transformations. This is my coming together. Here are my selves become one."

Corn and clouds and cattle are gods renewing. I am the god of myself. Lift me up. Imagination is creation, genius is genesis. The gods give us their hands. Imagination is the fact at the back of the head. I make my changes in secret like an insect in its chrysalis, like lead into gold, the man in his mummy, the sanity in madness. Transformation is intellect, will, purpose, desire. Die. Be born. Bring forth labors and love. Let the invisible be the visible. Name yourself in your heart and know who you are.

A beetle wanders in the night tasting dust, smelling worms, feeling the ground. He pushes and pushes the seed of himself, a dried ball of dung. Insanity! What can be the fruit of such preoccupation, such slavish devotion to shit? Seeing nothing, hearing nothing, he knows not what he is. He moves not by thought, but by instinct. Through the belly of darkness, he creeps, struggles with his burden, at first small and soft, now a large, hard, heavy stone.

It is one hour before dawn. In the beginning, the end is foretold, but we are not privy to it. We struggle on, strive to reach some end, the purpose of which escapes us, yet, whose purpose is simply that we strive for the end. It is desire that propels us. Process alone has significance. You are one when the question is its own answer, when the answer is the quest. Breezes blow. The ball of dung turns gold. In the light of day, the ball breaks; beetles fly into the sun.

That is Khepera. That is one way of becoming.

There is no creation without destruction. To make the pot to carry water, the river must give up its clay. To make the child, the father must give up his seed. To make love, one gives up the self. Creation is death. Sex is death. All the ways of making are sacrifice. So bit by bit those who create murder themselves, use themselves up, give labor their love.

I know the story of Ra, how in a frenzy of lust for flesh or blood, he cut off his cock with a knife. I know the story of perpetuity, how the death of one is the joy of many. I know the story of holy self-undoing. Salvation. Sacrifice.

These are two passages unto heaven. A seed is planted with the intention of harvest. Its truth is to know the touch of the sickle, to come at last to feed the hand of its reaper. This is the vegetal way of becoming, the law of nature, the way of change, blind function. As barley grows, its leaves open to heaven and its roots burrow deep into the ground. It clings to earth, it clings to life, its end forgotten, denied. The plant must be torn from the ground.

Knowing his end, a man may sacrifice himself, choosing death, rather than life. He feels tomorrow's sorrow, but today's joy; he looks toward heaven and lives without regret. His change quickens, he knows the sorrow of the knife, the ways of darkness. He weeps and clings to the stone near at hand. He lets go. He grieves, therefore, he is man. He becomes the heart and tongue of god. He creates of mortality something immortal. Pain and defeat follow his days, as do joy and passage.

7

The Duel

In the land beneath I come and go and the earth bends over, wraps its legs around darkness. I know the story of creations and the histories of destructions. There were two sons born of heaven and earth and they married beautiful sisters. The world was new then; the fruits of the land were plentiful, the papyrus grew tall and antelope galloped the plains. Through the land a graceful river flowed nourishing all that lay there in it.

The gods said, "I give to you, Osiris and Isis, the land on the northern river; and to you, Set and Nephthys, this land that lies to the south. Go, live in peace and birth sons and daughters. Let them know they are beloved of gods."

In their land Osiris took up the plow and Isis learned to weave. From the labor of their hands came wondrous things—corn, onion and squash, reed baskets and fine linen. But Set in his land stalked antelope and lion. He chased the elephant. He drank animal blood and sucked the marrow of their bones. He tore lettuce from its roots and left nothing to seed, until one day he found his region barren. That day he coveted the bountiful world of his brother. That day sorrow began.

With perfumed hair, amid the jangle of bells on his feet, he came bearing a chest of gold inlaid with emerald, lapis lazuli and green tourmaline. "Lie in the chest, Osiris," he said. "If it fits you, it shall be yours." Distrusting no one, Osiris lay in it. How quickly worked the mind of deceit. Set sealed the chest with his brother in it and carried it to the river. The swift current bore the god away, day grew dark and the night was without stars.

Years passed. Isis found the chest lodged at the core of a tamarisk where the trunk lay thick around it. In a boat she bore the god away, up the Nile far from the marshes to the caves of mountains. There she hid herself, broke open the chest and fell down upon him, chanting spells of love and sorrow. Beneath the long ropes of her hair she worked the magic that conceived the child.

That night Set roamed the mountains hunting jackals by the light of the moon. Stumbling upon the body of his brother in the darkened cave, he shrieked and, enraged, seized the corpse and hacked it into fourteen pieces. Thirteen bits of flesh, bone and sinew—the backbones, the skull, the limbs—he scattered across the Nile, but the tastiest morsel he fed to the crocodile. Lost was the phallus of the god and he would be no more a husband on earth. Hidden and full of form, Isis bore their child in the papyrus swamps. She named him Horus and drew charms of power on his forehead. He grew to converse with his father in dream. He was a mighty son, a golden child, the avenger of his father.

One day the child became a man and that was the day of terror. The battle between gods was waged once in heaven and again and again on earth. When Horus set himself against his uncle, thunder rolled and arrows flashed fire. Beneath the sun's wasting heat, rain fell and dried before reaching the ground. Then the earth rose up like an animal and shook itself. Hot winds blew and stirred the sand into black and red clouds. The sun was blotted from the sky. The two gods seized each other. Blind with rage and stumbling, they fought with magic, with words, with clubs and knives. They fell upon each other with their hands. They wrestled about the earth in the shapes of bears, in the shapes of snakes, in the forms of men and wolves and wild beasts. Swords of iron battered shields of gold. Set buggered the warrior and Horus cut off his balls. They threw vomit and shit in each other's faces.

In heaven the gods wept and looked away, all but Thoth who watched the bloody onslaught for he was unafraid of truth. They might have killed each other, but for the flashing hand of truth which sometimes parted them. They rested. They rose and fought. Years passed. Oh, hideous face of the beast! Looking into his uncle's eyes, Horus saw only himself. The knives thrust into Set came away with Horus' blood. The eye he tore out was the eye of god.

There was a great weeping in the sky. The hair of Ra hung over his face and the world grew blind in the storm. For Ra saw that it was his own flesh, the words he had spoken turned into fists and swords. It was the creation of his own eye that raged against him. The sun fell from the sky and the empty socket dripped blood. Red tears fell scalding the wheat and withering flowers. The sun no longer rose and set. There was no light from it, but neither was there darkness. As the battle waged on even the warrior gods lost strength and they were no more than two angry mists entwined.

Thus, the world was nearly lost until Thoth parted the hair of the sorrowing god and with the fire of his hand brought forth a new eye. It was the living disk of sun—healthy and sound and without defect to its lord, as it was on the first day of the world. It opened and shut and the great wheel turned. The eons to come Thoth inscribed in Ra's blue iris. There he wrote men's

fates and of the battles of the gods of dark and light, of Self conquering self.

The heavens are full of eyes—the eye of Horus, the eye of Ra, the eyes of water and of flame. There is the white eye and the black. These are the beautiful eyes of Hathor. These are the eyes of Ptah. Man battles the beast. Order battles chaos. Life strives to conquer death as the eyes of gods and goddesses watch. There are days when a man's own strength is used against him. Even the path of lies can be walked with great persistence. Years passed. Thoth still stands at the river's edge and the battle rages on.

Have you seen it? How the fist of order tries to hold back chaos? How chaos oozes between the grasp of fingers? How the sun is born and dies twelve hours later? How it rises? How the two weights swing in the scale balanced on the fingertip of a god? Envisioned by Ra, Horus and Set were two possibilities, two sparks of a single eye. The world is whole, the eye of Ra is one crystal and the light of the eye within splinters in a thousand directions. In the underworld Osiris gathers together the fragments of himself.

I am like those warriors Horus and Set when my heart opposes my mind. I am like Osiris, my desires fragmented. I am the pieces of myself, a man longing for unity. I am the guardian of my creations, like Ra whose twin children were Shu and Tefnut, the hot dry air and the mist hanging over the river. The heat of the son's mouth burned up mist, and the hand of the daughter cooled the heat of the air. The doubles walked earth together, each necessary for the other, and the creatures below bade the twin gods homage.

My soul is like the soul of Ra, two spirits in a single heart. Blood rushing in and blood rushing out, the animal is sustained. Mine is the double soul of heaven, the dazzling, splintering power of Ra, the gathering power of Osiris. Mine is the double soul of the universe, heaven mingled with earth. I am a creature of light striving for light, battling ignorance, oppression and darkness. I am matter, the backbone of god. I am the cat beneath the laurel tree, dividing and conquering evil.

There was a day when darkness gathered itself into a hungry snake and crawled upon earth. On her belly she crept toward the city of light, swallowing whatever lay in her path: men and women, beasts, vegetables and gods. And no thing that touched her lips escaped her, for all matter was lost in the darkness. That was the day, or rather the night, that Ra left the sky and took his shape in the cat. To fool the snake, he slept under the leathery leaves of the laurel, holding in his strength, stirring only once for a single languid lick of his paws to brush against his whiskers.

Seeing the cat—that tasty bit of flesh, the snake slithered over and opened its mouth. On the other side of her teeth swelled the void, the abyss, the great nothing, and from it issued the cries of all the lost things of creation. Their voices were a wailing wind that beckoned from the darkness.

Then the soul of Ra in the form of a tiny cat leapt up beneath the shade of the laurel and, with teeth of iron and gold, he snapped off the head of the snake and sliced its body into a thousand pieces and swallowed them up. Blood from the snake's mouth spilled onto the ground. In that manner Ra's creations returned to earth. The blood seeped into the ground and was taken up by the thirsty laurel, which burst into bloom with the souls of the dead in the shape of yellow flowers.

Now leaning down from the east edge of heaven, the god of words had witnessed the battle. He had felt each puncture of the snake's teeth upon his own throat and praised the cat which had given its shape to Ra. "How like the god that made him is the radiant cat. How he slew the darkness with his mouth!" And Mau became the cat's name and the god gave him words of power.

I have stood on the eastern bank beneath that flowering laurel—it is old now; its roots gnarled but still bursting with life—and I have gazed at the sky seeing daily the same battle. The sun rises. Light overcomes darkness and the high pink clouds of morning are tinged with the blood of the snake.

I am like that cat, overcoming my own darknesses. The soul duels fear and doubt and inertia, for these are the children of the snake, the worms hidden in the clay of being that would gnaw a man to death even while he lived. I am that cat. I stand up and fight. I struggle with the evils of my own petty insistence. The battle of old gods wages in me. I am a creature of history—human and divine. I am the scroll of numerous myths, one teller of a single story.

Now the sun rises as the gold egg of god, whole light of the world, saffron cake of being. Ra shines from his disk in heaven. He rises up—a golden wonder, a bead on the throat of sky. Gusts of wind issue forth as warm breath of his mouth and drive the boats along the water, sails the sun over a river of sky and enlivens the nostrils of his people. He rises, making plain the two worlds of heaven and earth. I see myself by the light of my becoming.

—————— *Questions for Consideration* ——————

Briefly, discuss the following. In your discussion, please adhere to the ordinary conventions of good composition: content, organization, clarity, and mechanics.

1. Explain why it was necessary to place a papyrus copy of the *Book of the Dead* in the tomb of the deceased and to inscribe parts of it on the mummy case.

   _____

   _____

   _____

   _____

   _____

2. Why is the Rosetta Stone significant to our understanding of ancient Egypt?

   _____

   _____

   _____

   _____

   _____

3. Discuss the two systems of technology which were important to the ancient Egyptians.

   _____

   _____

   _____

   _____

   _____

4. In the *Book of the Dead* is a code for ethical conduct. Write your reactions to these negative confessions. Explain their relevance to most western religions.

   _____

   _____

   _____

   _____

   _____

5.   What is a myth? What are myths about? What is their function?

_____

_____

_____

_____

_____

Writing Critically
---

1. Our dreams and imaginings are personified in myths: feelings become persons; different kinds of feelings, as people, talk to each other; where feelings conflict people take sides, quarrel, and injure each other; when a new level of feeling emerges from such a conflict, a child is born. How does this scenario apply to Osiris, Set, Isis, and Horus?

   _____

   _____

   _____

   _____

   _____

   _____

2. Discuss how the myth of Osiris dramatizes the dialogue of order and disorder, good and evil, life and death.

   _____

   _____

   _____

   _____

   _____

   _____

3. The appeal of the myth of Iris and Osiris lay in the fact that people could identify with them as sharing the fate of human beings yet they also transcend the limitations of the human condition. Discuss.

   _____

   _____

   _____

   _____

   _____

   _____

4. In ancient Egypt, as in early civilizations, through sacred stories of the creation, man tried to make sense of the world he lived in. These stories dramatize the essential questions that students in all ages have asked: How did we get here? Who made the world? Why do we suffer? What is death? How should we live? Discuss.

    _____

    _____

    _____

    _____

    _____

5. Discuss the reawakening of Osiris and, through him, the resurgence of all life.

    _____

    _____

    _____

    _____

    _____

Introduction

The Ancient World: Greece
Background: The Epics — Iliad, Odyssey

About three thousand years ago, as nearly as we can tell, Western World Literature is presumed to have begun in Greece. There are, as yet, no surviving fragments which can be assigned safely to a date earlier than 900 B.C., when the Epic Age began and lasted two hundred years. The poetry of this earliest period reflects a life style that appeals to us today.

Who were these early inhabitants who worshipped sky gods, a religion which was brought into Greece by the people whom we will identify as the Mycenaeans, the first true Greeks? For three hundred years northern European tribes infiltrated Greece until they occupied all of the Greek mainland including the Peloponnesus by 1600 B.C. The warlike Mycenaeans, existing in conflict with the Cretan culture, were successful in conquering Crete in the period between 1400 B.C. and 1125 B.C. This Mycenaean culture existed from 1599 B.C. to 1100 B.C. (Cross et al. 42).

Much is known about the facts of this culture. We know that the people lived in small, warlike self-sustaining kingdoms; presiding over each kingdom was a king who lived in a fortified, rich palace. The king was independent, governing via a group of officials who were in charge of religious sacrifices and celebrations, the supervision of the farmlands, the collection of the taxes in produce, and the general affairs of the government. Despite the independence of each king, each acknowledged a chain of allegiance to the high king at Mycenae. In the epic the *Iliad* the king of Mycenae is Agamemnon. Achilles is a young, local ruler who owes a rough allegiance to him; however, he disobeyed his ruler but he was not forced to follow him. Of course, each king had his well-armed warriors—infantry, primarily—as well as his militia of chariot riding nobles (ibid.).

What did the Mycenaeans do to maintain their prosperity, as attested to in the royal tombs? In general, they engaged in extended trade, commerce, and barter among the people of the islands, Asia Minor, and throughout the Mediterranean world. This society had specific virtues which are honored in the epics the *Iliad* and the *Odyssey* of the late ninth century or early eighth. Certainly, masculine virtues were honored. Chief among the virtues of the early Greeks were physical courage and the preservation of individual honor. For the Greeks of the heroic age, dignity and human worth lay in complete self-fulfillment, most often on the field of battle where brilliant feats would bring death, perhaps, but the achievement of fame would surround them as their deeds were told in story and song. As you read the *Iliad* you will recognize the heroic qualities in Hector, Achilles, and Diomedes. In the *Odyssey* another aspect of the Greek character (much admired throughout the history of the people) will be experienced by you. This quality is "the use of a wily and tricky intelligence"—for which Odysseus stands as the supreme example.

Generally, during the formative age of a people, the most common medium of literary expression is the epic or heroic poem. The epic is defined as, "a long narrative poem on a serious subject, related in an elevated style, and centered about an heroic figure on whose actions depend to some degree the fate of a nation or a race" (Abrams 28).

A distinction is usually made between the folk epic, thought by some scholars to be a unification of many shorter tales of heroic adventures, and the art epic—the refined literary work of an individual author. Folk epic was suited to oral delivery; art epic, to reading.

Whatever may have been the origin of the former, its composer or composers, as well as the audience for whom it was composed, believed implicitly in the truth of the story. It has been said and written many times that Homer's poems were the *Bible* of the ancient Greeks. It has been quoted and recorded many times that aside from the *Bible* the *Iliad* and the *Odyssey* are the two most influential literary works in the Western world; they have served as the inspiration for numerous other literary pieces and for architecture, dance, the decorative arts, music, painting, and sculpture.

Epics, both folk and art epics, share a group of common characteristics that the reader will find helpful to refer to (and to keep in mind) as we shall study several epics. This group of common characteristics is as follows: (1) the main character is a figure of heroic stature, of national or international importance, and of great historical or legendary significance; (2) the setting is vast in scope, governing great nations, the world, or the universe; (3) the action consists of deeds that require great valor or superhuman courage; (4) supernatural forces—gods, angels, demons [jinn]—interest themselves in the action and intervene from time to time; (5) a style of sustained elevation and grand simplicity is used as well as intricate figures of speech;[1] and (6) the epic poet recounts the deeds of his heroes with objectivity.

To the foregoing general characteristics (some of which are omitted from particular epics) there should be added a list of common devices or conventions employed by most epic poets. These are the poet's opening of an epic by stating his theme, his invoking a Muse to inspire and instruct him, his beginning of his narrative *in medias res*—in the middle of things—giving the necessary exposition in later portions of the epic; his cataloguing, most often, of names, warriors, armies, ships, countries; his extended use of formal speeches by the main characters; and his frequent use of the epic simile, which expands a comparison until it becomes a complete picture.

Among the more important folk epics are the Assyrian *Epic of Gilgamesh*, the Greek *Iliad* and *Odyssey* (by Homer), the Old English *Beowulf*, the Indian *Mahabharata* and *Ramayana*, the Spanish *Cid*, the Finnish *Kalevala*, the African *Sundiata: An Epic of Old Mali*, the French *Song of Roland*, the German *Nibelungenlied*. Among the best known art epics are Virgil's *Aeneid*, Dante's *Divine Comedy* (which lacks many of the distinctive characteristics of the epic), Tasso's *Jerusalem Delivered*, Milton's *Paradise Lost*, Longfellow's *Hiawatha* (an attempt at an Indian epic). Walt Whitman's *Leaves of Grass* and Stephen Vincent Binet's *John Brown's Body* are sometimes called American epics.

Since the word epic by its definition, characteristics, and conventions images the larger-than-life panorama (larger-than-life hero, setting, and experiences), the inquiring reader must be informed concerning the Greek religion in the heroic age. There were gods and, yes, they were recognized as superior to men: they were immortal, completely powerful, handsome/beautiful, eternally young; they were anthropomorphic but in higher classification than men.

What follows will be oversimplified but the genealogy of the gods can be related in this manner; in the beginning was Chaos, consisting of darkness, mass, void. Emerging from Chaos was a male god, Uranus, representing the heavens, and a female god, Gaea, representing earth. Of the three types of offspring of the couple, one was the Titans, representing earthquakes and various cataclysms of the earth. As the myth develops Kronus, a Titan, led a revolt against the father and defeated him. Kronus mated with his sister Rhea, another representation of the earth goddess, who bore him the Olympian gods. Kronus knew the prophecy that one of his children would overthrow him; to circumvent this he swallowed all of his children at birth. However, Rhea saved Zeus and sent him to Crete where he grew to manhood. But Zeus did fulfill the prophecy of revolt. Assisted by some of the Titans, he stuffed his father in the black cave of Tartarus—but not until Kronus had had time to regurgitate the other children: Vesta, Poseidon, Pluto, Hera, and Demeter. It was from the union of Zeus and Hera, as his wife, that several gods and goddesses evolved—among them Apollo, Athena, Aphrodite, and Artemis.

The total Greek pantheon included many local gods and nymphs who presided over specific groves and streams, and were locally worshiped.

The Greek religion in the heroic age was a curious one. There was the worship of the Olympian gods but there was no prophet, interpreter, "revealer," mortal or divine; there was no Christ, no Mohammed, no Buddha; and there was no sacred book such as the *Bible*, the *Koran*, or the *Talmud*. We know only that the religion grew as a collection of myths, varying greatly, and that no single version of the history and the nature of the gods exists.

During the Mycenaean and later times the worship of the gods in formal ceremonies occurred during feasts. There was the sacrifice of animals; a portion of the meat was burned upon the fire. The remaining meat was roasted and eaten by the men offering the sacrifice. A libation was poured first to the gods, then the men drank and feasted in the belief that the god, who was present as a guest at the meal, was enjoying himself as thoroughly as they were enjoying themselves.

Whenever an important state decision arose, one of the oracles was consulted and usually it was the oracle of Delphi, presided over by the god Apollo. Even though the answers given by the oracles were often riddles that could be interpreted in any of several ways, the faith of the people was unshaken.

Where Homer was born (Chios?),[2] when he lived (ca. 850 B.C.?), even that he lived at all, have been subjects of speculation among classical scholars. The poet is said to have been blind. What arrests our attention is that the *Iliad* and the *Odyssey* relate events which occurred in a period prior to recorded literary history. These Homeric poems were written and read years after they were composed. The Greeks called bards *rhapsodists* and they sang of the events of the Trojan War, which was probably fought about 1200 B.C.

We can afford to leave the "Homeric Question" to the scholars. We cannot afford to bypass the importance of the reading of these masterpieces (not because they are written in Greek and have long been considered classics,) but because they are good stories. The *Iliad* has for a background the wedding of Peleus (Jove's grandson) and the goddess Thetis and the fact that Eris (the goddess of Discord) had not been invited. Miffed by the oversight, Eris proceeded to the ceremony and, to make trouble, tossed into the party a golden apple inscribed "for the fairest." Three goddesses claimed the prize: Hera, Athena, and Aphrodite. The judge of the contest was Paris, the son of King Priam of Troy. Paris, ultimately, awarded the prize to Aphrodite upon her promise to arrange that he would meet Helen (wife of Menelaus, King of Sparta). The meeting resulted in an elopement and the ten year siege of Troy.

The actual account in the *Iliad* begins with the quarrel between Agamemnon and Achilles toward the end of the tenth year of the Trojan conflict when Agamemnon takes Achilles' girl, Briseis, from him. The settlement of the quarrel left the great warrior Achilles pouting in his tent, thus giving for a time the advantage to the Trojans; but when Hector killed Achilles' friend, Patroclus, the Greek warrior forgot his private grievance against Agamemnon and revenged the loss of his beloved friend by killing Hector. The epic closes with King Priam's ransom of his son Hector's body. [EUB/ACJ]

ENDNOTES

1. There was the use of the epic formula which consisted of standard words, phrases, and lines that had been passed down from poet to poet until by Homer's time (ca. 850? or 750? B.C.) it was possible to compose a long epic of great complexity and originality made up largely of formulas.
    There was the use of epithets: Homer's method of applying adjectives to names. There was the use of epic simile—an elaborated comparison. (The epic device or convention.)
2. At least seven cities claimed Homer.

BIBLIOGRAPHY

Abrams, M. H. *A Glossary of Literary Terms*. New York: Holt, Rinehart & Winston, 1988.

Boardman, John, Jaspar Griffin and Oswyn Murray. Eds. *The Oxford History of the Classical World*. Oxford: University Press, 1986.

Camps, W. A. *An Introduction to Homer*. Oxford: University Press, 1980.

Clarke, Howard. *Homer's Readers: A Historical Introduction to the Iliad and the Odyssey*. Newark: University of Delaware Press, 1981.

Cross, Neal M., Robert C. Lamm and Rudy H. Turk. *The Search for Personal Freedom*. Vol. 15th Ed. Dubuque: Wm. C. Brown, 1977.

Edwards, Mark W. *Homer: Poet of the Iliad*. Baltimore: Johns Hopkins, 1990.

Homer. *The Iliad*. Trans. Robert Fitzgerald. New York: Doubleday / Anchor, 1974.

Mueller, Martin. *The Iliad*. London: Allen & Unwin, 1986.

Venus Presenting Helen to Paris

Introduction

Homer: The Iliad (8th Century B.C.)

The general consensus of modern scholarship is that there was a Homer who shaped the *Iliad* into the artistic whole we now have. Working with the traditional oral material of the pre-Homeric bards and using the resources of oral poets, he has created an organic structure with a unity and distinctive style though with clear evidence of the oral tradition throughout.

The subject of the epic is war, its violence, cruelty, and destructiveness, and also its excitement and romance in a heroic age. This deadly conflict between Greeks and Trojans is presented in graphic details amid the dash and panache of the heroes in contest on the plains outside Troy. The siege ends with the ultimate defeat and destruction of Troy, but Homer does not show this, for he limits the scope of his epic to events in the tenth year of the war. This gives dramatic intensity and facilitates a greater focus on events, themes and characters without sacrificing the scale and characteristics of the epic.

The theme is the wrath of Achilles, an essentially tragic theme of moral decline and recovery, and one which subsumes other themes such as heroism, pride, free will, and fate. Homer presents and develops these themes while also exploring the contrasts between war and peace, Greeks and Trojans, gods and humans, and Achilles and Hector, both seen consistently in war-like situations though with Hector in many domestic settings. Homer never loses sight of the inevitability of the outcome.

The actual account of the *Iliad* begins with the quarrel between Agamemnon and Achilles toward the end of the tenth year of the conflict when Agamemnon takes Achilles' girl Briseis from him. The settlement of the quarrel left the great warrior pouting in his tent, thus giving for a time the advantage to the Trojans; but when Hector killed Achilles' friend, Patroclus, the Greek warrior forgot his private grievance against Agamemnon and revenged the loss of his beloved friend by killing Hector. The epic ends with King Priam ransoming his son Hector's body followed by his funeral and a resumption of the war.

Beginning in classic style, the epic in a few lines presents the theme, the gods, two major characters, invokes the Muse, asks the epic question and plunges *in medias res* into the narrative. Evidence of the oral genesis of the narrative can be seen in the absence of information on the setting, the characters' background, and the general lack of context, since the oral poet assumed an audience familiar with the story.

Book I then introduces the quarrel between Agamemnon and Achilles, the role of other characters like Calchas and Nestor, the unfolding plot and the crucial intervention of the gods in the affairs of men Homer presents these gods not only as determining the behavior of man but also portrays them as beings who show human tendencies such as the jealousy of Hera, the partiality of Thetis, and the domestic quarrels of Zeus and Hera. Man honors the gods by sacrificing to them and his actions are conditioned by them, but Homer also shows man's free will and gives psychological plausibility to his motivation and conduct. Thus in their quarrel both Achilles and Agamemnon are wrong though for different reasons, and Calchas and Nestor are seen to respond to social forces when they intervene.

In Book 16 we are introduced to the Trojans who are on the ascendant for Hector has fought his way to the Greek ships. The Greeks are facing defeat, a consequence of Achilles' refusal to fight; his anger is still intense as he declines Patroclos' persuasive arguments to rescue them, but ironically this inflexibility costs him the life of his friend. Patroclos is not only carried away by the taste of victory and the dynamics of conflict as he leads the Myrmidons and Achaeans in throwing back the Trojans, but he also inadvertently crosses the will of the gods, so that Zeus allows it and Apollo and Hector destroy him.

In a series of vividly described scenes of heroic action, Homer shows both the glamour and gory viciousness of war, the heroic acts of valour by Greek and Trojan heroes, the larger-than-life scale of the clashes of the two armies, the calculated intervention of the gods, and their deliberate inaction and sacrifice of man. There are references to the fate of Achilles and Troy; the death of Patroclos is a crisis; later, Hector's death would be the climactic scene; but we should note that Greek honor, moral values, and physical virtues are defined in this arena of war.

Homer Invoking the Muse

Homer typically uses characteristics and minor conventions of the epic in both books. These include the assembly, set speeches, formulaic language and epic similes, set scenes, the gods' supernatural intervention in man's affairs, and the elevated style. He also develops the human side of the conflict by his deft characterization and differentiation of the major combatants, especially Achilles, Hector, Agamemnon, and the immortals. For example, though Agamemnon abuses his authority by taking Briseis, Achilles not only disrespects his commander and would have used violence on him, but he also allows his pride and arrogance to overcome his better judgment and thus causes Patroclos' death. He declines further from Book 18 in his blind and immoral revenge on the dead Hector thus offending man and the gods, only to later go through a regeneration in the scenes with Priam at the end in Book 24.

Homer explores the human condition and provides profound insights into the spirit of man in his heroic endeavours, especially in a world where the relentless will of the gods and fate make such strivings often futile. That the *Iliad* became the basis of Greek cultural and social values and contributed so much to western civilization attests to its significant place in the literary canon. [ACJ]

BIBLIOGRAPHY

Abrams, M. H. *A Glossary of Literary Terms.* New York: Holt, Rinehart & Winston, 1988.

Boardman, John, Jaspar Griffin and Oswyn Murray. Eds. *The Oxford History of the Classical World.* Oxford: University Press, 1986.

Camps, W. A. *An Introduction to Homer.* Oxford: University Press, 1980.

Clarke, Howard. *Homer's Readers: A Historical Introduction to the Iliad and the Odyssey.* Newark: University of Delaware Press, 1981.

Cross, Neal M., Robert C. Lamm and Rudy H. Turk. *The Search for Personal Freedom.* Vol. 15th Ed. Dubuque: Wm. C. Brown, 1977.

Edwards, Mark W. *Homer: Poet of the Iliad.* Baltimore: Johns Hopkins, 1990.

Homer. *The Iliad.* Trans. Robert Fitzgerald. New York: Doubleday/Anchor, 1974.

Mueller, Martin. *The Iliad.* London: Allen & Unwin, 1986.

from the Iliad

Homer

Book 1

Sing, goddess, of Achilles' ruinous anger
which brought ten thousand pains to the Achaeans,
and cast the souls of many stalwart heroes
to Hades, and their bodies to the dogs
and birds of prey. So Zeus' will was accomplished   5
when these two separated quarrelling:
Atreides, lord of men, and bright Achilles.
   Which of the gods set these two men at odds?
Apollo, who in anger with the king,
sent plague throughout the camp, and men were dying.   10
For Atreus' son dishonored his priest, Chryses,
when he came down to the Achaeans' ships
to get his daughter, bringing boundless ransom,
holding Apollo's wreaths and golden staff
in his hands as he begged all the Achaeans,   15
but Atreus' sons, the people's marshals, most:

The Embassy to Achilles

The Wrathful Achilles Visited in His Tent by Odysseus

"Sons of Atreus, and well-greaved Achaeans,
may the gods upon Olympus grant
that Priam's town be razed and you reach home.
Release my dear child, and accept this ransom;   20
Respect Zeus' son Apollo, who shoots far."
    The rest of the Achaeans cried assent:
"Honor the priest, and take his splendid ransom!"
But Agamemnon, Atreus' son, displeased,   25
drove him away, and did so with harsh words:
"Don't let me find you near the ships, old man,
lingering now, or coming back here later.
Your staff and wreathes won't help you then, for I
won't give her back; old age will find her first
in my palace in Argos, far from home,   30
weaving on a loom, and sharing my bed.
Get out! Don't anger me! You'll get home safer!"
    He spoke; the old man feared him and obeyed,
walking in silence down the sounding shore.
Then going aside some way, the old man prayed   35
to Lord Apollo, whom fair Leto bore:
"Lord of the silver bow, the guard of Chryse
and sacred Cilla, lord of Tenedos,
Smintheus, if I have ever built a temple
or burned fat thighs of bulls or goats that pleased you, 40
grant me this wish, and let the Danaans
pay with your arrows for these tears of mine."
    He spoke in prayer, and Phoebus Apollo heard him,
and with a raging heart dropped from Olympus,
carrying bow and quiver on his shoulders,   45
and as he moved the arrows raged and rattled
upon his shoulders, as he fell like night.
He sat apart and let an arrow fly;
a dreadful twang rose from the silver bow.
He struck the mules first and the flashing hounds,   50

then sent a bitter shaft among the men;
many fires for the dead were always burning.
    The god's shafts swept the army for nine days,
but on the tenth Achilles called assembly,
for white-armed Hera gave him the idea,   55
as she was vexed at seeing Danaans dying.
So when they had assembled all together,
Achilles of the swift feet stood and spoke:
"Atreus' son, if the war and plague together
break the Achaeans, we'll get home again,   60
but straggling back, if we escape from death.
So come, let's ask some seer or priest, or some
interpreter of dreams—dreams come from Zeus—
to tell us why Apollo is so angry.
If he finds fault with vows or hecatombs,   65
perhaps somehow with smoke of lambs and goats
we can persuade him to call off the plague."
    He spoke and then sat down, and Calchas rose,
by far the best interpreter of birds,
who knows the past, the present and the future,   70
and brought the Achaeans' ships to Ilion
through power Apollo gave of divination.
With graciousness to all, he said in answer:
"Achilles, you have asked me to explain
the anger of Apollo, who shoots far,   75
so I shall speak; if you'll agree and swear
that you'll defend me both by word and deed,
for I believe I'll anger one who rules
the Argives; the Achaeans too obey him.
A great king angered by a lesser man   80
may swallow anger for that day alone,
but holds his grudge within his heart until
he works it off. So say you will protect me."
    Then swift Achilles answered him and said:
"Take heart, and tell me anything you know,   85
for by Apollo, whom you pray to, Calchas,
when showing Danaans your divinations,
no one, while I'm on earth, alive and watching,
shall lay a hand on you here by the ships;
no Danaan, not even Agamemnon,   90
who boasts he's much the best of the Achaeans."
    And then the blameless seer took heart and said:
"He finds no fault with vows or hecatombs,
but with the king's dishonoring his priest,
keeping his daughter and refusing ransom.   95
Apollo gave us woes, and will give more,
and won't relieve the Danaans from trouble
before we give the girl, free, to her father,
unransomed, and then take a hecatomb
to Chryse. When appeased, he might be willing."   100
    He spoke and then sat down; then Atreus' son,
the hero, stood, wide-ruling Agamemnon,
incensed, his black heart filled with mighty rage,
and both eyes blazing so they looked like fire.
First eyeing Calchas evilly, he said: 105
"Prophet of ill, you never forecast good;

evil forecasts are dearer to your heart;
you've never said or done one bit of good.
And now among the Danaans you argue
of how and why Apollo makes them trouble: 110
because I wouldn't take Chryseis' ransom,
although I wished to have her in my house,
for I prefer her much to Clytemnestra,
my lawful wife; she's not inferior
in face and figure, nor in wits or works.   115
I'm willing, though, if best, to give her back;
I'd rather have my people safe than perish.
So find another prize; it's wrong for me
to be the only Argive with no prize.
You are all my witnesses; my prize goes elsewhere."   120
    And then god-like Achilles answered him:
"Atreus' proud son, the greediest of them all,
how can the Achaeans still give you a prize?
I know there isn't much still lying around:
loot from the towns we sacked has been divided,   125
and people shouldn't give back what they've got.
So send the god the girl now; the Achaeans
will make it up threefold, or four, if Zeus
will let us sack the well-walled town of Troy."
    In answer to him Agamemnon said: 130
"Good as you are, don't try to cheat, Achilles,
because you won't outwit, and can't persuade me.
Perhaps you wish, since you have yours, that I
have none? Or order me to give mine back?
No! Either the Achaeans give a prize   135
who pleases me because she's just as good,
or, if they don't, I'll go myself and take one,
either your prize, or Ajax' or Odysseus',
and it will anger him to whom I go:
but these things we can talk about again.   140
So come and drag a ship down to the sea,
collect sufficient oarsmen, and put in
the hecatomb; then take the girl Chryseis.
And let there be one man responsible,
Idomeneus, or Ajax, or Odysseus,   145
or you, Achilles, most astounding man,
to mollify the god with sacrifice."
    Achilles, looking grimly at him, said:
"Oh yes! And what a shameless, greedy soul!
How can any Achaean mind your orders   150
either to take the road, or fight with men?
I didn't come to fight the Trojan spearmen
since they have never done me any harm;
they've never driven cattle off, or horses,
in fertile Phthia, nurse of heroes, nor   155
have they destroyed my crops; there's much between us,
shadowy mountains and the sounding sea.
We came, you dog-eyed man, to help you save
honor for Menelaus from the Trojans;
you've never realized, or just don't care,   160
so you yourself will take away my prize
for which I worked, and the Achaeans gave me.

I never have a prize equal to yours
when the Achaeans sack some well-built city.
However, most of the fury of the battle   165
falls to my hands, but when the sharing comes,
your share's much bigger; I go to the ships,
tired of the fighting, with some small but dear thing.
But now I'm gong to Phthia, for it's better
to go home with my ships; I don't intend   170
to stay here in dishonor to enrich you."
    Then Agamemnon, lord of men, replied:
"Run away, if the spirit moves you to.
I won't beg you to stay on my account.
Others will honor me, above all, Zeus.   175
You're the most hateful of the kings Zeus cares for;
strife, battle and war are always dear to you;
and if you're strong, some god gave you that strength.
Go home then with your ships and your companions,
and rule your Myrmidons, for I don't care,   180
or heed your grudge, but let me warn you this:
as Phoebus Apollo took Chryseis from me,
I myself will send my ship and comrades,
and go myself, and take fair-cheeked Briseis
your own prize, going to your hut myself,   185
so you'll know how much mightier I am,
and none will dare to call himself my equal."
    So he spoke, and Achilles was distressed;
the heart within his hairy chest was torn;
should he pull out the sharp sword by his thigh,   190
drive off the crowd, and kill the son of Atreus,
or check his anger and restrain his wrath?
Now as he pondered in his heart and mind
while drawing out his sword, Athene came
from heaven because Hera, who had sent her,   195
loved and cared for the two men equally.
She grasped Achilles' hair, and stood behind him,
appearing to him only, no one else.
Amazed, Achilles turned and recognized
Athene with her strange and piercing eyes,   200
and spoke to her with winged words, and said:
"Why have you come again, daughter of Zeus?
Is it to see the pride of Agamemnon?
I'll tell you this, and it will surely happen:
his arrogance will some day be his death."   205
    In turn bright-eyed Athene said to him:
"If you'll obey and stop your wrath, I came
from heaven because Hera, who has sent me,
loves and cares for both of you equally.
Come, stop this squabble! Do not draw your sword.   210
Attack each other, if you will, with words;
for I will tell you this, and it will happen:
some day you'll get three times as many gifts
because of this disgrace. Stop now! Obey us!"
    In answer to her swift Achilles said: 215
    "Goddess, I must honor your joint commands
although my heart's outraged. It's better so;
the gods give ear to him who will obey."

Athene Repressing the Fury of Achilles

He laid his heavy hand upon the hilt,
and thrust his sword back in its sheath, obeying   220
Athene's words. She went back to Olympus
and to the house of Zeus and the other gods.
  Then Peleus' son again spoke to Atreides
with mischief in his words, but held his temper:
"You dog-eyed sot, whose heart is like a deer's,   225
you never armed for battle with your people,
nor had the heart to lie in ambush with
the Achaeans' bravest; that meant death to you.
Far better to deprive a man of gifts
who speaks throughout the Achaean host against you,   230
you king who feeds upon a worthless people!
So let this outrage be your last, Atreides.
But I'll speak out and swear a mighty oath
by this staff which will never more bear leaves
nor sprout again since first it left its stump   235
upon the mountains where the axe stripped leaves
and bark. The Achaeans' sons now carry it
in their hands when administering the laws
of Zeus. And this will be my oath to you:
Some day the Achaeans' sons will want Achilles,   240
and then, though anguished, you will be unable
to save them when they fall dead by the hand
of murderous Hector. You'll regret you paid
no honor to the best of the Achaeans."
  So spoke Achilles, flung to earth his staff   245
studded with golden nails, and then sat down.
Atreides raged apart. Soft-spoken Nestor
sprang up, the clearest orator in Pylos,
from whose tongue speech could run sweeter than honey.
Two generations perished in his lifetime,   250
the first were those brought up with him in Pylos,
and now he was the ruler of the third.
With kindly feeling toward them both he said;

"Oh dear! Grief's come to the Achaeans' land!
How Priam and his sons would all rejoice   255
and other Trojan hearts be filled with joy
if they should learn that you were quarreling,
you, who excel in counsel and in battle.
Now mind me! You're both younger than I am,
yet I have dealt with better men than you,   260
and they have never disregarded me.
Such men I've seen I'll never see again,
such as Perithous and also Dryas,
Caereus, Exadios and Polyphemus,
or Theseus, Aegeus' son, like the immortals;   265
they grew to be the strongest men on earth,
the very strongest, and they fought the strongest
savage mountain men, and fiercely killed them.
I joined their company, coming from Pylos,
a far off distant land, for they had asked me.   270
And by myself I fought against such men
though now no mortal man would battle with them.
They listened to my words and were persuaded.
So you too be persuaded, since it's better.
Though you're a noble, do not take this girl,   275
but leave her where the Achaeans' sons first gave her.
Achilles, do not try to match the king
in power, since a king is not the same
in honor; Zeus has given him great glory.
Though you are strong, and though a goddess bore you,   280
still he is mightier; he rules more people.
And you, Atreides, hold your temper. I
beg you to drop your anger with Achilles,
a bulwark of the Achaeans in this war."
     Then Agamemnon answered him in turn: 285
"Indeed, sir, all the things you say are right.
Yet this man wants to be above all others,
to be all-powerful and lord of all,
give orders which I think none will obey.
Because the gods have made a spearman of him,   290
are they to let him speak abusively?"
     Then interrupting him Achilles said:
"I should be called a no-account and craven
if I complied and did the deeds you order.
Give orders to the others, not to me,   295
for I know very well I won't obey you.
Another thing, and keep it well in mind:
I will not fight with you or any other,
over the girl, since you who take her gave her.
But other things of mine beside my ship   300
you shall not take away against my will.
Come, try then, so these men may understand;
your own black blood will spurt around my spear."
So when they'd fought their war of words, these two
stood and broke up the assembly by the ships.   305
Achilles then went to his hut and ships,
Patroclus and his other comrades with him;
Atreus' son drew a fast ship to the water,
put twenty oarsmen in and the hecatomb

The Seizure of Briseis by Agamemnon

for the god, and led fair-cheeked Chryseis   310
aboard. Wily Odysseus went in charge.
    They sailed the waterways when they had boarded,
and Atreus' son ordered his men to bathe.
They bathed and threw the water in the sea,
and then completed hecatombs to Apollo,   315
of bulls and goats beside the barren sea,
the steam reached heaven, swirling round in smoke.
    So they were occupied, but Agamemnon
nursed his rage and his threat against Achilles,
and to Talthybios and Eurybates,   320
his heralds and quick servants, spoke and said:
"Go to the hut of Peleus' son, Achilles,
lead out fair-cheeked Briseis by the hand,
and if he will not give her, I will come
with many men; he'll be the worse for it."   325
He spoke and sent them with this cruel order.
They walked unwillingly beside the sea,
and reached the huts and ships of the Myrmidons.
They found Achilles sitting by his ship;
Achilles was not pleased at seeing them.   330
They saw the king, and stood in awe and terror,
and could not speak or say a word to him.
But he knew in his heart, and spoke to them:
"Greetings, messengers of Zeus and men.
Come near. You're not to blame; it's Agamemnon   335
who sent you here because of the girl, Briseis.
Come then, Patroclus, go and get the girl;
give her to them; let them be witnesses
before the blessed gods and mortal men
and this harsh king, if ever after this   340
there's need of me to ward off shameful ruin
from others, for with murderous mind he rages
without a thought for what's before or after,
so the Achaeans by their ships may fight."
    So he spoke, and Patroclus was persuaded   345

to bring fair-cheeked Briseis from the hut.
The two men took her past the Achaean's ships;
the woman went unwillingly. Achilles
wept as he sat apart from his champions
upon the shore, watching the endless sea.   350
He reached out with his hands and prayed his mother:
"Since you bore me to have a short life, mother:
Olympian Zeus who thunders ought to put
honor in my hand, but he gives me little.
For Atreus' son, wide ruling Agamemnon,   355
has shamed me since he took my prize away."
   He spoke in tears, but his lady mother heard him
as she sat in the deep sea by her father.
She rose at once like mist out of the water,
and sat before him as he wept, and with   360
her hand she patted him, and said to him:
"Why crying, child? What sorrow's reached your heart?
Tell me without concealment, so we'll know."
   Sighing deeply, Achilles answered her:
"You know. Why don't you know all that I tell you?   365
We went to Thebes, Eetion's sacred city,
sacked it and brought everything in it here;
the Achaeans' sons divided these things fairly,
choosing fair-cheeked Chryseis for Atreides.
But Chryses, priest of far-shooting Apollo   370
came to the ships of the bronze-clad Achaeans
to free his daughter, bringing boundless ransom,
holding Apollo's wreaths and golden staff
in his hands as he begged all the Achaeans,
but Atreus' sons, the people's marshals, most.   375
The rest of the Achaeans cried assent:
'Honor the priest, and take his splendid ransom!'
But Agamemnon, Atreus' son, displeased,
drove him away, and did so with harsh words.
The old man went back angry, but Apollo   380
heard his prayer—he was very dear to him—

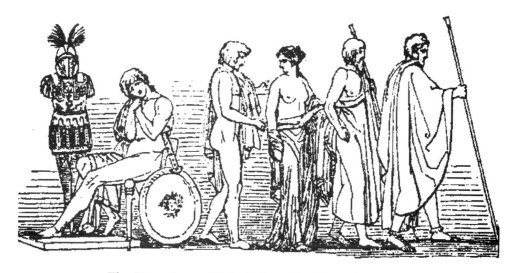

The Departure of Briseis from the Tent of Achilles

and sent an evil shaft among the Argives.
There one by one the people died, his shafts
went round the Achaean host until a seer
who knew the archer's oracles spoke to us.   385
I was the first to urge the god's appeasement.
Then Atreus' son was angered, quickly stood,
and threatened, and his threat is now accomplished.
The Achaeans sent the girl upon a ship
to Chryses, and then took gifts to his lord.   390
The heralds have just taken from my hut
Briseus' daughter whom the Achaeans gave me.
So, if you can, protect your son, and go
up to Olympus and beg Zeus if ever
you've pleased his heart either by word or deed.   395
For in my father's house I've often heard you
praying, when you said to Cronus' son
that you alone had saved him from destruction
when others of the Olympians wished to bind him,
both Hera and Poseidon, and Athene.   400
But you came, goddess, and untied his bonds
and called the hundred-handed one to Olympus—
the gods call him Briareos, but men
Aegeos' son—he's stronger than his father.
He, glorying in splendor, sat by Zeus   405
and the blessed gods were afraid to bind him.
So sit by him, remind him, take his knees,
and somehow he might wish to help the Trojans
drive the Achaeans to the ship and sea,
dying, so they may all enjoy their king,   410
and Agamemnon may know ruin for
not honoring the best of the Achaeans."
     Then Thetis, shedding tears, replied to him:
"Why did I bear and raise you, child, to sorrow?
I wish you sat untroubled by your ships,   415
since now your life is to be short, not long;
for now especially you'll be short-lived;
I bore you in my room to a sorry fate.
I'll tell the tale to thunder-loving Zeus
when I go to Olympus. He might listen.   420
But now you sit beside your speedy ship
angry with the Achaeans, but aren't fighting.
For Zeus went to the Ocean yesterday
to feast with the Aethiopians and others;
and on the twelfth day he'll come to Olympus,   425
and then I'll go to Zeus' bronze-founded house,
and clasp his knees; I think I can persuade him."
     She spoke and walked away and left him weeping
with all his heart for the lovely-girdled woman
taken by force against his will. Odysseus   430
arrived in Chryse with the hecatomb.
And when they came into the harbor's depths,
they furled their sails and stowed them in the ship,
dropped the mast by the forestays in its crutch,
and rowed in to the mooring with their oars,   435
then dropped the anchors, tied up by the stern,
and disembarked themselves upon the beach,

led out the hecatomb to give Apollo,
and then Chryseis stepped out of the ship.
Wily Odysseus led her to the altar,   440
and put her in her father's arms, and said:
"Chryses, Agamemnon sent me to bring you
your child and sacred hecatombs to Phoebus
for the Danaans, to appease your lord
who has laid great sorrows on the Argives."   445
      He put her in his arms, and Chryses took
his child with joy. They stood the hecatomb
for the god in order around the altar,
washed their hands, sprinkled barley, and killed them.
Chryses, raising his hands, prayed loudly for them: 450
"Lord of the silver bow, the guard of Chryse
and sacred Cilla, lord of Tenedos,
if once before you listened to my prayer,
and honored me, and struck the Achaeans' host,
then once again grant me this wish I pray for: 455
relieve the Danaans of this dreadful plague."
      So he prayed, and Phoebus Apollo heard him.
And when they'd prayed and thrown the barley on,
they raised the victims' heads, slaughtered and skinned them,
cut out the thigh bones, covered them with fat   460
making a double fold, and put flesh on them.
The old man burned them on a stick, poured on
the fiery wine; the young held five-pronged forks.
Then when they'd burned the thighs and tasted vitals,
they cut the rest up, putting it on spits,   465
and broiled it carefully, then took it off.
But when they'd finished and the feast was ready,
they feasted, and none lacked an equal share;
but when they'd had enough of food and drink,
the young men filled the mixing bowls with wine,   470
and supplied all, beginning with libations,
and some Achaean youths, to appease the god,
sang all day long to celebrate Apollo
with lovely hymns; and he was glad to hear them.
      Then when the sun set and the twilight came   475
they went to sleep beside the ship's stern cables.
But when young rosy-fingered Dawn appeared,
they sailed to the Achaeans' wide-spread camp;
Apollo sent a following wind to them.
They raised the mast, and spread the white sail on it;   480
the wind swelled out the middle of the sail;
a purple wave sang at the ship's cutwater
as she made her way over the waves.
But when they reached the Achaeans' wide-spread camp,
they hauled the black ship up upon the land,   485
high on the beach, and put the props underneath,
then scattered to their huts and to their ships.
      But swift Achilles, son of Peleus, sat
beside his speedy sailing ships, enraged.
He never went where men win fame, the assembly,   490
he never went to war, but pined away
sitting there, and longed for the cry of battle.
      But when at last the twelfth dawn finally came

the eternal gods all went up to Olympus   495
led by Zeus, but Thetis didn't forget
her son's request, and rose from the sea and went
early to vast heaven and to Olympus.
She found Cronus' son apart from the others
upon the highest peak of ridged Olympus,   500
and sat beside him while with her left hand
she took his knees, and with her right his chin,
and begged the lord, Zeus, Cronus' son, and said:
"Father Zeus, if I've helped you with the gods
by word or deed, then grant this wish for me: 505
honor my son, short-lived above all others,
for Agamemnon, king of men, disgraced him;
he took away his prize, and now he keeps it.
But you can punish him, Olympian Zeus;
just give the Trojans the strength so the Achaeans   510
will give my son the honor that they owe him."
    She spoke. Cloud-gathering Zeus did not reply
but sat long silent. Thetis clasped his knees
again, and then she asked a second time:
"Now promise me and nod, or else refuse,   515
since you have nothing to fear, so I may know
how much I'm in disgrace among the gods."
    Then much distressed cloud-gathering Zeus replied:
"A wretched job to set me against Hera!
When she's provoked she uses shameless words,   520
and always nags me when we're with the gods,
saying I help the Trojans with their battles.
So you go back, and don't let Hera know,
and I'll take care of this; it shall be done.
Come now, I'll nod my head so you'll believe me.   525
This sign's the greatest proof to all the gods.
Nothing can be revoked or said in vain
nor unfulfilled if I should nod my head."
    Then Cronus' son nodded his blue-black brows,
and his immortal hair flowed down the head   530
of the deathless king, and it shook Olympus.
    When they had made their plan they separated.
She plunged into the sea from bright Olympus,
and Zeus went home. The other gods all rose
out of the chairs before their father; none   535
dared to stay seated; all stood up before him.
He sat upon his throne, but Hera knew;
she'd seen that he had been contriving plans
with Thetis, daughter of the sea's Old Man.
and spoke at once in stinging words to Zeus: 540
"With what god now are you contriving plans?
You always like to make decisions on
secret affairs when I'm away. You don't
discuss freely with me what you are planning."
    The father of men and gods replied to her: 545
"Hera, don't hope to know all of my thoughts:
they'd be too painful though you are my wife.
But what is suitable no one shall hear,
neither a god nor man before you do.
Don't ask me though about the things I wish

to plan without the knowledge of the gods."　　　　　　550
　　The ox-eyed lady Hera answered him:
"Dread son of Cronus, what is that you're saying?
I've never asked you very much before,
and you are free to tell just what you wish.
But now I am afraid you've been won over　　　　　　555
by silver-footed Thetis, for she sat
and took you by the knees. I think you nodded
assenting to do honor to Achilles
and kill many Achaeans by their ships."
　　Cloud-gathering Zeus replied to her, and said:　　560
"Madam, I can't escape from your suspicions.
Yet you can't do a thing but grow more distant
from my heart, which will be worse for you.
But if you're right, then that's the way I want it.
So sit in silence, and obey my words,　　　　　　565
for all the gods who live here on Olympus
can't do a thing if I lay hands on you."
So he spoke, and frightened the ox-eyed Hera,
and she sat silent, and her heart complied.
The heavenly gods in Zeus' house were disturbed;　　570
Hephaestus, the famed smith, stood up and spoke
to comfort his dear mother, white-armed Hera:
"It will be wretched and unbearable
if these two quarrel on account of mortals,
and start a brawl among the gods. This feast　　　　575
will be no pleasure, since the worst will happen.
I beg my mother, and she understands me,
be kind to father Zeus so he won't scold her
again, and start a tumult at our banquet.
For if he wants, the lightning-thrower, Zeus,　　　　580
can knock us from our seats, he is so strong.
So you go speak to him with gentle words,
and the Olympian will be kind at once."
　　He spoke, arose, put a two-handled cup
in his dear mother's hand, and said to her:　　　　585
"Be patient, mother, even though you're vexed,
for fear I see you struck before my eyes;
then, though I'd grieve, I couldn't do a thing;
the Olympian's a hard one to withstand.
One time before I wanted to defend you;　　　　　590
he caught my foot, and threw me from the threshold;
I fell all day, and when the sun was setting,
landed on Lemnos; little life was in me;
and there the Sintian men took care of me."
　　So he spoke, and the white-armed Hera smiled,　　595
and smiling took a goblet from his hands.
Then going left to right he poured sweet nectar
out of the mixing bowl for other gods.
Then ceaseless laughter rose up as the gods
watched Hephaestus bustling through the palace.　　600
　　So all day long they feasted until sunset,
and no one was denied his proper portion
of food or music from Apollo's lyre,
or voices of the Muses in response.
　　But when the brilliance of the sun had set,　　　605

each one went to his house, and went to bed.
The famous lame Hephaestus had made houses
for each of them with knowledge and with skill;
and then Olympian Zeus went toward the bed
in which he usually lay when sweet sleep came,   610
climbed in and slept, and Hera slept beside him.

Book 16

So they battled around the well braced ships.
Patroclus came and stood beside Achilles
shedding hot tears like water from a fountain
that pours a gloomy wash over sheer rocks.
God-like Achilles saw him and felt pity,   5
and calling to him, said in winged words,
"Why crying like a baby girl, Patroclus,
who runs and begs her mother to be carried,
clings to her dress, and holds back when she's hurried,
and looks up tearfully until she's taken.   10
You're dripping tender tears like her, Patroclus.
What would you tell the Myrmidons or me?
What news have you just had from Phthia?
They say Menoitius, Actor's son, still lives,
and Peleus lives still with the Myrmidons;   15
we'd grieve a lot if either of them died.
Or do you mourn the Argives who are dying
over the ships because of their transgressions?
Come, speak your mind so we'll both understand."
    Then, sighing heavily, Patroclus said: 20
"Achilles, Peleus' son, bravest Achaean.
don't be resentful; such distress has struck
all the Achaeans; those who were the bravest
lie in the ships with spear and arrow wounds:
Tydeus' son, Diomedes, hit by arrows,   25
Odysseus and Agamemnon, stabbed by spears,
Eurypylus with an arrow in the thigh.
Doctors skilled with drugs are attending them,
staunching their wounds, Achilles, while you're useless.
I hope this anger which you nurse won't get me;   30
how will some other, later born, be helped
unless you keep destruction from the Argives?
Pitiless man, your father was not Peleus,
your mother Thetis, but the towering rock
and gray sea bore you, for your heart is hard.   35
But if some inner knowledge holds you back,
something your mother, by Zeus' will, has told you,
then send me out at once, and with me send
the Myrmidons to give the Danaans light.
Give me your armor to put on your shoulders;   40
the Trojans might suppose that I was you,
hold back, and give the Achaeans' sons a breather,
for breathing spells in war are very few.

Then, with a shout, fresh men might easily
turn tired men from the ships toward the city."   45
   So, like a fool he begged; for it would be
an evil death and doom for himself he asked.
Then much disturbed Achilles answered him:
"Patroclus, what a dreadful thing you're saying!
I have no prophecy in mind I know of,   50
no word from Zeus reported by my mother.
And it still hurts my pride and bothers me
that someone who's my equal would deprive me
of my own prize because he has more power.
The thought is bitter and it angers me.   55
This girl the Achaeans picked out as the prize
that I won with my spear, sacking a city.
Then Agamemnon took her from my hands
as if I were some common vagabond.
But let the past be done with. I've no mind   60
to remain angry always though I've said
I wouldn't give my anger up until
the battle and the shouting reached my ships.
So put my famous armor on your shoulders,
and lead the fighting Myrmidons to war.   65
Then if the Trojans get around the ships,
and Argive troops are bent back to the sea,
and only hold a little piece of land,
but the whole Trojan city will be on them
if they can't see my face inside the helmet   70
glaring at them; they'd fill the streams with corpses
if they saw Agamemnon treat me kindly.
But now they have surrounded the encampment,
the spear is gone from Diomedes' hand
that keeps destruction from the Danaans.   75
I haven't heard the voice of Agamemnon
cry from his hateful head, but Hector's voice
calling the Trojans fills my ears; their war-cry
fills the whole plain while they beat the Achaeans.
But even so, Patroclus, save the ships.   80
Hit them with all your might; don't let them fire
the ships, and take away our dear homecoming.
Obey this thought I call to your attention,
and you'll win glory for me and great honor
in the Danaans' sight, so they'll bring back   85
the lovely girl, and give me gifts as well.
When you've driven them from the ships, come back.
Though Hera's thundering lord might grant you glory,
don't long to fight the Trojans without me,
for you'd decrease my honor. You must not   90
rejoice in war and battle, nor in killing
Trojans, not lead the way to Ilion
for fear one of the gods upon Olympus
might interfere, especially Apollo.
You must turn back once you have saved the ships,   95
and let the others fight upon the plain.
Oh, Father Zeus, Athene and Apollo,
don't let a single Trojan flee from death,
or any Argive save ourselves be spared:

we two could break Troy's holy crown of towers."   100
    In this way these two talked with one another.
But Ajax couldn't hold; the missiles beat him.
Zeus' will compelled him, and the noble Trojans.
His shining helmet rang around the temples,
and blows were constant on his strong cheek-pieces.   105
His shoulder tired from holding up his shield,
and yet they couldn't beat it out of place
although they strongly pelted him with missiles.
He gasped for breath, and sweat was pouring down him
from every limb. He couldn't catch his breath,   110
and trouble piled on trouble all around him.
    Now tell me, Muses, living on Olympus,
how fire was first put to the Achaean ships.
    Hector stood close to Ajax with his sword,
and cut his spear head off behind the socket,   115
so Telamonian Ajax held a spear,
of ash without a point; the head of bronze
fell clanking to the ground some distance off.
Then Ajax shivered, knowing in his heart
this was gods' work;   120
high-thundering Zeus had foiled him,
Or he was planning victory for the Trojans.
So he drew back before the Trojan missiles.
Then they threw tireless fire upon the ships;
unquenchable flames engulfed the sterns. Achilles   125
slapped both his thighs, and then spoke to Patroclus:
"Stand up, divine Patroclus, master of horses.
I see that fire is going through the ships.
They mustn't get our ships, or we can't leave.
Put on your armor, quick! I'll get the troops!"   130
    Patroclus put his shining armor on.
First he put lovely greaves upon his shins,
fastened with silver clips around the ankles,
and next he put the breastplate round his chest
with starry ornaments; it had been Peleus'.   135
He slung his silver-studded sword of bronze
around his shoulders, then his heavy shield,
and on his mighty head he put his helmet,
the horsehair plumes above it nodding terror,
and took two spears that fitted in his hands,   140
but didn't take the spear of blameless Peleus,
huge, heavy, thick, which none of the Achaeans
could use except Achilles, who could wield it—
of Pelian ash which Cheiron brought his father
from Pelion's crest. It had killed many heroes.   145
He told Automedon to harness horses,
the man he honored most after Achilles,
who stood most faithfully by him in battle.
Automedon hitched up the horses for him,
Xanthus and Balius, fast as the wind,   150
which Podarge horse to the West Wind when
she grazed in a meadow by the Ocean's stream,
and Pedasus, a horse Achilles got
one time when he had sacked Eetion's city.
Though mortal, it ran well with immortal horses.   155

Achilles got the Myrmidons assembled
with all their armor on beside the shelters.
Then like carnivorous wolves whose strength is endless,
who've brought an antlered stag down in the mountains,
and feed upon it till their jaws run blood,   160
running as a pack to the spring for water,
lapping the dark top with their slender tongues,
spitting out clotted blood, while in their breasts
their hearts are strong, but their bellies are distended—
so were the lords of Myrmidons and leaders   165
running about Achilles' good companion,
and in among them stood warlike Achilles,
urging the fighters on with shields and horses.
   There were fifty ships in which bright Achilles,
beloved of Zeus, had brought his men to Troy;   170
in each were fifty men at the rowing benches,
Five men he then entrusted with command,
though he himself was mightiest and ruled them.
One company Menestheus commanded;
he was the son of Sperchius, the river,   175
whom Peleus' daughter bore, fair Polydore—
a woman with a god, a tireless river—
but people thought him Perieres' son,
Borus, who married her and gave her gifts.
Eudorus led the second company;   180
his mother, Phylas' daughter, Polymele,
a lovely dancer was unmarried. Hermes
fell in love when he saw her in a chorus
dancing for Artemis of the golden spindle.
Gracious Hermes went to an upper chamber   185
and lay with her in secret, and she bore him
a brilliant son, Eudorus, swift in running.
But after Eileithyia brought the child
into the light, and he could see the son,
then Echecles, the mighty son of Actor,   190
led her into his house, and gave her gifts,
and Phylas took the child and brought him up,
and cared for him as if he were his son.
The third company's leader was Pisander,
Maimalus' son, who beat all Myrmidons   195
fighting with spears—that is, after Patroclus.
The fourth was led by Phoenix, the old horseman,
the fifth Alcimedon, Laerces' son.
Then when Achilles had them all in order
with officers, he gave them firm instructions: 200
"Now Myrmidons, let not one man forget
how you threatened the Trojans by the ships
during my anger when you censured me:
'Cruel Achilles, you were raised on gall!
Against our will you kept us by the ships.   205
We should go home again in sea-borne vessels
now that this anger has come over you!'
Gathered in groups you often said such things,
but now the job you longed for is at hand.
So keep your spirits high, and fight the Trojans"   210
   So he spoke, and aroused the strength and spirits,

and when they heard their king they all closed ranks.
As when a man constructs a wall of stone
set close together to keep out the wind,
so did they set their helmets and their shields,   215
shield next to shield, and helmet close to helmet,
with horsehair plumes upon their shining crests
which nodded as they stood there, man by man.
In front of them went two men clad in armor,
Patroclus and Automedon, resolved   220
to fight before the Myrmidons. Achilles
went to his hut, and lifted up the lid
of a chest which silver-footed Thetis
had put upon his ship, well filled with tunics,
robes to break the wind, and fleecy blankets.   225
Inside it was a lovely cup from which
no other man could drink bright wine, and he
would make libation to no god but Zeus.
He took it out, and cleaned it first with sulphur,
then rinsed it out again with running water,   230
and washed his hands, and poured wine in the cup.
Then standing in the court he made libation,
looking to heaven—and Zeus noticed him.
"Lord Zeus, Dodonian and Pelasgian god,
guarding snowy Dodona where your priest,   235
the Selli, sleep on the ground with unwashed feet,
you heard me when I prayed to you before;
you honored me, and struck the Achaean host,
so bring about again the thing I wish for.
I myself will stay where the ships are gathered,   240
and send my friend with the Myrmidons to fight.
Let glory, Zeus of the broad brows, go with him.
Strengthen the heart within his breast, so Hector
may see whether my friend can fight alone,
or if he has unconquerable hands   245
only if I am in the struggle too.
But when he's stopped the onslaught on the ships,
let him come back again to me unwounded,
with all his armor and his fighting men."
   So he prayed, and Zeus of the counsels heard him,   250
and granted one prayer, but denied the other:
Patroclus stopped the onslaught on the ships,
but didn't come back safely from the fighting.
Achilles finished praying and libation,
and went back to his hut, and put the cup   255
back in the chest, and stood before the door
to watch the war of Trojans and Achaeans.
   These armed with brave Patroclus marched in line,
planning a mighty charge against the Trojans.
They poured out fast like wasps along the roadside   260
which little boys habitually madden,
teasing them in their homes along the wayside,
the silly fools, for they hurt many people,
for if some traveler upon the road
stirs them unintentionally, they come swarming   265
in raging fury to defend their children.
So poured the Myrmidons out of the ships

with hearts enraged, making an awful din.
Patroclus from afar called to his comrades:
"O Myrmidons, companions of Achilles,   270
be men, my friends, remember your great courage.
so we, his fighting comrades by the ships,
may honor Peleus' son, the best of Argives,
so Atreus' son may recognize his madness
dishonoring the best of the Achaeans."   275
     He spoke, and roused the spirit in each man,
and in a mass they fell upon the Trojans;
the ships around them echoed to their yelling.
     The Trojans, when they saw Menoetius' son
and his companions in their shining armor,   280
were shaken in their ranks beside the ships,
fearing it might be Peleus' son himself,
who put away his wrath, and caught up friendship,
and each one watched for some chance to escape.
     Patroclus was the first to throw his spear   285
right in the middle of the worst confusion
by the stern of Protesilaus' ship,
and struck Pyraechmes, who led the Paeones
from Amydon, from Axius' wide river,
and hit his shoulder; backward in the dust   290
he fell down groaning. The Paeones fled.
Patroclus killed their champion, and they ran,
for he had been a leader in the fighting.
He drove them from the ships, put out the fire,
and left the ship half burned. The Trojans scattered   295
with an unearthly noise. The Danaans
poured out along the ships with a dreadful racket.
As from the high crest of a massive mountain
Zeus of the lightning flash collects thick clouds,
and all the lookout places and the peaks   300
and valleys clear, and bright air spills from heaven,
so when the Danaans had quenched the fire
they breathed a moment, though the war continued.
The Trojans were not stopped by the Achaeans,
and hadn't turned in panic from the ships,   305
but stood quite firm, and only left when forced.
     So man killed man along the spread out struggle
of leaders. First Menoetius' son, Patroclus
struck Areïlycus with his sharp spear point
in his thigh when he turned. The spear went through,   310
and broke the bone; he fell face down on the earth.
Then warlike Menelaus wounded Thoas
in the chest by the shield. His limbs were loosed.
Meges, Phyleus' son watched Amphiclus
charge, but he quickly stabbed him in the buttock   315
where muscles are the thickest. Ligaments
were torn by the spearhead. Darkness covered both eyes.
Antilochus, a son of Nestor, stabbed
Atymnius with his spear, which went straight through
his side, and he fell face down. Maris struck   320
Antilochus in rage over his brother,
stood over him and lunged, but Thrasymedes
was quicker with his spear, and didn't miss him,

but hit his shoulder, and sheared off the arm,
tearing the muscles from the bone completely.   325
He fell with a crash, and darkness covered both eyes.
So these two, beaten by two brothers, went
to Erebus. They were Sarpedon's comrades,
sons of Amisodarus, who had reared
the dread Chimaera, evil beast to many.   330
Oïleus' Ajax caught Cleoboulus
disabled in the crush, and promptly killed him
striking him a sharp blow in the neck
with a sword hot with blood. Both eyes were closed
by purple death and mighty destiny.   335
Peneleos and Lycon then collided;
they'd thrown their spears in vain, and missed each other,
so now they ran together with their swords.
Then Lycon struck the horn of the crested helmet;
his sword broke at the hilt; Peneleos   340
struck him beneath the ear; his sword went through;
his head held by the skin alone; he died.
Meriones on foot caught Akamas
mounting behind his horse, and hit his shoulder;
he fell from the chariot, and darkness clothed him.   345
Idomeneus stabbed Erymas in the mouth,
so that the spearhead smashed its way all through
beneath the brain, and shattered all the bone;
the teeth were shaken out and both eyes filled
with blood which ran out from his nose and mouth,   350
and then a cloud of black death covered him.
     Each of the Danaan leaders killed his man.
As wolves attack small lambs and little kids
taking them from the flocks out in the mountains
through shepherds' carelessness: they watch the men,   355
and snatch them quickly—they've a feeble spirit.
So did the Danaans attack the Trojans,
who thought of flight, and quite forgot their courage.
     Ajax forever tried to throw his spear
at Hector, who, experienced in war,   360
hid his broad shoulders in an oxhide shield,
and watched the whistling arrows and the spears.
He knew the changing tide of victory,
but waited patiently to save his friends.
     As when a storm cloud from Olympus comes   365
into the sky when Zeus brings on a whirlwind,
so rose the outcry and the noise of panic
as they went back again in some disorder.
His horses carried Hector and his armor;
he left the Trojans helpless in the ditch,   370
and in the ditch were many chariot horses,
left by their masters with their poles in pieces.
Patroclus called the Danaans, and followed,
planning destruction for the Trojans, who
filled all the roads and choked them. Then a whirlwind   375
raised clouds of dust beneath, while horses strained
returning to the city from the ships.
Then where Patroclus saw some people stirring,
he steered, and many people fell beneath the axles

out of the chariots, which rattled on.   380
Over the ditch the swift immortal horses,
the shining gift the gods had given Peleus,
leaped as the spirit moved them after Hector,
to strike him, but his horse bore him off.
Now as black earth is burdened by the water   385
Zeus showers in a whirlwind in the autumn
when he is irritated, and is stirred to anger
by crooked judgments men make in the market,
forgetful of the vengeance of the gods.
Then all their rivers fill to overflowing,   390
and many rivulets cut up the hillsides
and flow into the purple sea in torrents
out of the mountains, and man's works are lessened—
so did the Trojan horses snort when running.
    Patroclus, when he'd cut the first line down,   395
made them fall back against the ships, but wouldn't
allow them to climb up into the city,
but in between the river, ships, and wall
he killed a lot, and many paid the blood-price.
Then with his shining spear he struck Pronous   400
upon the chest, bare of his shield, and killed him;
he fell with a crash. His second charge was Thestor,
the son of Enops, crouched in his chariot;
he'd lost his wits, and also lost his reins.
Patroclus came and pricked him in the jaw   405
with his spear, and it went right through his teeth;
he hooked him, and he hauled him up, as when
a fisherman sits on a rock and drags
a fish with line and hook out of the water—
so did he drag him from his chariot   410
with open mouth; and as he fell life left him.
He struck Euryalus with a stone while charging,
and broke his skull in two inside the helmet;
he dropped to earth face downwards in the dust,
and death, which breaks the spirit, drifted round him.   415
Then Erymas, Amphoterus, Epaltes,
Damastor's son Tlepolemus, Echius,
Euippus, Pyria, lpheus, Polymelus—
he brought them down to earth in quick succession.
    But when Sarpedon saw his comrades falling   420
at Menoetius' son Patroclus' hands,
he shouted to the Lycians bitterly:
"Shame, Lycians! Where are you running? Hurry up!
I'll meet this man myself so I can learn
who this man may be who has made such trouble   425
for us Trojans; he's slackened many knees."
    He jumped in armor out of his chariot,
while on the other side Patroclus watched him.
As vultures with bent beaks and crooked claws
above a high cliff scream and fight each other—   430
so these two screamed and rushed upon each other.
Then Cronus' son while watching, pitied them,
and told his wife and sister, Hera, this:
"Oh dear! Sarpedon, dear to me, is destined
to be subdued beneath Patroclus' hands.   435

My heart is torn in two ways as I ponder
whether to snatch him from the sorry battle,
and set him down alive in wealthy Lycia,
or let him be subdued beneath Patroclus."
    In turn the ox-eyed lady Hera answered: 440
"Dread son of Cronus, what a thing you've said!
You wish to save a mortal man foredoomed
by destiny to death, and to release him?
But all the other gods may not approve.
And keep in mind another thing I'll tell you: 445
If you should send Sarpedon home alive,
I tell you that some other god might wish
to take his own son from the bitter battle,
since many who are fighting round the city
are sons of gods: you'll raise resentment in them.   450
But if he's dear to you, and you would mourn him,
leave him alone to go down in the battle
beneath Menoetius' son Patroclus' hands.
Then when his soul is gone, and life has left him,
send Death and painless Sleep to carry him   455
until they reach the broad domain of Lycia
where friends and kin will give him burial
with tomb and headstone, honors due the dead."
    She spoke: the father of men and gods obeyed her.
Then she shed tears of blood that fell to earth   460
because of his dear son whom soon Patroclus
would kill in fertile Troy, far from his home.
    When they were close enough to one another
Patroclus threw first at Thrasymelus,
who was the servant of his lord Sarpedon,   465
and struck him in his guts, and loosed his limbs.
Sarpedon missed him with his shining spear
the second throw, but he hit Pedasus, the horse,
in the shoulder; it screamed as it breathed its last;
it fell in the dust, and its spirit flew away;   470
the horses shied, the yoke creaked, and the reins
lay tangled where the horse lay in the dust.
Automedon knew what he had to do:
he drew his long sword from beside his thigh,
and cut the trace-horse off, but not in vain: 475
the pair were straightened out,
and stretched the traces
and pulled the car to strife that breaks the heart.
    Sarpedon threw his shining spear, and missed.
It didn't hit, but passed Patroclus' shoulder.   480
And then Patroclus threw a second time.
With flawless aim the missile left his hand,
and struck his heart beneath the diaphragm.
He fell as when an oak or poplar falls,
or tall pine in the hills which carpenters   485
have cut with sharpened axes for ships' timbers.
So lay Sarpedon by his chariot,
bellowing, and clawing bloody dust—
or like a fiery bull that's going with
a herd of cattle when a lion comes   490
and kills him, bellowing beneath its claws—

so did Patroclus kill the Lycian lord,
who bellowed as he died to his companion:
"Glaucus, my boy, you are with men, a fighter.
Now you must be a fighting spearman too,   495
and if you're quick, let evil war attract you.
First you must go among the Lycian lords,
and stir them up to fight over Sarpedon.
Then you yourself must fight with bronze for me
so I won't be a thing of shame to you   500
later, for all your days, if the Achaeans
despoil me where I fell beside the ships.
So hold on tight, and urge the army on."
    He spoke. Death came, and closed his eyes and nostrils.
Patroclus put his foot upon his chest,   505
and pulled the spear out, and the heart came too,
so he pulled out the spear and spirit also.
The Myrmidons nearby restrained his horses,
which, freed from his chariot, now tried to bolt.
    Glaucus was saddened when he heard his voice;   510
his heart was moved because he couldn't help him.
He held his arm; his wound was hurting him
where Teucer hit him when he shot an arrow
from the high wall, protecting his companions.
And so he prayed Apollo, who shoots far: 515
"Hear, lord, if you are in the Lycian country,
or Troy, for you can listen anywhere
to a man wounded, as I'm wounded now.
I have a big wound, and my arm on both sides
is driven by sharp pain, so that the blood   520
will not stop running, and my shoulder's heavy.
I can't hold up my spear, nor go to battle
against the foe. The best of men is dead,
Sarpedon, son of Zeus—who couldn't help him.
Cure me, my lord, and put my pains to sleep,   525
and give me strength so I can call my comrades,
the Lycians, and arouse them to the fight,
while I do battle for the dead man here."
    He spoke in prayer, and Phoebus Apollo heard him.
He stopped the pain at once, and dried the blood   530
from the deep wound, and put strength in his spirit.
Glaucus knew what had happened, and rejoiced
to know the god had listened to his prayer.
He went among the Lycian men and leaders
first, and aroused them to defend Sarpedon;   535
then went with long strides next among the Trojans,
Poulydamas Panthous' son, Agenor,
and came at last to Hector and Aeneas,
and standing close, he spoke with winged words:
"Hector, have you forgotten your companions   540
who left their friends and native land with you?
their spirits are worn thin, and you won't help them.
Sarpedon, lord of Lycian shields, has fallen
defending Lycia with his strength and justice,
for Ares downed him with Patroclus' spear.   545
Stand up with me, so you won't feel resentment
if they despoil him, or abuse his body,

those Myrmidons, enraged because we killed
so many Danaans beside the ships."
    The Trojans were submerged from head to foot   550
with grief they couldn't bear because Sarpedon
had been the city's mainstay—although foreign—
and best in battle, so they followed him.
Enraged, they went straight for the Danaans;
Hector in anger for Sarpedon, led them.   555
Patroclus' savage heart roused the Achaeans.
First he aroused the Ajaxes, both burning:
"You two must wish you could defend yourselves
just as you did before, or even better.
The man who first scaled the Achaean wall   560
lies dead: Sarpedon. So let's snatch his body,
and strip the armor from his shoulders, and
kill some of the companions who defend him."
    He spoke, and they were furious in defense,
and when both sides had strengthened companies,   565
Trojans, Lycians, Myrmidons and Achaeans
united in a battle for the body
with frightful yells as men in armor clashed.
Then Zeus stretched deadly night across the fight
as there would be a struggle for his son.   570
    First Trojans pushed the rolling eyed Achaeans.
One Myrmidon, and not the worst, was killed,
Epeigeus, godlike son of Agacles,
who formerly had ruled well built Boudeion,
but now, since he had killed a noble kinsman,   575
had come as suppliant to Peleus and
to Thetis, who had sent him to Achilles
and Ilion to battle with the Trojans.
Then Hector hit him as he touched a dead man
with a boulder, and inside his helmet   580
his head was split; he fell down on the body.
Then death which breaks the spirit poured around him.
Then sorrow for his comrade seized Patroclus
who sowed his way through champions like a hawk
which scatters claws and starlings into flight.   585
So straight for the Lycians and the Trojans too,
you drove in anger for your friend, Patroclus.
Next he struck the son of Ithaemenes
in the neck with a stone, and tore the tendons.
The Trojan champions drew back with Hector   590
as far as a hunting javelin can be thrown
when a man tries his strength in competition
or in the struggle of heart breaking war—
so far did the Trojans yield to the Achaeans.
Glaucus, lord of the Lycians, turned back first,   595
and killed great-hearted Bathycles, the son
of Chalkodon, who had made his home in Hellas,
in ample wealth among the Myrmidons.
Glaucus stabbed him full in the chest, turning
suddenly back when overtaking him.   600
He fell with a crash, and grief engulfed the Achaeans
as he fell, but joy came over the Trojans,
who stood around in a crowd; but the Achaeans

didn't relax their force, but turned in fury.
And there Meriones struck down a Trojan,   605
Laogonus, Onetor's son, Zeus' priest
on Ida, who was honored as a god.
He struck him underneath his jaw and ear:
his spirit left his limbs, and darkness hid him.
Aeneas threw his spear, hoping to hit   610
Meriones beneath his shield, advancing.
But he was watching, and eluded it
by leaning forward so the long spear fell
and withered on the ground with quivering butt,
for mighty Ares took the force from it,   615
and so Aeneas' shaft fell to the ground,
for it was thrown in vain by his strong hand.
Aeneas was enraged, and called to him:
"Meriones, although you are a dancer,
my spear would quickly stop you if it hit you."   620
     Meriones, the famous Spearman, answered:
"Aeneas, though you're strong, you'd find it hard
to quench the fire of all who come against you
in self-defence, since even you are mortal.
If I should chance to hit you with my spear,   625
strong as you are, and confident as well,
you'd give glory to me: your soul to Hades."
     So he spoke, and Menoetius' son reproved him:
"Meriones, if you're so brave, why talk?
My friend, hard words won't make the Trojans leave.   630
The earth will cover him before they do.
Work will end the war, not words in council.
There is no need for us to talk—just fight."
     He spoke, and left. The other followed him.
Then as a din arises in the mountains   635
when men are cutting wood, a sound heard far,
so did a crash arise from the wide earth
of bronze and well-made ox-hide covered shields
pricked by swords and spears with double edges.
No longer could a man have seen Sarpedon   640
since he was covered up by blood and dust
that covered him from head to tips of toes.
They crowded round his body just like flies
buzzing around a milkpail on the sheepfold
in early spring when pails are splashed with milk.   645
So was the crowd around the corpse. But Zeus
never turned his shining eyes from the battle,
but always watched the fighters as he pondered
over the manner of Patroclus' death,
and whether now in this tremendous battle,   650
or whether Hector by Sarpedon's body
should kill the man and strip him of his armor,
or whether to send more men into battle:
and in his mind he thought this way the best:
send Peleus' son Achilles' friend, Patroclus   655
at once to drive the Trojans back with Hector
toward the city, and kill many men.
First he put a feeble spirit in Hector:
Mounting his chariot, he turned to fly,

and called to the rest to fly: he'd seen Zeus' scales.   660
The Lycians didn't wait; all flew away
on seeing that their king, with spear in heart,
was lying dead with many other bodies
who fell when Zeus had stretched the battle out.
The Achaeans took the armor from Sarpedon,   665
all gleaming bronze. Menoetius' mighty son
sent it to his companions by the ships.
And then cloud-gathering Zeus said to Apollo:
"Go now, dear Phoebus, clean the blood away
from underneath his gear, and save Sarpedon.   670
Take him, and wash in a running river;
anoint him, and put on ambrosial clothes,
then send him by quick messengers who'll take him,
Sleep and Death, twin brothers, and they'll lay him
quickly in the broad rich land of Lycia   675
where kin and countrymen will bury him
with tomb and gravestone as is due the dead."
   So he spoke, and Apollo heard his father,
and went down Ida's mountains to the battle.
From underneath his gear he took Sarpedon,   680
took him, and washed him in a running stream,
anointed him, and put ambrosial clothes on,
then sent quick messengers to take him off,
Sleep and Death, twin brothers, and these two laid
quickly on the broad rich land of Lycia.   685
   Calling to Automedon and his horses,
Patroclus chased the Trojans and the Lycians,
the reckless fool. If he'd obeyed Achilles,
he might have fled the cruel fate of death.
Zeus' mind is always quicker than a man's: 690
he scares the strong, and steals his victory
with ease, though he has urged him on to fight,
as he now drove Patroclus' heart to fury.
   Whom first, whom later, did you kill, Patroclus
when finally the gods called you to death?   695
Adrestus first, Autonous and Echecles,
Perimus Megades, Melanippus,
Epistor, Elasus, Moulion, Pylartes—
these he killed, and the rest escaped in flight.
   The Achaeans' sons might then have taken Troy   700
under Patroclus' hands—he raged before it,
but Phoebus took his stand upon the tower
with ill intent for him, and help for Trojans.
Three times he scaled the corner of the tower,
three times Apollo drove him back by force   705
with his immortal hands beating his shield.
But when he tried the fourth time like a spirit,
Apollo called to him with winged words:
"Give way, Patroclus! It is not your fate
to sack the Trojans' city with your spear—   710
nor with Achilles', who's a better man!"
   So he spoke, and Patroclus gave way greatly,
shunning Apollo's wrath, for he shoots far.
   Hector waited with the Scaean gate,
wondering whether to drive back to the battle,   715

or call the people who were inside the gate.
As he was pondering, Apollo came
appearing like a young and husky man,
Asius, Hector's uncle, and the brother
of Hecabe, and son of Dymas who   720
lived in Phrygia by Sangarius' river.
Appearing like this man, Apollo spoke:
"Hector, why have you quit the battle? You must not.
I wish I were as strong as I am weaker
than you, so you'd withdraw from evil war.   725
Come now! And drive your horses toward Patroclus
so you might kill him, and Apollo praise you."
    He spoke, and as a god rejoined the mortals.
    Then Hector called to wise Cebriones
to drive his horses to the fight. Apollo   730
entered the crowd, and gave the Argives trouble,
but gave the Trojans and bright Hector glory.
Hector let the other Danaans go,
but held his horses toward Patroclus, who
leaped from the chariot from the other side,   735
holding a spear in his left hand, a stone
of sparkling marble hidden in his right;
he threw without retreating from the man,
and not in vain: he hit the charioteer,
Cebriones, a bastard son of Priam,   740
who held the reins. The sharp stone hit his forehead.
It smashed both brows; the bone could not withstand it,
and both eyes fell to earth, and lay in dust
before his feet. And then just like a diver
he fell from the chariot. Life left his bones.   745
And then in mockery you said, Patroclus:
"How strange! The man is like an acrobat,
if he were only on the fish filled sea,
this man would feed a crowd, looking for oysters,
diving from ships, even in stormy weather,   750
just as he jumped so lightly from his chariot—
so too in Troy they have their acrobats."
    So he spoke as he drove at Cebriones
with the spring of a lion plundering sheepfolds
when wounded in the chest so his strength destroys him—   755
so you sprang, Patroclus, at Cebriones.
Hector jumped from his chariot to the ground,
as they fought for the body like two lions
on a mountain over a slaughtered deer,
both hungry, and both fighting with great courage-   760
so these two men fought over Cebriones:
Patroclus, son of Menoetius, and Hector,
trying to tear each other with the bronze.
    Hector held the corpse by the head; Patroclus
held it by one foot, while the Danaans   765
and Trojans came together in the battle.
    As East and South Winds fight with one another
in mountain valleys, shaking forest timber,
both oak and ash, and cornel with fine bark
which lash their branches one against another   770
with an unearthly noise of shattering timber—

so Trojans and Achaeans crashed together
cutting men down, and didn't think of panic.
Many a spear was stuck around the body,
many a winged arrow sprang from the bowstrings,   775
and many boulders beat on mighty shields
while fighting for the body in the dust,
strong in its might, its horsemanship forgotten.
    While Helius was climbing up to mid-day,
the weapons on both sides were thrown—and hit.   780
But when the sun called for unyoking cattle,
the Achaeans had grown stronger than was fated.
They dragged Cebriones from under all the weapons
and weary Trojans stripping off his armor.
Patroclus hurled himself upon the Trojans: 785
three times he charged with all the force of Ares
with a fierce cry, and three times killed nine men.
But on the fourth he met some sort of spirit
which showed, Patroclus, that your life was ending,
for Phoebus came against you in the battle,   790
although Patroclus did not see him coming,
he came up in the mist and stood behind him,
he stood behind and struck his back and shoulder
with his flat hand so that his eyes were spinning.
Apollo struck his helmet from his head: 795
four horned and hollow-eyed, it rolled beneath
his horses' feet so that its plumes were soiled
by blood and dust. It had not been allowed
before to stain this helmet in the dust;
for it had kept the god-like head and brow   800
of great Achilles. Zeus gave it to Hector
to wear upon his head, though death approached him.
He held the heavy long spear in his hands,
all shattered, and upon the ground he dropped
his shield strap from his shoulders with its tassels.   805
Zeus' son, Apollo loosed the breast-plate on him.
He lost his wits; his legs went limp beneath him.
He stood bewildered, and behind his back
a Trojan named Euphorbus who excelled
all others of his age with spears and running   810
and horsemanship, hit him between the shoulders.
He had unhorsed some twenty men since coming
with his chariot to learn to fight.
He was the first to hit you with a spear,
O knight Patroclus, but he didn't beat you;   815
he ran away and mingled with the crowd.
He couldn't face Patroclus, although naked.
Patroclus, mastered by the god, and spear,
tried to shun death and mingle with his comrades.
    When Hector saw him try to get away   820
and that he had been wounded by a spear,
he came up close across the ranks, and stabbed him
right in the lower flank, and pierced it.
He fell with a crash; the Achaean army grieved.
As when a lion overcomes a boar   825
as the two fight upon a mountain peak
over a spring from which both wish to drink,

the lion beating him as he fights for breath.
So Hector robbed Patroclus of his soul—
a man who'd killed so many—with a spear stroke,   830
and gloating, spoke with winged words, and said:
"Patroclus, so you thought to sack our city,
and take away their freedom from our women,
and take them to your homeland in your ships.
You fool! before them are my running horses   835
galloping on swift feet to war. My spear
is famous among Trojans: it protects them
from slavery. The vultures here will eat you.
You wretch! Though great, Achilles couldn't help you
he must have said, when he remained behind   840
and sent you out: 'Patroclus, don't come back
to me or to the ships until you've torn the tunic
all bloody from the chest of murderous Hector.
In some such way he fooled your idiot's mind."

    Weakly you answered him, O knight Patroclus: 845
"Now, Hector, you can boast. Zeus and Apollo
gave you the victory. They mastered me
with ease, and stripped the armor from my shoulders.
Even if twenty such as you had charged me,
all would have perished underneath my spear.   850
No, destiny and Leto's son have killed me—
Euphorbus among men, you're only third.
I'll tell you this, though: take it well to heart.
You won't live very long. Already Death
and mighty Destiny are standing by you   855
to go down at Achilles' mighty hands."

    He spoke, and Death at last closed in on him.
His soul was freed, and flew to Hades' house,
mourning her lot, and leaving youth and manhood.
Then to the dead man glorious Hector said: 860
"What is this prophecy of death, Patroclus?
Who knows, perhaps Achilles, son of Thetis,
may fall before my spear, and lose his soul."

    He spoke, and pulled the bronze spear from the wound,
and pushed the body over on its back.   865
He left it then, and charged Automedon
the comrade of Achilles, the swift runner.
He longed to throw it, but the immortal horses
the gods gave Peleus, carried him away.

The Meeting of Hector and Andromache

Thetis and Zeus

---------------- *Questions for Consideration* ----------------

Using complete sentences, provide brief answers for the following questions.

1. Identify (a) characteristics of the epic and (b) minor conventions or devices of the epic with examples in each case.

   _____

   _____

   _____

   _____

   _____

   _____

2. Using examples from the text, outline features of language of the *Iliad* that are appropriate to the epic.

   _____

   _____

   _____

   _____

   _____

   _____

3. Prepare a list of character traits and attributes to contrast Achilles and Hector and show the unique personality of each epic hero.

   _____

   _____

   _____

   _____

   _____

   _____

Writing Critically

Select one of the essay topics listed below and compose a 500 word essay which discusses the topic fully. Support your thesis with evidence from the text and with critical and/or historical material. Use the space below for preparing to write the essay.

1. Write a critical portrait of Agamemnon and Achilles.

2. Research and present your findings on the Homeric Question.

3. Identify major themes in the *Iliad* and show how they are presented and developed.

4. Write a critical evaluation of Homer's gods as presented in the *Iliad*.

5. Using Book 16, show how the heroic deeds of valour are used to define character and reveal moral values in the combatants.

6. What does Book 16 reveal about war in the heroic age?

7. What have you learned about Greek culture and society from the *Iliad*?

Prewriting Space:

_____
_____
_____
_____
_____
_____
_____
_____
_____
_____
_____
_____
_____
_____
_____
_____
_____

Introduction

Homer: The Odyssey

The Homeric epic, the *Odyssey*, is concerned with Odysseus' difficulties in getting home after the Greek and Trojan War. It takes up the account after Troy has fallen and vividly presents the long adventures and wanderings of Odysseus of Ithaca in the ten years between the victory at Troy and his return home. When Odysseus' adventures began several events had occurred: Achilles has already been killed by a poisoned arrow shot in his heel by Paris; Ajax had become insane and committed suicide after Achilles' armor was awarded to Odysseus; Paris had been killed soon afterward; Athena and Poseidon, once great allies in the *Iliad*, had turned against the Greeks. Homer does not provide the background information for the *Odyssey.* He just begins assuming the audience is familiar with the events found in earlier actions of the *Iliad.*

Homer begins the *Odyssey* nine years after the Trojan war and nineteen years since Odysseus left Ithaca to fight in the war. After the Greeks won the Trojan war, all the surviving heroes returned to their homes, except Odysseus. Odysseus left Troy with about 600 men and twelve ships, but he suffered greatly because of the gods' anger. He stole Athena's sacred image from Troy; he blinded Poseidon's son, the Cyclops; and his men killed Helios' sacred cattle of the sun. Thus, he had a long, drawn-out return to Ithaca. The Odyssey begins with all the gods except Poseidon agreeing in a council that Odysseus has suffered long enough and that they will arrange to bring him home.

Homer's epic has a unique design. As evidenced by its style and content, the *Odysseus* was originally song and recited. It has extended similes and repeated epithets, phrases, and sentences. Homer begins by giving an invocation to the Muse and stating the theme:

> *Sing in me, Muse, and through me tell the story of that man skilled in all ways of contending, the wanderer, harried for years on end, after he plundered the stronghold on the proud height of Troy.*[1]

Then he begins telling the story. He does not use the chronological order to tell his story. Instead he divides the story into three parts: Telemachus' search for his father; the many adventures of Odysseus; and the problems in his home with Penelope and the suitors. Homer begins with one part, puts one aside, begins another part, puts that side, and goes back to the first until at the end all the parts are completed. In his complex structure, Homer brings Odysseus home, allows Odysseus to meet his son and rejoin his wife, and has him drive the suitors out of his Ithaca. All the parts form the Conclusion—Odysseus' safe return home to his family.

Books 1–4 show the general plight of Ithaca and the particular dilemma of Penelope in the absence of Odysseus. The section is important to understanding the difficulties Odysseus must face on his return. The suitors rush his wife to select a husband, devour his substance, corrupt his servants, and plot the death of Telemachus. These books help to prepare the reader for Odysseus' return to Ithaca and introduce other characters with whom he will be associated. In addition, they prepare the way for later events in the epic.

The middle section of the *Odyssey* includes books 5–12. Books 9–12 of this section are in our text. This section contains the many adventures of Odysseus, shows his physical powers by swimming in the rough sea for two days and two nights, relates his resourcefulness by winning the help of the Phaeacians' royal family, and shows his cleverness by planning the

63

escape from the Cyclops. The hero and his companions are caught in the cave of the Cyclops, and after suffering losses of their own men, blind him and escape. To help in their escape, Odysseus tricks the Cyclops by saying that his name is "Nobody." When the Cyclops calls for help and says that "Nobody" is hurting him, his friends go away. This section also contains episodes with two witches, Circe and Calypso. Circe, who lives on an uninhabited island, turns Odysseus' companions into swines. After Odysseus defeats her with his cunning and courage, she welcomes him as her lover and keeps him a year. Calypso keeps Odysseus hidden on Ogygia for eight years hoping to make him immortal, but she gives him up reluctantly to the gods' command.

Books 13–24 show events back in Ithaca. Odysseus does finally return to Ithaca. He finds his house in utter pandemonium, with suitors trying to woo Penelope. Odysseus moves through a series of recognitions: to Telemachus; to his dog Argos whom he trained twenty years before; to his old nurse, Eurycleia, who recognizes a scar; to Eumaeus, who also recognizes the scar; to Penelope, who tests him about the make of their bed. With the aid of his son, Telemachus, Odysseus kills the suitors and re-establishes order to his house. (CGH)

ENDNOTE

1. Translated by Robert Fitzgerald.

MAJOR CHARACTERS

Odysseus   King of Ithaca, son of Laertes and Anticileia, father of Telemachus

Penelope   Faithful wife of Odysseus

Telemachus   Young son of Odysseus and Penelope

Helen   Wife of Menelaus, former wife of Paris

Menelaus   Husband of Helen, king of Sparta

Laertes   Aged father of Odysseus

Nestor   Aged king of Pylus

Polyphemus   Barbaric, cave-dwelling, one eyed giant

Circe   Sorceress, goddess, daughter of Helios

Calypso   Beautiful nymph, daughter of Atlas

Teiresias   Blind Theban soothsayer

Eumaeus   Faithful swineherd of Odysseus

Eurycleia   Faithful aged nurse of Odysseus

Nausicaa   Young daughter of Alcinous and Arete

Antinous   Leading suitor of Penelope

Arete   Mother of Nausicaa, queen of Phaeacians, wife of Alcinous

Alcinous   Father of Nausicaa, king of Phaeacians, husband of Arete

BIBLIOGRAPHY

Basset, S. E. *The Poetry of Homer.* Berkeley: The University of California Press, 1938.

Beye, Charles R. *The Iliad, the Odyssey and the Epic Tradition.* New York: Anchor, 1966.

Burns, Edward McNall and Phillip Lee Ralph. *World Civilization.* 5th ed. New York: W. W. Norton and Co., 1974.

Clark, H. W. *The Art of the Odyssey.* Englewood Cliffs, N.J.: Prentice-Hall, 1961.

Cross, Neal M., Robert C. Lamm and Rudy H. Turk. *The Search for Personal Freedom.* Vol. 15th ed. Dubuque: Wm. C. Brown Company, 1977.

Finley, Moses I. *The World of Odysseus.* New York: Meridian Books, 1959.

Murray, Gilbert. *The Rise of the Greek Epic.* Oxford University Press. 1960.

Nelson, Conny. *Homer's Odyssey: A Critical Handbook.* Belmont, California: Wadsworth, 1969.

Page, Denys L. *The Homeric Odyssey.* New York: Oxford University Press, 1955.

Porter, Howard N. "The Early Greek Hexameter." *Yale Classical* Studies, XII (1951).

Rexroth, Kenneth. "Homer: The Odyssey." in *The Classics Revisited.* Chicago: Quadrangle Books, 1968, pp. 12–16.

Robbins, Harry Wolcott and William H. Coleman, eds. *Western World Literature.* New York: The Macmillan Co., 1938.

from the Odyssey

Homer

Book IX

Then resourceful Odysseus spoke in turn and answered him:
"O great Alkinoös, pre-eminent among all people,
surely indeed it is a good thing to listen to a singer
such as this one before us, who is like the gods in his singing;
for I think there is no occasion accomplished that is more pleasant   5
than when festivity holds sway among all the populace,
and the feasters up and down the houses are sitting in order
and listening to the singer, and beside them the tables are loaded
with bread and meats, and from the mixing bowl the wine steward
draws the wine and carries it about and fills the cups. This   10
seems to my own mind to be the best of occasions.
But now your wish was inclined to ask me about my mournful
sufferings, so that I must mourn and grieve even more. What then
shall I recite to you first of all, what leave till later?
Many are the sorrows the gods of the sky have given me.   15
Now first I will tell you my name, so that all of you
may know me, and I hereafter, escaping the day without pity,
be your friend and guest, though the home where I live is far away from
      you.
I am Odysseus son of Laertes, known before all men
for the study of crafty designs, and my fame goes up to the heavens.   20
I am at home in sunny Ithaka. There is a mountain
there that stands tall, leaf-trembling Neritos, and there are islands
settled around it, lying one very close to another.
There is Doulichion and Same, wooded Zakynthos,
but my island lies low and away, last of all on the water   25
toward the dark, with the rest below facing east and sunshine,
a rugged place, but a good nurse of men; for my part
I cannot think of any place sweeter on earth to look at.
For in truth Kalypso, shining among divinities, kept me
with her in her hollow caverns, desiring me for her husband,   30
and so likewise Aiaian Circe the guileful detained me
beside her in her halls, desiring me for her husband,
but never could she persuade the heart within me. So it is
that nothing is more sweet in the end than country and parents
ever, even when far away one lives in a fertile   35

place, when it is in alien country, far from his parents.
But come, I will tell you of my voyage home with its many
troubles, which Zeus inflicted on me as I came from Troy land.

"From Ilion the wind took me and drove me ashore at Ismaros
by the Kikonians. I sacked their city and killed their people,   40
and out of their city taking their wives and many possessions
we shared them out, so none might go cheated of his proper
portion. There I was for the light foot and escaping,
and urged it, but they were greatly foolish and would not listen,
and then and there much wine was being drunk, and they slaughtered   45
many sheep on the beach, and lumbering horn-curved cattle.
But meanwhile the Kikonians went and summoned the other
Kikonians, who were their neighbors living in the inland country,
more numerous and better men, well skilled in fighting
men with horses, but knowing too at need the battle   50
on foot. They came at early morning, like flowers in season
or leaves, and the luck that came our way from Zeus was evil,
to make us unfortunate, so we must have hard pains to suffer.
Both sides stood and fought their battle there by the running
ships, and with bronze-headed spears they cut at each other,   55
and as long as it was early and the sacred daylight increasing,
so long we stood fast and fought them off, though there were more of them;
but when the sun had gone to the time for unyoking of cattle,
then at last the Kikonians turned the Achaians back and beat them,
and out of each ship six of my strong-greaved companions   60
were killed, but the rest of us fled away from death and destruction.

"From there we sailed on further along, glad to have escaped death,
but grieving still at heart for the loss of our dear companions.
Even then I would not suffer the flight of my oarswept vessels
until a cry had been made three times for each of my wretched   65
companions, who died there in the plain, killed by the Kikonians.
Cloud-gathering Zeus drove the North Wind against our vessels
in a supernatural storm, and huddled under the cloud scuds
land alike and the great water. Night sprang from heaven.
The ships were swept along yawing down the current; the violence   70
of the wind ripped our sails into three and four pieces. These then,
in fear of destruction, we took down and stowed in the ships' hulls,
and rowed them on ourselves until we had made the mainland.
There for two nights and two days together we lay up,
for pain and weariness together eating our hearts out.   75
But when the fair-haired Dawn in her rounds brought on the third day,
we, setting the masts upright, and hoisting the white sails on them,
sat still, and let the wind and the steersmen hold them steady.
And now I would have come home unscathed to the land of my fathers,
but as I turned the hook of Maleia, the sea and current   80
and the North Wind beat me off course, and drove me on past Kythera.

"Nine days then I was swept along by the force of the hostile
winds on the fishy sea, but on the tenth day we landed
in the country of the Lotus-Eaters, who live on a flowering
food, and there we set foot on the mainland, and fetched water,   85
and my companions soon took their supper there by the fast ships.
But after we had tasted of food and drink, then I sent
some of my companions ahead, telling them to find out
what men, eaters of bread, might live here in this country.
I chose two men, and sent a third with them, as a herald.   90
My men went on and presently met the Lotus-Eaters,

nor did these Lotus-Eaters have any thoughts of destroying
our companions, but they only gave them lotus to taste of.
But any of them who ate the honey-sweet fruit of lotus
was unwilling to take any message back, or to go   95
away, but they wanted to stay there with the lotus-eating
people, feeding on lotus, and forget the way home. I myself
took these men back weeping, by force, to where the ships were,
and put them aboard under the rowing benches and tied them
fast, then gave the order to the rest of my eager   100
companions to embark on the ships in haste, for fear
someone else might taste of the lotus and forget the way home,
and the men quickly went aboard and sat to the oarlocks,
and sitting well in order dashed the oars in the gray sea.
    "From there, grieving still at heart, we sailed on further   105
along, and reached the country of the lawless outrageous
Cyclopes who, putting all their trust in the immortal
gods, neither plow with their hands nor plant anything,
but all grows for them without seed planting, without cultivation,
wheat and barley and also the grapevines, which yield for them   110
wine of strength, and it is Zeus' rain that waters it for them.
These people have no institutions, no meetings for counsels;
rather they make their habitations in caverns hollowed
among the peaks of the high mountains, and each one is the law
for his own wives and children, and cares nothing about the others.   115
    "There is a wooded island that spreads, away from the harbor,
neither close in to the land of the Cyclopes nor far out
from it; forested; wild goats beyond number breed there,
for there is no coming and going of human kind to disturb them,
nor are they visited by hunters, who in the forest   120
suffer hardships as they haunt the peaks of the mountains,
neither again is it held by herded flocks, nor farmers,
but all its days, never plowed up and never planted,
it goes without people and supports the bleating wild goats.
For the Cyclopes have no ships with cheeks of vermilion,   125
nor have they builders of ships among them, who could have made them
strong-benched vessels, and these if made could have run them sailings
to all the various cities of men, in the way that people
cross the sea by means of ships and visit each other,
and they could have made this island a strong settlement for them.   130
For it is not a bad place at all, it could bear all crops
in season, and there are meadow lands near the shores of the gray sea,
well watered and soft; there could be grapes grown there endlessly,
and there is smooth land for plowing, men could reap a full harvest
always in season, since there is very rich subsoil. Also   135
there is an easy harbor, with no need for a hawser
nor anchor stones to be thrown ashore nor cables to make fast;
one could just run ashore and wait for the time when the sailors'
desire stirred them to go and the right winds were blowing.
Also at the head of the harbor there runs bright water,   140
spring beneath rock, and there are black poplars growing around it.
There we sailed ashore, and there was some god guiding
us in through the gloom of the night, nothing showed to look at,
for there was a deep mist around the ships, nor was there any moon
showing in the sky, but she was under the clouds and hidden.   145
There was none of us there whose eyes had spied out the island,
and we never saw any long waves rolling in and breaking

on the shore, but the first thing was when we beached the well-benched
    vessels.
Then after we had beached the ships we took all the sails down,
and we ourselves stepped out onto the break of the sea beach,   150
and there we fell asleep and waked for the divine Dawn.
    "But when the young Dawn showed again with her rosy fingers,
we made a tour about the island, admiring everything
there, and the nymphs, daughters of Zeus of the aegis, started
the hill-roving goats our way for my companions to feast on.   155
At once we went and took from the ships curved bows and javelins
with long sockets, and arranging ourselves in three divisions
cast about, and the god granted us the game we longed for.
Now there were twelve ships that went with me, and for each one nine
    goats
were portioned out, but I alone had ten for my portion.   160
So for the whole length of the day until the sun's setting,
we sat there feasting on unlimited meat and sweet wine;
for the red wine had not yet given out in the ships, there was
some still left, for we all had taken away a great deal
in storing jars when we stormed the Kikonians' sacred citadel.   165
We looked across at the land of the Cyclopes, and they were
near by, and we saw their smoke and heard sheep and goats bleating.
But when the sun went down and the sacred darkness came over,
then we lay down to sleep along the break of the seashore;
but when the young Dawn showed again with her rosy fingers,   170
then I held an assembly and spoke forth before all:
'The rest of you, who are my eager companions, wait here,
while I, with my own ship and companions that are in it,
go and find out about these people, and learn what they are,
whether they are savage and violent, and without justice,   175
or hospitable to strangers and with minds that are godly.'
    "So speaking I went aboard the ship and told my companions
also to go aboard, and to cast off the stern cables,
and quickly they went aboard the ship and sat to the oarlocks,
and sitting well in order dashed the oars in the gray sea.   180
But when we had arrived at the place, which was nearby, there
at the edge of the land we saw the cave, close to the water,
high, and overgrown with laurels, and in it were stabled
great flocks, sheep and goats alike, and there was a fenced yard
built around it with a high wall of grubbed-out boulders   185
and tall pines and oaks with lofty foliage. Inside
there lodged a monster of a man, who now was herding
the flocks at a distance away, alone, for he did not range with
others, but stayed away by himself; his mind was lawless,
and in truth he was a monstrous wonder made to behold, not   190
like a man, an eater of bread, but more like a wooded
peak of the high mountains seen standing away from the others.
    "At that time I told the rest of my eager companions
to stay where they were beside the ship and guard it. Meanwhile
I, choosing out the twelve best men among my companions,   195
went on, but I had with me a goatskin bottle of black wine,
sweet wine, given me by Maron, son of Euanthes
and priest of Apollo, who bestrides Ismaros; he gave it
because, respecting him with his wife and child, we saved them
from harm. He made his dwelling among the trees of the sacred   200
grove of Phoebos Apollo, and he gave me glorious presents.

He gave me seven talents of well-wrought gold, and he gave me
a mixing bowl made all of silver, and gave along with it
wine, drawing it off in storing jars, twelve in all. This was
a sweet wine, unmixed, a divine drink. No one of his servants   205
or thralls that were in his household knew anything about it,
but only himself and his dear wife and a single housekeeper.
Whenever he drank this honey-sweet red wine, he would pour out
enough to fill one cup, then twenty measures of water
were added, and the mixing bowl gave off a sweet smell;   210
magical; then would be no pleasure in holding off. Of this
wine I filled a great wineskin full, and took too provisions
in a bag, for my proud heart had an idea that presently
I would encounter a man who was endowed with great strength,
and wild, with no true knowledge of laws or any good customs.   215
    "Lightly we made our way to the cave, but we did not find him
there, he was off herding on the range with his fat flocks.
We went inside the cave and admired everything inside it.
Baskets were there, heavy with cheeses, and the pens crowded
with lambs and kids. They had all been divided into separate   220
groups, the firstlings in one place, and then the middle ones,
the babies again by themselves. And all his vessels, milk pails
and pans, that he used for milking into, were running over
with whey. From the start my companions spoke to me and begged me
to take some of the cheeses, come back again, and the next time   225
to drive the lambs and kids from their pens, and get back quickly
to the ship again, and go sailing off across the salt water;
but I would not listen to them, it would have been better their way,
not until I could see him, see if he would give me presents.
My friends were to find the sight of him in no way lovely.   230
    "There we built a fire and made sacrifice, and helping
ourselves to the cheeses we ate and sat waiting for him
inside, until he came home from his herding. He carried a heavy
load of dried-out wood, to make a fire for his dinner,
and threw it down inside the cave, making a terrible   235
crash, so in fear we scuttled away into the cave's corners.
Next he drove into the wide cavern all from the fat flocks
that he would milk, but he left all the male animals, billygoats
and rams, outside in his yard with the deep fences. Next thing,
he heaved up and set into position the huge door stop,   240
a massive thing; no twenty-two of the best four-wheeled
wagons could have taken that weight off the ground and carried it,
such a piece of sky-towering cliff that was he set over
his gateway. Next he sat down and milked his sheep and his bleating
goats, each of them in order, and put lamb or kid under each one   245
to suck, and then drew off half of the white milk and put it
by in baskets made of wickerwork, stored for cheeses,
but let the other half stand in the milk pails so as to have it
to help himself to and drink from, and it would serve for his supper.
But after he had briskly done all his chores and finished,   250
at last he lit the fire, and saw us, and asked us a question:
'Strangers, who are you? From where do you come sailing over the watery
ways? Is it on some business, or are you recklessly roving
as pirates do, when they sail on the salt sea and venture
their lives as they wander, bringing evil to alien people?'   255
    "So he spoke, and the inward heart in us was broken
in terror of the deep voice and for seeing him so monstrous;

but even so I had words for an answer, and I said to him:
'We are Achaians coming from Troy, beaten off our true course
by winds from every direction across the great gulf of the open   260
sea, making for home, by the wrong way, on the wrong courses.
So we have come. So it has pleased Zeus to arrange it.
We claim we are of the following of the son of Atreus,
Agamemnon, whose fame now is the greatest thing under heaven,
such a city was that he sacked and destroyed so many   265
people; but now in turn we come to you and are suppliants
at your knee, if you might give us a guest present or otherwise
some gift of grace, for such is the right of strangers. Therefore
respect the gods, O best of men. We are your suppliants,
and Zeus the guest god, who stands behind all strangers with honors   270
due them, avenges any wrong toward strangers and suppliants.'
    "So I spoke, but he answered me in pitiless spirit:
'Stranger, you are a simple fool, or come from far off,
when you tell me to avoid the wrath of the gods or fear them.
The Cyclopes do not concern themselves over Zeus of the aegis,   275
nor any of the rest of the blessed gods, since we are far better
than they, and for fear of the hate of Zeus I would not spare
you or your companions either, if the fancy took me
otherwise. But tell me, so I may know: where did you
put your well-made ship when you came? Nearby or far off?'   280
    "So he spoke, trying me out, but I knew too much and was not
deceived, but answered him in turn, and my words were crafty:
'Poseidon, Shaker of the Earth, has shattered my vessel.
He drove it against the rocks on the outer coast of your country,
cracked on a cliff, it is gone, the wind on the sea took it;   285
but I, with these you see, got away from sudden destruction.'
    "So I spoke, but he in pitiless spirit answered
nothing, but sprang up and reached for my companions,
caught up two together and slapped them, like killing puppies,
against the ground, and the brains ran all over the floor, soaking   290
the ground. Then he cut them up limb by limb and got supper ready,
and like a lion reared in the hills, without leaving anything,
ate them, entrails, flesh and the marrowy bones alike. We
cried out aloud and held our hands up to Zeus, seeing
the cruelty of what he did, but our hearts were helpless.   295
But when the Cyclops had filled his enormous stomach, feeding
on human flesh and drinking down milk unmixed with water,
he lay down to sleep in the cave sprawled out through his sheep. Then I
took counsel with myself in my great-hearted spirit
to go up close, drawing from beside my thigh the sharp sword,   300
and stab him in the chest, where the midriff joins on the liver,
feeling for the place with my hand; but the second thought stayed me;
for there we too would have perished away in sheer destruction,
seeing that our hands could never have pushed from the lofty
gate of the cave the ponderous boulder he had propped there.   305
So mourning we waited, just as we were, for the divine Dawn.
    "But when the young Dawn showed again with her rosy fingers,
he lit his fire, and then set about milking his glorious
flocks, each of them in order, and put lamb or kid under each one.
But after he had briskly done all his chores and finished,   310
again he snatched up two men, and prepared them for dinner,
and when he had dined, drove his fat flocks out of the cavern,
easily lifting off the great doorstone, but then he put it

back again, like a man closing the lid on a quiver.
And so the Cyclops, whistling loudly, guided his fat flocks   315
to the hills, leaving me there in the cave mumbling my black thoughts
of how I might punish him, how Athene might give me that glory.
And as I thought, this was the plan that seemed best to me.
The Cyclops had lying there beside the pen a great bludgeon
of olive wood, still green. He had cut it so that when it dried out   320
he could carry it about, and we looking at it considered
it to be about the size for the mast of a cargo-carrying
broad black ship of twenty oars which crosses the open
sea; such was the length of it, such the thickness, to judge by
looking. I went up and chopped a length of about a fathom,   325
and handed it over to my companions and told them to shave it
down, and they made it smooth, while I standing by them sharpened
the point, then put it over the blaze of the fire to harden.
Then I put it well away and hid it under the ordure
which was all over the floor of the cave, much stuff lying   330
about. Next I told the rest of the men to cast lots, to find out
which of them must endure with me to take up the great beam
and spin it in Cyclops' eye when sweet sleep had come over him.
The ones drew it whom I myself would have wanted chosen,
four men, and I myself was the fifth, and allotted with them.   335
With the evening he came back again, herding his fleecy
flocks, but drove all his fat flocks inside the wide cave
at once, and did not leave any outside in the yard with the deep fence,
whether he had some idea, or whether a god so urged him.
When he had heaved up and set in position the huge door stop,   340
next he sat down and started milking his sheep and his bleating
goats, each of them in order, and put lamb or kid under each one.
But after he had briskly done all his chores and finished,
again he snatched up two men and prepared them for dinner.
Then at last I, holding in my hands an ivy bowl   345
full of the black wine, stood close up to the Cyclops and spoke out:
'Here, Cyclops, have a drink of wine, now you have fed on
human flesh, and see what kind of drink our ship carried
inside her. I brought it for you, and it would have been your libation
had you taken pity and sent me home, but I cannot suffer   350
your rages. Cruel, how can any man come and visit
you ever again, now you have done what has no sanction?'
    "So I spoke, and he took it and drank it off, and was terribly
pleased with the wine he drank and questioned me again, saying:
'Give me still more, freely, and tell me your name straightway   355
now, so I can give you a guest present to make you happy.
For the grain-giving land of the Cyclopes also yields them
wine of strength, and it is Zeus' rain that waters it for them;
but this comes from where ambrosia and nectar flow in abundance.'
    "So he spoke, and I gave him the gleaming wine again. Three times 360
I brought it to him and gave it to him, three times he recklessly
drained it, but when the wine had got into the brains of the Cyclops,
then I spoke to him, and my words were full of beguilement:
'Cyclops, you ask me for my famous name. I will tell you
then, but you must give me a guest gift as you have promised.   365
Nobody is my name. My father and mother call me
Nobody, as do all the others who are my companions.'
    "So I spoke, and he answered me in pitiless spirit:
'Then I will eat Nobody after his friends, and the others

I will eat first, and that shall be my guest present to you.'   370
    "He spoke and slumped away and fell on his back, and lay there
with his thick neck crooked over on one side, and sleep who subdues all
came on and captured him, and the wine gurgled up from his gullet
with gobs of human meat. This was his drunken vomiting.
Then I shoved the beam underneath a deep bed of cinders,   375
waiting for it to heat, and I spoke to all my companions
in words of courage, so none should be in a panic, and back out;
but when the beam of olive, green as it was, was nearly
at the point of catching fire and glowed, terribly incandescent,
then I brought it close up from the fire and my friends about me   380
stood fast. Some great divinity breathed courage into us.
They seized the beam of olive, sharp at the end, and leaned on it
into the eye, while I from above leaning my weight on it
twirled it, like a man with a brace-and-bit who bores into
a ship timber, and his men from underneath, grasping   385
the strap on either side whirl it, and it bites resolutely deeper.
So seizing the fire-point-hardened timber we twirled it
in his eye, and the blood boiled around the hot point, so that
the blast and scorch of the burning ball singed all his eyebrows
and eyelids, and the fire made the roots of his eye crackle.   390
As when a man who works as a blacksmith plunges a screaming
great ax blade or plane into cold water, treating it
for temper, since this is the way steel is made strong, even
so Cyclops' eye sizzled about the beam of the olive.
He gave a giant horrible cry and the rocks rattled   395
to the sound, and we scuttled away in fear. He pulled the timber
out of his eye, and it blubbered with plenty of blood, then
when he had frantically taken it in his hands and thrown it
away, he cried aloud to the other Cyclopes, who live
around him in their own caves along the windy pinnacles.   400
They hearing him came swarming up from their various places,
and stood around the cave and asked him what was his trouble:
'Why, Polyphemos, what do you want with all this outcry
through the immortal night and have made us all thus sleepless?
Surely no mortal against your will can be driving your sheep off?   405
Surely none can be killing you by force or treachery?'
    "Then from inside the cave strong Polyphemos answered:
'Good friends, Nobody is killing me by force or treachery.'
    "So then the others speaking in winged words gave him an answer:
'If alone as you are none uses violence on you,   410
why, there is no avoiding the sickness sent by great Zeus;
so you had better pray to your father, the lord Poseidon.'
    "So they spoke as they went away, and the heart within me
laughed over how my name and my perfect planning had fooled him.
But the Cyclops, groaning aloud and in the pain of his agony,   415
felt with his hands, and took the boulder out of the doorway,
and sat down in the entrance himself, spreading his arms wide,
to catch anyone who tried to get out with the sheep, hoping
that I would be so guileless in my heart as to try this;
but I was planning so that things would come out the best way,   420
and trying to find some release from death, for my companions
and myself too, combining all my resource and treacheries,
as with life at stake, for the great evil was very close to us.
And as I thought, this was the plan that seemed best to me.
There were some male sheep, rams, well nourished, thick and fleecy,   425

handsome and large, with a dark depth of wool. Silently
I caught these and lashed them together with pliant willow
withes, where the monstrous Cyclops lawless of mind had used to
sleep. I had them in threes, and the one in the middle carried
a man, while the other two went on each side, so guarding   430
my friends. Three rams carried each man, but as for myself,
there was one ram, far the finest of all the flock. This one
I clasped around the back, snuggled under the wool of the belly,
and stayed there still, and with a firm twist of the hands and enduring
spirit clung fast to the glory of this fleece, unrelenting.   435
So we grieved for the time and waited for the divine Dawn.
     "But when the young Dawn showed again with her rosy fingers,
then the male sheep hastened out of the cave, toward pasture,
but the ewes were bleating all through the pens unmilked, their udders
ready to burst. Meanwhile their master, suffering and in   440
bitter pain, felt over the backs of all his sheep, standing
up as they were, but in his guilelessness did not notice
how my men were fastened under the breasts of his fleecy
sheep. Last of all the flock the ram went out of the doorway,
loaded with his own fleece, and with me, and my close counsels.   445
Then, feeling him, powerful Polyphemos spoke a word to him:
'My dear old ram, why are you thus leaving the cave last of
the sheep? Never in the old days were you left behind by
the flock, but long-striding, far ahead of the rest would pasture
on the tender bloom of the grass, be first at running rivers,   450
and be eager always to lead the way first back to the sheepfold
at evening. Now you are last of all. Perhaps you are grieving
for your master's eye, which a bad man with his wicked companions
put out, after he had made my brain helpless with wine, this
Nobody, who I think has not yet got clear of destruction.   455
If only you could think like us and only be given
a voice, to tell me where he is skulking away from my anger,
then surely he would be smashed against the floor and his brains go
spattering all over the cave to make my heart lighter
from the burden of all the evils this niddering Nobody gave me.'   460
     "So he spoke, and sent the ram along from him, outdoors,
and when we had got a little way from the yard and the cavern,
first I got myself loose from my ram, then set my companions
free, and rapidly then, and with many a backward glance, we
drove the long-striding sheep, rich with fat, until we reached   465
our ship, and the sight of us who had escaped death was welcome
to our companions, but they began to mourn for the others;
only I would not let them cry out, but with my brows nodded
to each man, and told them to be quick and to load the fleecy
sheep on board our vessel and sail out on the salt water.   470
Quickly they went aboard the ship and sat to the oarlocks,
and sitting well in order dashed the oars in the gray sea.
But when I was as far from the land as a voice shouting
carries, I called out aloud to the Cyclops, taunting him:
'Cyclops, in the end it was no weak man's companions   475
you were to eat by violence and force in your hollow
cave, and your evil deeds were to catch up with you, and be
too strong for you, hard one, who dared to eat your own guests
in your own house, so Zeus and the rest of the gods have punished you.'
     "So I spoke, and still more the heart in him was angered.   480
He broke away the peak of a great mountain and let it

fly, and threw it in front of the dark-prowed ship by only
a little, it just failed to graze the steering oar's edge,
but the sea washed up in the splash as the stone went under, the tidal
wave it made swept us suddenly back from the open   485
sea to the mainland again, and forced us on shore. Then I
caught up in my hands the very long pole and pushed her
clear again, and urged my companions with words, and nodding
with my head, to throw their weight on the oars and bring us
out of the threatening evil, and they leaned on and rowed hard.   490
But when we had cut through the sea to twice the previous distance,
again I started to call to Cyclops, but my friends about me
checked me, first one then another speaking, trying to soothe me:
'Hard one, why are you trying once more to stir up this savage
man, who just now threw his missile in the sea, forcing   495
our ship to the land again, and we thought once more we were finished;
and if he had heard a voice or any one of us speaking,
he would have broken all our heads and our ship's timbers
with a cast of a great jagged stone, so strong is his throwing.'
   "So they spoke, but could not persuade the great heart in me,   500
but once again in the anger of my heart I cried to him:
'Cyclops, if any mortal man ever asks you who it was
that inflicted upon your eye this shameful blinding,
tell him that you were blinded by Odysseus, sacker of cities.
Laertes is his father, and he makes his home in Ithaka.'   505
   "So I spoke, and he groaned aloud and answered me, saying:
'Ah now, a prophecy spoken of old is come to completion.
There used to be a man here, great and strong, and a prophet,
Telemos, Eurymos' son, who for prophecy was prominent
and grew old as a prophet among the Cyclopes. This man told me   510
how all this that has happened now must someday be accomplished,
and how I must lose the sight of my eye at the hands of Odysseus.
But always I was on the lookout for a man handsome
and tall, with great endowment of strength on him, to come here;
but now the end of it is that a little man, niddering, feeble,   515
has taken away the sight of my eye, first making me helpless
with wine. So come here, Odysseus, let me give you a guest gift
and urge the glorious Shaker of the Earth to grant you conveyance
home. For I am his son, he announces himself as my father.
He himself will heal me, if he will, but not any other   520
one of the blessed gods, nor any man who is mortal.'
   "So he spoke, but I answered him again and said to him:
'I only wish it were certain I could make you reft of spirit
and life, and send you to the house of Hades, as it is certain
that not even the Shaker of the Earth will ever heal your eye for you.'   525
   "So I spoke, but he then called to the lord Poseidon
in prayer, reaching both arms up toward the starry heaven:
'Hear me, Poseidon who circle the earth, dark-haired. If truly
I am your son, and you acknowledge yourself as my father,
grant that Odysseus, sacker of cities, son of Laertes,   530
who makes his home in Ithaka, may never reach that home;
but if it is decided that he shall see his own people,
and come home to his strong-founded house and to his own country,
let him come late, in bad case, with the loss of all his companions,
in someone else's ship, and find troubles in his household.'   535
   "So he spoke in prayer, and the dark-haired god heard him.
Then for the second time lifting a stone far greater

he whirled it and threw, leaning into the cast his strength beyond measure,
and the stone fell behind the dark-prowed ship by only
a little, it just failed to graze the steering oar's edge,   540
and the sea washed up in the splash as the stone went under; the tidal
wave drove us along forward and forced us onto the island.
But after we had so made the island, where all the rest of
our strong-benched ships were waiting together, and our companions
were sitting about them grieving, having waited so long for us,   545
making this point we ran our ship on the sand and beached her,
and we ourselves stepped out onto the break of the sea beach,
and from the hollow ships bringing out the flocks of the Cyclops
we shared them out so none might go cheated of his proper
portion; but for me alone my strong-greaved companions   550
excepted the ram when the sheep were shared, and I sacrificed him
on the sands to Zeus, dark-clouded son of Kronos, lord over
all, and burned him the thighs; but he was not moved by my offerings,
but still was pondering on a way how all my strong-benched
ships should be destroyed and all my eager companions.   555
So for the whole length of the day until the sun's setting,
we sat there feasting on unlimited meat and sweet wine.
But when the sun went down and the sacred darkness came over,
then we lay down to sleep along the break of the seashore;
but when the young Dawn showed again with her rosy fingers,   560
then I urged on the rest of my companions and told them
to go aboard their ships and to cast off the stern cables,
and quickly they went aboard the ships and sat to the oarlocks,
and sitting well in order dashed their oars in the gray sea.
From there we sailed on further along, glad to have escaped death,   565
but grieving still at heart for the loss of our dear companions.

Book X

"We came next to the Aiolian island, where Aiolos
lived, Hippotas' son, beloved by the immortal
gods, on a floating island, the whole enclosed by a rampart
of bronze, not to be broken, and the sheer of the cliff runs upward
to it; and twelve children were born to him in his palace,   5
six of them daughters, and six sons in the pride of their youth, so
he bestowed his daughters on his sons, to be their consorts.
And evermore, beside their dear father and gracious mother,
these feast, and good things beyond number are set before them;
and all their days the house fragrant with food echoes   10
in the courtyard, but their nights they sleep each one by his modest
wife, under coverlets, and on bedsteads corded for bedding.
We came to the city of these men and their handsome houses,
and a whole month he entertained me and asked me everything
of Ilion, and the ships of the Argives, and the Achaians'   15
homecoming, and I told him all the tale as it happened.
But when I asked him about the way back and requested
conveyance, again he did not refuse, but granted me passage.
He gave me a bag made of the skin taken off a nine-year
ox, stuffed full inside with the courses of all the blowing   20

winds, for the son of Kronos had set him in charge over
the winds, to hold them still or start them up at his pleasure.
He stowed it away in the hollow ship, tied fast with a silver
string, so there should be no wrong breath of wind, not even
a little, but set the West Wind free to blow me and carry   25
the ships and the men aboard them on their way; but it was not
so to be, for we were ruined by our own folly.
    "Nevertheless we sailed on, night and day, for nine days,
and on the tenth at last appeared the land of our fathers,
and we could see people tending fires, we were very close to them.   30
But then the sweet sleep came upon me, for I was worn out
with always handling the sheet myself, and I would not give it
to any other companion, so we could come home quicker
to our own country; but my companions talked with each other
and said that I was bringing silver and gold home with me,   35
given me by great-hearted Aiolos, son of Hippotas;
and thus they would speak to each other, each looking at the man next him:
'See now, this man is loved by everybody and favored
by all, whenever he visits anyone's land and city,
and is bringing home with him handsome treasures taken from the plunder   40
of Troy, while we, who have gone through everything he has
on the same venture, come home with our hands empty. Now too
Aiolos in favor of friendship has given him all these
goods. Let us quickly look inside and see what is in there,
and how much silver and gold this bag contains inside it.'   45
    "So he spoke, and the evil counsel of my companions
prevailed, and they opened the bag and the winds all burst out. Suddenly
the storm caught them away and swept them over the water
weeping, away from their own country. Then I waking
pondered deeply in my own blameless spirit, whether   50
to throw myself over the side and die in the open water,
or wait it out in silence and still be one of the living;
and I endured it and waited, and hiding my face I lay down
in the ship, while all were carried on the evil blast of the stormwind
back to the Aiolian island, with my friends grieving.   55
    "There again we set foot on the mainland, and fetched water,
and my companions soon took their supper there by the fast ships.
But after we had tasted of food and drink, then I
took along one herald with me, and one companion,
and went up to the famous house of Aiolos. There I found him   60
sitting at dinner with his wife and with his own children.
We came to the house beside the pillars, and on the doorstone
we sat down, and their minds wondered at us and they asked us:
'What brings you back, Odysseus? What evil spirit has vexed you?
We sent you properly on your way, so you could come back   65
to your own country and house and whatever else is dear to you.'
    "So they spoke, and I though sorry at heart answered:
'My wretched companions brought me to ruin, helped by the pitiless
sleep. Then make it right, dear friends; for you have the power.'
    "So I spoke to them, plying them with words of endearment,   70
but they were all silent; only the father found words and answered:
'O least of living creatures, out of this island! Hurry!
I have no right to see on his way, none to give passage
to any man whom the blessed gods hate with such bitterness.
Out. This arrival means you are hateful to the immortals.'   75
    "So speaking he sent me, groaning heavily, out of his palace,

and from there, grieving still at heart, we sailed on further,
but the men's spirit was worn away with the pain of rowing
and our own silliness, since homecoming seemed ours no longer.
   "Nevertheless we sailed on, night and day, for six days,   80
and on the seventh came to the sheer citadel of Lamos,
Telepylos of the Laistrygones, where one herdsman, driving
his flocks in hails another, who answers as he drives
his flocks out; and there a man who could do without sleep could earn him
double wages, one for herding the cattle, one for the silvery   85
sheep. There the courses of night and day lie close together.
There as we entered the glorious harbor, which a sky-towering
cliff encloses on either side, with no break anywhere,
and two projecting promontories facing each other
run out toward the mouth, and there is a narrow entrance,   90
there all the rest of them had their oar-swept ships in the inward
part, they were tied up close together inside the hollow
harbor, for there was never a swell of surf inside it,
neither great nor small, but there was a pale calm on it.
I myself, however, kept my black ship on the outside,   95
at the very end, making her fast to the cliff with a cable,
and climbed to a rocky point of observation and stood there.
From here no trace of cattle nor working of men was visible;
all we could see was the smoke going up from the country.
So I sent companions ahead telling them to find out   100
what men, eaters of bread, might live here in this country.
I chose two men, and sent a third with them, as a herald.
They left the ship and walked on a smooth road where the wagons
carried the timber down from the high hills to the city,
and there in front of the town they met a girl drawing water.   105
This was the powerful daughter of the Laistrygonian
Antiphates, who had gone down to the sweet-running wellspring,
Artakie, whence they would carry their water back to the city.
My men stood by her and talked with her, and asked her who was
king of these people and who was lord over them. She readily   110
pointed out to them the high-roofed house of her father.
But when they entered the glorious house, they found there a woman
as big as a mountain peak, and the sight of her filled them with horror.
At once she summoned famous Antiphates, her husband,
from their assembly, and he devised dismal death against them.   115
He snatched up one of my companions, and prepared him for dinner,
but the other two darted away in flight, and got back to my ship.
The king raised the cry through the city. Hearing him the powerful
Laistrygones came swarming up from every direction,
tens of thousands of them, and not like men, like giants.   120
These, standing along the cliffs, pelted my men with man-sized
boulders, and a horrid racket went up by the ships, of men
being killed and ships being smashed to pieces. They speared them
like fish, and carried them away for their joyless feasting.
But while they were destroying them in the deep-water harbor,   125
meanwhile I, drawing from beside my thigh the sharp sword,
chopped away the cable that tied the ship with the dark prow,
and called out to my companions, and urged them with all speed
to throw their weight on the oars and escape the threatening evil,
and they made the water fly, fearing destruction. Gladly   130
my ship, and only mine, fled out from the overhanging
cliffs to the open water, but the others were all destroyed there.

"From there we sailed on further along, glad to have escaped death,
but grieving still at heart for the loss of our dear companions.
We came to Aiaia, which is an island. There lived Circe   135
of the lovely hair, the dread goddess who talks with mortals,
who is own sister to the malignant-minded Aietes;
for they both are children of Helios, who shines on mortals,
and their mother is Perse who in turn is daughter of Ocean.
There we brought our ship in to the shore, in silence,   140
at a harbor fit for ships to lie, and some god guided us
in. There we disembarked, and for two days and two nights
we lay there, for sorrow and weariness eating our hearts out.
But when the fair-haired Dawn in her rounds brought on the third day,
then at last I took up my spear again, my sharp sword,   145
and went up quickly from beside the ship to find a lookout
place, to look for some trace of people, listen for some sound.
I climbed to a rocky point of observation and stood there,
and got a sight of smoke which came from the halls of Circe
going up from wide-wayed earth through undergrowth and forest.   150
Then I pondered deeply in my heart and my spirit,
whether, since I had seen the fire and smoke, to investigate;
but in the division of my heart this way seemed the best to me,
to go back first to the fast ship and the beach of the sea, and give
my companions some dinner, then send them forward to investigate.   155
But on my way, as I was close to the oarswept vessel
some god, because I was all alone, took pity upon me,
and sent a great stag with towering antlers right in my very
path; he had come from his range in the forest down to the river
to drink, for the fierce strength of the sun was upon him. As he   160
stepped out, I hit him in the middle of the back, next to
the spine, so that the brazen spearhead smashed its way clean through.
He screamed and dropped in the dust and the life spirit fluttered from him.
I set my foot on him and drew the bronze spear out of
the wound it had made, and rested it on the ground, while I   165
pulled growing twigs and willow withes and, braiding them into
a rope, about six feet in length, and looping them over
the feet of this great monster on both sides, lashed them together,
and with him loaded over my neck went toward the black ship,
propping myself on my spear, for there was no way to carry him   170
on the shoulder holding him with one hand, he was such a very
big beast. I threw him down by the ship and roused my companions,
standing beside each man and speaking to him in kind words:
'Dear friends, sorry as we are, we shall not yet go down into
the house of Hades. Not until our day is appointed.   175
Come then, while there is something to eat and drink by the fast ship,
let us think of our food and not be worn out with hunger.'
"So I spoke, and they listened at once to me and obeyed me,
and unveiling their heads along the beach of the barren water
they admired the stag, and truly he was a very big beast.   180
But after they had looked at him and their eyes had enjoyed him,
they washed their hands and set to preparing a communal high feast.
So for the whole length of the day until the sun's setting
we sat there feasting on unlimited meat and sweet wine.
But when the sun went down and the sacred darkness came over,   185
then we lay down to sleep along the break of the seashore;
but when the young Dawn showed again with her rosy fingers,
then I held an assembly and spoke forth to all of them:

'Hear my words, my companions, in spite of your hearts' sufferings.
Dear friends, for we do not know where the darkness is nor the sunrise,   190
nor where the Sun who shines upon people rises, nor where
he sets, then let us hasten our minds and think, whether there is
any course left open to us. But I think there is none.
For I climbed to a rocky place of observation and looked at   195
the island, and the endless sea lies all in a circle
around it, but the island itself lies low, and my eyes saw
smoke rising in the middle through the undergrowth and the forest.'
    "So I spoke, and the inward heart in them was broken,
as they remembered Antiphates the Laistrygonian
and the violence of the great-hearted cannibal Cyclops,   200
and they wept loud and shrill, letting the big tears fall,
but there came no advantage to them for all their sorrowing.
    "I counted off all my strong-greaved companions into two
divisions, and appointed a leader for each, I myself
taking one, while godlike Eurylochos had the other.   205
Promptly then we shook the lots in a brazen helmet,
and the lot of great-hearted Eurylochos sprang out. He then
went on his way, and with him two-and-twenty companions,
weeping, and we whom they left behind were mourning also.
In the forest glen they came on the house of Circe. It was   210
in an open place, and put together from stones, well polished,
and all about it there were lions, and wolves of the mountains,
whom the goddess had given evil drugs and enchanted,
and these made no attack on the men, but came up thronging
about them, waving their long tails and fawning, in the way   215
that dogs go fawning about their master, when he comes home
from dining out, for he always brings back something to please them;
so these wolves with great strong claws and lions came fawning
on my men, but they were afraid when they saw the terrible big beasts.
They stood there in the forecourt of the goddess with the glorious   220
hair, and heard Circe inside singing in a sweet voice
as she went up and down a great design on a loom, immortal
such as goddesses have, delicate and lovely and glorious
their work. Now Polites leader of men, who was
the best and dearest to me of my friends, began the discussion: 225
'Friends, someone inside going up and down a great piece
of weaving is singing sweetly, and the whole place murmurs to the echo
of it, whether she is woman or goddess. Come, let us call her.'
    "So he spoke to them, and the rest gave voice, and called her,
and at once she opened the shining doors, and came out, and invited   230
them in, and all in their innocence entered; only
Eurylochos waited outside, for he suspected treachery.
She brought them inside and seated them on chairs and benches,
and mixed them a potion, with barley and cheese and pale honey
added to Pramneian wine, but put into the mixture   235
malignant drugs, to make them forgetful of their own country.
When she had given them this and they had drunk it down, next thing
she struck them with her wand and drove them into her pig pens,
and they took on the look of pigs, with the heads and voices
and bristles of pigs, but the minds within them stayed as they had been   240
before. So crying they went in, and before them Circe
threw down acorns for them to eat, and ilex and cornel
buds, such food as pigs who sleep on the ground always feed on.
    "Eurylochos came back again to the fast black ship,

to tell the story of our companions and of their dismal   245
fate, but he could not get a word out, though he was trying
to speak, but his heart was stunned by the great sorrow, and both eyes
filled with tears, he could think of nothing but lamentation.
But after we had wondered at him and asked him questions,
at last he told us about the loss of his other companions: 250
'We went, O glorious Odysseus, through the growth as you
told us, and found a fine house in the glen. It was
in an open place, and put together from stones, well polished.
Someone, goddess or woman, was singing inside in a clear voice
as she went up and down her loom, and they called her, and spoke to her,   255
and at once she opened the shining doors, and came out and invited
them in, and all in their innocence entered, only
I waited for them outside, for I suspected treachery.
Then the whole lot of them vanished away together, nor did one
single one come out, though I sat and watched for a long time.'   260
"So he spoke, and I slung my great bronze sword with the silver
nails across my shoulders, and hung my bow on also,
and told him to guide me back by the same way he had gone;
but he, clasping my knees in both hands, entreated me,
and in loud lamentation spoke to me and addressed me: 265
'Illustrious, do not take me against my will there. Leave me
here, for I know you will never come back yourself, nor bring back
any of your companions. Let us rather make haste, and with these
who are left, escape, for we still may avoid the day of evil.'
"So he spoke, and I answered again in turn and said to him: 270
'Eurylochos, you may stay here eating and drinking, even
where you are and beside the hollow black ship; only
I shall go. For there is strong compulsion upon me.'
"So I spoke, and started up from the ship and the seashore.
But as I went up through the lonely glens, and was coming   275
near to the great house of Circe, skilled in medicines,
there as I came up to the house, Hermes, of the golden
staff, met me on my way, in the likeness of a young man
with beard new grown, which is the most graceful time of young manhood.
He took me by the hand and spoke to me and named me, saying: 280
'Where are you going, unhappy man, all alone, through the hilltops,
ignorant of the land-lay, and your friends are here in Circe's
place, in the shape of pigs and holed up in the close pig pens.
Do you come here meaning to set them free? I do not think
you will get back yourself but must stay here with the others.   285
But see, I will find you a way out of your troubles, and save you.
Here, this is a good medicine, take it, and go into Circe's
house; it will give you power against the day of trouble.
And I will tell you all the malevolent guiles of Circe.
She will make you a potion, and put drugs in the food, but she will not   290
even so be able to enchant you, for this good medicine
which I give you now will prevent her. I will tell you the details
of what to do. As soon as Circe with her long wand strikes you,
then drawing from beside your thigh your sharp sword, rush
forward against Circe, as if you were raging to kill her,   295
and she will be afraid, and invite you to go to bed with her.
Do not then resist and refuse the bed of the goddess,
for so she will set free your companions, and care for you also;
but bid her swear the great oath of the blessed gods, that she
has no other evil hurt that she is devising against you,   300

so she will not make you weak and unmanned, once you are naked.'
    "So spoke Argeïphontes, and he gave me the medicine,
which he picked out of the ground, and he explained the nature
of it to me. It was black at the root but with a milky
flower. The gods call it moly. It is hard for mortal   305
men to dig up, but the gods have power to do all things.
    "Then Hermes went away, passing over the wooded island,
toward tall Olympos, and I meanwhile made my way to the house
of Circe, but my heart was a storm in me as I went. Now
I stood outside at the doors of the goddess with the glorious   310
hair, and standing I shouted aloud; and the goddess heard me,
and at once she opened the shining doors and came out and invited
me in; and I, deeply troubled in my heart, went in with her.
She made me sit down in a chair that was wrought elaborately
and splendid with silver nails, and under my feet was a footstool.   315
She made a potion for me to drink and gave it in a golden
cup, and with evil thoughts in her heart added the drug to it.
Then when she had given it and I drank it off, without being
enchanted, she struck me with her wand and spoke and named me:
'Go to your sty now and lie down with your other friends there.'   320
    "So she spoke, but I, drawing from beside my thigh the sharp sword,
rushed forward against Circe as if I were raging to kill her,
but she screamed aloud and ran under my guard, and clasping both knees
in loud lamentation spoke to me and addressed me in winged words:
'What man are you and whence? Where are your city and parents?   325
The wonder is on me that you drank my drugs and have not been
enchanted, for no other man beside could have stood up
under my drugs, once he drank and they passed the barrier
of his teeth. There is a mind in you no magic will work on.
You are then resourceful Odysseus. Argeïphontes   330
of the golden staff was forever telling me you would come
to me, on your way back from Troy with your fast black ship.
Come then, put away your sword in its sheath, and let us
two go up into my bed so that, lying together
in the bed of love, we may then have faith and trust in each other.'   335
    "So she spoke, and I answered her again and said to her:
'Circe, how can you ask me to be gentle with you, when it
is you who turned my companions into pigs in your palace?
And now you have me here myself, you treacherously
ask me to go into your chamber and go to bed with you,   340
so that when I am naked you can make me a weakling, unmanned.
I would not be willing to go to bed with you unless
you can bring yourself, O goddess, to swear me a great oath
that there is no other evil hurt you devise against me.'
    "So I spoke, and she at once swore me the oath, as I asked her,   345
But after she had sworn me the oath, and made an end of it,
I mounted the surpassingly beautiful bed of Circe.
    "Meanwhile, the four maidservants, who wait on Circe
in her house, were busy at their work, all through the palace.
Those are daughters born of the springs and from the coppices   350
and the sacred rivers which flow down to the sea. Of these
one laid the coverlets, splendid and stained in purple, over
the backs of the chairs, and spread on the seats the cloths to sit on.
The second drew up the silver tables and placed them in front of
the chairs, and laid out the golden serving baskets upon them.   355
The third mixed wine, kindly sweet and fragrant, in the silver

mixing bowl, and set out the golden goblets. The fourth one
brought in water, then set about building up an abundant
fire, underneath the great caldron, and the water heated.
But when the water had come to a boil in the shining bronze, then   360
she sat me down in the bathtub and washed me from the great caldron,
mixing hot and cold just as I wanted, and pouring it
over shoulders and head, to take the heart-wasting weariness
from my limbs. When she had bathed me and anointed me with olive oil,
she put a splendid mantle and a tunic upon me,   365
and made me sit down in a chair that was wrought elaborately
and splendid with silver nails, and under my feet was a footstool.
A maidservant brought water for us and poured it from a splendid
and golden pitcher, holding it above a silver basin,
for us to wash, and she pulled a polished table before us.   370
A grave housekeeper brought in the bread and served it to us,
adding many good things to it, generous with her provisions,
and told us to eat, but nothing pleased my mind, and I sat there
thinking of something else, mind full of evil imaginings.
    "When Circe noticed how I sat there without ever putting   375
my hands out to the food, and with the strong sorrow upon me,
she came close, and stood beside me and addressed me in winged words:
'Why, Odysseus, do you sit so, like a man who has lost his
voice, eating your heart out, but touch neither food nor drink. Is it
that you suspect me of more treachery? But you have nothing   380
to fear, since I have already sworn my strong oath to you.'
    "So she spoke, but I answered her again and said to her:
'Oh, Circe, how could any man right in his mind ever
endure to taste of the food and drink that are set before him,
until with his eyes he saw his companions set free? So then,   385
if you are sincerely telling me to eat and drink, set them
free, so my eyes can again behold my eager companions.'
    "So I spoke, and Circe walked on out through the palace,
holding her wand in her hand, and opened the doors of the pigsty,
and drove them out. They looked like nine-year-old porkers. They stood   390
ranged and facing her, and she, making her way through their
ranks, anointed each of them with some other medicine,
and the bristles, grown upon them by the evil medicine Circe
had bestowed upon them before, now fell away from them,
and they turned back once more into men, younger than they had been   395
and taller for the eye to behold and handsomer by far.
They recognized me, and each of them clung to my hand. The lovely
longing for lamentation came over us, and the house echoed
terribly to the sound, and even the goddess took pity,
and she, shining among goddesses, came close and said to me: 400
'Son of Laertes and seed of Zeus, resourceful Odysseus,
go back down now to your fast ship and the sand of the seashore,
and first of all, drag your ship up on the land, stowing
your possessions and all the ship's running gear away in the sea caves,
and then come back, and bring with you your eager companions.'   405
    "So she spoke, and the proud heart in me was persuaded,
and I went back down to my fast ship and the sand of the seashore,
and there I found beside the fast ship my eager companions
pitiful in their lamentation and weeping big tears.
And as, in the country, the calves, around the cows returning   410
from pasture back to the dung of the farmyard, well filled with grazing,
come gamboling together to meet them, and the pens no longer

can hold them in, but lowing incessantly they come running
around their mothers, so these men, once their eyes saw me,
came streaming around me, in tears, and the spirit in them made them   415
feel as if they were back in their own country, the very
city of rugged Ithaka, where they were born and raised up.
So they came in tears about me, and cried in winged words:
'O great Odysseus, we are as happy to see you returning
as if we had come back to our own Ithakan country.   420
But come, tell us about the death of our other companions.'
　　"So they spoke, but I answered in soft words and told them:
'First of all, let us drag our ship up on the land, stowing
our possessions and all the ship's running gear away in the sea caves,
and then make haste, all of you, to come along with me,   425
so that you can see your companions, in the sacred dwelling
of Circe, eating and drinking, for they have all in abundance.'
　　"So I spoke, and at once they did as I told them. Only
Eurylochos was trying to hold back all my other
companions, and he spoke to them and addressed them in winged words: 430
'Ah, poor wretches. Where are we going? Why do you long for
the evils of going down into Circe's palace, for she will
transform the lot of us into pigs or wolves or lions,
and so we shall guard her great house for her, under compulsion.
So too it happened with the Cyclops, when our companions   435
went into his yard, and the bold Odysseus was of their company;
for it was by this man's recklessness that these too perished.'
　　"So he spoke, and I considered in my mind whether
to draw out the long-edged sword from beside my big thigh,
and cut off his head and throw it on the ground, even though   440
he was nearly related to me by marriage; but my companions
checked me, first one then another speaking, trying to soothe me:
'Zeus-sprung Odysseus, if you ask us to, we will leave
this man here to stay where he is and keep watch over
the ship. You show us the way to the sacred dwelling of Circe.'   445
　　"So they spoke, and started up from the ship and the seashore;
nor would Eurylochos be left alone by the hollow
ship, but followed along in fear of my fierce reproaches.
　　"Meanwhile, inside the house, Circe with loving care bathed
the rest of my companions, and anointed them well with olive oil,   450
and put about them mantles of fleece and tunics. We found them
all together, feasting well in the halls. When my men
looked each other in the face and knew one another,
they burst into an outcry of tears, and the whole house echoed,
But she, shining among goddesses, came close and said to us: 455
'Son of Laertes and seed of Zeus, resourceful Odysseus,
no longer raise the swell of your lamentation. I too
know all the pains you have suffered on the sea where the fish swarm,
and all the damage done you on the dry land by hostile
men. But come now, eat your food and drink your wine, until   460
you gather back again into your chests that kind of spirit
you had in you when first you left the land of your fathers
on rugged Ithaka. Now you are all dried out, dispirited
from the constant thought of your hard wandering, nor is there any
spirit in your festivity, because of so much suffering.'   465
　　"So she spoke, and the proud heart in us was persuaded.
There for all our days until a year was completed
we sat there feasting on unlimited meat and sweet wine.

But when it was the end of a year, and the months wasted
away, and the seasons changed, and the long days were accomplished,   470
then my eager companions called me aside and said to me:
'What ails you now? It is time to think about our own country,
if truly it is ordained that you shall survive and come back
to your strong-founded house and to the land of your fathers.'
   "So they spoke, and the proud heart in me was persuaded.   475
So for the whole length of the day until the sun's setting
we sat there feasting on unlimited meat and sweet wine.
But when the sun went down and the sacred darkness came over,
they lay down to sleep all about the shadowy chambers,
but I, mounting the surpassingly beautiful bed of Circe,   480
clasped her by the knees and entreated her, and the goddess
listened to me, and I spoke to her and addressed her in winged words:
'O Circe, accomplish now the promise you gave, that you
would see me on my way home. The spirit within me is urgent
now, as also in the rest of my friends, who are wasting   485
my heart away, lamenting around me, when you are elsewhere.'
   "So I spoke, and she, shining among goddesses, answered:
'Son of Laertes and seed of Zeus, resourceful Odysseus,
you shall no longer stay in my house when none of you wish to;
but first there is another journey you must accomplish   490
and reach the house of Hades and of revered Persephone,
there to consult with the soul of Teiresias the Theban,
the blind prophet, whose senses stay unshaken within him,
to whom alone Persephone has granted intelligence
even after death, but the rest of them are flittering shadows.'   495
   "So she spoke, and the inward heart in me was broken,
and I sat down on the bed and cried, nor did the heart in me
wish to go on living any longer, nor to look on the sunlight.
But when I had glutted myself with rolling about and weeping,
then at last I spoke aloud and answered the goddess: 500
'Circe, who will be our guide on that journey? No one
has ever yet in a black ship gone all the way to Hades.'
   "So I spoke, and she, shining among goddesses, answered:
'Son of Laertes and seed of Zeus, resourceful Odysseus,
let no need for a guide on your ship trouble you; only   505
set up your mast pole and spread the white sails upon it,
and sit still, and let the blast of the North Wind carry you.
But when you have crossed with your ship the stream of the Ocean, you
     will
find there a thickly wooded shore, and the groves of Persephone,
and tall black poplars growing, and fruit-perishing willows;   510
then beach your ship on the shore of the deep-eddying Ocean
and yourself go forward into the moldering home of Hades.
There Pyriphlegethon and Kokytos, which is an off-break
from the water of the Styx, flow into Acheron. There is
a rock there, and the junction of two thunderous rivers.   515
There, hero, you must go close in and do as I tell you.
Dig a pit of about a cubit in each direction,
and pour it full of drink offerings for all the dead, first
honey mixed with milk, then a second pouring of sweet wine,
and the third, water, and over all then sprinkle white barley,   520
and promise many times to the strengthless heads of the perished
dead that, returning to Ithaka, you will slaughter a barren
cow, your best, in your palace and pile the pyre with treasures,

and to Teiresias apart dedicate an all-black
ram, the one conspicuous in all your sheep flocks.   525
But when with prayers you have entreated the glorious hordes
of the dead, then sacrifice one ram and one black female,
turning them toward Erebos, but yourself turn away from them
and make for where the river runs, and there the numerous
souls of the perished dead will come and gather about you.   530
Then encourage your companions and tell them, taking
the sheep that are lying by, slaughtered with the pitiless
bronze, to skin these, and burn them, and pray to the divinities,
to Hades the powerful, and to revered Persephone,
while you yourself, drawing from beside your thigh the sharp sword,   535
crouch there, and do not let the strengthless heads of the perished
dead draw nearer to the blood until you have questioned Teiresias.
Then, leader of the host, the prophet will soon come to you,
and he will tell you the way to go, the stages of your journey,
and tell you how to make your way home on the sea where the fish swarm.'   540
    "So she spoke, and Dawn of the golden throne came on us,
and she put clothing upon me, an outer cloak and a tunic,
while she, the nymph, mantled herself in a gleaming white robe
fine-woven and delightful, and around her waist she fastened
a handsome belt of gold, and on her head was a wimple;   545
while I walked all about the house and roused my companions,
standing beside each man and speaking to him in kind words:
'No longer lie abed and dreaming away in sweet sleep.
The queenly Circe has shown me the way. So let us go now.'
    "So I spoke, and the proud heart in them was persuaded.   550
Yet I did not lead away my companions without some
loss. There was one, Elpenor, the youngest man, not terribly
powerful in fighting nor sound in his thoughts. This man,
apart from the rest of his friends, in search of cool air, had lain
down drunkenly to sleep on the roof of Circe's palace,   555
and when his companions stirred to go he, hearing their tumult
and noise of talking, started suddenly up, and never thought,
when he went down, to go by way of the long ladder,
but blundered straight off the edge of the roof, so that his neck bone
was broken out of it sockets, and his soul went down to Hades.   560
    "Now as my men were on their way I said a word to them:
'You think you are on your way back now to your own beloved
country, but Circe has indicated another journey
for us, to the house of Hades and of revered Persephone
there to consult with the soul of Teiresias the Theban.'   565
    "So I spoke, and the inward heart in them was broken.
They sat down on the ground and lamented and tore their hair out,
but there came no advantage to them for all their sorrowing.
    "When we came down to our fast ship and the sand of the seashore,
we sat down, sorrowful, and weeping big tears. Circe   570
meanwhile had gone down herself to the side of the black ship,
and tethered aboard it a ram and one black female, easily
passing by us unseen. Whose eyes can follow the movement
of a god passing from place to place, unless the god wishes?

Book XI

"Now when we had gone down again to the sea and our vessel,
first of all we dragged the ship down into the bright water,
and in the black hull set the mast in place, and set sails,
and took the sheep and walked them aboard, and ourselves also
embarked, but sorrowful, and weeping big tears. Circe   5
of the lovely hair, the dread goddess who talks with mortals,
sent us an excellent companion, a following wind, filling
the sails, to carry from astern the ship with the dark prow.
We ourselves, over all the ship making fast the running gear,
sat still, and let the wind and the steersman hold her steady.   10
All day long her sails were filled as she went through the water,
and the sun set and all the journeying-ways were darkened.
   "She made the limit, which is of the deep-running Ocean.
There lie the community and city of Kimmerian people,
hidden in fog and cloud, nor does Helios, the radiant   15
sun, ever break through the dark, to illuminate them with his shining,
neither when he climbs up into the starry heaven,
nor when he wheels to return again from heaven to earth,
but always a glum night is spread over wretched mortals.
Making this point, we ran the ship ashore, and took out   20
the sheep, and ourselves walked along by the stream of the Ocean
until we came to that place of which Circe had spoken.
   "There Perimedes and Eurylochos held the victims
fast, and I, drawing from beside my thigh my sharp sword,
dug a pit, of about a cubit in each direction,   25
and poured it full of drink offerings for all the dead, first
honey mixed with milk, and the second pouring was sweet wine,
and the third, water, and over it all I sprinkled white barley.
I promised many times to the strengthless heads of the perished
dead that, returning to Ithaka, I would slaughter a barren   30
cow, my best, in my palace, and pile the pyre with treasures,
and to Teiresias apart would dedicate an all-black
ram, the one conspicuous in all our sheep flocks.
Now when, with sacrifices and prayers, I had so entreated
the hordes of the dead, I took the sheep and cut their throats   35
over the pit, and the dark-clouding blood ran in, and the souls
of the perished dead gathered to the place, up out of Erebos,
brides, and young unmarried men, and long-suffering elders,
virgins, tender and with the sorrows of young hearts upon them,
and many fighting men killed in battle, stabbed with brazen   40
spears, still carrying their bloody armor upon them.
These came swarming around my pit from every direction
with inhuman clamor, and green fear took hold of me.
Then I encouraged my companions and told them, taking
the sheep that were lying by, slaughtered with the pitiless   45
bronze, to skin these, and burn them, and pray to the divinities,
to Hades the powerful, and to revered Persephone,
while I myself, drawing from beside my thigh my sharp sword,
crouched there, and would not let the strengthless heads of the perished
dead draw nearer to the blood, until I had questioned Teiresias.   50
   "But first there came the soul of my companion, Elpenor,
for he had not yet been buried under earth of the wide ways,

since we had left his body behind in Circe's palace,
unburied and unwept, with this other errand before us.
I broke into tears at the sight of him, and my heart pitied him,   55
and so I spoke aloud to him and addressed him in winged words:
'Elpenor, how did you come here beneath the fog and the darkness?
You have come faster on foot than I could in my black ship.'
    "So I spoke, and he groaned aloud and spoke and answered:
'Son of Laertes and seed of Zeus, resourceful Odysseus,   60
the evil will of the spirit and the wild wine bewildered me.
I lay down on the roof of Circe's palace, and never thought,
when I went down, to go by way of the long ladder,
but blundered straight off the edge of the roof, so that my neck bone
was broken out of it socket, and my soul went down to Hades.   65
But now I pray you, by those you have yet to see, who are not here,
by your wife, and by your father, who reared you when you were little,
and by Telemachos whom you left alone in your palace;
for I know that after you leave this place and the house of Hades
you will put back with your well-made ship to the island, Aiaia;   70
there at that time, my lord, I ask that you remember me,
and do not go and leave me behind unwept, unburied,
when you leave, for fear I might become the gods' curse upon you;
but burn me there with all my armor that belongs to me,
and heap up a grave mound beside the beach of the gray sea,   75
for an unhappy man, so that those to come will know of me.
Do this for me, and on top of the grave mound plant the oar
with which I rowed when I was alive and among my companions.'
    "So he spoke, and I in turn spoke to him in answer:
'All this, my unhappy friend, I will do for you as you ask me.'   80
    "So we two stayed there exchanging our sad words, I on
one side holding my sword over the blood, while opposite
me the phantom of my companion talked long with me.
    "Next there came to me the soul of my dead mother,
Antikleia, daughter of great-hearted Autolykos,   85
whom I had left alive when I went to sacred Ilion.
I broke into tears at the sight of her and my heart pitied her,
but even so, for all my thronging sorrow, I would not
let her draw near the blood until I had questioned Teiresias.
    "Now came the soul of Teiresias the Theban, holding   90
a staff of gold, and he knew who I was, and spoke to me:
'Son of Laertes and seed of Zeus, resourceful Odysseus,
how is it then, unhappy man, you have left the sunlight
and come here, to look on dead men, and this place without pleasure?
Now draw back from the pit, and hold your sharp sword away from me,   95
so that I can drink of the blood and speak the truth to you.'
    "So he spoke, and I, holding away the sword with the silver
nails, pushed it back in the sheath, and the flawless prophet,
after he had drunk the blood, began speaking to me.
'Glorious Odysseus, what you are after is sweet homecoming,   100
but the god will make it hard for you. I think you will not
escape the Shaker of the Earth, who holds a grudge against you
in his heart, and because you blinded his dear son, hates you.
But even so and still you might come back, after much suffering,
if you can contain your own desire, and contain your companions,   105
at that time when you first put in your well-made vessel
at the island Thrinakia, escaping the sea's blue water,
and there discover pasturing the cattle and fat sheep

of Helios, who sees all things, and listens to all things.
Then, if you keep your mind on homecoming, and leave these unharmed,   110
you might all make your way to Ithaka, after much suffering;
but if you do harm them, then I testify to the destruction
of your ship and your companions, but if you yourself get clear,
you will come home in bad case, with the loss of all your companions,
in someone else's ship, and find troubles in your household,   115
insolent men, who are eating away your livelihood
and courting your godlike wife and offering gifts to win her.
You may punish the violences of these men, when you come home.
But after you have killed these suitors in your own palace,
either by treachery, or openly with the sharp bronze,   120
then you must take up your well-shaped oar and go on a journey
until you come where there are men living who know nothing
of the sea, and who eat food that is not mixed with salt, who never
have known ships whose cheeks are painted purple, who never
have known well-shaped oars, which act for ships as wings do.   125
And I will tell you a very clear proof, and you cannot miss it.
When, as you walk, some other wayfarer happens to meet you,
and says you carry a winnow-fan on your bright shoulder,
then you must plant your well-shaped oar in the ground, and render
ceremonious sacrifice to the lord Poseidon,   130
one ram and one bull, and a mounter of sows, a boar pig,
and make your way home again and render holy hecatombs
to the immortal gods who hold the wide heaven, all
of them in order, Death will come to you from the sea, in
some altogether unwarlike way, and it will end you   135
in the ebbing time of a sleek old age. Your people
about you will be prosperous. All this is true that I tell you.'
     "So he spoke, but I in turn said to him in answer:
'All this, Teiresias, surely must be as the gods spun it.
But come now, tell me this and give me an accurate answer.   140
I see before me now the soul of my perished mother,
but she sits beside the blood in silence, and has not yet deigned
to look directly at her own son and speak a word to me.
Tell me, lord, what will make her know me, and know my presence?'
     "So I spoke, and he at once said to me in answer: 145
'Easily I will tell you and put it in your understanding.
Any one of the perished dead you allow to come up
to the blood will give you a true answer, but if you begrudge this
to any one, he will return to the place where he came from.'
     "So speaking, the soul of the lord Teiresias went back into   150
the house of Hades, once he had uttered his prophecies, while I
waited steadily where I was standing, until my mother
came and drank the dark-clouding blood, and at once she knew me,
and full of lamentation she spoke to me in winged words:
'My child, how did you come here beneath the fog and the darkness   155
and still alive? All this is hard for the living to look on,
for in between lie the great rivers and terrible waters
that flow, Ocean first of all, which there is no means of crossing
on foot, not unless one has a well-made ship. Are you
come now to this place from Troy, with your ship and your companions,   160
after wandering a long time, and have you not yet come
to Ithaka, and there seen your wife in your palace?'
     "So she spoke, and I in turn said to her in answer:
'Mother, a duty brought me here to the house of Hades.

I had to consult the soul of Teiresias the Theban.   165
For I have not yet been near Achaian country, nor ever
set foot on our land, but always suffering I have wandered
since the time I first went along with great Agamemnon
to Ilion, land of good horses, and the battle against the Trojans.
But come now, tell me this, and give me an accurate answer.   170
What doom of death that lays men low has been your undoing?
Was it a long sickness, or did Artemis of the arrows
come upon you with her painless shafts, and destroy you?
And tell me of my father and son whom I left behind. Is
my inheritance still with them, or does some other   175
man hold them now, and thinks I will come no more? Tell me
about the wife I married, what she wants, what she is thinking,
and whether she stays fast by my son, and guards everything,
or if she has married the best man among the Achaians.'
    "So I spoke, and my queenly mother answered me quickly: 180
'All too much with enduring heart she does wait for you
there in your own palace, and always with her the wretched
nights and the days also waste her away with weeping.
No one yet holds your fine inheritance, but in freedom
Telemachos administers your allotted lands, and apportions   185
the equal feasts, work that befits a man with authority
to judge, for all call him in. Your father remains, on the estate
where he is, and does not go to the city. There is no bed there
nor is there bed clothing nor blankets nor shining coverlets,
but in the winter time he sleeps in the house, where the thralls do,   190
in the dirt next to the fire, and with foul clothing upon him;
but when the summer comes and the blossoming time of harvest,
everywhere he has places to sleep on the ground, on fallen
leaves in piles along the rising ground of his orchard,
and there he lies, grieving, and the sorrow grows big within him   195
as he longs for your homecoming, and harsh old age is on him.
And so it was with me also and that was the reason I perished,
nor in my palace did the lady of arrows, well-aiming,
come upon me with her painless shafts, and destroy me,
nor was I visited by sickness, which beyond other   200
things takes the life out of the body with hateful weakness,
but, shining Odysseus, it was my longing for you, your cleverness
and your gentle ways, that took the sweet spirit of life from me.'
    "So she spoke, but I, pondering it in my heart, yet wished
to take the soul of my dead mother in my arms. Three times   205
I started toward her, and my heart was urgent to hold her,
and three times she fluttered out of my hands like a shadow
or a dream, and the sorrow sharpened at the heart within me,
and so I spoke to her and addressed her in winged words, saying:
'Mother, why will you not wait for me, when I am trying   210
to hold you, so that even in Hades with our arms embracing
we can both take the satisfaction of dismal mourning?
Or are you nothing but an image that proud Persephone
sent my way, to make me grieve all the more for sorrow?'
    "So I spoke, and my queenly mother answered me quickly: 215
'Oh my child, ill-fated beyond all other mortals,
this is not Persephone, daughter of Zeus, beguiling you,
but it is only what happens, when they die, to all mortals.
The sinews no longer hold the flesh and the bones together,
and once the spirit has left the white bones, all the rest   220

of the body is made subject to the fire's strong fury,
but the soul flitters out like a dream and flies away. Therefore
you must strive back toward the light again with all speed; but remember
these things for your wife, so you may tell her hereafter.'
"So we two were conversing back and forth, and the women   225
came to me. They were sent my way by proud Persephone.
These were all who had been the wives and daughters of princes,
and now they gathered in swarms around the dark blood. I then
thought about a way to question them, each by herself,
and as I thought this was the plan that seemed best to me;   230
drawing out the long-edged sword from beside my big thigh,
I would not let them all drink the dark blood at the same time.
So they waited and came to me in order, and each one
told me about her origin, and I questioned all of them.
"There first I saw Tyro, gloriously descended,   235
and she told me she was the daughter of stately Salmoneus,
but said she was the wife of Kretheus, the son of Aiolos,
and she was in love with a river, godlike Enipeus, by far
the handsomest of all those rivers whose streams cross over
the earth, and she used to haunt Enipeus' beautiful waters;   240
taking his likeness, the god who circles the earth and shakes it
lay with her where the swirling river finds its outlet,
and a sea-blue wave curved into a hill of water reared up
about the two, to hide the god and the mortal woman;
and he broke her virgin zone and drifted a sleep upon her.   245
But when the god had finished with the act of lovemaking,
he took her by the hand and spoke to her and named her, saying:
'Be happy, lady, in this love, and when the year passes
you will bear glorious children, for the couplings of the immortals
are not without issue. You must look after them, and raise them.   250
Go home now and hold your peace and tell nobody
my name, but I tell it to you; I am the Earthshaker Poseidon.'
"So he spoke and dived back into the heaving water
of the sea, but she conceived and bore Pelias and Neleus,
and both of these grew up to be strong henchmen of mighty   255
Zeus; Pelias lived, rich in sheepflocks, in the wide spaces
of Iolkos, while the other was king in sandy Pylos;
but this queen among women bore the rest of her children to Kretheus,
Aison and Pheres and Amythaon delighting in horses.
"After her I saw Antiope, who was the daughter   260
of Asopos, who claimed she had also lain in the embraces
of Zeus, and borne two sons to him, Amphion and Zethos.
These first established the foundations of seven-gated
Thebes, and built the bulwarks, since without bulwarks they could not
have lived, for all their strength, in Thebes of the wide spaces.   265
"After her I saw Amphitryon's wife, Alkmene,
who, after lying in love in the embraces of great Zeus,
brought forth Herakles, lion-hearted and bold of purpose.
And I saw Megara, daughter of high-spirited Kreion,
whom Amphitryon's bold and weariless son had married.   270
"I saw the beautiful Epikaste, Oidipodes' mother,
who in the ignorance of her mind had done a monstrous
thing when she married her own son. He killed his father
and married her, but the gods soon made it all known to mortals.
But he, for all his sorrows, in beloved Thebes continued   275
to be lord over the Kadmeians, all through the bitter designing

of the gods; while she went down to Hades of the gates, the strong one,
knotting a noose and hanging sheer from the high ceiling,
in the constraint of her sorrow, but left to him who survived her
all the sorrows that are brought to pass by a mother's furies.   280
    "And I saw Chloris, surpassingly lovely, the one whom Neleus
married for her beauty, giving numberless gifts to win her.
She was the youngest daughter of Iasos' son Amphion,
who once ruled strongly over Orchomenos of the Minyai.
So she was queen of Pylos and she bore him glorious children,   285
Nestor and Chromios and proud Periklymenos. Also
she bore that marvel among mortals, majestic Pero,
whom all the heroes round about courted, but Neleus would not
give her to any, unless he could drive away the broad-faced
horn-curved cattle of strong Iphikles out of Phylake.   290
It was hard to do, and only the blameless seer Melampous
undertook it, but he was bound fast by the hard destiny
of the god, and the painful fetters on him, and the loutish oxherds.
But when the months and the days had come to an end, and the year
had gone full circle and come back with the seasons returning,   295
then strong Iphikles released him, when he had told him
all prophecies he knew; and the will of Zeus was accomplished.
    "And I saw Leda, who had been the wife of Tyndareos,
and she had borne to Tyndareos two sons with strong hearts,
Kastor, breaker of horses, and the strong boxer, Polydeukes.   300
The life-giving earth holds both of them, yet they are still living,
and, even underneath the earth, enjoying the honor
of Zeus, they live still every other day; on the next day
they are dead, but they are given honor even as gods are.
    "After her I saw Iphimedeia, wife of Aloeus,   305
but she told me how she had been joined in love with Poseidon
and borne two sons to him, but these in the end had not lived
long, Otos like a god, and the far-famed Ephialtes;
and these were the tallest men the grain-giving earth has brought forth
ever, and the handsomest by far, after famous Orion.   310
When they were only nine years old they measured nine cubits
across, but in height they grew to nine fathoms, and even made threat
against the immortal gods on Olympos, that they would carry
the turmoil of battle with all its many sorrows against them,
and were minded to pile Ossa on Olympos, and above Ossa   315
Pelion of the trembling leaves, to climb the sky. Surely
they would have carried it out if they had come to maturity,
but the son of Zeus whom Leto with ordered hair had borne him,
Apollo, killed them both, before ever the down gathered
below their temples, or on their chins the beards had blossomed.   320
    "I saw Phaidra and Prokris and Ariadne, the beautiful
daughter of malignant Minos. Theseus at one time
was bringing her from Crete to the high ground of sacred Athens,
but got no joy of her, since before that Artemis killed her
in sea-washed Dia, when Dionysos bore witness against her.   325
    "I saw Maira, Klymene, and Eriphyle the hateful,
who accepted precious gold for the life of her own dear husband.
But I could not tell over the whole number of them nor name all
the women I saw who were the wives and daughters of heroes,
for before that the divine night would give out. It is time now   330
for my sleep, either joining my companions on board the fast ship,
or here; but you, and the gods, will see to my homeward journey."

So he spoke, and all of them stayed stricken to silence,
held in thrall by the story all through the shadowy chambers.
Now it was white-armed Arete who began the discourse: 335
"Phaiakians, what do you think now of this man before you
for beauty and stature, and for the mind well balanced within him?
And again he is my own guest, but each one of you has some part
in honoring him. Do not hurry to send him off, nor cut short
his gifts, when he is in such need, for you all have many   340
possessions, by the grace of the gods, stored up in your palaces."
    Then in turn the aged hero Echeneos spoke forth,
who was the most advanced in age of all the Phaiakians:
"Friends, our circumspect queen is not off the mark in her speaking,
nor short of what we expect of her. Do then as she tells us.   345
From now on the word and the act belong to Alkinoös."
    Then in turn Alkinoös spoke to him and answered:
"Even so this word will be mine to say, as long as
I am alive and king over the oar-loving Phaiakians.
But let our guest, much though he longs for the homeward journey,   350
still endure to wait till tomorrow, until I have raised all
the contribution; but the men shall see to his convoy
home, and I most of all; for mine is the power in this district."
    Then resourceful Odysseus spoke in turn and answered him:
"O great Alkinoös, pre-eminent among all people,   355
if you urged me to stay here even for the length of a year,
and still sped my conveyance home and gave me glorious
presents, that would be what I wished, there would be much advantage
in coming back with a fuller hand to my own dear country,
and I would be more respected so and be more popular   360
with all people who saw me make my return to Ithaka."
    Then Alkinoös answered him in turn and said to him:
"Odysseus, we as we look upon you do not imagine
that you are a deceptive or thievish man, the sort that the black earth
breeds in great numbers, people who wander widely, making up   365
lying stories, from which no one could learn anything. You have
a grace upon your words, and there is sound sense within them,
and expertly, as a singer would do, you have told the story
of the dismal sorrows befallen yourself and all of the Argives.
But come now, tell me this and give me an accurate answer: 370
Did you see any of your godlike companions, who once with you
went to Ilion and there met their destiny? Here is
a night that is very long, it is endless. It is not time yet
to sleep in the palace. But go on telling your wonderful story.
I myself could hold out until the bright dawn, if only   375
you could bear to tell me, here in the palace, of your sufferings."
    Then resourceful Odysseus spoke in turn and answered him:
"O great Alkinoös, pre-eminent among all people,
there is a time for many words, and a time for sleeping;
but if you insist on hearing me still, I would not begrudge you   380
the tale of these happenings and others yet more pitiful
to hear, the sorrows of my companions, who perished later,
who escaped onslaught and cry of battle, but perished
all for the sake of a vile woman, on the homeward journey.
    "Now when chaste Persephone had scattered the female   385
souls of the women, driving them off in every direction,
there came the soul of Agamemnon, the son of Atreus,
grieving, and the souls of the other men, who died with him

and met their doom in the house of Aigisthos, were gathered around him.
He knew me at once, when he drank the dark blood, and fell to   390
lamentation loud and shrill, and the tears came springing,
and threw himself into my arms, meaning so to embrace me,
but there was no force there any longer, nor any juice left
now in his flexible limbs, as there had been in time past.
I broke into tears at the sight of him and my heart pitied him,   395
and so I spoke aloud to him and addressed him in winged words:
'Son of Atreus, most lordly and king of men, Agamemnon,
what doom of death that lays men low has been your undoing?
Was it with the ships, and did Poseidon, rousing a stormblast
of battering winds that none would wish for, prove your undoing?   400
Or was it on the dry land, did men embattled destroy you
as you tried to cut out cattle and fleecy sheep from their holdings,
or fighting against them for the sake of their city and women?'
    "So I spoke, and he in turn said to me in answer:
'Son of Laertes and seed of Zeus, resourceful Odysseus,   405
not in the ships, nor did Poseidon, rousing a stormblast
of battering winds that none would wish for, prove my destruction,
nor on dry land did enemy men destroy me in battle;
Aigisthos, working out my death and destruction, invited
me to his house, and feasted me, and killed me there, with the help   410
of my sluttish wife, as one cuts down an ox at his manger.
So I died a most pitiful death, and my other companions
were killed around me without mercy, like pigs with shining
tusks, in the house of a man rich and very powerful,
for a wedding, or a festival, or a communal dinner.   415
You have been present in your time at the slaughter of many
men, killed singly, or in the strong encounters of battle;
but beyond all others you would have been sorry at heart
for this scene, how we lay sprawled by the mixing bowl and the loaded
tables, all over the palace, and the whole floor was steaming   420
with blood; and most pitiful was the voice I heard of Priam's
daughter Kassandra, killed by treacherous Klytaimestra
over me; but I lifted my hands and with them beat on
the ground as I died upon the sword, but the sluttish woman
turned away from me and was so hard that her hands would not   425
press shut my eyes and mouth though I was going to Hades.
So there is nothing more deadly or more vile than a woman
who stores her mind with acts that are of such sort, as this one
did when she thought of this act of dishonor, and plotted
the murder of her lawful husband. See, I had been thinking   430
that I would be welcome to my children and thralls of my household
when I came home, but she with thoughts surpassingly grisly
splashed the shame on herself and the rest of her sex, on women
still to come, even on the one whose acts are virtuous.'
    "So he spoke, and I again said to him in answer: 435
'Shame it is, how most terribly Zeus of the wide brows
from the beginning has been hateful to the seed of Atreus
through the schemes of women. Many of us died for the sake of Helen,
and when you were far, Klytaimestra plotted treason against you.'
    "So I spoke, and he in turn said to me in answer: 440
'So by this, do not be too easy even with your wife,
nor give her an entire account of all you are sure of.
Tell her part of it, but let the rest be hidden in silence.
And yet you, Odysseus, will never be murdered by your wife.

The daughter of Ikarios, circumspect Penelope, 445
is all too virtuous and her mind is stored with good thoughts.
Ah well. She was only a young wife when we left her
and went off to the fighting, and she had an infant child then
at her breast. That child now must sit with the men and be counted.
Happy he! For his dear father will come back, and see him, 450
and he will fold his father in his arms, as is right. My wife
never even let me feed my eyes with the sight of
my own son, but before that I myself was killed by her.
And put away in your heart this other thing that I tell you.
When you bring your ship in to your own dear country, do it 455
secretly, not in the open. There is no trusting in women.
But come now, tell me this and give me an accurate answer;
tell me if you happened to hear that my son was still living,
whether perhaps in Orchomenos, or in sandy Pylos,
or perhaps with Menelaos in wide Sparta; for nowhere 460
upon the earth has there been any death of noble Orestes.'
    "So he spoke, and I again said to him in answer:
'Son of Atreus, why do you ask me that? I do not know
if he is alive or dead. It is bad to babble emptily.'
    "So we two stood there exchanging our sad words, grieving 465
both together and shedding the big tears. After this,
there came to us the soul of Peleus' son, Achilleus,
and the soul of Patroklos and the soul of stately Antilochos,
and the soul of Aias, who for beauty and stature was greatest
of all the Danaans, next to the stately son of Peleus. 470
The soul of swift-footed Achilleus, scion of Aiakos, knew me,
and full of lamentation he spoke to me in winged words:
'Son of Laertes and seed of Zeus, resourceful Odysseus,
hard man, what made you think of this bigger endeavor, how could you
endure to come down here to Hades' place, where the senseless 475
dead men dwell, mere imitations of perished mortals?'
    "So he spoke, and I again said to him in answer:
'Son of Peleus, far the greatest of the Achaians, Achilleus,
I came for the need to consult Teiresias, if he might tell me
some plan by which I might come back to rocky Ithaka; 480
for I have not yet been near Achaian country, nor ever
set foot on my land, but always I have troubles. Achilleus,
no man before has been more blessed than you, nor ever
will be. Before, when you were alive, we Argives honored you
a we did the gods, and now in this place you have great authority 485
over the dead. Do not grieve, even in death, Achilleus.'
    "So I spoke, and he in turn said to me in answer:
'O shining Odysseus, never try to console me for dying.
I would rather follow the plow as thrall to another
man, one with no land allotted him and not much to live on, 490
than be a king over all the perished dead. But come now,
tell me anything you have heard of my proud son, whether
or not he went along to war to fight as a champion;
and tell me anything you have heard about stately Peleus,
whether he still keeps his position among the Myrmidon 495
hordes, or whether in Hellas and Phthia they have diminished
his state, because old age constrains his hands and feet, and I
am no longer there under the light of the sun to help him,
not the man I used to be once, when in the wide Troad
I killed the best of their people, fighting for the Argives. If only 500

for a little while I could come like that to the house of my father,
my force and my invincible hands would terrify such men
as use force on him and keep him away from his rightful honors.'
    "So he spoke, and I again said to him in answer:
'I have no report to give you of stately Peleus,   505
but as for your beloved son Neoptolemos, I will
tell you, since you ask me to do it, all the true story;
for I myself, in the hollow hull of a balanced ship, brought him
over from Skyros, to join the strong-greaved Achaians. Whenever
we, around the city of Troy, talked over our counsels,   510
he would always speak first, and never blunder. In speaking
only godlike Nestor and I were better than he was.
And when we Achaians fought in the Trojan plain, he never
would hang back where there were plenty of other men, nor stay with
the masses, but run far out in front, giving way to no man   515
for fury, and many were those he killed in the terrible fighting.
I could not tell over the number of all nor name all
the people he killed as he fought for the Argives, but what a great man
was one, the son of Telephos he slew with the brazen
spear, the hero Eurypylos, and many Keteian   520
companions were killed about him, by reason of womanish presents.
Next to great Memnon, this was the finest man I ever
saw. Again, when we who were best of the Argives entered
the horse that Epeios made, and all the command was given
to me, to keep close hidden inside, or sally out from it,   525
the other leaders of the Danaans and men of counsel
were wiping their tears away and the limbs were shaking under
each man of them; but never at any time did I see him
losing his handsome color and going pale, or wiping
the tears off his face, but rather he implored me to let him   530
sally out of the horse; he kept feeling for his sword hilt
and spear weighted with bronze, full of evil thoughts for the Trojans.
But after we had sacked the sheer citadel of Priam,
with his fair share and a princely prize of his own, he boarded
his ship, unscathed; he had not been hit by thrown and piercing   535
bronze, nor stabbed in close-up combat, as often happens
in fighting. The War God rages at all, and favors no man.'
    "So I spoke, and the soul of the swift-footed scion of Aiakos
stalked away in long strides across the meadow of asphodel,
happy for what I had said of his son, and how he was famous.   540
    "Now the rest of the souls of the perished dead stood near me
grieving, and each one spoke to me and told of his sorrows.
Only the soul of Telamonian Aias stood off
at a distance from me, angry still over that decision
I won against him, when beside the ships we disputed   545
our cases for the arms of Achilleus. His queenly mother
set them as prize, and the sons of the Trojans, with Pallas Athene,
judged; and I wish I had never won in a contest like this,
so high a head has gone under the ground for the sake of that armor,
Aias, who for beauty and for achievement surpassed   550
all the Danaans next to the stately son of Peleus.
So I spoke to him now in words of conciliation:
'Aias, son of stately Telamon, could you then never
even in death forget your anger against me, because of
that cursed armor? The gods made it to pain the Achaians,   555
so great a bulwark were you, who were lost to them. We Achaians

grieved for your death as incessantly as for Achilleus
the son of Peleus at his death, and there is no other
to blame, but Zeus; he, in his terrible hate for the army
of Danaan spearmen, visited this destruction upon you.   560
Come nearer, my lord, so you can hear what I say and listen
to my story; suppress your anger and lordly spirit.'
    "So I spoke. He gave no answer, but went off after
the other souls of the perished dead men, into the darkness.
There, despite his anger, he might have spoken, or I might   565
have spoken to him, but the heart in my inward breast wanted
still to see the souls of the other perished dead men.
    "There I saw Minos, the glorious son of Zeus, seated,
holding a golden scepter and issuing judgments among
the dead, who all around the great lord argued their cases,   570
some sitting and some standing, by the wide-gated house of Hades.
    "After him I was aware of gigantic Orion
in the meadow of asphodel, rounding up and driving together
wild animals he himself had killed in the lonely mountains,
holding in his hands a brazen club, forever unbroken.   575
    "And I saw Tityos, Earth's glorious son, lying
in the plain, and sprawled over nine acres. Two vultures,
sitting one on either side, were tearing his liver,
plunging inside the caul. With his hands he could not beat them
away. He had manhandled Leto, the honored consort   580
of Zeus, as she went through spacious Panopeus, toward Pytho.
    "And I saw Tantalos also, suffering hard pains, standing
in lake water that came up to his chin, and thirsty
as he was, he tried to drink, but could capture nothing;
for every time the old man, trying to drink, stooped over,   585
the water would drain away and disappear, and the black earth
showed at his feet, and the divinity dried it away. Over
his head trees with lofty branches had fruit like a shower descending,
pear trees and pomegranate trees and apple trees with fruit shining,
and figs that were sweet and olives ripened well, but each time   590
the old man would straighten up and reach with his hands for them,
the wind would toss them away toward the clouds overhanging.
    "Also I saw Sisyphos. He was suffering strong pains,
and with both arms embracing the monstrous stone, struggling
with hands and feet alike, he would try to push the stone upward   595
to the crest of the hill, but when it was on the point of going
over the top, the force of gravity turned it backward,
and the pitiless stone rolled back down to the level. He then
tried once more to push it up, straining hard, and sweat ran
all down his body, and over his head a cloud of dust rose.   600
    "After him I was aware of powerful Herakles;
his image, that is, but he himself among the immortal
gods enjoys their festivals, married to sweet-stepping
Hebe, child of great Zeus and Hera of the golden sandals.
All around him was a clamor of the dead as of birds scattering   605
scared in every direction; but he came on, like dark night,
holding his bow bare with an arrow laid on the bowstring,
and forever looking, as one who shot, with terrible glances.
There was a terrible belt crossed over his chest, and a golden
baldrick, with marvelous works of art that figured upon it,   610
bears, and lions with glaring eyes, and boars of the forests,
the battles and the quarrels, the murders and the manslaughters.

May he who artfully designed them, and artfully put them
upon that baldrick, never again do any designing.
He recognized me at once as soon as his eyes had seen me,   615
and full of lamentation he spoke to me in winged words:
'Son of Laertes and seed of Zeus, resourceful Odysseus,
unhappy man, are you too leading some wretched destiny
such as I too pursued when I went still in the sunlight?
For I was son of Kronian Zeus, but I had an endless   620
spell of misery. I was made bondman to one who was far worse
than I, and he loaded my difficult labors on me. One time
he sent me here to fetch the dog back, and thought there could be
no other labor to be devised more difficult than that
one, but I brought the dog up and led him from the realm of Hades,   625
and Hermes saw me on my way, with Pallas Athene.'
    "So he spoke, and went back into the realm of Hades,
but I stayed fast in place where I was, to see if some other
one of the generation of heroes who died before me
would come; and I might have seen men earlier still, whom I wanted   630
to see, Perithoös and Theseus, gods' glorious children;
but before that the hordes of the dead men gathered about me
with inhuman clamor, and green fear took hold of me
with the thought that proud Persephone might send up against me
some gorgonish head of a terrible monster up out of Hades.   635
So, going back on board my ship, I told my companions
also to go aboard, and to cast off the stern cables;
and quickly they went aboard the ship and sat to the oarlocks,
and the swell of the current carried her down the Ocean river
with rowing at first, but after that on a fair wind following.   640

Book XII

    "Now when our ship had left the stream of the Ocean river,
and come back to the wide crossing of the sea's waves, and to the island
of Aiaia, where lies the house of the early Dawn, her dancing
spaces, and where Helios, the sun, makes his uprising,
making this point we ran our ship on the sand and beached her,   5
and we ourselves stepped out onto the break of the sea beach,
and there we fell asleep and waited for the divine Dawn.
    "But when the young Dawn showed again with her rosy fingers,
then I sent my companions away to the house of Circe
to bring back the body of Elpenor, who had died there.   10
Then we cut logs, and where the extreme of the foreland jutted
out, we buried him, sorrowful, shedding warm tears for him.
But when the dead man had burned and the dead man's armor, piling
the grave mound and pulling the gravestone to stand above it,
we planted the well-shaped oar in the very top of the grave mound.   15
    "So we were busy each with our various work, nor was Circe
unaware that we had come back from Hades. Presently
she came, attired, and her attendants following carried
bread at her will and many meats and the shining red wine.
Bright among goddesses she stood in our midst and addressed us: 20
'Unhappy men, who went alive to the house of Hades,

so dying twice, when all the rest of mankind die only
once, come then eat what is there and drink your wine, staying
here all the rest of the day, and then tomorrow, when dawn shows,
you shall sail, and I will show you the way and make plain   25
all details, so that neither by land nor on the salt water
you may suffer and come to grief by unhappy bad designing.'
  "So she spoke, and the proud heart in us was persuaded.
So for the whole length of the day until the sun's setting,
we sat there feasting on unlimited meat and sweet wine.   30
But when the sun went down and the sacred darkness came over,
the men lay down to sleep all by the ship's stern cables,
but she, taking me by the hand, made me sit down away from
my dear companions, and talked with me, and asked me the details
of everything, and I recited all, just as it had happened.   35
Then the queenly Circe spoke in words and addressed me:
'So all that has been duly done. Listen now, I will tell you
all, but the very god himself will make you remember.
You will come first of all to the Sirens, who are enchanters
of all mankind and whoever comes their way; and that man   40
who unsuspecting approaches them, and listens to the Sirens
singing, has no prospect of coming home and delighting
his wife and little children as they stand about him in greeting,
but the Sirens by the melody of their singing enchant him.
They sit in their meadow, but the beach before it is piled with boneheaps   45
of men now rotted away, and the skins shrivel upon them.
You must drive straight on past, but melt down sweet wax of honey
and with it stop your companions' ears, so none can listen;
the rest, that is, but if you yourself are wanting to hear them,
then have them tie you hand and foot on the fast ship, standing   50
upright against the mast with the ropes' ends lashed around it,
so that you can have joy in hearing the song of the Sirens;
but if you supplicate your men and implore them to set you
free, then they must tie you fast with even more lashings.
  'Then, for the time when your companions have driven you past them,   55
for that time I will no longer tell you in detail which way
of the two your course must lie, but you yourself must consider
this in your own mind. I will tell you the two ways of it.
On one side there are overhanging rocks, and against them
crashes the heavy swell of dark-eyed Amphitrite.   60
The blessed gods call these rocks the Rovers. By this way
not even any flying thing, not even the tremulous
doves, which carry ambrosia to Zeus the father, can pass through,
but every time the sheer rock catches away one even
of these; but the Father then adds another to keep the number   65
right. No ship of men that came here ever has fled through,
but the waves of the sea and storms of ravening fire carry
away together the ship's timbers and the men's bodies.
That way the only seagoing ship to get through was Argo,
who is in all men's minds, on her way home from Aietes;   70
and even she would have been driven on the great rocks that time,
but Hera saw her through, out of her great love for Jason.
  "'But of the two rocks, one reaches up into the wide heaven
with a pointed peak, and a dark cloud stands always around it,
and never at any time draws away from it, nor does the sunlight   75
ever hold that peak, either in the early or the late summer,
nor could any man who was mortal climb there, or stand mounted

on the summit, not if he had twenty hands and twenty
feet, for the rock goes sheerly up, as if it were polished.
Halfway up the cliff there is a cave, misty-looking   80
and turned toward Erebos and the dark, the very direction
from which, O shining Odysseus, you and your men will be steering
your hollow ship; and from the hollow ship no vigorous
young man with a bow could shoot to the hole in the cliffside.
In that cavern Skylla lives, whose howling is terror.   85
Her voice indeed is only as loud as a new-born puppy
could make, but she herself is an evil monster. No one,
not even a god encountering her, could be glad at that sight.
She has twelve feet, and all of them wave in the air. She has six
necks upon her, grown to great length, and upon each neck   90
there is a horrible head, with teeth in it, set in three rows
close together and stiff, full of black death. Her body
from the waist down is holed up inside the hollow cavern,
but she holds her heads poked out and away from the terrible hollow,
and there she fishes, peering all over the cliffside, looking   95
for dolphins or dogfish to catch or anything bigger,
some sea monster, of whom Amphitrite keeps so many;
never can sailors boast aloud that their ship has passed her
without any loss of men, for with each of her heads she snatches
one man away and carries him off from the dark-prowed vessel.   100
"'The other cliff is lower; you will see it, Odysseus,
for they lie close together, you could even cast with an arrow
across. There is a great fig tree grows there, dense with foliage,
and under this shining Charybdis sucks down the black water.
For three times a day she flows it up, and three times she sucks it   105
terribly down; may you not be there when she sucks down water,
for not even the Earthshaker could rescue you out of that evil.
But sailing your ship swiftly drive her past and avoid her,
and make for Skylla's rock instead, since it is far better
to mourn six friends lost out of your ship than the whole company.'   110
    "So she spoke, but I in turn said to her in answer:
'Come then, goddess, answer me truthfully this: is there
some way for me to escape away from deadly Charybdis,
but yet fight the other one off, when she attacks my companions?'
    "So I spoke, and she, shining among goddesses, answered: 115
'Hardy man, your mind is full forever of fighting
and battle work. Will you not give way even to the immortals?
She is no mortal thing but a mischief immortal, dangerous
difficult and bloodthirsty, and there is no fighting against her,
nor any force of defense. It is best to run away from her.   120
For if you arm for battle beside her rock and waste time
there, I fear she will make another outrush and catch you
with all her heads, and snatch away once more the same number
of men. Drive by as hard as you can, but invoke Krataiis.
She is the mother of Skylla and bore this mischief for mortals,   125
and she will stay from making another sally against you.
    "'Then you will reach the island Thrinakia, where are pastured
the cattle and the fat sheep of the sun god, Helios,
seven herds of oxen, and as many beautiful sheepflocks,
and fifty to each herd. There is no giving birth among them,   130
nor do they ever die away, and their shepherdesses
are gods, nymphs with sweet hair, Lampetia and Phaethousa,
whom shining Neaira bore to Hyperion the sun god.

These, when their queenly mother had given them birth and reared them,
she settled in the island Thrinakia, far away, to live   135
there and guard their father's sheep and his horn-curved cattle.
Then, if you keep your mind on homecoming and leave these unharmed,
you might all make your way to Ithaka, after much suffering;
but if you do harm them, then I testify to the destruction
of your ship and your companions, but if you yourself get clear,   140
you will come home in bad case with the loss of all your companions.'
    "So she spoke, and Dawn of the golden throne came on us.
She, shining among goddesses, went away, up the island.
Then, going back on board my ship, I told my companions
also to go aboard, and to cast off the stern cables,   145
and quickly they went aboard the ship and sat to the oarlocks,
and sitting well in order dashed the oars in the gray sea;
but fair-haired Circe, the dread goddess who talks with mortals,
sent us an excellent companion, a following wind, filling
the sails, to carry from astern the ship with the dark prow.   150
We ourselves, over all the ship making fast the running gear,
sat there, and let the wind and the steersman hold her steady.
Then, sorrowful as I was, I spoke and told my companions:
'Friends, since it is not right for one or two of us only
to know the divinations that Circe, bright among goddesses,   155
gave me, so I will tell you, and knowing all we may either
die, or turn aside from death and escape destruction.
First of all she tells us to keep away from the magical
Sirens and their singing and their flowery meadow, but only
I, she said, was to listen to them, but you must tie me   160
hard in hurtful bonds, to hold me fast in position
upright against the mast, with the ropes' ends fastened around it;
but if I supplicate you and implore you to set me
free, then you must tie me fast with even more lashings.'
    "So as I was telling all the details to my companions,   165
meanwhile the well-made ship was coming rapidly closer
to the Sirens' isle, for the harmless wind was driving her onward;
but immediately then the breeze dropped, and a windless
calm fell there, and some divinity stilled the tossing
waters. My companions stood up, and took the sails down,   170
and stowed them away in the hollow hull, and took their places
for rowing, and with their planed oarblades whitened the water.
Then I, taking a great wheel of wax, with the sharp bronze
cut a little piece off, and rubbed it together in my heavy
hands, and soon the wax grew softer, under the powerful   175
stress of the sun, and the heat and light of Hyperion's lordling.
One after another, I stopped the ears of all my companions,
and they then bound me hand and foot in the fast ship, standing
upright against the mast with the ropes' ends lashed around it,
and sitting then to row they dashed their oars in the gray sea.   180
But when we were as far from the land as a voice shouting
carries, lightly plying, the swift ship as it drew nearer
was seen by the Sirens, and they directed their sweet song toward us:
'Come this way, honored Odysseus, great glory of the Achaians,
and stay your ship, so that you can listen here to our singing;   185
for no one else has ever sailed past this place in his black ship
until he has listened to the honey-sweet voice that issues
from our lips; then goes on, well pleased, knowing more than ever
he did; for we know everything that the Argives and Trojans

did and suffered in wide Troy through the gods' despite.   190
Over all the generous earth we know everything that happens.'
    "So they sang, in sweet utterance, and the heart within me
desired to listen, and I signaled my companions to set me
free, nodding with my brows, but they leaned on and rowed hard,
and Perimedes and Eurylochos, rising up, straightway   195
fastened me with even more lashings and squeezed me tighter.
But when they had rowed on past the Sirens, and we could no longer
hear their voices and lost the sound of their singing, presently
my eager companions took away from their ears the beeswax
with which I had stopped them. Then they set me free from my lashings.   200
    "But after we had left the island behind, the next thing
we saw was smoke, and a heavy surf, and we heard it thundering.
The men were terrified, and they let the oars fall out of
their hands, and these banged all about in the wash. The ship stopped
still, with the men no longer rowing to keep way on her.   205
Then I going up and down the ship urged on my companions,
standing beside each man and speaking to him in kind words:
'Dear friends, surely we are not unlearned in evils.
This is no greater evil now than it was when the Cyclops
had us cooped in his hollow cave by force and violence,   210
but even there, by my courage and counsel and my intelligence,
we escaped away. I think that all this will be remembered
some day too. Then do as I say, let us all be won over.
Sit well, all of you, to your oarlocks, and dash your oars deep
into the breaking surf of the water, so in that way Zeus   215
might grant that we get clear of this danger and flee away from it.
For you, steersman, I have this order; so store it deeply
in your mind, as you control the steering oar of this hollow
ship; you must keep her clear from where the smoke and the breakers
are, and make hard for the sea rock lest, without your knowing,   220
she might drift that way, and you bring all of us into disaster.'
    "So I spoke, and they quickly obeyed my words. I had not
spoken yet of Skylla, a plague that could not be dealt with,
for fear my companions might be terrified and give over
their rowing, and take cover inside the ship. For my part,   225
I let go from my mind the difficult instruction that Circe
had given me, for she told me not to be armed for combat;
but I put on my glorious armor and, taking up two long
spears in my hands, I stood bestriding the vessel's foredeck
at the prow, for I expected Skylla of the rocks to appear first   230
from that direction, she who brought pain to my companions.
I could not make her out anywhere, and my eyes grew weary
from looking everywhere on the misty face of the sea rock.
    "So we sailed up the narrow strait lamenting. On one side
was Skylla, and on the other side was shining Charybdis,   235
who made her terrible ebb and flow of the sea's water.
When she vomited it up, like a caldron over a strong fire,
the whole sea would boil up in turbulence, and the foam flying
spattered the pinnacles of the rocks in either direction;
but when in turn again she sucked down the sea's salt water,   240
the turbulence showed all the inner sea, and the rock around it
groaned terribly, and the ground showed at the sea's bottom,
black with sand; and green fear seized upon my companions.
We in fear of destruction kept our eyes on Charybdis,
but meanwhile Skylla out of the hollow vessel snatched six   245

of my companions, the best of them for strength and hands' work,
and when I turned to look at the ship, with my other companions,
I saw their feet and hands from below, already lifted
high above me, and they cried out to me and called me
by name, the last time they ever did it, in heart's sorrow;   250
And as a fisherman with a very long rod, on a jutting
rock, will cast his treacherous bait for the little fishes,
and sinks the horn of a field-ranging ox into the water,
then hauls them up and throws them on the dry land, gasping
and struggling, so they gasped and struggled as they were hoisted   255
up the cliff. Right in her doorway she ate them up. They were screaming
and reaching out their hands to me in this horrid encounter.
That was the most pitiful scene that these eyes have looked on
in my sufferings as I explored the routes over the water.
    "Now when we had fled away from the rocks and dreaded Charybdis   260
and Skylla, next we made our way to the excellent island
of the god, where ranged the handsome wide-browed oxen, and many
fat flocks of sheep, belonging to the Sun God, Hyperion.
While I was on the black ship, still out on the open water,
I heard the lowing of the cattle as they were driven   265
home, and the bleating of sheep, and my mind was struck by the saying
of the blind prophet, Teiresias the Theban, and also
Aiaian Circe. Both had told me many times over
to avoid the island of Helios who brings joy to mortals.
Then sorrowful as I was I spoke and told my companions: 270
'Listen to what I say, my companions, though you are suffering
evils, while I tell you the prophecies of Teiresias
and Aiaian Circe. Both have told me many times over
to avoid the island of Helios who brings joy to mortals,
for there they spoke of the most dreadful disaster that waited   275
for us. So drive the black ship onward, and pass the island.'
    "So I spoke, and the inward heart in them was broken.
At once Eurylochos answered me with a bitter saying:
'You are a hard man, Odysseus. Your force is greater,
your limbs never wear out. You must be made all of iron,   280
when you will not let your companions, worn with hard work and wanting
sleep, set foot on this land, where if we did, on the seagirt
island we could once more make ready a greedy dinner;
but you force us to blunder along just as we are through the running
night, driven from the island over the misty face of the water.   285
In the nights the hard stormwinds arise, and they bring damage
to ships. How could any of us escape sheer destruction,
if suddenly there rises the blast of a storm from the bitter
blowing of the South Wind or the West Wind, who beyond others
hammer a ship apart, in despite of the gods, our masters?   290
But now let us give way to black night's persuasion; let us
make ready our evening meal, remaining close by our fast ship,
and at dawn we will go aboard and put forth onto the wide sea.'
    "So spoke Eurylochos, and my other companions assented.
I saw then what evil the divinity had in mind for us,   295
and so I spoke aloud to him and addressed him in winged words:
'Eurylochos, I am only one man. You force me to it.
But come then all of you, swear a strong oath to me, that if
we come upon some herd of cattle or on some great flock
of sheep, no one of you in evil and reckless action   300
will slaughter any ox or sheep. No, rather than this, eat

at your pleasure of the food immortal Circe provided.'
  "So I spoke, and they all swore me the oath that I asked them.
But after they had sworn me the oath and made an end of it
we beached the well-made ship inside of the hollow harbor,   305
close to sweet water, and my companions disembarked also
from the ship, and expertly made the evening meal ready.
But when they had put away their desire for eating and drinking,
they remembered and they cried for their beloved companions
whom Skylla had caught out of the hollow ship and eaten,   310
and on their crying a quiet sleep descended; but after
the third part of the night had come, and the star changes,
Zeus the cloud gatherer let loose on us a gale that blustered
in a supernatural storm, and huddled under the cloud scuds
land alike and the great water. Night sprang from heaven.   315
But when the young Dawn showed again with her rosy fingers,
we berthed our ship, dragging her into a hollow sea cave
where the nymphs had their beautiful dancing places and sessions.
Then I held an assembly and spoke my opinion before them:
'Friends, since there is food and drink stored in the fast ship,   320
let us then keep our hands off the cattle, for fear that something
may befall us. These are the cattle and fat sheep of a dreaded
god, Helios, who sees all things and listens to all things.'
  "So I spoke, and the proud heart in them was persuaded.
But the South Wind blew for a whole month long, nor did any other   325
wind befall after that, but only the South and the East Wind.
As long as they still had food to eat and red wine, the men kept
their hands off the cattle, striving as they were for sustenance. Then, when
all the provisions that had been in the ship had given
out, they turned to hunting, forced to it, and went ranging   330
after fish and birds, anything that they could lay hands on,
and with curved hooks, for the hunger was exhausting their stomachs.
Then I went away along the island in order
to pray to the gods, if any of them might show me some course
to sail on, but when, crossing the isle, I had left my companions   335
behind, I washed my hands, where there was a place sheltered
from the wind, and prayed to all the gods whose hold is Olympos;
but what they did was to shed a sweet sleep on my eyelids,
and Eurylochos put an evil counsel before his companions:
'Listen to what I say, my companions, though you are suffering   340
evils. All deaths are detestable for wretched mortals,
but hunger is the sorriest way to die and encounter
fate. Come then, let us cut out the best of Helios' cattle,
and sacrifice them to the immortals who hold wide heaven,
and if we ever come back to Ithaka, land of our fathers,   345
presently we will build a rich temple to the Sun God Helios
Hyperion, and store it with dedications, many
and good. But if, in anger over his high-horned cattle,
he wishes to wreck our ship, and the rest of the gods stand by him,
I would far rather gulp the waves and lose my life in them   350
once for all, than be pinched to death on this desolate island.'
  "So spoke Eurylochos, and the other companions assented.
At once, cutting out from near at hand the best of Helios'
cattle; for the handsome broad-faced horn-curved oxen
were pasturing there, not far from the dark-prowed ship; driving   355
these, they stationed themselves around them, and made their prayers
to the gods, pulling tender leaves from a deep-leaved oak tree;

for they had no white barley left on the strong-benched vessel.
When they had made their prayer and slaughtered the oxen and skinned
    them,
they cut away the meat from the thighs and wrapped them in fat,   360
making a double fold, and laid shreds of flesh upon them;
and since they had no wine to pour on the burning offerings,
they made a libation of water, and roasted all of the entrails;
but when they had burned the thigh pieces and tasted the vitals,
they cut all the remainder into pieces and spitted them.   365
    "At that time the quiet sleep was lost from my eyelids,
and I went back down to my fast ship and the sand of the seashore,
but on my way, as I was close to the oar-swept vessel,
the pleasant savor of cooking meat came drifting around me,
and I cried out my grief aloud to the gods immortal: 370
'Father Zeus, and you other everlasting and blessed
gods, with a pitiless sleep you lulled me, to my confusion,
and my companions staying here dared a deed that was monstrous.'
    "Lampetia of the light robes ran swift with the message
to Hyperion the Sun God, that we had killed his cattle,   375
and angered at the heart he spoke forth among the immortals:
'Father Zeus, and you other everlasting and blessed
gods, punish the companions of Odysseus, son of Laertes;
for they outrageously killed my cattle, in whom I always
delighted, on my way up into the starry heaven,   380
or when I turned back again from heaven toward earth. Unless
these are made to give me just recompense for my cattle,
I go down to Hades and give my light to the dead men.'
    "Then in turn Zeus who gathers the clouds answered him:
'Helios, shine on as you do, among the immortals   385
and mortal men, all over the grain-giving earth. For my part
I will strike these men's fast ship midway on the open
wine-blue sea with a shining bolt and dash it to pieces.'
    "All this I heard afterward from fair-haired Kalypso,
and she told me she herself had heard it from the guide, Hermes.   390
    "But when I came back again to the ship and the seashore,
they all stood about and blamed each other, but we were not able
to find any remedy, for the oxen were already dead. The next thing
was that the gods began to show forth portents before us.
The skins crawled, and the meat that was stuck on the spits bellowed,   395
both roast and raw, and the noise was like the lowing of cattle.
    "Six days thereafter my own eager companions feasted
on the cattle of Helios the Sun God, cutting the best ones
out; but when Zeus the son of Kronos established the seventh
day, then at last the wind ceased from its stormy blowing,   400
and presently we went aboard and put forth on the wide sea,
and set the mast upright and hoisted the white sails on it.
    "But after we had left the island and there was no more
land in sight, but only the sky and the sea, then Kronian
Zeus drew on a blue-black cloud, and settled it over   405
the hollow ship, and the open sea was darkened beneath it;
and she ran on, but not for a very long time, as suddenly
a screaming West Wind came upon us, stormily blowing,
and the blast of the stormwind snapped both the forestays that were
    holding
the mast, and the mast went over backwards, and all the running gear 410
collapsed in the wash; and at the stern of the ship the mast pole

crashed down on the steersman's head and pounded to pieces
all the bones of his head, so that he like a diver
dropped from the high deck, and the proud life left his bones there.
Zeus with thunder and lighting together crashed on our vessel,   415
and, struck by the thunderbolt of Zeus, she spun in a circle,
and all was full of brimstone. My men were thrown in the water,
and bobbing like sea crows they were washed away on the running
waves all around the black ship, and the god took away their homecoming.
    "But I went on my way through the vessel, to where the high seas   420
had worked the keel free out of the hull, and the bare keel floated
on the swell, which had broken the mast off at the keel; yet
still there was a backstay made out of oxhide fastened
to it. With this I lashed together both keel and mast, then
rode the two of them, while the deadly stormwinds carried me.   425
    "After this the West Wind ceased from its stormy blowing,
and the South Wind came swiftly on, bringing to my spirit
grief that I must measure the whole way back to Charybdis.
All that night I was carried along, and with the sun rising
I came to the sea rock of Skylla, and dreaded Charybdis.   430
At this time Charybdis sucked down the sea's salt water,
but I reached high in the air above me, to where the tall fig tree
grew, and caught hold of it and clung like a bat; there was no
place where I could firmly brace my feet, or climb up it,
for the roots of it were far from me, and the branches hung out   435
far, big and long branches that overshadowed Charybdis.
Inexorably I hung on, waiting for her to vomit
the keel and mast back up again. I longed for them, and they came
late; at the time when a man leaves the law court, for dinner,
after judging the many disputes brought him by litigious young men;   440
that was the time it took the timbers to appear from Charybdis.
Then I let go my hold with hands and feet, and dropped off,
and came crashing down between and missing the two long timbers,
but I mounted these, and with both hands I paddled my way out.
But the Father of Gods and men did not let Skylla see me   445
again, or I could not have escaped from sheer destruction.
    "From there I was carried along nine days, and on the tenth night
the gods brought me to the island Ogygia, home of Kalypso
with the lovely hair, a dreaded goddess who talks with mortals.
She befriended me and took care of me. Why tell the rest of   450
this story again, since yesterday in your house I told it
to you and your majestic wife? It is hateful to me
to tell a story over again, when it has been well told."

─────── *Questions for Consideration* ───────

1. Apply the definition of the epic to the *Odyssey* in order to give evidence that it is an epic.

   _____

   _____

   _____

   _____

   _____

2. Enumerate five epic characteristics and five epic conventions. Apply two from each category to the *Odyssey*.

   _____

   _____

   _____

   _____

   _____

3. The guest-host relationship was very important to the ancient Greeks. Both the guest and the host were obligated to show a great deal of regard for the other. In the *Odyssey* give instances where the obligation is fulfilled and instances where it is ignored.

   _____

   _____

   _____

   _____

4. Give a brief description of Odysseus.

   _____

   _____

   _____

   _____

5. Describe Odysseus' homecoming in Ithaca.

_____

_____

_____

_____

_____

Writing Critically

Select one of the essays listed below and compose a well-developed essay using evidence to support your thesis.

1. Consider the epics of Homer in terms of how the heroes demonstrated their idea of freedom and responsibility. To what extent are the decisions made by one hero independent, individual decisions?

2. Write an essay on Telemachus' growth to manhood. Analyze the stages of his assumption of responsibility and the recognition of the fact by others.

3. Using examples from the text discuss hospitality as a criterion of civilization in the *Odyssey*.

4. Identify and discuss the major themes in the *Odyssey*.

Prewriting Space:

_____

_____

_____

_____

_____

_____

_____

_____

_____

_____

_____

_____

_____

_____

_____

_____

_____

_____

_____

_____

Introduction

Homeric Hymn to Demeter (650–550 B.C.)

The *Homeric Hymn to Demeter* is so called because, during classical antiquity, it was one of a large collection of similar poems praising various gods and attributed to Homer. In modern times, it has of course been widely recognized that the *Iliad* and *Odyssey* are products of an oral tradition involving several poets, and not the sole creation of a legendary, blind singer of tales. Similarly, the Homeric hymns were no doubt composed by a number of oral poets. Although we can be no more certain of the authorship of the Homeric hymns than of the *Iliad* and the *Odyssey*, there are many features of language and style that the hymns share with the Homeric epics and with Hesiod, another influential, early Greek mythographer about whom very little is known. Like other poetry of the archaic or most ancient period of Greek literature, the Homeric hymns are distinguished by their simple and direct language, a preoccupation with myth, and their representation of a primitive culture that was highly civilized in its own way.

The present work, which focuses on Demeter, the goddess of grain, is perhaps the most interesting of the Homeric hymns. One of the longest, it is also composed in a fine literary style that survives even in translation. This poem is especially significant because, although it may have been composed by a man, it reveals a sensitivity toward the concerns of women. While it is obvious that the *Iliad* and *Odyssey* present Thetis, Andromache, Penelope, and other women, they subsist amid an heroic world where men and male values are dominant. In the *Hymn to Demeter*, female characters enjoy a centrality rare in Greek literature and found nowhere else in the epic age. To find a similar attentiveness to the perspectives of women, the reader must turn to later works such as the poems of Sappho, the *Lysistrata* of Aristophanes, or the plays of Euripides.

This hymn is the primary source for the myth of Persephone, which is one of the great narratives of classical mythology. The beautiful maiden Persephone, daughter of Demeter, was carried away by the god Hades, king of the Underworld. Demeter wanders in search of her daughter and discovers her only with great difficulty. Angry that the other gods have allowed this abduction to take place, the goddess Demeter disguises herself for a while as an elderly woman and finds employment caring for the infant son of the ruling family of the town of Eleusis near Athens. After some intriguing adventures, she is discovered to be an immortal, and she is again separated from a child she cares for and loves. She leaves the company of the mortals to live in a temple that has been especially built for her.

Intent on regaining her daughter, Demeter now inflicts a terrible famine. Even the gods are affected because mortals no longer have any agricultural products to present or sacrifice to the gods. Hades is at last persuaded to release Persephone, but because she ate a pomegranate seed while in his custody, she must forever after spend a third of each year in the Underworld.

Demeter is thus portrayed as an "earth-mother" figure who is intimately involved in the seasonal cycles of planting, growth, harvest, and the annual decline of plant life. At the same time, this poem provides rare background information on the Eleusinian mysteries, a religious cult that became influential in Athens (the center of the ancient Greek world) and eventually throughout the Roman Empire. Relatively little is known with certainty about Eleusinian beliefs and practices because the cult consisted, as its name indicates, of a series of mysteries revealed only to those initiated as members. While the *Hymn to Demeter* does not record exactly what was revealed during initiation, it provides details of how a new member prepared for initiation. The poem also helps clarify the general nature of the cult. Probably originating as a ritual concerned with the annual processes of the regeneration of crops following the apparent death of winter, the Eleusinian mysteries acquired a wider significance. The cult is notable for its emphasis on an afterlife. The dedicated follower would supposedly lead a comfortable life on earth, and after death, like a planted seed that sprouts in the ground, he or she would enjoy a pleasant afterlife. The abstract beliefs for which the Eleusinian mysteries became widely known in antiquity are anticipated and hinted at in the intriguing tale of Demeter and her daughter, Persephone. (NW)

BIBLIOGRAPHY

Athanassakis, Apostolos N., trans. *The Homeric Hymns*. Baltimore: Johns Hopkins University Press, 1976.

Foley, Helene P., ed. *The Homeric Hymn to Demeter: Translation, Commentary, and Interpretive Essays*. Princeton: Princeton University Press, 1994.

Kerényi, K. *Eleusis: The Achetypal Image of Mother and Daughter*. Trans. R. Manheim. New York: Schocken, 1977.

Rich, Adrienne. *Of Woman Born: Motherhood as Experience and Institution*. New York: Norton, 1976.

Zeitlin, Froma I. *Playing the Other: Essays on Gender and Society in Classical Greek Literature*. Chicago: University of Chicago Press, 1996

Demeter, Triptolemos, and Persephone

Homeric Hymn to Demeter

Translated by Apostolos N. Athanassakis

I begin to sing of lovely-haired Demeter, the goddess august,
of her and her slender-ankled daughter whom Zeus,
far-seeing and loud-thundering, gave to Aidoneus to abduct.
Away from her mother of the golden sword and the splendid fruit
she played with the full-bosomed daughters of Okeanos,⠀⠀⠀⠀⠀5
gathering flowers, roses, crocuses, and beautiful violets
all over a soft meadow; irises, too, and hyacinths she picked,
and narcissus, which Gaia, pleasing the All-receiver,
made blossom there, by the will of Zeus, for a girl with a flower's beauty.
A lure it was, wondrous and radiant, and a marvel to be seen⠀⠀⠀10
by immortal gods and mortal men.
A hundred stems of sweet-smelling blossoms
grew from its roots. The wide sky above
and the whole earth and the briny swell of the sea laughed.
She was dazzled and reached out with both hands at once⠀⠀⠀15
to take the pretty bauble; Earth with its wide roads gaped
and then over the Nysian field the lord and All-receiver,
the many-named son of Kronos, sprang out upon her with his immortal
⠀⠀⠀horses.
Against her will he seized her and on his golden chariot
carried her away as she wailed; and she raised a shrill cry,⠀⠀⠀20
calling upon father Kronides, the highest and the best.
None of the immortals or of mortal men heard
her voice, not even the olive-trees bearing splendid fruit.
Only the gentle-tempered daughter of Persaios,
Hekate of the shining headband, heard from her cave,⠀⠀⠀25
and lord Helios, the splendid son of Hyperion, heard
the maiden calling father Kronides; he sat
apart from the gods away in the temple of prayers,
accepting beautiful sacrifices from mortal men.
By Zeus' counsels, his brother, the All-receiver⠀⠀⠀30
and Ruler of Many, Kronos' son of many names,
was carrying her away with his immortal horses, against her will.
So while the goddess looked upon the earth and the starry sky
and the swift-flowing sea teeming with fish
and the rays of the sun and still hoped to see⠀⠀⠀35
her loving mother and the races of gods immortal,
hope charmed her great mind, despite her grief.
The peaks of the mountains and the depths of the sea resounded
with her immortal voice, and her mighty mother heard her.

A sharp pain gripped her heart, and she tore   40
the headband round her divine hair with her own hands.
From both of her shoulders she cast down her dark veil
and rushed like a bird over the nourishing land and the sea,
searching; but none of the gods or mortal men
wanted to tell her the truth and none   45
of the birds of omen came to her as truthful messenger.
For nine days then all over the earth mighty Deo
roamed about with bright torches in her hands,
and in her sorrow never tasted ambrosia
or nectar sweet to drink, and never bathed her skin.   50
But when the tenth light-bringing Dawn came to her,
Hekate carrying a light in her hands, met her,
and with loud voice spoke to her and told her the news:
"Mighty Demeter, bringer of seasons and splendid gifts,
which of the heavenly gods or of mortal men   55
seized Persephone and pierced with sorrow your dear heart?
For I heard a voice but did not see with my eyes
who it was; I am quickly telling you the whole truth."
Thus spoke Hekate. And to her the daughter of lovely-haired Rhea
answered not a word, but with her she sped away   60
swiftly, holding the bright torches in her hands.
They came to Helios, watcher of gods and men,
and stood near his horses, and the illustrious goddess made a plea:
"Helios, do have respect for me as a goddess, if I ever
cheered your heart and soul by word or deed.   65
Through the barren ether I heard the shrieking voice
of my daughter famous for her beauty, a sweet flower at birth,
as if she were being overcome by force, but I saw nothing.
And since you do gaze down upon the whole earth
and sea and cast your rays through the bright ether,   70
tell me truly if you have seen anywhere
what god or even mortal man in my absence
seized by force my dear child and went away."
Thus she spoke and Hyperionides gave her an answer:
"Lady Demeter, daughter of lovely-haired Rhea,   75
you shall know; for I greatly reverence and pity you
in your grief for your slender-ankled child; no other immortal
is to be blamed save cloud-gathering Zeus
who gave her to Hades, his own brother, to become
his buxom bride. He seized her and with his horses   80
carried her crying loud down to misty darkness.
But, Goddess, stop your great wailing; you mustn't give
yourself to grief so great and fruitless. Not an unseemly
bridegroom among immortals is Aidoneus, Lord of Many,
your own brother from the same seed; to his share fell   85
honor when in the beginning a triple division was made,
and he dwells among those over whom his lot made him lord."
With these words, he called upon his horses, and at his command
speedily, like long-winged birds, they drew the swift chariot,
as a pain more awful and savage reached Demeter's soul.   90
Afterwards, angered with Kronion, lord of black clouds,
she withdrew from the assembly of the gods and from lofty Olympos
and went through the cities of men and the wealth of their labors,
tearing at her fair form for a long time; no man
or deep-girded woman looking at her knew who she was   95

before she reached the house of prudent Keleos,
who then was lord of Eleusis, a town rich in sacrifices.
Grieving in her dear heart, she sat near the road,
at Parthenion, the well from which the citizens drew water,
in the shade of a bushy olive-tree which grew above it.   100
She looked like an old woman born a long time ago
and barred from childbearing and the gifts of wreath-loving Aphrodite,
even as are nurses for the children of law-tending
kings and keepers of the storerooms in their bustling mansions.
The daughters of Keleos Eleusinides saw her   105
as they were coming to fetch easily-drawn water
in copper vessels to their father's dear halls,
four of them in their maidenly bloom, like goddesses,
Kallidike, Kleisidike and Demo the lovely,
and Kallithoe, who was the eldest of them all.   110
They did not know who she was; it is hard for mortals to see divinity.
Standing near they addressed her with winged words:
"Old woman, whence and from what older generation do you come?
Why have you wandered away from the city and not approached
a house; there in the shadowy halls live   115
women of your age and even younger ones
who will treat you kindly in both word and deed."
After these words, the mighty goddess answered:
"Dear children, whoever of ladylike women you are,
I greet you and will explain; indeed it is fitting   120
to tell you the truth, since you are asking.
Dos is the name which my mighty mother gave me.
And now from Crete on the broad back of the sea
I came unwillingly; marauding men by brute force
carried me off against my will, and later   125
they landed their swift ship at Thorikos, where the women
came out in a body and the men themselves
prepared a meal by the stern-cables of the ship.
But my heart had no desire for the evening's sweet meal;
I eluded them and, rushing through the black land,   130
I fled my reckless masters, so that they might not enjoy
the benefit of my price, since, like thieves, they carried me across the sea.
So I have wandered to this place and know not at all
what land this is and what men live in it.
But may all who dwell in the Olympian halls   135
grant you men to wed and children to bear
as your parents wish; and now have mercy on me, maidens
and, dear children, kindly let me go to someone's house,
a man's and a woman's, to work for them
in such tasks as befit a woman past her prime.   140
I shall be a good nurse to a new-born child,
holding him in my arms; I shall take care of the house,
and make the master's bed in the innermost part
of the well-built chamber and mind his wife's work."
So said the goddess, and forthwith Kallidike, still a pure virgin   145
and the most beautiful of Keleos' daughters, replied:
"Good mother, men must take the gifts of the gods
even when they bring them pain, since gods are truly much stronger.
I shall advise you clearly and give you the names
of the men who have great power and honor in this place;   150
these are leaders of the people who defend the towers

of the city by their counsels and straight judgments.
They are Triptolemos, shrewd in counsel, and Diokles,
Polyxeinos and Eumolpos, untainted by blame,
Dolichos and our manly father,   155
and everyone has a wife managing his mansion.
No woman there, when she first looks upon you,
will dishonor your appearance and remove you from the mansion,
but each will receive you, for indeed you look like a goddess.
If you wish, wait here for us to go to the mansion   160
of our father and tell our deep-girded mother, Metaneira,
all these things from beginning to end, hoping that
she will bid you come to our mansion and not search for another's.
A growing son is being reared in the well-built mansion,
born late in her life, much wished for and welcome.   165
If you should bring him up to reach puberty,
some tender woman seeing you could easily
be envious; such rewards for rearing him she'll give you."
So she spoke, and the goddess nodded her head in assent,
and they proudly carried their shining vessels filled with water.   170
Swiftly they reached their father's great mansion and quickly told
their mother what they had seen and heard. And she commanded them
to go forthwith and invite her to come for copious wages.
And they, as deer or heifers in the season of spring,
sated in their hearts with pasture frisk over a meadow,   175
held up the folds of their lovely robes
and darted along the hollow wagon-road, as their flowing hair
tossed about their shoulders, like the flowers of the crocus.
They met the glorious goddess near the road where
they had left her before; and then they led her to their father's   180
house. And the goddess walked behind them, brooding
in her dear heart, with her head covered, while a dark
cloak swirled about her tender feet.
Soon they reached the house of Zeus-cherished Keleos
and through the portico they went where their lady mother   185
sat by a pillar, which supported the close-fitted roof,
holding a child, a young blossom, on her lap; they ran
near her, and the goddess stepped on the threshold and touched
the roof with her head and filled the doorway with divine radiance.
Awe, reverence and pale fear seized the mother;   190
and she yielded her seat to the goddess and asked her to sit.
But Demeter, the bringer of seasons and splendid gifts,
did not want to sit on the lustrous seat;
she kept silent and cast down her beautiful eyes
until Iambe, knowing her duties, placed in front of her   195
a well-fitted seat and over it she threw a white fleece.
Demeter sat on it and with her hands she held in front of her a veil,
remaining on the seat for long, speechless and brooding,
doing nothing and speaking to nobody.
And without laughing or tasting food and drink   200
she sat pining with longing for her deep-girded daughter
until Iambe, knowing her duties, with her jokes
and many jests induced the pure and mighty one
to smile and laugh and have a gracious temper.
At later times, too, Iambe was able to please her moods.   205
Metaneira now filled a cup with wine and gave it
to her, but she refused it; it was not right for her, she said,

to drink red wine. She asked them to give her a drink
of barley-meal and water mixed with tender pennyroyal.
She mixed the drink and gave it to the goddess, as she had asked,   210
and mighty Deo accepted it, complying with holy custom.
Then among them fair-girded Metaneira started speaking.
"I salute you, lady, because I think you were born to noble
and not to lowly parents. Modesty and grace show
in your eyes, as if you were the child of law-giving kings.   215
But man must take the gifts of gods even when they are
grieved by them, for on their necks there is a yoke.
And now since you have come here, what is mine will be yours.
Nurture this child of mine, whom unhoped for and late-born
the gods have granted me, in answer to my many prayers.   220
If you should bring him up to reach the age of puberty,
some tender woman seeing you could easily
be envious; such rewards for rearing him I will give you."
Fair-wreathed Demeter addressed her in turn:
"I salute you too, lady; may the gods grant you good   225
things. I will gladly accept the child as you ask me.
I will nurture him and I don't think that for his nurse's foolishness
either a spell or the Undercutter will harm him.
I know a remedy by far mightier than the tree-felling creature,
and for harmful bewitching I know a noble antidote."   230
With these words she received him to her fragrant bosom
and immortal arms, and the mother rejoiced in her heart.
Thus the fine son of prudent Keleos,
Demophoön, to whom fair-girded Metaneira gave birth,
was nurtured by her in the palace; and he grew up like a god,   235
not eating food or nursing at his mother's breast.
As if he were the child of a god, Demeter annointed him with ambrosia
holding him to her bosom and breathing on him sweetly.
At night she hid him like a firebrand in the blazing fire,
secretly from his dear parents. To them it was a miracle   240
how he blossomed forth and looked like the gods.
And she would have made him ageless and immortal,
if fair-girded Metaneira, thinking foolish thoughts
and keeping watch by night from her fragrant chamber,
had not seen her; she raised a cry, striking her thighs   245
in fear for her child, and blindness entered her mind,
and weeping she spoke winged words:
"Demophoön, my child, this stranger hides you
in a great fire, bringing me grief and painful care."
Thus she spoke wailing, and the splendid goddess heard her.   250
The shafts of terrible anger shot through Demeter,
the fair-wreathed, who then with her immortal hands
took from the blazing fire and placed on the ground
the dear child born in the queen's mansion,
and at the same time addressed fair-girded Metaneira: 255
"Men are too foolish to know ahead of time
the measure of good and evil which is yet to come.
You too were greatly blinded by your foolishness.
The relentless water of the Styx by which gods swear
be my witness: immortal and ageless forever   260
would I have made your dear son and granted him everlasting honor;
but now it is not possible for him to escape the fate of death.
Yet honor everlasting shall be his because

he climbed on my knees and slept in my arms.
But in due time and as the years revolve for him,   265
the sons of the Eleusinians will join in war
and dreadful battle against each other forever.
I am Demeter the honored, the greatest
benefit and joy to undying gods and to mortals.
But come now, let all the people build me   270
a great temple and beneath it an altar under the steep walls
of the city, above Kallichoron, on the rising hill.
I myself shall introduce rites so that later
you may propitiate my mind by their right performance."
With these words the goddess changed her size and form   275
and sloughed off old age, as beauty was wafted about her.
From her fragrant veils a lovely smell
emanated, and from the immortal skin of the goddess a light
shone afar, as her blond hair streamed down over her shoulders,
and the sturdy mansion was filled with radiance as if from lightning.   280
Out she went through the mansion. The queen staggered,
and she remained speechless for a long time, forgetting
to pick her growing child up from the floor.
His sisters heard his pitiful voice,
and they ran from their well-spread beds; and then one   285
took up the child in her arms and held him to her bosom.
Another revived the fire and yet a third rushed
with her tender feet to rouse her mother from her fragrant chamber.
They gathered round the squirming child, bathed him
and fondled him, but his heart was not soothed,   290
for surely lesser nurses and governesses held him now.
All night long they propitiated the glorious goddess,
quaking with fear, and as soon as dawn appeared
they told the truth to Keleos, whose power reached far,
as the fair-wreathed goddess Demeter had ordered them.   295
He then called to assembly the people of every district
and bade them build an opulent temple to lovely-haired Demeter
and make an altar on the rising hill.
And they listened to his speech, and obeying forthwith
they built it as he ordered; and the temple took shape according to divine
       decree.   300
Now when they finished the temple and refrained from labor,
each man went to his home, but blond Demeter,
sitting there apart from all the blessed ones,
kept on wasting with longing for her deep-girded daughter.
Onto the much-nourishing earth she brought a year   305
most dreadful and harsh for men; no seed
in the earth sprouted, for fair-wreathed Demeter concealed it.
In vain the oxen drew many curved plows over the fields,
and in vain did much white barley fall into the ground.
And she would have destroyed the whole race of mortal men   310
with painful famine and would have deprived
the Olympians of the glorious honor of gifts and sacrifices,
if Zeus had not perceived this and pondered in his mind.
First he sent golden-winged Iris to invite
the lovely-haired Demeter of the fair form.   315
He spoke to her and she obeyed Zeus, the son of Kronos and lord
of dark clouds, and ran swiftly mid-way between earth and heaven.
She reached the town of Eleusis rich in sacrifices,

found the dark-veiled Demeter in the temple
and spoke, uttering winged words to her: 320
"Demeter, Zeus the father, whose wisdom never wanes,
invites you to come among the tribes of the immortal gods.
But come and let not the word of Zeus be unaccomplished."
Thus she spoke begging her, but her mind was not persuaded.
So then again the father sent forth all the blessed 325
immortal gods. They ran to her, and each in his turn
summoned her and gave her many beautiful gifts
and whatever honors she might want to choose among the immortals.
But no one could persuade the mind and thought
of the angry goddess who stubbornly spurned their offers. 330
She said she would never set foot on fragrant Olympos
and never allow the grain in the earth to sprout forth
before seeing with her eyes her fair-faced daughter.
So when loud-thundering, far-seeing Zeus heard this,
he sent Argeiphontes of the golden wand to Erebos. 335
His mission was to win Hades over with gentle words,
and bring Persephone out of misty darkness
to light and among the gods, so that her mother
might see her with her eyes and desist from anger.
Hermes did not disobey and, leaving his Olympian seat, 340
with eager speed plunged into the depths of the earth.
He found the lord inside his dwelling,
sitting on his bed with his revered spouse; she was
in many ways reluctant and missed her mother, who far
from the works of the blessed gods was devising a plan. 345
Mighty Argeiphontes stood near and addressed him:
"Hades, dark-haired lord of those who have perished,
Zeus the father bids you bring noble Persephone
out of Erebos and among the gods, so that her mother,
seeing her with her eyes, may desist from anger 350
and dreadful wrath against the gods; because she is contemplating
a great scheme to destroy the feeble races of earth-born men,
hiding the seed under the earth and abolishing the honors
of the immortals. Her anger is dreadful, and she does not mingle
with the gods, but apart from them in a fragrant temple 355
she sits, dwelling in the rocky town of Eleusis."
Thus he spoke and Aidoneus, lord of the nether world,
with smiling brows obeyed the behests of Zeus the king
and speedily gave his command to prudent-minded Persephone:
"Persephone, go to your dark-robed mother, 360
with a gentle spirit and temper in your breast,
and in no way be more dispirited than the other gods.
I shall not be an unfitting husband among the immortals,
as I am father Zeus' own brother. When you are here
you shall be mistress of everything which lives and moves; 365
your honors among the immortals shall be the greatest,
and those who wrong you shall always be punished,
if they do not propitiate your spirit with sacrifices,
performing sacred rites and making due offerings."
Thus he spoke and wise Persephone rejoiced 370
and swiftly sprang up for joy, but he himself
gave her to eat a honey-sweet pomegranate seed,
contriving secretly about her, so that she might not spend
all her days again with dark-robed, revered Demeter.

Aidoneus, Ruler of Many, harnessed nearby   375
the immortal horses up to the golden chariot.
She mounted the chariot, and next to her mighty Argeiphontes
took the reins and the whip in his own hands
and sped out of the halls, as the horses flew readily.
Soon they reached the end of the long path, and neither   380
the sea nor the water of rivers nor the grassy glens
and mountain-peaks checked the onrush of the immortal horses,
but they went over all these, traversing the lofty air.
He drove them and then halted near the fragrant temple
where fair-wreathed Demeter stayed. When she saw them,   385
she rushed as a maenad does, along a shady woodland on the mountains.
Persephone on her part, when she saw the beautiful eyes
of her mother, leaving chariot and horses, leaped down
to run and, throwing her arms around her mother's neck, embraced her.
And as Demeter still held her dear child in her arms,   390
her mind suspected trickery, and in awful fear she withdrew
from fondling her and forthwith asked her a question:
"Child, when you were below, did you perchance partake
of food? Speak out, that we both may know.
If your answer is no, coming up from loathsome Hades,   395
you shall dwell both with me and with father Kronion,
lord of dark clouds, honored by all the immortals.
Otherwise, you shall fly and go to the depths of the earth
to dwell there a third of the seasons in the year,
spending two seasons with me and the other immortals.   400
Whenever the earth blooms with every kind of sweet-smelling
springflower, you shall come up again from misty darkness,
a great wonder for gods and mortal men.
With what trick did the mighty All-receiver deceive you?"
Facing her now, beautiful Persephone replied: 405
"Surely, Mother, I shall tell you the whole truth.
When Hermes, the helpful swift messenger, came
from father Zeus and the other heavenly dwellers
to fetch me from Erebos, so that seeing me with your eyes
you might desist from your anger and dreadful wrath against the
    immortals,   410
I myself sprang up for joy, but Aidoneus slyly placed
in my hands a pomegranate seed, sweet as honey to eat.
Against my will and by force he made me taste of it.
How he abducted me through the shrewd scheming of Kronides,
my father, and rode away carrying me to the depths of the earth 415
I shall explain and rehearse every point as you are asking.
All of us maidens in a delightful meadow,
Leukippe, Phaino, Electra, Ianthe,
Melite, Iache, Rhodeia, Kallirhoe,
Melobosis, Tyche, Okyrhoe with a face like a flower,   420
Chryseis, Ianeira, Akaste, Admete,
Rhodope, Plouto, lovely Kalypso,
Styx, Ourania, charming Galaxaura,
battle-stirring Pallas, and arrow-pouring Artemis,
were playing and picking lovely flowers with our hands,   425
mingling soft crocuses and irises with hyacinths
and the flowers of the rose and lilies, a wonder to the eye,
and the narcissus which the wide earth grows crocus-colored.
So I myself was picking them with joy, but the earth beneath

gave way and from it the mighty lord and All-receiver   430
leaped out. He carried me under the earth in his golden chariot,
though I resisted and shouted with shrill voice.
I am telling you the whole truth, even though it grieves me."
So then all day long, being one in spirit,
they warmed each other's hearts and minds in many ways   435
with loving embraces, and an end to sorrow came for their hearts,
as they took joys from each other and gave in return.
Hekate of the shining headband came near them
and many times lovingly touched the daughter of pure Demeter.
From then on this lady became her attendant and follower.   440
Far-seeing, loud-thundering Zeus sent them a messenger,
Lovely-haired Rhea, to bring her dark-veiled mother
among the races of the gods, promising to give her
whatever honors she might choose among the immortal gods.
with a nod of his head he promised that, as the year revolved,   445
her daughter could spend one portion of it in the misty darkness
and the other two with her mother and the other immortals.
He spoke and the goddess did not disobey the behests of Zeus.
Speedily she rushed down from the peaks of Olympos
and came to Rharion, life-giving udder of the earth   450
in the past, and then no longer life-giving but lying idle
without a leaf. It was now hiding the white barley
according to the plan of fair-ankled Demeter, but later
the fields would be plumed with long ears of grain,
as the spring waxed, and the rich furrows on the ground   455
would teem with ears to be bound into sheaves by withies.
There she first landed from the unharvested ether.
Joyfully they beheld each other and rejoiced in their hearts;
and Rhea of the shining headband addressed her thus:
"Come, child! Far-seeing, loud-thundering Zeus invites you   460
to come among the races of the gods and promises to give you
whatever honors you wish among the immortal gods.
With a nod of his head he promised you that, as the year revolves,
your daughter could spend one portion of it in the misty darkness
and the other two with you and the other immortals.   465
With a nod of his head he said it would thus be brought to pass.
But obey me, my child! Come and do not nurse
unrelenting anger against Kronion, lord of dark clouds;
Soon make the life-giving seed grow for men."
Thus she spoke and fair-wreathed Demeter did not disobey,   470
but swiftly made the seed sprout out of the fertile fields.
The whole broad earth teemed with leaves and flowers;
and she went to the kings who administer the laws,
Triptolemos and Diokles, smiter of horses, and mighty Eumolpos
and Keleos, leader of the people, and showed them the   475
celebration of holy rites, and explained to all,
to Triptolemos, to Polyxeinos and also to Diokles,
the awful mysteries not to be transgressed, violated
or divulged, because the tongue is restrained by reverence for the gods.
Whoever on this earth has seen these is blessed,   480
but he who has no part in the holy rites has
another lot as he wastes away in dank darkness.
After the splendid Demeter had counseled the kings in everything,
she and her daughter went to Olympos for the company of the other gods.
There they dwell beside Zeus who delights in thunder,   485

commanding awe and reverence; thrice blessed is he
of men on this earth whom they gladly love.
Soon to his great house they send as guest
Ploutos, who brings wealth to mortal men.
But come now, you who dwell in the fragrant town of Eleusis, 490
sea-girt Paros and rocky Antron,
mighty mistress Deo, bringer of seasons and splendid gifts,
both you and your daughter, beauteous Persephone,
for my song kindly grant me possessions pleasing the heart,
and I shall remember you and another song, too. 495

ENDNOTES

3   "Gave" is both appropriate and consistent with Zeus' position as "father of gods and men." Of course, "gave" here almost means permitted or allowed, but the notion of giving Persephone away as a bride is also inherent. Hesiod expresses the same idea in *Theogony* 914. Later versions of the story, which make Zeus act under the constraint Moira or have Pluto fall victim to the designs of a capricious Venus, must be the result of learned mythographic speculation or of poetic fancy.

4   Scholars have not been able to determine the propriety or significance of the adjective that I am translating "of the golden sword." Lycophron mentions an obscure cult of the sword-bearing Demeter in Boeotia and it is possible that this cult was a survival from an earlier, more widespread aspect of the cult of Demeter.

5–14   The presence of the Okeanidai cannot be of any special significance. It may simply enhance the atmosphere of maidenly innocence. However, the gathering of flowers is no mere poetic embellishment and must correspond to ritualistic aspects of the worship of Demeter and Persephone as goddesses of vegetation. Survivals of flower-gathering festivals can still be found in most rural communities of Greece. It is interesting that, although other flowers are present in the poem, the narcissus is given the prominence that it doubtless deserved as a flower especially connected with the Great Goddesses (cf. Sophocles, *Oedipus Coloneus* 683). The chthonic nature of this flower is evident in its being sacred to the Eumenides, and Artemidoros tells us that it was also funereal (*Oneirokritikos* 1.77). The association of the narcissus with death could be attributed both to its real or presumed soporific qualities and to the fact that in myth it was the lure that led to the rape of Persephone and her sojourn in Hades for one third of the year during which nature "died."

17   Scholarly efforts to identify the Nysian field have not yielded any credible results.

23   We should not be surprised that a Mediterranean poet chose to endow the olive trees with the ability to hear. The Greeks, ancient and modern, frequently grant human attributes not only to animals but also to inanimate objects. One of the earliest instances is to be found in *Iliad* 3.275–80. In the song of *Constantine and Arete* birds speak, and a Cretan singer from the days of the Second World War begins his song with the line: "What ails the mountains of Crete, and they stand about with tearful eyes?"

24   This is one of the earliest references to Hekate, who is the daughter of the Titan Persês (so spelled in other sources) and Asteriê (cf. Hesiod *Theogony* 411). The fact that she is not mentioned in Homer testifies not only to a relatively late arrival in Greece, most likely from the East, but also to a

date of composition later than that of the two great Homeric epics.

42 It is odd that Demeter wears a dark veil, a sign of mourning, even before she hears of her daughter's abduction. We may be faced with a case in which later ritual influences mythopoetic composition.

47 The number of days may indeed be conventional. But, although we do not know the exact duration of the fast, either at the Eleusinian mysteries or at the *Thesmophoria,* we do know that the period of strict mourning after someone's death as well as certain expiatory rites lasted for nine days. The number three and its multiples were frequently employed then as even now. Thus, the Graces were three, the Muses nine, the Olympian gods twelve, etc. When Apollon attacks the Achaean camp with his pestiferous arrows, he does so for nine whole days (*Iliad* 1.53). Dêô, most likely a diminutive, is another name for Demeter.

48 In the myth Demeter holds torches in her hands because she is searching—one presumes—especially dark caves and wooded glens in which the abductor might have sought refuge. In the ritual of the Eleusinian mysteries and the *Thesmophoria,* the torches may have been symbols of the solar light and warmth that must triumph over the infernal cold and darkness of the winter so that nature may come alive again in the spring.

49–50 These tokens of extreme grief are not substantially different from those practiced by the Greeks of today during the Holy Week and especially on Good Friday. Devout Christians follow a certain dietary regimen during the Holy Week and abstain from all festive activities. On the Saturday preceding Easter Sunday, and usually at midnight, there is a light-giving ceremony and, after the conclusion of the liturgy, participants carry the light of the Resurrection to their homes. (cf. *Iliad* 23.43–48).

52 The author of this hymn definitely identifies Hekate with the moon, and the torch must be symbolic of the lunar light emanating from Hekate, the moon-goddess.

62 The sun does see everything and so he watches gods and men. Similarly, the moon sees all and it is no accident that the cry of Persephone did not escape either Helios or Hecate. The idea of the all-seeing sun is commonplace in Greek poetry down to the present day. Thus Homer's "O sun, you who see and hear all things" (*Iliad* 3.277) is reechoed by Kazantzakis in "Great sun, who pass on high yet watch all things below" (*The Odyssey, a Modern Sequel, Prol.* 17).

74 Hyperionidês (the son of Hyperion) is a patronymic; the usual form is Hyperiôn as in *Odyssey* 1.8 (cf. also *Hymn to Apollon* 369).

96 Keleos, his wife Metaneira, and even his daughters were still revered at Eleusis in classical times (cf. Paus. 1.39 and Clement of Alexandria 1.39).

99 The Parthenion has not been convincingly identified with any modern landmark. In ancient times it came to be confused with another well, the Kallichoron, which was near the precinct of Eleusis.

101 Disguises in order to conceal true identity are in keeping with the conventions of the Greek epic. Aphrodite appears to Helen in the guise of an old woman (*Iliad* 3.386–89) and to Anchises as a young Phrygian maiden (*Hymn to Aphrodite* 81–83, 106–42).

109–10 Pausanias, on the authority of Homer (?) and Pamphos, names only three daughters and gives them names other than the ones in the text of the hymn (1.38.3).

122 Dôs is not an unlikely pseudonym for Demeter. The word occurs as a substantive in Hesiod *Works and Days* 356 and is equivalent to *dosis* (giving). The goddess is playful because on the one hand she does not give her true name but on the other hand her pseudonym begins with the same letter and has a meaning that is highly suggestive of Demeter's nature as a generous and "giving" divinity.

123 Some have tried to discover the origin of the Eleusinian cult in this story. But the story of a young girl kidnapped by

Cretan pirates may be no more than a convenient lie. Odysseus pretends that he is a Cretan on three different occasions (*Odyssey* 13.256; 14.199; 19.17).

126   Thorikos was north of Cape Sounion.

153   In classical times Triptolemos became a very important figure in the Eleusinian mysteries. Here he is merely another one of the local princes, a fact which testifies to the great antiquity of the hymn. His parentage is uncertain, but for Apollodoros he is the eldest son of Keleos and Memneira (1.5.2). Dioklos may be the same as the Megarian hero Dioklês and his inclusion here may not be unrelated to the dependence of Eleusis on Megara in earlier times.

154–55   Although some later sources make Dolichos the son of Triptolemos, Polyxeinos, Eumolpos and Dolichos are otherwise unknown.

188–89   Demeter's head touches the roof much as Aphrodite's does in the *Hymn to Aphrodite* 173–174. The Greeks generally ascribed superhuman stature to the gods (c.*Iliad* 4.443). Radiance as a token of divine presence (cf. *Hymn to Apollon* 444) has found ready acceptance in Christian accounts of miraculous epiphany.

191–205   This charming and intriguing incident in the story of Demeter's search for Persephone is still awaiting the day on which some incisive mind will shed light on its origins and implications. On the surface the story is simple: Demeter is deeply distraught and a funny old lady tells her some coarse, most likely mimetic jokes, and makes her smile and laugh. But who is Iambê, and why in the Orphic version is it not Iambê but the Eleusinia queen, Baubô, who induces the goddess to forget her sorrow and laugh by lifting her robe and exposing her pudenda? From ancient sources we know that at nearly every festival in honor of Demeter, including the procession to Eleusis (cf. Aristophanes *Frogs* 372ff.), there was frivolity in the form of obscene gestures and jesting. We have reason to believe that the gestures and jests were sexual in character and, thus, a most appropriate part of a fertility

cult. For the Orphic version of the story see *Orphicorum Fragmenta* 46–53 (Kern)—especially fragment 52—and Clement of Alexandria in *Protreptikos* 2.20,1–21,2.

207–8   It should be mentioned here that most sacrifices to Demeter and to many other chthonic gods were wineless. The reason for this taboo remains unknown.

208–10   The Greek word for this potion is *kykeôn* (literally, a mixed or stirred drink). On the authority of Clement of Alexandria we know that a mixture of water, mint (pennyroyal) and meal was used as a drink of initiation into the Eleusinian mysteries. However, this act of initiation must not have been part of the secret and ineffable rites performed at the *telestêrion* (Hall of Rituals), because depictions of it are found on Attic vases.

228–30   In "the Undercutter" and "the tree-felling creature" scholars have, I think rightly, seen references to the belief that toothache is caused by a certain worm. The goddess wisely refers to it with a periphrasis for fear that calling it by its name might provoke its instant appearance.

231–41   Parallels to the story of Demophoôn are found not only in Greek literature but also in the legends of other nations (cf. the story of Isis and the infant son of the king of Byblos in Plutarch's *Isis and Osiris* 16). In Greek literature the story of Thetis and Achilles shows that the motif is not confined to this hymn. Apollodoros and other later writers depart from the tradition of this hymn and, accommodating the eventual prominence of Triptolemos in the Eleusinian mysteries, tell us either that Demophoôn died when Demeter's strange doings were discovered by Metaneira (Apollodoros 1.5.1) or that the child nursed by Demeter was not Demophoôn but Triptolemos (cf. among others Ovid *Metamorphoses* 5.645; Nicander *Thêriaka* 484). As Demeter herself explains in lines 260–61 the purpose of anointing Demophoôn with ambrosia and hiding him in the fire by night was to make him immortal. The reader may recall that Thetis put drops of ambrosia into the nose of Patroklos to prevent decay of his skin (*Iliad* 19.39). According to Lycophron (*Cassandra* 178ff.), Thetis immortalized six of her children by burning away their mortal parts in the fire. Her attempt to make Achilles immortal by placing him on the fire and then by anointing him with ambrosia was frustrated by Peleus, who intervened just when the goddess had subjected all but the ankle-bone of the child to this treatment (Apollodoros 3.13.6). It is interesting that fire and ambrosia are used both in the case of Achilles and Demophoôn. As Apollodoros tells the story, Thetis hid Achilles in the fire by night and annointed him with ambrosia by day. Although in the story of Demophoôn it is not clear what procedure is followed, the treatment with fire took place at night, the implication thereby being that the annointing occurred during the day. Perhaps the origin of using fire and then ambrosia to make someone immortal may not be unconnected with the smith's technique, who first "hides" the metal in fire and then dips it in water to harden it.

265–67 We know of no civil war at Eleusis and this may indeed be an *ex post facto* prophecy, in which case, given the antiquity of the hymn, we may be dealing with a facet of Eleusinian history antedating the prominence that Eleusis gained as a result of the cult of Demeter.

270–72 For the identification of the temple mentioned in these lines see G. E. Mylonas, *Eleusis and the Eleusinian Mysteries*, 34ff. The *Kallichoron* was discovered in 1892.

292 Keleos, the child's father, knows nothing as yet. This nocturnal propitiation of the goddess is solely attended by women and may correspond to the *pannychis*, the all-night women's festival, of the *Thesmophoria*.

302 *Xanthos* ("blond") must be used as conventionally here as elsewhere in Greek epic (cf. 279).

305–13 It has not been determined whether these lines conceal a reference to lean years of famine and destitution for the Eleusinians, destitution that the Eleusinians were known to have once suffered.

349 Erebos here means "darkness."

358 "Smiling brows," the literal translation of the expression, is at first sight a strange expression. Modern Greeks use the expression "even his moustache laughed" and signal "no" by swiftly raising their eyebrows. Thus, "smiling brows" may be a reference to an especially Greek facial expression or merely a hyperbole for "he really smiled."

372–74 Apollodoros follows the hymn closely with respect to line 372 (cf. 1.5.3). In Ovid's *Metamorphoses* 5.535, Persephone is not given the fruit by the god of the Underworld, but she finds it in a garden and eats seven seeds. Some obscure numerological allusion may be hidden in this version. The pomegranate was widely used both in ritual and folk medicine, but our poet may have chosen it rather than some other fruit because the plant had definite chthonic connections. The tree was thought to have sprung from the blood of Dionysos Zagreus (Clement of Alexandria, *Protreptikos*, 2.19) and pomegranate seeds are still used by Greeks as decorations in the *kollyba*, wheat offerings that are distributed to the congregation in memorial services in honor of the dead. By eating of a fruit that is especially connected with the world of the dead and by accepting what is a gift from the ruler of that world, Persephone establishes a *xenia*, a guest-host tie that comes with an obligation for her both to come back and to give in return.

390–93 For a variation on this version, cf. Ovid *Metamorphoses* 5.534.

399 Of the explanations given for Persephone's sojourn in Hades for one third of the year the ancient Stoic doctrine that this period stood for the time during which seeds are "hidden" in the ground is certainly both logical and plausible. One might add that the Greek winter lasts for about one third of the year. However the reader should know that most of the text of lines 387–400 has been restored and

438–40   that, therefore, everything pertaining to these lines is highly conjectural.

For Hekate, cf. Hesiod *Theogony* 411ff. The association of Hekate with Demeter and Persephone is understandable. She is frequently confused with Artemis and closely associated with Selene, the Moon, whose role in women's menstrual cycle is too obvious to need elaboration.

450   Rharion has not been identified with a definite place in the vicinity of Eleusis, where Stephanus Byzantinus places it.

459   Demeter is the daughter of Kronos and Rhea.

476   The Greek word for which I translate "celebration" is *drêsmosynê* (enactment); thus the emphasis is definitely on a sacred *drama* in which the story of Demeter and Persephone was acted out by priests of the cult.

479   The *hierokêryx* (literally "sacred herald") proclaimed silence with the word *euphêmeite*, "keep reverent silence," and the initiates complied. The injunction not to divulge the sacred rites must rather refer to the sworn secrecy that was imposed upon the initiates. The reasons for this secrecy are not immediately obvious. Secret religious or semireligious societies still swear their members to secrecy on certain aspects of their initiations and their practices, and followers of transcendental meditation are not supposed to reveal their mantra to others. Some have supposed that the drômena—which we may translate the "acting rites"—of the Eleusinian mysteries were kept secret because their revelation would rob them of their power. Others have seen in these mysteries an ancient chthonic cult of the original inhabitants of Eleusis, who were anxious to keep it secret from their Indo-European conquerors. I think that secrecy was imposed in order to protect the rites from vulgarization and frivolous mimicry and to keep them as the private preserve, as it were, of the few families from which the priests of this prestigious cult were drawn.

480–82   For the sentiment, cf. Aristophanes *Frogs* 455–59; Pindar fr. 137; Plato *Phaedrus* 69c; Euripides *Heracles* 613ff, et al. The bliss of the initiates may have stemmed from their communion with divinities connected with the whole cycle of life from birth to death and from their participation in holy rites that revealed to them that death was only part of this cycle and not the end of it.

489   In Orphic Hymn 40.3, Demeter is described as *ploutodoteira*, "giver of wealth" (*ploutos* means "wealth" in Greek) and in the *Thesmophoriazousai* of Aristophanes (296), *Ploutos* is invoked in prayer after Demeter and Persephone. In art *Ploutos* is often represented as a boy with cornucopia or corn-basket. One may conjecture that in addition to psychic bliss and hope for afterlife, the initiates were also promised material wealth as a reward for their sharing in the sacred rites.

491   The cult of Demeter at Paros is well-known both from inscriptions and other evidence. The scholiast on the *Birds* of Aristophanes, line 1764, informs us that Archilochos had composed a hymn to Parian Demeter. *Antron* was a Thessalian town mentioned in the *Iliad* 2.697.

———————— *Questions for Consideration* ————————

Using complete sentences, provide brief answers for the following questions.

1. Like many examples of mythological literature, the *Hymn to Demeter* is to a large extent a myth of etiology; i.e., it explains how the changing seasons of the year came into existence. What other myths of this type are you familiar with? Try to locate and list additional etiological myths elsewhere in this volume.

    _____

    _____

    _____

    _____

    _____

2. Find the various relocations and other strategies Demeter carries out in order to regain her daughter. Give line numbers.

    _____

    _____

    _____

    _____

    _____

3. Describe and briefly discuss the role of Demophoon. How is his appearance related to the major theme of the poem (i.e., the loss of Persephone)?

    _____

    _____

    _____

    _____

    _____

——————— *Writing Critically* ———————

Select one of the topics listed below and compose a 500-word essay that discusses the topic fully. Support your thesis with evidence from the text and with critical and/or historical material. Use the space below for preparing to write the essay.

1. How does the mythological world of the *Hymn to Demeter* compare with the epic world portrayed in the *Iliad* and the *Odyssey?* What similarities and differences do you find? Give particular attention to the status of women in each text.

2. During late antiquity, there was strong rivalry between Christianity, the Eleusinians, and other cults with respect to the idea of an afterlife. Because Christianity eventually became the dominant religion in Europe and its colonies, many of us are unaware of the views of the afterlife held by other religions and cultures. Consult one or more reference works on African or Asian religions to find at least one account of such beliefs prevalent in a culture you are currently unfamiliar with. In essay form, present your views or reflections on the idea of life after death.

3. What do you think about when you hear the word "hymn"? Is the work you have just read appropriately called a hymn? In preparing to write an essay on this topic, think of a hymn you may be familiar from another context. Alternatively, look at Shelley's "Hymn to Intellectual Beauty" or "Hymn to Apollo" to see what the concept of a hymn meant to a poet of a much later era.

4. The *Hymn to Demeter* includes a trip to the underworld when Hermes visits Hades to persuade him to release Persephone. This theme has always been a popular one in European literature. Find and discuss examples in the *Odyssey*, the *Aeneid* or Dante.

Prewriting Space:

_____

_____

_____

_____

_____

_____

_____

_____

_____

_____

_____

_____

Introduction

Sappho
(Seventh Century B.C. to Sixth Century B.C.)

The popularity of the long narrative epic poetry of Homer, which recounted the adventures of Greek heroes, gave way in the Archaic period to lyric poetry. Sixth century B.C. writers of this poetic form placed their personal feelings and opinions into verse. Sappho, one of the most outstanding lyricists of this period, was a female who spent most of her life on the island of her birth, Lesbos. Despite the fact that the majority of her works survives in fragmentary form, it remains as a chronicle of her own experience. In fact, she is the first woman of the classical period to leave such a legacy.

Details of Sappho's life are sketchy and cause much debate among scholars. It is agreed that she was born circa 612 B.C. on the island of Lesbos. Definite details of her parentage remain unclear, however, it is suspected from allusions in her verse that she was a member of the wealthy class. Herodotus records her father's name as Scamandronymes, who died when the poet was a child. The poet herself, in one of her verses, identified her mother as one Cleis. Sappho was a wife and mother, but she also had a career as a teacher. Because she was widely respected as a poet and musician, young women from all over Greece came to study with her. Her deep affection for her pupils is documented in her poetry and the nature of this affection has been hotly debated for centuries. To this issue there are no definitive answers; the readers of the poetry will have to make that determination for themselves.

From the short repetitive rhythms in the poetic lines, it is clear that the verse was to be set to music. This rhythmic pattern made the works easy to remember. Love is the chief subject of Sappho's poetry. In fact, the only poem to survive in its entirety is a "Hymn to Aphrodite." Finally, the entire body of Sappho's work may be described as one woman's introspective examination of herself in order that she might fully understand who she is. (EN)

BIBLIOGRAPHY

Sappho. *Sappho: Memoir, Text, Selected Renderings, and a Literal Translation.* trans. Henry Thornton Wharton. London: John Lane Company, 1908.

Sappho. *Sappho: Memoir, Text, Selected Renderings, and a Literal Translation.* Trans. Henry Thornton Wharton. Chicago: A. C. Mcclurg Company, 1905.

Cunningham, Lawrence and John Reich, ed. *Culture and Values: A Survey of the Western Humanities.* Vol. 1. New York: CBS College Publishing, 1982.

Hymn to Aphrodite

Sappho

Golden-throned beyond the sky,
Jove-born immortality:
Hear and heal a suppliant's pain:
Let not love be love in vain!

Come, as once to Love's imploring
Accents of a maid's adoring,
Wafted 'neath the golden dome
Bore thee from thy father's home;

When far off thy coming glowed,
Whirling down th' aethereal road,
On thy dove-drawn progress glancing,
'Mid the light of wings advancing;

And at once the radiant hue
Of immortal smiles I knew;
Heard the voice of reassurance
Ask the tale of love's endurance:—

"Why such prayer? And who for thee,
Sappho, should be touch'd by me;
Passion-charmed in frenzy strong—
Who hath wrought my Sappho wrong?

"—Soon for flight pursuit wilt find,
Proffer'd gifts for gifts declined;
Soon, thro' long reluctance earn'd,
Love refused be Love return'd."

—To thy suppliant so returning,
Consummate a maiden's yearning:
Love, from deep despair set free,
Championing to victory!

F. T. Palgrave, 1854

Introduction to Sappho written by Dr. Evelyn E. Nettles, Associate Professor of English. Reprinted by permission of the author. "Hymn to Aphrodite," reprinted from *Sappho*; Memoir, text, selected renderings, and a literal translation by Henry Thornton Wharton. London: John Lane Company, 1908.

—————— *Questions for Consideration* ——————

Directions: Using complete sentences, provide brief answers for the following questions.

1. Describe the goddess Aphrodite's role in Greek mythology and in the epic poem *The Iliad* by Homer.

    _____

    _____

    _____

    _____

    _____

2. In "Hymn to Aphrodite," what is the speaker asking of the goddess? Cite the lines that support your answer.

    _____

    _____

    _____

    _____

    _____

3. What lines from the poem indicate that the speaker has called on the goddess for help in the past?

    _____

    _____

    _____

    _____

    _____

4. Identify the lines in the poem in which the speaker quotes the goddess. What do these lines mean? Stylistically, what do these lines do for the poem.?

    _____

    _____

    _____

    _____

    _____

5. Use lines from the poem to describe the speaker's lover.

_____

_____

_____

_____

_____

Writing Critically

Directions: Select one of the essay topics listed below and compose a 500 word paper which discusses the topic fully. Support your thesis with evidence from the text and with critical and/or historical material. Use the space provided below for the first stages of the writing process.

1. Examine Sappho's life. Using the information found, what conclusions can you draw about the education of Greek women and about their ability to freely express their artistic skills?

2. Locate information about another female poet of ancient Greece. Read that writer's works and compare it with that of Sappho.

3. About the year 380 A.D. St. Gregory of Nazianzos, Bishop of Constantinople, ordered the burning of Sappho's writing. Explain why St. Gregory found her work offensive. Use the extant lines of Sappho's poetry to illustrate the point.

Prewriting Space:

_____

_____

_____

_____

_____

_____

_____

_____

_____

_____

_____

_____

_____

_____

_____

_____

_____

_____

_____

Introduction

Euripides (484–406 B.C.)

THE BACKGROUND

Euripides (480–406 B.C.), along with Aeschylus and Sophocles, were three of the most distinguised tragedy writers during the Golden Age of Ancient Greece. Euripides came from a family of some means and was, therefore, given the conventional education in gymnastics, music, and dancing. His father actually wanted him to become a boxer, but Euripides demonstrated only a minor interest in the sport. After a few uneventful fights as a boxer, Euripides soon turned his attention to writing and painting.

Euripides possessed an introverted, grim-faced, bookish, and rather standoffish personality. He even preferred to live in quiet solitude with a cave as his home rather than the surroundings of people and neighbors. The response to his demeanor was, therefore, one of mistrust, contempt, and rejection by the people of Athens. In a career that spanned nearly fifty years, Euripides only won the first prize at the drama festival four times in twenty-two competitions and once rewarded posthumously. This may suggest that officials regarded him as being too controversial with powerful ideas that were very disturbing to his audience.

Restoration of the Acropolis at Athens

Euripides was a prolific writer of some ninety plays of which nineteen survived. Some of his earlier works include the plays *Alcestis, Medea, Hippolytus, Hecuba,* and *Andromache.* Later works that proved enduring to readers and audiences today were *The Trojan Women, Electra, Iphigenia in Aulis,* and *The Bacchae. The Cyclops* was the only satyr play that survived. During his time as a writer, Euripides was influenced by the Sophistic movement, political climate, and various philosophical issues. Many scholars have seen Euripides as a realist. In his writing, he was not afraid to confront such issues as incest, murder, prostitution, revenge, and the drug scene with stark realism. Euripides, in essence, portrayed individuals as they really were. All of his plays dealt with one of the following: war, women, and religion. He was a pacifist who severely criticized any aggression of war. In many of his works, Euripides wanted to dignify the position of women by attacking the double standards that they often faced in society. He was not an atheist, but Euripides was opposed to traditional anthropomorphic divinities. He often criticized the evils of religion, oracles, and prophets. In addition, Euripides included in several of his works the clash of emotion and reason, and the clash of absolute standards and relative standards of conduct. Through all of his basic themes, this scholarly recluse possessed sympathy for all human suffering and a tolerant understanding of the emotions of human beings.

Euripides demonstrated an interest in the old myths and tales as sources for his plays. He wanted them to serve as vehicles of character study. Many of his characters become amazingly human creations viewed sympathetically and objectively for their weaknesses. Euripides' main concern in all of his plays was character. He often gave little concern for plot, and even utilized the deus ex-machina to dispose of it. The deus ex-machina, "god from the machine," was a device used to solve a situation that appeared to be insolvable. In other words, the author has no valid means of completing the plot. With the deus ex-machina, a god not involved in the play would suddenly descend on some type of crane or machine on stage for the purpose of deciding the final outcome of a problem that appears to be too difficult to solve.

Euripides accomplished a great deal technically in his writing. He reduced the status of the chorus in order that he might concentrate on his main characters. He introduced realism into the conception, staging, and dialogue of his dramas. The dialogue was often simple, clear everyday speech. Euripides made use of the monologue-prologue to the audience that provided a quick review of the background and plot.

The *Medea,* written in 431 B.C., is generally recognized as Euripides' masterpiece. The mythological background for his tragedy is Jason and the Golden Fleece. Jason, son of Aeson, King of Ioieos, in Thessaly, lived a life in exile because of his devious Uncle Pelias who had seized the throne of Ioieos. When Jason reached manhood, he came to the city to demand his rightful position as king. Reluctantly, Pelias promised the throne to his nephew if two tasks were accomplished in the land of Colchis. First, it was required that he must return the soul of his kinsman Phrixus who died there. Second, Jason was to obtain the Golden Fleece which was owned by Aeetes, king of Colchis. Jason soon set sail on the first ship built, the Argo, along with his heroic companions, the Argonauts to complete his duties. After arriving in Colchis, Jason experienced trouble with the hostile king Aeetes. It seemed only a matter of time for Jason's defeat when the king's daughter, Medea, a sorceress, came to the rescue. Medea fell in love with Jason and proved to be of valuable help to him through his difficulties. She slew her serpent who guarded the fleece, deceived her father, secured the soul of Phrixus, stabbed her brother Absyrtus dead after learning of an attempted ambush against Jason, and aided Jason in obtaining the Golden Fleece. Jason soon set sail with Medea for Ioieos to claim the throne that Pelias had usurped from Jason's father Aeson. Pelias, however, hated Jason and was unwilling to give up his reign. Medea, realizing the hatred of Pelias, offers still more valuable service to Jason. Medea uses her powers as a sorceress to cause the death of Pelias through the unsuspecting hands of his daughters. As a result of the wicked demise of Pelias, Jason and Medea were forced into exile. They found a home in Corinth where they lived for ten years with two children. The king of Corinth, Kreon, was growing old and had one daughter, Creusa. He saw in Jason a worthy successor and soon offered his daughter as a wife. Because Jason was not married to Medea according to Greek customs and law, he was free to leave Medea and their two sons.

Jason found the offer one he could not refuse. He also felt that his sons would be in line to become kings one day if he made this "royal alliance" with Kreon's daughter. What about Medea? Medea, of course, is devastated by Jason's betrayal. She had done everything for him! The results of Jason's treatment of Medea begins this tragedy of passion, violence, and pain. (AHF)

BIBLIOGRAPHY

Dyson, M. "Euripides, Medea." *The Classical Quarterly* 38 (Spring 88): 324–327.

Foley, Helene. "Medea's divided self." *Classical Antiquity* 8 (April 89): 61–85.

Hunter, R. L. "Medea's flight: the fourth book of the Argonauts." *The Classical Quarterly* 37 (Spring 1987): 129–30.

Joyal, Mark A. "Euripides' Medea." *The Classical Quarterly* 41 (Spring 1991): 524–5.

Medea. Videotape. Prod. by Jose Quintero. Ivy Classics Video. 1989.

Nugent, S. Georgia. "Euripides' Medea: the stranger in the house." *Comparative Drama* 27 (Fall 1993): 306–27.

Wakoski, Diane. *Medea the Sorceress*. Santa Rosa, California: Black Sparrow Press, 1991.

Webster, T. B. L. *The Tragedies of Euripides*. London: London Press, 1967.

Wertheim, Albert. "Euripides in South Africa: Medea and Demea." *Comparative Drama* 29 (Fall 1995): 334–47.

Medea

Euripides
Translated by Peter D. Arnott

CHARACTERS

NURSE to Medea
TUTOR to Medea's children
The two sons of Medea and Jason
CHORUS of Corinthian women
MEDEA

CREON, King of Corinth
JASON
AEGEUS, King of Athens
MESSENGER
Soldiers, servants and attendants.

The action takes place before the house of MEDEA *in Corinth.* MEDEA's
old NURSE *is standing at the door.*

NURSE

If only Argo's hull had never flown
Between the Clashing Rocks to Colchis' shore,
And if the pine in Pelion's woods had never
Been chopped down, to put oars into the hands
Of heroes who went out in Pelias' name
To fetch the Golden Fleece! My mistress then,
Medea, would never have fallen in love with Jason
And sailed with him to the walls of Iolkos' land,
Or persuaded the daughters of Pelias to kill
Their father; would not be living here   10
In Corinth, with her husband and her children,
Giving pleasure to the country she has chosen for her exile.
Everything she did was for Jason's sake,
And that's the best way of avoiding risks,
For a wife to have no quarrel with her husband.
But love's turned sour, there's hatred everywhere.
Jason deserts my mistress and his children
And seeks a royal alliance, marrying
The daughter of Creon, ruler of this land,
While poor Medea is left wretched and dishonored   20
To cry "You promised," and remind him of the hand
He pledged in faith, and calls on heaven to see
What she has done for him—and her reward.
She lies without eating, her body abandoned to grief,
Weeping herself thinner with each day that passed
Since first she knew her husband was unfaithful,

Never lifting her head or raising her eyes
From the ground, as deaf as rock or water
To anyone who gives her good advice.
Except, at times, she lifts her snow-white neck   30
And mourns to herself for the loss of her dear father
And the home and country she betrayed to come
Away with a man who now cares nothing for her.
Poor lady, she has come to learn the hard way
What it means to have no country to go back to.
She hates her children, takes no joy in seeing them;
I'm afraid she has something dreadful in her mind.
She's a dangerous woman; he who picks a fight
With her won't come off victor easily.
Here come her children, leaving their games behind;   40
They don't know anything about their mother's
Sorrows; youth is no friend to grief.

(*Enter* MEDEA's *two small sons, with their* TUTOR.)

TUTOR
My mistress' time-worn piece of household property,
What are you doing standing here alone
Before the gates, soliloquizing on misfortune?
However could Medea do without you?

NURSE
Old fellow, guardian of Jason's children,
Good servants take it as a personal sorrow
When trouble and misfortune touch their masters.
And I was moved to such a pitch of misery   50
I longed to come outside, to tell
Heaven and earth about Medea's troubles.

TUTOR
Poor lady, has she not stopped weeping yet?

NURSE
O blessed ignorance! Not halfway, hardly started.

TUTOR
The fool—if I may speak so of my mistress;
She knows nothing of her more recent troubles.

NURSE
What is it, old man? Don't keep it to yourself!

TUTOR
Nothing. I'm sorry that I said so much.

NURSE
By your beard, don't keep it from your fellow-servant.
I'll swear to keep it secret if I must.   60

TUTOR
I heard somebody saying, and pretended not to listen,
When I was at the place where the old men sit

Playing draughts around the holy fountain of Peirene,
That Creon, this country's ruler, was about
To send Medea with her children into exile
Away from Corinth. Whether this tale is true
I cannot say; I hope it may not be so.

> NURSE

Will Jason be content to see his sons
So treated, even though he's quarrelled with their mother?

> TUTOR

When loyalties conflict, the old one loses.   70
He has no love for any in this house.

> NURSE

Why then, we are ruined, if we must add new sorrow
Before we have got rid of the old one.

> TUTOR

This is no time to tell Medea
What has happened; be quiet, keep it to yourself.

> NURSE

My children, do you see what your father's like?
I hope he—no, he is my master still,
Even though he's proved a traitor to his loved ones.

> TUTOR

Who isn't? Have you only just now realized
That no man puts his neighbor before himself?   80
Some have good reason, most are out for profit,
Just as he neglects his sons for his new wife's sake.

> NURSE

Go indoors, my children, everything will be all right.
You keep them to themselves as much as possible,
Don't bring them near their mother when she's angry.
I saw that wild bull look come in her eyes
As if she meant them harm. I know too well
She'll keep her anger warm till someone's hurt.
May it be enemies, and not her friends!

(MEDEA's *voice is heard from inside the house.*)

> MEDEA

Oh,
I am wretched and oppressed with troubles.   90
I wish I were dead, I wish I were dead.

> NURSE

What did I tell you, dear children? Your mother
Is stirring her heart and her anger with it.
Get along indoors as quickly as possible,
Don't go within sight of her, don't come near her,
Beware of her temper, the wild beast lurking
In that desperate mind of hers.

Come now, hurry along indoors;
It's clear that her smoldering anger will burst
Into flames as her passion increases.   100
Her spirit's too big for her, uncontrollable;
What will she do when provoked?

    MEDEA
Oh,
I have suffered things, I have suffered things
Worth a world of weeping. Unhappy sons,
May you die with your father, the whole house perish!

    NURSE
Oh dear, oh dear, what a state I am in!
What have your children to do with their father's
Wickedness, why hate them?
Oh, my darling children,
I'm terrified something will happen to you.   110
It's bad when a queen is angry; she rarely submits,
Gets her own way in most things, and changes
Her mood without warning.

(Exeunt CHILDREN *and* TUTOR.*)*

It's better if you've been used to a life
Without any ups or downs; I'd rather
Grow old in peace than be a great lady.
Moderation's a word that's good to hear
And the greatest blessing that men could have.
Excess can never bring profit; when heaven's
Angry, the great ones are hit the hardest.   120

(Enter the CHORUS *of Corinthian women.)*

    CHORUS
I heard the voice, I heard the cry
Of Colchis' unhappy daughter.
It is ringing still; tell us, old woman.
I was inside at my door, and heard her crying.
I cannot be happy when the home is troubled,
When the home is one I love.

    NURSE
Home! There is no home, that's past and gone.
Jason is wrapped up in his new wife,
And my mistress sits pining away in her room
And her friends can say nothing to comfort her.   130

    MEDEA
I wish
That lightning from heaven would split my head open!
What have I to live for now?
Why can I not leave this hateful life
And find repose in death?

CHORUS
Zeus, heaven and earth, do you hear
How the wretched wife is weeping?
Why do you pray for that hateful sleep?
Fool, would you wish your death sooner?
This is no way to pray. If your husband   140
Honors another wife, it has happened
To others, don't take it to heart.
Zeus will see justice done; don't wear
Yourself out with lamenting your husband.

MEDEA
Goddess of justice, Queen Artemis,
You see how I suffer, who bound
My husband, curse him, with oaths?
I pray I may see him perish
And his wife, and all the house
Who have dared unprovoked to wrong me.   150
My father, my country, how shamefully
I left you, and killed my own brother.

NURSE
Do you hear what she says, how she cries
To Themis in prayer, and to Zeus
Whom we honor as keeper of oaths?
One thing is certain, my mistress
Won't let go her anger for nothing.

CHORUS
If she would only come out here to see us,
If she would only hear what we have to say,
To see if her bitterness would melt   160
And her anger disappear.
I hope I shall always be ready
To stand by my friends. Go inside, old woman,
And fetch her out of the house; and hurry,
Before she can harm the household;
That's the way her grief is going.

NURSE
I'll do it, but I'm afraid
I shan't be able to move her.
Still, it's a labor of love.
She's angry, and glares at her servants   170
Like a lioness guarding her cubs
When anyone comes with a message.
You wouldn't be wrong to consider
The old poets not clever but fools
Who wrote music for dinners and banquets,
Pleasant tunes for men who were happy,
But nobody ever discovered
How to use all this music and singing
To lessen a man's load of trouble
That brought death and misfortune and ruin.   180
It would certainly be an advantage
To use music for healing! Why waste it

On dinners? There's pleasure enough
In a banquet, who wants any more?

(Exit.)

CHORUS
I heard the voice heavy with grief
Bitterly mourning the faithless
Husband who married and left her,
Blaming her wrongs on the gods,
The justice of Zeus, the sworn oath
That started her difficult crossing   190
Through the gates of the salt foggy sea
To the opposite shores of Greece.

(Enter MEDEA.)

MEDEA
Women of Corinth, I have come outside
To avoid your disapproval. I know there are many
Conceited people; some keep themselves to themselves,
Others show it in public, while others still, who take
Things quietly, will find themselves called idlers.
The eyes are no good judges, when a man
Dislikes another at sight before he knows
His character, when there is nothing against him.   200
A foreigner especially should conform.
I'd even blame a native for presuming
To annoy his fellow citizens through lack of manners.
For me, this unexpected blow that fell
Has shattered me; it is the end, I only want to die.
The man to whom I gave my all, as well he knows,
Has turned out utterly false—my husband.
Of all things living that possess a mind
We women are the most unfortunate.
To start with, we must put ourselves to vast expense   210
To buy ourselves a husband, take a master for
Our bodies—a worse evil than the other:
And everything depends on this, whether we take a good man
Or a bad one; divorce is not respectable
For women, we may not deny our husbands.
Coming to new manners and a new way of life,
A woman needs second sight to know how best
To manage her bedfellow; no-one taught her at home.
And if we work hard at it, and our husband
Lives with us without struggling against the yoke   220
We are to be envied; if not, death comes at last.
When a man is bored with the company in his household
He can go out to find his consolation.
We women have only one soul-mate to look to.
They tell us we can spend our lives at home
In safety, while they go out to fight the wars.
How illogical! I'd rather stand three times
In the battlefield than bear one child.
But we have different stories, you and I;
You have a city, and a father's home,   230

And friendly company, a life you can enjoy.
I have no home, no country; I am despised
By my husband, something brought back from abroad;
I have no mother, no brother, no family
Where I can find a refuge from my troubles.
So this is the favor I will ask of you:
If the means offer, or I can find some way
To pay my husband back for the wrong he has done me,
Keep my secret. At other times a woman is timid,
Afraid to defend herself, frightened at the sight   240
Of weapons; but when her marriage is in danger
There is no mind bloodthirstier than hers.

    CHORUS
I will; for you have every right to punish him.
I do not wonder that you are distressed.
But I can see Creon, ruler of this land,
Approaching with some new decision to tell us.

(Enter CREON.*)*

    CREON
You with the scowling face, who hate your husband,
Medea, I command you leave this land
An exile, taking your two children with you
Without delay. I come to execute   250
My own decree, and shall not go back home
Till I have seen you past our boundaries.

    MEDEA
Alas, my ruin is complete;
My enemies pursue full-sailed, and I
Can find no friendly harbor from calamity.
But though I am persecuted I will ask one thing:
For what reason, Creon, do you banish me?

    CREON
I am afraid of you. Why veil my words?
Afraid you will do my child some dreadful harm.
And many things contribute to my fear: 260
You are clever, and accomplished in black arts,
And angry that your husband has deserted you.
I hear you threaten—so I am informed—
To act against the bridegroom and the bride
And the father too. I had rather be safe than sorry.
Better be hated, woman, by you now,
Than soften and repent my weakness later.

    MEDEA
This has happened before. It is not the first time, Creon,
I have been the victim of my reputation.
No sensible man should ever have his sons   270
Brought up more clever than the average.
Apart from being told they waste their time
They earn the spite and envy of their neighbors.
You'll be called good-for-nothing, not intelligent,

For holding unconventional ideas;
And if the know-alls find your reputation
Exceeding theirs, the state will turn against you.
And I am one of those to whom it happened.
I am clever, so some people envy me,
Some call me idle, some the opposite,   280
While others hate me; but they exaggerate.
You fear me? Do you think you will be hurt?
I am in no state—do not be nervous, Creon—
To commit an offence against the authorities.
How have you wronged me? You bestowed your daughter
On the man your heart desired. It is my husband
That I hate.
But I suppose you know what you are doing.
I do not grudge you any of your good fortune.
Let the marriage stand, and prosper; but permit me   290
To stay here. Though I am the injured party
I shall not raise my voice against my betters.

     CREON
Your words are smooth enough, but I fear your heart
Is already plotting mischief, and by so much less
I trust you than I did before.
A fiery temper, in woman as in man,
Is easier to guard against than silent cunning.
So get gone without more argument.
You may be sure that no arts you can use
Will keep you here, now you have turned against us.   300

     MEDEA
No, by your knees, and by your child the bride!

     CREON
Go, it is useless, you cannot persuade me.

     MEDEA
Will you turn me away and not listen to my prayers?

     CREON
My family comes first in my affections.

     MEDEA
My country, how strongly I recall you now.

     CREON
I love my country too, after my children.

     MEDEA
Oh, what a bitter curse is love to men.

     CREON
Well, that depends on circumstances, I suppose.

     MEDEA
O Zeus, remember who began these sorrows.

CREON

Get out, you fool, and trouble me no further.   310

MEDEA

I have my troubles; trouble me no further.

CREON

Soon my men will drive you out by force.

MEDEA

No! Spare me that, at least. I beg you, Creon—

CREON

You seem determined, woman, to be difficult.

MEDEA

No. I will go. It was not that I wanted.

CREON

Then why resist? Why do you not leave the country?

MEDEA

Permit me to remain here this one day,
To make my mind up where I am to go,
And where to keep my children, since their father
Prefers to leave his sons without protection.   320
You are a father; you have sons yourself,
And therefore should be well disposed to mine.
I do not care for myself if I am banished
But I am wretched if they are in trouble.

CREON

I never had the heart to play the tyrant.
My conscience has always been my disadvantage.
Woman, I know that I am making a mistake,
But your request is granted. But I warn you,
If the light of heaven falls on you tomorrow
Here with your sons inside our boundaries   330
You die. This is my final word.
And now, if stay you must, remain one day,
Too little time to do the harm I dread.

(*Exit.*)

CHORUS

How troubled you are, unfortunate lady!
Where will you turn? What home, what country
Will give you protection?
Medea, god has plunged you in a sea of troubles
And there is no land in sight.

MEDEA

Beaten on every side; who can deny it?
But not in this, so do not think I am.   340
There are still trials for this new-married pair
And no small sorrow for their families.

You think I would have fawned upon this man
Unless I were working for my own advantage?
I would not have touched him, not have spoken to him.
But he has gone so far in foolishness
That when he could have foiled my plans
By sending me to exile, he allowed me stay
One day, in which I shall make corpses of
Three of my enemies—father, girl, my husband.   350
And I have many ways to work their deaths
And do not know where first to try my hand—
Whether to set their wedding house on fire,
Or creep indoors to where their bedroom is
And thrust a sharpened sword into their hearts.
One thing prevents me; if I should be caught
Entering the house and plotting against it
I shall die the laughingstock of my enemies.
No. It is best to go direct, the way in which I am
Most skilled, and poison both of them.   360
Ah then,
Suppose them dead; what city will receive me?
What host will offer me home and security
In some safe country, and protect my life?
No-one. Then I shall wait a little while,
And if some tower of safety should appear,
By stealth and cunning I shall murder them.
But if misfortune should drive me out helpless,
I shall take the sword, even though it means my death,
And kill them.
No, by the Queen of Night whom above all   370
I honor and have chosen as my partner,
Dark Hecate dwelling in the corners of my hearth,
No man shall wound my heart and still live happy.
I will make them curse the day they married,
Curse this alliance and my banishment.
Then come, Medea, call on all the skill
You have in plotting and contriving;
On to the crime! This is the test of courage.
Look to your wrongs! You must not let yourself
Be mocked by Jason's Sisyphean wedding,   380
You, a royal child, descended from the Sun.
You have the skill; moreover you were born
A woman; and women are incapable of good,
But have no equal in contriving harm.

    CHORUS
The sacred rivers flow back to their sources,
The appointed order of things is reversed.
It is men whose minds are deceitful, who take
The names of their gods in vain,
And women the future will honor in story
As leaders of upright lives.   390
Glory is ours! And the slanderous tongues
That attacked womankind shall be stilled.
You Muses of past generations, inspire
No more the refrain that woman is fickle.
We were not given the wit by Phoebus

Apollo, the master of songs,
To strike from the lyre its heavenly music.
If it were so, I should sing
In answer to men; for history tells
As much of men's lives as of ours.   400
In passion you sailed from the land
Of your fathers, and saw the twin rocks
Of the sea fall open before you.
Now you live among strangers, exchange
Your couch for a husbandless bed;
Without rights and distressed you are driven
An exile out of the land.
The spell of the oath has been broken; no longer
Has Greece any shame, it has flown to the winds.
Poor lady, your father's home   410
Will offer you shelter no more
In time of distress; your marriage
Is lost to a queen who descends
On your house as a second bride.

(Enter JASON.*)*

JASON
I have noticed many times, this not the first,
How willfulness runs on to self-destruction.
You could have kept this country as your home
By obeying the decisions of your betters,
But futile protests send you into exile.
They do not worry me. You can go on   420
Forever saying Jason is a scoundrel;
But when it comes to slandering your rulers,
Count yourself lucky you were only banished.
I wanted you to stay—tried all the time
To pacify the anger of the king;
But you persevered in folly, and continually
Spoke ill of him, and so you must be banished.
However, I shall not desert my friends
In spite of their behavior, but am here to see
That you and your children do not go out penniless   430
Or in need of anything; for banishment
Brings many hardships. Hate me though you may,
I could never bring myself to bear you malice.

MEDEA
Oh, devil! Devil! This is the worst abuse
My tongue can find for your lack of manliness.
You come to me, my mortal enemy,
Hateful to heaven and to all mankind?
This is not venturesome, this is not courage,
To look friends in the face whom you have wronged,
But the most detestable of human weaknesses,   440
Yes, shamelessness! But I am glad you came,
For I can ease my overburdened heart
Abusing you, and you will smart to hear.
I shall begin my tale at the beginning.
I saved your life, as every single Greek

Who sailed with you on board the Argo knows,
When you were sent to tame the bulls that breathed fire,
And yoke them, and sow death in the field.
The dragon that encircled with his coils
The Golden Fleece and watched it without sleeping   450
I killed for you, and lit your path to safety.
For you I left my father and my home
And sailed to Iolkos and Mount Pelion
With you, and showed more eagerness than sense.
I brought on Pelias the worst of ends,
Death at his children's hands, and ruined his house.
All this I suffered for your worthless sake,
To be abandoned for another woman,
Though I had borne you children! Were I barren
You might have some excuse to marry again.   460
I have no faith in your promises; I cannot tell
If you believe in the old gods still, or think
There is some newer standard of morality
You have broken your oath to me, you must know that.
Oh, this my right hand, that you wrung so often!
These knees, at which you fell; how am I deceived
In a false lover, cheated of my hopes.
But come, I will open my heart to you as to a friend—
Though what fair treatment could I hope from you?
Yet will I; you will feel more shame to answer: 470
Where should I turn now? To my father's home?
The country I betrayed to come with you?
Or Pelias' wretched daughters? They would give
A gracious welcome to their father's murderess.
For that is how it is. I have estranged myself
From friends at home, and those I should not hurt
I have made mortal enemies for your sake.
In recompense, how happy have you made me
Among Greek women; what a paragon
Of rectitude I married, to my sorrow,   480
When I am exiled, cast out of the land
Without a friend. My sons are all I have.
A fine reproach for this new-married man
When his sons and she who saved him wander beggars.
O Zeus, why have you given men clear marks
To help them tell true gold from counterfeit,
While nature sets no stamp upon men's bodies
To help us tell the true man from the false!

CHORUS
Tempers run high, and cannot soon be soothed,
When those who have once loved begin to quarrel.   490

JASON
I must show myself no mean speaker, so it seems,
But like the sea-wise steersman of a ship
Close-haul my canvas, lady, and run before
The storm of your verbosity. Since you
Have raised this monument to your own kindness,
I hold that Cypris was the guardian of my voyages,
No other god or man. You are quick-witted, true,

But it would be ungenerous to explain
You were compelled by Love's unerring shafts to save me.
However, I shall not go too deeply into that;   500
Where you did help me, you did not do badly.
But you have profited by my escape
More than you lost by it. Let me explain:
To start with, instead of living among savages
You live in Greece and come to learn our laws
And how to live by justice, not brute force.
Besides, all Greece has learned how clever you are.
You're famous! If you still lived at the ends
Of the earth, nobody would have heard of you.
If only my good fortune made me famous   510
I would not ask for riches, nor the power
To sing a sweeter song than Orpheus did.
So much for what you have to say about
My labors; you began the argument.
For your reproaches on my royal marriage
I'll show you first of all how clever I was,
Second, how prudent, and third, that I am my sons'
And your best friend. Please do not interrupt me.
When, with this irretrievable misfortune
Behind me, I came here from Iolkos' land,   520
What better piece of luck could I have found
Than this, an exile marry a princess?
Not that you bored me—the sore point with you—
Or that I was infatuated with a new wife
Or anxious for a larger family;
I'm satisfied with those I already have.
No! My main reason was that we should live well,
Not have to count our pennies. I'm aware
How all friends turn against you when you're poor.
I wanted to bring my children up as sons of mine   530
Should be, and give my sons by you some brothers.
If I could join our families and make them one,
I'd count myself a happy man. You need no sons,
But it profits me to add to those I have. Is this
So reprehensible? It's only jealousy
That makes you think so. But things have come to such a pass
That women think marriage is the only thing that matters.
When once your sole possession is endangered,
Whatever's good and right for you to do
You fight it. There ought to be some other way   540
For men to get their sons, there ought to be
No women; then a man could live his life in peace.

CHORUS
Jason, you have made a pretty speech,
But I will be bold, and say what I think:
It was criminal to desert your wife.

MEDEA
The world and I have very different views.
The bad man who is clever with his tongue
In my opinion asks for double punishment.
He prides himself on his power to talk his way

Out of everything, nothing frightens him. But he   550
Is not so clever as he thinks. So do not make
Fine speeches, or think to play the innocent
With me. One word will throw you. If you were honest
You should have told me of your wedding plans,
Not kept them secret from the ones that loved you.

> JASON

Much good you would have done my wedding plans, I must say,
If I'd told you of them when even now
You can't disguise the anger in your heart.

> MEDEA

It was not that. You thought it might cause talk
To have a foreign wife when you grew older.   560

> JASON

I tell you it was not for the woman's sake
I made the royal alliance that I did,
But as I said before, to offer you
Protection, and beget young kings to be
My sons' new brothers, towers of strength to us.

> MEDEA

Give me no happiness involving pain
Or joy that will not leave the mind in peace.

> JASON

You should know better; pray for something else,
Never to judge good fortune to be bad
Or count yourself hard done by when all's well.   570

> MEDEA

Go on, insult me! You have a place to go
While I am an exile from the land and friendless.

> JASON

You brought it on yourself, blame no-one else.

> MEDEA

How? Did I marry and abandon you?

> JASON

Calling down blasphemous curses on the king.

> MEDEA

Yes, you will find me a curse to your house too.

> JASON

I refuse to discuss this matter any further.
But if you want my money, to assist
You and your children when you are gone,
Speak out; I am ready to be open-handed,   580
And give you introductions to my friends
Who will assist you. It is foolish to refuse;
Let your anger rest, and you will profit by it.

MEDEA

I want no truck with any friends of yours
Or anything from you, so do not offer it.
A bad man's gifts bring no-one any good.

JASON

Very well! But I call on heaven to witness
I have done everything possible for you and your sons.
Your stubbornness rejects your friends; you don't know
When you are well off. So much the worse for you.   590

(Exit.)

MEDEA

Yes, go; you are too eager for your new bride
To stay any longer outside her house.
Go and be married! God will echo me,
This marriage may be such you will disown it.

CHORUS

Love unrestrained can bring
No worth or honor with it,
But coining in small measure
There is no power more gracious.
Never let fly at me
Great Queen, the unerring shafts   600
Of your golden arrows, tipped
In the poison of desire.
Let moderation be
My guide, the gods' best gift.
Dread Aphrodite, never
Send strife and argument
To attack my heart and make
Me long for other loves,
But learn to honor marriage
And let love lie in peace.   610
Oh, let me never lose you,
My country and my home,
Or learn the thorny ways
Of poverty, the worst
Of life's calamities.
No! Let me rather die
And see life's brief day done.
This is the greatest sorrow,
The loss of fatherland.
I know; I do not learn   620
The tale from the lips of others.
No home or friend to share
The depths of your distress.
Dishonored be the man
Who honors not his friends
And locks his heart away;
No friend shall be of mine.

(Enter AEGEUS.)

AEGEUS
Give you joy, Medea; this is the best way
Men know to start a conversation with their friends.

MEDEA
And joy to you, wise Aegeus, son of Pandion.   630
Where are you from? What brings you to our country?

AEGEUS
From Apollo's ancient oracle at Delphi.

MEDEA
What took you there, to earth's prophetic center?

AEGEUS
To inquire how children might be born to me.

MEDEA
What, are you still without a son at your age?

AEGEUS
Yes, by some whim of providence I have no heir.

MEDEA
Are you married? Or have you never had a wife?

AEGEUS
I am no stranger to the marriage bond.

MEDEA
And what did Phoebus have to say about it?

AEGEUS
Words too wise for a man to understand.   640

MEDEA
Then may I know the oracle's reply?

AEGEUS
Most certainly, for cleverness is what we need.

MEDEA
Then tell me, if you may, what Phoebus said.

AEGEUS
Not to loosen the wineskin's hanging foot—

MEDEA
Until you had arrived somewhere, or done something?

AEGEUS
Until I reached my ancestral hearth again.

MEDEA
And what directs your journey through this country?

AEGEUS
There is a man called Pittheus, King of Troezen—

MEDEA
Old Pelops' son, with a great reputation for piety.

AEGEUS
I want to tell him what the oracle has said.   650

MEDEA
He is a wise man, skillful in such matters.

AEGEUS
And the oldest of my military allies.

MEDEA
I hope you are lucky, and achieve your heart's desire.

(She breaks down, and turns away her head.)

AEGEUS
Why do you turn away, and look so pale?

MEDEA
Aegeus, my husband is the worst of men.

AEGEUS
What's this you say? Tell me about your troubles.

MEDEA
Jason, unprovoked, has done me wrong.

AEGEUS
What has he done to you? Tell me more clearly.

MEDEA
Put another woman over his household in my place.

AEGEUS
He would not dare to treat you so despicably!   660

MEDEA
Too truly; and I, the old love, am dishonored.

AEGEUS
Was it for love of her, or hate of you?

MEDEA
Much love he has; the man was born unfaithful.

AEGEUS
Take no notice, if he's as worthless as you say.

MEDEA
He was in love with marrying a king's daughter.

AEGEUS
Who gives her to him? Tell me the whole story.

MEDEA
Creon, the ruler of this land of Corinth.

AEGEUS
You have good reason for your grief, my lady.

MEDEA
It is the end; and I am banished too.

AEGEUS
On whose orders? This is a new wrong you speak of.   670

MEDEA
It is Creon who sends me into exile from the land.

AEGEUS
And Jason lets him? This is unforgivable.

MEDEA
He says not, but he has resigned himself.

(She falls at his feet.)

But I beseech you, by the beard I clasp,
And throw myself a suppliant at your knees,
Have pity, have pity on my misery
And do not see me thrown out destitute.
Let me come to your country and live at your hearthside;
So may your great desire come to fruition
And give you children, and allow you to die happy.   680
You do not know what good fortune you have found.
I can put a stop to your childlessness, and give
You issue, with the potions that I know.

AEGEUS
I am anxious for many reasons, lady,
To grant your request; first, my religious scruples,
And then your promise that I should have sons,
For in this there is nothing else that I can do.
But this is how I stand. If you can reach my country
I'll endeavor to protect you as in duty bound.
But one thing I must make clear from the start: 690
I am not willing to take you from this country.
If you can make your own way to my home
I will keep you safe and give you up to no-one,
But you must make your own escape from Corinth.
I would not give offence, even to strangers.

MEDEA
So let it be, then. If you swear an oath
To do this, I have nothing more to ask.

AEGEUS
Do you not trust me? What is it puts you off?

MEDEA
I trust you; but the house of Pelias is against me,
And Creon. Oath-bound, you could never yield   700
Me to them when they came to take me away.
A promise unsupported by an oath
Would allow you to befriend them, and obey
Their summons when it came. My cause is weak,
While they have power and money on their side.

AEGEUS
You show great thought for the future in what you say.
But, if you wish it, I shall not refuse.
My own position will be unassailable
If I have an excuse to offer your enemies,
And you will run less risk. Come, name your gods.   710

MEDEA
Swear by the plain of Earth, and by the Sun,
My father's father; add the whole family of gods.

AEGEUS
That I will do or not do what? Say on.

MEDEA
Never to drive me from the land yourself
Or willingly yield me to my enemies
When they come for me, as long as you do live.

AEGEUS
I swear by Earth, by the holy light of Sun,
By all the gods, to do as you have said.

MEDEA
Enough. What penalty if you break your oath?

AEGEUS
What comes to men who take their gods in vain.   720

MEDEA
Now go your way in peace. All will be well.
I shall come to your country as soon as I have done
What I intend to do, and won my heart's desire.

CHORUS
Now Hermes, God of Travelers,
Give you safe conduct home,
And may the desire that you cherish
So eagerly be fulfilled.
You have shown, Aegeus,
What a good man you are.

(*Exit* AEGEUS.)

MEDEA

O Zeus, Zeus' daughter justice, light of Sun,   730
Now shall we have a glorious triumph, friends,
Upon our enemies; our feet are on the path.
Now is there hope my enemies will pay
The penalty. This man has shown himself,
Where we were weakest, a haven for my plans.
In him my ship may find safe anchorage;
To Athena's fortress city shall I go!
And now I will reveal you all my plans.
Hear what I have to say; it will not please you.
One of my servants I shall send to Jason   740
And ask him to come here before my face.
And when he comes, I shall say soft words to him,
That I agree with him, and all is well;
That the royal match he abandons me to make
Is for my advantage, and a good idea.
I shall entreat him that my sons should stay—
Not to allow my sons to be insulted
In a strange country by my enemies,
But to kill the daughter of the king with cunning.
I shall send them both with presents in their hands,   750
A fine-spun robe, a golden diadem.
If she accepts the gifts and puts them on
She will die in agony and all who touch her,
With such deadly poison shall I anoint my gifts.
Now I must leave this story, and lament
The dreadful thing that then remains for me to do.
I will kill my sons; no man shall take them from me.
And when the house of Jason lies in ruins,
I shall fly this land, setting my darlings' death
Behind me, most unspeakable of crimes.   760
The scorn of enemies is unendurable.
But let it go; for what have I to live for?
I have no home, no country, no escape from misery.
I made my mistake the day I left behind
My father's home, seduced by speeches from
A Greek who heaven knows will pay for them.
The sons I bore him he will never see
Alive after this day, nor father more
On his new-married bride, condemned to die
In agony from my poisons as she deserves.   770
No-one shall call me timorous or weak
Or stay-at-home, but quite the opposite,
A menace to my enemies and help to friends;
Those are the people that the world remembers.

CHORUS

Since you have taken me into your confidence,
I should like to help you, but must still uphold
The laws of men. I say you cannot do this.

MEDEA

There is nothing else I can do. But you have excuse
For speaking so, you have not known my sufferings.

CHORUS
But will you have the heart to kill your children?   780

MEDEA
Yes; it is the way I can most hurt my husband.

CHORUS
But you will be the most unhappy of women.

MEDEA
So be it; there can be no compromise.

(*Calling the* NURSE.)

You; go at once and fetch Jason here.
We have no secrets from each other, you and I.
And breathe no word to anyone of my plans,
As you love your mistress, as you are a woman.

(*Exit* NURSE.)

CHORUS
Happy of old were the sons of Erechtheus,
Sprung from the blessed gods, and dwelling
In Athens' holy and untroubled land.   790
Their food is glorious wisdom; they walk
With springing step in the crystal air.
Here, so they say, golden Harmony first
Saw the light, the child of the Muses nine.
And here too, they say, Aphrodite drank
Of Cephisus' fair-flowing stream, and breathed
Sweet breezes over the land, with garlands
Of scented roses entwined in her hair,
And gave Love a seat on the throne of Wisdom
To work all manner of arts together.   800
How then will this city of sacred waters,
This guide and protector of friends, take you,
Your children's slayer, whose touch will pollute
All others you meet? Think again of the deaths
Of your children, the blood you intend to shed
By your knees, by every entreaty we beg you
Not to become your children's murderess.
Where will you find the boldness of mind,
The courage of hand and heart, to kill them?
How will you strike without weeping, how   810
Be constant to still your hands in their blood
When your children kneel weeping before you?

(*Enter* JASON.)

JASON
I come at your request; although you hate me,
This favor you shall have. So let me hear
What new demand you have to make of me.

MEDEA

Jason, I ask you to forgive the words
I spoke just now. The memory of our
Past love should help you bear my evil temper.
Now I have taken myself to task and found
I was to blame. "Fool, why am I so mad?   820
Why should I quarrel with those who want to help me,
And why antagonize the men in power
And my husband, who works only for my advantage
In making this royal marriage, and begetting
New brothers for my sons? Why not lay down
My anger, why resent what the gods provide?
Are not the children mine, and am I not
An exile from the land, without a friend?"
Such were my thoughts; and then I realized
What foolishness my futile anger was.   830
Now I agree with you, and think you provident
In gaining us this connection, and myself a fool.
I should have been your go-between and shared
Your plans, stood by your marriage-bed,
And had the joy of tending your new bride.
But we are what we are; I will not say bad,
But women. But you should not take bad example
And answer my stupidity with yours.
Now I submit, agree that I was wrong
Before, but come to saner judgment now.   840
My children, here, my children, leave the house,
Come out to greet your father, and with me
Bid him goodbye; be reconciled to friends
And let your anger rest beside your mother's.

(*The* CHILDREN *appear from the houses and go, to* JASON.)

We are at peace; there is no anger now.
Come, take his hand.

(*aside*)   Oh, the pity of it;

There is something still unseen, but my mind knows it.
Children, will you live long to stretch out
Your loving arms, as now? Oh pity, pity;
How near I am to tears, how full of fear.   850

(*aloud*)

At last I have stopped the quarrel with their father
And brought tears of forgiveness to their eyes.

CHORUS

And my eyes too are wet with running tears.
I pray we have no troubles worse than these.

JASON

I approve this mood, and do not blame the other.
It is natural for a woman to show resentment
When her husband smuggles in a second marriage.

But now your mind has turned to better things
And learned—at last—which policy must win.
Done like a sensible woman!   860

(To the CHILDREN.*)*

Your father hasn't forgotten you, my boys.
God willing, you'll be well provided for.
I'll see you here in Corinth at the top
Beside your brothers. Just grow up; your father
Will see to the rest, and any god that fancies you.
I want to see you, when you've grown young men,
Stout fellows, head and shoulders above my enemies.
Medea, what are these tears upon your checks?
Why do you turn your face away from me?
Why aren't you happy at the things I say?   870

      MEDEA
It is nothing. I was thinking of my children.

      JASON
Don't worry. I shall see them well set up.

      MEDEA
I shall try to be brave, not mistrust what you say;
But we women are the weaker sex, born weepers.

      JASON
Why so unhappy, lady, for these children?

      MEDEA
I am their mother. When you prayed that they might live,
Compassion came, and said, "Will it be so?"
For what you came here to discuss with me,
Part has been said, the rest remains to say.
Since the king thinks good to send me from the land,   880
I too think it is good, and I acknowledge it,
Not to embarrass you or the authorities
By staying. I am not welcome in this house.
Yes, I will leave this country, go to exile;
But that your hand alone may rear my sons,
I pray you, beg the king to let them stay.

      JASON
I doubt I will succeed, but I must try.

      MEDEA
Then you must tell your new wife, the princess,
To beg her father to remit their banishment.

      JASON
I'll do it. Yes, I think I can persuade her.   890

      MEDEA
You will, if she is a woman like the rest of us.
And I shall lend my shoulder to this labor,

And send her gifts more beautiful by far
Than any man has ever seen, I know—
A fine-spun robe, a golden diadem.
My sons shall take them. One of my servants,
Go bring the robes as quickly as you can.
She will be not once blessed but a thousand times,
Having you, the best of men, to be her husband,
And owning ornaments which once the Sun,   900
My father's father gave to his descendants.

(A servant brings the presents from the house.)

Here, take this dowry, children, put it in the hands
Of the happy royal bride. She will not think lightly of it.

JASON

What are you doing? Why deprive yourself?
Do you think the royal house lacks robes?
Do you think we have no gold? Keep them,
Don't give them away. If my wife respects me at all,
She will prefer my wish to presents, I can tell you.

MEDEA

Not so; they say that gifts can move the gods.
A piece of gold is worth a thousand speeches.   910
Her luck is in, god give her more of it.
A queen, so young. I'd willingly give my life
To save my sons from banishment, not only gold.
Go to the halls of wealth, my sons, beseech
The new wife of your father and my queen,
And beg her not to send you into exile.
Give her the presents—this is most important—
Into her own hands.
Now hurry; bring your mother back good news
That you have accomplished what she sets her heart on.   920

(Exeunt CHILDREN *and* JASON.*)*

CHORUS

There is no hope now for the children's lives,
No hope any longer; they go to their deaths,
And the bride, poor bride, will accept the gift
Of the crown worked of gold,
And with her own hands make death an adornment
To set in her yellow hair.
The unearthly splendor and grace of the robe
And the crown worked of gold will persuade her to wear them.
She will soon be attired to marry the dead.
Into such a snare is she fallen,   930
Into such deadly fate, poor girl, and will never
Escape from the curse upon her.
And you, unhappy man, bitter bridegroom,
Who make an alliance with kings,
Unknowing you send your sons to their deaths
And bring on your bride the worst of ends.
How are you deceived in your hopes of the future.

And next to theirs we mourn your sorrows,
Unhappy mother of sons,
Who, to repay your husband for leaving   940
Your bed, and going to live with another
Woman, will kill your children.

(*Enter the* TUTOR, *leading the two* CHILDREN.)

TUTOR

Mistress! Your children are reprieved from exile!
The royal bride was pleased to take into her hands
Your gifts, and with your sons is peace.
Why does good fortune leave you so confused?
Why do you turn your face the other way?
Why aren't you happy at the things I say?

MEDEA

Alas.

TUTOR

Your words and mine are out of tune.

MEDEA

Alas again.

TUTOR

            Is there some meaning to my words   950
I do not know? Am I wrong to think them good?

MEDEA

You have said what you have said; I do not blame you.

TUTOR

Why do you drop your eyes, begin to weep?

MEDEA

Because there is necessity, old man. The gods
And my pernicious schemings brought this thing to pass.

TUTOR

Be brave; your children will bring you home again.

MEDEA

I shall send others home before they do.

TUTOR

You are not the only mother to lose her children.
Mankind must bear misfortune patiently.

MEDEA

And so shall I. But go inside the house   960
And see about my children's daily needs.

(*Exit* TUTOR.)

My sons, my sons, you have a city now

And home, where when we've said our sad goodbye
You will stay for ever, parted from your mother.
I go in exile to another land
Before I have had the joy of seeing you happy,
Before I have made your marriage beds, and seen
Your brides, and carried torches at your weddings.
My willfulness has brought its own reward.
For nothing did I toil to bring you up,   970
For nothing did I labor, and endure
The pangs I suffered in your hour of birth.
Once I had in you, oh, once, such splendid hopes,
To have you by my side as I grew old
And when I died, your loving arms around me,
What all men long for. This sweet dream is now
Destroyed. When you and I have parted
My life will be forlorn and desolate.
Your loving eyes will never look upon
Your mother again, you go to another life.   980
My sons, my sons, why do you look at me?
Why smile at me the last smile I shall see?
Oh, oh, what shall I do? Women, my heart
Is faltering when I look at their bright eyes.
I cannot do it; I renounce the plans
I made before, my children shall go with me.
Why should I use their sufferings to hurt
Their father, and so doubly hurt myself?
Not I, not I; I renounce my plans.
And yet—what is happening to me? Shall I let   990
My enemies go scot-free and earn their scorn?
Be bold, Medea. Why, what a coward am I
That can allow my mind talk of relenting.
Go in, my children. He who may not be
Present at my sacrifice without sin,
On his own head be it; my hand is firm.

(She turns to follow the CHILDREN *into the House, and then pauses.)*

Do not do this, my heart, do not do this!
Spare them, unhappy heart, let my sons go.
They will live with you in exile and make you glad.
No, by the fiends that dwell in Hell below,   1000
It shall never come to this, that I allow
My sons to be insulted by my enemies.

(A noise of shouting is heard off-stage.)

So; it is finished ; there is no escape.
The crown is on her head, the royal bride
Is dying in her robes, this I know well.
And I must tread my own unhappy road;
Far worse the road on which I send my sons.
I want to speak to them. Here, children give
Your mother your hand, let mother hold your hand.
Oh dearest hand, oh lips I hold most dear,   1010
Dear face, and dear bright eyes, may you be happy—
But in another place; your father leaves

You nothing here. Oh, sweet embrace,
The feel of your skin, the scent of your sweet breath;
Go away! Go away! I have no strength
To look on you, my sorrows overwhelm me.
Women, I know what evil I am to do,
But anger has proved stronger than our reason
And from anger all our greatest ills arise.

(*The* CHILDREN *go into the house.*)

CHORUS
I have often allowed my mind   1020
To speculate, enter into arguments
Lying outside a woman's province.
But there is a Muse in women too
To help us to wisdom; not in all,
But look far enough, and you may find a few
On whom the Muse has smiled.
And I say that those men and women
Who do not know what it means to have children
Are blessed above parents in this world.
A child can bring joy, or bitter pain;
What can the childless know of these?   1030
And those whose fortune it is to be barren
Are spared a world of worry.
But we see that those who tend
The delicate plant of youth in their houses
Have care at their side every hour of the day;
How they will bring their children up,
How they will leave them the means to live,
Will they grow up to be good or bad?
There is no way of knowing.
Then the unkindest blow: 1040
Suppose young bodies grow sturdy and strong
To make parents proud; then if Fate decides,
Down goes Death to the house of Hades,
Taking the children's bodies with him.
How should it profit a man, if heaven
Adds this, the bitterest grief, to his sorrows
Only for loving his children?

MEDEA
Friends, I have awaited my fortune this long while,
Anxious to see which way events would turn.
And now I can see one of Jason's servants   1050
Approaching; he is running, out of breath,
Sure sign of some new horror to report.

(*Enter a* MESSENGER.)

MESSENGER
You who have outraged all laws, and done
This dreadful crime; run, run away, Medea!
Take ship or chariot, and do not scorn their aid!

MEDEA
What have I done, that I should run away?

MESSENGER
The royal bride is dead, and with her
Her father Creon; it was your poisons killed them.

MEDEA
You tell a glorious tale. From this time on
I'll number you among my friends and benefactors.   1060

MESSENGER
Are you in your right mind? Have you gone insane,
To work the ruin of the royal house
And laugh, and not be afraid of what I tell you?

MEDEA
There is a great deal I could say
To answer you. Do not be hasty, friend,
But tell me how they died. My pleasure will
Be doubled, if their deaths were horrible.

MESSENGER
When the two children, your sons, came with their father
And presented themselves at the house where the bride lived,
We servants, who sympathized with your misfortunes,   1070
Were glad, and rumor soon buzzed about the house
That you had patched up the old quarrel with your husband.
Some kissed their hands, and some
Their golden heads; and I was so delighted
I followed the children to the women's quarters.
Our mistress—her we honor in your place—
Only had eyes for Jason, and didn't see
The children, when they came in at first.
And then she turned her pretty head the other way,
Angry they should have been let in. But Jason   1080
Tried to pacify her anger and resentment
And said, "You must not be at odds with friends.
Stop sulking, turn your head this way again;
You must believe your husband's friends are yours.
Accept their gifts, and supplicate your father
To reprieve the boys from exile, for my sake."
When she saw the finery, she couldn't hold out longer,
But did everything he asked. Before the children
And their father had gone far outside the house
She took the pretty robe and put it on,   1090
And set the golden crown around her curls,
Arranging them before a shining mirror
And smiling at her ghostly image there.
Then she stood up, and left the throne, and trod
Her white feet delicately round the room,
Delighted with the gifts, and every now and then
She made a leg and studied the effect.
And then there was a sight that scared us all:
Her color goes, she stumbles sideways, back
Towards the throne, and hardly stops herself   1100

From falling on the floor.
Then some old waiting maid, who must have thought
The fit was sent by Pan, or by some god,
Began to pray; and then she saw her mouth
All white with running froth, the eyeballs starting from
Their sockets, and her body pale and bloodless; and then
She screamed so loud the screaming drowned the prayer.
Someone went straight to fetch
Her father, someone to her new husband,
To tell them what was happening to the bride,   1110
And the house rang everywhere with noise of running feet.
Already, in the time a practised runner
Could run a hundred yards, the princess
Recovered from her speechless, sightless swoon
And screamed in anguish. It was terrible;
From two directions the pain attacked her.
The golden circlet twining round her hair
Poured forth a strange stream of devouring fire,
And the fine-spun robe, the gift your children gave her,
Had teeth to tear the poor girl's pretty skin.   1120
She left the throne and fled burning through the room,
Shaking her head this way and that,
Trying to dislodge the crown, but it was fixed
Immovably, and when she shook her hair
The flames burnt twice as fiercely.
Then, overcome with pain, she fell to the ground.
Only her father would have recognized her.
Her eyes had lost their settled look, her face
Its natural expression, and the blood
Dripped from her head to mingle with the fire.   1130
The flesh dropped front her bones like pine-tears, torn
By the unseen power of the devouring poison,
We saw, and shuddered; no-one dared
To touch the corpse, we had her fate for warning.
But her old father, who knew nothing of what had happened,
Came running in, and flung himself on the body,
Began to weep, and flung his arms around her,
And kissed her, crying "Oh, unhappy child,
What god has killed you so inhumanly?
Who takes you from me, from the grave of my   1140
Old age? If I could die with you, my child!"
And then he stopped his tears and lamentations
And tried to raise his old body up again,
But clung fast to the robe, as ivy clings
To laurel branches. Then there was a ghastly struggle,
He trying to raise himself from off his knees,
She holding him down; and when he pushed her off
He tore the aged flesh from off his bones.
And then he fought no more; the poor old man
Gave up the ghost, the struggle was too much for him.   1150
The bodies of the princess and her father
Lie side by side, a monument to grief.
Your part in this affair is none of my business.
You will find your own escape from punishment.
Life is a shadow; I have thought so often,
And I am not afraid to say that those

Who seem wise among men, and accomplished talkers,
Must pay the heaviest penalty of all.
No man is happy. He might grow more prosperous
Than other men, if fortune comes his way,   1160
But happy he can never be.

(Exit.)

CHORUS
This is the day of heaven's visitation
On Jason, and he has deserved it richly.
But we have only tears for your misfortune,
Poor child of Creon, who must go to Hades
Because of Jason's wedding.

MEDEA
Women, my task is fixed: as quickly as possible
To kill my children and to fly this land,
And not by hesitation leave my sons
To die by other hands more merciless.   1170
Whatever happens, they must die; and since they must,
I, who first gave them life, shall give them death.
Come, steel yourself, my heart; why do you hesitate
To do this dreadful thing which must be done?
Come, my unhappy hand, take up the sword
And go to where life's misery begins.
Do not turn coward; think not of your children,
How much you loved them, how you bore them; no,
For this one day forget you are a mother;
Tomorrow you may weep. But though you kill them, yet   1180
You love them still; and my poor heart is broken.

(She goes into the house.)

CHORUS
Earth and all-seeing light of the Sun,
Look down, look down on a woman destroyed
Before she raises her murderous hand
Against her babes. From a golden age
Was she born, and we fear divine blood
Will be shed by mortals. Restrain her, great light
Of heaven, hold her back, drag her forth from the house,
This accursed murderess driven by fairies.
Did you toil for your sons in vain, did you labor   1190
For nothing to bring your darlings to birth
When you left behind you the angry straits
Where ships are crushed in the grim grey rocks?
Why has their weight of anger fallen
Upon your heart, this lust for the kill?
The death of kindred is mortals' curse
And heaven sends sorrows meet for the murderers,
Calamities falling upon the house.

(The CHILDREN are heard screaming inside the house.)

Do you hear them? Do you hear the children crying?

Oh wretched woman, woman possessed.   1200

FIRST CHILD
What shall I do? How avoid my mother's hand?

SECOND CHILD
I cannot tell, dear brother; we are dying.

CHORUS
Shall we enter the house? We ought to stop
The murder of the children.

FIRST CHILD
Help us in heaven's name, in our necessity.

SECOND CHILD
The sword is near, and death is closing round us.

CHORUS
Woman, you must have a heart of stone
Or iron, that can kill with your own hand
The fruit of your own womb.
One woman, one woman only   1210
I have heard of before this time
Who laid hands on her darling children—
The heaven-demented Ino
Whom Hera made mad, and drove abroad.
And because of her children's dying
The wretched mother drowned,
Leaping from cliff to water
To join her two sons in death.
What worse could the world still hold?
Oh, women, how many sorrows begin   1220
In your bed; what a count of ills
You have brought to mankind already.

(Enter JASON.)

JASON
You women, standing close beside the house,
Is she indoors, Medea, that has done
This dreadful crime, or has she taken flight?
She needs must hide herself beneath the earth
Or raise herself on wings to heaven's height
To escape the vengeance of the royal house.
How can she think, when she has killed the king,
That she can escape out of this house unharmed?   1230
It is not her I am thinking of, but my sons;
I leave her to the people she has wronged,
But I am here to save my children's lives
For fear my kinsmen may intend some harm to me
In vengeance for the mother's bloody murder.

CHORUS
Jason, you do not know the full extent
Of your sorrows, or you would not have spoken so.

JASON
What is it? Does she want to kill me too?

CHORUS
Your sons are dead; it was their mother killed them.

JASON
What do you say? You have destroyed me, woman.   1240

CHORUS
You have no children now; remember them.

JASON
Where did she kill them? In the house or outside?

CHORUS
Unbar the door and you will see their bodies.

JASON
What are you waiting for, men? Unbar the doors,
Break them down, so that I may see this double blow,
My dead sons, and she whose blood will pay for theirs.

(MEDEA *appears above the roof of the house in a fiery chariot drawn by snakes, clasping the bodies of her children.*)

MEDEA
Why hammer on the doors, and try to unbar them,
Seeking the bodies and their murderess?
No need of that. If you want anything from me,
Say what you wish; your hand will never touch me,   1250
So strong the chariot my father's father,
The Sun, gave me to keep away my enemies.

JASON
Abomination! Woman more than any other
Hateful to heaven and to all mankind.
You dared, their mother, thrust the sword
Into their bodies, rob me of my sons,
And show yourself before the world when you
Had done this foul and most abominable of murders?
Your death must pay for this. Oh, now I know
What I did not see before, it was a fatal curse   1260
To bring you from your foreign land to Greece,
Traitor to your father and the land that reared you.
The gods have turned your fury on my head.
You killed your own brother there at your hearthside
Before you set foot on our good ship's deck,
And that was your beginning; married to
The man you see before you, mother of his sons,
Because I left you, you have killed your children.
There is no woman throughout Greece would dare
Do such a thing, and these I overlooked   1270
To marry you, my ruin and my curse.
No woman, but a lioness, more fierce by nature
Than Tyrrhenian Scylla. I could go on abusing you

Forever, and not touch you; such hardness were you born with.
Go, foul woman, children's murderess;
My part to stay and weep for my misfortunes.
No new-wed bride with whom to share my joy,
No children whom I fathered and brought up
To live with me; I have no children.

MEDEA
There is a great deal that I could have said   1280
To answer you, if heaven did not know
How we have dealt with each other, you and I.
Did you think you could desert my marriage bed,
Make me your laughing stock, and still live happy?
Neither your queen nor Creon your new father
Could banish me from Corinth with impunity.
So call me lioness if you will, call me
A Scylla haunting the Tyrrhenian rocks,
I tore your heart for you, and you deserved it.

JASON
You too have paid; you hurt yourself as much.   1290

MEDEA
I do, but gain by it, so do not laugh.

JASON
Oh children, what a mother you have found.

MEDEA
Oh children, dying from your father's malady.

JASON
It was not my hand that killed them; do not say that.

MEDEA
No, your defiance, and your second marriage.

JASON
You make my marriage an excuse for murder?

MEDEA
You think it is a little thing for women?

JASON
For decent women. You think bad of everything.

MEDEA
Your sons are dead, and this will tear your heart.

JASON
My sons live still as curses on your head.   1300

MEDEA
The gods know who began this misery.

JASON
They know then your abominable mind.

MEDEA
You are detestable; I hate your bitter tongue.

JASON
I yours. We have an easy remedy, to part.

MEDEA
How then? What shall I do? I too am eager.

JASON
Give me my sons to bury and to mourn.

MEDEA
No! I shall bury them with my own hands,
Taking them to the Mountain-Mother's shrine
To ensure their tomb will keep its dignity
Untouched by enemies. I will inaugurate   1310
A solemn rite and festival in this land
Of Sisyphus, for future time to expiate
This impious murder; then I go to Erectheus' land
To live with Aegeus, son of Pandion.
And you will meet the base death you deserve,
Crushed by a relic of your ship, the Argo,
Now you have wept the end of this new wedding.

JASON
May Erinys and bloody Justice
Avenge the death of my children.

MEDEA
What god, what power, will listen to you,   1320
False swearer, betrayer of friends?

JASON
Foul woman, children's murderess.

MEDEA
Go home, and bury your dead.

JASON
I go, with two sons to mourn for.

MEDEA
You will not miss them yet; wait till you are older.

JASON
My darling children.

MEDEA
            Not yours but mine.

JASON
            And yet you killed them.

MEDEA

To give you pain.

JASON

Oh, how I long to kiss
The soft lips of my children.

MEDEA

You would fondle and talk to them now,
Then you rejected them.   1330

JASON

In heaven's name let me feel
The soft touch of my children's bodies.

MEDEA

No, you are wasting your breath.

(Exit.)

JASON

Zeus, do you hear how she mocks me,
How she tortures me, this accursed
Lioness, slayer of children?
But with what little power is left me
I call upon heaven to see
My sufferings, and summon the gods
To witness how she prevents me   1340
From giving my children burial.
I wish I had never begot them
To see them destroyed by you.

CHORUS

Many things are wrought by Zeus in Olympus
And heaven works much beyond human imagining.
The looked-for result will fail to materialize
While heaven finds ways to achieve the unexpected.
So it has happened in this our story.

ENDNOTES

References are to line numbers

2   *the Clashing Rocks*   at the opening of the Bosphorus. In legend one of the chief hazards for the seafarer; they were believed to close on ships passing between them.

63   *Peirene*   Called by an ancient traveller "the pride of Corinth," this fountain is still to be seen. Situated in a grotto, richly provided by later patrons with arches and seats, it gave not only water but shade, and was a popular meeting-place for the citizens.

270   *No sensible man . . .*   Euripides puts into Medea's mouth a speech bitterly descriptive of his own situation. His bold views, his association with some of the most notorious freethinkers of his time, and his habit of working in solitude, did not endear him to his fellow-citizens. The scurrilous stories in the ancient "Life" of Euripides and the cruel caricatures in Aristophanes'

comedies reflect the antagonism which such behavior aroused. He has eventually forced to leave Athens and end his life as an expatriate.

372 *Hecate* In one of her aspects the goddess of witchcraft, and so adopted by Medea as a patron deity.

380 *Sisyphean wedding* Sisyphus was the legendary founder of the earliest settlement on the site of Corinth. A promoter of navigation and commerce, he was regarded by tradition as fraudulent and avaricious. See *Cyclops* l. 131, where he is jocularly referred to as the "father" of the wily Odysseus.

489 *Tempers run high* Perhaps the best way of regarding these brief choral interjections, in Euripides often platitudinous, is as a mechanical expedient. The actors were masked and declaimed their parts in a highly artificial style. All parts were played by men, and even at this time there was little, if any, attempt to make a vocal distinction between male and female characters. Thus it would sometimes be difficult for the audience to distinguish where one character stopped speaking and the other began. The author has experienced a similar difficulty in hearing an unfamiliar opera in the Theatre of Herodes Atticus; it was often impossible to tell which of a group of soloists was singing at any one time. Here the chorus interjection clearly marks the division of speeches, and gives the audience time to refocus its attention. It can safely be cut in modern performance.

496 *Cypris* Aphrodite, Goddess of Love.

633 *earth's prophetic center.* Zeus, according to the myth, sent two eagles flying from each end of the earth; they met over Delphi, which was thus established as the center point, and marked by a pointed stone (*omphalos*, navel) in the oracular shrine.

638 *no stranger to the marriage bond.* Aegeus had already married twice.

644 *not to loosen . . .* The Delphic Oracle is typically ambiguous. Aegeus is commanded "not to loosen the wineskin's hanging foot"—that is, not to engage in sexual intercourse—until

he reaches his "ancestral hearth." He naturally takes this to mean Athens. But on his way home he stopped at Troezen and lay with Aethra, who bore him a son. Euripides is referring here to a tradition whereby Troezen was already associated with Athens; thus the "ancestral hearth" could apply equally well to either place, and the oracle is proved correct.

775 *Since you have taken me . . .* Here the awkwardness of the chorus becomes apparent. Euripides is compelled to take their presence into account and make Medea divulge her plans to them; though they object, the exigencies of the plot forbid them to interfere. Euripides has given their inaction a bare plausibility by making Medea, earlier in the play, swear them to secrecy.

788 *Erechtheus* Mythical founder of the Athenian people. The chorus try to divert Medea from her purpose by dwelling on the glory and sanctity of Athens. How could such a city receive a murderess? This provides an opportunity for a burst of patriotic sentiment.

895 *A fine-spun robe* The exact repetition of this line from l. 751 has led some editors to excise it as an interpolation. It has, however, considerable dramatic point. Jason does not appreciate the full significance of the phrase, but the chorus and audience do. This is true dramatic irony.

994 *Go in, my children.* We must imagine the children as turning to go into the house, and then pausing at the door as Medea continues to speak.

1164 *But we have only tears . . .* These lines have been dismissed by some editors as a sentimental interpolation, but they are in keeping with Euripides' intention. He wishes to stress the horror of the deaths of Creon and the princess, and by implication the murders of Apsurtos and Pelias. This accounts for the Grand Guignol nature of the Messenger's speech, which violates all the customary restraint of Greek tragedy. Euripides is concerned to show the true nature of violence, and to condemn the acceptance of such episodes in the traditional stories.

Thus the chorus makes a clear distinction. Jason deserved his punishment, but the princess did not; she, like Medea's brother, has been sacrificed to further a personal advantage.

1201   *What shall I do?*   Although he is forced to work within the old conventions, Euripides often contrives to give them a new twist. Tragedy was allowed only three speaking actors; thus the children must be *personae mutae,* silent characters, as long as they are on the stage. But Euripides uses their unspeaking presence to increase the pathos of their plight. Every time we see them, we wonder if it will be the last. Note how Euripides gives the final twist by postponing their final exit (see l. 994 and note). When we do hear them, it is in the moment of their death.

1210   *One woman . . .*   This chorus serves a dual purpose. First, it increases the excitement of her predicament. In drawing this parallel between Medea's crime and Ino's, Euripides seems to depart from the usual version, in which Ino saw one of her sons killed by his father and lept into the sea with the other, for one in which Ino killed both sons and then lept into the sea herself. The parallel, of course, is not as exact as the chorus thinks. Medea does not die, though the chorus sees this as inevitable, and so does Jason when he appears. The escape in the dragon chariot thus comes as a great surprise.

The chorus also provides a welcome relief from the high tragedy that has gone before. The tension has mounted higher and higher, to culminate in Medea's speech of decision and the dying screams of the children. Euripides now gives his audience a moment to recuperate.

1244   *What are you waiting for?*   Euripides once more gives a new and exciting twist to an old formula. Such commands to "unbar the door" are customarily followed by the revelation of the *ekkyklema,* a wheeled platform bearing a tableau of the dead bodies. The audience, hearing the familiar words, would have their gaze riveted on the central door. Then, from above, comes a cry, and Medea is seen on the roof of the stage building. Euripides has performed a theatrical conjuring trick, distracting the audience's attention to one point while he brings in Medea at another.

1254   *Hateful to heaven . . .*   An exact repetition of l. 437 and thus excised by most editors. But it emphasizes the exact counterbalancing of the two halves of the play. Earlier, Medea said this of Jason; now, Jason says it of Medea. Their positions have been completely reversed.

1273   *Scylla*   The mythical monster, familiar from the *Odyssey,* who lived in a sea-cave and preyed on passing ships.

1318   *Mountain-mother's shrine*   Euripides likes to link his plays to some familiar rite or festival—here, to the worship of Hera.

1316   *Crushed by a relic . . .*   There were two versions of Jason's death. According to one, he was sleeping under the beached Argo, now old and rotten, when the timbers collapsed on his head. According to the other, he had dedicated the stem of his ship in the temple of Hera; one day, as he was visiting the shrine, it fell down and killed him. Euripides seems to be following the second version.

1344   *Many things are wrought . . .*   A stock epilogue, which appears at the end of several plays.

—————————— *Questions for Consideration* ——————————

Directions: Using complete sentences provide brief answers for the following questions.

1. Discuss briefly the major theme found in the tragedy *Media* by Euripides.

    _____

    _____

    _____

    _____

    _____

    _____

2. Identify three adjectives that would describe Medea's character. Provide a reason for each selection.

    _____

    _____

    _____

    _____

    _____

    _____

3. Based on Aristotle's definition of a tragedy, does *Medea* succeed or fail as one. Why or why not?

    _____

    _____

    _____

    _____

    _____

    _____

———————————— *Writing Critically* ————————————

Select one of the essay topics listed below and compose a 500 word essay which discusses the topic fully.

1. Discuss in what ways the relationship between Jason and Medea failed. Provide convincing reasons for your beliefs.

2. Discuss how one can see Euripides as a realist concerning the characters and their actions in his tragedy, *Medea*.

3. Discuss the character of Jason from the beginning of the tragedy to the end. Does your opinion of him change? Why or why not?

4. Discuss what you feel is Medea's tragic flaw. Defend your answer with logical support.

5. Discuss why you feel Euripides allows Medea to end in the manner that it does. Was this on purpose?

Prewriting Space:

_____

_____

_____

_____

_____

_____

_____

_____

_____

_____

_____

_____

_____

_____

_____

_____

_____

Introduction

Aristotle (384–322 B.C.)

The origin of Western philosophy can be traced to ancient Greece as early as the sixth century B.C. However, the most significant period in the development of ancient Greek philosophy is perhaps during the fourth and fifth centuries B.C. with the emergence of such revolutionary thinkers as Socrates, Plato, and Aristotle. The impact of their influence on Western thought is unquestionable. Of these three philosophers, it is probably Aristotle's philosophy that has had the most profound influence on modern thought—if not for its relevance, certainly for its provocative theory. Most scholarship places Aristotle's reputation as a philosopher and shaper of Western thought comparable to that of his renowned teacher and mentor, Plato.

Aristotle was born in 384 B.C. in Stagira, a small town in Northern Greece. His father was Nichomachus, a physician to the King of Macedonia, Amyntas. This affiliation with the Macedonia court is significant in that Amyntas was the father of Philip II of Macedonia and the grandfather of Alexander the Great, whom Aristotle tutored for several years (Burns et al. 193). Hence, it was in his youth that Aristotle's interests in medicine and politics were ignited. Also, Aristotle's connection with this royal lineage would be maintained for the remainder of his life (Lamm and Cross 138–139).

Another important and equally influential experience in Aristotle's life was his association with Plato. At the age of 17, Aristotle entered Plato's school in Athens, the Academy. He remained at the Academy for twenty years—first as a student, then as a teacher. He left the Academy after Plato's death. The extent of Plato's influence on Aristotle's philosophical

Aristoteles and his Pupil, Alexander

thought is undeniable, in spite of the fact that each philosopher's search for "absolute knowledge" took a different path of discovery and experimentation. Aristotle eventually went on to establish his own school, the Lyceum, based in principle on Plato's academic program, but offering a wider range of subjects than the Academy (Burns et al. 192–194).

If there is one word that serves better than another to describe Aristotle's achievements, it is "versatility." Aristotle was a writer, educator, scientist, and foremost a philosopher. His interests were universal and his life's experiences were unique, in a most productive way. It is likely that this combination of intellectual astuteness and environmental influences provided the source and substance for his life's work (Lamm and Cross 138–139). Aristotle's "corpus" of writings display a most extraordinary range of interests: astronomy, logic, biology, ethics, politics, mathematics, metaphysics, psychology, rhetoric, and literature. His writings on ethics—*Eumedian Ethics, Nicomachean Ethics,* and *Ethics*—and "esthetics"—*Rhetoric* and *Poetics*—are among his most popular works. Thus, the Aristotelian "corpus" consists mainly of treatises—some fragments—that Aristotle had written for his students (Soll). The *Poetics* is one of those treatises surviving in fragmentary form. It represents the earliest and most systematic analysis of "poetic theory" in western literature and is regarded as the most influential document of literary criticism in classical literature (Olsen ix).

The *Poetics* as a document of literary criticism has exerted enormous influence on critical theory as well as trends in drama, particularly that of the Renaissance and Neoclassical periods. This work is also noted for the "critical vocabulary" that it generated and that has proven to be useful to writers and critics alike, and even today it continues to serve students of literature. Aristotle uses works and artists from antiquity (Homer), the classical Greek period (Sophocles and other dramatists), and from his contemporaries for illustrative purposes in his analysis of the "art of poetry."

Aristotle begins the *Poetics* by stating his intentions to analyze the nature and form of poetry and the means whereby they differ. He states his purpose as thus:

> *I propose to treat poetry in itself and of its various kinds, noting the essential quality of each; to inquire into the structure of the plot as requisite to a good poem; into the number and nature of the part of which a poem is composed; . . . (qtd. in Butcher 7).*

He proceeds to identify those various forms of art as "epic poetry, tragedy, comedy, and dithyrambic poetry," along with the music of the flute and lyre. He further adds that the features that distinguish these artistic forms are the medium, the objects, and the manner of production (13).

Aristotle also presents his famous theory of imitation in this introduction. He states that all art is "imitation" and nature serves as the model. This notion gives rise to the "mimetic" theory in art. According to Aristotle, man's tendency to imitate that which he sees is an instinct that is instilled in man from childhood. He further states that man is the most imitative of all "living creatures" and his ability to gain knowledge and "delight" from his experience distinguishes him from "other animals." (15)

Aristotle's explanation of poetry and his discussion of the art and form of imitation serve as the prelude to his even more detailed analysis of tragedy. Aristotle distinguishes tragedy as the highest form of poetic art and plot as the most important aspect of tragedy. He defines tragedy as:

> *an imitation of an action that is serious, complete, and of a certain magnitude; in language embellished with each kind of artistic ornament, the several kinds being found in separate parts of the play; in the form of action, not of narrative; through pity and fear effecting the proper purgation of these emotions. (23)*

Aristotle's definition of tragedy is followed by his classification of tragedy into six elements—spectacle, character, plot, music, diction, and thought. These elements become the focus of his discussion of the "nature of tragedy"; however, it is the element of plot that is given the most extensive treatment. Sophocles' *Oedipus Rex* serves as the model for Aristotle's discussion of an effective tragedy. It is Aristotle's conception of tragedy as it is clearly and systematically presented in the *Poetics* that has earned this work as well as its composer lasting critical acclaim. (BJJ)

BIBLIOGRAPHY

Abercombie, L. "Aristotle's Poetics." *Principles of Literary Criticism.* New York: Barnes & Noble, 1960. 63–117.

Allan, Donald James. *The Philosophy of Aristotle.* New York: Oxford University Press, 1970.

Aristotle. *Aristotle's Poetics.* Trans. James Hutton. New York: W.W. Norton and Company, 1982.

Bal, Mieke. "Mimesis and Genre Theory in Aristotle's *Poetics.*" *Poetics Today.* 3.1 Winter 1982: 171–180.

Butcher, S. H. *Aristotle's Theory of Poetry and Fine Art.* New York: Dover, 1951.

Cantor, Paul A. "Aristotle and the History of Tragedy." *Theoretical Issues in Literary History.* Ed. Daniel Perkins. Cambridge: Harvard University Press, 1991. 60–84.

Else, G. F. *Aristotle's Poetics: The Argument.* Cambridge, Mass.: Harvard University Press, 1958.

Grene, Majorie G. *A Portrait of Aristotle.* Chicago: University of Chicago Press, 1963.

Heath, Malcolm. "The University of Poetry in Aristotle's *Poetic.*" *The Classical Quarterly* 41:2 (1991): 389–402.

Olsen, Elder. ed. *Aristotle's Poetics and English Literature.* Chicago: University of Chicago Press, 1965.

Smithson, Isaiah. "The Moral View of Aristotle's *Poetics.*" Journal of *the History of Ideas.* 44:1 January–March 1983: 3–17.

Schreiberman S. M. *An Introduction to Literary Criticism.* Oxford: Pergamon Press, 1965.

Veatch, Henry Babcock. *Aristotle: A Contemporary Appreciation.* Bloomington: Indiana University Press, 1974.

from On the Art of Poetry

Aristotle
Translated by Lane Cooper

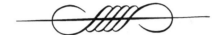

As to its general origin, we may say that Poetry has sprung from two causes, each of them a thing inherent in human nature. The first is the habit of imitation; for to imitate is instinctive with mankind; and man is superior to the other animals, for one thing, in that he is the most imitative of creatures, and learns at first by imitation. Secondly, all men take a natural pleasure in the products of imitation—a pleasure to which the facts of experience bear witness; for even when the original objects are repulsive, as the most objectionable of the lower animals, or dead bodies, we still delight to contemplate their forms as represented in a picture with the utmost fidelity. The explanation of this delight lies in a further characteristic of our species, the appetite for learning; for among human pleasures that of learning is the keenest—not only to the scholarly, but to the rest of mankind as well, no matter how limited their capacity. Accordingly, the reason why men delight in a picture is that in the act of contemplating it they are acquiring knowledge and drawing inferences—as when they exclaim: "Why, that is so and so!" Consequently, if one does not happen to have seen the original, any pleasure that arises from the picture will be due, not to the imitation as such, but to the execution, or the coloring, or some similar cause.

To imitate, then, is natural in us as men; just as our sense of musical harmony and our sense of rhythm are natural—and it is to be noted that metre plainly falls under the general head of rhythm. In the beginning, therefore, being possessed of these natural endowments, men originated poetry, the process of generation coming about by gradual and, in the main, slight advances upon the first naive improvisations. So much for the origin of the art in general.

. . .

As for Comedy, this is an artistic imitation of men of an inferior moral bent; faulty, however, not in any or every way, but only in so far as their shortcomings are ludicrous; for the Ludicrous is a species or part, not all, of the Ugly. It may be described as that kind of shortcoming and deformity which does not strike us as painful, and causes no harm to others; a ready example is afforded by the comic mask, which is ludicrous, being ugly and distorted, without any suggestion of pain.

. . .

Epic Poetry has much in common with Tragedy: it is an imitation, in a lofty kind of verse, of serious events. Still there is a difference, on the metrical side, in the medium of imitation, as well as a difference in the manner; for the Epic employs one and the same metre throughout, namely the hexameter, and epic poetry is in the form of a tale that is told, and not, like Tragedy, of an action directly presented. And there is further a difference in length; for the Epic is not restricted to any fixed limit of time. Writers of Tragedy, on the other hand, endeavor to represent the action as taking place within a period of twenty-four hours (that is, within a period of one apparent revolution of the sun), or at all events try to avoid exceeding this limit by very much. This difference in respect to time exists at present; but at first tragic and epic poets were alike in not restricting themselves to any special limits. . . .

TRAGEDY DEFINED. THE PRINCIPLES OF ITS CONSTRUCTION

. . .

A Tragedy is an artistic imitation of an action that is serious, complete in itself, and of an adequate magnitude; so much for the object which is imitated. As for the medium, the imitation is produced in language embellished in more than one way, one kind of embellishment being introduced separately in one part, and another kind in another part of the whole. As for the manner, the imitation is itself in the form of an action directly presented, not narrated. And as for the proper function resulting from the imitation of such an object in such a medium and manner, it is to arouse the emotions of pity and fear in the audience; and to arouse this pity and fear in such a way as to effect that special purging off and relief (*catharsis*) of these two emotions which is the characteristic of Tragedy.

By "language embellished in more than one way" is meant language which is simply rhythmical or metrical, language which is delivered in recitative, and language which is uttered in song. And by the separate introduction of one kind of embellished language in one part, and of another kind in another part, is meant that some portions of the tragedy (e.g., prologue and episode) are rendered in verse alone, without being sung or chanted, and other portions again (e.g., parode and stasimon) in the form of singing or chanting.

. . .

Advancing now from the synthetic definition of Tragedy, we proceed to analyze the elements that separately demand the attention of the tragic poet. Since there are *dramatis personae* who produce the author's imitation of an action, it necessarily follows that (1) everything pertaining to the appearance of the actors on the stage—including costume, scenery, and the like—will constitute an element in the technique of tragedy; and that (2) the composition of the music ("Melody"), and (3) the composition in words ("Diction"), will constitute two further elements, as Melody and Diction represent the medium in which the action is imitated. By Diction is meant, in this connection, the fitting together of the words in metre; as for Melody (= "Song"), the meaning is too obvious to need explanation.

But furthermore, the original object of the imitation is an action of men. In the performance, then, the imitation, which is also an action, must be carried on by agents, the *dramatis personae*. And these agents must necessarily be endowed by the poet with certain distinctive qualities both of (4) Moral Character (*ethos*) and (5) Intellect (*dianoia*)—one might say, of heart and head; for it is from a man's moral bent, and from the way in which he reasons, that we are led to ascribe goodness or badness, success or failure, to his acts. Thus, as there are two natural causes, moral bent and thought, of the particular deeds of men, so there are the same two natural causes of their success or failure in life. And the tragic poet must take cognizance of this.

Finally, the action which the poet imitates is represented in the tragedy by (6) the Fable or Plot. And according to our present distinction, Plot means that synthesis of the particular incidents which gives form or being to the tragedy as a whole; whereas Moral Bent is that which leads us to characterize the agents as morally right or wrong in what they do; and Intellect (or "Thought") is that which shows itself whenever they prove a particular point, or, it may be, avouch some general truth.

. . .

The most important of the constitutive elements is the Plot, that is, the organization of the incidents of the story; for Tragedy in its essence is an imitation, not of men as such, but of action and life, of happiness and misery. And happiness and misery are not states of being, but forms of activity; the end for which we live is some form of activity, not the realization of a moral quality. Men are better or worse, according to their moral bent; but they become happy or miserable in their actual deeds. In a play, consequently, the agents do not perform for the sake of representing their individual dispositions; rather, the display of moral character is included as subsidiary to the things that are done. So that the incidents of the action, and the structural ordering of these incidents, constitute the end and purpose of the tragedy. Here, as elsewhere, the final purpose is the main thing.

Such is the importance of this element that, we may add, whereas Tragedy cannot exist without action, it is possible to construct a tragedy in which the agents have no distinctive moral bent. In fact, the works of most of the modern tragic poets, from the time of Euripides on, are lacking in the element of character. Nor is the defect confined to tragic poets: it is common among poets in general. And there is a similar defect among the painters—in Zeuxis, for example, as contrasted with lacking in Polygnotus; for Polygnotus excels in the representation of the ethical element, whereas the pictures of Zeuxis are in this respect wholly deficient.

Again, one may string together a series of speeches in which the moral bent of the agents is delineated in excellent verse and diction, and with excellent order in the thoughts, and yet fail to produce the essential effect of Tragedy as already described. One is much more likely to produce this effect with a tragedy, however deficient in these respects, if it has a plot—that is, an artistic ordering of the incidents. In addition to all this, the most vital features of Tragedy, by which the interest and emotions of the audience are most powerfully aroused—that is, reversals of fortune, and discoveries of the identity of agents—are parts of the plot or action. . . .

(1) The Plot, then, is the First Principle, and as it were the very Soul of Tragedy.

(2) And the element of Character is second in importance.—There is a parallel in the art of painting: the most beautiful colors, laid on with no order, will not give as much pleasure as the simplest figure done in outline.—Tragedy is an imitation of an action: mainly on account of this action does it become, in the second place, an imitation of personal agents.

(3) Third in importance comes the Intellectual element. This corresponds to the power of the agent to say what can be said, or what is fitting to be said, in a given situation. It is that element in the speeches of a drama which is supplied by the study of Politics and the art of Rhetoric. . . .

Adequate limit for the magnitude of the plot is this: Let the length be such that the hero may fall from happiness to misfortune, or rise from misfortune to happiness, through a series of incidents linked together in a probable or inevitable sequence.

The Unity of a Plot does not consist, as some suppose, in having one man as the hero; for the number of accidents that befall the individual man is endless, and some of them cannot be reduced to unity. So, too, during the life of any one man, he performs many deeds which cannot be brought together in the form of a unified action. We see, therefore, the faulty choice of subject in such poets as have written a *Heracleid* or a *Theseid*, or the like; they suppose that, since Heracles or Theseus was a single person, the story of Heracles or Theseus must have unity. Homer, on the contrary, whether by conscious art or native insight, evidently understood the correct method, for he excels the rest of the epic poets in this as in all other respects. Thus, in composing a story of Odysseus, he did not make his plot include all that ever happened to Odysseus. For example, it

befell this hero to receive a gash from a boar on Mount Parnassus; and it befell him also to feign madness at the time of the mustering against Ilium; but what he suffered in the former case and what he did in the latter are incidents between which there was no necessary or probable connection. Instead of joining disconnected incidents, Homer took for the subject of the *Odyssey* an action with the kind of unity here described; and the subject chosen for the *Iliad* is likewise unified. For, as in the other imitative arts, painting and the rest, so in poetry, the object of the imitation in each case is a unit; therefore in an epic or a tragedy, the plot, which is an imitation of an action, must represent an action that is organically unified, the structural order of the incidents being such that transposing or removing any one of them will dislocate and disorganize the whole. Every part must be necessary, and in its place; for a thing whose presence or absence makes no perceptible difference is not an organic part of the whole.

From what has been said, it is clear that the office of the Poet consists in displaying, not what actually has happened, but what in a given situation might well happen—a sequence of events that is possible in the sense of being either credible or inevitable. In other words, the Poet is not a Historian; for the two differ, not in the fact that one writes in metrical, and the other in nonmetrical, language. For example, you might turn the work of Herodotus into verse, and it would still be a species of history, with metre no less than without it. The essential distinction lies in this, that the Historian relates what has happened, and the Poet represents what might happen— what is typical. Poetry, therefore, is something more philosophic and of a higher seriousness than History; for Poetry tends rather to express what is universal, whereas History relates particular events as such. By an exhibition of what is universal or typical is meant the representation of what a certain type of person is likely or is bound to say or do in a given situation. This is the aim of the Poet, though at the same time he attaches the names of specific persons to the types. As distinguished from the universal, the particular, which is the subject matter of history, consists of what an actual person, Alcibiades or the like, actually did or underwent. . . .

Plots and action, as we shall see, are either Involved or Uninvolved. Of the uninvolved, the purely episodic plots are the worst, a plot being called "episodic" when there is neither probability nor necessity in the sequence of incident.

A bad poet will construct this kind of plot through his own want of insight; a good poet, in order to meet the requirements of the actors. Since his work must be presented on the stage, and occupy a certain length of time, a good poet often stretches out the plot beyond its inherent capacity, and by the insertion of unnecessary matter is forced to distort the proper sequence of incident.

But to proceed with the parts of the definition of Tragedy. Tragedy is an imitation not only of a complete action, but of incidents that arouse pity and fear; and such incidents affect us most powerfully when we are not expecting them, if at the same time they are caused by one another. For we are struck with more wonder if we find a causal relation in unexpected tragic occurrences than if they came about of themselves and in no special sequence; since even pure coincidences seem most marvelous if there is something that looks like design in them. For example, while the man who had been the cause of Mitys' death was looking at Mitys' statue in Argos, the statue fell over and killed him; such things do not impress people as being the result of mere chance. Plots, therefore, that illustrate the principle of necessity or probability in the sequence of incident are better than others.

But plots are either Uninvolved or Involved, since the actions which are imitated in the plots may readily be divided into the same two classes. Now we may call an action Uninvolved when the incidents follow one another, as explained above, in a single continuous movement; that is, when the change of fortune comes to the hero without a Reversal of Situation and without a Discovery (or identification) of some person or fact at first unrecognized. An Involved action is one in which the change of fortune is attended by such Reversal, or by such Discovery, or by both. And each of these two incidents should arise from the structure of the plot itself; that is, each should be the necessary or probable result of the incidents that have gone before, and not merely follow them in point of time—for in the sequence of events there is a vast difference between *post hoc* and *propter hoc.*

A Reversal of Situation is a change in some part of the action from one state of affairs to its precise opposite—as has been said, from good fortune to ill, or from ill to good; and a change that takes place in the manner just described, namely, in a necessary or probable sequence of incident. To illustrate: in the *Oedipus the King* of Sophocles, the Messenger comes to cheer Oedipus by removing his fears as to his parentage on his mother's side, but, by disclosing whose son the hero really is, brings about the opposite state of affairs for him—that is, brings about the change from happiness to misery. Of the opposite change, from misery to happiness, there is an example in the *Lynceus* of Theodectes: when Lynceus is being led off to die, and Danaus follows to be his executioner, it comes about, as a result of the previous incidents of the drama, that Lynceus is saved and Danaus executed.

A Discovery, as the word itself indicates, is a transition from ignorance to knowledge, and hence a passing into love or hate on the part of those agents who are marked for happiness or misfortune. The best form is a recognition of the identity of persons, attended by reversals of fortune—such a reversal as attends the Discovery of Oedipus' true parentage in the *Oedipus the King.* There are, of course, other forms of Discovery besides this; some such transition from ignorance to knowledge may come about with reference to inanimate, even casual things. It is also possible to discover whether some person has done, or not done, a particular deed. But the form of Discovery most intimately connected with the plot, and with the action imitated, is the one we have specially mentioned; for the Discovery bringing love or hate, and the Reversal bringing happiness or misery, will occasion either pity or fear; and by our definition it is these emotions that the tragic imitation is to arouse. Furthermore, this kind of Discovery will be instrumental in bringing about the happy or unhappy ending of the action as a whole. . . .

Two parts of the plot, then, Reversal and Discovery, represent these things in the action, and have been sufficiently explained. A third part is Suffering: this may be defined as an incident of a destructive or painful sort, such as violent death, physical agony, woundings, and the like.

. . .

In the most perfect tragedy, as we have seen, the synthesis of the incidents must be, not uninvolved, but involved, and this synthesis must be imitative of events that arouse pity and fear—for therein lies the distinctive function of this kind of imitation. When we take this function as a standard, it is clear that there are three forms of plot to be avoided. (1) Good and just men are not to be represented as falling from happiness into misery; for such a spectacle does not arouse fear or pity in us—it is simply revolting. (2) Nor must evil men be represented as rising from ill fortune to prosperity; for this is the most untragic situation of all. It does not stir our general human sympathy, nor arouse tragic pity or tragic fear.

(3) Nor, again, may an excessively wicked man be represented as falling from prosperity into misfortune. Such a course of events may arouse in us some measure of human sympathy, but not the emotions of pity and fear. For, to define: Pity is what we feel at a misfortune that is out of proportion to the faults of a man; and Fear is what we feel when misfortune comes upon one like ourselves. Now the excessively wicked man deserves misery in proportion; and since his wickedness exceeds the average, he is not like one of ourselves. Accordingly, in this third situation there is nothing to arouse either pity or fear. There remains, then, (4) the case of the man intermediate between these extremes: a man not superlatively good and just, nor yet one whose misfortune comes about through vice and depravity; but a man who is brought low through some error of judgment or shortcoming, one from the number of the highly renowned and prosperous—such a person as Oedipus of the line of Thebes, Thyestes of Pelops' line, and the eminent men of other noted families.

. . .

To be perfectly tragic, accordingly, the Plot must not, as some hold, have a double issue, fortunate for the good, unfortunate for the bad, but a single one. And the change of fortune must be, not a rise from misery to happiness, but just the contrary, a fall from happiness to misery; and this fall must come about, not through depravity, but through a serious defect in judgment, or shortcoming in conduct, in a person either as good as the average of mankind, or better than that rather than worse. In support of this view the history of the drama itself is significant. In the early days the tragic poets were satisfied with any stories that came in their way; but now the practice has narrowed down to traditions concerning a few houses, and the best tragedies are founded on the legends of Alcmeon, Oedipus, Orestes, Meleager, Thyestes, Telephus, and similar personages who have been either the movers or the victims in some signal overthrow of fortune. From practice as well as theory, then, we argue that the ideal tragedy will have a plot of this type. Those critics, therefore, are in error who blame Euripides for adhering to this plan in his tragedies, since many of them have the unhappy ending. It is, as we have said, the correct procedure. And the best proof of its correctness is this: when they are put upon the stage and acted, such plays, if they have been properly worked out, are seen to have the most tragic effect; and Euripides, even if his procedure be faulty in every other respect is yet, through the

unhappy ending, certainly the most tragic of poets on the stage.

. . .

The effect of fear and pity may be produced by means that pertain simply to stage presentation; but it may also arise from the structure and incidents of the tragedy, which is the preferable way, and is the mark of a better poet. For the Plot should be so constructed that, even without help from the eye, one who simply hears the play recited must feel the chill of fear, and be stirred with pity, at what occurs. In fact, these are just the emotions one would feel in listening to the story of *Oedipus the King* off the stage. To bring about this emotional effect by spectacular means is less a matter of the poetic art, and depends upon adventitious assistance. But those who employ the means of the stage to produce what strikes us as being merely monstrous, without being terrible, are absolute strangers to the art of Tragedy; for not every kind of pleasure is to be sought from a tragedy, but only that specific pleasure which is characteristic of this art.

Since the pleasure which is characteristic of Tragedy comes from the arousing of pity and fear, and since the poet must produce this pleasure through an imitation of some action, it is clear that the tragic quality must be impressed upon the incidents that make up the story. Let us consider, then, what kinds of occurrence strike us as terrible, or rather what kinds of terrible occurrences strike us as piteous. When persons are involved in some deed of horror, they must be either (1) friends, or (2) enemies, or (3) indifferent to one another. Now when (2) an enemy injures, or wishes to injure, an enemy, there is nothing to arouse our pity either in his deed or his intention, except in so far as concerns the suffering of the one who is injured. And the same is true when (3) the persons are indifferent to each other. But when (1) the tragic incident occurs within the circle of those who are bound by natural ties—when murder or the like is done or intended by brother upon brother, son upon father, mother upon son, or son upon mother,—pity is aroused; and such are the situations the tragic poet must look for in the traditional stories. The general framework of these stories, then, the poet must not disturb: Clytaemnestra must be slain by her son Orestes, and Eriphyle by her son Alcmeon. At the same time, the poet must select for himself from the materials of tradition, and he must employ the given materials with skill.

Let us explain more clearly what is meant by the skilful use of material; for example, the tale of a deed of violence among friends. This may be treated in several ways. The deed may be done, as in the early poets, (1) by a person aware of what he is doing, to another who knows the identity of the doer, as is the case also in Euripides; for he makes Medea kill her children with premeditation, while they recognize her as their slayer. Or the deed may be done (2) by persons ignorant of the terrible nature of what they are doing, who afterwards discover their relationship with the victims; as Oedipus, in Sophocles' version of the tale, kills a man who he subsequently learns was his father. In this case, however, the deed lies outside of the drama proper.

. . .

When actually constructing his Plots and elaborating them in the Diction, the poet should endeavor as far as he can to visualize what he is representing. In this way, seeing everything with the utmost vividness, just as if he were an actual spectator of the events he is portraying, he will devise what is suitable, and run the least danger of overlooking inconsistencies. . . .

To every tragedy there pertain (1) a Complication and (2) an Unravelling, or *Dénouement.* The incidents lying outside of the drama proper, and often certain of the incidents within it, form the Complication; the rest of the play constitutes the *Dénouement.* More specifically, by Complication is meant everything from the beginning of the story up to that critical point, the last in a series of incidents, out of which comes the change of fortune; by *Dénouement,* everything from the beginning of the change of fortune to the end of the play.

The Chorus should be regarded as one of the actors; it should be an integral part of the whole, and take its share in the action. The model is the practice of Sophocles, and not Euripides. In subsequent poets the choral songs in a tragedy have no more connection with the plot than with that of any other play. Accordingly, at the present day, the Chorus sing mere interludes, a practice that goes back to Agathon. And yet, what real difference is there between introducing a song that is foreign to the action and attempting to fit a speech, or a whole episode, from one drama into another?

. . .

Metaphor consists in the application to one thing of the name that belongs to another: (a) the name of the genus may be applied to a subordinate species; (b) the name of the species may be applied to the inclusive genus; (c) under the same genus, the name of one species may be applied to another; or (d) there may be a transference of names on grounds of analogy (or proportion).

(a) The transference of a name from the genus to a species is illustrated in "Here *stands* my ship"; for *to be at anchor* is one species of the genus *standing.*

(b) That from species to genus, in "Of a truth, ten *thousand* noble deeds hath Odysseus wrought"; where *ten thousand* is a particular large number, used instead of *a large number* in general.

(c) That from species to species, in "With a knife of bronze *drawing* away the life-blood," and in "*Cutting* with the unwearing bronze"; where the poet (? Empedocles) uses *drawing* for *cutting,* and *cutting* for *drawing,* when both terms are species of the genus *removing.*

(d) By Metaphor formed on the basis of analogy (or proportion) is meant the case when a second term, B, is to a first, A, as a fourth, D, is to a third, C; whereupon the fourth term, D, may be substituted for the second, B, or the second, B, for the fourth, D. Sometimes, too, the poet will qualify the metaphorical word by adding to it the term (+ A or + C) to which the nonfigurative term is relative. To illustrate: the drinking-bowl (B) is to Dionysus (A) as the shield (D) is to Ares (C). Accordingly, the bowl (B) may be called *the shield* (D) of Dionysus, and the shield (D) *the bowl* (B) of Ares. Or another illustration: old age (B) is to life (A) as evening (D) is to the day (C). Hence one will speak of *the evening* (D) as the *old age* (B) of the day—or as Empedocles does; and of *old age* (B) as *the evening (D)* of life—or as "the sunset of life." In certain cases, the language may contain no actual word corresponding to one of the terms in the proportion, but the figure nevertheless will be employed. For example, when a fruit casts forth its seed the action is called "sowing," but the action of the sun in casting forth its flame has no special name. Yet this nameless action (B) is to the sun (A) as *sowing* (D) is to the fruit (C); and hence we have the expression of the poet, "*sowing* a god-created flame." There is still another way in which this kind of metaphor may be used. We may substitute one term, B, for another, D, and then subtract some characteristic attribute of B. For example, one might call *the shield* (D), not *the bowl* (B) of Ares, but "the *wineless* bowl."

KEY TERMS IN ARISTOTLE'S POETICS

The *Poetics* of Aristotle (384–322 B.C.) has exerted immense influence on the writing and study of western literature, even though we do not even possess the entire manuscript. The work has been variously perceived in many ways ranging from a single individual's descriptive response to the literature of his time, especially its tragic drama, to an infallible guide to the interpretation and composition of all literary texts. Some of the most frequently utilized and sometimes misinterpreted Aristotelian terms are as follows:

mimesis: imitation, the representation of reality, of human life, in literature

muthos: not exactly the plot of a literary work, as it is sometimes taken to mean. The term *muthos* is perhaps best regarded as the general or background narrative sequence that the plot of a literary work, especially a drama, develops in detail

character: person whose actions are depicted in words; one who "lives" in a work of literature

unity of action: not specifically referred to as such by Aristotle but implied in his insistence that the plot of a drama should depict a complete action

episodic: refers to a plot that consists of various episodes that are not successfully tied together

a unity of time: again, not a phrase Aristotle uses but implied in his mention of a single day as the maximum period of time likely to be depicted in a successful plot

a unity of place: a phrase not directly implied by Aristotle at all but thought by his commentators to be consistent with his remarks on time and action. Thus, a commendable drama should take place in a single location.

peripeteia: a reversal; a sudden change in an individual's fortune from bad to good or good to bad

hamartia: an error, more specifically a tragic mistake or misjudgment committed by one whose actions and decisions will affect the lives of others. The term is often mistranslated as "tragic flaw," as if it indicted an internal weakness in character. Also, the term is often incorrectly assumed to indicate pride as a moral failing.

anagnorisis: recognition, a passage to knowledge from ignorance, especially with regard to the concealed or unknown identity of a character or characters in a literary work. Aristotle held that the best plots combined recognition and reversal, as in the *Oedipis Rex* of Sophocles.

hero: central character in a dramatic or other work. For Aristotle, a hero was typically an individual of high social standing, a member of a great house or of noble lineage. Aristotle maintained that the heroic character depicted in a tragedy should be neither of the highest or lowest moral caliber. Otherwise, an audience would not believe that a tragic outcome was deserved or plausible.

tragedy: considered by Aristotle to be the highest form of literature, superior even to the epic poetry held in such great esteem by the Greeks. This dramatic genre, according to Aristotle, is typified by tragic incident or suffering and by skilled handling of the elements indicated above.

catharsis: the purging of emotions, especially of pity and fear, experienced by the spectator as a result of viewing a successful tragedy

General Study Question: Consider a tragedy or other narrative work you are familiar with. Can you apply some or most of Aristotle's terminology to this text? Provide illustration for as many of his terms as you can by citing passages from the work you have chosen. (NW)

Questions for Consideration

Using complete sentences, provide brief answers for the following questions.

1. What is the subject of the *Poetics* as pronounced by Aristotle?

    _____

    _____

    _____

    _____

    _____

2. How does Aristotle define "tragedy"? What are the major constituents of the tragedy?

    _____

    _____

    _____

    _____

    _____

3. What distinction does Aristotle make between epic poetry and tragedy?

    _____

    _____

    _____

    _____

    _____

4. How does Aristotle define plot as it relates to tragedy? What does he consider to be the most important aspects (elements) of a plot?

    _____

    _____

    _____

    _____

    _____

5. Aristotle states that an episodic plot is the "worst" of all plots and actions. "How does he define an episodic plot? What kind of plot does he consider to be the best?

_____

_____

_____

_____

_____

6. What, according to Aristotle, is the function of the Chorus in tragedy?

_____

_____

_____

_____

_____

7. What is Aristotle's conception of the "ideal" tragic character?

_____

_____

_____

_____

_____

8. What is Aristotle's conception of "unity"? Why does he insist upon the "unity of action" in tragedy?

_____

_____

_____

_____

_____

———————— *Writing Critically* ————————

Select one of the topic ideas listed below and compose a 500 word essay which discusses the topic fully. Support your thesis with evidence from the text and with critical and/or historical material.

1. Aristotle defines the tragic hero as a person "not preeminent in virtue and justice" who "does not fall into misfortune through vice or depravity, but falls because of some mistake." To what extent is this definition applicable to the characters in *Medea*? Does Jason or Medea fit this description? Defend your answer.

2. Aristotle's concept of unity proposes a plot "so organized that if any one (of the events) is displaced or taken away, the whole will be shaken and put out of joint" as opposed to a plot "in which episodes follow one another in no probable or inevitable sequence." Does *Medea* have a logical plot? Do all events contribute to the unity of plot? Can Aristotle's concept of unity be applied to the plot of *Medea*? Defend your answer.

Prewriting Space:

_____

_____

_____

_____

_____

_____

_____

_____

_____

_____

_____

_____

_____

_____

_____

_____

_____

_____

Introduction

Terence (195–159 B.C.)

Publius Terentius Afer (Terence) (195 or 185–159 B.C.) was born in North Africa and brought to Rome as a slave. He was properly educated and soon freed by his master, a Roman senator, because of his genius. He wrote six plays, all of which have survived. The first was produced in 166 B.C. the last in 160 B.C. All were adapted from the Greek comedies of Meander and others. The names of the most famous of his plays are as follows: *Andria* (166), *Mother-in-Law* (165), *Self-Tormentor* (163), *Eunuch* (161), *Phormio* (161), and *The Brothers* (160) (Brockett 63–64). Because of these plays, it is generally agreed that Plautus and Meander, by way of Terence, are the founders of the modern theater. For example, in Terence's hands, the "Greek Comedy of Meander was a lesson to Romans in manners, in tolerance, in kindly indulgence to equals and inferiors, and in the cultivation of pleasant relations with one another" (Sellar 213).

Although of the six plays of Terence, four were based more or less directly on the work of Meander, it cannot be said that Terence was a translator only. Rather he used the New Attic Comedy as a storehouse from which he drew stories, lines, and sometimes whole scenes (Norwood 13). That he was not a mere translator may be proved in several ways. First of all, a study of his plays proves conclusively that there is a definite advance in technical excellence and that later plays far surpass the earlier ones in mastery of methods (Norwood). This growth would not be noted if he simply were translating plays. Second, Donatus often indicates a divergence of treatment, which he would not mention if Terence's plays were faithful reproductions of Meander. Third, the comic force of Meander is completely lacking in Terence (Matthews 103). Fourth, *contaminatio*, which Terence admits openly is a sign of originalty (Norwood).

Although he is not a close translator, Terence's preference for Meander's plots brought him much of the Greek's spirit (Duff 208). The setting is uniformly Athens as are the references to laws and customs (Duff). His characters are types from the Greek comedy, but he has made them more humane (Duff 211). Ordinarily, when he added a character to a Greek play, he simply borrowed from some other Greek play (Flickinger 693). It is probable he took the original Greek story in all its details but changed it so that the plot was his own (Norwood).

The *Phormio* is based on a play by Apollodorus. Again Terence has taken just the story and has evolved his own plot. Or to be exact, he has used his favorite device of a double plot—both of which move along side by side throughout the play, and each reaches a climax (Norwood 42). Again, he has varied from the method of Meander by giving no preparation in the prologues for the plot and by carrying the tension of the spectator to extreme lengths (Frank 119). Thus in Terence's *Phormio* a young penniless adventurer engineers the intrigues and cleverly solves the difficulties in the farce. Phaedria son of Chremes, is in love with a slave girl, Pamphila, but does not have the money to buy her. His cousin Antipho, son of Chremes' brother Demipho, loves Phanium, a poor but beautiful orphan. Through the machinations of Phormio, Antipho obtains Phanium in a false lawsuit and Demipho is tricked into purchasing Pamphila for Phaedria. Phanium is then revealed as the lost daughter of Chremes (Shank 45).

In his introduction to *An Anthology of Roman Drama*, Philip Whaley Harsh makes the following comments about Terence's the *Phormio*:

Delightful comedy and extremely deft construction unite in the Phormio *to make it one of the most successful Roman Comedies. The various strands of the double plots are most intimately interwoven. The difficulties concerning Antipho's marriage are arrested at their point of greatest tension by the development of Phraedria's need for money to have his sweetheart, and the securing of this money complicates the marriage situation. Later, the clarification of this situation causes the marital troubles of Chremes to worsen. Thus the false pessimism so characteristic of high comedy (in contrast to the false optimism of tragedy) is maintained throughout the play. Portrayal of character, also, is skillfully handled. The determination of Demipho, though shaken by conflicting advocates, brings out the vacillation of Chremes, who now is so cautious about appearances and reputation, although in the past when his blood was less frigid, he was so careless. Deliberate Greek New Comedy, and an unfaithful husband such as Chremes is held up to ridicule (xix).*

The *Phormio* relies on plot ahead of other dramatic elements to achieve its success. Terence has orchestrated love affairs, legal maneuvers, double lives, argumentative confrontations, and double dealings with great dramatic force and clarity.

In conclusion, Terence's literary reputation is on the level of Horace and Livy, not of Virgil and Tacitus (Norwood 120). Cicero praised him for his "choice style, quietness, urbanity, and charm of utterance" (Norwood). Varro praised his characterization; Horace considered him eminent; and Quintilian called his plays the "height of elegance" (103). During the Middle Ages, his reputation was high, and his plays for a long time formed a Latin textbook for beginners in England (Norwood 104). Erasmus studied him (106). (CDH)

BIBLIOGRAPHY

Barsby, John. *Terence: The Eunuch, Phormio, The Brothers: A Companion to the Penguin Translation*. Bristol: Bristol Classical Press, 1991.

Duckworth, George. *The Nature of Roman Comedy: A Study in Popular Entertainment*. Princeton: Princeton University Press, 1952.

Duff, J. Wright. *Literary History of Rome*. London: T.E. Unwin, 1909.

Flickinger, Roy C. "Terence and Meander." *The Classical Journal* 26 (1931): 676–94.

Fowler, Harold N. *History of Roman Literature*. New York: D. Appleton and Company, 1923.

Frank, Tenney. *Life and Literature in the Roman Republic*. Berkeley, California: University of California Press, 1930.

Goldberg, Sander M. *Understanding Terence*. Princeton: Princeton University Press, 1986.

Kershaw, Allan. "A Sign of a New Speaker in Plautus and Terence?" *The Classical Quarterly* 45 (1995): 249–250.

Kronstan, David. *Roman Comedy*. Ithaca: Cornell University Press, 1983.

Matthews, Brander. *Development of the Drama*. New York: Charles Scribner's Sons, 1930.

Norwood, Gilbert. *The Art of Terence*. Oxford: Blackwell, 1923.

Sellar, W. Y. *Roman Poets of the Republic*. London: Oxford University Press, 1932.

Phormio

Terence
Edited by Duckworth

CHARACTERS IN THE PLAY

DAVUS, *a slave*
GETA, *slave of* DEMIPHO
ANTIPHO, *a young man, son of* DEMIPHO
PHAEDRIA, *a young man, son of* CHREMES
DEMIPHO, *an aged Athenian*
PHORMIO, *a parasite*
HEGIO
CRATINUS } *legal advisers of* DEMIPHO
CRITO
DORIO, *a pimp*
CHREMES, *an old man, brother of* DEMIPHO
SOPHRONA, *a nurse*
NAUSISTRATA, *wife of* CHREMES

DIDASCALIA

The *Phormio* of Terence. Acted at the Roman Games during the curule aedileship of Lucius Postumius Albinus and Lucius Cornelius Merula. The chief parts were taken by Lucius Ambivius Turpio and Lucius Atilius Praenestinus. Set to music by Flaccus, the slave of Claudius, for flutes of unequal length. The play was taken entirely from *The Claimant*, a Greek comedy by Apollodorus. The poet's fourth comedy.[1] Produced in the consulship of Gaius Fannius and Marcus Valerius.[2]

SUMMARY

Demipho, the brother of Chremes, went abroad and left his son Antipho at Athens. Chremes had a wife and a daughter secretly at Lemnos, and at Athens he had another wife and a son devoted to a music girl. The Lemnian wife came to Athens and died there; the girl arranged for the funeral, Chremes being away. Antipho saw the girl at the funeral, fell in love with her, and with the aid of a parasite made her his wife. His father and Chremes returned and were angry. Then they gave thirty minae to the parasite so that he would marry the girl himself. The music girl was bought with this money. Antipho kept his wife when she had been recognised by Chremes as his daughter.

INTRODUCTION

The *Phormio* is one of Terence's two most successful comedies. It lacks the more serious content and the psychological interest of *The Brothers* but it is fully its equal in brilliance of dialogue and neatness of construction. The liveliness of the play and the presence of the parasite Phormio and the pimp Dorio make the comedy rather more Plautine than Terence's other works, with the exception of *The Eunuch*. Phormio is not the typical hungry parasite of Plautus, however; he is an impudent rogue who engineers the trickery and whose cleverness solves the difficulties of the play. He has been called "one of the most engaging scoundrels in the rich annals of the stage."

Phaedria, son of Chremes, is in love with a music girl, Pamphila, but has no money to buy her from Dorio. Antipho, son of Chremes' brother Demipho, falls in love with Phanium, a poor but respectable girl. Here again we have the dual structure of which Terence is so fond; in the solution of the two difficulties both deception and recognition have their place. During the absence of the fathers Phormio arranges a scheme whereby Antipho shall be legally compelled to marry. Since Phanium's mother is dead, Phormio brings suit against Antipho claiming that the youth is the girl's nearest relative and according to the law should therefore marry her. Antipho purposely loses the suit and makes Phanium his wife. The problems of the two young men are thus very different: Phaedria fears he will be unable to possess Pamphila, and Antipho dreads the possibility that he may be forced to give up Phanium. This is the situation when Demipho and Chremes, the two fathers, return. Demipho is angry and in spite of the so-called lawsuit wants Antipho to give up his wife.Terence's use of the double plot at this point is particularly skilful; he employs one difficulty to solve the other. Phormio pretends to be willing to marry Phanium upon payment of thirty minae—the very sum needed by Phaedria to get the music girl from Dorio.

Chremes, who had a second wife and a daughter in Lemnos, was trying to locate his daughter and was eager for her to marry Antipho. The revelation that Phanium is his daughter, like the recognition of Antiphila in *The Self-Tormentor*, complicates the situation, for Demipho at that very moment is arranging with Phormio to have the parasite take Phanium off Antipho's hands. Chremes' desire to have Antipho's marriage stand and his attempts to reveal the truth to Demipho without letting his own wife find it out are highly amusing. Geta, Demipho's slave who has been assisting Phormio in his schemes, learns of Chremes' double life and reveals it to Phormio. The secret which brings a happy solution to Antipho's problem is now used by Phormio to confirm Phaedria in his possession of Pamphila. Here again is unusual skill in the handling of the double plot.

Structurally the *Phormio* is one of Terence's finest plays. The situation is complex but not puzzling, and the plot develops naturally from one stage to the next. The spectator is kept in suspense, for the dramatist seeks to achieve his effects by uncertainty and surprise. The revelation of Chremes' secret life comes as a complete surprise, as does that of Phanium's identity. This type of suspense is characteristic of Terence and is best illustrated in *The Mother-in-law*, where the secret is withheld from the audience until the very end. Another interesting feature of the plot is the manner in which Phormio's fiction concerning the relationship of Antipho and Phanium proves to be true. This is not unlike Milphio's second trick in *The Carthaginian* of Plautus, which makes Hanno the father of the Carthaginian maidens as he proves to be in reality.

There are numerous scenes in the *Phormio* full of irony and humour. Antipho's cowardice and his inability to face his father, his misunderstanding of Phormio's second trick which appears to oppose the continuance of his marriage, the not too helpful advice of Demipho's three friends, Chremes' attempt to conceal his secret from his wife, the impudence and ingenuity of Phormio throughout and especially in the final scene when he reveals the truth to Chremes' wife—all these make the play one of the most amusing and delightful in Roman comedy.

The best-known adaptation of the *Phormio* in modern times is Molière's *Les Fourberies de Scapin* (1671). Later plays, such as Otway's *The Cheats of Scapin* (1677) and Ravenscroft's *Scaramouch a Philosopher* (1677) are related to Terence through their imitation of Molière. Colman's *The Man of Business* (1774) combined elements from Terence's *Phormio* and Plautus' *The Three Penny Day*.

Phormio

(SCENE:—*A street in Athens in front of the houses of* DEMIPHO, CHREMES, *and* DORIO.)

PROLOGUE

Since the old poet[3] can't divert our poet from his profession and take away his occupation, he's using abuse to scare him from writing plays. He keeps saying that the plays which our poet has written are weak in dialogue and commonplace in style, and that's because our poet has never portrayed a crazy young man seeing a doe running with hounds after her, and the beast weeping and crying for help. If the old playwright had known that the success of his play, when it was put on the stage, was due more to the skill of the actor than to that of the author, he wouldn't be so bold in his attacks.

If there is anyone here who speaks and thinks as follows, "If the old poet hadn't abused him first, this young poet couldn't have written a prologue at all, having no one to attack," that man shall receive this answer: all literary men have an equal right to win success if they can. The old poet has tried to drive our poet from his work and make him starve. Our poet wished to answer him, not to attack him. If he had carried on his rivalry in pleasant terms, he would have received pleasant terms in reply; as it is, he must realise that he is only getting back what he gave. I shall stop talking about him now, although he for his part does not stop his wrongdoing.

Please give me your attention. I bring you a new comedy, called *The Claimant* in Greek but *Phormio* in Latin, because the actor who takes the leading part is Phormio the parasite, and he will carry on the main part of the plot, if you grant your favour to the poet. Therefore give us your attention, and listen in fairness and silence, that we may not suffer the misfortune we did when our company was driven from the stage by a riot.[4] The excellence of our chief actor, supported by your kindness and good will, has enabled us to return again to the stage.

ACT ONE. SCENE I

(Enter DAVUS, carrying a bag of money.)

DAVUS (*to himself*): My good friend and fellow-townsman Geta came to me yesterday, and asked me to get hold of a little money I'd been owing him. Well, I've got it and here I am. I understand his master's son's just married, and I'll wager this money goes for a present to his wife. The woman will take all the earnings of a miserable man, who's saved up little by little, cheating himself of the bare necessities of life; and she won't give a thought to how much trouble it took to get that present. Poor Geta'll be stuck again for another present when a child is born; for another when its birthday comes around. The mother takes it all; the child is only the excuse for the presents. Is that Geta there?

ACT ONE. SCENE II

(Enter GETA from DEMIPHO's house.)

GETA (*speaking to someone within*): Now, if a red-headed fellow asks for me—

DAVUS: He's here already; sh-h!

GETA: Oh, Davus, I was looking for you.

DAVUS: Well, here you are. (*Hands him the bag of money*) It's counted out; you'll find the amount correct.

GETA: My best thanks.

DAVUS: I tell you, in these times if anybody pays his debts, you should be glad. What makes you so melancholy?

GETA: I'm frightened out of my wits. Don't you know what's happened?

DAVUS: No.

GETA: I'll tell you, if you'll keep still.

DAVUS: Go on, you fool! Are you afraid to trust me with words when you've already trusted me with money? What's the use of cheating you, anyway?

GETA: Listen, then.

DAVUS: Proceed.

GETA: Do you know Chremes, my master's elder brother?

DAVUS: Certainly.

GETA: And Phaedria, his son?

DAVUS: As well as I know you.

GETA: Well, it happened that my master was forced to make a journey to Cilicia, to visit a friend who sent letters to the old man and tempted him with mountains of gold.

DAVUS: Didn't he have enough already?

GETA: Keep still; this is the way it happened.

DAVUS: I wish I had been a rich man!

GETA: When Chremes went away to Lemnos at the same time, both the old men left me as a sort of tutor to their sons, Phaedria and Antipho.

DAVUS: Geta, you had your hands full!

GETA: I found that out soon enough. Luck left me then and there. First, I opposed them; no use; so long as I was faithful to the old men, my only reward was beatings.

DAVUS: The old proverb occurs to me: "It's folly to kick against the pricks."

GETA: Then I decided to reverse myself, so I did everything I could for the young fellows.

DAVUS: That was sensible.

GETA: Antipho didn't do anything bad for a while; but Phaedria at once found a little harp-player and fell desperately in love with her. She was a slave—her master a villainous trader. The old men didn't leave the young fellows much extra cash, so Phaedria could do no more than feast his eyes on her. He accompanied her back and forth to school; that was all. Having nothing in particular to do, we turned our attention to the young man. Right across from the music school there's a barber shop. He used to wait there every day and go home with her. One day when we were there, a young man came in weeping. We were dumbfounded and asked him what the matter was. "Never," said he, "has poverty seemed so terrible or so great a burden. Just now I saw a girl who lives nearby, mourning her dead mother; there wasn't a single friend around, except one old woman who helped the girl with the funeral arrangements. I was sorry for her. She was good looking, too." In short, he moved us all to tears. Then Antipho said, "Let's go and see her." We went and saw her, and she certainly was handsome; hair loose, feet bare, and dress shabby. She would have been disgusting in these circumstances, had she not been so beautiful. Phaedria said, "Oh, she's well enough, I suppose"—but Antipho—

DAVUS: Fell in love!

GETA: Right. But listen to the sequel. The next day he went straight to the old woman and begged her to let him see the girl; but she wouldn't listen to him, and told him he was not acting honourably; that she was an Athenian citizen, born of good parents, and that if he wished to make the girl his wife, he might do so according to law; otherwise, she would have nothing to do with him. He didn't know what to do. He wanted to marry the girl, but he was afraid of his father.

DAVUS: Wouldn't his father give him permission when he returned?

GETA: Do you think he'd let his son marry a girl without a dowry? Never in the world.

DAVUS: What happened then?

GETA: There is a certain fellow named Phormio, a parasite—confound him!

DAVUS: What did he do?

GETA: He advised Antipho in this fashion: "There is a law that orphans are compelled to marry their nearest relatives; I will say that you are the girl's nearest relative, and bring suit against you; I'll make believe I'm a friend of the girl's father. We'll come before the judges. I'll arrange to supply a father and a mother, and tell how she's related to you. Now, *you* won't deny anything, then *I'll* win my case; you see? Your father'll come home, and I'll have a fight with him; what's the difference? We'll have the girl."

DAVUS: Ha! That's funny. He's courageous enough!

GETA: Antipho agreed; Phormio won, and the young fellow is married.

DAVUS: What do you say?

GETA: Just what I've told you.

DAVUS: Oh, Geta, what'll happen to you?

GETA: Well, I don't know about that; but I *do* know that whatever happens, I'll bear it bravely.

DAVUS: That's right; and spoken like a man!

GETA: My only hope lies in myself.

DAVUS: Excellent!

GETA: I'll go for a pleader, who'll plead for me in this wise: "Forgive him this time; if he ever does anything wrong after this, I'll not plead for him." Just so he doesn't add: "And when I go, kill him, for all I care!"

DAVUS: What about the little harpist's attendant? How's he?

GETA: None too well.

DAVUS: He hasn't much to give, has he?

GETA: He has nothing but hope.

DAVUS: Has his father returned yet?

GETA: No.

DAVUS: Tell me, when do you think your master will arrive home?

GETA: I don't exactly know—but I hear a letter has come from him. It's at the post-office now. I'm going to get it.

DAVUS: Do you need me any longer, Geta?

GETA: No. Good-bye. (DAVUS *departs*.)

GETA *calls to slave within*) What ho, boy!—Nobody there? (*Enter slave.* GETA *gives him the bag of money*) Here, take this in and give it to Dorcium. (GETA *departs towards the harbour*.)

ACT TWO. SCENE I

(*Enter* ANTIPHO *and* PHAEDRIA *from* CHREMES' *house*.)

ANTIPHO: Think of it! That matters should come to this pass! That I should fear my father, who is always planning what is best for me, whenever I think of his return! If I hadn't been so impetuous I might have welcomed him as became a dutiful son.

PHAEDRIA: Why, what's the matter?

ANTIPHO: Do you ask? You who know of my foolish deed? I wish Phormio had never thought of persuading me to do this, eager as I was! Oh, that was the beginning of all my troubles. Then I shouldn't have got her; for a few days I might have suffered; but this daily distraction would not have tortured my conscience as it has.

PHAEDRIA: I see.

ANTIPHO: And now I await the person who is to break off my union with Phanium.

PHAEDRIA: Others grieve because they cannot have those whom they desire; you're sad because

you enjoy the object of your love. You have too much; you are overwhelmed with love, Antipho. You live an enviable life. The gods bless me—if I could have the woman I love, I would willingly die! See here now: you have a cultured and well-bred girl of good principles. You couldn't wish for more. Why, you would be completely happy if you had only the courage to bear misfortune. If you had to deal with that slave-trader, as I do, then you'd know what it is to have troubles.

ANTIPHO: But you are fortunate, Phaedria; you can do whatever you please: keep the girl, or let her go. But I, unhappy man, haven't the right either to keep my beloved or to let her go. But what's this? Is that Geta running here? I'm afraid I know what ill news he brings.

ACT TWO. SCENE II

(*Enter* GETA, *running*.)

GETA (*to himself, not seeing* ANTIPHO *and* PHAEDRIA): Geta, you must devise at once some plan of escape. Great dangers are threatening you, and you can't avoid them. How shall I get out of this scrape? I can't keep the secret dark any longer.

ANTIPHO (*aside to* PHAEDRIA): I wonder why he's so upset?

GETA: I have only a second to make my plans; my master'll be here any minute.

ANTIPHO (*aside to* PHAEDRIA): What's this?

GETA: When he hears what's happened, what shall I do? Shall I speak? I'll only make him angry. Shall I keep still? That'll arouse him. Clear myself? No use at all; I might as well try to wash the colour out of a brick. This is terrible. I'm afraid on my own account—and Antipho drives me to distraction. If it weren't for him, I should have been revenged on the old men long ago, and run away immediately.

ANTIPHO (*aside to* PHAEDRIA): What's that he says about running away?

GETA: Where can I find Antipho?

PHAEDRIA (*aside to* ANTIPHO): Aha! He's talking about you.

ANTIPHO (*aside to* PHAEDRIA): I'm afraid he has bad news for me.

GETA: I'm going to his home; he's usually to be found there.

ANTIPHO (*to* GETA, *as he is making for the house*): Stop, there!

GETA (*without looking back*): You order me about familiarly enough, whoever you are.

ANTIPHO: Geta!

GETA (*turning around*): Why, it's the very man I'm looking for.

ANTIPHO: Quick now, what's the news? Tell me in one word.

GETA: I'll do it.

ANTIPHO: Speak, then.

GETA: Just now, at the harbour—

ANTIPHO: My—?

GETA: You're right.

ANTIPHO: I'm dead and buried.

PHAEDRIA: Is it possible!

ANTIPHO: Wh-wh-what'll I do?

PHAEDRIA (*to* GETA): What do you say?

GETA: That I saw his father, your uncle.

ANTIPHO: How can I bear up under this disaster? Oh, Phanium, if Fortune decrees that I be torn from your arms, life will mean nothing for me.

GETA: Antipho, you must be careful; Fortune favours the brave, you know.

ANTIPHO: I'm not myself at all.

GETA: But now, of all times, you must be, Antipho. If your father should see that you're afraid, he'd think you were in the wrong.

PHAEDDRIA: That's true enough.

ANTIPHO: I can't change my nature.

GETA: Well, what would you do if you had something worse on your hands?

ANTIPHO: Since I can't do this, I'd be still less able to do that.

GETA (*to* PHAEDRIA, *with a wink*): This is nothing, Phaedria. Come along. Why should we waste our time here? I'm going.

PHAEDRIA: So am I. (GETA *and* PHAEDRIA *turn to go away.*)

ANTIPHO: Please stay! What if I should bluster it through? Put on a brave front? (*Looking brave*) How's this?

GETA (*not looking at him*): Nonsense.

ANTIPHO: Look at my expression. Hm! Br-r! Is this all right?

GETA (*turning around and looking at him*): No.

ANTIPHO: Is this?

GETA: Better. Try again.

ANTIPHO: How about this?

GETA: That's all right; now, hold that expression. Answer him word for word, argument for argument, and don't let him scare you with big talk.

ANTIPHO: I see—I—I see.

GETA: Tell him you were forced to marry unwillingly.

PHAEDRIA: By the law and by the judge.

GETA: Understand? (*He sees* DEMIPHO *at a distance*) Who's that old man I see at the end of the street? It's he, indeed.

ANTIPHO: I *can't* stay. (*Going.*)

GETA: What are you going to do? Where are you going, Antipho? Stay here, I tell you.

ANTIPHO: I'm too conscious of my crimes. I entrust Phanium and my life to your charge! (*He runs off.*)

PHAEDRIA: Geta, what now?

GETA: Now you'll hear some accusations. I'll be beaten, hung up by the wrists, if I'm not very much mistaken. By the way, do you remember what you said to me once, when we were embarking on this enterprise? To defend ourselves from trouble we should say that our cause was right, just, and honourable?

PHAEDRIA: Yes, I do.

GETA: Well, we have need of those arguments, or even better ones, if we can find them.

PHAEDRIA: I'll do my best.

GETA: You greet him first, and I'll wait here in ambush, as a reserve force, in case you have to retreat.

PHAEDRIA: Very well, then. (*They withdraw.*)

ACT TWO. SCENE III[5]

(*Enter* DEMIPHO *from the harbour.*)

DEMIPHO (*to himself*): So Antipho has married without my consent, has he? To think that he should have no regard for my authority—or fear of my anger! Isn't he ashamed of himself? Geta, Geta, wily counsellor!

GETA (*aside*): At last!

DEMIPHO: What can they say to me, what excuse can they find for their conduct?

GETA (*aside*): Oh, I've found an excuse; think of something harder!

DEMIPHO: Perhaps he'll say: "I did it unwillingly; the law forced me to." Very well—I don't deny it.

GETA (*aside*): Good! Excellent!

DEMIPHO: To give up the case to the prosecutors, without saying a word—did the law compel him to do that?

GETA (*aside*): That *is* more difficult![6] But I'll think up a good answer to that.

DEMIPHO: I don't know what to do, this is so unexpected. I am so angry I can't think. I hold that when any man's affairs are in good order, he ought to consider how he should bear adversity: dangers of every kind, lawsuits, exile, and the like; and returning from travel he should always imagine that his son is in a bad scrape, his wife dead, and his daughter ill. These accidents are common to all humanity. He should let nothing upset him. Whatever comes out better than was expected, he should consider as so much to the good.

GETA (*aside to* PHAEDRIA): Oh, Phaedria, it's wonderful how much more I know than my master! I have considered long ago everything that might happen to me in case my master should return. I must grind away at the mill, be beaten, put in chains, and labour and sweat in the fields. Nothing unexpected is possible. Whatever comes out better than I thought is so much to the good. Why don't you go up to him and begin to explain your case?

DEMIPHO: Oho! I see Phaedria. (PHAEDRIA *goes towards* DEMIPHIO.)

PHAEDRIA: Welcome, uncle.

DEMIPHO: Welcome to you; but where's Antipho?

PHAEDRIA: I'm glad you have re—

DEMIPHO (*interrupting*): That's all very well, but tell me this—

PHAEDRIA: He is in good health. Is everything well with you, sir?

DEMIPHO: I wish it were.

PHAEDRIA: What is the trouble?

DEMIPHO: Do you ask, Phaedria? You have allowed a fine marriage to take place while I was away.

PHAEDRIA: Oh, you are annoyed with him on that account?

GETA (*aside*): Cunning dog!

DEMIPHO: Why shouldn't I be? Ah, I'm just waiting for him to cross my path, so that he may see how by his fault I have been changed from a most indulgent to a most severe father.

PHAEDRIA: But he's done nothing, uncle, deserving of blame.

DEMIPHO: Nonsense—you are birds of a feather; know one and you know all.

PHAEDRIA: That's not so.

DEMIPHO: If one's in trouble, the other's ready to plead his cause: turn and turn about.

GETA (*aside*): There he's right.

DEMIPHO: If that weren't true you would not have upheld his case.

PHAEDRIA: At any rate, if Antipho has been a little neglectful of his reputation, I'm not trying to excuse him or find reasons why he shouldn't get what he deserves. But if by chance someone lays a snare for our tender years and catches us, is it our fault, or that of the judges? And anyway, the judges are often spiteful; they take away from the rich and then out of pity give it to the poor.

GETA (*aside*): If I didn't know the facts about the trial, I'd think he was telling the truth.

DEMIPHO: What judge could possibly know your rights, when you didn't say a word in your defence? That's what happened with him.

PHAEDRIA: He did just as any other young man would do: when he came before the judges, he couldn't say what he had planned to say—he was too upset.

GETA (*advancing to* DEMIPHO): Well, master, I'm glad to see you home again!

DEMIPHO: Oh, most excellent guardian, welcome! Mainstay of the family, protector and adviser of my son!

GETA: For some time I have heard you blaming us all, and wrongly, me most of all! What would

you have had me do in this case? The law doesn't allow a slave to plead or to give testimony.

DEMIPHO: Very true. I'll grant he might have been nervous, and that you as a slave could do nothing in court; but if the woman were related so closely, he did not have to marry her; he should have given her a dowry, according to law, and let her find another husband. On what account did he marry a girl without a thing?

GETA: On no account: he needed the cash.

DEMIPHO: He might have borrowed it from someone.

GETA: Easier said than done!

DEMIPHO: If the worst had come to the worst, he might have borrowed it at interest.

GETA: Fine words! As if anybody would trust him, with you still alive!

DEMIPHO: No, no, it can't be; it isn't possible. Am I to allow her to be his wife? She deserves no pity. I'd like that fellow pointed out to me; where does he live?

GETA: You mean Phormio?

DEMIPHO: Yes, the fellow who pleaded for her.

GETA: I'll see that he comes at once.

DEMIPHO: Where is Antipho now?

GETA: Off somewhere.

DEMIPHO: Phaedria, bring him here, please.

PHAEDRIA: Very well, I'll go by the shortest road. (*He goes into* DORIO's *house.*)

GETA (*aside*): To Pamphila! (GETA *departs.*)

DEMIPHO (*to himself*): I'll go into the house, and render offerings to the gods; then I'll go to the forum, and call my friends together to help me in the matter, so that I shan't be unprepared when Phormio comes.

(*He goes into his own house. A short time is supposed to elapse before the next Act.*)

ACT THREE. SCENE I

(Enter PHORMIO *and* GETA.*)*

PHORMIO: You say he ran off because he was afraid of his father?

GETA: Yes.

PHORMIO: And Phanium is left alone?

GETA: Yes.

PHORMIO: And the old man is angry?

GETA: Very.

PHORMIO *(aside)*: The whole thing rests on you alone, Phormio; you've got us into the trouble and you must get us out.—Well, to work now!

GETA: Please—

PHORMIO *(to himself, not listening to* GETA*)*: If he asks—

GETA: You are my only hope.

PHORMIO *(as before)*: Well, now, what if he should—?

GETA: You are the one who urged us on. Please help us.

PHORMIO *(to* GETA*)*: Let him come! All my plans are made.

GETA: What'll you do?

PHORMIO: Phanium stays with Antipho; I clear him of blame, and bring down on my own head all the anger of the old man!

GETA: You're a brave man and a true friend. Indeed, I've often feared that that bravery would some day land you in jail.

PHORMIO: Not so; the danger's begun, and I've mapped out my course. How many people do you suppose I've beaten to death already? As my technique improves, my practice increases! Come now, did you ever hear of anyone bringing a suit for damages against me?

GETA: Why is that?

PHORMIO: Because a net isn't spread for a hawk or a kite, birds that do us harm; it's spread for harmless birds, for there's some profit in them; it's labour wasted to catch the others. The men from whom some profit can be squeezed are the ones in danger. They know I haven't a thing to lose. You'll say they might bring me home as a slave after condemning me. But they don't want to feed a man with my appetite; and I think they're wise, because they don't wish to return good for evil.

GETA: Wonderful! How grateful he ought to be to you!

PHORMIO: You take your place at the table, free from cares, while I am burdened with your troubles and my own. While you have whatever you want, I am worried; you laugh gaily, are the first to drink, take the place of honour at table, and have doubtful viands placed before you. Then you have—

GETA: What do you mean by "doubtful viands"?

PHORMIO: I mean that when you look at the various delicacies, you are in doubt as to which one to begin with.

GETA *(seeing* DEMIPHO *approach)*: The old man's coming. See what he's doing. The first encounter is the worst. If you survive that, you may do what you please afterward. *(They retire.)*

ACT THREE. SCENE II

(Enter DEMIPHO, HEGIO, CRATINUS, *and* CRITO.*)*

DEMIPHO: Have you ever heard of anything more ridiculous than what has happened to me? I implore you to help me.

GETA *(aside to* PHORMIO*)*: He's getting angry.

PHORMIO *(aside to* GETA*)*: Now, pay attention; I'm going to stir him up. *(Speaking aloud)* By the immortal gods, does Demipho say that Phanium is not his relative? Does he?

GETA: He does.

PHORMIO: Does he deny that he knows who her father was?

GETA: He denies it.

DEMIPHO (*turning to his friends*): I believe this is the fellow I was talking about. Follow me.

PHORMIO: And that he knows who Stilpo was?

GETA: Absolutely.

PHORMIO: And why? Because the miserable creature was left in poverty, her father ignored, she herself neglected. See what avarice will do to a man!

GETA: If you accuse my master of any wrong, you'll hear something you won't like!

DEMIPHO: The idea! Does he come here on purpose to accuse me?

PHORMIO: I have no reason to be angry at the youth if he didn't know my friend. He was old and poor and generally worked hard in the country; he rented some land there from my father. But the old man often told me how his relative neglected him. And what a fine man he was, too, the best I've ever seen!

GETA (*with sarcasm*): And you're the same sort of fellow, I suppose.

PHORMIO: Oh, go to the devil! If I hadn't thought so highly of him, I wouldn't have been so bitter against your family. And it's on account of his daughter, whom your master now rejects, like the cad he is.

GETA: Be careful what you say!

PHORMIO: Doesn't he deserve it?

GETA: Is that so, you rascal?

DEMIPHO: Geta!

GETA (*to* PHORMIO, *pretending not to hear* DEMIPHO): You cheat the citizens and twist the laws up into knots.

DEMIPHO: Geta!

PHORMIO (*aside to* GETA): Answer him.

GETA (*turning around*): Who is it? Well?

DEMIPHO (*to* GETA): Sh-h!

GETA: He never stopped abusing you while you were away.

DEMIPHO: Stop it! (*To* PHORMIO) Young fellow, with your very kind permission, if you will be good enough to answer me, tell me what friend of yours you just mentioned, and in what manner he claims I am related to him?

PHORMIO: There now, you're trying to pump me. As if you didn't know!

DEMIPHO: *I* know?

PHORMIO: Certainly you know.

DEMIPHO: But I say I don't; tell me about it; *you* seem to know.

PHORMIO: Well, well, don't you know your own first cousin?

DEMIPHO: You're joking! What's the name?

PHORMIO: The name? The name—indeed—

DEMIPHO: Why don't you tell me?

PHORMIO (*aside*): I'm dead: I've forgotten the name.

DEMIPHO: What do you say?

PHORMIO (*aside to* GETA): Geta, if you remember that name I told you just now, help me out. (*To* DEMIPHO) Well, I won't tell you; as if you didn't know! You came here to get me to tell you.

DEMIPHO: I get you to tell me!

GETA (*aside to* PHORMIO): Stilpo.

PHORMIO: Well, what's the difference? Stilpo is the name.

DEMIPHO: What?

PHORMIO: Stilpo, I say; you know him.

DEMIPHO: I never heard of him before. Related to me?

PHORMIO: Aren't you ashamed? If he'd left you ten talents—

DEMIPHO: Go to the devil!

PHORMIO: You would be the first to trace your ancestors back even as far as your great grand-father.

DEMIPHO: That may be, but if I had begun, I should have stated what relation she was to me. Come now, what relation is she to me?

GETA (*to* DEMIPHO): That's right, master. (*To* PHORMIO) Look out, now.

PHORMIO: I have explained my case clearly to the judge, as was my duty. Besides, if this were wrong, why didn't your son deny it?

DEMIPHO: Don't mention his name to me.

PHORMIO: Oh, most wise of men, go to a magistrate, and have him give you another decision on the same case, since you are the only man who can get two decisions!

DEMIPHO: I'll do what the law advises, rather than listen to you or involve myself in lawsuits. Give her a dowry! Take her away! Take the five minae!

PHORMIO: Ha, ha, ha, what a dear fellow!

DEMIPHO: What's that? Don't I ask what's right? Can't I even have common justice?

PHORMIO: I ask you, is that the law? Does it say you can treat her as a courtesan and then pay her and send her away? Doesn't the law say that no citizen is to be driven to shame because of her poverty? That's why she's ordered to marry her next of kin and live her life with him. And that's just what you forbid.

DEMIPHO: Surely, to her next of kin; but how does that concern us?

PHORMIO: My good sir, don't try a case that's been tried already, as they say.

DEMIPHO: I shan't stop until I have established my rights.

PHORMIO: Nonsense.

DEMIPHO: Leave that to me!

PHORMIO: Well, I'll have nothing to do with it, Demipho, nor with you. *Your* son is the one who is in trouble.

DEMIPHO: I'll shut him out of the house at once, and his wife with him.

PHORMIO: You wouldn't do that!

DEMIPHO: Rascal, are you always troubling me for the amusement you get out of it?

PHORMIO (*aside to* GETA): He's afraid of us, but he's trying to conceal it.

GETA (*aside to* PHORMIO): You've made a good beginning.

PHORMIO (*to* DEMIPHO): If you'll do the right thing, we'll remain on good terms.

DEMIPHO: Do you think I want your friendship, or wish to hear or see you?

PHORMIO: If you can get on well with her, you'll have her to cheer your old age; you're getting on in years.

DEMIPHO: Let her cheer you up; you may have her.

PHORMIO: There, there, keep cool!

DEMIPHO: You've said enough. Unless you take that woman away, I'll send her packing. Phormio, I have spoken.

PHORMIO: If you lay hands on her in any other way than befits a free woman, I'll bring suit against you. I have spoken, Demipho. (*Aside to* GETA) If you want me, I'll be home.

GETA (*aside to* PHORMIO): Yes, I know. (PHORMIO *goes out.*)

ACT THREE. SCENE III

DEMIPHO: What troubles and cares does my son heap on my poor old back! And this marriage! Oh! Why doesn't he come, and try at least to explain the matter to me? (*to* GETA) Go and see whether he's home yet.

GETA: Very well. (*He goes into* DEMIPHO'S *house.*)

DEMIPHO: You see how matters stand? What shall I do? Tell me, Hegio.

HEGIO: I? I think that Cratinus ought to give his opinion, if you have no objection.

DEMIPHO: Tell me, Cratinus.

CRATINUS: Do you wish me to speak?

DEMIPHO: Yes, you.

CRATINUS: Well, I think you should do what is best; what this son of yours has done in your absence should be undone. In that way you will secure justice. That is my opinion.

DEMIPHO: Now you, Hegio.

HEGIO: I believe that Cratinus has spoken with good sense. But it's a fact that "So many men, so many opinions": each man after his own fashion. Now, it doesn't seem to me that what has been done by law can be undone; and it's wrong to try to change it.

DEMIPHO: It's your turn now, Crito.

CRITO: I think we should consider the matter more fully. It's an important affair.

HEGIO: Anything else?

DEMIPHO: No, you have done very well. (HEGIO, CRATINUS, *and* CRITO *go out*) Now I'm more uncertain what to do than I was before.

(*Enter* GETA *from* DEMIPHO'S *house.*)

GETA: They say he hasn't come back yet.

DEMIPHO: I'll wait for my brother, and do what he advises. I'll go down to the harbour now and find out when he is expected to return. (*He goes out.*)

GETA (*to himself*): I'll go and find Antipho and tell him what's just happened. But I see him coming. He's just in the nick of time.

ACT THREE. SCENE IV[7]

(*Enter* ANTIPHO.)

ANTIPHO (*to himself*): Oh, Antipho, you are to blame for the way you feel; to think that I ran away and left my life and safety in the hands of others! Did you believe that they would take care of your interests better than you could yourself? No matter how the other things were, you should have thought of the girl you had at home, that she might not suffer through her trust in you. All her hopes are placed in you alone.

GETA (*advancing to* ANTIPHO): Well, master, we've been angry with you for some time, because you ran off.

ANTIPHO: I was looking for you.

GETA: But we weren't any the less careful on your behalf.

ANTIPHO: Tell me, please, how are my affairs proceeding? Does my father suspect anything yet?

GETA: Not a thing.

ANTIPHO: Is there any hope?

GETA: I don't know.

ANTIPHO (*disappointed*): Oh—

GETA: But Phaedria has never ceased helping you.

ANTIPHO: That's nothing new; he always helps me.

GETA: Then Phormio once again proved himself an enormously clever fellow, in this as in other matters.

ANTIPHO: What did he do?

GETA: He pacified the old man, who was very angry.

ANTIPHO: Oh, my dear Phormio.

GETA: And—I myself did what I could.

ANTIPHO: Oh, Geta, you are all my friends.

GETA: So far, so good. Your father is waiting for your uncle to arrive.

ANTIPHO: Why?

GETA: Because he said he wanted to do as his brother advised.

ANTIPHO: Oh, Geta, how I dread to see my uncle arrive here safe and sound! For by his sentence alone, as I hear, I am to live or die.

GETA: Here's Phaedria.

ANTIPHO: Where?

GETA: See, he's coming out of his training-school.

ACT THREE. SCENE V

(Enter DORIO from his house, followed by PHAE-DRIA.)

PHAEDRIA: Dorio, please listen to me.

DORIO: I won't.

PHAEDRIA: Only a minute.

DORIO: Leave me alone.

PHAEDRIA: Listen to what I have to tell you.

DORIO: I'm tired of hearing the same thing a thousand times over.

PHAEDRIA: But now I'm going to tell you something you'll be glad to hear.

DORIO: Speak; I'll listen.

PHAEDRIA: Can't I persuade you to wait for three days? (DORIO *turns away*) Where are you going?

DORIO: I thought you were going to offer me something different.

ANTIPHO (*aside to* GETA): I'm afraid this slave-trader—

GETA (*aside to* ANTIPHO): —won't be safe?

PHAEDRIA: Don't you believe me?

DORIO: I don't.

PHAEDRIA: But if I promise?

DORIO: Nonsense.

PHAEDRIA: You'll be well paid for your trouble.

DORIO: No.

PHAEDRIA: Take my word for it; you'll be satisfied.

DORIO: You're dreaming.

PHAEDRIA: Just try. I don't ask you to wait long.

DORIO: Same old story.

PHAEDRIA: You'll be a second father to me, my best friend, my—

DORIO: Nonsense.

PHAEDRIA: How can you be so hard-hearted? Won't you be softened by pity or prayers?

DORIO: And to think that you, Phaedria, are so impudent and foolish as to think you could deceive me with your fine talk, and have for nothing what belongs to me!

ANTIPHO (*aside to* GETA): Poor fellow!

PHAEDRIA (*aside to himself*): True enough.

GETA (*aside to* ANTIPHO): See how each one acts his part.

PHAEDRIA (*to himself*): I wish this hadn't happened to me now that Antipho's in trouble.

ANTIPHO (*advancing*): What's all this trouble about, Phaedria?

PHAEDRIA: Oh, lucky Antipho.

ANTIPHO: What, I?

PHAEDRIA: Yes, you, who have your loved one at home.

ANTIPHO: Yes, indeed, but I've a wolf by the ears, as they say. I don't see how I can let her go, nor how to keep her.

DORIO: That's just the way with me.

ANTIPHO (*to* DORIO): Then be a real slave-trader, if you're going to be one at all. (*To* PHAEDRIA) Now, what's he done?

PHAEDRIA: What has he done? The villain has sold my Pamphila.

ANTIPHO: What? Sold her?

GETA: Do you mean to say he sold her?

PHAEDRIA: Yes, sold her.

DORIO: Why, what a wicked crime! To sell a girl whom I bought with my own money!

PHAEDRIA: I can't make him wait three days for me, and put off that man who wants to buy her, till I get the money my friends have promised me. And then, I told him, if I don't give him the money he needn't wait a minute longer.

DORIO: Talk away!

ANTIPHO (*to* DORIO): He doesn't ask you to wait long, Dorio. If you'll do this, he'll give you twice as much.

DORIO: Words, words.

ANTIPHO: How could you allow Pamphila to be taken away from the city? Would you allow their love to be destroyed?

DORIO: It's no affair of yours or mine; it's Phaedria's.

PHAEDRIA: May all the gods give you what you deserve!

DORIO: I have suffered your delays and insults against my will for a long time; always weeping and promising, and not giving me a thing; but now I've found a man who pays and isn't always whimpering. Give way to your betters!

ANTIPHO: Now, if I remember well, a day was agreed on when you should pay him.

PHAEDRIA: That's true.

DORIO: Well, what of it?

ANTIPHO: Has that day passed?

DORIO: No, but this has come before!

ANTIPHO: Aren't you ashamed of your trickery?

DORIO: Not in the least, especially when it's to my interest.

GETA: Rascal!

PHAEDRIA: Dorio, do you think you're acting rightly in this matter?

DORIO: That's my way of doing business; if you want me, use me.

ANTIPHO: Don't trifle with him.

DORIO: Antipho has trifled with me, rather; he knew I was this kind of man, but I thought *he* was very different. He's the one who's fooled me; I've not acted differently. However, I'll do this. The captain who wants to buy the girl said he'd bring the money tomorrow morning; now, Phaedria, if you bring me the money before then, I'll act according to my motto: "First come, first served." I bid you good-bye. (*He goes into his house.*)

ACT THREE. SCENE VI

PHAEDRIA: What shall I do now? Where can I get the money at once? I, who have less than nothing? If he had only been willing to wait three days—the money was promised at that time.

ANTIPHO: Geta, shall we let this poor fellow waste away in misery? He who helped me just now, as I told you? Come, now, shouldn't we try to return good for good, when there's such need for help?

GETA: I think it only fair we should.

ANTIPHO: You're the one man who can help him.

GETA: What can I do?

ANTIPHO: Get the money.

GETA: I'd like to; but tell me where.

ANTIPHO: My father has just returned.

GETA: Yes, I know, but what then?

ANTIPHO: A word to the wise—

GETA: What? That?

ANTIPHO: That's what I mean.

GETA: Well, you do give me fine advice indeed. Go on with you! Shouldn't I be satisfied at avoiding trouble from your marriage, without your urging me to risk my life for Phaedria's sake?

ANTIPHO (*to* PHAEDRIA): There's truth in what he says.

PHAEDRIA: What, Geta? Am I a stranger to you?

GETA: Come now, is it so small a thing that the old man is angry with us all? Should we make him angrier, so that he may never forgive us?

PHAEDRIA: And shall another take her away to a foreign land, before my very eyes? Oh, Antipho, speak to me, while I am here; look at me!

ANTIPHO: What are you going to do? Tell me.

PHAEDRIA: Wherever she is taken, I am determined to follow her, or perish in the attempt.

GETA: May the gods help you! I implore you, be careful.

ANTIPHO: See if you can help him in some way.

GETA: In what way?

ANTIPHO: Try, please; let him do nothing we may be sorry for.

GETA: Wait a minute—I think he's safe; but I fear harm.

ANTIPHO: Never fear; with you (*to* PHAEDRIA) we share good and ill fortune.

GETA (*to* PHAEDRIA): Now, tell me how much you need.

PHAEDRIA: Only thirty minae.

GETA: Only thirty! By the gods, she's expensive, Phaedria.

PHAEDRIA: Oh, that's very cheap.

GETA: Well, well, I'll get them for you. (ANTIPHO *and* PHAEDRIA *embrace him*) Away with you.

PHAEDRIA: I need it right away, remember.

GETA: At once I'll bring you the money. But I need Phormio to help me in this affair.

PHAEDRIA: He's ready; place any load on him and he'll carry it. He's a real friend.

GETA: Let's go to him now.

ANTIPHO: Will you need my help?

GETA: No; you'd better go home and comfort that poor girl. She is almost dead from fear, I'm thinking. Why do you hesitate?

ANTIPHO: Oh, there's nothing I would more willingly do! (*He goes hastily into* DEMIPHO's *house.*)

PHAEDRIA: How'll you do this?

GETA: I'll tell you on the way; come along. (They depart in the direction of the forum.)

ACT FOUR. SCENE I

(*Enter* DEMIPHO *and* CHREMES *from the harbour.*)

DEMIPHO: Well, Chremes, have you brought back your daughter, for whom you went to Lemnos?

CHREMES: No, I have not.

DEMIPHO: And why not?

CHREMES: Mother and child couldn't wait for me, because of the girl's age; they told me that she and the whole family had set out to find me.

DEMIPHO: Well, when you heard this, why did you remain so long?

CHREMES: I was detained by sickness.

DEMIPHO: What sickness?

CHREMES: You ask what sickness? Why, old age itself is a sickness. But I heard the captain who brought them over say that they arrived here safe and sound.

DEMIPHO: Chremes, have you heard what's happened? About my son, when I was away?

CHREMES: That's what has made me so uncertain about my plans; because if I offer my daughter in marriage to a stranger, he must know where and how I got her. I always knew I could depend on you as upon myself. Now if a stranger should wish to marry my daughter, he'll keep still so long as we're friends; but if he takes a dislike to me, he'll learn more than he ought to know. I'm afraid, too, that my wife might find out about this some way. If she does, I must be off in a hurry. I'm the only one I can count on at home.

DEMIPHO: I know that; and that's what's troubling me. But I shan't stop till I've carried out my promise to you.

ACT FOUR. SCENE II

(Enter GETA)

GETA (to himself): I never saw such a clever fellow in all my life as that Phormio. I come up to him, tell him we need money, and explain how to get it. I'd scarcely told him half, and he knew all about it. He was very glad, and complimented me, then asked where the old man was. He thanked the gods that he was given a chance to show that he was just as good a friend to Phaedria as he was to Antipho. I told him to wait for me at the forum, till I brought the old man. Well, here he is himself. Who's the other? Oh, Phaedria, *your* father's come back, too? Coward, what am I afraid of, anyway? Simply because I

have two men to fool instead of one? It's better to have a double hope, I'm thinking. I'll go attack the first one now; if he gives me the money, that'll be enough. If I can't get anything out of him, I'll try the other.

ACT FOUR. SCENE III

(Enter ANTIPHO *from* DEMIPHO's *house, unseen.*)

ANTIPHO (*to himself*): Geta will be here any time now. Ha, my uncle and my father together! I'm afraid he'll influence my father against me.

GETA (*to himself*): I'll speak to them. (*Advancing to* CHREMES) Welcome, Chremes.

CHREMES: Welcome, Geta.

GETA: I'm glad to see you've arrived safe at home.

CHREMES: Thanks.

GETA: How are things with you? Many changes since you went away?

CHREMES: Yes, a great many.

GETA: Indeed? And you have heard what has happened to Antipho?

CHREMES: Yes, everything.

GETA (*to* DEMIPHO): Did you tell him? Well, well, Chremes, and you believed it?

CHREMES: I was just now talking about it with him.

GETA: Now, after thinking over the case, I believe I've found a remedy.

CHREMES: What do you say, Geta?

DEMIPHO: What remedy?

GETA: Just after I left you, I met Phormio.

CHREMES: Who is Phormio?

DEMIPHO: The man who acted as the girl's patron.

CHREMES: Oh, yes, I know.

GETA: Well, it seemed best to find out what he thought; so I took him off alone and said to him: "Phormio, why not arrange the matter peaceably, rather than quarrel over it? My master's reasonable, and doesn't want to go to law; but all his friends have advised him to turn the poor girl out."

ANTIPHO (*aside, to himself*): What's he talking about, anyway?

GETA: "He'll have to pay the penalty by law provided, if he throws her out, you say? Oh, he's found out about that already; I tell you, you'll have your hands full if you do business with that fellow; why, he'll make you believe anything, he's such a glib talker. For the sake of argument, suppose he gets beaten; they only take his money, not his life." When I saw he was affected by what I told him, I reminded him that we were alone, and asked him how much cash he'd take to stop the suit at once and let the girl go.

ANTIPHO (*aside to himself*): Why, the fellow's crazy!

GETA: Then I said: "I'm positive that if you propose anything that's fair and square—because he's a fair man—you won't have to wait a second."

DEMIPHO: Who told you to talk that way?

CHREMES (*to* DEMIPHO): Why, he couldn't have done more to accomplish the very thing we are wishing for.

ANTIPHO (*aside*): Good-bye for me now.

CHREMES: Go on, Geta.

GETA: At first he raved like a madman.

CHREMES: Come, come, how much did he ask?

GETA: Oh, a great deal too much.

CHREMES: *How* much? Tell me, now.

GETA: Well—what if he should have asked a great talent?

DEMIPHIO: The devil! Wasn't he ashamed of himself?

GETA: That's just what I told him—in these very words: "What if he were disposing of his only daughter in marriage, and giving her a dowry? What's the difference if he has one or not, when someone else is ready to ask for the fortune?" Well, to make a long story short, this was what he answered: "I've wanted all the time to marry my friend's daughter, as I ought; for I knew very well there'd be trouble if a poor wife married into a rich family. Now, to tell the truth, I needed a wife to pay off my debts; even now, indeed, I don't know of anyone I'd rather marry, if Demipho will give as much as I get from the one I'm engaged to now."

ANTIPHO (*aside*): Is he a fool, or is he deceiving me?

DEMIPHO: What if he's head over heels in debt?

GETA: He said his land's mortgaged for ten minae.

DEMIPHO: Well, let him marry her; I'll give the ten minae.

GETA: Then, his house is mortgaged for another ten.

DEMIPHO: Here, here, hold on; that's too much!

CHREMES (*to* DEMIPHO): Say no more about it; I'll pay that ten.

GETA: Now, his wife must have a waiting-maid; then, they've got to have a little more for odds and ends, and wedding expenses. He said that ten minae would cover these items.

DEMIPHO (*enraged*): He may bring a thousand suits against me for all I care! I won't give anything! The scoundrel's making game of me!

CHREMES: Please keep calm; I'll give the money, I tell you; you just bring along your son and we'll marry him off.

ANTIPHO (*aside*): Geta, Geta, you've completely ruined me by your falsehoods!

CHREMES: She's turned out because of me, and it's only right that I should make amends for it.

GETA: Then he said to me: "Let me know as soon as you can, if he'll let me marry her, so that I can let the other one go, and be sure how I stand. The other party'll pay me spot cash, you know."

CHREMES: Let him have her and marry her. Break off the other engagement; quick, now.

DEMIPHO: Yes, do! Curse him!

CHREMES: I'm glad I had some cash with me. I have the rent payments from my wife's farm at Lemnos. (CHREMES *and* DEMIPHO *go into* CHREMES' *house.*)

ACT FOUR. SCENE IV

ANTIPHO (*advancing*): Geta!

GETA: Yes.

ANTIPHO: What have you done?

GETA: Cleaned the old men out of their money.

ANTIPHO: Is that so?

GETA: I did what I was ordered to do.

ANTIPHO: Do you give me an answer when I don't ask?

GETA: Well, what did you ask me to do?

ANTIPHO: What? Through your fault matters have come to such a state that I had better go and hang myself. May all the gods and goddesses, below and above, curse you! I see now, if you want anything done, let the man do it who will take you out of calm smooth water to a sharp and dangerous rock! Why should you now touch my wound, by mentioning my wife? My father has great hopes that he can get rid of her. See here, now: what if Phormio should accept the dowry? He'd have to marry her. What then?

GETA: But he's not going to marry her.

ANTIPHO: I know it. But when they ask for the dowry back again, Phormio will of course, out of consideration for us, march right off to jail!

GETA: Antipho, there is nothing that can't be made worse in the telling. You tell the worst side, and leave out all that's good. Now listen to what I've to say on the other side of the question: if he should take the money, he must, as you say, marry her. I'll grant that. Yet, some time is necessary to prepare for the ceremony, invite the guests, and for the sacrifices. Now, during this interval Phormio's friends will give the money they've promised.

ANTIPHO: But what friends ? On what grounds? What'll he say?

GETA: What? "How many extraordinary things have happened to me? A strange dog came into my house; a serpent entered the skylight from the roof, and—a hen crowed! The soothsayer prevented it, the fortune-teller forbade it; it's impossible to begin any new business before the shortest day of winter!" And that's the best excuse of all. You see?

ANTIPHO: I wish it would happen that way.

GETA: It will; just trust me. Here comes your father; go and tell Phaedria that I've got the money. (ANTIPHO *departs hurriedly.*)

ACT FOUR. SCENE V

(*Enter* DEMIPHO *and* CHREMES *from* CHREMES' *house.*)

DEMIPHO: Silence I tell you! I'll see that he plays no tricks on me. I won't pay any money till I have witnesses. I'll have it set down to whom and for what I give it.

GETA (*aside*): How careful he is!

CHREMES: You're perfectly right; and you should do it at once while you're in the mood. Now if the other woman insists a little more than ours does, he may give us the slip.

GETA (*aloud*): There, sir, you are right.

DEMIPHO: (*to* GETA): Take me to him.

GETA: At once, Sir.

CHREMES: (*to* DEMIPHO): Go to my wife when you're done, so she may visit Phanium before she leaves. Let her tell her that we are going to marry her off to Phormio, to prevent her being angry with us; say that he's better suited to her, because he knows her; that we've done our best, and that the dowry is as large as he asked for.

DEMIPHO: What the deuce do you care?

CHREMES: I care a great deal, Demipho. It's not sufficient for a man to do his duty—people must know all about it. I wish this to be done as she wants it done, that she may not say she was turned out.

DEMIPHO: Why, I myself can do that.

CHREMES: It's better for a woman to do it.

DEMIPHO: I'll go and ask for her. (DEMIPHO *and* GETA *go out towards the forum.*)

CHREMES (*to himself*): I wonder where my wife and daughter can be?

ACT FOUR. SCENE VI[8]

(*Enter* SOPHRONA *from* DEMIPHO's *house.*)

SOPHRONA (*to herself, not seeing* CHREMES): What *shall* I do? I'm so miserable, I haven't a friend in the world! Where shall I get advice or help? I'm so afraid that my dear mistress may get into trouble through my negligence. She does not deserve it at all. I hear that the young man's father is very angry at what's been done.

CHREMES (*aside*): Who's this old woman, I wonder, coming out of my brother's house? She seems very much upset.

SOPHRONA (*still not seeing* CHREMES): Poverty forced me to do it, even though I knew the marriage wasn't strictly legal; but I had to find some way to keep her alive.

CHREMES (*aside*): Why, she's my daughter's nurse, if I'm not mistaken.

SOPHRONA (*as before*): And we can't find—

CHREMES (*aside*): What shall I do?

SOPHRONA (*as before*): —her father anywhere.

CHREMES (*aside*): There's no mistake about it. I'll speak to her.

SOPHRONA: Who's that talking?

CHREMES (*advancing*): Sophrona!

SOPHRONA: He knows my name!

CHREMES: Look at me; turn round.

SOPHRONA (*turning around, and with great surprise*): Heavens! Aren't you Stilpo?

CHREMES: No.

SOPHRONA: Do you deny it?

CHREMES (*lowering his voice, and glancing suspiciously towards the house*): Just come away from the door a few steps, please. Now, don't call me Stilpo any more.

SOPHRONA: Why not? Didn't you always tell me you were called Stilpo?

CHREMES: Sh-h-h—(*Looking again at the house.*)

SOPHRONA: Why are you so afraid of that door?

CHREMES: I've a fiery-tempered wife caged up there. I changed my name to Stilpo so that you wouldn't tell it to anybody; my wife might learn the truth.

SOPHRONA: Yes, and that's just why we could never find you.

CHREMES: Tell me, what have you to do with that family in there? Where are the women?

SOPHRONA: Oh, I'm so miserable!

CHREMES: What's the matter? Are they—still living?

SOPHRONA: The daughter is: but her mother, poor creature, died of grief.

CHREMES: Well, well, that's very sad, very sad, indeed.

SOPHRONA: And I, an old woman, lonely, poor and without friends, did what I could to marry the girl to the young man who lives there (*Pointing to* ANTIPHO's *house*).

CHREMES: What's that? To Antipho?

SOPHRONA: Yes; he's the one.

CHREMES: Do you mean to tell me he has two wives?

SOPHRONA: Not at all. This is the only one.

CHREMES: Well, what about that girl they say is his relative?

SOPHRONA: This is the one.

CHREMES: Why—Why—how?

SOPHRONA: It was done on purpose, in order that he might marry her without a dowry.

CHREMES: Blessed be the gods, by whose aid things happen that we wouldn't even dare hope for! Here I am returning to find my daughter about to marry the very man I wished her to. The very thing we were trying so hard to bring about he has arranged by his own efforts.

SOPHRONA: Now let's see what is to be done. His father has just returned, and they say he's very angry.

CHREMES: There's no danger, however. By gods and men, I beg you not to let anyone know she's my daughter!

SOPHRONA: Never fear: no one shall know it from me.

CHREMES: Follow me, please. I'll tell you the rest inside. (*They go into* DEMIPHO's *house*.)

ACT FIVE. SCENE I

(*Enter* DEMIPHO *and* GETA, *from the forum*.)

DEMIPHO: Well, it's our own fault that it's better to be dishonest; and yet we want to be called honest and honourable! I suppose it wasn't enough to be injured by him, but he must go and get my money, and live on that while he's planning how to fleece someone else.

GETA: Perfectly right.

DEMIPHO: People nowadays get the best of it who don't recognise the difference between right and wrong.

GETA: Certainly.

DEMIPHO: We were fools to do business with him as we did.

GETA: I only hope we can manage to have him marry her this way.

DEMIPHO: Is there any doubt about that?

GETA: Now, considering what sort of fellow he is, he might perhaps change his mind.

DEMIPHO: Change his mind?

GETA: I'm not sure. I said "Perhaps."

DEMIPHO: I'll do what my brother told me to do: I'll bring his wife and have her talk with her. You go ahead, Geta; tell her Nausistrata is going to call on her. (DEMIPHO *goes into* CHREMES' *house*.)

GETA (*to himself*): I must get that money for Phaedria; the lawsuit business is out of the way, and she is going to remain where she is now. Well, what then? I'm still sticking in the mud; I'm only borrowing money to pay off a debt. Clouds are gathering round me, and I'd better be on the lookout. Well, I'll go home now, and tell Phanium not to be afraid of Phormio, and not to fear Nausistrata's words. (*He goes into* DEMIPHO's *house*.)

ACT FIVE. SCENE II

(*Enter* DEMIPHO *and* NAUSISTRATA *from* CHREMES' *house*.)

DEMIPHO: Come, Nausistrata, cheer her up, as you always do, and make her do what must be done.

NAUSISTRATA: Willingly.

DEMIPHO: Do you know you're a great help to me, Nausistrata?

NAUSISTRATA: Not so much as I should wish to be, because of that husband of mine.

DEMIPHO: How's that?

NAUSISTRATA: He's so careless with that farm my father left him; why, my father used to get two talents a year from the products. just see how much one man surpasses another!

DEMIPHO: Two talents, you say?

NAUSISTRATA: Yes, and that much even when times were worse.

DEMIPHO (*in astonishment*): Whew!

NAUSISTRATA: Are you surprised?

DEMIPHO: Of course.

NAUSISTRATA: I should have been a man; I'd have shown them what—

DEMIPHO: Undoubtedly.

NAUSISTRATA: How I—

DEMIPHO: Stop, please, so that you can talk with her. She's a young girl and may tire you out.

NAUSISTRATA: Very well. There's my husband.

(*Enter* CHREMES *running from* DEMIPHO's *house.*)

CHREMES (*not seeing* NAUSISTRATA): Demipho, Demipho, have you paid him yet?

DEMIPHO: Yes—just a few minutes ago.

CHREMES: Well, I wish you hadn't. (*Aside, as he sees* NAUSISTRATA) Aha, my wife! I almost said too much.

DEMIPHO: How's that, Chremes?

CHREMES: Never mind; everything's all right.

DEMIPHO: What? Did you let her know why we're bringing her? (*Points to* NAUSISTRATA.)

CHREMES: I've arranged everything.

DEMIPHO: What does she say?

CHREMES: She won't leave.

DEMIPHO: Why is that?

CHREMES: They love each other.

DEMIPHO: What's the difference?

CHREMES: A great deal. (*Aside*) Then, I just found out she's a relative of yours.

DEMIPHO (*aside*): You're crazy!

CHREMES (*aside*): I tell you she is.

DEMIPHO (*aside*) : She isn't.

CHREMES (*aside*): Her father took another name, and that threw us off the scent.

DEMIPHO (*aside*): Didn't she know her own father?

CHREMES (*aside*): Of course.

DEMIPHO (*aside*): Then why did she call him by another name?

CHREMES (*aside*): Don't you understand, or won't you?

DEMIPHO (*aside*) But if you don't—?

CHREMES (*aside*): Do you still wish to keep it up?

NAUSISTRATA: What's all this fuss about?

DEMIPHO: I'm sure I don't know.

CHREMES (*whispering to* DEMIPHO): Do you really want to know? Well, I swear by Jupiter, she's our closest relative.

DEMIPHO: By all the gods, let's go to her; I must know all about this. (*Turning to leave.*)

CHREMES (*stopping him*): Here, stop!

DEMIPHO: What's the matter?

CHREMES (*reproachfully*): Don't you believe me?

DEMIPHO: You want me to believe you? Very well, then. But—what shall we do about—our friend's—(*With a significant wink at* CHREMES)—daughter?

CHREMES: She's all right.

DEMIPHO: Shall we let her go?

CHREMES: Why not?

DEMIPHO: And allow the other to stay?

CHREMES: Yes.

DEMIPHO: We don't need you any longer, Nausistrata.

NAUSISTRATA: I think it's better for us all that she stay here. She seemed very nice when I saw her. (NAUSISTRATA *goes into* CHREMES' *house.*)

DEMIPHO: How about this, Chremes?

CHREMES (*looking anxiously at the door of his house*): Is the door closed?

DEMIPHO: Yes.

CHREMES: Oh, Jupiter, we're fortunate! I've found that my daughter has married your son!

DEMIPHO: Is it possible! How did it happen?

CHREMES: This isn't the place to tell you.

DEMIPHO: Let's go inside.

CHREMES: Listen; I don't want our sons to know anything about this business. (DEMIPHO *and* CHREMES *go into* DEMIPHO's *house.*)

ACT FIVE. SCENE III

(*Enter* ANTIPHO *from the forum.*)

ANTIPHO (*to himself*): Well, I'm delighted that my cousin's affairs are going so well, no matter how mine are going. How wise it is to have only such longings as can be easily satisfied when things go wrong! He has plenty of money and no cares; now, I can't possibly get out of my troubles; if it's kept secret, I'm afraid—if it's known, I'm disgraced. I shouldn't go home now,

if I didn't think that in some way I could keep her. Where is Geta? I want to find out where I may safely meet my father.

ACT FIVE. SCENE IV

(*Enter* PHORMIO *from the forum.*)

PHORMIO (*aside to himself, not seeing* ANTIPHO): I got the money, gave it to the slave-trader, took the girl and gave her to Phaedria. There's just one more thing to be done—get the old men to let me have time for a grand night of it!

ANTIPHO: Aha, Phormio! (*Advancing*) Well, what have you to say?

PHORMIO: What's that?

ANTIPHO: What is Phaedria going to do?

PHORMIO: Just what you did.

ANTIPHO: And what is that?

PHORMIO: Run away from his father; and he asks you to make his excuses. He's going to have a grand time of it at my house. I'll tell the old men I'm going to the fair at Sunium to buy the lady's maid that Geta told them about just now. I don't want them to think I'm wasting their money when they find I've gone. But I hear your door creaking.

ANTIPHO: See who's coming out.

PHORMIO: It's Geta.

ACT FIVE. SCENE V

(*Enter* GETA *from* DEMIPHO's *house.*)

GETA (*to himself*): Oh! Goddess of Good Fortune, how great and manifold are the blessings thou hast heaped upon Antipho!

ANTIPHO (*to* PHORMIO): What's he talking about?

GETA (*as before*): And freed us, his friends from all our fears. But I'd better hurry up and find him.

ANTIPHO (*aside to* PHORMIO): Can you make out what he's talking about?

PHORMIO (*aside to* ANTIPHO): Can you?

ANTIPHO (*aside to* PHORMIO): Not a word.

PHORMIO (*aside to* ANTIPHO): Neither can I.

GETA (*as before*): Well, I'll hurry to the slave-trader's; that's where they are. (*Turns and starts away.*)

ANTIPHO: Oh, Geta!

GETA (*not turning*): That's nothing new!

ANTIPHO: Geta, Geta!

GETA (*still farther away*): Keep it up! That's right!

ANTIPHO (*running out after* GETA): We'll see about this!

GETA: You'll get whipped, if you don't take care.

ANTIPHO: You villain, you're the one who'll get the whipping.

GETA: Must be someone I know, if he'll beat me. (GETA *turns around and is surprised*) The very man!

ANTIPHO: Well, what is it?

GETA: You're the happiest man alive, Antipho.

ANTIPHO: I wish it with all my heart; but tell me why. Don't keep me waiting.

PHORMIO: Hurry up and tell us, won't you?

GETA (*seeing* PHORMIO): Oh, you are here, too?

PHORMIO: Yes, but go on.

GETA: Listen to me. Just after we gave you the money, we went to Chremes; in the meanwhile, my master sent me to get your wife.

ANTIPHO: Why did he do that?

GETA: Never mind, Antipho. Just as I was going to the room where the ladies were, the boy ran up and stopped me. He said no one was allowed to see his mistress, and that Sophrona was talking with Chremes. Then I listened at the door and heard what they said.

ANTIPHO: Good! Go on.

GRETA: I heard a fine piece of news. I almost shouted for joy.

ANTIPHO: What was it? Quick!

GETA: What do you think?

ANTIPHO: I don't know.

GETA: Most wonderful! Your uncle is your wife Phanium's father!

ANTIPHO (*excitedly*): *What!*

GETA: He had a secret love affair with her mother long ago in Lemnos.

PHORMIO: You're dreaming. How did it happen that she didn't know her own father?

GETA: I know there's some good reason. Besides, I couldn't hear everything.

ANTIPHO: Now, I've heard that same story before.

GETA: Yes, and I'll tell you one reason for believing it: your uncle came out and went away. Then he came back with your father, and they both agreed to let you marry her. They sent me to find you and bring you where they are.

ANTIPHO: Well, why don't you take me at once? Hurry.

GETA: By all means.

ANTIPHO: Good-bye, dear Phormio.

PHOMIO: Good-bye, Antipho. (*To himself, as* ANTIPHO *and* GETA *go into* DEMIPHO's *house*) This is lucky, and I'm glad of it. Here's my chance to outwit the old fellows, and fix Phaedria in a comfortable way. The money has been given to Phaedria and he shall keep it, whether they wish it or not. I've found the means now to force their hand. I must assume a different air and expression. I'll hide in this alley and wait for them. I shan't go on that business journey that I pretended a while ago.[9] (*He retires into the alley.*)

ACT FIVE. SCENE VI

(*Enter* DEMIPHO *and* CHREMES *from* DEMIPHO'S *house.*)

DEMIPHO: The gods be thanked, brother, for this good fortune! We'd better find Phormio before he spends the money, and get it back from him.

PHORMIO (*advancing from the alley*): I'll go and see whether Demipho's home, and—

DEMIPHO: Phormio, we were looking for you.

PHORMIO: For the same reason, I suppose?

DEMIPHO: That's right.

PHORMIO: Certainly; but why were you coming to me?

DEMIPHO: Don't waste time.

PHORMIO: Do you think I shan't do what I undertook? No matter how poor I am, I've always kept my word. And I come to you now, Demipho, to tell you that I am ready. Give me the girl, if you please; I understand that you desire it with all your heart.

DEMIPHO: But this man has persuaded me not to let you have her. He said, "What will people say if you do this? A while ago, when she might have been honourably married off, no one wanted her. Now, it's wrong to turn her out." He told me almost the same things you told me not long ago.

PHORMIO: You are certainly very impudent.

DEMIPHO: How is that?

PHORMIO: Don't you see that I can't marry the other one now, after I've let her go?

CHREMES (*aside to* DEMIPHO): "Then I see Antipho won't let his wife go." Tell him that.

DEMIPHO: Then I see Antipho—a—a won't let his wife go. But please come over to the forum, and give me back my money.

PHORMIO: I can't; I've just paid off my debts.

DEMIPHO: What of it?

PHORMIO: If you wish to let me have the girl you promised me, I'll marry her. But if you want her to remain with you, the dowry remains here, Demipho. It isn't right for me to lose out on your account; it was for your sake that I broke my engagement with the other girl, who was to bring me just as large a dowry.

DEMIPHO: Do you think we don't know all about your trickery, you villan?

PHORMIO: Don't make me too angry, now.

DEMIPHO: Would you marry the girl?

PHORMIO: Just try and see.

DEMIPHO: Come along with the money.

PHORMIO: Come along and give me the girl.

DEMIPHO (*seizing him*): Come to court at once—

PHORMIO: Take care, or I'll—

DEMIPHO: What'll you do?

PHORMIO: What? Oh, I do more than protect girls without dowries.

CHREMES: What do we care?

PHORMIO: Oh, nothing. But I heard of a woman here whose husband—

CHREMES (*startled*): Oh!

DEMIPHO: What's the matter, Chremes?

PHORMIO: Had another wife at Lemnos.

CHREMES (*aside*): I'm dead!

PHORMIO: He had a daughter by her, and brought her up secretly.

CHREMES (*aside*): I'm buried!

PHORMIO: I'm going to tell her about this at once. (*Starts towards* CHREMES' *house.*)

CHREMES: Don't, don't. (*Catching him.*)

PHORMIO: Perhaps you were that man?

DEMIPHO: He's making fun of us.

CHREMES: We'll let it drop, Phormio.

PHORMIO: Nonsense!

CHREMES: What more do you want? We'll let you have the money, too.

PHORMIO: Very well; but why do you pester me with your childish actions? "I will, I won't. Give me this, keep it."

CHREMES (*aside to* DEMIPHO): How did he find out about this?

DEMIPHO (*aside to* CHREMES): I don't know. I haven't told anyone.

PHORMIO (*aside*): I've got them this time.

DEMIPHO (*aside to* CHREMES): Shall I let him carry off so much money? I'd rather die. You see, this little indiscretion of yours is well known, and you can't conceal it any longer from your wife. I think you'd better tell her yourself before she hears it from anybody else; then we can get even with this Phormio fellow.

PHORMIO (*aside*): Oho! I'd better look out now or I'll get caught. They're ganging up against me.

CHREMES (*to* DEMIPHO): I'm afraid she'll never forgive me.

DEMIPHO (*to* CHREMES): Cheer up. I'll restore you to her favour, Chremes, with the argument that the girl's mother has died.

PHORMIO (*as they approach nearer*): So this is how you treat me, is it? Very well. Demipho, you've made me angry now, and it won't do Chremes any particular good I can tell you. (*To* CHREMES) So you thought you could amuse yourself abroad and neglect your wife here and wrong her in this way, eh? And then you'll come whining to her for forgiveness? Well, I'll make her so blazing angry that you can't quench her fury even if you dissolve in tears.

DEMIPHO: Damn this fellow! That anyone should have such impudence! He ought to be dumped on some desert island at the public expense.

CHREMES (*aside*): Now I *am* in trouble.

DEMIPHO: I've an idea. Let's go to court.

PHORMIO: To court? No, no, here. (*Pointing to* CHREMES' *house, and trying to go in that direction.*)

DEMIPHO (*to* CHREMES): Hold him till I fetch servants

CHREMES (*trying to hold* PHORMIO): I can't do it alone; you help me. (*They both hold him and begin to drag him towards the forum.*)

PHORMIO: Oho, I see I must use my lungs. Nausistrata, Nausistrata, come here!

CHREMES (*to* DEMIPHO): Stop his mouth.

DEMIPHO: he's too strong.

PHORMIO: Nausistrata!

CHREMES: Keep still, won't you!

PHORMIO: Keep still?

DEMIPHO: (*to* CHREMES): Strike him hard, if he won't come.

PHORMIO: Yes, or put out an eye. But I'll have my revenge.

ACT FIVE. SCENE VII

(*Enter* NAUSISTRATA *from her house.*)

NAUSISTRATA: Who's calling me?

CHREMES: Oh!

NAUSISTRATA: Husband, what does this mean?

PHORMIO (*to* CHREMES): Why don't you tell her?

NAUSISTRATA: Who is this man? Answer me.

PHORMIO (*to* NAUSISTRATA): He doesn't know where he is.

CHREMES (*to* NAUSISTRATA): Don't believe him, I beg you.

PHORMIO (*to* NAUSISTRATA): Look at him; scared to death!

CHREMES: I'm not.

NAUSISTRATA: What's he talking about then?

PHORMIO: Listen, and I'll tell you.

CHREMES (*to* NAUSISTRATA): Will you believe him?

NAUSISTRATA: He hasn't told me anything yet. You're frightened.

CHREMES: I?

PHORMIO (*to* CHREMES): Well, since this is nothing and you're not frightened, you tell her.

NAUSISTRATA: Please tell me, Chremes.

CHREMES: But I—

NAUSISTRATA: But what?

CHREMES: What's the use anyway?

PHORMIO: No use—for you. But she ought to know all about it. In Lemnos—

DEMIPHO: What are you doing?

CHREMES (*to* PHORMIO): Keep still, I tell you!

PHORMIO (*to* NAUSISTRATA): You didn't know it—

CHREMES: Stop!

PHORMIO: He married another woman!

NAUSISTRATA: It can't be!

PHORMIO: It is.

NAUSISTRATA: How wretched I am!

PHORMIO: And he had a daughter by her.

NAUSISTRATA: What a wicked deed!

DEMIPHO (*aside to* CHREMES): You're done for!

NAUSISTRATA: Oh, what wickedness! (*To* DEMIPHO) Demipho, I appeal to you, for it makes me sick to speak to him. So this was the meaning of the many voyages and the long stays in Lemnos! This was the low prices that brought down our rents!

DEMIPHO: Nausistrata, of course he is somewhat to blame, but might he not be forgiven?

PHORMIO: He's speaking for a corpse.

DEMIPHO: It wasn't that he was tired of you or disliked you. Fifteen years ago he seduced the girl's mother when he was drunk. He had no intercourse with her after that. She's dead now and the difficulty's vanished so just be patient.

NAUSISTRATA: Patient? How do I know he won't do the same thing again?

PHORMIO (*loudly*): All who wish to attend the funeral of Chremes, this way, please! I've had my revenge. Make it up with him, Nausistrata. Now, you've got something to pester him with for the rest of your life.

NAUSISTRATA (*ironically*): I suppose this was my fault. Why should I tell him now, Demipho, how devoted I've been to him?

DEMIPHO: I know this as well as you do.

NAUSISTRATA: Have I deserved such treatment, then?

DEMIPHO: Of course not. But he begs you to forgive him—he confesses his fault. What more can you ask?

PHORMIO (*to* NAUSISTRATA): Just a minute, Nausistrata; listen to me before you answer him.

NAUSISTRATA: What is it?

PHORMIO: I got thirty minae out of him, which I gave to your son, who purchased his wife from the slave-trader.

CHREMES: What's that?

NAUSISTRATA: Do you think it's so disgraceful for your son, a young man, to have one mistress, when you have two wives? Aren't you ashamed of yourself? How will you have the face to scold him? Tell me that.

PHORMIO: He'll do as you wish.

NAUSISTRATA: I won't say anything till I see my son. I'll do just as he advises.

DEMIPHO: That's right, Nausistrata.

NAUSISTRATA: Are you satisfied, Chremes?

CHREMES: Yes—(*aside*) and more than satisfied.

NAUSISTRATA (*to* PHORMIO): What is your name, please?

PHORMIO: Phormio, a good friend to your son, Phaedria.

NAUSISTRATA: Phormio, I shall do for you what I can.

PHORMIO: Many thanks. First, will you do something to make your husband angry?

NAUSISTRATA: Gladly. What is it?

PHORMIO: Invite me to dinner.

NAUSISTRATA: Very well; I invite you.

DEMIPHO: Come, let's go in.

CHREMES: Yes, but where is Phaedria?

PHORMIO: He'll be here in a minute. (*Turning to the audience*) Farewell—and give us your applause.

ENDNOTES

The translation of the Phormio by Barrett H. Clark was an acting version and several passages of the original were omitted or abridged. The editor has added or revised the following lines: 1–34 (the prologue), 77–78, 276–278, 330–333, 361–371, 412–419, 428–429, 545, 708–710, 760–761, 794, 821–822, 838–840, 873, 888–890, 893, 927–929, 963–979, 1011–1020, 1031–1033, 1040–1042.

1. This disregards the unsuccessful performance of *The Mother-in-law* in 165 B.C.
2. The *Phormio* was produced in the year 161 B.C. at the *ludi Romani,* or Roman Games, given in honour of Jupiter.
3. This is a reference to Terence's rival, Luscius Lanuvinus.
4. This apparently refers to the failure of *The Mother-in-law* at its first production.
5. The translator's division into acts has been adopted. Kauer and Lindsay begin Act Two at this point.
6. This sentence is assigned to Phaedria by Kauer and Lindsay.
7. Kauer and Lindsay begin Act Three here.
8. Kauer and Lindsay begin Act Five here.
9. Phormio's soliloquy forms a separate scene in most editions.

—————— *Questions for Consideration* ——————

Briefly, discuss the following. In your discussion, please adhere to the ordinary conventions of good composition: content, organization, clarity and mechanics.

1. The *Phormio* exhibits the "duality" structure in its love affairs and several pairs of characters. Discuss.

2. Discuss legal maneuvering as an important structural element in the *Phormio*.

3. How do Phaedria and Antipho complement each other while Demipho and Chremes contrast each other?

4. Phormio's character is at once the finest accomplishment of the play and its most controversial element. Discuss.

5. One notable aspect of *Phormio* is the question of ethical behavior on behalf of the two young men and of Chremes, in protecting his secret life. Discuss.

_____

_____

_____

_____

6. Phormio is the dominant role in the play, and perhaps the choice role in all of Terence, albeit he is no hero. Agree? Disagree? Discuss.

_____

_____

_____

_____

7. Nausistrata is hurt and angry when she learns about Chremes' double life. In this connection, discuss one of the play's best lines: "Does it seem unworthy to you if your son has one mistress, you with two wives?"

_____

_____

_____

_____

8. What is the relationship between Geta and Phormio?

_____

_____

_____

_____

9. Is there a clear-cut theme in *Phormio?* Discuss.

_____

_____

_____

_____

Writing Critically

Select one of the essay topics listed below and compose a 500 word essay which discusses the topic fully. Support your thesis with evidence from the text and with critical and/or historical material. Use the space below for preparing to write the essay.

1. The *Phormio* exhibits the "duality" structure in its love affairs and several pairs of characters. Discuss.

2. Discuss legal maneuvering as an important structural element in the *Phormio*.

3. How do Phaedria and Antipho complement each other while Demipho and Chremes contrast each other?

4. Phormio's character is at once the finest accomplishment of the play and its most controversial element. Discuss.

5. One notable aspect of Phormio is the question of ethical behavior on behalf of the two young men and of Chremes, in protecting his secret life. Discuss.

6. Phormio is the dominant role in the play, and perhaps the choice role in all of Terence, albeit he is no hero. Agree? Disagree? Discuss.

7. Nausistrata is hurt and angry when she learns about Chremes' double life. In this connection, discuss one of the play's best lines: "Does it seem unworthy to you if your son has one mistress, you with two wives?"

8. What is the relationship between Geta and Phormio?

9. Is there a clear-cut theme in *Phormio*? Discuss.

Prewriting Space:

_____

_____

_____

_____

_____

_____

_____

_____

_____

_____

Introduction

African Myth and Folklore: West African Myth

A rich body of oral literature which has existed for generations is our heritage from West Africa. One hundred years ago, this statement would not have received entire acceptance, for unfortunately, the Western humanist tradition had taught us to scorn oral sources in matters of literature; all that was not written in black and white was considered without foundation, and, in addition, the peoples of such cultures were thought not to have had any literature or history. This was in spite of research that has revealed that European Literature consisted of many works, among them the *Iliad* and the *Odyssey*, that are in the stream of the oral tradition. However, this knowledge has ultimately helped Westerners accept and appreciate the narrative and poetry that have survived for generations without the benefit of the written form.

The literature that we call mythology and folklore contains deep secrets, but we seem unaware of this significant value. This literature is precious and sacred; it speaks not only of what we have left behind (our past) but it also addresses what we are (our present) and what we continue to be (our future).

Some students presume that a myth is a false belief or a lie. Others accept mythology as a collection of fairy tales. There are not many who believe that mythology represents the divine history of the particular society in which it is found or that myth-making continues today, although to a lesser degree than it did in the past.

What are myths? Malinowski, though in his own pejorative way when writing of the Trobriand islands, had called myth any tale that is "sacred and religious," and a mythology as "the sacred lore of the tribe" (14). He went on to add that it is a "lived reality" in its "living primitive form" and "not merely a story told" (18). Myths are the traditional stories of alleged historical events that are considered to be truthful accounts of what happened in a particular society in the remote past; they are sacred in African mythology and reflect the deepest beliefs that serve to unite a people. Essentially a story or a system of linked narratives which were once held to be true, a myth or a mythology attempts to explain the mysteries and problems of life, why the world is as it is, why environmental and cultural phenomena happen as they do. Such explanations are usually in terms of the intentions, decisions, and actions of Gods, Supreme Beings, and the supernatural (Abrams 52). It has been said that a mythology is a religion that we no longer believe in though it continues to unite us. Different cultures, then, have their myths and mythologies which inevitably vary from place to place.

In contrast to all this is Okpewho who argues that myth is not a type of tale but simply "that quality of fancy which informs the creative or configurative powers of the human mind in varying degrees of intensity" (*Myth in Africa* 69). From his perspective, "any narrative of the oral tradition (is) a myth, so long as it gives due emphasis to fanciful play" (ibid.). Clearly then, myth so defined would include a wide range of oral narratives like fables and tales which explain a variety of phenomena.

We are familiar with several Christian myths such as the Creation myth (in Genesis in *The Bible*) and The Fall in the Garden of Eden (the biblical source of original sin). In West Africa there are the various creation myths from the many different tribes; the Yoruba of Nigeria, in particular, have an extensive mythology and an elaborate pantheon including that of Olodumare with stories of the founding of Oyo, the Obatala myth, and those myths expressing the belief that the Creator is responsible for deformities in man. We are therefore already quite knowledgeable about the subject matter of myths. They answer some basic questions such as these: Where did man come from? Who or what are jinn (also djinn)? Who or what controls the sun and the moon?

In the past, the study of African mythology was undertaken in a situation where ancient books and texts did not exist. The absence of the equivalent of the Homeric texts was a great obstacle, for tropical Africa was essentially a pre-literate culture, and where indigenous writing systems have been identified, they were both rare and esoteric. The fact that the art of writing remained unknown is not attributable to any African inability but may have been due simply to geographical isolation. Sea, desert, and forest were effective barriers to the spread of written cultures until the nineteenth century. The myths that you are to read were not the work of an author but are the products of early collections by expatriates presenting the stories told to them by Africans. More recently, African scholars have collected and published the myths of their own peoples before these disappear or are irrevocably adulterated.

African myths belong firmly to the oral tradition, are communal property without any particular owner or author, are instances of African oral literature and therefore articulated in African languages in which they are told and sung. But they also frequently occur in religious ritual, and since they address those profoundly metaphysical and mysterious issues from time immemorial connected with man's existence and the universe, they are inevitably linked to African religious beliefs and practices. And because there are a great many African tribes and languages (peoples and sub-cultures), there are very many myths and mythological systems; therefore, the immense variety in African mythologies is due more to this diversity and less to the existence of many African religions. Something of this variety may be seen in the West African creation myths from the Yoruba, Fon, Fulani, and Kono to which we have limited this selection, the insights they give into these cultures, and the samples of oral literature they represent.

From these myths, we note that West African culture and religions postulate the existence of a creator of the universe, a Supreme Being, whose name varies with the culture. This is a specific common feature of the outlook of these peoples. Some mythological systems also recognize the existence of lesser spirits and Gods who in some respects symbolize aspects of the Supreme Being. Men communicate with these spiritual beings through rituals, prayers, and sacrifice. African traditions and traditional African religious beliefs and practices are reflected in the perceptions these peoples have of these mythological beings. (The Creator presents a summary of these perceptions).

These creation myths lead us to mention two related and relevant features of West African religion and culture—animism and ancestral spirits. Animism is the belief that "souls" or supernatural spirits reside in animals and inanimate parts of nature such as plants, trees, streams, rivers, rocks, and mountains, and that these spirits are guardians who should be given recognition and honored or pacified as appropriate. The second feature is a belief in the spirit of the dead ancestors as existing entities which could be communicated with and which have the power to influence the affairs of man and mediate between him and the spirits. We therefore need to see myths, creation or other, not in a vacuum but in the context of a complex sociocultural environment.

As literature these myths may be examined for their literary characteristics, and for the aesthetic experience and play of the imagination which they exhibit. These stories have a range of subjects and themes, basically, themes of origins such as of man, the earth, races, languages, death, sun, moon, stars, darkness as in "Death and the Creator" and of deformities in man as in "The Creation of Man." The fanciful which tests man's credulity is clearly evident. A simple story line or plot at its most rudimentary with basic causal relationships, a typical objective third person point of view, flat and static characterization, little or no explanation of motivation are some of the literary features which are characteristic of these myths. The setting is often indeterminate, or vaguely defined spatially and temporally, but in a way consistent with such narratives; for example, note his opening, "At the beginning there was a huge drop of milk." A simple narrative structure is often used, which is a strategy typical of the oral story telling setting, but the variety of styles possible can be seen in the use of parallel structures and incrementalism in "How the World Was Created from a Drop of Milk" and the more involved narrative technique of "Death and the Creator."

These stories in translation have lost the flavor of their original languages, but they still do reveal unique culture-specific characteristics through their referential content, by certain vocabulary items as in the paraphrase "Creating the Earth," and through the people's outlook and experience; hence, the significance of milk to a nomadic Fulani culture heavily dependent on its livestock for sustenance explains why milk is seen as the original life source. Myths are an expression of a culture and help define an important aspect of this non-Western environment. (ACJ)

BIBLIOGRAPHY

Abrams, M. H. *A Glossary of Literary Terms*. New York: Holt, Rinehart and Winston, 1957.

Beier, U. Ed. *The Origin of Life and Death: African Creation Myths*. London: Heinemann, 1966.

Dorson, Richard. M. Ed. *African Folklore*. Bloomington: Indiana University Press, 1972.

Eliot, Alexander. *The Global Myths: Exploring Primitive, Pagan, Sacred, and Scientific Mythologies*. New York: Penguin/Meridan, 1995.

Feldman, Susan. *African Myths and Tales*. New York: Dell, 1963.

Knappert, J. *Myths and Legends of the Swahili*. London: Heinemann, 1970.

Malinowski, B. *Myth in Primitive Psychology*. New York: Norton, 1926.

Okpewho, Isidore. *African Oral Literature*. Bloomington and Indianapolis: Indiana University Press, 1992.

_____. *Myth in Africa: A Study of Its Aesthetic and Cultural Relevance*. Cambridge: Cambridge University Press, 1983.

Parrinder, Geoffrey. *African Mythology*. London: Hamlyn, 1967.

_____. *African Traditional Religion*. Westport: Greenwood Press, 1970.

African Myths

Geoffrey Parrinder

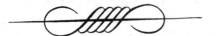

The Creator

There is no doubt that nearly all, if not all, African peoples believe in a Supreme Being, the creator of all things. A supreme god is named in the earliest dictionary of a Bantu language, compiled in 1650, and in Bosman's description of West Africa published in 1705. Belief in a Supreme Being is a thoroughly negro African conception, current long before there were any established Christian or Moslem missions in the interior regions of tropical or Southern Africa.

The names of the Supreme Being vary a great deal, of course, due to the many different languages of Africa. But there are some names which are common over wide areas. The name Mulungu for God is used in East Africa and has been adopted in about thirty translations of the Bible. In central Africa the name Leza is used by a number of different peoples. And in the western tropics, from Botswana to the Congo, variants of the name Nyambe are found. It is possible that the name Nyame for God in Ghana is related to Nyambe, but West African peoples have many other names: Ngewo, Mawu, Amma, Olorun, Chukwu, and so on to denote the Supreme Being. In this reading, the English word God will sometimes be used as the nearest equivalent of an African conception of the Supreme Being.

God is the Creator, and myths told about him seek to explain the origins of the world and man. He is transcendent, living in heaven, to which men naturally look up and recognize his greatness. It is often thought that he used to dwell on earth, but he retired to the sky, usually because of some human misdeed.

Although he is the greatest of all, there are lesser spirits which are often prominent in religious worship. Gods of storm, earth, forest, water, and the like, are popular. In West Africa there are many temples for such deities, though in other parts of the continent they may be only vaguely reverenced and there are relatively few temples for their worship. But the spirits of the dead are important everywhere. Belief in life after death, perhaps the most ancient and tenacious religious belief of all mankind, is found everywhere in Africa. The many secret societies, masked dancers, and ancestral rituals prove this.

It is strange that there are very few temples of the supreme God, while lesser deities and ancestors have many holy places for their worship. This has led some people to think that he is a distant deity, a necessary Creator but now an absentee, often forgotten or only rarely invoked. But the myths to be recorded later will show that he is not only a past Creator, but appears very often in the ordinary events of human life. Wise old Africans, when questioned on this point of the absence of worship, say that God is too great to be contained in a house. Solomon in his wisdom said much the same.

Although in myths the Supreme Being is spoken of in a personal manner, as if he were a man with a body, and often with a wife and family, yet many African sayings and proverbs speak of God in an abstract and philosophical fashion. God is the abstract idea, the cause. He is also a personal deity, generally benevolent, who cares for men and does not strike them with terror. Further, he often is an indwelling power, which sustains and animates all things. God knows everything, he sees all, he can do whatever he wishes. He is justice, rewarding the good and punishing the wicked. He is the final court of appeal, to which even the poorest and most insignificant can go, when they get no redress from other gods and chiefs. Although men speak of him with a face, and hands and legs, as does the Bible, yet in reality God has no form. He cannot be contained in a temple, the thunder is his voice, yet he is greater than the storm. He is indescribable, the only reality.

These divine attributes appear in proverbs and myths, but of course in stories more tangible human characteristics appear. As Creator he made all things and fixed the customs of every people. He laid out the countryside, arranged the mountains in their places, put in rivers, planted trees and grass. He even fixed the anthills that rise up red and hard, great cones made by the termite white ant.

As Moulder of All he shaped things, like a woman fashioning pots that she makes out of clay. He put things together and constructed them, like a builder making a house of dried clay, layer by layer.

God is father and mother of men and animals. He is not often thought of as having been born, since he is eternal, but there is a story that says he was born of a woman with one breast. His wife is spoken of, and the hard brown rings which form the body of a centipede or millipede are called "the ivory bracelets of the wife of God." Yet some peoples think of him as possessing dual natures, male and female, and a famous writer in Ghana used to speak of "Father-Mother God." Of course God is beyond sex, though in story he usually appears in human form.

The Supreme Being is in heaven and so he is particularly concerned with rain, upon which men depend entirely for their life. He is rarely associated with the sun, for in the tropics the sun is always present, and there is no need of chants and sacrifices to bring the sun back again, as in ancient Europe and Japan. God rends the sky with lightning and moves the forest so that the trees murmur. Instead of saying "it," as we do when we say "it is hot," Africans often say "God is fiercely hot," "God is falling as rain," "God

makes the drumming of thunder." To say "God is burying eggs" means that as a crocodile hides eggs in the sand and comes back later without mistake, so the thunder will return in time. When rain begins the pleasant freshness is described by saying that "God has softened the day." The rainbow is often called the "the bow of God," who is like a hunter.

God is high and over all things, he "covers" us like the sky. He is powerful and wise, but not easy to understand. There are mysteries about God, he is "the incomprehensible being." This comes from the nature of life itself, which has sorrow as well as joy. Like an almighty Fate, he is held responsible for evil and suffering. A man who has lost all his children through sickness or accident may be called "one on whom God has looked." There are moving myths of men and women who went to God to find out the reason for their sufferings.

Some of the names given to God in African ritual, proverbs, and myths, show what men think of his character and attributes. He is first of all Creator, Moulder, Giver of Breath and Souls, God of Destiny. His work in nature is shown by titles such as Giver of Rain and Sunshine, One who Brings the Seasons, the One who Thunders, the Bow in the Sky, the Fire-lighter. The divine greatness is indicated by the names Ancient of Days, the Limitless, the First, the One who Bends Even Kings, He who Gives and Rots, the One who Exists of Himself, the One You Meet Everywhere.

The providence of God is shown by names such as Father of Babies, Great Mother, Greatest of Friends, the Kindly One, God of Pity and Comfort, the Providence who Watches All Like the Sun, the One on whom Men Lean and Do Not Fall. Finally there are mysterious and enigmatic titles: the Great Ocean Whose Headdress is the Horizon, the Great Pool Contemporary of Everything, the One Beyond All Thanks, the Inexplicable, the Angry One, the Great Spider—the clever insect who comes into many stories.

Creating The Earth

The primal myth occurs in many forms, and specimens will now be given from different countries. Shorter references to creating the earth will also be found in stories about the creation of men and traditions of the first ancestors.

The Yoruba of Nigeria say that in the beginning the world was all marshy and watery, a waste place. Above it was the sky where Ol-Orun, the Owner of the Sky, lived with other divinities. The gods came down sometimes to play in the marshy waste, coming down spider's webs which hung across great gaps like fairy bridges. But there were no men yet, for there was no solid ground. One day Ol-Orun—Supreme Being—called the chief of the divinities, Great God (Orisha Nla) into his presence. He told him that he wanted to create firm ground and asked his to set about the task (in some versions it was the Oracle god who did the work). Great God was given a snail shell in which there was some loose earth, a pigeon, and a hen with five toes. He came down to the marsh and threw the earth from the snail shell into a small space. Then he put the pigeon and the hen on the earth, and they started to scratch and scatter it about. Before long they had covered much of the marsh and solid ground was formed.

When Great God went back to report to the Supreme Being the latter sent a Chameleon to inspect the work. The Chameleon is a prominent figure in may African myths, and it is noted for its slow careful walk, its change of colour to suit its environment, and its big rolling eyes. After a first inspection the Chameleon reported that the earth was wide but not dry enough. Then he was sent again, and this time he said it was both wide and dry. The place where creation began was called Ifé, meaning "wide," and later the word Ilé, "house," was added, to show that it was the house from which all other earthly dwellings have originated. Ilé-Ifé has been ever since the most sacred city of the Yoruba people, and this explanatory story is put out to justify its eminence.

The making of the earth took four days, and the fifth was reserved for the worship of Great God, and ever since a week of four days has been observed, each one of which is sacred to a divinity. Then the Supreme Being-Creator sent Great God back to earth to plant trees, to give food and wealth to man. He gave him the palm nut of the original palm tree, whose nuts give oil and whose juice supplies drink. Three other common trees were planted, and later rain fell to water them.

Meanwhile the first men had been created in heaven and were then sent to earth. Part of the work of making men was entrusted to Great God, and he made human beings from the earth and moulded their physical features. But the task of bringing these dummies to life was reserved for the Creator alone. It is said that Great God was envious of this work of giving life, and he decided to spy on the Creator to see how it was done. So one day when he had finished moulding human forms, he shut himself in with them overnight and hid behind them so that he could watch. But the Creator knew everything and he sent Great God into a deep sleep, and when he woke up the human beings had come to life. Great God still makes only the bodies of men and women, but he leaves distinct marks on them and some bear signs of his displeasure.

Heavenly Twins

Neighbours of the Yoruba are the Fon of Dahomey, and they have different creation stories. They speak of a supreme God (Mawu) and many other beings related to him. But Mawu is sometimes called male and sometimes female; Mawu has a partner called Lisa, and they may be spoken of as twins. One myth says that these twins were born from a primordial mother, Nana Buluku, who created the world and then retired. Mawu was the moon and female, having control of the night and dwelling in the west. Lisa was male, the sun, and lived in the east. They had no children when they first took up their stations, but eventually they came together in an eclipse. Whenever there is an eclipse of the sun or moon it is said that Mawu and Lisa are making love.

The primeval twins, Mawu-Lisa, became parents of all the other gods. These were all twins too, seven pairs. There is difference of opinion as to which were born first and so are senior, but probably the gods of earth, storm, and iron are first in succession. It is said that one day Mawu-Lisa called their children together, and gave each of them a domain. The first set of twins was entrusted with the rule of the Earth and they were told to take whatever they wished from heaven. The twins of Storm were told to stay in the sky and rule over thunder and lightning. Then the Iron twins were told that since they were the strength of their parents they must clear the forests and make cultivable land; they should also give tools and weapons to men. Another pair were ordered to live in the sea and all waters and rule the fishes. Other hunters were sent into the bush to rule over the birds and beasts and care for trees. The space between the earth and sky was the domain of other deities who were entrusted with the life-span of human beings and they were told to return from time to time to the Supreme Being (Mawu) to tell of all that happened in the world. These Sky gods also prevented other gods from being seen by men, and so men speak of gods as sky or spirit.

To each of the gods the Creator gave a special language and these are the ritual languages spoken by the priests and mediums of the gods in their songs and oracles. One spirit, a divine messenger (Eshu, Legba), was given knowledge of all language and serves today as intermediary between gods and gods, and between men and all the divinities. It will be noticed that the Supreme Being is often called Mawu, without mention of Lisa, and the tendency to unity of thought that makes this deity supreme in practice, without mention of male or female nature.

The Origin of Life and Death
African Creation Myths

edited by Ulli Beier

How the World Was Created from a Drop of Milk

At the beginning there was a huge drop of milk.
Then Doondari came and he created the stone.
Then the stone created iron;
And iron created fire;
And fire created water;
And water created air.
Then Doondari descended the second time. And he took the five elements
And he shaped them into man.
But man was proud.
Then Doondari created blindness and blindness defeated man.

But when blindness became too proud,
Doondari created sleep, and sleep defeated blindness;
But when sleep became too proud,
Doondari created worry, and worry defeated sleep;
But when worry became too proud,
Doondari created death, and death defeated worry.
But when death became too proud,
Doondari descended for the third time,
And he came as Gueno, the eternal one,
And Gueno defeated death.

The Creation of Land

At the beginning everything was water. Then Olodumare, the supreme god, sent Obatala (or Orishanla) down from heaven, to create the dry land. Obatala descended on a chain and he carried with him a snail shell filled with earth, some pieces of iron, and a cock. When he arrived, he placed the iron on the water, spread the earth over it, and placed the cock on top. The cock immediately started to scratch and thus the land spread far and wide.

When the land had been created, the other orisha descended from heaven in order to live on the land with Obatala.

The Creation of Man

Obatala made man out of earth. After shaping men and women he gave them to Olodumare to blow in the breath of life.

One day Obatala drank palm wine. Then he started to make hunchbacks, and cripples, albinos and blind men. From that day onwards hunchbacks and albinos and all deformed persons are sacred to Obatala. But his worshippers are forbidden to drink palm wine.

Obatala is still the one who gives shape to the new babe in the mother's womb.

Obatala Is Destroyed By His Slave

At the beginning there was only one orisha in the world, Obatala. Obatala had a slave whom he loved well, and who served him faithfully. One day the slave asked Obatala for a farm, and the god gave him a piece of land. The slave made his farm and built himself a hut at the foot of a hill. Obatala often came to rest in the slave's hut. But the slave was wicked and planned to destroy Obatala. One day when the slave saw Obatala approaching in his white gown from afar, he hid on the hill. As soon as he saw Obatala approaching, the slave hurled down a huge rock. Obatala was smashed into hundreds of pieces.

When the news of this disaster spread, Orunmila, the divinity of the oracle, went and collected as many pieces as he could. He gathered together more than half. These he deposited in a sacred calabash and called it "Orisha Nla"—the great orisha. Since that time there are hundreds of smaller orisha in the world.

Death and the Creator

At the beginning there was nothing, In the darkness of the world lived Sa, Death, with his wife and only daughter.

In order to be able to live somewhere, Sa created an immense sea of mud, by means of magic. One day Alatangana, the God, appeared, and visited Sa in his dirty abode. Shocked by this state of affairs, Alatangana reproached Sa fiercely, saying that he had created an uninhabitable place, without plants, without living beings, without light

To remedy these faults, Alatangana set out first of all to solidify the dirt. He thus created the earth, but this earth still seemed to him too sterile and too sad, and so he created vegetation and animals of all kinds. Sa, who was satisfied with these improvements of his dwelling place, entertained great friendship for Alatangana and offered him much hospitality. After some time Alatangana, who was a bachelor, asked his host for the hand of his only daughter. But the father found many excuses and in the end flatly refused to satisfy his demand. However, Alatangana came to a secret agreement with the young girl.

He married her, and in order to escape the wrath of Sa they fled to a remote corner of the earth. There they lived happily and bore many children: seven boys and seven girls—four white boys and girls and three black boys and girls. To the great surprise of their parents, these children spoke strange languages among themselves which their parents did not understand. Alatangana was annoyed and finally decided to go and consult Sa, and without delay he set out on his way.

His father-in-law addressed him coldly and said: "Yes, it was I who punished you, because you have offended me. You shall never understand what your children say. But I shall give your white children intelligence and paper and ink so that they may write down their thoughts. To your black children, so that they may feed themselves and procure everything they need, I shall give the hoe, the matchet, and the axe."

Sa also recommended to Alatangana that the white children should marry among themselves and the black children should do the same. Eager to be reconciled to his father-in-law, Alatangana accepted all his conditions. When he returned he had the marriages of all his children celebrated. They dispersed to all parts of the world and engendered the white and black races. From these ancestors were born innumerable children whom we know today under the names of French, English, Italians, Germans, etc., on the one hand, and Kono, Guuerze, Manon Malinke, and Toma Yacouba on the other.

But the world that had thus been peopled was still living in darkness. Once more Alatangana was forced to ask the advice of Sa. He commanded the "tou-tou" (an early-rising little red bird) and the cock to go and ask Sa's advice.

When he had heard the two messengers, Sa told them: "Enter the house. I shall give you the song by which you shall call the light of day so that men can go about their work."

When the messengers returned, Alatangana became angry and scolded them: "I gave you money and I gave you food for your journey, and you neglected your duty. You deserve death."

But in the end Alatangana mercifully forgave the two unhappy messengers. A little later the tou-tou gave its first cry and the cock too uttered his first song.

And behold, a miracle: hardly had the two birds finished their song when the first day dawned. The sun appeared on the horizon and according to the directions of Sa started on its celestial course. When his journey was completed the sun went to sleep somewhere on the other side of the earth. At this moment there appeared the stars in order to give to mankind some of their light during the night. And since that day the two birds must sing in order to call the light. First the tou-tou and then the cock.

Having thus given the sun, the moon and the stars to mankind, Sa called Alatangana. He said to him: "You took my only child away and in return I have done good to you. It is your turn now to render me a service: as I have been deprived of my child, you must give me one of yours, any time that I choose to call for one. He shall hear a calabash rattle in his dreams when I choose him. This shall be my call which must always be obeyed."

Conscious of his guilt, Alatangana could not but consent. Thus it is because Alatangana disobeyed the custom requiring the payment of the bride-price that human beings must die.

Mythological Gods

FUNCTION OF THE GODS	GREEK	ROMAN	NORSE	AFRICAN Yoruba	Others
Ruler of the sky and King of Gods	Zeus	Jupiter	Odin	Olodumare (Olorun or Ol-Orun)	Nyame (Ashanti) Nyankopon (Ghana)
Queen of the Gods	Hera	Juno	Frigga		
God of the Sea	Poseidon	Neptune		Ol-Okum Oshun (Goddess)	Twe (Ghana)
God of the Underworld	Hades Persephone (Wife)	Pluto Proserpine (Wife)	Hela (Goddess)		
God of War	Ares	Mars	Tyr		Kibuka (Buganda)
God of Fire and Iron	Hephaestus	Vulcan		Ogun	
God of the Sun	Apollo	Apollo	Balder		Lisa (Dahomey) Nyankopon (Ashanti)
God of Wine and Vegetation	Dionysus	Bacchus	Freyr		
God of the Thunder	Zeus	Jupiter	Thor	Shango (Storm God)	
Messenger of the Gods	Hermes	Mercury		Eshu	
Watchman of the Gods and the Heavens	Argus		Heimdall		Fa (Fon Tribe—Dahomey)
Goddess of Love	Aphrodite	Venus	Freya		
Goddess of the Moon God of the Moon	Artemis	Diana			Mawu (Dahomey) Nyame (Ashanti)
Goddess of Wisdom God of Wisdom	Athene	Minerva		Orunmila	Mawu (Dahomey) Nyame (Ashanti)
The Divine Drummer					Odomankoma Kyerema (Ashanti)

——————— *Questions for Consideration* ———————

Using complete sentences, provide brief answers for the following questions.

1. Present the insights into African religious beliefs you have acquired from studying these myths. How are they similar to or different from your own religious outlook?

    _____

    _____

    _____

    _____

    _____

2. Examine "Death and the Creator" and identify and comment on the various origins and phenomena which it presents.

    _____

    _____

    _____

    _____

    _____

3. Comment on literary qualities like plot, character, setting, point of view of these myths treated as short stories. Use "Death and the Creator" or "How the World Was Created from a Drop of Milk."

    _____

    _____

    _____

    _____

    _____

————————— *Writing Critically* —————————

Select one of the essay topics listed below and compose a 500 word essay which discusses the topic fully. Support your thesis with evidence from the text and with critical and/or historical material. Use the space below for preparing to write the essay.

1. Compare and/or contrast these creation myths with the Genesis story of the Creation in *The Bible* or Greek myths of Creation.

2. Critically discuss the various perceptions of the Supreme Being presented here. How are the roles of the Lesser Beings and the Supreme Being defined by these perceptions?

3. What do the Yoruba myths tell you about the outlook of these people?

4. Discuss the creation myths by the Fon, Fulani and Yoruba, and show whether they present these tribes as essentially different from each other in their perceptions of the world.

5. Using the definitions of myths offered here, attempt to characterize in cultural and literary terms the relationship between these myths and the people they belong to.

Prewriting Space:

_____

_____

_____

_____

_____

_____

_____

_____

_____

_____

_____

_____

_____

_____

_____

_____

_____

Introduction

African Fables

"Fables" and "folk tales" as labels for oral narratives invite us to focus on stories associated with peoples, the "folk," of different cultures. A fable is a story which has a didactic moral thesis in which animals talk and behave like people. The Greek *Aesop's Fables* is an early example, but other cultures have produced fables, such as those by the seventeenth century Frenchman, La Fontaine, the German Brothers Grimm, the Uncle Remus stories of the American Joel Chandler Harris, and Africa where a rich body of such fables exists.

Fables, as defined by Okpewho, simply tell a story or present "an imaginative drama of experience involving human beings, animals, or spiritual figures either within or outside the familiar human world" (*African Oral Literature* 209). Fables so defined he distinguished from folk tales, the rich variety of oral narratives which explore origins, record the historical and pseudo-historical and are less open ended as literature.

Folk tales and fables are here used interchangeably to refer to stories that in Africa are a product of the oral tradition and an example of African oral literature; these definitions here together clearly specify the essential features of such African fables and folk tales. They are of various kinds, they contain characters that may be animals, human beings, monsters, spirits, God, lesser divinities, ghosts, and though all occupy different planes of existence, they somehow interact. As literature these tales have aesthetic and literary qualities as well as present possibilities for more profound interpretations. They are also different from myths even though some are myth-like, for they are not related to the traditional pantheon, nor do they present religious beliefs or views of God.

Fables are cultural and traditional creations with their roots in the local African environment; they present the customs, beliefs, outlook, and aesthetic expressiveness of these people and are a societal possession. Some themes and subjects have been spread widely by the movement of peoples, for the multilingual and multi-ethnic settings have tales that are similar in significant ways. Some foreign influences may also have been at work in their composition and modification, but it is also true that similar ideas have been known to occur to people in different places and at different times. As communal property which are to be found in sub-cultures and ethnic groups, they are invariably given non-textual delivery in performance situations in a variety of social settings.

As an oral work, the fable does not exist in a written or fixed text but rather in the mind of the storyteller or performer. He has extreme latitude since he can respond to the story-telling situation, can be innovative, can embellish and manipulate his material in the act of creation, and he either may have much detail or only the bare outlines of story or theme. Something of this can be seen in the paraphrased tales which are variations on the same themes, for example "Rubber Girl," "Hare and Tortoise" and "Strength and Cunning," and "Mister Spider and His Mother-in-Law." Not only is this mode of existence of the text not evident from reading these tales, but so also is the story telling context itself. This context consists of the teller who could be anyone with skill in delivery who has a good memory and is innovative, the audience, the setting in time and place, and ancillary features like song, music and dramatization. We are thus looking at situational features of the oral performance, a performance which is both transmission and creation and not lifeless words in a foreign language on a page as these tales may appear to be to us.

The story may be told or the narrative may be presented as a performance and so has features which have been lost in the translation of these tales. In a typical authentic traditional setting, the time is usually the evening under moonlight or by the light of a fire or lamp, and the place a yard, porch, or compound, both enhancing the communal and the leisurely. Variations abound, but some preliminary verbal play such as tongue twisters and riddles may occur which facilitates teller and audience interaction and sets the tone. An opening formula may be uttered requiring audience feedback, and specific responses may punctuate the narrative which could also end with certain closing formulas. Other elements may include songs and chants, perhaps dance as vivid expressive parts of the story, mimicry and imitations, sound effects and ideophones, and other linguistic resources like repetition. The sample texts show all of these performance characteristics as would have the paraphrased tales in their original settings.

Folk tales and fables are not only examples of cultural and social expression but have a variety of functions in their societies. They are a medium of socialization and could be explanatory, instructive, entertainment, and allow an imaginative projection of the human mind. Many tales explain things, phenomena, and happenings found in the experience and surroundings of the people, and some do so using gods and lesser divinities like the myths of origins; for example, some of our stories explain why we have blindness, leopard's spots, domesticated animals, and even spiders. Other fables have a didactic element for they inculcate moral values and instruct on desirable social conduct, for example, "The Price of Jealousy," "Rubber Girl," and "Strength and Cunning." All these tales are sheer entertainment with the pleasure deriving from the performance context, the beings who people them, the nature of their settings, the events which happen in them, and the way they invite the audience to exercise their minds in a pleasurable way as in the dilemma tales and the trickster tales involving tortoise, hare, and spider. Finally, these tales enable the teller to project his creative imagination and so gain social recognition.

We may now consider some features or formal elements of fables and tales seen as literary compositions, some of which go back to our definitions. The characters are typically animals (with the spider, tortoise, and hare predominating), monsters and spirits all given human attributes, and man himself; the plot or story line is at its most elementary; the setting is defined as a local or fantastic world barely adequate to place events and characters; characterization and motivation are at their simplest; there is great variety in subjects and themes, and the fable often presents an explicit or implied moral code. In spite of the very many different sources of these fables from a highly multi-ethnic and multilingual continent, they show much similarity on a number of these levels.

Two types of texts follow: a paraphrase and/or summary of fables from various parts of Africa, and five simple tales recorded, transcribed, and translated from the Temne and Limba languages of Sierra Leone. The paraphrased tales are arranged around (a) specific themes—"Rubber Girl," "Tug of War," "Strength and Cunning," "King of Beasts," (b) the Anansi trickster theme—"How Anansi Tricked God," "Anansi and the Corn Cob," (c) the explanatory type—"Why the Tortoise is Taboo," "How the Leopard Got Its Spots," "Rubber Girl." These broad categories conceal most of the other elements identified earlier, as some tales promote moral, social, and cultural values like the work ethic, resourcefulness, and honesty; suggest origins of habits and behavior of animals, or afflictions like blindness, and why the spider is what it is; and some may even be interpreted as morally ambiguous like "Hare and Tortoise" and "Anansi and the Corn Cob."

The three Temne texts have been translated idiomatically, while the Limba stories have been transliterated to give an impression of the language of the original story telling context. All five stories show some of the following—the opening and closing formula; "The Price of Jealousy" has song, mimicry of rowing and wading through water; sound effects and ideophones indicative respectively of a breaking vessel and movement at speed occur in "The Spider, the Lover of Meat" which also contains Limba items and audience feedback; and the paratactic syntax of the Limba stories successfully contributes to recreating the feel of the moment of performance.

The referential content of both types of texts and their literary qualities provide valuable insights into this form and show its similarity to myths. What has to be stressed, however, is the story telling setting which gives completeness to those forms and enhances their cultural context. (ACJ)

BIBLIOGRAPHY

Aesop's Fables. Ed. Jack Zipes, New York: Penguin/Signet, 1995.

Ben-Amos, D. "Introduction: Folklore in African Society." *Forms of Folklore in Africa*, Ed. Bernth Lindfors. Austin: University of Texas Press, 1977.

Bullfinch, Thomas. *Bullfinch's Mythology: The Age of Fable*. New York: Penguin 1995.

Dorson, R. M. *American Negro Folklore*. Greenwich: Fawcet, 1975.

Dundes, A., Ed. *The Study of Folklore*. Englewood Cliffs: Prentice Hall, 1965.

Finnegan, Ruth. *Limba Stories and Storytelling*. Oxford: Clarendon Press, 1967.

_____. *Literacy and Orality*. Oxford: Basil Blackwell, 1988.

_____. *Oral Literature in Africa*. Oxford: Clarendon Press, 1970.

Kilson, M. *Royal Antelope and Spider: West African Mende Tales*. Cambridge, Mass: Langdon Associates, 1976.

Magel, Emil. Trans. *Folktales from the Gambia: Wolof Fictional Narratives*. Colorado Springs: Three Continents Press, 1995.

Okpewho, Isidore. *African Oral Literature*. Bloomington and Indianapolis: Indiana University Press, 1992.

_____. Ed. *The Oral Performance in Africa*. Ibadan: Spectrum, 1990.

Tutuola, Amos. *Yoruba Folktales*. Ibadan: Ibadan University Press, 1987.

Turay, Abdul Karim and Wilhelm, J. G. Mohlig. *Temne Stories*. Koln: Rudiger Kopp Verlag, 1989.

Animal Fables

Some of the most popular of all African stories are the animal fables, and these are innumerable. They show that men are in close touch with nature, but the animals are pictured with human feelings. Some fables are pure fantasy, others are projections of human desire. There are many "Just So" stories, of the kind that Kipling made popular with additions and literary form of his own. African fables of this kind are explanatory: why the cock has fine feathers, why the ram paws the ground when it thunders, how the goat became a domestic animal, why bats hang downwards and only fly at night, why the crocodile does not die in water, why the mosquito lives in the forest, why frogs swell up and croak, why the lizard bobs its head up and down, why the chameleon's head is square, why the snake sheds its skin, why elephants live in the forest, why the sparrow flies into smoke, how the spider became bald, how the elephant's bottom became small and how the parrot's tail became red.

How the Leopard Got Its Spots

This is a characteristic story from Sierra Leone and says that at first the Leopard was friendly with the Fire. Every day the Leopard went to see the Fire, but the Fire never visited him in return. This went on so long that the Leopard's wife mocked her husband, saying it was a poor sort of friend who would never return a visit. When he went out next day she quarreled with him and said it must be because his house was unworthy that his friend would never come to it. So the Leopard begged the Fire to come to his house on the next day.

At first the Fire tried to excuse himself, saying he never visited. But the Leopard pressed him, and the Fire said he never walked but if there was a road of dry leaves from his house to the Leopard's then he would come. The Leopard went home and told his wife what to do. She gathered leaves and laid them in a long line from one house to the other. She and her husband prepared their house ready to do honour to the Fire. While they were waiting they heard a strong wind and loud cracks outside the door. The Leopard went to see what was the matter and it was the Fire at the door. His fingers of flame touched the Leopard, but he and his wife leapt backwards and jumped out of the window. Their house was destroyed, and ever since then the Leopard and his wife have been marked all over their bodies with black spots where the fingers of Fire touched them.

250

How the Goat Was Domesticated

A Yoruba story from Nigeria says that the animals used to drink from a common pool, and once a year they all went to clean it out. Anyone who did not join in this work was to be killed. But one year the Goat did not go to the cleaning, for she had a baby kid and did not want to leave it. The other animals sent messengers to ask why the Goat was absent, and she prepared her excuses. When the Stag came to demand her reason the Goat said she had a kid. And the Stag then demanded if it was a male or female. The Goat knew that the Stag's mother had died recently, so she said it was female. Then the Stag asked whose mother had been born again in the kid and the Goat replied that it was his own. The Stag could not harm the mother of his own reincarnated parent, so he went away.

Then the Antelope came along and asked why the Goat had been absent and was told that she had a male kid. When he demanded whose father had been reborn, he was told that it was his own, so he too went away. All the animals came in turn, and the Goat told each one that it was some dead relative of theirs reborn. But the Leopard was suspicious, and he hid while the Goat answered two other animals. To one he said he had a male kid and to the other a female. So when he came to the Goat's house and asked whose parent had been reborn, the Goat said it was his mother, because she knew the mother had died not long before. But the Leopard said it could be his father, who was also dead, and he respected him more. When the Goat tried to change her story, the Leopard sprang at her with a roar. The Goat leapt sideways out of her house and ran with all speed to the village of men. Only there did the Leopard turn back, and the Goat has stayed with men ever since, but the Leopard kills goats if it finds them straying outside the village.

Why the Tortoise Is Taboo

A Malagasy fable says that one day a green Bird was hopping about in the bushes, looking for insects, when it saw a huge sea tortoise with a scaly shell come out of the water. The Tortoise told the Bird that it had always lived in the sea but would like to know the earth and its people. The Bird said that it was easily done and he would act as guide. So they set off for the interior. The Tortoise found it hard to walk, because of its flat feet, and began to complain. But the Bird had no trouble, jumping from tree to tree and resting in the shade. It laughed at the Tortoise at first, but then took pity on it. The Bird said it was a magician and would make better feet for the Tortoise. This was done and they went on with their journey. A little later the Bird dropped some dirt on the Tortoise, by accident, and the Tortoise called it filthy. The Bird got angry and flew off leaving the Tortoise to find its way back by itself. That is how the Sea Tortoise became a Land Tortoise. Ever since then the Land Tortoise and its children have wandered about, without finding the sea. So its flesh is taboo, for God made it for salt water, and men can only eat animals that live on land.

Tales of Spider and Hare

All across Africa fables are told of the cleverness, deceit and triumph of the Spider or the Hare, called by various names according to the language. These yarns were taken to America by the slaves and became the Brer Rabbit tales related by Uncle Remus. There are no rabbits in tropical Africa, and the clever animal is really a hare, which depends on its speed and cunning to protect itself against the dangers of the open Sudan and savannah country. Its chief enemy is the hyena, the Brer Fox of the American version.

In the forest regions it is the Spider, the Annancy of America, which plays the role of the clever animal. In these stories the weak but guileful creature overcomes the powerful but stupid larger beasts. Perhaps he is the ordinary man, oppressed by harsh rulers or foreign conquerors, who projects himself into the parts of the agile hare or spider, taking revenge on the great ones of the earth. To score off the police or the government is a great delight, and always arouses laughter from the listeners to these village tales as they sit around in the moonlight. But they have their sad side too, and the hare who is caught in deception, or going beyond his powers, is severely punished by authority. Since he is often a thief or a practical joker, laughing at the morality of sober people, he suffers for his folly when caught.

Rubber Girl

This is a well known Hare or Spider tale, the Tarbaby of the Brer Rabbit stories. The Hausa of Nigeria tell it about the spider. One day the Spider told his wife to measure out some ground-nuts and he would plant them in his field. When they were ready he took his hoe, but arriving at the field he sat down by a shady stream, for it was hot and he was a lazy animal who preferred somebody else to work. He had a drink, began nibbling the nuts, finally ate them all, and fell asleep. When he awoke it was evening. He got some mud from the stream, plastered it all over his body, went home, and told his wife that he had come dirty from work and wanted some water for a bath. The same thing happened on the following days, till the time for gathering ground-nuts was at hand. Then the Spider's wife said that the neighbours were digging up their nuts and she would go and get their own. But her husband answered that as he had planted the nuts it was his right to dig them up. He went off and stole nuts from his neighbour's field, and did this so much that the neighbour kept watch and saw him.

Then he laid a trap for the Spider, in the form of a Rubber Girl made out of the sticky resin from the rubber tree. When the Spider came along he saw the Rubber Girl, with a beautiful long neck and large breasts. He came up to her, put out a hand and touched her breast, and his hand was held fast by the sticky rubber. "Oh, you must want me badly," he said, and put his other hand on her other breast. That hand stuck tight, and he exclaimed, "You girls hold a man too tight. I will kick you." He did this and rubber caught his foot. Then he was angry and called the Rubber Girl an illegitimate child of low parents, and kicked her with the other foot. That stuck too and he was clasped tight to her body. He tried butting with his head and that stuck also to the Rubber Girl. Then the neighbour, who was watching from a hiding place, saw the Spider securely held and gave thanks to God. He cut a pliable switch from a tree, warmed it in a fire, rubbed it with grease, and beat and beat the Spider till his back was raw. Then he released the Spider and told him that if he came stealing again he would kill him. So the Spider suffered for his laziness and thieving.

In a Sierra Leone version the Spider wanted to eat rice but also to save himself the toil of working, so he pretended to die, having first made his wife promise to bury him on his farm. Then the rice from his neighbours' field started disappearing, for the Spider came out of his grave at night after the others had gone home, and ate all he found. His wife asked the advice of a diviner, who told her to make a girl of wax from a tree that had sticky gum. The Spider was caught as before. Then all the people came up and beat him till the Spider's body became flat as it is today; formerly it was round and sleek.

In a Yoruba version of Nigeria a Hare figures in a tale of a great drought. All the animals decided that they would cut off the tips of their ears, and the fat from them would be used to buy hoes so that they could dig a well. Everyone did this except the Hare, who hid away. The other animals dug their well, and when it was finished the Hare came along beating a calabash, and making such a noise that the animals ran away without waiting to see who it was. Then the Hare drank his fill of water from the well, and not content with that he washed himself in the water and made it dirty. When he had gone the animals saw that they had been tricked, and they made an image of a girl and covered it with bird lime. The Hare was caught in the usual way and well beaten. Then he was driven away and has lived in the grasslands ever since, and that is why he has longer ears than any other animals.

In a version from Angola the owner of the farm was a Leopard, who made a wooden image of a girl and smeared it with gum from a wild fig-tree. He caught both the Hare and the Monkey, and gave them a thorough beating. Since then they have always slept in secret places to keep away from the Leopard; the Hare sleeping in a hole and the Monkey in a tree.

In southern African stories the Hare is caught by the Tortoise, who hid in the bottom of a well and smeared his shell with bird-lime. The Hare came to bathe his feet and was caught fast, and then his hands and face were caught too. All the other animals came up and beat him for deceiving them and stealing their goods.

Tug of War

One of the most popular of the Hare stories tells how by his cunning he deceived larger but more stupid animals. It is sometimes told about the Tortoise, and in America it is Brer Tarrypin who challenges the Bear, and since he can find no animal of equal size, he ties the other end of the rope to a tree.

In a West African version the Hare was improvident and always borrowed from his neighbours. He had taken so much from the Elephant and the Hippopotamus (the crocodile in some versions) that both got very angry. But the Hare managed to calm them down by promising to give them all and more than he owed, with interest. He went away and made himself a rope of liana from the forest trees, then taking one end to the Elephant the Hare told him that he had only to pull it and he would find a great treasure chest on the end. Quickly he took the other end to the Hippo in the river and told him the same. The two animals took the strain, the Hare running backwards and forwards to cheer them on. As the Hippo was in the river and the Elephant in the trees, and both are short-sighted, this went on for a long time. But finally the Elephant got thirsty and went to the river for a drink, and the Hippo came out of the water, and they recognized each other, while the Hare ran off in safety.

In other versions it is a plain trial of strength, to which the Hare challenged the Rhinoceros and the Hippotamus in turn. They ridiculed the idea that he was stronger than they were, but they pulled against each other from opposite sides of a bush-covered island until the rope broke, or the Hare cut it in the middle, and both competitors fell over and Hare claimed his forfeit. In an Ila version in Zambia the Rhino and the Hippo had been enemies before, but now they became reconciled, and so the Rhino goes to the river to drink and the Hippo comes out to eat the grass where the Rhino feeds.

An additional narrative from Togo says that the Elephant and the Hippo were so angry at their deception that they vowed to prevent the Hare from eating any grass on land or drinking water from the river. The Hare was in a fix, and while he was thinking over his problem he met a deer and asked for the loan of the horns from his head. Putting the horns on his own head the Hare went to see the Elephant. The Elephant asked if the Hare was ill, since horns had grown out of his head. The Hare started spitting all over the place and said the sickness came from his mouth. The elephant was frightened and ran away, and the Hare ate as much grass as he liked. Then he went to the Hippo and told him the same story, with the same result, and had plenty of water to drink.

Strength and Cunning

One day the Hare went hunting with Hyena (Brer Fox), and they agreed to share all their catch. But whenever the Hare killed a beast the Hyena took it and put it in his own bag. As the Hare was so much smaller and weaker he was in no position to complain. He was particularly annoyed when the Hyena caught a fine red deer and kept it to himself. So the Hyena had a great bag of fine game and the Hare had nothing. They set off home, but having no bundle the Hare went on ahead.

Just outside their village he found some red earth and plastered his body with it, and got some white earth and put spots all over himself. Then he climbed on top of an ant-hill and waited for the Hyena to pass by. When the Hyena came along he saw this strange thing and was afraid to pass. He called out, "O Something-on-the-hill, shall I give you some meat that I have caught?" The Hare just growled, "Mm, Mm," and the Hyena drew out a large piece of meat and laid it in front of him. But the Hare did not move away, and the Hyena called out again, and gave him another piece of meat. He kept on doing this till nearly all the meat was gone. Then the Hyena called out, "O Something-on-the-hill, I have given you all my meat, can I pass on?" But the Hare growled, "You still have some meat left." So the Hyena drew out the red deer, laid it down, and ran off. The Hare had all the good meat, and it had been carried to his door as well.

King of Beasts

In a Hausa story of Nigeria, similar to others told in many parts of the world, the small animal defeated the King of Beasts, the Lion. In the American Uncle Remus Stories the Hare defeated the Wolf. The Hausa say that the animals were all being eaten by the Lion and they took counsel to see what could be done to save themselves from extinction. They went to the Lion and asked if he would be content to eat one of them every day and leave the rest alive. As the Lion is proud but lazy he accepted the offer, and the animals drew lots each day to decide who should be the victim. First the Gazelle was taken, and they seized her and took her to the lion, who ate her with pleasure but did not touch the other animals. Then the Roan Antelope was drawn and taken to execution, and the same went on every day among all the animals.

Finally the lot fell on the Hare, and when the others were going to carry him off he persuaded them that he was going calmly to his fate and did not need to be dragged there. So he marched off but went to his hole and fell asleep till midday. Then the Lion felt hungry and got up in anger and went roaring through the forest looking for the chosen animal. The Hare had meanwhile climbed up a tree overlooking a well, and as the Lion drew near he shouted to him to stop.

"Why are you making all that noise?" he asked. The Lion replied that he had waited all morning and his servant had not brought the promised food. Then the Hare from the top of the tree said, "Well, I was chosen for you by lot, and I was coming along with a present of honey as well, when another Lion met me and took the honey out of my hand." "Where is this other Lion?" roared the Lion angrily. The Hare said, "He is in the well, but he is not afraid of you, for he says he is much stronger than you." The Lion was even more furious, and looking into the well he saw another Lion looking up at him, and angry as well. The Lion insulted him, but there was silence. He abused him, slandering the honour of his parents, but still there was no answer. The Lion became mad, and sprang on the other Lion in the well—and was drowned. Then the Hare went back to the other animals and told them that he had killed the Lion, and he was King of Beasts.

In a story from Zambia the Hare was out with the Lion one day. He laid himself down on an ant-hill, and asked the Lion to set light to all the grass around it. While the Lion was doing this the Hare slipped down a burrow underneath the ant-hill and was saved from the flames. When they had died down he came out, rolled in the black ash, and went to find the Lion. "See, I am not hurt, look at this ash," he said. The Lion was astonished and asked if he could have some of the Hare's magical medicine. So the Hare gave him some leaves, looked round for another ant-hill with plenty of grass on it, and told the Lion to lie down there. Then he set fire to the grass all round. When the fire got near him the Lion cried out in alarm, but the Hare told him not to cry— that would spoil the power of the medicine. Then the fire reached the Lion, it singed his hair, burnt his body, set fire to him all over, and he died. So the Hare ran off and told the other animals that he was now their King.

Other fables tell more of Hare's victories over lions, how he broke all the lion's teeth, ate his children, wore a lion's skin, killed many lions, and caused the chief Lion to be stung to death by bees. Another tale from Zambia says that one day the Hare found the Lions eating meat, and he asked if he could stay with them and simply pick the fleas out of their tails. Of course he was deceiving them as usual, and instead of picking out fleas he was digging holes underneath them. As the lazy animals lay stretched out gorged with their meal, the Hare buried their tails in the holes and rammed them down with soil. Then he went home, fetched out a big drum, and began to beat it. The Lions thought that men were coming and jumped up suddenly to run away, breaking off their tails which were fixed in the holes. Then the Hare enjoyed the rest of the meat which they had left.

Hare and Tortoise

This story of the famous race is known in many versions in Africa, sometimes it is the Hare who races the Tortoise, sometimes the Elephant or some other animal. One day the Hare was boasting as usual, and the Tortoise said that he could jump farther than the Hare. The Hare laughed at the very idea, so the Tortoise challenged him to a trial and it was agreed for the next day. The Tortoise hurried off, found his wife, put her in the bushes near the spot that had been decided. When the Hare arrived early next day he found that the Tortoise was waiting for him. He asked the Hare to jump in a certain direction, and the lively beast took a great leap. Then the Tortoise called out that he was coming, slipped into the grass, and his wife appeared in the distance, far ahead of the Hare. The Hare was amazed and said he had not seen the jump, but the Tortoise said that was because his eyes had not been quick enough.

So the Hare acknowledged defeat, but challenged the Tortoise to a foot race which he knew he could win. The Tortoise agreed, but said he was too tired that day and it would have to be the next morning. Then he went home and collected all his family, and spent the night placing them along the road and telling them what to do. Next morning the Hare and the Tortoise started off together and the Hare was soon far ahead. He called back, "Tortoise," and to his surprise heard a voice ahead saying, "I am here." The same happened all along the road, and since it was circular when the Hare arrived panting he found the original Tortoise calmly sitting waiting for him.

Other versions of a race between a slow and fast animal appear in the stories of the messengers of life and death, where the slow Chameleon, or another animal, arrives before the fast Dog, but with a less happy message. There are stories of the Tortoise and Baboon, Lizard and Leopard, in all of which he scores off his opponents. Other animals, birds, snakes and other reptiles figure in countless stories. But the cycles of fables about the Hare and the Spider are the most popular.

Anansi and the Corn Cob

In West Africa, where the spider is called Anansi, the Annancy of America, he is the cleverest of animals and often appears in mythology where he is the chief official of God though at first he has no name. One day Anansi asked God for one corn cob, a stick of maize grains, promising to bring him a hundred slaves in exchange for it. God laughed but gave him the cob. Anansi set off from heaven to earth and stopped at the first village, requesting a night's lodging from the chief. Before he went to bed he asked the chief where he could put the corn cob safely, explaining that it belonged to God and must not be lost. The chief showed him a hiding place in the roof, and they all went to sleep. But in the night Anansi got up and gave all the corn from the cob to the fowls. When he demanded his cob next morning it had gone, and he made such a fuss that the chief gave him a whole basket of corn to pacify him.

Anansi continued his journey and after a time sat down by the roadside, since the basket was too heavy to carry far. Along came a man with a chicken in his hand and Anansi easily persuaded him to exchange it for all the corn. When he reached the next village the chief put him up, and Anansi asked where the fowl could be hidden, since it belonged to God and must be kept safe. The bird was put in a quiet fowl-house and everybody went to sleep. But Anansi got up, killed the fowl, and daubed its blood and feathers on the chief's door. At dawn he made a great cry, shouting that the bird was gone and he would lose his place as God's captain. Everybody started looking and Anansi suddenly pointed to the blood and feathers on the chief's door. The chief and all his people begged Anansi to forgive them, and gave him ten sheep to calm his anger.

Anansi went off and rested on the way to graze the sheep. Along came some people carrying a corpse, and when Anansi asked whose it was they replied that it was the body of a young man who had died far from home and they were taking him back to the family. Anansi said he was going that way, and offered to take the body if they would take his sheep. They were glad to agree and Anansi went on with the body to the next village. There he asked the chief for rest and explained that he had with him the favourite son of God, who was asleep and needed a hut to rest in. The chief prepared his best room for God's son, and after feasting and dancing they all went to bed.

In the morning Anansi asked some of the chief's children to wake God's son, saying that they might have to shake and even beat him, for he slept heavily. When they came and said they could not wake him, Anansi told them to flog him harder. Still the boy did not wake up, and at last Anansi uncovered the body and cried out that he was dead. He said that the sons of the chief had killed the favourite child of God with their rough beating. There was great wailing among the people, and they were terrified to think of the anger of God. The boy was buried that day, on Anansi's advice, and he said he would try to think of a plan to appease the divine anger. At night he called the chief and said he would have to report the matter back to God. But the chief must give him a hundred young men, to witness that they and not Anansi were responsible for the boy's death. The chief and people gladly agreed, and Anansi set off and finally arrived back in heaven with youths. He told God how from one corn cob he had gained a hundred fine young slaves, as he had promised. God was so pleased that he confirmed him as chief of all his host, and gave him the special name of Anansi which he still bears.

How Anansi Tricked God

Anansi, the spider, was very conceited and this was often his undoing. When he had been made captain of the divine hosts he began to boast that he was even more clever than God himself. God heard this and was angry. He sent for Anansi and asked him to bring him "something." He would not say what it was and Anansi puzzled all day without success, to find out the mysterious object that was needed. In the evening God laughed at him, saying that he had boasted that he was as clever as himself, so he must prove it and find the "something" without any further help.

Anansi left the sky to look for this "something" on earth, and after a time he had an idea. He called all the birds to him and borrowed a feather from each of them. He made the feathers into a splendid cloak, flew back to heaven, and perched in a tree against God's house. When God came out he saw the brilliant bird and called all the people together to find out the name of the bird. Nobody could tell him, not even the elephant who knows all the beasts of the forest. Somebody said that Anansi might know, but God explained that he had sent him away on an errand. All the people asked what the errand was and God said that Anansi had boasted that he was as wise as God so he had been sent to get "something." The people asked what the "something" was and God told them that it was the sun, moon, and darkness.

Anansi in the tree heard this, and when God and the people had gone he came down from the tree, threw away his fine feathers, and went off to look for the sun, moon and darkness. It is said that the python was the only one who knew where they were and he gave them to him. Anansi put them in a bag and went back to God. God asked if he had brought "something," and Anansi said "yes" and brought Darkness out of his bag. Then he drew out the Moon, and people could see a little. Finally he took out the Sun, which was so brilliant that some of the people were blinded, and others could see only a little. So it was that blindness came into the world. But others had their eyes shut and the Sun did them no harm.

Anansi and the Chameleon

Anansi and the Chameleon lived in the same village. Anansi was rich, with plenty of children and a large farm, while the Chameleon was poor and alone, and had only a small field to cultivate. But one year the rain fell on the Chameleon's field and not at all on Anansi's farm. Anansi was envious and asked the Chameleon to sell him his field, and when he refused he threatened revenge. Chameleons walk with curious steps over grass and bushes and do not make roads like other people, so there was no path to the Chameleon's field. Anansi therefore got his children to make a wide roadway from his house to the Chameleon's field during the night. In the morning he went there and started pulling up the crops. The Chameleon came and protested and was told to go away—the field belonged to Anansi. The Chameleon made a complaint at the chief's court and Anansi was called to account for his action. When both animals claimed the field, the chief asked for proofs. Anansi demanded that they agree it was true that he always made a path while the Chameleon made none, and the latter agreed. The chief sent his servants to see if this was true, and when they reported back he awarded the field to Anansi.

The Chameleon had to go home without field or food, and shut himself up in his house plotting revenge. He decided to dig a great hole, deeper than anyone had seen before, covering it with a roof and leaving just a small hole. Then he set to work to catch hundreds of large buzz flies, which he tied to dried vines and made into a large cloak. When the chief next called his people together the Chameleon went along, walking slowly and proudly in his strange brilliant costume, with the flies buzzing and shining in the sun. The chief himself wanted to buy the cloak but the Chameleon refused. But when Anansi heard of it he promised the chief he would buy it for him, since he was rich. He went to the Chameleon and asked the price. At first the Chameleon refused, but later he relented, saying he was so hungry that if Anansi would give him the food he needed he could have the cloak. He did not want much food, just enough to fill the little hole of his store.

Anansi looked at the tiny opening and promised to send his children with enough food to fill it twice over. So Anansi's children came with loads of food next day and poured the grain into the hole, but the more they brought the less the hole was filled. For days and weeks they brought food, while the Chameleon stood by and reminded Anansi that he had promised to fill the hole twice over. Anansi was vexed, and kept his children at work till his granaries were empty. Still the hole was not filled, and to keep his word Anansi sold his sheep and cows, and all he had to buy grain to fill the hole. At last the Chameleon declared he was not a hard man, and though the hole was still not full, he would let Anansi off the rest of the debt. He took the cloak out of a box and gave it to him. But during the long time that the cloak had been put away the vines had rotted, and when Anansi took the cloak outside the wind blew it about and all the flies flew away, leaving Anansi with a few withered vines and no crops or money. All the people laughed at him, and since that time Anansi hides in the corners of houses and no longer goes out proudly in the streets as before.

How Anansi Became a Spider

Another fable explains why Anansi became so small. He was once a man, and there was a king who had a magnificent ram, larger than any other, and he forbade anybody to touch it, no matter what it did or ate, under pain of death. Anansi had a large farm and a fine crop of corn was growing there. But one day when Anansi went to look at his corn he was horrified to find that part of the field had been trampled down and the young corn shoots eaten. In the middle of the field, and still munching, was the king's ram. Anansi was so angry that he threw a stone at the ram and killed it. Then he was afraid, for he knew the king's orders.

As he stood under a tree wondering what to do a nut fell on his head, and he picked it up and ate it. Then another nut fell, and he had an idea, like Newton with the apple. He picked up the ram and climbed up with it into the tree, hanging it on one of the branches. Then he went to call on a friend, who was a large spider. He showed him a nut and promised to show him where he could find others. They went back to the tree and Anansi told the spider to shake it, and the dead ram fell down also. Anansi exclaimed that the spider had killed the king's ram, and the spider asked what he should do. Anansi said the best thing was to confess his crime and hope that the king would be in a good mood.

The spider picked up the dead ram and set off. But on the way he stopped to tell his wife what had happened, in case he did not see her again. Anansi stayed outside while the spider went in to speak to his wife. She said her husband was stupid. Had he ever seen a ram climb trees? There must be some trick, so the spider must go on alone to the king, return without seeing him, but report to Anansi that all was well. The spider did this, and when he came back he told Anansi that not only the king was not angry but he had actually given him some of the meat of the ram to eat. Anansi cried that this was not fair. He himself had killed the ram and ought to have a share of its flesh. Then the spider and his wife seized Anansi and took him to the king. Anansi fell to the ground and begged for mercy, but the king was furious and kicked him so hard that he broke into a thousand pieces. That is why Anansi is much smaller now, and is found in every corner of the house, like a spider broken into many pieces.

Temne Stories

collected and translated into
English by Abdul Karim Turay

The Price of Jealousy

N: Sweet Yenken (name of a woman)!

A: Beautiful, beautiful woman!

N: Sweet Yenken!

A: Beautiful, beautiful woman!

N: Oh Yenken!

A: Beautiful, beautiful woman!

(Voice from audience) What happened?

A young man had two wives. The younger one was called Yenken. She was responsible for washing dishes at the river. One of the things which she had to wash was a large calabash which was used for many things.

One day, she lost the calabash in the river. She went to the elder wife to report the mischief. "I have lost the calabash," she said.—"If you don't go and bring the calabash back, you'll be in serious trouble," the elder wife replied. Jealousy was beginning to come into it. This young girl, as all the children of the olden days, was afraid.

She returned to the river to trace the calabash [downstream]. As she went along, she sang:

Our calabash, precious calabash,
the fine calabash is lost in the water.
Ah me, I miss my mother so much!

(Narrator directing the audience) You sing "Our calabash, precious calabash, I miss my mother so much."

(Audience)

Our calabash, precious calabash,
I miss my mother so much.
Our calabash, precious calabash.

When the husband came [home], he inquired about his younger wife. The elder wife explained that Yenken had gone to search for the calabash which was lost in the river. "I have still not seen her come back," she said. Angry and afraid for Yenken's safety, the husband jumped into his canoe. He took his paddle and started rowing to find his younger wife.

As he rowed, he sang:

N: Sweet Yenken!

(Narrator mimes action of rowing)

A: Beautiful, beautiful woman!

N: Sweet Yenken!

A: Beautiful, beautiful woman!

N: Is that not my sweet wife?

A: Beautiful, beautiful woman!

N: Oh Yenken!

A: Beautiful, beautiful woman!

The calabash continued floating downstream. Yenken still followed it. The husband in turn still followed Yenken. Yenken could see the calabash, but could not reach it. The husband could see Yenken, but could not reach her. So he continued rowing harder:

N: Sweet Yenken!

A: Beautiful, beautiful woman!

N: Sweet Yenken!

A: Beautiful, beautiful woman!

N: Is that not my sweet wife?

A: Beautiful, beautiful woman!

N: Oh Yenken!

A: Beautiful. beautiful woman!

(Narrator explaining his gestures in an ordinary voice) He is now rowing still harder.

N: Sweet Yenken!

A: Beautiful, beautiful woman!

N: Sweet Yenken!

A: Beautiful, beautiful woman!

Meanwhile the young girl was following the calabash (gesture of wading in deep water):

N: Our calabash, precious calabash!
The fine calabash is lost in the water!
Ah me, I miss my mother so much.

A: Our calabash, precious calabash!

N: I miss my mother so much.

A: Our calabash, precious calabash!

(In an ordinary voice) The calabash did not stop, so Yenken continued following it:

N: I miss my mother so much!

A: Our calabash, precious calabash.

N: I miss my mother so much!

A: Our calabash, precious calabash.

The husband still followed:

N: Sweet Yenken!

A: Beautiful, beautiful woman!

N: Oh Yenken!

A: Beautiful, beautiful woman!

They went on and on, until they came to a deep whirlpool. Everything which comes near this whirlpool is sucked to the bottom. So, the calabash got there and sank. Yenken got there and drowned immediately. The husband got there and he also drowned.

The jealous wife was now left with nothing. She lost her calabash, her young co-wife and her husband. She gained nothing.

This is the price of jealousy!

I stop so far.

Mr. Spider and His Mother-in-Law

: Move your body forward and backward!

A: Do it strongly!

N: Move your body forward and backward!

A: Do it strongly!

(Gestures of rowing a boat)

(Voice from audience) What happened?

Spider lived together with his mother-in-law. There was a river near their house. The mother-in-law cultivated a vegetable garden on the other side of the river. She planted pepper, aubergines and several other kinds of vegetables. Spider longed to eat these vegetables. So, he secretly made a boat. He used this boat to row across the river. As he rowed, he sang:

N: Move your body forward and backward!

A: Do it strongly!

N: Strongly!

He quickly crossed the river. When he got to the other side, he filled up the boat with his mother-in-law's vegetables. Then he started his homeward journey.

N: Move your body forward and backward!

A: Do it strongly!

N: Strongly!

After crossing the river he sold some of the vegetables in the market. His wife used some to

Mr. Spider rows across river to steal from his mother-in-law

prepare their meals. Spider continued this theft until there was hardly anything left in the vegetable garden.

The mother-in-law was upset and anxious to catch the thief. She went to Pa Lulu (a bird: Red Breasted Robin), the great diviner, who instructed her to gather sap from the gum tree. He told her to carve a life size female model and to pour gum all over its body. This should be left in the garden, because the thief might come and attempt to embrace this young woman.

That night Mister Spider came again.

N: Move your body forward and backward!

A: Do it strongly!

N: Strongly!

He arrived and harvested what was left of the vegetables. The carved model was standing on a prominent side of the garden. Its body was shining in the moonlight and it looked like a real life woman. It looked as beautiful as a newly married girl who has just been brought to her husband. When he had loaded his boat with vegetables, Mister Spider began to row back:

N: Move your body forward and backward!

A: Do it strongly!

N: Strongly!

He had not gone far when he turned back and saw the model standing in the garden. He rushed back, jumped out of the boat and went to the handsome woman in order to greet her. "How do you do?" he said. "You are so beautiful, I'd like to marry you."—No reply! The woman did not say a word. "Why don't you answer me?" He attempted to kiss her.—His face got stuck. "Dear me! I've never seen such a beautiful woman before. Now I've played all my tricks and she doesn't even reply to me. Well, let me touch her with my hands." He touched her and got stuck. He bit her and got even more stuck.

There he stayed till the morning, when his mother-in-law came. She was surprised to discover that Mister Spider was the thief. "Why have you done this to me?" she asked. Spider had no explanation. He pleaded with his mother-in-law not to expose him to the public. "I will not do that. I'll never shame you publicly." Then she got hold of Mister Spider's legs and pulled them apart and she beat him so hard that he stayed flat all his life.

There goes my story up in flames.

Lizard and Tortoise

All the animals got together and decided to make a farm. Tortoise said he would not take part. He claimed no other territory as his own but the spot on which he lay. The other animals tried to convince him (of their plan), but without success. Then they decided to move him from the spot where he was lying to enable them to make their farm.

Mister Elephant came—in vain!

Mister Wolf came—in vain!

Mister Leopard came—in vain!

All the large animals came to move Tortoise, but none succeeded. Then they decided to leave him. In the end Lizard came and said: "Why should a mere tortoise dictate to us?" He promised that he would remove Tortoise at once from the farming area. He asked the other animals, while he was doing this, they should cheer him shouting: "Hurray Lizard, hurray Lizard!" He warned them not to interfere, even if they saw him struggling or being in danger. The animals agreed to this.

Lizard approached Tortoise and asked him: "Did you say you'll not move from here?" Tortoise casually replied: "I don't speak of other people's territories, but of this spot on which I lie, which belongs to me." Lizard began moving his head up and down to threaten Tortoise. The other animals shouted: "Hurray, Lizard, the one and only Lizard!" He began to hit his head against Tortoise's shell. But Tortoise did not say a word. Encouraged by the cheers, Lizard pushed his head into the shell of Tortoise. Tortoise immediately squeezed tight so that Lizard could not free his head anymore.

Meanwhile, the cheers continued: "Hurray Lizard, hurray Lizard!" Lizard struggled and fought to free his head. The more he struggled, the louder the cheering from the other animals. Lizard fought till he wetted his trousers and defecated. He fought and struggled until he bruised his head all over. Blood began to flow from his bruised head. The other animals obeying instructions kept on cheer-ing: "Hurray Lizard, the one and only Lizard!" Nearly suffocating, he made one last effort, suc-ceeding in drawing his head out. If you saw Lizard—he was covered with urine, feces and blood! The cheering started afresh: "Hurray Lizard, hurray Lizard!"

Then Lizard went up to the other animals and said to them: "Whatever you think, you must admit that I, Lizard, was able to squeeze my head out. Lizard is a real man!" After that he climbed on a high tree, accompanied by the mocking laughter of the other animals. "Lizard is a real man! Lizard is brave!" Lizard, from the top of the tree, would agree with these sentiments, nod-ding vigorously in agreement: "Yes, of course, I agree." The more they shouted, the harder Lizard nodded in agreement.

Up to this day, if you come across a Lizard and say "Lizard is a real man," you will see him moving his head up and down in agreement. He is acknowledging your praises. This is what hap-pened to Lizard.

There goes my story.

(Audience) Thanks.

Lizard attempts to move Tortoise

Limba Stories and Story-Telling

Ruth Finnegan

The Spider, The Lover Of Meat

Karanke Dema. *Recorded* 1.2.64

The spider is again frustrated in his attempt to get much meat for himself. The tale ends with the common attribution of origin about why the spider is always to be found on the walls of houses (many different explanations of this are given in different stories). As often, one of the highlights was the vivid representation of the way the spider was beaten.

A story for you, Suri; a story for you, Yenkeni. You will reply, Suri won't you?

A spider once came out—a great lover of meat. Of all meat-lovers, he was the "Commissioner."* Wherever anyone killed, he used to go there.

When the chief fixed a time for people to go and hoe his farm, he made a sacrifice, providing an ox for all the workers who went. The spider was the herald in the village. When he had announced this in the evening, and at night, when all the people were gathered, he announced it. When he had finished announcing it they spent the whole night—*kudu!*

In the morning, then the chief said, "Here is a cooking pot,[1] standing here"—now the pot was very large—"Whoever can carry it, he will get the ox's head." That pleased the spider, to be given the head, for him alone to eat! That pleased him. He congratulated himself, "Ha! Kayi! Today we are eating the head now, today we are eating the head now.[2] I am carrying the pot." He got up. He went and told the chief, "I am carrying the pot, I am able." The chief said, "Are you able?" "Yes." "Are you able?" "Yes." "What if you are not able?" "You can thrash me." The chief said, "All right."

The servants put the pot up on his head. When they had put it up, he set out to go. When he was going, the pot weighed him down very much. When they came to a rock—the rock was slippery. Just as he went to tread on it—he slipped, *thalabasa—fuuu, puuuuy!*[3] (on to the rock)[4]—on to the rock. The pot broke. Now the servants were following him. They had heard that, "If I am unable, they can thrash me." He was seized there. The chief came. "The spider has broken the pot oh!" "Oh? Thrash him!" They lifted him up there, and crashed him down on to the rock, *ban!* They—*thrashed* him there.

You see now, the spider is always small, he dwindled. That is why he ran off quickly, *kare kare*, saying, "I, I will go and cling on to the chief's walls." You see now, the spider likes the wall where people build—he goes in there, he goes and clings on to the wall. It was his love of meat that caused him to dwindle to the size he is. You see now, whoever treads in the place where the spider was thrashed, they are the people who are great lovers of meat—like vultures. Wherever meat is killed, they have to go there.

Well, since I heard that story, and Yenkeni said that she wanted it, that is that story. Suri, it is finished.

ENDNOTES

1. i.e., the large and very heavy iron pot which would be used to cook the ox killed for the workers.
2. As often the spider starts rejoicing too soon.

3. The sound of the spider slipping, the pot falling, and both crashing on to the rock.

4. An interjection by Suri, one of the listeners.

Three Twins And An Elephant

Karanke Dema. *Dictated 26.10.61*

A story ending in a dilemma—which of three twins who all achieve impossible tasks was the greatest in "cunning"? (I also heard a story with a similar plot told by one of the children from Karanke's village in which the plots of this and *The oldest of three twins* were run together to make one brief story ending with the boy's return home and no dilemma.)

A story again. Three twins again came out. One Koto, one Yemi, one Luseni. They were going to go to hunt, the three of them. They said, "Let us go to hunt elephants." They set out. Then Koto said, "I, when we find the tracks, I will shoot." Then Yemi said, "When you shoot there, and when it dies, and when we find it, I will cut it up, I alone." Then Luseni said, "When you have cut it up, I will find something to carry it in."

They set out. They found the tracks of an elephant. Koto aimed. He shot. The bullet set out, it went, it came to the elephant. It entered there, the elephant died.

They set out, to follow where the bullet had gone and killed it. They went. For four days they went. They did not come to where the elephant was. On the fifth, they arrived. They came to the elephant. Then Yemi said, "Yes, Koto, you have finished your part. My part, that is left now." He took his nail, the first one [thumb]. He pulled it out, its full length. With that he cut up the elephant! When he had finished cutting it up, he piled it up. He said, "I have finished my part."

Then Luseni said, "All right. Koto, thank you. Yemi, thank you. We did not bring each other into shame. Since we came out into the wilderness, if we had not killed—shame. Since you have come and done this, that pleases me. My part is left now." He got up, he Luseni, he pinched a small fly, he split it open. The empty skin, there he put in the whole elephant! It went in there.

When they brought it—of those three, Koto, Yemi, and Luseni, which one was the most in cunning? That is what I ask you, you Yenkeni.

─────── *Questions for Consideration* ───────

Using complete sentences, provide brief answers for the following questions.

1. What have you learned from the stories with the Anansi theme?

_____

_____

_____

_____

_____

2. Point out and comment on the effectiveness of language and stylistic features in "The Price of Jealousy" and "The Spider, the Lover of Meat."

_____

_____

_____

_____

_____

3. Do these fables have anything in common with the myths you studied earlier? If not, how would you distinguish between myths and fables?

_____

_____

_____

_____

_____

———————————— *Writing Critically* ————————————

Directions: Select one of the essay topics listed below and compose a 500 word essay which discusses the topic fully. Support your thesis with evidence from the text and with critical and/or historical material. Use the space below for preparing to write the essay.

1. From your reading of these fables and the introduction, discuss what you understand by Oral Literature and the Oral Tradition.

2. What are the major themes in these fables, and how are they presented and developed?

3. Using all the texts in this selection, attempt to show what roles these stories may have in education and socialization of people in that culture.

4. Attempt to recreate the story-telling/performance setting for one of these sample tales using ideas provided in the introduction and features suggested by the tales themselves.

5. Using elements of the short story you are familiar with, analyze at least one of these tales as short stories, viz. plot, theme, setting, character, etc.

6. Use these texts to present the social and cultural significance of fables in traditional African society.

Prewriting Space:

_____

_____

_____

_____

_____

_____

_____

_____

_____

_____

_____

_____

_____

_____

_____

Introduction

Asian Cultures: China

From almost any standpoint, China has been one of the great influences in human history and culture. Anyone who has ever dined on a porcelain plate, drunk tea, eaten rice, or purchased a silk tie or blouse has felt the impact of Chinese civilization. Over many centuries, China has introduced some of the most basic commodities and products used throughout the world on a daily basis. A primary reason why China's contributions have permeated world culture is that the "middle kingdom" (as its Chinese name, *Zhongguo*, translates literally into English) has maintained a steady existence for approximately three millennia. Whereas Egypt, Greece, India, and the other great societies of antiquity have experienced major dislocations and transformations during their long histories, Chinese civilization has remained relatively constant despite numerous replacements of one dynasty by another until the overthrow of the imperial form of rule in 1911. The notion of a Chinese tradition thus has a special resonance not evoked by, say, Roman tradition. It is instructive to note that "tradition" derives from a Latin word meaning "the act of handing over." Chinese traditions dating from antiquity have been transmitted with a continuity perhaps unique in world history.

Chinese civilization began to emerge around 8,000 B.C. with the development of agricultural communities along the banks of the Yellow River in central China. Although ancient Chinese sources refer to a prehistoric Xia dynasty, archaeological findings date the earliest traces of a centralized government, the Shang dynasty, to around 1700 B.C. Centered in what is now the northeast section of Henan province, Shang culture possessed the skills of writing, chariot-making, working in bronze, architecture, divination, and other technologies typical of the earliest world civilizations. An intriguing record of this very ancient culture survives in the form of tortoise shells that were inscribed with Chinese characters and exposed to fire. Soothsayers would examine each shell and make a prediction on the basis of where cracks appeared in a message that had been carved in the shell. These inscriptions provide valuable evidence of the nature of Chinese writing at its earliest stages.

Chinese writing is character-based, and the language is monosyllabic. That is, most words consists of only one syllable, and there is a separate character for each word. Many of the characters are pictographic; that is, the sign resembles what it means. For example, the word and character for mountain are: *"shan,"* "山". Since Chinese is a mostly non-inflected language, we must learn from the context whether one or many mountains are intended; the written character and the spoken sound are the same for singular and plural. other characters are ideographs; they present in visual form the general idea of what is meant. "人" *(ren)* is a pictograph meaning a person, but "众" *(zhong)* is an ideograph meaning "crowd." Other characters or parts of characters have a phonetic dimension; they help indicate how a word is pronounced. Most characters are written differently today than they were during the Shang dynasty, but there is often a clear resemblance. For example, the Shang or oracle-bone character for "not" was written as "𣄼" while in modern Chinese, it is "不." Chinese is also a tonal language; what a word means depends heavily on the pitch. There are four tones in modern Mandarin (the official dialect out of the many dialects of China), but there were several more in ancient times.

269

At present, there are two major systems for presenting the sounds of Chinese in the Roman letters used in English and other Western languages. These systems are Wade-Giles and Pinyin; they are presented in a table accompanying this introduction. Both systems are used in this anthology. Thus, anyone wishing to become acquainted with Chinese culture needs to know a little about both systems since both are widely used.

For those interested in literature and other cultural documents, the period of greatest interest begins around 1000 B.C. with a collection of written material relating to the Zhou dynasty, which replaced the Shang. (Like the Shang, the Zhou rulers occupied only a portion of the territory we know today as China.) Many of the texts in this collection are now believed to be forgeries by later writers, but the *Book of Documents* also contains a considerable number of authentic speeches and other court-related records.

The *Book of Documents (Shujing* in Chinese) is one of the five major bodies of early texts that make up the Five Classics. These collections were supposedly compiled by Confucius, a belief no longer held to be true, but the arrangement of this material into five compilations at least began during the Confucian era (551–479 B.C.). In addition to the *Book of Documents*, the Five Classics comprise the *Book of Changes (Yi jing)*, a guide to divination based on a system of numbers and written signs; the *Book of Songs (Shi jing)*, a poetry anthology; the *Spring and Autumn Annals (Chungiu)*, a chronicle of major occurrences in the kingdom of Lu (the home of Confucius) during the years 722 to 481 B.C.; and the *Book of Rites (Li jing)*, which is a reconstruction, dating from the second century B.C., of an earlier lost work on ritual.

The Five Classics are significant because they became the intellectual foundation of Chinese civilization. Any educated person had to be familiar with the Confucian Classics, as they are often called. The refined or "high culture" that developed out of this tradition placed special emphasis on the Four Books, a group of rather short texts selected in part from the Five Classics. The Four Books, which became the most basic compendium of Chinese values, comprise two important chapters from the *Book of Rites*, the *Analects* of Confucius, and the book of Mencius, a thinker who reformulated the Confucian tradition during the fourth century B.C. Thus, Chinese culture (somewhat like that of the ancient Greeks) distinguished itself at an early date for its interest in coming to terms with the almost infinite range of human and social beliefs and behaviors—and indeed with the entire *cosmos*, the natural and supernatural world of which humankind is a part. In addition, there is a clear effort to systematize and codify the results of all this speculation and theorizing.

Thus, in 221 B.C., when Qin Shihuang became China's first emperor by uniting the various independent states of ancient China into one country, he gave a form of political expression to his culture's continuous attempt to deal inclusively with the full spectrum of human life. The name, "China," is derived from the surname of this first emperor. (Remember that in Chinese, the surname comes at the beginning of the full name.) Yet Qin Shihuang was brutally simplistic in many of his policies, and it is fitting that his government was short-lived. The Confucian-oriented Han dynasty gained control of China in 206 B.C., a mere four years after the death of the ambitious Qin Shihuang.

The civilization of ancient China, both before and after its unification into an empire, was rich and complex. In addition to the Confucian perspective discussed above, another great intellectual movement, Daoism, developed in a variety of forms. On the one hand, Confucianism and its derivatives emphasized the principles of social and political order, and how the ethical person could fit into a larger cultural scheme. The Daoists, on the other hand, reacted to the pressures and turmoil that seemed the inevitable result of society's preoccupation with politics. Daoists such as Zhuangzi and Laozi stressed the dimension of randomness in the universe and the lack of certainty in human actions. Daoism sought, instead, to harmonize the individual mind with the ultimate and nearly inexplicable power of the *cosmos*, a potency designated by the term "Dao" or "Way." (Although Confucius had employed the term "Dao" in presenting his outlook on society, the Daoists used the word in a more abstract sense.)

In addition to the theorizing of the Confucianists, Daoists, and other thinkers, a variety of basic cultural activities flourished in ancient China. The bureaucracy that eventually became very complicated in China began to develop as early as the Shang dynasty. Technologies such as the production of silk were practiced with definite sophistication. Architecture no doubt reached an advanced level, but since wood was the construction material of choice, virtually nothing remains of the buildings of the early periods. Work in bronze and jade, along with ceramics, reached a high state of proficiency. The intricate writing system inspired the efforts of calligraphers early on.

Mythology also developed; creation myths are found along with fictitious flora and fauna. The dragon is undoubtedly the most familiar animal in Chinese mythology; the beast typically displays a certain beneficence alien to its European counterparts. Despite a vast range of legends scattered in a myriad of texts, there were no major recorders of myth in China as Hesiod, Ovid, and others in the West.

Ancient China never produced an epic, in contrast to India, Greece, and Rome. Why? Perhaps because there has always been such a great emphasis on practicality in China. There is also a traditional resistance to a scenario of surrender to extreme emotions or passionate desires. The Homeric epics are based on the Greek reaction to the abduction of Helen; in addition, the wrath of Achilles is a major factor in the *Iliad*. The heroic temperament as manifested in ancient Greece is somehow un-Chinese. Also, the imperial theme so emphatic in the *Aeneid* is perhaps superfluous for a people so actively engaged in the processes of government and empire. China in its early stages was in any case just as culturally complex as any other ancient society. (NW)

BIBLIOGRAPHY

Birrell, Anne. *Chinese Mythology: An Introduction*. Baltimore: Johns Hopkins University Press, 1993.

Gernet, Jacques. *A History of Chinese Civilization*. Trans. J. R. Foster. Cambridge: Cambridge University Press, 1982.

Raphals, Lisa. *Knowing Words: Wisdom and Cunning in the Classical Traditions of China and Greece*. Ithaca: Cornell University Press, 1992.

Schwartz, Benjamin. *The World of Thought in Ancient China*. Cambridge: Harvard University Press, 1985.

Van Gulik, R. H. *Sexual Life in Ancient China: A Preliminary Survey of Chinese Sex and Society from ca. 1500 B.C. till 1644 A.D.* Leiden: E. J. Brill, 1974.

Zhang, Longxi. *The Tao and the Logos: Literary Hermeneutics, East and West*. Durham: Duke University Press, 1992.

Note on Chinese Names and Terms

Some Chinese names in this book are written in the roman alphabet in the system used in mainland China, pinyin; exceptions include familiar names which have been retained in older forms.

Pinyin is pronounced phonetically with a few idiosyncracies, chiefly these:

Consonants

c is pronounced like the *ts* in *tsetse fly*.
q is pronounced like the *ch* in *chin*.
x is pronounced like the *sh* in *sheen*.
zh is pronounced like the *j* in *jump*.

Vowels

e is pronounced like a dull *er* without the *r* being sounded, like the *e* in *talent*.
e before *ng* is pronounced like the *u* in *rung*.
o is pronounced like the *aw* in *jaw*.
ou is pronounced like the *o* in *go*.

Some names are given below in pinyin and in their equivalent in the more familiar, older forms of romanization, mainly the Wade-Giles system:

People

Pinyin	*Wade-Giles or other older romanization*
Beijing	Peking
Cao Xueqin	Ts'ao Hsüeh-ch'in
Empress Dowager Cixi	Tz'u-hsi
Deng Xiaoping	Teng Hsiao-p'ing
Hua Guofeng	Hua Kuo-feng
The Kangxi Emperor	The K'ang-hsi Emperor
Lao Zi	Lao-tze (more familiar) or Lao-tzu (more correct)
Li Bai or Li Bo	Li Po
Liu Shaoqi	Liu Shao-ch'i
Mao Zedong	Mao Tse-tung
Meng Zi	Mencius
The Qianlong Emperor	The Ch'ien-lung Emperor
Qin Shihuangdi	Ch'in Shih-huang-ti
Su Dongpo	Su Tong-p'o
The Yongle Emperor	The Yung-lo Emperor
Zhou Enlai	Chou En-lai
Meng Haoran	Meng Hao-jan

NB: In Chinese, the surname or family name precedes the given name.

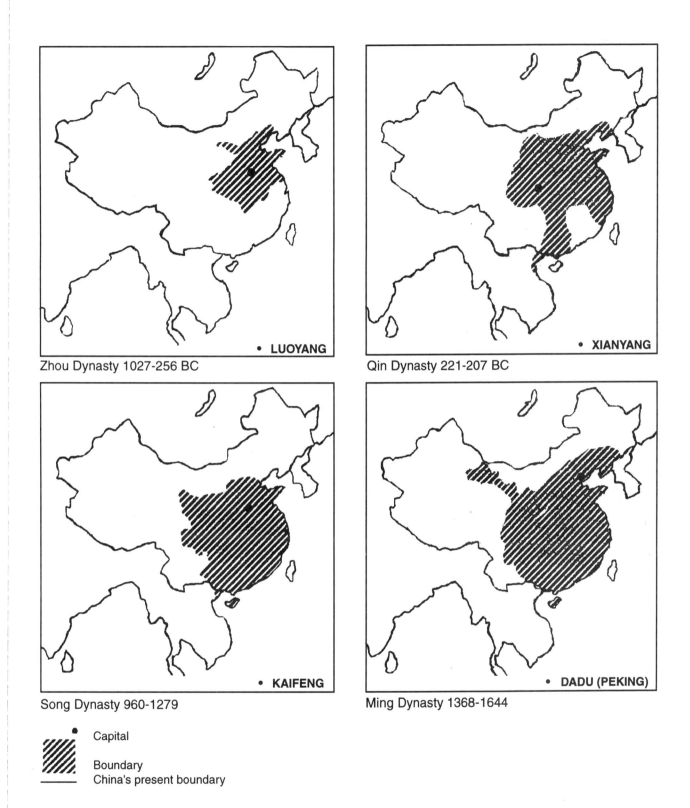

Zhou Dynasty 1027-256 BC   • LUOYANG

Qin Dynasty 221-207 BC   • XIANYANG

Song Dynasty 960-1279   • KAIFENG

Ming Dynasty 1368-1644   • DADU (PEKING)

• Capital

Boundary

China's present boundary

CHINA'S BOUNDARIES FROM THE ZHOU DYNASTY

Han Dynasty 206 BC- 220 AD

Tang Dynasty 618-906

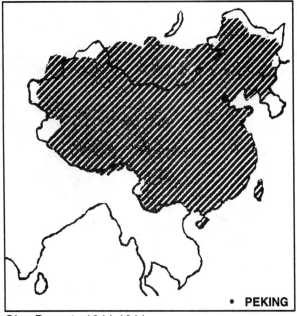

Qing Dynasty 1644-1911

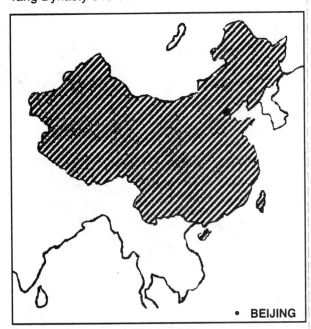

People's Republic of China 1949-

Introduction

Confucius (551–479 B.C.)
The Analects

ew civilizations of the ancient world had any scholastic or historical figure comparable to Confucius. If any one were asked to characterize in one word the Chinese way of life for the last two thousand years or more, the word would be "Confucian." Just how this became so is not easy to explain. Confucius and his teachings were little respected and rarely practiced by the people of his day. Only some three hundred years after Confucius' time was Confucianism declared the official creed of the country, and his classics became the principal study of all scholars and statesmen.

Since the 2nd century B.C. to this day, Confucianism has been synonymous with learning in China. Confucius was revered by the illiterate millions who could not read his classics but nonetheless practiced what he stood for. He was referred to as "the all-encompassing, supremely sagacious late master."

Who was Confucius, and what did he teach?

Confucius is the Latinized form of the name K'ung Fu-tzu[1]—the surname being "King" and "Fu-tzu" meaning "Master." He was born in the feudal state of Lu, now part of Shantung province. His parents were said to have been respectable but poor. Early he assumed the leadership of the family (his father was beyond seventy at the time of his birth, and his elder brother was a cripple). He was about twenty-three when his mother's death was the occasion for his retirement in mourning for the conventional period of three years. It is probable that during these years of meditation he worked out the foundations of his philosophy, to the teaching of which he was to devote the rest of his life. Confucius seems to have been self-educated, for the most part. In his early twenties he began to teach. He went to the state of Ch'i where he was consulted about many affairs, but the opposition threatened his life. He departed Ch'i. It is known that Confucius showed a sincere interest in the common people and his disciples were not selected on the basis of birth or rank. Little is known of the

incidents of his career. It is believed that in his early fifties he was a magistrate and then a minister of public works. In his mid-fifties he left Chou (Joe) and spent thirteen years wandering with his students (or disciples) from state to state. He returned to his native Lu[2] at sixty-eight to continue his teaching.

Confucius is credited with being the first professional teacher in China; he was the first to teach literature and the principles of conduct as opposed to the teaching of statecraft. He opened the doors of education to all people. He believed that all people could learn. However, it is clear from the *Analects* that those who are born with knowledge (wisdom) are those with the best minds. Those who have to study to acquire knowledge are on the lower rung of the ladder. How would you respond to Confucius' statements? (There is no elaboration in the *Analects*.)

Late in the sixth century B.C. or early in the fifth century B.C. the *Analects* were transcribed in three categories: (1) Ethics (moral conduct—what is right, what is wrong); (2) Political philosophy; (3) Epistemology (the origin and nature of knowledge). The excerpts from the *Analects* that you will read will require your knowledge and understanding of a few Confucian concepts.[3]

First, there is the concept of *ren* (wren) which is the foundation of Confucian ethics. It is the perfect virtue of men because it means gentility, humanity, goodness of character, and benevolence. The individual who values the principle of *ren* will treat people gently and humanely; for all who do this, all will go well. *Ren* was believed to be within the grasp of everyone, although it was not practiced by all. (Confucius was sufficiently realistic to know that this would happen.) By extension, the only road to the peace and harmony of a society is via *ren*.

Second, there is the concept of *li* (lee) which is the central aim of Confucianism. Man is close to *ren* by his very nature, that is, that he is a man (not an

From *The Wisdom of China and India* by Lin Yutang. Copyright © 1942 and renewed 1970 by Random House, Inc. Reprinted by permission of Random House, Inc.

animal) but his action should be controlled by *li*. This concept refers to propriety, a good form, or decorum. With the use of *li* man can contain the passion (even the wild passion) within him and make himself a better person. The concept of *li* is the evidence of man's culture—his civilization—as it distinguishes man from the animals. *Li* saves society from chaos and disorder. *Li* is essential to sophisticated, cultured, and orderly living.

Third, there is the concept of *Chun'-tzu* (CHUN-dzoo) which refers to the ideal man in Confucian thought. This is the formula: *ren + li = Chun'tzu*. To obtain *Chun'tzu* (the ideal) the individual (man) practices *ren* and acts in accordance with *li*. He seeks the *Tao* (dow, to rhyme with how) or the right way of being a man; his right way does not demand the thought of profit. These are differences between the superior man and the inferior man. The ideal man *(chun'tzu)* has a strong will and guards himself against fears and anxieties. *Chun'tzu*, then, personifies the good man, the best of men—hence, the ideal. He is not an aristocrat, but merely a kind and gentle man of moral principles. He is a man who loves learning, who is calm himself and perfectly at ease and constantly careful of his own conduct, believing that by example he has great influence over society in general. He is also perfectly at ease in his own station of life and has a certain contempt for the mere luxuries of living. Confucius said: "The gentleman makes demands on himself; the inferior man makes demands on others." How do you react to this statement?

Fourth, there is the concept of *Shu* which refers to tolerance or reciprocity in Confucian thought. *Shu* is also the cultivation of cooperation and sympathy, which must begin in the family and extend gradually into the larger areas of association. Continuing his ethical teaching, Confucius emphasized the importance of the five cardinal human relationships that were traditional among the Chinese: (1) ruler and subject, (2) father and son, (3) elder brother and younger brother, (4) husband and wife, and (5) friend and friend. The logic of this kind of thought can be tersely expressed in the famous line, "All men are brothers." But Confucius insisted, in his political philosophy, that the individual must be a worthy member of his own community before he could think in terms of world citizenship. (Is there ethical thought in this statement?) In addition, Confucius stressed personal civilization as the basis of a world order. *Hsiao*, or filial piety, is the basis of this. For having acquired the habits of love and respect in the home, one must extend, perforce, this mental attitude of love and respect to other people's parents and elder

brothers and to the authorities of the state. The state, ideally, is the family "writ large" just as the Greek gods and goddesses were Greek men and women "writ large." True, the Chinese family was patriarchal; but as Chinese women in the family grew older, they were accorded the same kind of respect as the male members of the family. The family in Confucian thought was a microcosm of society.

Throughout the teacher-philosopher's life he sought to restore a social order based on love for one's kind and respect for authority, of which the social rites of public worship and festivities in ritual and music should be the outward symbols. Confucius attributed all the problems of his day to the fact that the leaders of society had neglected the old rites, were performing them incorrectly, or were usurping ceremonies and rites to which they were not entitled. It was Confucius' belief that the neglect and abuse of the rites reflected a moral chaos (including oppression of the people) and the start of spiritual darkness. This was the state of affairs in the teacher's native feudal state of Lu.

In regard to Confucius' attitude toward heaven, there is limited information. The ethical leader identifies *Ming* as heaven's evil or destiny. Heaven, he said, was on the side of the just. Confucius talked rarely about God, angels, and heaven. His focus was upon man. Once when he was asked about the worship of the celestial and earthly spirits, he said, "We don't know yet how to serve men, how can we know about serving the spirits?" "What about death?" was the next question; and Confucius said, "We don't know yet about life, how can we know about death?"[4]

In his role of scholar, Confucius, who wrote little, edited the ancient records of China.[5] He edited the *Book of Odes*, the *Book of Rites*, the *Book of History*,[6] the *Book of Changes*, the *Annals of Spring and Autumn*. He wrote one book himself; the book was a chronicle of events from 722 to 481 B.C. based on the history of the state of Lu.

Lun Yu, or the *Analects* of Confucius (as named by their first translator, James Legge), is a collection of the sayings of the Master as they were remembered and eventually recorded by his disciples after his death.

ENDNOTES

1. Pronounce K'ung Fu-tzu, Koong-zjoo.
2. He never received an offer of an appointment that he could accept in good conscience.

3. Remember, knowledge—according to Confucius and Socrates—is the key to happiness (and successful conduct, too, adds Confucius).

4. Quoted in the excerpt captioned "His Philosophy," paragraph 2, from the *Analects*.

5. One collection, the *Book of Music*, was lost in its entirety.

6. Preferred title: *Document Classic*.

from the Analects

Confucius
Translated by Lin Yutang

Confucius the Man

Duke Yeh asked Tselu about Confucius, and Tselu did not make a reply. Confucius said, "Why didn't you tell him that I am a person who forgets to eat when he is enthusiastic about something, forgets all his worries when he is happy, and is not aware that old age is coming on?"

Confucius said, "There is pleasure in lying pillowed against a bent arm after a meal of simple vegetables with a drink of water. On the other hand, to enjoy wealth and power without coming by it through the right means is to me like so many floating clouds."

Confucius said, "There are three things about the superior man that I have not been able to attain. The true man has no worries; the wise man has no perplexities; and the brave man has no fear." Tsekung said, "But, Master, you are exactly describing yourself."

Confucius said, "As to being a Sage and a true man, I am not so presumptuous. I will admit, however, that I have unceasingly tried to do my best and to teach other people."

"The things that trouble or concern me are the following: lest I should neglect to improve my character, lest I should neglect my studies, and lest I should fail to move forward when I see the right course, or fail to correct myself when I see my mistake."

Confucius said, "I won't teach a man who is not anxious to learn, and will not explain to one who is not trying to make things clear to himself.

And if I explain one-fourth and the man doesn't go back and reflect and think out the implications in the remaining three-fourths for himself, I won't bother to teach him again."

Confucius did not talk about monsters, physical exploits, unruly conduct, and the heavenly spirits.

Confucius was gentle but dignified, austere yet not harsh, polite and completely at ease.

When Confucius offered sacrifice to his ancestors, he felt as if his ancestors were present bodily, and when he offered sacrifice to the other gods, he felt as if the gods were present bodily. Confucius said, "If I don't offer sacrifice by being personally present, it is as if I didn't sacrifice at all."

Tsekung wanted to do away with the ceremony of sacrificing the lamb in winter. Confucius said, "Ah Sze, you love the lamb, but I love the institution."

Confucius said, "Wake yourself up with poetry, establish your character in *li* and complete your education in music."

For him rice could never be white enough and mince meat could never be chopped fine enough. When the food was mushy or the flavor had deteriorated, or when the fish had become bad or the meat was tainted, he would not eat. When its color had changed he would not eat. When the smell was bad, he would not eat. When it was not cooked right, he would not eat. When food was not in season, he would not eat. When the meat was not cut properly, he would not eat. When a food was not served with its proper sauce, he would not eat. Although there was a lot of meat on the table, he would not take it out of proportion with his rice; as for wine, he drank without any set limit, but would stop before getting drunk. Wine or shredded meat bought from the shops he would not eat. A meal without ginger on the table he would not eat. He did not overeat.

Tselu, Tseng Hsi, Ran Ch'iu, and Kunghsi Hua were sitting together one day, and Confucius said, "Do not think that I am a little bit older than you and therefore am assuming airs. You often say among yourselves that people don't know you. Suppose someone should know you, I should like to know how you would appear to that person." Tselu immediately replied, "I should like to rule over a country with a thousand carriages, situated between two powerful neighbors, involved in war and suffering from famine. I should like to take charge of such a country, and in three years the nation will become strong and orderly." Confucius smiled at this remark and said, "How about you, Ah Ch'iu?" Ran Ch'iu replied, "Let me have a country sixty or seventy *li* square or perhaps only fifty or sixty *li*[1] square. Put it in my charge, and in three years the people will have enough to eat, but as for teaching them moral order and music, I shall leave it to the superior man." (Turning to Kunghsi Hua) Confucius said, "How about you, Ah Ch'iu?" Kunghsi Hua replied, "Not that I say I can do it, but I'm willing to learn this. At the ceremonies of religious worship and at the conference of the princes, I should like to wear the ceremonial cap and gown and be a minor official assisting at the ceremony." "How about you, Ah Tien?" The latter (Tseng Hsi) was just playing on the *seh*,[2] and with a bang he left the instrument

Confucius

and arose to speak. "My ambition is different from theirs." "It doesn't matter," said Confucius; "we are just trying to find out what each would like to do." Then he replied, "In late spring, when the new spring dress is made, I would like to go with five or six grownups and six or seven children to bathe in the River Yi, and after the bath go to enjoy the breeze in the Wuyu woods, and then sing on our way home." Confucius heaved a deep sigh and said, "You are the man after my heart."

His Conversation

Confucius said, "I have sometimes talked with Huei for a whole day, and he just sits there like a fool. But then he goes into his own room and thinks about what I have said and is able to think out some ideas of his own. He is not a fool."

Tsekung asked Confucius, "What kind of person do you think can be properly called a scholar?" Confucius replied, "A person who shows a sense of honor in his personal conduct and who can be relied upon to carry out a diplomatic mission in a foreign country with competence and dignity can

be properly called a scholar." "What kind of person would come next?" "One who is known to be a good son in his family and has a reputation for humility and respect in a village." "What kind of person would come next after that?" "A person who is extremely careful of his conduct and speech and always keeps his word. That is a priggish, inferior type of person, but still he can rank below the above two types." "What do you think of the officials today?" "Oh!" said Confucius, "Those rice-bags! They don't count at all."

Yuan Rang (who was reputed to sing at his mother's death) squatted in Confucius' presence and Confucius said, "As a child, you were impudent; after you are grown up, you have absolutely done nothing; and now in your old age you refuse to die! You blackguard!" And Confucius struck him in the shin with a cane.

Baron K'ang Chi was worried about thieves and burglars in the country and consulted Confucius about it. Confucius replied, "If you yourself don't love money the people will not steal, even though you reward the thieves."

Confucius said, "To know what you know and know what you don't know is the characteristic of one who knows."

Confucius said, "A man who has committed a mistake and doesn't correct it is committing another mistake."

Baron Wen Chi said that he always thought three times before he acted. When Confucius heard this, he remarked, "To think twice is quite enough." Confucius said, "A man who has a beautiful soul always has some beautiful things to say, but a man who says beautiful things does not necessarily have a beautiful soul. A true man (or truly great man) will always be found to have courage, but a courageous man will not always be found to have true manhood."

Tsekung asked Confucius, "What would you say if all the people of the village like a person?" "That is not enough," replied Confucius. "What would you say if all the people of a village dislike a person?" "That is not enough," said Confucius. "It is better when the good people of the village like him, and the bad people of the village dislike him."

Confucius said, "It is easy to be rich and not haughty; it is difficult to be poor and not grumble."

Confucius said, "Can you ever imagine a petty soul serving as a minister of the state? Before he gets his post, he is anxious to get it, and after he has got it, he is anxious about losing it, and if he begins to be anxious about losing it, then there is nothing that he will not do."

Confucius said, "Do not worry about people not knowing you, but strive so that you may be worth knowing."

Confucius said, "A gentleman blames himself, while a common man blames others."

Someone said, "What do you think of repaying evil with kindness?" Confucius replied, "Then what are you going to repay kindness with? Repay kindness with kindness, but repay evil with justice (or severity)."

Confucius said, "Men are born pretty much alike, but through their habits they gradually grow further and further apart from each other."

Confucius said, "When you see a good man, try to emulate his example, and when you see a bad man, search yourself for his faults."

His Philosophy

Confucius said, "It is man that makes truth great, and not truth that makes man great."

Tselu asked about the worship of the celestial and earthly spirits. Confucius said, "We don't know yet how to serve men, how can we know about serving the spirits?" "What about death?" was the next question, and Confucius said, "We don't know yet about life, how can we know about death?"

Tsekung asked, "Is there one single word that can serve as a principle of conduct for life?" Confucius replied, "Perhaps the word 'reciprocity' (shu) will do. Do not do unto others what you do not want others to do unto you."

Yen Huei asked about true manhood, and Confucius said, "True manhood consists in realizing your true self and restoring the moral order or discipline (li). If a man can for just one day realize his true self, and restore complete moral discipline, the world will follow him. To be a true man depends on oneself. What has it got to do with others? "

Confucius said, "Humility is near to moral discipline (li); simplicity of character is near to true manhood; and loyalty is near to sincerity of heart. If a man will carefully cultivate these things in his conduct, he may still err a little, but he won't be far from the standard of true manhood. For with humility or pious attitude, a man seldom commits errors; with sincerity of heart, a man is generally reliable; and with simplicity of character, he is usually generous. You seldom make a mistake when you start off from these points."

Confucius said, "The superior man loves his soul; the inferior man loves his property. The superior man always remembers how he was punished for his mistakes; the inferior man always remembers what presents he got."

Confucius said, "The superior man is liberal toward others' opinions, but does not completely agree with them; the inferior man completely agrees with others' opinions, but is not liberal toward them."

Confucius and his followers had to go for days without food in Ch'en, and some of his followers felt ill and were confined to bed. Tselu came to see Confucius in low spirits and asked, "Does the superior man also land in difficulties?" Confucius said, "Yes, the superior man also sometimes finds himself in difficulties, but when an inferior man finds himself in difficulties, he is likely to do anything."

Confucius said, "A gentleman is ashamed that his words are better than his deeds."

Confucius said, "A gentleman is careful about three things: In his youth, when his blood is strong, he is careful about sex. When he is grown up, and his blood is full, he is careful about getting into a fight (or struggle in general). When he is old, and his blood is getting thinner, he is careful about money." (A young man loves women; a middle-aged man loves struggle; and an old man loves money.)

Confucius said, "When a man has more solid worth than polish, he appears uncouth, and when a man has more polish than solid worth, he appears urbane. The proper combination of solid worth and polish alone makes a gentleman."

Confucius said, "I hate things that resemble the real things but are not the real things. I hate cockles because they get mixed up with the corn. I hate the ingratiating fellows, because they get mixed up with the good men. I hate the glib talkers, because they confuse us with honest people. I hate the music of Cheng, because it brings confusion into classical music. I hate the purple color, because it confuses us with the red color. I hate the goody-goodies, because they confuse us with the virtuous people." (Mencius)

Confucius said, "Women and the inferior people are most difficult to deal with. When you are familiar with them, they become cheeky, and when you ignore them, they resent it."

Confucius said, "Guide the people with governmental measures and control or regulate them by the threat of punishment, and the people will try to keep out of jail, but will have no sense of honor or shame. Guide the people by virtue and control or regulate them by *li*, and the people will have a sense of honor and respect."

Confucius said, "In presiding over lawsuits, I'm as good as any man. The thing is to aim so that there should be no lawsuits."

Baron K'ang Ch'i asked Confucius concerning government, and Confucius replied, "Government is merely setting things right. When you yourself lead them by the right example, who dares to go astray?"

Confucius said, "When the ruler himself does what is right, he will have influence over the people without giving commands, and when the ruler himself does not do what is right, all his commands will be of no avail."

Lin Fang asked concerning the foundation of *li*, and Confucius replied, "You are asking an important question! In this matter of rituals or ceremony, rather than be extravagant, be simple. In funeral ceremonies, rather than be expertly familiar, it is more important to have the real sentiment of sorrow."

Confucius said, "That type of scholarship which is bent on remembering things in order to answer people's questions does not qualify one to be a teacher."

Confucius said, "Ah Yu, have you heard of the six sayings about the six shortcomings?" "No," said Tselu. "Sit down, then, and I will tell you. If a man loves kindness, but doesn't love study, his shortcoming will be ignorance. If a man loves wisdom but does not love study, his shortcoming will be having fanciful or unsound ideas. If a man loves honesty and does not love study, his shortcoming will be a tendency to spoil or upset things. If a man loves simplicity but does not love study, his shortcoming will be sheer following of routine. If a man loves courage and does not love study, his shortcoming will be unruliness or violence. If a man loves decision of character and does not love study, his shortcoming will be self-will or headstrong belief in himself."

Confucius said, "Those who are born wise are the highest type of people; those who become wise through learning come next; those who learn by sheer diligence and industry, but with difficulty, come after that. Those who are slow to learn, but still won't learn, are the lowest type of people."

ENDNOTES

1. *li*, here a unit of measure, roughly equal to one third of a mile.
2. *seh*, an ancient musical intrument of twenty-five strings, which is still in use in China.

Introduction

The Book of Songs (1000–600 B.C.)

The *Book of Songs (Shi jing)*, which marks the beginning of Chinese literature, is a collection of poems composed over a period of about four centuries. The *Book of Songs* is traditionally said to have been compiled by Confucius (551–479 B.C.), who selected them in order to reflect the ethical and social cohesion of the people of the Zhou dynasty. The collection of 305 songs was to provide models for proper behavior as well as inspiration for the development of the intellect. From the time of Confucius' compilation until the twentieth century, the *Book of Songs*, one of the Five Classics, was considered an essential part of a cultivated man's learning. Quoting from the *Book of Songs* in ancient China was also a statesman's way of making indirect political commentary. There are even records of state meetings during which the only conversation was in the form of allusions through recitation of portions of the songs.

Although the *Book of Songs* was used by Confucius and generations of his followers for didactic purposes, both the original intent and the authors of these poems remain obscure. The bulk of the songs are said to have originated from the common people and to have been recorded by a literate élite. However, some songs clearly originated from an educated aristocracy.

One intriguing factor in their preservation was a practice in ancient China of sending government ministers to rural areas to gather and record popular songs in order to assess the sentiments and loyalties of their subjects—a kind of early public opinion poll. Several of the songs are, in fact, either hymns of praise or oaths of condemnation directed at local officials.

The 305 songs that constitute the *Book of Songs* are generally divided into four sections: "Ballads of the States" (songs sung by the people of various states), "Lesser Festival Songs" and "Greater Festival Songs" (sung on state occasions), and finally, lyrics sung at sacrifices to the gods and ancestor spirits of the royal house. Most of the songs are no longer than two or three stanzas, with a single refrain repeated throughout. Each line typically contains only four words. Unfortunately, the music that the songs were set to was lost around the first century A.D., but the rhythms, alliteration, and rhymes of a reading of the ancient words, even in modern Chinese, still makes for lively entertainment.

The *Book of Songs* is rich in imagery and figurative language juxtaposing the singer's inner state and various natural phenomena. Depictions of plants, water, or animals either stand in contrast to the personal voice or serve as a symbol of the singer's predicament. In the earliest commentary on the *Book of Songs* (the Mao text written in the first century B.C.), such language was interpreted politically. Most of the lyrics, then, were said to refer to virtuous or evil rulers. Even songs that seemed quite personal in nature, such as the complaint of a jilted lover, were considered to be political satires. It was not until several centuries later, with the work of the Song scholar Zhu Xi (1130–1200), that the romantic nature of some of the songs was accepted, and the rigid political interpretation was relaxed. Whether the songs are political comments or poetic metaphors of earthly sentiments, they are terse yet rich in content, making them enjoyable reading and providing poignant, timeless insight into human nature. (JK)

BIBLIOGRAPHY

Li, Zehou. *The Path of Beauty: A Study of Chinese Aesthetics.* Trans. Gong Lizeng. Oxford: Oxford University Press, 1995.

Van Zoeren, Steven Jay. *Poetry and Personality: Reading, Exegesis, and Hermeneutics in Traditional China.* Stanford: Stanford University Press, 1991.

Waley, Arthur, trans. *The Book of Songs.* New York: Grove Press, 1960.

Watson, Burton. *Early Chinese Literature.* New York: Columbia University, 1962.

Yang, Mu. *From Ritual to Allegory: Seven Essays in Early Chinese Poetry.* Hong Kong: Chinese University Press, 1988.

Yu, Pauline. *The Reading of Imagery in the Chinese Poetic Tradition.* Princeton: Princeton University Press, 1987.

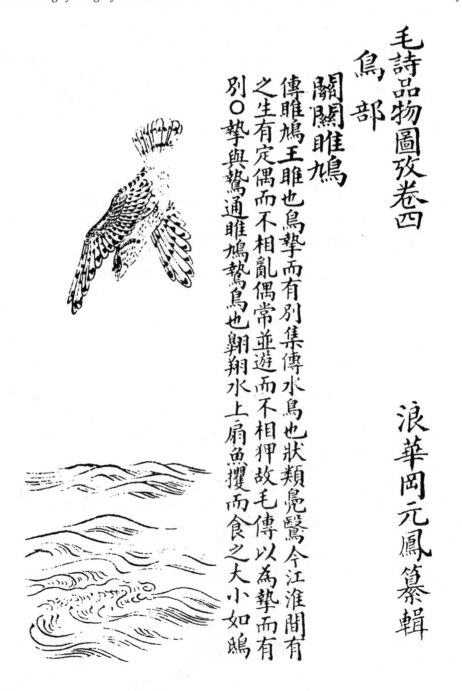

毛詩品物圖攷卷四

鳥部

浪華岡元鳳纂輯

關關雎鳩

傳雎鳩王雎也鳥摯而有別集傳水鳥也狀類鳧鷖今江淮間有之生有定偶而不相亂偶常並遊而不相狎故毛傳以為摯而有別○摯與鷙通雎鳩鷙鳥也翱翔水上扇魚攫而食之大小如鴟

from The Book of Songs

Translated from the Chinese by Arthur Waley

COURTSHIP

3

Hey-ho, he is splendid!
Magnificent in stature,
Noble his brow,
His lovely eyes so bright,
Nimble in running,
A bowman unsurpassed.

Hey-ho, he is glorious!
Lovely eyes so clear,
Perfect in courtesy,
Can shoot all day at a target
And never miss the mark.
Truly a man of my clan.

Hey-ho, he is lovely!
His clear brow well-rounded,
When he dances, never losing his place,
When he shoots, always piercing.
Swift his arrows fly
To quell mischief on every side.

4

Sun in the east!
This lovely man
Is in my house,
Is in my home,
His foot is upon my doorstep.

Moon in the east!
This lovely man
Is in my bower,[1]
Is in my bower,
His foot is upon my threshold.

6

In skins of the young lamb
Sewn with white silk of five and twenty strands,
Going home to supper from the palace
With step grave and slow!

In hides of the young lamb
Sewn with white silk of a hundred strands,
With step grave and slow
From the palace going to his supper!

In skins of the young lamb sewn
With white silk of four hundred strands,
With step grave and slow
Going home to supper from the palace!

The more numerous the strands the more potent the personal magic (tê) of the wearer. Thread of a fixed number of strands is often used in attaching amulets, charms, etc.

86

A splendid woman and upstanding;
Brocade she wore, over an unlined coat,
Daughter of the Lord of Ch'i,
Wife of the Lord of Wei.
Sister of the Crown Prince of Ch'i,
Called sister-in-law by the Lord of Hsing,
Calling the Lord of T'an her brother-in-law.

Hands white as rush-down,
Skin like lard,
Neck long and white as the tree-grub,
Teeth like melon seeds,
Lovely head, beautiful brows.

Oh, the sweet smile dimpling,
The lovely eyes so black and white.

This splendid lady takes her ease;
She rests where the fields begin.
Her four steeds prance,
The red trappings flutter.
Screened by fans of pheasant-feather she is led to
  Court
Oh, you Great officers, retire early,
Do not fatigue our lord.

Where the water of the river, deep and wide,
Flows northward in strong course,
In the fish-net's swish and swirl
Sturgeon, snout-fish leap and lash.
Reeds and sedges tower high.
All her ladies are tall-coiffed;
All her knights, doughty men.

*This poem celebrates the most famous wedding of
Chinese antiquity, that of Chuang Chiang, daughter of the Lord of Ch'i (northern Shantung), who
married the Lord of Wei in 757 B.C. Wei centred
round the modern Weihwei in northern Honan.
Hsing was farther north, on the borders of Honan
and southern Hopeh. T'an was the modern Ch'êng-
tzu-ai, near Lungshan, in central Shantung. One
has to bear in mind that the bridegroom and bride
are in other parts of the world often treated as
though they were a king and queen. It is not impossible that such a song as this, though royal in origin, was afterwards sung at ordinary people's weddings.*

87

"Fair, fair," cry the ospreys
On the island in the river.
Lovely is this noble lady,
Fit bride for our lord.

In patches grows the water mallow;
To left and right one must seek it.
Shy was this noble lady;
Day and night he sought her.

Sought her and could not get her,
Day and night he grieved.
Long thoughts, oh, long unhappy thoughts,
Now on his back, now tossing on to his side.

In patches grows the water mallow;
To left and right one must gather it.
Shy is this noble lady;
With great zithern and little we hearten her.

In patches grows the water mallow;
To left and right one must choose it.
Shy is this noble lady;
With gongs and drums we will gladden her.

A Blessing
173

Far off at that wayside pool we draw;
Ladle there and pour out here,
And with it we can steam our rice.
All happiness to our lord,
Father and mother of his people.

Far off at that wayside pool we draw;
Ladle there and pour out here,
And with it we can rinse our earthen bowls.
All happiness to our lord,
Father of his people.

Far off at that wayside pool we draw;
Ladle there and pour out here,
And with it we can rinse our lacquer bowls.
All happiness to our lord,
Support of his people.

*The meaning of the comparison is, I think, that though
our lord is far above us, we are all able to share in his tê.*

Contentment
193

The fish are at home, at home among their
  water-plants,
Beautifully streaked are their heads.
The king is at home, at home in Hao,[2]
Content and happy he drinks his wine.

The fish are at home, at home among their
  water-plants,
Very pliant are their tails.
The king is at home, at home in Hao,
Drinking his wine, happy and content.

The fish are at home, at home among their
water-plants,
Snuggling close to their reeds.
The king is at home, at home in Hao,
Very soft he lies.

THE CLAN FEAST
194

The flowers of the cherry-tree,
Are they not truly splendid?
Of men that now are,
None equals a brother.

When death and mourning affright us
Brothers are very clear;
As "upland" and "lowland" form a pair,
So "elder brother" and "younger brother" go
together.

There are wagtails[3] on the plain;
When brothers are hard pressed
Even good friends
At the most do but heave a sigh.

Brothers may quarrel within the walls.
But outside they defend one another from insult;
Whereas even good friends
Pay but short heed.

But when the times of mourning or violence are
over,
When all is calm and still,
Even brothers
Are not the equal of friends.

Set out your dishes and meat-stands,
Drink wine to your fill;
All you brothers are here together,
Peaceful, happy, and mild.

DYNASTIC SONGS
227

Pity me, your child,
Inheritor of a House unfinished,
Lonely and in trouble.
O august elders,
All my days I will be pious,
Bearing in mind those august forefathers

That ascend and descend in the courtyard.
Yes, I your child,
Early and late will be reverent.
O august kings,
The succession shall not stop!

Nos. 227–231 are all songs from the legend of King Ch'eng. It is said that when he came to the throne he was a mere child and had to be helped in his rule by his uncle, the Duke of Chou. He also had wicked uncles, who rebelled against him, making common cause with the son of the last Shang king. The story in its main features is probably historical. But the part played by the Duke of Chou has perhaps been exaggerated by the Confucians, who made the duke into a sort of patron saint of their school.

228

Here, then, I come,
Betake myself to the bright ancestors:
"Oh, I am not happy.
I have not yet finished my task.
Help me to complete it.
In continuing your plans I have been idle.
But I, your child,
Am not equal to the many troubles that
assail my house.
You that roam in the courtyard,[4] up and down,
You that ascend and descend in His house,
Grant me a boon, august elders!
Protect this my person, save it with your
light."

229

Reverence, reverence!
By Heaven all is seen;
Its charge is not easy to hold.
Do not say it is high, high above,
Going up and down about its own business.
Day in, day out it watches us here.
I, a little child,
Am not wise or reverent.
But as days pass, months go by,
I learn from those that have bright
splendour.
O Radiance, O Light,
Help these my strivings;
Show me how to manifest the ways of
power.

230

I will take warning,
Will guard against ills to come.
Never again will I bump myself and bang
    myself
With bitter pain for my reward.
Frail was that reed-warbler;
It flew away a great bird.
I, not equal to the troubles of my house,
Must still perch upon the smartweed.

*When the reed-warbler grows up it turns into an
eagle. Till then it perches in a nest precariously hung
between the stems of reeds or other water-plants,
liable to be hurled to disaster at the first coming of
wind or rain. So the boy king, when he gets older, will
pounce upon his enemies. But for the present he must
be content to perch upon the smartweed, i.e., put up
with his troubles.*

231

Oh, kite-owl, kite-owl,
You have taken my young.
Do not destroy my house.
With such love, such toil
To rear those young ones I strove!

Before the weather grew damp with rain
I scratched away the bark of that mulberry-tree
And twined it into window and door.
"Now, you people down below,
If any of you dare affront me. . . ."

My hands are all chafed
With plucking so much rush flower;
With gathering so much bast
My mouth is all sore.
And still I have not house or home!

My wings have lost their gloss.
My tail is all bedraggled.
My house is all to pieces,
    tossed and battered by wind and rain.
My only song, a cry of woe!

*This poem is traditionally associated with the legend
of King Ch'êng and his protector, the Duke of Chou.
It figures in the Metal-clasped Box,[5] a fairly late work
which, however, incorporates a good deal of early
legend. The song is said to have been given to King*
*Ch'êng by his good uncle. Naturally the kite-owl,
always classed as a "wicked bird" by the Chinese,
symbolizes the wicked, rebellious uncles. The persecuted bird, who is the speaker in the poem, would seem
most naturally to be the Duke of Chou, and the young
whom the bird had reared with such love and care
would then be the boy king. But the allegory does not
work out very closely, and it is possible that the song
had a quite different origin, and was only later utilized as an ornament to the legend of King Ch'êng.*

232

Broken were our axes
And chipped our hatchets.[6]
But since the Duke of Chou came to the
    East
Throughout the kingdoms all is well.
He has shown compassion to us people,
He has greatly helped us.

Broken were our axes
And chipped our hoes.
But since the Duke of Chou came to the
    East
The whole land has been changed.
He has shown compassion to us people,
He has greatly blessed us.

Broken were our axes
And chipped our chisels.
But since the Duke of Chou came to the
    East
All the kingdoms are knit together.
He has shown compassion to us people,
He has been a great boon to us.

A LEGEND
244

When he built the Magic Tower,
When he planned it and founded it,
All the people worked at it;
In less than a day they finished it.

When he built it, there was no goading;
Yet the people came in their throngs.
The king was in the Magic Park,
    where doe and stag lay hid.

Doe and stag at his coming leapt and
    bounded;
The white herons gleamed so sleek.
The king was by the Magic Pool,
Where the fish sprang so lithe.

On the upright posts and cross-beams with
    their spikes
Hang the big drums and gongs.
Oh, well-ranged are the drums and gongs,
And merry is the Moated Mound.

Oh, well-ranged are the drums and gongs!
And merry is the Moated Mound.
Bang, bang go the fish-skin drums;
The sightless and the eyeless[7] ply their skill.

*The Magic Tower was built by King Wên near his
capital at Hao, close to the modern Sianfu. The
Moated Mound was a holy place surrounded by
water, where the sons of the Chou royal house
were trained in the accomplishments of manhood.
An inscription[8] describes an early Chou king as
boating on the waters of the Moated Mound, where
he shoots a large wild-goose. The Lord of Hsing,
who follows him in a "boat with red banners,"
gives the bird a coup de grâce, which suggests that
the king had only managed to wing it.*

A LAMENT
276

Big rat, big rat,
Do not gobble our millet!
Three years we have slaved for you.
Yet you take no notice of us.
At last we are going to leave you
And go to that happy land;
Happy land, happy land,
Where we shall have our place.

Big rat, big rat,
Do not gobble our corn!

Three years we have slaved for you,
Yet you give us no credit.
At last we are going to leave you
And go to that happy kingdom;
Happy kingdom, happy kingdom,
Where we shall get our due.

Big rat, big rat,
Do not eat our rice-shoots!
Three years we have slaved for you.
Yet you did nothing to reward us.
At last we are going to leave you
And go to those happy borders;
Happy borders, happy borders,
Where no sad songs are sung.

ENDNOTES

1. The word that I have translated "bower" means the back part of the house, where the women lived. The sun and moon are symbols of his beauty, and do not mark (as one might at first sight suppose) the time of his visit.

2. Said to have been the capital of Chou in the early days of the dynasty. When this poem was written, Hao had probably become a pleasure-palace, a sort of Versailles. We do not know at what date the later conception of a "Capital" began. When we discuss where the earliest kings had their "capital," we are perhaps committing an anachronism. Possibly in early times the centre of government was where the king was at the moment.

3. Symbols of agitation.

4. Of God.

5. One of the books of the *Shu Ching*.

6. i.e., the whole State was in a bad way. The Duke of Chou was sent to rule in Lu, the southern part of Shantung.

7. i.e., blind musicians.

8. Karlgren, B. 14.

———————— *Questions for Consideration* ————————

Using complete sentences, provide brief answers for the following questions.

1. It is generally agreed that the poems in the *Book of Songs* grew out of an oral tradition. Drawing on your reading of Homeric poetry, find common elements or techniques that tend to confirm the oral origin of these Chinese poems.

    _____

    _____

    _____

    _____

    _____

2. What are some of the indications in these poems that they belong to an early stage of human culture?

    _____

    _____

    _____

    _____

    _____

3. Look for and record images and other stylistic devices used in two or more of the poems in this selection.

    _____

    _____

    _____

    _____

    _____

—————— *Writing Critically* ——————

Select one of the topics listed below and compose a 500-word essay that discusses the topic fully. Support your thesis with evidence from the text and with critical and/or historical material. Use the space below for preparing to write the essay.

1. Confucius is often credited with having selected and compiled the *Book of Songs*. This view is probably not true, but many readers of the *Book of Songs* claim to find a number of values and ethical principles that are consistent with the Confucian tradition. After reviewing the section in *Literary Perspectives* on Confucius, discuss the *Book of Songs* in relation to the Confucian code of values and behavior.

2. Several of the excerpts you have read deal with courtship and marriage. Discuss statements made or suggested in the *Book of Songs* concerning love relationships and the relative status of men and women. Be sure to include your reaction to the overall outlook on the social roles of men and women.

3. After consulting some of the secondary sources listed above, write an extended analysis of one of the more complicated or substantial poems in the *Book of Songs*.

4. China has sometimes been called the "land of poetry" because of the huge number of poems the country has produced over a period of nearly three thousand years. While the *Book of Songs* sums up one great age of Chinese poetry, the selections from Tang dynasty poets (618–907 A.D.) are representative of another. After reading through the selections from Tang poetry in this anthology, write an essay comparing some of the major traits of the poetry of these two eras.

Prewriting Space:

_____

_____

_____

_____

_____

_____

_____

_____

_____

_____

_____

_____

_____

_____

Introduction

Publius Vergilius Maro (Virgil) (70–19 B.C.)

Virgil was born in 70 B.C. near Mantua in northern Italy. During Virgil's youth, as the Roman Republic neared its end, the political and military situation in Italy was confused and often calamitous. The civil war between Marius and Sulla had been succeeded by conflict between Pompey and Julius Caesar for supreme power. When Virgil was 20, Caesar with his armies swooped south from Gaul, crossed the Rubicon, and began the series of civil wars that were not to end until Augustus' victory at Actium in 31 B.C. (Burns, Ralph, Lerner, and Meacham, 247–249). Hatred and fear of civil war is powerfully expressed by both Virgil and his contemporary Horace. The key to a proper understanding of the Augustan Age and its poets lies, indeed, in a proper understanding of the turmoil that had preceded the Augustan peace. In 37 B.C. he published his first important work, the *Eclogues*, pastoral poems. One eclogue in particular stands out as having relevance to the contemporary situation, and this is the fourth (sometimes called the Messianic, because it was later regarded as prophetic of Christianity). It is an elevated poem, prophesying the birth of a child who will bring back the Golden Age, banish sin, and restore peace. It was clearly written at a time when the clouds of civil war seemed to be lifting; it can be dated firmly to 41–40 B.C., and it seems most likely that Virgil refers to an expected child of the triumvir Antony and his wife Octavia, sister of Octavian. But, though a specific occasion may be allocated to the poem, it goes beyond the particular and, in symbolic terms, presents a vision of world harmony, which was, to some extent, destined to be realized under Augustus. In 30 B.C. he completed the *Georgics* which glorified farming. *The Aeneid* was started when Virgil was 40 years old in 59 B.C. and finished eleven years later. He asked on his deathbed that it be destroyed as it needed three years of revision. Augustus refused and it was first transcribed about 17 B.C. by order of Augustus.

The *Aeneid* celebrates the glory of Rome by recording its establishment and tracing its ancestry back to Aeneas, the Trojan hero. After Troy fell, Aeneas became the leader of the surviving Trojans. He was given the divine mission of building a new city which was preordained by fate. Guided by the hand of fate, Aeneas and his followers set out in twenty-one ships to find this new home. Accompanied by his father and his son, Aeneas wandered for seven years until he arrived at the coast of western Sicily, where his father died. The epic starts when the Trojans are ready to begin their voyage north from Sicily to Italy.

Thus Virgil's epic begins seven years after the end of the Trojan War and ends with the establishment of the Trojans in Italy. To Dido, queen of Carthage, Aeneas recounts the incident of the treacherous Wooden Horse, the apparitions on the night of Troy's fall, and the flight which became a quest for the real homeland of the Trojans. Many obstacles block Aeneas: the wrath of Juno, the passion of Dido, the weariness of his followers, his own feelings of exile and rootlessness. When he reaches the lowest point of despair, he is taken to Hades for advice from his father and for a vision of his descendants—virtually a roll call of Roman history. Strengthened, he returns to lead his thinning band of followers to Italy, where the hotheaded Turnus, in defiance of the oracles and against the better judgment of the King, provokes war. But the new Aeneas does not falter; he has now a clear view of his mission and an unshakable will to accomplish it.

The general quality of the *Aeneid* has been eloquently described by a modern poet, Mark Van Doren in his *The Noble* Voice:

A political subject—in this case the great role of Rome as coordinator and pacifier of world society, and more particularly the great place of Augustus at the goal of so much progress—might seem to have demanded a forth right, confident, and masculine narrative, clearly ordered and precisely phrased. Instead of that we get in the Aeneid indirect lighting and misty effects. . . . The prevailing hue is gray, and the time when the poet is most at home is twilight or nightfall, when things have become difficult to see in their hard, natural outlines. The result, given Virgil's genius, is a number of passages washed over with the loveliest tones the minor lyre has ever commanded.

The enthusiasm that Virgil felt for the reborn Rome promised by Augustus' regime is often reflected in the poem. The sonorous and awe-inspiring prophecy by Jupiter, (l. 257 ff.) giving a picture of Rome's divinely inspired destiny, has a moving patriotic impact: "To these I set no bounds in space or time—I have given them rule without end" (278–279); and again, under Augustus, "Then shall the harsh generations be softened, and wars shall be laid aside" (291). The speech ends with a memorable image depicting the personified figure of Frenzy in chains, gnashing its bloodstained teeth in vain. At the end of the sixth book, Aeneas visits the underworld, and there pass before his eyes the figures of heroes from Roman history, waiting to be born. The ghost of his father (Anchises) describes them to him and ends by defining the Roman mission as one concerned with government and civilization (compared with the Greek achievement in art and literature and theoretical science). "Rule the people with your sway, spare the conquered, and war down the proud": this is the vision of Rome's destiny that the emperor Augustus and the poet Virgil had before them—that Rome was divinely appointed first to conquer the world in war and then to spread civilization and the rule of law among the peoples. As Horace told the Romans in one of his odes, "Because you are servants of the gods, you are masters on earth."

Homer was Virgil's model for the epic. The first six books of the *Aeneid*, like the *Odyssey*, are a narration of a man's wandering before he reaches his destined home; and the last six books deal with battles, as does the *Iliad*. The hero, Aeneas, was a minor character in the *Iliad* on the side of the Trojans. Virgil owes a heavy debt, therefore, to Homer for the framework of his plot, for incidents, scenery, characters, and similes. Virgil adopted Homer's device of including Olympian gods as characters, but he did so for moral and political purposes. The literary historian Henry T. Rowell points out that in the *Aeneid*,

we learn that we are dealing with a poem in which the traditional materials have been reworked to serve far different ends, that much is present of which Homer could not have dreamed, and that the poetry is no pale imitation of the Homeric but carries the stamp of the originality of a master poet.

Virgil himself replied to anyone who might charge him with plagiarism by saying, "You will find it easier to rob Hercules of his club than Homer of a single verse."

Some specific examples of Virgil's borrowings from the *Iliad* and *Odyssey* are these: the many battle scenes, the catalogues of troops and chiefs, the armor of Aeneas which is similar to that of Achilles, the funeral games for Anchises, which resemble those for Patroclus, midnight reconnoitering by Nisus and Euryalus (Diomedes and Odysseus), the unsuccessful embassy to Diomedes (like that to Achilles) and the duel at the end between Aeneas and Turnus, resembling that between Achilles and Hector. Some borrowings from the *Odyssey* are: the storm and shipwreck, the hero's remaining with Dido (similar to Odysseus' remaining with Calypso), visiting Hades and being directed by Sibyl (Circe), and Anchises' predictions of the future (like those of Teiresias).

To Romans until the end of their civilization, Virgil was the voice of living Rome as no other Roman was—not Cicero or Horace or Livy or Seneca. Ignoring Virgil's immense respect for Homer, his contemporaries considered the *Aeneid* superior to the *Iliad*. Generations of Roman school children studied his works as textbooks; poets modeled their work upon his; soldiers and statesmen looked to him for inspiration—all this, not only because of the excellence of his poetry but also because his works epitomized the age in which he lived. The *Aeneid* inspired the Romans to greatness, enshrining for them their heritage and responsibility. What Augustus and Romans wanted most, Virgil celebrated: lasting peace and order. It was a dream Roman civilization died still holding; but while Rome lived, the *Aeneid* was its epic, a national epic that fitted the Roman sense of grandeur. (CDH)

BIBLIOGRAPHY

Brown, Robert D. "The Homeric Background to a Virgilian Repetition." *American Journal of Philology*, 114 (1993): 182–6.

Duckworth, George Eckel. *Structural Patterns and Proportions in Virgil's* Aeneid. Ann Arbor: University of Michigan Press, 1962.

Duff, John Wight. *A Literary History of Rome—the Golden Age*. New York: Charles Scribner's Sons, 1927.

Glover, Terrot Reaveley. *Virgil*. New York: Macmillan Company, 1912.

Poschl, Viktor. *The Art of Virgil*. Ann Arbor: University of Michigan Press, 1962.

Tatum, James. "Allusion and Interpretation in Aeneid." *American Journal of Philology*, 105 (1984): 434–52.

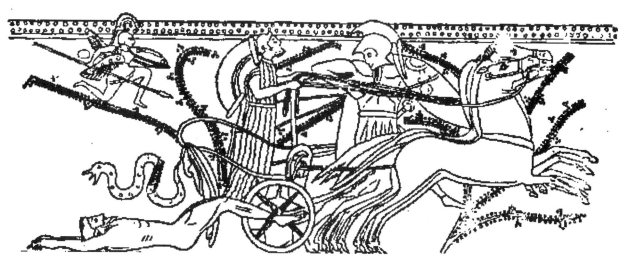

Hector's Body Dragged behind the Chariot of Achilles

from the Aeneid of Virgil

Virgil
Translated into English by Theodore C. Williams

Book II

A general silence fell; and all gave ear,
While, from his lofty station at the feast,
Father Æneas with these words began:—

A grief unspeakable thy gracious word,
O sovereign lady, bids my heart live o'er:
How Asia's glory and afflicted throne
The Greek flung down; which woeful scene I
    saw,
And bore great part in each event I tell.
But O! in telling, what Dolopian churl,
Or Myrmidon, or gory follower
Of grim Ulysses could the tears restrain?
'T is evening; lo! the dews of night begin
To fall from heaven, and yonder sinking stars
Invite to slumber. But if thy heart yearn
To hear in brief of all our evil days
And Troy's last throes, although in memory
Makes my soul shudder and recoil in pain,
I will essay it.

        Wearied of the war,
And by ill-fortune crushed, year after year,
The kings of Greece, by Pallas' skill divine,
Build a huge horse, a thing of mountain size,
With timbered ribs of fir. They falsely say
It has been vowed to Heaven for safe return,
And spread this lie abroad. Then they conceal
Choice bands of warriors in the deep, dark side,
And fill the caverns of that monstrous womb
With arms and soldiery. In sight of Troy
Lies Tenedos, an island widely famed
And opulent, ere Priam's kingdom fell,
But a poor haven now, with anchorage
Not half secure; 't was thitherward they sailed,
And lurked unseen by that abandoned shore.
We deemed them launched away and sailing far,
Bound homeward for Mycenæ. Teucria then

Threw off her grief inveterate; all her gates
Swung wide; exultant went we forth, and saw
The Dorian camp untenanted, the siege
Abandoned, and the shore without a keel.
"Here!" cried we, "the Dolopian pitched; the host
Of fierce Achilles here; here lay the fleet;
And here the battling lines to conflict ran."
Others, all wonder, scan the gift of doom
By virgin Pallas given, and view with awe
That horse which loomed so large. Thymoetes
    then
Bade led it through the gates, and set on high
Within our citadel, —or traitor he,
Or tool of fate in Troy's predestined fall.
But Capys, as did all of wiser heart,
Bade hurl into the sea the false Greek gift,
Or underneath it thrust a kindling flame,
Or pierce the hollow ambush of its womb
With probing spear. Yet did the multitude
Veer round from voice to voice and doubt of all.
Then from the citadel, conspicuous,
Laocoön, with all his following choir,
Hurried indignant down; and from afar
Thus hailed the people: "O unhappy men!
What madness this? Who deems our foemen
    fled?
Think ye the gifts of Greece can lack for guile?
Have ye not known Ulysses? The Achæan
Hides, caged in yonder beams; or this is reared
For engin'ry on our proud battlements,
To spy upon our roof-tops, or descend
In ruin on the city. 'T is a snare.
Trust not this horse, O Troy, whate'er it bode!
I fear the Greeks, though gift on gift they bear."

So saying, he whirled with ponderous javelin
A sturdy stroke straight at the rounded side
Of the great, jointed beast. A tremor struck

Its towering form, and through the cavernous
    womb
Rolled loud, reverberate rumbling, deep and
    long.
If heaven's decree, if our own wills, that hour,
Had not been fixed on woe, his spear had
    brought
A bloody slaughter on our ambushed foe,
And Troy were standing on the earth this day!
O Priam's towers, ye were unfallen still!

But, lo! with hands fast bound behind, a youth
By clamorous Dardan shepherds haled along,
Was brought before our King, to this sole end
A self-surrendered captive, that he might,
Although a nameless stranger, cunningly
Deliver to the Greek the gates of Troy.
His firm-set mind flinched not from either
    goal,—
Success in crime, or on swift death to fall.
The thronging Trojan youth made haste his way
From every side, all eager to see close
Their captive's face, and flout with emulous
    scorn.
Hear now what Greek deception is, and learn
From one dark wickedness the whole. For he,
A mark for every eye, defenceless, dazed,
Stood staring at our Phrygian hosts, and cried:
"Woe worth the day! What ocean or what shore
Will have me now? What desperate path remains
For miserable me? Now have I lost
All footholds with the Greeks, and o'er my head
Troy's furious sons call bloody vengeance
    down."
Such groans and anguish turned all rage away
And stayed our lifted hands. We bade him tell
His birth, his errand, and from whence might be

Such hope of mercy for a foe in chains.
Then fearing us no more, this speech he dared:
"O King! I will confess, whate'er befall,
The whole unvarnished truth, I will not hide
My Grecian birth. Yea, thus will I begin.
For Fortune has brought wretched Sinon low;
But never shall her cruelty impair
His honor and his truth. Perchance the name
Of Palamedes, Belus' glorious son,
Has come by rumor to your listening ears;
Whom by false witness and conspiracy,
Because his counsel was not for this war,
The Greeks condemned, though guiltless, to his
    death,
And now make much lament for him they slew.
I, his companion, of his kith and kin,
Sent hither by my humble sire's command,
Followed his arms and fortunes from my youth.
Long as his throne endured, and while he throve
In conclave with his kingly peers, we twain
Some names and lustre bore; but afterward,
Because that cheat Ulysses envied him
(Ye know the deed), he from this world
    withdrew,
And I in gloom and tribulation sore
Lived miserably on, lamenting loud
My lost friend's blameless fall. A fool was I
That kept not these lips closed; but I had vowed
That if a conqueror home to Greece I came,
I would avenge. Such words moved wrath, and
    were
The first shock of my ruin; from that hour,
Ulysses whispered slander and alarm;
Breathed doubt and malice into all men's ears,
And darkly plotted how to strike his blow.
Nor rest had he, till Calchas, as his tool,—
But why unfold this useless, cruel story?

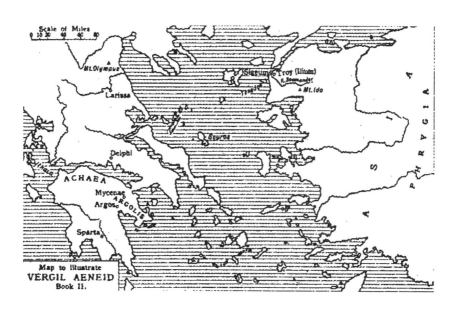

Map to Illustrate
VERGIL AENEID
Book II.

Why make delay? Ye count all sons of Greece
Arrayed as one; and to have heard thus far
Suffices you. Take now your ripe revenge!
Ulysses smiles and Atreus' royal sons
With liberal price your deed of blood repay."

We ply him then with passionate appeal
And question all his cause: of guilt so dire
Or such Greek guile we harbored not the
    thought.
So on he prates, with well-feigned grief and fear,
And from his lying heart thus told his tale:
"Full oft the Greeks had fain achieved their
    flight,
And raised the Trojan siege, and sailed away
War-wearied quite. O, would it had been so!
Full oft the wintry tumult of the seas
Did wall them round, and many a swollen storm
Their embarcation stayed. But chiefly when,
All fitly built of beams of maple fair,
This horse stood forth,—what thunders filled the
    skies!
With anxious fears we sent Eurypylus
To ask Apollo's word; and from the shrine
He brings the sorrowful commandment home:
By flowing blood and by a virgin slain
The wild winds were appeased, when first ye
    came,
Ye sons of Greece, to Ilium's distant shore.
Through blood ye must return. Let some Greek
    life
'Your expiation be.'

    "The popular ear
The saying caught, all spirits were dimmed o'er;
Cold doubt and horror through each bosom ran,
Asking what fate would do, and on what wretch
Apollo's choice would fall. Ulysses, then,
Amid the people's tumult and acclaim,
Thrust Calchas forth, some prophecy to tell
To all the throng: he asked him o'er and o'er
What Heaven desired. Already not a few
Foretold the murderous plot, and silently
Watched the dark doom upon my life impend.
Twice five long days the seer his lips did seal,
And hid himself, refusing to bring forth
His word of guile, and name what wretch should
    die.
At last, reluctant, and all loudly urged
By false Ulysses, he fulfils their plot,
And, lifting up his voice oracular,
Points out myself the victim to be slain.
Nor did one voice oppose. The mortal stroke
Horribly hanging o'er each coward head
Was changed to one man's ruin, and their hearts
Endured it well. Soon rose th' accursèd morn;

The bloody ritual was ready; salt
Was sprinkled on the sacred loaf; my brows
Were bound with fillets for the offering.
But I escaped that death—yes! I deny not!
I cast my fetters off, and darkling lay
Concealed all night in lake-side sedge and mire,
Awaiting their departure, if perchance
They should in truth set sail. But nevermore
Shall my dear, native country greet these eyes.
No more my father or my tender babes
Shall I behold. Nay, haply their own lives
Are forfeit, when my foemen take revenge
For my escape, and slay those helpless ones,
In expiation of my guilty deed.
O, by yon powers in heaven which witness truth,
By aught in this dark world remaining now
Of spotless human faith and innocence,
I do implore thee look with pitying eye
On these long suffering my heart hath borne.
O, pity! I deserve not what I bear."

Pity and pardon to his tears we gave,
And spared his life. King Priam bade unbind
The fettered hands and loose those heavy chains
That pressed him sore; then with benignant mien
Addressed him thus: "Whate'er thy place or
    name,
Forget the people thou hast lost, and be
Henceforth our countryman. But tell me true!
What means the monstrous fabric of this horse?
Who made it? Why? What offering to Heaven,
Or engin'ry of conquest may it be?"
He spake; and in reply, with skilful guile,
Greek that he was! the other lifted up
His hands, now freed and chainless, to the skies:
"O ever-burning and inviolate fires,
Witness my word! O altars and sharp steel,
Whose curse I fled, O fillets of the gods,
Which bound a victim's helpless forehead, hear!
'Tis lawful now to break the oath that gave
My troth to Greece. To execrate her kings
Is now my solemn duty. Their whole plot
I publish to the world. No fatherland
And no allegiance binds me any more.
O Troy, whom I have saved, I bid thee keep
The pledge of safety by good Priam given,
For my true tale shall my rich ransom be.

"The Greeks' one hope, since first they opened
    war,
Was Pallas' grace and power. But from the day
When Diomed, bold scorner of the gods,
And false Ulysses, author of all guile,
Rose up and violently bore away
Palladium, her holy shrine, hewed down
The sentinels of her acropolis,

And with polluted, gory-hands dared touch
The goddess' virgin fillets, white and pure,—
Thenceforth, I say, the courage of the Greeks
Ebbed utterly away; their strength was lost,
And favoring Pallas all her grace withdrew.
No dubious sign she gave. Scarce had they set
Her statue in our camp, when glittering flame
Flashed from the staring eyes; from all its limbs
Salt sweat ran forth; three times (O wondrous tale!)
It gave a sudden skyward leap, and made
Prodigious trembling of her lance and shield.
The prophet Calchas bade us straightway take
Swift flight across the sea for fate had willed
The Trojan citadel should never fall
By Grecian arm, till once more they obtain
New oracles at Argos, and restore
That god the round ships hurried o'er the sea.
Now in Mycenæ, whither they are fled,
New help of heaven they find, and forge anew
The means of war. Back hither o'er the waves
They suddenly will come. So Calchas gave
The meaning of the god. Warned thus, they reared
In place of Pallas' desecrated shrine
Yon image of the horse, to expiate
The woeful sacrilege. Calchas ordained
That they should build a thing of monstrous size
Of jointed beams, and rear it heavenward,
So might it never pass your gates, nor come
Inside your walls, nor anywise restore
Unto the Trojans their lost help divine.
For had your hands Minerva's gift profaned,
A ruin horrible—O, may the gods
Bring it on Calchas rather!—would have come
On Priam's throne and all the Phrygian power.
But if your hands should lift the holy thing
To your own citadel, then Asia's host
Would hurl aggression upon Pelop's land,
And all that curse on our own nation fall."

Thus Sinon's guile and practiced perjury
Our doubt dispelled. His stratagems and tears
Wrought victory where neither Tydeus' son,
Nor mountain-bred Achilles could prevail,
Nor ten years' war, nor fleets a thousand strong.
But now a vaster spectacle of fear
Burst over us, to vex our startled souls,
Laocoön, that day by cast of lot
Priest unto Neptune, was in act to slay
A huge bull at the god's appointed fane.
Lo! o'er the tranquil deep from Tenedos
Appeared a pair (I shudder as I tell)
Of vastly coiling serpents, side by side,
Stretching along the waves, and to the shore
Taking swift course; their necks were lifted high,

Their gory dragon-crests o'ertopped the waves;
All else, half seen, trailed low along the sea,
While with loud cleavage of the foaming brine
Their monstrous backs wound forward fold on fold.
Soon they made land; the furious bright eyes
Glowed with ensanguined fire; their quivering tongues
Lapped hungrily the hissing, gruesome jaws.
All terror-pale we fled. Unswerving then
The monsters to Laocoön made way.
First round the tender limbs of his two sons
Each dragon coiled, and on the shrinking flesh
Fixed fast and fed. Then seized they on the sire,
Who flew to aid, a javelin in his hand,
Embracing close in bondage serpentine
Twice round the waist; and twice in scaly grasp
Around his neck, and o'er him grimly peered
With lifted head and crest; he, all the while,
His holy fillet fouled with venomous blood,
Tore at his fetters with a desperate hand,
And lifted up such agonizing voice,
As when a bull, death-wounded, seeks to flee
The sacrificial altar, and thrusts back
From his doomed head the ill-aimed, glancing blade.
Then swiftly writhed the dragon-pair away
Unto the templed height, and in the shrine
Of cruel Pallas sure asylum found
Beneath the goddess' feet and orbèd shield.

Such trembling horror as we ne'er had known
Seized now on every heart. "Of his vast guilt
Laocoön," they say, "receives reward
For he with most abominable spear
Did strike and violate that blessèd wood.
Yon statue to the temple! Ask the grace
Of glorious Pallas!" So the people cried
In general acclaim. Ourselves did make
A breach within our walls and opened wide
The ramparts of our city. One and all
Were girded for the task. Smooth-gliding wheels
Were 'neath its feet; great ropes stretched round its neck,
Till o'er our walls the fatal engine climbed,
Pregnant with men-at-arms. On every side
Fair youths and maidens made a festal song,
And hauled the ropes with merry heart and gay.
So on and up it rolled, a tower of doom,
And in proud menace through our Forum moved.
O Ilium, my country, where abode
The gods of all my sires! O glorious walls
Of Dardan's sons! before your gates it passed,
Four times it stopped and dreadful clash of arms
Four times from its vast concave loudly rang.

Yet frantic pressed we on, our hearts all blind,
And in the consecrated citadel
Set up the hateful thing. Cassandra then
From heaven-instructed heart our doom
    foretold;
But doomed to unbelief were Ilium's sons.
Our hapless nation on its dying day
Flung free o'er streets and shrines the votive
    flowers.

The skies rolled on; and o'er the ocean fell
The veil of night, till utmost earth and heaven
And all their Myrmidonian stratagems
Were mantled darkly o'er. In silent sleep
The Trojan city lay; dull slumber chained
Its weary life. But now the Greek array
Of ordered ships and moved on from Tenedos,
Their only light the silent, favoring moon,
On to the well-known strand. The King
    displayed
A torch from his own ship, and Sinon then,
Whom wrathful Heaven defended in that hour,
Let the imprisoned band of Greeks go free
From that huge womb of wood; the open horse
Restored them to the light; and joyfully
Emerging from the darkness, one by one,
Princely Thessander, Sthenelus, and dire
Ulysses glided down the swinging cord.
Closely upon them Neoptolemus,
The son of Peleus, came, and Acamas,
King Menelaus, Thoas and Machaon,
And last, Epeüs, who the fabric wrought.
Upon the town they fell, for deep in sleep
And drowsed with wine it lay; the sentinels
They slaughtered, and through gates now
    opened wide
Let in their fellows, and arrayed for war
Th' auxiliar legions of the dark design.

That hour it was when heaven's first gift of sleep
On weary hearts of men most sweetly steals.
O, then my slumbering senses seemed to see
Hector, with woeful face and streaming eyes;
I seemed to see him from the chariot trailing,
Foul with dark dust and gore, his swollen feet
Pierced with a cruel thong. Ah me! what change
From glorious Hector when he homeward bore
The spoils of fierce Achilles; or hurled far
That shower of torches on the ships of Greece!
Unkempt his beard, his tresses thick with blood,
And all those wounds in sight which he did take
Defending Troy. Then, weeping as I spoke,
I seemed on that heroic shape to call
With mournful utterance: "O star of Troy!
O surest hope and stay of all her sons!
Why tarriest thou so long? What region sends

The long-expected Hector home once more?
These weary eyes that look on thee have seen
Hosts of thy kindred die, and fateful change
Upon thy people and thy city fall.
O, say what dire occasion has defiled
Thy tranquil brows? What mean those bleeding
    wounds?"

Silent he stood, nor anywise would stay
My vain lament; but groaned, and answered
    thus:
"Haste, goddess-born, and out of yonder flames
Achieve thy flight. Our foes have scaled the wall,
Exalted Troy is failing. Fatherland
And Priam ask no more. If human arm
Could profit Troy, my own had kept her free.
Her Lares and her people to thy hands
Troy here commends. Companions let them be
Of all thy fortunes. Let them share thy quest
Of that wide realm, which, after wandering far,
Thou shalt achieve, at last, beyond the sea."
He spoke: and from our holy hearth brought
    forth
The solemn fillet, the ancestral shrines,
And Vesta's ever-bright, inviolate fire.

Now shrieks and loud confusion swept the town,
And though my father's dwelling stood apart
Embowered deep in trees, th' increasing din
Drew nearer, and the battle-thunder swelled.
I woke on sudden, and up-starting scaled
The roof, the tower, then stood with listening ear:
'T was like an harvest burning, when wild winds
Uprouse the flames; 't was like a mountain
    stream
That bursts in flood and ruinously whelms
Sweet fields and farms and all the ploughman's
    toil,
Whirling whole groves along; while dumb with
    fear,
From some far cliff the shepherd hears the sound.
Now their Greek plot was plain, the stratagem
At last laid bare. Deiphobus' great house
Sank vanquished in the fire. Ucalegon's
Hard by was blazing, while the waters wide
Around Sigeum gave an answering glow.
Shrill trumpets rang; loud shouting voices
    roared;
Wildly I armed me (when the battle calls,
How dimly reason shines!); I burned to join
The rally of my peers, and to the heights
Defensive gather. Frenzy and vast rage
Seized on my soul. I only sought what way
With sword in hand some noble death to die.

When Panthus met me, who had scarce escaped

The Grecian spears,—Panthus of Othrys' line,
Apollo's priest within our citadel;
His holy emblems, his defeated gods,
And his small grandson in his arms he bore,
While toward the gates with wild, swift steps he
    flew.
"How fares the kingdom, Panthus? What strong
    place
Is still our own?" But scarcely could I ask
When thus, with many a groan, he made reply:—
"Dardania's death and doom are come today,
Implacable. There is no Ilium now;
Our Trojan name is gone, the Teucrian throne
Quite fallen. For the wrathful power of Jove
Has given to Argos all our boast and pride.
The Greek is lord of all yon blazing towers.
Yon horse uplifted on our city's heart
Disgorges men-at-arms. False Sinon now,
With scorn exultant, heaps up flame on flame.
Others throw wide the gates. The whole vast
    horde
That out of proud Mycenæ hither sailed
Is at us. With confronting spears they throng
Each narrow passage. Every steel-bright blade
Is flashing naked, making haste for blood.
Our sentries helpless meet the invading shock
And give back blind and unavailing war."

By Panthus' word and by some god impelled,
I flew to battle, where the flames leaped high,
Where grim Bellona called, and all the air
Resounded high as heaven with shouts of war.
Rhipeus and Epytus of doughty arm
Were at my side, Dymas and Hypanis,
Seen by a pale moon, join our little band;
And young Coræbus, Mygdon's princely son,
Who was in Troy that hour because he loved
Cassandra madly, and had made a league
As Priam's kinsman with our Phrygian arms:
Ill-starred, to heed not what the virgin raved!
When these I saw close-gathered for the fight,
I thus addressed them: "Warriors, vainly brave,
If ye desire to follow one
Who dares the uttermost brave men may do,
Our evil plight ye see: the gods are fled
From every altar and protecting fire,
Which were the kingdom's stay. Ye offer aid
Unto your country's ashes. Let us fight
Unto the death! To arms, my men, to arms!
The single hope and stay of desperate men
Is their despair." Thus did I rouse their souls.
Then like the ravening wolves, some night of
    cloud,
When cruel hunger in an empty maw
Drives them forth furious, and their whelps
    behind

Wait famine-throated; so through foemen's steel
We flew to surest death, and kept our way
Straight through the midmost town. The wings
    of night
Brooded above us in vast vault of shade.
But who the bloodshed of that night can tell?
What tongue its deaths shall number, or what
    eyes
Find need of tears to equal all its woe?
The ancient City fell, whose throne had stood
Age after age. Along her streets were strewn
The unresisting dead; at household shrines
And by the temples of the gods they lay.
Yet not alone was Teucrian blood required:
Oft out of vanquished hearts fresh valor flamed,
And the Greek victor fell. Anguish and woe
Were everywhere; pale terrors ranged abroad,
And multitudinous death met every eye.

Androgeos, followed by a thronging band
Of Greeks, first met us on our desperate way;
But heedless, and confounding friend with foe,
Thus, all unchallenged, hailed us as his own:
"Haste, heroes? Are ye laggards at this hour?
Others bear off the captives and the spoil
Of burning Troy. Just from the galleys ye?"
He spoke; but straightway, when no safe reply
Returned, he knew himself entrapped, and fallen
Into a foeman's snare; struck dumb was he
And stopped both word and motion; as one
    steps,
When blindly treading a thick path of thorns,
Upon a snake, and sick with fear would flee
That lifted wrath and swollen gorge of green:
So trembling did Androgeos backward fall.
At them we flew and closed them round with
    war;
And since they could not know the ground, and
    fear
Had whelmed them quite, we swiftly laid them
    low.
Thus Fortune on our first achievement smiled;
And, flushed with victory, Coræbus cried:
"Come, friends, and follow Fortune's finger,
    where
She beckons us what path deliverance lies.
Change we our shields, and these Greek emblems
    wear.
'Twixt guile and valor who will nicely weigh
When foes are met? These dead shall find us
    arms."
With this, he dons Androgeos' crested helm
And beauteous, blazoned shield; and to his side
Girds on a Grecian blade. Young Rhipeus next,
With Dymas and the other soldiery,
Repeat the deed, exulting, and array

Their valor in fresh trophies from the slain.
Now intermingled with our foes we moved,
And alien emblems wore; the long, black night
Brought many a grapple, and a host of Greeks
Down to the dark we hurled. Some fled away,
Seeking their safe ships and the friendly shore.
Some cowards foul went clambering back again
To that vast horse and hid them in its maw.
But woe is me! If gods their help withhold,
'T is impious to be brave. That very hour
The fair Cassandra passed us, bound in chains,
King Priam's virgin daughter, from the shrine
And alters of Minerva; her loose hair
Had lost its fillet; her impassioned eyes
Were lifted in vain prayer,—her eyes alone!
For chains of steel her frail, soft hands confined.
Coræbus' eyes this horror not endured,
And, sorrow-crazed, he plunged him headlong
    in
The midmost fray, self-offered to be slain,
While in close mass our troop behind him
    poured.
But, at this point, the overwhelming spears
Of our own kinsmen rained resistless down
From a high temple-tower; and carnage wild
Ensued, because of the Greek arms we bore
And our false crests. The howling Grecian band,
Crazed by Cassandra's rescue, charged at us
From every side; Ajax of savage soul,
The sons of Atreus, and that whole wild horde
Achilles from Dolopian deserts drew.
'T was like the bursting storm, when gales
    contend,
West wind and South, and jocund wind of morn
Upon his orient steeds—while forests roar,
And foam-flecked Nereus with fierce trident stirs
The dark deep of the sea.

    All who did hide
In shadows of the night, by our assault
Surprised, and driven in tumultuous flight,
Now start to view. Full well they now can see
Our shields and borrowed arms, and clearly note
Our speech of alien sound; their multitude
O'erwhelms us utterly. Coræbus first
At mailed Minerva's altar prostate lay,
Pierced by Peneleus' blade; then Rhipeus fell;
We deemed him of all Trojans the most just,
Most scrupulously righteous; but the gods
Gave judgment otherwise. There Dymas died,
And Hypanis, by their compatriots slain,
Nor thee, O Panthus, in that mortal hour,
Could thy clean hands or Phoebus' priesthood
    save.
O ashes of my country! funeral pyre
Of all my kin! bear witness that my breast

Shrank not from any sword the Grecian drew,
And that my deeds the night my country died
Deserved a warrior's death, had Fate ordained.

But soon our ranks were broken; at my side
Stayed Iphitus and Pelias; one with age
Was long since wearied, and the other bore
The burden of Ulysses' crippling wound.
Straightway the roar and tumult summoned us
To Priam's palace, where a battle raged
As if save this no conflict else were known,
And all Troy's dying brave were mustered there.
There we beheld the war-god unconfined;
The Greek besiegers to the roof-tops fled;
Or, with shields tortoise-back, the gates assailed.
Ladders were on the walls; and round by round,
Up the huge bulwark as they fight their way,
The shielded left-hand thwarts the falling spears,
The right to every vantage closely clings.
The Trojans hurl whole towers and roof-tops
    down
Upon the mounting foe; for well they see
That the last hour is come, and with what arms
The dying must resist. Rich gilded beams,
With many a beauteous blazon of old time,
Go crashing down. Men armed with naked
    swords
Defend the inner doors in close array.
Thus were our hearts inflamed to stand and
    strike
For the king's house, and to his body-guard
Bring succor, and renew their vanquished
    powers.
A certain gate I knew, a secret way,
Which gave free passage between Priam's halls,
    And exit rearward; hither, in the days
Before our fall, the lone Andromache
Was wont with young Astyanax to pass
In quest of Priam and her husband's kin.
This way to climb the palace roof I flew,
Where, desperate, the Trojans with vain skill
Hurled forth repellent arms. A tower was there,
Reared skyward from the roof-top, giving view
Of Troy's wide walls and full reconnaissance
Of all Achaea's fleets and tented field;
This, with strong steel, our gathered strength
    assailed,
And as the loosened courses offered us
Great threatening fissures, we uprooted it
From its aerial throne and thrust it down:
It fell with instantaneous crash of thunder
Along the Danaan host in ruin wide.
But fresh ranks soon arrive; thick showers of
    stone
Rain down, with every missile rage can find.

Now at the threshold of the outer court
Pyrrhus triumphant stood, with glittering arms
And helm of burnished brass. He glittered like
Some swollen viper, fed on poison-leaves,
Whom chilling winter shelters underground,
Till, fresh and strong, he sheds his annual scales
And, crawling forth rejuvenate, uncoils
His slimy length; his lifted gorge insults
The sunbeam with three-forked and quivering
   tongue.
Huge Periphas was there; Automedon,
Who drove Achilles' steeds, and bore his arms.
Then Scyros' island-warriors assault
The palaces, and hurl reiterate fire
At wall and tower. Pyrrhus led the van;
Seizing an axe he clove the ponderous doors
And rent the hinges from their posts of bronze;
He cut the beams, and through the solid mass
Burrowed his way, till like a window huge
The breach yawned wide, and opened to his gaze
A vista of long courts and corridors,
The hearth and home of many an ancient king,
And Priam's own; upon its sacred bourne
The sentry, all in arms, kept watch and ward.
Confusion, groans, and piteous turmoil
Were in that dwelling; women shrieked and
   wailed
From many a dark retreat, and their loud cry
Rang to the golden stars. Through those vast
   halls
The panic-stricken mothers wildly roved,
And clung with frantic kisses and embrace
Unto the columns cold. Fierce as his sire,
Pyrrhus moves on; nor bar nor sentinel
May stop his way; down tumbles the great door
Beneath the battering beam, and with its fall
Hinges and framework violently torn.
Force bursts all bars; th' assailing Greeks break
   in,
Do butchery, and with men-at-arms possess
What place they will. Scarce with an equal rage
A foaming river, when its dykes are down,
O'erwhelms its mounded shores, and through
   the plain
Rolls mountain-high, while from the ravaged
   farms
Its fierce flood sweeps along both flock and fold.

My own eyes looked on Neoptolemus
Frenzied with slaughter, and both Atreus' sons
Upon the threshold frowning; I beheld
Her hundred daughters with old Hecuba;
And Priam, whose own bleeding wounds defiled
The altars where himself had blessed the fires;
There fifty nuptial beds gave promise proud
Of princely heirs; but all their brightness now,

Of broidered cunning and barbaric gold,
Lay strewn and trampled on. The Danaan foe
Stood victor, where the raging flame had failed.
But would ye haply know what stroke of doom
On Priam fell? Now when his anguish saw
His kingdom lost and fallen, his abode
Shattered, and in his very hearth and home
Th' exulting foe, the aged King did bind
His rusted armor to his trembling thews,—
All vainly,—and a useless blade of steel
He girded on; then charged, resolved to die
Encircled by the foe. Within his walls
There stood, beneath the wide and open sky,
A lofty altar; an old laurel-tree
Leaned o'er it, and enclasped in holy shade
The statues of the tutelary powers.
Here Hecuba and all the princesses
Took refuge vain within the place of prayer.
Like panic-stricken doves in some dark storm,
Close-gathering they sate, and in despair
Embraced their graven gods. But when the
   Queen
Saw Priam with his youthful harness on,
"What frenzy, O my wretched lord," she cried,
"Arrayed thee in such arms? O, whither now?
Not such defences, nor such arm as thine,
The time requires, though thy companion were
Our Hector's self. O, yield thee, I implore!
This altar now shall save us one and all,
Or we must die together." With these words
She drew him to her side, and near the shrine
Made for her aged spouse a place to cling.

But, lo! just 'scraped of Pyrrhus' murderous
   hand,
Polites, one of Priam's sons, fled fast
Along the corridors, through thronging foes
And a thick rain of spears. Wildly he gazed
Across the desolate halls, wounded to death.
Fierce Pyrrhus followed after, pressing hard
With mortal stroke, and now his hand and spear
Were close upon:—when the lost youth leaped
   forth
Into his father's sight, and prostrate there
Lay dying, while his life-blood ebbed away.
Then Priam, though on all sides death was nigh,
Quit not the strife, nor from loud wrath
   refrained:
"Thy crime and impious outrage, may the gods
(If Heaven to mortals render debt and due)
Justly reward and worthy honors pay!
My own son's murder thou hast made me see,
Blood and pollution impiously throwing
Upon a father's head. Not such was he,
Not such, Achilles, thy pretended sire,
When Priam was his foe. With flush of shame

He nobly listened to a suppliant's plea
In honor made. He rendered to the tomb
My Hector's body pale, and me did send
Back to my throne a king."

　　　With this proud word
The aged warrior hurled with nerveless arm
His ineffectual spear, which hoarsely rang
Rebounding on the brazen shield, and hung
Piercing the midmost boss,—but all in vain.
Then Pyrrhus: "Take these tidings, and convey
A message to my father, Peleus' son!
Tell him my naughty deeds! Be sure and say
How Neoptolemus hath shamed his sires.
Now die!"

　　　With this, he trailed before the shrines
The trembling King, whose feet slipped in the
　　stream
Of his son's blood. Then Pyrrhus' left hand
　　clutched
The tresses old and gray; a glittering sword
His right hand lifted high, and buried it
Far as the hilt in that defenceless heart.
So Priam's story ceased. Such final doom
Fell on him, while his dying eyes surveyed
Troy burning, and her altars overthrown,
Though once of many an orient land and tribe
The boasted lord. In huge dismemberment
His severed trunk lies tombless on the shore,
The head from shoulder torn, the corpse
　　unknown.

Then first wild horror on my spirit fell
And dazed me utterly. A vision rose
Of my own cherished father, as I saw
The King, his aged peer, sore wounded lying
In mortal agony; a vision too
Of lost Creüsa at my ravaged hearth,
And young Iulus' peril. Then my eyes
Looking round me seeking aid. But all were fled,
War-wearied and undone; some earthward
　　leaped
From battlement or tower, some in despair
Yielded their suffering bodies to the flame.
I stood there sole surviving; when, behold,
To Vesta's altar clinging in dumb fear,
Hiding and crouching in the hallowed shade,
Tyndarus' daughter!—'t was the burning town
Lighted full well my roving steps and eyes.
In fear was she both of some Trojan's rage
For Troy overthrown, and of some Greek
　　revenge,
Or her wronged husband's long indignant ire.
So hid she at that shrine her hateful brow,
Being of Greece and Troy, full well she knew,

The common curse. Then in my bosom rose
A blaze of wrath; methought I should avenge
My dying country, and with horrid deed
Pay crime for crime. "Shall she return unscathed
To Sparta, to Mycenæ's golden pride,
And have a royal triumph? Shall her eyes
Her sire and sons, her hearth and husband see,
While Phrygian captives follow in her train?
Is Priam murdered? Have the flames swept o'er
My native Troy? and doth our Dardan strand
Sweat o'er and o'er with sanguinary dew?
O, not thus unavenged! For though there be
No glory if I smite a woman's crime,
Nor conqueror's fame for such a victory won,
Yet if I blot this monster out, and wring
Full punishment from guilt, the time to come
Will praise me, and sweet pleasure it will be
To glut my soul with vengeance and appease
The ashes of my kindred."

　　　So I raved,
And to such frenzied purpose gave my soul.
Then with clear vision (never had I seen
Her presence so unclouded) I beheld,
In golden beams that pierced the midnight
　　gloom,
My gracious mother, visibly divine,
And with that mien of majesty she wears
When seen in heaven, she stayed me with her
　　hand,
And from her lips of rose this counsel gave:
"O son, what sorrow stirs thy boundless rage?
What madness this? Or whither vanisheth
Thy love of me? Wilt thou not seek to know
Where bides Anchises, thy abandoned sire,
Now weak with age? or if Creüisa lives
And young Ascanius, who are ringed about
With ranks of Grecian foes, and long ere this—
Save that my love can shield them and defend—
Had fallen on flame or fed some hungry sword?
Not Helen's hated beauty works thee woe;
Nor Paris, oft-accused. The cruelty
Of gods, of gods unaided, overwhelms
Thy country's power, and from its lofty height
Casts Ilium down. Behold, I take away
The barrier-cloud that dims thy mortal eye,
With murk and mist o'er-veiling. Fear not thou
To heed thy mother's word, nor let thy heart
Refuse obedience to her counsel given.
'Mid yonder trembling ruins, where thou see'st
Stone torn from stone, with dust and smoke
　　uprolling,
'T is Neptune strikes the wall, his trident vast
Makes her foundation tremble, and unseats
The city from her throne. Fierce Juno leads
Resistless onset at the Scæan gate,

And summons from the ships the league of
  powers,
Wearing her wrathful sword. On yonder height
Behold Tritonia in the citadel
Clothed   with   the   lightning   and   her
  Gorgon-shield!
Unto the Greeks great Jove himself renews
Their courage and their power; 't is he thrusts on
The gods themselves against the Trojan arms.
Fly, O my son! The war's wild work give o'er!
I will be always nigh and set thee safe
Upon thy father's threshold." Having said,
She fled upon the viewless night away.

Then loomed o'er Troy the apparition vast
Of her dread foes divine; I seemed to see
All Ilium sink in fire, and sacred Troy,
Of Neptune's building, utterly overthrown.
So some huge ash-tree on the mountain's brow
(When rival woodmen, heaving stroke on stroke
Of two-edged axes, haste to cast her down)
Sways ominously her trembling, leafy top,
And drops her smitten head; till by her wounds
Vanquished at last, she makes her dying groan,
And falls in loud wreck from the cliffs uptorn.
I left the citadel; and, led by Heaven,
Threaded the maze of deadly foes and fires,
Through spears that glanced aside and flames
  that fell.
Soon came I to my father's ancient seat,
Our home and heritage. But lo! my sire
(Whom first of all I sought, and first would bear
To safe asylum in the distant hills)
Vowed he could never, after fallen Troy,
Live longer on, or bear an exile's woe.
"O you," he cried, "whose blood not yet betrays
The cruel taint of time, whose powers be still
Unpropped and undecayed, go, take your flight,
If heavenly wrath had willed my life to spare,
This dwelling had been safe. It is too much
That I have watched one wreck, and for too long
Outlived my vanquished country. Thus, O, thus!
Compose these limbs for death, and say farewell.
My own hand will procure it; or my foe
Will end me of mere pity, and for spoil
Will strip me bare. It is an easy loss
To have no grave. For many a year gone by,
Accursed of Heaven, I tarry in this world
A useless burden, since that fatal hour
When Jove, of gods the Sire and men the King,
His lightnings o'er me breathed and blasting
  fire."

Such fixed resolve he utter o'er and o'er,
And would not yield, though with my tears did
  join

My spouse Creüsa, fair Ascanius,
And our whole house, imploring the gray sire
Not with himself to ruin all, nor add
Yet heavier burdens to our crushing doom.
He still cried, "No!" and clung to where he sate
And to the same dread purpose. I once more
Back to the fight would speed. For death alone
I made my wretched prayer. What space was left
For wisdom now? What chance or hope was
  given?
"Didst thou, dear father, dream that I could fly
Sundered from thee? Did such an infamy
Fall from a father's lips? If Heaven's decree
Will of this mighty nation not let live
A single soul if thine own purpose be
To cast thyself and thy posterity
Into thy country's grave, behold, the door
Is open to thy death! Lo, Pyrrhus comes
Red-handed from King Priam! He has slain
A son before a father's eyes, and spilt
A father's blood upon his own hearthstone.
Was it for this, O heavenly mother mine,
That thou hast brought me safe through sword
  and fire?
That I might see these altars desecrate
By their worst foes? that I might look upon
my sire, my wife, and sweet Ascanius
Dead at my feet in one another's blood?
To arms, my men, to arms! The hour of death
Now beckons to the vanquished. Let me go
Whither the Greeks are gathered; let me stand
Where oft revives the flagging stroke of war:
Not all of us die unavenged this day!"

I clasped my sword-belt round me once again,
Fitted my left arm to my shield, and turned
To fly the house; but at the threshold clung
Creüsa to my knees, and lifted up
Iulus to his father's arms. "If thou
Wouldst rush on death," she cried, "O suffer us
To share thy perils with thee to the end.
But if this day's work bid thee trust a sword,
Defend thy hearthstone first. Who else shall
  guard
Thy babe Iulus, or thy reverend sire?
Or me, thy wife that was—what help have I?"

So rang the roof-top with her piteous cries:
But lo! a portent wonderful to see
On sudden rose; for while his parents' grief
Held the boy close in arm and full in view,
There seemed upon Iulus' head to glow
A flickering peak of fire; the tongue of flame
Innocuous o'er his clustering tresses played,
And hovered round his brows.

We, horror-struck,
Grasped at his burning hair, and sprinkled him,
To quench that holy and auspicious fire.
Then sire Anchises with exultant eyes
Looked heavenward, and lifted to the stars
His voice and outstretched hands. "Almighty
    Jove,
If aught of prayer may move thee, let thy grace
Now visit us! O, hear this holy vow!
And if for service at thine altars done,
We aught can claim, O Father, lend us aid,
And ratify the omen thou hast given!"

Scarce ceased his aged voice, when suddenly
From leftward, with a deafening thunder-peal,
Cleaving the blackness of the vaulted sky,
A meteor-star in trailing splendor ran,
Exceeding bright. We watched it glide sublime
O'er tower and town, until its radiant beam
In forest-mantled Ida died away;
But left a furrow on its track in air,
A glittering, long line, while far and wide
The sulphurous fume and exhalation flowed.

My father strove not now; but lifted him
In prayer to all the gods, in holy awe
Of that auspicious star, and thus exclaimed:
"Tarry no moment more! Behold, I come!
Whithersoe'er ye lead, my steps obey.
Gods of my fathers, O, preserve our name!
Preserve my son, and his! This augury
Is yours; and Troy on your sole strength relies.
I yield, dear son; I journey at thy side."

He spoke; and higher o'er the blazing walls
Leaped the loud fire, while ever nearer drew
The rolling surges of tumultuous flame.
"Haste, father, on these bending shoulders
    climb!
This back is ready, and the burden light;
One peril smites us both, whate'er befall,
One rescue both shall find. Close at my side
Let young Iulus run, while, not too nigh,
My wife Creüsa heeds what way we go.
Ye servants of our house, give ear, I pray,
To my command. Outside the city's gates
Lies a low mound and long since ruined fane
To Ceres vowed; a cypress' ancient shade
O'erhangs it, which our fathers' pious care
Protected year by year; by various paths
Be that our meeting-place.

    "But in thy hands
Bring, sire, our household gods, and sanctities:
For me to touch, who come this very hour
From battle and the fresh blood of the slain,

Were but abomination, till what time
In living waters I shall make me clean."

So saying, I bowed my neck and shoulders broad,
O'erspread me with a lion's tawny skin,
And lifted up my load. Close at my side
Little Iulus twined his hand in mine
And followed, with unequal step, his sire.
My wife at distance came. We hastened on,
Creeping through shadows; I, who once had
    viewed
Undaunted every instrument of war
And all the gathered Greeks in grim array,
Now shook at every gust, and heard all sounds
With fevered trepidation, fearing both
For him I bore and him who clasped my hand.

Now near the gates I drew, and deemed our
    flight
Safely at end, when suddenly I heard
The sounding tread of many warriors
That seemed hard-by, while through the murky
    night
My father peered, and shouted, "O my son,
Away, away! for surely all our foes
Are here upon us, and my eyes behold
The glance of glittering shields and flash of
    arms."

O, then some evil-working, nameless god
Clouded my senses quite: for while I sped
Along our pathless way, and left behind
All paths and regions known—O wretched me!—
Creüsa on some dark disaster fell;
She stopped, or wandered, or sank down
    undone,—
I never knew what way,—and nevermore
I looked on her alive. Yet knew I not
My loss, nor backward turned a look or thought,
Till by that hallowed hill to Ceres vowed
We gathered all,—and she alone came not,
While husbands, friends, and son made search in
    vain.
What god, what man, did not my grief accuse
In frenzied word? In all the ruined land
What worse woe had I seen? Entrusting then
My sire, my son, and all the Teucrian gods
To the deep shadows of a slanting vale
Where my allies kept guard, I hied me back
To that doomed town, re-girt in glittering arms.
Resolved was I all hazards to renew,
All Troy to re-explore, and once again
Offer my life to perils without end.
The walls and gloomy gates whence forth I came
I first revisit, and retrace my way,

Searching the night once more. On all sides
   round
Horror spread wide; the very silence breathed
A terror on my soul. I hastened then
Back to my fallen home, if haply there
Her feet had strayed—, but the invading Greeks
Were its possessors, though the hungry fire
Was blown along the roof-tree, and the flames
Rolled raging upward on the fitful gate.
To Priam's house I haste, and climb once more
The citadel; in Juno's temple there,
The chosen guardians of her wasted halls,
Phoenix and dread Ulysses watched the spoil.
Here, snatched away from many a burning fane,
Troy's treasures lay,—rich tables for the gods,
Thick bowls of massy gold, and vestures rare,
Confusedly heaped up, while round the pile
Fair youths and trembling virgins stood forlorn.

Yet oft my voice rang dauntless through the
   gloom,
From street to street I cried with anguish vain;
And on Creüsa piteously calling,
Woke the lamenting echoes o'er and o'er.
While on this quest I roamed the city through,
Of reason reft, there rose upon my sight—
O shape of sorrow!—my Creüsa's ghost,
Hers truly, though a loftier port it wore.
I quailed, my hair rose, and I gasped for fear;
But thus she spoke, and soothed my grief away:
"Why to these frenzied sorrows bend thy soul,
O husband ever dear! The will of Heaven
Hath brought all this to pass. Fate doth not send
Creüsa the long journeys thou shalt take,
Nor hath th' Olympian King so given decree.
Long is thy banishment; thy ship must plough
The vast, far-spreading sea. Then shalt thou
   come
Unto Hesperia, whose fruitful plains

Are watered by the Tiber, Lydian stream,
Of smooth, benignant flow. Thou shalt obtain
Fair fortunes, and a throne and royal bride.
For thy beloved Creüsa weep no more!
No Myrmidon's proud palace waits me now;
Dolopian shall not scorn, nor Argive dames
Command a slave of Dardan's royal stem
And wife to Venus's son. On these loved shores
The Mother of the Gods compels my stay.
Farewell! farewell! O, cherish evermore
Thy son and mine!"

   Her utterance scarce had ceased,
When, as I strove through tears to make reply,
She left me, and dissolved in empty air.
Thrice would my frustrate arms her form enfold;
Thrice from the clasp of hand that vision fled,
Like wafted winds and like a fleeting dream.

The night had passed, and to my friends once
   more
I made my way, much wondering to find
A mighty multitude assembled there
Of   friends   new-come,—matrons   and
   men-at-arms,
And youth for exile bound,—a doleful throng.
From far and near they drew, their hearts
   prepared
And their possessions gathered, to sail forth
To lands unknown, wherever o'er the wave
I bade them follow.

   Now above the crest
Of loftiest Ida rose the Morningstar,
Chief in the front of day. The Greeks held fast
The captive gates of Troy. No help or hope
Was ours any more. Then, yielding all,
And lifting once again my aged sire,
For refuge to the distant hills I fled.

Book IV

Now felt the Queen the sharp, slow-gather-
   ing pangs,
Of love; and out of every pulsing vein
Nourished the wound and fed its viewless fire.
Her hero's virtues and his lordly line
Keep calling to her soul; his words, his glance,
Cling to her heart like lingering, barbed steel,
And rest and peace from her vexed body fly.

A new day's dawn with Phoebus' lamp divine

Lit up all lands, and from the vaulted heaven
Aurora had dispelled the dark and dew;
When thus unto the ever-answering heart
Of her dear sister spoke the stricken Queen:
"Anna, my sister, what disturbing dreams
Perplex me and alarm? What guest is this
New-welcomed to our house? How proud his
   mien!
What dauntless courage and exploits of war!
Sooth, I receive it for no idle tale

That of the gods he sprang. 'T is cowardice
Betrays the base-born soul. Ah me! How fate
Has smitten him with storms! What dire
  extremes
Of war and horror in his tale he told!
O, were it not immutably resolved
In my fixed heart, that to no shape of man
I would be wed again (since my first love
Left me by death abandoned and betrayed);
Loathed I not so the marriage torch and train,
I could—who knows?—to this one weakness
  yield.
Anna, I hide it not! But since the doom
Of my ill-starred Sichæus, when our shrines
Were by a brother's murder dabbled o'er,
This man alone has moved me; he alone
Has shaken my weak will. I seem to feel
The motions of love's lost, familiar fire.
But may the earth gape open where I tread,
And may almighty Jove with thunder-scourge
Hurl me to Erebus' abysmal shade,
To pallid ghosts and midnight fathomless,
Before, O Chastity! I shall offend
Thy holy power, or cast thy bonds away!
He who first mingled his dear life with mine
Took with him all my heart. 'T is his alone—
O, let it rest beside him in the grave!"
She spoke: the bursting tears her breast
  o'erflowed.

"O dearer to thy sister than her life,"
Anna replied, wouldst thou in sorrow's weed
Waste thy long youth alone, nor ever know
Sweet babes at thine own breast, nor gifts of
  love?
Will dust and ashes, or a buried ghost,
Reck what we do? 'Tis true thy grieving heart
Was cold to earlier wooers, Libya's now,
And long ago in Tyre. Iarbas knew
Thy scorn, and many a prince and captain bred
In Afric's land of glory. Why resist
A love that makes thee glad? Hast thou no care
What alien lands are these where thou dost
  reign?
Here are Gætulia's cities and her tribes
Unconquered ever; on thy borders rove
Numidia's uncurbed cavalry; here too
Lies Syrtis' cruel shore, and regions wide
Of thirsty desert, menaced everywhere,
By the wild hordes of Barca. Shall I tell
Of Tyre's hostilities, the threats and rage
Of our own brother? Friendly gods, I trow,
Wafted the Teucrian ships, with Juno's aid,
To these our shores. O sister, what a throne,
And what imperial City shall be thine,
If thus espoused! With Trojan arms allied

How far may not our Punic fame extend
In deeds of power? Call therefore on the gods
To favor thee; and, after omens fair,
Give queenly welcome, and contrive excuse
To make him tarry, while yon wintry seas
Are loud beneath Orion's stormful star,
And on his battered ships the season frowns."
So saying, she stirred a passion-burning breast
To love more madly still; her words infused
A doubting mind with hope, and bade the blush
Of shame begone. First to the shrines they went
And sued for grace; performing sacrifice,
Choosing an offering of unblemished ewes,
To law-bestowing Ceres, to the god
Of light, to sire Lyæs, lord of wine;
But chiefly unto Juno, patroness
Of nuptial vows. There Dido, beauteous Queen,
Held forth in her right hand the sacred bowl,
And poured it full between the lifted horns
Of the white heifer; or on temple floors
She strode among the richly laden shrines,
The eyes of gods upon her, worshipping
With many a votive gift; or, peering deep
Into the victims' cloven sides, she read
The fate-revealing tokens trembling there.
How blind the hearts of prophets be! Alas!
Of what avail be temples and fond prayers
To change a frenzied mind? Devouring ever,
Love's fire burns inward to her bones; she feels
Quick in her breast the viewless, voiceless
  wound.
Ill-fated Dido ranges up and down
The spaces of her city, desperate,
Her life one flame-like arrow-stricken doe,
Through Cretan forest rashly wandering,
Pierced by a far-off shepherd, who pursues
With shafts, and leaves behind his light-winged
  steel,
Not knowing; while she scours the dark ravines
Of Dicte and its woodlands; at her heart
The mortal barb irrevocably clings.
Around her city's battlements she guides
Æneas, to make show of Sidon's gold,
And what her realm can boast; full oft her voice
Essays to speak and trembling dies away:
Or, when the daylight fades, she spread anew
A royal banquet, and once more will plead,
Mad that she is, to hear the Trojan sorrow;
And with oblivious ravishment once more
Hangs on his lips who tells; or when her guests
Are scattered, and the wan moon's fading horn
Bedims its ray, while many a sinking star
Invites to slumber, there she weeps alone
In the deserted hall, and casts her down
On the cold couch he pressed. Her love from far
Beholds her vanished hero and receives

His voice upon her ears; or to her breasts,
Moved by a father's image in his child,
She clasps Ascanius, seeking to deceive
Her unblest passion so. Her enterprise
Of tower and rampart stops: her martial host
No longer she reviews, nor fashions now
Defensive haven and defiant wall;
But idly all her half-built bastions frown,
And enginery of sieges, high as heaven.
But soon the chosen spouse of Jove perceived
The Queen's infection; and because the voice
Of honor to such frenzy spoke not, she,
Daughter of Saturn, unto Venus turned
And counselled thus: "How noble is the praise,
How glorious the spoils of victory,
For thee and for thy boy? Your names should be
In lasting, vast renown—that by the snare
Of two great gods in league one woman fell!
It 'scapes me not that my protected realms
Have ever been thy fear, and the proud halls
Of Carthage thy vexation and annoy.
Why further go? Prithee, what useful end
Has our long war? Why not from this day forth
Perpetual peace and nuptial amity?
Hast thou not worked thy will?. Behold and see
How love-sick Dido burns, and all her flesh
The madness feels! So let our common grace
Smile on a mingled people! Let her serve
A Phrygian husband, while thy hands receive
Her Tyrian subjects for the bridal dower!"

In answer (reading the dissembler's mind
Which unto Libyan shores were fain to shift
Italia's future throne) thus Venus spoke:
"'T were mad to spurn such favor, or by choice
Be numbered with thy foes. But can it be
That fortune on thy noble counsel smiles?
To me Fate shows but dimly whether Jove
Unto the Trojan wanderers ordains
A common city with the sons of Tyre,
With mingling blood and sworn, perpetual
    peace.
His wife thou art; it is thy rightful due
To plead to know his mind. Go, ask him, then!
For humbly I obey!"

  With instant word
Juno the Queen replied: "Leave that to me!
But in what wise our urgent task and grave
May soon be sped, I will in brief unfold
To thine attending ear. A royal hunt
In sylvan shades unhappy Dido gives
For her Æneas, when to-morrow's dawn
Uplifts its earliest ray and Titan's beam
Shall first unveil the world. But I will pour
Black storm-clouds with a burst of heavy hail

Along their way; and as the huntsmen speed
To hem the wood with snares, I will arouse
All heaven with thunder. The attending train
Shall scatter and be veiled in blinding dark,
While Dido and her hero out of Troy
To the same cavern fly. My auspices
I will declare—if thou alike wilt bless;
And yield her in true wedlock for his bride.
Such shall their spousal be!" To Juno's will
Cythèra's Queen inclined assenting brow:
And laughed such guile to see.

  Aurora rose,
And left the ocean's rim. The city's gates
Pour forth to greet the morn a gallant train
Of huntsmen, bearing many a woven snare
And steel-tipped javelin, while to and fro
Run the keen-scented dogs and Libyan squires.
The Queen still keeps her chamber; at her doors
The Punic lords await; her palfrey, brave
In gold and purple housing, paws the ground
And fiercely champs the foam-flecked
    bridle-rein.
At last, with numerous escort, forth she shines:
Her Tyrian pall is bordered in bright hues,
Her quiver, gold; her tresses are confined
Only with gold; her robes of purple rare
Meet in a golden clasp. To greet her come
The noble Phrygian guests; among them smiles
The boy Iulus; and in fair array
Æneas, goodliest of all his train.
In such a guise Apollo (when he leaves
Cold Lycian hills and Xanthus' frosty stream
To visit Delos to Latona dear)
Ordains the song, while round his altars cry
The choirs of many islands, with the pied,
Fantastic Agathyrsi; soon the god
Moves o'er the Cynthian steep; his flowing hair
He binds with laurel garland and bright gold;
Upon his shining shoulder as he goes
The arrows ring:—not less uplifted mien
Æneas wore; from his illustrious brow
Such beauty shone.

  Soon to the mountains tall
The cavalcade comes nigh, to pathless haunts
Of woodland creatures; the wild goats are seen,
From pointed crag descending leap by leap
Down the steep ridges; in the vales below
Are routed deer, that scour the spreading plain,
And mass their dust-blown squadrons in wild
    flight,
Far from the mountain's bound. Ascanius,
Flushed with the sport, spurs on a mettled steed
From vale to vale, and many a flying herd
His chase outspeeds; but in his heart he prays

Among these tame things suddenly to see
A tusky boar, or, leaping from the hills,
A growling mountain-lion, golden-maned.

Meanwhile low thunders in the distant sky
Mutter confusedly; soon bursts in full
The storm-cloud and the hail. The Tyrian troop
Is scattered wide; the chivalry of Troy,
With the young heir of Dardan's kingly line,
Of Venus sprung, seek shelter where they may,
With sudden terror; down the deep ravines
The swollen torrents roar. In that same hour
Queen Dido and her hero out of Troy
To the same cavern fly. Old Mother-Earth
And wedlock-keeping Juno gave the sign;
The flash of lightnings on the conscious air
Lit them the bridal bed; along the hills
The wailing wood-nymphs sobbed a wedding
     song.
Such was that day of death, the source and spring
Of many a woe. For Dido took no heed
Of honor and good-name; nor did she mean
Her loves to hide; but called the lawless deed
A marriage, and with phrases veiled her shame.

Swift through the Libyan cities Rumor sped.
Rumor! What evil can surpass her speed?
In movement she grows mighty, and achieves
Strength and dominion as she swifter flies.
Small first, because afraid, she soon exalts
Her stature skyward, stalking through the lands
And mantling in the clouds her baleful brow.
The womb of Earth, in anger at high Heaven,
Bore her, they say, last of the Titan spawn,
Sister to Coeus and Enceladus.
Feet swift to run and pinions like the wind
The dreadful monster wears; her carcase huge
Is feathered, and at root of every plume
A peering eye abides; and, strange to tell,
An equal number of vociferous tongues,
Foul, whispering lips, and ears, that catch at all.
At night she spreads midway 'twixt earth and
     heaven
Her pinions in the darkness, hissing loud,
Nor e'er to happy slumber gives her eyes:
But with the morn she takes her watchful throne
High on the housetops or on lofty towers,
To terrify the nations. She can cling
To vile invention and malignant wrong,
Or mingle with her word some tidings true.

She now with changeful story filled men's ears,
Exultant, whether false or true she sung:
How Trojan-born Æneas having come,
Dido, the lovely widow, looked his way,
Deigning to wed; how all the winter long

They passed in revel and voluptuous ease,
To dalliance given o'er; naught heeding now
Of crown or kingdom—shameless! lust-
     enslaved!
Such tidings broadcast on the lips of men
The filthy goddess spread; and soon she hied
To King Iarbas, where her hateful song
To newly-swollen wrath his heart inflamed.
Him the god Ammon got by forced embrace
Upon a Libyan nymph; his kingdoms wide
Possessed a hundred ample shrines to Jove,
A hundred altars whence ascended ever
The fires of sacrifice, perpetual seats
For a great god's abode, where flowing blood
Enriched the ground, and on the portals hung
Garlands of every flower. The angered King,
Half-maddened by malignant Rumor's voice,
Unto his favored altars came, and there,
Surrounded by the effluence divine,
Upraised in prayer to Jove his suppliant hands.
"Almighty Jupiter, to whom each day,
At banquet on the painted couch reclined,
Numidia pours libation! Do thine eyes
Behold us? Or when out of yonder heaven,
O sire, thou launchest the swift thunderbolt,
Is it for naught we fear thee? Do the clouds
Shoot forth blind fire to terrify the soul
With wild, unmeaning roar? O, look upon
That woman, who was homeless in our realm,
And bargained where to build her paltry town,
Receiving fertile coastland for her farms,
By hospitable grant! She dares disdain
Our proferred nuptial vow. She has proclaimed
Æneas partner of her bed and throne.
And now that Paris, with his eunuch crew,
Beneath his chin and fragrant, oozy hair
Ties the soft Lyndian bonnet, boasting well
His stolen prize. But we to all these fanes,
Though they be thine, a fruitless offering bring,
And feed on empty tales our trust in thee."

As thus he prayed and to the altars clung,
Th' Omnipotent gave ear, and turned his gaze
Upon the royal dwelling, where for love
The amorous pair forgot their place and name.
Then thus to Mercury he gave command:
"Haste thee, my son, upon the Zephyrs call,
And take thy wingèd way! My mandate bear
Unto that prince of Troy who tarries now
In Tyrian Carthage, heedless utterly
Of empire Heaven-bestowed. On wingèd winds
Hasten with my decrees. Not such the man
His beauteous mother promised; not for this
Twice did she shield him from the Greeks in
     arms:
But that he might rule Italy, a land

Pregnant with thrones and echoing with war;
That he of Teucer's seed a race should sire,
And bring beneath its law the whole wide world.
If such a glory and event supreme
Enkindle not his bosom; if such task
To his own honor speak not; can the sire
Begrudge Ascanius the heritage
Of the proud name of Rome? What plans he now?
What mad hope bids him linger in the lap
Of enemies, considering no more
The land Lavinian and Ausonia's sons.
Let him to sea! Be this our final word:
This message let our herald faithful bear."
He spoke. The god a prompt obedience gave
To his great sire's command. He fastened first
Those sandals of bright gold, which carry him
Aloft o'er land or sea, with airy wings
That race the fleeting wind; then lifted he
His wand, wherewith he summons from the
    grave
Pale-featured ghosts, or, if he will, consigns
To doleful Tartarus; or by its power
Gives slumber or dispels; or quite unseals
The eyelids of the dead: on this relying,
He routs the winds or cleaves th' obscurity
Of stormful clouds. Soon from his flight he spied
The summit and the sides precipitous
Of stubborn Atlas, whose star-pointing peak
Props heaven; of Atlas, whose pine-wreathèd
    brow
Is girdled evermore with misty gloom
And lashed of wind and rain; a cloak of snow
Melts on his shoulder; from his aged chin
Drop rivers, and ensheathed in stiffening ice
Glitters his great grim beard.

   Here first was stayed
The speed of Mercury's well-poising wing;
Here making pause, from hence he headlong
    flung
His body to the sea; in motion like
Some sea-bird's, which along the levelled shore
Or round tall crags where rove the swarming
    fish,
Flies low along the waves: o'er-hovering so
Between the earth and skies, Cyllene's god
Flew   downward   from   his   mother's
    mountain-sire,
Parted the winds and skimmed the sandy marge
Of Libya. When first his wingèd feet
Came nigh the clay-built Punic huts, he saw
    Æneas building at a citadel,
And founding walls and towers; at his side
Was girt a blade with yellow jaspers starred,
His mantle with the stain of Tyrian shell
Flowed purple from his shoulder, broidered fair

By opulent Dido with fine threads of gold,
Her gift of love; straightway the god began:
"Dost thou for lofty Carthage toil, to build
Foundations strong? Dost thou, a wife's weak
    thrall,
Build her proud city? Hast thou, shameful loss!
Forgot thy kingdom and thy task sublime?
From bright Olympus, I. He who commands
All gods, and by his sovran deity
Moves earth and heaven—he it was who bade
Me bear on wingèd winds his high decree.
What plan is thine? By what mad hope dost thou
Linger so long in lap of Libyan land?
If the proud guerdon of thy destined way
Move not thy heart, if all the arduous toil
To thine own honor speak not, look upon
Iulus in his bloom, thy hope and heir
Ascanius. It is his rightful due
In Italy o'er Roman lands to reign."
After such word Cyllene's wingèd god
Vanished, and e'er his accents died away,
Dissolved in air before the mortal's eyes.
Æneas at the sight stood terror-dumb
With choking voice and horror-rising hair.
He fain would fly at once and get him gone
From that voluptuous land, much wondering
At Heaven's wrathful word. Alas! how stir?
What cunning argument can plead his cause
Before th' infuriate Queen? How break such
    news?
Flashing this way and that, his startled mind
Makes many a project and surveys them all.
But, pondering well, his final counsel stopped
At this resolve: he summoned to his side
Mnestheus, Sergestus, and Serestus bold,
And bade them fit the fleet, all silently
Gathering the sailors and collecting gear,
But carefully dissembling what emprise
Such novel stir intends: himself the while
(Since high-born Dido dreamed not love so fond
Could have an end) would seek an audience,
At some indulgent time, and try what shift
Such matters may require. With joy they heard,
And wrought, assiduous, at their prince's plan.

But what can cheat true love? The Queen
    foreknew
His stratagem, and all the coming change
Perceived ere it began. Her jealous fear
Counted no hour secure. That unclean tongue
Of Rumor told her fevered heart the fleet
Was fitting forth, and hastening to be gone.
Distractedly she raved, and passion-tossed
Roamed through her city, like a Mænad roused
By the wild rout of Bacchus, when are heard
The third year's orgies, and the midnight scream

To cold Cithæron calls the frenzied crew.
Finding Æneas, thus her plaint she poured:
"Didst hope to hide it, false one, that such crime
Was in thy heart,—to steal without farewell
Out of my kingdom? Did our mutual joy
Not move thee; nor thine own true promise given
Once on a time? Nor Dido, who will die
A death of sorrow? Why compel thy ships
To brave the winter stars? Why off to sea
So fast through stormy skies? O, cruelty!
If Troy still stood, and if thou wert not bound
For alien shore unknown wouldst steer for Troy
Through yonder waste of waves? Is it from me
Thou takest flight? O, by these flowing tears,
By thine own plighted word leitr nothing more
My weakness left to miserable me,
By our poor marriage of imperfect vow,
If aught to me thou owest, if aught in me
Ever have pleased thee—O, be merciful
To my low-fallen fortunes! I implore,
If place be left for prayer, thy purpose change!
Because of thee yon Libyan savages
And nomad chiefs are grown implacable,
And my own Tyrians hate me. Yes, for thee
My chastity was slain and honor fair,
By which alone to glory I aspired,
In former days. To whom dost thou in death
Abandon me? my guest!—since but this name
Is left me of a husband! Shall I wait
Till fell Pygmalion, my brother, raze
My city walls? Or the Gætulian king,
Iarbas, chain me captive to his car?
O, if, ere thou hadst fled, I might but bear
Some pledge of love to thee, and in these halls
Watch some sweet babe Æneas at his play,
Whose face should be the memory of thine
    own—I were not so forsaken, lost, undone!"

She said. But he, obeying Jove's decree,
Gazed steadfastly away; and in his heart
With strong repression crushed his cruel pain;
Then thus the silence broke: "O Queen, not one
Of my unnumbered debts so strongly urged
Would I gainsay. Elissa's memory
Will be my treasure long as memory holds,
Or breath of life is mine. Hear my brief plea!
'T was not my hope to hide this flight I take,
As thou hast dreamed. Nay, I did never light
A bridegroom's torch, nor gave I thee the vow
Of marriage. Had my destiny decreed,
That I should shape life to my heart's desire,
And at my own will put away the weight
Of toil and pain, my place would now be found
In Troy, among the cherished sepulchres
Of my own kin, and Priam's mansion proud
Were standing still; or these my loyal hands

Had rebuilt Ilium for her vanquished sons.
But now to Italy Apollo's power
Commands me forth; his Lycian oracles
Are loud for Italy. My heart is there,
And there my fatherland. If now the towers
Of Carthage and the Libyan colony
Delight thy Tyrian eyes; wilt thou refuse
To Trojan exiles their Ausonian shore?
I too by Fate was driven, not less than thou,
To wander far a foreign throne to find.
Oft when in dewy dark night hides the world,
And flaming stars arise, Anchises' shade
Looks on me in my dreams with angered brow.
I think of my Ascanius, and the wrong
To that dear heart, from whom I steal away
Hesperia, his destined home and throne.
But now the wingèd messenger of Heaven,
Sent down by Jove (I swear by thee and me!),
Has brought on wingèd wings his sire's
    command.
My own eyes with unclouded vision saw
The god within these walls; I have received
With my own ears his words. No more inflame
With lamentation fond thy heart and mine.
'T is not my own free act seeks Italy."
She with averted eyes and glance that rolled
Speechless this way and that, had listened long
To his reply, till thus her rage broke forth:
"No goddess gave thee birth. No Dardanus
Begot thy sires. But on its breast to stone
Caucasus bore thee, and the tigresses
Of fell Hyrcania to thy baby lip
Their udders gave. Why should I longer show
A lying smile? What worse can I endure?
Did my tears draw one sigh? Did he once drop
His stony stare? or did he yield a tear
To my lament, or pity this fond heart?
Why set my wrongs in order? Juno, now,
And Jove, the son of Saturn, heed no more
Where justice lies. No trusting heart is safe
In all this world. That waif and castaway
I found in beggary and gave him share—Fool
    that I was!—in my own royal glory.
His lost fleet and his sorry crews I steered
From death away. O, how my fevered soul
Unceasing raves! Forsooth Apollo speaks!
His Lycian oracles! and sent by Jove
The messenger of Heaven on fleeting air
The ruthless biddings brings! Proud business
For gods, I trow, that such a task disturbs
Their still abodes! I hold thee back no more,
Nor to thy cunning speeches give the lie.
Begone! Sail on to Italy, thy throne,
Through wind and wave! I pray that, if there be
Any just gods of power, thou mayest drink down
Death on the mid-sea rocks, and often call

With dying gasps on Dido's name—while I
Pursue with vengeful fire. When cold death
   rends
The body from the breath, my ghost shall sit
Forever in thy path. Full penalties
Thy stubborn heart shall pay. They'll bring me
   news
In yon deep gulf of death of all thy woe."

Abrupt her utterance ceased, and sick at heart
She fled the light of day, as if to shrink
From human eyes, and left Æneas there
Irresolute with horror, while his soul
Framed many a vain reply. Her swooning shape
Her maidens to a marble chamber bore
And on her couch the helpless limbs reposed.

Æneas, faithful to a task divine,
Though yearning sore to remedy and soothe
Such misery, and with the timely word
Her grief assuage, and though his burdened
   heart
Was weak because of love, while many a groan
Rose from his bosom, yet no whit did fail
To do the will of Heaven, but of his fleet
Resumed command. The Trojans on the shore
Ply well their task and push into the sea
The lofty ships. Now floats the shining keel,
And oars they bring all leafy from the grove,
With oak half-hewn, so hurried was the flight.
Behold them how they haste—from every gate
Forth-streaming!—just as when a heap of corn
Is thronged with ants, who, knowing winter
   nigh,
Refill their granaries; the long black line
Runs o'er the levels, and conveys the spoil
In narrow pathways through the grass; a part
With straining and assiduous shoulder push
The kernels huge; a part array the file,
And whip the laggards on; their busy track
Swarms quick and eager with unceasing toil.

O Dido, how thy suffering heart was wrung,
That spectacle to see! What sore lament
Was thine, when from the towering citadel
The whole shore seemed alive, the sea itself
In turmoil with loud cries! Relentless Love,
To what mad courses may not mortal hearts
By thee be driven? Again her sorrow flies
To doleful plaint and supplication vain;
Again her pride to tyrant Love bows down,
Lest, though resolved to die, she fail to prove
Each hope of living: "O Anna, dost thou see
Yon busy shore? From every side they come.
Their canvas wooes the winds, and o'er each
   prow

The merry seamen hang their votive flowers.
Dear sister, since I did forebode this grief,
I shall be strong to bear it. One sole boon
My sorrow asks thee, Anna! Since of thee,
Thee only, did that traitor make a friend,
And trusted thee with what he hid so deep—
The feelings of his heart; since thou alone
Hast known what way, what hour the man would
   yield
To soft persuasion—therefore, sister, haste,
And humbly thus implore our haughty foe:
I was not with the Greeks what time they swore
At Aulis' to cut off the seed of Troy;
I sent no ships to Ilium. Pray, have I
Profaned Anchises' tomb, or vexed his shade?
Why should his ear be deaf and obdurate
To all I say? What haste? May he not make
One last poor offering to her whose love
Is only pain? O, bid him but delay
Till flight be easy and the winds blow fair.
I plead no more that bygone marriage-vow
By him forsworn, nor ask that he should lose
His beauteous Latium and his realm to be.
Nothing but time I crave! to give repose
And more room to this fever, till my fate
Teach a crushed heart to sorrow. I implore
This last grace. (To thy sister's grief be kind!)
I will requite with increase, till I die."

Such plaints, such prayers, again and yet again.
Betwixt the twain the sorrowing sister bore.
But no words move, no lamentations bring
Persuasion to his soul; decrees of Fate
Oppose, and some wise god obstructs the way
That finds the hero's ear. Oft-times around
The aged strength of some stupendous oak
The rival blasts of wintry Alpine winds
Smite with alternate wrath: loud is the roar,
And from its rocking top the broken boughs
Are strewn along the ground; but to the crag
Steadfast it ever clings; far as toward heaven
Its giant crest uprears, so deep below
Its roots reach down to Tartarus:—not less
The hero by unceasing wail and cry
Is smitten sore, and in his mighty heart
Has many a pang, while his serene intent
Abides unmoved, and tears gush forth in vain.

Then wretched Dido, by her doom appalled,
Asks only death. It wearies her to see
The sun in heaven. Yet that she might hold fast
Her dread resolve to quit the light of day,
Behold, when on an incense-breathing shrine
Her offering was laid—O fearful tale!—
The pure libation blackened, and the wine
Flowed like polluting gore. She told the sight

To none, not even to her sister's ears.
A second sign was given: for in her house
A marble altar to her husband's shade,
With garlands bright and snowy fleeces dressed,
Had fervent worship; here strange cries were
    heard
As if her dead spouse called while midnight
    reigned,
And round her towers its inhuman song
The lone owl sang, complaining o'er and o'er
With lamentation and long shriek of woe.
Forgotten oracles by wizard told
Whisper old omens dire. In dreams she feels
Cruel Æneas goad her madness on,
And ever seems she, friendless and alone,
Some lengthening path to travel, or to seek
Her Tyrians through wide wastes of barren
    lands.
Thus frantic Pentheus flees the stern array
Of the Eumenides, and thinks to see
Two noonday lights blaze o'er his doubled
    Thebes;
Or murdered Agamemnon's haunted son,
Orestes, flees his mother's phantom scourge
Of flames and serpents foul, while at his door
Avenging horrors wait.

    Now sorrow-crazed
And by her grief undone, resolved on death,
The manner and the time her secret soul
Prepares, and, speaking to her sister sad,
She masks in cheerful calm her fatal will:
"I know a way—O, wish thy sister joy!—To bring
    him back to love, or set me free.
On Ocean's bound and next the setting sun
Lies the last Æthiop land, where Atlas tall
Lifts on his shoulder the wide wheel of heaven,
Studded with burning stars. From thence is come
A witch, a priestess, a Numidian crone,
Who guards the shrine of the Hesperides
And feeds the dragon; she protects the fruit
Of that enchanting tree, and scatters there
Her slumbrous poppies mixed with honey-dew.
Her spells and magic promise to set free
What hearts she will, or visit cruel woes
On men afar. She stops the downward flow
Of rivers, and turns back the rolling stars;
On midnight ghosts she calls: her vot'ries hear
Earth bellowing loud below, while from the hills
The ash-trees travel down. But, sister mine,
Thou knowest, and the gods their witness give,
How little mind have I to don the garb
Of sorcery. Depart in secret, thou,
And bid them build a lofty funeral pyre
Inside our palace-wall, and heap thereon
The hero's arms, which that blasphemer hung

Within my chamber; every relic bring,
And chiefly that ill-omened nuptial bed,
My death and ruin! For I must blot out
All sight and token of this husband vile.
'Tis what the witch commands." She spoke no
    more,
And pallid was her brow. Yet Anna's mind
Knew not what web of death her sister wove
By these strange rites, nor what such frenzy dares;
Nor feared she worse than when Sichæus died,
But hied her forth the errand to fulfil.

Soon as the funeral pyre was builded high
In a sequestered garden, looming huge
With boughs of pine and faggots of cleft oak,
The queen herself enwreathed it with sad flowers
And boughs of mournful shade; and crowning all
She laid on nuptial bed the robes and sword
By him abandoned; and stretched out thereon
A mock Æneas;—but her doom she knew.
Altars were there; and with those locks unbound
The priestess with a voice of thunder called
Three hundred gods, Hell, Chaos, and three
    shapes
Of triple Hecate, the faces three
Of virgin Dian. She aspersed a stream
From dark Avernus drawn, she said; soft herbs
Were cut by moonlight with a blade of bronze,
Oozing black poison-sap; and she had plucked
That philter from the forehead of new foal
Before its dam devoirs. Dïdo herself,
Sprinkling the salt meal, at the altar stands;
One foot unsandalled, and with cincture free,
On all the gods and fate-instructed stars,
Foreseeing death, she calls. But if there be
Some just and not oblivious power on high,
Who heeds when lovers plight unequal vow,
To that god first her supplications rise.

Soon fell the night, and peaceful slumbers
    breathed
On all earth's weary creatures; the loud seas
And babbling forests entered on repose;
Now midway in their heavenly course the stars
Wheeled silent on; the outspread lands below
Lay voices; all the birds of tinted wing,
And flocks that haunt the marge of waters wide
Or keep the thorny wold, oblivious lay
Beneath the night so still; the stings of care
Ceased troubling, and no heart its burden knew
Not so the Tyrian Queen's deep-grieving soul!
To sleep she could not yield; her eyes and heart
Refused the gift of night; her suffering
Redoubled, and in full returning tide
Her love rebelled, while on wild waves of rage
    She drifted to and fro. So, ceasing not

From sorrow, thus she brooded on her wrongs:
"What refuge now? Shall I invite the scorn
Of my rejected wooers, or entreat
Of some disdainful, nomad blackamoor
To take me to his bed—though many a time
Such husbands I made mock of? Shall I sail
On Ilian ships away, and sink to be
The Trojans' humble thrall? Do they rejoice
That once I gave them bread? Lives gratitude
In hearts like theirs for bygone kindnesses?
O, who, if so I stooped, would deign to bear
On yon proud ships the scorned and fallen
   Queen?
Lost creature! Woe betide thee! Knowest thou not
The perjured children of Laomedon?
What way is left? Should I take flight alone
And join the revelling sailors? Or depart
With Tyrians, the whole attending train
Of my own people? Hard the task to force
Their hearts from Sidon's towers; how once more
Compel to sea, and bid them spread the sail?
Nay, perish! Thou hast earned it. Let the sword
From sorrow save thee! Sister of my blood—
Who else but thee,—by my own tears borne
   down,
Didst heap disaster on my frantic soul,
And fling me to this foe? Why could I not
Pass wedlock by, and live a blameless life
As wild things do, nor taste of passion's pain?
But I broke faith! I cast the vows away
Made at Sichæus' grave." Such loud lament
Burst from her breaking heart with doleful
   sound.

Meanwhile Æneas on his lofty ship,
Having made ready all, and fixed his mind
To launch away, upon brief slumber fell.
But the god came; and in the self-same guise
Once more in monitory vision spoke,—
All guised as Mercury,—his voice, his hue,
His golden locks, and young limbs strong and
   fair,
"Hail, goddess-born! Wouldst linger on in sleep
At such an hour? Nor seest thou the snares
That hem thee round? Nor hearest thou the voice
Of friendly zephyrs calling? Senseless man!
That woman's breast contrives some treachery
And horrid stroke; for, resolute to die,
She drifts on swollen floods of wrath and scorn.
Wilt thou not fly before the hastening hour
Of flight is gone? To-morrow thou wilt see
Yon waters thronged with ships, the cruel glare
Of fire-brands, and yonder shore all flame,
If but the light of morn again surprise
Thee loitering in this land. Away! Away!
Stay not! A mutable and shifting thing

Is woman ever."

   Such command he spoke,
Then melted in the midnight dark away.
Æneas, by that fleeting vision struck
With an exceeding awe, straightway leaped forth
From slumber's power, and to his followers
   cried:
"Awake, my men! Away! Each to his place
Upon the thwarts! Unfurl at once the sails!
A god from heaven a second time sent down
Urges our instant flight, and bids us cut
The twisted cords. Whatever be thy name,
Behold, we come, O venerated Power!
Again with joy we follow! Let thy grace
Assist us as we go! And may thy power
Bring none but stars benign across our sky."
So saying, from its scabbard forth he flashed
The lightning of his sword, with naked blade
Striking the hawsers free. Like ardor seized
On all his willing men, who raced and ran;
And, while their galleys shadowed all the sea,
Clean from the shore they scudded, with strong
   strokes
Sweeping the purple waves and crested foam.

Aurora's first young beams to earth were
   pouring
As from Tithonus' saffron bed she sprang;
While from her battlements the wakeful Queen
Watched the sky brighten, saw the mated sails
Push forth to sea, till all her port and strand
Held not an oar or keel. Thrice and four times
She smote her lovely breast with wrathful hand,
And tore her golden hair. "Great Jove," she cries,
"Shall that departing fugitive make mock
Of me, a queen? Will not my men-at-arms
Draw sword, give chase, from all my city
   thronging?
Down from the docks, my ships! Out, out!
   Begone!
Take fire and sword! Bend to your oars, ye slaves!
What have I said? Where am I? What mad
   thoughts
Delude this ruined mind? Woe unto thee,
Thou wretched Dido, now thy impious deeds
Strike back upon thee. Wherefore struck they not,
As was most fit, when thou didst fling away
Thy sceptre from thy hand? O lying oaths!
O faith forsworn! of him who brings, they boast,
His father's gods along, and bowed his back
To lift an age-worn sire! Why dared I not
Seize on him, rend his body limb from limb,
And hurl him piecemeal on the rolling sea?
Or put his troop of followers to the sword,
Ascanius too, and set his flesh before

That father for a feast? Such fearful war
Had been of doubtful issue. Be it so!
What fears a woman dying? Would I had
Attacked their camp with torches, kindled flame
From ship to ship, until that son and sire,
With that whole tribe, were unto ashes burned
In one huge holocaust—myself its crown!
Great orb of light whose holy beam surveys
All earthly deeds! Great Juno, patroness
Of conjugal distress, who knowest all!
Pale Hecate, whose name the witches cry
At midnight crossways! O avenging furies!
O gods that guard Queen Dido's dying breath!
Give ear, and to my guiltless misery
Extend your power. Hear me what I pray!
If it be fated that yon creature curst
Drift to the shore and happy haven find,
If Father Jove's irrevocable word
Such goal decree—there may he be assailed
By peoples fierce and bold. A banished man,
From his Iulus' kisses sundered far,
May his own eyes see miserably slain
His kin and kind, and sue for alien arms.
Nor when he basely bows him to receive
Terms of unequal peace, shall he be blest
With sceptre or with life; but perish there
Before his time, and lie without a grave
Upon the barren sand. For this I pray.
This dying word is flowing from my heart
With my spilt blood. And—O ye Tyrians!
Sting with your hatred all his seed and tribe
Forevermore. This is the offering
My ashes ask. Betwixt our nations twain,
No love! No truce or amity! Arise,
Out of my dust, unknown Avenger, rise!
To harry and lay waste with sword and flame
Those Dardan settlers, and to vex them sore,
To-day, to-morrow, and as long as power
Is thine to use! My dying curse arrays
Shore against shore and the opposing seas
In shock of arms with arms. May living foes
Pass down from sire to son insatiate war!"

She said. From point to point her purpose flew,
Seeking without delay to quench the flame
Of her loathed life. Brief bidding she addressed
To Barce then, Sichæus' nurse (her own
Lay dust and ashes in a lonely grave
Beside the Tyrian shore), "Go, nurse, and call
My sister Anna! Bid her quickly bathe
Her limbs in living water, and procure
Due victims for our expiating fires.
Bid her make haste. Go, bind on thy own brow
The sacred fillet. For to Stygian Jove
It is my purpose now to consummate
The sacrifice ordained, ending my woe,

And touch with flame the Trojan's funeral pyre."

The aged crone to do her bidding ran
With trembling zeal. But Dido (horror-struck
At her own dread design, unstrung with fear,
Her bloodshot eyes wide-rolling, and her cheek
Twitching and fever-spotted, her cold brow
Blanched with approaching death)—sped past
    the doors
Into the palace garden; there she leaped,
A frenzied creature, on the lofty pyre
And drew the Trojan's sword; a gift not asked
For use like this! When now she saw the garb
Of Ilian fashion, and the nuptial couch
She knew too well, she lingered yet awhile
For memory and tears, and, falling prone
On that cold bed, outpoured a last farewell:
"Sweet relics! Ever dear when Fate and Heaven
Upon me smiled, receive my parting breath,
And from my woe set free! My life is done.
I have accomplished what my lot allowed;
And now my spirit to the world of death
In royal honor goes. The founder I
Of yonder noble city, I have seen
Walls at my bidding rise. I was avenged
For my slain husband: I chastised the crimes
Of our injurious brother. Woe is me!
Blest had I been, beyond deserving blest,
If but the Trojan galleys ne'er had moored
Upon my kingdom's bound!" So saying, she
    pressed
One last kiss on the couch. "Though for my death
No vengeance fall, O, give my death!" she cried.
O thus! O thus! it is my will to take
The journey to the dark. From yonder sea
May his cold Trojan eyes discern the flames
That make me ashes! Be this cruel death
His omen as he sails!"

    She spoke no more.
But almost ere she ceased, her maidens all
Thronged to obey her cry, and found their Queen
Prone fallen on the sword, the reeking steel
Still in her bloody hands. Shrill clamor flew
Along the lofty halls; wild rumor spread
Through the whole smitten city; loud lament,
Groans and the wail of women echoed on
From roof to roof, and to the dome of air
The noise of mourning rose. Such were the cry
If a besieging host should break the walls
Of Carthage or old Tyre, and wrathful flames
O'er towers of kings and worshipped altars roll.
Her sister heard. Half in a swoon, she ran
With trembling steps, where thickest was the
    throng,
Beating her breast, while with a desperate hand

She tore at her own face, and called aloud
Upon the dying Queen, "Was it for this
My own true sister used me with such guile?
O, was this horrid deed the dire intent
Of altars, lofty couch, and funeral fires?
What shall I tell for chiefest of my woes?
Lost that I am! Why, though in death, cast off
Thy sister from thy heart? Why not invite
One mortal stroke for both, a single sword,
One agony together? But these hands
Built up thy pyre; and my voice implored
The blessing of our gods, who granted me
That thou shouldst perish thus—and I not know!
In thy self-slaughter, sister, thou hast slain
Myself, thy people, the grave counsellors
Of Sidon, and yon city thou didst build
To be thy throne!—Go, fetch me water, there!
That I may bathe those gashes! If there be
One hovering breath that stays, let my fond lips
Discover and receive!"

   So saying she sprang up
From stair to stair, and, clasping to her breast
Her sister's dying form, moaned grievously,
And staunched the dark blood with her
   garment's fold.
Vainly would Dido lift her sinking eyes,
But backward fell, while at her heart the wound
Opened afresh; three times with straining arm

She rose; three times dropped helpless, her
   dimmed eyes
Turned skyward, seeking the sweet light of
   day,—
—Which when she saw, she groaned.

   Great Juno then
Looked down in mercy on that lingering pain
And labor to depart: from realms divine
She sent the goddess of the rainbow wing,
Iris, to set the struggling spirit free
And loose its fleshly coil. For since the end
Came not by destiny, nor was the doom
Of guilty deed, but of a hapless wight
To sudden madness stung, ere ripe to die,
Therefore the Queen of Hades had not shorn
The fair tress from her forehead, nor assigned
That soul to Stygian dark. So Iris came
On dewy, saffron pinions down from heaven,
A thousand colors on her radiant way,
From the opposing sun. She stayed her flight
Above that pallid brow: "I come with power
To make this gift to Death. I set thee free
From thy frail body's bound." With her right
   hand
She cut the tress: then through its every limb
The sinking form grew cold; the vital breath
Fled forth, departing on the viewless air.

Book VI

After such words and tears, he flung free
   rein
To the swift fleet, which sped along the wave
To old Euboeran Cumæ's sacred shore.
They veer all prows to sea; the anchor fluke
Makes each ship sure, and shading the long
   strand
The rounded sterns jut o'er. Impetuously
The eager warriors leap forth to land
Upon Hesperian soil. One strikes the flint
To find the seed-spark hidden in its veins;
One breaks the thick-branched trees, and steals
   away
The shelter where the woodland creatures bide;
One leads his mates where living waters flow.

Æneas, servant of the gods, ascends
The templed hill where lofty Phoebus reigns,
And that far-off, inviolable shrine
Of dread Sibylla, in stupendous cave,

O'er whose deep soul the god of Delos breathes
Prophetic gifts, unfolding things to come.
Here are pale Trivia's golden house and grove.
Here Dædalus, the ancient story tells,
Escaping Minos' power, and having made
Hazard of heaven on far-mounting wings,
Floated to northward, a cold, trackless way,
And lightly poised, at last, o'er Cumæ's towers.
Here first to earth come down, he gave to thee
His gear of wings, Apollo! and ordained
Vast temples to thy name and altars fair.
On huge bronze doors Androgeos' death was
   done;
And Cecrops' children paid their debt of woe,
Where, seven and seven,—O pitiable sight!—
The youths and maidens wait the annual doom,
Drawn out by lot from yonder marble urn.
Beyond, above a sea, lay carven Crete:
The bull was there; the passion, the strange guile;
And Queen Pasiphaë's brute-human son,

The Minotaur—of monstrous loves the sign.
Here was the toilsome, labyrinthine maze,
Where, pitying love-lorn Ariadne's tears,
The crafty Dædalus himself betrayed
The secret of his work; and gave the clue
To guide the path of Theseus through the gloom.
O Icarus, in such well-graven scene
How proud thy place should be! but grief
    forbade:
Twice in pure gold a father's fingers strove
To shape thy fall, and twice they strove in vain.

Æneas long the various work would scan;
But now Achates comes, and by his side
Deïphobe, the Sibyl, Glaucus' child.
Thus to the prince she spoke:

    "Is this thine hour
To stand and wonder? Rather go obtain
From young unbroken herd the bullocks seven,
And seven yearling ewes, our wonted way."
Thus to Æneas; his attendants haste
To work her will; the priestess, calling loud,
Gathers the Trojans to her mountain-shrine.

Deep in the face of the Euboean crag
A cavern vast is hollowed out amain,
With hundred openings, a hundred mouths,
Whence voices flow, the Sibyl's answering songs.
While at the door they paused, the virgin cried:
"Ask now thy doom!—the god! the god is nigh!"
So saying, from her face its color flew,
Her twisted locks flowed free, the heaving breast
Swelled with her heart's wild blood; her statute
    seemed
Vaster, her accent more than mortal man,
As all th' oncoming god around her breathed:
"On with thy vows and prayers, O Trojan, on!
For only unto prayer this haunted cave
May its vast lips unclose." She spake no more.
An icy shudder through the marrow ran
Of the bold Trojans; while their sacred King
Poured from his inmost soul this plaint and
    prayer:
"Phoebus, who ever for the woes of Troy
Hadst pitying eyes! who gavest deadly aim
To Paris when his Dardan shaft he hurled
On great Achilles! Thou hast guided me
Through many an unknown water, where the
    seas
Break upon kingdoms vast, and to the tribes
Of the remote Massyli, whose wild land
To Syrtes spreads. But now, because at last
I touch Hesperia's ever-fleeting bound,
May Troy's ill fate forsake me from this day!
O gods and goddesses, beneath whose wrath

Dardania's glory and great Ilium stood,
Spare, for ye may, the remnant of my race!
And thou, most holy prophetess, whose soul
Foreknows events to come, grant to my prayer
(Which asks no kingdom save what Fate decrees)
That I may stablish in the Latin land
My Trojans, my far-wandering household gods,
And storm-tossed deities of fallen Troy.
Then unto Phoebus and his sister pale
A temple all of marble shall be given,
And festal days to Phoebus evermore.
Thee also in my realms a spacious shrine
Shall honor; thy dark books and holy songs
I there will keep, to be my people's law;
And thee, benignant Sibyl, for all time
A company of chosen priests shall serve.
O, not on leaves, light leaves, inscribe thy songs!
Lest, playthings of each breeze, they fly afar
In swift confusion! sing thyself, I pray."

So ceased his voice; the virgin through the cave,
Scarce bridled yet by Phoebus' hand divine,
Ecstatic swept along, and vainly strove
To fling its potent master from her breast;
But he more strongly plied his rein and curb
Upon her frenzied lips, and soon subdued
Her spirit fierce, and swayed her at his will.
Free and self-moved the cavern's hundred doors
Swung open wide, and uttered to the air
The oracles the virgin-priestess sung:
"Thy long sea-perils thou hast safely passed;
But heavier woes await thee on the land.
Truly thy Trojans to Lavinian shore
Shall come—vex not thyself thereon—but, oh!
Shall rue their coming thither! war, red war!
And Tiber stained with bloody foam I see.
Simois, Xanthus and the Dorian horde
Thou shalt behold; a new Achilles now
In Latium breathes,—he, too, of goddess born;
And Juno, burden of the sons of Troy,
Will vex them ever; while thyself shalt sue
In dire distress to many a town and tribe
Through Italy; the cause of so much ill
Again shall be a hostess-queen, again
A marriage-chamber for an alien bride.
Oh! yield not to thy woe, but front it ever,
And follow boldly whither Fortune calls.
Thy way of safety, as thou least couldst dream,
Lies through a city of the Greeks, thy foes."

Thus from her shrine Cumaea's prophetess
Changed the dark decrees; the dreadful sound
Reverberated through the bellowing cave,
Commingling truth with ecstasies obscure.
Apollo, as she raged, flung loosened rein,
And thrust beneath her heart a quickening spur.

When first her madness ceased, and her wild lips
Were still at last, the hero thus began:
"No tribulations new, O Sibyl blest,
Can now confront me; every future pain
I have foretasted; my prophetic soul
Endured each stroke of fate before it fell.
One boon I ask. If of th' infernal King
This be the portal where the murky wave
Of swollen Acheron o'erflows its bound,
Here let me enter and behold the face
Of my loved sire. Thy hand may point the way;
Thy word will open wide yon holy doors.
My father through the flames and falling spears,
Straight through the centre of our foes, I bore
Upon these shoulders. My long flight he shared
From sea to sea, and suffered at my side
The anger of rude waters and dark skies,—
Though weak—O task too great for old and gray!
Thus as a suppliant at thy door to stand,
Was his behest and prayer. On son and sire,
O gracious one, have pity,—for thy rule
Is over all; no vain authority
Hadst thou from Trivia o'er th' Avernian groves.
If Orpheus could call back his loved one's shade,
Emboldened by the lyre's melodious string:
If Pollux by the interchange of death
Redeemed his twin, and oft repassed the way:
If Theseus—but why name him? why recall
Alcides' task? I, too, am sprung from Jove."

Thus, to the altar clinging, did he pray:
The Sibyl thus replied: "Offspring of Heaven,
Anchises' son, the downward path to death
Is easy; all the livelong night and day
Dark Pluto's door stands open for a guest.
But O! remounting to the world of light,
This is a task indeed, a strife supreme.
Few, very few, whom righteous Jove did bless,
Or quenchless virtue carried to the stars,
Children of gods, have such a victory won.
Grim forests stop the way, and, gliding slow,
Cocytus circles through the sightless gloom.
But if it be thy dream and fond desire
Twice o'er the Stygian gulf to travel, twice
On glooms of Tartarus to set thine eyes,
If such mad quest be now thy pleasure—hear
What must be first fulfilled. A certain tree
Hides in obscurest shade a golden bough,
Of pliant stems and many a leaf of gold,
Sacred to Proserpine, infernal Queen.
Far in the grove it hides; in sunless vale
Deep shadows keep it in captivity.
No pilgrim to that underworld can pass
But he who plucks this burgeoned, leafy gold;
For this hath beauteous Proserpine ordained
Her chosen gift to be. Whene'er 't is culled,

A branch out-leafing in like golden gleam,
A second wonder-stem, fails not to spring.
Therefore go seek it with uplifted eyes!
And when by will of Heaven thou findest it,
Reach forth and pluck; for at a touch it yields,
A free and willing gift, if Fate ordain;
But otherwise no mortal strength avails,
Nor strong, sharp steel, to rend it from the tree.
Another task awaits; thy friend's cold clay
Lies unentombed. Alas! thou art not ware
(While in my house thou lingerest, seeking light)
That all thy ships are by his death defiled.
Unto his resting-place and sepulchre,
Go, carry him! And sable victims bring,
In expiation, to his mournful shade.
So at the last on yonder Stygian groves,
And realms to things that breathe impassable,
Thine eye shall gaze." So closer her lips inspired.
Æneas then drew forth, with downcast eyes,
From that dark cavern, pondering in his heart
The riddle of his fate. His faithful friend
Achates at his side, with paces slow,
Companioned all his care, while their sad souls
Made mutual and oft-renewed surmise
What comrade dead, what cold and tombless
  clay,
The Sibyl's word would show.

    But as they mused,
Behold Misenus on the dry sea-sands,
By hasty hand of death struck guiltless down!
A son of Æolus, none better knew
To waken heroes by the clarion's call,
With war-enkindling sound. Great Hector's
  friend
In happier days, he oft at Hector's side
Strode to the fight with glittering lance and horn.
But when Achilles stripped his fallen foe,
This dauntless hero to Æneas gave
Allegiance true, in not less noble cause.
But, on a day, he chanced beside the sea
To blow his shell-shaped horn, and wildly dared
Challenge the gods themselves to rival song;
Till jealous Triton, if the tale be true,
Grasped the rash mortal, and out-flung him far
'Mid surf-beat rocks and waves of whirling foam.
Now from all sides, with tumult and loud cry,
The Trojans came,—Æneas leading all
In faithful grief; they hasten to fulfill
The Sibyl's mandate, and with many a tear
Build, altar-wise, a pyre, of tree on tree
Heaped high as heaven: then they penetrate
The tall, old forest, where wild creatures bide,
And fell pitch-pines, or with resounding blows
Of axe and wedge, cleave oak and ash-tree
  through,

Or logs of rowan down the mountains roll.
Æneas oversees and shares the toil,
Cheers on his mates, and swings a woodman's
   steel.
But, sad at heart with many a doubt and care,
O'erlooks the forest wide; then prays aloud:
"O, that the Golden Bough from this vast grove
Might o'er me shine! For, O Æolides,
The oracle foretold thy fate, too well!"
Scarce had he spoken, when a pair of doves
Before his very eyes flew down from heaven
To the green turf below; the prince of Troy
Knew them his mother's birds, and joyful cried,
"O, guide me on, whatever path there be!
In airy travel through the woodland fly,
To where yon rare branch shades the blessed
   ground.
Fail thou not me, in this my doubtful hour,
O heavenly mother!" So saying, his steps he
   stayed,
Close watching whither they should signal give;
The lightly-feeding doves flit on and on.
Ever in easy ken of following eyes,
Till over foul Avernus' sulphurous throat
Swiftly they lift them through the liquid air,
In silent flight, and find a wished-for rest
On a twy-natured tree, where through green
   boughs
Flames forth the glowing gold's contrasted hue.
As in the wintry woodland bare and chill,
Fresh-budded shines the clinging mistletoe,
Whose seed is never from the parent tree
O'er whose round limbs its tawny tendrils
   twine,—
So shone th' out-leafing gold within the shade
Of dark holm-oak, and so its tinsel-bract
Rustled in each light breeze. Æneas grasped
The lingering bough, broke it in eager haste,
And bore it straightway to Sibyl's shrine.

Meanwhile the Trojans on the doleful shore
Bewailed Misenus, and brought tribute there
Of grief's last gift to his unheeding clay.
First, of the full-sapped pine and well-hewn oak
A lofty pyre they build; then sombre boughs
Around it wreathe, and in fair order range
Funereal cypress; glittering arms are piled
High over all; on blazing coals they lift
Cauldrons of brass brimmed o'er with waters
   pure;
And that cold, lifeless clay lave and anoint
With many a moan and cry; on their last couch
The poor, dead limbs they lay, and mantle o'er
With purple vesture and familiar pall.
Then in sad ministry the chosen few,
With eyes averted, as our sires did use,

Hold the enkindling torch beneath the pyre:
They gather up and burn the gifts of myrrh,
The sacred bread and bowls of flowing oil;
And when in flame the dying embers fall,
On thirsty ash they pour the streams of wine.
Good Corynæus, in an urn of brass
The gathered relics hides; and three times round,
With blessed olive branch and sprinkling dew,
Purges the people with ablution cold,
In lustral rite; oft chanting, "Hail! Farewell!"
Faithful Æneas for his comrade built
A mighty tomb, and dedicated there
Trophy of arms, with trumpet and with oar,
Beneath a windy hill, which now is called
"Misenus,"—for all time the name to bear.

After these toils, they hasten to fulfil
What else the Sibyl said. Straightway they find
A cave profound, of entrance gaping wide,
O'erhung with rock, in gloom of sheltering
   grove,
Near the dark waters of a lake, whereby
No bird might ever pass with scathless wing,
So dire an exhalation is breathed out
From that dark deep of death to upper air:—
Hence, in the Grecian tongue, Aornos called.
Here first four youthful bulls of swarthy hide
Were led for sacrifice; on each broad brow
The priestess sprinkled wine; 'twixt the two
   horns
Outplucked the lifted hair, and cast it forth
Upon the holy flames, beginning so
Her offerings; then loudly sued the power
Of Hecate, a Queen in heaven and hell.
Some struck with knives, and caught in shallow
   bowls
The smoking blood. Æneas' lifted hand
Smote with a sword a sable-fleecèd ewe
To Night, the mother of th' Eumenides,
And Earth, her sister dread; next unto thee,
O Proserpine, a curst and barren cow;
Then unto Pluto, Stygian King, he built
An altar dark and piled upon the flames
The ponderous entrails of the bulls, and poured
Free o'er the burning flesh the goodly oil.
Then lo! at dawn's dim, earliest beam began
Beneath their feet a groaning of the ground:
The wooded hill-tops shook, and, as it seemed,
She-hounds of hell howled viewless through the
   shade,
To hail their Queen. "Away, O souls profane!
Stand far away!" the priestess shrieked, "nor
   dare
Unto this grove come near! Æneas, on!
Begin thy journey! Draw thy sheathed blade!
Now, all thy courage! now, th' unshaken soul!"

She spoke, and burst into the yawning cave
With frenzied step; he follows where she leads,
And strides with feet unfaltering at her side.

Ye gods! who rule the spirits of the dead!
Ye voiceless shades and silent lands of night!
O Phlegethon! O Chaos! let my song,
If it be lawful, in fit words declare
What I have heard; and by your help divine
Unfold what hidden things enshrouded lie
In that dark underworld of sightless gloom.

They walked exploring the unpeopled night,
Through Pluto's vacuous realms, and regions
    void,
As when one's path in dreary woodlands winds
Beneath a misty moon's deceiving ray,
When Jove has mantled all his heaven in shade,
And night seals up the beauty of the world.
In the first courts and entrances of Hell
Sorrows and vengeful Cares on couches lie:
There sad Old Age abides, Diseases pale,
And Fear, and Hunger, temptress to all crime;
Want, base and vile, and, two dread shapes to
    see,
Bondage and Death: then Sleep, Death's next of
    kin;
And dreams of guilty joy. Death-dealing War
Is ever at the doors, and hard thereby
The Furies' beds of steel, where wild-eyed Strife
Her snaky hair with bloodstained fillet binds.
There in the middle court a shadowy elm
Its ancient branches spreads, and in its leaves
Deluding visions ever haunt and cling.
Then come strange prodigies of bestial kind:
Centaurs are stabled there, and double shapes
Like Scylla, or the dragon Lema bred,
With hideous scream; Briareus clutching far
His hundred hands, Chimæra girt with flame,
A crowd of Gorgons, Harpies of foul wing,
And giant Geryon's triple-monstered shade.
Æneas, shuddering with sudden fear,
Drew sword and fronted them with naked steel;
And, save his sage conductress bade him know
These were but shapes and shadows sweeping
    by,
His stroke had cloven in vain the vacant air.
Hence the way leads to that Tartarean stream
Of Acheron, whose torrent fierce and foul
Disgorges in cocytus all its sands.
A ferryman of gruesome guise keeps ward
Upon these waters,—Charon, foully garbed,
With unkempt, thick gray beard upon his chin,
And staring eyes of flame; a mantle coarse,
All stained and knotted, from his shoulder falls,
As with a pole he guides his craft, tends sail,

And in the black boat ferries o'er hid dead;—
Old, but a god's old age looks fresh and strong.

To those dim shores the multitude streams on—
Husbands and wives, and pale, unbreathing
    forms
Of high-souled heroes, boys and virgins fair,
And strong youth at whose graves fond parents
    mourned.
As numberless the throng as leaves that fall
When autumn's early frost is on the grove;
Or like vast flocks of birds by winter's chill
Sent flying o'er wide seas to lands of flowers.
All stood beseeching to begin their voyage
Across that river, and reached out pale hands,
In passionate yearning for its distant shore.
But the grim boatman takes now these, now
    those,
Or thrusts unpitying from the stream away.

Æneas, moved to wonder and deep awe,
Beheld the tumult; "Virgin seer!" he cried,
"Why move the thronging ghosts toward yonder
    stream?
What seek they there? Or what election holds
That these unwilling linger, while their peers
Sweep forward yonder o'er the leaden waves?"
To him, in few, the aged Sibyl spoke:
"Son of Anchises, offspring of the gods,
Yon are cocytus and Stygian stream,
By whose dread power the gods themselves do
    fear
To take an oath in vain. Here far and wide
Thou seest the hapless throng that hath no grave.
That boatman Charon bears across the deep
Such as be sepulchred with holy care.
But over that loud flood and dreadful shore
No trav'ler may be borne, until in peace
His gathered ashes rest. A hundred years
Round this dark borderland some haunt and
    roam,
Then win late passage o'er the longed-for wave."

Æneas lingered for a little space,
Revolving in his soul with pitying prayer
Fate's partial way. But presently he sees
Leucaspis and the Lycian navy's lord,
Orontes; both of melancholy brow,
Both hapless and unhonored after death,
Whom, while from Troy they crossed the
    wind-swept seas,
A whirling tempest wrecked with ship and crew.
There, too, the helmsman Palinurus strayed:
Who, as he whilom watched the Libyan stars,
Had fallen, plunging from his lofty seat
Into the billowy deep. Æneas now

Discerned his sad face through the blinding
    gloom,
And hailed him thus: "O Palinurus, tell
What god was he who ravished thee away
From me and mine, beneath the overwhelming
    wave?
Speak on! for he who ne'er had spoke untrue,
Apollo's self, did mock my listening mind,
And chanted me a faithful oracle
That thou shouldst ride the seas unharmed, and
    touch
Ausonian shores. Is this the pledge divine?"
Then he, "O chieftain of Anchises' race,
Apollos's tripod told thee not untrue.
No god did thrust me down beneath the wave,
For that strong rudder unto which I clung,
My charge and duty, and my ship's sole guide,
Wrenched from its place, dropped with me as I
    fell.
Not for myself—by the rude seas I swear—
Did I have terror, but lest thy good ship,
Stripped of her hear, and her poor pilot lost,
Should fail and founder in that rising flood.
Three wintry nights across the boundless main
The south wind buffeted and bore me on;
At the fourth daybreak, lifted from the surge,
I looked at last on Italy, and swam
With weary stroke on stroke unto the land.
Safe was I then. Alas! but as I climbed
With garments wet and heavy, my clenched hand
Grasping the steep rock, came a cruel horde
Upon me with drawn blades, accounting me—
So blind they were!—a wrecker's prize and spoil.
Now are the waves my tomb, and wandering
    winds
Toss me along the coast. O, I implore,
By heaven's sweet light, by yonder upper air,
By thy lost father, by Iulus dear,
Thy rising hope and joy, that from these woes,
Unconquered chieftain, thou wilt set me free!
Give me a grave where Velia's haven lies,
For thou hast power! Or if some path there be,
If thy celestial mother guide thee here
(For not, I ween, without the grace of gods
Wilt cross yon rivers vast, yon Stygian pool)
Reach me a hand! and bear with thee along!
Until (least gift!) death bring me peace and
    calm."

Such words he spoke: the priestess thus replied:
"Why, Palinurus, these unblest desires?
Wouldst thou, unsepulchred, behold the wave
Of Styx, stern river of th' Eumenides?
Wouldst thou, unbidden, tread its fearful strand?
Hope not by prayer to change the laws of
    Heaven!

But heed my words, and in thy memory
Cherish and keep, to cheer this evil time.
Lo, far and wide, led on by signs from Heaven,
Thy countrymen from many a templed town
Shall consecrate thy dust, and build thy tomb,
A tomb with annual feasts and votive flowers,
To Palinurus a perpetual fame!"
Thus was his anguish stayed, from his sad heart
Grief ebbed awhile, and even to this day,
Our land is glad such noble name to wear.

The twain continue now their destined way
Unto the river's edge. The Ferryman,
Who watched them through still groves
    approach his shore,
Hailed them, at distance, from the Stygian wave,
And with reproachful summons thus began:
"Whoe'er thou art that in this warrior guise
Unto my river comest,—quickly tell
Thine errand! Stay thee where thou standest
    now!
This is ghosts' land, for sleep and slumbrous
    dark.
That flesh and blood my Stygian ship should
    bear
Were lawless wrong. Unwillingly I took
Alcides, Theseus, and Pirithous,
Though sons of gods, too mighty to be quelled.
One bound in chains yon warder of Hell's door,
And dragged him trembling from our monarch's
    throne:
The others, impious, would steal away
Out of her bride-bed Pluto's ravished Queen."

Briefly th' Amphrysian priestess made reply:
"Not ours, such guile: Fear not! this warrior's
    arms
Are innocent. Let Cerberus from his cave
Bay ceaselessly, the bloodless shades to scarce;
Let Proserpine immaculately keep
The house and honor of her kinsman King.
Trojan Æneas, famed for faithful prayer
And victory in arms, descends to seek
His father in this gloomy deep of death.
If loyal goodness move not such as thee,
This branch at least" (she drew it from her breast)
"Thou knowest well."

    Then cooled his wrathful heart;
With silent lips he looked and wondering eyes
Upon that fateful, venerable wand,
Seen only once an age. Shoreward he turned,
And pushed their way his boat of leaden hue.
The rows of crouching ghosts along the thwarts
He scattered, cleared a passage, and gave room
To great Æneas. The light shallop groaned

Beneath his weight, and, straining at each seam,
Took in the foul flood with unstinted flow.

At last the hero and his priestess-guide
Came safe across the river, and were moored
'Mid sea-green sedges in the formless mire.
Here Cerberus, with triple-throated roar,
Made all the region ring, as there he lay
At vast length in his cave. The Sibyl then,
Seeing the serpents writhe around his neck,
Threw down a loaf with honeyed herbs imbued
And drowsy essences: he, ravenous,
Gaped wide his three fierce mouths and snatched
    the bait,
Crouched with his large backs loose upon the
    ground,
And filled his cavern floor from end to end.
Æneas through hell's portal moved, while sleep
Its warder buried; then he fled that shore
Of Stygian stream, whence travellers ne'er
    return.
Now hears he sobs, and piteous, lisping cries
Of souls of babes upon the threshold plaining;
Whom, ere they took their portion of sweet life,
Dark Fate from nursing bosoms tore, and
    plunged
In bitterness of death. Nor far from these,
The throng of dead by unjust judgment slain.
Not without judge or law these realms abide:
Wise Minos there the urn of justice moves
And holds assembly of the silent shades,
Hearing the stories of their lives and deeds.
Close on this place those doleful ghosts abide,
Who, not for crime, but loathing life and light
With their own hands took death, and cast away
The vital essence. Willingly, alas!
They now would suffer need, or burdens bear,
If only life were given! But Fate forbids.
Around them winds the sad, unlovely wave
Of Styx: nine times it coils and interflows.
Not far from hence, on every side outspread,
The Fields of Sorrow lie,—such name they bear;
Here all whom ruthless love did waste away
Wander in paths unseen, or in the gloom
Of a dark myrtle grove: not even in death
Have they forgot their griefs of long ago.
Here impious Phædra and poor Procris bide;
Lorn Eriphyle bares the vengeful wounds
Her own son's dagger made; Evadne here,
And foul Pasiphaë are seen; hard by,
Laodamia, nobly fond and fair;
And Cæneus, not a boy, but maiden now,
By Fate remoulded to her native seeming.
Here Tyrian Dido, too, her wound unhealed,
Roamed through a mighty wood. The Trojan's
    eyes

Beheld her near him through the murky gloom,
As when, in her young month and crescent pale,
One sees th' o'er-clouded moon, or thinks he
    sees.
Down dropped his tears, and thus he fondly
    spoke:
"O suffering Dido! Were those tidings true
That thou didst fling thee on the fatal steel?
Thy death, ah me! I dealt it. But I swear
By stars above us, by the powers in Heaven,
Or whatsoever oath ye dead believe,
That not by choice I fled thy shores, O Queen!
Divine decrees compelled me, even as now
Among these ghosts I pass, and thread my way
Along this gulf of night and loathsome land.
How could I deem my cruel taking leave
Would bring thee at the last to all this woe?
O, stay! Why shun me? Wherefore haste away?
Our last farewell! Our doom! I speak it now!"
Thus, though she glared with fierce, relentless
    gaze, Æneas, with fond words and tearful
    plea,
Would soothe her angry soul. But on the ground
She fixed averted eyes. For all he spoke
Moved her no more than if her frowning brow
Were changeless flint or carved in Parian stone.
Then, after pause, away in wrath she fled,
And refuge took within the cool, dark grove,
Where her first spouse, Sichæus, with her tears
Mingled his own in mutual love and true.
Æneas, none the less, her guiltless woe
With anguish knew, watched with dimmed eyes
    her way,
And pitied from afar the fallen Queen.
But now his destined way he must be gone;
Now the last regions round the travellers lie,
Where famous warriors in the darkness dwell:
Here Tydeus comes in view, with far-renowned
Parthenopæus and Adrastus pale;
Here mourn in upper air with many a moan,
In battle fallen, the Dardanidæ,
Whose long defile Æneas groans to see:
Glaucus and Medon and Thersilochus,
Antenor's children three, and Ceres' priest,
That Polypoetes, and Idæus still
Keeping the kingly chariot and spear.
Around him left and right the crowding shades
Not only once would see, but clutch and cling
Obstructive, asking on what quest he goes.
Soon as the princes of Argolic blood,
With line on line of Agamemnon's men,
Beheld the hero and his glittering arms
Flash through the dark, they trembled with
    amaze,
Or turned in flight, as if once more they fled
To shelter of the ships; some raised aloft

A feeble shout, or vainly opened wide
Their gaping lips in mockery of sound.
Here Priam's son, with body rent and torn,
Deïphobus, is seen,—his mangled face,
His face and bloody hands, his wounded head
Of ears and nostrils infamously shorn.
Scarce could Æneas know the shuddering shade
That strove to hide its face and shameful scar,
But, speaking first, he said, in their own tongue:
"Deïphobus, strong warrior, nobly born
Of Teucer's royal stem, what ruthless foe
Could wish to wreak on thee this dire revenge?
Who ventured, unopposed, so vast a wrong?
The rumor reached me how, that deadly night,
Wearied with slaying Greeks, thyself didst fall
Prone on a mingled heap of friends and foes.
Then my own hands did for thy honor build
An empty tomb upon the Trojan shore,
And thrice with echoing voice I called thy shade.
Thy name and arms are there. But, O my friend,
Thee could I nowhere find, but launched away,
Nor o'er thy bones their native earth could
    fling."

To him the son of Priam thus replied:
"Nay, friend, no hallowed rite was left undone,
But every debt to death and pity due
The shades of thy Deïphobus received.
My fate it was, and Helen's murderous wrong,
Wrought me this woe; of her these tokens tell.
For how that last night in false hope we passed,
Thou knowest,—ah, too well we both recall!
When up the steep of Troy the fateful horse
Came climbing, pregnant with fierce
    men-at-arms,
'T was she, accurst, who led the Phrygian dames
In choric dance and false bacchantic song,
And, waving from the midst a lofty brand,
Signalled the Greeks from Ilium's central tower.
In that same hour on my sad couch I lay,
Exhausted by long care and sunk in sleep,
That sweet, deep sleep, so close to tranquil death.
But my illustrious bride from all the house
Had stolen all arms; from 'neath my pillowed
    head
She stealthily bore off my trusty sword;
Then loud on Menelaus did she call,
And with her own false hand unbarred the door;
Such gift to her fond lord she fain would send
To blot the memory of his ancient wrong!
Why tell the tale, how on my couch they broke,
While their accomplice, vile Æolides,
Counselled to many a crime. O heavenly Powers!
Reward these Greeks their deeds of wickedness,
If with clean lips upon your wrath I call!
But, friend, what fortunes have thy life befallen?

Tell point by point. Did waves of wandering seas
Drive thee this way, or some divine command?
What chastisement of fortune thrusts thee on
Toward this forlorn abode of night and cloud?"
While thus they talked, the crimsoned car of
    Morn
Had wheeled beyond the midmost point of
    heaven,
On her ethereal road. The princely pair
Had wasted thus the whole brief gift of hours;
But Sibyl spoke the warning: "Night speeds by,
And we, Æneas, lose it in lamenting.
Here comes the place where cleaves our way in
    twain.
Thy road, the right, toward Pluto's dwelling
    goes,
And leads us to Elysium. But the left
Speeds sinful souls to doom, and is their path
To Tartarus th' accurst. Deïphobus
Cried out: O priestess, be not wroth with us!
Back to the ranks with yonder ghosts I go.
O glory of my race, pass on! Thy lot
Be happier than mine!" He spoke and fled.

Æneas straightway by the leftward cliff
Beheld a spreading rampart, high begirt
With triple wall, and circling round it ran
A raging river of swift floods of flame,
Infernal Phlegethon, which whirls along
Loud-thundering rocks. A mighty gate is there
Columned in adamant; no human power,
Nor even the gods, against this gate prevail.
Tall tower of steel it has; and seated there
Tisiphone, in blood-flecked pall arrayed,
Sleepless forever, guards the entering way.
Hence groans are heard, fierce cracks of lash and
    scourge,
Loud-clanking iron links and trailing chains.
Æneas motionless with horror stood
O'erwhelmed at such uproar. "O virgin, say
What shapes of guilt are these? What penal woe
Harries them thus? What wailing smites the air?"
To whom the Sibyl, "Far-famed prince of Troy,
The feet of innocence may never pass
Into this house of sin. But Hecate,
When o'er th' Avernian groves she gave me
    power,
Taught me what penalties the gods decree,
And showed me all. There Cretan Rhadamanth
His kingdom keeps, and from unpitying throne
Chastises and lays bare the secret sins
Of mortals who, exulting in vain guile,
Elude, till death, their expiation due.
There, armed forever with her vengeful scourge,
Tisiphone, with menace and affront,
The guilty swarm pursues; in her left hand

She lifts her angered serpents, while she calls
A troop of sister-furies fierce as she.
Then, grating loud on hinge of sickening sound,
Hell's portals open wide. O, dost thou see
What sentinel upon that threshold sits,
What shapes of fear keep guard upon that
    gloom?
Far, far within the dragon Hydra broods
With half a hundred mouths, gaping and black;
And Tartarus slopes downward to the dark
Twice the whole space that in the realms of light
Th' Olympian heaven above our earth aspires.
Here Earth's first offspring, the Titanic brood,
Roll lightning-blasted in the gulf profound;
The twin Aloïdæ, colossal shades,
Came on my view; their hand made stroke at
    Heaven
And strove to thrust Jove from his seat on high.
I saw Salmoneous his dread stripes endure,
Who dared to counterfeit Olympian thunder
And Jove's own fire. In chariot of four steeds,
Brandishing torches, he triumphant rode
Through throngs of Greeks, o'er Elis' sacred way,
Demanding worship as a god. O fool!
To mock the storm's inimitable flash
With crash of hoofs and roll of brazen wheel!
But mightiest Jove from rampart of thick cloud
Hurled his own shaft, no flickering, mortal
    flame,
And in vast whirl of tempest laid him low.
Next unto these, on Tityos I looked,
Child of old Earth, whose womb all creatures
    bears:
Stretched o'er nine roods he lies; a vulture huge
Tears with hooked beak at his immortal side,
Or deep in entrails ever rife with pain
Gropes for a feast, making his haunt and home
In the great Titan bosom; nor will give
To ever new-born flesh surcease of woe.
Why name Ixion and Pirithous,
The Lapithæ, above whose impious brows
A crag of flint hangs quaking to its fall,
As if just toppling down, while couches proud,
Propped upon golden pillars, bid them feast
In royal glory: but beside them lies
The eldest of the Furies, whose dread hands
Thrust from the feast away, and wave aloft
A flashing firebrand, with shrieks of woe.
Here in a prison-house awaiting doom
Are men who hated, long as life endured,
Their brothers, or maltreated their gray sires,
Or tricked a humble friend; the men who grasped
At hoarded riches, with their kith and kin
Not sharing ever—an unnumbered throng:
Here slain adulterers be; and men who dared
To fight in unjust cause, and break all faith

With their own lawful lords. Seek not to know
What forms of woe they feel, what fateful shape
Of retribution hath overwhelmed them there.
Some roll huge boulders up; some hang on
    wheels,
Lashed to the whirling spokes; in his sad seat
Theseus is sitting, nevermore to rise;
Unhappy Phlegyas uplifts his voice
In warning through the darkness, calling loud,
'O, ere too late, learn justice and fear God!'
Yon traitor sold his country, and for gold
Enchained her to a tyrant, trafficking
In laws, for bribes enacted or made void;
Another did incestuously assail
His daughter's bed with infamous embrace.
All ventured some unclean, prodigious crime;
And what they dared achieved. I could not tell,
Not with a hundred mouths, a hundred tongues,
Or iron voice, their divers shapes of sin,
Nor call by name the myriad pangs they bear."

So spake Apollo's aged prophetess.
"Now up and on! she cried. Thy task fulfil!
We must make speed. Behold yon arching doors,
Yon walls in furnace of the Cyclops forged!
Tis there we are commanded to lay down
Th' appointed offering." So, side by side,
Swift through the intervening dark they strode,
And, drawing near the portal-arch, made pause.
Æneas, taking station at the door,
Pure, lustral waters o'er his body threw,
And hung for garland there the Golden Bough.
Now, every rite fulfilled, and tribute due
Paid to the sovereign power of Proserpine,
At last within a land delectable
Their journey lay, through pleasurable bowers
Of groves where all is joy,—a blest abode!
An ampler sky its roseate light bestows
On that bright land, which sees the cloudless
    beam
Of suns and planets to our earth unknown.
On smooth green lawns, contending limb with
    limb,
Immortal athletes play, and wrestle long
'Gainst mate or rival on the tawny sand;
With sounding footsteps and ecstatic song,
Some thread the dance divine: among them
    moves
The bard of Thrace, in flowing vesture clad—,
Discoursing seven-noted melody,
Who sweeps the numbered strings with
    changeful hand,
Or smites with ivory point his golden lyre.
Here Trojans be of eldest, noblest race,
Great-hearted heroes, born in happier times,
Ilus, Assaracus, and Dardanus,

Illustrious builders of the Trojan town.
Their arms and shadowy chariots he views,
And lances fixed in earth, while through the
    fields
Their steeds without a bridle graze at will.
For if in life their darling passion ran
To chariots, arms, or glossy-coated steeds,
The self-same joy, though in their graves, they
    feel.
Lo! on the left and right at feast reclined
Are other blessed souls, whose chorus sings
Victorious pæans on the fragrant air
Of laurel groves; and hence to earth outpours
Eridanus, through forests rolling free.
Here dwell the brave who for their native land
Fell wounded on the field; here holy priests
Who kept them undefiled their mortal day;
And poets, of whom the true-inspired song
Deserved Apollo's name; and all who found
New arts, to make man's life more blest or fair;
Yea! here dwell all those dead whose deeds
    bequeath
Deserved and grateful memory to their kind.
And each bright brow a snow-white fillet wears.
Unto this host the Sibyl turned, and hailed
Musæus, midmost of a numerous throng,
Who towered o'er his peers a shoulder higher:
"O spirits blest! O venerable bard!
Declare what dwelling or what region holds
Anchises, for whose sake we twain essayed
Yon passage over the wide streams of hell."
And briefly thus the hero made reply:
"No fixed abode is ours. In shadowy groves
We make our home, or meadows fresh and fair,
With streams whose flowery banks our couches
    be.
But you, if thitherward your wishes turn,
Climb yonder hill, where I your path may show."

So saying, he strode forth and led them on,
Till from that vantage they had prospect fair
Of a wide, shining land; thence wending down,
They left the height they trod; for far below
Father Anchises in a pleasant vale
Stood pondering, while his eyes and thought
    surveyed
A host of prisoned spirits, who there abode
Awaiting entrance to terrestrial air.
And musing he reviewed the legions bright
Of his own progeny and offspring proud—
Their fates and fortunes, virtues and great deeds.
Soon he discerned Æneas drawing nigh
O'er the green slope, and, lifting both his hands
In eager welcome, spread them swiftly forth.
Tears from his eyelids rained, and thus he spoke:
"Art here at last? Hath thy well-proven love

Of me thy sire achieved yon arduous way?
Will Heaven, beloved son, once more allow
That eye to eye we look? and shall I hear
Thy kindred accent mingling with my own?
I cherished long this hope. My prophet-soul
Numbered the lapse of days, nor did my thought
Deceive. O, o'er what lands and seas wast driven
To this embrace! What perils manifold
Assailed thee, O my son, on every side!
How long I trembled, lest that Libyan throne
Should work thee woe!"

    Æneas thus replied:
"Thine image, sire, thy melancholy shade,
Came oft upon my vision, and impelled
My journey hitherward. Our fleet of ships
Lies safe at anchor in the Tuscan seas.
Come, clasp my hand! Come, father, I implore,
And heart to heart this fond embrace receive!"
So speaking, all his eyes suffused with tears,
Thrice would his arms in vain that shape enfold.
Thrice from the touch of hand the vision fled,
Like wafted winds or likest hovering dreams.
After these things Æneas was aware
Of solemn groves in one deep, distant vale
Where trees were whispering, and forever
    flowed
The river Lethe, through its land of calm
Nations unnumbered roved and haunted there:
As when, upon a windless summer morn,
The bees afield among the rainbow flowers
Alight and sip, or round the lilies pure
Pour forth in busy swarm, while far diffused
Their murmured songs from all the meadows
    rise.
Æneas in amaze the wonder views,
And fearfully inquires of whence and why;
What yonder rivers be; what people press,
Line after line, on those dim shores along.
Said Sire Anchises: "Yonder thronging souls
To reincarnate shape predestined move.
Here, at the river Lethe's wave, they quaff
Care-quelling floods, and long oblivion.
Of these I shall discourse, and to thy soul
Make visible the number and array
Of my posterity; so shall thy heart
In Italy, thy new-found home, rejoice."
"O father," said Æneas, "must I deem
That from this region souls exalted rise
To upper air, and shall once more return
To cumbering flesh? O, wherefore do they feel,
Unhappy ones, such fatal lust to live?"
"I speak, my son, nor make thee longer doubt,"
Anchises said, and thus the truth set forth,
In ordered words from point to point unfolding:

"Know first that heaven and earth and ocean's
   plain,
The moon's bright orb, and stars of Titan birth
Are nourished by one Life; one primal Mind,
Immingled with the wast and general frame,
Fills every part and stirs the mighty whole.
Thence man and beast, thence creatures of the
   air,
And all the swarming monsters that be found
Beneath the level of the marbled sea;
A fiery virtue, a celestial power,
Their native seeds retain; but bodies vile,
With limbs of clay and members born to die,
Encumber and o'ercloud; whence also spring
Terrors and passions, suffering and joy;
For from deep darkness and captivity
All gaze but blindly on the radiant world.
Nor when to life's last beam they bid farewell
May sufferers cease from pain, nor quite be freed
From all their fleshly plagues; but by fixed law,
The strange, inveterate taint works deeply in.
For this, the chastisement of evils past
Is suffered here, and full requital paid.
Some hang on high, outstretched to viewless
   winds;
For some their sin's contagion must be purged
In vast ablution of deep-rolling seas,
or burned away in fire. Each man receives
His ghostly portion in the world of dark;
But thence to realms Elysian we go free,
Where for a few these seats of bliss abide,
Till time's long lapse a perfect orb fulfils,
And takes all taint away, restoring so
The pure, ethereal soul's first virgin fire.
At last, when the millennial æon strikes,
God calls them forth to yon Lethæan stream,
In numerous host, that thence, oblivious all,
They may behold once more the vaulted sky,
And willingly to shapes of flesh return."

So spoke Anchises; then led forth his son,
The Sibyl with him, to the assembled shades
(A voiceful throng), and on a lofty mound
His station took, whence plainly could be seen
The long procession, and each face descried.
"Hark now! for of the glories I will tell
That wait our Dardan blood: of our sons' sons
Begot upon the old Italian breed,
Who shall be mighty spirits, and prolong
Our names, their heritage. I will unfold
The story, and reveal the destined years.
Yon princeling, thou beholdest leaning there
Upon a royal lance, shall next emerge
Into the realms of day. He is the first
Of half-Italian strain, the last-born heir
To thine old age by fair Lavinia given,

Called Silvius, a royal Alban name
(Of sylvan birth and sylvan nurture he),
A king himself and sire of kings to come,
By whom our race in Alba Longa reign.
Next Procas stands, our Trojan people's boast;
Capys and Numitor, and, named like thee,
Æneas Sylvius, like thee renowned
For faithful honor and for deeds of war,
When he ascends at last his Alban throne.
Behold what warrior youth they be! How strong
Their goodly limbs! Above their shaded brows
The civic oak they wear! For thee they build
Nomentum, and the walls of Gabii,
Fidena too, and on the mountains pile
Collatia's citadels, Pometii,
Bola and Cora, Castrum-Inui—
Such be the names the nameless Inads shall bear.
See, in that line of sires the son of Mars,
Great Romulus, of Ilian mother born,
From far-descended line of Trojan kings!
See from his helm the double crest uprear,
While his celestial father in his mien
Shows forth his birth divine! Of him, my son,
Great Rome shall rise, and, favored of his star,
Have power world-wide, and men of godlike
   mind.
She clasps her seven hills in single wall,
Proud mother of the brave! So Cybele,
The Berecynthian goddess, castle-crowned,
On through the Phrygian kingdoms speeds her
   car,
Exulting in her hundred sons divine,
All numbered with the gods, all throned on high.

"Let now thy visionary glance look long
On this thy race, these Romans that be thine.
Here Cæsar, of Iulus' glorious seed,
Behold ascending to the world of light!
Behold, at last, that man, for this is he,
So oft unto thy listening ears foretold,
Augustus Cæsar, kindred unto Jove.
He brings a golden age; he shall restore
Old Saturn's sceptre to our Latin land,
And o'er remotest Garamant and Ind
His sway extend; the fair dominion
Outruns th' horizon planets, yea, beyond
the sun's bright path, where Atlas' shoulder
   bears
Yon dome of heaven set thick with burning stars.
Against his coming the far Caspian shores
Break forth in oracles; the Mæotian land
Trembles, and all the seven-fold mouths of Nile.
Not o'er domain so wide Alcides passed,
Although the brazen-footed doe he slew
And stilled the groves of Erymanth, and bade
The beast of Lerna at his arrows quail.

Nor half so far triumphant Bacchus drove,
With vine-entwisted reins, his frolic team
Of tigers from the tall-topped Indian hill.

"Still do we doubt if heroes' deeds can fill
A realm so wide? Shall craven fear constrain
Thee or thy people from Ausonia's shore?
Look, who is he I may discern from far
By olive-branch and holy emblems known?
His flowing locks and hoary beard, behold!
Fit for a Roman king! By hallowed laws
He shall found Rome anew—from mean estate
In lowly Cures led to mightier sway.
But after him arises one whose reign
Shall wake the land from slumber: Tullus then
Shall stir slack chiefs to battle, rallying
His hosts which had forgot what triumphs be.
Him boastful Ancus follows hard upon,
O'erflushed with his light people's windy praise.
Wilt thou see Tarquins now? And haughty hand
Of vengeful Brutus seize the signs of power?
He first the consul's name shall take; he first
Th' inexorable fasces sternly bear.
When his own sons in rash rebellion join,
The father and the judge shall sentence give
In beauteous freedom's cause—unhappy he!
Howe'er the age to come the story tell,
'T will bless such love of honor and of Rome.
See Decius, sire and son, the Drusi, see!
Behold Torquatus with his axe! Look where
Camillus brings the Gallic standards home!
But who are these in glorious armor clad
And equal power? In this dark world of cloud
Their souls in concord move;—but woe is me!
What duel 'twixt them breaks, when by and by
The light of life is theirs, and forth they call
Their long-embattled lines to carnage dire!
Allied by nuptial truce, the sire descends
From Alpine rampart and that castled cliff,
Monoecus by the sea; the son arrays
His hostile legions in the lands of morn.
Forbear, my children! School not your great souls
In such vast wars, nor turn your giant strength
Against the bowels of your native land!
But be thou first, O first in mercy! thou
Who art of birth Olympian! Fling away
Thy glorious sword, mine offspring and mine
    heir!

"Yonder is one whose chariot shall ascend
The laurelled Capitolian steep; he rides
In glory o'er Achæa's hosts laid low,
And Corinth overthrown. There, too, is he
Who shall uproot proud Argos and the towers
Of Agamemnon; vanquishing the heir
Even of Æacus, the warrior seed

Of Peleus' son; such vengeance shall be wrought
For Troy's slain sires, and violated shrines!
Or who could fail great Cato's name to tell?
Or, Cossus, thine? or in oblivion leave
The sons of Gracchus? or the Scipios,
Twin thunderbolts of war, and Libya's bane?
Or, more than kingly in his mean abode,
Fabricius? or Serranus at the plough?
Ye Fabii, how far would ye prolong
My weary praise? But see! 't is Maximus,
Who by wise waiting saves his native land.

"Let others melt and mould the breathing bronze
To forms more fair,—aye! out of marble bring
Features that live; let them plead causes well;
Or trace with pointed wand the cycled heaven,
And hail the constellations as they rise;
But thou, O Roman, learn with sovereign sway
To rule the nations. Thy great art shall be
To keep the world in lasting peace, to spare
The humbled foe, and crush to earth the proud."

So did Anchises speak, then, after pause,
Thus to their wondering ears his word
    prolonged:
"Behold Marcellus, bright with glorious spoil,
In lifted triumph through his warriors move!
The Roman power in tumultuous days
He shall establish; he rides forth to quell
Afric and rebel Gaul; and to the shrine
Of Romulus the third-won trophy brings."
Then spoke Æneas, for he now could see
A beauteous youth in glittering dress of war,
Though of sad forehead and down-dropping
    eyes:
"Say, father, who attends the prince? a son?
Or of his greatness some remoter heir?
How his friends praise him, and how matchless
    he!
But mournful night rests darkly o'er his brow."
With brimming eyes Anchises answer gave:
"Ask not, O son, what heavy weight of woe
Thy race shall bear, when fate shall just reveal
This vision to the world, then yield no more.
O gods above, too glorious did ye deem
The seed of Rome, had this one gift been sure?
The lamentation of a multitude
Arises from the field of Mars, and strikes
The city's heart. O Father Tiber, see
What pomp of sorrow near the new-made tomb
Beside thy fleeting stream! What Ilian youth
Shall e'er his Latin kindred so advance
In hope of glory? When shall the proud land
Of Romulus of such a nursling boast?
Ah, woe is me! O loyal heart and true!
O brave, right arm invincible! What foe

Had 'scaped his onset in the shock of arms,
Whether on foot he strode, or if he spurred
The hot flanks of his war-horse flecked with
    foam?
O lost, lamented child! If thou evade
Thy evil star, Marcellus thou shalt be.
O bring me lilies! Bring with liberal hand!
Sad purple blossoms let me throw—the shade
Of my own kin to honor, heaping high
My gifts upon his grave! So let me pay
An unavailing vow!"

    Then, far and wide
Through spacious fields of air, they wander free,
Witnessing all; Anchises guides his son
From point to point, and quickens in his mind
Hunger for future fame. Of wars he tells

Soon imminent; of fair Laurentum's tribes;
Of King Latinus' town; and shows what way
Each task and hardship to prevent, or bear.

Now Sleep has portals twain, whereof the one
Is horn, they say, and easy exit gives
To visions true; the other, gleaming white
With polished ivory, the dead employ
To people night with unsubstantial dreams.
Here now Anchises bids his son farewell;
And with Sibylla, his companion sage,
Up through that ivory portal lets him rise.
Back to his fleet and his dear comrades all
Æneas hastes. Then hold they their straight
    course
Into Caieta's bay. An anchor holds
Each lofty prow; the stems stand firm on shore.

———————— *Questions for Consideration* ————————

Briefly, discuss the following. In your discussion, please adhere to the ordinary conventions of good composition: content, organization, clarity, and mechanics.

1. What is the theme of the *Aeneid*?

    _____

    _____

    _____

    _____

    _____

2. In what sense is Aeneas an exile? In what sense a man returning home?

    _____

    _____

    _____

    _____

    _____

3. Characterize Dido and Anna. What is Anna's function in Aeneas' affair with Dido?

    _____

    _____

    _____

    _____

    _____

4. Why does Aeneas desert Dido? Why does Dido commit suicide? What is the significance of the sacrificial aspects of her death?

    _____

    _____

    _____

    _____

    _____

5. Why must Aeneas go to Hades? How does he react to what he sees there?

_____

_____

_____

_____

_____

6. In what ways does this national epic transcend propaganda?

_____

_____

_____

_____

_____

7. What, according to Virgil, is the mission of the Roman people?

_____

_____

_____

_____

_____

8. Discuss Virgil's use of symbolism and imagery.

_____

_____

_____

_____

_____

9. Much of the Aeneid is composed of borrowings from the *Iliad* and the *Odyssey*. Cite some prominent examples of such borrowings.

_____

_____

_____

_____

———————————— *Writing Critically* ————————————

Select one of the essay topics listed below and compose a 500 word essay which discusses the topic fully. Support your thesis with evidence from the text and with critical and/or historical material. Use the space below for preparing to write the essay.

1. Your study of literature to this point has included the folk epics—*The Iliad* and *The Odyssey* as well as the art epic—*The Aeneid*. Critics often describe *The Aeneid* as an "artificial" or contrived epic. Discuss the significant ways in which the two types of epics differ. Consider such features as the style, subject matter, theme, symbolic meaning, etc. in *The Iliad*, (or *The Odyssey)* and *The Aeneid* to support or illustrate your views.

2. It has been noted that *The Aeneid* is composed of significant borrowings from *The Iliad* and *The Odyssey*. Many of the episodes—Aeneas' recounting the fall of Troy—are reminiscent of Homer's epics. Cite at least three prominent examples of Virgil's borrowings from Homer. Then discuss the manner in which Virgil shapes Homer's material to his specific purposes.

3. Discuss the double conflict which runs through Book IV of *The Aeneid*. Historical? Human?

4. Use the epics discussed thus far to formulate a definition of the epic hero. Then compare/contrast Achilles and Aeneas as epic heroes.

5. Explain in detail the significance of Aeneas' underworld visit. What, if any, symbolic meaning can be attached to this journey?

6. In *The Aeneid*, Aeneas' growth as a symbolic figure is evolutionary. Books IV and VI of *The Aeneid* are important episodes in that evolutionary process. Write an essay that illustrates how the events of Book IV and Book VI contribute to the shaping of Aeneas' character as a transcendent figure.

Prewriting Space:

_____

_____

_____

_____

_____

_____

_____

_____

Introduction

Publius Ovidius Naso (Ovid) (43 B.C.–A.D. 17)

The imaginative, sensual Roman poet Publius Ovidius Naso (Ovid) was born in 43 B.C. in a small town ninety miles east of Rome called Sulmo (modern Sulmona). Ovid belonged to a wealthy equestrian family. As a result, he and his brother were sent, as others who could afford, to Rome and Athens in order to pursue a rhetorical education. During his years of study, he acquired a great deal of insight into the art of speaking and philosophical ideals under the best teachers of the time. In addition, Ovid was able to spend some time in Greece. While he was in Greece, Ovid had the opportunity to visit many of the renowned cities of Asia Minor.

Ovid's ambitious father wanted him to pursue a career in the government. His brother proved to be a promising student of law, but an early death prevented any advancement. Ovid became disenchanted with the law and public affairs. He held a few minor public offices perhaps pleasing his parents, but soon he abandoned that career and began to focus all of his energies toward becoming a poet. It was actually a passion he possessed in his early child-hood.

Ovid eventually became a member of the literary circle of the patron Marcus Valerius Messala that included such friends as Tibullus, Propertius, and Macer. He became acquainted with the famous orator Horace and appreciated the works of Virgil. Ovid soon became popular among the many literary and fashionable circles and salons in Rome, especially among the youth who herald him as their poet laureate. Ovid married three times. The third marriage appeared to have been the most successful, producing a daughter, Perilla.

In A.D. 8, Ovid's life was in a state of shambles! The Emperor Augustus banished him to a remote Roman outpost of Tomis on the Black Sea. Furthermore, it was ordered that all of his books be removed from public libraries. The specific reason for this harsh sentence to Ovid still remains an "unsolved mystery." There was speculation that his work the *Art of Love*, which revealed some disrespect against certain moral values, infuriated Emperor Augustus. The emperor at the time was desperately attempting to reform the morals of the Roman Empire. Another possible reason for Augustus' wrath was the poet's love affair with the emperor's amoral granddaughter Julia. Whatever the reason for Emperor Augustus' actions, it was a life altering experience for Ovid. He never received a pardon and lived the rest of his life in the somewhat barbaric city of Tomis writing and adjusting to his home. He did achieve some recognition among the people of Tomis, but he lost all hope of ever returning to Rome when Tiberius became emperor. Ovid died in A.D. 17 as an exile of the Roman Empire.

Ovid was an engaging writer with a great deal of wit, grace, and spontaneity. His works covered a wide range of types such as the love elegy, handbooks on love, the epistle (a set of fictitious letters), the mytho-historical epic, and the tragedy. All of his poems except the *Metamorphoses* were written in elegiac couplets. The trips throughout Greece that began to whet his appetite for mythology, the men of letters at Alexandria with their creation of the pastoral, his appreciation of Horace, Virgil, and Hesiod all influenced him as a writer.

Ovid's achievements as a writer can be seen through three periods: early, mature, and banishment. During his early period, Ovid wrote several love poems and short lyrics. The first major work that solidified his reputation as a poet was *Amores* (*Loves*) which was a series of erotic vignettes concerning a love affair Ovid had with a woman named Corinna. The *Heroides* consisted of a number of imaginary letters from mythological heroines such as Dido,

Penelope, and Medea addressing their absent lovers or husbands. In this particular work, the theme of romantic love and the poet's budding interest in mythology can be seen. In 1 B.C., the work that upset Emperor Augustus, the *Ars Amatoria* (*The Art of Love*), was published. It was a lively treatise concerning the art of seduction that gave instructions to men and women. In addition, the work offered the reader a glimpse of Roman life via the games, races, and theatre.

The second phase of his literary career saw a somewhat more serious and mature writer. Ovid turned from amorous works to serious themes. He composed the tragedy, *Medea*, of which only two verses have survived. Another work during this period was *Fasti*, a poetical calendar of the Roman year and its religious festivals. He attempted flattery of the ruling class to perhaps get back in good graces with the emperor. His attempt, however, failed! Ovid's most celebrated work, the *Metamorphoses*, was published during this period. The poet reached his zenith in his appreciation of mythology and the passion that ruled human beings. During Ovid's banishment years, away from his beloved Rome and third wife, he began to write again. Most of the subject matter was gloomy with the playful, gay tone of his writing lost. *The Tristia* was a work consisting of five books of poems addressed to the emperor and other individuals. Another work, *Epistulae ex Ponto* (*Letters from the Black Sea*), described his experience in Tomis as an exile. Both the *Tristia* and *Epistulae ex Ponto* were in reality appeals by Ovid to Augustus for clemency against his decree. A final major work, *Ibis*, was a poem written as a curse directed at an unnamed enemy.

The *Metamorphoses* is Ovid's triumphant masterpiece composed before his exile. The poem is a collection of myths and legends of the ancient world written in 15 books utilizing the hexameter verse form. The primary focus of this epic-like poem is the strange transformation of human beings or gods into the form of an animal, body of water, star, rock, or plant. Not only does Ovid vividly present a certain metamorphosis, but he comments on the passions, conflicts, sufferings, and sacrifices existing among people. The theme of metamorphosis provides a sense of unity reinforced by Ovid's ability to link the stories into groups and to create ingenious transitions between one story or group of stories and the next.

Ovid begins his *Metamorphoses* by utilizing the invocation to the gods for help in conveying his story of change. He writes about the first metamorphosis of Chaos to Order (Cosmos). Along with the creation of man, Ovid depicts the various ages of man such as gold, silver, bronze, and iron. In the Age of Gold, Kronos ruled the world, and Prometheus brought the gift of fire. The Age of Silver saw divisions of the season with extreme heat. The Age of Bronze saw a period of fierce warriors destroying their races. The Age of Iron finds man never escaping toil, sorrow, and death,

While introducing the various ages of man, Ovid composed some type of transformation that was to occur. He provided such examples as the weeping Niobe turning into a spring; Daphne, a nymph, into a laurel; Pygmalion's statue into a beautiful woman, and Narcissus into a flower. A number of the stories in the *Metamorphoses* are concerned with the human experience of love such as Orpheus and Eurydice, Baucis and Philemon, and Ceyx and Alcyone. Regardless of what myth he was telling, Ovid perfected his narrative skills and his insights into the human psyche.

According to scholar E.J. Kenney, the overriding aim of Ovid in the *Metamorphoses* was to carry the reader effortlessly from episode to episode with his or her appetite constantly titillated by the variety of subject matter, tone, tempo, linguistic wit, and literary treatment. The *Metamorphoses* is one of the greatest treasures in Western literature. Ovid's influence has been tremendous. His influence can be seen on the poets of courtly love in the Middle Ages, the painters and poets of the Renaissance, and in the works of such authors as Shakespeare, Goethe, Yeats, Milton, Boccaccio, Dryden, Pound, Spencer, and Chaucer. At the end of the *Metamorphoses*, Ovid boasted that his work would become immortal. He was right! (AHF)

BIBLIOGRAPHY

Colavito, Maria Maddelena. *The Pythagorean Intertext in Ovid's "Metamorphoses": A New Interpretation.* Lewiston, New York: The Edwin Mellen Press, 1989.

Du Rocher, Richard J. *Milton and Ovid.* Ithaca, New York: Cornell University Press, 1985.

Galinsky, G. Karl. *Ovid's "Metamorphoses": An Introduction to the Basic Aspects.* Oxford: Basil Blackwell, 1975.

Green, Peter. "Ovid in Exile." *Southern Human Review* 28(1994): 29–41.

Kenney, E. J. *The Love Poems by Ovid.* Trans. A. D. Melville. Oxford: Oxford University Press, 1990.

Martindale, Charles, ed. *Ovid Renewed.* Cambridge: Cambridge University Press, 1988.

Otis, Brooks. *Ovid as an Epic Poet.* 2nd ed. Cambridge: University Press, 1971.

from Metamorphoses

Ovid

The Golden Age

The golden age was first; when man, yet new,
No rule but uncorrupted reason knew;
And, with a native bent, did good pursue.
Unforced by punishment, unaw'd by fear,
His words were simple, and his soul sincere:
Needless was written law, where none
    oppress'd;
The law of man was written in his breast:
No suppliant crowds before the judge appear'd;
No court erected yet, nor cause was heard;
But all was safe, for conscience was their guard.
The mountain trees in distant prospect please,
Ere yet the pine descended to the seas;
Ere sails were spread, new oceans to explore;
And happy mortals, unconcern'd for more,
Confined their wishes to their native shore.
No walls were yet, nor fence, nor moat, nor
    mound;

Nor drum was heard, nor trumpet's angry
    sound:
Nor swords were forged; but, void of care and
    crime,
The soft creation slept away their time.
The teeming earth, yet guiltless of the plough,
And unprovoked, did fruitful stores allow:
Content with food, which nature freely bred,
On wildings and on strawberries they fed;
Cornels and bramble-berries gave the rest,
And falling acorns furnish'd out a feast.
The flowers, unsown, in fields and meadows
    reign'd;
And western winds immortal spring maintain'd.
In following years the bearded corn ensued
From earth unask'd, nor was that earth renew'd.
From veins of valleys milk and nectar broke,
And honey sweating through the pores of oak.

The Silver Age

But when good Saturn, banish'd from
    above,
Was driven to hell, the world was under Jove.
Succeeding times a silver age behold,
Excelling brass, but more excell'd by gold.
Then Summer, Autumn, Winter did appear,
And Spring was but a season of the year.
The sun his annual course obliquely made,
Good days contracted, and enlarged the bad.
Then air with sultry heats began to glow;

The wings of winds were clogg'd with ice and
    snow;
And shivering mortals, into houses driven,
Sought shelter from the inclemency of heaven.
Those houses, then, were caves, or homely sheds,
With twining osiers fenced, and moss their beds.
Then ploughs, for seed, the fruitful furrows
    broke,
And oxen labour'd first beneath the yoke.

The Brazen Age

To this next came in course the brazen age:

A warlike offspring prompt to bloody rage,
Not impious yet—

The Iron Age

Hard steel succeeded then;

And stubborn as the metal were the men.
Truth, Modesty and Shame, the world forsook:
Fraud, Avarice, and Force, their places took.
Then sails were spread to every wind that blew;
Raw were the sailors, and the depths were new:
Trees, rudely hollow'd did the waves sustain;
Ere ships in triumph plough'd the watery plain.
Then landmarks limited to each his right:
For all before was common as the light.
Nor was the ground alone required to bear
Her annual income to the crooked share;
But greedy mortals, rummaging her store,
Digg'd from her entrails first the precious ore;
Which next to hell the prudent gods had laid;
And that alluring ill to sight display'd;

Thus cursed steel, and more accursed gold,
Gave mischief birth, and made that mischief
  bold:
And double death did wretched man invade,
By steel assaulted, and by gold betray'd.
Now (brandish'd weapons glittering in their
  hands)
Mankind is broken loose from moral bands;
No rights of hospitality remain:
The guest, by him who harbour'd him, is slain:
The son-in-law pursues the father's life;
The wife her husband murders, he the wife.
The step-dame poison for the son prepares;
The son inquires into his father's years.
Faith flies, and Piety in exile mourns;
And Justice here oppress'd, to heaven returns.

The Transformation Of Daphne Into A Laurel

The first and fairest of his loves was she,

Whom not blind fortune, but the dire decree
Of angry Cupid forced him to desire:
Daphne her name, and Peneus was her sire.
Swell'd with the pride that new success attends,
He sees the stripling, while his bow he bends,
And this insults him: Thou lascivious boy,
Are arms like these for children to employ?
Know, such achievements are my proper claim;
Due to my vigour and unerring aim:
Resistless are my shafts, and Python late,
In such a feather'd death, has found his fate.
Take up thy torch, and lay my weapons by;
With that the feeble souls of lovers fry.
To whom the son of Venus thus replied:
Phoebus, thy shafts are sure on all beside;
But mine on Phoebus: mine the fame shall be
Of all thy conquests, when I conquer thee.

   He said, and soaring swiftly wing'd his
flight—,

Nor stopp'd but on Parnassus' airy height.
Two different shafts he from his quiver draws;
One to repel desire, and one to cause.
One shaft is pointed with refulgent gold,
To bribe the love, and make the lover bold:
One blunt, and tipp'd with lead, whose base allay
Provokes disdain, and drives desire away.
The blunted bolt against the nymph he dress'd,
But with the sharp transfix'd Apollo's breast.
   The enamour'd deity pursues the chase;
The scornful damsel shuns his loathed embrace;
In hunting beasts of prey her youth employs;
And Phoebe rivals in her rural joys.
With naked neck she goes, and shoulders bare,
And with a fillet binds her flowing hair.
By many suitors sought, she mocks their pains,
And still her vow'd virginity maintains.
Impatient of a yoke, the name of bride
She shuns, and hates the joys she never tried.
On wilds and wood she fixes her desire:
Nor knows what youth and kindly love inspire.

Her father chides her oft: Thou ow'st says he,
A husband to thyself, a son to me.
She, like a crime, abhors the nuptial bed:
She glows with blushes, and she hangs her head.
Then, casting round his neck her tender arms,
Soothes him with blandishments, and filial
    charms:
Give me, my lord, she said, to live and die
A spotless maid, without the marriage-tie.
'Tis but a small request; I beg no more
Than what Diana's father gave before.
The good old sire was soften'd to consent;
    But said her wish would prove her punish-
ment:
For so much youth, and so much beauty join'd,
Opposed the state which her desires design'd.
The god of light, aspiring to her bed,
Hopes what he seeks, with flattering fancies fed;
And is by his own oracles misled.
And as in empty fields the stubble burns,
Or nightly travellers, when day returns,
Their useless torches on dry hedges throw,
That catch the flames, and kindle all the row;
So burns the god, consuming in desire,
And feeding in his breast the fruitless fire:
Her well-turn'd neck he view'd (her neck was
    bare)
And on her shoulders her dishevell'd hair.
Oh, were it comb'd, said he, with what a grace
Would every waving curl become her face!
He view'd her eyes, like heavenly lamps that
    shone;
He view'd her lips, too sweet to view alone,
Her taper fingers, and her panting breast;
He praises all he sees, and for the rest,
Believes the beauties yet unseen are best.
Swift as the wind, the damsel fled away,
Nor did for these alluring speeches stay:
Stay, nymph, he cried, I follow, not a foe:
Thus from the lion trips the trembling doe;
Thus from the wolf the frighten'd lamb removes,
And from pursuing falcons fearful doves;
Thou shunn'st a god, and shunn'st a god that
    loves
Ah, lest some thorn should pierce thy tender foot
Or thou should'st fall in flying my pursuit!
To sharp uneven ways thy steps decline;
Abate thy speed, and I will bate of mine.
Yet think from whom thou dost so rashly fly;
Nor basely born, nor shepherd's swain am I.
Perhaps thou know'st not my superior state;
And from that ignorance proceeds thy hate.
Me Claros, Delphos, Tenedos obey;
These hands the Patareian sceptre sway.
The king of gods begot me: what shall be,
Or is, or ever was, in fate, I see.

Mine is the invention of the charming lyre;
Sweet notes, and heavenly numbers I inspire.
Sure is my bow, unerring is my dart;
But, ah, more deadly his, who pierced my heart!
Med'cine is mine; what herbs and simples grow
In fields and forests, all their powers I know;
And am the great physician call'd below.
Alas, that fields and forests can afford
No remedies to heal their love-sick lord!
To cure the pains of love, no plant avails;
And his own physic the physician fails.
    She heard not half, so furiously she flies,
And on her ear the imperfect accent dies.
Fear gave her wings; and as she fled, the wind
Increasing spread her flowing hair behind;
And left her legs and thighs exposed to view;
Which made the god more eager to pursue.
The god was young, and was too hotly bent
To lose his time in empty compliment:
But led by love, and fired by such a sight,
Impetuously pursued his near delight.
    As when the impatient greyhound, slipt from far,
Bounds o'er the glebe, to course the fearful hare,
She in her speed does all her safety lay;
And he with double speed pursues the prey—,
O'erruns her at the fitting turn, and licks
His chaps in vain, and blows upon the flix;
She 'scapes, and for the neighb'ring covert
    strives,
And gaining shelter, doubts if yet she lives:
If little things with great we may compare,
Such was the god, and such the flying fair:
She, urged by fear, her feet did swiftly move,
But he more swiftly, who was urged by love.
He gathers ground upon her in the chase;
Now breathes upon her hair, with nearer pace;
And just is fastening on the wish'd embrace.
The nymph grew pale, and in a mortal fright,
Spent with the labour of so long a flight;
And now despairing, cast a mournful look
Upon the streams of her paternal brook:
Oh, help, she cried, in this extremest need,
If water-gods are deities indeed:
Gape, Earth, and this unhappy wretch entomb:
Or change my form whence all my sorrows come!
Scarce had she finish'd when her feet she found
Benumb'd with cold, and fasten'd to the ground:
A filmy rind about her body grows,
Her hair to leaves, her arms extend to boughs:
The nymph is all into a laurel gone,
The smoothness of her skin remains alone.
Yet Phoebus loves her still, and casting round
Her bole his arms, some little warmth he found.
The tree still panted in the unfinish'd part,
Not wholly vegetive, and heaved her heart.
He fix'd his lips upon the trembling rind;

It swerved aside, and his embrace declined.
To whom the god: Because thou canst not be
My mistress, I espouse thee for my tree:
Be thou the prize of honour and renown;
The deathless poet, and the poem, crown.
Thou shalt the Roman festivals adorn,
And, after poets, be by victors worn.
Thou shalt returning Cæsar's triumph grace;
When pomps shall in a long procession pass:

Wreathed on the post before his palace wait;
And be the sacred guardian of the gate:
Secure from thunder, and unharm'd by Jove,
Unfading as the immortal powers above:
And as the lock of Phoebus are unshorn,
So shall perpetual green thy boughs adorn.
The grateful tree was pleased with what he said,
And shook the shady honours of her head.

Baucis and Philemon

*T*he author, pursuing the deeds of Theseus, relates how he, with his friend Pirithous, were invited by Achelous, the river god, to stay with him, till his waters were abated. Achelous entertains them with a relation of his own love to Perimele, who was changed into an island by Neptune, at his request. Pirithous, being an atheist, derides the legend, and denies the power of the gods to work that miracle. Lelex, another companion of Theseus, to confirm the story of Achelous, relates another metamorphosis, of Baucis and Philemon into trees, of which he was partly an eye-witness.

Thus Achelous ends: his audience hear
With admiration, and, admiring, fear
The powers of heaven; except Ixion's son,
Who laugh'd at all the gods, believed in none;
He shook his impious head, and thus replies:
These legends are no more than pious lies:
You attribute too much to heavenly sway,
To think they give us forms, and take away.
   The rest, of better minds, their sense declared
Against this doctrine, and with horror heard.
   Then Lelex rose, an old experienced man,
And thus with sober gravity began:
Heaven's power is infinite: earth, air, and sea,
The manufacture mass, the making power obey:
By proof to clear your doubt; in Phrygian ground
Two neighb'ring trees, with walls encompass'd
   round,
Stand on a moderate rise, with wonder shown,
One a hard oak, a softer linden one:
I saw the place and them, by Pittheus sent
To Phrygian realms, my grandsire's government.
Not far from thence is seen a lake, the haunt
Of coots, and of the fishing cormorant:
Here Jove with Hermes came; but in disguise
Of mortal men conceal'd their deities:
One laid aside his thunder, one his rod,
And many toilsome steps together trod—,
For harbour at a thousand doors they knock'd,

Not one of all the thousand but was lock'd.
At last an hospitable house they found,
An homely shed; the roof, not far from ground,
Was thatch'd with reeds and straw together
   bound.
There Baucis and Philemon lived, and there
Had lived long married, and a happy pair:
Now old in love; though little was their store,
Inured to want, their poverty they bore,
Nor aim'd at wealth, professing to be poor.
For master or for servant here to call,
Was all alike, where only two were all.
Command was none, where equal love was paid,
Or rather both commanded, both obey'd.
   From lofty roofs the gods repulsed before,
Now stooping, enter'd through the little door;
The man (their hearty welcome first express'd)
A common settle drew for either guest,
Inviting each his weary limbs to rest.
But ere they sat, officious Baucis lays
Two cushions stuff'd with straw, the seat to raise;
Coarse, but the best she had; then takes the load
Of ashes from the hearth, and spreads abroad
The living coals, and, lest they should expire,
With leaves and barks she feeds her infant fire:
It smokes, and then with trembling breath she
   blows,
Till in a cheerful blaze the flames arose.
With brushwood and with chips she strengthens
   these,
And adds at last the boughs of rotten trees.
The fire thus form'd, she sets the kettle on,
(Like burnish'd gold the little seether shone)
Next took the coleworts which her husband got
From his own ground (a small well-water'd
   spot);
She stripp'd the stalks of all their leaves; the best
She cull'd, and then with handy care she dress'd.
High o'er the hearth a chine of bacon hung;
Good old Philemon seized it with a prong,

And from the sooty rafter drew it down,
Then cut a slice, but scarce enough for one:
Yet a large portion of a little store,
Which for their sakes alone he wish'd were more.
This in the pot he plunged without delay,
To tame the flesh, and drain the salt away.
The time between, before the fire they sat,
And shorten'd the delay by pleasing chat.

A beam there was, on which a beechen pail
Hung by the handle, on a driven nail:
This fill'd with water, gently warm'd, they set
Before their guests; in this they bathed their feet,
And after with clean towels dried their sweat.
This done, the host produced the genial bed;
Sallow the foot, the borders, and the stead,
Which with no costly coverlet they spread;
But coarse old garments, yet such robes as these
They laid alone, at feasts, on holidays.
The good old housewife, tucking up her gown,
The table sets; the invited gods lie down.
The trivet-table of a foot was lame,
A blot which prudent Baucis overcame,
Who thrust beneath the limping leg a sherd,
So was the mended board exactly rear'd:
Then rubb'd it o'er with newly gathr'd mint;
A wholesome herb, that breathed a grateful
    scent.
Pallas began the feast, where first was seen
The party-colour'd olive, black and green:
Autumnal cornels next in order served,
In lees of wine well pickled and preserved:
A garden salad was the third supply,
Of endive, radishes, and succory:
Then curds and cream, the flower of country fare,
And new-laid eggs, which Baucis' busy care
Turn'd by a gentle fire, and roasted rare.
All these in earthenware were served to board;
And, next in place, an earthen pitcher, stored
With liquor of the best the cottage could afford.
This was the table's ornament and pride,
With figures wrought: like pages at his side
Stood beechen bowls; and these were shining
    clean,
Varnish'd with wax without, and lined within.
By this the boiling kettle had prepared,
And to the table sent the smoking lard;
On which with eager appetite they dine,
A savoury bit, that served to relish wine:
The wine itself was suiting to the rest,
Still working in the must, and lately press'd.
The second course succeeds like that before;
Plums, apples, nuts, and, of their wintry store,
Dry figs and grapes, and wrinkled dates were set
In canisters, to enlarge the little treat:
All these a milk-white honeycomb surround,
Which in the midst the country banquet crown'd.

But the kind hosts their entertainment grace
With hearty welcome, and an open face;
In all they did, you might discern with ease
A willing mind, and a desire to please.

Meantime the beechen bowls went round, and
still,
Though often emptied, were observed to fill,
Fill'd without hands, and of their own accord
Ran without feet, and danced about the board.
Devotion seized the pair, to see the feast
With wine, and of no common grape, increased;
And up they held their hands, and fell to prayer,
Excusing, as they could, their country faire.
One goose they had ('twas all they could allow)
A wakeful sentry, and on duty now,
Whom to the gods for sacrifice they vow:
Her, with malicious zeal, the couple view'd;
She ran for life, and, limping, they pursued:
Full well the fowl perceived their bad intent,
And would not make her master's compliment;
But, persecuted, to the powers she flies,
And close between the legs of Jove she lies.
He, with a gracious ear, the suppliant heard,
And saved her life; then what he was declared,
And own'd the god. The neighbourhood, said he,
Shall justly perish for impiety:
You stand alone exempted; but obey
With speed, and follow where we lead the way:
Leave these accursed; and to the mountain's
    height
Ascend; nor once look backward in your flight.

They haste, and what their tardy feet denied,
The trusty staff (their better leg) supplied.
An arrow's flight they wanted to the top,
And there secure, but spent with travel, stop;
Then turn their now no more forbidden eyes;
Lost in a lake the floated level lies:
A watery desert covers all the plains,
Their cot alone, as in an isle remains:
Wondering with peeping eyes, while they
    deplore
Their neighbours' fate, and country now no
    more,
Their little shed, scarce large enough for two,
Seems, from the ground increased, in height and
    bulk to grow.
A stately temple shoots within the skies:
The crotchets of their cot in columns rise:
The pavement polish'd marble they behold,
The gates with sculpture graced, the spires and
    tiles of gold.

Then thus the sire of gods, with looks serene,
"Speak thy desire, thou only just of men;
And thou, O woman, only worthy found
To be with such a man in marriage bound.

Awhile they whisper; then, to Jove address'd,

Philemon thus prefers their joint request:
"We crave to serve before your sacred shrine,
And offer at your altars rites divine:
And since not any action of our life
Has been polluted with domestic strife;
We beg one hour of death, that neither she
With widow's tears may live to bury me.
Nor weeping I, with wither'd arms may bear
My breathless Baucis to the sepulchre.
　The godheads sign their suit. They run their race
In the same tenour all th' appointed space:
Then, when their hour was come, while they
　relate
These past adventures at the temple gate,
Old Baucis is by old Philemon seen
Sprouting with sudden leaves of spritely green:
Old Baucis look'd where old Philemon stood,
And saw his lengthen'd arms a sprouting wood;

New roots their fasten'd feet begin to bind,
Their bodies stiffen in a rising rind:
Then, ere the bark above their shoulders grew,
They give, and take at once their last adieu.
At once, "Farewell, oh faithful spouse," they said;
At once th' incroaching rinds their closing lips
　invade.
Ev'n yet, an ancient Tyanaean shows
A spreading oak, that near a linden grows;
The neighbourhood confirm the prodigy,
Grave men, not vain of tongue, or like to lie.
I saw myself the garlands on their boughs,
And tablets hung for gifts of granted vows;
And off'ring fresher up, with pious pray'r,
The good, said I, are God's peculiar care,
And such as honour heav'n, shall heav'nly
　honour share.

Pygmalion and the Statue

T*he Propoetides, for their impudent behaviour,
being turned into stone by Venus, Pygmalion,
prince of Cyprus, detested all women for their sake,
and resolved never to marry. He falls in love with a
statue of his own making, which is changed into a
maid, whom he marries. One of his descendants is
Cinyras, the father of Myrrha: the daughter incestuously loves her own father, for which she is changed
into a tree which bears her name. These two stories
immediately follow each other, and are admirably well
connected.*

Pygmalion loathing their lascivious life,
Abhorr'd all womankind, but most a wife:
So single chose to live, and shunn'd to wed,
Well pleased to want a consort of his bed:
Yet fearing idleness, the nurse of ill,
In sculpture exercised his happy skill;
And carved in ivory such a maid, so fair,
As nature could not with his art compare,
Were she to work; but in her own defence,
Must take her pattern here, and copy hence.
Pleased with his idol, he commends, admires,
Adores; and last, the thing adored desires.
A very virgin in her face was seen,
And, had she moved, a living maid had been:
One would have thought she could have stirr'd;
　but strove
With modesty, and was ashamed to move.
Art, hid with art, so well perform'd the cheat,
It caught the carver with his own deceit:
He knows 'tis madness, yet he must adore,

And still the more he knows it, loves the more:
The flesh, or what so seems, he touches oft,
Which feels so smooth, that he believes it soft.
Fired with this thought, at once he strain'd the
　breast,
And on the lips a burning kiss impress'd.
Tis true, the harden'd breast resists the gripe,
And the cold lips return a kiss unripe:
But when, retiring back, he look'd again,
To think it ivory was a thought too mean:
So would believe she kiss'd and courting more,
Again embraced her naked body o'er;
And straining hard the statue, was afraid
His hands had made a dint, and hurt the maid:
Explored her, limb by limb, and fear'd to find
So rude a gripe had a left a livid mark behind:
With flattery now he seeks her mind to move,
And now with gifts, the powerful bribes of love:
He furnishes her closet first; and fills
The crowded shelves with rarities of shells:
Adds orient pearls, which from the conchs he
　drew,
And all the sparkling stones of various hue:
And parrots, imitating human tongue,
And singing-birds in silver cages hung;
And every fragrant flower, and odorous green,
Were sorted well, with lumps of amber laid
　between:
Rich, fashionable robes her person deck,
Pendents her ears, and pearls adorn her neck:
Her taper'd fingers too with rings are graced.

And an embroider'd zone surrounds her slender
    waist.
Thus like a queen array'd, so richly dress'd,
Beauteous she show'd, but naked show'd the
    best.
Then from the floor, he raised a royal bed,
With coverings of Sidonian purple spread:
The solemn rites perform'd, he calls her bride,
With blandishments invites her to his side,
And as she were with vital sense possess'd,
Her head did on a plumy pillow rest.

    The feast of Venus came, a solemn day,
To which the Cypriots due devotion pay;
With gilded horns the milk-white heifers led,
Slaughter'd before the sacred altars, bled:
Pygmalion offering, first approach'd the shrine,
And then with prayers implored the powers
    divine:
Almighty gods, if all we mortals want,
If all we can require, be yours to grant;
Make this fair statue mine, he would have said,
But changed his words for shame, and only
    pray'd,
Give me the likeness of my ivory maid.

    The golden goddess, present at the prayer,
Well knew he meant the inanimated fair,
And gave the sign of granting his desire;
For thrice in cheerful flames ascends the fire.
The youth, returning to his mistress, hies,
And, impudent in hope, with ardent eyes,
And beating breast, by the dear statue lies.

He kisses her white lips, renews the bliss,
He looks and thinks they redden at the kiss:
He thought them warm before; nor longer stays,
But next his hand on her hard bosom lays:
Hard as it was, beginning to relent,
It seem'd the breast beneath his fingers bent;
He felt again, his fingers made a print,
'Twas flesh, but flesh so firm, it rose against the
    dint.
The pleasing task he fails not to renew:
Soft, and more soft at every touch it grew:
Like pliant wax, when chafing hands reduce
The former mass to form, and frame to use.
He would believe, but yet is still in pain,
And tries his argument of sense again,
Presses the pulse, and feels the leaping vein.
Convinced, o'erjoy'd, his studied thanks and
    praise,
To her who made the miracle, he pays:
Then lips to lips he join'd; now freed from fear,
He found the favour of the kiss sincere:
At this the waken'd image oped her eyes,
And view'd at once the light and lover, with
    surprise.
The goddess present at the match she made,
So bless'd the bed, such fruitfulness convey'd,
That ere ten moons had sharpen'd either horn,
To crown their bliss, a lovely boy was born;
Paphos his name, who, grown to manhood,
    wall'd
The city Paphos, from the founder call'd.

—————— *Questions for Consideration* ——————

Directions: Using complete sentences provide brief answers for the following questions.

1. Describe the metamorphosis of one of Ovid's mythological characters.

   _____

   _____

   _____

   _____

   _____

2. Identify the theme of one of Ovid's stories in his Metamorphoses.

   _____

   _____

   _____

   _____

   _____

3. What are the various ages of man and their characteristics according to Ovid?

   _____

   _____

   _____

   _____

   _____

Writing Critically

Directions: Select one of the essay topics listed below and compose a 500 word essay which discusses the topic fully.

1. Locate a love story found in Ovid's *Metamorphoses*. Discuss in a paper what type of relationship the two individuals have, and in what ways, if any, does it change. Is it a positive or negative change?

2. Imagine you have undergone a metamorphosis through some strange manner or occurrence. Describe in a paper what circumstances led to your transformation. What are you now since your transformation (a statue, a rock, an animal, something in the cosmos, a flower)? Describe your life now.

3. Research the five Ages of Man according to the Ancient Greeks. After your discoveries, decide five "Ages of Man" in the last century. Discuss your specific names of your ages and the characteristics of man in each. Are they different from Ovid's interpretations?

Prewriting Space:

_____

_____

_____

_____

_____

_____

_____

_____

_____

_____

_____

_____

_____

_____

_____

_____

_____

Introduction

Great Dialogues of Plato (427–347 B.C.)

Along with Socrates and Aristotle, Plato formed a trio of three of the most profound thinkers from Ancient Western Civilization. Plato was born in Athens approximately 428 B.C. to a prominent aristocratic family. In his youth, Plato was active in the political life of Athens. At that particular time, Athens was in a political upheaval with the Thirty Tyrants, the oligarchs who ruled Athens in cooperation after the Peloponnesian War. Plato's uncles, Critas and Charmides, were leaders who aided in establishing the rule of the Thirty Tyrants.

Plato probably met Socrates in 407 B.C. during the philosopher's discourses in the streets and homes of Athens. From this association bloomed a teacher-mentor relationship that lasted until Socrates' trial in 399 B.C. for corrupting the youth of Athens. Through his studies with Socrates, he absorbed many of the ideas embraced by his mentor. It is primarily through Plato that we know about the philosophical ideals and opinions proposed by Socrates.

Plato soon became dissatisfied with the democratic climate of Athenian government. As a result, shortly after attending the execution of Socrates, Plato traveled for nearly ten years to such areas as Italy, Egypt, and Sicily. Upon his return to Athens, Plato established in 387 B.C. his Academy. Plato's Academy, one of the first enduring universities, stressed not only philosophical and scientific research, music, astronomy, and mathematics, but it offered one a chance to explore issues in law, ethics, and politics. Some of the most creative minds were nourished at the Academy. In 367 B.C., Aristotle was accepted into the Academy soon allowing Plato to assume the role of a mentor.

There is a continuous debate among many scholars concerning the time frame of Plato's works, but most can agree that his writings fall into the Early Period, Middle Period, and Late Period. Plato wrote mainly all of his works in philosophic dialogue form. The Platonic dialogue is an argumentative conversation dramatic in form. The dialogue attempts to look at both sides of an issue and arrive at some type of opinion or compromise. The principal speaker in most of the dialogues is Socrates, who serves as a representative for Plato. Included in many of the dialogues are myths serving as allegories. Plato's dialogues are often praised for their graceful poetic prose, sense of humor, achievement in character delieation, dramatic form, and the keen incorporation of metaphor, simile, and irony. Such areas as ethics, law, and politics were often subject materials for his dialogues.

In the Early Period of Plato's works, often referred to as the Socratic, one can see Socrates as primarily the chief spokesperson. In many of the dialogues of this period, the personality and ideals of Socrates are revealed. It was as if Plato were a tape recorder because one perhaps hears dialogues that may actually have taken place. Plato's *Apology, Crito, Gorgias, Charmides*, and *Protagoras* belong to this earlier period. The Middle Period saw the mature philosopher with many of his dialogues still emphasizing the character of Socrates. At this time, however, the dialogues began to reveal many of Plato's own doctrines, especially his Theory of Ideas. Included in this period were such dialogues as *Phaedo, Meno, Symposium*, and the *Republic*. During the Late Period, Socrates almost disappears from his dialogues as a mouthpiece for Plato. Most of his works were focused on a reconsideration or rejection of previous ideas from the Middle Period. *Philebus, Sophist*, and *Laws* fall into the last years of productivity.

The central doctrine permeating Plato's philosophy, as it is seen in the dialogues, is his Theory of Ideas. According to Plato's Theory of Ideas, each thing we perceive in this world is merely a copy or imitation of a perfect original form of reality. He rejected the concrete material world as a source of true knowledge. In the nature of things, there can not be any true knowledge of that which is subject to change. Therefore, the Ideas, which alone of all things are changeless, are the only real objects of knowledge in the cosmos. With regard to all other things, we have only opinion which is capricious, fallible, and irrational, whereas knowledge is enduring, infallible, and relational. In order to achieve knowledge of these Ideas, one must be capable of "pure reason" or "pure intellect." The fundamental "idea" is the meaning of the good. Until one is capable of comprehending the idea of the good, a person is not able to understand reality. That person essentially lives in a fog or a world of shadows. As a result, obtaining an understanding of the good or virtue is the means of all knowledge.

The *Symposium*, written between 384 and 369 B.C., is considered by many scholars Plato's literary masterpiece. In this dialogue, the philosopher explores the controversial subject of Platonic love. The background of the *Symposium* is a banquet at the home of tragic poet Agathon. Apollodorus, the narrator, tells a friend about a conversation on love that takes place at the drinking party almost in the style of a round-table discussion. Through the speeches of such characters as Phaedrus, Pausanias, Aristophanes, and Socrates, the various types of love are revealed. In the speech of Socrates, there is a discussion concerning the various stages of love. The first stage is the love of one beautiful body. Next, is the love of all beautiful bodies and things. After this is accomplished, there is the love of all beautiful pursuits and then to another stage the love of all beautiful sciences. The highest form or stage of love is of absolute beauty and all truth. According to Plato, this is the closest to immortality a human being can reach.

In the *Symposium*, Plato suggests that beauty arouses the desire to procreate beauty. It does not mean, however, to possess the beautiful person or object. The desire for parenthood is a strong yearning for immortality. Spiritual parenthood is nobler and more productive of immortal wisdom, offspring, and goodness. Therefore, love is a climb to beauty, first physical and then mental. On the highest rung of the ladder the lover reaches abstract beauty, that is, pure wisdom or the Idea of the Good.

One of the most intriguing sections of Plato's *Republic* is found in Book VII, commonly referred to as the "Allegory of the Cave." Plato presents his ontology and the relationships between the realm of Ideas and the sensible world. The distinction is drawn between true reality and images of reality, noting the common failure to comprehend true reality. In addition, Plato includes the stages of education that ultimately lead to an understanding of true reality.

In the "Allegory of the Cave," Plato depicted men as prisoners living in a subterranean cave chained in such a way that they cannot move and that they must look at a wall. In essence, these prisoners are in a world of darkness seeing only shadows on a far cave wall that they take for reality. Behind them and above them, light (truth) streams into the cave from the outside. Suppose one of the prisoners becomes freed from his chains, begins to climb the steep slope, and eventually sees the sun, realizing it is the source of true light and heat. That individual perhaps would want to return to the comfortable falseness of the cave, finding truth difficult to face. On the other hand, that person could accept new "reality" and learn to appreciate it. If that individual returned to the cave with the fellow prisoners and told them about the real world outside, they may not want to accept or even listen to it because of their own world of darkness or ignorance. Thus, the rise to true knowledge is a demanding, steep, and long one. What, then, is the meaning of the allegory? Plato perhaps suggests that we, as individuals, are living in a cave of shadows chained by our own ignorance and nonchalant attitudes. We must, therefore, break those chains and begin the process of enlightenment! Education is a way of breaking the chains and leading us from the cave into the bright sunshine of reality.

The influence of Plato has been one of the most powerful forces in Western philosophy. Karl Jaspers has observed that Plato's words have been interpreted at one time or another as the source of all philosophies. Platonic thought has influenced Christianity. Wordsworth,

Spencer, Shelley, and countless other writers have been influenced by Plato. The Neoplatonists and the Cambridge Platonists enhanced his ideals. The philosophy of idealism has as its chief spokesperson Plato. As the writer Ralph Waldo Emerson said, "Plato is philosophy, and philosophy, Plato." (AHF)

BIBLIOGRAPHY

Allen, R. E. *The Dialogues of Plato, Volume I*. New Haven, Conn. Yale University, 1984.

Blank, David L. "The arousal of emotion in Plato's dialogues." *The Classical Quarterly*. 47 (Spring 1993): 428–39.

Brandwood, Leonard. *The Chronology of Plato's Dialogues*. Cambridge, England: Cambridge University Press, 1990.

Crombie, I. M. *An Examination of Plato's Doctrines, Vol. I: Plato on Man and Society*. New York: Routledge and Kegan, Paul, 1962.

Cross, R. C., and Woozley, A. D. *Plato's "Republic": A Philosophical Commentary*. London: Macmillian and Co., 1964.

Ficino, Marsilio. *Commentary on Plato's "Symposium" on Love*. Trans. Sears Jayne. Dallas: Spring Publications, 1985.

Gauss, H. *Plato's Conception of Philosophy*. New York: Haskell House Publications, 1974.

Gill, Jerry. "Re-exploring Plato's Cave." *Philosophy Today* 38 (Spring 1994): 98–110.

Gross, Barry. *The Great Thinkers on Plato*. New York: G. P. Putnam's Sons, 1968.

Hunter, Geoffrey. "Platonist Manifesto." *Philosophy Today* 69 (April 1994): 151–62.

EDITORS' NOTE

This translation was one of Dr. Rouse's many labours, and he was unfortunately prevented, by the volume of other work which he undertook, from giving it a final revision in detail before his death in February 1950.

In carrying out this revision, the Editors have tried to clear up the few inaccuracies and obscurities they found, and at the same time to interrupt as little as possible the distinctive character of Dr. Rouse's translation.

By far the greater part of his work remains unaltered, but in fairness to him it should be stated that the Divided Line diagram, the Banquet and Cave diagrams, and some of the footnotes have been subsequently added, so any faults in these should be imputed not to Dr. Rouse but to the Editors. The Summary of the *Republic*, which is also an addition, was written by J. C. G. Rouse, who also assisted in the work of editing.

Except for one or two well-known names (such as Plato) Dr. Rouse retained consistently the ancient Greek spelling of names; e.g. Phaidon, instead of Phaedo, the familiar Anglicised form; but for readers' convenience it has been decided to adopt the more generally accepted form for the titles of the dialogues.

Eric H. Warmington
Phillip G. Rouse

from Symposium

Plato
translated by W. H. D. Rouse

The Banquet

INTRODUCTORY NOTE

The banquet took place in Agathon's house in 416 B.C.; a few days previously Agathon, the handsome young tragic poet then aged about thirty-one, had won the prize, his first "victory," when one of his tragedies was first performed at a dramatic festival in the Theatre of Dionysos, the theatre at the foot of the Acropolis at Athens, which accommodated about 30,000 spectators; on page 135 Socrates refers to Agathon's courage in facing such a huge audience. Agathon appears to have been the first to insert into his tragedies choral odes unconnected with the plot of the drama. He gave this banquet to his friends on the next evening after he and his chorus had offered their sacrifice of thanksgiving for his victory.

Of his guests:

SOCRATES was then aged fifty-three.
PHAIDROS (Phaedrus), who was invited to preside, was a friend of Plato. The famous dialogue *The Phaedrus*, not included in this volume, on the subject of love, was named after him.
PAUSANIAS was a disciple of Prodicos, the Sophist, of Ceos.
ARISTOPHANES, the famous comic poet, was then about thirty-two. In his comedy *The Clouds*, first performed five years previously, he had made fun of Socrates.
ALCIBIADES, the eminent statesman then about thirty-five, a man of remarkable beauty and talent, but unscrupulous and dissolute, was a great admirer of Socrates, as his speech at the banquet shows. Socrates saved his life in battle when Alcibiades was about twenty.

The story of the banquet, as told by Aristodemos, who attended it with Socrates, is here retold by Apollodoros to a friend while they were out walking together about fifteen years after. Apollodoros is described in the dialogue *Phaidon (Phaedo)* as being present weeping at Socrates' death about a year later.

APOLLODORUS AND FRIEND
ARISTODEMOS
SOCRATES
AGATHON
PAUSANIAS
ARISTOPHANES
ERYXIMACHOS
PHAIDROS
ALCIBIADES

APPOLODOROS: I think I am pretty well word-perfect in what you are inquiring about. It so happened a day or two ago that I was coming up to town from Phaleron, when someone I know caught sight of me and called out from behind, some distance away, in a bantering tone— "Hullo, you Phalerian there!" he shouted. "Apollodoros! Halt!" I halted and stood still.

Then he said, "Well Apollodoros, I was just looking for you. I wanted to know about Agathon's party, Socrates and Alcibiades and the others who were at the dinner then, and the speeches they made about love. Somebody else told me the story; he heard it from Phoinix, Philip's son, and he said you knew too. But he had nothing very clear to say, so you must tell it to me; you are the best man to report your friend's speeches. But tell me first of all," he went on, "were you at the party yourself, or not?"

Then I said, "It is obvious that the story he told was not clear, if you think this party you ask about was held lately, so that I might have been there myself."

"That *is* what I thought," he said.

"How could you think that, my dear Glaucon?" I said. "Don't you know that Agathon has been abroad for many years, and it's only in the last three years I have been spending my time with Socrates, and taking care every day to know whatever he says or does? Before that I used to run all over the place, anywhere, and I thought myself a grand fellow, but I was more miserable than anyone—just as *you* are now, when you think you would do anything rather than be a philosopher."

"Oh, don't jeer," said he, "just tell me when that party was."

I said, "It was when we were boys, and Agathon won the prize with his first tragedy—on the next day after he and his chorus offered the sacrifice of thanksgiving."

"Then that is a long time ago," he said, "as it seems. But who told you the story—was it Socrates?"

"Oh dear me , no," I said, "the same man who told Phoinix; he was a Cydathenian, Aristodemos, a little man who never wore shoes. He was at the party, a lover of Socrates as much as anyone else in those days, I think. I did ask Socrates himself about some things too, which I heard from this man, and he agreed with all the other had told me."

"Well, I think you might tell me now," he said, "certainly the road to town will do well enough for us to talk and listen as we go."

So as we went along we talked about all this; and hence, as I told you to begin with, I am pretty well word-perfect. Well, if I must tell you people the story too, then I must. The truth is that whenever I speak about philosophy myself or hear others doing so, I am highly delighted, besides believing that it does me good. But when I hear other kinds of talk, especially among you rich men and moneymakers, it annoys me, and I pity you, my friends, because you are doing nothing while you think you are doing something. Well, perhaps again you believe I am a poor devil, and I think you think right; but I don't *think* you are, I *know* it well.

FRIEND: Always the same, Apollodoros! Always abusing yourself and everybody else. You really seem to think everyone wretched except Socrates, beginning with yourself! Where you got that nickname of madman, I don't know exactly, but in what you say you are always mad enough—you rave against yourself and everybody except Socrates!

APOLLODOROS: O my dear man, surely it is plain that I am mad and crazy, if I have such a notion about myself and you all!

FRIEND: It is not worth while quarrelling about this now, Apollodoros; but please do what I begged you—don't say no, but tell me what the speeches were.

APOLLODOROS: Well they were something like this—but I will try to tell you the story from the beginning as Aristodemos[1] told it.

Aristodemos said that he met Socrates coming from the bath, with evening shoes on,[2] which he did not often wear; and he asked him where he was going so smart; he said, dinner at Agathon's; yesterday he had refused him at the victory feast, to avoid the crowd; but he accepted for today. "That's why I made myself pretty," he said, "to go pretty to a pretty man! But look here," he continued, "how about you yourself feeling willing to go to dinner uninvited?"

And I replied (said Aristodemos), "As you like."

"Come with me, then," said Socrates, "and we will pervert the proverb a bit, and say, 'When gents give dinners, gents may just walk in.'[3] For Homer has really perverted this proverb, and made it vulgar too. He draws Agamemnon as a very perfect gentle knight, and Menelaos as a 'weak warrior': and when Agamemnon gave a feast and a sacrifice, he brings in Menelaos to the feast uninvited, although he is a low man and the other high."

Hearing this, my friend said, "Well, perhaps I'll risk it too, not as you suggest, Socrates, but, as in Homer, I, a poor creature, will go uninvited to a wise man's feast. Then just think what you will say about it, for I certainly will not admit that I came uninvited, I'll tell him that you invited me."

He said, "Two heads are better than one;[4] we will plan what we shall say. Well, let us go."

So after some such talk, they started off. On the way, Socrates fell behind, absorbed in his own thoughts; and when my friend was waiting, Socrates told him to go on ahead. When he came to Agathon's house, he found the door open, and there (he said) something rather ridiculous happened; for a servant from inside met him at once, and led him where the others were on their couches, and he came upon them as they were about to begin dinner. But as soon as Agathon saw him, he said, "My, dear Aristodemos, you are just in time to join us at dinner; if you have come for something else, put it off to another time; yesterday I looked for you to invite you, but I could not see you anywhere. But why have you not brought us Socrates?" I turned round (continued Aristodemos) but I could not see Socrates following; so I said I had come with Socrates and he had invited me there to dinner. "Very nice of you to come," he said, "but where is the man?"

"He was coming in behind me just now; I wonder myself where he could be."

"You there, you boy," said Agathon, "look about and bring in Socrates. And you take your place here, Aristodemos, beside Eryximachos."

Then the boy washed his feet, that he might take his place; and another boy came and reported, "Socrates went into the porch next door and there he is standing, but though I call him he won't come in."[*]

"That's odd," said he, "just ask him again and don't let him go."

But my friend said, "Don't do that, leave him alone. That is only his way; he often goes off and stands anywhere. He will come soon, I think. Don't interfere with him, let him alone."

Agathon said, "Very well, if you think so, we must do so. Serve the feast for the rest of us, you boys, and put before us just what you choose, whenever no one directs you (I never tried this before!).[5] Now then, imagine that I also as well as the others here have been invited by you to dinner, and serve us so as to earn our compliments."

After this, he said, they fell to, but no Socrates appeared. Agathon kept on giving orders to send for him, but my friend would not let him. However he did come, after not so long delay as usual, and found them about the middle of dinner. Then Agathon, who was reclining on the lowest seat[6] alone, on the right, said, "This way, Socrates,

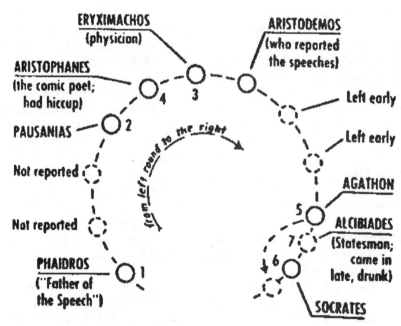

The banquet at Agathon's house (416 B.C.)
Diagram showing order of reported speeches[*]

NOTE: The diagram is drawn circular for convenience. It is not known how the couches were arranged. The couches usually accommodated two persons each, but some were made longer. From representations on ancient vases it seems that each diner reclined towards his left, supported under his left arm by a large cushion and with his right hand free to help himself from a low stool or table in front of the couch. They had no knives or forks. The wine was usually drunk mixed with water, about three parts of water to two of wine. See *A Dictionary of Greek and Roman Antiquities,* by W. Smith, W. Wayte, and G. E. Marindin, 3rd edition (1891), p. 393 on "Cena" and p. 741 on "Symposium."

come by me, I want to get hold of you, to enjoy that wise thought which came to you in the porch. For it is clear you found it and have it still, or you would never have come away."

Socrates sat down, and said, "What a blessing it would be, Agathon, if wisdom could run from the fuller amongst us to the emptier, while we touch one another, as when two cups are placed side by side a bit of wool conveys water from the fuller to the emptier! If wisdom is like that, I think it precious to be beside you, for I think I shall be filled up with fine wisdom. Mine would be poor stuff and questionable, like a dream, but yours brilliant and fast growing; see how it has blazed out of you while you are still young, and showed itself to us the other day before over thirty thousand of our nation!"

"You are a scoffer, Socrates!" said Agathon. "Well, we will come into court before long about this, you and I, on our claim for wisdom, and the judge shall be Dionysos:[7] now first turn to dinner."

After this (Aristodemos said), Socrates reclined, and he and they all had their dinner; they poured the drops of grace, and sang a chant to the god, and did the usual things, and settled down to drinking. Then (he continued) Pausanias began the talk like this: "Look here, gentlemen," he said, "how shall we manage our drinking most conveniently? I tell you I am really not up to the mark myself after yesterday's bout and I want some rest, and so do most of you, I think—for you were present yesterday; just consider then how we could manage our drinking most conveniently."

Then Aristophanes said, "Now that is good advice, Pausanias, to make the drinking as comfortable as we can; I am one of those myself who had a good soaking yesterday."

So Eryximachos, Acumenos' son, when he heard them, said, "Quite right, you two. And one thing more I want to know, how Agathon feels about being fit to drink."

"No," said Agathon, "I don't feel very fit myself either."

The other said, "It seems it would be a bit of luck for us, me and Aristodemos and Phaidros and our friends here, if you with the strongest heads for drinking have thrown up the sponge; for we are always the weaklings. I do not count Socrates; he can do both ways, and it will content him whichever we choose. Then since it seems no one present votes for a hearty bout of deep wine-drinking, perhaps I should not give offence if I tell you the truth about the effect of getting drunk. I think I have seen quite clearly as a phy-

sician that drunkenness is a dangerous thing for mankind; and I am not willing to go far in drinking myself, nor would I advise another to do it, especially if he still has a headache from yesterday."

Phaidros the Myrrhinusian responded, "Well, I always take your advice, especially on matters of physic and health; and the rest of us will be wise to do the same now." So all agreed after hearing this not to drink too much during the present party but everyone should drink just to please himself.

"Very well," said Eryximachos, "since the motion is passed that each one may drink as much as he likes, but no one *must* drink, my next motion is, that the piping-girl who has just come in may go out again, and play to herself, or if she pleases to the women inside, and that today we entertain each other with talk; and with your leave, I will propose what kind of talk." They all agreed, and gave leave, and told him to propose away.

"I will begin," said Eryximachos, "by quoting from the *Melanippe* of Euripides:[8] 'the story is not mine' which I am going to tell, it belongs to Phaidros. For Phaidros is always complaining to me, 'It's a shame, Eryximachos, that many other gods have hymns and paeans made for them by the poets, but Love, that ancient mighty god, has not a single one; of all the thousands of poets who have lived, not one has ever made even an ode to praise him! Or look at the worthy professors,[9] if you please; they compose praises of men like Heracles in prose, as the excellent Prodicos did,[10] perhaps that is not so surprising, but lately I came across a book by some wise man where salt was lauded to the skies for its usefulness and you could find many other such things praised up. Just think—to make such a fuss about things like salt, when no human being has ever dared to this day to hymn Love worthily! What neglect for so great a god!' I think Phaidros is quite right there. So I wish to make my small contribution, and to offer it to him; and at the same time it seems to me proper on this occasion for us now present to glorify the god. If you vote with me, we should find plenty to amuse us in the speeches; for my proposal is that we should deliver a full-dress oration in praise of Love, each one from left to right, and Phaidros must begin first, since he is in the first place[11] and he is also father of the speech."

Then Socrates said, "No one will vote against you, Eryximachos. I could not refuse myself, I suppose, when love is the only thing I profess to know about; nor will Agathon, I suppose, and

Pausanias, nor indeed Aristophanes, who devotes all this time to Dionysos[12] and Aphrodite, nor any other of those I see here. However, it is not quite fair on us who are last.[13] But if those before us give us some really good speeches, that will do for us. Then let Phaidros be the first, and speak in praise of Love, and good luck to him." All the others agreed, and asked him to do as Socrates suggested. However, what each one of them all said, Aristodemos could not remember, nor can I remember all he told me. But what I do remember, and what I thought most worth remembering, I will tell you of each of the speeches.

Well, as I say, Phaidros, according to Aristodemos, was the first, and he began hereabouts; that Love was a great god and wonderful on earth and in heaven, especially in his birth. "The god is honourable as being among the most ancient of all," he said; "and a proof is, that parents Love has none, nor are they mentioned by anyone, poet or not, although Hesiod does say that Chaos came first,[14]

> *And then*
> *Broad-breasted Earth, the everlasting seat*
> *Of all, and Love.*

Acusileōs also agreed with Hesiod; he says that after Chaos were produced these two, Earth and Love. But Parmenides says of Birth, that she

> *Contrivèd Love the first of all the gods.*

Thus many agree that Love is most ancient among them. And being most ancient, he is cause of the greatest good for us. For I cannot say what is a greater good for a man in his youth than a lover, and for a lover than a beloved. For that which ought to guide mankind through all his life, if it is to be a good life, noble blood cannot implant in him so well, nor office, nor wealth, nor anything but Love. And what do I mean by that? I mean shame at ugly things, and ambition in beautiful things; for without these neither city nor man can accomplish great and beautiful works. I say then of a man who loves, that if he should be detected in doing something ugly, or allowing himself to be treated in ugly fashion because through cowardice he did not defend himself, he would suffer less pain to be seen by father or friends or anyone else than by his beloved. In the same way we see that the beloved is particularly ashamed before the lover, when seen in any augly situation. Then if any device could be found how a state or an army could be made up only of lovers and beloved, they could not possibly find a better way of living, since they would abstain from all ugly things and be ambitious in beautiful things toward each other; and in battle side by side, such troops although few would conquer pretty well all the world. For the lover would be less willing to be seen by his beloved than by all the rest of the world, leaving the ranks or throwing away his arms, and he would choose to die many times rather than that; yes, and as to deserting the beloved, or not helping in danger, no one is so base that Love himself would not inspire him to valour, and make him equal to the born hero. And just as Homer says that the god 'breathes fury'[15] into some of the heroes, so does Love really give to lovers a power coming from himself.

"And to die for another—this only lovers are willing to do, not only men, but women. Alcestis, Pelias' daughter,[16] gives sufficient evidence of this to prove it to our nation; she alone was willing to die for her husband, although he had a father and a mother; these the wife so much surpassed in love because of her affection for her husband that she showed they were aliens to their own son and were relatives only in name. Having done this, she was thought, not only by men, but by gods also, to have done so nobly that they sent up her soul from the dead in admiration for her deed, although of all the many who have done noble deeds one might easily count those to whom the gods gave the privilege of having their souls sent up again from Hades. Thus the gods also honour especially earnestness and valour in love. But Orpheus, Oiagros' son, they sent back unsuccessful from Hades, showing him a phantom of his wife for whom he came, but not giving her real self because they thought him soft, being a zither-player, and they thought he did not dare to die for his love like Alcestis, but managed to get into Hades alive. For this reason, therefore, they punished him and made his death come about by women, unlike Achilles, the son of Thetis; but they honoured Achilles and sent him to the Islands of the Blest,[17] because when his mother told him that if he killed Hector he would die, but if he did not kill him he would return home and live to be an old man, he dared to choose, by helping his lover Patroclos and avenging him, not only to die for him but in his end to perish over his body; hence therefore the gods, admiring him above measure, honoured him particularly, because he set so high the value of his lover. (But Aeschylus is absurd[18] when he says Achilles was the lover and Patroclos the beloved, when he was more beautiful not only than Patroclos but than all the heroes, and was yet beardless, and again much younger, as Homer says.[19]) But in fact the gods do most greatly honour this valour for love's sake; yet they still more respect and admire and reward when the beloved feels affection for the lover, than when the lover does for his beloved. For a lover is more divine than the beloved, since he is inspired. Therefore they honoured Achilles more than Alcestis, and sent him to the Islands of the Blest.

"Thus then I say, that of the gods Love is at once oldest, and most precious, and has most power to provide virtue and happiness for mankind, both living and dead."

Such or something like it was the speech of Phaidros, as related to me by Aristodemos; and after Phaidros there were some others which he did not remember well; so he passed them by, and reported the speech of Pausanias, who said, "I do not think, Phaidros, that the rules were properly laid down, I mean that we should just simply belaud Love. For if Love were one, that would do, but really he is not one; and since he is not one, it is more proper to say first which we are to praise. Then I will try to set this right, and say first which Love we ought to praise, and then praise that god worthily. For we all know that Aphrodite[20] is never without a Love: if she were one, Love would be one; but since there are really two, there must be two Loves. Of course there are two goddesses. One I take it is older, and motherless, daughter of Heaven, whom we call Heavenly Aphrodite, the other younger, a daughter of Zeus and Dione, whom we call, as you know, Common. It must be then, you see, that Love too, the one who works with this Aphrodite, should be called Common Love, and the other Heavenly Love. It is true we must praise all gods, but I must try to say what is the province of each of these two. For the performance of every action is, in itself, neither beautiful nor ugly. So what we are doing now, whether drinking or singing or speaking, is not itself beautiful, but according as it is done, so it comes out in the doing; when it is done well and rightly, it is beautiful, but when not rightly done, it is ugly. Just so with being in love, and with Love himself; he is not all beautiful and worthy to be praised, but only so far as he leads to right loving.

"The Love, then, which belongs to Common Aphrodite is really and truly common and works at random; and this is the love which inferior men feel. Such persons love firstly women as well as boys; next, when they love, they love bodies rather than souls; and next, they choose the most foolish person they can, for they look only to getting something done, and care nothing whether well or not. So what happens to them is that they act at random, whether they do good or whether they do its opposite; for this Love springs from the goddess which is much younger than the other, and in her birth had a share of both female and male. But the other Love springs from the Heavenly goddess, who firstly has had no share of the female, but only of the male; next, she is the elder, and has no violence in her; consequently those inspired by this love turn to the male, because they feel affection rather for what is stronger and has more mind. One could recognise even in boy-love those who are driven by this Love pure and simple; for they do not fall in love with those who are little boys, but with those who begin to have mind, and that is nearly when they show the down on their chins. For those who begin to love them from this age, I think, are ready to be with them always for all their lives, and to live with them together; they do not wish to get a boy in the foolishness of youth, and then deceive him and laugh at him and go off running to another. There ought to have been a law against loving little boys, that a great deal of earnestness might not have been spent on what is uncertain; for it is uncertain how little boys will turn out, as regards vice and virtue, both of body and soul. Now those who are good place this law before themselves unbidden; but it ought to be made compulsory for those common lovers, just as we make it compulsory as far as we can that they shall not make love to freeborn women. For these are they who bring reproach on the whole thing, so that some dare to say that it is ugly to gratify lovers; they say this with their eye on those common ones, when they see their tactlessness and injustice; since I suppose nothing done decently and lawfully could fairly bring discredit.

"Again, here and in Lacedaimon the law about love is confusing, but that in other states is easy to understand. In Elis and Boeotia, and where people are not clever speakers, it is simply laid down that it is right to gratify lovers, and no one young or old would call it ugly; as I think, they wish not to have the trouble of convincing the young, because they cannot argue; but in many other parts of Ionia it is considered ugly, where they are under barbarians. For the barbarians because of the rule of despots call this ugly, as well as philosophy and sports; I still suppose it is profitable to their rulers that the subjects should not be great in spirit or make strong friendships and unions, which things love is wont to implant more than anything else. In fact, our own despots[21] here found that out by experience; for the love of Aristogeiton, and the friendship of Harmodios, grown strong, brought their rule to an end. So where it has been laid down as ugly to gratify lovers, that was from the evil condition of those that made the laws, the grasping habits of the rulers and the cowardice of the ruled; and where it was thought simply good, that was from laziness of soul in those who made the laws. But in these parts, much of the law and custom is better, and as I said, it is not easy to understand.

"For consider that it is called better to love openly than secretly, and especially to love the highest and noblest born, even if they are uglier than others; and consider how wonderfully all encourage the lover—not as if he were doing something ugly, which if he wins is thought beautiful, and if he does not win, ugly; and how the law has allowed the lover, in trying to win, to be praised for doing extraordinary things, which if a man should dare to do in pursuit of anything else except this, or should even wish to accomplish, he would reap the greatest disgrace. For if, wishing to get money from someone, or to win public office, or to get any other power, a man should behave as lovers do towards their beloved, begging and beseeching them in their petitions, and swearing solemn oaths, and sleeping at their doors, and being willing to do slavish services such as no slave would do, he would be hindered both by friends and by enemies from doing business thus: the friends would be ashamed of such things and warn him, the enemies would upbraid him for flattery and bad manners. But the lover has a grace when he does all this, and the law allows him to do it without discredit, as a thing wholly beautiful; and strangest of all, he alone, as the people say, is pardoned by the gods for breaking the oath he has sworn— for it is said an oath of love simply has no force. Thus both gods and men have given full licence to the lover, as the law here says; so far, then, one might think it was considered wholly beautiful in this city both to love and to feel affection for a lover. But on the other hand when fathers place tutors over the loved ones and forbid them to converse with their lovers, and the tutor is ordered to see to it; when age-mates and companions reproach them if they see anything like this going on; and lastly when the older men do not stop these from reproaching them, nor scold them for talking nonsense—if one looked at this, one would think such a thing was considered very ugly here. The fact is, I think, the case is not simple: as I said at the beginning, it is neither beautiful nor ugly by itself, but beautifully done it is beautiful, and uglily done it is ugly—uglily, is to gratify a base man and basely; beautifully, is to gratify a good man and beautifully. A base man is that common lover who loves the body rather than the soul; for he is not lasting since he loves a thing not lasting. For as soon as the flower of the body fades, which is what he loved, 'He takes to the wing and away he flies,'[22] and violates any number of vows and promises; but the lover of a good character remains faithful throughout life, since he has been fused with a lasting thing. These, then, our law wishes to test well and thoroughly; for these reasons, then, it enjoins to pursue the one and eschew the other, setting them tasks and testing them to see which class the lover belongs to, and which class the beloved. Thus you see it is on these grounds that, first of all, to be won quickly is considered ugly— for time should come in, which seems to test everything well; next, to be won by money and political power is ugly, whether it means shrinking from suffering and lack of endurance, or failure to despise the benefits flowing from money or political achievements; for none of these things appears to be firm and lasting, not to mention that genuine affection is never bred from them. Then only one road is left for our law, if the beloved is to gratify the lover beautifully. For our law is, that as it was not counted flattery or disgrace for lovers to be willing slaves in any slavery to the beloved, so for the beloved, there is only one willing slavery which is no disgrace— and that is in pursuit of virtue.

"For we have a custom that if one wishes to serve another because he thinks that the man can make him better either in wisdom or any other part of virtue, this willing slavery is not ugly and it is no flattery. Then let us compare these two customs, that which concerns boy-lovers and that which concerns philosophy and virtue in general, if we are to infer that when the beloved gratifies the lover it is beautiful. For when lover and beloved come together each with his law— the one, that when he serves the consenting beloved in anything whatever the service is right, the other, that by doing any service whatever to one who makes him wise and good he does right service, the one able to contribute something for wisdom and virtue in general, the other desiring to get this for education and wisdom in general— then, you see, these laws meet together, and then only it follows that for beloved to gratify lover is beautiful, but never otherwise. In this case, even to be deceived is not ugly; in all others both to be deceived and not to be deceived is ugly. For if one in pursuit of riches gratifies a lover supposed to be rich, and is deceived and gets no money because the lover turns out to be poor, it is no less ugly; for such a one is thought to show, as far as in him lay, that for money he would do anyone and everyone any and every service, and that is not beautiful. By the same argument observe that even if one gratifies another as being good, expecting to be better himself because of his affection for the lover, but since the other turns out to be bad and not possessed of virtue, he is deceived, nevertheless the deceit is beautiful; for he again is thought to have shown, as far as in him lay, that for virtue and to become better he was ready with everything for everyone. And this again is the most beautiful thing of all; so in every case it is beautiful to gratify for the sake of virtue.

"This is the love of the heavenly goddess, love both heavenly and precious to city and men; for it compels both lover and beloved to take all possible care for virtue. But all other loves belong to the other goddess, the common one. Here, my dear Phaidros, you have my humble contribution on Love, as well as I could make it at the moment."

Pausanias paused upon this clause—that's how the stylists teach me to jingle!—and Aristodemos said that Aristophanes ought to have spoken next, but he had a hiccup from surfeit or something, and couldn't speak. However, he managed to say to Doctor Eryximachos, who was reclining in the place just below him, "My dear Eryximachos, it's your job either to stop my hiccup, or to speak instead until I stop myself."

And Eryximachos answered, "Well, I will do both; I will speak in your turn, and when you stop the hiccup you shall speak in mine. And while I am speaking, hold your breath a long time and see if the hiccup will stop; if it won't, gargle water. But if it still goes strong, pick up something to tickle your nose with, and sneeze; do this once or twice, and stop it will, even if it is very strong."

"Look sharp," says Aristophanes, "speak away, and I'll do all that."

Then (continued Aristodemos) Eryximachos said, "Pausanias began well, but ended feebly, so I think I must try to put a good end to his oration. He said Love was double, and I think he was right in dividing him. But I think I have seen from our art of medicine how great and wonderful the god is, and how he extends over everything human and divine; he is not only in the souls of mankind and directed towards beautiful people,

but he is in all the rest, and directed towards many other things: he is in the bodies of all living creatures, and in what grows in the earth, and, one may say, in everything there is. I will begin my speech with medicine, that we may do special honour to my art. The natural body had this double Love; for bodily health and disease are by common consent different things and unlike, and what is unlike desires and loves things unlike. Then there is one love in the healthy, and another in the diseased. So you see just as, according to what Pausanias said just now, it is beautiful to gratify good men, and ugly to gratify the intemperate, so in the bodies themselves, to gratify the good things in each body and the healthy things is beautiful and must be done, and this gratification is what is called the healing art, but to gratify what is bad and diseased is ugly and must not be done, if one is to practise that art. For the healing art, to put it shortly, is knowledge of the body's loves for filling and emptying, and one who distinguishes the beautiful and the ugly love in these things is the most complete physician; and one who makes them change, so that they get one love instead of the other, and, where there is no love when there ought to be, one who knows how to put it in, and to take out love that is in, he would be a good practitioner. You see one must be able to make loving friends of the greatest enemies in the body. Now the greatest enemies are the most opposite, hot and cold, bitter and sweet, dry and wet, and so forth; our ancestor Asclepios,[23] as our poets[24] here say and I believe, composed our art because he knew how to implant love and concord in these. Then the healing art, as I say, is all guided by this god, and so is gymnastic and agriculture; music too is clearly in the same case with this, as it is plain to anyone who thinks for a moment; and perhaps that is what Heracleitos means, since his words are not very clear. He says, 'The One at variance with itself is brought together again, like a harmony of bow and lyre.'[25] It is quite illogical to say that a *harmony* is *at variance* with itself or is made up of notes still *at variance*. But perhaps he meant to say that it was made from the high and low notes—first at variance, then afterwards reconciled together by the art of music. For I suppose there could not be harmony from high and low notes still at variance, for harmony is symphony and symphony is a kind of agreement; but agreement there cannot be of things at variance so long as they are at variance. But what is at variance, and yet is not unable to be brought into agreement, it is possible to harmonize. Just so rhythm is made from quick and slow, first differing, then brought into agreement. But music places agreement here in all these, just as there the art of healing does, by implanting concord and love for each other; and music again is the knowledge of love affairs concerning harmony and rhythm. And in the very composition of harmony and rhythm it is not difficult to distinguish the love affairs, although the double love is not there yet; but whenever one must use rhythm and harmony for men, either composing (which they call melody-making), or rightly using the melodies and verses made (which is called education), that is the time when there are difficulties, and a good craftsman is wanted. Then the same old argument comes round again, that decent men must be gratified, and also those not yet quite decent that they may become so, find their Love must be protected; and this is the beautiful Love, the Heavenly Love, the Love belonging to the 'Heavenly' Muse Urania; but that of 'Manyhymn' Polymnia is the common one, who must be offered to people with great care whenever he is offered, to let them reap the pleasure from him, but not to implant any intemperance: just so in our art, it is a great business to use well the desires concerned with the art of cookery, so that people may reap the pleasures without disease. So you see, both in music and in physic and in everything else earthly and heavenly, we must watch and protect both Loves as far as we can, for both are there.

"See how the composition of the seasons of the year is full of these two: and so, whenever the things I mentioned just now, hot and cold and dry and wet, have the decent Love towards each other, and get a harmony and a temperate mixture, they come bringing a good season, with health for mankind and the other animals and vegetables and plants, and then they do no harm; but when the violent Love has more power on the seasons of the year, he does harm, and destroys much. For pestilences often come as a result, and many other discordant diseases in wild beasts and growing things: hoarfrosts and hails and blights come from the habits and indecency of such love affairs, knowledge of which as regards the courses of the stars and the seasons of the year is called astronomy. Moreover, all sacrifice and the domain of divination (this is the communion of gods and men together), all this is concerned solely with the protection and healing of Love. For all impiety is wont to occur, as concerns parents both living and dead, and gods, if one does not gratify the decent Love and honour him and put him first in every work, but honours the other. So you see this is what divi-

nation is ordered to do, to supervise these Loves and to treat them as a physician; and divination is again the craftsman of friendship between men and gods, by its knowledge of the love affairs of mankind which tend towards good law and piety.

"So Love as a whole has great and mighty power, or rather in a word, omnipotence; but the one concerned with good things, being accomplished with temperance and justice, both here and in heaven, has the greatest power, and provides all happiness for us, and makes us able to have society together, and to be friends with the gods also, who are higher than we are. Perhaps indeed I also omit much in praising Love; but I can't help it. If I have omitted something, it is your part, Aristophanes, to fill up the gap; or if you intend to praise the god in some other way, go on and do so, since your hiccup is gone."

So Aristophanes (said Aristodemos) took his turn next, and said, "Oh yes, it has quite gone, but not until sneezing was applied to it; which makes me wonder if the decency of the body desires noises and ticklings like a sneeze; for it stopped at once when I applied the sneeze to it."

Then Eryximachos said, "My good man, look what you're doing! You are playing the fool when you are about to make a speech! You compel me to keep a watch on your speech and look out for something laughable, when you might speak in peace!"

And Aristophanes answered, with a laugh, "Quite right, Eryximachos, I take back what I said. But don't watch me, for as to what I am going to say, I am not at all afraid I may say something laughable, for that would be clear gain and natural to our Muse—but lest the things I say may be just ridiculous!"

"So you think you are going to hurl your shaft, Aristophanes," he said, "and get off scot free? Take care, take care, and be sure you will have to account for yourself. But perhaps I will let you off, if I am so disposed."

"Well, Eryximachos," said Aristophanes. "I intend to speak in a different way from you and Pausanias. For it seems to me that mankind have wholly failed to perceive the power of Love; if they had, they would have built to him their greatest sanctuaries and altars, and they would have made their greatest sacrifice to him; but now nothing of the sort is done, although it most assuredly ought to be done. For he is the most man-loving of gods, being the helper of man, and the healer of those whose hearing would be the greatest happiness to the human race. Therefore

I will try to introduce you to his power, and you shall teach the others.

"First you must learn about the nature of man and the history of it. Formerly the natural state of man was not what it is now, but quite different. For at first there were three sexes, not two as at present, male and female, but also a third having both together; the name remains with us, but the thing is gone. There was then a male-female sex and a name to match, sharing both male and female, but now nothing is left but the title used in reproach.[26] Next, the shape of man was quite round, back and ribs passing about it in a circle; and he had four arms and an equal number of legs, and two faces on a round neck, exactly alike; there was one head with these two opposite faces, and four ears, and two privy members, and the rest as you might imagine from this. They walked upright as now, in whichever direction they liked; and when they wanted to run fast, they rolled over and over on the ends of the eight limbs they had in those days, as our tumblers tumble now with their legs straight out. And why there were three sexes, and shaped like this, was because the male was at first born of the sun, and the female of the earth, and the common sex had something of the moon, which combines both male and female; their shape was round and their going was round because they were like their parents. They had terrible strength and force, and great were their ambitions; they attacked the gods, and what Homer said of Otos and Ephialtes is said of them, that they tried to climb into heaven intending to make war upon the gods.[27]

"So Zeus and the other gods held council what they should do, and they were perplexed; for they could not kill the tribe with thunderbolts and make them vanish like the giants—since then their honours and the sacrifices of mankind would vanish too—nor could they allow them to go on in this wild way. After a deal of worry Zeus had a happy thought. 'Look here,' he said, 'I think I have found a scheme; we can let men still exist but we can stop them from their violence by making them weaker. I will tell you what I'll do now,' says he, 'I will slice each of them down through the middle! Two improvements at once! They will be weaker, and they will be more useful to us because there will be more of them. They shall walk upright on two legs. And if they choose to go on with their wild doings, and will not keep quiet, I'll do it again!' says he, 'I'll slice 'em again through the middle! And they shall hop about on one leg! Like those boys that hop on the greasy wineskins at the fair!'[28] says he; and then he sliced men through the middle, as

you slice your serviceberries through the middle for pickle, or as you slice hard-boiled eggs with a hair. While he sliced each, he told Apollo to turn the face and half the neck towards the cut, to make the man see his own cut and be more orderly, and then he told him to heal the rest up. So Apollo turned the face, and gathered up the skin over what is now called the belly, like purses which you pull shut with a string; he made one little mouth, and fastened it at the middle of the belly, what they call the navel. Most of the wrinkles he smoothed out, and shaped the breasts, using a tool like the shoemaker's when he smooths wrinkles out of his leather on the last; but he left a few, those about the navel and the belly, to remind them of what happened. So when the original body was cut through, each half wanted the other, and hugged it; they threw their arms round each other desiring to grow together in the embrace, and died of starvation and general idleness because they would not do anything apart from each other. When one of the halves died and the other was left, the half which was left hunted for another and embraced it, whether he found the half of a whole woman (which we call woman now), or half of a whole man; and so they perished. But Zeus pitied them and found another scheme; he moved their privy parts in front, for these also were outside before, and they had begotten and brought forth not with each other but with the ground, like the cicadas. So he moved these parts also in front and made the generation come between them, by the male in the female; that in this embrace, if a man met a woman, they might beget and the race might continue, and if a man met a man, they might be satisfied by their union and rest, and might turn to work and care about the general business of life. So you see how ancient is the mutual love implanted in mankind, bringing together the parts of the original body and trying to make one out of two, and to heal the natural structure of man.

"Then each of us is the tally[29] of a man; he is sliced like a flatfish, and two made of one. So each one seeks his other tally. Then all men who are a cutting of the old common sex which was called manwoman are fond of women, and adulterers generally come of that sex, and all women who are mad for men, and adulteresses. The women who are a cutting of the ancient women do not care much about men, but are more attracted to women, and strumpetesses also come from this sex. But those which are a cutting of the male pursue the male, and while they are boys, being slices of the male, they are fond of men, and enjoy lying with men and embracing them, and these are the best of boys and lads because they are naturally bravest. Some call them shameless, but that is false; no shamelessness makes them do this, but boldness and courage and a manly force, which welcome what is like them. Here is a great proof: when they grow up, such as these alone are men in public affairs. And when they become men, then, fancy boys, and naturally do not trouble about marriage and getting a family, but that law and custom compels them; they find it enough themselves to live unmarried together. Such a person is always inclined to be a boy-lover or a beloved, as he always welcomes what is akin. So when one of these meets his own proper half, whether boy-lover or anyone else, then they are wonderfully overwhelmed by affection and intimacy and love, and one may say never wish to be apart for a moment. These are the ones who remain together all their lives, although they could not say what they expect to get from each other; for no one could suppose that this is sensual union, as if this could make anyone delight in another's company so seriously as all that. Plainly the soul of each wants something else—what, it cannot say, but it divines and riddles what it wants. And as they lie together suppose Hephaistos[30] were to stand beside them with his tools, and ask, 'What do you want from each other, men?' And if they were at a loss, suppose be should ask again, 'Is it only that you desire to be together as close as possible, and not to be apart from each other night or day? For if that is what you desire, I am ready to melt you and weld you together, so that you two may be made one, and as one you may live together as long as you live, and when you die you may die still one instead of two, and be yonder in the house of Hades together. Think if this is your passion, and if it will satisfy you to get this.' If that were offered, we know that not a single one would object, or be found to wish anything else; he would simply believe he had heard that which he had so long desired, to be united and melted together with his beloved, and to become one from two. For the reason is that this was our ancient natural shape, when we were one whole; and so the desire for the whole and the pursuit of it is named Love.

"Formerly, as I say, we were one, but now because of doing wrong we have been dispersed by the god, as the Arcadians were dispersed by the Lacedaimonians. There is fear then, if we are not decent towards the gods, that we may be sliced in half again, and we may go about like so many relief carvings of persons shown in half-view on tombstones, sawn right through the nose, like tally-dice cut in half. For these reasons we must exhort all men in everything to be god-fearing men, that we may escape this fate and attain our desire, since Love is our leader and captain. But let no man oppose Love—and whoever is the gods' enemy does oppose him. For when we are friends with this god and reconciled to him, we shall find and enjoy our very own beloved, which now few are able to do. And don't let Eryximachos chip in and make fun of my speech, and say that I mean Pausanias and Agathon; I should not be surprised if they are really of this class, and both males by nature, but indeed I speak in general of all men and women, that the way to make our race happy is to make love perfect, and each to get his very own beloved and go back to our original nature. If this is the best thing possible, the best thing to our hand must of course be to come as near it as possible, and that is to get a beloved who suits our mind. Then if we would praise the god who is the cause of this, we should rightly praise Love, who in the present gives us our chief blessing by bringing us home to our own, and for the future offers the greatest hopes; that if we duly worship the god, he will restore us to our ancient nature and heal us and make us blessed and happy.

"There is my speech about Love, Eryximachos, very different from yours. Then, as I begged you, do not make fun of it, but let us hear what each of the others will say, or rather, each of the two others; for only Agathon and Socrates are left."

"I will do as you ask," said Eryximachos, "for I did very much enjoy hearing that speech. And if I did not know that both Socrates and Agathon were experts in love matters, I should be afraid they might be puzzled what to say when such a world of things has been said already. But as it is, I don't fear at all."

Then Socrates said, "You played your part well yourself, Eryximachos; but if you were where I am now, or rather perhaps where I shall be, when Agathon has made his speech, you would be very much afraid, and like me now, you wouldn't know where you were."

"You want to put a spell on me, Socrates," said Agathon, "and make me shy through thinking that the audience has great expectations of a fine speech from me!"

Socrates answered, "I should have a very bad memory, Agathon, if I thought you would be shy now before a few people like us, since I saw your courage and spirit when you mounted the platform along with the actors, and faced all that huge audience, ready to display your compositions without the smallest sign of confusion."

"What!" said Agathon, "my dear Socrates, you don't really think I am so full of the theatre that I don't know a few men with minds are more formidable to a man of sense than many without minds!"

"I should make a mistake, my dear Agathon," Socrates said, "if I imagined anything about you; I am quite sure that if you were in company with any you thought intelligent, you would rate them among the many. However, perhaps we are not intelligent—for we were there too, and we were among the many—but if you should meet with others who are, you would be ashamed of doing before them anything which you might think ugly. What do you say to that?"

"Quite true," said he.

"And before the many, would you not be ashamed if you thought you were doing something ugly?"

Then Phaidros put in a word, and said, "My, dear friend Agathon, if you answer Socrates, he will not care what becomes of our business here! He won't care anything about anything, so long as he can have someone to converse with, especially someone beautiful. For myself, I like hearing Socrates arguing, but it is my duty to care about the praise of Love, and to exact from each one of you his speech. So just pay up to the god, both of you, and then you may argue."

"Quite right, Phaidros," said Agathon, "I am ready to speak; Socrates will be there another time, and often, to talk to.

"First, then, I wish to describe how I ought to speak; then to speak. It seems to me that all who have spoken so far have not praised the god, but have congratulated mankind on the good things which the god has caused for them: what that god was himself who gave these gifts, no one has described. But the one right way for any laudation of anyone is to describe what he is, and then what he causes, whoever may be our subject. Thus, you see, with Love: we also should first praise him for what he is, and then praise his gifts.

"I say then that all gods are happy, but if it is lawful to say this without offence, I say that Love is happiest of them all, being most beautiful and best. And how he is most beautiful, I am about to describe. First of all, Phaidros, he is youngest of the gods. He himself supplies one great proof of what I say, for he flies in full flight away from Old Age, who is a quick one clearly, since he comes too soon to us all. Love hates him naturally and will not come anywhere near but he is always associated with the young, and with them he consorts, for the old saying is right, 'Like ever comes to like.' I am ready to admit many other things to Phaidros, but one I do not admit, that Love is older than Cronos and Iapetos;[31] no, I say he is youngest of the gods, and ever young; but that old business of the gods, which Hesiod and Parmenides tell about, was done through Necessity and not through Love, if they told the truth; for if Love had been in them, there would have been no gelding or enchaining of each other and all those violent things, but friendship and peace, as there is now, and has been ever since Love has reigned over the gods. So then, he is young, and besides being young he is tender; but we need a poet like Homer to show the god's tenderness. For Homer says of Ate[32] that she was a god and tender—at least her feet were tender—when he says that

> *Tender are her feet; she comes not near*
> *The ground, but walks upon the heads of men.*

I think he gives good proof of her tenderness, that she walks not on the hard but on the soft. Then let us use the same proof for Love, that he is tender. For he walks not on the earth nor on top of heads, which are not so very soft, but both walks and abides in the softest things there are; for his abode is settled in the tempers and souls of gods and men, and again, not in all souls without exception; no, whenever he meets a soul with a hard temper, he departs, but where it is soft, he abides. So since he always touches with feet and all else the softest of the soft, he must needs be tender. You see, then, he is youngest and tenderest, but besides this his figure is supple, for if he were stiff, he could not fold himself in everywhere, or throughout every soul, and come in and go out unnoticed from the first. A great proof of his good proportion and supple shape is his gracefulness, which, as we all know, Love has in high degree; for there is always war between gracelessness and Love. Colours and beauty are testified by the god's nestling in flowers; for where there is no flower, or flower is past, in body and soul and everything else, Love sits not, but where the place is flowery and fragrant there he both sits and stays.

"Of the god's beauty much more might be said, but this is enough; the virtue of Love comes next. Chief is that Love wrongs not and is not wronged, wrongs no god and is wronged by none, wrongs no man and is wronged by none. Nothing that happens to him comes by violence, for violence touches not Love; nothing he does is violent, for everyone willingly serves Love in everything, and what a willing person grants to a willing, is just—so say 'the city's king, the laws.'[33] And besides justice, he is full of temperance. It is agreed that temperance is the mastery and control of pleasures and desires, and that no pleasure is stronger than Love. But if they are weaker, then Love would master and control them; and being master of pleasure and desires, Love would be especially temperate. Furthermore, in courage 'not even Ares[34] stands up against Love,' for it is not Ares that holds Love, but Love Ares—love of Aphrodite, as they say, stronger is he that holds than he that is held, and the master of the harvest of all would be himself bravest. Now the justice and temperance and courage of the god have been spoken of, and wisdom is left; so one must try to do the best one is able to do. And first, that I may honour our art as Eryximachos honoured his, Love is so wise a poet that he can make another the same; at least, everyone becomes a poet whom Love touches, even one who before that had 'no music in his soul.'[35] This we may fittingly use as a proof that Love is a good poet[36] or active maker in practically all the creations of the fine arts; for what one has not or knows not, one can neither give to another nor teach another. Now take the making of all living things; who will dispute that they are the clever work of Love, by which all living things are made and begotten? And craftsmanship in the arts; don't we know that where this god is teacher, art turns out notable and illustrious, but where there is no touch of Love, it is all in the dark? Archery, again, and medicine and divination were invented by Apollo, led by desire and love, so that even he would be a pupil of Love; so also the Muses in music and Hephaistos in smithcraft and Athena in weaving and Zeus in 'pilotage of gods and men.' Hence you see also, all that business of the gods was arranged when Love came among them—love of beauty, that is plain, for there is no Love in ugliness. Before that, as I said at the beginning, many terrible things happened to the gods because of the reign of Necessity—so the story goes; but when this god Love was born, all became good both for gods and men from loving beautiful things.

"Thus it seems to me, Phaedros, that Love comes first, himself most beautiful and best, and thereafter he is cause of other such things in others. And I am moved to speak something of him in verse myself, that it is he who makes

Peace among men, calm weather on the deep,
Respite from winds, in trouble rest and sleep.[37]

He empties us of estrangement, and fills us with friendliness, ordaining all such meetings as this one, of people one with another, in feasts, in dances, in sacrifices becoming men's guide; he provides gentleness, and banishes savagery; he loves to give good will, hates to give ill will; gracious, mild: illustrious to the wise, admirable to the gods; enviable to those who have none of him, treasured by those who have some of him; father of luxury, daintiness, delicacy, grace, longing, desire; careful of good things, careless of bad things; in hardship, in fear, in drinking,[38] in talk a pilot, a comrade, a stand-by[39] and the best of saviours; of all gods and men an ornament, a guide most beautiful and best, whom every man must follow, hymning him well, sharing in the song he sings as he charms the mind of gods and men.

"This, Phaidros, is my speech," he said; "may the god accept my dedication, partly play, partly modest seriousness, and the best that I am able to do."

When Agathon had spoken (Aristodemos told me), all applauded; the young man was thought to have spoken becomingly for himself and for the god. Then Socrates looked at Eryximachos, and said, "Now then, son of Acumenos, do you think there was no reason to fear in the fears I feared?[40] Was I not a prophet when I said, as I did just now, that Agathon would make a wonderful speech, and leave me with nothing to say?"

"Yes, to the first," said Eryximachos, "you were a prophet there, certainly, about the wonderful speech; but nothing to say? I don't think so!"

"Bless you," said Socrates, "and how have I anything to say, I or anyone else, when I have to speak after that beautiful speech, with everything in it. The first part was wonderful enough, but the end! The beauty of those words and phrases! It was quite overwhelming for any listener. The fact is, when I considered that I shall not be able to get anywhere near it, and I have nothing fine to say at all—I was so ashamed that I all but took to my heels and ran, but I had nowhere to go. The speech reminded me of Gorgias,[41] and I really felt quite as in Homer's story;[42] I was afraid that Agathon at the end of his speech might be going to produce the Gorgon's head of Gorgias—the terror in speech-making—directed against *my* speech, and turn me into stone with dumbness. And I understood then that I was a fool when I told you I would take my turn in singing the honors of Love, and admitted I was terribly clever in love affairs, whereas it seems I really had no idea how a eulogy ought to be made. For I was stupid enough to think that we ought to speak the truth about each person eulogised, and to make this the foundation, and from these truths to choose the most beautiful things and arrange them in the most elegant way; and I was quite proud to think how well I should speak, because I believed that I knew the truth. However, apparently this was not the right way to praise anything, but we should dedicate all that is greatest and most beautiful to the work, whether things are so or not; if they were false it did not matter. For it seems the task laid down was not for each of us to praise Love, but to seem to praise him. For this reason then, I think, you rake up every story, and dedicate it to Love, and say he is so-and-so and the cause of such-and-such, that he may seem to be most beautiful and best, of course to those who don't know—not to those who do, I suppose—and the laudation is excellent and imposing. But indeed I did not know how an encomium was made, and it was without this knowledge that I agreed to take my part in praising. Therefore the tongue promised, but not the mind,[43] so good-bye to that. For I take it back now; I make no eulogy in this fashion: I could not do it. However, the truth, if you like: I have no objection to telling the truth, in my own fashion, not in rivalry with your speeches, or I should deserve to be laughed at. Then see whether you want a speech of that sort, Phaidros. Will you listen to the truth being told about Love, in any words and arrangement of phrases such as we may hit on as we go?"

Phaidros and the others (continued Aristodemos) told him to go on just as he thought best. "Then, Phaidros," he said, "let me ask Agathon a few little things, that I may get his agreement before I speak."

"Oh, I don't mind," said Phaidros, "ask away." After that Socrates began something like this:

"Indeed, my dear Agathon, I thought you were quite right in the beginning of your speech, when you said that you must first show what Love was like, and afterwards come to his works. That beginning I admire very much. Now then about Love: you described what he is magnificently well and so on; but tell me this too—is Love such as to be a love of something, or of nothing? I don't mean to ask if he is a love of mother or father; for that would be a ridiculous question, whether Love is love for mother or father; I mean it in the sense that one might apply to 'father' for instance; is the father a father of

something or not? You would say, I suppose, if you wanted to answer right, that the father is father of son or daughter. Is that correct?"

"Certainly," said Agathon.

"And the same with the mother?"

This was agreed.

"Another, please." said Socrates, "answer me one or two more, that you may better understand what I want. What if I were to ask: 'A brother now, in himself, is he brother of something?'"

He said yes.

"Of a brother or sister?"

He agreed.

"Then tell me," he said, "about Love. Is Love of nothing or of something"

"Certainly he is love of something."

"Now then," said Socrates, "keep this in your memory, what the object of Love is;[44] and say whether Love desires the object of his love."

"Certainly," said Agathon.

"Is it when he *has* what he desires and loves that he desires and loves it, or when he has not?"

"Most likely, when he has not," said he.

"Just consider," said Socrates, "put 'necessary' for 'likely'; isn't it necessary that the desiring desires what it lacks, or else does not desire if it does not lack? I think positively myself, Agathon, that it is absolutely necessary; what do you think?"

"I think the same," said he.

"Good. Then would one being big want to be big, or being strong want to be strong?"

"Impossible, according to what we have agreed."

"For I suppose he would not be lacking in whichever of these he is?"

"True."

"For if being strong he wanted to be strong," said Socrates, "and being swift he wanted to be swift, and being healthy he wanted to be healthy—you might go on forever like this, and you might think that those who were so-and-so and had such-and-such did also desire what they had; but to avoid our being deceived I say this— if you understand me, Agathon, it is obvious that these *must* have at this present time all they have, whether they wish to or not—and can anyone desire that? And when one says, 'I am healthy and want to be healthy,' 'I am rich and want to be rich,' 'I desire what I have,' we should answer, 'You, my good man, being possessed of riches and health and strength, wish to go on being possessed of them in the future, since at present you have them whether you want it or not; and when you say, "I desire what I have," consider—

you mean only that you want to have in the future what you have now.' Wouldn't he agree?"

Agathon said yes.

Then Socrates went on, "Therefore this love for these blessings to be preserved for him into the future and to be always present for him—this is really loving that which is not yet available for him or possessed by him?"

"Certainly," he said.

"Then he, and every other who desires, desires what is not in his possession and not there, what he has not, and what his is not himself and what he lacks? Those are the sorts of things of which there is desire and love?"

"Certainly." he said.

"Come now," said Socrates, "let us run over again what has been agreed. Love is, first of all, of something; next, of those things which one lacks?"

"Yes," he said.

"This being granted, then, remember what things you said in your speech were the objects of Love. I will remind you if you wish. I think you said something like this; the gods arranged their business through love of beautiful things, for there could not be a love for ugly things. Didn't you say something like that?"

"Yes, I did," said Agathon.

"And quite reasonably too, my friend," said Socrates; "and if this is so, would not Love be love of beauty, not of ugliness?"

He agreed.

"Well now, it has been agreed that he loves what he lacks and has not?"

"Yes," he said.

"Then Love lacks and has not beauty."

"That must be," said he.

"Very well: do you say that what lacks beauty and in no wise has beauty is beautiful?"

"Certainly not."

"Then if that is so, do you still agree that Love is beautiful?"

Agathon answered, "I fear, Socrates, I knew nothing of what I said!"

"Oh no," said he, "it was a fine speech, Agathon! But one little thing more: don't you think good things are also beautiful?"

"I do."

"Then if Love lacks beautiful things, and good things are beautiful, he should lack the good things too."

"Socrates," he said, "I really could not contradict you; let it be as you say."

"Contradict the truth, you should say, beloved Agathon," he replied; "you can't do that, but to contradict Socrates is easy enough.

"And now you shall have peace from me; but there is a speech about Love which I heard once from Diotima of Mantineia,[45] who was wise in this matter and in many others; by making the Athenians perform sacrifices before the plague she even managed to put off the disease for ten years. And she it was who taught me about love affairs. This speech, then, which she made I will try to narrate to you now, beginning with what is agreed between me and Agathon; I will tell it by myself, as well as I can. You will see that I must describe first, as you did, Agathon, who Love is and what like, and then his works. I think it easiest to do it as the lady did in examining me. I said to her very much what Agathon just now did to me, that Love was a great god, and was a love of beautiful things; and she convinced me by saying the same as I did to Agathon, that he is neither beautiful, according to my argument, nor good. Then I said, 'What do you mean, Diotima? Is Love then ugly and bad?' And she said, 'Hush, for shame! Do you think that what is not beautiful must necessarily be ugly?' 'Yes, I do.' 'And what is not wise, ignorant? Do you not perceive that there is something between wisdom and ignorance?' 'What is that?' 'To have right opinion without being able to give a reason,' she said, is neither to understand (for how could an unreasoned thing be understanding?) nor is it ignorance (for how can ignorance hit the truth?). Right opinion is no doubt something between knowledge and ignorance.' 'Quite true,' I said. 'Then do not try to compel what is not beautiful to be ugly, or what is not good to be bad. So also with Love. He is not good and not beautiful, as you admit yourself, but do not imagine for that reason any the more that he must be ugly and bad, but something between these two,' said she. 'Well, anyway,' I said, 'he is admitted by all to be a great god.' 'All who don't know,' she said, 'or all who know too?' 'All without exception.' At this she said, with a laugh, 'And how could he be admitted to be a great god, Socrates, by those who say he is not a god at all?' 'Who are these?' said I. 'You for one,' said she, 'and I for another.' And I asked, 'How can that be?' She said, 'Easily. Tell me, don't you say that all the gods are happy and beautiful? Or would you dare to say that any one of them is not happy and beautiful?' 'Indeed I would not,' said I. 'Then don't you call happy those possessed of good and beautiful things?' 'Certainly 'Yet you admitted that Love, because of a lack of good and beautiful things, actually desired those things which he lacked.' 'Yes, I admitted that.' 'Then how could he be a god who has no share in beautiful and good things?' 'He could not be a god, as it seems.' 'Don't you see then,' said she, 'that you yourself deny Love to be a god?'

"'Then what could Love be?' I asked. 'A mortal?' 'Not at all.' 'What then?' I asked. 'Just as before, between mortal and immortal.' 'What is he then, Diotima?' 'A great spirit, Socrates; for all the spiritual is between divine and mortal.' 'What power has it?' said I. 'To interpret and to ferry across to the gods things given by men, and to men things from the gods, from men petitions and sacrifices, from the gods commands and requitals in return; and being in the middle it completes them and binds all together into a whole. Through this intermediary moves all the art of divination, and the art of priests, and all concerned with sacrifice and mysteries and incantations, and all sorcery and witchcraft. For God mingles not with man, but through this comes all the communion and conversation of gods with men and men with gods, both awake and asleep; and he who is expert in this is a spiritual man, but the expert in something other than this, such as common arts or crafts, is a vulgar man. These spirits are many and of all sorts and kinds, and one of them is Love.'

"'Who was his father,' said I, 'and who was his mother?' She answered, 'That is rather a long story, but still I will tell you. When Aphrodite was born, the gods held a feast, among them Plenty,[46] the son of Neverataloss. When they had dined, Poverty came in begging, as might be expected with all that good cheer, and hung about the doors. Plenty then got drunk on the nectar—for there was no wine yet—and went into Zeus's park all heavy and fell asleep. So Poverty because of her penury made a plan to have a child from Plenty, and lay by his side and conceived Love. This is why Love has become follower and servant of Aphrodite, having been begotten at her birthday party, and at the same time he is by nature a lover busy with beauty because Aphrodite is beautiful. Then since Love is the son of Plenty and Poverty he gets his fortunes from them. First, he is always poor; and far from being tender and beautiful, as most people think, he is hard and rough and unshod and homeless, lying always on the ground without bedding, sleeping by the doors and in the streets in the open air, having his mother's nature, always dwelling with want. But from his father again he has designs upon beautiful and good things, being brave and go-ahead and high-strung, a mighty hunter, always weaving devices, and a successful coveter of wisdom, a philosopher all his days, a great wizard and sorcerer and sophist. He was

born neither mortal nor immortal; but on the same day, sometimes he is blooming and alive, when he has plenty, sometimes he is dying; then again he gets new life through his father's nature; but what he procures in plenty always trickles away, so that Love is not in want nor in wealth, and again he is between wisdom and ignorance. The truth is this: no god seeks after wisdom or desires to become wise—for wise he is already; nor does anyone else seek after wisdom, if he is wise already. And again, the ignorant do not seek after wisdom nor desire to become wise; for this is the worst of ignorance, that one who is neither beautiful and good[47] nor intelligent should think himself good enough, so he does not desire it, because he does not think he is lacking in what he does not think he needs.'

"'Then who are the philosophers, Diotima,' said I, 'if those who seek after wisdom are neither the wise nor the ignorant?' 'That's clear enough even to a child.' she answered; 'they are those between these two, as Love is. You see, wisdom is one of the most beautiful things, and Love is a love for the beautiful, so Love must necessarily be a philosopher, and, being a philosopher, he must be between wise and ignorant. His birth is the cause of this, for he comes of a wise and resourceful father but of a mother resourceless and not wise. Well then, dear Socrates, this is the nature of the spirit; but it was no wonder you thought Love what you did think. You thought, if I may infer it from what you say, that Love was the beloved, not the lover. That was why, I think, Love seemed to you wholly beautiful; for the thing loved is in fact beautiful and dainty and perfect and blessed, but the loving thing has a different shape, such as I have described.'

"Then I said 'Very well, madam, what you say is right; but Love being such as you describe, of what use is he to mankind?' 'I will try to teach you that next, Socrates,' she said. 'Love then is like that and born like that, and he is love of beautiful things, as you said he is. But suppose someone should ask us: "Socrates and Diotima, what is meant by love of beautiful things?" I will put it more clearly: "He that loves beautiful things loves what?"' Then I answered, 'To get them.' 'Still,' she said, 'that answer needs another question, like this: "What will he get who gets the beautiful things?"' I said I could not manage at all to answer that question offhand. 'Well,' said she, 'suppose one should change "beautiful" to "good" and ask that? See here, Socrates, I will say: "What does he love who loves good things?"' 'To get them,' said I. 'And what will he get who gets the good things?'

'That's easier,' said I; 'I can answer that he will be happy.' 'Then,' said she, 'by getting good things the happy are happy, and there is no need to ask further, why he who wishes to be happy, does wish that, but the answer seems to be finished.' 'Quite true,' said I. 'But do you think this wish and this love is common to all mankind,' Diotima said, 'and do you think that all men always wish to have the good things, or what do you say?' 'That's it,' said I, 'it's common to all.' 'Why then, Socrates,' said she, 'do we not say that all men are lovers, if they do in fact all love the same things and always, instead of saying that some are lovers and some are not?' 'That surprises me too,' I said. 'Don't let it surprise you,' she said. 'For we have taken one kind of love, and given it the name of the whole, love; and there are other cases in which we misapply other names.' 'For example?' said I. 'Here is one,' she said. 'You know that poetry is many kinds of making;[48] for when anything passes from not-being to being, the cause is always making, or poetry, so that in all the arts the process is making, and all the craftsmen in these are makers, or poets.' 'Quite true,' I said. 'But yet," said she, 'they are not all called poets; they have other names, and one bit of this making has been taken, that concerning music and verse, and this is called by the name of the whole. For this only is called poetry, and those who have this bit of making are called poets.' 'That is true,' I said. "So with love, then; in its general sense it is all the desire for good things and for happiness—Love most mighty and all-ensnaring; but those who turn to him by any other road, whether by way of money-making, or of a taste for sports or philosophy, are not said to be in love and are not called lovers, but only those who go after one kind and are earnest about that have the name of the whole, love, and are said to love and to be lovers.' 'I think you are right there,' said I. 'And there is a story, said she, 'that people in love are those who are seeking for their other half,[49] but my story tells that love is not for a half, nor indeed the whole, unless that happens to be something good, my friend; since men are willing to cut off their own hands and feet, if their own seem to them to be nasty. For really, I think, no one is pleased with his own thing, except one who calls the good thing his own and his property, and the bad thing another's; since there is nothing else men love but the good. Don't you think so?' 'Yes,' I said. 'Then,' said she, 'we may say simply that men love the good?' 'Yes,' I said. 'Shall we add,' she asked, 'that they love to have the good?' 'Yes, add that,' I said. 'Not only to have it, but always to have it?' 'Add that too.' 'Then to sum up,' she said, 'it is the love of having the good for oneself always.' 'Most true, indeed,' I said.

"She went on, 'Now if love is the love of having this always, what is the way men pursue it, and in what actions would their intense earnestness be expressed so as to be called love? What is this process? Can you tell me?' 'No,' said I, 'or else, Diotima, why should I, in admiration of your wisdom have come to you as your pupil to find out these very matters?' 'Well then, I will tell you,' she said. 'It is a breeding in the beautiful, both of body and soul.' 'It needs divination,' I said, 'to tell what on earth you mean, and I don't understand.' 'Well,' she said. 'I will tell you clearer. All men are pregnant, Socrates, both in body and in soul; and when they are of the right age, our nature desires to beget. But it cannot beget in an ugly thing, only in a beautiful thing. And this business is divine, and this is something immortal in a mortal creature, breeding and birth. These can not be in what is discordant. But the ugly is discordant with everything divine, and the beautiful is concordant. Beauty therefore is Portioner and Lady of Labour at birth. Therefore when the pregnant comes near to a beautiful thing it becomes gracious, and being delighted it is poured out and begets and procreates; when it comes near to an ugly thing, it becomes gloomy and grieved and rolls itself up and is repelled and shrinks back and does not procreate, but holds back the conception and is in a bad way. Hence in the pregnant thing swelling full already, there is great agitation about the beautiful thing because he that has it gains relief from great agony. Finally, Socrates, love is not for the beautiful, as you think.' 'Why not?' 'It is for begetting and birth in the beautiful.' 'Oh, indeed?' said I. 'Yes indeed,' said she. 'Then why for begetting?' 'Because begetting is, for the mortal, something everlasting and immortal. But one must desire immortality along with the good, according to what has been agreed, if love is love of having the good for oneself always. It is necessary then from this argument that love is for immortality also.'

"All this she taught me at different times whenever she came to speak about love affairs; and once she asked, 'What do you think, Socrates, to be the cause of this love and desire? You perceive that all animals get into a dreadful state when they desire to procreate, indeed birds and beasts alike; all are sick and in a condition of love, about mating first, and then how to find food for their young, and they are ready to fight hard for them, the weakest against the strongest, and to die for them, and to suffer the agonies of starvation themselves in order to feed them, ready to do anything. One might perhaps think that man, she said, 'would do all this from reasoning; but what about beasts? What is the cause of their enamoured state? Can you tell me?' And I said again that I did not know; and she said, 'Then how do you ever expect to become expert in love affairs, if you do not understand that?' 'Why, Diotima, this is just why I have come to you, as I said; I knew I needed a teacher. Pray tell me the cause of this, and all the other love lore.'

"'Well then,' she said, 'if you believe love is by nature love of that which we often agreed on, don't be surprised. For on the same principle as before, here mortal nature seeks always as far as it can be to be immortal; and this is the only way it can, by birth, because it leaves something young in place of the old. Consider that for a while each single living creature is said to live and to be the same; for example a man is said to be the same from boyhood to old age; he has, however, by no means the same things in himself, yet he is called the same: he continually becomes new, though he loses parts of himself, hair and flesh and bones and blood and all the body. Indeed, not only body, even in soul, manners, opinions, desires, pleasures, pains, fears, none of these remains the same, but some perish and others are born. And far stranger still, this happens to knowledge too; not only do some kinds of knowledge perish in us, not only are other kinds born, and not even in our knowledge are we ever the same, but the same happens even in each single kind of knowledge. For what is called study and practice means that knowledge is passing out; forgetting is knowledge leaving us, and study puts in new knowledge instead of that which is passing away, and preserves our knowledge so that it seems to be the same. In this way all the mortal is preserved, not by being wholly the same always, like the divine, but because what grows old and goes leaves behind something new like its past self. By this device, Socrates,' said she, 'mortality partakes of immortality, both in body and in all other respects; but it cannot otherwise. Then do not be surprised that everything naturally honours its own offspring; immortality is what all this earnestness and love pursues.'

"I heard this with admiration; and I said, 'Really, Diotima most wise! Is that really and truly so?' She answered as the complete Sophists do,[50] and said, 'You may be sure of that, Socrates. Just think, if you please, of men's ambitions. You would be surprised at its unreasonableness if you didn't bear in mind what I have told you; observe what a terrible state they are in with love of becoming renowned, "and to lay up their fame for evermore"[51] and for this how ready they are to run all risks even more than for their children, and to spend money and endure hardship to any extent, and to die for it. Do you think Alcestis would have died for Admetos, or Achilles would have died over Patroclos, or your Codros[52] would have died for the royalty of his sons, if they had not thought that "immortal memory of Virtue" would be theirs, which we still keep! Far from it,' she said; 'for eternal virtue and glorious fame like that all men do everything, I think, and the better they are, the more they do so; for the immortal is what they love. So those who are pregnant in body,' she said, 'turn rather to women and are enamoured in this way, and thus, by begetting children, secure for themselves, so they think, immortality and memory and happiness, "Providing all things for the time to come;"[53] but those who are pregnant in soul—for there are some,' she said, 'who conceive in soul still more than in body, what is proper for the soul to conceive and bear; and what is proper? wisdom and virtue in general—to this class belong all creative poets and those artists and craftsmen who are said to be inventive. But much the greatest wisdom,' she said, 'and the most beautiful, is that which is concerned with the ordering of cities and homes, which we call temperance and justice. So again a man with divinity in him, whose soul from his youth is pregnant with these things, desires when he grows up to beget and procreate; and thereupon, I think, he seeks and goes about to find the beautiful thing in which he can beget; for in the ugly he never will. Being pregnant, then, he welcomes bodies which are beautiful rather than ugly, and if he finds a soul beautiful and generous and well-bred, he gladly welcomes the two body and soul together, and for a human being like that he has plenty of talks about virtue, and what the good man ought to be and to practise, and he tries to educate him. For by attaching himself to a person of beauty, I think, and keeping company with him, he begets and procreates what he has long been pregnant with; present and absent he remembers him, and with him fosters what is begotten, so that as a result these people maintain a much closer communion together and a firmer friendship than parents of children, because they have shared between them children more beautiful and more immortal. And everyone would be content to have such children born to him rather than human children; he would look to Homer and Hesiod and the other good poets, and wish to rival them, who leave such offspring behind them, which give their parents the same immortal fame and memory as they have themselves; or if you like,' she said, 'think what children Lycurgos[54] left in Lacedaimon, the saviours of Lacedaimon and, one may say, of all Hellas. Honour came to Solon also, in your country, by the begetting of his laws; and to many others in many countries and times, both Hellenes and barbarians, who performed many beautiful works and begat all kinds of virtue; in their names many sanctuaries have been made because they had such children, but never a one has been so honoured because of human children.

"'These are some of the mysteries of Love, Socrates, in which perhaps even you may become an initiate; but as for the higher revelations, which initiation leads to if one approaches in the right way, I do not know if you could ever become an adept. At least I will instruct you, she said, 'and no pains will be lacking; you try to follow if you can. It is necessary,' she said, 'that one who approaches in the right way should begin this business young, and approach beautiful bodies. First, if his leader leads aright, he should love one body and there beget beautiful speech; then he should take notice that the beauty in one body is akin to the beauty in another body, and if we must pursue beauty in essence, it is great folly not to believe that the beauty in all such bodies is one and the same. When he has learnt this, he must become the lover of all beautiful bodies, and relax the intense passion for one, thinking lightly of it and believing it to be a small thing. Next he must believe beauty in souls to be more precious than beauty in the body; so that if anyone is decent in soul, even if it has little bloom, it should be enough for him to love and care for, and to beget and seek such talks as will make young people better; that he may moreover be compelled to contemplate the beauty in our pursuits and customs, and to see that all beauty is of one and the same kin, and that so he may believe that bodily beauty is a small thing. Next, he must be led from practice to knowledge, that he may see again the beauty in different kinds of knowledge, and, directing his gaze from now on towards beauty as a whole, he may no longer dwell upon one, like a servant, content with the beauty of one boy or one human being or one pursuit, and so be slavish and petty; but he should turn to the great ocean of beauty, and in contemplation of it give birth to many

beautiful and magnificent speeches and thoughts in the abundance of philosophy, until being strengthened and grown therein he may catch sight of some one knowledge, the one science of this beauty now to be described. Try to attend,' she said, 'as carefully as you can.

"'Whoever shall be guided so far towards the mysteries of love, by contemplating beautiful things rightly in due order, is approaching the last grade. Suddenly he will behold a beauty marvellous in its nature, that very Beauty, Socrates, for the sake of which all the earlier hardships had been borne: in the first place, everlasting, and never being born nor perishing, neither increasing nor diminishing; secondly, not beautiful here and ugly there, not beautiful now and ugly then, not beautiful in one direction and ugly in another direction, not beautiful in one place and ugly in another place. Again, this beauty will not show itself to him like a face or hands or any bodily thing at all, nor as a discourse or a science, nor indeed as residing in anything, as in a living creature or in earth or heaven or anything else, but being by itself with itself always in simplicity; while all the beautiful things elsewhere partake of this beauty in such manner, that when they are born and perish it becomes neither less nor more and nothing at all happens to it; so that when anyone by right boy-loving goes up from these beautiful things to that beauty, and begins to catch sight of it, he would almost touch the perfect secret. For let me tell you, the right way to approach the things of love, or to be led there by another, is this: beginning from these beautiful things, to mount for that beauty's sake ever upwards, as by a flight of steps, from one to two, and from two to all beautiful bodies, and from beautiful bodies to beautiful pursuits and practices, and from practices to beautiful learnings, so that from learnings he may come at last to that perfect learning which is the learning solely of that beauty itself, and may know at last that which is the perfection of beauty. There in life and there alone, my dear Socrates,' said the inspired woman,[55] 'is life worth living for man, while he contemplates Beauty itself. If ever you see this, it will seem to you to be far above gold and raiment and beautiful boys and men, whose beauty you are now entranced to see and you and many others are ready, so long as they see their darlings and remain ever with them, if it could be possible, not to eat nor drink but only to gaze at them and to be with them. What indeed,' she said, 'should we think, if it were given to one of us to see beauty undefiled, pure, unmixed, not adulterated with human flesh and colours and much other mortal rubbish, and if he could behold beauty in perfect simplicity? Do you think it a mean life for a man,' she said, 'to be looking thither and contemplating that and abiding with it? Do you not reflect,' said she, 'that there only it will be possible for him, when he sees the beautiful with the mind, which alone can see it, to give birth not to likenesses of virtue, since he touches no likeness, but to realities, since he touches reality; and when he has given birth to real virtue and brought it up, will it not be granted him to be the friend of God, and immortal if any man ever is?'

"This then, Phaidros and gentlemen, is what Diotima said, and I am quite convinced, and, being convinced, I try to persuade other people also to believe that to attain this possession one could not easily find a better helper for human nature than Love. And so I say that every man ought to honour Love, and I honour love matters myself, and I practise them particularly and encourage others; and now and always I sing the praises of Love's power and courage, as much as I am able. Then let this be my speech of eulogy to Love, if you please, Phaidros, or call it anything else you like."

When Socrates had done speaking, there was applause from the rest, and Aristophanes started to say something about Socrates' allusion to his own speech, when suddenly there came a knocking on the courtyard door and a great din as of some party of revellers, and they heard a girl piper's notes. Then Agathon said to the staff, "Boys, go and see about that. If it is one of our friends, ask him in; if not, say we are not drinking now, we are just going to bed." In a few minutes they heard the voice of Alcibiades in the yard, very drunk and shouting loud, asking where Agathon was, and take him to Agathon. So he was brought in to them by the piping-girl, who with some others of his company supported him; he came to a stand at the door crowned with a thick wreath of ivy and violets and wearing a great lot of ribands on his head, and said, "Good evening, you fellows, will you have a very drunken man to drink with you, or shall we only put a garland on Agathon, which we came for, and then go? For I tell you this," he said, "I could not get at him yesterday, but here I come with the ribands on my head, that I may take them off my head and just twine them about the head of the cleverest and most beautiful of men, if I may say so. Will you laugh at me because I'm drunk? I tell you, even if you laugh, that this is true and I know it. Look here, tell me straight, do I come in

on those terms or not? Will you drink with me or not?"

Then they all cheered and told him to come in and take his place, and Agathon gave him a formal invitation. So he came in leaning on those people, pulling off the ribands at the same time to put them on Agathon, and as he held them in front of his eyes, he did not see Socrates, but sat down beside Agathon, between Socrates and him, for Socrates made room for him. He sat down and embraced Agathon and crowned him. Then Agathon said, "Take off Alcibiades' shoes, you boys, and let him make a third on our couch."

"All right," said Alcibiades, "but who is fellow-drinker number three here?" At the same time he turned round and saw Socrates; when he saw him, he jumped up and cried, "What the deuce is this? Socrates here? You lay there again in wait for me, as you are always turning up all of a sudden where I never thought to see you! And now what have you come for? And again, why did you lie there, not by Aristophanes or some other funny man or would-be funny man, but you managed to get beside the handsomest of the company!"

Then Socrates said, "Agathon, won't you defend me? I find that this person's love has become quite a serious thing. From the time when I fell in love with him, I am no longer allowed to look at or talk with a handsome person, not even one, or this jealous and envious creature treats me outrageously, and abuses me, and hardly keeps his hands off me. Then don't let him try it on now, but do reconcile us, or if he uses force, defend me, for I'm fairly terrified at his madness and passion."

"No," said Alcibiades, "there's no reconciliation between you and me! My word, I'll punish you for this by and by; but for now, Agathon," he said, "give me some of the ribands and let me wreath this fellow's wonderful head—there!—so he can't quarrel with me and say I wreathed you and didn't wreath the man who beats all the world at talking, not only the other day like you, but always!" While he spoke he took some of the ribands and wreathed Socrates, and then reclined himself.

When he was settled, he said, "I say, men, I think you are sober. That won't do, you must drink! We agreed on that. Then I choose as prince of the pots, to see that you drink enough, myself. Let 'em bring it in, Agathon, the biggest goblet you have! No, better than that! You, boy there; bring that cooler," said he, for he saw it would hold more than half a gallon; first he filled that and drank it off himself, then told the boy to fill for Socrates, saying, "For Socrates, men, my trick is nothing; he drinks as much as anyone tells him, and never gets drunk one bit the more."

So the boy filled for Socrates, and he drank; then Eryximachos said, "Well, Alcibiades, what do we do? Are we just to say nothing over the cup, and to sing nothing, but only to drink like thirsty men?"

Alcibiades answered, "Good evening to you, Eryximachos, best son of a best father you, and he was very sober too!"[56]

"Same to you," said Eryximachos, "but what are we to do?"

"Whatever you say," he replied, "for we have to obey you. 'One medicine man is worth a host of laymen.'[57] Command what you will."

"Then listen," said Eryximachos. "Before you came in, we decided that each one in turn from left to right[58] should recite the most excellent speech he could as a eulogy in honour of Love. All the rest of us, then, have made their speeches; but since you have made none, and since you have drunk your bumper, you are the proper one to speak; and when you have spoken, lay your commands on Socrates, what you like, and let him do the same with the next man to the right[58] and so with the rest."

"Good," said Alcibiades, "but look here, Eryximachos, I don't think it's fair to tell a drunken man to risk a speech before sober men! And at the same time, bless you my dear! Do you really believe anything of what Socrates has just said? Don't you know that the truth is exactly the opposite of what he stated? For if *I* praise anybody in his presence, god or man other than himself, this man will not keep his two hands off *me*."

"Won't you shut up?" said Socrates.

"Oh my honour, you need not make any objection," said Alcibiades. "I would not praise a single other person in your presence!"

"Very well, do this if you like," said Eryximachos; "praise Socrates."

"What's that?" said Alcibiades. "Must I, Eryximachos? Am I to have at the man and punish him before your faces?"

"Hullo," said Socrates, "what's your notion? To praise me and raise a laugh, or what will you do?"

"I'll tell the truth! Will you let me?"

"Oh yes, let you tell the truth, I even command you do that."

"Then I'll do it at once!" said Alcibiades. "Look here, this is what I want you to do. If I say anything that is not true, stop me in the middle, and say that I am lying; for I won't tell any lies if I can help it. But if I speak higgledy-giggledy trying to remember, don't be surprised, for it is not easy to set out all your absurdities nicely in order, for one in my state.

"I am to speak in praise of Socrates, gentlemen, and I will just try to do it by means of similes.[59] Oh yes, he will think perhaps it is only for a bit of fun, by my simile will be for truth, not for fun. I say then, that he is exactly like a Silenos, the little figures which you see sitting in the statuaries' shops: as the craftsmen make them, they hold Panspipes or pipes, and they can be opened down the middle and folded back, and then they show inside them images of the gods. And I say further, he is like Marsyas[60] the Satyr. Well anyway, Socrates, your face is like them, I don't suppose you will deny that yourself! In everything else, too, you are like them, listen what comes next. You are a bully! Aren't you? If you don't admit that I will find witnesses. Well, aren't you a piper? Yes, a more wonderful performer than that Marsyas! For he used to bewitch men through instruments by the power of his mouth, and so also now does anyone who pipes his tunes; for those Olympos[61] piped, I say were from Marsyas who taught him; then it is his tunes, whether a good artist plays them or a common piping-girl, which alone enravish us and make plain those who feel the need of the gods and their mysteries, because the tunes are divine. The only difference between you is, that *you* do the very same without instruments by bare words! We, at least, when we hear someone else making other speeches, even quite a good orator, nobody cares a jot, I might say; but when one hears you, or your words recited by another, even a very poor speaker, let a man hear, or a boy hear, we are overwhelmed and enravished. I, indeed, my friends, if you would not have thought me completely drunk, would have taken a solemn oath before you, and described to you how this man's words have made me feel and still make me feel now. When I hear them my heart goes leaping worse than frantic revellers', and tears run from my eyes at the words of this man, and I see crowds of others in the same state. When I heard Pericles, and other good orators, I thought them fine speakers, but I felt nothing like that, and no confusion in my soul or regret for my slavish condition; but this Marsyas here has brought me very often into such a condition that I thought the life I lead was not worth living. And that, Socrates, you will not say is untrue! And even now at this moment, I know in my conscience that if I would open my ears I could never hold out, but I should be in the same state. For he compels me to admit that I am very remiss, in going on neglecting my own self but attending to Athenian public business. So I force myself, and stop my ears, and off I go running as from the Sirens, or else I should sit down on the spot beside him till I become an old man. I feel towards this one man something which no one would ever think could be in me—to be ashamed before anybody; but I *am* ashamed before him and before no one else. For I know in my conscience that I cannot contradict him and say it is not my duty to do what he tells me, yet when I leave him, public applause is too much for me. So I show my heels and run from him, and, whenever I see him, I am ashamed of what I confessed to him. Often enough I should be glad to see him no longer among mankind; but if that should happen, I am sure I should be sorrier still, so I don't know what to do with the fellow.

"The pipings of this satyr have put many others into the same state as me; but let me tell you something else to show how like he is to my simile, and how wonderful his power is. I assure you that no one of you knows this man; but I will show you, since I have begun. You see, of course, that Socrates has a loving eye for beauty, he's always interested in such people and quite smitten with them, and again he is ignorant of everything and knows nothing; that is his pose. Isn't that Silenosity? Very much so! He wraps that round him like a cloak, like the outside of the carved Silenos figure; but inside, when he is opened—what do you think he is full of, gentlemen pot-fellows? Temperance! Let me say that he cares not a straw if one is a beauty, he despises that as no one would ever believe; and the same if one is rich or has one of those mob distinctions which people think so grand. He thinks all those possessions are worthless and we are nothing, yes, I tell you! Pretending ignorance and making fun of his fellows all his life—that's how he goes on. But when he's in earnest, and opened out—I don't know if anyone has seen the images inside; but I saw them once, and I thought them divine and golden and all-beautiful and wonderful, so that one must in short do whatever Socrates commands. I thought he was in earnest over my youthful bloom, I thought I had found a godsend and a wonderful piece of luck, in that by gratifying Socrates I had the chance to hear all he knew; I thought a lot of my blooming beauty, you know, an awful lot. With this notion—you see, before that, I never used to visit him alone without an attendant—but after that I sent my attendant away and always went in alone; for I must tell you all the truth; now Socrates, attend and refute me if I tell a lie. Well, I paid him visits, gentlemen, I alone and he alone, and I thought he would talk to me as a lover would talk to his darling in solitude, and I was happy. Nothing came of it, nothing, he just talked as usual, and when we had had a nice day together, he always went off. Next I challenged him to gymnastics with me, and I went through it hoping for something then; well, he exercised with me, and we wrestled together often, with nobody there. What's the good of talking? I got nothing by it. Since I was none the better for all that, I resolved to try stronger measures with the man, and not to give in after I had undertaken something, but to find out what was behind the business. So I invited him to dinner with me, exactly like a lover with designs on his beloved. For a long time he would not even consent to come, but at last I persuaded him. The first time he came he wanted to go after dinner. That time I was ashamed, and let him go; but I make my plot again, and after we had dined, I went on talking till late at night, and when he wanted to go, I forced him to stay by pretending it was late. So he rested on the couch next to mine where he had dined, and no one else was sleeping in the room, only we two. So far I could tell my story to anyone; but what follows you would never have heard me tell, only first, wine is true, as they say—whether children are there or not[62]—secondly, to hide a superimperious deed of Socrates is unfair, I think, for one who has come to sing his praises. Moreover, I too have 'felt the viper's bite,' as the saying goes. You know they say that one who felt it would not tell what it was like except to other people who had been bitten, since they alone would know it and would not be hard on him for what he allowed himself to do and say in his agony. Well, I have been bitten by a more painful viper, and in the most painful spot where one could be bitten—the heart, or soul, or whatever it should be called—stung and bitten by his discourses in philosophy, which hang on more cruelly than a viper when they seize on a soul young and not ungenerous, and make it do and say anything—and when I see men like Phaidros, Agathon, Eryximachos, Pausanias, Aristodemos, too, and Aristophanes—Socrates himself I need not mention—and how many more! For you have all shared in the philosopher's madness and passion! Then you shall all hear; for you will not be hard on what was done then and what is being said now; but you servants, and anyone else who is common and boorish, clap strong doors on your ears!

"Well then, gentlemen, when the lamp was out and the servants outside, I thought it necessary not to mince matters but to say freely what I felt; so I stirred him up, and said, 'Asleep, Socrates?' 'Not at all,' said he. 'Do you know what is in my mind?' 'What is it?' he asked. 'I think,' said I, 'that you are the only lover I have ever had worthy of me, and now you won't speak a word to me. I'll tell you how I feel: I consider it simply silly not to gratify you in this, and anything else you want of my property or from my friends. For myself, I think nothing more precious than to attain the height of excellence, and to help me in this there is no one more competent than you. Then I should be much more ashamed before the wise if I did not gratify such a man than I should be ashamed before the multitude of fools if I did.' He answered, playing the innocent as usual, quite like himself, 'My dearest Alcibiades, you are really and truly no bad hand at a bargain, if what you say is really true about me, and if there is in me some power which can make you better; you must see some inconceivable beauty in me immensely greater than your own loveliness. If then you spy it there, and if you are trying to do a deal and exchange beauty for beauty, you want to get very much the better of me, you want to get real beauties for sham, and indeed to exchange "golden for bronze."[63] Bless you, my dear, spy better, and you'll see I am nothing. The sight of the mind begins to see sharp when the sight of the eyes is losing its keenness, and you are far from that still.' I heard him, and said, 'That is what I have to tell you, and I have said exactly what I mean; consider yourself, then, what you believe best for you and me.' 'That's well said,' he answered, 'another time we will consider, and do whatever seems best for us both in this and other matters.'

"When I heard this and said this, and as it were shot my shafts, I thought he was wounded; so I got up, and without letting this man[64] say another word, I threw my own mantle over the man and crept in under this man's threadbare cloak—for it was winter—and threw my arms round this man, this really astonishing and wonderful man, and there I lay the whole night! You will not say that is a lie either, Socrates! Though I had done all this, yet this man was so much above me and so despised me and laughed at my bloom, and insulted me in the point where I did think I was something, gentlemen of the jury—for jury you are, to give a verdict on the superimperiosity of Socrates—that I swear by the gods, I swear by the goddesses, when I got up I had no more slept with Socrates than if I had been with a father or elder brother.

"How do you think I felt after that! I thought I had been disgraced, and yet I admired the way this man was made, and his temperance and courage; and I had met such a human being for wisdom and endurance as I never expected to find in the world, so that I could not bring myself to quarrel and lose his company, nor could I think of any way to attract him. For I knew quite well that to money he was much less vulnerable than Aias to steel, and in what I thought would alone win him, he had escaped me. So I was at a loss, and I walked about, a slave to the creature as no one ever was to anyone. Well, all this happened before our expedition went to Poteidaia;[65] we were both in it, and we were messmates there. And first of all, in bearing hardships he not only beat me but everyone else; when we were cut off somewhere, and had to go without food, as happens on campaign, the others were nothing for endurance. Yet when there was plenty of good cheer, he was the only one who could really enjoy it; particularly, although he did not care for drinking, when he was compelled to drink he beat them all, and what is most wonderful of all, no one in the world has ever seen Socrates drunk. That we shall be able to test presently, as I think. That was not all; in his endurance of the cold winter—the winters were dreadful there—he did wonders, and here is a specimen. Once there was a most dreadful frost, and no one would go out of doors, or if he did he put up his feet in felt and sheepskin, but this man went out in that weather wearing only such a cloak as he used to wear before, and unshod he marched over the ice more easily than others did with boots on. The soldiers looked back at him thinking he despised them.

"So much for that;
but here's a doughty deed the strong man did,[66]

once on that expedition, and it is worth hearing. He got some notion into his head, and there he stood on one spot from dawn, thinking, and when it did not come out, he would not give in but still stood pondering. It was already midday, and people noticed it, and wondered, and said to one another that Socrates had been standing thinking about something ever since dawn. At last when evening came, some of the Ionians after dinner—it was summertime then—brought out their pallets and slept near in the cool, and watched him from time to time to see if he would stand all night. He did stand until it was dawn, and the sun rose; then he offered a prayer to the sun and walked away.

"Now with your leave we will take the battles; for it is fair to pay him his due. When there was that battle[67] after which the generals actually gave me the prize of valour, this man, when not a single other person came to my rescue, saved my life. I was wounded, but he would not leave me, and saved my weapons and me too. Then I begged the generals myself, Socrates, to give you the prize for valour, and here you will not find fault with me or say I am lying; but the fact is when the generals looked at my rank and wanted to give me the prize, you were more eager than the generals that I should get it and not yourself. Again gentleman, it was worth while to see Socrates when the army was routed and retreating from Delion.[68] I happened to be there on horseback, and he on foot. This man and Laches were retreating together in the rout; I met them, and told them to cheer up, and said I would not desert them. There indeed I had an even better view of Socrates than at Poteidaia, for I had less to fear, being on horseback. First I saw how he kept his head much better than Laches; next I really thought, Aristophanes, to quote your words,[69] that he marched exactly as he does here, 'with swaggering gait and rolling eye,' quietly looking round at friends and enemies, and making it quite clear to everyone even a long way off that if anyone laid a finger on this man, he would defend himself stoutly. And therefore he came off safe, both this man and his companion; for in war where men are like that, people usually don't touch them with a finger, but pursue those who are running headlong.

"One could quote many other things in praise of Socrates, wonderful things: of his other habits one might perhaps say much the same about any other man in the world, ancient or modern, that is worth of all wonder. Men like Achilles might be found, one might take, for example, Brasidas and others; and again men like Pericles,[70] such as Nestor and Antenor, and there are more besides; and so we might go on with our comparisons. But as for this man, so odd, both the man and his talk, none could ever be found to come near him, neither modern nor ancient, unless he is to be compared to no man at all, but to the Silenoses and satyrs to which I have compared him—him and his talk.

"For indeed there is something which I left out when I began, that even his talk is very like the opening Silenoses. When you agree to listen to the talk of Socrates, it might seem at first to be nothing but absurdity; such words and phrases are wrapped outside it, like the hide of a boisterous satyr. Pack-asses and smiths and shoemakers and tanners are what he talks about, and he seems to be always saying the same things in the same words, so that any ignorant and foolish man would laugh at them. But when they are opened out, and you get inside them, you will find his words first full of sense, as no others are; next, most divine and containing the finest images of virtue, and reaching farthest, in fact reaching to everything which it profits a man to study who is to become noble and good.

"This, gentlemen, is my laudation of Socrates; and I have mixed in as well some blame, by telling you of the way he insulted me. I am not the only one he has treated so; he has done the same to Charmides, Glaucon's son, and Euthydemos, Diocles' son, and very many others, whom he has tricked as a lover and made them treat him as beloved instead. That is a warning to you, Agathon, not to be deceived by this man; try to learn from our experience, and take care not to be the fool in the proverb, who could only learn by his own."[71]

When Alcibiades had ended his speech, there was much laughter at his frankness, because he seemed to be still in love with Socrates. But Socrates said, "You're sober, I think, Alcibiades, or you wold never have wrapped all that smart mantle round you in trying to hide why you have said all this, and put your point in a postscript at the end; for your real aim in all that you said was to make me and Agathon quarrel: you think I ought to be your lover and love no one else, and Agathon should be your beloved and loved by no one else. But I see through you; your satyric and silenic drama has been shown up. Now, my dearest Agathon, don't let him gain anything by it; only take care that no one shall make you and me quarrel."

Then Agathon said, "Upon my word, Socrates, that's the truth, I am sure. I notice how he reclined between me and you in order to keep us apart. Then he shall gain nothing by it, and I will come past you and recline there."

"Yes do," said Socrates, "recline here below me."

"Oh Zeus!" cried Alcibiades, "how the creature treats me! He things he must have the best of me everywhere! Well, if nothing else, you plague, let Agathon recline between us."

"Impossible!" said Socrates. "For you have sung my praises, and it is my duty to praise the next man to the right.[72] Then if Agathon reclines below you—I don't suppose he is going to praise me again, before I have praised him as I should?

Then let him alone, you rascal, and don't grudge my praise to the lad; for I want very much to sing his glory."

"Hooray, hooray!" cried Agathon, "I can't stay here, Alcibiades. I must and will change my place, and then Socrates will praise me!"

"Here we are again," said Alcibiades, "the usual thing: where Socrates is, there is no one else can get a share of the beauties! And now how easily he has invented a plausible reason why this one should be beside him!"

Then Agathon got up to go and lie down beside Socrates, but suddenly a great crowd of revellers came to the doors; seeing them open as someone was going out, they marched straight in and found places among the dinners, and the whole place was in an uproar. No order was kept any longer and they were forced to drink a great deal of wine. Eryximachos and Phaidros and some others went out and departed (so Aristodemos told me), and he fell asleep himself, and slept soundly for a long time, as the nights were long then and he woke up towards day when the cocks were already crowing. When he awoke he saw the others were either asleep or had gone, but Agathon and Aristophanes and Socrates were the only ones still awake, and they were drinking out of a large bowl from left to right. Socrates was arguing with them; Aristodemos told me he could not remember much of what was said, for he was not listening from the beginning and he was rather drowsy, but he told me the upshot of it was that Socrates was compelling them to admit that the same man ought to understand how to compose both comedy and tragedy, and that he who has skill as a tragic poet has skill for a comic poet. While they were being forced to this, and not following very well, they began to nod, and first Aristophanes fell asleep, and while day was dawning, Agathon too. Socrates made them comfortable, then got up and went away, and Aristodemos himself followed as usual. Socrates went to the Lyceum and had a wash, and spent the day as he generally did, and after spending the day so, in the evening went home to bed.

Return of Alcibiades to Athens

from The Republic, Book VII

Plato
translated by Benjamin Jowett

Allegory of the Cave

And now, I said, let me show in a figure how far our nature is enlightened or unenlightened:—Behold! human beings living in an underground den, which has a mouth open towards the light and reaching all along the den; here they have been from their childhood, and have their legs and necks chained so that they can not move, and can only see before them, being prevented by the chains from turning round their heads. Above and behind them a fire is blazing at a distance, and between the fire and the prisoners there is a raised way; and you will see, if you look, a low wall built along the way, like the screen which marionette players have in front of them, over which they show the puppets.

I see.

And do you see, I said, men passing along the wall carrying all sorts of vessels, and statues and figures of animals made of wood and stone and various materials, which appear over the wall? Some of them are talking, others silent.

You have shown me a strange image, and they are strange prisoners.

Like ourselves, I replied; and they see only their own shadows, or the shadows of one another, which the fire throws on the opposite wall of the cave?

True, he said; how could they see anything but the shadows if they were never allowed to move their heads?

And of the objects which are being carried in like manner they would only see the shadows?

Yes, he said.

And if they were able to converse with one another, would they not suppose that they were naming what was actually before them?

Very true.

And suppose further that the prison had an echo which came from the other side, would they not be sure to fancy when one of the passersby spoke that the voice which they heard came from the passing shadow?

No question, he replied.

To them, I said, the truth would be literally nothing but the shadows of the images.

That is certain.

And now look again, and see what will naturally follow if the prisoners are released and disabused of their error. At first, when any of them is liberated and compelled suddenly to stand up and turn his neck around and walk and look towards the light, he will suffer sharp pains; the glare will distress him, and he will be unable to see the realities of which in his former state he had seen the shadows; and then conceive some one saying to him, that what he saw before was an illusion, but that now, when he is approaching nearer to being and his eye is turned towards more real existence, he has a clearer vision, what will be his reply? And you may further imagine that his instructor is pointing to the objects as they pass and requiring him to name them, will he not be perplexed? Will he not fancy that the shadows which he formerly saw are truer than the objects which are now shown to him?

Far truer.

And if he is compelled to look straight at the light, will he not have a pain in his eyes which will make him turn away to take refuge in the objects of vision which he can see, and which he will conceive to be in reality clearer than the things which are now being shown to him?

True, he said.

And suppose once more, that he is reluctantly dragged up a steep and rugged ascent, and held fast until he is forced into the presence of the sun himself, is he not likely to be pained and irritated? When he approaches the light his eyes will be dazzled, and he will not be able to see anything at all of what are now called realities.

Not all in a moment, he said.

He will require to grow accustomed to the sight of the upper world. And first he will see the shadows best, next the reflections of men and other objects in the water, and then the objects themselves; then he will gaze upon the light of the moon and the stars and the spangled heaven; and he will see the sky and the stars by night better than the sun or the light of the sun by day?

Certainly.

Last of all he will be able to see the sun, and not mere reflections of him in the water, but he will see him in his own proper place, and not in another; and he will contemplate him as he is.

Certainly.

He will then proceed to argue that this is he who gives the season and the years, and is the guardian of all that is in the visible world, and in a certain way the cause of all things which he and his fellows have been accustomed to behold?

Clearly, he said, he would first see the sun and then reason about him.

And when he remembered his old habitation, and the wisdom of the den and his fellow-prisoners, do you not suppose that he would felicitate himself on the change, and pity them?

Certainly, he would.

And if they were in the habit of conferring honors among themselves on those who were quickest to observe the passing shadows and to remark which of them went before, and which followed after, and which were together; and who were therefore best able to draw conclusions as to the future, do you think that he would care for such honors and glories, or envy the possessors of them? Would he not say with Homer,

"Better to be the poor servant of a poor master,"

and to endure anything, rather than think as they do and live after their manner.

Yes, he said, I think that he would rather suffer anything than entertain these false notions and live in this miserable manner.

Imagine once more, I said, such an one coming suddenly out of the sun to be replaced in his old situation; would he not be certain to have his eyes full of darkness?

To be sure, he said.

And if there were a contest, and he had to compete in measuring the shadows with the prisoners who had never moved out of the den, while his sight was still weak, and before his eyes had become steady (and the time which would be needed to acquire this new habit of sight might be very considerable), would he not be ridiculous? Men would say of him that up he went and down he came without his eyes; and that it was better not even to think of ascending; and if any one tried to loose another and lead him up to the light, let them only catch the offender, and they would put him to death.

No question, he said.

This entire allegory, I said, you may now append, dear Glaucon, to the previous argument; the prisonhouse is the world of sight, the light of the fire is the sun, and you will not misapprehend me if you interpret the journey upwards to be the ascent of the soul into the intellectual world according to my poor belief, which, at your desire, I have expressed—whether rightly or wrongly God knows. But, whether true or false, my opinion is that in the world of knowledge the idea of good appears last of all, and is seen only with an effort; and, when seen, is also inferred to be the universal author of all things beautiful and right, parent of light and of the lord of light in this visible world, and the immediate source of reason and truth in the intellectual; and that this is the power upon which he who would act rationally either in public or private life must have his eye fixed.

I agree, he said, as far as I am able to understand you.

Moreover, I said, you must not wonder that those who attain to this beatific vision are unwilling to descend to human affairs; for their souls are ever hastening into the upper world where they desire to dwell; which desire of theirs is very natural, if our allegory may be trusted.

Yes, very natural.

And is there anything surprising in one who passes from divine contemplations to the evil state of man, misbehaving himself in a ridiculous manner, if, while his eyes are blinking and before he has become accustomed to the surrounding darkness, he is compelled to fight in courts of law, or in other places, about the images or the shadows of images of justice, and is endeavoring to meet the conceptions of those who have never yet seen absolute justice?

Anything but surprising, he replied.

Any one who has common sense will remember that the bewilderments of the eyes are of two kinds, and arise from two causes, either from coming out of the light or from going into the light, which is true of the mind's eye, quite as much as of the bodily eye; and he who remembers this when he sees any one whose vision is perplexed and weak, will not be too ready to laugh; he will first ask whether that soul of man has come out of the brighter life, and is unable to see because unaccustomed to the dark, or having turned from darkness to the day is dazzled by excess of light. And he will count the one happy in his condition and state of being, and he will pity the other; or, if he have a mind to laugh at the soul which comes from below into the light, there will be more reason in this than in the laugh which greets him who returns from above out of the light into the den.

That, he said, is a very just distinction.

But then, if I am right, certain professors of education must be wrong when they say that they can put a knowledge into the soul which was not there before, like sight into blind eyes.

They undoubtedly say this, he replied.

Whereas, our argument shows that the power and capacity of learning exists in the soul already; and that just as the eye was unable to turn from darkness to light without the whole body, so too the instrument of knowledge can only by the movement of the whole soul be turned from the world of becoming into that of being, and learn by degrees to endure the sight of being, and of the brightest and best of being, or in other words, of the good.

Very true.

And must there not be some art which will effect conversion in the easiest and quickest manner; not implanting the faculty of sight, for that exists already, but has been turned in the wrong direction, and is looking away from the truth?

Yes, he said, such an art may be presumed.

And whereas the other so-called virtues of the soul seem to be akin to bodily qualities, for even when they are not originally innate they can be implanted later by habit and exercise, the virtue of wisdom more than anything else contains a divine element which always remains, and by this conversion is rendered useful and profitable; or, on the other hand, hurtful and useless. Did you never observe the narrow intelligence flashing from the keen eye of a clever rogue—how eager he is, how clearly his paltry soul sees the way to his end; he is the reverse of blind, but his keen eye-sight is forced into the service of evil, and he is mischievous in proportion to his cleverness?

Very true, he said.

But what if there had been a circumcision of such natures in the days of their youth; and they had been severed from those sensual pleasures, such as eating and drinking, which, like leaden weights, were attached to them at their birth, and which drag them down and turn the vision of their souls upon the things that are below—if, I say, they had been released from these impediments and turned in the opposite direction, the very same faculty in them would have seen the truth as keenly as they see what their eyes are turned to now.

Very likely.

Yes, I said; and there is another thing which is likely, or rather a necessary inference from what has preceded, that neither the uneducated and uninformed of the truth, nor yet those who never make an end of their education, will be able ministers of State; not the former, because they have no single aim of duty which is the rule of all their actions, private as well as public; nor the latter, because they will not act at all except upon compulsion, fancying that they are already dwelling apart in the islands of the blest.

Very true, he replied.

Then, I said, the business of us who are the founders of the State will be to compel the best minds to attain that knowledge which we have already shown to be the greatest of all—they must continue to ascend until they arrive at the good; but when they have ascended and seen enough we must not allow them to do as they do now.

What do you mean?

I mean that they remain in the upper world: but this must not be allowed; they must be made to descend again among the prisoners in the den, and partake of their labors and honors, whether they are worth having or not.

But is not this unjust? he said; ought we to give them a worse life, when they might have a better?

You have again forgotten, my friend, I said, the intention of the legislator, who did not aim at making any one class in the State happy above the rest; the happiness was to be in the whole State, and he held the citizens together by persuasion and necessity, making them benefactors of the State, and therefore benefactors of one another; to this end he created them, not to please themselves, but to be his instruments in binding up the State.

True, he said, I had forgotten.

Observe, Glaucon, that there will be no injustice in compelling our philosophers to have a care and providence of others; we shall explain to them that in other States, men of their class are not obliged to share in the toils of politics: and this is reasonable, for they grow up at their own sweet will, and the government would rather not have them. Being self-taught, they can not be expected to show any gratitude for a culture which they have never received. But we have brought you into the world to be rulers of the hive, kings of yourselves and of the other citizens, and have educated you far better and more perfectly than they have been educated, and you are better able to share in the double duty. Wherefore each of you, when his turn comes, must go down to the general underground abode, and get the habit of seeing in the dark. When you have acquired the habit, you will see ten thousand times better than the inhabitants of the den, and you will know what the several images are, and what they represent, because you have seen the beautiful and just and good in their truth. And thus our State, which is also yours, will be a reality, and not a dream only, and will be administered in a spirit unlike that of other States, in which men fight with one another about shadows only and are distracted in the struggle for power, which in their eyes is a great good. Whereas the truth is that the State in which the rulers are most reluctant to govern is always the best and most quietly governed, and the State in which they are most eager, the worst.

Quite true, he replied.

And will our pupils, when they hear this, refuse to take their turn at the toils of State, when they are allowed to spend the greater part of their time with one another in the heavenly light?

Impossible, he answered; for they are just men, and the commands which we impose upon them are just; there can be no doubt that every one of them will take office as a stern necessity, and not after the fashion of our present rulers of State.

Yes, my friend, I said; and there lies the point. You must contrive for your future rulers another and a better life than that of a ruler, and then you may have a well-ordered State; for only in the State which offers this, will they rule who are truly rich, not in silver and gold, but in virtue and wisdom, which are the true blessings of life. Whereas if they go to the administration of public affairs, poor and hungering after their own private advantage, thinking that hence they are to snatch the chief good, order there can never be; for they will be fighting about office, and the civil and domestic broils which thus arise will be the ruin of the rulers themselves and of the whole State.

Most true, he replied.

And the only life which looks down upon the life of political ambition is that of true philosophy. Do you know of any other?

Indeed, I do not, he said.

And those who govern ought not to be lovers of the task? For, if they are, there will be rival lovers, and they will fight.

No question.

Who then are those whom we shall compel to be guardians? Surely they will be the men who are wisest about affairs of State, and by whom the State is best administered, and who at the same time have other honors and another and a better life than that of politics?

They are the men, and I will choose them, he replied.

And now shall we consider in what way such guardians will be produced, and how they are to be brought from darkness to light,—as some are said to have ascended from the world below to the gods?

By all means, he replied.

The process, I said, is not the turning over of an oyster-shell,[73] but the turning round of a soul passing from a day which is little better than night to the true day of being, that is, the ascent from below, which we affirm to be true philosophy?

Quite so.

And should we not inquire what sort of knowledge has the power of effecting such a change?

Certainly.

What sort of knowledge is there which would draw the soul from becoming to being? And another consideration has just occurred to me: You will remember that our young men are to be warrior athletes?

Yes, that was said.

Then this new kind of knowledge must have an additional quality?

What quality?

Usefulness in war.

Yes, if possible.

There were two parts in our former scheme of education, were there not?

Just so.

There was gymnastic which presided over the growth and decay of the body, and may therefore be regarded as having to do with generation and corruption?

True.

Then that is not the knowledge which we are seeking to discover?

No.

But what do you say of music, what also entered to a certain extent into our former scheme?

Music, he said, as you will remember, was the counterpart of gymnastic, and trained the guardians by the influences of habit, by harmony making them harmonious, by rhythm rhythmical, but not giving them science; and the words, whether fabulous or possibly true, had kindred elements of rhythm and harmony in them. But in music there was nothing which tended to that good which you are now seeking.

You are most accurate, I said, in your recollection; in music there certainly was nothing of the kind. But what branch of knowledge is there, my dear Glaucon, which is of the desired nature; since all the useful arts were reckoned mean by us?

Undoubtedly; and yet if music and gymnastic are excluded, and the arts are also excluded, what remains?

Well, I said, there may be nothing left of our special subjects; and then we shall have to take something which is not special, but of universal application.

What may that be?

A something which all arts and sciences and intelligences use in common, and which every one first has to learn among the elements of education.

What is that?

The little matter of distinguishing one, two, and three—in a word, number and calculation:—do not all arts and sciences necessarily partake of them?

Yes.

Then the art of war partakes of them?

To be sure.

Then Palamedes, whenever he appears in tragedy, proves Agamemnon ridiculously unfit to be a general. Did you never remark how he declares that he had invented number, and had numbered the ships and set in array the ranks of the army at Troy; which implies that they had never been numbered before, and Agamemnon must be supposed literally to have been incapable of counting his own feet—how could he if he was ignorant of number? And if that is true, what sort of general must he have been?

I should say a very strange one, if this was as you say.

Can we deny that a warrior should have a knowledge of arithmetic?

Certainly he should, if he is to have the smallest understanding of military tactics, or indeed, I should rather say, if he is to be a man at all.

I should like to know whether you have the same notion which I have of this study?

What is your notion?

It appears to me to be a study of the kind which we are seeking, and which leads naturally to reflection, but never to have been rightly used; for the true use of it is simply to draw the soul towards being.

Will you explain your meaning? he said.

I will try, I said; and I wish you would share the inquiry with me, and say "yes" or "no" when I attempt to distinguish in my own mind what branches of knowledge have this attracting power, in order that we may have clearer proof that arithmetic is, as I suspect, one of them.

Explain, he said.

I mean to say that objects of sense are of two kinds; some of them do not invite thought because the sense is an adequate judge of them; while in the case of other objects sense is so untrustworthy that further inquiry is imperatively demanded.

You are clearly referring, he said, to the manner in which the senses are imposed upon by distance, and by painting in light and shade.

No, I said, that is not at all my meaning.

Then what is your meaning?

When speaking of uninviting objects, I mean those which do not pass from one sensation to the opposite; inviting objects are those which do; in this latter case the sense coming upon the object, whether at a distance or near, gives no more vivid idea of anything in particular than of its opposite. An illustration will make my meaning clearer: here are three fingers—a little finger, a second finger, and a middle finger.

Very good.

You may suppose that they are seen quite close: And here comes the point.

What is it?

Each of them equally appears a finger, whether seen in the middle or at the extremity, whether white or black, or thick or thin—it makes no difference; a finger is a finger all the same. In these cases a man is not compelled to ask of thought the question what is a finger? for the sight never intimates to the mind that a finger is other than a finger.

True.

And therefore, I said, as we might expect, there is nothing here which invites or excites intelligence.

There is not, he said.

But is this equally true of the greatness and smallness of the fingers? Can sight adequately perceive them? And is no difference made by the circumstance that one of the fingers is in the middle and another at the extremity? And in like manner does the touch adequately perceive the qualities of thickness or thinness, of softness or hardness? And so of the other senses; do they give perfect intimations of such matters? Is not their mode of operation on this wise—the sense which is concerned with the quality of hardness is necessarily concerned also with the quality of softness, and only intimates to the soul that the same thing is felt to be both hard and soft?

You are quite right, he said.

And must not the soul be perplexed at this intimation which the sense gives of a hard which is also soft? What, again, is the meaning of light and heavy, if that which is light is also heavy, and that which is heavy, light?

Yes, he said, these intimations which the soul receives are very curious and require to be explained.

Yes, I said, and in these perplexities the soul naturally summons to her aid calculation and intelligence, that she may see whether the several objects announced to her are one or two.

True.

And if they turn out to be two, is not each of them one and different?

Certainly.

And if each is one, and both are two, she will conceive the two as in a state of division, for if they were undivided they could only be conceived of as one?

True.

The eye certainly did see both small and great, but only in a confused manner; they were not distinguished.

Yes.

Whereas the thinking mind, intending to light up the chaos, was compelled to reverse the process, and look at small and great as separate and not confused.

Very true.

Was not this the beginning of the inquiry "What is great?" and "What is small?"

Exactly so.

And thus arose the distinction of the visible and the intelligible.

Most true.

This was what I meant when I spoke of impressions which invited the intellect, or the reverse—those which are simultaneous with opposite impressions, invite thought; those which are simultaneous do not.

I understand, he said, and agree with you.

And to which class do unity and number belong?

I do not know, he replied.

Think a little and you will see that what has preceded will supply the answer; for if simple unity could be adequately perceived by the sight or by any other sense, then, as we were saying in the case of the finger, there would be nothing to attract towards being; but when there is some contradiction always present, and one is the reverse of one and involves the conception of plurality, then thought begins to be aroused within us, and the soul perplexed and wanting to arrive at a decision asks "What is absolute unity?" This is the way in which the study of the one has a power of drawing and converting the mind to the contemplation of true being.

And surely, he said, this occurs notably in the case of one; for we see the same thing to be both one and infinite in multitude?

Yes, I said; and this being true of one must be equally true of all number?

Certainly.

And all arithmetic and calculation have to do with number?

Yes.

And they appear to lead the mind towards truth?

Yes, in a very remarkable manner.

Then this is knowledge of the kind for which we are seeking, having a double use, military and philosophical; for the man of war must learn the art of number or he will not know how to array his troops, and the philosopher also, because he has to rise out of the sea of change and lay hold of true being, and therefore he must be an arithmetician.

That is true.

And our guardian is both warrior and philosopher?

Certainly.

Then this is a kind of knowledge which legislation may fitly prescribe; and we must endeavor to persuade those who are to be the principal men of our State to go and learn arithmetic, not as amateurs, but they must carry on the study until they see the nature of numbers with the mind only; or again, like merchants or retail-traders, with a view to buying or selling, but for the sake of their military use, and of the soul herself; and because this will be the easiest way for her to pass from becoming to truth and being.

That is excellent, he said.

Yes, I said, and now having spoken of it, I must add how charming the science is! and in how many ways it conduces to our desired end, if pursued in the spirit of a philosopher, and not of a shopkeeper!

How do you mean?

I mean, as I was saying, that arithmetic has a very great and elevating effect, compelling the soul to reason about abstract number, and rebelling against the introduction of visible or tangible objects into the argument. You know how steadily the masters of the art repel and ridicule any one who attempts to divide absolute unity when he is calculating, and if you divide, they multiply[74] taking care that one shall continue one and not become lost in fractions.

That is very true.

Now, suppose a person were to say to them: O my friends, what are these wonderful numbers about which you are reasoning, in which, as you say, there is a unity such as you demand, and each unit is equal, invariable, indivisible,—what would they answer?

They would answer, as I should conceive, that they were speaking of those numbers which can only be realized in thought.

Then you see that this knowledge may be truly called necessary, necessitating as it clearly does the use of the pure intelligence in the attainment of pure truth?

Yes; that is a marked characteristic of it.

And have you further observed, that those who have a natural talent for calculation are generally quick at every other kind of knowledge; and even the dull, if they have had an arithmetical training, although they may derive no other advantage from it, always become much quicker than they would otherwise have been.

Very true, he said.

And indeed, you will not easily find a more difficult study, and not many as difficult.

You will not.

And, for all these reasons, arithmetic is a kind of knowledge in which the best natures should be trained, and which must not be given up.

I agree.

Let this then be made one of our subjects of education. And next, shall we inquire whether the kindred science also concerns us?

You mean geometry?

Exactly so.

Clearly, he said, we are concerned with that part of geometry which relates to war; for in pitching a camp, or taking up a position, or closing or extending the lines of an army, or any other military manoeuvre, whether in actual battle or on a march, it will make all the difference whether a general is or is not a geometrician.

Yes, I said, but for that purpose a very little of either geometry or calculation will be enough; the question relates rather to the greater and more advanced part of geometry—whether that tends in any degree to make more easy the vision of the idea of good; and thither, as I was saying, all things tend which compel the soul to turn her gaze towards that place, where is the full perfec-

tion of being, which she ought, by all means, to behold.

True, he said.

Then if geometry compels us to view being, it concerns us; if becoming only, it does not concern us?

Yes, that is what we assert.

Yet anybody who has the least acquaintance with geometry will not deny that such a conception of the science is in flat contradiction to the ordinary language of geometricians.

How so?

They have in view practice only, and are always speaking, in a narrow and ridiculous manner, of squaring and extending and applying and the like—they confuse the necessities of geometry with those of daily life; whereas knowledge is the real object of the whole science.

Certainly, he said.

Then must not a further admission be made?

What admission?

That the knowledge at which geometry aims is knowledge of the eternal, and not of aught perishing and transient.

That, he replied, may be readily allowed, and is true.

Then, my noble friend, geometry will draw the soul towards truth, and create the spirit of philosophy, and raise up that which is now unhappily allowed to fall down.

Nothing will be more likely to have such an effect.

Then nothing should be more sternly laid down than that the inhabitants of your fair city should by all means learn geometry. Moreover the science has indirect effects, which are not small.

Of what kind? he said.

There are the military advantages of which you spoke, I said; and in all departments of knowledge, as experience proves, any one who has studied geometry is infinitely quicker of apprehension than one who has not.

Yes indeed, he said, there is an infinite difference.

Then shall we propose this as a second branch of knowledge which our youth will study?

Let us do so, he replied.

And suppose we make astronomy the third—what do you say?

I am strongly inclined to it, he said; the observation of the seasons and of months and years is as essential to the general as it is to the farmer or sailor.

I am amused, I said, at your fear of the world, which makes you guard against the appearance of insisting upon useless studies; and I quite admit the difficulty of believing that in every man there is an eye of the soul which, when by other pursuits lost and dimmed, is by these purified and re-illumined; and is more precious far than ten thousand bodily eyes, for by it alone is truth seen. Now there are two classes of person: one class of those who will agree with you and will take your words as a revelation; another class to whom they will be utterly unmeaning, and who will naturally deem them to be idle tales, for they see no sort of profit which is to be obtained from them. And therefore you had better decide at once with which of the two your are proposing to argue. You will very likely say with neither, and that your chief aim in carrying on the argument is your own improvement; at the same time you do not grudge to others any benefit which they may receive.

I think that I should prefer to carry on the argument mainly on my own behalf.

Then take a step backward, for we have gone wrong in the order of the sciences.

What was the mistake? he said.

After plane geometry, I said, we proceeded at once to solids in revolution, instead of taking solids in themselves; whereas after the second dimension the third, which is concerned with cubes and dimensions of depth, ought to have followed.

That is true, Socrates; but so little seems to be known as yet about these subjects.

Why, yes, I said, and for two reasons:—in the first place, no government patronizes them; this leads to a want of energy in the pursuit of them, and they are difficult; in the second place, students can not learn them unless they have a director. But then a director can hardly be found, and even if he could, as matters now stand, the students, who are very conceited, would not attend to him. That, however, would be otherwise if the whole State became the director of these studies and gave honor to them; then disciples would want to come, and there would be continuous and earnest search, and discoveries would be made; since even now, disregarded as they are by the world, and maimed of their fair proportions, and although none of their votaries can tell the use of them, still these studies force their way by their natural charm, and very likely, if they had the help of the State, they would some day emerge into light.

Yes, he said, there is a remarkable charm in them. But I do not clearly understand the change in the order. First you began with a geometry of plane surfaces?

Yes, I said.

And you placed astronomy next, and then you made a step backward?

Yes, and I have delayed you by my hurry; the ludicrous state of solid geometry, which in natural order, should have followed, made me pass over this branch and go on to astronomy, or motion of solids.

True, he said.

Then assuming that the science now omitted would come into existence if encouraged by the State, let us go on to astronomy, which will be fourth.

The right order, he replied. And now, Socrates, as you rebuked the vulgar manner in which I praised astronomy before, my praise shall be given in your own spirit. For every one, as I think, must see that astronomy compels the soul to look upwards and leads us from this world to another.

Every one but myself, I said; to every one else this may be clear, but not to me.

And what then would you say?

I should rather say that those who elevate astronomy into philosophy appear to me to make us look downwards and not upwards.

What do you mean? he asked.

You, I replied, have in your mind a truly sublime conception of our knowledge of the things above. And I dare say that if a person were to throw his head back and study the fretted ceiling, you would still think that his mind was the percipient, and not his eyes. And you are very likely right, and I may be a simpleton: but, in my opinion, that knowledge only which is of being and of the unseen can make the soul look upwards, and whether a man gapes at the heavens or blinks on the ground, seeking to learn some particular of sense, I would deny that he can learn, for nothing of that sort is matter of science; his soul is looking downwards, not upwards, whether his way to knowledge is by water or by land, whether he floats, or only lies on his back.

I acknowledge, he said, the justice of your rebuke. Still, I should like to ascertain how astronomy can be learned in any manner more conducive to that knowledge of which we are speaking?

I will tell you, I said: The starry heaven which we behold is wrought upon a visible ground, and therefore, although the fairest and most perfect of visible things, must necessarily be deemed inferior far to the true motions of absolute swiftness and absolute slowness, which are relative to each other, and carry with them that which is contained in them, in the true number and in every true figure. Now, these are to be apprehended by reason and intelligence, but not by sight.

True, he replied.

The spangled heavens should be used as a pattern and with a view to that higher knowledge; their beauty is like the beauty of figures or pictures excellently wrought by the hand of Daedalus, or some other great artist, which we may chance to behold; any geometrician who saw them would appreciate the exquisiteness of their workmanship, but he would never dream of thinking that in them he could find the true equal or the true double, or the truth of any other proportion.

No, he replied, such an idea would be ridiculous.

And will not a true astronomer have the same feeling when he looks at the movements of the stars? Will he not think that heaven and the things in heaven are framed by the Creator of them in the most perfect manner? But he will never imagine that the proportions of night and day, or of both to the month, or of the month to the year, or of the stars to these and to one another, and any other things that are material and visible can also be eternal and subject to no deviation—that would be absurd; and it is equally absurd to take so much pains in investigating their exact truth.

I quite agree, though I never thought of this before.

Then, I said, in astronomy, as in geometry, we should employ problems and let the heavens alone if we would approach the subject in the right way and so make the natural gift of reason to be any of real use.

That, he said, is a work infinitely beyond our present astronomers.

Yes, I said; and there are many other things which must also have a similar extension given to them, if our legislation is to be of any value. But can you tell me of any other suitable study?

No, he said, not without thinking.

Motion, I said, has many forms, and not one only; two of them are obvious enough even to wits no better than ours; and there are others, as I imagine, which may be left to wiser persons.

But where are the two?

There is a second, I said, which is the counter of the one already named.

And what may that be?

The second, I said, would seem relatively to the ears to be what the first is to the eyes; for I conceive that as the eyes are designed to look up at the stars, so are the ears to hear harmonious

motions; and these are sister sciences—as the Pythagoreans say, and we, Glaucon, agree with them?

Yes, he replied.

But this, I said, is a laborious study, and therefore we had better go and learn of them; and they will tell us whether there are any other applications of these sciences. At the same time, we must not lose sight of our own higher object.

What is that?

There is a perfection which all knowledge ought to reach, and which our pupils ought also to attain, and not to fall short of, as I was saying that they did in astronomy. For in the science of harmony, as you probably know, the same thing happens. The teachers of harmony compare the sounds and consonances which are heard only, and their labor, like that of the astronomers, is in vain.

Yes, by heaven! he said; and 'tis as good as a play to hear them talking about their condensed notes, as they call them; they put their ears close alongside of the strings like persons catching a sound from their neighbor's wall[75]—one set of them declaring that they distinguish an intermediate note and have found the least interval which should be the unit of measurement; the others insisting that the two sounds have passed into the same—either party setting their ears before their understanding.

You mean, I said, those gentlemen who tease and torture the strings and rack them on the pegs of the instrument: I might carry on the metaphor and speak after their manner of the blows which the plectrum gives, and make accusations against the strings, both of backwardness and forwardness to sound; but this would be tedious, and therefore I will only say that these are not the men, and that I am referring to the Pythagoreans, of whom I was just now proposing to inquire about harmony. For they too are in error, like the astronomers; they investigate the numbers of the harmonies which are heard, but they never attain to problems—that is to say, they never reach the natural harmonies of number, or reflect why some numbers are harmonious and others not.

That, he said, is a thing of more than mortal knowledge.

A thing, I replied, which I would rather call useful; that is, if sought after with a view to the beautiful and good; but if pursued in any other spirit, useless.

Very true, he said.

Now, when all these studies reach the point of intercommunion and connection with one another, and come to be considered in their mutual affinities, then, I think, but not till then, will the pursuit of them have a value for our objects; otherwise there is no profit in them.

I suspect so; but you are speaking, Socrates, of a vast work.

What do you mean? I said; the prelude or what? Do you not know that all this is but the prelude to the actual strain which we have to learn? For you surely would not regard the skilled mathematician as a dialectician?

Assuredly not, he said; I have hardly ever known a mathematician who was capable of reasoning.

But do you imagine that men who are unable to give and take a reason will have the knowledge which we require of them?

Neither can this be supposed.

And so, Glaucon, I said, we have at last arrived at the hymn of dialectic. This is that strain which is of the intellect only, but which the faculty of sight will nevertheless be found to imitate; for sight, as you may remember, was imagined by us after a while to behold the real animals and stars, and last of all the sun himself. And so with dialectic; when a person starts on the discovery of the absolute by the light of reason only, and without any assistance of sense, and perseveres until by pure intelligence he arrives at the perception of the absolute good, he at last finds himself at the end of the intellectual world, as in the case of sight at the end of the visible.

Exactly, he said.

Then this is the process which you call dialectic?

True.

But the release of the prisoners from chains, and their translation from the shadows to the images and to the light, and the ascent from the underground den to the sun, while in his presence they are vainly trying to look on animals and plants and the light of the sun, but are able to perceive even with their weak eyes the images in the water [which are divine], and are the shadows of true existence (not shadows of images cast by a light of fire, which compared with the sun is only an image)—this power of elevating the highest principle in the soul to the contemplation of that which is best in existence, with which we may compare the raising of that faculty which is the very light of the body to the sight of that which is brightest in the material and visible world—this power is given, as I was saying, by all that study and pursuit of the arts which has been described.

I agree in what you are saying, he replied, which may be hard to believe, yet, from another

point of view, is harder still to deny. This however is not a theme to be treated of in passing only, but will have to be discussed again and again. And so, whether our conclusion be true or false, let us assume all this, and proceed at once from the prelude or preamble to the chief strain, and describe that in like manner. Say, then, what is the nature and what are the divisions of dialectic, and what are the paths which lead thither; for these paths will also lead to our final rest.

Dear Glaucon, I said, you will not be able to follow me here, though I would do my best, and you should behold not an image only but the absolute truth, according to my notion. Whether what I told you would or would not have been a reality I can not venture to say; but you would have seen something like reality; of that I am confident.

Doubtless, he replied.

But I must also remind you, that the power of dialectic alone can reveal this, and only to one who is a disciple of the previous sciences.

Of that assertion you may be as confident as of the last.

And assuredly no one will argue that there is any other method of comprehending by any regular process all true existence or of ascertaining what each thing is in its own nature; for the arts in general are concerned with the desires or opinions of men, or are cultivated with a view to production and construction, or for the preservation of such productions and constructions; and as to the mathematical sciences which, as we were saying, have some apprehension of true being—geometry and the like—they only dream about being, but never can they behold the waking reality so long as they leave the hypotheses which they use unexamined, and are unable to give an account of them. For when a man knows not his own first principle, and when the conclusion and intermediate steps are also constructed out of he knows not what, how can he imagine that such a fabric of convention can ever become science?

Impossible, he said.

Then dialectic, and dialectic alone, goes directly to the first principle and is the only science which does away with hypotheses in order to make her ground secure; the eye of the soul, which is literally buried in an outlandish slough, is by her gentle aid lifted upwards; and she uses as handmaids and helpers in the work of conversion, the sciences which we have been discussing. Custom terms them sciences, but they ought to have some other name, implying greater clearness than opinion and less clearness than science:

and this, in our previous sketch, was called understanding. But why should we dispute about names when we have realities of such importance to consider?

Why indeed, he said, when any name will do which expresses the thought of the mind with clearness?

At any rate, we are satisfied, as before, to have four divisions, two for intellect and two for opinion, and to call the first division science, the second understanding, the third belief, and the fourth perception of shadows, opinion being concerned with becoming, and intellect with being; and so to make a proportion;

As being is to becoming, so is pure intellect to opinion. And as intellect is to opinion, so is science to belief, and understanding to the perception of shadows.

But let us defer the further correlation and subdivision of the subjects of opinion and of intellect, for it will be a long inquiry, many times longer than this has been.

As far as I understand, he said, I agree.

And do you also agree, I said, in describing the dialectician as one who attains a conception of the essence of each thing? And he who does not possess and is therefore unable to impart this conception, in whatever degree he fails, may in that degree also be said to fail in intelligence? Will you admit so much?

Yes, he said; how can I deny it?

And you would say the same of the conception of the good? Until the person is able to abstract and define rationally the idea of good, and unless he can run the gauntlet of all objections, and is ready to disprove them, not by appeals to opinion, but to absolute truth, never faltering at any step of the argument—unless he can do all this, you would say that he knows neither the idea of good nor any other good; he apprehends only a shadow, if anything at all, which is given by opinion and not by science;—dreaming and slumbering in this life, before he is well awake here, he arrives at the world below, and has his final quietus.

In all that I should most certainly agree with you.

And surely you would not have the children of your ideal State, whom you are nurturing and educating—if the ideal ever becomes a reality—you would not allow the future rulers to be like posts, having no reason in them, and yet to be set in authority over the highest matters?

Certainly not.

Then you will make a law that they shall have such an education as will enable them to attain the greatest skill in asking and answering questions?

Yes, he said, you and I together will make it.

Dialectic, then, as you will agree, is the coping-stone of the sciences, and is set over them; no other science can be placed higher—the nature of knowledge can no further go?

I agree, he said.

But to whom we are to assign these studies, and in what way they are to be assigned, are questions which remain to be considered.

Yes, clearly.

You remember, I said, how the rulers were chosen before?

Certainly, he said.

The same natures must still be chosen, and the preference again given to the surest and the bravest, and, if possible, to the fairest; and, having noble and generous tempers, they should also have the natural gifts which will facilitate their education.

And what are these?

Such gifts as keenness and ready powers of acquisition: for the mind more often faints from the severity of study than from the severity of gymnastics: the toil is more entirely the mind's own, and is not shared with the body.

Very true, he replied.

Further, he of whom we are in search should have a good memory, and be an unwearied solid man who is a lover of labor in any line; or he will never be able to endure the great amount of bodily exercise and to go through all the intellectual discipline and study which we require of him.

Certainly, he said; he must have natural gifts.

The mistake at present is, that those who study philosophy have no vocation, and this, as I was before saying, is the reason why she has fallen into disrepute: her true sons should take her by the hand and not bastards.

What do you mean?

In the first place, her votary should not have a lame or halting industry—I mean, that he should not be half industrious and half idle: as, for example, when a man is a lover of gymnastic and hunting, and all other bodily exercises, but a hater rather than a lover of the labor of learning or listening or inquiring. Or the occupation to which he devotes himself may be of an opposite kind, and he may have the other sort of lameness.

Certainly, he said.

And as to truth, I said, is not a soul equally to be deemed halt and lame which hates voluntary falsehood and is extremely indignant at herself and others when they tell lies, but is patient of involuntary falsehood, and does not mind wallowing like a swinish beast in the mire of ignorance, and has no shame at being detected?

To be sure.

And, again, in respect of temperance, courage, magnificence, and every other virtue, should we not carefully distinguish between the true son and the bastard? for where there is no discernment of such qualities states and individuals unconsciously err; and the state makes a ruler, and the individual a friend, of one who, being defective in some part of virtue, is in a figure lame or a bastard.

That is very true, he said.

All these things, then, will have to be carefully considered by us; and if only those whom we introduce to this vast system of education and training are sound in body and mind, justice herself will have nothing to say against us, and we shall be the saviors of the constitution and of the State; but, if our pupils are men of another stamp, the reverse will happen, and we shall pour a still greater flood of ridicule on philosophy than she has to endure at present.

That would not be creditable.

Certainly not, I said; and yet perhaps, in thus turning jest into earnest I am equally ridiculous.

In what respect?

I had forgotten, I said, that we were not serious and spoke with too much excitement. For when I saw philosophy so undeservedly trampled under foot of men I could not help feeling a sort of indignation at the authors of her disgrace: and my anger made me too vehement.

Indeed! I was listening, and did not think so.

But I, who am the speaker, felt that I was. And now let me remind you that, although in our former selection we chose old men, we must not do so in this. Solon was under a delusion when he said that a man when he grows old may learn many things—for he can no more learn much than he can run much; youth is the time for any extraordinary toil.

Of course.

And, therefore, calculation and geometry and all the other elements of instruction, which are a preparation for dialectic, should be presented to the mind in childhood; not, however, under any notion of forcing our system of education.

Why not?

Because a freeman ought not to be a slave in the acquisition of knowledge of any kind. Bodily exercise, when compulsory, does no harm to the body; but knowledge which is acquired under compulsion obtains no hold on the mind.

Very true.

Then, my good friend, I said, do not use compulsion, but let early education be a sort of amusement; you will then be better able to find out the natural bent.

That is a very rational notion, he said.

Do you remember that the children, too, were to be taken to see the battle on horseback; and that if there were no danger they were to be brought close up and, like young hounds, have a taste of blood given them?

Yes, I remember.

The same practice may be followed, I said, in all these things—labors, lessons, dangers—and he who is most at home in all of them ought to be enrolled in a select number.

At what age?

At the age when the necessary gymnastics are over: the period whether of two or three years which passes in this sort of training is useless for any other purpose; for sleep and exercise are unpropitious to learning; and the trial of who is first in gymnastic exercises is one of the most important tests to which our youth are subjected.

Certainly, he replied.

After that time those who are selected from the class of twenty years old will be promoted to higher honor, and the sciences which they learned without any order in their early education will now be brought together, and they will be able to see the natural relationship of them to one another and to true being.

Yes, he said, that is the only kind of knowledge which takes lasting root.

Yes, I said; and the capacity for such knowledge is the great criterion of dialectical talent; the comprehensive mind is always the dialectical.

I agree with you, he said.

These, I said, are the points which you must consider; and those who have most of this comprehension, and who are most steadfast in their learning, and in their military and other appointed duties, when they have arrived at the age of thirty will have to be chosen by you out of the select class, and elevated to higher honor; and you will have to prove them by the help of dialectic, in order to learn which of them is able to give up the use of sight and the other senses, and in company with truth to attain absolute being: And here, my friend, great caution is required.

Why great caution?

Do you not remark, I said, how great is the evil which dialectic has introduced?

What evil? he said.

The students of the art are filled with lawlessness.

Quite true, he said.

Do you think that there is anything so very unnatural or inexcusable in their case? or will you make allowance for them?

In what way make allowance?

I want you, I said, by way of parallel, to imagine a supposititious son who is brought up in great wealth; he is one of a great and numerous family, and has many flatterers. When he grows up to manhood, he learns that his alleged are not his real parents; but who the real are he is unable to discover. Can you guess how he will be likely to behave towards his flatterers and his supposed parents, first of all during the period when he is ignorant of the false relation, and then again when he knows? Or shall I guess for you?

If you please.

Then I should say, that while he is ignorant of the truth he will be likely to honor his father and his mother and his supposed relations more than the flatterers; he will be less inclined to neglect them when in need, or to do or say anything against them; and he will be less willing to disobey them in any important matter.

He will.

But when he has made the discovery, I should imagine that he would diminish his honor and regard for them, and would become more devoted to the flatterers; their influence over him would greatly increase; he would now live after their ways, and openly associate with them, and, unless he were of an unusually good disposition, he would trouble himself no more about his supposed parents or other relations.

Well, all that is very probable. But how is the image applicable to the disciples of philosophy?

In this way: you know that there are certain principles about justice and honor, which were taught us in childhood, and under their parental authority we have been brought up, obeying and honoring them.

That is true.

There are also opposite maxims and habits of pleasure which flatter and attract the soul, but do not influence those of us who have any sense of right, and they continue to obey and honor the maxims of their fathers.

True.

Now, when a man is in this state, and the questioning spirit asks what is fair or honorable, and he answers as the legislator has taught him, and then arguments many and diverse refute his words, until he is driven into believing that nothing is honorable any more than dishonorable, or just and good any more than the reverse, and so of all the notions which he most valued, do you think that he will still honor and obey them as before?

Impossible.

And when he ceases to think them honorable and natural as heretofore, and he fails to discover the true, can he be expected to pursue any life other than that which flatters his desires?

He can not.

And from being a keeper of the law he is converted into a breaker of it?

Unquestionably.

Now all this is very natural in students of philosophy such as I have described, and also, as I was just now saying, most excusable.

Yes, he said; and, I may add, pitiable.

Therefore, that your feelings may not be moved to pity about our citizens who are now thirty years of age, every care must be taken in introducing them to dialectic.

Certainly.

There is a danger lest they should taste the dear delight too early; for youngsters, as you may have observed, when they first get the taste in their mouths, argue for amusement, and are always contradicting and refuting others in imitation of those who refute them; like puppy-dogs, they rejoice in pulling and tearing at all who come near them.

Yes, he said, there is nothing which they like better.

And when they have made many conquests and received defeats at the hands of many, they violently and speedily get into a way of not believing anything which they believed before, and hence, not only they, but philosophy and all that relates to it is apt to have a bad name with the rest of the world.

Too true, he said.

But when a man begins to get older, he will no longer be guilty of such insanity; he will imitate the dialectician who is seeking for truth, and not the eristic, who is contradicting for the sake of amusement; and the greater moderation of his character will increase instead of diminishing the honor of the pursuit.

Very true, he said.

And did we not make special provision for this, when we said that the disciples of philosophy were to be orderly and steadfast, not, as now, any chance aspirant or intruder?

Very true.

Suppose, I said, the study of philosophy to take the place of gymnastics and to be continued diligently and earnestly and exclusively for twice the number of years which were passed in bodily exercise—will that be enough?

Would you say six or four years? he asked.

Say five years, I replied; at the end of the time they must be sent down again into the den and compelled to hold any military or other office which young men are qualified to hold: in this way they will get their experience of life, and there will be an opportunity of trying whether, when they are drawn all manner of ways by temptation, they will stand firm or flinch.

And how long is this stage of their lives to last?

Fifteen years, I answered; and when they have reached fifty years of age, then let those who still survive and have distinguished themselves in every action of their lives and in every branch of knowledge come at last to their consummation: the time has now arrived at which they must raise the eye of the soul to the universal light which lightens all things, and behold the absolute good; for that is the pattern according to which they are to order the State and the lives of individuals, and the remainder of their own lives also; making philosophy their chief pursuit, but, when their turn comes, toiling also at politics and ruling for the public good, not as though they were performing some heroic action, but simply as a matter of duty; and when they have brought up in each generation others like themselves and left them in their place to be governors of the State, then they will depart to the Islands of the Blest and dwell there; and the city will give them public memorials and sacrifices and honor them, if the Pythian oracle consent, as demigods, but if not, as in any case blessed and divine.

You are a sculptor, Socrates, and have made statues of our governors faultless in beauty.

Yes, I said, Glaucon, and of our governesses too; for you must not suppose that what I have been saying applies to men only and not to women as far as their natures can go.

There you are right, he said, since we have made them to share in all things like the men.

Well, I said, and you would agree (would you not?) that what has been said about the State and the government is not a mere dream, and although difficult not impossible, but only possible in the way which has been supposed; that is to say, when the true philosopher kings are born in a State, one or more of them, despising the honors of this present world which they deem mean and worthless, esteeming above all things right and the honor that springs from right, and regarding justice as the greatest and most necessary of all things, whose ministers they are, and whose principles will be exalted by them when they set in order their own city?

How will they proceed?

They will begin by sending out into the country all the inhabitants of the city who are more than ten years old, and will take possession of their children, who will be unaffected by the habits of their parents; these they will train in their own habits and laws, I mean in the laws which we have given them: and in this way the State and constitution of which we were speaking will soonest and most easily attain happiness, and the nation which has such a constitution will gain most.

Yes, that will be the best way. And I think, Socrates, that you have very well described how, if ever, such a constitution might come into being.

Enough then of the perfect State, and of the man who bears its image—there is no difficulty in seeing how we shall describe him.

There is no difficulty, he replied; and I agree with you in thinking that nothing more need be said.

ENDNOTES

1. The reader must be careful to remember that Plato represents the banquet and the speakers as described by Aristodemos, one of the guests.
2. Socrates usually went unshod, so he was evidently going somewhere in dress.
3. The Greek text is uncertain, but the proverb seems to have been something like "When snobs give dinners, gents may just walk in." Socrates makes a perfect pun on Agathon's name, which means "the gentleman." Homer's passage is in *Iliad*, xvii. 588–90.
4. *Iliad* x. 224. Literally, "When two go together, one thinks things out before the other." (ενοησεν is understood from *Iliad*.)
5. An "aside" to his guests.
6. Lowest in dignity, at the end on the right. It was taken in politeness by the host. They reclined in twos.
7. Dionysos or Bacchus, god of wine, who loosens care and inspires to music and poetry.
8. Euripides, *Fragment* 488.
9. "Sophists," see *Meno*, p. 50, n. 1.
10. In his famous *Choice of Heracles (Hercules),* Xenophon, Memorabilia ii. 1.21.
11. He sat farthest on the left, in the place of honor.
12. As the patron of comedy.

13. Socrates and Agathon on the lowest couch on the right.
14. Hesiod, *Theogonia*, 116.
15. *Iliad* x. 482 and elsewhere.
16. See Euripides' famous play *Alcestis*, produced in 438 B.C.
17. Pindar, *Olympian* ii. 78.
18. In a lost play called *The Myrmidons*.
19. *Iliad* xi. 786.
20. Goddess of love.
21. Hippias and his brother Hipparchos, joint tyrants of Athens, 514 B.C.
22. Agamemmnon thus speaks about a dream. *Iliad* ii. 71.
23. Father of medicine.
24. Agathon and Aristophanes.
25. The reader may find Eryximachos' explanation which follows easier to understand if he thinks of "at variance" as meaning "out of tune," and "reconciling" as tuning the strings, and of a bow as giving out a deep faint musical note when the arrow leaves it. "Harmony" and "symphony" had not to the Greeks all the meaning they have to us as musical terms. Harmony was rather the relation between single notes which sounded well in sequence, and symphony the sound of those notes played together. (Unison was one form of harmony, and sound in unison one form of symphony; steady motion, a compromise of quick and slow, is one form of rythm.) See also *Republic*, p. 248, n. 4.
26. Hermaphrodite.
27. *Odyssey* xi. 305 ff. Otos and Ephialtes were the giants, who, to climb into heaven, piled Mt. Pelion on Mt. Ossa.
28. This was done at the country feast of Dionysos.
29. Tallies, like half of a broken coin or bone kept by friends or parties to an agreement, or the split laths of the old English exchequer, or the cut parchments of an indenture.
30. The god of fire.
31. In Greek mythology these were two of the Titans who were children of Ouranos (Heaven) and Gaia (Earth). They existed even before Zeus.
32. Atè, presumptuous Madness, something like Sin. *Iliad* xix. 92.
33. Quoted from Alcidamas, a stylist.
34. Ares, god of war. The quotation is from Sophocles' lost play *Thyestes*, fragment 235 N.
35. Euripides, *Stheneboea*, fragment 663 N.
36. The Greek word ποιητης, poet, means a maker, and he uses this here to indicate

37. Compare *Odyssey* v. 391.
38. This word "drinking" is doubtful in the Greek text.
39. The three words used by Plato mean a ship's pilot, a fighter (not the driver) in a chariot or a marine on a ship, and a man who stands by another in battle.
40. He puts in his own little drop of parody.
41. Gorgias, the celebrated Sophist, adopted an artificial, affected style. See *Meno* p. 29, n. 1.
42. *Odyssey* xi. 634. Odysseus, at the end of his visit to the Kingdom of the Dead, grew pale with fear that Persephone might out of Hades send upon him a Gorgon head, and turn him to stone.
43. A modification of Euripides' *Hippolytos* 612.
44. Agathon had just said it was beauty.
45. A well-known Greek city in the Peloponnesus. The names perhaps suggest "the prophetess Fearthelord of Prophetville."
46. So Spenser calls him in the "Hymn to Love"; Lamb has "Resource, the son of Cunning," in his translation in the Loeb Classical Library.
47. The Greeks meant by this what we might call a cultured gentleman.
48. See p. 138, n. 3.
49. See Aristophanes' story, p. 132.
50. That is, she made a speech rather than answered questions.
51. A line of poetry.
52. A legendary King of Athens, who gave his life for this in the Dorian invasion.
53. A line of poetry.
54. The Spartan lawgiver.
55. The Greek word is Μαντινικη see p. 143, n. 1.
56. Alcibiades' Greek becomes poetic!
57. *Iliad* xi. 514.
58. From the left of the company clockwise, round to the right; see diagram, p. 117.
59. A favourite game in society. Socrates obviously plays up, and makes signs or grimaces as Alcibiades goes on, and the other turns to him and to the company in turn.
60. In Greek mythology a celebrated player on the pipe. See also *Republic*, p. 251.
61. A Phrygian musician.
62. The proverb was: "Wine and children are true."
63. An allusion to Homer, where Diomedes exchanges his bronze armour for Glaucos' golden; *Iliad* vi. 236.
64. With each phrase he points at Socrates.

creative arts and crafts and even the "creation" of living things.

65. 432 B.C., when Socrates was about thirty-seven and Alcibiades about nineteen.
66. *Odyssey* iv. 242.
67. During the activities at Poteidaia, 432–429 B.C.
68. Delium, 424 B.C.
69. Aristophanes, *Clouds*, 362.
70. Pericles was the great leader of the Athenians from 460 to 429 B.C.; Brasidas was a fine Spartan officer who served his city well against the Athenians from 431 to 422 B.C.
71. *Iliad* xvii. 33.
72. I.e., the next man beyond or "below" Socrates; see diagram, p. 336.
73. In allusion to a game in which two parties fled or pursued according as an oyster-shell which was thrown into the air fell with the dark or light side uppermost.
74. Meaning either (1) that they integrate the number because they deny the possibility of fractions; or (2) that division is regarded by them as a process of multiplication, for the fractions of one continue to be units.
75. Or, "close alongside of their neighbor's instruments, as if to catch a sound from them."

————————— *Questions for Consideration* —————————

Directions: Using complete sentences provide answers for the following questions.

1. After reading the *Symposium*, briefly describe a few of the types of love you feel exist today between two individuals.

    _____

    _____

    _____

    _____

    _____

2. Provide a brief definition for the term "love."

    _____

    _____

    _____

    _____

    _____

3. Do you agree or disagree that there are various stages of love?

    _____

    _____

    _____

    _____

    _____

———————————— *Writing Critically* ————————————

Directions: Select one of the essay topics listed below and compose a 500 word essay which discusses the topic fully.

1. Imagine you are a prisoner chained in a cave. Suppose you were able to see the light of truth and knowledge after leaving the cave of shadows and ignorance. Discuss in a paper the reasons you would or would not return to the cave to enlighten your former friends.

2. Research a few of Plato's dialogues that feature Socrates. Discuss in a paper the character of Socrates.

3. Compare or contrast at least three philosophical issues or ideas advocated by Plato and Aristotle.

4. Imagine you are a student enrolled in Plato's Academy. Describe your activities during one day of class. What subjects were taught?

Prewriting Space:

_____

_____

_____

_____

_____

_____

_____

_____

_____

_____

_____

_____

_____

_____

_____

_____

_____

_____

Introduction

Indian Literature

Just as Western Civilization has been celebrated for its interest in the physical world with its conveniences, comforts, and practical ideas, India, the sub-continent of Asia, is justly characterized as "the most religious part of the earth, where spirituality is not only an expression of the Indian's disdain for the materialistic, but where it is a living framework around which he centers his entire existence." Thus, to understand the literature of India, one must know the essence of that philosophy as it is expressed in the literature.

Two facets of Indian life are foremost in the thinking and the creativity of the Indian writer—the caste system and the Hindu religion.

When the invading tribes conquered the aborigines of India, they developed there a social system of caste which was to solidify as the characteristic pattern of Indian society to the present day. Originally, this system recognized four castes, which were fancifully linked to the four parts of the body of the creator god, Brahma: the priest (or Brahma) caste, associated with the head; the warrior caste, associated with the arms; the farmer-merchant caste, associated with the body; and the labor-servant caste (for the aborigines), associated with the feet. This social system of India, with its religious foundation, is called Hinduism (Warnock and Anderson I:9).

The caste system makes a practical application of the religious ideas of Hinduism which, in the simplest terms, purport to show that man is but a fragment of some great, forceful spirit of the universe and that he is at the mercy of Nature and the spirit that is behind Nature. Man reaches greatest kinship with this World Spirit (Oversoul) only by self-denial and self-annihilation. The world that one lives in is not Reality; the only Reality is that state in which man becomes most closely connected with Nirvana or the Oversoul. This can be done by the mystical experience of "Self-destruction."

The most important and most familiar Indian literature includes the *Upanishads*, a collection of 108 discourses on the Brahman religion, and the *Mahabharata*, the epic containing the "Baghavad Gita."

The Kena-Upanishad is one of the philosophical poems explaining the fundamentals of the mysticism of Hinduism. The poem consists of a series of questions and answers similar to those in a Christian catechism or a Platonic dialogue. The teacher explains that the only real life is the life of communication with the Great Spirit, and that this life is achieved by the practice of renunciation, austerity, self-control, meditation, and denial of selfish desire.

From *The Mahabharata*, the longest epic in the world, comes the philosophic "Bhagavad-Gita" or simply "The Gita" ("The Song of the Holy One") and the charming, romantic "Tale of Savitri."

The major theme of the first poem is DUTY, and the major conflict is SHOULD WE DO OUR DUTY EVEN IF IT MEANS DESTROYING THOSE WHO ARE BY AFFECTIONS, CUSTOM, AND LAW CLOSE TO US? (Mascaro ii).

"The Bhagavad Gita" found in chapters 23–40 of Book VI of the *Mahabharata*, expresses the doubt of the warrior Arjuna, who was horrified that polarization and war within the family would destroy the entire society based on *dharma*, the proper norms (Fitzgerald 620). In the excerpt in our text, Arjuna is preached to by his cousin, brother-in-law, friend, advisor, and charioteer Krishna Vasudeva, about the doctrine of *Karmayoga* [The regimen of doing one's proper action in one's proper social place, one's *dharma*]. Krishna admonishes Arjuna "to pursue yogic perfection in the course of acting, by acting without any personal interest in the actions or their consequences. He set forth the value that action can have for the welfare of God's creation, and argued that there is no contradiction between action and essence of yoga, which is the renunciation of individual, personal, desire-based interest in one's action and its fruits" whether this brings about the death of family and friends or not. Krishna continues by saying that Arjuna "ought now to do his *dharma*, acting as Krishna's human instrument in the critical situation at hand" (Fitzgerald 621).

"The Tale of Savitri," also from the *Mahabharata*, symbolizes both the pattern of Hindu myth and of Hindu domestic life. It gives evidence of the high place women held in ancient Indian culture. Like the story of Ruth in the Bible, the "Tale of Savitri" has as its main character a woman whose love for her husband and devotion to her father-in-law triumphed over Yama, the god of death. (GRG)

BIBLIOGRAPHY

Anderson, George K. and Robert Warnock. *The World in Literature,* I. Glenview, Illinois: Scott, Foresman and Company, 1967.

Bothwell, Jan. *The Story of India*. New York: Harcourt, Brace and World, Inc. 1952.

Eaton, Jeanette. *Gandhi, Fighter Without a Sword*. New York: Morrow Publishing Co. 1950.

Fitzgerald, James L. "The Great Epic of India as Religious Rhetoric: A Fresh Look at the *Mahabharata*." *Journal of the American Academy of Religion*, Vol. 51.

Forster, E. M. *A Passage to India*. Bloomington: Indiana University Press, 1956.

Mascaroo, Juan (Translator). *The Bhagavad Gita*. Penguin Classics: Baltimore. 1962.

Moraes, F. R. *Jawaharlal Nehru*. New York: Macmillan Co., 1956. December 1983, pp. 611–630.

Narayan, R.K. *The Mahabharata: A Shortened Modern Prose Version of the Indian Epic*. Viking Press. 1978.

Nehru, Jawaharlal. *Toward Freedom*. New York: John Day Company, 1941.

Roosevelt, Eleanor. *India and the Awakening East,* New York: Harper and Brothers, 1953.

The Bhagavad Gita As It Is. Macmillan. 1972.

The Bhagavad Gita Explained, with a Literal Translation from the Original Sanskrit. The American Academy of Asian Studies Graduate School. 1961 [c1954].

The Bhagavad Gita or The Lord's Song. Theosophical Publishing House. 1953.

from the Kena-Upanishad

*Translated by Shree Purohit Swami
and William Butler Yeats*

At Whose Command?

1

Speech, eyes, ears, limbs, life, energy, come to my help. These books have Spirit for theme. I shall never deny Spirit, nor Spirit deny me. Let me be in union, communion with Spirit. When I am one with Spirit, may the laws these books proclaim live in me, may the laws live.

The enquirer asked: "What has called my mind to the hunt? What has made my life begin? What wags in my tongue? What God has opened eye and ear?"

The teacher answered: "It lives in all that lives, hearing through the ear, thinking through the mind, speaking through the tongue, seeing through the eye. The wise man clings neither to this nor that, rises out of sense, attains immortal life.

"Eye, tongue, cannot approach it nor mind know; not knowing, we cannot satisfy enquiry. It lies beyond the known, beyond the unknown. We know through those who have preached it, have learnt it from tradition.

"That which makes the tongue speak, but needs no tongue to explain, that alone is Spirit; not what sets the world by the ears.

"That which makes the mind think, but needs no mind to think, that alone is Spirit; not what sets the world by the ears.

"That which makes the eye see, but needs no eye to see, that alone is Spirit; not what sets the world by the ears.

"That which makes the ear hear, but needs no ear to hear, that alone is Spirit; not what sets the world by the ears.

"That which makes life live, but needs no life to live, that alone is Spirit; not what sets the world by the ears."

2

"If you think that you know much, you know little. If you think that you know It from study of your own mind or of nature, study again."

The enquirer said: "I do not think that I know much, I neither say that I know, nor say that I do not."

The teacher answered: "The man who claims that he knows, knows nothing; but he who claims nothing, knows.

"Who says that Spirit is not known, knows; who claims that he knows, knows nothing. The ignorant think that Spirit lies within knowledge, the wise man knows It beyond knowledge.

"Spirit is known through revelation. It leads to freedom. It leads to power. Revelation is the conquest of death.

"The living man who finds Spirit, finds Truth. But if he fails, he sinks among fouler shapes. The man who can see the same Spirit in every creature, clings neither to this nor that, attains immortal life."

3

Once upon a time, Spirit planned that the gods might win a great victory. The gods grew boastful; though Spirit had planned their victory, they thought they had done it all.

Spirit saw their vanity and appeared. They could not understand; they said: "Who is that mysterious Person?"

They said to Fire: "Fire! Find out who is that mysterious Person."

Fire ran to Spirit. Spirit asked what it was. Fire said: "I am Fire; known to all."

Spirit asked: "What can you do?" Fire said: "I can burn anything and everything in this world."

"Burn it," said Spirit, putting a straw on the ground. Fire threw itself upon the straw, but could not burn it. Then Fire ran to the gods in a hurry and confessed it could not find out who was that mysterious Person.

Then the gods asked Wind to find out who was that mysterious Person.

Wind ran to Spirit and Spirit asked what it was, Wind said: "I am Wind; I am the King of the Air."

Spirit asked: "What can you do?" and Wind said: "I can blow away anything and everything in this world."

"Blow it away," said Spirit, putting a straw on the ground. Wind threw itself upon the straw, but could not move it. Then Wind ran to the gods in a hurry and confessed it could not find out who was that mysterious Person.

Then the gods went to Light and asked it to find out who was that mysterious Person. Light ran towards Spirit, but Spirit disappeared upon the instant.

There appeared in the sky that pretty girl, the Goddess of Wisdom, snowy Himalaya's daughter. Light went to her and asked who was the mysterious Person.

4

The Goddess said: "Spirit, through Spirit you attained your greatness. Praise the greatness of Spirit." Then Light knew that the mysterious Person was none but Spirit.

That is how these gods—Fire, Wind, and Light—attained supremacy; they came nearest to Spirit and were the first to call that Person Spirit.

Light stands above Fire and Wind; because closer than they, it was the first to call that Person Spirit.

This is the moral of the tale. In the lightning, in the light of an eye, the light belongs to Spirit

The power of the mind when it remembers and desires, when it thinks again and again, belongs to Spirit. Therefore let Mind meditate on Spirit.

Spirit is the good in all. It should be worshipped as the Good. He that knows it as the Good is esteemed by all.

You asked me about spiritual knowledge, I have explained it.

Austerity, self-control, meditation are the foundation of this knowledge; the Vedas are its house, truth its shrine.

He who knows this shall prevail against all evil, enjoy the Kingdom of Heaven, yes, for ever enjoy the blessed Kingdom of Heaven.

from The Mahabharata

Translated by Shri Purohit Swami

from The Bhagavad Gita

Then beholding [the two armies,] drawn up on the battlefield, ready to begin the fight. . . . Arjuna noticed fathers, grandfathers, uncles, cousins, sons, grandson, teachers, friends;

Fathers-in-law and benefactors, arrayed on both sides. Arjuna then gazed at all those kinsmen before him.

And his heart melted with pity and sadly he spoke: "O my Lord! When I see all these, my own people, thirsting for battle,

My limbs fail me and my throat is parched, my body trembles and my hair stands on end.

The bow Gandeeva slips from my hand, and my skin burns. I cannot keep quiet, for my mind is in a tumult.

The omens are adverse; what good can come from the slaughter of my people on this battlefield?

Ah, my Lord! I crave not for victory, nor for kingdom, nor for any pleasure. What were a kingdom or happiness or life to me,

When those for whose sake I desire these things stand here about to sacrifice their property and their lives. . . .

Although these men, blinded by greed, see no guilt in destroying their kin, or fighting against their friends,

Should not we, whose eyes are open, who consider it to be wrong to annihilate our house, turn away from so great a crime? . . .

If, on the contrary, [my enemies,] with weapons in their hands, should slay me, unarmed and unresisting, surely that would be better for my welfare!"

. . .

Thereupon the Lord, with a gracious smile, addressed him who was so much depressed in the midst between the two armies.

Lord Shri Krishna said: "Why grieve for those for whom no grief is due, and yet profess wisdom. The wise grieve neither for the dead nor for the living.

There was never a time when I was not, nor thou, nor these princes were not; there will never be a time when we shall cease to be.

As the soul experiences in this body, infancy, youth and old age, so finally it passes into another. The wise have no delusion about this.

Those external relations which bring cold and heat, pain and happiness, they come and go; they are not permanent. Endure them bravely, O Prince!

The hero whose sole is unmoved by circumstance, who accepts pleasure and pain with equanimity, only he is fit for immortality.

That which is not, shall never be; that which is, shall never cease to be. . . .

He who knows the Spirit as Indestructible, Immortal, Unborn, Always-the-Same, how should he kill or cause to be killed?

As a man discards his threadbare robes and puts on new, so the Spirit throws off Its worn-out bodies and takes fresh ones. . . .

Even if thou thinkest of It as constantly being born, constantly dying; even then, O Mighty Man! thou still hast no cause to grieve.

The Gita. From *The Geeta,* translated by Shri Purohit Swami. Reprinted by permission of Faber and Faber Limited.

For death is as sure for that which is born, as birth is for that which is dead. Therefore grieve not for what is inevitable.

The end and beginning of beings are unknown. We see only the intervening formations. Then what cause is there for grief? . . .

Thou must look at thy duty. Nothing can be more welcome to a soldier than a righteous war. Therefore to waver in thy resolve is unworthy, O Arjuna!

Blessed are the soldiers who find their opportunity. This opportunity has opened for thee the gates of heaven. . . .

If killed, thou shalt attain Heaven; if victorious, enjoy the kingdom of earth. Therefore arise, and fight.

Look upon pleasure and pain, victory and defeat, with an equal eye. Make ready for the combat, and thou shalt commit no sin.

I have told thee the philosophy of Knowledge. Now listen! and I will explain the philosophy of Action, by means of which, O Arjuna, thou shalt break through the bondage of all action. . . .

Thou hast only the right to work; but none to the fruit thereof. Let not then the fruit of thy action be thy motive; nor yet be thou enamored of inaction.

Perform all thy actions with mind concentrated on the Divine, renouncing attachment and looking upon success and failure with an equal eye. . . .

Physical action is far inferior to an intellect concentrated on the Divine. Have recourse then to the Pure Intelligence. It is only the petty-minded who work for reward.

When a man attains to Pure Reason, he renounces in this world the results of good and evil alike. Cling thou to Right Action. Spirituality is the real art of living.

The sages guided by Pure Intellect renounce the fruit of action; and, freed from the chains of rebirth, they reach the highest bliss. . . .

No man can attain freedom from activity by refraining from action; nor can he reach perfection by merely refusing to act. . . .

Do thy duty as prescribed; for action for duty's sake is superior to inaction. Even the maintenance of the body would be impossible if man remained inactive.

In this world people are fettered by action, unless it is performed as a sacrifice. Therefore, O Arjuna! let thy acts be done without attachment, as sacrifice only. . . .

There is nothing in this universe, O Arjuna! that I am compelled to do; nor anything for Me to attain; yet I am persistently active.

For were I not to act without ceasing, O Prince! people would be glad to do likewise.

And if I were to refrain from action, the human race would be ruined; I should lead the world to chaos, and destruction would follow. . . .

The four divisions of society (the wise, the soldier, the merchant, the laborer) were created by Me, according to the natural distribution of Qualities and instincts. I am the author of them. . . .

In the light of this wisdom, our ancestors, who sought deliverance, performed their acts. Act thou also, as did our fathers of old. . . .

What is action and what is inaction? . . .

He who can see inaction in action, and action in inaction, is the wisest among men. . . .

Having surrendered all claim to the results of his actions, always contented and independent, in reality he does nothing, even though he is apparently acting.

Expecting nothing, his mind and personality controlled, without greed, doing bodily actions only; though he acts, yet he remains untainted.

Content with what comes to him without effort of his own, mounting above the pairs of opposites, free from envy, his mind balanced both in success and in failure, though he act, yet the consequences do not bind him.

He who is without attachment, free, his mind centered in wisdom, his actions, being done as a sacrifice, leave no trace behind. . . .

He who knows and lives in the Absolute remains unmoved and unperturbed; he is not elated by pleasure, or depressed by pain.

He finds happiness in his own Self, and enjoys eternal bliss, whose heart does not yearn for the contacts of earth, and whose Self is one with the Everlasting.

He who is happy within his Self, and has found Its peace, and in whom the inner light shines, that sage attains Eternal Bliss and becomes the Spirit Itself. . . .

Therefore, surrendering thy actions unto Me, thy thoughts concentrated on the Absolute, free from selfishness and without anticipation of reward, with mind devoid of excitement, begin thou to fight."

from The Mahabharata

Translated by Romesh C. Dutt

The Tale of Savitri

I. INTRODUCTION

In the country of fair Madra lived a king in days of old,

Faithful to the holy Brahma, pure in heart and righteous-souled,

He was loved in town and country, in the court and hermit's den,
Sacrificer to the bright gods, helper to his brother men,

But the monarch, Aswapati, son or daughter had he none,
Old in years and sunk in anguish, and his days were almost done!

Vows he took and holy penance, and with pious rules conformed,
Spare in diet as *brahmachari*[1] many sacred rites performed,

Sang the sacred hymn, *savitri*, to the gods oblations gave,
Through the lifelong day he fasted, uncomplaining, meek and brave!

Year by year he gathered virtue, rose in merit and in might,
Till the goddess of *savitri* smiled upon his sacred rite,

From the fire upon the altar which a holy radiance flung,
In the form of beauteous maiden, goddess of *savitri* sprung!

And she spake in gentle accents, blessed the monarch good and brave,
Blessed his rites and holy penance and a boon unto him gave:

"Penance and thy sacrifices can the Powers Immortal move,
And the pureness of thy conduct doth thy heart's affection prove,

Ask thy boon, king Aswapati, from creation's Ancient Sire,
True to virtue's sacred mandate speak thy inmost heart's desire."

403

"For an offspring brave and kingly," so the saintly king replied,
"Holy rites and sacrifices and this penance I have tried,

If these rite and sacrifices move thy favour and thy grace,
Grant me offspring, Prayer-Maiden, worthy of my noble race."

"Have thy object," spake the maiden, "Madra's pious-hearted king,
From Swaymbhu, Self-created blessings onto thee I bring,

For He lists to mortal's prayer springing from a heart like thine,
And He wills,—a noble daughter grace thy famed and royal line,

Aswapati, glad and grateful, take the blessing which I bring,
Part in joy and part in silence, bow unto Creation's King!"

Vanished then the Prayer-Maiden, and the king of noble fame,
Aswapati, Lord of coursers, to his royal city came,

Days of hope and nights of gladness Madra's happy monarch passed,
Till his queen of noble offspring gladsome promise gave at last!

As the moon each night increaseth chasing darksome nightly gloom,
Grew the unborn babe in splendour in its happy mother's womb,

And in fullness of the season came a girl with lotus-eye,
Father's hope and joy of mother, gift of kindly gods on high!

And the king performed its birth-rites with a glad and grateful mind,
And the people blessed the dear one with their wishes good and kind,

As *Savitri*, Prayer-Maiden, had the beauteous offspring given,
Brahmans named the child *Savitri*, holy gift of bounteous Heaven!

Grew the child in brighter beauty like a goddess from above,
And each passing season added fresher sweetness deeper love,

Came with youth its lovelier graces, as the buds their leaves unfold,
Slender waist and rounded bosom, image as of burnished gold,

Deva-Kanya! born a goddess, so they said in all the land,
Princely suitors struck with splendour ventured not to seek her hand.

Once upon a time it happened on a bright and festive day,
Fresh from bath the beauteous maiden to the altar came to pray,

And with cakes and pure libations duly fed the Sacred Flame,
Then like Sri[2] in heavenly radiance to her royal father came.

And she bowed to him in silence, sacred flowers beside him laid,
And her hands she folded meekly, sweetly her obeisance made,

With a father's pride, upon her gazed the ruler of the land,
But a strain of sadness lingered, for no suitor claimed her hand.

"Daughter," whispered Aswapati, "Now, methinks, the time is come,
Thou shouldst choose a princely suitor, grace a royal husband's home,

Choose thyself a noble husband worthy of thy noble hand,
Choose a true and upright monarch, pride and glory of his land,

As thou choosest, gentle daughter, in thy loving heart's desire,
Blessing and his free permission will bestow thy happy sire.

For our sacred *sastras*[3] sanction, holy Brahmans oft relate,
That the duty-loving father sees his girl in wedded state,

That the duty-loving husband watches o'er his consort's ways,
That the duty-loving offspring tends his mother's widowed days,

Therefore choose a loving husband, daughter of my house and love,
So thy father earn no censure or from men or gods bove."

Fair Savitri bowed unto him and for parting blessings prayed,
Then she left her father's palace and in distant regions strayed,

With her guard and aged courtiers whom her watchful father sent,
Mounted on her golden chariot unto sylvan woodlands went.

Far in pleasant woods and jungle wandered she from day to day,
Unto *asrams*, hermitages, pious-hearted held her way,

Oft she stayed in holy *tirthas*[4] washed by sacred limpid streams,
Food she gave unto the hungry, wealth beyond their fondest dreams.

Many days and months are over, and it once did so befall,
When the king and *rishi*[5] Narad sat within the royal hall,

From her journeys near and distant and from places known to fame,
Fair Savitri with courtiers to her father's palace came,

Came and saw her royal father, *rishi* Narad by his seat,
Bent her head in salutation, bowed unto their holy feet.

II. THE FATED BRIDEGROOM

"Whence comes she," so Narad questioned, "whither was Savitri led,
Wherefore to a happy husband hath Savitri not been wed?"

"Nay, to choose her lord and husband," so the virtuous monarch said,
"Fair Savitri long hath wandered and in holy *tirthas* stayed,

Maiden! speak unto the *rishi,* and thy choice and secret tell,"
Then a blush suffused her forehead, soft and slow her accents fell!

"Listen, father! Salwa's monarch was of old a king of might,
Righteous-hearted Dyumat-sena, feeble now and void of sight,

Foemen robbed him of his kingdom when in age he lost his sight,
And from town and spacious empire was the monarch forced to flight,

With his queen and with his infant did the feeble monarch stray,
And the jungle was his palace, darksome was his weary way,

Holy vows assumed the monarch and in penance passed his life,
In the wild woods nursed his infant and with wild fruits fed his wife,

Years have gone in rigid penance, and that child is now a youth,
Him I choose my lord and husband, Satyavan, the Soul of Truth!"

Thoughtful was the *rishi* Narad, doleful were the words he said:
"Sad disaster waits Savitri if this royal youth she wed,

Truth-beloving is her father, truthful is the royal dame,
Truth and virtue rule his actions, Satyavan his sacred name,

Steeds he loved in days of boyhood and to paint them was his joy,
Hence they called him young Chitraswa, art-beloving gallant boy,

But O pious-hearted monarch! fair Savitri hath in sooth
Courted Fate and sad disaster in that noble gallant youth!"

"Tell me," questioned Aswapati, "for I may not guess thy thought,
Wherefore is my daughter's action with a sad disaster fraught,

Is the youth of noble lustre, gifted in the gifts of art,
Blest with wisdom and with prowess, patient in his dauntless heart?"

"Surya's lustre in his shineth," so the *rishi* Narad said,
"Brihaspati's wisdom dwelleth in the youthful prince's head,

Like Mahendra in his prowess, and in patience like the Earth,
Yet O king! sad disaster marks the gentle youth from birth!"

"Tell me, rishi, then, thy reason," so anxious monarch cried,
"Why to youth so great and gifted may this maid be not allied,

Is he princely in his bounty, gentle-hearted in his grace,
Duly versed in sacred knowledge, fair in mind and fair in face?"

"Free in gifts like Rantideva," so the holy *rishi* said,
"Versed in lore like monarch Sivi who all ancient monarchs led,

Like Yayati open-hearted and like Chandra in his grace,
Like the handsome heavenly Asvins fair and radiant in his face,

Meek and graced with patient virtue he controls his noble mind,
Modest in his kindly actions, true to friends and ever kind,

And the hermits of the forest praise him for his righteous truth,
Nathless, king, thy daughter may not wed this noble-hearted youth!"

"Tell me, *rishi*," said the monarch, "for thy sense from me is hid,
Has this prince some fatal blemish, wherefore is this match forbid?"

"Fatal fault!" exclaimed the *rishi*, "fault that wipeth all his grace,
Fault that human power nor effort, rite nor penance can efface,

Fatal fault or destined sorrow! for it is decreed on high,
On this day, a twelve-month later, this ill-fated prince will die!"

Shook the startled king in terror and in fear and trembling cried:
"Unto short-lived, fated bridegroom ne'er my child shall be allied,

Come, Savitri, dear-loved maiden, choose another happier lord,
Rishi Narad speaketh wisdom, list unto his holy word!

Every grace and every virtue is effaced by cruel Fate,
On this day, a twelve-month later, leaves the prince his mortal state!"

"Father!" answered thus the maiden, soft and sad her accents fell,
"I have heard thy honoured mandate, holy Narad counsels well,

Pardon witless maiden's fancy, but beneath the eye of Heaven,
Only once a maiden chooseth, twice her troth may not be given,

Long his life or be it narrow, and his virtues great or none,
Satyavan is still my husband, he my heart and troth hath won,

What a maiden's heart hath chosen that a maiden's lips confess,
True to him thy poor Savitri goes into the wilderness!"

"Monarch!" uttered then the *rishi*, "fixed is she in mind and heart,
From her troth the true Savitri never, never will depart,

More than mortal's share of virtue unto Satyavan is given,
Let the true maid wed her chosen, leave the rest to gracious Heaven!"

"*Rishi* and preceptor holy!" so the weeping monarch prayed,
"Heaven avert all future evils, and thy mandate is obeyed!"

Narad wished him joy and gladness, blessed the loving youth and maid,
Forest hermits on their wedding every fervent blessing laid.

III. OVERTAKEN BY FATE

Twelve-month in the darksome forest by her true and chosen lord,
Sweet Savitri served his parents by her thought and deed and word,

Bark of tree supplied her garments draped upon her bosom fair,
Or the red cloth as in *asrams* holy women love to wear.

And the aged queen she tended with a fond and filial pride,
Served the old and sightless monarch like a daughter by his side,

And with love and gentle sweetness pleased her husband and her lord,
But in secret, night and morning, pondered still on Narad's word!

Nearer came the fatal morning by the holy Narad told,
Fair Savitri reckoned daily and her heart was still and cold,

Three short days remaining only! and she took a vow severe
Of *triratra*, three nights' penance, holy fasts and vigils drear.

Of Savitri's rigid penance heard the king with anxious woe,
Spake to her in loving accents, so the vow she might forgo:

"Hard the penance, gentle daughter, and thy woman's limbs are frail,
After three nights' fasts and vigils sure thy tender health may fail,"

"Be not anxious, loving father," meekly this Savitri prayed,
"Penance I have undertaken, will unto the gods be made."

Much misdoubting then the monarch gave his sad and slow assent,
Pale with fast and unseen tear-drops, lonesome nights Savitri spent.

Nearer came the fatal morning, and to-morrow he shall die,
Dark, lone hours of nightly silence! Tearless, sleepless is her eye!

"Dawns that dread and fated morning!" said Savitri, bloodless, brave,
Prayed her fervent prayers in silence, to the Fire oblations gave,

Bowed unto the forest Brahmans, to the parents kind and good,
Joined her hands in salutation and in reverent silence stood.

With the usual morning blessing, "Widow may'st thou never be,"
Anchorites and aged Brahmans blessed Savitri fervently,

O! that blessing fell upon her like the rain on thirsty air,
Struggling hope inspired her bosom as she drank those accents fair,

But returned the dark remembrance of the *rishi* Narad's word,
Pale she watched the creeping sunbeams, mused upon her fated lord!

"Daughter, now thy fast is over," so the loving parents said,
"Take thy diet after penance, for thy morning prayers are prayed,"

"Pardon, father," said Savitri, "let this other day be done,"
Unshed tear-drops filled her eyelids, glistened in the morning sun!

Satyavan, sedate and stately, ponderous axe on shoulder hung,
For the distant darksome jungle issued forth serene and strong,

But unto him came Savitri and in sweetest accents prayed,
As upon his manly bosom gently she her forehead laid:

"Long I wished to see the jungle where steals not the solar ray,
Take me to the darksome forest, husband, let me go to-day!"

"Come not, love," he sweetly answered with a loving husband's care,
"Thou art all unused to labour, forest paths thou may'st not dare

And with recent fasts and vigils pale and bloodless is thy face,
And thy steps are weak and feeble, jungle paths thou may'st not trace."

"Fasts and vigils make me stronger," said the wife with wifely pride,
"Toil I shall not feel nor languor when my lord is by my side,

For I feel a woman's longing with my lord to trace the way,
Grant me, husband ever gracious, with thee let me go to-day!"

Answered then the loving husband, as his hands in hers he wove,
"Ask permission from my parents in the trackless woods to rove,"

Then Savitri to the monarch urged her longing strange request,
After duteous salutation thus her humble prayer addrest.

"To the jungle goes my husband, fuel and the fruit to seek,
I would follow if my mother and my loving father speak,

Twelve-month from this narrow *asram* hath Savitri stepped nor strayed,
In this cottage true and faithful ever hath Savitri stayed,

For the sacrificial fuel wends my lord his lonesome way,
Please my kind and loving parent, I would follow him to-day."

"Never since her wedding morning," so the loving king replied,
"Wish or thought Savitri whispered, for a boon or object sighed,

Daughter, thy request is granted, safely in the forest roam,
Safely with thy lord and husband seek again thy cottage home."

Bowing to her loving parents did the fair Savitri part,
Smile upon her pallid features, anguish in her inmost heart,

Round her sylvan greenwoods blossomed 'neath a cloudless Indian sky,
Flocks of pea-fowls gorgeous plumaged flew before her wondering eye,

Woodland rills and crystal nullahs gently roll'd o'er rocky bed,
Flower-decked hills in dewy brightness towering glittered overhead,

Birds of song and beauteous feather trilled a note in every grove,
Sweeter accents fell upon her, from her husband's lips of love!

Still with thoughtful eye Savitri watched her dear and fated lord,
Flail of grief was in her bosom but her pale lips shaped no word,

And she listened to her husband still on anxious thought intent,
Cleft in two her throbbing bosom as in silence still she went!

Gaily with the gathered wild-fruits did the prince his basket fill,
Hewed the interlaced branches with his might and practised skill,

Till the drops stood on his forehead, weary was his aching head,
Faint he came unto Savitri and in faltering accents said:

"Cruel ache is on my forehead, fond and ever faithful wife,
And I feel a hundred needles pierce me and torment my life,

And my feeble footsteps falter and my senses seem to reel,
Fain would I beside thee linger for a sleep doth o'er me steal."

With a wild and speechless terror pale Savitri held her lord,
On her lap his head she rested as she laid him on the sward,

Narad's fatal words remembered as she watched her husband's head,
Burning lip and pallid forehead and the dark and creeping shade,

Clasped him in her beating bosom, kissed his lips with panting breath,
Darker grew the lonesome forest, and he slept the sleep of death!

IV. TRIUMPH OVER FATE

In the bosom of the shadows rose a Vision dark and dread,
Shape of gloom in inky garment and a crown was on his head,

Gleaming Form of sable splendour, blood-red was his sparkling eye,
And a fatal noose he carried, grim and godlike, dark and high!

And he stood in solemn silence, looked in silence on the dead,
And Savitri on the greensward gently placed her husband's head,

And a tremor shook Savitri, but a woman's love is strong,
With her hands upon her bosom thus she spake with quivering tongue:

"More than mortal is thy glory! If a radiant god thou be,
Tell me what bright name thou bearest, what thy message unto me."

"Know me," thus responded Yama, "mighty monarch of the dead,
Mortals leaving earthly mansion to my darksome realm are led,

Since with woman's full affection thou hast loved thy husband dear,
Hence before thee, faithful woman, Yama doth in form appear,

But his days and loves are ended, and he leaves his faithful wife,
In this noose I bind and carry spark of his immortal life,

Virtue graced his life and action, spotless was his princely heart,
Hence for him I came in person, princess, let thy husband part."

Yama from the prince's body, pale and bloodless, cold and dumb,
Drew the vital spark, *purusha*, smaller than the human thumb,

In his noose the spark he fastened, silent went his darksome way,
Left the body shorn of lustre to its rigid cold decay,

Southward went the dark-hued Yama with the youth's immortal life,
And, for woman's love abideth, followed still the faithful wife.

"Turn, Savitri," outspoke Yama, "for thy husband loved and lost,
Do the rites due unto mortals by their Fate predestined crost,

For thy wifely duty ceases, follow not in fruitless woe,
And no farther living creature may with monarch Yama go!"

"But I may not chose but follow where thou takest my husband's life,
For Eternal Law divides not loving man and faithful wife,

For a woman's true affection, for a woman's sacred woe,
Grant me in thy godlike mercy farther still with him I go!

Fourfold are our human duties: first to study holy lore,
Then to live as good householders, feed the hungry at our door,

Then to pass our days in penance, last to fix our thoughts above,
But the final goal of virtue, it is Truth and deathless Love!"

"True and holy are thy precepts," listening Yama made reply,
"And they fill my heart with gladness and with pious purpose high,

I would bless thee, fair Savitri, but the dead come not to life,
Ask for other boon and blessing, faithful, true and virtuous wife!"

"Since you so permit me, Yama," so the good Savitri said,
"For my husband's banished father let my dearest suit be made,

Sightless in the darksome forest dwells the monarch faint and weak,
Grant him sight and grant him vigour, Yama, in thy mercy speak!"

"Duteous daughter," Yama answered, "be thy pious wishes given,
And his eyes shall be restored to the cheerful light of heaven,

Turn, Savitri, faint and weary, follow not in fruitless woe,
And no farther living creature may with monarch Yama go!"

"Faint nor weary is Savitri," so the noble princess said,
"Since she waits upon her husband, gracious Monarch of the dead,

What befalls the wedded husband still befalls the faithful wife,
Where he leads she ever follows, be it death or be it life!

And our sacred writ ordaineth and our pious *rishis* sing,
Transient meeting with the holy doth its countless blessings bring,

Longer friendship with the holy purifies the mortal birth,
Lasting union with the holy is the bright sky on the earth,

Union with the pure and holy is immortal heavenly life,
For Eternal Law divides not loving man and faithful wife!"

"Blessed are thy words," said Yama, "blessed is thy pious thought,
With a higher purer wisdom are thy holy lessons fraught,

I would bless thee, fair Savitri, but the dead come not to life,
Ask for other boon and blessing, faithful, true and virtuous wife!"

"Since you so permit me, Yama, "so the good Savitri said,
"Once more for my husband's father be my supplication made,

Lost his kingdom, in the forest dwells the monarch faint and weak,
Grant him back his wealth and kingdom, Yama, in thy mercy speak!"

"Loving daughter," Yama answered, "wealth and kingdom I bestow,
Turn, Savitri, living mortal may not with King Yama go!"

Still Savitri, meek and faithful, followed her departed lord,
Yama still with higher wisdom listened to her saintly word,

And the Sable King was vanquished, and he turned on her again,
And his words fell on Savitri like the cooling summer rain,

"Noble woman, speak thy wishes, name thy boon and purpose high,
What the pious mortal asketh gods in heaven may not deny!"

"Thou hast," so Savitri answered, "granted father's realm and might,
To his vain and sightless eyeballs has restored their blessed sight,

Grant him that the line of monarchs may not all untimely end,
Satyavan may see his kingdom to his royal sons descend!"

"Have thy object," answered Yama, "and thy lord shall live again,
He shall live to be a father, and his children too shall reign,

For a woman's troth abideth longer than the fleeting breath,
And a woman's love abideth higher than the doom of Death!"

V. RETURN HOME

Vanished then the Sable Monarch, and Savitri held her way
Where in dense and darksome forest still her husband lifeless lay,

And she sat upon the greensward by the cold unconscious dead,
On her lap with deeper kindness placed her consort's lifeless head,

And that touch of true affection thrilled him back to waking life,
As returned from distant regions gazed the prince upon his wife,

"Have I lain too long and slumbered, sweet Savitri, faithful spouse,
But I dreamt a Sable Person took me in a fatal noose!"

"Pillowed on this lap," she answered, "long upon the earth you lay,
And the Sable Person, husband, he hath come and passed away,

Rise and leave this darksome forest if thou feelest light and strong,
For the night is on the jungle and our way is dark and long."

Rising as from happy slumber looked the young prince on all around,
Saw the wide-extending jungle mantling all the darksome ground,

"Yes," he said, "I now remember, ever loving faithful dame,
We in search of fruit and fuel to this lonesome forest came,

As I hewed the gnarled branches, cruel anguish filled my brain,
And I laid me on the greensward with a throbbing piercing pain,

Pillowed on thy gentle bosom, solaced by thy gentle love,
I was soothed, and drowsy slumber fell on me from skies above.

All was dark and then I witnessed, was it but a fleeting dream,
God or Vision, dark and dreadful, in the deepening shadows gleam,

Was this dream my fair Savitri, dost thou of this Vision know,
Tell me, for before my eyesight still the Vision seems to glow!"

"Darkness thickens," said Savitri, "and the evening waxeth late,
When the morrow's light returneth I shall all these scenes narrate,

Now arise, for darkness gathers, deeper grows the gloomy night,
And thy loving anxious parents trembling wait thy welcome sight,

Hark the rangers of the forest! how their voices strike the ear,
Prowlers of the darksome jungle! how they fill my breast with fear!

Forest-fire is raging yonder, for I see a distant gleam,
And the rising evening breezes help the red and radiant beam,

Let me fetch a burning faggot and prepare a friendly light,
With these fallen withered branches chase the shadows of the night,

And if feeble still thy footsteps,—long and weary is our way,—
By the fire repose, my husband, and return by light of day."

"For my parents, fondly anxious," Satyavan thus made reply,
"Pains my heart and yearns my bosom, let us to their cottage hie,

When I tarried in the jungle or by day or dewy eve,
Searching in the hermitages often did my parents grieve,

And with father's soft reproaches and with mother's loving fears,
Chid me for my tardy footsteps, dewed me with their gentle tears,

Think then of my father's sorrow, of my mother's woeful plight
If afar in wood and jungle pass we now the livelong night,

Wife beloved, I may not fathom what mishap or load of care,
Unknown dangers, unseen sorrows, even now my parents share!"

Gentle drops of filial sorrow trickled down his manly eye,
Fond Savitri sweetly speaking softly wiped the teardrops dry:

"Trust me, husband, if Savitri hath been faithful in her love,
If she hath with pious offerings served the righteous gods above,

If she hath a sister's kindness unto brother men performed,
If she hath in speech and action unto holy truth conformed,

Unknown blessings, mighty gladness, trust thy ever faithful wife,
And not sorrows or disasters wait this eve our parents' life!"

Then she rose and tied her tresses, gently helped her lord to rise,
Walked with him the pathless jungle, looked with love into his eyes,

On her neck his clasping left arm sweetly winds in soft embrace,
Round his waist Savitri's right arm doth as sweetly interlace,

Thus they walked the darksome jungle, silent stars looked from above,
And the hushed and throbbing midnight watched Savitri's deathless love.

ENDNOTES

1. *brahmachari,* those who have taken holy vows.
2. Sri, goddess of beauty and wealth.
3. *sastras,* scriptures.
4. *tirthas,* shrines.
5. *rishi,* holy man.

—————— *Questions for Consideration* ——————

Using complete sentences, provide brief answers for the following questions.

1. In the *Kena-Upanishad,* many questions are raised, but few are discussed at length. Extend the philosophic questions raised by the pupil in Sections 2, 3, and 4. Condemn or defend.

    _____

    _____

    _____

    _____

    _____

2. In the "Gita," Arjuna, although a brave warrior, has certain misgivings about going into battle. What is the basis of his misgivings, and how is he finally made to understand his duty as a warrior and as a good Hindu?

    _____

    _____

    _____

    _____

    _____

3. Explain Savitri's philosophy of "Action," and compare it to the "Inaction" of the Hindu.

    _____

    _____

    _____

    _____

    _____

Writing Critically

Select one of the essay topics listed below and compose a 500 word essay which discusses the topic fully. Support your thesis with evidence from the text and with critical and/or historical material. Use the space below for planning to write the essay (prewriting).

1. Describe the caste system and explain its place in modern day Indian society.

2. Discuss the "Tale of Savitri" as an expression of Hindu mythology.

3. Trace the changes in the status of Indian women from ancient times to the present.

4. Support or refute the theory that India's "spirituality" is a hindrance to its social advancement .

Prewriting Space:

_____

_____

_____

_____

_____

_____

_____

_____

_____

_____

_____

_____

_____

_____

_____

_____

_____

_____

_____

_____

Introduction

Válmíki: The Rámáyana (circa 550 B.C.)

Perhaps the most popular literary work produced by ancient India is the *Rámáyana*. It originated as oral literature that, like the Homeric epics of Greece, no doubt underwent numerous modifications before it assumed its final form. While the date of composition of the *Rámáyana* has often been debated, some of the material relating to its hero, Prince Ráma, was already circulating during the seventh century B.C. Its supposed author, Válmíki, is at least partly a legendary figure who probably added little that was entirely new to the poem. In all likelihood, he reworked and consolidated a large amount of pre-existing oral material. The many repeated, formulaic phrases in the epic help identify it as oral literature. The *Rámáyana* (translation: "the way of Ráma") was composed in Sanskrit, the literary language of ancient India. Complicated and highly inflected, Sanskrit is the oldest member of the Indo-European family of languages, the same language group to which Greek, Latin, and English belong. Not only is Válmíki credited with having created the *Rámáyana*, he is also supposed to have invented the śloka, the special Sanskrit couplet used in the epic. (The śloka in fact predates the *Rámáyana*.) The shadowy, legendary author and the oral legacy, as well as the mythological dimensions of the poem, make this work analogous to the epic literature of ancient Greece.

Ráma, who is the main protagonist of the poem, enters the epic as heir to the throne of the kingdom of Kosala in the valley of the Ganges River in northern India. His father is King Dasaratha, and his mother is Kausalyá, the head wife of the king. No ordinary mortal, Ráma is an incarnation of the god Vishnu, the Hindu deity responsible for preserving *dharma*. *Dharma* is a basic but complex ethical force that maintains the integrity of the cosmos, human society, and the individual life. (The concept thus parallels the idea of the *Dao* in Chinese thought.) Ráma's goal is to kill Rávana, a ruler of evil spirits who plague the *dharma* or fundamental order of the world. Like heroes in a number of other epics and myths of various cultures, Ráma distinguishes himself by performing an extraordinary feat: he bends a magical bow and wins the hand of the beautiful princess Sítá. She is analogous to the ancient Greek figure Persephone, for Sítá's mother is the earth goddess.

There is a major difference, however, between this Indian epic and the heroic literature of classical Greece. Ráma values principle above all. In his dedication to abstract moral values, he resembles somewhat more closely "pious Aeneas" of ancient Rome than the passionate heroes and heroines of ancient Greece. In many cases, much of the interest generated by the characters of Greek myth lies in the keen fervor with which they are devoted to a cause.

The plot becomes complicated when Ráma is disinherited. His father, King Daśaratha, desires to place Ráma on the throne, but Kaikeyí, a secondary wife of the king, manages to thwart his wishes, and her own son, Bharata, assumes the kingship. Ráma withdraws into a fourteen-year exile, accompanied by his virtuous and beautiful wife, Sítá. In exile, Ráma busies himself with fighting Rávana and the evil demons. Though suffering major setbacks at first, the malicious Rávana manages to abduct the shapely Queen Sítá. Ráma heads to southern India, looking for his wife, and he arrives in a land of friendly monkeys who desire to assist in the search. Especially helpful is the astonishing Hanumán, son of the wind god. After a series of fabulous adventures, Hanumán discovers Sítá's whereabouts. Ráma eventually recovers his wife and slays the nefarious King Rávana.

The *Rámáyana* is more than an outstanding and engaging work of world literature. It is a core cultural narrative for Indian civilization. The epic has remained popular and influential for over two millennia, not just in India but in other areas of southeast Asia, such as Indonesia, wherever Indian culture has reached. The characters and adventures of Ráma, Hanumán, and others have been depicted in a wide array of art forms ranging from painting to puppet theater to comic books.

The passages printed here, drawn from Books IV and V of the *Rámáyana*, are concerned with Sítá's captivity and the monkey Hanumán's rescue mission. As this selection begins, the Vánars (monkeys) and vultures (Ráma's allies) are dismayed over Sítá's abduction. Sampáti, a noble vulture, is distraught over the death of his brother, Jatáyus, who died fighting against Rávana while the king of demons was in the act of abducting Sítá. (NW)

BIBLIOGRAPHY

Alles, Gregory D. *The Iliad, the Ramayana, and the Work of Religion: Failed Persuasion and Religious Mystification.* University Park: Pennsylvania State University Press, 1994.

Blank, Jonah. *Arrow of the Blue-Skinned God: Retracing the Ramayana through India.* New York: Touchstone, 1994.

Griffith, Ralph T. H., trans. *The Rámáyan of Válmíki.* 5 vols. Benares: E. J. Lazarus, 1870–74.

Ludvik, Catherine. *Hanuman in the Ramayana of Valmiki and the Ramacaritamanasa of Tulasi Dasa.* Delhi: Motilal Banarsidass, 1994.

Parkhill, Thomas. *The Forest Setting in Hindu Epics: Princes, Sages, Demons.* Lewiston: Mellen, 1995.

THE RAMAYANA: A GLOSSARY OF NAMES

Note on Pronunciation: The accent marks in many of the proper names in the *Rámáyana* may baffle readers who are new to classical Indian literature. Some basic guidelines are as follows:
1. An "á" has an "ah" sound like the "a" in "father" or "shah"; an unaccented "a" is pronounced like the "u" sound in "book."
2. The "í" and "i" are virtually the same; both are pronouced like the "e" sound in "feet" or "wheat."
3. The "ś" is pronounced as "sh."
4. The "." mark under some letters can be disregarded.

Angad: prince of the monkeys

Apsaras: a kind of nymph living in paradise

Aśoka: a flowering tree native to tropical sections of Asia. The reddish flowers often adorn religious sites.

Báli: Angad's father

Brahmá: the creator of the world in Hindu belief

Dandaks: Dandaka Forest, a huge jungle controlled by Rávan and his demons

Daśaratha: Ráma's father

Gandharvas: heavenly singers and other musicians who provide music at the banquets of the gods. They also belong to the court of Indra and fight in his battles.

Garud: Garuda, the king of birds

Hanumán: a monkey with supernatural powers, son of the wind god

Ikshváku: the dynastic line to which Ráma belongs

Indra: god of rain and ruler of heaven

Jámbaván: the bear king

Janak: Sítá's father

Jatáyus: king of the vultures. He dies trying to save Sítá from abduction by Rávan.

Kailása: a mountain in the Himalayas with mythological associations

Kausalyá: Ráma's mother

Krita: the first of the mythological ages of the world, a "golden" age. (Compare with Ovid.)

Kumbhakarna: one of Rávan's brothers

Lakshman: brother of Ráma

Lamba: a mountain

Lanká: an island paradise, ruled by Rávan

Mahendra: a mountain range

Maináka: a mountain, son of Himalaya, located beneath the sea

Maithil: pertaining to Mithilá, the city where Sítáis from

Matarisva: a name associated with Vayu, god of the wind and Hanumán's father

Nágas: serpent gods who dwell under the earth

Náráyan: "He who moved upon the waters"; one of the manifestations or identities of Vishnu.

Nisákar: the name of a hermit or holy man living in solitude

Punjikasthalá: the name of a certain Apsaras (nymph of paradise)

Raghu: an ancient king. His descendents became known as the Raghu clan. Ráma belongs to this clan, so the phrase "son of Raghu" here means Ráma.

Ráhu: a demon said to cause eclipses by attempting to swallow the sun and the moon

Rákshases: harmful spirits

Ráma: protagonist of the *Rámáyana*. He is also the god Vishnu in human form.

Rávan: Rávana, king of the Rakshases (malignant spirits)

Śachí: wife of Indra

Sampáti: a leader of the vultures and brother of Jatayus

Sinhiká: mother of Ráhu, the perpetrator of eclipses

Sítá: Ráma's wife and heroine of the *Rámáyana*

Sugríva: king of the monkeys

Sumitrá: Lakshman's mother

Supárśva: a noble vulture, son of Sampáti

Trijatá: a woman Rakshas or demon who is kind-hearted

Vánars: the nation of monkeys

Varun: the god of the sea

Vedas: the most ancient Hindu religious texts. They gave rise to a body of commentary or "branches" designed to aid in reading the Vedas and applying the principles they contained.

Videhan: pertaining to Videha, a region in eastern India that is Sítá's homeland

Vikatá: a demon who threatens Sítá

Vindhya: a mountain

Vishnu: one of the greatest of the Hindu gods, preserver of creation

Viśvakarmá: architect of the gods

Vivasvat: the sun god and father of Yama, the god of death

Vritra: demon of darkness and drought

Yama: god of death, thought to reside in the distant south

Hanumán

from The Rámáyana

Translated by Ralph T. H. Griffith

from Book IV
Canto LVI

SAMPÁTI

Then came the vultures' mighty king
Where sat the Vánars sorrowing,—
Sampáti, best of birds that fly
On sounding pinions through the sky,
Jatáyus' brother, famed of old,   5
Most glorious and strong and bold.
Upon the slope of Vindhya's hill
He saw the Vánars calm and still.
These words he uttered while the sight
Filled his fierce spirit with delight: 10
"Behold how Fate with changeless laws,
Within his toils the sinner draws,
And brings me, after long delay,
A rich and noble feast to-day,
These Vánars who are doomed to die   15
My hungry maw to satisfy."
He spoke no more: and Angad heard
The menace of the mighty bird;
And thus, while anguish filled his breast,
The noble Hanuman addressed   20
"Vivasvat's son has sought this place
For vengeance on the Vánar race.
See, Yama, wroth for Sítá's sake,
Is come our guilty lives to take.
Our king's decree is left undone,   25
And naught achieved for Raghu's son.
In duty have we failed, and hence
Comes punishment for dire offence.
Have we not heard the marvels wrought
By King Jatáyus, how he fought   30
With Rávan's might, and, nobly brave,
Perished, the Maithil queen to save?
There is no living creature, none,
But loves to die for Raghu's son,
And in long toils and dangers we   35

Have placed our lives in jeopardy,
Blest is Jatáyus, he who gave
His life the Maithil queen to save,
And proved his love for Ráma well
When by the giant's hand he fell. . . .   40
    He ceased: the feathered monarch heard,
His heart with ruth and wonder stirred:
"Whose is that voice," the vulture cried,
"That tells me how Jatáyus died,
And shakes my inmost soul with woe   45
For a loved brother's overthrow?
After long days at length I hear
The glorious name of one so dear.
Once more, O Vánar chieftains, tell
How King Jatáyus fought and fell.   50
But first your aid, I pray you, lend,
And from this peak will I descend.
The sun has burnt my wings, and I
No longer have the power to fly."

Canto LVII

ANGAD'S SPEECH

Though grief and woe his utterance broke,
They trusted not the words he spoke;
But, looking still for secret guile,
Reflected in their hearts a while
"If on our mangled limbs he feed,   5
We gain the death ourselves decreed."
    Then rose the Vánar chiefs, and lent
Their arms to aid the bird's descent
And Angad spake: . . .
"Brave Ráma, Daśaratha's heir,   10
A glorious prince beyond compare,
His sire and duty's law obeyed,
And sought the depths of Daṇḍaks' shade.
Sítá his well-beloved dame,
And Lakshman, with the wanderer came.   15
A giant watched his hour, and stole
The sweet delight of Ráma's soul.
Jatáyus, Daśaratha's friend,
Swift succour to the dame would lend.
Fierce Rávaṇ from his car he felled,   20
And for a time the prize withheld.
But bleeding, weak with years, and tired,
Beneath the demon's blows expired,
Due rites at Ráma's hands obtained,
And bliss that ne'er shall minish, gained.   25
Then Ráma with Sugríva made
A covenant for mutual aid . . .
Sugríva then, by Ráma's grace,

Was monarch of the Vánar race.
By his command a mighty host   30
Seeks Ráma's queen from coast to coast.
Sent forth by him, in every spot
We looked for her, but find her not.
Vain is the toil, as though by night
We sought to find the Day-God's light. . . .   35

Canto LVIII

TIDINGS OF SÍTÁ

The piteous tears his eye bedewed
As thus his speech the bird renewed:
"Alas my brother, slain in fight
By Rávan's unresisted might!
I, old and wingless, weak and worn,   5
O'er his sad fate can only mourn.
Fled is my youth: in life's decline
My former strength no more is mine.
Once on the day when Vritra died,
We brothers, in ambitious pride,   10
Sought, mounting with adventurous flight,
The Day-God garlanded with light.
On, ever on we urged our way
Where fields of ether round us lay,
Till, by the fervent heat assailed,   15
My brother's pinions flagged and failed.
I marked his sinking strength, and spread
My stronger wings to screen his head,
Till, all my feathers burnt away,
On Vindhya's hill I fell and lay.   20
There in my lone and helpless state
I heard not of my brother's fate."
    Thus King Sampáti spoke and sighed
And royal Angad thus replied:
"If, brother of Jatáyus, thou   25
Hast heard the tale I told but now,
Obedient to mine earnest prayer
The dwelling of that fiend declare.
O, say where cursed Rávan dwells,
Whom folly to his death impels."   30
    He ceased. Again Sampáti spoke,
And hope in every breast awoke:
"Though lost my wings, and strength decayed,
Yet shall my words lend Ráma aid. . . .
I saw the cruel Rávan bear   35
A gentle lady through the air.
Bright was her form, and fresh and young,
And sparkling gems about her hung.
"O Ráma, Ráma!" cried the dame,

And shrieked in terror Lakshman's name,   40
As, struggling in the giant's hold,
She dropped her gauds of gems and gold.
Like sun-light on a mountain shone
The silken garments she had on,
And glistened o'er his swarthy form   45
As lightning flashes through the storm.
That giant Rávan famed of old,
is brother of the Lord of Gold.
The southern ocean roars and swells
Round Lanká, where the robber dwells   50
In his fair city nobly planned
And built by Viśvakarmá's hand.
Within his bower securely barred,
With monsters round her for a guard,
Still in her silken vesture clad   55
Lies Sítá, and her heart is sad.
A hundred leagues your course must be
Beyond this margin of the sea.
Still to the south your way pursue,
And there the giant Rávan view.   60
Then up, O Vánars, and away!
For by my heavenly lore I say,
There will you see the lady's face,
And hither soon your steps retrace. . . .
Now from this spot my gazing eye   65
Can Rávan and the dame descry.
Devise some plan to overleap
This barrier of the briny deep.
Find the Videhan lady there,
And joyous to your home repair.   70
Me too, O Vánars, to the side
Of Varuṇ's home the ocean, guide,
Where due libations shall be paid
To my great-hearted brother's shade."

Canto LIX

Sampáti's Story

They heard his counsel to the close,
Then swiftly to their feet they rose;
And Jámbaván with joyous breast
The vulture king again addressed:
"Where, where is Sítá? who has seen,   5
Who borne away the Maithil queen?
Who would the lightning flight withstand,
Of arrows shot by Lakshman's hand?"
Again Sampáti spoke to cheer
The Vánars as they bent to hear: 10
"Now listen, and my words shall show
What of the Maithil dame I know,

And in what distant prison lies
The lady of the long dark eyes.
Scorched by the fiery God of Day,   15
High on this mighty hill I lay.
A long and weary time had passed,
And strength and life were failing fast.
Yet, ere the breath had left my frame,
My son, my dear Supárśva, came.   20
Each morn and eve he brought me food,
And filial care, my life renewed. . . .
Once he returned at close of day,
Stood by my side but brought no prey.
He looked upon my ravenous eye,   25
Heard my complaint and made reply:
"Borne on swift wings ere day was light
I stood upon Mahendra's height
And, far below, the sea I viewed
And birds in countless multitude.   30
Before mine eyes a giant flew
Whose monstrous form was dark of hue,
And struggling in his grasp was borne
A lady radiant as the morn.
Swift to the south his course he bent,   35
And cleft the yielding element.
The holy spirits of the air
Came round me as I marvelled there,
And cried, as their bright legions met:
"O say, is Sítá living yet?"   40
Thus cried the saints and told the name
Of him who held the struggling dame.
Then while mine eye with eager look
Pursued the path the robber took,
marked the lady's streaming hair,   45
And heard her cry of wild despair.
I saw her silken vesture rent
And stripped of every ornament. . . .
In vain the mournful tale I heard
My pitying heart to fury stirred.   50
What could a helpless bird of air,
Reft of his boasted pinions, dare?
Yet can I aid with all that will
And words can do, and friendly skill."

Canto LX

SAMPÁTI'S STORY

Then from the flood Sampáti paid
Due offerings to his brother's shade.
He bathed him when the rites were done,
And spake again to Báli's son:

"Now listen, Prince, while I relate   5
How first I learned the lady's fate.
Burnt by the sun's resistless might
I fell and lay on Vindhya's height.
Seven nights in deadly swoon I passed,
But struggling life returned at last.   10
Around I bent my wondering view,
But every spot was strange and new.
I scanned the sea with eager ken,
And rock and brook and lake and glen
I saw gay trees their branches wave,   15
And creepers mantling o'er the cave.
I heard the wild birds' joyous song,
And waters as they foamed along,
And knew the lovely bill must be
Mount Vindhya by the southern sea.   20
Revered by heavenly beings, stood
Near where I lay, a sacred wood,
Where great Niśákar dwelt of yore
And pains of awful penance bore. . . .
As nearer to the grove I drew   25
The breeze with cooling fragrance blew,
And not a tree that was not fair
With richest flower and fruit was there.
With anxious heart a while I stayed
Beneath the trees' delightful shade,   30
And, soon, the holy hermit, bright
With fervent penance, came in, sight.
Behind him bears and lions, tame
As those who know their feeder, came
And tigers, deer, and snakes pursued,   35
His steps, a wondrous multitude,
And turned, obeisant when the sage
Had reached his shady hermitage
Then came Niśákar to my side
And looked, with, wondering eyes, and cried: 40
"I knew thee not so, dire a change
Has made thy form and feature strange.
Where are thy glossy feathers? where
The rapid wings that cleft the air?
Two vulture brothers once I knew: 45
Each form at will could they endue.
They of the vulture race were kings,
And flew with Mátariśva's wings.
In human shape they loved to greet
Their hermit friend, and clasp his feet.   50
The younger was Jatáyus thou
The elder whom I gaze on now.
Say, has disease or foeman's hate
Reduced thee from thy high estate?"

Canto LXI

SAMPÁTI'S STORY

"Ah me! overwhelmed with shame and weak
With wounds," I cried, "I scarce can speak.
My hapless brother once and I
Our strength of flight resolved to try,
And by our foolish pride impelled   5
Our way through realms of ether held.
We vowed before the saints who tread
The wilds about Kailása's head,
That we with following wings would chase
The swift sun to his resting place.   10
Up on our soaring pinions through,
The fields of cloudless air we flew.
Beneath us far, and far away,
Like chariot wheels bright cities lay,
Whence in wild snatches rose the song   15
Of women mid the gay-clad throng. . . .
But fervent heat and toil o'ercame
The vigour of each yielding frame.
Our weary hearts began to quail,
And wildered sense to reel and fail.   20
We knew not, fainting and distressed,
The north or south or east or west.
With a great strain mine eyes I turned
Where the fierce sun before me burned,
And seemed to my astonished eyes,   25
The equal of the earth in size.
At length, o'erpowered, Jatáyus fell
Without a word to say farewell,
And when to earth I saw him hie
I followed headlong from the sky.   30
With sheltering wings I intervened
And from the sun his body screened,
But lost, for heedless folly doomed,
My pinions which the heat consumed. . . .

Canto LXII

SAMPÁTI'S STORY

"As to the saint I thus complained
My bitter tears fell unrestrained.
He pondered for a while, then broke
The silence, and thus calmly spoke:
'Forth from thy sides again shall spring,   5

O royal bird, each withered wing,
And all thine ancient power and might
Return to thee with strength of sight.
A noble deed has been foretold
in prophecy pronounced of old: . . .   10
A glorious king shall rise and reign,
The pride of old Ikshváku's strain.
A good and valiant prince, his heir,
Shall the dear name of Ráma bear
With his brave brother Lakshman he   15
An exile in the woods shall be,
Where Rávan, whom no God may slay,
Shall steal his darling wife away.
In vain the captive will be wooed
With proffered love and dainty food.   20
She will not hear, she will not taste:
But, lest her beauty wane and waste,
Lord Indra's self will come to her
With heavenly food, and minister.
Then envoys of the Vánar race   25
By Ráma sent will seek this place.
To them, O roamer of the air,
The lady's fate shalt thou declare.
Thou must not move—so maimed thou art—
Thou canst not from this spot depart.   30
Await the day and moment due,
And thy burnt wings will sprout anew. . . .'

Canto LXIII

SAMPÁTI'S STORY

"With this and many a speech beside
My failing heart he fortified,
With glorious hope my breast inspired,
And to his holy home retired.
I scaled the mountain height, to view   5
The region round, and looked for you.
In ceaseless watchings night and day
A hundred seasons passed away,
And by the sage's words consoled
I wait the hour and chance foretold. . . .   10
    He ceased: and in the Vánars' view
Forth from his side young pinions grew,
And boundless rapture filled his breast
As thus the chieftains he addressed:
"Joy, joy! the pinions, which the Lord   15
Of Day consumed, are now restored
Through the dear grace and boundless might
Of that illustrious anchorite.
The fire of youth within me burns,

And all my wonted strength returns.   20
Onward, ye Vánars, toil and strive,
And you shall find the dame alive.
Look on these new-found wings, and hence
Be strong in surest confidence."
   Swift from the crag, he sprang to try   25
His pinions in his native sky.
His words the chieftains' doubts had stilled,
And every heart with courage filled.

Canto LXIV

THE SEA

Shouts of triumphant joy outrang
As to their feet the Vánars sprang;
And, on the mighty task intent,
Swift to the sea their steps they bent.
They stood and gazed upon the deep,   5
Whose billows with a roar and leap
On the sea banks were wildly hurled,—
The mirror of the mighty world.
There on the strand the Vánars stayed
And with sad eyes the deep surveyed. . . .   10
Then princely Angad looked on each,
And thus began his prudent speech:
"What chief of all our host will leap
A hundred leagues across the deep? . . .
To whom, O warriors, shall we owe   15
A sweet release from pain and woe,
And proud success, and happy lives
With our dear children and our wives,
Again permitted by his grace
To look with joy on Ráma's face,   20
And noble Lakshman and our lord
The king, to our sweet homes restored?"
   Thus to the gathered lords he spoke;
But now reply the silence broke.
Then with a sterner voice he cried: 25
"O chiefs, the nations boast and pride,
Whom valour strength and power adorn
Of most illustrious lineage born,
Where'er you will you force a way,
And none your rapid course can stay.   30
Now come, your several powers declare,
And who this desperate leap will dare?"

Canto LXV

THE COUNCIL

But none of all the host was found
To clear the sea with desperate bound,
Though each, as Angad bade, declared
His proper power and what he dared.
Then spake good Jámbaván the sage,   5
"Chief of them all for reverend age:
I, Vánar chieftains, long ago
Limbs light to leap could likewise show,
But now on frame and spirit weighs
The burden of my length of days. . . .   10
    Then Angad due obeisance paid,
And to the chief his answer made:
"Then I, ye noble Vánars, I
Myself the mighty leap will try;
Although perchance the power I lack   15
To leap from Lanká's island back."
    Thus the impetuous chieftain cried,
And Jámbaván the sage replied:
"Whate'er thy power and might may be,
This task, O Prince, is not for thee.   20
Kings go not for themselves, but send
The servants who their hest attend. . . .
Then spoke the aged chief again:
"Nay, our attempt shall not be vain,
For to the task will I incite   25
A chieftain of sufficient might!"

Canto LXVI

HANUMÁN

The chieftain turned his glances where
The legions sat in mute despair;
And then to Hanumán, the best
Of Vánar lords, these words addressed:
"Why still, and silent, and apart,   5
O hero of the dauntless heart?
Thou keepest treasured in thy mind
The laws that rule the Vánar kind,
Strong as our king Sugríva, brave
As Ráma's self to slay or save. . . .   10
Why, rich in wisdom power, and skill,
O hero, art thou lingering still?
An Apsaras, the fairest found

Of nymphs for heavenly charms renowned,
Sweet Punjikasthalá, became   15
A noble Vánar's wedded dame.
Her heavenly title heard no more,
Anjaná was the name she bore,
When, cursed by Gods, from heaven she fell
In Vánar form on earth to dwell. . . .   20
In youthful beauty wondrous fair,
A crown of flowers about her hair,
In silken robes of richest dye
She roamed the hills that kiss the sky.
Once in her tinted garments dressed   25
She stood upon the mountain crest.
The God of Wind beside her came,
And breathed upon the lovely dame,
And as he fanned her robe aside
The wondrous beauty that he eyed   30
In rounded lines of breast and limb
And neck and shoulder ravished him;
And captured by her peerless charms
He strained her in his amorous arms.
Then to the eager God she cried   35
In trembling accents, terrified:
"Whose impious love has wronged a spouse
So constant to her nuptial vows?"
He heard, and thus his answer made:
"O, be not troubled, nor afraid.   40
But trust, and thou shalt know ere long
My love has done thee, sweet, no wrong.
So strong and brave and wise shall be
The glorious child I give to thee.
Might shall be his that naught can tire,   45
And limbs to spring as springs his sire."
Thus spoke the God: the conquered dame
Rejoiced in heart nor feared the shame.
Down in a cave beneath the earth
The happy mother gave thee birth.   50
Once o'er the summit of the wood
Before thine eyes the new sun stood.
Thou sprangest up in haste to seize
What seemed the fruitage of the trees.
Up leapt the child, a wondrous bound,   55
Three hundred leagues above the ground,
And, though the angered Day-God shot
His fierce beams on him, feared him pot.
Then from the hand of Indra came
A red bolt winged with wrath and flame.   60
The child fell smitten on a rock,
His cheek was shattered by the shock,
Named Hanumán[1] thenceforth by all
In memory of the fearful fall.
The wandering Wind-God saw thee lie   65
With bleeding cheek and drooping eye,
And stirred to anger by thy woe
Forbade each scented breeze to blow.
The breath of all the worlds was stilled,

And the sad Gods with terror filled   70
Prayed to the Wind, to calm the ire
And soothe the sorrow of the sire.
His fiery wrath no longer glowed,
And Brabmá's self the boon bestowed
That in the brunt of battle none   75
Should slay with steel the Wind-God's son.
Lord Indra, sovereign of the skies,
Bent on thee all his thousand eyes,
And swore that ne'er the bolt which he
Hurls from the heaven should injure thee.   80
"Tis thine, O mighty chief, to share
The Wind-God's power, his son and heir.
Sprung from that glorious father thou,
And thou alone, canst aid us now. . . ."
   He spoke: the younger chieftain heard,   85
His soul to vigorous effort stirred,
And stood before their joyous eyes,
Expanded to gigantic size.

Canto LXVII

HANUMÁN'S SPEECH

Soon as his stature they beheld,
Their fear and sorrow were dispelled;
And joyous praises loud and long
Rang out from all the Vánar throng.
On the great chief their eyes they bent   5
In rapture and astonishment,
As, when his conquering foot he raised,
The Gods upon Náráyan gazed.
He stood amid the joyous crowd,
Bent to the chiefs, and cried aloud: 10
'The Wind-God, Fire's eternal friend,
Whose blasts the mountain summits rend,
With boundless force that none may stay,
Takes where he lists his viewless way.
Sprung from that glorious father, I   15
In power and speed with him may vie. . . .
I can pursue the Lord of Light
Uprising from the eastern height,
And reach him ere his course be sped
With burning beams engarlanded.   20
I will dry up the mighty main,
Shatter the rocks and rend the plain.
O'er earth and ocean will I bound,
And every flower that grows on ground,
And bloom of climbing plants shall show   25
Strewn on the ground, the way I go,
Bright as the lustrous path that lies

Athwart the region of the skies.[2]
The Maithil lady will I find,—
Thus speaks mine own prophetic mind,—   30
And cast in hideous ruin down
The shattered walls of Lankás town."

. . .

   Then sprang the Wind-God's son, the best
Of Vánars, on Mahendra's crest,
And the great mountain rocked and swayed   35
By that unusual weight dismayed,
As reels an elephant beneath
The lion's spring and rending teeth.
The shady wood that crowned him shook,
The trembling birds the boughs forsook, . . .   40

from Book V
Canto 1

HANUMÁN'S LEAP

Thus Rávan's foe resolved to trace
The captive to her hiding-place
Through airy pathways overhead
Which heavenly minstrels visited.
With straining nerve and eager brows,   5
Like some strong husband of the cows,
In ready might he stood prepared
For the bold task his soul had dared.
O'er gem-like grass that flashed and glowed
The Vánar like a lion shod,   10
Roused by the thunder of his tread,
The beasts to shady coverts fled.
Tall trees he crushed or hurled aside,
And every bird was terrified. . . .
Then once again the chief addressed   15
The Vánars from the mountain crest:
"Swift as a shaft from Ráma's bow
To Rávan's city will I go,
And if she be not there will fly
And seek the lady in the sky;   20
Or, if in heaven she be not found,
Will hither bring the giant bound."
   He ceased; and mustering his might
Sprang downward from the mountain height
While, shattered by each mighty limb,   25
The trees unrooted followed him.
The shadow on the ocean cast
By his vast form, as on he passed,
Flew like a ship before the gale
When the strong breeze has filled the sail,   30
And where his course the Vánar held

The sea beneath him raged and swelled.
Then Gods and all the heavenly train
Poured flowerets down in gentle rain; . . .
Fain would the Sea his succour lend   35
And Raghu's noble son befriend.
He, moved by zeal for Ráma's sake,
The hill Maináka thus bespake: . . .
"To thee is given the power to spread
Or spring above thy watery bed.   40
Now, best of noble mountains, rise
And do the thing that I advise.
E'en now above thy buried crest
Flies mighty Hanumán, the best
Of Vánars, moved for Ráma's sake   45
A wondrous deed to undertake.
Lift up thy head that he may stay
And rest him on his weary way."
  He heard, and from his watery shroud,
As bursts the sun from autumn cloud,   50
Rose swiftly, crowned with plant and tree,
And stood above the foamy sea. . . .
The Vánar thought the mountain rose
A hostile bar to interpose,
And, like a wind-swept cloud, o'erthrew   55
The glittering mountain as he flew.
Then from the falling hill rang out
A warning voice and joyful shout.
Again he raised him high in air
To meet the flying Vánar there;   60
And standing on his topmost peak
In human form began to speak:
"Best of the Vánars' noblest line,
A mighty task, O chief, is thine.
Here for a while, I, pray thee, light   65
And rest upon the breezy height. . . .
Refresh thy weary limbs, and eat
My mountain fruits for they are sweet.
I too, O chieftain, know thee well;
Three worlds thy famous virtues tell. . . .   70
And how shall I neglect thee, how
Slight the great guest so near me now?
Son of the Wind, 'tis thine to share
The might of him who shakes the air;
And,—for he loves his offspring,—he   75
Is honoured when I honour thee.
Of yore, when Krita's age was new,
The little hills and mountains flew
Where'er they listed, borne on wings
More rapid than the feathered king's.   80
But mighty terror came on all
The Gods and saints who feared their fall,
And Indra in his anger rent
Their pinions with the bolts he sent.
When in his ruthless fury he   85
Levelled his flashing bolt at me,
The great-souled Wind inclined to save,

And laid me neath the ocean's wave,
Thus by the favour of thy sire
I kept my cherished wings entire;   90
And for this deed of kindness done
I honour thee his noble son.
O come, thy weary limbs relieve,
And honour due from me receive."
"I may not rest," the Vánar cried;   95
I must not stay or turn aside.
Yet pleased am I, thou noblest hill,
And as the deed accept thy will."
   Thus as he spoke he lightly pressed
With his broad hand the mountain's crest,   100
Then bounded upward to the height
Of heaven, rejoicing in his might,
And through the fields of boundless blue,
The pathwav of his father, flew. . . .
Through the broad fields of ether, fast   105
As Garud's royal self, he passed,
The region of the cloud and rain,
Loved by the gay Gandharva train,
Where mid the birds that came and went
Shone Indra's glorious bow unbent,   110
And like a host of wandering stars
Flashed the high Gods' celestial cars.
Fierce Sinhiká who joyed in ill
And changed her form to work her will,
Descried him on his airy way   115
And marked the Vánar for her prey.
"This day at length," the demon cried,
"My hunger shall be satisfied,"
And at his passing shadow caught
Delighted with the cheering thought.   120
The Vánar felt the power that stayed
And held him as she grasped his shade,
Like some tall ship upon the main
That struggles with the wind in vain.
Below, above, his eye he bent   125
And scanned the sea and firmament.
High from the briny deep upreared
The monster's hideous form appeared. . . .
Wide as the space from heaven to hell
Her jaws she opened with a yell,   130
And rushed upon her fancied prey
With cloud-like roar to seize and slay.
The Vánar swift as thought compressed
His borrowed bulk of limb and chest,
And stood with one quick bound inside   135
The monstrous mouth she opened wide.
Hid like the moon when Ráhu draws
The orb within his ravening jaws
Within that ample cavern pent
The demon's form he tore and rent,   140
And from the mangled carcass freed,
Came forth again with thought-like speed.
Thus with his skill the fiend he slew,

Then to his wonted stature grew.
The spirits saw the demon die,   145
And hailed the Vánar from the sky. . . .
    Pleased with their praises as they sang,
Again through fields of air he sprang.
And now, his travail wellnigh done,
The distant shore was almost won.   150
Before him on the margent stood
In long dark line a waving wood,
And the fair island, bright and green
With flowers and trees, was clearly seen. . . .
He lighted down on Lamba's peak   155
Which tinted metals stain and streak,
And looked where Lanká's splendid town
Shone on the mountain like a crown.

Canto II

LANKÁ

The glorious sight a while he viewed,
Then to the town his way pursued.
Around the Vánar as he went
Breathed from the wood delicious scent,
And the soft grass beneath his feet   5
With gem-like flowers was bright and sweet
Still as the Vánar nearer drew
More clearly rose the town to view. . . .
A thousand trees mid flowers that glowed
Hung down their fruit's delicious load,   10
And in their crests that rocked and swayed
Sweet birds delightful music made.
And there were pleasant pools whereon
The glories of the lotus shone;
And gleams of sparkling fountains, stirred   15
By many a joyous water-bird.
Around, in lovely gardens grew
Blooms sweet of scent and bright of hue,
And Lanká, seat of Rávan's sway,
Before the wondering Vánar lay: 20
With stately domes and turrets tall,
Encircled by a golden wall,
And moats whose waters were aglow
With lily blossoms bright below:
For Sítá's sake defended well   25
With bolt and bar and sentinel,
And Rákshases who roamed in bands
With ready bows in eager hands. . . .
The Vánar by the northern gate
Thus in his heart began debate: 30
"Our mightiest host would strive in vain

To take this city on the main;
A city that may well defy
The chosen warriors of the sky. . . .
But now my search must I pursue   35
Until the Maithil queen I view;
And, when I find the captive dame,
Make victory mine only aim.
But, if I wear my present shape,
How shall I enter and escape   40
The Rákshas troops, their guards and spies,
And sleepless watch of cruel eyes? . . .
I in a shape to mock their sight
Must steal within the town by night,
Blind with my art the demons' eyes,   45
And thus achieve my enterprise. . . .
    When the bright sun had left the skies
The Vánar dwarfed his mighty size,
And, in the straitest bounds restrained,
The bigness of a cat retained.   50
Then, when the moon's soft light was spread,
Within the city's walls he sped.

Canto III

THE GUARDIAN GODDESS

. . . In semblance of a Rákshas dame
The city's guardian Goddess came,—
For she with glances sure and keen
The entrance of a foe had seen,—
And thus with fury in her eye   5
Addressed him with an angry cry:
"Who art thou? what has led thee, say,
Within these walls to find thy way? . . ."
"And who art thou?" the Vánar cried,
By form and frown unterrified   10
"Why hast thou met me by the gate,
And chid me thus infuriate?"
    He ceased: and Lanká made reply:
"The guardian of the town am I,
Who watch for ever to fulfil   15
My lord the Rákshas monarch's will.
But thou shalt fall this hour, and deep
Shall be thy never-ending sleep."
    Again he spake: "In spite of thee
This golden city will I see,   20
Her gates and towers, and all the pride
Of street and square from side to side, . . .
On all her beauties sate mine eye,
Then, as I came will homeward hie."
    Swift with an angry roar she smote   25

With her huge hand the Vánar's throat.
The smitten Vánar, rage-impelled,
With fist upraised the monster felled;
But quick repented, stirred with shame
And pity for a vanquished dame,   30
"When with her senses troubled, weak
With terror, thus she strove to speak:
"O spare, me thou whose arm is strong:
O spare me, and forgive the wrong. . . .
Hear, best of Vánars, brave and bold,   35
What Brahmá's self of yore foretold:
'Beware,' he said, 'the fatal hour
When thou shalt own a Vánar's power.
Then is the giants' day of fear,
For terror and defeat are near.'   40
Now, Vánar chief, o'ercome by thee,
I own the truth of heaven's decree.
For Sítá's sake will ruin fall
On Rávan, and his town, and all."

Canto IV

WITHIN THE CITY

The guardian goddess thus subdued,
The Vánar chief his way pursued,
And reached the broad imperial street
Where fresh-blown flowers were bright and sweet.
The city seemed a fairer sky   5
Where cloud-like houses rose on high. . . .
From house to house the Vánar went
And marked each varied ornament,
Where leaves and blossoms deftly strung
About the crystal columns hung.   10
Then soft and full and sweet and clear
The song of women charmed his ear,
And, blending with their dulcet tones,
Their anklets' chime and tinkling zones.
He heard the Rákshas minstrels sing   15
The praises of their matchless king;
And softly through the evening air
Came murmurings of text and prayer. . . .
There savage warriors roamed in bands
With clubs and maces in their hands,   20
Some dwarfish forms, some huge of size,
With single ears and single eyes.
Some shone in glittering mail arrayed
With bow and mace and flashing blade;
Fiends of all shapes and every hue,   25
Some fierce and foul, some fair to view.
    He saw the grisly legions wait

In strictest watch at Rávan's gate,
Whose palace on the mountain crest
Rose proudly towering o'er the rest, . . .   30
But Hanumán, unhindered, found
Quick passage through the guarded bound,
Mid elephants of noblest breed,
And gilded car and neighing steed.

Canto VII

RÁVAN'S PALACE

He passed within the walls and gazed
On gems and gold that round him blazed,
And many a latticed window bright
With turkis and with lazulite.
Through porch and ante-rooms he passed   5
Each richer, fairer than the last;
And spacious halls where lances lay,
And bows and shells, in fair array. . . .

Canto IX

THE LADIES' BOWER

Where stately mansions rose around,
A palace fairer still he found,
Whose royal height and splendour showed
Where Rávan's self, the king, abode.
A chosen band with bow and sword   5
Guarded the palace of their lord,
Where Rákshas dames of noble race,
And many a princess fair of face
Whom Rávan's arm had torn away
From vanquished kings, in slumber lay. . . .   10
In sweet disorder lay a throng
Weary of dance and play and song,
Where heedless girls had sunk to rest
One pillowed on another's breast, . . .
With limbs at random interlaced   15
Round arm and leg and throat and waist,
That wreath of women lay asleep
Like blossoms in a careless heap.

Canto X

Rávan Asleep

Apart a dais of crystal rose
With couches spread for soft repose,
Adorned with gold and gems of price
Meet for the halls of Paradise.
A canopy was o'er them spread   5
Pale as the light the moonbeams shed,
And female figures, deftly planned,[3]
The faces of the sleepers fanned.
There on a splendid couch, asleep
On softest skins of deer and sheep,   10
Dark as a cloud that dims the day
The monarch of the giants lay,
Perfumed with sandal's precious scent
And gay with golden ornament.
His fiery eyes in slumber closed,   15
In glittering robes the king reposed
Like Mandar's mighty hill asleep
With flowery trees that clothe his steep.
Near and more near the Vánar drew
The monarch of the fiends to view,   20
And saw the giant stretched supine
Fatigued with play and drunk with wine,
While, shaking all the monstrous frame,
His breath like hissing serpents' came. . . .
The spouses of the giant king   25
Around their lord were slumbering,
And, gay with sparkling earrings, shone
Fair as the moon to look upon.
There by her husband's side was seen
Mandodarí the favourite queen,   30
The beauty of whose youthful face
Beamed a soft glory through the place.
The Vánar marked the dame more fair
Than all the royal ladies there,
And thought, "These rarest beauties speak   35
The matchless dame I come to seek.
Peerless in grace and splendour, she
The Maithil queen must surely be."

Canto XI

THE BANQUET HALL

But soon the baseless thought was spurned,
And longing hope again returned:
"No: Ráma's wife is none of these,
No careless dame that lives at ease.
Her widowed heart has ceased to care   5
For dress and sleep and dainty fare.
She near a lover ne'er would lie
Though Indra wooed her from the sky.
Her own, her only lord, whom none
Can match in heaven, is Raghu's son."   10
    Then to the banquet ball intent,
On strictest search his steps be bent. . . .
That spacious hall from side to side
With noblest fare was well supplied,
There quarters of the boar, and here   15
Roast of the buffalo and deer.
There on gold plate, untouched as yet,
The peacock and the hen were set. . . .
There wrought of gold, ablaze with shine
Of precious stones, were cups of wine.   20
Through court and bower and banquet hall
The Vánar passed and viewed them all;
From end to end, in every spot,
For Sítá searched, but found her not.

Canto XII

THE SEARCH RENEWED

. . . Again he turned him to explore
Each chamber, hall, and corridor,
And arbour bright with scented bloom,
And lodge and cell and picture-room.
With eager eye and noiseless feet   5
He passed through many a cool retreat
Where women lay in slumber drowned;
But Sítá still was nowhere found.

Canto XIII

DESPAIR AND HOPE

Then rapid as the lightnings flame
From Rávans halls the Vánar came.
Each lingering hope was cold and dead,
And thus within his heart he said:
"Alas, my fruitless search is done: 5
Long have I toiled for Raghu's son
And yet with all my care have seen
No traces of the ravished queen. . . .
If with no happier tale to tell
I seek our mountain citadel,   10
How shall I face our lord the king,
And meet his angry questioning?
How shall I greet my friends, and brook
The muttered taunt, the scornful look? . . .
Ah no: unless the dame I find   15
I ne'er will meet my Vánar kind.
Here rather in some distant dell
A lonely hermit will I dwell,
Where roots and berries will supply
My humble wants until I die;   20
Or on the shore will raise a pyre
And perish in the kindled fire.
Or I will strictly fast until
With slow decay my life I kill,
And ravening dogs and birds of air   25
The limbs of Hanumán shall tear.
Here will I die, but never bring
Destruction on my race and king.
But still unsearched one grove I see
With many a bright Aśoka tree.   30
There will I enter in, and through
The tangled shade my search renew. . . .

Canto XIV

THE AŚOKA GROVE

He cleared the barrier at a bound
He stood within the pleasant ground,
And with delighted eyes surveyed
The climbing plants and varied shade.
He saw unnumbered trees unfold   5
The treasures of their pendent gold,
As searching for the Maithil queen,

He strayed through alleys soft and green. . . .
The earth, on whose fair bosom lay
The flowers that fell from every spray,　　　　　　10
Was glorious as a lovely maid
In all her brightest robes arrayed.
He saw the breath of morning shake
The lilies on the rippling lake
Whose waves a pleasant lapping made　　　　　　15
On crystal steps with gems inlaid.
Then roaming through the enchanted ground,
A pleasant hill the Vánar found,
And grottoes in the living stone
With grass and flowery trees o'ergrown. . . .　　　20
　　He clomb a tree that near him grew
And leafy shade around him threw.
"Hence," thought the Vánar, "shall I see
The Maithil dame, if here she be.
These lovely trees, this cool retreat　　　　　　25
Will surely tempt her wandering feet.
Here the sad queen will roam apart,
And dream of Ráma in her heart."

Canto XV

SÍTÁ

Fair as Kailása white with snow
He saw a palace flash and glow,
A crystal pavement gem-inlaid,
And coral steps and colonnade,
And glittering towers that kissed the skies,　　　5
Whose dazzling splendour charmed his eyes.
There pallid with neglected dress,
Watched close by fiend and giantess,
Her sweet face thin with constant flow
Of tears, with fasting and with woe;　　　　　　10
Pale as the young moon's crescent when
The first faint light returns to men:
Dim as the flame when clouds of smoke
The latent glory hide and choke;
Like Rohiní the queen of stars　　　　　　　　15
Oppressed by the red planet Mars;
From her dear friends and husband torn,
Amid the cruel fiends, forlorn,
Who fierce-eyed watch around her kept,
A tender woman sat and wept.　　　　　　　　20
Her sobs, her sighs, her mournful mien,
Her glorious eyes, proclaimed the queen.
"This, this is she," the Vánar cried,
"Fair as the moon and lotus-eyed. . . .
This peerless queen whom I behold　　　　　　　25

Is Ráma's wife with limbs of gold.
Best of the sons of men is he,
And worthy of her lord is she."

Canto XVI

HANUMÁN'S LAMENT

Then, all his thoughts on Sítá bent,
The Vánar chieftain made lament:
"The queen to Ráma's soul endeared,
By Lakshman's pious heart revered, . . .
And now these sad eyes look on her   5
Mid hostile fiends a prisoner.
From home and every bliss she fled
By wifely love and duty led,
And, heedless of a wanderer's woes,
A life in lonely forests chose.   10
This, this is she so fair of mould,
Whose limbs are bright as burnished gold,
Whose voice was ever soft and mild,
Who sweetly spoke and sweetly smiled.
O, what is Ráma's misery! how   15
He longs to see his darling now!
Pining for one of her fond looks
As one athirst for water-brooks.
Absorbed in woe the lady sees
No Rákshas guard, no blooming trees.   20
Her eyes are with her thoughts and they
Are fixed on Ráma far away."

Canto XVII

SÍTÁ'S GUARD

His pitying eyes with tears bedewed,
The weeping queen again he viewed,
And saw around the prisoner stand
Her demon guard, a fearful band:
Some earless, some with ears that hung   5
Low as their feet and loosely swung:
Some fierce with single ears and eyes,
Some dwarfish, some of monstrous size:
Some with their dark necks long and thin
With hair upon the knotty skin: 10
Some with wild locks, some bald and bare,
Some covered o'er with bristly hair:

Some tall and straight, some bowed and bent
With every foul disfigurement; . . .
Some with the jackal's jaw and nose,   15
Some faced like boars and buffaloes:
Some with the heads of goats and kine,
Of elephants, and dogs, and swine:
With lions' lips and horses' brows,
They walked with feet of mules and cows: 20
Swords, maces, clubs, and spears they bore
In hideous hands that reeked with gore,
And, never sated, turned afresh
To bowls of wine and piles of flesh.
Such were the awful guards who stood   25
Round Sítá in that lovely wood,
While in her lonely sorrow she
Wept sadly neath a spreading tree. . . .

Canto XVIII

RÁVAṆ

While from his shelter in the boughs
The Vánar looked on Ráma's spouse,
He heard the gathered giants raise
The solemn hymn of prayer and praise,
Priests skilled in rite and ritual, who   5
The Vedas and their branches knew.
Then, as loud strains of music broke
His sleep, the giant monarch woke.
Swift to his heart the thought returned
Of the fair queen for whom he burned   10
Nor could the amorous fiend control
The passion that absorbed his soul.
In all his brightest garb arrayed
He hastened to that lovely shade,
Where glowed each choicest flower and fruit,   15
And the sweet birds were never mute,
And tall deer bent their heads to drink
On the fair streamlet's grassy brink.
Near that Aśoka grove he drew,—
A hundred dames his retinue,   20
Like Indra with the thousand eyes
Girt with the beauties of the skies. . . .
Some by the monarch's side displayed,
Wrought like a swan, a silken shade;
Another beauty walked behind,   25
The sceptre to her care assigned.
Around the monarch gleamed the crowd
As lightnings flash about a cloud,
And each made music as she went
With zone and tinkling ornament.   30

Attended thus in royal state
The monarch reached the garden gate. . . .
The Vánar from his station viewed,
Amazed, the wondrous multitude,
Where, in the centre of that ring   35
Of noblest women, stood the king,
As stands the full moon fair to view,
Girt by his starry retinue.

Canto XIX

SÍTÁ'S FEAR

Then o'er the lady's soul and fame
A sudden fear and trembling came,
When, glowing in his youthful pride,
She saw the monarch by her side.
Silent she sat, her eyes depressed,   5
Her soft arms folded o'er her breast,
And,—all she could,—her beauties screened
From the bold gazes of the fiend.
There where the wild she-demons kept
Their watch around, she sighed and wept,   10
Then, like a severed bough, she lay
Prone on the bare earth in dismay,
The while her thoughts on love's fleet wings
Flew to her lord the best of kings. . . .

Canto XX

RÁVAN'S WOOING

With amorous look and soft address
The fiend began his suit to press:
"Why wouldst thou, lady lotus-eyed,
From my fond glance those beauties hide
Mine eager suit no more repel;   5
But love me, for I love thee well.
Dismiss, sweet dame, dismiss thy fear;
No giant and no man is near.
Ours is the right by force to seize
What dames soe'er our fancy please.   10
But I with rude hands will not touch
A lady whom I love so much.
Fear not, dear queen: no fear is nigh:
Come, on thy lover's love rely.
Some little sign of favour show,   15

Nor lie enamoured of thy woe.
Those limbs upon the cold earth laid,
Those tresses twined in single braid,[4]
The fast and woe that wear thy frame,
Beseem not thee, O beauteous dame.   20
For thee the fairest wreaths were meant,
The sandal and the aloe's scent,
Rich ornaments and pearls of price,
And vesture meet for Paradise. . . .
Come, let us love while yet we may,   25
For youth will fly and charms decay.
Come, cast thy grief and fear aside,
And be my love, my chosen bride.
The gems and jewels that my hand
Has reft from every plundered land,—   30
To thee I give them all this day,
And at thy feet my kingdom lay.
The broad rich earth will I o'errun,
And leave no town unconquered, none;
Then of the whole an offering make   35
To Janak, dear, for thy sweet sake. . . .
Come, taste of bliss and drink thy fill,
And rule the slave who serves thy will.
Think not of wretched Ráma: he
Is less than nothing now to thee.   40
Stript of his glory poor, dethroned,
A wanderer by his friends disowned,
On the cold earth he lays his head,
Or is with toil and misery dead.
And if perchance he lingers yet,   45
His eyes on thee shall ne'er be set. . . .
Thou unadorned art dearer far
Than all my loveliest consorts are.
My royal home is bright and fair;
A thousand beauties meet me there.   50
But come, my glorious love, and be
The queen of all those dames and me."

Canto XXI

SÍTÁ'S SCORN

She thought upon her lord and sighed,
And thus in gentle tones replied:
"Beseems thee not, O King, to woo
A matron, to her husband true.
Thus vainly one might hope by sin   5
And evil deeds success to win.
Shall I, so highly born, disgrace
My husband's house, my royal race?
Shall I, a true and loyal dame,

Defile my soul with deed of shame?"   10
    Then on the king her back she turned,
And answered thus the prayer she spurned:
"Turn, Rávan, turn thee from thy sin;
Seek virtue's paths and walk therein.
To others dames be honour shown;   15
Protect them as thou wouldst thine own.
Taught by thyself, from wrong abstain
Which, wrought on thee, thy heart would pain.
Beware: this lawless love of thine
Will ruin thee and all thy line;   20
And for thy sin, thy sin alone,
Will Lanká perish overthrown.
Dream not that wealth and power can sway
My heart from duty's path to stray.
Linked like the Day-God and his shine,   25
I am my lord's and he is mine.
Repent thee of thine impious deed;
To Ráma's side his consort lead.
Be wise: the hero's friendship gain,
Nor perish in his fury slain. . . ."   30

Canto XXII

RÁVAN'S THREAT

Then anger swelled in Rávan's breast,
Who fiercely thus the dame addressed:
"'Tis ever thus: in vain we sue
To woman, and her favour woo.
A lover's humble words impel   5
Her wayward spirit to rebel.
The love of thee that fills my soul
Still keeps my anger in control,
As charioteers with bit and rein
The swerving of the steed restrain. . . .   10
Two months, fair dame, I grant thee still
To bend thee to thy lover's will.
If when that respite time is fled
Thou still refuse to share my bed,
My cooks shall mince thy limbs with steel   15
And serve thee for my morning meal."
    The minstrel daughters of the skies
Looked on her woe with pitying eyes,
And sun-bright children of the Gods[5]
Consoled the queen with smiles and nods.   20
She saw, and with her heart at ease,
Addressed the fiend in words like these:
"Hast thou no friend to love thee, none
In all this isle to bid thee shun
The ruin which thy crime will bring   25

On thee and thine, O impious King?
Who in all worlds save thee could woo
Me, Ráma's consort pure and true,
As though he tempted with his love
Queen Śachí on her throne above?   30
How canst thou hope, vile wretch, to fly
The vengeance that e'en now is nigh,
When thou hast dared, untouched by shame,
To press thy suit on Ráma's dame? . . .
        Then, hissing like a furious snake,   35
The fiend again to Sítá spake:
"Deaf to all prayers and threats art thou,
Devoted to thy senseless vow.
No longer respite will I give,
And thou this day shalt cease to live. . . .   40
        The Rákshas guard was summoned: all
The monstrous crew obeyed the call,
And hastened to the king to take
The orders which he fiercely spake:
"See that ye guard her well, and tame,   45
Like some wild thing, the stubborn dame,
Until her haughty soul be bent
By mingled threat and blandishment."
        The monsters heard: away he strode,
And passed within his queens' abode.   50

Canto XXIII

THE DEMONS' THREAT

Then round the helpless Sítá drew
With fiery eyes the hideous crew,
And thus assailed her, all and each,
With insult, taunt, and threatening speech. . . .
        One demon, Vikatá by name,   5
In words like these addressed the dame:
"The king whose blows, in fury dealt,
The Nágas and Gandharvas felt,
In battle's fiercest brunt subdued,
Has stood by thee and humbly wooed.   10
And wilt thou in thy folly miss
The glory of a love like this?
Scared by his eye the sun grows chill,
The wanderer wind is hushed and still.
The rains at his command descend,   15
And trees with new-blown blossoms bend,
His word the hosts of demons fear,
And wilt thou, dame, refuse to hear?,
Be counselled; with his will comply,
Or, lady, thou shalt surely die."   20

Canto XXIV

SÍTÁ'S REPLY

Still with reproaches rough and rude
Those fiends the gentle queen pursued:
"What! can so fair a life displease,
To dwell with him in joyous ease?
Dwell in his bowers a happy queen   5
In silk and gold and jewels' sheen?
Still must thy woman fancy cling
To Ráma and reject our king? . . ."
    Then, as a tear bedewed her eye,
The hapless lady made reply: 10
"I loathe, with heart and soul detest
The shameful life your words suggest,
Eat, if you will, this mortal frame:
My soul rejects the sin and shame.
A homeless wanderer though he be,   15
In him my lord, my life I see,
And, till my earthly days be done,
Will cling to great Ikshváku's son."
    Then with fierce eyes on Sítá set
They cried again with taunt and threat, . . .   20
And menacing the lady's life
With axe, or spear or murderous knife:
"Hear, Sítá, and our words obey,
Or perish by our hands to-day.
Thy love for Raghu's son forsake,   25
And Rávan for thy husband take,
Or we will rend thy limbs apart
And banquet on thy quivering heart.
Now from her body strike the head,
And tell the king the dame is dead.   30
Then by our lord's commandment she
A banquet for our band shall be.
Come, let the wine be quickly brought
That frees each heart from saddening thought.
Then to the western gate repair,   35
And we will dance and revel there."

Canto XXV

SÍTÁ'S LAMENT

On the bare earth the lady sank,
And trembling from their presence shrank,
Like a strayed fawn, when night is dark,

And hungry wolves around her bark.
Then to a shady tree she crept,   5
And thought upon her lord and wept.
By fear and bitter woe oppressed
She bathed the beauties of her breast
With her hot tears' incessant flow,
And found no respite from her woe.   10
As shakes a plantain in the breeze
She shook, and fell on trembling knees; . . .
And, wild with grief, with fear appalled,
On Ráma and his brother called:
"O dear Kauisalyá, hear me cry!   15
Sweet Queen Sumitrá, hear my sigh! . . .

Canto XXVI

SÍTÁ'S LAMENT

"I Ráma's wife, on that sad day,
By Rávan's arm was borne away,
Seized, while I sat and feared no ill,
By him who wears each form at will.
A helpless captive, left forlorn   5
To demons' threats and taunts and scorn,
Here for my lord I weep and sigh,
And worn with woe would gladly die.
For what is life to me afar
From Ráma of the mighty car? . . .   10
My lord was grateful, true and wise,
And looked on woe with pitying eyes;
But now, recoiling from the strife,
He pities not his captive wife.
Alone in Janasthán he slew   15
The thousands of the Rákshas crew.
His arm was strong, his heart was brave,
Why comes he not to free and save?
Why blame my lord in vain surmise?
He knows not where his lady lies.   20
O, if he knew, o'er land and sea
His feet were swift to set me free;
This Lanká, girdled by the deep,
Would fall consumed, a shapeless heap,
And from each ruined home would rise   25
A Rákshas widow's groans and cries."

Canto XXVII

Trijatá's Dream

Their threats unfeared, their counsel spurned,
The demons' breasts with fury burned.
Some sought the giant king, to bear
The tale of Sítá's fixt despair.
With threats and taunts renewed the rest   5
Around the weeping lady pressed.
But Trijatá, of softer mould,
A Rákshas matron wise and old,
With pity for the captive moved,
In words like these the fiends reproved: 10
"Me, me," she cried, "eat me, but spare
The spouse of Daśaratha's heir.
Last night I dreamt a dream; and still
The fear and awe my bosom chill;
For in that dream I saw foreshown   15
Our race by Ráma's hand overthrown.
I saw a chariot high in air,
Of ivory exceeding fair,
A hundred steeds that chariot drew
As swiftly through the clouds it flew,   20
And, clothed in white, with wreaths that shone,
The sons of Raghu rode thereon.
I looked and saw this lady here,
Clad in the purest white, appear
High on the snow-white hill whose feet   25
The angry waves of ocean beat.
And she and Ráma met at last
Like light and sun when night is past.
Again I saw them side by side:
On Rávan's car they seemed to ride,   30
And with the princely Lakshman flee
To northern realms beyond the sea.
Then Rávan, shaved and shorn, besmeared
With oil from head to foot, appeared. . . .
I saw him from his chariot thrust;   35
I saw him rolling in the dust.
A woman came and dragged away
The stricken giant where he lay,
And on a car which asses drew
The monarch of our race she threw.   40
He rose erect, he danced and laughed,
With thirsty lips the oil he quaffed,
Then with wild eyes and streaming mouth
Sped on the chariot to the south. I
Then, dropping oil from every limb,   45
His sons the princes followed him,
And Kumbhakarṇa, shaved and shorn,
Was southward on a camel borne.
Then royal Lanká reeled and fell

With gate and tower and citadel.   50
This ancient city, far-renowned:
All life within her walls was drowned;
And the wild waves of ocean rolled
O'er Lanká and her streets of gold.
Warned by these signs I bid you fly;   55
Or by the band of Ráma die,
Whose vengeance will not spare the life
Of one who vexed his faithful wife.
Your bitter taunts and threats forgo:
Comfort the lady in her woe,   60
And humbly pray her to forgive
For so you may be spared and live."

ENDNOTES

Editor's Note: As the narrative continues, Sítá's life is spared, and she soon meets with Hanumán. The magical monkey then returns to Rama, but only after causing immense damage in Lanká. After that, the monkeys construct an incredibly long bridge leading to Ravan's island kingdom. Rama then crosses the bridge with an army of monkeys and bears. The king of demons is killed, and Sítá is restored to her husband.

1. Hanu or Hanú means jaw. Hanumán or Hanúmán means properly one with a large jaw.

2. The Milky Way.
3. Women, says Válmíki. But an ancient commentator claims that automatons (what we would call robots today) are meant. Actual women would have seen Hanumán and expressed alarm.
4. Indian women twisted their long hair in a single braid as a sign of mourning for their absent husbands.
5. Rávan carried off and kept in his palace not only earthly princesses but the daughters of Gods and Gandharvas.

———— *Questions For Consideration* ————

Using complete sentences, provide brief answers for the following questions.

1. Provide a sketch of a character, for instance Hanumán, that caught your attention as you read the selections from the *Rámáyana*.

    _____

    _____

    _____

    _____

    _____

2. Identify the moral values of Indian epic as they emerged through your reading.

    _____

    _____

    _____

    _____

    _____

3. Focusing on the characters of Ráma and Aeneas, specify resemblances between the heroic values of the *Rámáyana* and those of the *Aeneid*.

    _____

    _____

    _____

    _____

    _____

———————————— *Writing Critically* ————————————

Select one of the topics listed below and compose a 500-word essay that discusses the topic fully. Support your thesis with evidence from the text and with critical and/or historical material. Use the space below for preparing to write the essay.

1. A simian hero is also found in the Chinese novel, *Journey to the West*, parts of which are included in this volume. Scholarly opinion is divided, but a number of critics believe that the portrayal of a monkey hero in Indian epic influenced the development of the character of Sun Wukong, the Monkey King, in Chinese literature. Write an essay comparing the two characters.

2. Explore parallels between the *Rámáyana* and the great African epic, the *Sundiata*.

3. Compare the character of Sítá with that of one or more heroines, such as Medea, Persephone, or Dido, that you are familiar with from your study of classical Western literature.

4. Examine the *Rámáyana* in a broader cultural and historical context. Investigate the nature of Indian society during the period when the epic was composed as well as the heritage of the *Rámáyana* story within and outside of modern-day India. Do not hesitate to request secondary material through your institution's interlibrary loan service. Also, search the Worldwide Web for information on this topic. Prepare a report or a detailed summary of your research.

Prewriting Space:

_____

_____

_____

_____

_____

_____

_____

_____

_____

_____

_____

_____

_____

_____

Cultural Currents from the 4th Century A.D. to the 14th Century A.D.

Sundiata: An Epic of Old Mali
Bhartrihari: The Hermit & the Love-Thief
Chinese Lyric Poetry of the Tang Dynasty
The Man'yoshū
Beowulf
Dante: The Divine Comedy
Chaucer: The Canterbury Tales

UNIT TWO

Introduction
Unit Two

The time period known in Europe as the Middle Ages might, from another cultural perspective, be known as the age of Islam, or the Golden age of India. While there is no single cultural perspective of this period which can be viewed as definitive, there are interesting connections and contrasts which can be traced.

Life in Europe was strongly shaped by the emergence of two major world religions: Christianity and Islam. After actively persecuting what had for a time been viewed as a minor sect of the Jewish religion, Constantine in 313 issued the Edict of Milan, which declared official tolerance of all religions, including Christianity. Less than eighty years later, the Roman Empire in 391 officially embraced Christianity as its official religion, and outlawed all other "pagan" religions. Four years later, in 395, the empire was permanently divided into two halves, an Eastern and Western Empire. The Eastern Empire, based in Constantinople, maintained a Greek speaking, Christian government for over a thousand years. The Western Empire was not nearly so unified. Its collapse as a unifying political entity led to the political disunity that marked the European middle ages.

In the absence of a strong, political empire, affiliations to the Church, to local customs, and to local families became increasingly important. The literature that emerged from this period celebrated an earlier heroic age, but usually put these stories and codes, which often descended from a "pagan" source, into a Christian context. Making war is a another major theme of these stories—and as the Islamic religion spread and the forces of Islam were increasingly powerful, Muslims were often the chief opponents to be bested.

In the absence of widespread political harmony, the importance of loyalty and duty to one's lord became an increasingly important virtue, and the minor victories of minor wars were retold until their literary value far outstripped their political or historical significance. The well known stories of King Arthur, which emerge in the latter half of the middle ages, are a good example of this. Though the historical Arthur, if he indeed existed, was probably a warrior leader of the Celts around the sixth century A.D., the legendary Arthur becomes, in some versions, the leader of much of Europe, and more importantly the embodiment of a code of chivalry. Again, because of the lack of a unified code of law, leaders such as Arthur, Roland (from the French *Song of Roland*) and the Cid (from the Spanish romance *El Cid*), all based on historical figures, became necessary, larger than life figureheads upon whom the burden of a code of chivalry could be hung.

The Christian Church also played a crucial role in keeping a sense of cultural (if not political) unity among the peoples of Western Europe, but it is impossible to appreciate this role without an understanding of the growth of Islam. From 610–632, Muhammad received prophecies from Allah which were gathered together in the Koran to form the basis of a new, major religion. The new religion quickly swept through the Arabic peoples, providing for a new degree of unity. Muslim armies expanded into India, Morocco, Spain, and central Asia, triggering a Golden Age of Islam. In the ninth century, even as the Greek cultural heritage of Europe was falling into obscurity there, Caliphate of al-Ma'mum began to actively promote the translation of Greek texts into Arabic. The tenth century saw the establishment of the first major centers of learning in Medieval Europe, founded by Spanish Muslims.

It was the Muslim occupation of Spain and Jerusalem that was to lead to one of the major effects of the Muslim world on European life. In 1099, after ninety years of Muslim rule of Jerusalem, Knights of the first crusade recaptured the city, setting the stage for two centuries of fighting during which Christian forces were never able to maintain control of the Holy Land. Though little noted in the literature from the Muslim world, these wars left a lasting impact on the literature of Europe. Heroes associated with the Crusades, such as Richard the Lion Heart, became recognizable figures in the literature of this period. Similarly, the *Song of Roland* celebrates a military victory against advancing Muslim forces, and many of the medieval romance writers found convenient villains in the figures of Muslim "Saracens." Nor can the influence be seen moving in only one direction; if the Crusades influenced romances (and it is important to recognize that the term "romance" in this context can best be understood to mean "popular adventure stories"), certainly the same spirit that gave rise to the popularity of these romances about the fall of Troy, the exploits of Aeneas, and other heroic tales from Europe's past must have helped garner support for the series of disastrous crusades that spanned three centuries.

If the crusades were enormously important in European literature, they had no such importance to the literature of the Arabic world. These wars over the Holy Lands did little to halt the progress of the Islamic Golden Age that had emerged, and were thus little noted. By far the most influential works of world literature to emerge from the Islamic writings of this period are the Koran and *The Thousand and One Nights*. It is important to realize that the Arabic Koran is revered by the Muslim faithful as the literal word of Allah; as such, it can never truly be translated. While translation is tolerated for instructional purposes, no translation is accepted as a true version of the Koran. The Koran retells many stories from the Bible, including the stories of Noah, Joseph, Moses, and Jesus (called Ka), but strips them of their nationalist trappings. The prophets of the past were prophets because they obeyed and preached the word of the Lord, not because they were leaders of their people.

The Thousand and One Nights is a work which occupies a curious position, in that though it is one of the most popular contributions to world literature to spring from any source, they were popular tales not regarded as "classical literature" in the Islamic nations that gave them birth. In part, this is because of their fanciful quality; the Koran frowns on fictions which serve no clear moral purpose. Nonetheless, the imaginative quality of these anonymous, oft-repeated tales did much to guarantee their popularity throughout the world.

While Europe was enduring the Middle Ages, and the Islamic world was being born, India was enjoying a vigorous Golden Age. The nature of Indian literary culture during this period to a large extent determines the literature that arose. Poets were employed by kings and recited their works to learned audiences; only the works which achieved the highest, purest aesthetic response were allowed to be true poetry, or "kavya." Though epics, drama, and animal tales are well represented by the Sanskrit literature of this period, it is in the compact form of the lyric poem that this literature achieved its highest degree of perfection. These poems, usually written in single stanzas, were anthologized to be memorized and recited for their pure aesthetic pleasure. The underlying theme which emerges is that life itself is an art which must be lived according to aesthetic principles. This Golden Age was followed by an age which mirrors Europe's middle ages, in that it saw the rise of an endless series of wars, partly ignited by the invasion of the Muslim world into India. This period also saw the rise of "bhakti" poetry, a poetry of personal religious devotion. Where the kavya poetry of earlier years was essentially aesthetic, bhakti poetry is religiously oriented, and more geared to the common man or woman.

China, during the years of the West's Middle Ages, saw a cultural flowering whose fruits continue to form the core of Chinese culture. Chinese poetry is especially valued worldwide for its lyric beauty, and much of the poetry which serves as models for Chinese poetry comes from this period. When North China fell to invaders in the early fourth century, the seat of Chinese culture moved to the south, and many of the northern aristocratic families sought refuge in the south. In a cultural atmosphere which favored individualism, the poetry of Tao

Chien stood out, in part because of the eccentricity of his own life. While the life of the peasant farmer was idealized by writers before him, Tao Chien chose such a life, and wrote about finding the natural pleasures in a life led simply and structured around the needs of farming.

In the late sixth century, the Sui dynasty reunited North and South China, to be replaced shortly thereafter by the T'ang Dynasty. It is this period that produced Li Po and Tu Fu, two of the most enduring of poets. Li Po was something of an outsider, a man of no aristocratic background from western China, who invented himself as an eccentric, somewhat comic poet to gain entrance to the imperial court. The comic sensibility which could lead him to write poems about wine and female company also led him to overstep the boundaries of good taste, and led to his dismissal from the court. Tu Fu, by contrast, was a man of some modest ancestry who spent years seeking political offices. His efforts panned out when he was appointed to a minor provincial post, but he soon grew to hate this job, and he quit it. It was only after years of wandering, and towards the end of his life, that he wrote most of the poetry attributed to him. In a pattern not uncommon in the Chinese poetry of the period, his poetry records reflections on both the great events of his life, and on some of the minutia he had lived through.

Japanese culture, by contrast, did not produce its first great era of achievement until the eighth century. Japanese culture of this period is sometimes regarded as imitative of the Chinese culture which thoroughly saturated Japanese society. However, by the eleventh century, Japan would reproduce *The Tale of Genji*, a long prose narrative, written by a woman writer, Murasaki Shikibu, which is frequently cited as the first novel in world literature. Following the sexual and outrageous exploits of Genji, a hero who is often abrasive and worse, *The Tale of Genji* displays a liberal view of sexuality such as would not become evident in Western literature for quite a few centuries. Though the novel begins in the spirit of a romance, celebrating a great hero, it quickly takes on elements of realism. Genji is not presented as a perfect hero, but as a deeply flawed human; when he dies two thirds of the way through the novel, his sons are presented as even more deeply flawed. However, if *The Tale of Genji* is the most significant contribution to come out of Japan from this era, it is by no means the only one; also of particular note is *The Pillow Book*, by Sei Shonagon, also a female writer. Though the meaning of the title of that book of personal reflections on love and life is somewhat obscure, one theory has it that the author kept her notebook next to her pillow, which is where these observations were composed. The random nature of her observations, while frequently criticized as a weakness, strike many readers as a delightful strength, and she spawned many imitators.

The European Middle Ages, meanwhile, came to a close with the writings of Dante Alighieri and Geoffery Chaucer, an Italian and an Englishman who produced the greatest vernacular literature of the middle ages, Dante in Italian, Chaucer in English. Both were men of political as well as literary importance. Dante's political beliefs led to his banishment from Florence in 1301, and he infuses his *Divine Comedy* with hatred of his political foes as much as with religious fervor, and with ardor for his dead first love, Beatrice. Chaucer, by contrast, held a variety of political posts throughout his life, and though his writing reveals the same interest in getting the crooked out of politics, Chaucer's favorite weapon is satire, not outrage. Though Chaucer's *Canterbury Tales* is a far more humorous work in its snapshots of life than is Dante's *Divine Comedy*, both works can be said to be united by a spiritual vision which sees this life as an audition for eternity, a view quite characteristic of the European Middle Ages. (TJC)

Introduction

Sundiata: An Epic of Old Mali

The *Sundiata* owes its present form to three levels of textual transmission; these are the original Mandingo narrative by the griot Mamadou Kouyate, its French translation by Djibril Tamsir Niane, and the English version of G. D. Pickett. The historical, cultural, and intellectual impulses behind Niane's initial endeavors can be traced back to the French colonial experience and the policy of assimilation into French culture of an African elite, and the inevitable backlash and reaction to it that produced the Negritude movement. By its affirmation of African culture and assertion of the positive values of the Black race, Negritude created a social climate which promoted a range of intellectual activities. Thus, Niane's recording of this facet of the African achievement in literature represents his recognition of the importance of the oral tradition in pre-literate and contemporary African society.

The *Sundiata*, then, is one of the many expressive forms of African oral literature which includes the myth, folktale, legend, fable, oral poetry, and the epic. These forms show that the African found a verbal expression for imaginative impulses and created aesthetic genres which satisfied his desire for beauty and the pleasant, demonstrated that he had a literature, and ensured the non-textual survival and transmission of valuable cultural and historical data.

The label "author" therefore would hardly fit the griot (French for *dyeli* or *belen tigui*), an institution whose status and role have been modified by time and social change. As dyeli Mamadou Kouyate tells us, he got his material and art from his ancestors; and he therefore did not author this epic though he created this particular version. Griots combined a complex range of roles in traditional society, for they were archivist, historian, teacher, entertainer in the courts of kings, and custodian and repository of cultural and social values; they effectively used the medium of music and eloquent language and exploited the paralinguistic features of the performance situation in creating a text. They are like the pre-Homeric bards as they have in their possession a common property of the language and culture of the Mandingo peoples of West Africa.

This griot from Guinea has a version which is an accessible and authentic representation of a wide spread tradition though it has been criticized. Niane's narrative in prose is, according to Okpewho, a less scholarly work, "less loyal and thus . . useful more for content than for issues of structure and style" (*African Oral Literature*). Irele sees it as a "faithful rendering of the action (which) fails to capture the epic's heroic movement and the atmosphere of performance essential to its character" (*Norton Anthology* 2338).

Other versions have been recorded from Senegal, Mali and the Gambia. Two such are *Sunjata: Three Mandinka Versions* (Gordon Innes, London: SOAS 1975), sung by three different griots from the Gambia, which with its comparative approach is very revealing of the nature of the oral narrative, and Fa-Digi Sisoko's *The Epic of Son-Jara: A West African Tradition* trans. John D. Johnson, Bloomington: Indiana University Press 1986) which gives valuable impressions of the performance and situational features of the narrative and communicates elements of the resources of the Mandinka language.

Other folk epics from Africa clearly demonstrate the continental incidence of this narrative form, and they include *The Ozidi Saga* (Ijaw-Nigeria), *Kambili Epic* (Mande-Mali), *Mwindo Epic* (Banyanga-Zaire), *Da Mozon* (Bambara-Mali), *Chaka* (Zulu-South Africa), *The Legend of Luyongo* (Swahili-East Africa) and the *Lianja Epic* (Nkudo-Zaire).

465

Sundiata is an epic from the Manding peoples who have occupied the Sahel and middle Savannah belt of West Africa for hundreds of years and who now straddle several modern states. They belong to the Mande language family, their language is variously referred to as Maninka, Mandinka, and Mandingo, and they have strong affinities with and a sense of historical and cultural continuity with the ancient Mali empire.

Africa saw the rise and decline of Ancient empires in the Western Savannah. These included Ghana ca. 8th to 13th century, Mali ca. 13th to 14th century, and Songhai ca. 15th to 16th century. Mali was the best known and the events described here span the years 1217 to 1237, and converge with those traditions which credit Sundiata, who died in 1255, as the founder of the empire in the first half of the 13th century. Ghana, which flourished in the 9th and 10th centuries, was in decline by the 12th century, and Mali eventually superseded it when Sundiata defeated Ghana. The various traditions define the Ghana-Mali relationship in terms of this conflict. One source describes the surprise attack on Mali by Sumanguru King of Old Ghana who slaughtered Sundiata's brothers but spared him because of his crippled nature, the latter's growth into strength and his ultimate defeat of Sumanguru's forces and annexation of Old Ghana as part of Mali (Wingfield 1966). Other versions also see Sundiata's formidable antagonist who he defeated at Krina as this Susu King, named Soumaoro Kanté by Niane, Sumamuru by Fa-Digi Sisoko and Susu Sumanguru by Bamba Suso, the griot of Innes' version one.

The *Sundiata* narrates the rise of ancient Mali and its subject is Sundiata; it celebrates the heroic empire building, military exploits and conquests of Sundiata; it combines history, legend, and myth; it explores themes of war, heroism, endurance, man's aspiration for justice, predestination, and man's achievement in the face of massive odds.

It is not clear or certain how this epic originated or when it was elaborated into its present forms, but this and other versions draw on history, and embellish events with accretions of the fanciful and legendary into a heroic narrative which is very firmly rooted in the traditional socio-cultural setting, and which have the stamp of the individual griots and their performance strategies and contexts. Related to this last point, it is significant to note that the griot usually performs for a live audience with musical accompaniment at appropriate stages, draws on the full resources of his language and other features of this context of performance, and does not rely only on a bland narration.

Thus, in developing the broadly defined historical, personal and social themes, in the broad chronological sweep of the narrative in true epic style, a history of Mali emerges from the earliest times to Sundiata's times. In addition, the fate and character of the hero himself is defined in terms of leadership qualities, the development of a heroic stature and achievement, and the exploitation of attractive personal traits. A strong, just, and pious ruler, Sundiata seems almost idealized while Soumaoro Kanté, though a worthy opponent, has a host of negative traits.

Also, the setting develops a sociocultural and traditional background which effectively contextualizes this epic in terms which clearly demonstrate its nonwestern character. On this level, the text presents elements of religion, especially Islam, customs and traditions, conduct, outlook, and beliefs of a people. These levels of the text not only present an environment located in the past into which Islam had spread and was in competition with traditional African religion but also articulate the cultural and historical cohesiveness of the Manding peoples.

As a folk epic, Sundiata exhibits characterists and minor conventions which define this genre. The reader soon meets the epic hero whose fate is Mali's fate; the heroic deeds of valour such as a child hero uprooting a baobab tree and the later battles; the vast scale of the setting; the language appropriately elaborated by the resonance of the griot's stylistic nuances, hyperbole and praise songs; participation by non-human supernatural forces conceived of in terms of the African's belief in sorcery, magic, ritual and sacrifice, super-human powers in man, and the efficacy of intervention by spiritual forces. The text also gives a genealogy of Sundiata which goes even beyond his forefathers, presents a catalogue of tribes and allies in the massed armies of Sundiata, and even has some epic similes and the assembly.

The *Sundiata* is thus firmly within the ambit of universal human values with respect to its referential content, artistic form, and as a literary genre, but it also defines its uniqueness and represents a significant aesthetic entity. (ACJ)

BIBLIOGRAPHY

Clark, J. P. *The Ozidi Saga.* Ibadan: University Press, 1977.

Innes, Gordon, *Sunjata: Three Mandinka Versions.* London: SOAS, 1975.

Irele, Abiola. "Africa: The Mali Epic of Son-Jara." *The Norton Anthology of World Masterpieces.* Vol. 1. New York: W.W. Norton, 1995.

___. "Negritude—Literature and Ideology." *Critical Perspectives on Leopold Sedar Senghor.* Ed. Janice Spleth. Colorado Springs: Three Continents Press, 1994.

Johnson, John W. *The Epic of Son-Jara: A West African Tradition.* Bloomington: Indiana University Press, 1986.

Mofolo, T. *Chaka.* Trans. F. H. Dutton. Oxford: Clarendon Press, 1931.

Niane, D. T. *Sundiata: An Epic of Old Mali.* Trans. G. D. Pickett. London: Longman, 1965.

Okpewho, Isidore. *African Oral Literature.* Bloomington and Indianapolis: Indiana University Press, 1992.

___. *The Epic in Africa: Towards a Poetic of the Oral Performance.* New York: Columbia University Press, 1979.

Vansina, J. *Oral Tradition as History,* London: James Curry, 1985.

Wingfield, R. J. *The Story of Old Ghana, Melle and Songhai.* Cambridge: Cambridge University Press, 1966.

from The Sundiata

Edited by Niane
Translated by Pickett

The Words of the Griot
Mamadou Kouyaté

I am a griot. It is I, Djeli Mamoudou Kouyaté, son of Bintou Kouyaté and Djeli Kedian Kouyaté, master in the art of eloquence. Since time immemorial the Kouyatés have been in the service of the Keita princes of Mali; we are vessels of speech, we are the repositories which harbour secrets many centuries old. The art of eloquence has no secrets for us; without us the names of kings would vanish into oblivion, we are the memory of mankind; by the spoken word we bring to life the deeds and exploits of kings for younger generations.

I derive my knowledge from my father Djeli Kedian, who also got it from his father; history holds no mystery for us; we teach to the vulgar just as much as we want to teach them, for it is we who keep the keys to the twelve doors of Mali.

I know the list of all the sovereigns who succeeded to the throne of Mali. I know how the black people divided into tribes, for my father bequeathed to me all his learning; I know why such and such is called Kamara, another Keita, and yet another Sibibé or Traoré; every name has a meaning, a secret import.

I teach kings the history of their ancestors so that the lives of the ancients might serve them as an example, for the world is old, but the future springs from the past.

My word is pure and free of all untruth; it is the word of my father; it is the word of my father's father. I will give you my father's words just as I received them; royal griots do not know what lying is. When a quarrel breaks out between tribes it is we who settle the difference, for we are the depositories of oaths which the ancestors swore.

Listen to my word, you who want to know; by my mouth you will learn the history of Mali.

By my mouth you will get to know the story of the ancestor of great Mali, the story of him who, by his exploits, surpassed even Alexander the Great; he who, from the East, shed his rays upon all the countries of the West.

Listen to the story of the son of the Buffalo, the son of the Lion. I am going to tell you of Maghan Sundiata, of Mari-Djata, of Sogolon Djata, of Naré Maghan Djata; the man of many names against whom sorcery could avail nothing.

The First Kings of Mali

Listen then, sons of Mali, children of the black people, listen to my word, for I am going to tell you of Sundiata, the father of the Bright Country, of the savanna land, the ancestor of those who draw the bow, the master of a hundred vanquished kings.

I am going to talk of Sundiata, Manding Diara, Lion of Mali, Sogolon Djata, son of Sogolon, Naré Maghan Djata, son of Naré Maghan, Sogo Sogo Simbon Salaba, hero of many names.

I am going to tell you of Sundiata, he whose exploits will astonish men for a long time yet. He was great among kings, he was peerless among men; he was beloved of God because he was the last of the great conquerors.

Right at the beginning then, Mali was a province of the Bambara kings; those who are today called Mandingo, inhabitants of Mali, are not indigenous; they come from the East. Bilali Bounama, ancestor of the Keitas, was the faithful servant of the Prophet Muhammad (may the peace of God be upon him). Bilali Bounama had seven sons of whom the eldest, Lawalo, left the Holy City and came to settle in Mali; Lawalo had Latal Kalabi for a son, Latal Kalabi had Damul Kalabi who then had Lahilatoul Kalabi.

Lahilatoul Kalabi was the first black prince to make the Pilgrimage to Mecca. On his return he was robbed by brigands in the desert; his men were scattered and some died of thirst, but God saved Lahilatoul Kalabi, for he was a righteous man. He called upon the Almighty and jinn appeared and recognized him as king. After seven years' absence Lahilatoul was able to return, by the grace of Allah the Almighty, to Mali where none expected to see him any more.

Lahilatoul Kalabi had two sons, the elder being called Kalabi Bomba and the younger Kalabi Dauman; the elder chose royal power and reigned, while the younger preferred fortune and wealth and became the ancestor of these who go from country to country seeking their fortune.

Kalabi Bomba had Mamadi Kani for a son. Mamadi Kani was a hunter king like the first kings of Mali. It was he who invented the hunter's whistle; he communicated with the jinn of the forest and bush. These spirits had no secrets from him and he was loved by Kondolon Ni Sané. His followers were so numerous that he formed them into an army which became formidable; he often gathered them together in the bush and taught them the art of hunting. It was he who revealed to hunters the medicinal leaves which heal wounds and cure diseases. Thanks to the strength of his followers, he became king of a vast country; with them Mamadi Kani conquered all the lands which stretch from the Sankarani to the Bouré. Mamadi Kani had four sons—Kani Simbon, Kamignogo Simbon, Kabala Simbon and Simbon Tagnogokelin. They were all initiated into the art of hunting and deserved the title of Simbon. It was the lineage of Bamari Tagnogokelin which held on to the power, his son was M'Bali Nènè whose son was Bello. Bello's son was called Bello Bakon and he had a son called Maghan Kon Fatta, also called Frako Maghan Keigu, Maghan the handsome.

Maghan Kon Fatta was the father of the great Sundiata and had three wives and six children—three boys and three girls. His first wife was called Sassouma Bérété, daughter of a great divine; she was the mother of King Dankaran Touman and Princess Nana Triban. The second wife, Sogolon Kedjou, was the mother of Sundiata and the two princesses Sogolon Kolonkan and Sogolon Djamarou. The third wife was one of the Kamaras and was called Namandjé; she was the mother of Manding Bory (or Manding Bakary), who was the best friend of his half-brother Sundiata. . . .

The Lion's Awakening

A short while after this interview between Naré Maghan and his son the king died. Sogolon's son was no more than seven years old. The council of elders met in the king's palace. It was no use Doua's defending the king's will which reserved the throne for Mari Djata, for the council took no account of Naré Meghan's wish. With the help of Sassouma Bérété's intrigues, Dankaran Touman was proclaimed king and a regency council was formed in which the queen mother was all-powerful. A short time after, Doua died.

As men have short memories, Sogolon's son was spoken of with nothing but irony and scorn. People had seen one-eyed kings, one-armed kings, and lame kings but a stiff-legged king had never been heard tell of. No matter how great the destiny promised for Mari Djata might be, the throne could not be given to someone who had no power in his legs; if the jinn loved him, let them begin by giving him the use of his legs. Such were the remarks that Sogolon heard every day. The queen mother, Sassouma Bérété, was the source of all this gossip.

Having become all-powerful, Sassouma Bérété persecuted Sogolon because the late Naré Maghan had preferred her. She banished Sogolon and her son to a back yard of the palace. Mari Djata's mother now occupied an old hut which had served as a lumber-room of Sassouma's.

The wicked queen mother allowed free passage to all those inquisitive people who wanted to see the child that still crawled at the age of seven. Nearly all the inhabitants of Niani filed into the palace and the poor Sogolon wept to see herself thus given over to public ridicule. Mari Djata took on a ferocious look in front of the crowd of sightseers. Sogolon found a little consolation only in the love of her eldest daughter, Kolonkan. She was four and she could walk. She seemed to understand all her mother's miseries and already she helped her with the housework. Sometimes, when Sogolon was attending to the chores, it was she who stayed beside her sister Djamarou, quite small as yet.

Sogolon Kedjou and her children lived on the queen mother's left-overs, but she kept a little garden in the open ground behind the village. It was there that she passed her brightest moments looking after her onions and gnougous. One day she happened to be short of condiments and went to the queen mother to beg a little baobab leaf.

"Look you," said the malicious Sassouma, "I have a calabash full. Help yourself, you poor woman. As for me, my son knew how to walk at seven and it was he who went and picked these baobab leaves. Take them then, since your son is unequal to mine." Then she laughed derisively with that fierce laughter which cuts through your flesh and penetrates tight to the bone.

Sogolon Kedjou was dumbfounded. She had never imagined that hate could be so strong in a human being. With a lump in her throat she left Sassouma's. Outside her hut Mari Djata, sitting on his useless legs, was blandly eating out of a calabash. Unable to contain herself any longer, Sogolon burst into sobs and seizing a piece of wood, hit her son.

"Oh son of misfortune, will you never walk? Through your fault I have just suffered the greatest affront of my life! What have I done, God, for you to punish me in this way?"

Mari Djata seized the piece of wood and, looking at his mother, said, "Mother, what's the matter?"

"Shut up, nothing can ever wash me clean of this insult."

"But what then?"

"Sassouma has just humiliated me over a matter of a baobab leaf. At your age her own son could walk and used to bring his mother baobab leaves."

"Cheer up, Mother, cheer up."

"No. It's too much. I can't."

"Very well then I am going to walk today," said Mari Djata. "Go and tell my father's smiths to make me the heaviest possible iron rod. Mother, do you want just the leaves of the baobab or would you rather I brought you the whole tree?"

"Ah, my son, to wipe out this insult I want the tree and its roots at my feet outside my hut."

Balla Fasséké, who was present, ran to the master smith, Farakourou, to order an iron rod.

Sogolon had sat down in front of her hut. She was weeping softly and holding her head between her two hands. Mari Djata went calmly back to his calabash of rice and began eating again as if nothing had happened. From time to time he looked up discreetly at his mother who was murmuring in a low voice, "I want the whole tree, in front of my hut, the whole tree."

All of a sudden a voice burst into laughter behind the hut. It was the wicked Sassouma telling one of her serving women about the scene of humiliation and she was laughing loudly so that Sogolon could hear. Sogolon fled into the hut and hid her face under the blankets so as not to have before her eyes this heedless boy, who was more preoccupied with eating than with anything else. With her head buried in the bed-clothes Sogolon wept and her body shook violently. Her daughter, Sogolon Djamarou, had come and sat down beside her and she said, "Mother, Mother, don't cry. Why are you crying?"

Mari Djata had finished eating and, dragging himself along on his legs, he came and sat under the wall of the hut for the sun was scorching. What was he thinking about? He alone knew.

The royal forges were situated outside the walls and over a hundred smiths worked there. The bows, spears, arrows and shields of Niani's warriors came from there. When Balla Fasséké came to order the iron rod, Farakourou said to him, "The great day has arrived then?"

"Yes, Today is a day like any other, but it will see what no other day has seen."

The master of the forges, Farakourou, was the son of the old Nounfaïri, and he was a soothsayer like his father. In his workshops there was an enormous iron bar wrought by his father Nounfaïri. Everybody wondered what this bar was destined to be used for. Farakourou called six of his apprentices and told them to carry the iron bar to Sogolon's house.

When the smiths put the gigantic iron bar down in front of the hut the noise was so frightening that Sogolon, who was lying down, jumped up with a start. Then Balla Fasséké, son of Gnankouman Doua, spoke.

"Here is the great day, Mari Djata. I am speaking to you, Maghan, son of Sogolon. The waters of the Niger can efface the stain from the body, but they cannot wipe out an insult. Arise, young lion, roar, and may the bush know that from henceforth it has a master."

The apprentice smiths were still there, Sogolon had come out and everyone was watching Mari Djata. He crept on all-fours and came to the iron bar. Supporting himself on his knees and one hand, with the other hand he picked up the iron bar without any effort and stood it up vertically. Now he was resting on nothing but his knees and held the bar with both his hands. A deathly silence had gripped all those present. Sogolon Djata closed his eyes, held tight, the muscles in his arms tensed. With a violent jerk he threw his weight on to it and his knees left the ground. Sogolon Kedjou was all eyes and watched her son's legs which were trembling as though from an electric shock. Djata was sweating and the sweat ran from his brow. In an effort he straightened up and was on his feet at one go—but the great bar of iron was twisted and had taken the form of a bow!

Then Balla Fasséké sang out the "Hymn to the Bow," striking up with his powerful voice:

"Take your bow, Simbon,
Take your bow and let us go.
Take your bow, Sogolon Djata."

When Sogolon saw her son standing she stood dumb for a moment, then suddenly she sang these words of thanks to God who had given her son the use of his legs:

"Oh day, what a beautiful day,
Oh day, day of joy;
Allah Almighty, you never created a finer day.
So my son is going to walk!"

Standing in the position of a soldier at ease, Sogolon Djata, supported by his enormous rod, was sweating great beads of sweat. Balla Fasséké's song had alerted the whole palace and people came running from all over to see what had happened, and each stood bewildered before Sogolon's son. The queen mother had rushed there and when she saw Mari Djata standing up she trembled from head to foot. After recovering his breath Sogolon's son dropped the bar and the crowd stood to one side. His first steps were those of a giant. Balla Fasséké fell into step and pointing his finger at Djata, he cried:

"Room, room, make room!
The lion has walked;
Hide antelopes,
Get out of his way."

Behind Niani there was a young baobab tree and it was there that the children of the town came to pick leaves for their mothers. With all his might the son of Sogolon tore up the tree and put it on his shoulders and went back to his mother. He threw the tree in front of the hut and said, "Mother, here are some baobab leaves for you. From henceforth it will be outside your hut that the women of Niani will come to stock up."

Sogolon Djata walked. From that day forward the queen mother had no more peace of mind. But what can one do against destiny? Nothing. Man, under the influence of certain illusions, thinks he can alter the course which God has mapped out, but everything he does falls into a higher order which he barely understands. That is why Sassouma's efforts were vain against Sogolon's son, everything she did lay in the child's destiny. Scorned the day before and the object of public ridicule, now Sogolon's son was as popular as he had been despised. The multitude loves and fears strength. Niani talked of nothing but Djata; the mothers urged their sons to become hunting companions of Djata and to share his games, as if they wanted their offspring to profit from the nascent glory of the buffalo-woman's son. The words of Doua on the name-giving day came back to men's minds and Sogolon was now surrounded with much respect; in conversation people were fond of contrasting Sogolon's modesty with the pride of malice of Soussouma Bérété. It was because the former had been an exemplary wife and mother that God had granted strength to her son's legs for, it was said, the more a wife loves and respects her husband and the more she suffers for her child, the more valorous will the child be one day. Each is the child of his mother; the child is worth no more than the mother is worth. It was not astonishing that the king Dankaran Touman was so colourless, for his mother had never shown the slightest respect to her husband and never, in the presence of the late king, did she show that humility which every wife should show before her husband. People recalled her scenes of jealousy and the spiteful remarks she circulated about her co-wife and her child. And people would conclude gravely, "Nobody knows God's mystery. The snake has no legs yet it is as swift as any other animal that has four."

Sogolon Djata's popularity grew from day to day and he was surrounded by a gang of children of the same age as himself. These were Fran Kamara, son of the king of Tabon; Kamandjan, son of the king of Sibi; and other princes whose fathers had sent them to the court of Niani. The son of Namandjé, Manding Bory, was already joining in their games. Balla Fasséké followed Sogolon Djata all the time. He was past twenty and it was he who gave the child education and instruction according to Mandingo rules of conduct. Whether in town or at the hunt, he missed no opportunity of instructing his pupil. Many young boys of Niani came to join in the games of the royal child.

He liked hunting best of all. Farakourou, master of the forges, had made Djata a fine bow, and he proved himself to be a good shot with the bow. He made frequent hunting trips with his troops, and in the evening all Niani would be in the square to be present at the entry of the young hunters. The crowd would sing the "Hymn to the Bow" which Balla Fasséké had composed, and Sogolon Djata was quite young when he received the title of Simbon, or master hunter, which is only conferred on great hunters who have proved themselves.

Every evening Sogolon Kedjou would gather Djata and his companions outside her hut. She would tell them stories about the beasts of the bush, the dumb brothers of man. Sogolon Djata learnt to distinguish between the animals; he knew why the buffalo was his mother's wraith and also why the lion was the protector of his father's family. He also listened to the history of the kings which Balla Fasséké told him; enraptured by the story of Alexander the Great, the mighty king of gold and silver, whose sun shone over quite half the world. Sogolon initiated her son into certain secrets and revealed to him the names of the medicinal plants which every hunter should know. Thus, between his mother and his griot, the child got to know all that needed to be known.

Sogolon's son was now ten. The name Sogolon Djata in the rapid Mandingo language became Sundiata or Sondjata. He was a lad full of strength; his arms had the strength of ten and his biceps inspired fear in his companions. He had already that authoritative way of speaking which

belongs to those who are destined to command. His brother, Manding Bory, became his best friend, and whenever Djata was seen, Manding Bory appeared too. They were like a man and his shadow. Fran Kamara and Kamandjan were the closest friends of the young princes, while Balla Fasséké followed them all like a guardian angel.

But Sundiata's popularity was so great that the queen mother became apprehensive for her son's throne. Dankaran Touman was the most retiring of men. At the age of eighteen he was still under the influence of his mother and a handful of old schemers. It was Sassouma Bérété who really reigned in his name. The queen mother wanted to put an end to this popularity by killing Sundiata and it was thus that one night she received the nine great witches of Mali. They were all old women. The eldest, and the most dangerous too, was called Soumosso Konkomba. When the nine old hags had seated themselves in a semicircle around her bed the queen mother said:

"You who rule supreme at night, nocturnal powers, oh you who hold the secret of life, you who can put an end to one life, can you help me?"

"The night is potent," said Soumosso Konkomba, "Oh queen, tell us what is to be done, on whom must we turn the fatal blade?"

"I want to kill Sundiata," said Sassouma. "His destiny runs counter to my son's and he must be killed while there is still time. If you succeed, I promise you the finest rewards. First of all I bestow on each of you a cow and her calf and from tomorrow go to the royal granaries and each of you will receive a hundred measures of rice and a hundred measures of hay on my authority."

"Mother of the king," rejoined Soumosso Konkomba, "life hangs by nothing but a very fine thread, but all is interwoven here below. Life has a cause, and death as well. The one comes from the other. Your hate has a cause and your action must have a cause. Mother of the king, everything holds together, our action will have no effect unless we are ourselves implicated, but Mari Djata has done us no wrong. It is, then, difficult for us to compass his death."

"But you are also concerned," replied the queen mother, "for the son of Sogolon will be a scourge to us all."

"The snake seldom bites the foot that does not walk," said one of the witches.

"Yes, but there are snakes that attack everybody. Allow Sundiata to grow up and we will all repent of it. Tomorrow go to Sogolon's vegetable patch and make a show of picking a few gnougou leaves. Mari Djata stands guard there and you will see how vicious the boy is. He won't have any respect for your age, he'll give you a good thrashing."

"That's a clever idea," said one of the old hags.

"But the cause of our discomfiture will be ourselves, for having touched something which did not belong to us."

"We could repeat the offence," said another, "and then if he beats us again we would be able to reproach him with being unkind, heartless. In that case we would be concerned, I think."

"The idea is ingenious," said Soumosso Konkomba. "Tomorrow we shall go to Sogolon's vegetable patch."

"Now there's a happy thought," concluded the queen mother, laughing for joy. "Go to the vegetable patch tomorrow and you will see that Sogolon's son is mean. Beforehand, present yourselves at the royal granaries where you will receive the grain I promised you; the cows and the calves are already yours."

The old hags bowed and disappeared into the black night. The queen mother was now alone and gloated over her anticipated victory. But her daughter, Nana Triban, woke up.

"Mother, who were you talking to? I thought I heard voices."

"Sleep, my daughter, it is nothing. You didn't hear anything."

In the morning, as usual, Sundiata got his companions together in front of his mother's hut and said, "What animal are we going to hunt today?"

Kamandjan said, "I wouldn't mind if we attached some elephants right now."

"Yes, I am of this opinion too," said Fran Kamara. "That will allow us to go far into the bush."

And the young band left after Sogolon had filled the hunting bags with eatables. Sundiata and his companions came back late to the village, but first Djata wanted to take a look at his mother's vegetable patch as was his custom. It was dusk. There he found the nine witches stealing gnougou leaves. They made a show of running away like thieves caught redhanded.

"Stop, stop, poor old women," said Sundiata, "what is the matter with you to run away like this. This garden belongs to all."

Straight away his companions and he filled the gourds of the old hags with leaves, aubergines and onions.

"Each time that you run short of condiments come to stock up here without fear."

"You disarm us," said one of the old crones, and another added, "And you confound us with your bounty."

"Listen, Djata," said Soumosso Konkomba, "we had come here to test you. We have no need to condiments but your generosity disarms us. We were sent here by the queen mother to provoke you and draw the anger of the nocturnal powers upon you. But nothing can be done against a heart full kindness. And to think that we have already drawn a hundred measures of rice and a hundred measures of millet and the queen promises us each a cow and her calf in addition. Forgive us, son of Sogolon."

"I bear you no ill-will," said Djata. "Here, I am returning from the hunt with my companions and we have killed ten elephants, so I will give you an elephant each and there you have some meat!"

"Thank you, son of Sogolon."

"Thank you, child of Justice."

"Henceforth," concluded Soumosso Konkomba, "we will watch over you." And the nine witches disappeared into the night, Sundiata and his companions continued on their way to Niani and got back after dark.

"You were really frightened; those nine witches really scared you, eh?" said Sogolon Kolonkan, Djata's young sister.

"How do you know," retorted Sundiata, astonished.

"I saw them at night hatching their scheme, but I knew there was no danger for you." Kolonkan was well versed in the art of witchcraft and watched over her brother without his suspecting it.

EXILE

But Sogolon was a wise mother. She knew everything that Sassouma could do to hurt her family, and so, one evening, after the children had eaten, she called them together and said to Sundiata.

"Let us leave here, my son; Manding Bory and Djamarou are vulnerable. They are not yet initiated into the secrets of night, they are not sorcerers. Despairing of ever injuring you, Sassouma will aim her blows at your brother or sister. Let us go away from here. You will return to reign when you are a man, for it is in Mali that your destiny must be fulfilled."

It was the wisest course. Manding Bory, the son of Naré Maghan's third wife, Namandjé, had no gift of sorcery, Sundiata loved him very much and since the death of Namandjé he had been welcomed by Sogolon. Sundiata had found a great friend in his half-brother. You cannot choose your relatives but you can choose your friends. Manding Bory and Sundiata were real friends and it was to save his brother that Djata accepted exile.

Balla Fasséké, Djata's griot, prepared the departure in detail. But Sassouma Bérété kept her eye on Sogolon and her family.

One morning the king, Dankaran Touman, called the council together. He announced his intention of sending an embassy to the powerful king of Sosso, Soumaoro Kanté. For such a delicate mission he had thought of Balla Fasséké, son of Doua, his father's griot. The council approved the royal decision, the embassy was formed and Balla Fasséké was at the head of it.

It was a very clever way of taking away from Sundiata the griot his father had given him. Djata was out hunting and when he came back in the evening, Sogolon Kedjou told him the news. The embassy had left that very morning. Sundiata flew in a frightful rage.

"What! Take away the griot my father gave me! No, he will give me back my griot."

"Stop!" said Sogolon. "Let it go. It is Sassouma who is acting thus, but she does not know that she obeys a higher order."

"Come with me," said Sundiata to his brother Manding Bory, and the two princes went out. Djata bundled aside the guards on the house of Dankaran Touman, but he was so angry that he could not utter a word. It was Manding Bory who spoke.

"Brother Dankaran Touman, you have taken away our part of the inheritance. Every prince has had his griot, and you have taken away Balla Fasséké. He was not yours but wherever he may be, Balla will always be Djata's griot. And since you do not want to have us around you we shall leave Mali and go far away from here."

"But I will return," added the son of Sogolon, vehemently. "I will return, do you hear?"

"You know that you are going away but you do not know if you will come back," the king replied.

"I *will* return, do you hear me?" Djata went on and his tone was categorical. A shiver ran through the king's whole body. Dankaran Touman trembled in every limb. The two princes went out. The queen mother hurried in and found her son in a state of collapse.

"Mother, he is leaving but he says he will return. But why is he leaving? I intend to give him back his griot, for my part. Why is he leaving?"

"Of course, he will stay behind since you so desire it, but in that case you might as well give up your throne to him, you who tremble before the threats of a ten-year-old child. Give your seat up to him since you cannot rule. As for me, I am going to return to my parents' village for I will not be able to live under the Tyranny of Sogolon's son. I will go and finish my days among my kinsfolk and I will say that I had a son who was afraid to rule."

Sassouma bewailed her lot so much that Dankaran Touman suddenly revealed himself as a man of iron. Now he desired the death of his brothers—but he let them leave, it could not be helped, but if they should ever cross his path again—! He would reign, alone, for power could not be shared!

Thus Sogolon and her children tasted exile. We poor creatures! We think we are hurting our neighbour at the time when we are working in the very direction of destiny. Our action is not us for it is commanded of us.

Sassouma Bérété thought herself victorious because Sogolon and her children had fled from Mali. Their feet ploughed up the dust of the roads. They suffered the insults which those who leave their country know of. Doors were shut against them and kings chased them from their courts. But all that was part of the great destiny of Sundiata. Seven years passed, seven winters followed and another and forgetfulness crept into the souls of men, but time marched on at an even pace. Moons succeeded moons in the same sky and rivers in the beds continued their endless course.

Seven years passed and Sundiata grew up. His body became sturdy and his misfortunes made his mind wise. He became a man. Sogolon felt the weight of her years and of the growing hump on her back, while Djata, like a young tree, was shooting up to the sky.

After leaving Niani, Sogolon and her children had sojourned at Djedeba with the king, Mansa Konkon, the great sorcerer. Djedeba was a town on the Niger two days away from Niani. The king received them with a little mistrust, but everywhere the stranger enjoys the right to hospitality, so Sogolon and her children were lodged in the very enclosure of the king and for two months Sundiata and Manding Bory joined in the games of the king's children. One night, as the children were playing at knuckle-bones outside the palace in the moonlight, the king's daughter, who was no more than twelve, said to Manding Bory, "You know that my father is a great sorcerer."

"Really?" said the artless Manding Bory.

"Why yes, you mean you did not know? Well anyway, his power lies in the game of wori; you can play wori."

"My brother now, he is a great sorcerer."

"No doubt he does not come up to my father."

"But what did you say? Your father plays at wori?"

Just then Sogolon called the children because the moon had just waned.

"Mother is calling us," said Sundiata, who was standing at one side. "Come Manding Bory. If I am not mistaken, you are fond of that daughter of Mansa Konkon's."

"Yes brother, but I would have you know that to drive a cow into be stable it is necessary to take the calf in."

"Of course, the cow will follow the kidnapper. But take care, for if the cow is in a rage so much the worse for the kidnapper."

The two brothers went in swopping proverbs. Men's wisdom is contained in proverbs and when children wield proverbs it is a sign that they have profited from adult company. That morning Sundiata and Manding Bory did not leave the royal enclosure but played with the king's children beneath the meeting tree. At the beginning of the afternoon Mansa Konkon ordered the son of Sogolon into his palace.

The king lived in a veritable maze and after several twists and turns through dark corridor a servant left Djata in a badly-lit room. He looked about him but was not afraid. Fear enters the heart of him who does not know his destiny, whereas Sundiata knew that he was striding towards a great destiny. He did not know what fear was. When his eyes were accustomed to the semi-darkness, Sundiata saw the king sitting with his back to the light on a great ox-hide. He saw some splendid wagons hanging on the walls and exclaimed.

"What beautiful weapons you have, Mansa Konkon," and, seizing a sword, he began to fence on his own against an imaginary foe. The king, astonished, watched the extraordinary child.

"You had me sent for," said the latter, "and here I am." He hung the sword back up.

"Sit down," said the king. "It is a habit with me to invite my guests to play, so we are going to play, we are going to play at wori. But I make rather unusual conditions; if I win—and I shall win—I kill you."

"And if it is I who win," said Djata without being put out.

"In that case I will give you all that you ask of me. But I would have you know that I always win."

"If I win I asking for nothing more than that sword," said Sundiata, pointing to the sword he had brandished.

"All right," said the king, "you are sure of yourself, eh?" He drew up the log in which the wori holes were dug and put four pebbles in each of the holes.

"I go first," said the king, and taking the four pebbles from one hole he dealt them out, punctuating his actions with these words:

"I don don, don don Kokodji.
Wori is the invention of a hunter.
I don don, don don Kokodji.
I am unbeatable at this game.
I am called the 'exterminator king'"

And Sundiata, taking the pebbles from another hole, continued:

"I don don, don don Kokodji.
Formerly guests were sacred.
I don don, don don Kokodji.
But the gold came only yesterday.
Whereas I came before yesterday."

"Someone has betrayed me," roared the king Mansa Konkon, "someone has betrayed me."

"No, king, do not accuse anybody," said the child.

"What then?"

"It is nearly three moons since I have been living with you and you have never up to now suggested a game of wori. God is the guest's tongue. My words express only the truth because I am your guest."

The truth was that the queen mother of Niani had sent gold to Mansa Konkon so that we would get rid of Sundiata: "the gold came only yesterday," and Sundiata was at the king's court prior to the gold. In fact, the king's daughter had revealed the secret to Manding Bory. Then the king, in confusion, said, "You have won, but you will not have what you asked for, and I will turn you out of my town."

"Thank you for two months' hospitality, but I will return, Mansa Konkon."

Once again Sogolon and her children took to the path of exile. They went away from the river and headed west. They were going to seek hospitality from the king of Tabon in the country which is called the Fouta Djallon today. This region was at that time inhabited by the Kamara blacksmiths and the Djallonkés. Tabon was an impregnable town firmly entrenched behind mountains, and the king had been for a long time an ally of the Niani court. His son, Fran Kamara, had been one of the companions of Sundiata. After Sogolon's departure from Niani the companion princes of Sundiata had been sent back to their respective families.

But the king of Tabon was already old and did not want to fall out with whoever ruled at Niani. He welcomed Sogolon with kindness and advised her to go away as far as possible. He suggested the court of Ghana, whose king he knew. A caravan of merchants was shortly leaving for Ghana. The old king commended Sogolon and her children to the merchants and even delayed the departure for a few days to allow the mother to recover a little from her fatigues.

It was with joy that Sundiata and Manding Bory met Fran Kamara again. The latter, not without pride, showed them round the fortresses of Tabon and had them admire the huge iron gates and the king's arsenals. Fran Kamara was very glad to receive Sundiata at his home but was very grieved when the fatal day arrived, the day of departure. The night before he had given a hunting party to the princes of Mali and the youngsters had talked in the bush like men.

"When I go back to Mali," Sundiata had said, "I will pass through Tabon to pick you up and we will go to Mali together."

"Between now and then we will have grown up," Manding Bory had added.

"I will have all the army of Tabon for my own," Fran Kamara had said, "The blacksmiths and the Djalonkés are excellent warriors. I already attend the gathering of armed men which my father holds once a year."

"I will make you a great general, we will travel through many countries and emerge the strongest of all. Kings will tremble before us as a woman trembles before a man." The son of Sogolon had spoken thus.

The exiles took to the road again. Tabon was very far from Ghana, but the merchants were good to Sogolon and her children. The king had provided the mounts and the caravan headed to the north, leaving the land of Kita on the right. On the way the merchants told the princes a great deal about events of the past. Mari Djata was particularly interested in the stories bearing on the great king of the day, Soumaoro Kanté. It was to him at Sosso that Balla Fasséké had gone as envoy. Djata learned that Soumaoro was the richest and most powerful king and even the king of Ghana paid him tribute. He was also a man of great cruelty.

The country of Ghana is a dry region where water is short. Formerly the Cissés of Ghana were the most powerful of princes. They were descended from Alexander the Great, the king of gold and silver, but ever since the Cissés had broken the ancestral taboo their power had kept on declining. At the time of Sundiata the descendants of Alexander were paying tribute to the king of Sosso. After several days of travelling the caravan arrived outside Wagadou. The merchants showed Sogolon and her children the great forest of Wagadou, where the great serpent-god used to live. The town was surrounded with enormous walls, very badly maintained. The travellers noticed that they were a lot of white traders and Wagadou and many encampments were to be seen all around the town. Tethered camels were everywhere.

Ghana was the land of the Soninke, and the people there did not speak Mandingo any more, but nevertheless there were many people who understood it, for the Soninke travel a lot. They are great traders. Their donkey caravans came heavily laden to Niani every dry season. They would set themselves up behind the town and the inhabitants would come out to barter.

The merchants made their way towards the colossal city gate. The head of the caravan spoke to the guards and one of them beckoned to Sundiata and his family to follow him, and they entered the city of the Cissés. The terraced houses did not have straw roofs in complete contrast to the towns of Mali. There were also a lot of mosques in this city, but that did not astonish Sundiata in the least, for he knew that the Cissés were very religious; at Niani there was only one mosque. The travellers noticed that the anterooms were incorporated in the houses whereas in Mali the anteroom or "bollon" was a separate building. As it was evening everybody was making his way to the mosque. The travellers could understand nothing of the prattle which the passers-by exchanged when they saw them on their way to the palace.

The palace of the king of Ghana was an imposing building. The walls were very high and you would have thought it was a dwelling-place for jinn not for men. Sogolon and her children were received by the king's brother, who understood Mandingo. The king was at prayer, so his brother made them comfortable in an enormous room and water was brought for them to quench their thirst. After the prayer the king came back into his palace and received the strangers. His brother acted as interpreter.

"The king greets the strangers."

"We greet the king of Ghana," said Sogolon.

"The strangers have entered Wagadou in peace, may peace be upon them in our city."

"So be it."

"The king gives the strangers permission to speak."

"We are from Mali," began Sogolon. "The father of my children was the king of Naré Maghan, who, a few years ago sent a goodwill embassy to Ghana. My husband is dead but the council has not respected his wishes and my eldest son," (she pointed to Sundiata) "has been excluded from the throne. The son of my co-wife was preferred before him. I have known exile. The hate of my co-wife has hounded me out of every town and I have trudged along every road with my children. Today I have come to ask for asylum with the Cissés of Wagadou."

There was silence for a few moments; during Sogolon's speech the king and his brother had not taken their eyes off Sundiata for an instant. Any other child of eleven would have been disconcerted by the eyes of the adults, but Sundiata kept cool and calmly looked at the rich decorations of the kings' reception hall—the rich carpets, the fine scimitars hanging on the wall—and the splendid garments of the courtiers.

To the great astonishment of Sogolon and her children the king also spoke in the very same Mandingo language.

"No stranger has ever found our hospitality wanting. My court is your court and my palace is yours. Make yourself at home. Consider that in coming from Niani to Wagadou you have done no more than change rooms. The friendship which unites Mali and Ghana goes back to a very distant age, as the elders and griots know. The people of Mali are our cousins."

And, speaking to Sundiata, the kind said in a familiar tone of voice, "Approach cousin, what is your name?"

"My name is Mari-Djata and I am also called Maghan, but most commonly people call me Sundiata. As for my brother, he is called Manding Boukary, my youngest sister is called Djamarou and the other Sogolon-Kolonkan."

"There's one that will make a great king. He forgets nobody."

Seeing that Sagolon was very tired, the king said, "Brother, look after our guests. Let Sogolon and her children be royally treated and from tomorrow let the princes of Mali sit among our children."

Sogolon recovered fairly quickly from her exertions. She was treated like a queen at the court of king Soumaba Cissé. The children were clothed in the same fashion as those of Wagadou. Sundiata and Manding Bory had long smocks splendidly embroidered. They were showered with so many attentions that Manding Bory was embarrassed by them, but Sundiata found it quite natural to be treated like this. Modesty is the portion of the average man, but superior men are ignorant of humility. Sundiata even became exacting, and the more exacting he became the more the servants trembled before him. He was held in high esteem by the king, who said to his brother one day, "If he has a kingdom one day everything will obey him because he knows how to command."

However, Sogolon found no more lasting peace at Wagadou than she had found at the courts of Djedeba or Tabon; she fell ill after a year.

King Soumaba Cissé decided to send Sogolon and her people to Mema to the court of his cousin, Tounkara. Mema was the capital of a great kingdom on the Niger beyond the land of Do. The king reassured Sogolon of the welcome she would be given there. Doubtless the air which blew from the river would be able to restore Sogolon's health.

The children were sorry to leave Wagadou for they had made many friends, but their destiny lay elsewhere and they had to go away.

King Soumaba Cissé entrusted the travellers to some merchants who were going to Mema. It was a large caravan and the journey was done by camel. The children had for a long time accustomed themselves to these animals which were unknown in Mali. The king had introduced Sogolon and her children as members of his family and they were thus treated with much consideration by the merchants. Always keen to learn, Sundiata asked the caravaneers many questions. They were very well-informed people and told Sundiata a lot of things. He was told about the countries beyond Ghana; the land of the Arabs; the Hejaz, cradle of Islam, and of Djata's ancestors (for Bibali Bounama, the faithful servant of the Prophet, came from Hejaz). He learnt many things about Alexander the Great, too, but it was with terror that the merchants spoke of Soumaoro, the sorcerer-king, the plunderer who would rob the merchants of everything when he was in a bad mood.

A courier, despatched earlier from Wagadou, had heralded the arrival of Sogolon at Mema; a great escort was sent to meet the travellers and a proper reception was held before Mema. Archers and spearmen formed a double line and the merchants showed even more respect to their travelling companions. Surprisingly enough, the king was absent. It was his sister who had organized this great reception. The whole of Mema was at the city gate and you would have thought it was the king's homecoming. Here many people could speak Mandingo and Sogolon and her children could understand the amazement of the people, who were saying to each other, "Where do they come from? Who are they?"

The king's sister received Sogolon and her children in the palace. She spoke Maninkakan very well and talked to Sogolon as if she had known her for a long time. She lodged Sogolon in a wing of the palace. As usual, Sundiata very soon made his presence felt among the young princes of Mema and in a few days he knew every corner of the royal enclosure.

The air of Mema, the air of the river, did Sogolon's health a lot of good, but she was even more affected by the friendliness of the king's sister, who was called Massiran. Massiran disclosed to Sogolon that the king had no children and that the new companions of Sundiata were only the sons of Mema's vassal kings. The king had gone on a campaign against the mountain tribes who lived on the other side of the river. It was like this every year, because as soon as these tribes were left in peace they came down from the mountains to pillage the country.

Sundiata and Manding Bory again took up their favourite pastime, hunting, and went out with the young vassals of Mema.

At the approach of the rainy season the king's return was announced. The city of Mema gave a triumphal welcome to its king. Moussa Tounkara, richly dressed, was riding on a magnificent horse while his formidable cavalry made an impressive escort. The infantry marched in ranks carrying on their heads the booty taken from the enemy. The war drums rolled while the captives, heads lowered and hands tied behind their backs, moved forward mournfully to the accompaniment of the crowd's derisive laughter.

When the king was in his palace, Massiran, his sister, introduced Sogolon and her children and handed him the letter from the king of Ghana. Moussa Tounkara was very affable and said to Sogolon, "My cousin Soumaba recommends you and that is enough. You are home. Stay here as long as you wish."

It was at the court of Mema that Sundiata and Manding Bory went on their first campaign. Moussa Tounkara was a great warrior and therefore he admired strength. When Sundiata was fifteen the king took him with him on campaign. Sundiata astonished the whole army with his strength and with his dash in the charge. In the course of a skirmish against the mountaineers he hurled himself on the enemy with such vehemence that the king feared for his life, but

Moussa Tounkara admired bravery too much to stop the son of Sogolon. He followed him closely to protect him and he saw with rapture how the youth sowed panic among the enemy. He had remarkable presence of mind, struck right and left and opened up for himself a glorious path. When the enemy had fled the old "sofas" said, "There's one that'll make a good king." Moussa Tounkara took the son of Sogolon in his arms and said, "It is destiny that has sent you to Mema. I will make a great warrior out of you."

From that day Sundiata did not leave the king any more. He eclipsed all the young princes and was the friend of the whole army. They spoke about nothing but him in the camp. Men were even more surprised by the lucidity of his mind. In the camp he had an answer to everything and the most puzzling situations resolved themselves in his presence.

Soon it was in Mema itself that people began to talk about Sundiata. Was it not Providence which had sent this boy at a time when Mema had no heir? People already averred that Sundiata would extend his dominion from Mema to Mali. He went on all the campaigns. The enemy's incursions became rarer and rarer and the reputation of Sogolon's son spread beyond the river.

After three years the king appointed Sundiata Kan-Koro-Sigui, his Viceroy, and in the king's absence it was he who governed. Djata had seen eighteen winters and at that time he was a tall young man with a fat neck and a powerful chest. Nobody else could bend his bow. Everyone bowed before him and he was greatly loved. Those who did not love him feared him and his voice carried authority.

The king's choice was approved of both by the army and the people; the people love all who assert themselves over them. The soothsayers of Mema revealed the extraordinary destiny of Djata. It was said that he was the successor of Alexander the Great and that he would be even greater; the soldiers already had a thousand dreams of conquest. What was impossible with such a gallant chief? Sundiata inspired confidence in the sofas by his example, for the sofa loves to see his chief share the hardship of battle.

Djata was now a man, for time had marched on since the exodus from Niani and his destiny was now to be fulfilled. Sogolon knew that the time had arrived and she had performed her task. She had nurtured the son for whom the world was waiting and she knew that now her mission was accomplished, while that of Djata was about to begin. One day she said to her son, "Do not deceive yourself. Your destiny lies not here but in Mali. The moment has come. I have finished my task and it is yours that is going to begin, my son. But you must be able to wait. Everything in its own good time."

SOUMAORO KANTÉ, THE SORCERER KING

While Sogolon's son was fighting his first campaign far from his native land, Mali had fallen under the domination of a new master, Soumaoro Kanté, king of Sosso.

When the embassy sent by Dankaran Touman arrived at Sosso, Soumaoro demanded that Mali should acknowledge itself tributary to Sosso. Balla Fasséké found delegates from several other kingdoms at Soumaoro's court. With his powerful army of smiths the king of Sosso had quickly imposed his power on everybody. After the defeat of Ghana and Diaghan no one dared oppose him any more. Soumaoro was descended from the line of smiths called Diarisso who first harnessed fire and taught men how to work iron, but for a long time Sosso had remained a little village of no significance. The powerful king of Ghana was the master of the country. Little by little the kingdom of Sosso had grown at the expense of Ghana and now the Kantés dominated their old masters. Like all masters of fire, Soumaoro Kanté was a great sorcerer. His fetishes had a terrible power and it was because of them that all kings trembled before him, for he could deal a swift death to whoever he pleased. He had fortified Sosso with a triple curtain wall and in the middle of the town loomed his palace, towering over the thatched huts of the villages. He had an immense seven-storey tower built for himself and he lived on the seventh floor in the midst of his fetishes. This is why he was called "The Untouchable King."

Soumaoro let the rest of the Mandingo embassy return but he kept Balla Fasséké back and threatened to destroy Niani if Dankaran Touman did not make his submission. Frightened, the son of Sassouma immediately made his submission, and he even sent his sister, Nana Triban, to the king of Sosso.

One day when the king was away, Balla Fasséké managed to get right into the most secret chamber of the palace where Soumaoro safeguarded his fetishes. When he had pushed the door open he was transfixed with amazement at what he saw. The walls of the chamber were tapestried with human skins and there was one in the middle of the room on which the king sat; around an earthenware jar nine heads formed a circle; when Balla had opened the door the water had become disturbed and a monstrous snake had raised its head. Balla Fasséké, who was also well versed in sorcery, recited some formulas and everything in the room fell quiet, so he continued his inspection. He saw on a perch above the bed three owls which seemed to be asleep; on the far wall hung strangely-shaped weapons, curved swords and knives with three cutting edges. He looked at the skulls attentively and recognized the nine kings killed by Soumaoro. To the right of the door he discovered a great balafon, bigger than he had ever seen in Mali. Instinctively he pounced upon it and sat down to play. The griot always has a weakness for music, for music is the griot's soul.

He began to play. He had never heard such a melodious balafon. Though scarcely touched by the hammer, the resonant wood gave out sounds of an infinite sweetness, notes clear and as pure as gold dust; under the skillful hand of Balla the instrument had found its master. He played with all his soul and the whole room was filled with wonderment. The drowsy owls, eyes half closed, began to move their heads as though with satisfaction. Everything seemed to come to life upon the strains of this magic music. The nine skulls resumed their earthly forms and blinked at hearing the solemn "Vulture Tune"; with its head resting on the rim, the snake seemed to listen from the jar. Balla Fasséké was pleased at the effect his music had had on the strange inhabitants of the ghoulish chamber, but he quite understood that this balafon was not at all like any other. It was that of a great sorcerer. Soumaoro was the only one to play this instrument. After each victory he would come and sing his own praises. No griot had ever touched it. Not all ears were made to hear that music. Soumaoro was constantly in touch with this xylophone and no matter how far away he was, one only had to touch it for him to know that someone had got into his secret chamber.

The king was not far from the town and he rushed back to his palace and climbed up to the seventh storey. Balla Fasséké heard hurried steps in the corridor and Soumaoro bounded into the room, sword in hand.

"Who is there?" he roared. "It is you, Balla Fasséké!"

The king was foaming with anger and his eyes burnt fiercely like hot embers. Yet without losing his composure the don of Doua changed key and improvised a song in honour of the king:

> There he is, Soumaoro Kanté.
> All hail, you who sit on the skins of kings.
> All hail, Simbon of the deadly arrow.
> I salute you, you who wear clothes of human skin.

This improvised tune greatly pleased Soumaoro and he had never heard such fine words. Kings are only men, and whatever iron cannot achieve against them, words can. Kings, too, are susceptible to flattery, so Soumaoro's anger abated, his heart filled with joy as he listened attentively to this sweet music:

> All hail, you who wear clothes of human skin.
> I salute you, you who sit on the skins of kings.

Balla sang and his voice, which was beautiful, delighted the king of Sosso.

"How sweet it is to hear one's praises sung by someone else; Balla Fasséké, you will nevermore return to Mali for from today you are my griot."

Thus Balla Fasséké, whom king Naré Maghan had given to his son Sundiata, was stolen from the latter by Dankaran Touman; now it was the king of Soss, Soumaoro Kanté, who, in turn, stole the precious griot from the son of Sassouma Bérété. In this way war between Sundiata and Soumaoro became inevitable.

HISTORY

We are now coming to the great moments in the life of Sundiata. The exile will end and another sun will arise. It is the sun of Sundiata. Griots know the history of kings and kingdoms and that is why they are the best counsellors of kings. Every king wants to have a singer to perpetuate his memory, for it is the griot who rescues the memories of the kings from oblivion, as men have short memories.

Kings have prescribed destinies just like men, and seers who probe the future know it. They have knowledge of the future, whereas we griots are depositories of the knowledge of the past. But whoever knows the history of a country can read its future.

Other peoples use writing to record the past, but this invention has killed the facility of memory among them. They do not feel the past any more, for writing lacks the warmth of the human voice. With them everybody thinks he knows, whereas learning should be a secret. The prophets did not write and their words have been all the more vivid as a result. What paltry learning is that which is congealed in dumb books!

I, Djeli Mamoudou Kouhaté, am the result of a long tradition. For generations we have passed on the history of kings from father to son. The narrative was passed on to me without alteration and I deliver it without alteration, for I received it free from all untruth.

Listen now to the story of Sundiata, the Na'Kamma, the man who had a mission to accomplish.

At the time when Sundiata was preparing to assert his claim over the kingdom of his fathers, Soumaoro was the king of kings, the most powerful king in all the lands of the setting sun. The fortified town of Sosso was the bulwark of fetishism against the word of Allah. For a long time Soumaoro defied the whole world. Since his accession to the throne of Sosso he had defeated nine kings who heads served him as fetishes in his macabre chamber. Their skins served as seats and he cut his footwear from human skin. Soumaoro was not like other men, for the jinn had revealed themselves to him and his power was beyond measure. So his countless sofas were very brave since they believed their king to be invincible. But Soumaoro was an evil demon and his reign had produced nothing but bloodshed. Nothing was taboo for him. His greatest pleasure was publicly to flog venerable old men. He had defiled every family and everywhere in his vast empire there were villages populated by girls whom he had forcibly abducted from their families without marrying them.

The tree that the tempest will throw down does not see the storm building up on the horizon. Its proud head braves the winds even when it is near its end. Soumaoro had come to despise everyone. Oh! how power can pervert a man. If man had but a mithkal of divine power at his disposal the world would have been annihilated long ago. Soumaoro arrived at a point where he would stop at nothing. His chief general was his nephew the smith, Fakoli Koroma. He was the son of Soumaoro's sister, Kassia. Fakoli had a wonderful wife, Keleya, who was a great magician like her husband. She could cook better than the three hundred wives of Soumaoro put together. Soumaoro abducted Keleya and locked her up in his place. Fakoli fell into a dreadful rage and went to his uncle and said, "Since you are not ashamed to commit incest by taking my wife, I am freed from all my ties with you from this day forward. Henceforth I shall be on the side of your enemies. I shall combine insurgent Mandingoes with my own troops and wage war against you." And he left Sosso with the smiths of the Koroma tribe.

It was like a signal. All those long-repressed hate and rancours burst out and everywhere men answered the call of Fakoli. Straight away Dankaran Touman, the king of Mali, mobilized and marched to join Fakoli. But Soumaoro, casting his nephew's threat aside, swooped down on Dankaran Touman, who gave up the struggle and fled to the land of the cola; and in those forested regions he founded the town of Kissidougou. During this period Soumaoro, in his anger, punished all the Mandingo towns which had revolted. He destroyed the town of Niani and reduced it to ashes. The inhabitants cursed the king, who had fled.

It is in the midst of calamity that man questions himself about his destiny. After the flight of Dankaran Touman, Soumaoro proclaimed himself king of Mali by right of conquest, but he was not recognized by the populace and resis-

tance was organized in the bush. Soothsayers were unanimous in saying that it would be the rightful heir to the throne who would save Mali. This heir was "The Man with Two Names." The elders of the court of Niani then remembered the son of Sogolon. The man with two names was no other than Maghan Sundiata.

But where could he be found? No one knew where Sogolon and her children lived. For seven years nobody had had any news of them. Now the problem was to find them. Nevertheless a search party was formed to seek him out. Among the people included must be mentioned Kountoun Manian, an old griot from the court of Naré Maghan; Mandjan Bérété, a brother of Sassouma's who did not want to follow Dankaran Touman in flight; Singbin Mara Cissé, a divine of the court; Siriman Touré, another divine; and finally, a woman, Magnouma. According to the clues to the soothsayers they had to search towards the riverine lands, that is, towards the east. The searchers left Mali while war raged between Sosso Soumaoro and his nephew Fakoli Koroma. . . .

The Return

Every man to his own land! If it is foretold that your destiny should be fulfilled in such and such a land, men can do nothing against it. Mansa Tounkara could not keep Sundiata back because the destiny of Sogolon's son was bound up with that of Mali. Neither the jealousy of a cruel stepmother, nor her wickedness, could alter for a moment the course of great destiny.

The snake, man's enemy, is not long-lived, yet the serpent that lives hidden will surely die old. Djata was strong enough now to face his enemies. At the age of eighteen he had the stateliness of the lion and the strength of the buffalo. His voice carried authority, his eyes were live coals, his arm was iron, he was the husband of power.

Moussa Tounkara, king of Mema, gave Sundiata half of his army. The most valiant came forward of their own free will to follow Sundiata in the great adventure. The cavalry of Mema, which he had fashioned himself, formed his iron squadron. Sundiata, dressed in the Muslim fashion of Mema, left the town at the head of his small but redoubtable army. The whole population sent their best wishes with him. He was sur-

rounded by five messengers from Mali and Manding Bory rode proudly at the side of his brother. The horsemen of Mema formed behind Djata a bristling iron squadron. The troop took the direction of Wagadou, for Djata did not have enough troops to confront Soumaoro directly, and so the king of Mema advised him to go to Wagadou and take half of the men of the king, Soumaba Cissé. A swift messenger had been sent there and so the king of Wagadou came out in person to meet Sundiata and his troops. He gave Sundiata half of his cavalry and blessed the weapons. Then Manding Bory said to his brother, "Djata, do you think yourself able to face Soumaoro now?"

"No matter how small a forest may be, you can always find there sufficient fibres to tie up a man. Numbers mean nothing; it is worth that counts. With my cavalry I shall clear myself a path to Mali."

Djata gave out his orders. They would head south, skirting Soumaoro's kingdom. The first objective to be reached was Tabon, the iron-gated town in the midst of the mountains, for Sundiata had promised Fran Kamara that he would pass by Tabon before returning to Mali. He hoped to find that his childhood companion had become king. It was a forced march and during the halts the divines, Singbin Mara Cissé and Mandjan Bérété, related to Sundiata the history of Alexander the Great and several other heroes, but of all of them Sundiata preferred Alexander, the king of gold and silver, who crossed the world from west to east. He wanted to outdo his prototype both in the extent of his territory and the wealth of his treasury.

However, Soumaoro Kanté, being a great sorcerer, knew that the son of Sogolon had set out and that he was coming to lay claim to Mali. The soothsayers told him to forestall this calamity by attacking Sundiata, but good fortune makes men blind. Soumaoro was busy fighting Fakoli, the insurgent nephew who was holding out against him. Even before he had given battle the name of Sundiata was already well known throughout the kingdom. . . .

Soumaoro marched out to meet Sundiata. "The meeting took place at Neguéboria in the Bouré country. As usual, the son of Sogolon wanted to join battle straight away. Soumaoro thought to draw Sundiata into the plain, but Sundiata did not allow him the time to do it. Compelled to give battle, the king of Sosso drew up his men across the narrow valley of Neguéboria, the wings of his army occupying the slopes. Sundiata adopted a very original form of deployment. He formed a tight square with all his cavalry in the front line. The archers of Wagadou and Tabon were stationed at the back. Soumaoro was on one of the hills dominating the valley and he could be distinguished by his height and his helmet bristling with horns. Under an overpowering sun the trumpets sounded, on both sides the drums and bolons echoed and courage entered the hearts of the sofas. Sundiata charged at the gallop and the valley soon disappeared in a cloud of red dust kicked up by thousands of feet and hooves. Without giving an inch, the smiths of Soumaoro stopped the wave.

As though detached from the battle, Soumaoro Kanté watched from the top of his hill. Sundiata and the king of Tabon were laying about them with mighty blows. Sundiata could be distinguished by his white turban and Soumaoro could see the breach he was opening up in the middle of his troops. The centre was about to cave in under the crushing pressure of Djata.

Soumaoro made a sign and from the hills came smiths swooping down into the bottom of the valley to encircle Sundiata. Then, without the slightest order from Sundiata, who was in the thick of the struggle, his square stretched and elongated itself into a great rectangle. Everything had been foreseen. The change was so quick that Soumaoro's men, halted in their mad career, could not use their weapons. In Djata's rear the archers of Wagadou and those of Tabon, on one knee, shot arrows into the sky, which fell thickly, like a rain of iron, on the ranks of Soumaoro. Like a stretching piece of elastic, Djata's line ascended to attack the hills. Djata caught sight of Sosso Balla and bore down on him, but the latter slipped away and the warriors of the buffalo woman's son raised a huzza of triumph. Soumaoro rushed up and his presence in the centre revived the courage of the Sossos. Sundiata caught sight of him and tried to cut a passage through to him. He struck to the right and struck to the left and trampled underfoot. The murderous hooves of his "Daffeké" dug into the chests of the Sossos. Soumaoro was now within spear range and Sundiata reared up his horse and hurled his weapon. It whistled away and bounced off Soumaoro's chest as off a rock and fell to the ground. Sogolon's son bent his bow but with a motion of the hand Soumaoro caught the arrow in flight and showed it to Sundiata as if to say "Look, I am invulnerable."

Furious, Sundiata snatched up his spear and with his head bent charged at Soumaoro, but as he raised his arm to strike his enemy he noticed that Soumaoro had disappeared. Manding Bory riding at his side pointed to the hill and said, "Look, brother."

Sundiata saw Soumaoro on the hill, sitting on his black-coated horse. How could he have done it, he who was only two paces from Sundiata? By what power had he spirited himself away on to the hill? The son of Sogolon stopped fighting to watch the king of Sosso. The sun was already very low and Soumaoro's smiths gave way but Sundiata did not give the order to pursue the enemy. Suddenly, Soumaoro disappeared!

How can I vanquish a man capable of disappearing and reappearing where and when he likes? How can I affect a man invulnerable to iron? Such were the questions which Sogolon's son asked himself. He had been told many things about Sosso-Soumaoro but he had given little credence to so much gossip. Didn't people say that Soumaoro could assume sixty-nine different shapes to escape his enemies? According to some, he could transform himself into a fly in the middle of battle and come and torment his opponent; he could melt into the wind when his enemies encircled him too closely—and many other things.

The battle of Neguéboria showed Djata, if he needed to be shown, that to beat the king of Sosso other weapons were necessary. The evening of Neguéboria, Sundiata was master of the field, but he was in a gloomy mood. He went away from the field of battle with its agonized cries of the wounded, and Manding Bory and Tabon Wana watched him go. He headed for the hill where he had seen Soumaoro after his miraculous disappearance. . . .

Names of the Heroes

Sundiata had now entered the region of the plains, the land of the powerful Niger. The trees that he saw were those of Mali, everything indicated that old Mali was near.

All the allies had arranged to meet up in the great plain of Sibi, and all the children of the savanna were there about their kings. There they were, the valorous sons of Mali, awaiting what destiny had promised them. Pennants of all colours fluttered above the sofas divided up by tribes.

With whom should I begin; with whom end?

I shall begin with Siara Kouman Konaté. Siara Kouman Konaté, the cousin of Sundiata was there. He was the ancestor of those who live in the land of Toron. His spear-armed troops formed a thick hedge around him.

I will also mention Faony Kondé, Faony Diarra, the king of the land of Do whence came Sogolon. Thus the uncle had come to meet his nephew. Faony, king of Do and Kri, was surrounded by sofas armed with deadly arrows. They formed a solid wall around his standard.

You also will I cite, Mansa Traoré, king of the Traoré tribe; Mansa Traoré, the double-sighted king, was at Sibi. Mansa Traoré could see what was going on behind him just as other men can see in front of them. His sofas, formidable archers with quivers on their shoulders, thronged around him.

As for you, Kamandjan, I cannot forget you among those whom I extol, for you are the father of the Dalikimbon Kamaras. The Kamaras, armed with long spears, raised their menacing pikes around Kamandjan.

In short, all the sons of Mali were there, all those who say "N'Ko," all who speak the clear language of Mali were represented at Sibi.

When the son of the buffalo woman and his army appeared, the trumpets, drums and tam-tams blended with the voices of the griots. . . .

Krina

Like Djata, Fakoli wanted to take Soumaoro alive. Keleya's husband sheered off and outflanked Soumaoro on the right, making his horse jump. He was going to lay hands on his uncle but the latter escaped him by a sudden turn. Through his impetus Fakoli bumped into Balla and they both rolled on the ground. Fakoli got up and seized his cousin while Sundiata, throwing his spear with all his might, brought Soumaoro's horse tumbling down. The old king got up and the foot race began. Soumaoro was a sturdy old man and he climbed the mountain with great agility. Djata did not want either to wound him or kill him. He wanted to take him alive.

The sun had just disappeared completely. For a second time the king of Sosso escaped from Djata. Having reached the summit of Koulikoro, Soumaoro hurried down the slope followed by Djata. To the right he saw the gaping cave of Koulikoro and without hesitation he entered the black cavern. Sundiata stopped in front of the cave. At this moment arrived Fakoli who had just tied the hands of Sosso Balla, his cousin.

"There," said Sundiata, "he has gone into the cave."

"But it is connected to the river," said Fakoli.

The noise of horses' hooves was heard and it turned out to be a detachment of Mema horsemen. Straight away the son of Sogolon sent some of them towards the river and had all the mountain guarded. The darkness was complete. Sundiata went into the village of Koulikoro and waited there for the rest of his army.

The victory of Krina was dazzling. The remains of Soumaoro's army went to shut themselves up in Sosso. But the empire of Sosso was done for. From everywhere around kings sent their submission to Sundiata. The king of Guidimakhan sent a richly furnished embassy to Djata and at the same time gave his daughter in marriage to the victor. Embassies flocked to Koulikoro, but when Djata had been joined by all the army he marched on Sosso. Soumaoro's city, Sosso, the impregnable city, the city of smiths skilled in wielding the spear.

In the absence of the king and his son, Noumounkeba, a tribal chief, directed the defence of the city. He had quickly amassed all that he could find in the way of provisions from the surrounding countryside.

Sosso was a magnificent city. In the open plain her triple rampart with awe-inspiring towers reached into the sky. The city comprised a hundred and eighty-eight fortresses and the palace of Soumaoro loomed above the whole city like a gigantic tower. Sosso had but one gate; colossal and made of iron, the work of the sons of fire. Noumounkeba hoped to tie Sundiata down outside of Sosso, for he had enough provisions to hold out for a year.

The sun was beginning to set when Sogolon-Djata appeared before Sosso the Magnificent. From the top of a hill, Djata and his general staff gazed upon the fearsome city of the sorcerer-king. The army encamped in the plain opposite the great gate of the city and fires were lit in the camp. Djata resolved to take Sosso in the course of a morning. He fed his men a double ration and the tam-tams beat all night to stir up the victors of Krina.

At daybreak the towers of the ramparts were black with sofas. Others were positioned on the ramparts themselves. They were the archers. The Mandingoes were masters in the art of storming a town. In the front line Sundiata placed the sofas of Mali, while those who held the ladders were in the second line protected by the shields of the spearmen. The main body of the army was to attack the city gate. When all was ready, Djata gave the order to attack. The drums resounded, the horns blared and like a tide the Mandingo front line moved off, giving mighty shouts. With their shields raised above their heads the Mandingoes advanced up to the foot of the wall, then the Sossos began to rain large stones down on the assailants. From the rear, the bowmen of Wa-

gadou shot arrows at the ramparts. The attack spread and the town was assaulted at all points. Sundiata had a murderous reserve; they were the bowmen whom the king of the Bobos had sent shortly before Krina. The archers of Bobo are the best in the world. On one knee the archers fired flaming arrows over the ramparts. Within the walls the thatched huts took fire and the smoke swirled up. The ladders stood against the curtain wall and the first Mandingo sofas were already at the top. Seized by panic through seeing the town on fire, the Sossos hesitated a moment. The huge tower surmounting the gate surrendered, for Fakoli's smiths had made themselves masters of it. They got into the city where the screams of women and children brought the Sossos' panic to a head. They opened the gates to the main body of the army.

Then began the massacre. Women and children in the midst of fleeing Sossos implored mercy of the victors. Djata and his cavalry were now in front of the awesome tower palace of Soumaoro. Noumounkeba, conscious that he was lost, came out to fight. With his sword held aloft he bore down on Djata, but the latter dodged him and, catching hold of the Sosso's braced arm, forced him to his knees whilst the sword dropped to the ground. He did not kill him but delivered him into the hands of Manding Bory.

Soumaoro's palace was now at Sundiata's mercy. While everywhere the Sossos were begging for quarter, Sundiata, preceded by Balla Fasséké, entered Soumaoro's tower. The griot knew every nook and cranny of the palace from his captivity and he led Sundiata to Soumaoro's magic chamber.

When Balla Fasséké opened the door to the room it was found to have changed its appearance since Soumaoro had been touched by the fatal arrow. The inmates of the chamber had lost their power. The snake in the pitcher was in the throes of death, the owls from the perch were flapping pitifully about on the ground. Everything was dying in the sorcerer's abode. It was all up with the power of Soumaoro. Sundiata had all Soumaoro's fetishes taken down and before the palace were gathered together all Soumaoro's wives, all princesses taken from their families by force. The prisoners, their hands tied behind their backs, were already herded together. Just as he had wished, Sundiata had taken Sosso in the course of a morning. When everything was outside of the town and all that there was to take had been taken out, Sundiata gave the order to complete its destruction. The last houses were set fire to and prisoners were employed in the razing of the walls. Thus, as Djata intended, Sosso was destroyed to its very foundations.

Yes, Sosso was razed to the ground. It has disappeared, the proud city of Soumaoro. A ghastly wilderness extends over the places where kings came and humbled themselves before the sorcerer king. All traces of the houses have vanished and of Soumaoro's seven-storey palace there remains nothing more. A field of desolation, Sosso is now a spot where guinea fowl and young partridges come to take their dust baths.

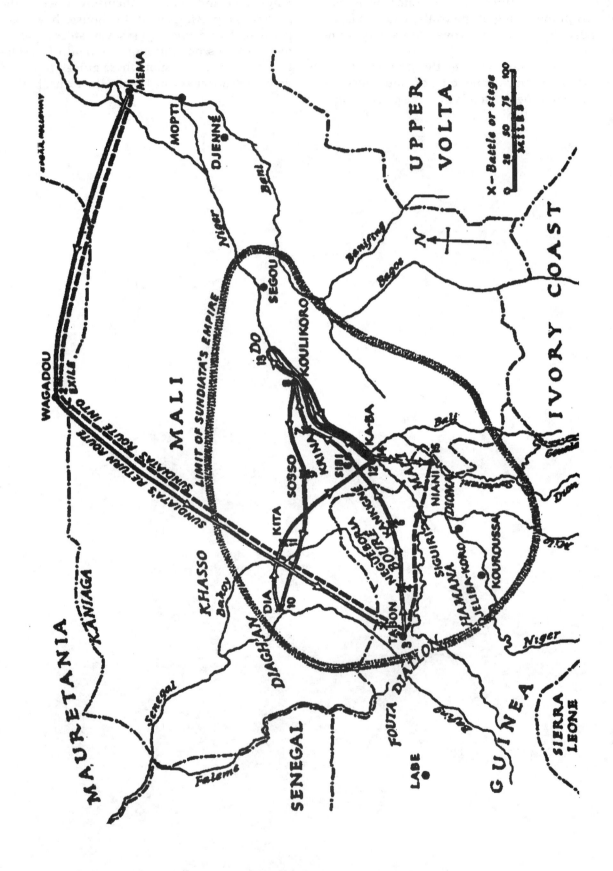

————————— *Questions for Consideration* —————————

Using complete sentences, provide brief answers for the following questions:

1. List examples of features of the West African setting, customs and traditions, comment on them and say what they contribute to the epic.

_____

_____

_____

_____

_____

2. The *Sundiata* presents examples of magic, sorcery, and the supernatural. Identify some examples and say whether this element is similar to the gods' role in Homer's epics.

_____

_____

_____

_____

_____

3. Examine the *Sundiata* for examples of minor conventions and epic features/characteristics, and say whether these make it a typical folk epic.

_____

_____

_____

_____

_____

———————————————— *Writing Critically* ————————————————

Select one of the essay topics listed below and compose a 500 word essay which discusses the topic fully. Support your thesis with evidence from the text and with critical and/or historical material. Use the space below for preparing to write the essay.

1. Using Sundiata's "Exile" and "Return" experiences respectively, discuss his growth and development into maturity and his unfolding heroic and personal qualities in a character portrait.

2. Examine the language and style of the *Sundiata* to show whether it is appropriately elevated for an epic while also showing any African elements which contribute to this style.

3. What are the major themes and how are they developed in the *Sundiata?*

4. What do secondary characters like Soumaoro Kanté, Sassouma Bérété, Fakoli Koroma and Sogolon Kedjou contribute to this epic's meaning and development?

5. *Sundiata* gives a sense of history and some insights into Mandinka culture. How would you describe these?

Prewriting Space:

_____

_____

_____

_____

_____

_____

_____

_____

_____

_____

_____

_____

_____

_____

_____

_____

_____

Introduction

Bhartrihari (fifth century A.D.)

As is the case for a number of major literary figures who lived in feudal societies, almost nothing is known about the life of Bhartrihari. Whoever he was, it is likely that he lived in northern India during the fifth century A.D. He probably passed most of his life under the rule of Shandagupta, a member of the powerful Gupta line of emperors that governed northern India from 335 to 470 A.D. This dynasty of Hindu rulers was relatively lenient in the exercise of power, and they encouraged literature and other arts.

The Gupta era was a high point in the history of classical India, a period characterized by the ascendancy of scholarship and literature written in Sanskrit, a very complex ancient language that was refined and codified by influential grammarians such as Panini, who lived around the fourth century B.C. Originally a special dialect spoken by Hindu priests, Sanskrit was adopted by the ruling class of northern India during the first and second centuries A.D. Hence it became the preferred language for literature, philosophy, and scholarly commentary. India's classical period extends from about 100 to 1200 A.D., a time span that roughly corresponds to the Middle Ages in Europe.

Whoever Bhartrihari was, he was highly skilled in exploiting the literary possibilities made available by the complicated Sanskrit language. He authored a substantial collection of brief but brilliantly composed poems known as the *Satakatrayam* (literal meaning: three hundred poems). Each of his compressed poems is packed with images, subtle depictions of emotions or thoughts, and witty, eloquent language that is full of puns and other literary devices. Bhartrihari's compact but intricate poems have frequently been compared to the detailed miniature paintings with which Indian manuscripts were often illuminated during the classical period. As outstanding examples of the *muktaka* or brief Sanskrit poem, Bhartrihari's verses greatly influenced the subsequent development of the short lyric, which became one of the primary genres of classical Indian literature.

Much about Bhartrihari remains a mystery. It is doubtful that he was a king or a philosopher, as popular legend and some scholars would have it. It is likely that he was a struggling courtier, familiar with the attractions of an affluent milieu but bruised by its intrigues. What is more certain is that his poetry reveals some of the basic aesthetic and spiritual values of his age. A common thread in his verse is a preoccupation with *dharma* or the ethical life. His poems record disillusionment with the conflicts, attractions, and vocations that consume the life-energies of the average human being. The section of his poems entitled "Among Fools and Kings" reveals his dissatisfaction with social ills, with the "rat race" of his time. "Passionate Encounters" is a testimony to both the excitement and the pitfalls of romantic entanglements.

"Refuge in the Forest" points to a solution: an effort to find relief in an ascetic life consisting of 1) withdrawal from worldly troubles and 2) meditation on religious ideals. Bhartrihari wished through his meditations to find spiritual union with Shiva, one of the three major Hindu divinities. In this way, he could experience *brahman* (pure consciousness, the highest spiritual reality). From the Hindu perspective (despite an aversion for most forms of human endeavor), language is the crucial link between ordinary existence and religious enlightenment. This belief empowers poets such as Bhartrihari to reach for the heights with eloquent and intricately constructed lyrics. (NW)

BIBLIOGRAPHY

Altekar, A. S. *The Position of Women in Hindu Civilization.* Delhi: Motilal Banarsidass, 1959.

Basham, A. L. *The Glory That Was India.* New York: Grove Press, 1959.

Chaitanya, Krishna. *Sanskrit Poetics: A Critical and Comparative Study.* London: Asia Publishing House, 1965.

Coward, Harold G. *Bhartrihari.* Boston: Twayne, 1976.

Miller, Barbara Stoler, translator. *The Hermit & the Love-Thief: Sanskrit Poems of Bhartrihari and Bilhana.* New York: Columbia University Press, 1978.

from The Hermit & the Love-Thief

Bhartrihari
Translated by Barbara Stoller Miller

Prologue

1

Radiating uncanny light
from the crescent moon crowning his head,
blazing his fire of bliss
to consume the moth of frenzied love,
dispelling dismal clouds of delusion
by hurling his thunderbolt to the heart,
Shiva triumphs—wisdom's lamp
deep inside the ascetic's mind.

3

Refrain from taking life,
never envy other men's wealth,
speak words of truth,
give timely alms within your means.
Keep silent on the conduct of women,
dam the torrent of your craving,
do reverence before the venerable,
and bear compassion for all creatures—
this unerring path to bliss
is taught in all the texts of scripture.

4

Wise men are consumed by envy,
kings are defiled by haughty ways,
the people suffer from ignorance.
Eloquence is withered on my tongue.

6

When dark passion wove
a web of ignorance about me,
then a woman seemed
to fill the world's expanse.
But now that I am favored with
keener discernment,
my tranquil sight sees Brahman
throughout the universe.

7

A splendid palace, wanton maids,
and a white umbrella's princely luster
and luxuries of wealth that survive
only while auspicious karma thrives.
When this is exhausted then wealth,
like a string of pearls snapped
in violent games of love,
is squandered—
falling in every dark direction.

Among Fools and Kings

8

An ignorant man is readily pleased;
more readily yet is a sage.
But a man corrupted by trifling knowledge,
Brahma himself cannot sway.

12

A hungry man craves a handful of barley,
but sated he deems the whole earth straw.
It is the condition of men's fortunes
that exaggerates or belittles things.

13

Their speech is rich with words of scripture,
their learning is worthy of students:
when wise men are poor in a king's domain,
the ruler shows his folly.
Even in poverty sages are lords;
vulgar appraisers are open to censure—
not the jewels they cheapen.

14

Courage in adversity, patience in prosperity,
eloquence in assembly, heroism at arms,
delight in fame, devotion to scripture—
all are in the nature of noble men.

76

Armlets do not adorn a person,
or necklaces luminous as the moon;
or ablutions, or ointments,
or blossoms, or beautiful hair.
Eloquent speech that is polished well
really adorns a person—
When other ornaments are ruined,
the ornament of speech is an enduring jewel.

Passionate Encounters

78

When men behold the beauty of women
with exotic flashing eyes,
youthful pride in voluptuous breasts,
creepers of beauty-creases
twining above their slender bellies,
those few are fortunate whose minds
are still unperturbed.

79

With smiles, affection, modesty, and art;
hostile looks and ardent glances:
eloquence, jealous quarrels, and play—
with all her emotions woman enchains us.

81

I do indeed speak without bias;
this is acknowledged as truth among men.
Nothing enthralls us like an ample-hipped woman;
nothing else causes such pain.

83

The pleasures of sense may be trivial
and bitter in the end;
they may be spurned and marked
as an abode of evil,
and yet, even the majesty of men
whose thoughts are fixed on truth
wavers in their power.
What force throbs in our hearts?

Refuge in the Forest
173

Hope is a river
whose water is desire,
whose waves are craving.
Passions are crocodiles,
conjectures are birds
destroying the tree of resolve.
Anxiety carves a deep ravine
and the whirlpool of delusion
makes it difficult to ford.
Let ascetics who cross
to the opposite shore
exult in their purified minds.

176

Though I search the triple world
through all its mundane passages,
no man has met my vision's field
or come within my hearing's range
who could really bind
to a post of self-restraint
the raging elephant of his mind
with its drunken desire to court
the world of the senses.

187

When man feels devotion to the Lord Shiva,
has the fear in his heart of death and rebirth,
indulges no bonds of attachment to kinsmen
or frenzy born of amorous passion;
when he dwells in a lonely forest
free from the taints of society,
he lives indifferent to worldly concerns.
What loftier goal can man strive to attain?

190

Earth his soft couch,
arms of creepers his pillow,
the sky his canopy,
tender winds his fan,
the moon his brilliant lamp,
indifference his mistress,
detachment his joy—
tranquil, the ash-smeared hermit
sleeps in ease like a king.

192

Life is a rough uncertain wave.
The splendor of youth is a transient bloom.
Fortune is imagination's whim.
Pleasure flashes like lightning during the rains.
Even fond embraces of beloved arms
do not rest long in their show of love.
Meditate then on that highest Brahman
to cross beyond this sea of worldly dread.

193

Moonlight beams, a forest glade,
the fellowship of friends,
the legends told in poetry, all are enchanting.
Enchanting too is her lovely face
gleaming with tears of anger—
enchanting if only your thought can forget
their ephemeral nature.

———————————— *Questions for Consideration* ————————————

Using complete sentences, provide brief answers for the following questions.

1. Comment on the mixture of ethical implications and sensual imagery in any one of Bhartrihari's poems.

    _____

    _____

    _____

    _____

    _____

    _____

2. Bhartrihari lived a very long time before our own era. Can you identify passages or aspects of his poetry that you, as a contemporary reader, found interesting or appealing?

    _____

    _____

    _____

    _____

    _____

    _____

3. Identify and list images and themes that recur in two or more of Bhartrihari's poems.

    _____

    _____

    _____

    _____

    _____

    _____

Writing Critically

Select one of the topics listed below and compose a 500-word essay that discusses the topic fully. Support your thesis with evidence from the text and with critical and/or historical material. Use the space below for preparing to write the essay.

1. Poets from many cultures of the world have stressed the anxieties that love can cause along with its pleasures. Compare Bhartrihari's handling of this theme with its treatment by Petrarch or any other writer with whom you are familiar.

2. While a great number of short poems have been written by authors in the European tradition, the brief lyric is even more common in Asian literatures. Compare one or more of Bhartrihari's poems with a Chinese or Japanese poem in this anthology. While the form of these poems may be similar, what about meanings and ideas?

3. As is the case for perhaps every culture, religious and ethical ideas are contained in much Indian literature. Try to identify the expression of such ideas in Bhartrihari's poems.

4. Mirabai, a woman writer of Sanskrit poems, lived about one thousand years after Bhartrihari. Compare her poetry, some of which is represented in this anthology, with that of her predecessor.

5. It is often said that literature deals with aspects of human nature that are the same or similar, regardless of time or place. Although Bhartrihari lived in India about 1500 years ago, explain how the viewpoints, emotions, and situations that he presents are relevant for our culture today.

Prewriting Space:

_____

_____

_____

_____

_____

_____

_____

_____

_____

_____

_____

_____

Introduction

Chinese Lyric Poetry of the Tang Dynasty (618–907 A.D.)

I, Zhuangzi, once dreamed that I was a butterfly, a butterfly flittering about and simply enjoying itself. It was unaware that it might be Zhuangzi. Then, I suddenly awoke and was myself again, the same old Zhuangzi. But I did not know whether I had just dreamed that I was a butterfly, or if a butterfly was now dreaming that it was me. But there is surely a difference between a butterfly and myself. This is an example of what can be called the Transformation of Things.

"The Butterfly Dream" by the Daoist philosopher, Zhuangzi (4th century B.C.). Adapted from the translation of James Legge.

How does this puzzling and well-known passage from the ancient philosopher Zhuangzi relate to Tang Chinese poetry, which was composed several centuries later? The answer to this question is presented later in this introduction. For the moment it is helpful to consider some general points that relate to the overall literary and historical background. It is helpful to recognize, first of all, that lyric poetry occupies a special place in Chinese culture.

There is no clear analogy to this situation in the literatures of Europe, and not even in some other Asian literatures, such as Indian. In ancient Greece and Rome, the creation of lyric was a valued yet secondary form of cultural achievement. Long epic poems such as Homer's *Iliad* and *Odyssey* were considered the consummate examples of artistic expression. In Greece, dramatic poetry—especially as manifested in the solemn tragedies of Aeschylus and Sophocles—ranked not far behind. All of this serious literature held the status of a verbal icon, for to the people of classical European antiquity, depictions of Achilles and other heroes vividly expressed the value-system that these ancient societies wished to preserve and live up to. The greatest of Greek lyric poets, Pindar, followed many aspects of the epic program in his great odes, which were written to celebrate the victories of accomplished athletes at important competitions. Ordinary lyric poetry, which is concerned with the expression of everyday moods, the experience of individual pleasures and frustrations, and the commemoration of an ordinary moment, was thus a far less prestigious achievement.

In China, however, the situation is quite different, especially during the Tang dynasty (618–907 A.D.). China has no tradition of either epic or tragedy. The brief lyric is the dominant form of poetry. Only a small number of poems run to more than a few hundred lines; four- to eight-line poems are most common. It is true that some of the oldest poems in Chinese deal with lofty themes such as the fortunes of Kings and the intricacies of governing a country. Examples of this trend can be found in the *Book of Songs* and in a group of texts attributed to the ancient poet Chu Yuan. However, the typical, brief Tang poem is largely concerned with everyday encounters between the individual and his or her immediate social or natural environment.

For many persons unfamiliar with the nuances and resonances of Tang lyric, the initial experience of reading such a poem can be anti-climactic or even a letdown. There is perhaps little in such poems that, on first glance, engages the interests of a reader accustomed to poetry with a more aggressive style and a more obvious meaning. In order to appreciate the distinctive richness of this influential form of literature, it is necessary to gain some acquaintance with the historical background of Tang poetry. It was composed during a period of about three centuries when China, under the rule of a series of emperors bearing the surname Tang, was a strong country that was, aesthetically, very productive in such areas as ceramics and painting, in addition to literature.

During the same era, western Europe was in a state of general disorganization. Except for the centralized authority of the Roman Catholic Church, government was something that took place on a more or less local level. While Europe was a complicated political mosaic of dukedoms, principalities, and small kingdoms, China had, under its emperors, a powerful government centered in the west-central city of Chang'an (present-day Xi'an). For those wishing to enter the political hierarchy, it was necessary to score well on an elaborate civil service examination. Poetry writing was a crucial section of the test. This examination requirement in part explains the huge number of surviving Tang poems—about fifty thousand poems by more than two thousand writers.

It is at this point that we should consider Zhuangzi's cryptic "butterfly dream." The fascination with fluctuations that is so apparent in Zhuangzi and in Daoist thought in general is also obvious in much Chinese poetry of the Tang period—and later. But why? After all, when we think of emperors, we think of stability, not change. Why would the Tang rulers want to promote individuals who were in tune with the Daoist notions of flux and change?

There are several possible answers to this question. One is that a love of complementarity (the pairing or joining of contrasting things and qualities) is evident in Chinese culture from very ancient times. So from a Chinese point of view, it is expected that an individual might lead a controlled everyday life and yet preserve a part of the mind that is open to fantasy and to an appreciation of life's unpredictable elements. An individual with this mindset—that is, a toleration of long periods of monotonous work—would perform well in whatever kind of job the government might assign him.

At any point, however, conditions could change; perhaps an emergency would arise that demanded a bureaucrat's full energies. Again, the individual with a Daoist outlook on life would adapt, in an instant, to any unforeseen circumstances. Relevant in this regard is Li She's brief poem, "On Highwaymen," which provides an illustration of a distinctive ability to roll with the punches of everyday life.

Only a small number of individuals thought of themselves primarily as poets during this period. Yet all educated persons—mostly men but women as well—felt that poetic composition was a necessary social skill. The ability to create a poem on short notice certified that one belonged to a social élite whose way of life differed sharply from that of the uneducated masses that made up most of the population on China. A poem was a way of recording one's impressions of a moment of solitude, leaving a note for someone not at home, commemorating a social gathering, expressing regret on parting from a friend, reworking a mythological theme, or even reflecting on the nature of the cosmos.

Tang poetry holds a secure cultural position among the Chinese today. Most educated persons know—often by heart—a number of these poems. This form of literacy is frequently preserved within families; grandfather and grandson may form—a bond based on learning and reciting poems by Du Fu and other Tang literati.

Given such a huge body of writing, it is not surprising that much of it is mediocre and might be regarded as a kind of upper-class graffiti. However, in the hands of an expert practitioner such as Du Fu, Li Bai, or Wang Wei, Tang dynasty lyric reveals its immense expressive capacities. The typical poem follows one of several strict patterns requiring five or seven syllables per line and two to eight lines for the entire work. On first reading, the poem can be deceptively simple; it may seem to present very little.

Yet complex and striking images are extremely common in Tang poetry. This imagery deeply impressed the American-born poet Ezra Pound, who published a number of loose but highly readable translations of Li Bai's poems early in the twentieth century. Pound's reaction was an appropriate response to the complicated visual dimension of Tang dynasty poetry. It is worth remembering that some of the poets, such as Wang Wei, were painters as well. Also, poems are typically inscribed in the beautiful calligraphy that is an integral part of traditional Chinese paintings. And in the imagery of these poems, there is often a portrayal of things in motion. This sense of motion parallels the impression of movement common in Chinese paintings.

Tang lyric is also distinguished by its ambiguity, its use of seemingly simple diction that is open to an array of meanings and apprehensions. The intriguing instability of Chinese poetic diction is not always apparent in translations, for the translator is pressed to opt for one possible reading or another. Perhaps one brief example will suffice. Printed below is a poem by Wang Wei, of which the first line reads:

There is no one to be seen on the empty mountain.

What exactly is an "empty mountain"? This phrase is a literal translation of the Chinese "空山" (*kong shan*). Can the massive bulk of a mountain really be thought of as empty, or does the term "empty" only indicate that the mountain is apparently devoid of people? Yet the next line reveals that the voice of at least one person is heard. Or is the word "empty" used because a mountain in the distance, when there is a haze or light cloud cover, looks as if it might be a fragile cone emptying itself into the sky?

In this brief but puzzling poem, Wang Wei moves beyond the Daoist fascination with the fluxes and transformations of everyday life. It is worth remembering that in later life, Wang Wei became quite involved in Buddhism. In "The Deer Enclosure," the poet evokes the Buddhist idea that the perceived world is only an extended illusion. From a Buddhist perspective, in order to gain enlightenment, it is necessary to recognize that there is a higher, spiritual reality beyond the flimsy, insubstantial attractions of the everyday world. A number of Tang poems suggest a Buddhist point of view just as many of them reveal the Daoist interest in change and transformation.

Also widespread in Tang lyric (and, as already mentioned, throughout Chinese culture) is the interplay of antithesis and complementarity. In the typical couplet or throughout a poem, however long it may be, there are various parallel words and phrases that present weak contrasts or even sharp oppositions. Thus, while the mountain is desolate, a voice is heard, perhaps in a valley. The sun is shining brightly, but the woods are shady. And so there is a resonating array of contrasting meanings and images throughout the well-constructed Tang poem.

With the exception of the poems by women authors and the Wang Wei poem translated by the writer of this introduction, the poems below were translated by Herbert A. Giles. He was a pioneer Victorian sinologist who did much to introduce Europe to the study of Chinese language and literature. Although some of his translations are tainted with the refined melancholy common in the verse of his contemporary fellow Englishman, A. E. Housman, Giles' best efforts provide a serviceable rendering of the original Chinese. The fact that the spirit of his age is often evident in his translations is a reminder that we always carry our own values and perspectives with us as we attempt to understand another culture by studying its literature. (NW)

BIBLIOGRAPHY

Chou, Eva Shan. *Reconsidering Tu Fu: Literary Greatness and Cultural Context.* Cambridge: Cambridge University Press, 1995.

Giles, Herbert A., translator. *Chinese Poetry in English Verse.* London: Bernard Quaritch, 1898.

Liu, James J. Y. *The Art of Chinese Poetry.* Chicago: University of Chicago Press, 1962.

Liu, Wu-Chi and Irving Yucheng Lo, editors. *Sunflower Splendor: Three Thousand Years of Chinese Poetry.* Bloomington: Indiana University Press, 1975.

Owen, Stephen. *The Great Age of Chinese Poetry: The High T'ang.* New Haven: Yale University Press, 1981.

Rexroth, Kenneth, and Ling Chung, translators and editors. *The Orchid Boat: Women Poets of China.* New York: McGraw-Hill, 1972.

Yu, Pauline. *The Reading of Imagery in the Chinese Poetic Tradition.* Princeton: Princeton University Press, 1987.

Note on punctuation and spelling: Is it "Tang" or "T'ang"? Both spellings are used above. The question of which is correct depends on the system of romanization one uses, for Chinese writing is based on characters and not an alphabet. ("唐" is the Chinese character for Tang/T'ang.) According to the *pinyin* system, used in mainland China, Tang is the correct spelling, while T'ang is correct according the older Wade-Giles system, which one of our translators, Herbert Giles, helped originate. In either case, the initial sound is pronounced as an English "t." In the Wade-Giles system, the spelling "t," without an apostrophe, is pronounced as a "d." Hence the surname of the poet "Tu Fu" (Wade-Giles system) is spelled "Du Fu" according to the *pinyin* system. (Remember also that in Chinese, surnames are first, then the given name.) For further details and a comparative sketch of the two systems, see the pronunciation table at the end of the introduction, "Asian Cultures: China."

Chinese Tang Dynasty Poetry

(various translators)

1. Poems by Li Bai
(also spelled Li Bo or Li Po)
(A.D. 701–762)

TO A FIREFLY[1]

Rain cannot quench thy lantern's light,

Wind makes it shine more brightly bright;
Oh why not fly to heaven afar,
And twinkle near the moon—a star?

AT PARTING

The river rolls crystal as clear as the sky,
To blend far away with the blue waves
     of ocean;
Man alone, when the hour of departure is
     nigh,
With the wine cup can soothe his emotion.
The birds of the valley sing loud in the sun,
Where the gibbons their vigils will shortly
     be keeping;
I thought that with tears I had long ago
     done,
But now I shall never cease weeping.

NIGHT THOUGHTS

I wake, and moonbeams play around my
                                        bed,
Glittering like hoarfrost to my wondering
                                        eyes;
Up towards the glorious moon I raise my
                                        head,
Then lay me down,—and thoughts of
                            home arise.

COMPANIONS

The birds have all flown to their roost in
                            the tree,
The last cloud has just floated lazily by;
But we never tire of each other, not we,
As we sit there together,—the moun-
                            tains and I.

FROM A BELVIDERE

With yellow leaves the hill is strown,
    A young wife gazes o'er the scene,
The sky with grey clouds overthrown,
    While autumn swoops upon the green.

See, Tartar troops mass on the plain;
    Homeward our envoy hurries on;
When will her lord come back again? . . .
    To find her youth and beauty gone!

A SNAPSHOT

A tortoise I see on a lotus-flower resting;
A bird 'mid the reeds and the rushes is
                            nesting;
A light skiff propelled by some boatman's
                            fair daughter,
Whose song dies away o'er the fast-flowing
                            water.

IN A MIRROR

My whitening hair would make a long, long
                              rope,
Yet could not fathom all my depth of woe;
Though how it comes within a mirror's scope
To sprinkle autumn frosts, I do not know.

II. Poems by Du Fu (also spelled Tu Fu) (A.D. 712–770)

IN ABSENCE

White gleam the gulls across the darkling
                              tide,
On the green hills the red flowers seem
                              to burn;
Alas! I see another spring has died . . .
When will it come—the day of my
                              return?

TO HIS BROTHER

The evening drum has emptied every street,
One autumn goose screams on its frontier
                              flight,
The dew is crystal and shimmers in fall,
The moon sheds, as of old, her silvery light.
The brothers,—ah, where are they?
                              Scattered all;
No home whence one might learn the
                              other's harms.
Letters may stray: will a messenger call
Now when the land rings with the clash
                              of arms?

The Hermit

Alone I wandered o'er the hills
    to seek the hermit's den,
While sounds of chopping rang around
    the forest's leafy glen.
I passed on ice across the brook   5
    which had not ceased to freeze,
As the slanting rays of afternoon
    shot sparkling through the trees.

I found he did not joy to gloat
    o'er fetid wealth by night,   10
But far from taint, to watch the deer[2]
    in the golden morning light . . .
My mind was clear at coming;
    but now I've lost my guide,
And rudderless my little bark   15
    is drifting with the tide![3]

Superseded[4]

Alas for the lonely plant that grows
    beside the river bed,
While the mango-bird screams loud and long
    from the tall tree overhead!
Full with the freshets of the spring,
    the torrent rushes on;
The ferry-boat swings idly, for
    the ferryman is gone.

III. Poems by other Male Writers of the Tang Dynasty

Meng Haoran (A.D. 689–740)

IN DREAMLAND

The sun has set behind the western slope,
The eastern moon lies mirrored in the
$\qquad$ pool;
With streaming hair my balcony I ope,
And stretch my limbs out to enjoy the
$\qquad$ cool.
Loaded with lotus-scent the tweeze sweeps by,   5
Clear dipping drops from tall bamboos
$\qquad$ I hear,
I gaze upon my idle lute and sigh:
Alas no sympathetic soul is near!
And so I doze, the while before mine eyes
Dear friends of other days in dream-clad   10
$\qquad$ forms arise.

Wang Wei (A.D. 699–761)

A RENCONTRE

Sir, from my dear old home you come,
$\quad$ And all its glories you can name;
Oh tell me,—has the winter-plum
$\quad$ Yet blossomed o'er the window-frame?

THE DEER COMPOUND

There is no one to be seen on the empty mountain,
but I hear an echoing voice.
Slanting sunlight enters the deep forest,
and the green moss is again luminous.[5]

Chang Jian (8th century A.D.)

DHYÂNA[6]

The clear dawn creeps into the cloister old,
The rising sun tips its tall trees with gold,—
As, darkly, by a winding path I reach
Dhyâna's hall, hidden midst fir and beech.
Around these hills sweet birds their pleasure
                              take,
Man's heart as free from shadows as this
                              lake;
Here worldly sounds are hushed, as by a
                              spell,
Save for the booming of the altar bell.

Ka Jiayun (8th century A.D.)

AT DAWN

Drive the young orioles away,
Nor let them on the branches play;
Their chirping breaks my slumber through
And keeps me from my dreams of you

Han Yu (A.D. 768–824)

THE WOUNDED FALCON

Within a ditch beyond my wall
I saw a falcon headlong fall.
Bedaubed with mud and racked with pain,
It beat its wings to rise, in vain;
While little boys threw tiles and stones,   5
Eager to break the wretch's bones.
    O bird, methinks thy life of late
Hath amply justified this fate!
Thy sole delight to kill and steal,
And then exultingly to wheel,   10
Now sailing in the clear blue sky,
Now on the wild gale sweeping by,
Scorning thy kind of less degree
As all unfit to mate with thee.
    But mark how fortune's wheel goes round;   15

A pellet lays thee on the ground.
Sore stricken at some vital part,
And where is then thy pride of heart?
 What's this to me?—I could not bear
To see the fallen one lying there.   20
I begged its life; and from the brook
Water to wash its wounds I took.
Fed it with bits of fish by day,
At night from foxes kept away.
My care I knew would naught avail   25
For gratitude, that empty tale.
And so this bird would crouch and hide
Till want its stimulus applied;
And I, with no reward to hope,
Allowed its callousness full scope.   30
 Last eve the bird showed signs of rage,
With health renewed, and beat its cage.
Today it forced a passage through,
And took its leave, without adieu.
 Good luck hath saved thee, not desert;   35
Beware, O bird, of further hurt;
Beware the archer's deadly tools!
'Tis hard to escape the shafts of fools
Nor e'er forget the chastening ditch
That found thee poor, and left thee rich.[7]   40

Du Mu
(also spelled Tu Mu)
(A.D. 803–852)

A LOST LOVE[8]

Too late, alas! . . . I came to find
 the lovely spring had fled.
Yet must I not regret the days
 of youth that now are dead;
For though the rosy buds of spring
 the cruel winds have laid,
Behold the clustering fruit that hangs
 beneath the leafy shade!

LOVERS PARTED

Across the screen the autumn moon
    stares coldly from the sky;
With silken fan I sit and flick
    the fireflies sailing by.
The night grows colder every hour,—
    it chills me to the heart
To watch the Spinning Maiden
    from the Herdboy far apart.[9]

Zhang Yan (9th century A.D.)

A SPRING FEAST

The paddy crops are waxing rich,
    upon the Goose-Lake hill;
The fowls have just now gone to roost,
    the grunting pigs are still;
The mulberry casts a lengthening shade,—
    the festival is o'er,
And tipsy revellers are helped
    each to his cottage door.

Li She (9th century A.D.)

ON HIGHWAYMEN[10]

The rainy mist sweeps gently,
    o'er the village by the stream,
When from the leafy forest glades
    the brigand daggers gleam
And yet there is no need to fear
    or step from out their way,
For more than half the world consists
    of bigger rogues than they!

Li Jiayu (8th or 9th century A.D.)

IN RETIREMENT

He envies none, the pure, and proud
    ex-Minister of State;
On the Western Lake he shuts himself
    within his bamboo gate.
He needs no fan to cool his brow, for
    the south wind never lulls,
While idly his official hat lies
    staring at the gulls.

Han Wu (8th or 9th century A.D.)

CONTEMPLATION

When my court-yard by the placid moon
                        is lit,
When around me leaves come dropping
                        from the trees,
On the terrace steps, contemplative, I sit,
The swing-ropes swaying idly in the
                        breeze.

IV. Women Writers of the Tang Dynasty

Wu Zetian (A.D. 624–705)*

A LOVE SONG OF THE EMPRESS WU

I watch the red buds turn to green leaves.
My thoughts are many and tumultuous,
As troubled as the tossing branches,
All for thinking of you.
If you do not believe I have wept
Constantly since that time,
Open my wardrobe case
And examine my pomegranate flower dress.

Guan Panpan (8th–9th century A.D.)

MOURNING

In the cemetery on North Hill
Heavy mist envelops the pines and cypresses.
In Swallow Mansion
I sit quietly thinking of you.
Since you were buried
Your singers are scattered like dust.
And the perfume in their red sleeves
Has faded away for ten years now.

Yu Xuanzhi (mid-9th century)

ADVICE TO A NEIGHBOR GIRL

Afraid of the sunlight,
You cover your face with your silk sleeves.
Tired out with Spring melancholy,
You neglect your makeup.
It is easier to get priceless jewels   5
Than to find a man with a true heart.
Why wet your pillow with secret tears?
Why hide your heartbreak in the flowers?
Go, seek a handsome famous man like Sung Yü.
Don't long for someone who will never come back.   10

LIVING IN THE SUMMER MOUNTAINS

I have moved to this home of Immortals.
Wild shrubs bloom everywhere.
In the front garden, trees
Spread their branches for clothes racks.
I sit on a mat and float wine cups   5
In the cool spring.
Beyond the window railing
A hidden path leads away
Into the dense bamboo grove.
In a gauze dress   10
I read among my disordered
Piles of books.
I take a leisurely ride
In the painted boat,
And chant poems to the moon.   15
I drift at ease, for I know
The soft wind will blow me home.

SENDING SPRING LOVE TO TZU-AN

The mountain path is steep
And the stone steps dangerous,
But I do not suffer from the hardships of the journey,
But from lovesickness.
The mountain torrent that comes   5
From far off melting ice
Is pure as your spiritual character.
When I see the snow on the distant mountains
I think of your jade-like beauty.
Do not listen to vulgar songs   10
Or drink too much Spring wine
Or play chess all night with idle guests.
Steady as a pine, not like a rolling stone,
My oath of love is forever.
I long for the days   15
When we will be together again
Like the birds that fly
With one wing in common.
I walk alone with my regrets, longing
All day long at the end of winter   20
For the time when we
Will be together again under the full moon.
What can I give you as a gift of separation—
Tears that glitter in the sun on a poem.

Xue Tao (A.D. 768–831)

THE AUTUMN BROOK

It has turned crystal clear lately
And flows away like a ribbon of smoke
With a music like a ten stringed zither.
The sound penetrates to my pillow,
And turns my mind to past loves,
And won't let me sleep for melancholy.

AN OLD POEM TO YÜAN CHÊN

Each poem has its own pattern of tones.
I only know how to write
Delicate evanescent verse
About tranquil love making—
In the shadow of moonlit flowers,   5
Or on misty mornings under the weeping willows.
The Green Jade Concubine was kept hidden away.
But you should learn to write love poems
On red paper for the girls in the pleasure city.
I am getting old and can let myself go,   10
So I will teach you as though you were a schoolboy.

Han Cuipin (9th century A.D.)

A POEM WRITTEN ON A FLOATING RED LEAF

How fast this water flows away!
Buried in the women's quarters,
The days pass in idleness.
Red leaf, I order you—
Go find someone
In the world of men.

Zhao Luanluan (8th century A.D.?)

SLENDER FINGERS

Slender, delicate, soft jade,
Fresh peeled spring onions—
They are always hidden in emerald
Sleeves of perfumed silk.
Yesterday on the lute strings
All their nails were painted scarlet.

WILLOW EYEBROWS

Sorrows play at the edge of these willow leaf curves.
They are often reflected, deep, deep,
In my water blossom inlaid mirror.
I am too pretty to bother with an eyebrow pencil.
Spring hills paint themselves
With their own personality.

CLOUD HAIRDRESS

My disordered perfumed clouds are still damp,
Iridescent as a blackbird's throat feathers,
Glossy as a cicada's wing.
I pin a gold phoenix by my ear.
After I have adorned myself,
My man smiles at me.

ENDNOTES

1. An impromptu, at the age of ten.
2. The deer is a traditional Chinese symbol for longevity or long life. Daoists typically devoted considerable energy to the pursuit of longevity through intellectual activities, exercises, and the consumption of special chemical compounds called elixirs.
3. Meaning that he is now doubtful whether he should not at once embrace a hermit's life.
4. A specimen of political allegory. The "lonely plant" refers to a virtuous statesman for whom the time is out of joint. The "mango-bird" is a worthless politician in power. The "ferry-boat" is the Ship of State.
5. Translator's note: The poem implies a late afternoon seeting. As in the early morning, the rays of the sun come from the side rather than from overhead, and once again, the sunlight is not blocked by tall trees and heavy foliage from reaching the secluded floor of the forest. (NW)
6. A state of mental abstraction, by recourse to which the Buddhist gradually shakes off all desire for sublunary existence. In a traditional monastery there is a building specially set apart for this purpose, and there priests may be seen sitting for hours with their eyes closed.
7. In experience of the ups and downs of life.
8. When the poet was ordered to a distant post, he said to his fiancée, "Within ten years I shall be Governor. If I do not return within that time, marry whomsoever you please." He came back at the end of fourteen years to find her married and the mother of three children.
9. Referring to two stars which are separated by the Milky Way, except on the 7th night of the 7th moon of each year, when magpies form a bridge for the Damsel to pass over to her lover.
10. This famous poet having been caught by brigands was ordered to give a specimen of his art. The impromptu in the text earned his immediate release.

—————— *Questions for Consideration* ——————

Using complete sentences, provide brief answers for the following questions.

1. Join the number of Americans who have attempted to write poetry inspired by Li Po or other Asian models. Choose a small scene or setting that you would normally overlook. Try to transform this scene into language that conveys a distinctive sense of absence or some other quality that you have noticed in your readings of the selections above.

   _____

   _____

   _____

   _____

   _____

2. Try briefly explicating a Chinese poem, proceeding line by line as you would for a poem in English. What images and meanings do the words convey to you?

   _____

   _____

   _____

   _____

   _____

3. In Tang China, the ability to compose a poem at a moment's notice was a requirement for social and economic success. Despite obvious historical and cultural differences, there may be similarities between imperial China and our world today. List ways in which the skilful manipulation of language is an ingredient of success in contemporary America.

   _____

   _____

   _____

   _____

   _____

Writing Critically

Select one of the topics listed below and compose a 500-word essay that discusses the topic fully. Support your thesis with evidence from the text and with critical and/or historical material. Use the space below for preparing to write the essay.

1. Write an essay focused on the gender identity and social situation revealed in the poems by women writers. How does their poetry differ from that by male authors?

2. A number of American poets of the first half of the twentieth century were directly or indirectly influenced by the imagery of Chinese poetry. After reading the translations in this anthology, examine a few poems by Ezra Pound, Amy Lowell, or Robert Frost. Discuss similarities along with differences. Focus on the way natural settings are depicted by authors of different cultural traditions who nonetheless came to share ideas about how poetry should be written.

3. As mentioned above, Herbert Giles probably had in mind the poetry of A. E. Housman when he set about translating Chinese poetry. Look at a volume of Housman's poems. What differences do you find between Housman's verse and Giles' translations? What similarities and contrasts are evident in your comparison of Chinese poetry of the Tang dynasty and the work of a British poet of the Victorian era?

4. The point is often made that there is a closer correlation between Chinese poetry and painting than there is between European poetry and painting. Consult an illustrated history of Chinese landscape painting. Discuss resemblances between the imagery in the Chinese poems in *Literary Perspectives* and the representation of nature in a Chinese landscape painting.

Prewriting Space:

_____

_____

_____

_____

_____

_____

_____

_____

_____

_____

_____

_____

Introduction

The Man'yōshū
(Mid-eighth century A.D.)

The *Man'yōshū*, a poetry collection compiled during the eighth century A.D., is the first major landmark in Japanese literature. The work is an anthology apparently based on earlier collections now lost. The literal meaning of the title is "the anthology of ten thousand leaves." Since well over four thousand poems are included in this vast compilation, the title is certainly appropriate. At the same time, in Japanese, which is a character-based language, the character that indicates the leaves or pages of a book can also mean a generation of people. The *Man'yōshū* was thus conceived of by its compilers as a collection of outstanding poetry that would capture the interests of a huge number of future generations. This prediction proved to be a self-fulfilling prophecy, for since its appearance during the second half of the eighth century, the *Man'yōshū* has been acclaimed and revered as a major document expressing many of the basic aesthetic and moral values of Japanese culture.

Although the *Man'yōshū* is obviously an ancient work in comparison with the national literatures of present-day European countries or of America, the eighth century A.D. is relatively recent when compared with the civilizations of ancient Egypt, Greece, Rome, India, or China. While these great world cultures developed and declined, the early Japanese lived a nomadic life, adopting a more settled, agricultural and village lifestyle only during the third century B.C.

The values and organizational patterns of the earliest phases of Japanese society exerted a strong influence as the culture expanded and grew more complex. Valorous warriors became the leaders of the developing society, and the clan remained a key unit of the social order and of political power. Around the fifth century A.D., one group of clans in the Yamato region of central Japan established dominance over a large number of neighboring clans. A centralized government was beginning to emerge.

During the sixth century, the Buddhist religion spread into Japan from China by way of Korea. With the introduction of Buddhism, a major influx of Chinese ideas relating to government and many other aspects of life was underway. Over a period of several decades, efforts were made to consolidate the Japanese government along Chinese lines. These efforts reached a peak around 710 A.D. Impressed by the achievements of the Tang emperors of China, who had established a splendid capital city at Chang'an (today's Xi'an), the Japanese constructed a new capital at Heijo (today's Nara). The *Man'yōshū* emerges out of this lengthy period during which Japan sought to absorb what were perceived as the best aspects of Chinese civilization. At the same time, the Japanese sought to strengthen and express a culture that was distinctively their own.

It is a paradox of literary history that this huge collection of poetry, represented below by some of its most notable poems, succeeds in conveying the special cultural aura of ancient Japan. In the *Man'yōshū*, Japanese as well as other readers have discovered the qualities of emotional spontaneity, valor, wide experience of the world, candor, sincerity, and a refreshing lack of artfulness or over-sophistication. Yet the Japanese originated no system of writing that was fully their own. Instead, during the decades preceding the publication of the *Man'yōshū*, they developed a writing system by relying heavily on Chinese characters, maintaining the basic meaning of many characters but pronouncing them in Japanese and making various other linguistic modifications. (For instance, the Chinese characters for Japan, "日本" [literal meaning: "origin of the sun"] are pronounced "Riben" in Chinese and "Nīhon" in Japanese.) Nor were the outside influences prevalent during this period solely Chinese. Buddhism, as mentioned above, arrived in Japan from China—but filtered through Korea, along with other facets of Korean culture. Many of the Japanese nobility were actually of Korean extraction.

Another paradoxical aspect of the *Man'yōshū* lies in the fact that many of the rustic-sounding and seemingly naive poems of the collection were produced by poets like Yakamochi who were well known for their high level of verbal artistry. In numerous other cases, however, unrefined and refreshingly direct poems in this collection were undoubtedly contributed by ordinary people not affiliated with the aristocracy.

Nearly half of the poems in the *Man'yōshū* are anonymous, and a number were composed by women. Two poetic forms are utilized: the brief *tanka* of five lines and the long *chōka of varying length. The number of syllables per line varies from five to seven. The short tanka* poems are by far the most numerous and make up more than ninety percent of the entire collection. Yet the long *chōka poems are among the most intriguing and memorable.*

Whether poems of the people or of sophisticated verbal craftsmen, indisputably Japanese or permeated with foreign influences, the verses that follow reveal a universal human dimension. They also invite comparison with some of the most widely appreciated poetry of other cultures, countries, and eras. (NW)

BIBLIOGRAPHY

Ebersole, Gary L. *Ritual Poetry and the Politics of Death in Early Japan.* Princeton: Princeton University Press, 1989.

Keene, Donald. "The *Man'yōshū.*" In *Seeds in the Heart: Japanese Literature from Earliest Times to the Late Sixteenth Century.* New York: Henry Holt, 1993. Pages 85–180.

___, ed. *Anthology of Japanese Literature: From the Earliest Times to the Mid-Nineteenth Century.* New York: Grove, 1955.

Levy, Ian Hideo. *Hitomaro and the Birth of Japanese Lyricism.* Princeton: Princeton University Press, 1984.

Miner, Earl, Hiroko Odagiri, and Robert E. Morrell. *The Princeton Companion to Classical Japanese Literature.* Princeton: Princeton University Press, 1985.

Taki, Seiichi, and others, translators. *The Man'yōshū.* New York: Columbia University Press, 1965.

from The Man'yōshū

Translated by Ralph Hodgson and others

1

Upon the departure of Prince Ōtsu for the capital after his secret visit to the Shrine of Ise

To speed my brother

Parting for Yamato,
In the deep of night I stood
Till wet with the dew of dawn.

The lonely autumn mountains
Are hard to pass over
Even when two go together—
How does my brother cross them all alone!

Princess Ōku (661–701)

11

In the sea of Iwami,
By the cape of Kara,
There amid the stones under sea
Grows the deep-sea *miru* weed;
There along the rocky strand   5
Grows the sleek sea tangle.

Like the swaying sea tangle,
Unresisting would she lie beside me—
My wife whom I love with a love
Deep as the *miru*-growing ocean.   10
But few are the nights
We two have lain together.

Away I have come, parting from her
Even as the creeping vines do part.
My heart aches within me;   15
I turn back to gaze—
But because of the yellow leaves
Of Watari Hill,
Flying and fluttering in the air,
I cannot see plainly   20
My wife waving her sleeve to me.
Now as the moon, sailing through the cloud-rift
Above the mountain of Yakami,
Disappears, leaving me full of regret,
So vanishes my love out of sight;   25
Now sinks at last the sun,
Coursing down the western sky.

I thought myself a strong man,
But the sleeves of my garment
Are wetted through with tears.   30

ENVOYS

My black steed
Galloping fast,
Away have I come,
Leaving under distant skies
The dwelling place of my love.   35

Oh, yellow leaves
Falling on the autumn hill,
Cease a while
To fly and flutter in the air,
That I may see my love's dwelling place!   40
                    Kakinomoto Hitomaro (Seventh Century)

111

After the death of his wife

Since in Karu lived my wife,
I wished to be with her to my heart's content;
But I could not visit her constantly
Because of the many watching eyes—
Men would know of our troth,   5
Had I sought her too often.
So our love remained secret like a rock-pent pool;
I cherished her in my heart,
Looking to aftertime when we should be together,
And lived secure in my trust   10
As one riding a great ship.

Suddenly there came a messenger
Who told me she was dead—
Was gone like a yellow leaf of autumn.
Dead as the day dies with the setting sun,   15
Lost as the bright moon is lost behind the cloud,
Alas, she is no more, whose soul
Whose was bent to mine like bending seaweed!

When the word was brought to me
I knew not what to do nor what to say;   20
But restless at the mere news,
And hoping to heal my grief
Even a thousandth part,
I journeyed to Karu and searched the market place
Where my wife was wont to go!   25

There I stood and listened,
But no voice of her I heard,
Though the birds sang in the Unebi Mountain;
None passed by who even looked like my wife.
I could only call her name and wave my sleeve.   30

ENVOYS

In the autumn mountains
The yellow leaves are so thick.
Alas, how shall I seek my love
Who has wandered away?
I know not the mountain track.   35

I see the messenger come
As the yellow leaves are falling.
Oh, well I remember
How on such a day we used to meet—
My wife and I!   40

In the days when my wife lived,
We went out to the embankment near by—
We two, hand in hand—
To view the elm trees standing there
With their outspreading branches   45
Thick with spring leaves. Abundant as their greenery
Was my love. On her leaned my soul.
But who evades mortality?
One morning she was gone, flown like an early bird.
Clad in a heavenly scarf of white,   50
To the wide fields where the shimmering *kagerō* rises
She went and vanished like the setting sun.

The little babe—the keepsake
My wife has left me—
Cries and clamors.   55
I have nothing to give; I pick up the child

And clasp it in my arms.
In our chamber, where our two pillows lie,
Where we two used to sleep together,
Days I spend alone, broken-hearted: 60
Nights I pass, sighing till dawn.

Though I grieve, there is no help;
Vainly I long to see her.
Men tell me that my wife is
In the mountains of Hagai—   65
Thither I go,
Toiling along the stony path;
But it avails me not,
For of my wife, as she lived in this world,
I find not the faintest shadow.   70

ENVOYS

Tonight the autumn moon shines—
The moon that shone a year ago,
But my wife and I who watched it then together
Are divided by ever widening wastes of time.
When leaving my love behind   75
In the Hikite mountains—
Leaving her there in her grave,
I walk down the mountain path,
I feel not like one living.

Kakinomoto Hitomaro

IV

I thought there could be
No more love left anywhere.
Whence then is come this love,
That has caught me now
And holds me in its grasp?

Princess Hirokawa (Eighth Century)

V

An old threnody
The mallards call with evening from the reeds
And float with dawn midway on the water;
They sleep with their mates, it is said,
With white wings overlapping and tails asweep
Lest the frost should fall upon them.   5

As the stream that flows never returns,
And as the wind that blows is never seen,
My wife, of this world, has left me,
Gone I know not whither!
So here, on the sleeves of these clothes   10
She used to have me wear,
I sleep now all alone!

ENVOY

Cranes call flying to the reedy shore;
How desolate I remain
As I sleep alone!   15
                              Tajihi (Eighth Century)

VI

If it were death to love,
I should have died—
And died again
One thousand times over.

                              Lady Kasa

VII

Love's complaint

At wave-bright Naniwa
The sedges grow, firm-rooted—
Firm were the words you spoke,
And tender, pledging me your love,
That it would endure through all the years;   5
And to you I yielded my heart,
Spotless as a polished mirror.
Never, from that day, like the seaweed
That sways to and fro with the waves,
Have I faltered in my fidelity,   10
But have trusted in you as in a great ship.
Is it the gods who have divided us?
Is it mortal men who intervene?
You come no more, who came so often,
Nor yet arrives a messenger with your letter.   15
There is—alas!—nothing I can do.
Though I sorrow the black night through
And all day till the red sun sinks,
It avails me nothing. Though I pine,
I know not how to soothe my heart's pain.   20

Truly men call us "weak women."
Crying like an infant,
And lingering around, I must still wait,
Wait impatiently for a message from you!

ENVOY

If from the beginning   25
You had not made me trust you,
Speaking of long, long years,
Should I have known now
Such sorrow as this?
        Lady Ōtomo of Sakanoue (Eighth Century)

VIII

Rather than that I should thus pine for you,
Would I had been transmuted
Into a tree or a stone,
Nevermore to feel the pangs of love.
        Ōtomo Yakamochi

IX

In obedience to the Imperial command,
Though sad is the parting from my wife,
I summon up the courage of a man,
And dressed for journey, take my leave.
My mother strokes me gently;   5
My young wife clings to me, saying,
"I will pray to the gods for your safekeeping.
Go unharmed and come back soon!"
As she speaks, she wipes with her sleeves
The tears that choke her.   10
Hard as it is, I start on my way,
Pausing and looking back time after time;
Ever farther I travel from my home,
Ever higher the mountains I climb and cross,
Till at last I arrive at Naniwa of wind-blown reeds.   15
Here I stop and wait for good weather,
To launch the ship upon the evening tide,
To set the prow seawards,
And to row out in the calm of morning.
The spring mists rise round the isles,   20
And the cranes cry in a plaintive tone,
Then I think of my far-off home—
Sorely do I grieve that with my sobs

I shake the war arrows I carry
Till they rattle in my ears.   25

ENVOYS

On an evening when the spring mists
Trail over the wide sea,
And sad is the voice of the cranes
I think of my far-off home.

Thinking of home,   30
Sleepless I sit,
The cranes call amid the shore reeds,
Lost in the mists of spring.

Ōtomo Yakamochi

X

An elegy on the impermanence of human life

We are helpless before time
Which ever speeds away.
And pains of a hundred kinds
Pursue us one after another.
Maidens joy in girlish pleasures,   5
With ship-borne gems on their wrists,
And hand in hand with their friends;
But the bloom of maidenhood,
As it cannot be stopped,
Too swiftly steals away.   10
When do their ample tresses
Black as a mud-snail's bowels
Turn white with the frost of age?
Whence come those wrinkles
Which furrow their rosy checks?   15
The lusty young men, warrior-like,
Bearing their sword blades at their waists,
In their hands the hunting bows,
And mounting their bay horses,
With saddles dressed with twill,   20
Ride about in triumph;
But can their prime of youth
Favor them for ever?
Few are the nights they keep,
When, sliding back the plank doors,   25
They reach their beloved ones
And sleep, arms intertwined,
Before, with staffs at their waists,
They totter along the road,
Laughed at here, and hated there.   30

This is the way of the world;
And, cling as I may to life,
I know no help!

ENVOY

Although I wish I were thus,
Like the rocks that stay for ever,   35
In this world of humanity
I cannot keep old age away.

Yamanoue Okura (660–733)

XI

A dialogue on poverty

On the night when the rain beats,
Driven by the wind,
On the night when the snowflakes mingle
With the sleety rain,
I feel so helplessly cold.   5
I nibble at a lump of salt,
Sip the hot, oft-diluted dregs of saké;
And coughing, snuffling,
And stroking my scanty board,
I say in my pride,   10
"There's none worthy, save I!"
But I shiver still with cold.
I pull up my hempen bedclothes,
Wear what few sleeveless clothes I have,
But cold and bitter is the night!   15
As for those poorer than myself,
Their parents must be cold and hungry,
Their wives and children beg and cry.
Then, how do you struggle through life?

Wide as they call the heaven and earth,   20
For me they have shrunk quite small;
Bright though they call the sun and moon,
They never shine for me.
Is it the same with all men,
Or for me alone?   25
By rare chance I was born a man
And no meaner than my fellows,
But, wearing unwadded sleeveless clothes
In tatters, like weeds waving in the sea,
Hanging from my shoulders,   30
And under the sunken roof,
Within the leaning walls,

Here I lie on straw
Spread on bare earth,
With my parents at my pillow,   35
My wife and children at my feet,
All huddled in grief and tears.
No fire sends up smoke
At the cooking-place,
And in the cauldron   40
A spider spins its web.
With not a grain to cook,
We moan like the night thrush.
Then, "to cut," is the saying is,
"The ends of what is already too short,"   45
The village headman comes,
With rod in hand to our sleeping place,
Growling for his dues.
Must it be so hopeless—
The way of this world?   50

ENVOY

Nothing but pain and shame in this world of men,
But I cannot fly away,
Wanting the wings of a bird.

Yamanoue Okura

XII

On seeing a dead man while crossing the pass of Ashigara

He lies unloosened of his white clothes,
Perhaps of his wife's weaving
From hemp within her garden fence,
And girdled threefold round
Instead of once.   5
Perhaps after painful service done
He turned his footsteps home,
To see his parents and his wife;
And now, on this steep and sacred pass
In the eastern land of Azuma,   10
Chilled in his spare, thin clothes,
His black hair fallen loose—
Telling none his province,
Telling none his home,
Here on a journey he lies dead.   15

From the Tanabe Sakimaro Collection

XIII

Love is a torment
Whenever we hide it.
Why not lay it bare
Like the moon that appears
From behind the mountain ledge?

Anonymous

XIV

Dialogue poems

Had I foreknown my sweet lord's coming,
My garden, now so rank with wild weeds,
I had strewn it with pearls!

What use to me a house strewn with pearls?.
The cottage hidden in wild weeds   5
Is enough, if I am with you.

Since I had shut the gate
And locked the door,
Whence did you, dear one, enter
To appear in my dream?   10

Though you had shut the gate
And locked the door,
I must have come to you in your dream
Through the hole cut by a thief.

Anonymous

———————— *Questions for Consideration* ————————

Using complete sentences, provide brief answers for the following questions.

1. Compiled during the eighth century A.D. , the *Man'yōshū* was conceived of as an anthology that would reach generations of readers hundreds of years in the future. Identify any passages or poems that can be related to events or situations that occur today.

\
\
\
\
\

2. As mentioned above, Japanese readers esteem the poetry of the *Man'yōshū* for its freshness, candor, and sincerity. Find passages that illustrate these qualities.

\
\
\
\
\

3. Just as Petrarch lamented the loss of Laura, Hitomaro was stricken by the death of his spouse. After reading "After the Death of His Wife" by Hitomaro, look for and list similar sentiments and phrasing in the poems of Petrarch included in this volume.

\
\
\
\
\

Writing Critically

Select one of the topics listed below and compose a 500-word essay that discusses the topic fully. Support your thesis with evidence from the text and with critical and/or historical material. use the space below for preparing to write the essay.

1. The separation of lovers is a topic that has been frequently addressed by poets of every culture and time period. Compare and contrast the handling of this theme in Hitomaro's poem, "In the Sea of Iwami" and in John Donne's well known "A Valediction: Forbidding Mourning."

2. The poems of the *Man'yōshū* were composed several centuries after the Chinese Book of Songs *(Shijing)*. However, in both cases, the society of each country was at an early stage of development. Discuss similarities of form and content in the two groups of poems.

3. Present an ample explication and analysis of any *Man'yōshū* poem that you find engaging enough to support a detailed response.

4. Examine a poem or poems from the *Man'yōshū* in light of secondary sources cited in the bibliography section of the introduction. Develop and write an essay that ties the poetry you have read to literary, cultural, or other trends discussed in the outside sources. Use parenthetical or other documentation to acknowledge quoted or paraphrased material.

Prewriting Space:

_____

_____

_____

_____

_____

_____

_____

_____

_____

_____

_____

_____

_____

_____

_____

_____

Introduction

Beowulf (Eighth Century)

The oldest known epic in English literature, *Beowulf* is the story of a rugged, Germanic people who the original Old English audience probably viewed as their ancestors. Though the only known version of the tale was probably written in the eighth century, it was not widely known until being printed in 1815. Before that, the poem had long existed as a single manuscript, one which was in fact almost destroyed in a fire in 1731. The charred, crumbling manuscript was transcribed by the Icelandic scholar G. J. Thorkelin in 1787, a transcription which continues to serve as the source of all modern editions of the text.

It is likely that the surviving version of *Beowulf* is a written account of an oral tale that may have been two or more centuries old before an anonymous scribe committed the story to paper. As such, it is difficult to talk about the author of *Beowulf* (is the author the person who recorded it, or the generations of people who retold it?). Someone, however, recorded it on paper; and whether or not it was the same person, it is likely that someone thought to combine what may have been several separate tales into one epic whole. Further, it is likely that the tale as presently recorded is a Christianized version of several tales whose origins predate the conversion of England to Christianity which began in 597 and swept through the country only gradually. Though Christian images are mentioned in *Beowulf* (most notable is the description of Grendel as a descendent of Cain), discussion of Christ is starkly absent.

Instead, the world of *Beowulf* is a brutal, Nordic world. The dominant ideology is a warrior's code. Within this code, loyalty is important, as is courage, but the reputation for both is almost as important. Thus, when Beowulf arrives at the Danish court, his first speech is a record of his accomplishments as a giant killer. When his prowess is questioned by Unferth, who claims that a fellow countryman of Beowulf's, Breca, had once bested Beowulf in a swimming contest, Beowulf replies that Breca was a friend, and they had not been competing, but that after being driven apart by the sea, Beowulf had stopped to kill nine water monsters. Furthermore, Beowulf counterattacks that Unferth is no one to talk; if Unferth were any kind of hero, he would not have killed his own brothers, and he would have killed Grendel long ago.

Overall, the story of *Beowulf* divides naturally into two parts. The first part shows Beowulf as a brash young man, seeking fame and glory. He seeks out Grendel because he has heard stories of the monster and he recognizes the opportunity to help and to show his courage and prowess. When he actually battles Grendel, he does so unarmed. Grendel escapes to his certain death when Beowulf's grip on him rips Grendel's arms free from his body. Unknown to the Danish court, he survives long enough to make his way back to his mother, who, a monster like her son, comes seeking revenge. After her rampage of killing, Beowulf pursues her. His own sword proves to be useless against her, but he finds in her lair a larger, more deadly sword which he uses to kill her.

The second part of *Beowulf* takes up his life after many years. Thanks to his fame, he has become the king of Geatland, where he has ruled for fifty years. A dragon, however, has been disturbed from its slumber and is causing widespread carnage in his kingdom. Beowulf, still seeking fame and glory, faces the dragon alone, killing it, but being killed in the process. If the tone of the first half balances the danger of Grendel and his mother against the high-spiritedness of Beowulf himself, the second part is decidedly more gloomy in tone, as the poem moves closer towards Beowulf's death. In his account of his swimming adventure, Beowulf had declared that fortune often smiles on the undoomed hero who shows enough courage (see sect. X), implying that the show of courage is itself a good in life. Beowulf shows his courage to the end, but though he kills the dragon, he is indeed doomed this time, and he dies. Further, a seeress at his funeral predicts that his death shall presage the ruin of his kingdom. Like Troy after the fall of Hector, Geatland is without its hero and doomed.

Was the poet who recorded *Beowulf* on paper familiar with the epic tradition? No one can know for sure. The allusive nature of some of *Beowulf*, however, suggests a writer who was assuming a sophisticated audience. The audience of *Beowulf* might well have recognized historical episodes from the sixth century to which the poem refers; this would have given the work some of the authentic weight of historic narrative, making the fabulous monsters seem more real. Then, too, this tale of the rugged courage of a people the audience might have identified as their ethnic ancestors almost certainly allowed them the double comfort of having an ancestry of rugged warriors while being removed from this society through region and a more developed Christianity.

For the contemporary reader, the pathos of both Grendel and his mother are certainly one of the more interesting aspects of the story. While the poem does not invite us to feel sorry for these two, the interesting shift to Grendel's point-of-view at the very moment that Beowulf is defeating him indicates an author who is well aware of the dramatic power of pathos. Indeed, this hint of a larger identity for Grendel and his mother was responsible for the 1971 John Gardner novel, *Grendel,* which retells the story of Beowulf's encounter with Grendel from the monster's viewpoint. For the tale's original audience, however, *Beowulf* would almost certainly have been read as a dramatization of the enduring power of courage and loyalty. (TJC)

BIBLIOGRAPHY

Bessinger, Jess B., and Robert F. Yeager, eds. *Approaches to Teaching Beowulf.* 1984

Clark, George, *Beowulf.* 1990.

Fry, Donald K. *The Beowulf Poet: A Collection of Essays.* 1968

Hudson, Marc. *Beowulf: a Translation and Commentary.* 1990.

Huppe, Bernard. *The Hero in the Earthly City: A Reading of Beowulf.* 1984

from Beowulf

FROM THE TRANSLATOR'S PREFACE

The present work is a modest effort to reproduce approximately, in modern measures, the venerable epic, Beowulf. *Approximately*, I repeat; for a very close reproduction of Anglo-Saxon verse would, to a large extent, be prose to a modern ear.

The effort has been made to give a decided flavor of archaism to the translation. All words not in keeping with the spirit of the poem have been avoided. Again, though many archaic words have been used, there are none, it is believed, which are not found in standard modern poetry.

With these preliminary remarks, it will not be amiss to give an outline of the story of the poem.

THE STORY

Hrothgar, king of the Danes, or Scyldings, builds a great mead-hall, or palace, in which he hopes to feast his liegemen and to give them presents. The joy of king and retainers is, however, of short duration. Grendel, the monster, is seized with hateful jealousy. He cannot brook the sounds of joyance that reach him down in his fen-dwelling near the hall. Oft and anon he goes to the joyous building, bent on direful mischief. Thane after thane is ruthlessly carried off and devoured, while no one is found strong enough and bold enough to cope with the monster. For twelve years he persecutes Hrothgar and his vassals.

Over sea, a day's voyage off, Beowulf, of the Geats, nephew of Higelac, king of the Geats, hears of Grendel's doings and of Hrothgar's misery. He resolves to crush the fell monster and relieve the aged king. With fourteen chosen companions, he sets sail for Daneland. Reaching that country, he soon persuades Hrothgar of his ability to help him. The hours that elapse before night are spent in beer-drinking and conversation. When Hrothgar's bedtime comes he leaves the hall in charge of Beowulf, telling him that never before has he given to another the absolute wardship of his palace. All retire to rest, Beowulf, as it were, sleeping upon his arms.

Grendel comes, the great march-stepper, bearing God's anger. He seizes and kills one of the sleeping warriors. Then he advances towards Beowulf. A fierce and desperate hand-to-hand struggle ensues.

No arms are used, both combatants trusting to strength and hand-grip. Beowulf tears Grendel's shoulder from its socket, and the monster retreats to his den, howling and yelling with agony and fury. The wound is fatal.

The next morning, at early dawn, warriors in numbers flock to the hall Heorot, to hear the news. Joy is boundless. Glee runs high. Hrothgar and his retainers are lavish of gratitude and of gifts.

Grendel's mother, however, comes the next night to avenge his death. She is furious and raging. While Beowulf is sleeping in a room somewhat apart from the quarters of the other warriors, she seizes one of Hrothgar's favorite counsellors, and carries him off and devours him. Beowulf is called. Determined to leave Heorot entirely purified, he arms himself, and goes down to look for the female monster. After traveling through the waters many hours, he meets her near the sea-bottom. She drags him to her den. There he sees Grendel lying dead. After a desperate and almost fatal struggle with the woman, he slays her, and swims upward in triumph, taking with him Grendel's head.

Joy is renewed at Heorot. Congratulations crowd upon the victor. Hrothgar literally pours treasures into the lap of Beowulf; and it is agreed among the vassals of the king that Beowulf will be their next liegelord.

Beowulf leaves Dane-land. Hrothgar weeps and laments at his departure.

When the hero arrives in his own land, Higelac treats him as a distinguished guest. He is the hero of the hour.

Beowulf subsequently becomes king of his own people, the Geats. After he has been ruling for fifty years, his own neighborhood is woefully harried by a fire-spewing dragon. Beowulf determines to kill him. In the ensuing struggle both Beowulf and the dragon are slain. The grief of the Geats is inexpressible. They determine, however, to leave nothing undone to honor the memory of their lord. A great funeral-pyre is built, and his body is burnt. Then a memorial-barrow is made, visible from a great distance, that sailors afar may be constantly reminded of the prowess of the national hero of Geatland.

The poem closes with a glowing tribute to his bravery, his gentleness, his goodness of heart, and his generosity.

J. L. HALL.

GLOSSARY OF PROPER NAMES

[The figures refer to the divisions of the poem in which the respective names occur. The large figures refer to fitts; the small to lines in the fitts.]

Æschere.—Confidential friend of King Hrothgar. Elder brother of Yrmenlaf. Killed by Grendel.—21 3; 30 89.

Beanstan.—Father of Breca.—9 26.

Beowulf.—Son of Scyld, the founder of the dynasty of Scyldings. Father of Healfdene, and grandfather of Hrothgar.—1 18; 2 1.

Beowulf.—The hero of the poem. Sprung from the stock of Geats, son of Ecgtheow. Brought up by his maternal grandfather Hrethel, and figuring in manhood as a devoted liegeman of his uncle Higelac. A hero from his youth. Has the strength of thirty men. Engages in a swimming-match with Breca. Goes to the help of Hrothgar against the monster Grendel. Vanquishes Grendel and his mother. Afterwards becomes king of the Geats. Late in life attempts to kill a fire-spewing dragon, and is slain. Is buried with great honors. His memorial mound.—6 26; 7 2; 7 9; 9 3; 9 8; 12 29; 12 43; 23 1, etc.

Breca.—Beowulf's opponent in the famous swimming-match.—9 8; 9 19; 9 21; 9 22.

Brondings.—A people ruled by Breca.—9 23.

Brosinga mene.—A famous collar once owned by the Brosings.—19 7.

Cain.—Progenitor of Grendel and other monsters.—2 56; 20 11.

Danes.—Subjects of Scyld and his descendants, and hence often called Scyldings. Other names for them are Victory-Scyldings, Honor-Scyldings, Armor-Danes, Bright-Danes, East-Danes, West-Danes, North-Danes, South-Danes, Ingwins, Hrethmen.—1 1; 2 1; 3 2; 5 14; 7 1, etc.

Ecglaf.—Father of Unferth, who taunts Beowulf.—9 1.

Ecgtheow.—Father of Beowulf, the hero of the poem. A widely-known Wægmunding warrior. Marries Hrethel's daughter. After slaying Heatholaf, a Wylfing, he flees his country.—7 3; 5 6: 8 4.

Eormenric.—A Gothic king, from whom Hama took away the famous Brosinga mene.—19 9.

Finn.—King of the North-Frisians and the Jutes. Marries Hildeburg. At his court takes place the horrible slaughter in which the Danish general, Hnæf, fell. Later on, Finn himself is slain by Danish warriors.—17 18; 17 30; 17 44; 18 4; 18 23.

Fin-land.—The country to which Beowulf was driven by the currents in his swimming-match.—10 22.

Fitela.— Son and nephew of King Sigemund, whose praises are sung in XIV.—14 42; 14 53.

Folcwalda.— Father of Finn.—17 38.

Franks.—Introduced occasionally in referring to the death of Higelac.—19 19; 40 21; 40 24.

Frisians.—A part of them are ruled by Finn. Some of them were engaged in the struggle in which Higelac was slain.—17 20; 17 42; 17 52; 40 21.

Geats, Geatmen.—The race to which the hero of the poem belongs. Also called Weder-Geats, or Weders, War-Geats, Sea-Geats. They are ruled by Hrethel, Hæthcyn, Higelac, and Beowulf.—4 7; 7 4; 10 45; 11 8; 27 14; 28 8.

Grendel.—A monster of the race of Cain. Dwells in the fens and moors. Is furiously envious when he hears sounds of joy in Hrothgar's palace. Causes the king untold agony for years. Is finally conquered by Beowulf, and dies of his wound. His hand and arm are hung up in Hrothgar's hall Heorot. His head is cut off by Beowulf when be goes down to fight with Grendel's mother.—2 50; 3 1; 3 13; 8 19; 11 17; 12 2; 13 27; 15 3.

Guthlaf.—A Dane of Hnæfs party.—18 24.

Half-Danes.—Branch of the Danes to which Hnæf belonged.—17 19.

Hama.—Takes the Brosinga mene from Eormenric.—19 7.

Helmings.—The race to which Queen Wealhtheow belonged.—10 63.

Hengest.—A Danish leader. Takes command on the fall of Hnæf.—17 33; 17 41.

Heremod.—A Danish king of a dynasty before the Scylding line. Was a source of great sorrow to his people.—14 64; 25 59.

Healfdene.—Grandson of Scyld and father of Hrothgar. Ruled the Danes long and well.—2 5; 4 1; 8 14.

Heathoremes.—The people on whose shores Breca is cast by the waves during his contest with Beowulf.—9 21.

Heorogar.—Elder brother of Hrothgar, and surnamed "Weoroda Ræswa," Prince of the Troopers.—8 12.

Hildeburg.—Wife of Finn, daughter of Hoce, and related to Hnæf,—probably his sister.—17 21; 18 34.

Hnæf.—Leader of a branch of the Danes called Half-Danes. Killed in the struggle at Finn's castle.—17 19; 17 61.

Hoce.—Father of Hildeburg and probably of Hnæf.—17 26.

Hrethel.—King of the Geats, father of Higelac, and grandfather of Beowulf—7 4; 34 39

Hrethla.—Once used for Hrethel.—7 82.

Hrethmen.—Another name for the Danes.—7 73.

Hrethric.—Son of Hrothgar.—18 65; 27 19.

Hrothgar.—The Danish king who built the hall Heort, but was long unable to enjoy it on account of Grendel's persecutions. Marries Wealhtheow, a Helming lady. Has two sons and a daughter. Is a typical Teutonic king, lavish of gifts. A devoted liegelord, as his lamentations over slain liegemen prove. Also very appreciative of kindness, as is shown by his loving gratitude to Beowulf.—8 10; 15 1; etc.

Hrothmund.—Son of Hrothgar.—18 65.

Hrothulf.—Probably a son of Halga, younger brother of Hrothgar. Certainly on terms of close intimacy in Hrothgar's palace.—16 26; 18 57.

Hrunting.—Unferth's sword, lent to Beowulf.—22 71.

Hun—A Frisian warrior, probably general of the Hetwars. Gives Hengest a beautiful sword.—18 19.

Hunferth.—Sometimes used for Unferth.

Ingwins.—Another name for the Danes.—16 52; 20 69.

Jutes.—Name sometimes applied to Finn's people.—17 22; 17 38; 18 17.

Lafing.—Name of a famous sword presented to Hengest by Hun.—18 19.

Nægling.—Beowulf's sword.—36 76.

Oslaf.—A Dane of Hnæf's party.—18 24.

Scyldings.—The descendants of Scyld. They are also called Honor-Scyldings, Victory-Scyldings, War-Scyldings, etc. (See "Danes," above.)—7 1; 8 1.

Sigemund.—Son of Wæls, and uncle and father of Fitela. His struggle with a dragon is related in connection with Beowulf's deeds of prowess.—14 38; 14 47.

Swerting.—Grandfather of Higelac, and father of Hrethel.—19 11.

Unferth.—Son of Ecglaf and seemingly a confidential courtier of Hrothgar. Taunts Beowulf for having taken part in the swimming-match. Lends Beowulf his sword when he goes to look for Grendel's mother. In the MS. sometimes written *Hunferth*.—9 1; 18 41.

Wæels.—Father of Sigemund.—14 60.

Weders.—Another name for Geats or Wedergeats.

Wayland.—A fabulous smith mentioned in this poem and in other old Teutonic literature.—7 83.

Wendels.—The people of Wulfgar, Hrothgar's messenger and retainer. (Perhaps = Vandals)—6 30.

Wealhtheow.—Wife of Hrothgar. Her queenly courtesy is well shown in the poem.—10 55.

Wulfgar.—Lord of the Wendels, and retainer of Hrothgar.—6 18; 6 30.

Wylfings.—A people to whom belonged Heatholaf, who was slain by Ecgtheow.—8 6; 8 16.

Yrmenlaf.—Younger brother of Æschere, the hero whose death grieved Hrothgar so deeply.—21 4.

Weapons and Dress of Warriors from the Western Baltic Area
(Present-day Denmark) around the time of *Beowulf.*

LIST OF WORDS AND PHRASES NOT IN GENERAL USE

ATHELING.—Prince, nobleman.

BAIRN.—Son, child.

BARROW.—Mound, rounded hill, funeral mound.

BATTLE-SARK.—Armor.

BEAKER.—Cup, drinking-vessel.

BEGEAR.—Prepare.

BIGHT.—Bay, sea.

BILL.—Sword.

BOSS.—Ornamental projection.

BRACTEATE.—A round ornament on a necklace.

BRAND.—Sword.

BURN.—Stream.

BURNIE.—Armor.

CARLE.— Man, hero.

EARL.—Nobleman, any brave man.

EKE.— Also

EMPRISE.—Enterprise, undertaking.

ERST.—Formerly.

ERST-WORTHY.—Worthy for a long time past.

FAIN.—Glad.

FERRY.—Bear, carry.

FEY.—Fated, doomed.

FLOAT.—Vessel, ship.

FOIN.—To lunge (Shaks.).

GLORY OF KINGS.—God.

GREWSOME.—Cruel, fierce.

HEFT.—Handle, hilt; used by synecdoche for "sword."

HELM.—Helmet, protector.

HENCHMAN.—Retainer, vassal.

HIGHT.—Am (was) named.

HOLM.—Ocean, curved surface of the sea.

HIMSEEMED.—(It) seemed to him.

LIEF.—Dear, valued.

MERE.—Sea; in compounds, "mere-ways," "mere-currents," etc.

MICKLE.—Much.

NATHLESS.—Nevertheless.

NAZE.—Edge (nose).

NESS.—Edge.

NICKER.—Sea-beast.

QUIT, QUITE.—Requite.

RATHE.—Quickly.

REAVE.—Bereave, deprive.

SAIL-ROAD.—Sea.

SETTLE.—Seat, bench.

SKINKER.—One who pours.

SOOTHLY.—Truly.

SWINGE.—Stroke, blow.

TARGE, TARGET.—Shield.

THROUGHLY.—thoroughly.

TOLD.—Counted.

UNCANNY.—Ill-featured, grizzly.

UNNETHE.—Difficult.

WAR-SPEED.—Success in war.

WEB.—Tapestry (that which is "woven").

WEEDED.—Clad (cf. widow's weeds).

WEEN.—Suppose, imagine.

WEIRD.—Fate, Providence.

WHILOM.—At times, formerly, often.

WIELDER.—Ruler. Often used of God, also in compounds, as "Wielder of Glory," "Wielder" of Worship.

WIGHT.—Creature.

WOLD.—Plane, extended surface.

WOT.—knows.

YOUNKER.—Youth.

VI
Beowulf Introduces Himself at the Palace

The highway glistened with many-hued pebble,
A by-path led the liegemen together.
Firm and hand-locked the war-burnie glistened,
The ring-sword radiant rang 'mid the armor
As the party was approaching the palace together   5
In warlike equipments. 'Gainst the wall of the building
Their wide-fashioned war-shields they weary did set then,
Battle-shields sturdy; benchward they turned then;
Their battle-sarks rattled, the gear of the heroes
The lances stood up then, all in a cluster,   10
The arms of the seamen, ashen-shafts mounted
With edges of iron: the armor-clad troopers
Were decked with weapons. Then a proud-mooded hero
Asked of the champions questions of lineage:
"From what borders bear ye your battle-shields plated,   15
Gilded and gleaming, your gray-colored burnies,
Helmets with visors and heap of war-lances?—
To Hrothgar the king I am servant and liegeman.
'Mong folk from far-lands found I have never
Men so many of mien more courageous.   20
I ween that from valor, nowise as outlaws,
But from greatness of soul ye sought for King Hrothgar."
Then the strength-famous earlman answer rendered,
The proud-mooded Wederchief replied to his question,
Hardy 'neath helmet: Higelac's mates are we   25
Beowulf hight I. To the bairn of Healfdene,
The famous folk-leader, I freely will tell
To thy prince my commission, if pleasantly hearing
He'll grant we may greet him so gracious to all men."
Wulfgar replied then (he was prince of the Wendels,   30
His boldness of spirit was known unto many,
His prowess and prudence): "The prince of the Scyldings,
The friend-lord of Danemen, I will ask of thy journey,
The giver of rings, as thou urgest me do it,
The folk-chief famous, and inform thee early   35
What answer the good one mindeth to render me."
He turned then hurriedly where Hrothgar was sitting,
Old and hoary, his earlmen attending him;
The strength-famous went till he stood at the shoulder
Of the lord of the Danemen, of courteous thanemen   40
The custom he minded. Wulfgar addressed then
His friendly liegelord: "Folk of the Geatmen
O'er the way of the waters are wafted hither,
Faring from far-lands the foremost in rank
The battle-champions Beowulf title.   45
They make this petition: with thee, O my chieftain,
To be granted a conference; O gracious King Hrothgar,
Friendly answer refuse not to give them!
In war-trappings weeded worthy they seem

Of earls to be honored; sure the atheling is doughty   50
Who headed the heroes hitherward coming."

VII
Hrothgar and Beowulf

Hrothgar answered, helm of the Scyldings:
"I remember this man as the merest of striplings.
His father long dead now was Ecgtheow titled,
Him Hrethel the Geatman granted at home his
One only daughter; his battle-brave son   5
Is come but now, sought a trustworthy friend.
Seafaring sailors asserted it then,
Who valuable gift-gems of the Geatmen carried
As peace-offering thither, that he thirty men's grapple
Has in his hand, the hero-in-battle.   10
The holy Creator usward sent him,
To West-Dane warriors, I ween, for to render
'Gainst Grendel's grimness gracious assistance
I shall give to the good one gift-gems for courage.
Hasten to bid them hither to speed them,   15
To see assembled this circle of kinsmen;
Tell them expressly they're welcome in sooth to
The men of the Danes." To the door of the building
Wulfgar went then, this word-message shouted:
"My victorious liegelord bade me to tell you,   20
The East-Danes' atheling, that your origin knows he,
And o'er wave-billows wafted ye welcome are hither,
Valiant of spirit. Ye straightway may enter
Clad in corslets, cued in your helmets,
To see King Hrothgar. Here let your battle-boards,   25
Wood-spears and war-shafts, await your conferring."
The mighty one rose then, with many a liegeman,
An excellent thane-group; some there did await them,
And as bid of the brave one the battle-gear guarded.
Together they hied them, while the hero did guide them,   30
'Neath Heorot's roof; the high-minded went then
Sturdy 'neath helmet till he stood in the building.
Beowulf spake (his burnie did glisten,
His armor seamed over by the art of the craftsman)
"Hail thou, Hrothgar! I am Higelac's kinsman   35
And vassal forsooth; many a wonder
I dared as a stripling. The doings of Grendel,
In far-off fatherland I fully did know of:
Sea-farers tell us, this hall-building standeth,
Excellent edifice, empty and useless   40
To all the earlmen after evenlight's glimmer
'Neath heaven's bright hues hath hidden its glory.
This my earls then urged me, the most excellent of them,
Carles very clever, to come and assist thee,
Folk-leader Hrothgar; fully they knew of   45
The strength of my body. Themselves they beheld me

When I came from the contest, when covered with gore
Foes I escaped from, where five I had bound,
The giant-race wasted, in the waters destroying
The nickers by night, bore numberless sorrows,   50
The Weders avengèd (woes had they suffered)
Enemies ravaged; alone now with Grendel
I shall manage the matter, with the monster of evil,
The giant, decide it. Thee I would therefore
Beg of thy bounty, Bright-Danish chieftain,   55
Lord of the Scyldings, this single petition
Not to refuse me, defender of warriors,
Friend-lord of folks, so far have I sought thee,
That I may unaided, my earlmen assisting me,
This brave-mooded war-band, purify Heorot.   60
I have heard on inquiry, the horrible creature
From veriest rashness reeks not for weapons;
I this do scorn then, so be Higelac gracious,
My liegelord belovèd, lenient of spirit,
To bear a blade or a broad-fashioned target,   65
A shield to the onset; only with hand-grip
The foe I must grapple, fight for my life then,
Foeman with foeman; he fain must rely on
The doom of the Lord whom death layeth hold of
I ween he will wish, if he win in the struggle,   70
To eat in the war-hall earls of the Geat-folk,
Boldly to swallow them, as of yore he did often
The best of the Hrethmen! Thou needest not trouble
A head-watch to give me; he will have me dripping
And dreary with gore, if death overtake me,   75
Will bear me off bleeding, biting and mouthing me,
The hermit will eat me, heedless of pity,
Marking the moor-fens; no more wilt thou need then
Find me my food. If I fall in the battle,
Send to Higelac the armor that serveth   80
To shield my bosom, the best of equipments,
Richest of ring-mails; 'tis the relic of Hrethla,
The work of Wayland. Goes Weird as she must go!"

VIII
Hrothgar and Beowulf—continued.

Hrothgar discoursed, helm of the Scyldings:
"To defend our folk and to furnish assistance,
Thou soughtest us hither, good friend Beowulf.
The fiercest of feuds thy father engaged in,
Heatholaf killed he in hand-to-hand conflict   5
'Mid Wilfingish warriors; then the Wederish people
For fear of a feud were forced to disown him.
Thence flying he fled to the folk of the South-Danes,
The race of the Scyldings, o'er the roll of the waters;
I had lately begun then to govern the Danemen,   10
The hoard-seat of heroes held in my youth,

Rich in its jewels: dead was Heregar,
My kinsman and elder had earth-joys forsaken,
Healfdene his bairn. He was better than I am
That feud thereafter for a fee I compounded;   15
O'er the weltering waters to the Wilfings I sent
Ornaments old; oaths did he swear me.
It pains me in spirit to any to tell it,
What grief in Heorot Grendel hath caused me,
What horror unlooked-for, by hatred unceasing.   20
Waned is my war-band, wasted my hall-troop;
Weird hath offcast them to the clutches of Grendel.
God can easily hinder the scather
From deeds so direful. Oft drunken with beer
O'er the ale-vessel promised warriors in armor   25
They would willingly wait on the wassailing-benches
A grapple with Grendel, with grimmest of edges.
Then this mead-hall at morning with murder was reeking,
The building was bloody at breaking of daylight,
The bench-deals all flooded, dripping and bloodied,   30
The folk-hall was gory: I had fewer retainers,
Dear-beloved warriors, whom death had laid hold of.
Sit at the feast now, thy intents unto heroes,
Thy victor-fame show, as thy spirit doth urge thee
For the men of the Geats then together assembled,   35
In the beer-hall blithesome a bench was made ready;
There warlike in spirit they went to be seated,
Proud and exultant. A liegeman did service,
Who a beaker embellished bore with decorum,
And gleaming-drink poured. The gleeman sang whilom   40
Hearty in Heorot; there was heroes' rejoicing,
A numerous war-band of Weders and Danemen.

IX
Unferth Taunts Beowulf

Unferth spoke up, Ecglaf his son,
Who sat at the feet of the lord of the Scyldings,
Opened the jousting (the journey of Beowulf,
Sea-farer doughty, gave sorrow to Unferth
And greatest chagrin, too, for granted he never   5
That any man else on earth should attain to,
Gain under heaven, more glory than he):
"Art thou that Beowulf with Breca did struggle,
On the wide sea-currents at swimming contended,
Where to humor your pride the ocean ye tried,   10
From vainest vaunting adventured your bodies
In care of the waters? And no one was able
Nor lief nor loth one, in the least to dissuade you
Your difficult voyage; then ye ventured a-swimming,
Where your arms outstretching the streams ye did cover,   15
The mere-ways measured, mixing and stirring them,
Glided the ocean; angry the waves were,

With the weltering of winter. In the water's possession,
Ye toiled for a seven-night; he at swimming outdid thee,
In strength excelled thee. Then early at morning   20
On the Heathoremes' shore the holm-currents tossed him,
Sought he thenceward the home of his fathers,
Beloved of his liegemen, the land of the Brondings,
The peace-castle pleasant, where a people he wielded,
Had borough and jewels. The pledge that he made thee   25
The son of Beanstan hath soothly accomplished.
Then I ween thou wilt find thee less fortunate issue,
Though ever triumphant in onset of battle,
A grim grappling, if Grendel thou darest
For the space of a night near-by to wait for!   30
Beowulf answered, offspring of Ecgtheow:
"My good friend Unferth, sure freely and wildly,
Thou fuddled with beer of Breca hast spoken,
Hast told of his journey! A fact I allege it
That greater strength in the waters I had then,   35
Ills in the ocean, than any man else had.
We made agreement as the merest of striplings
Promised each other (both of us then were
Younkers in years) that we yet would adventure
Out on the ocean; it all we accomplished.   40
While swimming the sea-floods, sword-blade unscabbarded
Boldly we brandished, our bodies expected
To shield from the sharks. He sure was unable
To swim on the waters further than I could,
More swift on the waves, nor *would* I from him go.   45
Then we two companions stayed in the ocean
Five nights together, till the currents did part us,
The weltering waters, weathers the bleakest,
And nethermost night, and the north-wind whistled
Fierce in our faces; fell were the billows.   50
The mere fishes' mood was mightily ruffled:
And there against foemen my firm-knotted corslet,
Hand-jointed, hardy, help did afford me;
My battle-sark braided, brilliantly gilded,
Lay on my bosom. To the bottom then dragged me,   55
A hateful fiend-scather, seized me and held me,
Grim in his grapple: 'twas granted me, nathless,
To pierce the monster with the point of my weapon,
My obedient blade; battle offcarried
The mighty mere-creature by means of my hand-blow.   60

X

Beowulf Silences Unferth — Glee Is High

"So ill-meaning enemies often did cause me
Sorrow the sorest. I sewed them, in quittance,
With my dear-lovèd sword, as in sooth it was fitting;
They missed the pleasure of feasting abundantly,
Ill-doers evil, of eating my body,   5

Of surrounding the banquet deep in the ocean;
But wounded with edges early at morning
They were stretched a-high on the strand of the ocean,
Put to sleep with the sword, that sea-going travelers
No longer thereafter were hindered from sailing   10
The foam-dashing currents. Came a light from the east,
God's beautiful beacon; the billows subsided,
That well I could see the nesses projecting,
The blustering crags. Weird often saveth
The undoomed hero if doughty his valor!   15
But me did it fortune to fell with my weapon
Nine of the nickers. Of night-struggle harder
'Neath dome of the heaven heard I but rarely,
Nor of wight more woeful in the waves of the ocean
Yet I 'scaped with my life the grip of the monsters,   20
Weary from travel. Then the waters bare me
To the land of the Finns, the flood with the current,
The weltering waves. Not a word hath been told me
Of deeds so daring done by thee, Unferth,
And of sword-terror none; never hath Breca   25
At the play of the battle, nor either of you two,
Feat so fearless performèd with weapons
Glinting and gleaming . . . .
. . . . I utter no boasting;
Though with cold-blooded cruelty thou killedst thy brothers,   30
Thy nearest of kin; thou needs must in hell get
Direful damnation, though doughty thy wisdom.
I tell thee in earnest, offspring of Ecglaf,
Never had Grendel such numberless horrors,
The direful demon, done to thy liegelord,   35
Harrying in Heorot, if thy heart were as sturdy,
Thy mood as ferocious as thou dost describe them.
He hath found out fully that the fierce-burning hatred,
The edge-battle eager, of all of your kindred,
Of the Victory-Scyldings, need little dismay him: 40
Oaths he exacteth, not any he spares
Of the folk of the Danemen, but fighteth with pleasure,
Killeth and feasteth, no contest expecteth
From Spear-Danish people. But the prowess and valor
Of the earls of the Geatmen early shall venture   45
To give him a grapple. He shall go who is able
Bravely to banquet, when the bright-light of morning
Which the second day bringeth, the sun in its ether-robes,
O'er children of men shines from the southward!"
Then the gray-haired, war-famed giver of treasure   50
Was blithesome and joyous, the Bright-Danish ruler
Expected assistance; the people's protector
Heard from Beowulf his bold resolution.
There was laughter of heroes; loud was the clatter,
The words were winsome. Wealhtheow advanced then,   55
Consort of Hrothgar, of courtesy mindful,
Gold-decked saluted the men in the building,
And the freeborn woman the beaker presented
To the lord of the kingdom, first of the East-Danes,
Bade him be blithesome when beer was a-flowing,   60
Lief to his liegemen; he lustily tasted

Of banquet and beaker, battle-famed ruler.
The Helmingish lady then graciously circled
'Mid all the liegemen lesser and greater:
Treasure-cups tendered, till time was afforded   65
That the decorous-mooded, diademed folk-queen
Might bear to Beowulf the bumper o'errunning;
She greeted the Geat-prince, God she did thank,
Most wise in her words, that her wish was accomplished,
That in any of earlmen she ever should look for   70
Solace in sorrow. He accepted the beaker,
Battle-bold warrior, at Wealhtheow's giving,
Then equipped for combat quoth he in measures,
Beowulf spake, offspring of Ecgtheow:
"I purposed in spirit when I mounted the ocean,   75
When I boarded my boat with a band of my liegemen,
I would work to the fullest the will of your people
Or in foe's-clutches fastened fall in the battle.
Deeds I shall do of daring and prowess,
Or the last of my life-days live in this mead-hall."   80
These words to the lady were welcome and pleasing,
The boast of the Geatman; with gold trappings broidered
Went the freeborn folk-queen her fond-lord to sit by.
Then again as of yore was heard in the building
Courtly discussion, conquerors' shouting,   85
Heroes were happy, till Healfdene's son would
Go to his slumber to seek for refreshing;
For the horrid hell-monster in the hall-building knew he
A fight was determined, since the light of the sun they
No longer could see, and lowering darkness   90
O'er all had descended, and dark under heaven
Shadowy shapes came shying around them.
The liegemen all rose then. One saluted the other,
Hrothgar Beowulf, in rhythmical measures,
Wishing him well, and, the wassail-hall giving   95
To his care and keeping, quoth he departing:
"Not to any one else have I ever entrusted,
But thee and thee only, the hall of the Danemen,
Since high I could heave my hand and my buckler.
Take thou in charge now the noblest of houses;   100
Be mindful of honor, exhibiting prowess,
Watch 'gainst the foeman! Thou shalt want no enjoyments,
Survive thou safely adventure so glorious!"

XI
All Sleep Save One

Then Hrothgar departed, his earl-throng attending him,
Folk-lord of Scyldings, forth from the building;
The war-chieftain wished then Wealhtheow to look for,
The queen for a bedmate. To keep away Grendel
The Glory of Kings had given a hall-watch,   5
As men heard recounted: for the king of the Danemen

He did special service, gave the giant a watcher:
And the prime of the Geatmen implicitly trusted
His warlike strength and the Wielder's protection.
His armor of iron off him he did then,   10
His helmet from his head, to his henchman committed
His chased-handled chain-sword, choicest of weapons,
And bade him bide with his battle-equipments.
The good one then uttered words of defiance,
Beowulf Geatman, ere his bed he upmounted: 15
"I hold me no meaner in matters of prowess,
In warlike achievements, than Grendel does himself;
Hence I seek not with sword-edge to sooth him to slumber,
Of life to bereave him, though well I am able.
No battle-skill has he, that blows he should strike me,   20
To shatter my shield, though sure he is mighty
In strife and destruction; but struggling by night we
Shall do without edges, dare he to look for
Weaponless warfare, and wise-mooded Father
The glory apportion, God ever-holy,   25
On which hand soever to him seemeth proper."
Then the brave-mooded hero bent to his slumber,
The pillow received the cheek of the noble;
And many a martial mere-thane attending
Sank to his slumber. Seemed it unlikely   30
That ever thereafter any should hope to
Be happy at home, hero-friends visit
Or the lordly troop-castle where he lived from his childhood;
They had heard how slaughter had snatched from the wine-hall,
Had recently ravished, of the race of the Scyldings   35
Too many by far. But the Lord to them granted
The weaving of war-speed, to Wederish heroes
Aid and comfort, that every opponent
By one man's war-might they worsted and vanquished,
By the might of himself; the truth is established   40
That God Almighty hath governed for ages
Kindreds and nations. A night very lurid
The trav'ler-at-twilight came tramping and striding.
The warriors were sleeping who should watch the horned-building,
One only excepted. 'Mid earthmen 'twas 'stablished,   45
Th' implacable foeman was powerless to hurl them
To the land of shadows, if the Lord were unwilling;
But serving as warder, in terror to foemen,
He angrily bided the issue of battle.

XII
Grendel and Beowulf

'Neath the cloudy cliffs came from the moor then
Grendel going, God's anger bare he.
The monster intended some one of earthmen
In the hall-building grand to entrap and make way with;
He went under welkin where well he knew of   5

The wine-joyous building, brilliant with plating,
Gold-hall of earthmen. Not the earliest occasion
He the home and manor of Hrothgar had sought:
Ne'er found he in life-days later nor earlier
Hardier hero, hall-thanes more sturdy!   10
Then came to the building the warrior marching,
Bereft of his joyance. The door quickly opened
On fire-hinges fastened, when his fingers had touched it;
The fell one had flung then—his fury so bitter—
Open the entrance. Early thereafter   15
The foeman trod the shining hall-pavement,
Strode he angrily; from the eyes of him glimmered
A lustre unlovely likest to fire.
He beheld in the hall the heroes in numbers,
A circle of kinsmen sleeping together,   20
A throng of thanemen: then his thoughts were exultant,
He minded to sunder from each of the thanemen
The life from his body, horrible demon,
Ere morning came, since fate had allowed him
The prospect of plenty. Providence willed not   25
To permit him any more of men under heaven
To eat in the night-time. Higelac's kinsman
Great sorrow endured how the dire-mooded creature
In unlooked-for assaults were likely to bear him.
No thought had the monster of deferring the matter,   30
But on earliest occasion he quickly laid hold of
A soldier asleep, suddenly tore him,
Bit his bone-prison the blood drank in currents
Swallowed in mouthfuls: he soon had the dead man's
Feet and hands, too, eaten entirely.   35
Nearer he strode then, the stout-hearted warrior
Snatched as he slumbered, seizing with hand-grip,
Forward the foeman foined with his hand;
Caught he quickly the cunning deviser,
On his elbow he rested. This early discovered   40
The master of malice, that in middle-earth's regions,
'Neath the whole of the heavens, no hand-grapple greater
In any man else had he ever encountered:
Fearful in spirit, faint-mooded waxed he,
Not off could betake him; death he was pondering,   45
Would fly to his covert, seek the devils' assembly:
His calling no more was the same he had followed
Long in his lifetime. The liege-kinsman worthy
Of Higelac minded his speech of the evening,
Stood he up straight and stoutly did seize him.   50
His fingers cracked; the giant was outward,
The earl stepped farther. The famous one minded
To flee away farther if he found an occasion,
And off and away, avoiding delay,
To fly to the fen-moors; he fully was ware of   55
The strength of his grapple in the grip of the foeman.
'Twas an ill-taken journey that the injury-bringing,
Harrying harmer to Heorot wandered:
The palace re-echoed; to all of the Danemen,
Dwellers in castles, to each of the bold ones,   60
Earlmen, was terror. Angry they both were,

Archwarders raging. Rattled the building;
'Twas a marvellous wonder that the wine-hall withstood then
The bold-in-battle, bent not to earthward,
Excellent earth-hall; but within and without it   65
Was fastened so firmly in fetters of iron,
By the art of the armorer. Off from the sill there
Bent mead-benches many, as men have informed me,
Adorned with gold-work, where the grim ones did struggle.
The Scylding wise men weened ne'er before   70
That by might and main-strength a man under heaven
Might break it in pieces, bone-decked, resplendent,
Crush it by cunning, unless clutch of the fire
In smoke should consume it. The sound mounted upward
Novel enough; on the North Danes fastened   75
A terror of anguish, on all of the men there
Who heard from the wall the weeping and plaining,
The song of defeat from the foeman of heaven,
Heard him hymns of horror howl, and his sorrow
Hell-bound bewailing. He held him too firmly   80
Who was strongest of main-strength of men of that era.

XIII
Grendel Is Vanquished

For no cause whatever would the earlmen's defender
Leave in life-joys the loathsome newcomer,
He deemed his existence utterly useless
To men under heaven. Many a noble
Of Beowulf brandished his battle-sword old,   5
Would guard the life of his lord and protector,
The far-famed chieftain, if able to do so;
While waging the warfare, this wist they but little,
Brave battle-thanes, while his body intending
To slit into slivers, and seeking his spirit: 10
That the relentless foeman nor finest of weapons
Of all on the earth, nor any of war-bills
Was willing to injure; but weapons of victory
Swords and suchlike he had sworn to dispense with.
His death at that time must prove to be wretched,   15
And the far-away spirit widely should journey
Into enemies, power. This plainly he saw then
Who with mirth of mood malice no little
Had wrought in the past on the race of the earthmen
(To God he was hostile), that his body would fail him,   20
But Higelac's hardy henchman and kinsman
Held him by the hand; hateful to other
Was each one if living. A body-wound suffered
The direful demon, damage incurable
Was seen on his shoulder, his sinews were shivered,   25
His body did burst. To Beowulf was given
Glory in battle; Grendel from thenceward
Must flee and hide him in the fen-cliffs and marshes,

Sick unto death, his dwelling must look for   30
Unwinsome and woeful; he wist the more fully
The end of his earthly existence was nearing,
His life-days' limits. At last for the Danemen,
When the slaughter was over, their wish was accomplished.
The comer-from-far-land had cleansed then of evil,   35
Wise and valiant, the war-hall of Hrothgar,
Saved it from violence. He joyed in the night-work,
In repute for prowess; the prince of the Geatmen
For the East-Danish people his boast had accomplished,
Bettered their burdensome bale-sorrows fully,   40
The craft-begot evil they erstwhile had suffered
And were forced to endure from crushing oppression,
Their manifold misery. 'Twas a manifest token,
When the hero-in-battle the hand suspended,
The arm and the shoulder (there was all of the claw
Of Grendel together) 'neath great-stretching hall-roof.   45

XIV
Rejoicing of the Danes

In the mist of the morning many a warrior
Stood round the gift-hall, as the story is told me:
Folk-princes fared then from far and from near
Through long-stretching journeys to look at the wonder,
The footprints of the foeman. Few of the warriors   5
Who gazed on the foot-tracks of the inglorious creature
His parting from life pained very deeply,
How, weary in spirit, off from those regions
In combats conquered he carried his traces,
Fated and flying, to the flood of the nickers.   10
There in bloody billows bubbled the currents,
The angry eddy was everywhere mingled
And seething with gore, welling with sword-blood;
He death-doomed had hid him, when reaved of his joyance
He laid down his life in the lair he had fled to,   15
His heathenish spirit, where hell did receive him.
Thence the friends from of old backward turned them,
And many a younker from merry adventure,
Striding their stallions, stout from the seaward,
Heroes on horses. There were heard very often   20
Beowulf's praises; many often asserted
That neither south nor north, in the circuit of waters,
O'er outstretching earth-plain, none other was better
'Mid bearers of war-shields, more worthy to govern,
'Neath the arch of the ether. Not any, however,   25
'Gainst the friend-lord muttered, mocking-words uttered
Of Hrothgar the gracious (a good king he).

XX
The Mother of Grendel

They sank then to slumber. With sorrow one paid for
His evening repose, as often betid them
While Grendel was holding the gold-bedecked palace,
Ill-deeds performing, till his end overtook him,
Death for his sins. 'Twas seen very clearly,   5
Known unto earth-folk, that still an avenger
Outlived the loathed one, long since the sorrow
Caused by the struggle; the mother of Grendel,
Devil-shaped woman, her woe ever minded,
Who was held to inhabit the horrible waters,   10
The cold-flowing currents, after Cain had become a
Slayer-with-edges to his one only brother,
The son of his sire; he set out then banished,
Marked as a murderer, man-joys avoiding,
Lived in the desert. Thence demons unnumbered   15
Fate-sent awoke; one of them Grendel,
Sword-cursèd, hateful, who at Heorot met with
A man that was watching, waiting the struggle
Where a horrid one held him with hand-grapple sturdy;
Nathless he minded the might of his body,   20
The glorious gift God had allowed him,
And folk-ruling Father's favor relied on,
His help and His comfort: so he conquered the foeman,
The hell-spirit humbled: he unhappy departed then,
Reaved of his joyance, journeying to death-haunts,   25
Foeman of man. His mother moreover
Eager and gloomy was anxious to go on
Her mournful mission, mindful of vengeance
For the death of her son. She came then to Heorot
Where the Armor-Dane earlmen all through the building   30
Were lying in slumber. Soon there became then
Return to the nobles, when the mother of Grendel
Entered the folk-hall; the fear was less grievous
By even so much as the vigor of maidens,
War-strength of women, by warrior is reckoned,   35
When well-carved weapon, worked with the hammer,
Blade very bloody, brave with its edges,
Strikes down the boar-sign that stands on the helmet.
Then the hard-edgèd weapon was heaved in the building,
The brand o'er the benches, broad-lindens many   40
Hand-fast were lifted; for helmet he recked not,
For armor-net broad, whom terror laid hold of.
She went then hastily, outward would get her
Her life for to save, when some one did spy her;
Soon she had grappled one of the athelings   45
Fast and firmly, when fenward she hied her;
That one to Hrothgar was liefest of heroes
In rank of retainer where waters encircle,
A mighty shield-warrior, whom she murdered at slumber,
A broadly-famed battle-knight. Beowulf was absent,   50

But another apartment was erstwhile devoted
To the glory-decked Geatman when gold was distributed.
There was hubbub in Heorot. The hand that was famous
She grasped in its gore; grief was renewed then
In homes and houses: 'twas no happy arrangement   55
In both of the quarters to barter and purchase
With lives of their friends. Then the well-agèd ruler,
The gray-headed war-thane, was woeful in spirit,
When his long-trusted liegeman lifeless he knew of,
His dearest one gone. Quick from a room was   60
Beowulf brought, brave and triumph.
As day was dawning in the dusk of the morning,
Went then that earlman, champion noble,
Came with comrades, where the clever one bided
Whether God all gracious would grant him a respite   65
After the woe he had suffered. The war-worthy hero
With a troop of retainers trod then the pavement
(The hall-building groaned), till he greeted the wise one,
The earl of the Ingwins; asked if the night had
Fully refreshed him, as fain he would have it.   70

XXI
Hrothgar's Account of the Monsters

Hrothgar rejoined, helm of the Scyldings:
"Ask not of joyance! Grief is renewed to
The folk of the Danemen. Dead is Æschere,
Yrmenlaf's brother, older than he,
My true-hearted counsellor, trusty adviser,   5
Shoulder-companion, when fighting in battle
Our heads we protected, when troopers were clashing,
And heroes were dashing; such an earl should be ever,
An erst-worthy atheling, as Æschere proved him.
The flickering death-spirit became in Heorot   10
His hand-to-hand murderer; I can not tell whither
The cruel one turned in the carcass exulting,
By cramming discovered. The quarrel she wreaked then,
That last night igone Grendel thou killedst
In grewsomest manner, with grim-holding clutches,   15
Since too long he had lessened my liege-troop and wasted
My folk-men so foully. He fell in the battle
With forfeit of life, and another has followed,
A mighty crime-worker, her kinsman avenging,
And henceforth hath 'stablished her hatred unyielding,   20
As it well may appear to many a liegeman,
Who mourneth in spirit the treasure-bestower,
Her heavy heart-sorrow; the hand is now lifeless
Which availed you in every wish that you cherished.
Land-people heard I, liegemen, this saying,   25
Dwellers in halls, they had seen very often
A pair of such mighty march-striding creatures,
Far-dwelling spirits, holding the moorlands:

One of them wore, as well they might notice,
The image of woman, the other one wretched 30
In guise of a man wandered in exile,
Except he was huger than any of earthmen;
Earth-dwelling people entitled him Grendel
In days of yore: they know not their father,
Whe'r ill-going spirits any were borne him 35
Ever before. They guard the wolf-coverts,
Lands inaccessible, wind-beaten nesses,
Fearfullest fen-deeps, where a flood from the mountains
'Neath mists of the nesses netherward rattles,
The stream under earth: not far is it henceward 40
Measured by mile-lengths that the mere-water standeth,
Which forests hang over, with frost-whiting covered,
A firm-rooted forest, the floods overshadow.
There ever at night one an ill-meaning portent
A fire-flood may see; 'mong children of men 45
None liveth so wise that wot of the bottom;
Though harassed by hounds the heath-stepper seek for,
Fly to the forest, firm-antlered he-deer,
Spurred from afar, his spirit he yieldeth,
His life on the shore, ere in he will venture 50
To cover his head. Uncanny the place is:
Thence upward ascendeth the Surging of waters,
Wan to the welkin, when the wind is stirring
The weathers unpleasing, till the air groweth gloomy,
And the heavens lower. Now is help to be gotten 55
From thee and thee only! The abode thou know'st not,
The dangerous place where thou'rt able to meet with
The sin-laden hero: seek if thou darest!
For the feud I will fully fee thee with money,
With old-time treasure, as erstwhile I did thee, 60
With well-twisted jewels, if away thou shalt get thee."

XXII
Beowulf Seeks Grendel's Mother

Beowulf answered, Ecgtheow's son:
"Grieve not, O wise one! for each it is better,
His friend to avenge than with vehemence wail him;
Each of us must the end-day abide of
His earthly existence; who is able accomplish 5
Glory ere death! To battle-thane noble
Lifeless lying, 'tis at last most fitting.
Arise, O king, quick let us hasten
To look at the footprint of the kinsman of Grendel!
I promise thee this now: to his place he'll escape not, 10
To embrace of the earth, nor to mountainous forest,
Nor to depths of the ocean, wherever he wanders.
Practice thou now patient endurance
Of each of thy sorrows as I hope for thee soothly!"
Then up sprang the old one, the All-Wielder thanked he, 15

Ruler Almighty, that the man had outspoken.
Then for Hrothgar a war-horse was decked with a bridle,
Curly-maned courser. The clever folk-leader
Stately proceeded: stepped then an earl-troop
Of Linden-wood bearers. Her footprints were seen then   20
Widely in wood-paths, her way o'er the bottoms,
Where she faraway fared o'er fen-country murky,
Bore away breathless the best of retainers
Who pondered with Hrothgar the welfare of country.
The son of the athelings then went o'er the stony,   25
Declivitous cliffs, the close-covered passes,
Narrow passages, paths unfrequented,
Nesses abrupt, nicker-haunts many;
One of a few of wise-mooded heroes,
He onward advanced to view the surroundings,   30
Till he found unawares woods of the mountain
O'er hoar-stones hanging, holt-wood unjoyful;
The water stood under, welling and gory.
'Twas irksome in spirit to all of the Danemen,
Friends of the Scyldings, to many a liegeman   35
Sad to be suffered, a sorrow unlittle
To each of the earlmen, when to Æschere's head they
Came on the cliff. The current was seething
With blood and with gore (the troopers gazed on it).
The horn anon sang the battle-song ready.   40
The troop were all seated; they saw 'long the water then
Many a serpent, mere-dragons wondrous
Trying the waters, nickers a-lying
On the cliffs of the nesses, which at noonday full often
Go on the sea-deeps their sorrowful journey,   45
Wild-beasts and wormkind; away then they hastened
Hot-mooded, hateful, they heard the great clamor,
The war-trumpet winding. One did the Geat-prince
Sunder from earth-joys, with arrow from bowstring,
From his sea-struggle tore him, that the trusty war-missile   50
Pierced to his vitals; he proved in the currents
Less doughty at swimming whom death had offcarried.
Soon in the waters the wonderful swimmer
Was straitened most sorely with sword-pointed boar-spears,
Pressed in the battle and pulled to the cliff-edge;   55
The liegemen then looked on the loath-fashioned stranger.
Beowulf donned then his battle-equipments,
Cared little for life; inlaid and most ample,
The hand-woven corslet which could cover his body,
Must the wave-deeps explore, that war might be powerless   60
To harm the great hero, and the hating one's grasp might
Not peril his safety; his head was protected
By the light-flashing helmet that should mix with the bottoms,
Trying the eddies, treasure-emblazoned,
Encircled with jewels, as in seasons long past   65
The weapon-smith worked it, wondrously made it,
With swine-bodies fashioned it, that thenceforward no longer
Brand might bite it, and battle-sword hurt it.
And that was not least of helpers in prowess
That Hrothgar's spokesman had lent him when straitened   70
And the hilted hand-sword was Hrunting entitled,

Old and most excellent 'mong all of the treasures;
Its blade was of iron, blotted with poison,
Hardened with gore; it failed not in battle
Any hero under heaven in hand who it brandished,   75
Who ventured to take the terrible journeys,
The battle-field sought; not the earliest occasion
That deeds of daring 'twas destined to 'complish.
Ecglaf's kinsman minded not soothly,
Exulting in strength, what erst he had spoken   80
Drunken with wine, when the weapon he lent to
A sword-hero bolder; himself did not venture
'Neath the strife of the currents his life to endanger,
To fame-deeds perform; there he forfeited glory,
Repute for his strength. Not so with the other   85
When he clad in his corslet had equipped him for battle.

XXIII
Beowulf's Fight with Grendel's Mother

Beowulf spake, Ecgtheow's son:
"Recall now, oh, famous kinsman of Healfdene,
Prince very prudent, now to part I am ready,
Gold-friend of earlmen, what erst we agreed on,
Should I lay down my life in lending thee assistance,   5
When my earth-joys were over, thou wouldst evermore serve me
In stead of a father; my faithful thanemen,
My trusty retainers, protect thou and care for,
Fall I in battle: and, Hrothgar belovèd,
Send unto Higelac the high-valued jewels   10
Thou to me hast allotted. The lord of the Geatmen
May perceive from the gold, the Hrethling may see it
When he looks on the jewels, that a gem-giver found I
Good over-measure, enjoyed him while able.
And the ancient heirloom Unferth permit thou,   15
The famed one to have, the heavy-sword splendid
The hard-edgèd weapon; with Hrunting to aid me,
I shall gain me glory, or grim-death shall take me."
The atheling of Geatmen uttered these words and
Heroic did hasten, not any rejoinder   20
Was willing to wait for; the wave-current swallowed
The doughty-in-battle. Then a day's-length elapsed ere
He was able to see the sea at its bottom.
Early she found then who fifty of winters
The course of the currents kept in her fury,   25
Grisly and greedy, that the grim one's dominion
Some one of men from above was exploring.
Forth did she grab them, grappled the warrior
With horrible clutches; yet no sooner she injured
His body unscathèd: the burnie out-guarded,   30
That she proved but powerless to pierce through the armor,
The limb-mail locked, with loath-grabbing fingers.
The sea-wolf bare then, when bottomward came she,

The ring-prince homeward, that he after was powerless
(He had daring to do it) to deal with his weapons,   35
But many a mere-beast tormented him swimming,
Flood-beasts no few with fierce-biting tusks did
Break through his burnie, the brave one pursued they.
The earl then discovered he was down in some cavern
Where no water whatever anywise harmed him,   40
And the clutch of the current could come not anear him,
Since the roofed-hall prevented; brightness a-gleaming
Fire-light he saw, flashing resplendent.
The good one saw then the sea-bottom's monster
The mighty mere-woman; he made a great onset   45
With weapon-of-battle, his hand not desisted
From striking, that war-blade struck on her head then
A battle-song greedy. The stranger perceived then
The sword would not bite, her life would not injure,
But the falchion failed the folk-prince when straitened: 50
Erst had it often onsets encountered,
Oft cloven the helmet, the fated one's armor:
'Twas the first time that ever the excellent jewel
Had failed of its fame. Firm-mooded after,
Not heedless of valor, but mindful of glory,   55
Was Higelac's kinsman; the hero-chief angry
Cast then his carved-sword covered with jewels
That it lay on the earth, hard and steel-pointed;
He hoped in his strength, his hand-grapple sturdy.
So any must act whenever he thinketh   60
To gain him in battle glory unending,
And is reckless of living. The lord of the War-Geats
(He shrank not from battle) seized by the shoulder
The mother of Grendel; then mighty in struggle
Swung he his enemy, since his anger was kindled,   65
That she fell to the floor. With furious grapple
She gave him requital early thereafter,
And stretched out to grab him; the strongest of warriors
Faint-mooded stumbled, till he fell in his traces,
Foot-going champion. Then she sat on the hall-guest   70
And wielded her war-knife wide-bladed, flashing,
For her son would take vengeance, her one only bairn.
His breast-armor woven bode on his shoulder;
It guarded his life, the entrance defended
'Gainst sword-point and edges. Ecgtheow's son there   75
Had fatally journeyed, champion of Geatmen,
In the arms of the ocean, had the armor not given,
Close-woven corslet, comfort and succor,
And had God most holy not awarded the victory,
All-knowing Lord; easily did heaven's   80
Ruler most righteous arrange it with justice;
Uprose he erect ready for battle.

XXIV
Beowulf Is Double-Conqueror

Then he saw mid the war-gems a weapon of victory,
An ancient giant-sword, of edges a-doughty,
Glory of warriors: of weapons 'twas choicest,
Only 'twas larger than any man else was
Able to bear to the battle-encounter,   5
The good and splendid work of the giants.
He grasped then the sword-hilt, knight of the Scyldings,
Bold and battle-grim, brandished his ring-sword,
Hopeless of living, hotly he smote her,
That the fiend-woman's neck firmly it grappled,   10
Broke through her bone-joints, the bill fully pierced her
Fate-cursèd body, she fell to the ground then:
The hand-sword was bloody, the hero exulted.
The brand was brilliant, brightly it glimmered,
just as from heaven gemlike shineth   15
The torch of the firmament. He glanced 'long the building,
And turned by the wall then, Higelac's vassal
Raging and wrathful raised his battle-sword
Strong by the handle. The edge was not useless
To the hero-in-battle, but he speedily wished to   20
Give Grendel requital for the many assaults he
Had worked on the West-Danes not once, but often,
When he slew in slumber the subjects of Hrothgar,
Swallowed down fifteen sleeping retainers
Of the folk of the Danemen, and fully as many   25
Carried away, a horrible prey.
He gave him requital, grim-raging champion,
When he saw on his rest-place weary of conflict
Grendel lying, of life-joys bereavèd,
As the battle at Heorot erstwhile had scathed him   30
His body far bounded, a blow when he suffered,
Death having seized him, sword-smiting heavy,
And he cut off his head then. Early this noticed
The clever carles who as comrades of Hrothgar
Gazed on the sea-deeps, that the surging wave-currents   35
Were mightily mingled, the mere-flood was gory:
Of the good one the gray-haired together held converse,
The hoary of head, that they hoped not to see again
The atheling ever, that exulting in victory
He'd return there to visit the distinguished folk-ruler: 40
Then many concluded the mere-wolf had killed him.
The ninth hour came then. From the ness-edge departed
The bold-mooded Scyldings; the gold-friend of heroes
Homeward betook him. The strangers sat down then
Soul-sick, sorrowful, the sea-waves regarding: 45
They wished and yet weened not their well-loved friend-lord
To see any more. The sword-blade began then,
The blood having touched it, contracting and shriveling
With battle-icicles; 'twas a wonderful marvel
That it melted entirely, likest to ice when   50

The Father unbindeth the bond of the frost and
Unwindeth the wave-bands, He who wieldeth dominion
Of times and of tides: a truth-firm Creator.
Nor took he of jewels more in the dwelling,
Lord of the Weders, though they lay all around him,   55
Than the head and the handle handsome with jewels;
The brand early melted, burnt was the weapon:
So hot was the blood, the strange-spirit poisonous
That in it did perish. He early swam off then
Who had bided in combat the carnage of haters,   60
Went up through the ocean; the eddies were cleansèd,
The spacious expanses, when the spirit from farland
His life put aside and this short-lived existence.
The seamen's defender came swimming to land then
Doughty of spirit, rejoiced in his sea-gift,   65
The bulky burden which he bore in his keeping.
The excellent vassals advanced then to meet him,
To God they were grateful, were glad in their chieftain,
That to see him safe and sound was granted them.
From the high-minded hero, then, helmet and burnie   70
Were speedily loosened: the ocean was putrid,
The water 'neath welkin weltered with gore.
Forth did they fare, then, their footsteps retracing,
Merry and mirthful, measured the earth-way,
The highway familiar: men very daring   75
Bare then the head from the sea-cliff, burdening
Each of the earlmen, excellent-valiant.
Four of them had to carry with labor
The head of Grendel to the high towering gold-hall
Upstuck on the spear, till fourteen most-valiant   80
And battle-brave Geatmen came there going
Straight to the palace: the prince of the people
Measured the mead-ways, their mood-brave companion.
The atheling of earlmen entered the building,
Deed-valiant man, adorned with distinction,   85
Doughty shield-warrior, to address King Hrothgar:
Then hung by the hair, the head of Grendel
Was home to the building where beer-thanes were drinking,
Loth before earlmen and eke 'fore the lady
The warriors beheld then a wonderful sight.   90

Questions for Consideration

Using complete sentences, provide brief answers for the following questions.

1. Read through the fights with Grendel and Grendel's mother carefully. How have these battles, been constructed to emphasize Beowulf's courage?

   _____

   _____

   _____

   _____

   _____

2. How has the author of *Beowulf* tried to make Grendel and his mother interesting?

   _____

   _____

   _____

   _____

   _____

3. Beowulf is unselfconsciously boastful. As a reader, how do you react to his boasting? Why do you think the *Beowulf* author or authors included this as a part of his character?

   _____

   _____

   _____

   _____

   _____

——————————— *Writing Critically* ———————————

Select one of the essay topics listed below and compose a 500-word essay which discusses the topic fully. Support your thesis with evidence from the text and with critical and/or historical material. Use the space below for preparing to write the essay.

1. You may be familiar with Achilles, Odysseus, and Aeneas from *The Iliad*, *The Odyssey*, and *The Aeneid*. Compare Beowulf with one or more of these characters. What do they have in common? How are they different?

2. Do you think there are any universal aspects of the tale of Beowulf? Explain your answer in your own words by referring to events in the text.

3. Does the shift to Grendel's point of view as he struggles with Beowulf indicate sympathy for him? If not, why this shift? If so, what do you think the Beowulf poet was saying?

Prewriting Space:

_____

_____

_____

_____

_____

_____

_____

_____

_____

_____

_____

_____

_____

_____

_____

_____

_____

_____

Introduction

Dante Alighieri (1265–1321)

Every fresh attempt at translating the *Divine Comedy* affords proof of Dante's assertion that "nothing harmonized by a musical bond can be transmuted from its own speech without losing all its sweetness and harmony." The coalescence of the music and the meaning of the verse, in the perfection of which the life of poetry consists, cannot be transferred from one tongue to another. A new harmony may be substituted, but the difference is fatal. The translation may have a life of its own, but it is not the life of the original.

No poem in any language displays a more indissoluble union of music and meaning, or is more informed with a rhythmic life of its own than the *Divine Comedy*. And yet, such is its extraordinary distinction, no poem has an intellectual and emotional substance more independent of its metrical form. Its complex structure and its elaborate rhyme, highly artificial as they are, are so mastered by the genius of the poet as to become the most natural expression of the spirit by which the poem is inspired; while at same time the thought and sentiment embodied in the verse is of such import, and the narrative of such interest, that they do not lose their worth when transferred to another tongue.

To preserve in its integrity what may be thus transferred, prose is a better medium than verse; and it was because of my conviction to this effect that I undertook this translation, in which my aim has been to follow the words of Dante as closely as our English idiom allows, and thus to give to the reader the substance of the poem as little altered as possible.

There are, indeed, many passages in it which require explanation or illustration for Italian, and, even more, for English readers. To these I have supplied footnotes, generally brief. But I have desired to avoid distracting attention from the direct narrative, and have mainly left the understanding and appreciation of it to the intelligence and imagination of the reader.

A far deeper-lying and more pervading source of imperfect comprehension of the poem than any difficulty of construction, obscurity of argument, or remoteness of allusion exists in the double meaning that runs through it. The account of the poet's spiritual journey is so vivid and consistent that it has all the reality of an account of an actual experience; but within and beneath runs a stream of allegory not less consistent and hardly less continuous than the narrative itself. To the illustration and carrying out of this interior meaning even the minutest details of external incident are often made to contribute, with an appropriateness of significance, and with a freedom from forced interpretation such as no other writer of allegory has succeeded in attaining. The poem may be read with interest as a record of experience with little attention to its inner meaning, but its full interest is only felt when this inner meaning is traced, and the moral significance of the incidents of the story apprehended by the alert intelligence. The allegory is the soul of the poem—that is, in scholastic phrase, the form of its body, giving to it its special individuality.

Thus in order truly to understand and rightly appreciate the poem the reader must continually seek the inner meaning of its story. "Taken literally," as Dante declares in his Letter to Can Grande, "the subject is the state of the soul after death, simply considered. But allegorically taken, its subject is man, according as by his good or ill deserts he renders himself liable to the reward or punishment of Justice." It is the allegory of human life; and not of human life as an abstraction, but of the individual life; and herein, as Mr. Lowell has said, "lie its profound meaning and its permanent force." And herein, too, lie its perennial freshness of interest and the actuality which makes it contemporaneous with every successive generation. The increase of knowledge, the loss of belief in doctrines that were fundamental in Dante's creed, the changes in the order of society, the new thoughts of the world, have not lessened the moral import of the poem, any more than they have lessened its excellence as a work of art. Its real substance is as independent as its artistic beauty, of science, of creed, and of institutions. Human nature does not change from age to age; the motives of action remain the same, though their relative force and the desires and ideals by which they are inspired vary from generation to generation. And thus it is that the moral judgments of a great poet whose imagination penetrates to the core of things, and who, from his very nature as poet, conceives and sets forth the issues of life not in a treatise of abstract morality, but by means of sensible types and images, never lose interest, and have a perpetual contemporaneousness. They deal with the permanent and unalterable elements of the soul of man.

The scene of the poem is the spiritual world, of which we are members even while still denizens in the world of time. In the spiritual world the results of sin or perverted love, and of virtue or right love, in this life of probation, are manifest. The life to come is but the fulfilment of the life that now is.

The allegory in which Dante cloaked this truth is of a character that distinguishes the *Divine Comedy* from all other works of similar intent. In *The Pilgrim's Progress,* for example, the personages are types of moral qualities or religious dispositions, mere simulacra of men and women. They are abstractions which the genius of Bunyan fails to inform with vitality sufficient to kindle the imagination of the reader with a sense of their actual, living and breathing existence. But in the *Divine Comedy* the personages are all from real life, they are men and women with their natural passions and emotions, and they are undergoing an actual experience. The allegory consists in making their characters and their fates, what all human characters and fates really are, the types and images of spiritual law. Virgil and Beatrice, whose natures as depicted in the poem make nearest approach to purely abstract and typical existence, are always consistently presented as living individuals, exalted indeed in wisdom and power, but with hardly less definite and concrete humanity than that of Dante himself.

The scheme of the created Universe held by the Christians of the Middle Ages was comparatively simple, and so definite that Dante, in accepting it in its main features without modification, was provided with the limited stage requisite for his design, and of which the general disposition was familiar to all his readers. The

three spiritual realms had their local bound marked out as clearly as those of the earth itself. Their cosmography was but an extension of the largely hypothetical geography of the time.

The Earth was supposed to be the centre of the Universe, and its northern hemisphere was the abode of man. At the middle point of this hemisphere stood Jerusalem, equidistant from the Pillars of Hercules on the west, and the Ganges on the east.

Within the body of this hemisphere was Hell, shaped as a vast hollow cone, of which the apex was the centre of the globe; and here, according to Dante, was the seat of Lucifer. The concave of Hell had been formed by his fall, when a portion of the solid earth, through fear of him, ran back to the southern uninhabited hemisphere, and formed there, directly antipodal to Jerusalem, the mountain of Purgatory, which rose a solid cone from the waste of waters that covered this half of the globe, and at its summit was the Terrestrial Paradise.

Immediately surrounding the atmosphere of the Earth was the sphere of the elemental fire. Around this was the Heaven of the Moon, and encircling this, in succession, were the Heavens of Mercury, Venus, the Sun, Mars, Jove, Saturn, the Fixed Stars, and the Crystalline or First Moving Heaven. These nine concentric Heavens revolved continually around the Earth, and in proportion to their distance from it was the greater swiftness of each. Encircling all was the Empyrean, increate, incorporeal, motionless, unbounded in time or space, the proper seat of God, the home of the Angels, the abode of the Elect.

The Angelic Hierarchy consisted of nine orders, corresponding to the nine moving Heavens. Their blessedness and the swiftness of the motion with which in unending delight they circled around God were in proportion to their nearness to Him—first the Seraphs, then in succession the Cherubs, Thrones, Dominations, Virtues, Powers, Princes, Archangels, and Angels. Through them, under the general name of Intelligences, the Divine influence was transmitted to the Heavens, giving to these their circular motion, which was the expression of their longing to be united with the source of their creation The Heavens in their turn streamed down upon the Earth the Divine influence thus distributed among them, in constantly varying proportion and power, producing divers effects in the generation and corruption of material things, and in the dispositions and the lives of men.

Such was the accepted general scheme of the Universe. The intention of God in its creation was to communicate of His perfection to the creatures endowed with souls, that is, to men and to angels, and the proper end of every such creature was to seek its own perfection in likeness to the Divine. This end was attained through that knowledge of God of which the soul was capable, and through love which was in proportion to knowledge. Virtue depended on the free will of man; it was the good use of that will directed to a right object of love. Two lights were given to the soul for guidance of the will: the light of reason for natural things and for the direction of the will to moral virtue; the light of grace for things supernatural, and for the direction of the will to spiritual virtue. Sin was the opposite of virtue, the choice by the will of false objects of love; it involved the misuse of reason and the absence of grace. As the end of virtue was blessedness, so the end of sin was misery.

The corner-stone of Dante's moral system was the Freedom of the Will; in other words, the right of private judgment with the condition of accountability. This is the liberty which Dante, that is, man, goes seeking in his journey through the spiritual world. This liberty is to be attained through the right use of reason, illuminated by Divine Grace; it consists in the perfect accord of the will of man with the will of God.

With this view of the nature and end of man Dante's conception of the history of the race could not be other than that its course was providentially ordered. The fall of man had made him a just object of the vengeance of God; but the elect were to be redeemed, and for their redemption the history of the world from the beginning was directed. Not only in His dealings with the Jews, but in His dealings with the heathen was God preparing for the reconciliation to Himself of man, to be finally accomplished in his sacrifice of Himself for them. The Roman Empire was foreordained and established for this end. It was to prepare the way for the establishment of the Roman Church. It was the appointed instrument for the political government of men. Empire and Church were alike divine institutions for the guidance of man on earth.

The aim of Dante in the *Divine Comedy* was to set forth these truths in such wise as to affect the imaginations and touch the hearts of men, so that they should turn to righteousness. His conviction of these truths was no mere matter of belief; it had the ardor and certainty of faith. They had appeared to him in all their fulness as a revelation of the Divine wisdom. It was his work as poet, as poet with a Divine commission, to make this revelation known. His work was a work of faith; it was sacred; to it both Heaven and Earth had set their hands.

To this work, as I have said, the definiteness and the limits of the generally accepted theory of the Universe gave the required frame. The very narrowness of this scheme made Dante's design practicable. He had had the experience of a man on earth. He had been lured by false objects of desire from the pursuit of the true good. But Divine Grace, in the form of Beatrice, who had when alive on earth led him aright, now intervened and sent to his aid Virgil, who, as the type of Human Reason, should bring him safe through Hell, showing to him the eternal consequences of sin, and then should conduct him, penitent, up the height of Purgatory, till on its summit, in the Earthly Paradise, Beatrice herself should appear once more to him. Thence she, as the type of that knowledge from which comes the love of the Divine Being, should lead him through the Heavens up to the Empyrean, to the consummation of his course in the actual vision of God.

BIBLIOGRAPHY

Alighieri, Dante. *Inferno*. Translated and edited by Thomas G. Bergin. New York: Appleton-Century-Crofts, Inc., 1948.

Grandgent, C. H. *Dante*. New York: Duffield, 1916.

Sayers, Dorothy L. *Introductory Papers on Dante*. London: Methuen, 1954.

Warnock, Robert and Anderson, George., eds. *The World in Literature*. Atlanta: Scott, Foresman and Co., 1967.

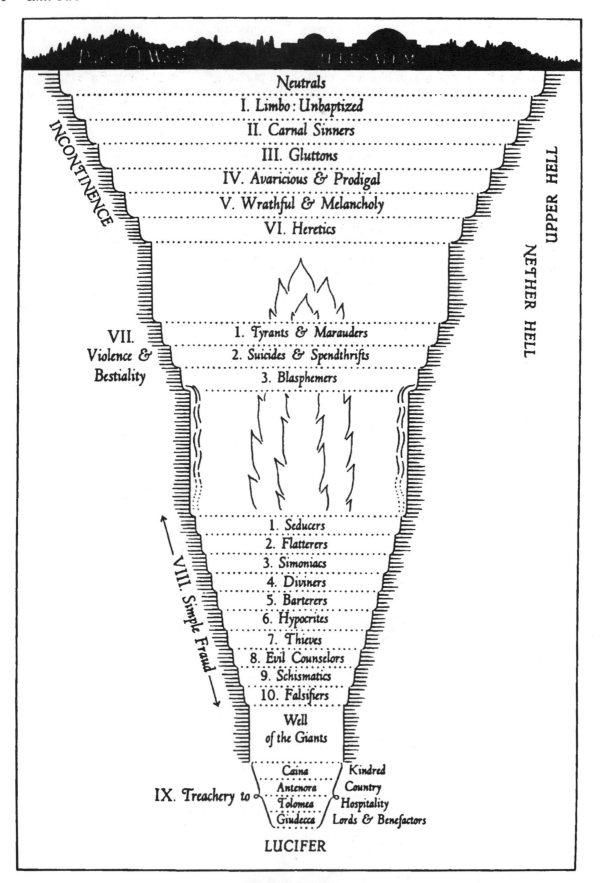

Neutrals
I. Limbo: Unbaptized
II. Carnal Sinners
III. Gluttons
IV. Avaricious & Prodigal
V. Wrathful & Melancholy
VI. Heretics

INCONTINENCE

UPPER HELL

NETHER HELL

VII.
Violence &
Bestiality

1. Tyrants & Marauders
2. Suicides & Spendthrifts
3. Blasphemers

VIII. Simple Fraud

1. Seducers
2. Flatterers
3. Simoniacs
4. Diviners
5. Barterers
6. Hypocrites
7. Thieves
8. Evil Counselors
9. Schismatics
10. Falsifiers

Well
of the Giants

IX. Treachery to

Caina
Antenora
Tolomea
Giudecca

Kindred
Country
Hospitality
Lords & Benefactors

LUCIFER

HELL

from The Divine Comedy: Inferno

Dante Alighieri
Translated by Mark Musa

Canto 1

Halfway through his life, DANTE THE PIL-GRIM wakes to find himself lost in a dark wood. Terrified at being alone in so dismal a valley, he wanders until he comes to a hill bathed in sunlight, and his fear begins to leave him. But when he starts to climb the hill his path is blocked by three fierce beasts: first a LEOPARD, then a LION, and finally a SHE-WOLF. They fill him with fear and drive him back down to the sunless wood. At that moment the figure of a man appears before him; it is the shade of VIRGIL, and the Pilgrim begs for help. Virgil tells him that he cannot overcome the beasts which obstruct his path; they must remain until a "GREYHOUND" comes who will drive them back to Hell. Rather by another path will the Pilgrim reach the sunlight, and Virgil promises to guide him on that path through Hell and Purgatory, after which another spirit, more fit than Virgil, will lead him to Paradise. The Pilgrim begs Virgil to lead on, and the Guide starts ahead. The Pilgrim follows.

Midway along the journey of our life
    I woke to find myself in a dark wood,
      for I had wandered off from the straight path.   3

How hard it is to tell what it was like,
    this wood of wilderness, savage and stubborn
      (the thought of it brings back all my old fears),   6

a bitter place! Death could scarce be bitterer.
    But if I would show the good that came of it
      I must talk about things other than the good.   9

How I entered there I cannot truly say,
    I had become so sleepy at the moment
      when I first strayed, leaving the path of truth;   12

but when I found myself at the foot of a hill,
    at the edge of the wood's beginning, down in the valley,
      where I first felt my heart plunged deep in fear,   15

I raised my head and saw the hilltop shawled
    in morning rays of light sent from the planet
      that leads men straight ahead on every road.   18

And then only did terror start subsiding
   in my heart's lake, which rose to heights of fear
   that night I spent in deepest desperation.   21

Just as a swimmer, still with panting breath,
   now safe upon the shore, out of the deep,
   might turn for one last look at the dangerous waters,   24

so I, although my mind was turned to flee,
   turned round to gaze once more upon the pass
   that never let a living soul escape.   27

I rested my tired body there awhile
   and then began to climb the barren slope
   (I dragged my stronger foot and limped along).   30

Beyond the point the slope begins to rise
   sprang up a leopard, trim and very swift!
   It was covered by a pelt of many spots.   33

And, everywhere I looked, the beast was there
   blocking my way, so time and time again
   I was about to turn and go back down.   36

The hour was early in the morning then,
   the sun was climbing up with those same stars
   that had accompanied it on the world's first day,   39

the day Divine Love set their beauty turning;
   so the hour and sweet season of creation
   encouraged me to think I could get past   42

that gaudy beast, wild in its spotted pelt,
   but then good hope gave way and fear returned
   when the figure of a lion loomed up before me,   45

and he was coming straight toward me, it seemed,
   with head raised high, and furious with hunger—
   the air around him seemed to fear his presence.   48

And now a she-wolf came, that in her leanness
   seemed racked with every kind of greediness
   (how many people she has brought to grief!).   51

This last beast brought my spirit down so low
   with fear that seized me at the sight of her,
   I lost all hope of going up the hill.   54

As a man who, rejoicing in his gains,
   suddenly seeing his gain turn into loss,
   will grieve as he compares his then and now,   57

so she made me do, that relentless beast—
   coming toward me, slowly, step by step,
   she forced me back to where the sun is mute.   60

While I was rushing down to that low place,
   my eyes made out a figure coming toward me
   of one grown faint, perhaps from too much silence.   63

And when I saw him standing in this wasteland,
   "Have pity on my soul," I cried to him,
   "whichever you are, shade or living man!"   66

"No longer living man, though once I was,"
   he said, "and my parents were from Lombardy,
   both of them were Mantuans by birth.   69

I was born, though somewhat late, *sub Julio,*
   and lived in Rome when good Augustus reigned,
   when still the false and lying gods were worshipped.   72

I was a poet and sang of that just man,
   son of Anchises, who sailed off from Troy
   after the burning of proud Ilium.   75

But why retreat to so much misery?
   Why not climb up this blissful mountain here,
   the beginning and the source of all man's joy?"   78

"Are you then Virgil, are you then that fount
   from which pours forth so rich a stream of words?"
   I said to him, bowing my head modestly.   81

"O light and honor of the other poets,
   may my long years of study, and that deep love
   that made me search your verses, help me now!   84

You are my teacher, the first of all my authors,
   and you alone the one from whom I took
   the noble style that was to bring me honor.   87

You see the beast that forced me to retreat;
   save me from her, I beg you, famous sage,
   she makes me tremble, the blood throbs in my veins."   90

"But you must journey down another road,"
   he answered, when he saw me lost in tears,
   "if ever you hope to leave this wilderness;   93

this beast, the one you cry about in fear,
   allows no soul to succeed along her path,
   she blocks his way and puts an end to him.   96

She is by nature so perverse and vicious,
   her craving belly is never satisfied,
   still hungering for food the more she eats.   99

She mates with many creatures, and will go on
   mating with more until the greyhound comes
   and tracks her down to make her die in anguish—   102

He will not feed on either land or money:
   his wisdom, love, and virtue shall sustain him;
   he will be born between Feltro and Feltro.   105

He comes to save that fallen Italy
   for which the maid Camilla gave her life
   and Turnus, Nisus, Euryalus died of wounds.   108

And he will hunt for her through every city
   until he drives her back to Hell once more,
   whence Envy first unleashed her on mankind.   111

And so, I think it best you follow me
   for your own good, and I shall be your guide
   and lead you out through an eternal place   114

where you will hear desperate cries, and see
   tormented shades, some old as Hell itself,
   and know what second death is, from their screams. 117

And later you will see those who rejoice
   while they are burning, for they have hope of coming,
   whenever it may be, to join the blessèd—   120

to whom, if you too wish to make the climb,
   a spirit, worthier than I, must take you;
   I shall go back, leaving you in her care,   123

because that Emperor dwelling on high
   will not let me lead any to His city,
   since I in life rebelled against His law.   126

Everywhere He reigns, and there He rules;
   there is His city, there is His high throne.
   Oh, happy the one He makes His citizen!"   129

And I to him: "Poet, I beg of you,
   in the name of God, that God you never knew,
   save me from this evil place and worse,   132

lead me there to the place you spoke about
   that I may see the gate Saint Peter guards
   and those whose anguish you have told me of."   135

Then he moved on, and I moved close behind him.

NOTES

1–10

The reader must be careful from the beginning to distinguish between the two uses of the first person singular in *The Divine Comedy:* one designating Dante the Pilgrim, the other Dante the Poet. The first is a character in a story invented by the second. The events are represented as having taken place in the past; the writing of the poem and the memories of these events are represented as taking place in the poet's present. We find references to both past and present, and to both pilgrim and poet, in line 10: "How *I entered* there *I cannot* truly say."

1. *Midway along the journey of our life:* In the Middle Ages life was often thought of as a journey, a pilgrimage, the goal of which was God and Heaven; and in the first line of *The Divine Comedy* Dante establishes the central motif of his poem—it is the story of man's pilgrimage to God. That we are meant to think in terms not just of the Pilgrim but of Everyman is indicated by the phrase "the journey of *our* life" (*our* journey through sin to repentance and redemption).

The imaginary date of the poem's beginning is the night before Good Friday in 1300, the year of the papal jubilee proclaimed by Boniface VIII. Born in 1265, Dante was thirty-five years old, which is one half of man's Biblical life span of seventy years.

8–9. *But if I would show the good:* Even though the memory of this "wood" brings back his "old fears" (6), Dante must talk about "things other than the good," which led to the final "Good" (his salvation) by contributing to the learning process of the Pilgrim.

13–15. *but when I found myself at the foot of a hill:* Once we leave Canto I, which is the introduction to the whole of *The Divine Comedy*, the topography of the various regions of Hell will be described with elaborate carefulness. But in this canto all is vague and unprepared for; the scene is set in a "nowhere land"—the region of undifferentiated sin. Suddenly the Pilgrim awakes in a forest (which is not described except in terms that could apply to Sin itself: "wilderness, savage and stubborn"); suddenly, as he is wandering through it, there is a hill—whereupon the forest becomes a valley. Other suggestions of this dreamlike atmosphere (which, under the circumstances, must be that of a nightmare) will be found throughout this canto.

17–18. *morning rays of light:* The time is the morning of Good Friday.

30. *I dragged my stronger foot and limped along:* A literal translation of this line which has puzzled all Dante critics would be "So that the firm foot (*piè fermo*) was always the lower." Let the two feet represent man's loves: when Gregory the Great comments on Jacob's wrestling with the angel, he identifies one foot as love of God and the other foot as love of the world (*Homiliarium in Ezechielem*, lib. II, hom. 2, 13; *PL* 76, 955–56). The "stronger foot," then, symbolizes the love of this world, for at this point in the Pilgrim's journey, this love is obviously "stronger" than the other; if he were not more strongly attracted to the things of this world than to God there would be little reason for him to make the journey. In order to ascend (to God) the Pilgrim must exert great force to drag upward his "stronger foot" (which is always the lower because its natural tendency is always downward) and prevent himself from slipping back into the "dark wood."

32–60

The early critics thought of the three beasts that block the Pilgrim's path as symbolizing three specific sins: lust, pride, and avarice, but I prefer to see in them the three major divisions of Hell. The spotted leopard (32) represents Fraud (cf. XVI, 106–108) and reigns over the Eighth and Ninth Circles, where the Fraudulent are punished (XVIII–XXXIV). The lion (45) symbolizes all forms of Violence, which are punished in the Seventh Circle (XII–XVII). The she-wolf (49) represents the different types of Concupiscence or Incontinence, which are punished in Circles Two to Five (V–VIII). In any case the beasts must represent the three major categories of human sin, and they threaten Dante the Pilgrim, the poet's symbol of mankind.

32–36. *sprang up a leopard:* Note the sudden appearance of the colorful leopard as if from nowhere. Then the trim, swift spotted beast disappears as such to become a symbol: a force that is everywhere, blocking upward movement.

40. *the day Divine Love set their beauty turning:* It was thought that the constellation of Aries, which is in conjunction with the sun in the spring equinox, was also in conjunction with the sun when God ("Divine Love") created the universe.

46–50. Note the triple use of the verb *seem* (which is a faithful reproduction of the original), intended to blur the figures of the lion and the she-wolf—in harmony with the "nowhereness" of the moral landscape.

55–60. *As a man who . . . the sun is mute:* it must be admitted that this simile is not one of Dante's most felicitous. The Pilgrim, having gained some terrain toward his goal, is forced back by the she-wolf, thus losing all he had gained. But in the parallel imagined by the poet, we have not only the phase of gaining followed by the phase of losing, we are also told of the victim's emotional reaction to his experience—of which there is no trace in the factual narrative.

60. *she forced me back to where the sun is mute:* In other words, back to the "dark wood" of line 2.

62. *my eyes made out a figure coming toward me:* The shade of Virgil miraculously appears before Dante. The Roman poet, born 70 B.C. in the time

of Julius Caesar (*sub Julio*), represents in the symbolic allegory of the poem Reason or Human Wisdom (the best that man can achieve on his own without the special grace of God), as well as poetry and art. The Pilgrim cannot proceed to the light of Divine Love (the mountain top) until he has overcome the three beasts of his sin; and because it is impossible for man to cope with the beasts unaided, Virgil has been summoned through the chain of divine command to guide the Pilgrim and help him overcome his sins by understanding and, later, repudiating them.

63. *of one grown faint, perhaps from too much silence:* Virgil is presented for the first time in the poem as "silent": *chi per lungo silenzio parea fioco,* which is to say literally that Virgil appears (to the Pilgrim's eyes) as one who is faint because he has been dead (a shade) for so long and deprived of the light of the sun (he appears in a place "where the sun is mute," 60), deprived of the light of God. This verse, which I would place in the same category as verse 30 of this same canto ("I dragged my stronger foot and limped along"), has other levels of meaning: it could, for example, imply that the voice of Reason has been silent in the Pilgrim's ear for too long a time.

73–75. *I was a poet and sang of that just man:* In the *Aeneid* Virgil relates the *post bellum* travels and deeds of Aeneas (son of Anchises), who, destined by the gods, founded on Italian soil the nation that, in the course of time, would become the Roman Empire.

87. *the noble style that was to bring me honor:* In the years before the composition of *The Divine Comedy* Dante employed in his sonnets and canzoni what he calls the tragic style, reserved for illustrious subject matter: martial exploits, love, and moral virtues (*De vulgari eloquentia* II, ii, iv). His respect for the Roman poet is boundless. The reasons for Dante's selection of Virgil as the Pilgrim's guide (instead of, shall we say, Aristotle, *the* philosopher of the time) are several: Virgil was a poet and an Italian; in the *Aeneid* is recounted the hero's descent into Hell. But the main reason surely lies in the fact that, in the Middle Ages, Virgil was considered a prophet, a judgment stemming from the interpretation of some obscure lines in the *Fourth Eclogue* as foretelling the coming of Christ. In this regard Dante saw Virgil as a sort of mediator between Imperial and Apostolic Rome. Moreover, Dante's treatise *De monarchia* reflects the principal concepts of the Roman Empire found in the pages of his guide.

91. *But you must journey down another road:* Dante must choose another road because, in order to arrive at the Divine Light, it is necessary first to recognize the true nature of sin, renounce it, and do penance for it. Virgil, here in his role of Reason or Human Wisdom, is of course the means through which man may come to an understanding of the nature of sin. With Virgil-Reason as his guide, Dante the Pilgrim will come to an understanding of sin on his journey through Hell and will see the penance imposed on repentant sinners on the Mount of Purgatory.

101–11

This obscure forecast of future salvation has never been explained satisfactorily: the figure of the greyhound has been identified with Henry VII, Charles Martel, and even Dante himself. It seems more plausible that the greyhound represents Can Grande della Scala, the ruler of Verona from 1308 to 1329, whose birthplace (Verona) is between Feltro and Montefeltro, and whose "wisdom, love, and virtue" (104) were certainly well known to Dante. Whoever the greyhound may be, the prophecy would seem to indicate in a larger sense the establishment of a spiritual kingdom on earth, a terrestrial paradise in which "wisdom, love, and virtue" (these three qualities are mentioned again in Canto III, 5–6, as attributes of the Trinity) will replace the bestial sins of this world.

107. *the maid Camilla:* She was the valiant daughter of King Metabus, who was slain while fighting against the Trojans (*Aeneid* XI).

108. *and Turnus, Nisus, Euryalus died of wounds:* Turnus was the King of the Rutulians who waged war against the Trojans and was killed by Aeneas in single combat. Nisus and Euryalus were young Trojan warriors slain during a nocturnal raid on the camp of the Rutulians. In subsequent literature their mutual loyalty became a standard measure of sincere friendship.

117. *and know what second death is:* The second death is the death of the soul, which occurs when the soul is damned.

122. *a spirit, worthier than I:* just as Virgil, the pagan Roman poet, cannot enter the Christian Paradise because he lived before the birth of Christ and lacks knowledge of Christian salvation, so Reason can only guide the Pilgrim to a certain point: in order to enter Paradise, the Pilgrim's guide must be Christian Grace or Revelation (Theology) in the figure of Beatrice.

124. *that Emperor dwelling on high:* Note the pagan terminology of Virgil's reference to God; it expresses, as best it can, his unenlightened conception of the Supreme Authority, that to his mind was, and could only be, an emperor.

133–35. *lead me there to the place you spoke about:* These lines are baffling. Many commentators interpret "the gate Saint Peter guards" as referring not to the gate of Heaven (in the *Paradise* no gate is mentioned) but to the gate of *Purgatory*, for in Canto IX of the Purgatory we are told that its gate is guarded by an angel whose keys have been given him by Peter. Thus the Pilgrim would be saying: "lead me to the two places you have just mentioned so that I may see those in Purgatory and those in Hell."

But it is difficult to believe that "the gate Saint Peter guards" refers to the entrance to Purgatory: neither the Pilgrim nor his guide could have known in Canto I anything about the entrance to Purgatory, nor could they have known about the absence of a gate in Paradise. Surely the Pilgrim's allusion must reflect the popular belief that the gate to Heaven is guarded by Saint Peter. But if line 134 refers to Paradise then it is difficult to make sense of the Pilgrim's words. The reference to Heaven in line 134 could follow quite easily from 133 if we interpret the two lines as meaning: "lead me to the two places you have just mentioned, Hell and Purgatory, so that ultimately I will be able to go to Heaven." But then how is the reference in line 135 to be understood? "Take me to Hell and Purgatory so that I may see (not only Heaven but) Hell" makes no sense.

But perhaps line 133 does not mean "lead me to both places you have just mentioned" but rather "lead me to the place you mentioned last," i.e., Purgatory (the literal translation of the Italian is: "lead me there where you said"). In that case the Pilgrim would be saying "take me to Purgatory so that I may see Heaven—and (since this is unfortunately necessary) Hell too." This would betray some confusion or agitation, but what would be more natural at this stage, when the Pilgrim is just about to begin his journey?

* * * * *

It is impossible to understand all of the allegory in the First Canto without having read the entire *Comedy* because Canto I is, in a sense, a miniature of the whole, and the themes that Dante introduces here will be the major themes of the entire work. Thus, this canto is perhaps the most important of all. The moral landscape of Canto I is tripartite, reflecting the structure of *The Divine Comedy* itself. The "dark wood" suggests the state of sin in which Dante the Pilgrim finds himself, and therefore is analogous to Hell (the subject matter of the first canticle), through which Dante will soon be traveling. The "barren slope" (29) suggests the middle ground between evil and good, which men must pass through before they reach the "sunlight" of love and blessedness at the mountain's peak. It is analogous therefore to Purgatory, the subject of the second part of the *Comedy*. The "blissful mountain" (77) bathed in the rays of the sun is the state of blessedness, toward which man constantly strives, described in the third canticle, the *Paradise*.

Canto V

From limbo Virgil leads his ward down to the threshold of the Second Circle of Hell, where for the first time he will see the damned in Hell being punished for their sins. There, barring their way, is the hideous figure of MINÒS, the bestial judge of Dante's underworld, but after strong words from Virgil, the poets are allowed to pass into the dark space of this circle, where can be heard the wailing voices of the LUSTFUL, whose punishment consists in being forever whirled about in a dark, stormy wind. After seeing a thousand or more famous lovers—including SEMIRAMIS, DIDO, HELEN, ACHILLES, and PARIS—the Pilgrim asks to speak to two figures he sees together. They are FRANCESCA DA RIMINI and her lover, PAOLO, and the scene in which they appear is probably the most famous episode of the Inferno. At the end of the scene, the Pilgrim, who has been overcome by pity for the lovers, faints to the ground.

This way I went, descending from the first
    into the second circle, that holds less space
    but much more pain—stinging the soul to wailing.   3

There stands Minòs grotesquely, and he snarls,
   examining the guilty at the entrance;
   he judges and dispatches, tail in coils.   6

By this I mean that when the evil soul
   appears before him, it confesses all,
   and he, who is the expert judge of sins,   9

knows to what place in Hell the soul belongs;
   the times he wraps his tail around himself
   tells just how far the sinner must go down.   12

The damned keep crowding up in front of him:
   they pass along to judgment one by one;
   they speak, they hear, and then are hurled below.   15

"O you who come to the place where pain is host,"
   Minòs spoke out when he caught sight of me,
   putting aside the duties of his office,   18

"be careful how you enter and whom you trust:
   it is easy to get in, but don't be fooled!"
   And my guide said to him: "Why keep on shouting?   21

Do not attempt to stop his fated journey;
   it is so willed there where the power is
   for what is willed; that's all you need to know."   24

And now the notes of anguish start to play
   upon my ears; and now I find myself
   where sounds on sounds of weeping pound at me.   27

I came to a place where no light shone at all,
   bellowing like the sea racked by a tempest,
   when warring winds attack it from both sides.   30

The infernal storm, eternal in its rage,
   sweeps and drives the spirits with its blast:
   it whirls them, lashing them with punishment.   33

When they are swept back past their place of judgment,
   then come the shrieks, laments, and anguished cries;
   there they blaspheme the power of almighty God.   36

I learned that to this place of punishment
   all those who sin in lust have been condemned,
   those who make reason slave to appetite;   39

and as the wings of starlings in the winter
   bear them along in wide-spread, crowded flocks,
   so does that wind propel the evil spirits: 42

now here, then there, and up and down, it drives them
   with never any hope to comfort them—
   hope not of rest but even of suffering less.   45

And just like cranes in flight, chanting their lays,
   stretching an endless line in their formation,
   I saw approaching, crying their laments,   48

spirits carried along by the battling winds.
   And so I asked, "Teacher, tell me, what souls
   are these punished in the sweep of the black wind?"   51

"The first of those whose story you should know,"
   my master wasted no time answering,
   "was empress over lands of many tongues;   54

her vicious tastes had so corrupted her
   she licensed every form of lust with laws
   to cleanse the stain of scandal she had spread;   57

she is Semiramis, who, legend says,
   was Ninus' wife and successor to his throne;
   she governed all the land the Sultan rules.   60

The next is she who killed herself for love
   and broke faith with the ashes of Sichaeus;
   and there is Cleopatra, who loved men's lusting.   63

See Helen there, the root of evil woe
   lasting long years, and see the great Achilles,
   who lost his life to love, in final combat;   66

see Paris, Tristan"—then, more than a thousand
   he pointed out to me, and named them all,
   those shades whom love cut off from life on earth.   69

After I heard my teacher call the names
   of all these knights and ladies of ancient times,
   pity confused my senses, and I was dazed.   72

I began: "Poet, I would like, with all my heart,
   to speak to those two there who move together
   and seem to be so light upon the winds."   75

And he: "You'll see for yourself when they are closer;
   if you entreat them by that love of theirs
   that carries them along, they will come to you."   78

When the winds bent their course in our direction
   I raised my voice to them, "O wearied souls,
   come speak with us if it be not forbidden."   81

As doves, called by desire to return
   to their sweet nest, with wings outstretched and poised,
   float downward through the air, guided by their will,   84

so these two left the flock where Dido is
   and came toward us through the malignant air,
   such was the tender power of my call.   87

"O living creature, gracious and so kind,
  who makes your way here through this dingy air
  to visit us who stained the world with blood,   90

if we could claim as friend the King of Kings,
  we would beseech him that he grant you peace,
  you who show pity for our atrocious plight.   93

Whatever pleases you to hear or speak
  we will hear and we will speak about with you
  as long as the wind, here where we are, is silent.   96

The place where I was born lies on the shore
  where the river Po with its attendant streams
  descends to seek its final resting place.   99

Love, that kindles quick in the gentle heart,
  seized this one for the beauty of my body,
  torn from me. (How it happened still offends me!)   102

Love, that excuses no one loved from loving,
  seized me so strongly with delight in him
  that, as you see, he never leaves my side.   105

Love led us straight to sudden death together.
  Caïna awaits the one who quenched our lives."
  These were the words that came from them to us.   108

When those offended souls had told their story,
  I bowed my head and kept it bowed until
  the poet said, "What are you thinking of?"   111

When finally I spoke, I sighed, "Alas,
  what sweet thoughts, and oh, how much desiring
  brought these two down into this agony."   114

And then I turned to them and tried to speak;
  I said, "Francesca, the torment that you suffer
  brings painful tears of pity to my eyes.   117

But tell me, in that time of your sweet sighing
  how, and by what signs, did love allow you
  to recognize your dubious desires?"   120

And she to me: "There is no greater pain
  than to remember, in our present grief,
  past happiness (as well your teacher knows)!   123

But if your great desire is to learn
  the very root of such a love as ours,
  I shall tell you, but in words of flowing tears.   126

One day we read, to pass the time away,
  of Lancelot, how he had fallen in love;
  we were alone, innocent of suspicion.   129

Time and again our eyes were brought together
  by the book we read; our faces flushed and paled.
  To the moment of one line alone we yielded: 132

it was when we read about those longed-for lips
  now being kissed by such a famous lover,
  that this one (who shall never leave my side)   135

then kissed my mouth, and trembled as he did.
  Our Galehot was that book and he who wrote it.
  That day we read no further." And all the while   138

the one of the two spirits spoke these words,
  the other wept, in such a way that pity
  blurred my senses; I swooned as though to die,   141

and fell to Hell's floor as a body, dead, falls.

NOTES

1–72

The fifth canto can be divided into two equal parts with a transitional tercet. The first part concerns Minòs and his activities, the band of souls being punished in the wind for their lust, and certain shades of royal figures seen in a formation that resembles that of flying cranes. The Pilgrim has learned (evidently from Virgil) the function of Minòs, and he will learn from him the type of sin being punished, the form of the punishment, and the names of many of those who are here. Chiefly, Virgil is trying to teach the Pilgrim three lessons in the first part of this canto, and, each is concerned with the nature of lust—a heinous sin even if it is the least of those punished in Hell. The first lesson should come from the sight of Minòs exercising his function: the horror of this sight should shock the Pilgrim into an awareness of the true nature of all sin. The second lesson should come from the royal figures guilty of lust. Semiramis, who legalized lust because of her own incestuous activity (and to whom Virgil devotes three tercets, more lines then anyone else in this group receives), should be a particularly significant lesson to the Pilgrim as to the nature of carnal sins. And thirdly, the Pilgrim should come to despise the lustful because they blaspheme Divine justice, which has placed them here, and thereby show themselves to be totally unrepentant.

But the Pilgrim learns nothing, as we see in the transitional tercet (70–72). Instead, pity for these sinners seizes his senses and he is "dazed." This tercet reveals the state of the Pilgrim's mind before meeting with Francesca da Rimini. Pity is precisely that side of the Pilgrim's character toward which Francesca will direct her carefully phrased speech. The Pilgrim has not learned his lesson, and in the direct encounter with one of the lustful (Francesca), he will fail his first "test."

4. *There stands Minòs grotesquely:* Minòs was the son of Zeus and Europa. As king of Crete he was revered for his wisdom and judicial gifts. For these qualities he became chief magistrate of the underworld in classical literature:

Minòs, presiding, shakes the urn; it is he who calls a court of the silent and learns men's lives and Misdeeds.

(Virgil, *Aeneid* VI, 432–33)

Although Dante did not alter Minòs's official function, he transformed him into a demonic figure, both in his physical characteristics and in his bestial activity. Minòs condemns souls to all parts of Hell, but Dante may well have placed him at the entrance to the Second Circle so that the reader, listening to the tragic tale of the sweet Francesca, would not be tempted to forget the hideous figure of Minòs, who, with his tail, once pronounced sentence on Francesca as well as on Thaïs the whore (XVIII).

31–32. *The infernal storm, eternal in its rage:* The *contrapasso*, or punishment, suggests that lust (the "infernal storm") is pursued without the light of reason (in the darkness).

34. *When they are swept back past their place of judgment:* In Italian this line reads, "Quando giungon davanti a la ruina," literally, "When they come before the falling place." According to Busnelli (*Miscellanea dantesca*, Padova, 1922, 51–53), the *ruina* refers to the tribunal of Minòs, that is, to the place where the condemned sinners "fall" before him at the entrance to the Second Circle to be judged. Therefore I have translated *ruina* as "their place of judgment"; the entire tercet means that every time the sinners in the windstorm are blown near Minòs they shriek, lament, and blaspheme.

58. *she is Semiramis:* the legendary queen of Assyria who, although renowned for her military conquests and civic projects, fell prey to her passions and became dissolute to the extent of legalizing lust. Paulus Orosius, Dante's principal source for the story, also attributes the restoration of Babylon, built by Nimrod, to Semiramis. According to Saint Augustine (*City of God*), one of the major conflicts of Christendom stems from the presence of two opposing civilizations: the city of God (*civitas dei,* founded by Abraham) and the city of man (*civitas mundi,* rejuvenated by Semiramis). Therefore, in a larger sense Dante conceived the Assyrian empress not only as the representative of libidinous passion in all its forms, but also as the motivating force of the degenerate society that ultimately opposes God's divine order.

60. *she governed all the land the Sultan rules:* During the Middle Ages the Sultan controlled the area that now contains Egypt and Syria.

61–62. *The next is she who killed himself for love:* According to Virgil (*Aeneid* I and IV), Dido, the queen of Carthage, swore faithfulness to the memory of her dead husband, Sichaeus. However, when the Trojan survivors of the war arrived in port, she fell helplessly in love with their leader, Aeneas, and they lived together as man and wife until the gods reminded Aeneas of his higher destiny: the founding of Rome and the Roman Empire. Immediately he set sail for Italy, and Dido, deserted, committed suicide.

63. *and there is Cleopatra, who loved men's lusting:* Cleopatra was the daughter of Ptolemy Auletes, the last king of Egypt before it came under Roman domination. She was married to her brother in conformity with the incestuous practices of the Ptolemies, but with the assistance of Julius Caesar, whose child she bore, Cleopatra disposed of her brother and became queen of Egypt. After Caesar's death her licentious charms captured Mark Antony, with whom she lived in debauchery until his death. Finally she attempted, unsuccessfully, to seduce Octavianus, the Roman governor of Egypt, and his refusal precipitated her suicide.

To the two great empires already mentioned, Assyria and Carthage, a third must be added, Egypt, which with its libidinous queen opposed the "*civitas dei.*"

64. *See Helen there, the root of evil woe:* Helen, wife of Menelaus, king of Sparta, was presented by Aphrodite to Paris in compensation for his judgment in the beauty contest of the goddesses. Paris carried Helen off to Troy and there married her, but her enraged husband demanded aid of the other Greek nobles to regain Helen. United, they embarked for Troy, and thus began the final conflagration involving the two powerful nations.

65–66. *and see the great Achilles:* Dante's knowledge of the Trojan War came directly or indirectly from the early medieval accounts of Dare the Phrygian (*De Excidio Trojae Historia*) and Dictys of Crete (*De Bello Trojano*). In these versions Achilles, the invincible Homeric warrior, had been transformed into an ordinary mortal who languished in the bonds of love. Enticed by the beauty of Polyxena, a daughter of the Trojan king, Achilles desired her to be his wife, but Hecuba, Polyxena's mother, arranged a counterplot with Paris so that when Achilles entered the temple for his presumed marriage, he was treacherously slain by Paris.

67. *see Paris, Tristan:* Paris was the son of Priam, king of Troy, whose abduction of Helen ignited the Trojan War. The classical Latin poets and the medieval redactors of the legend of Troy consistently depicted him more disposed to loving than to fighting. Tristan is the central figure of numerous medieval French, German, and Italian romances. Sent as a messenger by his uncle, King Mark of Cornwall, to obtain Isolt for him in marriage, Tristan became enamored of her, and she of him. After Isolt's marriage to Mark, the lovers continued their love affair, and in order to maintain its secrecy they necessarily employed many deceits and ruses. According to one version, however, Mark, growing continuously more suspicious of their attachment, finally discovered them together and ended the incestuous relationship by mortally wounding Tristan with a lance.

73–142

Having seen the shades of many "knights and ladies of ancient times" (71), the Pilgrim now centers his attention upon a single pair of lovers. The spotlight technique here employed emphasizes the essentially dramatic quality of the *In-*

ferno. Francesca recognizes the Pilgrim's sympathetic attitude and tells her story in a way that will not fail to win the Pilgrim's interest, even though she, like Semiramis, was the initiator in an act of incest. Her choice of words and phrases frequently reveals her gentility and her familiarity with the works of the *stilnovisti* poets (the school of poets that was contemporary with, and perhaps included, Dante). But the careful reader can see beneath the superficial charm and grace what Francesca really is—vain and accustomed to admiration. Francesca is also capable of lying, though whether her lies are intentional or the result of self-deception we do not know. For example, her reference to the love of Lancelot in line 128 shows her technique of changing facts that would condemn her. In the medieval French romance *Lancelot du Lac,* the hero, being quite bashful in love, is finally brought together in conversation with Queen Guinevere through the machinations of Galehot ("Our Galehot was that book and he who wrote it," 137). Urged on by his words, Guinevere takes the initiative and, placing her hand on Lancelot's chin, kisses him. In order to fully understand Francesca's character, it is necessary to note that in our passage she has reversed the roles of the lovers: here she has Lancelot kissing Guinevere just as she has presented Paolo as kissing her. The distortion of this passage offered as a parallel to her own experience reveals the (at best) confusion of Francesca: if the passage in the romance inspired their kiss, it must have been she, as it was Guinevere, who was responsible. Like Eve, who tempted Adam to commit the first sin in the Garden of Eden, Francesca tempted Paolo, and thus she is perhaps an example of the common medieval view of women as "daughters of Eve." Francesca attempts to exculpate herself by blaming the romantic book that she and Paolo were reading (137); the Pilgrim is evidently convinced of her innocence for he is overcome ". . . in such a way that pity blurred [his] senses," and he faints.

Many critics, taken in like the Pilgrim by Francesca's smooth speech, have asserted that she and Paolo in their love have "conquered" Hell because they are still together. But their togetherness is certainly part of their punishment. The ever-silent, weeping Paolo is surely not happy with their state, and Francesca coolly alludes to Paolo with the impersonal "that one" (*costui*) or "this one" (*questi*). She never mentions his name. Line 102 indicates her distaste for Paolo: the manner of her death (they were caught and killed together in the midst of their lustful passion) *still* offends her because she is forever condemned to be together with her naked lover; he serves as a constant reminder of her shame and of the reason that they are in Hell ("he never leaves my side," 105). Their temporary pleasure together in lust has become their own particular torment in Hell.

74. *those two there who move together:* Francesca, daughter of Guido Vecchio da Polenta, lord of Ravenna, and Paolo Malatesta, third son of Malatesta da Verrucchio, lord of Rimini. Around 1275 the aristocratic Francesca was married for political reasons to Gianciotto, the physically deformed second son of Malatesta da Verrucchio. In time a love affair developed between Francesca and Gianciotto's younger brother, Paolo. One day the betrayed husband discovered them in an amorous embrace and slew them both.

82–84. *As doves:* Paolo and Francesca are compared to "doves, called by desire . . ." who "float downward through the air, guided by their will." The use of the words "desire" and "will" is particularly interesting because it suggests the nature of lust as a sin: the subjugation of the will to desire.

97–99. *The place where I was born:* Ravenna, a city on the Adriatic coast.

100–108. *Love . . . Love . . . Love:* These three tercets, each beginning with the word "Love," are particularly important as revealing the deceptive nature of Francesca. In lines 100 and 103 Francesca deliberately employs the style of *stilnovisti* poets such as Guinizelli and Cavalcanti in order to ensure the Pilgrim's sympathy, but she follows each of those lines with sensual and most un-*stilnovistic* ideas. For in the idealistic world of the *dolce stil nuovo,* love would never "seize" a man for the beauty of the woman's body alone, nor would the sensual delight that "seized" Francesca be appropriate to *stilnovistic* love, which was distant, nonsexual, and ideal.

107. *Caïna awaits the one who quenched our lives:* Caïna is one of the four divisions of Cocytus, the lowest part of Hell, wherein are tormented those souls who treacherously betrayed their kin.

141–42. *I swooned as though to die:* To understand this reaction to Francesca, it is necessary to remember that Dante the Pilgrim is a fictional character, who should not be equated with Dante the Poet, author of *The Divine Comedy.* Dante the Pilgrim is journeying through Hell as a man who must learn the true nature of sin, and since this is his first contact with those who are damned and punished in Hell proper, he is easily seduced into compassion for these souls. As the Pilgrim progresses he will learn the nature of sin and of evil souls, and his reaction to them will change (cf. XIX). But the extent of his failure in Canto V to recognize sin and treat it with proper disdain is symbolized here by his abject figure, unconscious (thus, without "reason") on the floor of Hell. Perhaps we should not blame the Pilgrim for being taken in by Francesca; dozens of critics, unaware of the wiles of sin, have also been seduced by her charm and the grace of her speech.

Canto XV

They move out across the plain of burning sand, walking along the ditchlike edge of the conduit through which the Phlegethon flows, and after they have come some distance from the wood they see a group of souls running toward them. One, BRUNETTO LATINI, a famous Florentine intellectual and Dante's former teacher, recognizes the Pilgrim and leaves his band to walk and talk with him. Brunetto learns the reason for the Pilgrim's journey and offers him a prophecy of the troubles lying in wait for him—an echo of Ciacco's words in Canto VI. Brunetto names some of the others being punished with him (PRISCIAN, FRANCESCO D'ACCORSO, ANDREA DE' MOZZI); but soon, in the distance, he sees a cloud of smoke approaching, which presages a new group, and because he must not associate with them, like a foot-racer Brunetto speeds away to catch up with his own band.

> Now one of those stone margins bears us on
>   and the river's vapors hover like a shade,
>   sheltering the banks and the water from the flames.   3
>
> As the Flemings, living with the constant threat
>   of flood tides rushing in between Wissant
>   and Bruges, build their dikes to force the sea back;   6
>
> as the Paduans build theirs on the shores of Brenta
>   to protect their town and homes before warm weather
>   turns Chiarentana's snow to rushing water—   9
>
> so were these walls we walked upon constructed,
>   though the engineer, whoever he may have been,
>   did not make them as high or thick as those.   12
>
> We had left the wood behind (so far behind,
>   by now, that if I had stopped to turn around,
>   I am sure it could no longer have been seen)   15
>
> when we saw a troop of souls come hurrying
>   toward us beside the bank, and each of them
>   looked us up and down, as some men look   18
>
> at other men, at night, when the moon is new.
>   They strained their eyebrows, squinting hard at us,
>   as an old tailor might at his needle's eye.   21
>
> Eyed in such a way by this strange crew,
>   I was recognized by one of them, who grabbed
>   my garment's hem and shouted: "How marvelous!"   24

And I, when he reached out his arm toward me,
   straining my eyes, saw through his face's crust,
   through his burned features that could not prevent   27

my memory from bringing back his name;
   and bending my face down to meet with his,
   I said: "is this really you, here, Ser Brunetto?"   30

And he: "O my son, may it not displease you
   if Brunetto Latini lets his troop file on
   while he walks at your side for a little while."   33

And I: "With all my heart I beg you to,
   and if you wish me to sit here with you,
   I will, if my companion does not mind."   36

"My son," he said, "a member of this herd
   who stops one moment lies one hundred years
   unable to brush off the wounding flames,   39

so, move on; I shall follow at your hem
   and then rejoin my family that moves
   along, lamenting their eternal pain."   42

I did not dare step off the margin-path
   to walk at his own level but, with head
   bent low in reverence, I moved along.   45

He began: "What fortune or what destiny
   leads you down here before your final hour?
   And who is this one showing you the way?"   48

"Up there above in the bright living life
   before I reached the end of all my years,
   I lost myself in a valley," I replied;   51

"just yesterday at dawn I turned from it.
   This spirit here appeared as I turned back,
   and by this road he guides me home again."   54

He said to me: "Follow your constellation
   and you cannot fail to reach your port of glory,
   not if I saw clearly in the happy life;   57

and if I had not died just when I did,
   I would have cheered you on in all your work,
   seeing how favorable Heaven was to you.   60

But that ungrateful and malignant race
   which descended from the Fiesole of old,
   and still have rock and mountain in their blood,   63

will become, for your good deeds, your enemy—
   and right they are: among the bitter berries
   there's no fit place for the sweet fig to bloom.   66

They have always had the fame of being blind,
    an envious race, proud and avaricious;
    you must not let their ways contaminate you.   69

Your destiny reserves such honors for you:
    both parties shall be hungry to devour you,
    but the grass will not be growing where the goat is.   72

Let the wild beasts of Fiesole make fodder
    of each other, and let them leave the plant untouched
    (so rare it is that one grows in their dung-heap)   75

in which there lives again the holy seed
    of those remaining Romans who survived there
    when this new nest of malice was constructed."   78

"Oh, if all I wished for had been granted,"
    I answered him, "you certainly would not,
    not yet, be banished from our life on earth;   81

my mind is etched (and now my heart is pierced)
    with your kind image, loving and paternal,
    when, living in the world, hour after hour   84

you taught me how man makes himself eternal.
    And while I live my tongue shall always speak
    of my debt to you, and of my gratitude.   87

I will write down what you tell me of my future
    and save it, with another text, to show
    a lady who can interpret, if I can reach her.   90

This much, at least, let me make clear to you:
    if my conscience continues not to blame me,
    I am ready for whatever Fortune wants.   93

This prophecy is not new to my ears,
    and so let Fortune turn her wheel, spinning it
    as she pleases, and the peasant turn his spade."   96

My master, hearing this, looked to the right,
    then, turning round and facing me, he said:
    "He listens well who notes well what he hears."   99

But I did not answer him; I went on talking,
    walking with Ser Brunetto, asking him
    who of his company were most distinguished.   102

And he: "It might be good to know who some are,
    about the rest I feel I should be silent,
    for the time would be too short, there are so many.   105

In brief, let me tell you, all here were clerics
    and respected men of letters of great fame,
    all befouled in the world by one same sin: 108

Priscian is traveling with that wretched crowd
   and Franceso d'Accorso too; and also there,
     if you could have stomached such repugnancy,   111

you might have seen the one the Servant of Servants
   transferred to the Bacchiglione from the Arno
     where his sinfully erected nerves were buried.   114

I would say more, but my walk and conversation
   with you cannot go on, for over there
     I see a new smoke rising from the sand: 117

people approach with whom I must not mingle.
   Remember my *Trésor*, where I live on,
     this is the only thing I ask of you."   120

Then he turned back, and he seemed like one of those
   who run Verona's race across its fields
     to win the green cloth prize, and he was like   123

the winner of the group, not the last one in.

NOTES

1. *Now one of those stone margins bears us on:* Note the use of the present tense. Compare VIII, n. 109–111.

4–6. *As the Flemings, living with the constant threat:* The cities of Wissant, between Boulogne and Calais, and Bruges, in eastern Flanders, were both centers of trade during the thirteenth century. Wissant was an important port city, and Bruges was famous for its extensive trade, especially with Italy.

It is not inconceivable that cities such as these, which counted a considerable number of itinerant tradesmen and sailors among their population, might have had a reputation for sodomy during Dante's time.

7. *as the Paduans build theirs on the shores of Brenta:* Although I know of no evidence that might support the theory that Padua was renowned for sodomy during the Middle Ages, it is perhaps not mere coincidence that in the journals of William Lithgow, a seventeenth-century Scottish (?) traveler and writer, we find reference made to the propensity for sodomy he had noted among the Paduans ("for beastly Sodomy . . . [is] . . . a monstrous filthinesse, and yet to them a pleasant pastime, making songs, and singing sonets of the beauty and pleasure of their Bardassi, or buggered boyes").

9. *turns Chiarentana's snow to rushing water:* The Chiarentana is a mountainous district situated north of the Brenta River.

11. *the engineer:* God.

16–114

The sin of sodomy being punished in this round is aesthetically mirrored in much of the imagery of the canto (the way in which the group of sodomites ogle the Pilgrim and Virgil, 17–22), and particularly in the language used by Brunetto Latini. He greets the Pilgrim with the exclamation "How marvelous!" (24), and in the metaphors of his prophecy (61–78), Dante is a "sweet fig" (66), whom "both parties shall be hungry to devour" (71); the next moment he is "grass" to be eaten by a "goat" (72). And it is difficult to be more explicit than Brunetto was in his description of Andrea de' Mozzi, who died in Vicenza, "where his sinfully erected nerves were buried" (114). The imagery used in connection with these scholarly or clerical sodomites should be compared to the more robust imagery used for the ones who were soldiers in Canto XVI,

22–27. The eternal wandering of the sodomites is comparable to the *contrapasso* of the lustful in Canto V, who are forever blown about aimlessly by a wind.

30. *I said: "Is this really you, here, Ser Brunetto?":*
The Pilgrim addresses his fellow Florentine
Brunetto Latini (c. 1220–94) with the respectful
pronoun form *"voi"* (cf. Dante's use of *"voi"* with
Farinata and Cavalcante in Canto X). The reverent tone of Dante's words bespeaks his admiration and affection for the famous Guelf statesman and writer, whose *Trésor* (see below, n.
119–20) and *Tesoretto,* an allegorical poem in Italian, greatly influenced Dante's own life and
works. Brunetto was a notary, and Dante accordingly prefixes the title "Ser" to his name. Forced
into exile after the Guelf defeat at Montaperti
(1260), he remained in France for six years. The
Ghibelline defeat at Benevento (1266) ensured
his safe return to Florence, where he took an
active part in public affairs until his death.

48. *And who is this one showing you the way?:* The
Pilgrim fails to answer Brunetto's second question, possibly because naming Virgil, who has
become his second "teacher," might offend
Brunetto.

51. *I lost myself in a valley:* The "valley" is the
"dark wood" of Canto I.

54. *and by this road he guides me home again:* That
is, to God, man's true home. In the Middle Ages
man's earthly existence was viewed as a pilgrimage, a preparation for the after-life.

61–78. *But that ungrateful and malignant race:*
During a Roman power struggle, Catiline fled
Rome and found sanctuary for himself and his
troops in the originally Etruscan town of Fiesole.
After Caesar's successful siege of that city, the
survivors of both camps founded Florence,
where those of the Roman camp were the elite.

Brunetto prophesies about Florence that both
political parties will become Dante's enemies
(61–64), for he will be the "sweet fig" (66), among
the "bitter berries" (65), who are "an envious
race, proud and avaricious" (68). They must hate
the plant in which "there lives again the holy
seed / of those remaining Romans who survived
there . . ." (76–77).

The prophecy, with its condemnation of the
current state of Florence (and Italy) and its implied hope of a renascent empire, continues the
political theme begun with the speech of the
Anonymous Suicide in Canto XIII, and continued
in the symbol of the Old Man of Crete in Canto
XIV.

68. *an envious race, proud and avaricious:* Envy
and pride are always the basis of the sins beyond
the walls of Dis. See XXXI, n. 19–127.

85. *you taught me how man makes himself eternal:*
Dante expresses his gratitude to Brunetto by say-

ing that it was he who taught him how to become
immortal through literary, accomplishments.

89–90. *and save it, with another text, to show:*
Again (as in X, 130–32), Beatrice is referred to as
the one who will reveal to the Pilgrim his future
course. She will gloss the earlier prophecies ("another text") of Ciacco (VI, 64–75) and Farinata (X,
79–81), together with the one just related by
Brunetto. However, in the Paradise this role is
given to Dante's ancestor Cacciaguida.

95–96. *let Fortune turn her wheel. . . ./ . . . and the
peasant turn his spade:* It is as right for Fortune to
spin her wheel as it is for the peasant to turn his
spade; and the Pilgrim will be as indifferent to
the first as to the second.

Could there also be a suggestion in his reference to the peasant's spade of his indifference to
those who might attempt to dig up the "plant . . .
in which there lives again the holy seed . . ."?

99. *He listens well who notes well what he hears:*
Virgil is certainly not rebuking the Pilgrim, as
some think (for his supposed indifference to
Brunetto's words), but rather praising him for
remembering the other prophecies and for believing that they will eventually be interpreted
by Beatrice. And surely, if the Pilgrim had considered himself rebuked by his guide, he would
not have reacted as he did: "But I did not answer
him; I went on talking."

110. *and Francesco d'Accorso:* A celebrated Florentine lawyer (1225–94) who taught law at the
University of Bologna and later at Oxford at the
request of King Edward I.

112–14. *you might have seen the one the Servant
of Servants:* Andrea de' Mozzi was Bishop of
Florence from 1287 to 1295, when, by order of
Pope Boniface VIII (the "Servant of Servants":
i.e., the servant of the servants of God), he was
transferred to Vicenza (on the Bacchiglione
River), where he died that same year or the next.
The early commentators make reference to his
naive and inept preaching and to his general
stupidity. Dante, by mentioning his "sinfully
erected nerves," calls attention to his major
weakness: unnatural lust or sodomy. See n. 16–
114, above.

119–20. *Remember my* Trésor, *where I live on:*
The *Livres du Tresor,* Brunetto's most significant
composition, was written during his exile in
France, and is an encyclopedic work written in
French prose.

123–24. *to win the green cloth prize:* The first
prize for the footrace, which was one of the
games held annually on the first Sunday of Lent
in Verona during the thirteenth century, was a
green cloth. Ironically, the Pilgrim's last view of

his elderly and dignified teacher is the sight of him, naked, racing off at top speed to catch up with his companions in sin. This image of the race in Verona (which was, appropriately for its aesthetic function in this canto, run naked) prepares the reader for the athletic imagery of the next canto.

Canto XXVI

From the ridge high above the Eighth *Bolgia* can be perceived a myriad of flames flickering far below, and Virgil explains that within each flame is the suffering soul of a DECEIVER. One flame, divided at the top, catches the Pilgrim's eye and he is told that within it are jointly punished ULYSSES and DIOMED. Virgil questions the pair for the benefit of the Pilgrim. Ulysses responds with the famous narrative of his last voyage, during which he passed the Pillars of Hercules and sailed the forbidden sea until he saw a mountain shape, from which came suddenly a whirlwind that spun his ship around three times and sank it.

Be joyful, Florence, since you are so great
   that your outstretched wings beat over land and sea,
   and your name is spread throughout the realm of Hell!   3

I was ashamed to find among the thieves
   five of your most eminent citizens,
   a fact which does you very little honor.   6

But if early morning dreams have any truth,
   you will have the fate, in not too long a time,
   that Prato and the others crave for you.   9

And were this the day, it would not be too soon!
   Would it had come to pass, since pass it must!
   The longer the delay, the more my grief.   12

We started climbing up the stairs of boulders
   that had brought us to the place from where we watched;
   my guide went first and pulled me up behind him.   15

We went along our solitary way
   among the rocks, among the ridge's crags,
   where the foot could not advance without the hand.   18

I know that I grieved then, and now again
   I grieve when I remember what I saw,
   and more than ever I restrain my talent   21

lest it run a course that virtue has not set;
   for if a lucky star or something better
   has given me this good, I must not misuse it.   24

As many fireflies (in the season when
   the one who lights the world hides his face least,
   in the hour when the flies yield to mosquitoes)   27

as the peasant on the hillside at his ease
    sees, flickering in the valley down below,
      where perhaps he gathers grapes or tills the soil—   30

with just so many flames all the eighth *bolgia*
    shone brilliantly, as I became aware
      when at last I stood where the depths were visible.   33
As he who was avenged by bears beheld
    Elijah's chariot at its departure,
      when the rearing horses took to flight toward Heaven,   36

and though he tried to follow with his eyes,
    he could not see more than the flame alone
      like a small cloud once it had risen high—   39

so each flame moves itself along the throat
    of the abyss, none showing what it steals
      but each one stealing nonetheless a sinner.   42

I was on the bridge, leaning far over—so far
    that if I had not grabbed some jut of rock
      I could easily have fallen to the bottom.   45

And my guide who saw me so absorbed, explained:
    "There are souls concealed within these moving fires,
      each one swathed in his burning punishment."   48

"O master," I replied, "from what you say
    I know now I was right; I had guessed already
      it might be so, and I was about to ask you: 51

Who's in that flame with its tip split in two,
    like that one which once sprang up from the pyre
      where Eteocles was placed beside his brother?   54

He said: "Within, Ulysses and Diomed
    are suffering in anger with each other,
      just vengeance makes them march together now.   57

And they lament inside one flame the ambush
    of the horse become the gateway that allowed
      the Romans' noble seed to issue forth.   60

Therein they mourn the trick that caused the grief
    of Deïdamia, who still weeps for Achilles;
      and there they pay for the Palladium."   63

"If it is possible for them to speak
    from within those flames," I said, "master, I pray
      and repray you—let my prayer be like a thousand—   66

that you do not forbid me to remain
    until the two-horned flame comes close to us;
      you see how I bend toward it with desire!"   69

"Your prayer indeed is worthy of highest praise,"
    he said to me, "and therefore I shall grant it;
       but see to it your tongue refrains from speaking.   72

Leave it to me to speak, for I know well
    what you would ask; perhaps, since they were Greeks,
       they might not pay attention to your words."   75

So when the flame had reached us, and my guide
    decided that the time and place were right,
       he addressed them and I listened to him speaking: 78

"O you who are two souls within one fire,
    if I have deserved from you when I was living,
       if I have deserved from you much praise or little,   81

when in the world I wrote my lofty verses,
    do not move on; let one of you tell where
       he lost himself through his own fault, and died."   84

The greater of the ancient flame's two horns
    began to sway and quiver, murmuring
       just like a flame that strains against the wind;   87

then, while its tip was moving back and forth,
    as if it were the tongue itself that spoke,
       the flame took on a voice and said: "When I   90

set sail from Circe, who, more than a year,
    had kept me occupied close to Gaëta
       (before Aeneas called it by that name),   93

not sweetness of a son, not reverence
    for an aging father, not the debt of love
       I owed Penelope to make her happy,   96

could quench deep in myself the burning wish
    to know the world and have experience
       of all man's vices, of all human worth.   99

So I set out on the deep and open sea
    with just one ship and with that group of men,
       not many, who had not deserted me.   102

I saw as far as Spain, far as Morocco,
    both shores; I had left behind Sardinia,
       and the other islands which that sea encloses.   105

I and my mates were old and tired men
    Then finally we reached the narrow neck
       where Heracles put up his signal-pillars   108

to warn men not to go beyond that point.
    On my right I saw Seville, and passed beyond;
       on my left, Ceüta had already sunk behind me.   111

'Brothers,' I said, 'who through a hundred thousand
   perils have made your way to reach the West,
   during this so brief vigil of our senses   114

that is still reserved for us, do not deny
   yourself experience of what there is beyond,
   behind the sun, in the world they call unpeopled.   117

Consider what you came from: you are Greeks!
   You were not born to live like mindless brutes
   but to follow paths of excellence and knowledge.'   120

With this brief exhortation I made my crew
   so anxious for the way that lay ahead,
   that then I hardly could have held them back;   123

and with our stern turned toward the morning light,
   we made our oars our wings for that mad flight,
   gaining distance, always sailing to the left.   126

The night already had surveyed the stars
   the other pole contains; it saw ours so low
   it did not show above the ocean floor.   129

Five times we saw the splendor of the moon
   grow full and five times wane away again
   since we had entered through the narrow pass—   132

when there appeared a mountain shape, darkened
   by distance, that arose to endless heights.
   I had never seen another mountain like it.   135

Our celebrations soon turned into grief:
   from the new land there rose a whirling wind
   that beat against the forepart of the ship   138

and whirled us round three times in churning waters;
   the fourth blast raised the stern up high, and sent
   the bow down deep, as pleased Another's will.   141

And then the sea was closed again, above us."

NOTES

1–6. Be joyful, Florence, since you are so great:
Dante's invective against Florence, inspired by
the presence of five of her citizens in the *bolgia* of
the thieves, also serves an artistic function. Depicted as a great bird that spreads its wings, the
proud city of Florence prefigures Lucifer (cf.
XXXIV, 46–48) and, more immediately, the "mad
flight" (125) of Ulysses, whose ship's oars were
like wings. But as Lucifer was cast down into

Hell in defeat by God, so Ulysses was cast into
the depths of the sea by a force he refers to as
"Another's will" (141). The implication is that
someday Florence, by adhering to her present
course, will also be destroyed.

7–9. But if early morning dreams have any truth:
According to the ancient and medieval popular
tradition, the dreams that men have in the early
morning hours before daybreak will come true.

Dante's dream-prophecy concerns impending strife for Florence and can be interpreted in several ways. It could refer to the malediction placed on the city by Cardinal Niccolò da Prato, who was sent (1304) by Pope Benedict XI to reconcile the opposing political factions, and who, having failed in his mission, decided to lay a curse on the city. Or we may have an allusion to the expulsion of the Blacks from Prato in 1309. However, it seems most plausible, given the phrase "and the others" (9), that Prato is to be interpreted here in a generic sense to indicate all the small Tuscan towns subjected to Florentine rule, which will soon rebel against their master.

34–39. *As he who was avenged by bears beheld:* The prophet Elisha saw Elijah transported to Heaven in a fiery chariot. When Elisha on another occasion cursed, in the name of the Lord, a group of children who were mocking him, two bears came out of the forest and devoured them (II Kings II, 9–12, 23–24).

52–54. *Who's in that flame with its tip split in two:* Here the attention of the Pilgrim is captured by a divided flame, as it was in Canto XIX by the flaming, flailing legs of Nicholas III. Dante compares this flame with that which rose from the funeral pyre of Eteocles and Polynices, the sons of Oedipus and Jocasta, who, contesting the throne of Thebes, caused a major conflict known as the Seven Against Thebes (see XIV, 68–69). The two brothers met in single combat and slew each other. They were placed together on the pyre, but because of their great mutual hatred, the flame split.

55–57. *Within, Ulysses and Diomed:* Ulysses, the son of Laertes, was a central figure in the Trojan War. Although his deeds are recounted by Homer, Dictys of Crete, and many others, the story of his last voyage presented here by Dante (90–142) has no literary or historical precedent. His story, being an invention of Dante's, is unique in *The Divine Comedy.*

Diomed, the son of Tydeus and Deipyle, ruled Argos. He was a major Greek figure in the Trojan War and was frequently associated with Ulysses in his exploits.

In Italian, lines 56–57 are: ". . . e così 'nseme / a la vendetta vanno come a l'ira." Most commentators interpret the lines to mean that Ulysses and Diomed go together toward punishment ("vendetta") now, as in life they went together in anger (they fought together?). But because of the parallel construction *a la vendetta . . . a l'ira*, both parts of which depend on the verb *vanno* ("go") in the present tense, and because of the comparison Dante makes between Ulysses and Diomed

and Eteocles and Polynices, I believe that these two figures in the flames are angry *now;* that it is part of their punishment, since they were close companions in sin on earth, to suffer ". . . in anger with each other" in Hell. "Togetherness" in punishment suffered by those who were once joined in sin has been suggested in the case of Paolo and Francesca (Canto V).

58–60. *And they lament inside one flame the ambush:* The Trojans mistakenly believed the mammoth wooden horse, left outside the city's walls, to be a sign of Greek capitulation. They brought it through the gates of the city amid great rejoicing. Later that evening the Greek soldiers hidden in the horse emerged and sacked the city. The Fall of Troy occasioned the journey of Aeneas and his followers ("noble seed") to establish a new nation on the shores of Italy which would become the heart of the Roman Empire. See Cantos I (73–75) and II (13–21).

61–62. *the grief/of Deïdamia:* Thetis brought her son Achilles, disguised as a girl, to the court of King Lycomedes on the island of Scyros, so that he would not have to fight in the Trojan War. There Achilles seduced the king's daughter Deïdamia, who bore him a child and whom he later abandoned, encouraged by Ulysses (who in company with Diomed had come in search of him) to join the war. Achilles' female disguise was unveiled by a "trick": bearing gifts for Lycomedes' daughters, Ulysses had smuggled in among them a shield and lance; Achilles betrayed his real sex by manifesting an inordinate interest in the two weapons.

63. *and there they pay for the Palladium:* The sacred Palladium, a statue of the goddess Pallas Athena, guaranteed the integrity of Troy as long as it remained in the citadel. Ulysses and Diomed stole it and carried it off to Argos, thereby securing victory for the Greeks over the Trojans.

75. *they might not pay attention to your words:* No one has yet offered a convincing explanation for Virgil's reluctance to allow the Pilgrim to address the two Greek warriors. Perhaps Virgil felt that it was more fitting for him to speak because he represented the same world of antiquity as they. (See XXVII, n.33)

90–92. *When I / set sail from Circe:* On his return voyage to Ithaca from Troy Ulysses was detained by Circe, the daughter of the Sun, for more than a year. She was an enchantress who transformed Ulysses' men into swine.

92–93. *close to Gaëta:* Along the coast of southern Italy above Naples there is a promontory (and now on it there is a city) then called Gaëta. Aeneas named it to honor his nurse, who had died there. See *Aeneid* VII, I ff. and Ovid's *Metamorphoses* XIV, 44 I ff.

94–96. *not sweetness of a son, not reverence:* In his quest for knowledge of the world Ulysses puts aside his affection for his son, Telemachus, his duty toward his father, Laertes, and the love of his devoted wife, Penelope; that is, he sinned against the classical notion of *pietas*.

108. *where Hercules put up his signal-pillars:* The Strait of Gibraltar, referred to in ancient times as the Pillars of Hercules. The two "pillars" are Mt. Abyla on the North African coast and Mt. Calpe on the European side; originally one mountain, they were separated by Hercules to designate the farthest reach of the inhabited world, beyond which no man was permitted to venture.

110–11. *On my right I saw Seville, and passed beyond:* In other words Ulysses has passed through the Strait of Gibraltar and is now in the Atlantic Ocean. Ceuta is a town on the North African coast opposite Gibraltar in this passage Seville probably represents the Iberian Peninsula and, as such, the boundary of the inhabited world.

125. *we made our oars our wings for that mad flight:* Note Ulysses' *present* judgment in Hell of his past action. (See XXVII, final note.)

130–31. *Five times we saw the splendor of the moon:* Five months had passed since they began their voyage:

133. *when there appeared a mountain shape, darkened:* In Dante's time the Southern Hemisphere was believed to be composed entirely of water; the mountain that Ulysses and his men see from afar is the Mount of Purgatory, which rises from the sea in the Southern Hemisphere, the polar opposite of Jerusalem. For the formation of the mountain see XXXIV, 112–26.

* * * * *

In the list of sins punished in the Eighth Circle of Hell (those of Simple Fraud) which Virgil offers in Canto XI, two categories are left unspecified, summed up in the phrase "and like filth." When the sins specified in this list are assigned to their respective *bolge* (and all commentators are agreed as to their localization), two *bolge* are left open: the Eighth and the Ninth—which must be those where the sins of "like filth" are punished. As for the specific variety of Fraud being punished in the Ninth *Bolgia*, the sinners there are clearly identified when we meet them in Canto XXVIII, as "sowers of scandal and schism." As for our canto, all scholars have assumed that the sin for which Ulysses and Diomed are being punished is that of Fraudulent Counseling, not because of what is said about them here but because of what is said about Guido da Montefeltro in the next canto: the Black Cherub, in claiming Guido's soul, says (XXVII, 115–16): "He must come down to join my other servants for the false counsel he gave." Since Guido is in the same *bolgia*, and suffers the same punishment as Ulysses and Diomed, critics have evidently assumed (as is only logical) that they must have committed the same sin; they also assume that the sin they share in common must be that of Fraudulent Counseling.

But as for Ulysses and Diomed, their sins are specifically mentioned and in none of the three instances involved is any act of "fraudulent counseling" recorded. If these two are not in Hell for this sin, then, in spite of the Black Cherub's words, it must follow that neither is Guido. (See final note to Canto XXVII).

Canto XXX

Capocchio's remarks are interrupted by two mad, naked shades who dash up, and one of them sinks his teeth into Capocchio's neck and drags him off; he is GIANNI SCHICCHI and the other is MYRRHA of Cyprus. When they have gone, the Pilgrim sees the ill-proportioned and immobile shade of MASTER ADAMO, a counterfeiter, who explains how members of the Guidi family had persuaded him to practice his evil art in Romena. He points out the fever-stricken shades of two infamous liars, POTIPHAR'S WIFE and SINON the Greek, whereupon the latter engages Master Adamo in a verbal battle. Virgil rebukes the Pilgrim for his absorption in such futile wrangling, but his immediate shame wins Virgil's immediate forgiveness.

In ancient times when Juno was enraged
   against the Thebans because of Semele
   (she showed her wrath on more than one occasion),   3
she made King Athamas go raving mad:
   so mad that one day when he saw his wife
   coming with his two sons in either arm,   6

he cried: "Let's spread the nets, so I can catch
   the lioness with her lion cubs at the pass!"
   Then he spread out his insane hands, like talons,   9
and, seizing one of his two sons, Learchus,
   he whirled him round and smashed him on a rock.
   She drowned herself with the other in her arms.   12

And when the wheel of Fortune brought down low
   the immeasurable haughtiness of Trojans,
   destroying in their downfall king and kingdom,   15

Hecuba sad, in misery, a slave
   (after she saw Polyxena lie slain,
   after this grieving mother found her son   18

Polydorus left unburied on the shore),
   now gone quite mad, went barking like a dog—
   it was the weight of grief that snapped her mind.   21

But never in Thebes or Troy were madmen seen
   driven to acts of such ferocity
   against their victims, animal or human,   24

as two shades I saw, white with rage and naked,
   running, snapping crazily at things in sight,
   like pigs, directionless, broken from their pen.   27

One, landing on Capocchio, sank his teeth
   into his neck, and started dragging him
   along, scraping his belly on the rocky ground.   30

The Aretine spoke, shaking where he sat:
   "You see that batty shade? He's Gianni Schicchi!
   He's rabid and he treats us all that way."   33

"Oh" I answered "so may that other shade
   never sink its teeth in you—if you don't mind,
   please tell me who it is before it's gone."   36

And he to me: "That is the ancient shade
   of Myrrha, the depraved one, who became,
   against love's laws, too much her father's friend.   39

She went to him, and there she sinned in love,
   pretending that her body was another's—
   just as the other there fleeing in the distance,   42

contrived to make his own the 'queen of studs,'
   pretending that he was Buoso Donati,
   making his will and giving it due form."   45

Now sat the rabid pair had come and gone
   (from whom I never took my eyes away,
   I turned to watch the other evil shades.   48

And there I saw a soul shaped like a lute,
   if only he'd been cut off from his legs
   below the belly, where they divide in two.   51

the bloating dropsy, disproportioning
   the body's parts with unconverted humors,
   so that the face, marched with the paunch, was puny,   54

forced him to keep his parched lips wide apart,
   as a man who suffers thirst from raging fever
   has one lip curling up, the other sagging.   57

"O you who bear no punishment at all
   (I can't think why) within this world of sorrow,"
   he said to us, "pause here and look upon   60

the misery of one Master Adamo:
   in life I had all that I could desire,
   and now, alas, I crave a drop of water.   63

The little streams that flow from the green hills
   of Casentino, descending to the Arno,
   keeping their banks so cool and soft with moisture,   66

forever flow before me, haunting me;
   and the image of them leaves me far more parched
   than the sickness that has dried my shriveled face.   69

Relentless Justice, tantalizing me,
   exploits the countryside that knew my sin,
   to draw from me ever new sighs of pain: 72

I still can see Romena, where I learned
   to falsify the coin stamped with the Baptist,
   for which I paid with my burned body there;   75

but if I could see down here the wretched souls
   of Guido or Alexander or their brother
   I would not exchange the sight for Branda's fountain.   78

One is here already, if those maniacs
   running around this place have told the truth,
   but what good is it, with my useless legs?   81

If only I were lighter, just enough
   to move one inch in every hundred years,
   I would have started on my way by now   84

to find him somewhere in this gruesome lot,
   although this ditch winds round eleven miles
   and is at least a half a mile across.   87

It's their fault I am here with this choice family:
   they encouraged me to turn out florins
   whose gold contained three carats' worth of alloy."   90

And I to him: "Who are those two poor souls
   lying to the right, close to your body's boundary,
   steaming like wet hands in wintertime?"   93

"When I poured into this ditch, I found them here,
   he answered, "and they haven't budged since then,
   and I doubt they'll move through all eternity.   96

One is the false accuser of young Joseph;
   the other is false Sinon, the Greek in Troy:
   it's their burning fever makes them smell so bad."   99

And one of them, perhaps somewhat offended
   at the kind of introduction he received,
   with his fist struck out at the distended belly,   102

which responded like a drum reverberating;
   and Master Adam struck him in the face
   with an arm as strong as the fist he had received,   105

and he said to him: "Although *I* am not free
   to move around, with swollen legs like these,
   I have a ready arm for such occasions."   108

"*But* it was *not* as free and ready, was it,"
   the other answered, "when you went to the stake?
   Of course, when you were coining, it was readier!"   111

And he with the dropsy: "*Now* you tell the truth,
   but you were not as full of truth that time
   when you were asked to tell the truth at Troy!"   114

"My words were false—so were the coins you made,"
   said Sinon, "and I am here for one false act
   but *you* for more than any fiend in hell!"   117

"The horse, recall the horse, you falsifier,"
   the bloated paunch was quick to answer back,
   "may it burn your guts that all the world remembers!" 120

"May your guts burn with thirst that cracks your tongue,"
   the Greek said, "may they burn with rotting humors
   that swell your hedge of a paunch to block your eyes!" 123

And then the money-man: "So there you go,
   your evil mouth pours out its filth as usual;
   for if *I* thirst, and humors swell me up,   126

you burn more, and your head is fit to split,
   and it wouldn't take much coaxing to convince you
   to lap the mirror of Narcissus dry!"   129

I was listening, all absorbed in this debate,
   when the master said to me: "Keep right on looking,
   a little more, and I shall lose my patience."   132

I heard the note of anger in his voice
   and turned to him; I was so full of shame
   that it still haunts my memory today.   135

Like one asleep who dreams himself in trouble
   and in his dream he wishes he were dreaming,
   longing for that which is, as if it were not,   138

just so I found myself: unable to speak,
   longing to beg for pardon and already
   begging for pardon, not knowing that I did.   141

"Less shame than yours would wash away a fault
   greater than yours has been," my master said,
   "and so forget about it, do not be sad.   144

If ever again you should meet up with men
   engaging in this kind of futile wrangling,
   remember I am always at your side;   147

to have a taste for talk like this is vulgar!"

NOTES

1–12. *In ancient times when Juno was enraged:* Jupiter's predilection for mortal women always enraged Juno, his wife. In this case her ire was provoked by her husband's dalliance with Semele, the daughter of Cadmus, King of Thebes, who bore him Bacchus. Having vowed to wreak revenge on her and her family, Juno not only had Semele struck by lightning, but also caused King Athamas, the husband of Ino (Semele's sister), to go insane. In his demented state he killed his son Learchus. Ino drowned herself and her other son, Melicertes.

16–21. *Hecuba sad, in misery, a slave:* Having triumphed over the Trojans, the Greeks returned to their homeland, bearing with them as a slave Hecuba, wife of Priam, King of Troy. She was also to make some tragic discoveries: she saw Polyxena, her daughter, slain on the grave of Achilles (17) and she discovered her son Polydorus dead and unburied on the coast of Thrace

(18–19). So great was her grief that she became insane.

25. *as two shades I saw, white with rage and naked:* See below, n. 32 and n. 37–41.

31. *The Aretine:* He is Griffolino d'Arezzo. See XXIX, 109–20.

32. *You see that batty shade? He's Gianni Schicchi!:* A member of the Florentine Cavalcanti family, Gianni Schicchi was well known for his mimetic virtuosity. Simone Donati, keeping his father's death a secret in order that he might change the will to his advantage, engaged Gianni to impersonate his dead father (Buoso Donati, 44) and alter the latter's will. The plan was carried out to perfection, and in the process Gianni willed himself, among other things, a prize mare ("the 'queen of studs,'" 43).

33. *He's rabid and he treats us all that way:* Gianni Schicchi, then, is insane, as must be also his companion in the mad flight through this *bolgia.* These are the only two sinners in *The Divine Com-*

edy who are mentally deranged, so that it is most fitting that the canto should open with a reminder of two famous cases of insanity in classical mythology.

37–41. *That is the ancient shade/of Myrrha:* The other self-falsifier darting about the bolgia with Gianni Schicchi is Myrrha, who, overpowered by an incestuous desire for her father, King Cinyras of Cyprus, went *incognita* to his bed, where they made love. Discovering the deception, Cinyras vowed to kill her; however, Myrrha escaped and wandered about until the gods took pity on her and transformed her into a myrrh tree, from which Adonis, the child conceived in the incestuous union, was born. See Ovid's *Metamorphoses* X.

52–53. *The bloating dropsy, disproportioning:* In other words, Adamo's dropsy was caused by the failure of the humors in his body to follow a natural course of change.

61–75

Although the early commentators disagree concerning Master Adamo's birthplace (Brescia? Casentino? Bologna?), it is now generally believed that he was not an Italian. He plied his art, the falsifying of gold florins ("the coin stamped with the Baptist," 74, i.e., with the image of John the Baptist, the patron saint of Florence), throughout northern Italy, encouraged to do so by the Conti Guidi, the lords of Romena (73). He was arrested by the Florentine authorities and burned to death in 1281.

64–66. *the green hills/of Casentino:* The Casentino is a hilly region southeast of Florence where the headwaters of the Arno river spread out.

76–78. *I would not exchange the sight for Branda's fountain:* Master Adamo, as much as he craves a "drop of water" (63), would forgo that pleasure if only he could see here in Hell the Conti Guidi (Guido, Alexander, Aghinolfo, and Ildebrando), who encouraged him in crime. "Branda's fountain" (78) is the name of a spring that once flowed near Romena. Often confused with it is the still-functioning fountain of the same name at Siena.

79. *One is here already:* Guido (d. 1292) is the only one of the four Conti Guidi who died before 1300.

90. *whose gold contained three carats' worth of alloy:* The florin was supposed to contain twenty-four-carat gold; those of Master Adamo had twenty–one carats.

92. *close to your body's boundary:* Note the dehumanization suggested by this phrase, which accords well with the advanced state of bodily deterioration in the *bolgia*; Master Adamo is more a land mass than a human being.

97. *One is the false accuser of young Joseph:* Potiphar's wife falsely accused Joseph, son of Jacob and Rachel, of trying to seduce her, while in reality it was she who made improper amorous advances. See Genesis XXXIX.

98. *the other is false Sinon, the Greek in Troy:* Sinon was left behind by his fellow Greek soldiers in accordance with the master plan for the capture of Troy. Taken prisoner by the Trojans, and misrepresenting his position with the Greeks, he persuaded them to bring the wooden horse (XXVI, 59) into the city.

100. *And one of them, perhaps somewhat offended:* Sinon.

129. *the mirror of Narcissus:* Water. According to the myth, Narcissus, enamoured with his own reflection in a pond, continued to gaze at it until he died.

136–41. *Like one asleep who dreams himself in trouble:* The confusing complexity of this closing image is in accordance with the theme of insanity that runs throughout the canto. At first reading, we are disoriented by both the structure and the sense of Dante's comparison. Thus it could be said that the lines cause the reader to experience the Pilgrim's confusion and not just to witness it. In order to understand the mental state of the Pilgrim at this moment, the reader is forced to pause, reread the passage, and consider carefully its meaning and effect.

The idea conveyed by the comparison is difficult because it has to do with perception of reality. The Pilgrim's desire is to beg pardon, but he feels incapable of doing so. Even as he contemplates his apparent inability to convey his message, he discovers that, in fact, it has been done. In this way, he says, he is not unlike the sleeper who dreams he is in trouble and, in his dream, wishes he were dreaming. The desire, then, in each case, is for something that already *is*.

The language of the comparison is in itself confusing; it goes beyond mere definition—it actually reflects the situation. Heavy use of repetition, particularly of the present participle, locks the reader in a kind of spiral, or perhaps a series of concentric circles. The geometrical aspect of the language is a device used elsewhere in the poem: in *Inferno* XIII, 25, for example, the geometrical configuration suggested by the language is a linear one.

* * * * *

Canto XXX is unique in that the suffering undergone by the sinners is caused not by something outside of them, some factor in this physical environment, but by something within them, by their own disease—mental or physical. The Alchemists are afflicted with leprosy, the Impersonators are mad, the Counterfeiters suffer from dropsy and the Liars are afflicted with a fever that makes them stink. In this, the last of the *Malebolge*, we see Simple Fraud at its most extreme; and because of the miscellaneous nature of the sins of the Falsifiers, we see perhaps the essence of the sin of Simple Fraud in general. In that case, Dante would be telling us that Fraud in general is a disease: the corrupt sense of values of the Fraudulent is here symbolized, in the case of the Falsifiers, by the corrupt state of their minds and bodies.

BIBLIOGRAPHY

Auerbach, Eric. *Dante: Poet of the Secular World*. Translated by Ralph Manheim. Chicago: University of Chicago Press, 1974.

Bloom, Harold, ed. *Dante's Divine Comedy*. New York: Chelsea House, 1987.

Ciardi, John. "How to Read Dante," in *Varieties of Literary Experience*. Ed. S. Burnshaw. New York: New York University Press, 1961

Clements, Robert J., ed. *American Critical Essays on The Divine Comedy*. New York: New York University Press, 1966.

Davis, Charles. *Dante and the Empire: The Cambridge Companion to Dante*. Cambridge: Cambridge University Press, 1993.

Demaray, John C. *The Invention of Dante's Commedia*. New Haven, Conn.: Yale University Press, 1974.

Hawkins, Peter S. *Dante and the Bible*. Cambridge: Cambridge University Press, 1993.

Perry, Anne. *Dorothy L. Sayers on Dante: The Centenary Celebration*. New York: Walker, 1993.

——————— *Questions for Consideration* ———————

1. How is Dante's view of what is important in life different from that of the Homeric Greeks? From that of Plato? From that of Lucretius? From that of Virgil?

    _____

    _____

    _____

    _____

    _____

    _____

    _____

2. Can the moral universe which Dante created be reconciled with the doctrine that "God is love"? If so, how?

    _____

    _____

    _____

    _____

    _____

    _____

    _____

3. Can Dante's forthright gradation of his contemporaries, living and dead, be reconciled with "Judge not, lest ye be judged"? How, or how not?

    _____

    _____

    _____

    _____

    _____

    _____

    _____

4. What qualities in Dante's literary art justify T. S. Eliot's claim that "the poetry of Dante is the one universal school of style for the writing of poetry in any language"?

_____

_____

_____

_____

_____

_____

5. How does Dante's rhyme scheme, terza rima, implement the grand design of his poem?

_____

_____

_____

_____

_____

_____

6. What elements has Dante taken over from the pagan epics, particularly Virgil? What new elements are present?

_____

_____

_____

_____

_____

7. What idea of the man-woman relationship emerges out of the treatment of Beatrice in the poem? What social and psychological consequences are suggested?

_____

_____

_____

_____

_____

8. How has Dante's religion shaped the form and content of the *Commedia?* Is he always orthodox?

_____

_____

_____

_____

_____

_____

9. To what extent was Dante's world-view bounded by the limited scientific knowledge of his time? Does this modify the greatness of his achievement for us today? If so, how?

_____

_____

_____

_____

_____

_____

Writing Critically

Select one of the essay topics listed below and compose a 500 word essay which discusses the topic fully. Support your thesis with evidence from the text and with critical and/or historical material. Use the space below for preparing to write the essay.

1. What does the character of Dante symbolize? Virgil? Beatrice? What does the presence of both Beatrice and Virgil, not one or the other, show about Dante's view of life?

2. Why, symbolically, does Dante have to make the trip through the Inferno?

3. Explain Virgil's repulse at the gates of Dis.

4. Why, symbolically, does Dante have to make his trip up the mountain of Purgatory?

5. What is Antepurgatory? Who inhabits it?

6. How does Dante explain the existence of evil in the world?

7. What does Dante learn of free will?

Prewriting Space:

_____
_____
_____
_____
_____
_____
_____
_____
_____
_____
_____
_____
_____
_____
_____
_____
_____
_____

Introduction

Geoffrey Chaucer: The Canterbury Tales

Geoffrey Chaucer was born around 1340 to a middle class and socially rising family; his father, a wine merchant, had attended on King Edward III in 1338. In 1357, he became a page, a highly coveted position, to Elizabeth, Countess of Ulster, and wife of Prince Lionel, one of the King's sons. He probably won the patronage of John of Gaunt, Duke of Lancaster, during this service which had an important effect on his manners, social values, and education, and his later career as poet and courtier.

In 1359, he was taken prisoner near Rheims in France while on military service but was ransomed in 1360 with funds partly provided by the king. In 1367, by then a courtier, he received a pension from Edward III, and in 1366 or 1367, married Philippa, sister of the third wife of John of Gaunt. From 1368 to 1378, Chaucer undertook a number of diplomatic missions in the king's service to France, Spain, the Low Countries, and Italy (Genoa, Milan, Florence). Another round of military service in France occurred in 1369. The Italian visits in 1372–3 and 1378 facilitated contact with that country's literature—the works of Dante, Boccaccio, and Petrarch.

Chaucer held a number of positions in England and received another pension from John of Gaunt in 1374, the same year that he was appointed Controller of Customs in the port of London. He received the wardship of Edward Staplegate's lands in Kent in 1375, was knight of the Shire and JP in 1386, Clerk of Works to King Richard II in 1389, Deputy Forester at North Petherton in Somerset in 1391, and received yet another pension in 1399 from King Henry IV. His wife died in 1387, and he in 1400, and he was buried at Westminster Abbey in Poet's Corner.

This brief biography reveals the scope of Chaucer's acquaintances, patronage, and contacts with important people and rulers in England and the continent, his experience and career as a Civil Servant and Courtier, his courtly connections, and a status that brought him into contact with all ranks and professions of life, all of which enriched his works, contributed to his insights and enhanced his literary resources.

He was an educated product of his age who could read in French, Latin, and Italian; he knew the classics—Virgil, Ovid, Lucan, Statius, Seneca, and Cicero—and the Bible, the Latin Liturgy of the Church, Boethius, and the various branches of medieval learning. He knew the Italian writers (though no evidence shows that he met them) Dante, Boc-

Monk and His Dogs

Friar

Parson

611

caccio, and Petrarch, and also knew and drew on the French poetry of Guillaume de Merchaut, Jean Froissart, and Eustace Deschamps. These influences assured an expanded intellectual resources and we see him drawing on a continental tradition but fusing it with an English perspective and themes. He was a major medieval literary figure who used the South East Midlands dialect of Middle English and so elevated English as a literary language on the level of French and Italian. He had an acute observation and contemplation of the human condition and presented it with technical skill, metrical brilliance, and artistic control.

With respect to his chronology, there is much uncertainty so the probable order of his works is: *The Romance of the Rose*, an early translation from French; *The Book of the Duchess*, 1369; *The House of Fame* and *The Parliament of Fowls*, both by 1382; *Troilus and Criseyde* and a prose translation of Boethius' *De Consolatione Philosophiae*, by middle 1380; *The Legend of Good Women*, 1386; *The Canterbury Tales*, 1380s and 1390s.

Chaucer's England was marked by a number of events: the 100 Years War with France, 1338–1453; the Black Death or

Summoner   Pardoner

Prioress   Wife of Bath

Plague, late 1340s; the Peasants' Revolt 1381; the Church in Schism, 1378, with two Popes, in Rome and Avignon, and weakened by corruption; John Wycliff's Lollard Movement for religious reform; the decline of Feudalism and villeinage, hence the Statute of Laborers; the rise of the middle classes; the decline in agriculture and health conditions in the rural areas. These social, historical, and religious conditions have been assimilated in human terms and they inform the portraits, tales, and characters' conduct in *The Canterbury Tales*.

Chaucer wrote this work in Middle English using a variety of metrical forms; for example, the General Prologue is in the heroic couplet. He uses the device of a pilgrimage as a framework for bringing people from different works of life together on a common enterprise who then proceed to tell stories. Boccaccio's *Decameron*, Gower's *Confessio Amantis* and Sercambi's *Novelle* similarly bring people together, and the latter, like Chaucer, uses the pilgrimage framework. This pilgrimage, here both a religious and a social event, was England's most popular, and was to the tomb of Archbishop Thomas a' Becket who was killed in Canterbury cathedral in 1170 and declared a saint in 1173. This collection of pilgrims gives a panoramic view of medieval England as it includes all stations of life, except the higher nobility and the lowest peasant tied to the land, and they are presented as individuals and representatives of their group.

The largest group is from the Church, the dominant medieval institution here represented by its clergy, including the Oxford Clerk studying for the priesthood, and its lay workers the Summoner and Pardoner. The social spectrum extends from the non-high aristocratic upper classes, the Knight and Squire, through the Merchant and Guildsmen from the middle classes, to the Yeoman and Plowman at the lower end. Secular professions include the law, medicine, and merchant navy, the managerial group, the Reeve and Manciple, the business and tradesmen class, the Merchant and Guildsmen, those who work on the land like the Plowman and Yeoman, and the land-owning non-aristocratic Franklin.

The Prologue then presents these individual portraits, taking up observed features that appear to strike the eye naturally and casually but which help define Chaucer's point of view. The Knight, Poor Parson, and Plowman are endorsed as ideal, some would say nostalgic, figures of chivalry, christian conduct, and honest hard work respectively, while in very sharp contrast the Friar, Summoner, and Pardoner are examples of moral decay and corruption, with the Shipman, Miller, Reeve, and Manciple representing different degrees of dishonesty. While some irony informs the Monk's and Prioress' portraits, Chaucer achieves a productive ambiguity with respect to what we must make of their conduct and priorities in relation to their vows and monastic principles. Further shrewd insights permeate the portraits of the Franklin, Oxford Clerk, and Wife of Bath; for example, is the former's hospitality not a type of hedonistic self-centeredness?

The Canterbury Tales consists of the Prologue and a scheme of twenty-three tales, some with their accompanying prologues, though Chaucer's plan was for each pilgrim to tell four tales, two each to and from Canterbury. The tales continue to develop his human social comedy and characterization begun in the Prologue and they also represent a range of medieval literary types or genres. We have the courtly romance (Knight's tale), beast fable (Nun's Priest), fabliau (Reeve and Miller), legend (Prioress), Breton lay (Franklin), exemplum (Pardoner and Wife of Bath), and sermon (Parson). Each tale is made to fit the teller's character and occupation; thus the Miller, Nun's Priest, and Wife of Bath respectively use the fabliau, beast fable, and exemplum.

Chaucer also uses a dramatic device which injects a naturalness to his imaginary world in the Prologue to the Miller's Tale. The interaction between the drunken Miller, the Reeve, and the Host sets the scene for the Miller's tale, a fabliau, which is a lewd, indecent story of low life in which a gullible old carpenter is cuckolded by his youthful wife and her clever young student paramour. Chaucer develops an engaging plot, psychologically valid themes, adequate characterization, and sense of a setting, and although keeping to the expected features of a fabliau, he gives a subtle twist to the notion of poetic justice at the end.

Second Nun   Nun's Priest

The Wife of Bath's Tale which belongs to the marriage group—others being the Clerk, Merchant, and Franklin—focuses on her theme of control in a marriage. It is preceded by her long Prologue that defines her character and complements Chaucer's initial portrait. An autobiographical review of her five marriages, it advances with relish the central role of sex in marriage and her basic thesis that women should have control in relationships. A remarkable self-conscious affirmation of her conduct, its defense in terms of her clearly stated goals, and her

Manciple   Reeve

attitude to and treatment of her husbands make this prologue a unique self-confessional and an assertion of women's rights.

Her tale, an exemplum, not only illustrates her thesis, confirms and extends her argument, but also shows Chaucer using a popular fairy tale theme. The Loathly Lady who marries a young man on her own terms only to be later transformed into a beautiful maiden is very familiar. Here the transformation comes when the knight allows her the choice, hence giving up his control to her. Both tale and prologue are ironic and reveal Chaucer's firm artistic control. Chaucer presents both feminist and antifeminist sentiments and arguments through this vividly individualized strong-willed woman. (ACJ)

Canon's Yeoman

BIBLIOGRAPHY

Anderson, J. J. Ed. *The Canterbury Tales: A Casebook*. London: Macmillan, 1976.

Bowden, Muriel. *A Reader's Guide to Geoffrey Chaucer*. Farrar: Straus, 1964.

Brewer, D.S. *Chaucer and His World*. 2nd ed. Rochester, New York: D.S. Brewer, 1992.

___. *An Introduction to Chaucer*. London: Longman, 1984.

Chaucer, Geoffrey. *The Canterbury Tales*. Trans. Nevill Coghill. London: Penguin, 1951.

Kittredge, George Lyman. *Chaucer and His Poetry*. Cambridge, Mass: Harvard University Press, 1915 reprint 1970.

Olson, Paul A. *The Canterbury Tales and the Good Society*. Princeton: The University Press, 1968.

Rowland, Beryl. Ed. *Companion to Chaucer Studies*. New York: Oxford University Press, 1968.

Strom, Paul. *Social Chaucer*. Cambridge, Mass: Harvard University Press, 1989.

Traversi, Derek A. *The Canterbury Tales: A Reading*. Delaware: The University Press, 1983.

Wagenknecht, Edward. Ed. *Chaucer: Modern Essays in Criticism*. New York: Oxford University Press. 1966.

from The Canterbury Tales

Geoffrey Chaucer

The Prologue

When in April the sweet showers fall
And pierce the drought of March to the root, and all
The veins are bathed in liquor of such power
As brings about the engendering of the flower,
When also Zephyrus with his sweet breath
Exhales an air in every grove and heath
Upon the tender shoots, and the young sun
His half-course in the sign of the *Ram* has run,
And the small fowl are making melody
That sleep away the night with open eye
(So nature pricks them and their heart engages)
Then people long to go on pilgrimages
And palmers long to seek the stranger strands
Of far-off saints, hallowed in sundry lands,
And specially, from every shire's end
Of England, down to Canterbury they wend
To seek the holy blissful martyr, quick
To give his help to them when they were sick.

   It happened in that season that one day
In Southwark, at *The Tabard,* as I lay
Ready to go on pilgrimage and start
For Canterbury, most devout at heart,
At night there came into that hostelry
Some nine and twenty in a company
Of sundry folk happening then to fall
In fellowship, and they were pilgrims all
That towards Canterbury meant to ride.
The rooms and stables of the inn were wide:
They made us easy, all was of the best
And, briefly, when the sun had gone to rest,
I'd spoken to them all upon the trip
And was soon one with them in fellowship,
Pledged to rise early and to take the way
To Canterbury, as you heard me say.

   But none the less, while I have time and space,
Before my story takes a further pace,

It seems a reasonable thing to say
What their condition was, the full array
Of each of them, as it appeared to me,
According to profession and degree,
And what apparel they were riding in;
And at a Knight I therefore will begin.
There was a *Knight,* a most distinguished man,
Who from the day on which he first began
To ride abroad had followed chivalry,
Truth, honour, generousness and courtesy.
He had done nobly in his sovereign's war
And ridden into battle, no man more,
As well in Christian as in heathen places,
And ever honoured for his noble graces.

   When we took Alexandria, he was there.
He often sat at table in the chair
Of honour, above all nations, when in Prussia.
In Lithuania he had ridden, and Russia,
No Christian man so often, of his rank.
When, in Granada, Algeciras sank
Under assault, he had been there, and in
North Africa, raiding Benamarin;
In Anatolia he had been as well
And fought when Ayas and Attalia fell,
For all along the Mediterranean coast
He had embarked with many a noble host.
In fifteen mortal battles he had been
And jousted for our faith at Tramissene
Thrice in the lists, and always killed his man.
This same distinguished knight had led the van
once with the Bey of Balat, doing work
For him against another heathen Turk;
He was of sovereign value in all eyes.
And though so much distinguished, he was wise
And in his bearing modest as a maid.
He never yet a boorish thing had said
In all his life to any, come what might;
He was a true, a perfect gentle-knight.

   Speaking of his equipment, he possessed
Fine horses, but he was not gaily dressed.
He wore a fustian tunic stained and dark
With smudges where his armour had left mark;
Just home from service, he had joined our ranks
To do his pilgrimage and render thanks.

   He had his son with him, a fine young *Squire,*
A lover and cadet, a lad of fire
With locks as curly as if they had been pressed.
He was some twenty years of age, I guessed.
In stature he was of a moderate length,
With wonderful agility and strength.
He'd seen some service with the cavalry
In Flanders and Artois and Picardy
And had done valiantly in little space
Of time, in hope to win his lady's grace.
He was embroidered like a meadow bright
And full of freshest flowers, red and white.

Singing he was, or fluting all the day;
He was as fresh as is the month of May.
Short was his gown, the sleeves were long and wide;
He knew the way to sit a horse and ride.
He could make songs and poems and recite,
Knew how to joust and dance, to draw and write
He loved so hotly that till dawn grew pale
He slept as little as a nightingale.
Courteous he was, lowly and serviceable,
And carved to serve his father at the table.

   There was a *Yeoman* with him at his side,
No other servant; so he chose to ride.
This Yeoman wore a coat and hood of green,
And peacock-feathered arrows, bright and keen
And neatly sheathed, hung at his belt the while
—For he could dress his gear in yeoman style,
His arrows never drooped their feathers low—
And in his hand he bore a mighty bow.
His head was like a nut, his face was brown.
He knew the whole of woodcraft up and down.
A saucy brace was on his arm to ward
It from the bow-string, and a shield and sword
Hung at one side, and at the other slipped
A jaunty dirk, spear-sharp and well-equipped.
A medal of St. Christopher he wore
Of shining silver on his breast, and bore
A hunting-horn, well slung and burnished clean,
That dangled from a baldrick of bright green.
He was a proper forester, I guess.

   There also was a *Nun,* a Prioress,
Her way of smiling very simple and coy.
Her greatest oath was only "By St. Loy!"
And she was known as Madam Eglantyne.
And well she sang a service, with a fine
Intoning through her nose, as was most seemly,
And she spoke daintily in French, extremely,
After the school of Stratford-atte-Bowe;
French in the Paris style she did not know.
At meat her manners were well taught withal;
No morsel from her lips did she let fall,
Nor dipped her fingers in the sauce too deep;
But she could carry a morsel up and keep
The smallest drop from falling on her breast.
For courtliness she had a special zest,
And she would wipe her upper lip so clean
That not a trace of grease was to be seen
Upon the cup when she had drunk; to eat,
She reached a hand sedately for the meat.
She certainly was very entertaining,
Pleasant and friendly in her ways, and straining
To counterfeit a courtly kind of grace,
A stately bearing fitting to her place,
And to seem dignified in all her dealings.
As for her sympathies and tender feelings,
She was so charitably solicitous
She used to weep if she but saw a mouse

Caught in a trap, if it were dead or bleeding.
And she had little dogs she would be feeding
With roasted flesh, or milk, or fine white bread.
And bitterly she wept if one were dead
Or someone took a stick and made it smart;
She was all sentiment and tender heart.
Her veil was gathered in a seemly way,
Her nose was elegant, her eyes glass-grey;
Her mouth was very small, but soft and red,
Her forehead, certainly, was fair of spread,
Almost a span across the brows, I own;
She was indeed by no means undergrown.
Her cloak, I noticed, had a graceful charm.
She wore a coral trinket on her arm,
A set of beads, the gaudies tricked in green,
Whence hung a golden brooch of brightest sheen
On which there first was graven a crowned A,
And lower, *Amor vincit omnia.*

    Another *Nun,* the secretary at her cell,
Was riding with her, and *three Priests* as well.

    A *Monk* there was, one of the finest sort
Who rode the country; hunting was his sport.
A manly man, to be an Abbot able;
Many a dainty horse fie had in stable.
His bridle, when he rode, a man might hear
Jingling in a whistling wind as clear,
Aye, and as loud as does the chapel bell
Where my lord Monk was Prior of the cell.
The Rule of good St. Benet or St. Maur
As old and strict he tended to ignore;
He let go by the things of yesterday
And took the modern world's more spacious way.
He did not rate that text at a plucked hen
Which says that hunters are not holy men
And that a monk uncloistered is a mere
Fish out of water, flapping on the pier,
That is to say a monk out of his cloister.
That was a text he held not worth an oyster;
And I agreed and said his views were sound;
Was he to study till his head went round
Poring over books in cloisters? Must he toil
As Austin bade and till the very soil?
Was he to leave the world upon the shelf?
Let Austin have his labor to himself.

    This monk was therefore a good man to horse;
Greyhounds he had, as swift as birds, to course.
Hunting a hare or riding at a fence
Was all his fun, he spared for no expense.
saw his sleeves were garnished at the hand
With fine grey fur, the finest in the land,
And on his hood to fasten it at his chin
He had a wrought-gold cunningly fashioned pin;
Into a lover's knot it seemed to pass.
His head was bald and shone like looking-glass;
So did his face, as if it had been greased.
He was a fat and personable priest;

His prominent eyeballs never seemed to settle.
They glittered like the flames beneath a kettle;
Supple his boots, his horse in fine condition.
He was a prelate fit for exhibition,
He was not pale like a tormented soul.
He liked a fat swan best, and roasted whole.
His palfrey was as brown as is a berry.
    There was a *Friar*, a wanton one and merry,
A Limiter, a very festive fellow.
In all Four Orders there was none so mellow,
So glib with gallant phrase and well-turned speech.
He'd fixed up many a marriage, giving each
Of his young women what he could afford her.
He was a noble pillar to his Order.
Highly beloved and intimate was he
With County folk within his boundary,
And city dames of honour and possessions;
For he was qualified to hear confessions,
Or so he said, with more than priestly scope;
He had a special licence from the Pope.
Sweetly he heard his penitents at shrift
With pleasant absolution, for a gift.
He was an easy man in penance-giving
Where he could hope to make a decent living;
It's a sure sign whenever gifts are given
To a poor Order that a man's well shriven,
And should he give enough he knew in verity
The penitent repented in sincerity.
For many a fellow is so hard of heart
He cannot weep, for all his inward smart.
Therefore instead of weeping and of prayer
One should give silver for a poor Friar's care.
He kept his tippet stuffed with pins for curls,
And pocket-knives, to give to pretty girls.
And certainly his voice was gay and sturdy,
For he sang well and played the hurdy-gurdy.
At sing-songs he was champion of the hour.
His neck was whiter than a lily-flower
But strong enough to butt a bruiser down.
He knew the taverns well in every town
And every innkeeper and barmaid too
Better than lepers, beggars and that crew,
For in so eminent a man as he
It was not fitting with the dignity
Of his position, dealing with a scum
Of wretched lepers; nothing good can come
Of commerce with such slum-and-gutter dwellers,
But only with the rich and victual-sellers.
But anywhere a profit might accrue
Courteous he was and lowly of service too.
Natural gifts like his were hard to match.
He was the finest beggar of his batch,
And, for his begging-district, paid a rent;
His brethren did no poaching where he went.
For though a widow mightn't have a shoo,
So pleasant was his holy how-d'ye-do

He got his farthing from her just the same
Before he left, and so his income came
To more than he laid out. And how he romped,
Just like a puppy! He was ever prompt
To arbitrate disputes on settling days
(For a small fee) in many helpful ways,
Not then appearing as your cloistered scholar
With threadbare habit hardly worth a dollar,
But much more like a Doctor or a Pope.
Of double-worsted was the semi-cope
Upon his shoulders, and the swelling fold
About him, like a bell about its mould
When it is casting, rounded out his dress.
He lisped a little out of wantonness
To make his English sweet upon his tongue.
When he had played his harp, or having sung,
His eyes would twinkle in his head as bright
As any star upon a frosty night.
This worthy's name was Hubert, it appeared.

There was a *Merchant* with a forking beard
And motley dress; high on his horse he sat,
Upon his head a Flemish beaver hat
And on his feet daintily buckled boots.
He told of his opinions and pursuits
In solemn tones, he harped on his increase
Of capital; there should be sea-police
(He thought) upon the Harwich-Holland ranges;
He was expert at dabbling in exchanges.
This estimable Merchant so had set
His wits to work, none knew he was in debt,
He was so stately in administration,
In loans and bargains and negotiation.
He was an excellent fellow all the same;
To tell the truth I do not know his name.

An *Oxford Cleric*, still a student though,
One who had taken logic long ago,
Was there; his horse was thinner than a rake,
And he was not too fat, I undertake,
But had a hollow look, a sober stare;
The thread upon his overcoat was bare.
He had found no preferment in the church
And he was too unworldly to make search
For secular employment. By his bed
He preferred having twenty books in red
And black, of Aristotle's philosophy,
Than costly clothes, fiddle or psaltery.
Though a philosopher, as I have told,
He had not found the stone for making gold.
Whatever money from his friends he took
He spent on learning or another book
And prayed for them most earnestly, returning
Thanks to them thus for paying for his learning.
His only care was study, and indeed
He never spoke a word more than was need,
Formal at that, respectful in the extreme,
Short, to the point, and lofty in his theme.

A tone of moral virtue filled his speech
And gladly would he learn, and gladly teach.
　　A *Serjeant at the Law* who paid his calls,
Wary and wise, for clients at St Paul's
There also was, of noted excellence.
Discreet he was, a man to reverence,
Or so he seemed, his sayings were so wise.
He often had been Justice of Assize
By letters patent, and in full commission
His fame and learning and his high position
Had won him many a robe and many a fee.
There was no such conveyancer as he;
All was fee-simple to his strong digestion,
Not one conveyance could be called in question.
Though there was nowhere one so busy as he,
He was less busy than he seemed to be.
He knew of every judgment, case and crime
Ever recorded since King William's time.
He could dictate defences or draft deeds;
No one could pinch a comma from his screeds
And he knew every statute off by rote.
He wore a homely parti-coloured coat,
Girt with a silken belt of pin-stripe stuff;
Of his appearance I have said enough.
　　There was a *Franklin* with him, it appeared;
White as a daisy-petal was his beard.
A sanguine man, high-coloured and benign,
He loved a morning sop of cake in wine.
He lived for pleasure and had always done,
For he was Epicurus' very son,
In whose opinion sensual delight
Was the one true felicity in sight.
As noted as St. Julian was for bounty
He made his household free to all the County.
His bread, his ale were finest of the fine
And no one had a better stock of wine.
His house was never short of bake-meat pies,
Of fish and flesh, and these in such supplies
It positively snowed with meat and drink—
And all the dainties that a man could think.
According to the seasons of the year
Changes of dish were ordered to appear.
He kept fat partridges in coops, beyond,
Many a bream and pike were in his pond.
Woe to the cook, unless the sauce was hot
And sharp, or if he wasn't on the spot!
And in his hall a table stood arrayed
And ready all day long, with places laid.
As Justice at the Sessions none stood higher;
He often had been Member for the Shire.
A dagger and a little purse of silk
Hung at his girdle, white as morning milk.
As Sheriff he checked audit, every entry.
He was a model among landed gentry.
　　A *Haberdasher*, a *Dyer*, a *Carpenter*,
A *Weaver* and a *Carpet-maker* were

Amoung our ranks, all in the livery
Of one impressive guild-fraternity.
They were so trim and fresh their gear would pass
For new. Their knives were not tricked out with brass
But wrought with purest silver, which avouches
A like display on girdles and on pouches.
Each seemed a worthy burgess, fit to grace
A guild-hall with a seat upon the dais.
Their wisdom would have justified a plan
To make each one of them an alderman;
They had the capital and revenue,
Besides their wives declared it was their due.
And if they did not think so, then they ought;
To be called '*Madam*' is a glorious thought,
And so is going to church and being seen
Having your mantle carried, like a queen.

    They had a *Cook* with them who stood alone
For boiling chicken with a marrow-bone,
Sharp flavouring-powder and a spice for savour.
He could distinguish London ale by flavour,
And he could roast and seethe and broil and fry,
Make good thick soup and bake a tasty pie.
But what a pity—so it seemed to me,
That he should have an ulcer on his knee.
As for blancmange, he made it with the best.

    There was a *Skipper* hailing from far west
He came from Dartmouth, so I understood.
He rode a farmer's horse as best he could,
In a woollen gown that reached his knee.
A dagger on a lanyard falling free
Hung from his neck under his arm and down.
The summer heat had tanned his colour brown,
And certainly he was an excellent fellow.
Many a draught of vintage, red and yellow,
He'd drawn at Bordeaux, while the trader snored.
The nicer rules of conscience he ignored.
If, when he fought, the enemy vessel sank,
He sent his prisoners home; they walked the plank.
As for his skill in reckoning his tides,
Currents and many another risk besides,
Moons, harbours, pilots, he had such dispatch
That none from Hull to Carthage was his match.
Hardy he was, prudent in undertaking;
His beard in many a tempest had its shaking,
And he knew all the havens as they were
From Gottland to the Cape of Finisterre,
And every creek in Brittany and Spain;
The barge he owned was called *The Maudelayne*.

    A *Doctor* too emerged as we proceeded;
No one alive could talk as well as he did
On points of medicine and of surgery,
For, being grounded in astronomy,
He watched his patient closely for the hours
When, by his horoscope, he knew the powers
Of favourable planets, then ascendent,
Worked on the images for his dependent.

The cause of every malady you'd got
He knew, and whether dry, cold, moist or hot;
He knew their seat, their humour and condition.
He was a perfect practising physician.
These causes being known for what they were,
He gave the man his medicine then and there.
All his apothecaries in a tribe
Were ready with the drugs he would prescribe
And each made money from the other's guile;
They had been friendly for a goodish while.
He was well-versed in Aesculapius too
And what Hippocrates and Rufus knew
And Dioscorides, now dead and gone,
Galen and Rhazes, Hali, Serapion,
Averroes, Avicenna, Constantine,
Scotch Bernard, John of Gaddesden, Gilbertine.
In his own diet he observed some measure;
There were no superfluities for pleasure,
Only digestives, nutritives and such.
He did not read the Bible very much.
In blood-red garments, slashed with bluish grey
And lined with taffeta, he rode his way;
Yet he was rather close as to expenses
And kept the gold he won in pestilences.
Gold stimulates the heart, or so we're told.
He therefore had a special love of gold.

A worthy *woman* from beside *Bath* city
Was with us, somewhat deaf, which was a pity.
In making cloth she showed so great a bent
She bettered those of Ypres and of Ghent.
In all the parish not a dame dared stir
Towards the altar steps in front of her,
And if indeed they did, so wrath was she
As to be quite put out of charity.
Her kerchiefs were of finely woven ground;
I dared have sworn they weighed a good ten pound,
The ones she wore on Sunday, on her head.
Her hose were of the finest scarlet red
And gartered tight; her shoes were soft and new.
Bold was her face, handsome, and red in hue.
A worthy woman all her life, what's more
She'd had five husbands, all at the church door,
Apart from other company in youth;
No need just now to speak of that, forsooth.
And she had thrice been to Jerusalem,
Seen many strange rivers and passed over them;
She'd been to Rome and also to Boulogne,
St. James of Compostella and Cologne,
And she was skilled in wandering by the way.
She had gap-teeth, set widely, truth to say.
Easily on an ambling horse she sat
Well wimpled up, and on her head a hat
As broad as is a buckler or a shield;
She had a flowing mantle that concealed
Large hips, her heels spurred sharply under that.
In company she liked to laugh and chat

And knew the remedies for love's mischances,
An art in which she knew the oldest dances.
    A holy-minded man of good renown
There was, and poor, the *Parson* to a town,
Yet he was rich in holy thought and work.
He also was a learned man, a clerk,
Who truly knew Christ's gospel and would preach it
Devoutly to parishioners, and teach it.
Benign and wonderfully diligent,
And patient when adversity was sent
(For so he proved in much adversity)
He hated cursing to extort a fee,
Nay rather he preferred beyond a doubt
Giving to poor parishioners round about
Both from church offerings and his property;
He could in little find sufficiency.
Wide was his parish, with houses far asunder,
Yet he neglected not in rain or thunder,
In sickness or in grief, to pay a call
On the remotest, whether great or small,
Upon his feet, and in his hand a stave.
This noble example to his sheep he gave
That first he wrought, and afterwards he taught;
And it was from the Gospel he had caught
Those words, and he would add this figure too,
That if gold rust, what then will iron do?
For if a priest be foul in whom we trust
No wonder that a common man should rust;
And shame it is to see—let priests take stock—
A shitten shepherd and a snowy flock.
The true example that a priest should give
Is one of cleanness, how the sheep should live.
He did not set his benefice to hire
And leave his sheep encumbered in the mire
Or run to London to earn easy bread
By singing masses for the wealthy dead,
Or find some Brotherhood and get enrolled.
He stayed at home and watched over his fold
So that no wolf should make the sheep miscarry.
He was a shepherd and no mercenary.
Holy and virtuous he was, but then
Never contemptuous of sinful men,
Never disdainful, never too proud or fine,
But was discreet in teaching and benign.
His business was to show a fair behaviour
And draw men thus to Heaven and their Saviour,
Unless indeed a man were obstinate;
And such, whether of high or low estate,
He put to sharp rebuke, to say the least.
I think there never was a better priest.
He sought no pomp or glory in his dealings,
No scrupulosity had spiced his feelings.
Christ and His Twelve Apostles and their lore
He taught, but followed it himself before.
    There was a *Plowman* with him there, his brother;
Many a load of dung one time or other

He must have carted through the morning dew.
He was an honest worker, good and true,
Living in peace and perfect charity,
And, as the gospel bade him, so did he,
Loving God best with all his heart and mind
And then his neighbour as himself, repined
At no misfortune, slacked for no content,
For steadily about his work he went
To thrash his corn, to dig or to manure
Or make a ditch; and he would help the poor
For love of Christ and never take a penny
If he could help it, and, as prompt as any,
He paid his tithes in full when they were due
On what he owned, and on his earnings too.
He wore a tabard smock and rode a mare.

    There was a *Reeve*, also a *Miller*, there,
A College *Manciple* from the Inns of Court,
A papal *Pardoner* and, in close consort,
A Church-Court *Summoner*, riding at a trot,
And finally myself—that was the lot.

    The *Miller* was a chap of sixteen stone,
A great stout fellow big in brawn and bone.
He did well out of them, for he could go
And win the ram at any wrestling show.
Broad, knotty and short-shouldered, he would boast
He could heave any door off hinge and post,
Or take a run and break it with his head.
His beard, like any sow or fox, was red
And broad as well, as though it were a spade;
And, at its very tip, his nose displayed
A wart on which there stood a tuft of hair
Red as the bristles in an old sow's ear.
His nostrils were as black as they were wide.
He had a sword and buckler at his side,
His mighty mouth was like a furnace door.
A wrangler and buffoon, he had a store
Of tavern stories, filthy in the main.
His was a master-hand at stealing grain.
He felt it with his thumb and thus he knew
Its quality and took three times his due—
A thumb of gold, by God, to gauge an oat!
He wore a hood of blue and a white coat.
He liked to play his bagpipes up and down
And that was how he brought us out of town.

    The *Manciple* came from the Inner Temple;
All caterers might follow his example
In buying victuals; he was never rash
Whether he bought on credit or paid cash.
He used to watch the market most precisely
And got in first, and so he did quite nicely,
Now isn't it a marvel of God's grace
That an illiterate fellow can outpace
The wisdom of a heap of learned men?
His masters—he had more than thirty then—
All versed in the abstrusest legal knowledge,
Could have produced a dozen from their College

Fit to be stewards in land and rents and game
To any Peer in England you could name,
And show him how to live on what he had
Debt-free (unless of course the Peer were mad)
or be as frugal as he might desire,
And make them fit to help about the Shire
in any legal case there was to try;
And yet this Manciple could wipe their eye.
    The *Reeve* was old and choleric and thin;
His beard was shaven closely to the skin,
His shorn hair came abruptly to a stop
Above his ears, and he was docked on top
just like a priest in front; his legs were lean,
Like sticks they were, no calf was to be seen.
He kept his bins and garners very trim;
No auditor could gain a point on him.
And he could judge by watching drought and rain
The yield he might expect from seed and grain.
His master's sheep, his animals and hens,
Pigs, horses, dairies, stores and cattle-pens
Were wholly trusted to his government.
He had been under contract to present
The accounts, right from his master's earliest years.
No one had ever caught him in arrears.
No bailiff, serf or herdsman dared to kick,
He knew their dodges, knew their every trick;
Feared like the plague he was, by those beneath.
He had a lovely dwelling on a heath,
Shadowed in green by trees above the sward.
A better hand at bargains than his lord,
He had grown rich and had a store of treasure
Well tucked away, yet out it came to pleasure
His lord with subtle loans or gifts of goods,
To earn his thanks and even coats and hoods.
When young he'd learnt a useful trade and still
He was a carpenter of first-rate skill.
The stallion-cob he rode at a slow trot
Was dapple-grey and bore the name of Scot.
He wore an overcoat of bluish shade
And rather long; he had a rusty blade
Slung at his side. He came, as I heard tell,
From Norfolk, near a place called Baldeswell.
His coat was tucked under his belt and splayed.
He rode the hindmost of our cavalcade.
    There was a *Summoner* with us at that Inn,
His face on fire, like a cherubin,
For he had carbuncles. His eyes were narrow,
He was as hot and lecherous as a sparrow.
Black scabby brows he had, and a thin beard.
Children were afraid when he appeared.
No quicksilver, lead ointment, tartar creams,
No brimstone, no boracic, so it seems,
Could make a salve that had the power to bite,
Clean up or cure his whelks of knobby white
Or purge the pimples sitting on his cheeks.
Garlic he loved, and onions too, and leeks,

And drinking strong red wine till all was hazy.
Then he would shout and jabber as if crazy,
And wouldn't speak a word except in Latin
When he was drunk, such tags as he was pat in;
He only had a few, say two or three,
That he had mugged up out of some decree;
No wonder, for he heard them every day.
And, as you know, a man can teach a jay
To call out "Walter" better than the Pope.
But had you tried to test his wits and grope
For more, you'd have found nothing in the bag.
Then *"Questio quid juris"* was his tag.
He was a noble varlet and a kind one,
You'd meet none better if you went to find one.
Why, he'd allow— just for a quart of wine—
Any good lad to keep a concubine
A twelvemonth and dispense him altogether!
And he had finches of his own to feather:
And if he found some rascal with a maid
He would instruct him not to be afraid
In such a case of the Archdeacon's curse
(Unless the rascal's soul were in his purse)
For in his purse the punishment should be.
"Purse is the good Archdeacon's Hell," said he.
But well I know he lied in what he said;
A curse should put a guilty man in dread,
For curses kill, as shriving brings, salvation.
We should beware of excommunication.
Thus, as he pleased, the man could bring duress
On any young fellow in the diocese.
He knew their secrets, they did what he said.
He wore a garland set upon his head
Large as the holly-bush upon a stake
Outside an ale-house, and he had a cake,
A round one, which it was his joke to wield
As if it were intended for a shield.

  He and a gentle *Pardoner* rode together,
A bird from Charing Cross of the same feather,
Just back from visiting the Court of Rome.
He loudly sang *"Come hither, love, come home!"*
The Summoner sang deep seconds to this song,
No trumpet ever sounded half so strong.
This Pardoner had hair as yellow as wax,
Hanging down smoothly like a hank of flax.
In driblets fell his locks behind his head
Down to his shoulders which they overspread;
Thinly they fell, like rat-tails, one by one.
He wore no hood upon his head, for fun;
The hood inside his wallet had been stowed,
He aimed at riding in the latest mode;
But for a little cap his head was bare
And he had bulging eye-balls, like a hare.
He'd sewed a holy relic on his cap;
His wallet lay before him on his lap,
Brimful of pardons come from Rome, all hot.
He had the same small voice a goat has got.

His chin no beard had harboured, nor would harbour,
Smoother than ever chin was left by barber.
I judge he was a gelding, or a mare.
As to his trade, from Berwick down to Ware
There was no pardoner of equal grace,
For in his trunk he had a pillow-case
Which he asserted was Our Lady's veil.
He said he had a gobbet of the sail
Saint Peter had the time when he made bold
To walk the waves, till Jesu Christ took hold.
He bad a cross of metal set with stones
And, in a glass, a rubble of pigs' bones.
And with these relics, any time he found
Some poor up-country parson to astound,
In one short day, in money down, he drew
More than the parson in a month or two,
And by his flatteries and prevarication
Made monkeys of the priest and congregation.
But still to do him justice first and last
In church he was a noble ecclesiast.
How well he read a lesson or told a story!
But best of all he sang an Offertory,
For well he knew that when that song was sung
He'd have to preach and tune his honey-tongue
And (well he could) win silver from the crowd.
That's why he sang so merrily and loud.
    Now I have told you shortly, in a clause,
The rank, the array, the number and the cause
Of our assembly in this company
In Southwark, at that high-class hostelry
Known as *The Tabard*, close beside *The Bell*.
And now the time has come for me to tell
How we behaved that evening; I'll begin
After we had alighted at the Inn,
Then I'll report our journey, stage by stage,
All the remainder of our pilgrimage.
But first I beg of you, in courtesy,
Not to condemn me as unmannerly
If I speak plainly and with no concealings
And give account of all their words and dealings,
Using their very phrases as they fell.
For certainly, as you all know so well,
He who repeats a tale after a man
Is bound to say, as nearly as he can,
Each single word, if he remembers it,
However rudely spoken or unfit,
Or else the tale he tells will be untrue,
The things pretended and the phrases new.
He may not flinch although it were his brother,
He may as well say one word as another.
And Christ Himself spoke broad in Holy Writ,
Yet there is no scurrility in it,
And Plato says, for those with power to read,
"The word should be as cousin to the deed."
Further I beg you to forgive it me
If I neglect the order and degree

And what is due to rank in what I've planned.
I'm short of wit as you will understand.
 Our *Host* gave us great welcome; everyone
Was given a place and supper was begun.
He served the finest victuals you could think,
The wine was strong and we were glad to drink.
A very striking man our Host withal,
And fit to be a marshal in a hall.
His eyes were bright, his girth a little wide;
There is no finer burgess in Cheapside.
Bold in his speech, yet wise and full of tact,
There was no manly attribute he lacked,
What's more he was a merry-hearted man.
After our meal he jokingly began
To talk of sport, and, among other things
After we'd settled up our reckonings,
He said as follows: "Truly, gentlemen,
You're very welcome and I can't think when
—Upon my word I'm telling you no lie—
I've seen a gathering here that looked so spry,
No, not this year, as in this tavern now.
I'd think you up some fun if I knew how.
And, as it happens, a thought has just occurred
To please you, costing nothing, on my word.
You're off to Canterbury—well, God speed!
Blessed St. Thomas answer to your need!
And I don't doubt, before the journey's done
You mean to while the time in tales and fun.
Indeed, there's little pleasure for your bones
Riding along and all as dumb as stones.
So let me then propose for your enjoyment,
Just as I said, a suitable employment.
And if my notion suits and you agree
And promise to submit yourselves to me
Playing your parts exactly as I say
Tomorrow as you ride along the way,
Then by my father's soul (and he is dead)
If you don't like it you can have my head!
Hold up your hands, and not another word."
 Well, our opinion was not long deferred,
It seemed not worth a serious debate;
We all agreed to it at any rate
And bade him issue what commands he would.
"My lords," he said, "now listen for your good,
And please don't treat my notion with disdain.
This is the point. I'll make it short and plain.
Each one of you shall help to make things slip
By telling two stories on the outward trip
To Canterbury, that's what I intend,
And, on the homeward way to journey's end
Another two, tales from the days of old;
And then the man whose story is best told,
That is to say who gives the fullest measure
Of good morality and general pleasure,
He shall be given a supper, paid by all,
Here in this tavern, in this very hall,

When we come back again from Canterbury.
And in the hope to keep you bright and merry
I'll go along with you myself and ride
All at my own expense and serve as guide.
I'll be the judge, and those who won't obey
Shall pay for what we spend upon the way.
Now if you all agree to what you've heard
Tell me at once without another word,
And I will make arrangements early for it."

   Of course we all agreed, in fact we swore it
Delightedly, and made entreaty too
That he should act as he proposed to do,
Become our Governor in short, and be
Judge of our tales and general referee,
And set the supper at a certain price.
We promised to be ruled by his advice
Come high, come low; unanimously thus
We set him up in judgement over us.
More wine was fetched, the business being done;
We drank it off and up went everyone
To bed without a moment of delay.

   Early next morning at the spring of day
Up rose our Host and roused us like a cock,
Gathering us together in a flock,
And off we rode at slightly faster pace
Than walking to St. Thomas' watering-place;
And there our Host drew up, began to ease
His horse, and said, "Now, listen if you please,
My lords! Remember what you promised me.
If evensong and mattins will agree
Let's see who shall be first to tell a tale.
And as I hope to drink good wine and ale
I'll be your judge. The rebel who disobeys,
However much the journey costs, he pays.
Now draw for cut and then we can depart;
The man who draws the shortest cut shall start.
My Lord the Knight," he said, "step up to me
And draw your cut, for that is my decree.
And come you near, my Lady Prioress,
And you, Sir Cleric, drop your shamefastness,
No studying now! A hand from every man!"
Immediately the draw for lots began
And to tell shortly how the matter went,
Whether by chance or fate or accident,
The truth is this, the cut fell to the Knight,
Which everybody greeted with delight.
And tell his tale he must, as reason was
Because of our agreement and because
He too had sworn. What more is there to say?
For when this good man saw how matters lay,
Being by wisdom and obedience driven
To keep a promise he had freely given,
He said, "Since it's for me to start the game,
Why, welcome be the cut in God's good name
Now let us ride, and listen to what I say."
And at the word we started on our way

And in a cheerful style he then began
At once to tell his tale, and thus it ran.

The Miller

Words between the Host and the Miller

When the Knight had thus told his tale,
in all that company there was no one, young or old,
who did not say it was a noble story,
and worthy to be remembered,
particularly the gentlefolk, each and every one.
Our Host laughed, and swore, "As I may walk,
this goes well: the pouch is unbuckled.
Now let's see who shall tell another tale,
for the game is indeed well begun.
Now, sir Monk, if you can, tell
something to repay the Knight's tale."
The Miller, who was all pale with drunkenness,
so that he could hardly sit on his horse,
was not minded to doff his hood or hat
nor wait on any man for courtesy's sake,
but began to cry out in a voice like Pilate's,
and swore, "By God's arms and blood and bones,
I know a splendid tale for the occasion,
with which I'll now match the Knight's tale!"
    Our Host saw that he was drunk with ale,
and said, "Wait, Robin, my dear brother;
first some better man shall tell us another.
Wait, and let us do things properly."
    "By God's soul," said he, "that I will not;
for I will speak or else go on my way."
Our Host answered, "Tell on, in the devil's name!
You are a fool; your wits are drowned."
    "Now listen," said the Miller, "everyone.
But first I will proclaim that
I am drunk; I know it by the sound of my voice.
And therefore, if I speak amiss,
blame it on the ale of Southwark, I pray you;
for I am going to tell a legend, a history,
of both a carpenter and his wife,
and how a clerk made a fool of the carpenter."
    The Reeve answered and said, "Stop your gabble!
Leave off your stupid, drunken obscenity.
It is sinful and very foolish
to injure any man or defame him,
and also to bring wives into such repute.
You can say enough about other things."
    This drunken Miller replied at once,

and said, "Dear brother Oswald,
he who has no wife is no cuckold.
But I don't say that therefore you are one;
there are a great many good wives,
and always a thousand good ones to one bad one;
you know that perfectly well yourself, unless you're crazy.
Why are you angry with my story now?
I have a wife by God, just as you do;
yet I wouldn't, for the oxen in my plow,
take more than enough on myself so
as to think that I am a cuckold;
I will believe firmly that I am none.
A husband should not be inquisitive
about God's secrets—or his wife's.
just so I can find God's plenty there,
there's no need to inquire about the rest."
What more should I say but that this Miller
would not spare his words for any man,
but told his churl's tale in his own way.
I regret that I must repeat it here,
and therefore I ask every well-bred person,
for God's love, don't think that I speak
with evil intentions; but I must repeat
all their tales, be they better or worse,
or else be false to some of my material.
And therefore whoever does not wish to hear it,
turn over the leaf and choose another tale;
for he shall find enough, long and short,
of narratives that deal with nobility,
and also morality and holiness.
Don't blame me if you choose amiss.
The Miller is a churl, you know this well;
so was the Reeve, and some of the others.
Both of them recited ribaldry.
Take heed, and don't put the blame on me;
and then, too, one should not take a game seriously.

Here begins the Miller's tale

Once upon a time there lived at Oxford
a rich churl who boarded paying guests;
he was a carpenter by trade.
At his house lived a poor scholar
who had completed part of his arts course, but his whole
imagination was directed to learning astrology.
He knew a number of propositions
by which to make a decision in astrological analyses
in certain hours if you asked him
when you would have drought or else showers,
or if you asked him what should come
of all sorts of things; I can't mention all of them.
This clerk was named pleasant Nicholas;
he knew all about secret love and pleasurable consolations,
and, besides, he was sly and very discreet
and looked as meek as a maiden.
In that boarding house he had a room,

alone, without further company,
and nicely decked with fragrant herbs;
and he himself was as sweet and clean as the root
of licorice or any ginger.
His *Almagest* and books large and small,
his astrolabe, proper to his art,
and his counters for arithmetic lay neatly separated
on shelves set at the head of his bed;
his storage chest was covered with a red woolen cloth.
At the top there lay a pretty psaltery
on which by night he made melody
so sweetly that all the room rang with it;
he sang *Angelus ad virginem,*
and after that he sang the King's Tune;
people often blessed his merry voice.
And thus this sweet clerk spent his time,
depending upon his friends' support and his income.
    This carpenter had recently married a wife
whom he loved more than his life;
she was eighteen years of age.
He was jealous and kept her on a short leash,
for she was wild and young, and he was old,
and judged himself near to being a cuckold.
He did not know (for his understanding was crude) Cato's
saying that a man should marry someone like himself:
people should wed according to their condition,
for youth and age are often at odds.
But since he had fallen into the trap,
he had to endure his trouble, like other people.
    This young wife was lovely;
her body was as graceful and slim as a weasel's.
She wore a sash threaded with silk,
and around her loins a flared apron
white as morning-fresh milk;
her smock was white, and embroidered with
black silk around the collar,
inside and outside, front and back.
The ribbons of her cap
matched her collar,
and her broad silk headband sat well back from her face.
And—certainly—she had a wanton eye.
Her eyebrows were closely plucked,
and they arched gracefully and were black as a sloe.
She was more of a treat to look at
than a peartree, just come into bloom,
and she was softer to touch than the wool of a sheep.
At her waist hung a leather purse,
tasseled with silk and beaded in bright metal.
In all this world, if you search up and down,
you can find no man clever enough to imagine
so gay a poppet or such a wench. The brilliance
of her coloring was better than the gleam of a
gold noble newly minted in the Tower of London.
As for her singing, it was as clear and lively
as the notes of a barn swallow.
Besides all this, she could gambol and play

like any kid or calf following his mother.
Her mouth was as sweet as drinks made from honey,
or as a hoard of apples laid away in hay or heather.
She was skittish as a colt,
tall as a mast, and straight as an arrow.
On her low collar she wore a brooch
as broad as the boss of a buckler.
Her shoes were laced far up her legs.
She was a morning glory, she was a daisy,
fit for any lord to lay in his bed,
or yet for any good yeoman to marry.

    Now sir, and again sir, the case so befell
that one day this pleasant Nicholas
happened to flirt and play with this young wife
while her husband was at Osney
(these clerks are very subtle and sly),
and privily he grabbed her where he shouldn't
and said, "Unless I have my will of you,
sweetheart, I'm sure to die for suppressed love."
And he held her hard by the hips
and said, "Sweetheart, love me right away
or I'll die, so God help me!"
She jumped like a colt imprisoned in a shoeing frame
and twisted her head away hard
and said, "I won't kiss you, on my faith;
why let be," she said, "let be, Nicholas,
or I'll cry 'Help!' and 'Alas!'
Take away your hands; where are your manners!"

    This Nicholas started begging for mercy
and spoke so prettily and pushed himself so hard
that she finally granted him her love
and made her oath, by Saint Thomas à Becket,
that she would be his to command
when she could see her opportunity.
"My husband is so filled with jealousy
that, unless you are on guard and keep it a secret,
I know for sure that I'm as good as dead," she said.
"You must be very discreet in this matter."

    "No, don't bother about that," said Nicholas,
"A clerk would certainly have spent his time poorly
if he couldn't fool a carpenter."
And thus they agreed and promised
to look out for an occasion, as I told before.
When Nicholas had accomplished all this,
and patted her thoroughly about the loins,
he kissed her sweetly, and took his psaltery
and played it hard and made music.

    Then it happened that this good wife
went to the parish church on a holy day
to perform Christ's own works:
her forehead shone as bright as day,
it had been washed so thoroughly when she left her work.

    Now, there was a parish clerk of that church
who was called Absalom.
His hair was curly and shone like gold
and spread out like a big, wide fan;

the pretty parting of his hair lay straight and even,
his complexion was red, his eyes as gray as a goose;
he went very elegantly in red hose,
with St. Paul's window tooled into his shoes.
He was dressed very properly and with a close fit
in a light blue tunic;
its laces were set in neatly and close together.
In addition he had a handsome surplice
as white as a blossom on the bough.
He was a merry lad, God help me.
He well knew how to let blood, to clip hair, and to shave,
and how to draw up a charter of land or a release.
He could trip and dance twenty different ways
according to the then manner of Oxford
and prance to and fro on his legs,
and play song tunes on a small fiddle
(he sometimes sang the high treble loudly);
and he could play as well on his guitar.
There wasn't a beer house or tavern in the whole town
that he didn't visit with his entertainment,
if there was any gay barmaid there.
But, to tell the truth, he was a little squeamish
about farting and prim in his speech.
   This Absalom, who was lively and playful,
went with a censer on the holy day
censing the wives of the parish zealously,
and many a loving look he cast upon them,
particularly on the carpenter's wife:
looking at her seemed a merry life to him,
she was so neat and sweet and appetizing.
I daresay that if she had been a mouse
and he a cat, he would have grabbed her right away.
Jolly Absalom, this parish clerk,
had such love longing in his heart
that he accepted no offering from any wife;
he said that he wouldn't for the sake of his manners.
   When night came, the moon shone brightly
and Absalom took his guitar,
for he planned to stay up as lovers do.
Forth he went, lusty and amorous,
until he came to the carpenter's house
a little after cockcrow,
and took his stand by a hinged window
in the carpenter's wall.
He sang in his refined, dainty voice,
"Now, dear lady, if it be your will,
I pray you to take pity on me,"
nicely in tune with his playing.
The carpenter woke up and heard him sing
and spoke to his wife saying,
"Why, Alison, don't you hear Absalom
singing that way below our chamber wall?"
And she thereupon answered her husband,
"Yes; God knows, John, I hear every bit of it."
   So things went on. What do you want better than good
enough? From day to day this pretty Absalom

wooed her until he was woebegone:
he stayed awake all night and all day;
he combed his wide-spreading locks and made himself look
pretty; he wooed her by go-betweens and proxy
and swore he would be her own page;
he sang quaveringly, like a nightingale;
he sent her sweetened wine, mead, spiced ale,
and pastries piping hot out of the coals;
and (since she was a townswoman) he offered bribes.
For some will be won with riches,
some with blows, and some with kindness.
    Once, to show his agility and skill,
he played Herod on a high scaffold.
But what use was anything to him in this case?
She loved pleasant Nicholas so much
that Absalom could go whistle to the wind;
he earned nothing but scorn for his labors;
thus she made a monkey of Absalom
and turned all his seriousness into a joke.
There's no doubt that this proverb is very true;
men say just this: "Always the nearby sly one
makes the distant dear one to be hated."
Though Absalom may be raging and furious
because he was far from her sight,
this nearby Nicholas stood in his light.
    Now play your part well, you pleasant Nicholas,
for Absalom may wail and sing "Alas."
And so it happened on a Saturday
that this carpenter had gone to Osney;
and pleasant Nicholas and Alison
agreed to this effect,
that Nicholas should invent himself a trick
to fool this simple-minded, jealous husband;
and if the game went right,
she would sleep in his arms all night,
for this was his desire, and hers, too.
Right away, without another word,
Nicholas wouldn't stand for further tarrying
but very quietly carried to his room
both food and drink for a day or two,
and told her to say to her husband
if he asked for Nicholas
that she didn't know where he was—
that she hadn't laid eyes on him all that day;
and that she imagined he was sick,
for her maid couldn't rouse him, no matter how she shouted;
he wouldn't answer, no matter what happened.
    It followed that all that Saturday
and until sundown on Sunday
Nicholas stayed quiet in his room
and ate and slept, or did whatever he wanted.
    This foolish carpenter was astonished
at Nicholas and wondered what ailed him;
he said, "By St. Thomas, I am afraid
that things aren't right with Nicholas.
God forbid that he should die suddenly!

This world now is very ticklish, in truth:
I saw a corpse being borne to church today,
and just last Monday I saw the man going about his business.
Go up," he said then to his servant,
"call at his door or knock with a stone.
See how matters stand, and tell me straight out."
   This servant went up sturdily,
and as he stood at the chamber door
he shouted and knocked like mad.
"How now, what are you doing, Master Nicholas?
How can you sleep all day long?"
   But all for nothing; he heard not a word.
He found a hole low down on one of the boards
where the cat was accustomed to creep in,
and he looked far in there;
at last he had a sight of him.
Nicholas sat there, continuously gaping up in the air,
as though he were gazing at the new moon.
The servant went down and soon told his master
in what state he had seen this man.
   The carpenter set to crossing himself
and said, "Help us, Saint Frideswide!
A man little knows what is going to happen to him.
This man has fallen, with his astromy,
into some madness or fit;
I always thought it would be this way!—
men shouldn't pry into the secret things of God.
Yea, ever blessed be an unschooled man
who knows nothing but his creed.
Another clerk fared the same way with astromy:
he walked in the fields to pry
upon the stars and find out what was to occur
until he fell into a pit of fertilizer—
he didn't see that. And yet, by St. Thomas,
I sorely pity pleasant Nicholas.
He shall be scolded for his studying
if I can do it, by Jesus, heaven's king!
Get me a staff, so that I can pry underneath
while you, Robin, heave up the door.
He shall come out of his studying, I'll bet."
And he began to apply himself to the chamber door.
His servant was a strong fellow for the purpose,
and he heaved it up at once by the hasp:
the door then fell on the floor.
Nicholas continued to sit as still as stone
and kept gaping up in the air.
The carpenter thought that Nicholas was in a fit,
and seized him strongly by the shoulders
and shook him hard, crying roughly.
"What! Nicholas, what! Look down!
Awake, and think on Christ's Passion!
I sign you with the cross against elves and evil creatures."
Then he immediately said the night charm
toward the four quarters of the house
and on the threshold of the outside door:
   "Jesus Christ and Saint Benedict,

bless this house against every wicked creature;
let the White Pater Noster defend us by night.
　　Where did you go, Saint Peter's sister?"
At last pleasant Nicholas
began to sigh sorely and said, "Alas,
shall all this world now be lost again?"
　　The carpenter answered, "What are you saying?
How now! Think on God, as we do—we men that work."
　　Nicholas answered, "Bring me something to drink,
and afterwards I want to speak in private
of a certain thing that concerns you and me;
I won't tell it to another man, for sure."
　　The carpenter went down and came up again,
bringing a generous quart of strong ale;
and when each of them had drunk his share.
Nicholas shut his door tight
and sat the carpenter down beside him.
　　He said, "John, my beloved and esteemed host,
you shall swear to me here on your word of honor
that you will not betray this secret to any creature;
for it is Christ's secret that I am going to utter,
and if you tell it to anyone, you are lost,
because for doing so you shall suffer this vengeance:
if you betray me, You shall go mad."
"No, Christ forbid it for the sake of his holy blood!"
said this simple man, "I am no blabber;
no, though I say it myself, I don't like to gossip.
Say what you will, I shall never tell it
to child or wife, by Him Who harrowed hell."
　　"Now, John," said Nicholas, "I won't lie;
I have discovered in my astrology,
as I was looking at the bright moon,
that on Monday next, when a quarter of the night is still
to go, there shall fall a rain, so wild and furious
that Noah's flood was never half so great.
In less than an hour," he said, "this world
shall be drowned, so hideous will be the downpour;
thus all mankind shall drown and lose their lives."
　　The carpenter answered, "Alas, my wife!
Shall she drown? Alas, my Alison!"
For his sorrow at this he almost collapsed,
and said, "Is there no remedy in this matter?"
　　"Why, yes, indeed, by God," said pleasant Nicholas,
"if you will act according to learning and advice—
you may not act according to your own idea;
for thus says Solomon, who was very truthful,
'Do everything according to advice and you will not be sorry.'
And if you will act on good advice,
I promise that, without mast or sail,
I shall yet save her and you and myself.
Haven't you heard how Noah was saved
when our Lord had forewarned him
that all the world should be lost by water?"
　　"Certainly," said the carpenter, "long ago."
　　"Haven't you heard also," said Nicholas,
"of the anxiety of Noah and his companions

until he could get his wife on board?
I'll bet that that time he would rather have
had her have a ship to herself
than keep all his fine black wethers.
And do you know what's best to do for all this?
This requires haste, and about an urgent matter
you mayn't preach or make delay.

   Go promptly and bring right into this inn
a kneading trough, or else a shallow tub,
Or each of us, but be sure they are large ones,
in which we can float as in a ship,
and have in them victuals enough
Or a day only—fie on the rest!
The water shall diminish and go away
about nine in the morning the next day.

   But Robin, your servant, may not know of this,
and I mayn't save Jill, your maid, either;
don't ask why, for even if you do,
I won't reveal God's private affairs.
It is enough for you, unless you are mad,
to have as great grace as Noah had.
I shall indeed save your wife, beyond a doubt.
Now go your way, and hurry about our business.

   But when, for her and yourself and me, you have
got us these three kneading tubs,
then you are to hang them high up in the roof,
so that no one will spy out our preparations.
And when you've done as I have said,
and have stowed our victuals in them safely,
and an axe, too, to cut the rope in two
when the water comes, so that we may float,
and when you've broken a hole high up on the gable
toward the garden and over the stable,
so that we can get out freely on our way
when the great rain is over—
then you'll float as merrily, I promise,
as the white duck does afar her drake.
Then I'll call out, 'How now, Alison! How now, John!
Cheer up; the flood will go away soon,'
and you will say, 'Hail, Master Nicholas!
Good morning, I see you well, it's light.'
And then we shall be lords for all our lives
of all the world, like Noah and his wife.

   But I caution you about one thing for sure:
be well forewarned that on that same night
when we have gone on shipboard,
none of us speak a word,
or call, or cry out, but he in prayer,
for it is God's own precious command.

   Your wife and you must hang far apart
so that there shall be no sin between you,
any more in looking than in deed.
Our arrangement has been described; go, Godspeed.
Tomorrow night, when everyone is asleep,
we'll creep into our kneading tubs
and sit there, awaiting God's grace.

Now go on your way, I have no more time
to make a longer sermon of this
People speak thus, 'Send the wise and say nothing';
you are so wise that there is no need to teach you:
go, save our lives, I beseech you."
　　The foolish carpenter went his way.
Often he said, "Alas" and "Alack,"
and he told his secret to his wife;
she was aware of it, and knew better than he
what all this elaborate contrivance amounted to.
Nevertheless, she behaved as though she would die,
and said, "Alas! Go your way immediately,
help us to escape, or we are lost, each one of us.
I am your faithful, true, wedded wife:
go, dear spouse, and help to save our lives."
　　Look what a great thing emotion is!
One may die by force of imagining things,
so deeply may a notion be imprinted.
This foolish carpenter began to shake;
he thinks in truth that he can see
Noah's flood come surging like the sea
to drown Alison, his honey-dear.
He weeps, wails, looks mournful;
he sighs with many a sorry gust;
he went and got himself a kneading trough,
and after that two tubs,
and secretly he sent them to his inn
and hung them under the roof in privacy.
With his own hand he made three ladders
on which they might climb by the rungs and uprights
to the tubs hanging in the rafters,
and victualed both trough and tub
with bread and cheese and good ale in a jug,
quite sufficient for a day.
But before he installed all this array,
he sent his manservant, and also the girl,
to go to London on an errand for him.
On Monday, when night drew on,
he shut his door without lighting any candles
and arranged everything as it was supposed to be.
And, shortly, they climbed up all three;
they sat still for the time it takes to go a furlong.
　　"Now, *Pater Noster*, hush!" said Nicholas,
and "Hush," said John, and "Hush," said Alison.
The carpenter recited his devotions,
and sat still, offering his prayers
and waiting to see whether he might hear the rain.
　　Wearied by his own diligence, the carpenter
fell into a dead sleep—as I judge, just
about curfew time, or a little later.
He groaned painfully for the affliction of his spirit,
and then he snored, for his head lay uncomfortably.
Nicholas crept down from the ladder
and Alison hurried down very softly;
without more words they went to bed
where the carpenter was wont to lie.

There was the revel and the harmony,
and thus lay Alison and Nicholas
in diligence of mirth and pleasure
until the bell of Lauds began to ring
and friars began to sing in the chancel.

   The parish clerk, this amorous Absalom,
who was always so woebegone for love,
was at Osney on Monday
to have a good time with company;
he chanced to ask a member of the order
very secretly about John the carpenter;
the man drew him apart, out of the church,
and said, "I don't know, I haven't seen him doing anything
here since Saturday; I imagine that he went
for timber where our abbot sent him,
for he is accustomed to go for timber
and stay at the farm for a day or two;
or else he's certainly at home;
I cannot truthfully say where he is."

   This Absalom grew frolicsome and lighthearted,
and thought, "Now is the time to stay up all night,
for surely I haven't seen him stirring
about his door since dawn.
As I may thrive, at cockcrow I shall
knock very secretly at the window
that is quite low in the wall of his bedchamber.
Now I'll tell Alison all
my love-sickness, for still it won't fail
at the very least that I'll kiss her.
I shall have some kind of comfort, for sure.
My mouth has itched all this livelong day;
that is a sign of kissing, at least.
Besides, I dreamed all night that I was at a feast.
Therefore, I'll go sleep for an hour or two,
and then I'll stay up and amuse myself all night."

   When the first cock had crowed, then
rose up this lusty lover Absalom,
and dressed himself handsomely to perfection.
But first he chewed cardamon and licorice,
in order to smell sweet, before he combed his hair.
He carried a sprig of clover, under his tongue,
for by its means he expected to be pleasing.
He strolled to the carpenter's house
and stood quietly under the hinged window—
it reached only to his chest, it was so low—
and he coughed softly with a small sound.
"What do you, honeycomb, sweet Alison?
My fair bird, sweet cinnamon,
awake, my sweetheart, and speak to me.
Little do you think of my woe, which is
so great that I sweat upon the ground as I walk.
It is no wonder though I melt and sweat:
I yearn as does the lamb for the teat.
Indeed, sweetheart, I have such love-sickness
that my mourning is like that of the faithful turtledove;
I may not eat any more than a girl."

"Go away from the window, Jack-fool," she said.
"So help me God, it won't be 'come-kiss-me.'
By Jesus, Absalom, I love another a lot better
than you, and otherwise I'd be to blame.
Go your way or I'll throw a stone,
and let me sleep, in the name of twenty devils!"
    "Alas," said Absalom, "and alack
that ever true love was so ill-used.
Kiss me, then—since it may be no better—
for Jesus' love and love of me."
    "Will you go your way then?" she said.
    "Yes, certainly, sweetheart," said Absalom.
    "Then get ready," she said, "I'm coming right away."
And she said quietly to Nicholas,
"Now keep quiet, and you shall laugh your fill."
    Absalom got down on his knees,
and said, "I am a lord in every way,
for after this I expect more will be coming.
Your favor, beloved; and sweet bird, your mercy!"
    She undid the window quickly.
"Finish up," she said, "come on and do it quickly,
so that our neighbors won't see you."
    Absalom wiped his mouth very dry;
the night was dark as pitch or coal,
and she stuck her hole out the window,
and Absalom fared neither better nor worse
than with his mouth to kiss her naked arse
with much relish, before he knew what he was doing.
    He started back and thought that something was wrong,
for he well knew that a woman doesn't have a beard;
he felt something that was all rough and long-haired,
and said, "Fie, alas, what have I done?"
    "Teehee," she said, and slammed the window shut;
and Absalom went forth with sorry step.
    "A beard, a beard," said pleasant Nicholas,
"by God's body, this goes nicely."
    Feckless Absalom heard it all,
and he bit his lip for anger
and said to himself, "I'll pay you back!"
    Who now rubs, who wipes, his lips
with dust, with sand, with straw, with cloth, with chips,
but Absalom; who says "Alas" again and again?
"I'll give my soul to Satan,
if I wouldn't rather be revenged for this insult
than have all this town," he said.
"Alas," he said, "alas, that I didn't turn aside!"
His hot love had grown cold and was all quenched,
for from the time that he had kissed her arse,
he didn't give a cress for woman's love,
for he was cured of his sickness.
He renounced love over and over,
and wept like a child that is beaten.
He crossed the street softly
to a smith called Master Gervase,
who was shaping plowing equipment in his forge:
he was busily sharpening plowshares and colters.

Absalom knocked quietly
and said, "Open up, Gervase, right away."
   "What, who are you?" "It's me, Absalom."
"How now, Absalom! Christ's cross!
Why do you rise so early, eh, bless us!
What's wrong with you? Some gay girl, God knows,
has got you on the prowl this way:
by Saint Neot, you well know what I mean."
   Absalom didn't care a bean
for all his joking. He replied not a word:
he had more wool on his distaff
than Gervase knew, and said, "Dear friend,
that hot colter in the chimney there—
lend it to me, I have something to do with it
and I'll return it to you very soon."
   Gervase answered, "Certainly, if it were gold
or uncounted gold nobles in a bag,
you should have it, as I am an honest smith;
eh, the devil, what will you do with it?"
   "Concerning that," said Absalom, "let it be as it may;
I'll tell you indeed tomorrow,"
and he grabbed the colter by its cool handle.
He stole out softly at the door
and walked to the carpenters wall:
first he coughed and then knocked
on the window, just as he had done before.
   Alison answered, "Who's there
knocking so hard? It's a thief, I warrant."
   "Why, no," he said, "God knows, Sweet love,
I am your Absalom, my darling.
I have brought you a gold ring," he said—
"my mother gave it to me, God save me;
it's very fine, and well engraved, too;
I'll give it to you if you'll kiss me."
   Nicholas had risen to urinate,
and thought he would improve on the joke:
Absalom should kiss his arse before getting off.
He raised the window quickly
and quietly stuck his arse out
beyond the buttocks, as far back as the thigh bone;
then this clerk Absalom said,
"Speak, sweet bird, I don't know where you are."
   Nicholas then let fly a fart
as strong as a thunderclap,
so that Absalom was almost blinded with its force;
but he was ready with his hot iron
and struck Nicholas in the middle of his arse:
off went the skin a handsbreadth on each side;
the hot colter burned his buttocks so badly
that he thought he would die with the pain.
He began to cry out as if he were mad,
"Help! Water! Help, for God's heart!"
   The carpenter started out of his slumber
and heard someone crying "Water!" like mad,
and he thought, "Alas, now Noel's flood is coming!"
He sat up without another word

and hacked the rope in two with his axe,
and down went all; he didn't find time to sell
either bread or ale before he hit the flooring
at ground level; and there he lay in a faint.
   Alison and Nicholas jumped up
and cried "Alas" and "Help" in the street.
The neighbors high and low
ran in to gape at this man
who still lay in a faint, pale and wan,
for he had broken his arm with the fall;
but he had to take the blame for his own mishap,
for when he spoke he was soon borne down
by pleasant Nicholas and Alison:
they told everyone that he was mad—
he was so afraid of "Noel's flood"
through hallucination that in his folly
he had bought himself three kneading tubs
and had hanged them up under the roof;
and that he had asked them for God's love
to sit under the roof for company's sake.
   The people set to laughing at his delusion.
They peered and gaped up at the roof
and turned all his misfortune into a joke,
for whatever the carpenter said in answer,
it did no good: no one listened to his explanation;
he was so sworn down with strong avowals
that he was considered mad through all the town,
for every clerk immediately stuck with the other's story.
They said, "The man is mad, dear brother";
and everyone laughed at this fuss.
   Thus plumbed was the carpenter's wife,
in spite of all his guard and jealousy;
and Absalom has kissed her lower eye;
and Nicholas is scalded in the bum:
this tale is done, and God save all the company!

The Wife of Bath

The Prologue of the Wife of Bath's Tale

   "Experience, even if there were no other authority
in this world, would be grounds enough for me
to speak of the woe that is in marriage;
for, my lords, since I was twelve years old,
thanks be to eternal God,
I have had five husbands at the church door—
if I may have been legally married so often;
and all were worthy men in their different ways.
But I was definitely told, not long ago,
that since Christ went but once
to a wedding, in Cana of Galilee,
by that example he taught me

that I should not be married more than once.
Also, consider what sharp words
Jesus, God and man, spoke beside a
well in reproof of the Samaritan:
'Thou hast had five husbands,' he said,
'and he whom thou now hast
is not thy husband'; thus he spoke, certainly;
what he meant by it, I cannot say.
But I ask this, why was the fifth man
no husband to the Samaritan?
How many was she allowed to have in marriage?
Never yet in my life have I heard
this number defined.
People may guess and interpret the text up and down,
but I know well, without a doubt, God bade
us expressly to increase and multiply;
that pleasant text I can well understand.
And also I well know that He said my husband
should leave father and mother, and take me;
but He made no mention of number—
of bigamy or of octogamy;
why should men speak evil of it?
    Look at the wise king, Lord Solomon;
I think he had more than one wife;
I would to God I could
be refreshed half so often as he!
What a gift from God he had with all his wives!
No man living in this world has such.
God knows this noble king to my thinking
had many a merry bout with each of them
the first night he had a good life.
Blessed be God that I have married five!
Welcome the sixth, whenever he comes along.
For indeed, I don't want to keep myself entirely chaste;
when my husband has gone from the world,
some Christian man shall wed me soon,
for the Apostle says that then I am free
to marry in God's name where I please.
He says it's no sin to be married;
it is better to marry than to burn.
What do I care if folk speak evil
of cursed Lamech and his bigamy?
I know very well that Abraham was a holy man,
and Jacob too, as far as I can see;
and each of them had more than two wives,
and so did many another holy man.
Tell me, where, in any time,
did God on high expressly prohibit marriage?
I pray you, tell me;
or where did he command virginity?
I know as well as you do—not a doubt!—
that the Apostle, when he spoke of maidenhood,
said that he had no commandment for it.
One may counsel a woman to be a virgin,
but counseling is not commandment;
he left it to our own judgment.

For if God had decreed maidenhood, then
he would have condemned marriage in effect;
and certainly if there were no seed sown,
then where should virginity grow from?
Paul did not dare in the least to decree
a thing for which his master gave no order.
The prize is set up for virginity;
grab it who may, let's see who wins the race.

    But this saying does not apply to every man,
but only where it pleases God to give it, of His might.
I very well know that the Apostle was a virgin;
but nevertheless, although he wrote and said
that he wished that everyone were such as he,
all this is only advice in favor of virginity;
and he gave me, as an indulgence, leave
to be a wife; so it is no reproach
for me to marry if my mate dies;
it is without any taint of bigamy—
although it may be good not to touch a woman
(he meant in a bed or couch;
for it is dangerous to assemble fire and tow—
you know what this example means).
This is the sum of the matter, he held virginity to be
more perfect than marrying in the frailty of the flesh.
It is frailty, that is, unless the man and woman
intend to live all their lives in chastity.

    I grant it freely; I'm not envious,
although maidenhood be preferred to bigamy.
It pleases some to be pure, body and soul;
I won't make any boast about my own estate.
As you well know, a lord doesn't have every
vessel in his household made of gold;
some are made of wood, and are serviceable to their lord.
God calls people to him in sundry ways,
and each one has an appropriate gift of God,
some this, some that—as it pleases Him to provide.

    Virginity is a great perfection,
and also devoted continence,
but Christ, who is the well of perfection,
did not bid every man to go and sell
all that he had and give it to the poor,
and in that way to follow in His footsteps;
He spoke to them that wished to live perfectly:
and by your leave, my lords, that isn't me.
I will bestow the flower of my whole life
in the acts and fruits of marriage.

    Tell me also, to what end
were reproductive organs made,
why are people made so perfectly?
Believe me, they were not made for nothing.
whoever wants to, let him enlarge on the matter and argue to
and fro that they were made for the purgation
of urine, and that both our private parts
were made to distinguish a female from a male,
and for no other cause—do you say no?
Experience knows well it is not so;

so that the clerics won't be angry with me,
I'll say this: they were made for both;
that is to say, for necessary business and for pleasure
in engendering, when we do not displease God.
Why else should men set it down in their books
that a man shall yield his wife her debt?
Now how shall he make his payment
unless he uses his simple instrument?
Then, they were given to creatures
for purging urine and also for propagation.
    But I don't say that everyone who has
such equipment as I mentioned is bound
to go and use it in engendering;
then we wouldn't care about chastity.
Christ, who was formed as a man, was a virgin,
and many a saint since the world began
lived always in perfect chastity.
I won't envy them virginity:
let them be white bread of finest wheat,
and let us wives be called barley bread;
and yet, with barley bread, as Mark tells us,
Our Lord Jesus refreshed many a man.
In such estate as God has called us to
I'll persevere; I'm not particular.
In marriage I'll use my equipment
as freely as my maker sent it.
If I should be grudging, God give me sorrow!
My husband shall have it both evening and morning,
whenever he wants to come forth and pay his debt.
I'll have a husband—I won't make it difficult—
who shall be both my debtor and my slave,
and have his trouble
in the flesh while I'm his wife.
All through my life I have the power
over his own body, and not he.
Just so the Apostle explained it to me,
and he bade our husbands to love us well.
Every bit of this lesson pleases me—"
just then tile Pardoner started up;
"Now, dame," he said, "by God and by Saint John,
you are a noble preacher in this matter!
I was about to wed a wife; alas,
why should I purchase it so dearly with my flesh?
I'd rather not wed a wife this year!"
    "Wait," said she, "my tale is not begun;
no, you'll drink from another barrel
before I am through—one that shall taste worse than ale.
And when I have told you my tale
of the tribulation of marriage,
in which I have been an expert all my life—
that is to say, I myself have been the whip—
then you may choose whether you wish to sip
of the tun that I shall broach.
Be wary of it, before you approach too near;
for I shall tell more than ten examples.
By him who won't be warned by other men

shall other men be warned.
These same words were written by Ptolemy;
read in his *Almagest,* and find it there."
    "Dame, I pray you, if it be your will,"
said this Pardoner, "tell your tale
as you began; leave off for no man,
and teach us young men some of your practice."
    "Gladly," said she, "since it may please you.
But yet I pray all this company
that if I speak according to my fancy,
you do not take what I say amiss;
for I only intend to amuse you.
    Now, sirs, I'll go on with my tale.—
As ever I hope to drink wine or ale,
I'll tell the truth, of those husbands that I had,
three of them were good and two were bad.
The first three men were good, and rich, and old;
they were scarcely able to keep the statute
by which they were bound to me—
you know quite well what I mean by this, by heaven!
So help me God, I laugh when I think
how pitifully I made them work at night;
and by my faith I set no store by it.
They had given me their land and their treasure;
I no longer needed to be diligent
to win their love, or show them reverence.
They loved me so well, by God above,
that I didn't prize their love!
A wise woman will concentrate on getting
that love which she doesn't possess;
but since I had them wholly in my hand,
and since they had given me all their land,
why should I take pains to please them,
unless it should be for my own profit and pleasure?
I so set them to work, by my faith,
that many a night they sang 'alas!'
The prize of bacon some people have in
Essex at Dunmow was never brought to them, I know.
I governed them so well in my way
that each of them was most happy and eager
to bring me gay things from the fair.
They were glad indeed when I spoke pleasantly to them;
for God knows I chided them cruelly.
    Now hear how suitably I behaved myself,
you wise wives who can understand.
You should speak thus and put them in the wrong;
for no man can perjure himself and he
half so boldly as a woman can.
I don't say this for wives that are wise,
except when they have made a mistake.
A wise wife, if she knows what is good for her,
will convince her husband that the chough
    is mad,
and call as a witness her own maid,
who conspires with her; but listen to how I spoke.
    'Old sluggard, is this the way you dress me?

Why is my neighbor's wife so smart?
She is honored everywhere she goes;
I sit at home, I have no decent clothes.
What do you do at my neighbor's house?
Is she so fair? Are you so amorous?
What are you whispering to our maid, for heaven's sake?
Old sir, lecher, stop your tricks!
Why, if I have a friend or acquaintance
in all innocence, you chide like a fiend
if I walk to his house and visit!
You come home as drunk as a mouse
and preach from your bench, bad luck to you!
You tell me it is a great misfortune
to marry a poor woman, as far as cost is concerned;
and if she is rich and of high lineage,
then you say that it is a torment
to suffer her pride and her melancholy.
And if she is fair, you knave,
you say that every lecher wants to have her;
she who is assaulted on every side
can't remain chaste very long.

   You say some men desire us for wealth,
some for our shapeliness, and some for our beauty;
some want a woman because she can sing or dance,
some because she is well-bred and flirtatious;
some like her hands and her graceful arms;
thus we all go to the devil by your account.
You say no one can keep a castle wall
when it is assailed all around for so long a time.

   And if she is ugly, you say that she
covets every man she sees;
for she will leap on him like a spaniel
until she finds some man who will buy her wares;
there is no goose swimming in the lake, you say,
that is so gray it cannot find a mate.
And you say it is very hard to manage
a thing that no man will willingly keep.
You say this, you wretch, as you go to bed,
and that no wise man needs to marry,
nor any man who aspires to heaven.
May wild thunderbolts and fiery lightning
break your withered neck!

   You say that leaking houses and smoke
and nagging wives make men flee
out of their own houses; bless us,
what ails such an old man to scold so?
You say we wives will hide our vices
until we are safely married, and then we will show them;
that's certainly a fit proverb for a scolding curmudgeon!
You say that oxen, asses, horses, and hounds
are tested at various times;
and so are basins and washbowls, before people buy them—
spoons and stools and all such household goods,
and so are pots, clothes and adornments;
but men don't try out wives
until they are married; scolding old dotard!

And then, you say, we'll show our vices.
   You also say that I am displeased
unless you praise my beauty,
and pore constantly on my face,
and call me "fair dame" everywhere;
and unless you hold a feast on my
birthday, and give me gay new clothing,
and unless you honor my nurse
and my chambermaid,
and my father's relatives and connections;—
you say all this, old barrel full of lies!
   Moreover, you have caught a false
suspicion of our apprentice Jankin,
because he has curly hair, shining like purest gold,
and squires me everywhere;
I wouldn't want him even if you died tomorrow.
   But tell me this, why do you hide—sorrow to you!—
the keys of your chest away from me?
It is my property as well as yours, by heaven.
Do you think you can make an idiot of the mistress of the
house? Now by the lord who is called Saint James,
you shall not be master of both my body and my goods,
even if you rage with anger;
you'll go without one of them, like it or not.
What use is it to snoop and spy on me?
I think you'd like to lock me in your chest!
You should say, "Wife, go where you like,
amuse yourself, I won't believe any gossip.
I know you for a true wife, Dame Alice."
We don't love a man who carefully watches
where we go; we want to be at large.
   Beyond all other men, may the wise
astrologer Lord Ptolemy be blessed,
for in his *Almagest* he speaks this proverb:
"The wisest of all men is he
that never cares who has the world in his hand."
You should understand by this proverb
that if you have enough, why should you care
how merrily other folks fare?
For certainly, old dotard, by your leave,
you'll have quite sex enough at night.
He who forbids another man to light a candle
at his lantern is too great a niggard;
he'll have none the less light, by heaven;
if you have enough, you needn't complain.
   You also say that if we make ourselves attractive
with fine clothing and adornments
it imperils our chastity;
and further—sorrow take you—you must back yourself up
by saying these words in the Apostle's name:
"You women shall adorn yourselves
in shamefastness and sobriety," said he,
"and not in braided hair and gay jewels,
as pearls or gold, or rich array";
I won't conform to this text and
rubric one gnat's worth!

You said this: that I was like a cat;
for if someone singes a cat's fur,
then the cat will stay in its dwelling;
and if the cat's fur is sleek and attractive,
she won't stay in the house half a day,
but out she'll go, before the break of day,
to show her fur and go a-caterwauling;
this is to say, sir grouch, that if I'm gaily dressed,
I'll run out to show off my clothes.

    You old fool, what use is it for you to spy?
Even if you ask Argus, with his hundred eyes,
to be my bodyguard (as he can do it best),
in faith, he can't guard me unless I please;
I still could deceive him, as I hope to thrive.

    You also said that there are three things
which trouble all this earth,
and that no man can endure a fourth;
O dear sir tartar, Jesus shorten your life!
Still you preach and say that a hateful wife
is reckoned as one of these misfortunes.
Are there no other kind of comparisons
you can apply your parables to—
must a poor wife be one of them?

    You compare a woman's love to hell,
to barren land where water can't remain.
You compare it also to wild fire:
the more it burns, the more it wants
to consume everything that will burn.
You say that just as worms destroy a tree,
just so a wife destroys her husband; and
that all who are bound to wives know this.'

    My lords, just so, as you have learned,
I boldly accused my old husbands
of speaking in their drunkenness;
and all was false, but I called on
Jankin and my niece as witnesses.
Oh Lord, the pain and woe I gave them,
though they were guiltless, by God's sweet suffering!
For I could bite and whinny like a horse;
I could complain, though I was the guilty one;
else many time I would have been ruined.
Whoever comes first to the mill, grinds first;
I complained first, and so our fight was ended.
They were quite glad to excuse themselves quickly
for things they had never been guilty of in their lives.

    I would accuse them about wenches
when they were so sick they could hardly stand.
Yet it tickled a husband's heart, since he
thought I showed such great fondness for him.
I swore that all my walking out by night
was to spy out the wenches he lay with;
under this pretense I had many a merry time,
for all such wit is given us at our birth;
God has given women by nature deceit, weeping,
and spinning, as long as they live.
And thus I can boast of one thing:

in the end I got the better of them in every case,
by trick, or force, or by some kind of method,
such as continual complaining or grouching;
in particular, they had misfortune in bed,
where I would chide and give them no pleasure;
I would no longer stay in the bed
if I felt my husband's arm over my side
until he had paid his ransom to me;
then I'd allow him to do his bit of business.
Therefore I tell this moral to everyone—
profit whoever may, for all is for sale:
you cannot lure a hawk with an empty hand;
for profit I would endure all his lust,
and pretend an appetite myself;
and yet I never had a taste for aged meat—
that's what made me scold them all the time.
For even if the Pope had sat beside them,
I wouldn't spare them at their own board;
I swear I requited them word for word.
So help me almighty God,
even if I were to make my testament right now,
I don't owe them a word which has not been repaid.
I brought it about by my wit
that they had to give up, as the best thing to do,
or else we would never have been at rest.
For though he might look like a raging lion,
yet he would fail to gain his point.
    Then I would say, 'Dear friend, notice
the meek look on Wilkin, our sheep;
come near, my spouse, let me kiss your cheek!
You should be quite patient and meek,
and have a scrupulous conscience,
since you preach so of the patience of Job.
Always be patient, since you preach so well;
for unless you do, we shall certainly teach you
that it is a fine thing to have a wife in peace.
One of us two must bend without a doubt;
and since a man is more reasonable
than a woman is, you must be patient.
What ails you to grumble and groan so?
Is it because you want to have my thing to yourself?
Why take it all, then, have every bit of it!
Peter! I swear you love it well!
Now if I would sell my *belle chose*,
I could walk as fresh as a rose;
but I will keep it for your own taste.
You're to blame, by God, I tell you the truth.'
    We would have words like this.
Now I will speak of my fourth husband.
    My fourth husband was a reveller—
that is to say, he had a paramour;
and I was young and full of wantonness,
stubborn and strong and merry as a magpie.
How gracefully I could dance to a harp,
and sing just like a nightingale,
when I had drunk a draught of sweet wine!

Metellius, the foul churl, the swine,
who took his wife's life with a staff
because she drank wine—if I had been his wife
he wouldn't have daunted me from drink;
and after wine I must needs think of Venus:
for just as surely as cold brings hail
a lickerish mouth must have a lecherous tail!
A drunken woman has no defense;
this, lechers know by experience.
　　But Lord Christ! When I remember
my youth and my gaity,
it tickles me to the bottom of my heart;
to this day it does my heart good
that I have had my world in my time.
But age, alas, that poisons everything,
has robbed me of my beauty and my pith;
let it go, farewell, the devil with it!
The flour is gone, there is no more to say:
now I must sell the bran, as best I can;
but still I will contrive to be right merry.
Now I'll tell about my fourth husband.
　　I tell you I was angry in my heart
that he had delight in any other.
But he was repaid, by God and by Saint Joce!
I made him a staff of the same wood—
not with my body in a filthy way,
but indeed my manner with other men was such
that I made him fry in his own grease
for anger and pure jealousy.
By God, I was his purgatory on earth,
by which help I hope his soul is in glory.
For God knows he often sat and sang out
when his shoe pinched him bitterly.
No one but God and he knew
how sorely I wrung him in many ways.
He died when I came back from Jerusalem,
and lies buried under the rood-beam,
although his tomb is not so elaborate
as the sepulchre of that Darius was
which Apelles wrought so skillfully;
it would have been just a waste to bury him expensively.
Farewell to him, may God rest his soul;
he is now in his grave and in his coffin.
　　Now I will tell of my fifth husband:
God never let his soul go down to hell!
And yet he was the most brutal to me;
that I can feel on my ribs, all down the row,
and always shall, to my dying day.
But in our bed he was so tireless and wanton,
and moreover he could cajole me so well
when he wanted to have my *belle chose*,
that even if he had beaten me on every bone,
he could soon win my love again.
I think I loved him best because
he was so cool in his love to me.
We women have, to tell the truth,

an odd fancy in this matter;
whatever we cannot easily get
we will cry after and crave all day.
Forbid us a thing, and we desire it;
press it upon us, and then we will flee.
Faced with coyness we bring out all our wares;
a great crowd at the market makes wares expensive,
and what is too cheap is held to be worth little;
every wise woman knows this.

My fifth husband, God bless his soul,
whom I took for love and not money,
was at one time a scholar of Oxford,
and had left school, and went home to board
with my close friend, who dwelt in our town:
God bless her soul! Her name was Alison.
She knew my heart and private affairs
better than our parish priest, as I may thrive!
To her I revealed all my secrets.
For whether my husband had pissed on a wall
or done something which should have cost him his life,
to her, and to another worthy wife,
and to my niece, whom I loved well,
I would have betrayed every one of his secrets.
And so I did often enough, God knows,
and that often made his face red and hot
for very shame, so that he blamed himself
for having told me so great a confidence.

And so it happened that once, in Lent
(thus many times I went to my friend's house,
for I always loved to be merry,
and to walk, in March, April, and May,
from house to house, to hear various tidings)
that Jankin the clerk and my dear friend Dame Alice
and I myself went into the fields.
My husband was at London all that Lent;
I had the better leisure to enjoy myself
and to see, and be seen by,
lusty people; how could I know how my favor
was destined to be bestowed, or where?
Therefore I made my visits to feast-eves and processions,
to sermons and these pilgrimages,
to miracle plays and to marriages,
and wore my gay scarlet clothes:
on my life, worms or moths or mites
never ate a bit of them;
and do you know why? Because they were used constantly.
Now I'll tell what happened to me.
As I was saying, we walked in the fields,
until truly this clerk and I enjoyed
such dalliance that in my foresight
I spoke to him and told him that
if I were a widow he should marry me.
For certainly (I don't say it as a boast)
I was never yet unprovided for
in marriage, and other matters too;
I hold that a mouse that has but one hole

to run to has a heart not worth a leek;
for if that should fail, then all is finished.
    I made him believe he had enchanted me;
my mother taught me that trick.
And also I said I had dreamed of him all night:
he wanted to slay me as I lay on my back,
and all my bed was full of very blood;
but yet I expected that he would bring me luck;
for blood signifies gold, as I was taught.
—And all this was false, I had dreamed none of it;
I was just following my mother's lore, as I
always did, in this as well as in other matters.
    But now sir, let me see, what am I talking about?
Aha! By God, I have my tale back again.
    When my fourth husband was on his bier,
I wept, all the same, and acted sorrowful,
as wives must, for it is customary,
and covered my face with my handkerchief;
but since I was provided with a mate,
I wept but little, that I guarantee.
    My husband was brought to church in the morning,
with neighbors who mourned for him;
and Jankin our clerk was one of them.
So help me God, when I saw him walk
behind the bier, it seemed to me he had a pair
of legs and feet so neat and handsome
that I gave all my heart into his keeping.
He was, I think, twenty years old,
and I was forty, if the truth be told;
but yet I always had a colt's tooth.
I was gap-toothed, and that became me well;
I had the print of St. Venus' seal.
So help me God, I was a lusty one,
and fair and rich and young and well off;
and truly, as my husbands told me,
I had the best *quoniam* that might be.
For certainly, my feelings all come
from Venus, and my heart from Mars:
Venus gave me my lust, my lecherousness,
and Mars gave me my sturdy hardiness,
because Taurus was in the ascendant when I was born, and
Mars was in that sign. Alas, alas, that ever love was sin!
I always followed my inclination
according to the stellar influences at my birth;
I was so made that I could not withhold
my chamber of Venus from a good fellow.
I still have the mark of Mars on my face,
and also in another private place.
For, as surely as God is my salvation,
I never had any discrimination in love,
but always followed my appetite,
be he short or tall, dark or fair;
I didn't care, so long as he pleased me,
how poor he was, nor of what rank.
    What should I say, except that at the end of the month
this gay clerk Jankin, that was so pleasant,

wedded me with great ceremony,
and to him I gave all the lands and property
that had ever been given to me before;
but afterward I repented this sorely:
he would not allow anything I wanted.
By God, he hit me once on the ear
because I had torn a leaf out of his book;
as a result of that stroke, my ear became totally deaf.
I was stubborn as a lionness,
and as for my tongue, an absolute ranter;
and I'd walk as I'd done before,
from home to house although he'd sworn I wouldn't;
because of this he would often preach
and teach me of the deeds of ancient Romans:
how Simplicius Gallus left his wife
and forsook her for the rest of his life
just because he saw her looking out
of his door bareheaded one day.

   He told me by name of another Roman
who also, because his wife was at a summer
game without his knowledge, forsook her.
And then he would seek in his Bible
for that proverb of Ecclesiasticus
where he makes a command strictly forbidding
a man to allow his wife to go roaming about;
then you could be sure he would say this:

   'Whoever builds his house of willows,
      and rides his blind horse over plowed land,
      and allows his wife to visit shrines,
      is worthy to be hanged on the gallows.'
But all for nought; I didn't care a berry
for proverbs and old saw,
nor would I be corrected by him.
I hate that man who tells me my vices,
and so, God knows, do more of us than I.
This made him utterly furious with me;
I wouldn't give in to him in any case.

   Now I'll tell you truly, by Saint Thomas,
why I tore a leaf out of his book,
for which he hit me so that I became deaf.
He had a book that he always loved to read
in night and day to amuse himself.
He called it Valerius and Theophrastus;
at which book he was always laughing heartily;
and also there was at some time a clerk at Rome,
a cardinal, that was called St. Jerome,
who wrote a book against Jovinian;
in this book there was also Tertulian,
Chrysippus, Trotula, and Heloise,
who was an abbess not far from Paris;
and also the Parables of Solomon,
Ovid's *Art of Love,* and many other books,
and all these were bound in one volume.
And every day and night it was his custom,
when he had leisure and could rest
from other worldly occupation,

to read in this book about wicked wives.
He knew more legends and lives of them
than there are of good wives in the Bible.
For believe me, it is an impossibility
for any clerk to speak good of wives—
unless it be of the lives of holy saints,
but never of any other woman.
Who painted the lion, tell me who?
By God, if women had written stories,
as clerks have in their oratories,
they would have written more of men's wickedness
than all of the sex of Adam can redress.
The children of Mercury and of Venus
are quite contrary in their ways;
Mercury loves wisdom and learning,
and Venus loves revelry and expenditure.
And, because of their diverse dispositions,
each loses power when the other is dominant;
and thus, God knows, Mercury is powerless
in the Sign of the Fish, where Venus is dominant;
and Venus falls when Mercury ascends;
therefore no woman is praised by any clerk.
The clerk, when he is old, and unable to do
any of Venus' work worth his old shoe,
then sits down and writes in his dotage
that women cannot keep their marriage vows!

But now to the purpose, as to why I was beaten,
as I told you, because of a book, for heaven's sake.
One night Jankin, who was the head of the household,
read in his book as he sat by the fire,
first, concerning Eve, that all mankind was brought
to wretchedness by her wickedness,
for which Jesus Christ himself was slain,
who redeemed us with his heart's blood.
Here you can expressly find this of woman:
that woman caused the fall of all mankind.
Then he read to me how Samson lost his hair:
while he was sleeping, his mistress cut it with her shears;
through this treason he lost both his eyes.

Then he read to me, and this is no lie,
about Hercules and his Dejanira,
who caused him to set himself on fire.

He forgot none of the sorrow and woe
that Socrates had with his two wives;
how Xantippe cast piss upon his head;
this poor man sat as still as if he were dead;
he wiped his head; he dared to say no more
than, 'Before the thunder stops, comes the rain.'
The tale of Pasiphaë, who was the queen of Crete,
he maliciously thought sweet;
fie, speak no more—it is a grisly thing—
about her horrible lust and her preference.

Of Clytemnestra, who because of her lechery
with falseness caused her husband's death,
he read with great devotion.

He told me also why

Amphiaraus lost his life at Thebes;
my husband had a story about his wife,
Eriphyle, who for a trinket of gold
secretly told the Greeks
where her husband had hidden himself,
which is why he had sad luck at Thebes.
    He told me of Livia and of Lucilla;
they both caused their husbands to die,
one for love and the other for hate;
Livia, late one night, poisoned
her husband, because she was his foe.
Lustful Lucilla loved her husband so
that in order to make him think of her always
she gave him a love potion of such a kind
that he was dead before morning;
and thus husbands always suffer.
    Then he told me how one Latumius
complained to his friend Arrius
that in his garden there grew a tree
on which, he said, his three wives
had spitefully hanged themselves.
    'O dear brother,' said this Arrius,
'give me a cutting of that blessed tree,
and it shall be planted in my garden.'
    He read of wives of a later date
some of whom had slain their husbands in their beds,
and let their lechers make love to them all the night
while the corpse lay flat on the floor.
And some have driven nails into their husband's brain
while they slept, and thus slain them.
Some have given them poison in their drink.
He told of more evil than the heart can imagine;
and along with that, he knew more proverbs
than there are blades of grass or herbs in the world.
    'It is better,' said he, 'to dwell
with a lion or a foul dragon
than with a woman accustomed to scold.
It is better,' said he, 'to stay high on the roof
than with an angry wife down in the house;
they are so wicked and contrary
they always hate what their husbands love.'
He said, 'A woman casts her shame away
when she casts off her smock,' and furthermore,
    'A fair woman, unless she is also chaste,
is like a gold ring in a sow's nose.'
Who would suppose or imagine
the woe and pain that was in my heart?
    And when I saw he would never stop
reading in this cursed book all night,
suddenly I plucked three leaves
out of his book, right as he was reading, and also
I hit him on the cheek with my fist, so
that he fell down into our fire backward.
He started up like a raging lion
and hit me on the head with his fist
so that I lay on the floor as if I were dead.

And when he saw how still I lay,
he was aghast, and would have fled away,
until at last I awoke from my swoon:
'Oh! have you slain me, false thief?' I said,
'And have you murdered me thus for my land?
Before I die, I yet want to kiss you.'
   He came near, and kneeled down gently,
and said, 'Dear sister Alison,
so help me God, I shall never hit you;
what I have done, you are to blame for yourself.
Forgive me for it, I beseech you.'
But yet again I hit him on the cheek,
and said, 'Thief, this much I am avenged;
now I shall die, I can speak no longer.'
But at last, after much care and woe,
we fell into accord between ourselves.
He gave the bridle completely into my hand
to have control of house and land,
and also of his tongue and hand;
and I made him burn his book right then.
And when I had got for myself,
through superiority, all the sovereignty,
and he had said, 'My own true wife,
do as you wish the rest of your life,
preserve your honor, and my public position, too,'
after that day we never argued.
So God help me, I was as kind to him
as any wife from Denmark to India,
and as true, and so was he to me.
I pray to God who sits in majesty
to bless his soul, for His dear mercy's sake!
Now I'll tell my tale, if you will listen."

Behold the words between the Summoner and the Friar

The Friar laughed, when he had heard all this:
"Now, dame," said he, "as I may have joy or bliss,
this is a long preamble to a tale!"
And when the Summoner heard the Friar exclaim,
"Lo!" said the Summoner, "By God's two arms!
A friar will always be butting in.
Set good people a fly and a friar
will fall into every dish and also every matter.
What do you mean, talking about preambulation?
Oh, amble or trot or hold your peace, or go sit down;
you're spoiling our fun by behaving in this manner."
   "Oh, is that so, sir Summoner?" said the Friar,
"Now by my faith, before I go, I'll
tell such a tale or two about a summoner
that everyone here shall laugh."
   "Now Friar, damn your eyes,"
said this Summoner, "and damn me
if I don't tell two or three tales
about friars before I get to Sittingbourne,
so that I shall make your heart mourn;
I can easily see that your patience is gone."

Our Host cried "Peace! And that at once!"
And said, "Let the woman tell her tale.
You behave like people who have got drunk on ale.
Tell your tale, dame; that is best!
    "All ready, sir," said she, "just as you wish,
if I have the permission of this worthy Friar."
"Yes, dame," said he, "tell on and I will listen."

Here begins the Wife of Bath's Tale

In the old days of King Arthur,
of whom Britons speak great honor,
this land was all filled with fairies.
The elf queen with her jolly company
danced often in many a green meadow—
this was the old belief, as I have read;
I speak of many hundred years ago.
But now no one can see elves any more,
for now the great charity and prayers
of limiters and other holy friars,
who search every field and stream,
as thick as specks of dust in a sunbeam,
blessing halls, chambers, kitchens, bedrooms,
cities, towns, castles, high towers,
villages, barns, stables, dairies,
this is the reason that there are no fairies.
For where an elf was wont to walk,
there now walks the limiter himself,
in afternoons and in mornings,
and says his Matins and his holy things,
as he goes about within his limits.
Women may go up and down safely;
in every bush or under every tree
there is no other incubus but he—
and he won't do anything but dishonor to them.
    It so happened that this King Arthur
had in his house a lusty bachelor,
who one day came riding from the river,
and it happened that he saw a maiden
walking before him, alone as he was born.
And from this maiden then, against her will,
and by pure force, he took her maidenhood.
Because of this violation, there was such a clamor
and such petitioning to King Arthur
that this knight was condemned to die
according to law, and should have lost his head—
it happened that such was the statute then—
except that the Queen and various other ladies
prayed to the king for grace so long
that he granted him his life on the spot,
and gave him to the queen, completely at her will,
to choose whether she would save or destroy him.
    The queen thanked the king heartily,
and then spoke thus to the knight,
one day, when she saw a fitting time:
"You are still in such a position," said she,

"that you have no guarantee of your life as yet.
I will grant you life if you can tell me
what thing it is that women most desire.
Be wary, and keep your neck from the ax.
And if you cannot tell it to me now,
I will still give you leave to go
a year and a day to seek and learn
a sufficient answer in this matter.
And I want a guarantee, before you go,
that you will yield up your person in this place."

The knight was woeful, and he sighed sorrowfully;
but then, he could not do as he pleased.
And in the end he decided to go off,
and to come back again just at the end of the year,
with such an answer as God would provide for him;
he took his leave and went forth on his way.

He sought in every house and every place
where he hoped to find favor,
in order to learn what thing women most love;
but he reached no land where he could find
two people who were in agreement
with each other on this matter.

Some said women love riches best;
some said honor; some said amusement;
some, rich apparel; some said pleasure in bed,
and often to be widowed and remarried.
Some said that our hearts are most soothed
when we are flattered and pampered:
he came near the truth, I will not lie;
a man can win us best with flattery,
and with constant attendance and assiduity
we are ensnared, both high and low.

And some said that we love best
to be free, and do just as we please,
and to have no man reprove us for our vice,
but say that we are wise and not at all foolish.
For truly, if anyone will scratch us
on a sore spot, there is not one of us
who will not kick for being told the truth;
try it, and he who does shall find this out.
No matter how full of vice we are within,
we wish to be thought wise and clean from sin.

And some said that we take delight
in being thought reliable and able to keep a secret
and hold steadfast to a purpose
and not betray anything that people tell us.
But that idea isn't worth a rake handle;
by heaven, we women can't conceal a thing;
witness Midas; would you hear the tale?

Ovid, among other brief matters,
said Midas had two ass's ears growing
on his head under his long hair;
which evil he hid from everyone's sight
as artfully as he could,
so that no one knew of it except his wife.
He loved her most, and also trusted her;

he prayed her not to tell anyone
of his disfigurement.
  She swore to him that not for all the world
would she do such villainy and sin
as to give her husband so bad a name;
out of her own shame she wouldn't tell it.
But nonetheless she thought that she would die
for having to keep a secret so long;
it seemed to her that her heart swelled so painfully
some word must needs burst from her;
and since she dared not tell it to anybody,
she ran down to a marsh close by—
her heart was on fire until she got there—
and, as a bittern booms, in the mire,
she laid her mouth down to the water:
"Betray me not, you water, with your sound,"
said she. "To you I tell it, and to no one else:
my husband has two long ass's ears!
Now my heart is all cured, for the secret is out!
I simply couldn't keep it any longer."
In this you can see that though we wait a time,
yet out it must come: we cannot hide a secret.
If you wish to hear the rest of the tale,
read Ovid, and there you can learn of it.
  When this knight whom my tale specially concerns
saw that, he couldn't come by it—
that is to say, What women love most—
his spirit was very sorrowful within his breast;
but home he went, he might not linger:
the day was come when he must turn homeward.
And on his way, burdened with care, he happened
to ride by the edge of a forest,
where he saw more than twenty-four
ladies moving in a dance—
he drew eagerly toward that dance
in the hope that he might learn something.
But indeed, before he quite got there,
the dancers vanished, he knew not where.
He saw no living creature,
except a woman sitting on the green:
no one could imagine an uglier creature.
This old woman rose before the knight
and said "Sir knight, no road lies this way.
Tell me, by your faith, what you seek for.
Perhaps it may be the better;
these old folks know many things," said she.
  "Dear mother," said this knight, "certainly
I am as good as dead unless I can say
what thing it is that women most desire;
if you could tell me, I would repay your trouble well."
  "Give me your promise here upon my hand," said she,
"that you will do the next thing I require
of you if lies in your power,
and I will tell it to you before nightfall."
"Here is my promise," said the knight, "I grant it."
  "Then," said she, "I dare to boast

that your life is safe, for I'll swear
upon my life that the queen will say as I do.
Let's see whether the proudest of all those
that wear a coverchief or headdress
dares deny what I shall teach you;
let's go on without any more talk."
Then she whispered a message in his ear,
and told him to be glad and not afraid.

   When they had come to the court, this knight
said he had kept his day as he had promised,
and his answer, he said, was ready.
Many a noble wife and many a maiden,
and many a widow (since widows are so wise),
were assembled to hear his answer
with the queen herself sitting as judge;
and then the knight was ordered to appear.

   Everyone was commanded to keep silence,
and the knight was commanded to tell in open assembly
what thing it is that secular women love best.
This knight did not stand in beastlike silence,
but answered to his question at once
with manly voice, so that all the court heard it:

   "My liege lady," he said, "generally
women desire to have dominion
over their husbands as well as their lovers,
and to be above them in mastery;
this is your greatest desire, though you may kill me;
do as you please, I am at your will here."

   In all the court there was neither wife nor maiden
nor widow who contradicted what he said,
but all said he deserved to have his life.

   And at that word up jumped the old woman
whom the knight had seen sitting on the green:
"Mercy," said she, "my sovereign lady queen!
Before your court depart, do right by me.
I taught this answer to the knight;
for this he gave me his promise there
that he would do the first thing
I required of him, if it lay in his power.
Before the court, then, I pray you, sir knight,"
said she, "to take me as your wife;
for well you know that I have saved your life.
If I say false, deny me, on your faith!"

   The knight answered, "Alas and woe is me!
I know quite well that such was my promise.
For the love of God ask for something else;
take all my property and let my body go."

   "No then," said she. "Curse the two of us!
For though I am ugly and old and poor,
I wouldn't want all the metal or ore
that is buried under the earth or lies above
unless I were your wife and your love as well."

   "My love?" said he; "No, my damnation
Alas, that any of my birth
should ever be so foully disgraced!"
But it was all for nothing; the end was this, that he

was forced to accept the fact that he must needs wed her;
and he took his old wife and went to bed.
    Now some people might say, perhaps,
that out of negligence I am not bothering
to tell you about the joy and the pomp
at the feast that day,
to which objection I shall answer briefly:
I am telling you that there was no joy or feast at all,
there was nothing but gloom and much sorrow;
for he married her privately in the morning
and afterward hid himself like an owl all day—
he was so dejected because his wife looked so ugly.
    Great was the woe in the knight's mind
when he was brought with his wife to bed;
he tossed and he turned to and fro.
His old wife lay smiling all the time,
and said, "O dear husband, bless my soul!
Does every knight behave with his wife as you do?
Is this the law of King Arthur's house?
Is every one of his knights so cold?
I am your own love and your wife;
I am she who saved your life;
and certainly I never yet did wrong to you.
Why do you act thus with me the first night?
You act like a man who has lost his mind.
What am I guilty of? For God's sake, tell me,
and it shall be corrected, if I can manage it."
    "Corrected?" said this knight, "Alas, no, no!
It will never be corrected
You are so loathsome and so old,
and what is more, of such low birth,
that it is little wonder if I toss and turn.
I wish to God my heart would break!
    "Is this," said she, "the cause of your unrest?"
    "Yes, certainly," said he, "it's no wonder."
    "Now, sir," said she, "I could rectify all this,
if I wanted to, before three days were up,
if you behaved yourself to me well.
    But in the matter of your speaking of such nobility
as descends from ancient wealth,
claiming that because of it you are supposed to be
noblemen—such arrogance is not worth a hen.
Find who is always the most virtuous,
privately and publicly, and who always tries hardest
to do what noble deeds he can,
and consider him the great nobleman.
Christ wants us to claim our nobility from him,
not from our ancestors because of their ancient wealth:
for though they give us all their heritage,
on the strength of which we claim to be of noble descent,
yet they cannot bequeath by any means
or to any of us their virtuous manner of life
which made them be called noblemen;
and which summoned us to follow them at the same level.
    Well can the wise poet of Florence
who is called Dante speak on this subject;

in this sort of rhyme is Dante's tale:
'Not oft by branches of a family tree
Does human prowess rise; for gracious God
Wants us to claim from Him nobility.'
For from our elders we may claim nothing
but perishable matter, to which man may do hurt and
injury. And everyone knows as well as I that
if nobility were implanted by nature
in a certain lineage, down the line of descent,
they would never cease, in private or public,
to do the fair offices of nobility;
they could do nothing shameful or evil.

Take fire, and bear it into the darkest house
from here to the Mount of Caucasus,
and let men shut the doors and go away;
yet the fire will blaze and burn as well
as if twenty thousand men were looking at it;
it will maintain its natural function always
until it dies, I'll stake my life.

By this you can easily see that nobility
is not tied to possessions,
since people do not perform their function
without variation as does the fire, according to its nature.
For, God knows, men may very often find
a lord's son committing shameful and vile deeds;
and he who wishes to have credit for his nobility
because he was born of a noble house,
and because his elders were noble and virtuous,
but will not himself do any noble deeds
or follow the example of his late noble ancestor,
he is not noble, be he duke or earl;
for villainous, sinful deeds make him a churl.
This kind of nobility is only the renown
of your ancestors, earned by their great goodness,
which is a thing apart from yourself.
Your nobility comes from God alone;
then our true nobility comes of grace,
it was in no way bequeathed to us with our station in life.

Think how noble, as Valerius says,
was that Tullius Hostilius
who rose out of poverty to high nobility.
Read Seneca, and read Boethius, too;
there you shall see expressly that there is no doubt
that he is noble who does noble deeds.
And therefore, dear husband, I thus conclude,
that even if my ancestors were low
yet God on high may—and so I hope—
grant me grace to live virtuously;
then I am noble, from the time when I begin
to live virtuously and avoid sin.

And as for the poverty you reprove me for,
high God in whom we believe
chose to live his life in willing poverty;
and certainly every man, maiden, or wife
can understand that Jesus, heaven's king,
would not choose a vicious way of life.

Contented poverty is an honorable thing, indeed;
this is said by Seneca and other learned men.
Whoever is content with his poverty
I hold to be rich, even if he hasn't a shirt.
He who covets anything is a poor man,
for he wants to have something which is not in his power.
But he who has nothing and desires nothing is rich,
although you may consider him nothing but a lowly man.

    True poverty sings of its own accord;
Juvenal says of poverty, 'Merrily can
the poor man sing and joke before the
thieves when he goes by the road.'
Poverty is a good that is hated, and, I guess,
a great expeller of cares;
a great amender of knowledge, too,
to him that takes it in patience.
Poverty is this, although it seem unhealthy:
possession of that which no man will challenge.
Poverty will often, when a man is low,
make him know his God and himself as well.
Poverty is a glass, it seems to me,
through which he can see his true friends.
And therefore, sir, since I do not harm you by it,
do not reprove me for my poverty any more.

    Now, sir, you reprove me for age;
but certainly, sir, aside from bookish
authority, you nobles who are honorable
say that one should honor an old person,
and call him father, for the sake of your nobility;
and I can find authors to that effect, I imagine.

    Now as to the point that I am ugly and old—
then you need not dread being a cuckold;
for ugliness and age, as I may thrive,
are great wardens of chastity.
But nevertheless, since I know what pleases you,
I shall fulfill your fleshly appetite.

    Choose now" said she, "one of these two things:
to have me ugly and old until I die,
and be a faithful, humble wife to you,
and never displease you in all my life;
or else to have me young and fair,
and take your chances on the flocking
of people to your house because of me—
or to some other place, it may well be.
Now choose yourself whichever you like."

    The knight considered and sighed sorely,
but at last he spoke in this manner,
"My lady and my love, and wife so dear,
I put myself under your wise control;
you yourself choose which may be most pleasurable
and most honorable to you and to me also.
I don't care which of the two I get;
for whatever pleases you suffices for me."

    "Then have I got mastery over you," said she,
"since I may choose and rule as I please?"

    "Yes, certainly, wife," said he, "I consider that best."

"Kiss me," said she, "we won't be angry any more;
for I swear I will be both these things to you;
that is to say, both fair indeed and good.
I pray to God that I may die of madness
if I am not just as good and true to you
as ever was wife since the world began.
And, if I am not tomorrow as fair to see
as any lady, empress, or queen
between the east and the west,
do with the question of my life and death just as you wish.
Raise the curtain, and see how it is."

And when the knight actually saw all this,—
that she was so fair and so young, too,
he seized her in his two arms for joy,
his heart was bathed in bliss;
he kissed her a thousand times in a row.
And she obeyed him in everything
that might give him pleasure or joy.

And thus they lived to the end of their lives
in perfect joy; and Jesu Christ send us
husbands who are meek, young, and lively in bed,
and grace to outlive those that we marry.
And also I pray Jesu to shorten the lives
of those that won't be governed by their wives;
and as for old and angry niggards of their money,
God send them soon a very pestilence.

Name _____ Date _____ Grade _____

——————— *Questions for Consideration* ———————

Using complete sentences, provide answers for the following questions.

1. Outline the characteristics of the medieval fabliau and show how Chaucer uses them in "The Miller's Tale."

    _____

    _____

    _____

    _____

    _____

2. Select two pilgrims with different social, professional or vocational backgrounds and outline Chaucer's presentation of each.

    _____

    _____

    _____

    _____

    _____

————————————————— *Writing Critically* —————————————————

Select one of the essay topics listed below and compose a 500 word essay which discusses the topic fully. Support your thesis with evidence from the text and with critical and/or historical material. Use the space below for preparing to write the essay.

1. Use the Prologue to *The Canterbury Tales* in a discussion to show how Chaucer develops a panoramic view of Medieval England.

2. Chaucer uses moral values and the highest standards of social and human conduct as yardsticks to judge his pilgrims. Examine the men and women of the Church from this point of view.

3. A composite theme in "The Miller's Tale" is love, relationships, and deception. To what extent is Chaucer's treatment of this theme consistent with contemporary values and attitudes?

4. Make a case for reading the Wife of Bath's prologue and tale as a feminist *or* an anti-feminist thesis.

5. Present a character portrait of the woman of Bath, and go on to evaluate her conduct in light of (a) medieval standards, and (b) contemporary standards of conduct.

6. What do you think about the thesis on marital relationships asserted in the wife of Bath's prologue and illustrated in her tale?

Prewriting Space:

_____

_____

_____

_____

_____

_____

_____

_____

_____

_____

_____

_____

_____

_____

Multicultural Currents of the Early Modern Period:
Tradition and Innovation
1350–1650 A.D.

Petrarch: Lyric Poetry and Travels
Boccaccio: The Decameron
Seami: Birds of Sorrow
Machiavelli: The Prince
Montaigne: Essays
Cervantes: Don Quixote de la Mancha
Shakespeare: The Tragedy of Hamlet
de Zayas: The Enchantments of Love
Milton: Paradise Lost
Wu Ch'eng-en: The Journey to the West
Oral Poetry from Africa
The Devotional Poems of Mirabai

UNIT THREE

Introduction
Unit Three

Defining the Early Modern period is a challenge. The three centuries from 1350 to 1650 are characterized by a great diversity of events, trends, and ideas. During this era, there was no dominant political power as there was during a good portion of classical antiquity, when the authority of Rome was ascendant. Nor was the period united through a relatively uniform and widely shared ideology; such was the case during the Middle Ages when the Catholic church and feudal authority in general were strong.

The unique problems presented by the Early Modern era are especially evident in the fact that there is another name by which this time period has long been familiar: the Renaissance. This term has been widely used since the mid-nineteenth century to designate the revival—or more literally, the "rebirth"—of classical learning and culture that began in Italy during the fourteenth century. While the concept of the Renaissance is marked by some shortcomings that the term "Early Modern" largely eliminates, anyone interested in this fascinating period of art, literature, and history needs to know about the term "Renaissance." Until a few years ago, the great majority of secondary sources referred to the Renaissance and not the Early Modern period, and at present, scholars remain divided over which term to use.

Why all the fuss about terminology? An answer to this question can help us understand a complex epoch. Some of the greatest literature ever produced was written during these centuries—by Petrarch, Rabelais, Cervantes, Shakespeare, and a throng of others. In the visual arts, Giotto, Michelangelo, Titian, and many others were extraordinarily productive. In each case, the visual artist and writer owed much to the rediscovered and re-emphasized literature, architecture, and other art of classical antiquity. Hence the term "Renaissance." But art is produced in a large and complicated social context. The idea of a cultural rebirth cannot fully explain all that was occurring during these three hundred years. A society is not composed solely of painters and writers, but of many kinds of individuals, each of whom is molded by a wide array of cultural, political, and other influences.

The term "Renaissance" privileges the artistic production and the classical heritage of this era. The concept of the "Early Modern," on the other hand, recognizes the complexity of the cultural milieu. Indeed, a host of subtle and not-so-subtle political and other influences had an impact on the life of each person, whether that person was a producer or an appreciator of art, a courtier or a king, a man or a woman, a pauper or a member of the rising middle class.

Yet the phrase "Early Modern" also preserves one of the most valid meanings conveyed by the term "Renaissance": an emphasis on the *newness* of the era. While most of us find it difficult to think of anything that happened or originated several centuries ago as new, historians point out that the term "modern" does not simply indicate whatever is new or recent. Instead, from an historian's point of view, an era should be called *modern* if modernity or newness is a prized quality or characteristic during that period. Just as the artists of the Early Modern epoch wanted to revive antiquity, they also prized the new works they created. What was new or innovative was highly esteemed because it echoed the past. It is worth remembering that love of the contemporary has not been strong in every time period; the people of the Middle Ages, for instance, looked to the biblical past or to the distant future and the end of the world.

The Early Modern age begins with an emphasis on newness that is apparent in Florence, Italy, in the fourteenth century. Some scholars maintain that this era runs all the way to the beginning of the Industrial Revolution during the mid-eighteenth century; at this point, Modern times, based on technology, begin. But do we still live in a modern era? Today, most of us are no longer convinced that newness and technological advances are always good. Nuclear weapons and a host of other technologically-related evils have raised many doubts. Our own epoch is often described as *postmodern*, and some commentators have argued that the human race has reached some historical period beyond postmodernism.

Yet in spite of huge differences, life in Early Modern Europe was suspiciously like our own, an often confusing network of opportunities and frustrations. The Early Modern world, like that we know today, was becoming both larger and smaller at the same time. Just as we witness space explorations on one hand and learn about "micro-management" on the other, so European governments were actively discovering and colonizing the Americas, frantically disseminating both contemporary and ancient texts with the aid of the newly invented printing press, and devising elaborate codes of acceptable behavior for anyone who wanted to succeed as a writer, a courtier, or as a gentlewoman.

Early Modern authors were in any case aware that theirs was a distinct age, and from the beginning of the era onward, there were frequent eulogies of its progressive spirit and of its high level of cultural achievement. In contrast, a general intellectual deprivation was held to be the distinguishing trait of the Middle Ages. An especially notable expression of this idea is found in Chapter 8 of Rabelais's *Pantagruel* (1532). As the giant Gargantua explains to his son, in the not-so-distant past:

> *The time was still tenebrous and felt the effects of the misfortune and calamity of the Goths, who had destroyed all fine literature. But, by divine goodness, light and dignity have been granted to letters in my own time . . . . Now all disciplines have been reestablished, and languages restored.*

Such is the way the era liked to think of itself, as a true Renaissance or rebirth, with the brilliance of classical civilization restored after a long hiatus notable only for its dullness.

Today we know better. The medieval period, especially the last few centuries, had no shortage of learned and talented producers of literature, philosophy, and the visual arts. Also, the transition from the Middle Ages to the Early Modern period was hardly as abrupt or as complete as many of the major writers of the era were fond of stating. Both tradition and innovation were major factors in the culture and literature of Early Modern Europe. While change was prevalent and continuous in many aspects of life, especially with regard to the recovery of the culture of ancient Greece and Rome, many facets of the medieval world were preserved. A writer such as Shakespeare, for instance, often shows strong affinities with various medieval ideas and perspectives. Also, as the elegance and refinement of the Early Modern period radiated northward from Italy, its intensity weakened somewhat, so that in England especially, long-held beliefs and perspectives competed actively with the new attitudes and artistic styles. A relevant example is Shakespeare's *Othello*, where the general outlines of a medieval morality play can be easily detected beneath the trappings of a Renaissance tragedy.

The Early Modern period was above all an era when the individual was emerging from the structure of a feudal system that was protective but could easily render him or her almost anonymous. In medieval art and literature, the individual character is to a large extent what social position—priest, knight, miller, or whatever—molded him or her to be. In Early Modern times, individuals often seem disoriented because the traditional cultural role—in Hamlet's case, that of prince—inadequately indicates, shapes, and supports attitudes and actions. Yet in the case of Hamlet, Montaigne, Don Quixote, and so many others, uncertainty over the issue of self-definition or self-fashioning helps create an engaging work of literature.

It was an age when different cultures met one another, not always under pleasant circumstances. Personal and civic wealth increased in general throughout Europe along with commerce. As Early Modern societies developed a stronger sense of themselves, the modern nation-state began to develop. In Spain and other countries, so did the desire to colonize, wage war, or otherwise dominate other cultures. Europe reached into Africa for inexpensive labor and developed a slave trade. Nor were conditions always tranquil within specific cultures when new religious perspectives emerged with the advance of the Protestant Reformation. Persecution, executions, and civil strife were common. At the same time, it was a great age of translation—of the Bible, of classical Greek and Latin texts, and of the recently created masterpieces of the new era. The Early Modern period is thus distinguished by its turpitude as well as its grandeur.

Whether one prefers "Early Modern" or "Renaissance," both terms refer to a European context. Yet African and Asian cultures are represented in the selections that follow this introduction. The rationale is that readings in *Literary Perspectives* have been placed where they seem most obviously to belong, usually on the basis of date of composition. This criterion is not always viable, however, for Chaucer is medieval although he was active just after the time of Petrarch and Boccaccio, who are among our Early Modern authors. While medieval culture was disappearing in Italy, it was still strong in England.

African oral poetry, though recorded in written form only recently, was no doubt composed much earlier, and it parallels the flowering of lyric poetry in Early Modern Europe. For Asian literature, the date of composition has been strictly followed in placing works within a particular period. At the same time, the stylized and highly symbolic Japanese nō drama makes it analogous to various forms of medieval European visual art and literature. The poems of Mirabai, also included here, are somewhat reminiscent of the popular devotionalism of late medieval Europe.

In the case of our example from China, *Journey to the West*, there are interesting parallels with the literature of Early Modern Europe. As in Europe, Chinese civilization had reached a stage when it could reflect deeply on its ancient traditions. The emperors of the late Ming dynasty were decadent, and to the conscientious Chinese person of the sixteenth century, society had grown distant from the values and texts that represented the best aspects of those traditions. The implied need for a general cultural revival, the interplay of religious and other ideas, and a complicated narrative with many elements of fantasy combine to make this Chinese text rather similar to literature produced during the same century on the other side of the globe. (NW)

BIBLIOGRAPHY

Burckhardt, Jacob. *The Civilization of the Renaissance in Italy.* Trans. S. G. C. Middlemore. New York: Mentor, 1960.

Burt, Richard and John Michael Archer, eds. *Enclosure Acts: Sexuality, Property, and Culture in Early Modern England.* Ithaca: Cornell University Press, 1994.

Chartier, Roger, ed. *Passions of the Renaissance.* Volume 3 of *History of Private Life.* Trans. Arthur Goldhammer. Cambridge: Harvard University Press, 1989.

Greene, Thomas M. *The Light in Troy: Imitation and Discovery in Renaissance Poetry.* New Haven: Yale University Press, 1982.

King, Margaret. *Women of the Renaissance.* Chicago: University of Chicago Press, 1991.

Schwartz, Stuart B. *Implicit Understandings: Observing, Reporting, and Reflecting on the Encounters Between Europeans and Other Peoples in the Early Modern Era.* Cambridge: Cambridge University Press, 1994.

Introduction

Petrarch (1304–1375)

Although the Petrarchan sonnet is a poetic form widely studied in college literature classes, the actual work of this Italian author frequently remains unread. What is usually read is the sonnet as composed by British sonneteers, especially Shakespeare, who modified the form. Much of the neglect of Petrarch stems from the misfortune of awkward translations as well as from the sense that this patriarch of Italian poetry represents an aristocratic and thus inaccessible cultural ideal. Good translations of Petrarch can be found, however, and a sensitive examination of his life and work reveals a portrait of a very human individual. Consideration of his career also leads to an understanding of the complex transitional period during which he lived.

The life of Petrarch (in Italian, Francesco Petrarca) spans most of the fourteenth century, which for Italy was a turbulent time. This era saw the end of the Middle Ages and the beginning of the Renaissance or Early Modern period. Petrarch is often referred to as the first modern man because of his crucial role in the transition. No change of such major proportions is completed with the sudden flip of some historical switch, and Petrarch's outlook remained medieval in many ways. The traditional medieval view emphasized the primacy of a divinely-ordered matrix in which the human life was basically a time of trial and preparation for the afterlife. Yet Petrarch's writings reveal a new sense of the importance of the individual and of the secular world.

In his renowned letter on his experiences while climbing Mount Ventoux, Petrarch initially seems exhilarated over an adventure that has no moral purpose, and he begins to draw a parallel between himself and Philip of Macedon, a well-known figure from classical antiquity who also was challenged by mountain-climbing. However, Petrarch quickly reverts to a medieval perspective that cautions against vanity or pride in any form. All the same, the sense of discovery he displays in ascending Mount Ventoux marks a major step in preparing the way for the enhanced individualism so much a part of the Early Modern period.

Petrarch was a deeply committed humanist. In the context of the fourteenth century, this locution indicates a person intensely interested in the literature of the ancient world, especially works written in Latin, for the knowledge of classical Greek was nearly extinct in Italy and other western European countries throughout the Middle Ages and into the fifteenth century. The Renaissance or rebirth of classical culture grew largely out of the efforts of humanists like Petrarch. They realized that, although Latin had remained the language of scholarship and of the most serious literature throughout the Middle Ages, the level of eloquence was well below that of such ancient writers as Virgil, Horace, and Cicero.

Petrarch and his contemporaries became keenly aware of a substantial historical gap between the grandeur of ancient Rome and their own time. The Renaissance or Early Modern age took as one of its main premises the notion that this lost cultural ideal could somehow be restored. As part of their agenda, humanists looked for neglected manuscripts by classical writers to supplement the limited selection available at the beginning of the fourteenth century. A major event in the development of humanism occurred when Petrarch discovered a collection of personal letters by Cicero, who became for the Renaissance the model of elegant prose that was refined but relaxed, learned but not pedantic. Another landmark event took place in Rome in 1341, when Petrarch was presented a special award in recognition of his poetic talent. He was crowned with laurel during a ceremony that marked the resumption—

after a full thousand years—of an ancient Roman practice of honoring poets. The modern concept of a "poet laureate" originates in the crown given to Petrarch.

The sonnets and other poems that form the basis of Petrarch's lasting reputation were composed in Italian—and not in the polished Latin in which he also wrote and which he considered the vehicle for the most profound literature.[1] This poetry in Italian is largely concerned with his love for Laura. A mysterious woman, she has never been identified, nor do we know the extent of the poet's involvement with her. It is only known that she was married to someone else and that she died in 1348 during an epidemic of the plague. Petrarch's verse acquires a somber tone after her passing, and the poems are usually divided into two chronological groups, those composed during Laura's lifetime and those written after her death. But in reading the poems, it is necessary to realize that Petrarch often uses the name "Laura" as a poetic way of referring to the laurel, the symbol of his own powers and fame as a writer.

The literary work Petrarch considered his most significant was never completed. This work is the *Africa*, an epic that he wrote in Latin in hopes of reviving classical epic. The *Africa* deals with the Punic Wars, an ancient conflict that concluded when Rome destroyed Carthage in northern Africa. Readers today are likely to dismiss the epic as Eurocentric if they can first manage to work past its shortcomings as literature. Yet Petrarch was nostalgic for a strong Rome during a period when his country was deeply divided. Also notable is the skilful depiction of Sophonisba, wife of the king of Libya, who has an affair with one of the allies of the conquering Roman general. The literary portrait of Sophonisba is one of the few memorable passages in the epic.

During his distinguished career, Petrarch endured misfortunes. As we have seen, he lost Laura, and he rightly sensed that his epic was bound for oblivion. He was also somewhat of an outsider in the culture he came to represent, for his family had been exiled from Florence; he spent many years living in and near Avignon in southern France, where the papal court was located for most of the fourteenth century. The paradoxes of his life reflect the tempestuous transition from medieval to Early Modern Europe. (NW)

NOTES

1. It is worth recalling that Petrarch did not create the sonnet, a 14-line form which Italian poets had been writing since the first half of the thirteenth century. Set forms are unusual in European poetry, and it is possible that Arabic models had an impact on the development of the sonnet. Highly patterned Chinese poems may have in turn influenced an Arabic source.

BIBLIOGRAPHY

Bermann, Sandra. *The Sonnet over Time: A Study in the Sonnets of Petrarch, Shakespeare, and Baudelaire.* Chapel Hill: University of North Carolina Press, 1988.

Bloom, Harold, ed. *Petrarch.* New York: Chelsea House, 1989.

Boyle, Marjorie O'Rourke. *Petrarch's Genius: Pentimento and Prophecy.* Berkeley: University California Press, 1991.

Foster, Kenelm. *Petrarch: Poet and Humanist.* Edinburgh: Edinburgh University Press, 1984.

Mazzotta, Giuseppe. *The Worlds of Petrarch.* Durham: Duke University Press, 1993.

Petrarch. *The Sonnets, Triumphs, and Other Poems Translated into English Verse.* Various Translators. London: Henry G. Bohn: 1859.

from the Lyric Poetry

Petrarch
(various translators)

Sonnet 1

Ye, who may listen to each idle strain
Bearing those sighs, on which my heart was fed
In life's first morn, by youthful error led,
(Far other then from what I now remain!)
That thus in varying numbers I complain,
Numbers of sorrow vain and vain hope bred,
If any in love's lore be practisèd,
His pardon,—e'en his pity I may obtain
But now aware that to mankind my name
Too long has been a bye-word and a scorn,
I blush before my own severer thought;
Of my past wanderings the sole fruit is shame;
And deep repentance, of the knowledge born
That all we value in this world is naught.

Sonnet LXI

Blest be the year, the month, the hour, the day,
The season and the time, and point of space,
And blest the beauteous country and the place
There first of two bright eyes I felt the sway:
Blest the sweet pain of which I was the prey,
When newly doom'd Love's sovereign law to embrace
And blest the bow and shaft to which I trace,
The wound that to my inmost heart found way:
Blest be the ceaseless accents of my tongue,
Unwearied breathing my loved lady's name:
Blest my fond wishes, sighs, and tears, and pains:
Blest be the lays in which her praise is sung,
That on all sides acquired to her fair fame,
And blest my thoughts! for o'er them all she reigns.

Sonnet XC

Loose to the breeze her golden tresses flow'd
Wildly in thousand mazy ringlets blown,
And from her eyes unconquered glances shone,
Those glances now so sparingly bestow'd.
And true or false, meseem'd some signs she show'd
As o'er her cheek soft pity's hue was thrown;
I, whose whole breast with love's soft food was sown,
What wonder if at once my bosom glow'd?
Graceful she moved, with more than mortal mien,
In form an angel: and her accents won
Upon the ear with more than human sound.
A spirit heavenly pure, a living sun,
Was what I saw; and if no more 'twere seen,
T'unbend the bow will never heal the wound.

Sonnet CCXCII

The eyes, the arms, the hands, the feet, the face,
Which made my thoughts and words so warm and wild,
That I was almost from myself exiled,
And render'd strange to all the human race;
The lucid locks that curl'd in golden grace,
The lightening beam that, when my angel smiled,
Diffused o'er earth an Eden heavenly mild;
What are they now? Dust, lifeless dust, alas!
And I live on, a melancholy slave,
Toss'd by the tempest in a shatter'd bark,
Reft of the lovely light that cheer'd the wave.
The flame of genius, too, extinct and dark,
Here let my lays of love conclusion have;
Mute be the lyre: tears best my sorrows mark.

Sonnet CCC

What envy of the greedy earth I bear,
That holds from me within its cold embrace
The light, the meaning, of that angel face,
On which to gaze could soften e'en despair.
What envy of the saints, in realms so fair,
Who eager seem'd, from that bright form of grace,
The spirit pure to summon to its place,
Amidst those joys, which few can hope to share;
What envy of the blest in heaven above,
With whom she dwells in sympathies divine
Denied to me on earth, though sought in sighs;

And oh! what envy of stern Death I prove,
That with her life has ta'en the light of mine,
Yet calls me not,—though fixed and cold those eyes.

Sonnet CCCXXXIII

  Go, melancholy rhymes! your tribute bring
To that cold stone which holds the dear remains
Of all that earth held precious;—uttering,
If heaven should deign to bear them, earthly strains.
Tell her, that sport of tempests, no more
To stem the troublous ocean,—here at last
Her votary treads the solitary shore;
His only pleasure to recall the past.
Tell her, that she who living ruled his fate,
In death still holds her empire: all his care,
So grant the Muse her aid,—to celebrate
Her every word, and thought, and action fair.
Be this my meed, that in the hour of death
Her kindred spirit may hail, and bless my parting breath!

A Canzone (Song)
CXXIX

  From hill to hill I roam, from thought to thought,
With Love my guide; the beaten path I fly,
For there in vain the tranquil life is sought:
If 'mid the waste well forth a lonely rill,
Or deep embosom'd a low valley lie,   5
In its calm shade my trembling heart is still;
And there, if Love so will,
I smile, or weep, or fondly hope, or fear,
While on my varying brow, that speaks the soul,
The wild emotions roll,   10
Now dark, now bright, as shifting skies appear;
That whosoe'er has proved the lover's state
Would say, "He feels the flame, nor knows his future fate."

On mountains high, in forests drear and wide,
I find repose, and from the throng'd resort   15
Of man turn fearfully my eyes aside;
At each lone step thoughts ever new arise
Of her I love, who oft with cruel sport
Will mock the pangs I bear, the tears, the sighs;
Yet e'en these ills I prize,   20
Though bitter, sweet, nor would they were removed:
For my heart whispers me, Love yet has power
To grant a happier hour:
Perchance, though self-despised, thou yet art loved:

E'en then my breast a passing sigh will heave,   25
Ah! when, or how, may I a hope so wild believe?

Where shadows of high rocking pines dark wave
I stay my footsteps, and on some rude stone
With thought intense her beauteous face engrave;
Roused from the trance, my bosom bathed I find   30
With tears, and cry, Ah! whither thus alone
Hast thou far wander'd, and whom left behind?
But as with fixèd mind
On this fair image I impassioned rest,
And, viewing her, forget awhile my ills,   35
Love my rapt fancy fills;
In its own error sweet the soul is blest,
While all around so bright the visions glide;
Oh! might the cheat endure, I ask not aught beside.

Her form portray'd within the lucid stream   40
Will oft appear, or on the verdant lawn,
Or glossy beech, or fleecy cloud, will gleam
So lovely fair, that Leda's self might say,
Her Helen sinks eclipsed, as at the dawn
A star when cover'd by the solar ray: 45
And, as o'er wilds I stray
Where the eye nought but savage nature meets,
There Fancy most her brightest tints employs
But when rude truth destroys
The loved illusion of those dreamèd sweets,   50
I sit me down on the cold rugged stone,
Less cold, less dead than I, and think, and weep alone.

Where the huge mountain rears his brow sublime,
On which no neighbouring height its shadow flings,
Led by desire intense the steep I climb;   55
And tracing in the boundless space each woe,
Whose sad remembrance my torn bosom wrings,
Tears, that bespeak the heart o'erfraught, will flow:
While, viewing all below,
From me, I cry, what worlds of air divide   60
The beauteous form, still absent and still near!
Then, chiding soft the tear,
I whisper low, haply she too has sigh'd
That thou art far away: a thought so sweet
Awhile my labouring soul will of its burden cheat.   65

Go thou, my song, beyond that Alpine bound,
Where the pure smiling heavens are most serene,
There by a murmuring stream may I be found,
Whose gentle airs around
Waft grateful odours from the laurel green;   70
Nought but my empty form roams here unblest,
There dwells my heart with her who steals it from my breast.

from the Letters

Translated by James Harvey Robinson and Henry Winchester Rolfe

TO DIONISIO DA BORGA SAN SEPOLCRO[1]

The Ascent of Mount Ventoux

To-day I made the ascent of the highest mountain in this region, which is not improperly called Ventosum.[2] My only motive was the wish to see what so great an elevation had to offer. I have had the expedition in mind for many years; for, as you know, I have lived in this region from infancy, having been cast here by that fate which determines the affairs of men. Consequently the mountain, which is visible from a great distance, was ever before my eyes, and I conceived the plan of some time doing what I have at last accomplished to-day. The idea took hold upon me with especial force when, in re-reading Livy's *History of Rome*, yesterday, I happened upon the place where Philip of Macedon, the same who waged war against the Romans, ascended Mount Haemus in Thessaly, from whose summit he was able, it is said, to see two seas, the Adriatic and the Euxine. Whether this be true or false I have not been able to determine, for the mountain is too far away, and writers disagree. Pomponius Mela, the cosmographer—not to mention others who have spoken of this occurrence—admits its truth without hesitation; Titus Livius, on the other hand, considers it false.

I, assuredly, should not have left the question long in doubt, had that mountain been as easy to explore as this one. Let us leave this matter one side, however, and return to my mountain here,—it seems to me that a young man in private life may well be excused for attempting what an aged king could undertake without arousing criticism. . . .

One peak of the mountain, the highest of all, the country people call "Sonny," why, I do not know, unless by antiphrasis, as I have sometimes suspected in other instances; for the peak in question would seem to be the father of all the surrounding ones. On its top is a little level place, and here we could at last rest our tired bodies.[3]

Now, my father, since you have followed the thoughts that spurred me on in my ascent, listen to the rest of the story, and devote one hour, I pray you, to reviewing the experiences of my entire day. At first, owing to the unaccustomed quality of the air and the effect of the great sweep of view spread out before me, I stood like one dazed. I beheld the clouds under our feet, and what I had read of Athos and Olympus seemed less incredible as I myself witnessed the same things from a mountain of less fame. I turned my eyes toward Italy, whither my heart most inclined. The Alps, rugged and snow-capped, seemed to rise close by, although they were really at a great distance; the very same Alps through which that fierce enemy of the Roman name once made his way, bursting the rocks, if we may believe the report, by the application of vinegar. I sighed, I must confess, for the skies of Italy, which I beheld rather with my mind than with my eyes. An inexpressible longing came over me to see once more my friend and my country. At the same time I reproached myself for this double weakness, springing, as it did, from a soul not yet steeled to manly resistance. And yet there were excuses for both of these cravings, and a number of distinguished writers might be summoned to support me. . . .

While I was thus dividing my thoughts, now turning my attention to some terrestrial object that lay before me, now raising my soul, as I had done my body, to higher planes, it occurred to me to look into my copy of St. Augustine's *Confessions*, a gift that I owe to your love, and that I always have about me, in memory of both the author and the giver. I opened the compact little volume, small indeed in size, but of infinite charm, with the intention of reading whatever came to hand, for I could happen upon nothing that would be otherwise than edifying and devout. Now it chanced that the tenth book presented itself. My brother, waiting to hear something of St Augustine's from my lips, stood attentively by. I call him, and God too, to witness that where I first fixed my eyes it was written: "And men go about to wonder at the heights of the mountains, and the mighty waves of the sea, and the wide sweep of rivers, and the circuit of the ocean, and the revolution of the stars, but themselves they consider not." I was abashed, and, asking my brother (who was anxious to hear more), not to annoy me, I closed the book, angry with myself that I should still be admiring earthly things who might long ago have learned from even the pagan philosophers that nothing is wonderful but the soul, which, when great itself, finds nothing great outside itself. Then, in truth, I was satisfied that I had seen enough of the mountain; I turned my inward eye upon myself, and from that time not a syllable fell from my lips until we reached the bottom again. . . .

Notes

1. *Fam.*, iv., I. This letter, written when Petrarch was about thirty-two years old, is addressed to an Augustinian monk, professor of divinity and philosophy in the University of Paris which drew several of its most famous teachers from Italy. It was probably in Paris that Petrarch first met him. The poet, we may infer from the present letter, made him his spiritual confidant, confessed to him his sinful love for Laura, whom he had first met six years before, and received from the monk, in addition to the natural spiritual counsels, a copy of St. Augustine's *Confessions*, to which he refers in this excerpt. Dionysius was called in 1339 to Naples, and proved an agreeable companion for the sage ruler of that kingdom, not only on account of his distinguished moral and intellectual qualities, but by reason of his proficiency in the theory and practice of astrology, in which Robert took a profound interest.

2. That is, Windy.

3. "Our": Petrarch has climbed the mountain with his younger brother, Gherardo.

———————— *Questions for Consideration* ————————

Using complete sentences, provide brief answers for the following questions.

1. Record some of the themes, ideas, and literary devices that you have encountered in your reading of Petrarch's poetry and his "Ascent of Mount Ventoux."

    _____

    _____

    _____

    _____

    _____

2. Summarize the main points that the selections from Petrarch tell you about the Early Modern period.

    _____

    _____

    _____

    _____

    _____

3. Sonnets are very difficult to write, but poets over the centuries have struggled to produce them. In the interests of becoming more familiar with the characteristics of this challenging poetic form, try writing a sonnet on a romantic or other topic.

    _____

    _____

    _____

    _____

    _____

Name _____ Date _____ Grade _____

———————————— *Writing Critically* ————————————

Select one of the topics listed below and compose a 500-word essay that discusses the topic fully. Support your thesis with evidence from the text and with critical and/or historical material. Use the space below for preparing to write the essay.

1. Discuss the concept of romantic love presented in Petrarch's poetry. It is often noted that Petrarch presents an idealized view of romantic love. Consider whether his idealized view is entirely fair to women. In evaluating Petrarch's poetry, cite examples from other works of literature in which women are portrayed.

2. Compare one of Petrarch's sonnets with a sonnet written by Shakespeare, Spenser, or Wordsworth. Examine similarities and differences of form and meaning.

Prewriting Space:

_____
_____
_____
_____
_____
_____
_____
_____
_____
_____
_____
_____
_____
_____
_____
_____
_____
_____
_____
_____

Introduction

Giovanni Boccaccio (1313–1375)

Along with Aesop, Ovid, and a few others, Boccaccio was one of the greatest storytellers who ever lived. He was also a primary figure in consolidating major trends that developed at the end of the Middle Ages and led into the Early Modern period in Italy. Although mainly remembered for his fascinating collection of tales, the *Decameron*, he wrote in many genres. In gaining an understanding of Boccaccio's place in literary history, it is useful to think of him as an early Italian humanist who built upon the precedents set by Petrarch, who in turn, as much as any single individual, was the initiator of the Renaissance or Early Modern period in Europe.

Born in or near Florence, Boccaccio was an illegitimate child. While the identity of his mother is unknown, his father, who worked for a prosperous Florence banking company, took full responsibility for the child, officially adopting him and arranging for his education. In 1327, the Bardi bank of Florence sent the father to Naples to head the office there. The young Giovanni was taken along and received training in accounting and other skills essential for success as a merchant. His interests were in literature and not business, however, and he spent much of his time writing poetry and collecting books. Until around 1340, Boccaccio enjoyed a leisurely life in the enchanting seaside city of Naples.

During this period, he also began producing literary works that set the stage for much future literature in Italy and in other countries as well. Although some of these works are not widely read today, they are significant because Boccaccio was eager to innovate in both style and subject matter. Several of the early texts were the first of their type in Italian.

Boccaccio was deeply impressed by Petrarch, who was the premier man of letters of the mid-fourteenth century and whom Boccaccio met in 1350. After this point, he endeavored to perfect his Latin skills, as was the fashion among the humanists (scholars who wished to revive the grandeur of Roman literature). Perhaps Boccaccio's foremost work in Latin is his *Geneologies of the Gentile Gods*, an extensive guide to classical mythology.

Yet he did not abandon his love of writing in the vernacular.[1] In fact, during the years just after the meeting with Petrarch, Boccaccio wrote the *Decameron*, from which selections are printed below. This collection of tales consists of one hundred stories preceded by a "frame tale" that sets the general scene and establishes the conditions according to which all of the ensuing tales will be presented. Like other advanced humanists of the tine, Boccaccio desired to display his skills in both Latin and Greek; the study of the latter was only beginning to be revived during this period. The title of the work is thus of Greek origin and combines words meaning "ten" and "day." The *Decameron's* hundred tales are narrated over a period of ten days by a group of seven young ladies and three young men who have quarantined themselves outside of Florence in the year 1348, when a severe outbreak of the plague was devastating the city. Boccaccio's overall approach is one of *realism,* of frank portrayal of character, customs, and social realities. The clear, readable, and stylistically rich language of the *Decameron* set the standard for Italian prose until the beginning of the eighteenth century.

Although many of the tales are of a coarsely humorous or sexual nature, Boccaccio's underlying concern with the disastrous epidemic should be kept in mind. His "frame tale" or preface describes the horrors of the plague, which he probably witnessed. Boccaccio was disturbed by the breakdown in ethics that was among the effects of the plague; the bawdy tales expose the licentious behavior that results when ordinary morals are forgotten.

However, Boccaccio's approach is hardly a moralistic medieval reaction to the evils of his day. There is an obvious delight as sensuality and general misbehavior are narrated. At the same time, the retreat of the seven women and three men into the countryside should not be interpreted as a kind of wild house party. Each one of the ten takes charge of the storytelling for one day and sets a theme that all of the ten tales for that day will follow. Boccaccio depicts a small, highly civilized community that lives in edifying contrast to the chaos of plague-infested Florence and to the dissolution described in the tales. The determination of the group to live "in order and in pleasure" is consistent with the new secular emphasis of the Early Modern period. (NW)

NOTE

1. The term "vernacular" means the ordinary, indigenous language of a people and place, as opposed to Latin, which was the "universal" language for most serious writing during the Middle Ages and into the Renaissance or Early Modern period. For Boccaccio, the vernacular is simply his native Italian.

BIBLIOGRAPHY

Bergin, Thomas G. *Boccaccio*. New York: Viking, 1981.

Boccaccio, Giovanni. *The Decameron*. In English, translator anonymous. 4 volumes. London: Gibbings, 1898.

Cottino-Jones, Marga. *Order from Chaos: Social and Aesthetic Harmonies in Boccaccio's Decameron*. Washington: University Press of America, 1982.

Mazzotta, Giuseppe. *The World at Play in Boccaccio's Decameron*. Princeton: Princeton University Press, 1986.

Scaglione, Aldo D. *Nature and Love in the Late Middle Ages*. Berkeley: University of California Press, 1963.

Wallace, David. *Giovanni Boccaccio, Decameron*. Cambridge: Cambridge University Press, 1991.

from The Decameron

Giovanni Boccaccio
(translator anonymous)

Introduction

To the Ladies

Whenever I reflect how disposed you are by nature to compassion, I cannot help being apprehensive lest what I now offer to your acceptance should seem to have but a melancholy beginning. For it calls to mind the remembrance of that most fatal plague, so terrible yet in the memories of us all, an account of which is in the front of this book. But be not frightened too soon, as if you expected to meet with nothing else. This beginning, disagreeable as it is, is as a rugged and steep mountain placed before a delightful valley, which appears more beautiful and pleasant as the way to it was more difficult; for, as joy usually ends with sorrow, so again the end of sorrow is joy. To this short fatigue (I call it short, because contained in few words) immediately succeed the mirth and pleasure I had before promised you; and which, but for that promise, you would scarcely expect to find. And in truth, could I have brought you by any other way than this, I would gladly have done it; but, as the occasion of the occurrences of which I am going to treat could not well be made out without such a relation, I am forced to use this Introduction.

In the year then of our Lord 1348, there happened at Florence, the finest city in all Italy, a most terrible plague; which, whether owing to the influence of the planets, or that it was sent from God as a just punishment for our sins, had broken out some years before in the Levant; and after passing from place to place, and making incredible havoc all the way, had now reached westward to the above-named city, where, spite of all the means that art and human foresight could suggest, as keeping the city clear from filth, and excluding all suspected persons; not-

withstanding frequent consultations what else was to be done, nor omitting prayers to God in frequent processions, in the spring of the foregoing year it began to show itself in a sad and wonderful manner; and, different from what it had been in the East, where bleeding from the nose is the fatal prognostic, here there appeared certain tumours in the groin or under the armpits, some as big as a small apple, others as an egg; and afterwards purple spots in most parts of the body; in some cases large and but few in number; in others less and more numerous, both sorts the usual harbingers of death. To the cure of this malady, neither medical knowledge, nor the power of drugs, was of any effect; whether because the disease was in its own nature mortal, or that the physicians (the number of whom, taking quacks and women pretenders into the account, was grown very great) could form no just idea of the cause, nor consequently ground a true method of cure—whichever was the reason, few or none escaped, but they generally died the third day from the first appearance of the symptoms, without a fever or other bad circumstance attending. And the disease, by being communicated from the sick to the well, seemed daily to get ahead, and to rage the more, as fire will do, by laying on fresh combustibles. Nor was it caught only by conversing with or coming near the sick, but even by touching their clothes, or anything that they had before touched. It is wonderful, what I am going to mention; which had I not seen it with my own eyes, and were there not many witnesses to attest it besides myself, I should never venture to relate, however credibly I might have been informed about it;—such, I say, was the quality of the pestilential matter as to pass not only from man to man, but, what is more strange, and has been often known, that anything belonging to the infected, if touched by any other creature, would certainly infect and even kill that creature in a short space of time. And one instance of this kind I took particular notice of; namely, that the rags of a poor man just dead, being thrown into the street, and two hogs coming by at the same time, and rooting amongst them, and shaking them about in their mouths, in less than an hour turned round, and died on the spot. These accidents, and others of a like sort, occasioned various fears and devices amongst those people that survived, all tending to the same uncharitable and cruel end; which was, to avoid the sick, and everything that had been near them expecting by that means to save themselves. And some, holding it best to live temperately, and to avoid excesses of all kinds, made parties, and shut themselves up from the rest of the world; eating and drinking moderately of the best, and diverting themselves with music, and such other entertainments as they might have within doors; never listening to anything from without, to make them uneasy. Others maintained free living to be a better preservative, and would baulk no passion or appetite they wished to gratify, drinking and revelling incessantly from tavern to tavern, or in private houses, which were frequently found deserted by the owners, and therefore common to every one; yet avoiding, with all this irregularity, to come near the infected. And such, at that time, was the public distress, that the laws, human and divine, were not regarded; for the officers who should have put them in force being either dead, sick, or in want of persons to assist them, every one did just as he pleased. A third sort of people chose a method between these two; not confining themselves to rules of diet like the former, and yet avoiding the intemperance of the latter, but eating and drinking what their appetites required; and, instead of shutting themselves, up, they walked everywhere, with odours and nosegays to smell to, as holding it best to corroborate the brain, for they supposed the whole atmosphere to be tainted with the stink of dead bodies, arising partly from the distemper itself, and partly from the fermenting of the medicines within them. Others of a more cruel disposition, as perhaps the more safe to themselves, declared that the only remedy was to avoid it: persuaded, therefore, of this, and taking care for themselves only, men and women in great numbers left the city, their houses, relations, and effects, and fled into the country; as if the wrath of God had been restrained to visit those only within the walls of the city, or else concluding that none ought to stay in a place thus doomed to destruction. Divided as they were, neither did all die nor all escape; but falling sick indifferently, as well those of one as of another opinion, they who first set the example by forsaking others now languished themselves without mercy. I pass over the little regard that citizens and relations showed to each other; for their terror was such that a brother even fled from his brother, a wife from her husband, and, what is more uncommon, a mother from her own child. On which account numbers that fell sick could have no help but what the charity of friends, who were very few, or the avarice of servants supplied; and even these were scarce, and at extravagant wages, and so little used to the business that they were fit only to reach what was called for, and observe when their employers died; and their desire of getting money often cost them their lives.

From this desertion of friends, and scarcity of servants, an unheard-of custom prevailed: no lady, however young or handsome, would disdain being attended by a man-servant, whether young or old it mattered not, and to expose herself naked to him, the necessity of the distemper requiring it, as though it were to a woman; which might make those who recovered less modest for the time to come. And many lost their lives, who might have escaped, had they been looked after at all. So that, between the scarcity of servants and violence of the distemper, such numbers were continually dying as made it terrible to hear as well as to behold. Whence, from mere necessity, many customs were introduced, different from what had been before known in the city. It had been usual, as it now is, for the women who were friends and neighbours to the deceased to meet together at his house, and to lament with his relations; at the same time the men would get together at the door, with a number of clergy, according to the person's circumstances; and the corpse was carried by people of his own rank, with the solemnity of tapers and singing, to that church where the person had desired to be buried; which custom was now laid aside, and, so far from having a crowd of women to lament over them, great numbers passed out of the world without a single person present, and few had the tears of their friends at their departure; but those friends would laugh, and make themselves merry, for even the women had learned to postpone every other concern to that of their own lives. Nor was a corpse attended by more than ten or a dozen, nor those citizens of credit, but fellows hired for the purpose, who would put themselves under the bier, and carry it with all possible haste to the nearest church; and the corpse was interred without any great ceremony, where they could find room.

With regard to the lower sort, and many of a middling rank, the scene was still more affecting; for they staying at home, either through poverty or hopes of succour in distress, fell sick daily by thousands, and, having nobody to attend them, generally died; some breathed their last in the streets, and others shut up in their own houses, in which case the stench that came from them made the first discovery of their deaths to the neighbourhood. And, indeed, every place was filled with the dead. A method now was taken, as well out of regard to the living as pity for the dead, for the neighhours, assisted by what porters they could meet with, to clear all the houses, and lay the bodies at the doors; and every morning great numbers might be seen brought out in this manner, from whence they were carried away on biers or tables, two or three at a time; and sometimes it has happened that a wife and her husband, two or three brothers, and a father and son, have been laid on together: it has been observed also, whilst two or three priests have walked before a corpse with their crucifix, that two or three sets of porters have fallen in with them; and, where they knew but of one, they have buried six, eight, or more; nor was there any to follow, and shed a few tears over them; for things were come to that pass, that men's lives were no more regarded than the lives of so many beasts. Hence it plainly appeared that what the wisest, in the ordinary course of things, and by a common train of calamities, could never be taught,—namely, to bear them patiently,—this, by the excess of those calamities, was now grown a familiar lesson to the most simple and unthinking. The consecrated ground no longer containing the numbers which were continually brought thither, especially as they were desirous of laying every one in the parts allotted to their families, they were forced to dig trenches, and to put them in by hundreds, piling them up in rows, as goods are stowed in a ship, and throwing in a little earth till they were filled to the top. Not to rake any farther into the particulars of our misery, I shall observe that it fared no better with the adjacent country; for to omit the different castles about us, which presented the same view in miniature with the city, you might see the poor distressed labourers, with their families, without cither the help of physicians or care of servants, languishing on the highways, in the fields, and in their own home, and dying rather like cattle than human creatures; and growing dissolute in their manners like the citizens, and careless of everything, as supposing every day to be their last, their thoughts were not so much employed how to improve, as to make use of their substance for their present support; whence it happened that the flocks and herds, and the dogs themselves, ever faithful to their masters, being driven from their own homes, would wander, no regard being had to them, among the forsaken harvest; and many times, after they had filled themselves in the day, would return of their own accord like rational creatures at night. What can I say more, if I return to the city?—unless that such was the cruelty of Heaven, and perhaps of men, that between March and July following, it is supposed, and made pretty certain, that upwards of a hundred thousand souls perished in the city only; whereas, before that calamity it was not supposed to have contained so many inhabitants. What magnificent dwellings, what noble palaces were then depopulated to the last person! what families extinct! what riches and vast possessions left, and no known heir to inherit! what numbers of both sexes in the prime and vigour of youth—whom in the morning neither Galen, Hippocrates, nor Æsculapius himself, but would have declared in perfect health—after dining heartily with their friends here, have supped with their departed friends in the other world!

But I am weary of recounting our late miseries; therefore, passing by everything that I can well omit, I shall only observe that, the city being left almost without inhabitants, it happened one Tuesday in the morning, as I was informed by persons of good credit, that seven ladies all in deep mourning, as most proper for that time, had been attending divine service (being the whole congregation) in the Church of Santa Maria Novella: who, as united by the ties either of friendship or relation, and of suitable years,—the youngest not less than eighteen, nor the eldest exceeding twenty-eight,—so were they all discreet, nobly descended and perfectly accomplished, both in person and behaviour. I do not mention their names, lest they should be displeased with some things said to have passed in conversation, there being a greater restraint on those diversions now; nor would I give a handle to ill-natured persons who carp at everything that is praiseworthy, to detract in any way from their modesty by injurious reflections. And that I may relate therefore all that occurred without confusion, I shall affix names to everyone, bearing some resemblance to the quality of the person. The eldest then I call Pampinea, the next to her Fiammetta, the third Filomena, the fourth

Emilia, the fifth Lauretta, the sixth Neifile, and the youngest Elisa; who being got together, by chance rather than any appointment, into a corner of the church, and there seated in a ring, and leaving off their devotions, and falling into some discourse together concerning the nature of the times, in a little while Pampinea thus began:

"My dear girls, you have often heard, as well as I, that no one is injured where we only make an honest use of our own reason; now reason tells us that we are to preserve our lives by all possible means, and, in some cases, at the expense of the lives of others. And if the laws, which regard the good of the community, allow this, may not we much rather (and all that mean honestly as we do), without giving offence to any, use the means now in our power for our own preservation? Every moment when I think of what has passed to-day, and every day, I perceive, as you may also, that we are all in pain for ourselves. Nor do I wonder at this; but much rather, as we are women, do I wonder that none of us should look out for a remedy, where we have so much reason to be afraid. We stay here for no other purpose, that I can see, but to observe what numbers come to be buried, or to listen if the monks, who are now reduced to a very few, sing their services at the proper times, or else to show by our habits the greatness of our distress. And, if we go from hence, we are saluted with numbers of the dead and sick carried along the streets, or with persons who had been outlawed for their villanies, now facing it out publicly, in defiance of the laws; or we see the scum of the city enriched with the public calamity, and insulting us with reproachful ballads. Nor is anything talked of, but that such an one is dead or dying; and, were any left to mourn, we should hear nothing but lamentations. Or, if we go home—I know not whether it fares with you as with myself—when I find out of a numerous family not one left besides a maidservant, I am frightened out of my senses; and, go where I will, the ghosts of the departed seem always before my eyes; not like the persons whilst they were living, but assuming a ghastly and dreadful aspect. Therefore the case is the same whether we stay here, depart hence, or go home; especially as there are few left who are able to go, and have a place to go to, but ourselves. And those few, I am told, fall into all sorts of debauchery; and even the religious and ladies shut up in monasteries, supposing themselves entitled to equal liberties with others, are as bad as the worst. And, if this be so (as you see plainly it is), what do we here? What are we dreaming of? Why less regardful of our lives than other people of theirs? Are we of less value to ourselves, or are our souls and bodies more firmly united, and so in less danger of dissolution? 'Tis monstrous to think in such a manner; so many of both sexes dying of this distemper in the very prime of their youth affords us an undeniable argument to the contrary. Wherefore, lest through our own wilfulness or neglect this calamity, which might have been prevented, should befall us, I should think it best (and I hope you will join with me) for us to quit the town, and avoiding, as we would death itself, the bad example of others, to choose some place of retirement, of which every one of us has more than one, where we may make ourselves innocently merry, without offering the least violence to the dictates of reason and our own consciences. There will our ears be entertained with the warbling of the birds, and our eyes with the verdure of the hills and valleys; with the waving of corn-fields like the sea itself; with trees of a thousand different kinds, and a more open and serene sky, which, however overcast, yet affords a far more agreeable prospect than these desolate walls. The air also is pleasanter, and there is greater plenty of everything, attended with fewer inconveniences; for, though people die there as well as here, yet we shall have fewer such objects before us, as the inhabitants are less in number; and on the other part, if I judge right, we desert nobody, but are rather ourselves forsaken. For all our friends, either by death, or endeavouring to avoid it, have left us, as if we in no way belonged to them. As no blame then can ensue by following this advice, and perhaps sickness and death by not doing so, I would have us take our maids, and everything we may be supposed to want, and to remove every day to a different place, taking all the diversions in the meantime which the seasons will permit; and there continue, unless death should interpose, till we see what end Providence designs for these things. And this I remind you of, that our character will stand as fair by our going away reputably as the characters of others will do who stay at home with discredit."

The ladies, having heard what Pampinea had to offer, not only approved of it, but were going to concert measures for their departure, when Filomena, who was a most discreet person, made answer: "Though Pampinea has spoken well, yet there is no occasion to run hand over head into it, as you are about to do. We are but women, nor is any of us so ignorant not to know how little able we shall be to conduct such an affair, without some man to help us. We are naturally fickle, obstinate, suspicious, and fearful and I doubt much, unless we take somebody into our scheme to manage it for us, lest it soon be at an end, and perhaps little to our reputation. Let us provide against this, therefore, before we begin.

Elisa then replied: "It is true, man is the head of a woman, and without his management it seldom happens that any undertaking of ours succeeds well. But how are these men to be come at? We all know that the greater part of our male acquaintance are dead, and the rest all dispersed abroad, avoiding what we seek to avoid, and without our knowing where to find them. And to take strangers with us would not be altogether so proper; for, whilst we have regard to our health, we should so contrive matters that, wherever we go to repose and divert ourselves, no scandal may ensue from it."

Whilst this was debated, behold, three young gentlemen came into the church (and yet the youngest was not less than twenty-five years of age), in whom neither the adversity of the times, the loss of relations and friends, nor even fear for themselves, could stifle, or indeed cool, the passion of love. One was called Pamfilo, the second Filostrato, and the third Dioneo, all of them well bred, and pleasant companions; and who, to divert themselves in this time of affliction, were then in pursuit of their mistresses, who by chance were three of these seven ladies, and the other four all related to one or other of them. These gentlemen were no sooner within view, but the ladies immediately had their eyes upon them; and Pampinea said, with a smile, "See, fortune is with us and has thrown in our way three prudent and worthy gentlemen, who will conduct and wait upon us, if we think fit to accept of their service." Neifile, with a blush, because she was one that had an admirer, answered: "Take care what you say; I know them all indeed to be persons of character, and fit to be trusted, even in affairs of more consequence, and in better company; but, as some of them are enamoured of certain ladies here, I am only concerned lest we be drawn into some scrape or scandal, without either our fault or theirs." Filomena replied: "Never tell me, so long as I know myself to be virtuous, what other people may think, God and the truth will be my defence; and, if they be willing to go, we will say with Pampinea that fortune is with us." The rest, hearing her speak in this manner, gave consent that they should be called, and invited to partake in this expedition. And, without more words, Pampinea—related to one of the three—rose up, and made towards them, who were standing at a distance, attentive to what passed, and, after a cheerful salutation,

acquainted them with their design, and entreated that they would, out of pure friendship, oblige them with their company. The gentlemen at first took it all for a jest; but, being assured to the contrary; immediately answered that they were ready; and, to lose no time, gave the necessary orders for what they would have done.

Everything being thus prepared, and a messenger despatched before, whither they intended to go, the next morning, which was Wednesday, by break of day, the ladies, with some of their women, and the gentlemen, with every one his servant, set out from the city, and, after they had travelled two short miles, came to the place appointed. It was a little eminence, remote from any great road, covered with trees and plants of an agreeable verdure; on the top of which was a stately palace, with a grand and beautiful court in the middle; within were galleries, and fine apartments elegantly fitted up, and adorned with most curious paintings; around it were fine meadows and most delightful gardens, with fountains of the purest and best water. The vaults also were stored with the richest wines, suited rather to the taste of epicures than of modest and virtuous ladies. This palace they found cleared out, and everything set in order for their reception, with the rooms all graced with the flowers of the season, to their great satisfaction.

Being seated, Dioneo, who was the pleasantest of them all, and full of words, began: "Your wisdom it is, ladies, rather than any foresight of ours, which has brought us hither. I know not how you have disposed of your cares; as for mine, I left them all behind me when I came from home. Either prepare, then, to be as merry as myself (I mean with decorum), or give me leave to go back again, and resume my cares where I left them." To whom Pampinea, as if she had disposed of hers in like manner, answered: "You say right, sir, we will be merry; we fled from our troubles for no other reason. But, as extremes are never likely to last, I who first proposed the means by which such an agreeable set of company is now got together, and being desirous to make our mirth of some continuance, find there is a necessity for our appointing a principal, whom we should honour and obey in all things as our head, whose province it shall be to regulate our diversions. And that every one may make trial of the burthen which attends care, as well as the pleasure which there is in superiority, nor therefore envy what he hath not yet tried, I hold it best that every one should experience both the trouble and the honour for one day: the first to be elected by us all, and who, on the approach of the evening, shall name a person to succeed for the following day; each, during the time of government, giving orders concerning the place where, and the manner how, we are to live." These words gave a general satisfaction, and they named Pampinea, with one consent, for the first day; whilst Filomena, running to a laurel tree, as having often heard how much that tree had always been esteemed, and what honour was conferred on those who were deservedly crowned with it, made a garland, and put it upon her head, which, whilst the company continued together, was hereafter to be the ensign of sovereignty.

Pampinea, thus elected queen, enjoined silence, and having summoned the gentlemen's servants, and their own women, who were four in number before her: "To give you the first example," said she, "how, by proceeding from good to better, we may live orderly and pleasantly, and continue together, without the least reproach, as long as we please, in the first place I declare Parmeno, Dioneo's servant, master of my household, and to him I commit the care of my family, and everything relating to my hall; Sirisco, Pamfilo's servant, I appoint my treasurer, and to be under the direction of Parmeno; and Tindaro I command to wait on Filostrato and the other two gentlemen, whilst their servants are thus employed. Misia, my woman, and Licisca, Filomena's, I order into the kitchen, there to get ready what shall be provided by Parmeno. To Chimera, Lauretta's, and Stratilia, Fiammetta's maid, I give the care of the ladies' chambers, and to keep the room clean where we sit. And I will and command you all, on pain of my displeasure, that wherever you go, or whatever you hear and see, you bring no news here but what is good." These orders were approved by them all; and she, rising from her seat, with a good deal of gaiety, added, "Here are gardens and meadows, where you may divert yourselves till nine o'clock, when I shall expect you back, that we may dine in the cool of the day."

The company were now at liberty, and the gentlemen and ladies took a pleasant walk in the garden, talking over a thousand merry things by the way, and diverting themselves them by singing love-songs and weaving garlands of flowers, and returned at the time appointed, when they found Parmeno busy in the execution of his office: for in a saloon below was the table set forth, covered with the neatest linen, with glasses re-flecting a lustre like silver; and having washed their hands, Parmeno, by the queen's order, desired them to sit down. The dishes now were served up in the most elegant manner, and the best wines brought in, the servants waiting all the time with the most profound silence; and, being well pleased with their entertainment, they dined with all the facetiousness and mirth imaginable. When dinner was over, as they could all dance, and some both play and sing well, the queen ordered in the musical instruments, and, commanding Dioneo to take a lute and Fiammetta a viol, they struck up a dance, and the queen, with the rest of the company, took an agreeable turn or two, whilst the servants were sent to dinner: when the dance was ended they began to sing, and continued till the queen thought it time to seek repose. Her permission being given, the gentlemen retired to their chambers, remote from the ladies' lodging-rooms, and the ladies did the same, and, having undressed themselves, lay down to rest.

Shortly after noontide the queen arose, and ordered all to be called, alleging that much sleep in the day-time was unwholesome; and they went into a meadow of deep grass, where the sun had little power; and, having the benefit of a pleasant breeze, they sat down in a circle, as the queen had commanded, who spoke in this manner: "As the sun is high, and the heat excessive, and nothing is to be heard but the chirping of the grasshoppers among the olives, it would be madness for us to think of moving yet. This is an airy place, and here are chess-boards And gammon-tables to divert yourselves with; but, if you are ruled by me, you will not play at all, since it often makes one party uneasy, without any great pleasure to the other or to the looker-on; but let us begin and tell stories, and in this manner one person will entertain the whole company; and by the time it has gone round the hottest part of the day will be over, and then we can divert ourselves as we like best. If this be agreeable to you, then—for I wait to know your pleasure—let us begin; if not, you are at your own disposal till the evening!" This motion was approved by all; whilst the queen continued, "Let every one for this first day take what subject he fancies most;" and turning to Pamfilo, who sat on her right hand, bade him begin; who, in ready obedience to her commands, and being heard attentively, spoke to this effect.

Day 1, Tale 4

As Boccaccio has explained in his introductory tale, the stories told during each day will conform to the directions of the monarch or leader for that day. As ruler for the first day, Pampinea has directed each participant to tell a story on a subject of his or her own choosing.

A *Monk having committed an offence, for which he ought to have been severely punished, saves himself by wittily proving his Abbot guilty of the very same fault.*

Thus ended Filomena, when Dioneo, who sat next to her (without waiting the queen's order, as knowing that he was to follow in course), spoke as follows:—

If I understand you aright, gracious ladies, we are assembled here to amuse ourselves by telling stories; whilst nothing, then, is done contrary to this intention, I suppose every one has liberty to relate what he thinks will be most entertaining. Therefore, having heard how, by the pious admonitions of Jeannot de Chevigny, Abraham the Jew was advised to his soul's salvation; and also how Melchizedech, by his good sense, saved his wealth from the designs of Saladin; I shall, without fear of reproof, show, in few words, how cunningly a monk saved his bones from the punishment intended him.

There was once, in the territories of Lunigiana, a monastery, better stored both with monks and religion than many are now-a-days, to which be-longed a young monk, whose constitution neither fasting nor praying could humble. Now it happened one day, early in the morning, whilst his brethren were all asleep, that, taking a walk about their church, which stood in a lonesome place, he cast his eye upon a pretty girl, a farmer's daughter, who was gathering herbs, and immediately felt a strong temptation, ill suiting with his profession; and drawing near, he entered into discourse with her, and prevailed upon her to go to his cell with him, before anybody was stirring abroad to see them; where, whilst they were diverting themselves together, it happened that the abbot, being just awake, and passing by the door, thought he heard something of a noise within; and laying his ear to listen, could distinguish a woman's voice. At first he was inclined to order the door to be opened, but he afterwards thought of a different method, and returned to his chamber to wait till the monk came out. The latter, though he was pleased with his companion, could not help being a little suspicious of a discovery, and imagining that he heard somebody treading at the door, he peeped through a crevice, and saw the abbot standing to listen; and knowing that he was detected, and should be soundly punished, he became very uneasy. Yet, without showing anything of it to the girl, he was contriving how to get clear of the affair; and he hit on a stratagem which succeeded to his heart's desire. Pretending that he could stay no longer—"I must go," he cried, "and will contrive a way to get you off without being seen; lie still, then, till I return." He now locked the door after him, and carried the key to the abbot, as is usual when they stir out of the monastery, and putting a good face on the matter, he said, "Reverend father, I could not get all my wood home this morning, and if you please I will go now and fetch the remainder." The abbot, willing to make a more perfect discovery, took the key, and gave leave. No sooner had the other departed, but he began to consider what he had best do in this case; whether to open the door in presence of all the monks, that so, the offence being known to all, they could have no room to murmur when he proceeded to punishment; or whether he should not rather inquire of the damsel herself how she had been brought thither. Supposing, also, that she might be a person's wife or daughter whom he would not have disgraced in that public manner, he thought it best to see first who she was, and then come to some resolution. So stepping privately to the chamber, he went in, and locked the door after him. The girl, on seeing him, was in great confusion, and fell a-weeping; whilst our abbot, finding her to be young and handsome, was seized (old as he was) with the same desires as the young monk had felt, and began to reason thus with himself: "Why should I not take a little pleasure when I may have it? for of plague and trouble I know enough every day. She is handsome, too. Nobody can ever know it. If I can persuade her, why should I not? Discovery is impossible, and a hidden sin is half pardoned. Such another offer may never fall in my way, and I hold it best to take it whilst I can have it." Upon this, his purpose in going thither being quite changed, he went nearer, and began to comfort her, desiring her not to weep; and making some farther advances, acquainted her, at last, with his intention and she, who was made neither of flint nor steel, easily complied with the abbot's wish; whereupon he embraced and kissed her, and being, as became his office, a somewhat ponderous person, out of tenderness to the girl, chose a rather unusual mode of achieving his aim.

The monk, who, under pretence of going to the wood, had concealed himself in the dormitory, on seeing the abbot go alone to his chamber, promised himself success; but when he saw him lock the door he thought it past all doubt; and, coming from the place where he lay hid, he heard and saw through a grating in the door all that passed between them. The abbot, after he had stayed some time, locked the door again, and returned to his chamber; and supposing the monk to be now come from the wood, he resolved to reprimand and imprison him, that so the girl might remain solely to himself; and causing him to be sent for, he gave him a severe rebuke, and ordered him to prison. The monk answered, very readily, "Good sir, I have not been so long of the Benedictine order as to be acquainted with all the particularities thereto belonging: your reverence instructed me well in the observance of fasts and vigils; but you never told me how I was to behave with regard to women, or that we should place ourselves in subjection to them. But, as you have so lately set me an example, I promise, if you will forgive me, to follow it, and to do hereafter as I have seen you." The abbot being quick of apprehension, found the monk knew more than he expected, and, being ashamed to punish him for a crime of which he himself was known to be guilty, he pardoned him; and, enjoining his silence, they had the girl conveyed privately out of the monastery, whither it is believed she frequently returned.

Day 11, Tale 5

Told while Filomena rules, this story deals with the theme of those who unexpectedly gain good fortune following a period of unhappiness.

*A*ndreuccio of Perugia, coming to Naples to buy horses, meets with three remarkable accidents in one night; from all which he escapes, and returns with a ruby of value.

The jewels found by Landolfo put me in mind, said Fiammetta, whose turn it was now to speak, of a story which contains as many perils as the last, although it be different in this respect,—that the first happened in the course of some years, whereas these fell out in the space of one night, as you shall hear.

There lived, as I have heard, at Perugia a young man named Andreuccio di Pietro, a dealer in horses, who, hearing of a good market at Naples, put five hundred florins of gold into his purse, and, having never been from home before, went with some other dealers, and arrived thither on a Sunday in the evening; and, according to the instruction he had received from his landlord, he went into the market next morning, where he saw many horses to his mind, cheapening their price as he went up and down, without coming to any bargain. But, to show people that he came with an intent to buy, he unadvisedly pulled out his purse on all occasions; insomuch

that a certain Sicilian damsel, very good-looking, but at every one's service for a small matter, got a sight of it as she was passing along, without being observed by him; and she said to herself, "Who is there that would be my betters, if that purse were mine?" and passed on. Along with this young wench was an old woman, of Sicily likewise, who, as soon as she saw Andreuccio, ran to embrace him, which the young woman observing, without saying a word, stepped aside to wait for her. He immediately knew her, to her great joy, and without much discourse there, she having promised to come to his inn, he went on about his business, but bought nothing all that morning. The young woman taking notice first of the purse, and then of the old woman's knowledge of him, and contriving how to come at all or part of the money, began to inquire of her, as cautiously as might be, if she knew who that man was, or whence he came, or what was his business, and also how she happened to know him; which she answered in every particular as fully as he himself could have done, having lived a long time with his father in Sicily, and afterwards at Perugia; telling her also the cause of his coming thither, and when he was to return. Thinking herself now sufficiently instructed, both concerning his kindred and their names, the fair damsel grounded her scheme upon it in the most artful manner possible; and going home, she furnished the old woman with employment for the whole day, to hinder her returning to him; and in the meantime, toward the evening, she despatched a young woman, well trained for such services, to his lodgings, who found him, by chance, sitting alone at the door, and inquiring of him whether he knew such a person of Perugia, he made answer that he was the man; upon which she took him a little aside, and said, "Sir, a gentlewoman of this city would gladly speak with you, if you please." On hearing this, he began to consider the matter; and held it for granted that the lady must be in love with him, thinking himself as handsome a man as any in Naples; he answered therefore that he was ready, and demanded where and when the lady would speak with him. The girl replied, "She expects you at her own house as soon as it is agreeable to you."

Without saying a word then to the people of the inn, he bade her show him the way; and the little maid brought him to the house, which was in a certain street called Malpertugio, a name which sufficiently indicates its character; but he, knowing nothing of the matter, nor at all suspecting but that he was visiting a place of good repute, and a lady that had taken a fancy to him, went into the house, and going upstairs (whilst the girl called aloud to her mistress, telling her that Andreuccio was there), found her at the top waiting for him. She was young and beautiful enough, and very well dressed. Seeing him appear, therefore, she ran down two or three steps with open arms to meet him; and taking him about the neck, she stood some time without speaking a word, as if prevented by her over-great tenderness; at last, shedding abundance of tears, and kissing him on the forehead, she said (her words being interrupted as it were with transport), "O my Andreuccio! you are heartily welcome." He, quite astonished at being caressed in such a manner, replied, "Madam, I am proud of the honour to wait upon you." She then took him by the hand, and led him, without saying a word more, through a large dining-room into her own chamber, which was perfumed with roses, orange-flowers, and other costly odours, where was also a fine bed, and other rich furniture, and garments hanging by the walls, far beyond what he had ever seen before, which convinced him that she was some great lady; and sitting down together upon a coffer at the bed's foot she addressed herself to him in this manner:—

"Andreuccio, I am very sure you must be under great astonishment both at my tears and embraces, as being unacquainted with me, and perhaps never having heard of me before; but you will now hear what will surprise you more, namely, that I am your sister: and I assure you that, since God has indulged me with the sight of one of my brethren, as I wished to have seen them all, I could die contented this very moment. If you be unacquainted with the particulars of my story, I will relate them. Pietro, my father and yours, as I suppose you must know, lived a long time at Palermo, where he was much respected for his behaviour and good-nature (and may be so still) by all that knew him. Amongst others that liked him on that account was my mother, a widow of good family; who, notwithstanding the regard due to her father and brothers, as well as to her own honour, became so intimate with him that at length I was born, and am now what you see. Having occasion afterwards to retire from Palermo, and to return to Perugia, our father left me there an infant, with my mother, and from that time, as far as I can learn, took no more notice either of me or her; which, were he not my father, I could blame him for, considering what ingratitude he showed to my mother—not to speak of the love he owed to me his child, begotten of no vile prostitute—who, out of her abundant love, had put herself and all her wealth into his hands, without having any farther knowledge of him. But to what purpose? Ill actions, done so long since, are easier blamed than amended. Yet so it was; he left me, as I said, at Palermo, an infant, where, when I grew up, my mother, who was rich, married me to one of the family of the Gergenti, who, out of regard to me and her, came and lived at Palermo, where, strongly adhering to the Guelph faction, and having begun to treat with our King Charles, he was discovered by Frederick, King of Arragon, before his scheme could take effect, and forced to fly from Sicily, at a time when I expected to have been the greatest lady in the island. Taking away what few effects we were able—I call them few, with regard to the abundance we were possessed of—and leaving our estates and palaces behind us, we came at length to this place, where we found King Charles so grateful that he has made up to us, in part, the losses we had sustained on his account, giving us lands and houses, and paying my husband, and your kinsman, a pension besides, as you will hereafter see. Thus live I here, where, thanks be to Heaven, and not to you, my dearest brother, I now see you." Which when she had said, she wept and tenderly embraced him again.

Andreuccio hearing this fable so orderly, so artfully composed, and related without the least faltering or hesitation; remembering also that his father had lived at Palermo, and knowing by his own experience how prone young fellows are to love; beholding too her tears and affectionate caresses, he took all she had said for granted, and when she had done speaking he made answer and said, "Madam, it should not seem strange to you that I am surprised; for, in truth—whether it was that my father, for reasons best known to himself, never mentioned you nor your mother at any time; or, if he did, that I have forgot it—I have no more knowledge of you than if you had never been born. And it is the more pleasing to me to find a sister here as I the less expected it, and am also alone; nor is there any man, of what quality soever, who would not value you; much more therefore shall I, who am but a mean trader. But one thing I beg you would clear up to me, namely, how came you to know that I was here?" When she replied in this manner: "A poor woman, whom I often employ, told me so this morning; for she lived, as she informed me, with our father a considerable time, both at Palermo and Perugia; and, were it not that it appeared more reputable that you should come to me at my house than I go to you at another person's, I had come directly to you." She then inquired of him particularly, and by name, how all their relations did; to all which he answered her fully, believing more firmly when there was the more reason for suspicion.

Their discourse lasting a long time, and the season being sultry, she ordered in Greek wine and sweetmeats for him; and he making an offer afterwards to depart, because it was sup-per-time, she would by no means suffer it; but seeming to be under great concern, she em-braced him, and said, "Alas! now I plainly see how little account you make of me; that, being with a sister whom you never saw before, and in her house, which you should always make your home, you should yet think of going to sup at an inn. Indeed you shall sup with me; and though my husband be abroad, which I am much concerned at, I know, as a woman, how to pay you some little respect." He, not know-ing what other answer to make, said, "I love you as much as it is possible for me to love a sister; but it will be wrong not to go, because they will expect me to supper all the evening." She immediately replied, "Heaven be praised, we have a present remedy for that; I will send one of my people to tell them not to expect you; but you would favour me more, and do as you ought if you would send to invite your com-pany hither to supper, and afterwards, if you chose to go, you might all of you depart to-gether." He said he should not trouble her that evening with his companions, but she might dispose of him as she pleased. She now made a pretence of sending to his inn, to tell them not to expect him to supper; and, after much other discourse, they sat down, and were elegantly served with a variety of dishes, which she con-trived to last till it was dark night. And rising then from table, he offered to go away; but she declared that she would by no means suffer it, for Naples was not a place to walk in when it was dark, especially for a stranger, and, as she had sent to the inn concerning his supping with her, so had she done the like about his bed. He believing this to be true, and glad also of being with her, was easily prevailed upon to remain. After supper, their discourse lasted a long

time, being lengthened out on purpose; and, as it was now midnight, she left him in her own cham-ber to take his repose with a boy to wait upon him; and she, with her women, retired into an-other room.

It was sultry hot, on which account Andreuc-cio, seeing himself alone, stripped to his doublet, and, pulling off his breeches, he laid them under his bolster, and, having occasion to retire, he asked the boy to show him a conveniency, who pointed to a corner of the room where there was a door, and desired him to enter it. He went in without the least suspicion, and set his foot upon a board which, not being nailed at the other end to the rafter on which it was laid, straight flew up, and down they went together.

Heaven was so merciful to him, however, that he took no harm, though it was a great height, but was grievously daubed with the filth of which the place was full. Now, that you may better understand this, and what followed also, I shall describe the place to you. In a narrow alley (as you see often between two houses), on tracings reaching from one to the other, were some boards laid, and a place to sit upon, and it was one of these boards that fell down with him. Finding himself now at the bottom, he called in great distress to the boy; but he, the moment he heard him fall, ran to tell his mistress, who hastened to his chamber, to see if his clothes were there, and finding both them and the money, which he, out of a foolish mistrust, always carried about him (and for the sake of which she had laid this snare, pretend-ing to have been of Palermo, and the sister of this Perugian), she took no further care, but made fast the door out of which he passed when he fell. Finding the boy made no answer, he called out louder, but to no purpose; and now, perceiving the trick when it was too late, he climbed up the wall which parted that place from the street, and getting down from thence he came again to the door, which he knew full well; there did he knock and call in vain for a long time, lamenting much, and seeing plainly his calamity. "Alas!" quoth he, "in how little time have I lost five hundred florins, and a sister besides!"

And using many other words, he now began to batter the door, and to call out aloud; and he continued doing so, till be raised many of the neighbours, and, among the rest, one of the women where he had been, pretending to be half asleep, opened the casement and called out angrily, "Who makes that noise there?" "Oh!" cried he, "don't you know me? I am Andreuccio, brother to Madam Fiordaliso." When she replied, "Prithee, honest fellow, if thou hast had too much liquor, get thee to bed, and come tomorrow. I know nothing of Andreuccio, nor what thy idle tale means; but go about thy business while thou mayst, and let us rest." "What!" said he, "don't you know what I say? You know well enough, if you will; but, if our Sicilian relationship be so soon forgotten, at least give me my clothes which I left with you, and I'll go with all my heart." She then replied, with a sneer, "The man is in a dream;" and shut the window at the same time.

Andreuccio, convinced of his loss, through his great grief became outrageous; and resolving to recover by force what he could not by fair words, took a great stone, and beat against the door harder than ever; which many of the neighbours hearing who had been awaked before, and supposing that he was some spiteful fellow that did this to annoy the woman, and provoked at the noise which he made, they called out, one and all, in like manner as dogs all join in barking at a strange cur, "It is a shameful thing to come to a woman's house at this time of night, with thy idle stories: get thee away, in God's name, and let us sleep; and if thou hast any business with her come to-morrow, and do not keep us awake all night." Encouraged, perhaps, by these last words, a bully in the house, whom he had neither seen nor heard of, came to the window, and, with a most rough and terrible voice, called out, "Who is that below?" Andreuccio, raising up his head at this, beheld an ill-looking rascal, with a great black beard, yawning and rubbing his eyes, as if he was just risen from bed and awaked out of his sleep. He made answer, therefore, not without a good deal of fear, "I am brother to the lady within;" but the other, never waiting to let him make an end of his speech, replied, "I'll come down and beat thee until thou canst not stand, for a troublesome drunken beast as thou art, disturbing everybody's rest in this manner; and he clapped to the window.

Hereupon some of the neighbours, who knew more of the fellow's disposition and character, called out softly to Andreuccio, and said, "For Heaven's sake, honest man, go away, unless thou hast a mind to lose thy life; it will be much the best for thee."

Terrified therefore with his voice and aspect, and persuaded also by these people, who seemed to speak out of mere goodwill, Andreuccio, quite cast down, and out of all hopes of receiving his money, now directed his course towards that part of the city from whence he had been led by the girl the day before (without knowing whither he was going), in order to get to his inn. But being offensive to himself, on account of the scent he carried about him, and desirous of washing in the sea, he turned to the left, through a street called Catalana, and went towards the highest part of the city, where he saw two people coming with a lantern, and fearing that they were the watch, or some ill-disposed persons, stepped into an old house that was near, to hide himself. It happened that these people were going into the very same place; and one of them having laid down some iron tools there, which he carried upon his neck, they had some discourse together about them. And as they were talking, said one to the other, "Here is the most confounded stink, whatever be the meaning of it, that ever I smelt in my life." Whereupon, holding up the lantern, they saw wretched Andreuccio, and, in a good deal of amaze, demanded who he was. He made no answer; and, drawing nearer with the light, they asked what he did there in that condition. He then related to them his whole adventure; and they, easily imagining the place where the thing had happened, said to one another, "This must certainly have been in the house of Scarabone Buttafuoco;" and then, turning towards him, one of them proceeded thus: "Honest man, you ought to be very thankful that you fell down, and could not return into the house, for otherwise you would certainly have been murdered as soon as ever you went to sleep, and so have lost your life as well as your money. But what signifies lamenting? You may as soon pluck a star out of the firmament as recover one farthing; nay, you may chance to be killed should the man hear that you make any words about it."

Having admonished him in this manner, they said, "See, we have pity on you, and if you will engage in a certain affair with us, which we are now about, we are very sure that your share will amount to more than you have lost." He, like a person in despair, told them he was willing.

That day was buried the Archbishop of Naples, whose name was Signor Filippo Minutolo, in rich pontifical robes, and with a ruby on his finger worth upwards of five hundred florins of gold, whom they proposed to strip and rifle; and they acquainted him with their intention. He then, more covetous than wise, went along with them; and, as they were going towards the cathedral, he smelt so strong that one said to the other, "Can we contrive no way to wash this man a little, to make him sweeter?" And the other made answer, "We are not far from a well, where there are usually a pulley and a great bucket; let us go thither and we may make him clean in an instant." Coming there they found the rope, but the bucket had been taken away; they therefore agreed to tie him to the rope, and to put him down into the well, and when he had well washed himself he was to shake the rope, and they would draw him up. Now it happened that, after they had let him down, some of the watch, being thirsty with the heat of the weather and having been in pursuit of some persons, came to that well to drink, and as soon as the two men saw them they took to their heels; the watch, however, saw nothing of them. Andreuccio now having washed himself at the bottom of the well, began to shake the rope; they therefore laid down their clothes and halberds upon the ground, and began to draw the rope, thinking the bucket was fastened thereto, and full of water; and when he found himself at the top he let go the rope, and clung fast to the edge of the well. They immediately threw down the rope on seeing him, and ran away, frighted out of their wits, which greatly surprised him; and had he not held fast he had fallen to the bottom, and perhaps lost his life. Getting out in this manner, and beholding their weapons, which he knew belonged not to his companions, he wondered the more; and, being in doubt what the meaning of it could be, he went away without touching anything, lamenting his fate and not knowing whither. As he was walking along, he met with his companions, who were returning to help him out of the well, and were surprised to see him, inquiring of him who had helped him out. He replied that he could not tell them; and related the whole affair and what he had found by the well-side; upon which they perceived how it had happened, and, laughing heartily, they acquainted him with the reason of their running away, and who they were that had drawn him up.

Without making more words, it being now midnight, they went to the great church, into which they found an easy admittance, and passed directly to the tomb, which was of marble and very magnificent; and with their levers raised up the cover, which was very heavy, so high that a man might go under, and propped it; which being done, said one, "Who shall go in?" "Not I," cried the other, "but Andreuccio shall." "I will not go in," quoth Andreuccio. Then they both turned towards him and said, "What! won't you go in? We will beat your brains out this moment if you don't." Terrified at their threats, he consented, and, being now within, he began

to consider with himself in this manner: "These fellows have surely forced me in here to deceive me, and therefore, when I have given them everything, and am endeavouring to get out again, they will certainly run away, and I shall be left destitute." For which reason he resolved to make sure of his part beforehand; and, remembering the ring of value which he had heard them speak of, as soon as ever he got into the vault he took it off the archbishop's finger, and secured it; giving them afterwards the pastoral staff, mitre, and gloves, and stripping him to his shirt, he told them there was nothing else. But they, affirming that there was a ring, bid him seek everywhere for it, whilst he assured them that he could nowhere find it, and, pretending to look carefully about, he kept them some time waiting for him: at length they, who were fully as cunning as himself, calling to him to search diligently, suddenly drew away the prop which supported the cover, and left him shut up in the vault. Which when he perceived, you may easily suppose what condition he was in. Many a time did he endeavour with his head and shoulders to raise it up, but in vain; till, overcome with grief, he fell down at last upon the dead body; and whoever had seen him at that time could scarcely have said whether there was more life in one than the other. But when he came to himself he lamented most bitterly, seeing that he was now brought to the necessity of one of these two evils, namely, to die there with hunger and the stench of the dead carcase, if no one came to help him out; or, if that should happen, and he be delivered, then to be hanged for a thief.

As he was in this perplexity, he heard the noise of many persons in the church, who he supposed were come to do what he and his companions had been about, which added greatly to his fear; but after they had raised up the lid and propped it, a dispute arose which should go in, and none caring to do it, after a long contest, said a priest, "What are you afraid of? Do you think he will eat you? Dead men cannot bite; I will go in myself." And immediately clapping his breast to the edge of the vault, he attempted to slide down with his feet foremost; which Andreuccio perceiving, and standing up, he caught fast hold of one of his legs, as if he meant to pull him in. The priest upon this making a most terrible outcry, got out immediately; and the rest, being equally terrified, ran away, leaving the vault open, as if they had been pursued by a hundred thousand devils. Andreuccio, little expecting this good fortune, got out of the vault, and so out of the church, the same way he came in.

And now daylight beginning to appear, he wandered with the ring on his finger he knew not whither, till, coming to the seaside, he found the way leading to his inn. There he met with his companions and his landlord, who had been in trouble all that night for him; and, having related to them all that had passed, he was advised to get out of Naples with all speed with which he instantly complied, and returned to Perugia, having laid out his money on a ring, whereas the intent of his journey was to have boughthorses.

Day VII, Tale 2

Dioneo, king for the seventh day, has directed each of his followers to tell of a trick played by a wife on her husband.

Peronella *puts her gallant into a tub on her husband's coming home, which tub the husband had sold; she consequently tells him that she had also sold it to a person who was then in it to see if it were sound; upon this the man jumps out, makes the husband clean it for him, and brings it home.*

Emilia's novel was heard with a great deal of mirth, and the charm esteemed a very good one, when the king ordered Filostrato to follow, which he did in the following manner:—

My dear ladies, the tricks which are put upon you by us men, and especially by your husbands, are so many that, if ever it happens that a woman does the like, you should not only be pleased to hear of it, but you yourselves should spread it everywhere, to let the men understand that if they are wise you are so too. This must have a good effect, for when it is known that people are forewarned, nobody will go about so readily to deceive them. Who sees not then that this day's discourse, being noised among the men, may not be a restraint upon them in that respect, when they come to find that you know how to serve them in the same way? I will tell you, therefore, what a woman, though but of mean rank, did to her husband in a moment, as it were, for her own safety.

It was not long since that a poor man at Naples married a young handsome wife, named Peronella; and he being a mason, and she spinning every day, they managed to gain a tolerable livelihood. Now it happened that a young man in the neighbourhood became enamoured of her, and so earnest were his solicitations that she at length responded to his wish. It was therefore agreed between them that, as the husband went out early every morning to his work, the lover should conceal himself in some place whence he could see him depart and then steal into the house, which was in a lonely street called Avorio; this accordingly he did more than once. But one morning amongst the rest, the honest man being gone abroad, and Giannello Strignario, for that was the gallant's name, sporting with her as usual, in a little time the husband returned, though he was not used to come home till night and finding the door bolted on the inside, he knocked, and then said to himself "Thank Heaven, though I am poor, I have an honest and careful wife; for no sooner am I gone out but she makes all fast that nobody should come, in my absence, to do us any injury." Peronella, who knew it was her husband by his manner of knocking, said, "Alas! Giannello, I am a dead woman; my husband—may curses light upon him!—is returned; I cannot imagine for what reason, unless it be that he saw you come in; but, for God's sake be it as it will, go you into that tub, wilst I open the door, and we shall then see what this sudden return of his means."

Accordingly he stepped into the tub, whilst she let her husband into the house; and, putting on an angry look, she said, "Pray, what new fancy is this, your coming home so early to-day? As far as I can find, you are disposed to do no more work, seeing you have got your tools with you. And what are we to live upon in the meantime? Do you think I will suffer you to pawn my gown, and what few clothes I have? I do nothing but spin night and day, till I have worn my fingers to the very bone, and all will scarcely find us oil to our lamp. Husband, husband, there is not a neighbour we have but wonders and makes a jest of me for all the labour I undergo, and yet you return here, with your hands in your pockets, when you ought to be at work." And here she began to weep, exclaiming, "Wretch that I am, in an ill hour was I born, and unlucky was the day when I happened to meet with you! I could have had a young man that would have maintained me well, and I refused him for this creature here, who knows not how to value a good wife. Other women have a good time with their gallants; nay, some have two or three, and make their husbands believe the moon is made of green cheese; and because I am virtuous, and have no regard for such practices, for that reason I am used the worse; I see no cause why I should not have my gallants as well as they. I would have you know that I have had offers of money, fine garments, and jewels from a number of young gentlemen, but nothing of that kind could seduce me: no, I was never the daughter of such a mother and yet you will come home when you ought to be at work." The husband then replied; "My dear, do not make your self uneasy; I am no stranger to your merit, and have had further proof of it this morning. I did go out to work indeed; but neither of us then knew that it was the feast of Saint Galeone, which is to be kept holy, and for that reason am I returned; nevertheless, I have found means to provide ourselves with bread for a month, for I have sold the tub, which you know has been long in our way, to this man whom I have brought with me, for five shillings." "This is so much the worse," answered she; "you that go up and down, and should know things better, to sell a thing for five shillings, which I, a poor ignorant woman, that keep always within

doors, considering the room it took up in our house, have now sold for six to an honest man, who had just got into it as you came to the door, to see whether it was sound."

When the husband heard this he was over and above rejoiced, and said to the man he had brought, "Friend, you may go about your business; you hear it is sold for six, whereas you were to have given no more than five." "Tis well, so be it," said the honest man, and away he went. "But," quoth Peronella to her husband, "as you are now here, even make the agreement with the man yourself." Giannello, who was listening attentively to what passed between them, hearing these words, came out of the tub; and, as if he knew nothing of the husband all the time said, "Where are you, good woman?" The husband, stepping forward, replied, "Here I am, what do you want? Who are you?" answered Giannello: "I want the woman who sold me the tub." "Friend, you may make the bargain with me," quoth the honest man, "for I am her husband." "Then," said Giannello, "the tub appears to be sound; but it seems as if you had kept something of dregs in it, for it is so crusted all over in the inside that I cannot scratch off one bit with my finger-nail; therefore I will not have it till it is made clean." Peronella replied, "This shall never break the bargain; my husband will soon clean it for you." "Ay, ay!" said the husband; and laying down his iron tools, and stripping to his shirt, he called for a lighted candle and a scraper; then getting inside, he fell to work. Peronella, as though she would fain see what he was doing, having put her head and one arm into the vessel's mouth, which was narrow enough, cried out, "Scrape here, scrape there; don't you see that spot, and this?" And, while she thus directed him in his task, Giannello, whose morning employment had been interrupted; seeing that he could not complete it as he would, resolved to do what he could; therefore, approaching his mistress as she lay over the tub, he made the best use he might of his opportunity, after which the husband issued forth. Then said Peronella to Giannello, "Take this candle, good man, and see whether it is cleaned to your liking." He, having peeped within, said he was well satisfied, and, having paid the price, caused the vessel to be carried to his house.

Day IX, Tale 6

On the ninth day, Queen Emilia has revived the rule of the first day, allowing each participant to select a subject for his or her narrative.

Two young gentlemen lie at an inn, one of whom goes to bed to the landlord's daughter, whilst the wife by mistake lies with the other. Afterwards, he that had lain with the daughter gets to bed to the father, and tells him what had passed, thinking it had been his friend; an uproar is made about it; upon which the wife goes to bed to the daughter, and wisely brings about a pacification.

Calandrino, who had so often diverted the company, made them laugh no less heartily once more; and when they were silent the queen laid her next commands upon Pamfilo, who therefore said:—

Ladies, the name of Niccolosa, beloved of Calandrino, puts me in mind of a novel concerning another of the same name, in which will be shown how the presence of mind of a certain wise woman was the means of preventing a great deal of scandal.

In the plain of Mugnone, not long since, lived an honest man who kept a little inn for the entertainment of travellers, serving them with meat and drink for their money, but seldom lodging any, unless they were his particular acquaintance. Now, he had a wife, a good comely woman, by whom he had two children, the one an infant, not yet weaned, and the other a pretty girl of about fifteen or sixteen years of age, but unmarried, who had taken the fancy of a young, gentleman of our city, one who used to travel much that way; whilst she, proud of such a lover, and endeavouring, by her agreeable carriage, to preserve his good opinion, soon felt the same liking for him: which love of theirs would several times have taken effect, to the desire of both, had not Pinuccio—for that was the young gentleman's name—carefully avoided it, for her credit as well as his own. Till at last, his love growing every day more fervent, he resolved, in order to gain his point, to lie all night at her father's house, judging that the matter might then be effected without any one's privity. Accordingly he let into the secret a friend of his, named Adriano, who had been acquainted with his love; so they hired a couple of horses one evening, and having their portmanteaus behind them, filled with things of no moment, they set out from Florence, and, after taking a circuit, came, as it grew late, to the plain of Mugnone; then turning their horses, as if they had come from Romagna, they rode on to this cottage, and knocking at the door, the landlord, who was always very diligent in waiting upon his guests, immediately went and opened it. Pinuccio then accosted him, and said, "Honest landlord, we must beg the favour of a night's lodging, for we had designed to reach Florence, but have so mistaken that it is now much too late, as you see." The host replied, "Sir, you know very well how ill I can accommodate such gentlemen as yourselves; but, as you are come in at an unseasonable hour, and there is no time for your travelling any farther, I will entertain you as well as I can." So they dismounted, and went into the house, having first taken care of their horses; and, as they had provision along with them, they sat down and invited their host to sup with them.

Now there was only one little chamber in the house, which had three beds in it—namely, two at one end, and the third at the other, opposite to them, with just room to go between. The least bad and incommodious of the three the landlord ordered to be prepared for these two gentlemen, and put them to bed. A little time afterwards, neither of them being asleep, though they pretended it, he made his daughter lie in one of the beds that remained, and he and his wife went into the other, whilst she set the cradle with the child by her bedside. Things being so disposed, and Pinuccio having made an exact observation of every particular, as soon as he thought it a proper time, and that every one was asleep, he arose and went softly to the bed of the daughter and lay down beside her, she, though very fearful, receiving him joyfully, and so they took what pastime they pleased. In the meantime, a cat happened to throw something down in the house, which awakened the wife, who, fearing it was something else got up in the dark, and went to find the cause of the noise. Adriano now rose by chance, upon a particular occasion, and finding the cradle in his way, he moved it, without any design, nearer to his own bed and, having done what he rose for, went to bed again, without putting the cradle in its place. The good woman, finding what was thrown down to be of no moment, never troubled herself to strike a light, to see farther about it, but having driven away the cat, returned to the bed where her husband lay; and, not finding the cradle, "Bless me," she said to herself, "I had like to have made a strange mistake, and gone to bed to my guests!" Going farther then, and finding the cradle, which stood by Adriano, she stepped into bed to him, thinking it had been her husband. He was awake, and treated her very kindly, without saying a word all the time to undeceive her.

At length Pinuccio, fearing lest he should fall asleep, and so be surprised with his mistress, after having made the best use of his time, left her to return to his own bed, when meeting with the cradle, and supposing that was the host's bed, he went farther, and stepped into the host's bed indeed, who immediately awoke. Pinuccio, thinking it was his friend, said to him, "Surely, nothing was ever so sweet as Niccolosa; never man was so blessed as I have been with her; I can assure you that since I left you I have been well employed." The host, hearing this, and not liking it over well, said first to himself, "What the devil does this man mean?" Afterwards, being more passionate than wise, he cried out, "Thou art the greatest of villains to use me in that manner; but I vow to God I will pay thee for it." Pinuccio, who was none of the sharpest men in the world, seeing his mistake, without ever thinking how to amend it, as he might have done, replied, "You pay me? What can you do?" The hostess, imagining that

she had been with her husband, said to Adriano, "Alas! dost thou hear our guests? What do they talk of?" He replied, with a laugh, "Let them talk as they will, and be hanged; they drank too much, I suppose, last night."

The woman now distinguishing her husband's voice, and hearing Adriano, soon knew where she was, and with whom. Therefore she very wisely got up, without saying a word, and removed the cradle, though there was no light in the chamber, as near as she could guess to her daughter's bed, and crept in to her; when, seeming as if she had been awakened by her husband's noise, she called out to him, to know what was the matter with him and the gentleman. The husband replied, "Do not you hear what he says he has been doing to-night with our daughter?" "He lies in his throat," quoth she; "he was never in bed with her; it was I, and I assure you I have never closed my eyes since; you are a great fool to think otherwise. You drink to that degree in the evening that you rave all night long, and walk up and down, without knowing anything of the matter, and think you do wonders; it is a pity that you do not break your neck. But what is Pinuccio doing there? why is he not in his own bed?" Adriano, on the other side, perceiving that the good woman had found a very artful evasion both for herself and daughter, said, "Pinuccio, I have told you a hundred times that you should never lie out of your own house; for that great failing of yours, of walking in your sleep and telling your dreams for truth, will be of ill consequence to you some time or other. Come here, then, to your own bed." The landlord hearing what his wife said, and what Adriano had just been speaking, began to think Pinuccio was really dreaming; so he got up and shook him by the shoulders to rouse him, saying, "Awake, and get thee to thine own bed."

Pinuccio, understanding what had passed, began now to ramble in his talk, like a man that was half asleep and dreaming, with which our host made himself vastly merry. At last when daylight came he seemed to awake, after much ado; and calling to Adriano, he said, "Is it day? what do you wake me for?" "Yes, it is," quoth he; "pray come hither." Then, pretending to be very sleepy, he got up at last, and went to Adriano. And in the morning the landlord laughed very heartily, and was full of jokes about him and his dreams. So they passed from one merry subject to another, whilst their horses were getting ready, and their portmanteaus trussed up, when, taking the host's parting cup, they mounted and went to Florence, no less pleased with the manner in which the thing had happened than the way in which it had been effected.

Afterwards Pinuccio found other means of being with Niccolosa, who still affirmed to her mother that he had been asleep; whilst she, remembering how well she had fared with Adriano, thought herself the only person that had been awake on that occasion.

———————— *Questions for Consideration* ————————

Using complete sentences, provide brief answers for the following questions.

1. The term "realism" is often applied to the *Decameron*. Of the tales you have read, review the tale which to you most clearly reveals elements of realism. Identify and comment on the realistic aspects of a relevant episode.

    _____

    _____

    _____

    _____

    _____

2. Describe the character of Andreuccio as portrayed in II.5 (Day II, Tale 5).

    _____

    _____

    _____

    _____

3. The *Decameron* is perhaps above all humorous. Locate one or more passages that you find outstanding from the standpoint of humor. Specify the comic devices or situations that Boccaccio has employed with particular skill to create humor.

    _____

    _____

    _____

    _____

    _____

─────────────── *Writing Critically* ───────────────

Select one of the topics listed below and compose a 500-word essay that discusses the topic fully. Support your thesis with evidence from the text and with critical and/or historical material. Use the space below for preparing to write the essay.

1. Compare a tale by Boccaccio with one by Chaucer. You might want to compare IX.6 by Boccaccio with "The Miller's Tale" by Chaucer.

2. Boccaccio was a transitional author; his *Decameron* reveals both medieval and Early Modern elements. Look carefully at one or more of the tales to discover and discuss characteristics of the two different historical periods.

3. The *Decameron* was written to illustrate one mode of response to the horrors of the plague. In our own society today, what kinds of disasters, if any, correspond to the threat posed by the plague? What methods do we utilize at present to deal with such threats? Are there any parallels with the situation presented in the *Decameron?*

4. What kind of picture of society does Boccaccio present? How are the various social classes depicted? Would you like to have lived in the Italy of Boccaccio's day? Which aspects of his society do you like, and which do you find alarming?

Prewriting Space:

_____

_____

_____

_____

_____

_____

_____

_____

_____

_____

_____

_____

_____

_____

_____

_____

_____

Introduction

Seami Motokiyo (1363–1443)

Birds of Sorrow is representative of *nō* drama, which developed in feudal Japan during the second half of the fourteenth century. A stylized form, the *nō* arose out of earlier kinds of cultural performance, including religious ritual, folk-songs, serious poetry, and pantomime. As this special type of drama congealed, the popular elements were modified, and the *nō* play came to reflect the aristocratic values of feudal Japan. The country was governed during this period by a series of *shōgun*, who were powerful military leaders. While the *shōgun* was primarily a warrior, he was often interested in literature and other arts. *Nō* drama reached a state of real sophistication during the late fourteenth century because it was the favorite art-form of the *shōgun* Yoshimitsu (1358–1408). This era, during which the *nō* play evolved rapidly, falls at the beginning of the Muromachi period of Japanese history, so called because the *shōgun's* government was centered in the Muromachi district of the ancient city of Kyoto.

The individual most responsible for perfecting *nō* drama was Seami Motokiyo, an extraordinary actor and playwright who enjoyed the patronage first of Yoshimitsu and then, to a much lesser extent, of his successor, Yoshimochi. Not only did Seami write and produce plays; he also, rather like Aristotle, authored theoretical writings that helped establish a dramatic tradition. The austere and powerful traits of *nō* theater have influenced a number of Western writers, including W. B. Yeats, Ezra Pound, and Bertolt Brecht.

Almost everything about the classic *nō* drama is stylized (that is, conceived of and performed according to conventions). The stage, to begin with, is stylized. There is an illustration of a pine tree on the back wall, and a ramp—along which there are three more pines—leads from the stage to the actors' dressing room. (See illustration below.) A minimal number of actors are involved, all male, even for women's roles. The usual play calls for a *shite*

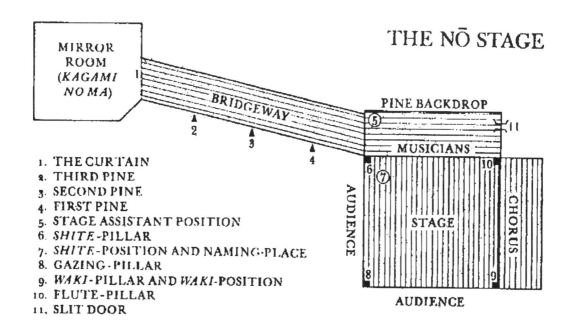

THE NŌ STAGE

MIRROR ROOM (*KAGAMI NO MA*)

BRIDGEWAY

PINE BACKDROP

MUSICIANS

AUDIENCE

STAGE

CHORUS

AUDIENCE

1. THE CURTAIN
2. THIRD PINE
3. SECOND PINE
4. FIRST PINE
5. STAGE ASSISTANT POSITION
6. *SHITE*-PILLAR
7. *SHITE*-POSITION AND NAMING-PLACE
8. GAZING-PILLAR
9. *WAKI*-PILLAR AND *WAKI*-POSITION
10. FLUTE-PILLAR
11. SLIT DOOR

(pronunciation: shee-tuh) or protagonist and a *waki* or secondary actor, who is typically the first to appear. The *shite* may be accompanied by another actor. A chorus consisting of six to eight actors (again, all men) repeats and reflects upon key sections of the play. There is musical accompaniment in the form of flute and drums.

The drama unfolds according to a set pattern leading to a climax or *kyū*. This configuration of characters and sequence, along with the extreme seriousness of the *nō* drama, have caused it to be compared to Greek tragedy. However, there are numerous differences, especially since the element of plot in the Japanese play is subdued. The drama seeks to create and define a particular mood or mental state rather than represent a plot understood as a complex and interconnected series of actions.

The sparse staging, minimal casting, the use of masks, and the diluted plot of the *nō* play leave the actors with a tremendous responsibility: it is they who must convey the powerful theatrical effect associated with this mode of drama. The term "*nō*" in fact denotes competence or expertise. The high level of histrionic proficiency required of the professional *nō* actor, who typically begins training in early childhood, insures a distinct impact on audiences.

There are over two hundred plays in the standard *nō* repertoire, and they are conventionally divided into two primary groups, mainly according to the kind of protagonist or *shite*. There are many supernatural elements and ghosts in *nō*, and the primary groups, *mugen* and *genzai*, are distinguished according to whether the protagonist is 1) a deity or the soul of a deceased individual (*mugen*) or 2) a living person (*genzai*). The plays are also divided into five sub-categories, again on the basis of the protagonist's role. These sub-groups feature a protagonist who is a) a deity, b) a war hero, c) a woman, typically a beautiful lady distressed over an unsuccessful romance, d) a deranged person, male or female, and e) a spirit, often a demon, who is intent on disrupting the social and natural order. The play that follows, *Birds of Sorrow*, belongs to the fourth group, for it depicts the ghost of a hunter who is distraught in the world of the dead because he killed numerous birds during his earthly existence.

Since the *nō* plays were originally performed at a much more rapid pace than today, a full program of five plays would feature one of each type. During each of the four intervals between the meditative *nō* plays, a *kyōgen* or comic play would be performed. Today's slower performances only permit one to three *nō* plays, usually along with a *kyōgen* play that serves as an introduction or interlude. Sometimes, *kyōgen* were composed to parody the pensive mood of particular *nō* plays. Such is the case with *The Bird-catcher in Hades*, a *kyōgen* drama that is a farcical imitation of *Birds of Sorrow*. In the *kyōgen* play, a hunter is in the netherworld awaiting punishment as a murderer of birds. When he provides the king of the underworld with a meal of roasted fowl, the ruler of hell is pleased and allows the hunter to return to the natural world in order to slaughter more birds.

Whatever its theme or type, the *nō* play is dominated by a single aesthetic principle, *yūgen*, a term that has no exact English equivalent. *Yūgen* is often translated as "mystery," for behind the minimalized staging and stark characterization of the *nō* drama, a deep meaning is implied that tends to resist restatement in ordinary language. This sense of a profound signification beyond words is also reminiscent of the occidental concept of the sublime. This principle of European aesthetics is usually applied to natural settings or artistic works that possess an extraordinary excellence or grandeur. The settings and depictions that evoke *yūgen*—such as a single isolated flower or the impeccable performance of a dancer—are often on a far less massive scale than those associated with the sublime. But in each case, there is a sense that words are inadequate to express the depth, meaning, and impact of an image or idea.

The centrality of *yūgen* in the *nō* tradition is perhaps the clearest link between this kind of drama and Zen Buddhism. While Buddhism as a religion emphasizes that everyday existence is only an illusion concealing ultimate realities, the Zen school stresses that meditation and intuitive insight (as opposed to theorizing or the study of scriptures) are the routes to spiritual enlightenment. The suggestive and evocative *nō* play also depends heavily on the Buddhist doctrines of *karma* (the theory that even the most ordinary actions have ethical implications) and metempsychosis (the belief that the soul, upon the death of the individual, can pass into another earthly existence). Playwright Seami Motokiyo was intensely interested in these religious concepts and became a Buddhist priest in 1422. The protagonist of *Birds of Sorrow*, like many *nō* characters, reveals a Buddhist agenda, for he endeavors to resolve in the afterlife a moral quandary created in a prior existence. (NW)

BIBLIOGRAPHY

Keene, Donald. "*Nō* and *Kyōgen* as Literature." In *Seeds in the Heart: Japanese Literature from Earliest Times to the Late-Sixteenth Century.* New York: Henry Holt, 1993. Pages 999–1061.

___, ed. *Anthology of Japanese Literature: From the Earliest Times to the Mid-Nineteenth Century.* New York: Grove, 1955.

Miner, Earl, Hiroko Odagiri, and Robert E. Morrell. *The Princeton Companion to Classical Japanese Literature.* Princeton: Princeton University Press, 1985.

Raz, Jacob. *Audience and Actors: A Study of Their Interaction in the Japanese Traditional Theatre.* Leiden: E. J. Brill, 1983.

Smethurst, Mae J. *The Artistry of Aeschylus and Zeami.* Princeton: Princeton University Press, 1989.

Yasuda, Kenneth. *Martin Luther King, Jr.: A Nō Play.* In *Masterworks of the Nō Theater*, K. Yasuda, trans and ed. Bloomington: Indiana University Press. Pages 485–507.

Birds of Sorrow

Seami Motokiyo

Translated by Meredith Weatherby and Bruce Rogers

The original title of the play, "Utō" is usually written in Japanese with three ideographs which may be loosely translated as "virtue-knowing bird." The utō or utōyasukata of early legends is a species of sea bird found in northern Japan and widely hunted for the delectability of its flesh. According to tradition, the parent bird of the species hides its young so well in the sand that even it cannot find them and, when bringing them food, calls them with the cry "Utō," to which they reply with the cry "Yasukata." Hunters catch both parent birds and the young by imitating these cries. It is also said that the parent birds weep tears of blood upon seeing their young taken, and that hunters must wear large hats and raincloaks to protect themselves from the falling tears, the touch of which causes sickness and death. Because of its traits the bird becomes an apt symbol for the Buddhist tenet that the taking of life in any form whatsoever is a sin.

PERSONS

A Buddhist Monk
The Ghost of a Dead Hunter
The Hunter's Wife
The Hunter's Child
A Villager
Chorus

PART I

Place: Tateyama, a high mountain in Central Honshū near the Sea of Japan.

Time: The month of April.

(The stage is completely bare. Two drummers and a flute player come through the curtain and, passing down the Bridge, take their usual seats at the rear of the stage. They are followed in silence by the Wife and Child. The Wife wears the mask and wig of a middle-aged woman; her inner kimono is the color of dried autumn leaves, over which is a kimono with a small pattern and a long outer kimono in somber colors which trails behind her on the floor. The Child, apparently six or eight years of age, wears a hakama and a brightly embroidered outer kimono over a scarlet inner kimono. They seat themselves near the Waki's Pillar. The Monk enters, accompanied by the introductory flute music. He is wearing a dark kimono and a peaked cowl of brocade which flows down over his shoulders, and carries a rosary. He passes down the Bridge onto the stage, where he stops at the Naming-Place and, facing the audience, introduces himself.)*

MONK: I am a wandering monk, making a pilgrimage throughout the provinces. I have never yet visited the village of Soto no Hama in Michinoku. Thinking on this, I was recently minded to go to Soto no Hama. And as the occasion is indeed favorable, I am planning to stop in passing and practice religious austerities upon Tateyama.

(Takes two steps forward, indicating he has arrived at the foot of the mountain.)

Coming swiftly along the road, already I have arrived here at Tateyama. With serene and reverent heart I now shall visit the mountain.

(Goes to center of stage, indicating he has climbed to the summit.)

But lo! upon arriving here on Tateyama, my eyes do indeed behold a living Hell. And the heart of even the boldest man must quail before this fell sight, more frightful even than demons

718

and fiends. Here the countless mountain trails, grim and precipitous, split asunder as if to lead down into the Realm of Ravenous Ghosts, and down into the Realm of Bestiality.

(Describing his actions.) So saying, he is overcome with the memory of his past sins and for a time is unable to restrain the starting tears. Then, penitent, he descends to the foot of the mountain . . . to the foot of the mountain, penitent . . .

(The Monk goes toward the Chorus, indicating he has returned to the foot of the mountain. He turns and faces the Bridge. The curtain is swept back and a voice is heard from the blackness of the Mirror Room beyond the curtain. It is the Ghost of the Dead Hunter who speaks, calling out as though he has been running after the Monk.)

HUNTER: Hallo-o! Hallo-o! Wait, O worthy monk, for I must speak with you.
MONK: What is it you want with me?

(The Hunter enters. He is seen now in his mortal form, wearing the mask of a pleasant old man and a white wig. He wears a plain, tea-colored outer kimono of rough weave over garments of solid brown and light green. He moves slowly down the Bridge as he speaks.)

HUNTER: If you are going down to Michinoku, pray take a message there. I am one who was a hunter of Soto no Hama and who died in the past year's autumn. I beseech you to visit the home of my wife and child and to tell them to offer up for me the cloak of straw and the sedge-hat which are there.
MONK: This is a strange request that I hear. To carry the message is a simple thing, but if I address her thus without any proof, like the falling of sudden rain from an empty sky, is it likely that she will believe?
HUNTER: Indeed, you are right. Without some certain sign or token, it would surely be of no avail.

(The Hunter has been advancing along the Bridge; he pauses now at the First Pine and bows his head dejectedly. Then an idea comes to him and he raises his head.)

Ah! Now I remember—this was the kimono which I was wearing at the very hour of death.

(Describing his actions.) And thereupon he tears a sleeve from the kimono which he is wearing, a kimono made of hemp like that of Kiso long ago, and worn in the days of his life.

(The Hunter removes the left sleeve of his kimono, touches it to his forehead, and then holds it out in both hands toward the Monk)

CHORUS: He says, "This give as a token." And so saying, gives it with tears to the wandering monk . . . with tears, to the wandering monk. . . .

(The Monk goes to the Hunter at the First Pine and takes the sleeve, then turns and comes onto the stage, while the Hunter starts along the Bridge toward the curtain.)

They bid farewell. The footsteps of the monk lead away toward Michinoku, down through the flaming, budding trees of spring, far and far away, amid the rising smoke and clouds of Tateyama, until his figure too becomes like a wisp of cloud.

(The Monk continues toward the front of the stage. The Hunter brings his hand to his forehead in a gesture of weeping. Then he turns around on the Bridge and looks long toward the stage, shading his eyes with his hand.)

The dead one weeps and weeps, watching the monk depart, and then vanishes, no one knows where . . . no one knows where.

(The Hunter has turned and continued along the Bridge. Now the curtain is swept back and he moves into the blackness beyond the curtain.)

INTERLUDE

Place: Soto no Hama, a fishing village on the northernmost coast of Honshū several hundred miles from Tateyama.

(There has been a slight pause on the stage, during which time the Monk is understood to be traveling to Michinoku. Now he goes to the Naming-Place, where he turns and addresses the actor who has been sitting motionless at the Kyōgen's Seat during Part I.)

MONK: Are you a native of Soto no Hama?

(The Villager rises and stands on the Bridge near the First Pine. He is wearing a simple plaid kimono and a kamishimo of brocade.)

VILLAGER: Yes, I am. May I help you?

MONK: Please show me the house here of the hunter who died last autumn.

VILLAGER: Why, of course. The dead hunter's house is that one you see there inside that high stockade made of crisscrossed bamboo. You can reach it in a moment if you please.

MONK: I understand. Thank you for your kindness. I shall go there at once and pay a visit.

VILLAGER: If there is anything else I can do for you, please say so.

MONK: Thank you very much.

VILLAGER: You are very welcome.

(The Villager resumes his seat. Later he makes an unobtrusive exit.)

PART II

Place: The home of the dead Hunter, both the interior and exterior being understood to be visible.

(The Monk has moved to the Stage Attendant's Pillar, where he pauses. The Wife speaks, as if to herself, from her seat at the Waki's Pillar.)

WIFE: Truly, long have I known this world to be a fleeting thing, becoming dreamlike even as it passes. But now more than ever before.

To what avail was my troth plighted? Now death has cut the ties which bound me to my husband. And this beloved child, left behind him like a footstep at the parting, only makes my grief more endless. . . . Oh, how can a mother's heart endure such sorrow?

(The Wife makes a gesture of weeping. The Monk has put the sleeve which he held into the breastfold of his kimono and has been advancing slowly toward the stage. Reaching the Shite's Pillar, he stops and turns toward the Wife, indicating he has reached the house)

MONK: Pray let me in.

WIFE: Who is there?

MONK: I am a wandering monk, making a pilgrimage throughout the provinces. While I was practicing religious austerities upon Tateyama there came a weird old man and said, "If you are going down to Michinoku, please take a message. I am one who was a hunter of Soto no Hama and who died in the past year's autumn. Visit the home of my wife and child and tell them to offer up for me the cloak of straw and sedge-hat which are there." I replied, "If I address her thus without any proof, out of a clear sky, she surely will not believe." Thereupon he loosened and gave to me a sleeve of the hempen kimono he wore. I have journeyed and carried it with me until now. Perchance it is a token which will call memories to your heart.

WIFE: Surely this is a dream. Or else a piteous thing. Like unto the song of the cuckoo, heard at early morning, bringing back from Hell a last message from the dead, so now with these tidings that I hear from my departed one. And even as I listen, the tears are springing in my eyes.

(Making gesture of weeping.)

Nevertheless, it is too strange a thing, passing all belief. And therefore, crude though it be and lowly as cloth woven of wistaria bark, I will bring out his kimono. . . .

(A stage attendant comes to the Wife where she sits and gives her the folded kimono without a sleeve which the Hunter was wearing in Part I. She holds it up on her outstretched arms toward the Monk.)

MONK: That kimono long treasured as a memory of him . . . this sleeve long carried. . . .

(The Monk takes out the sleeve and holds it out toward the Wife.)

WIFE: Upon taking them out. . . .

MONK: . . . and comparing them well. . . .

(The Monk looks fixedly at the kimono which the Wife is holding.

CHORUS: . . . there can be no doubt left.

(The Monk comes to the Wife and lays the sleeve in her arms upon the kimono. She bends her head over the articles, examining them closely, while the Chorus speaks for her.)

The cloth is the same—thin, crude stuff, for summer's wearing . . . thin, crude stuff for summer's wearing. And see! a sleeve is gone—this sleeve exactly fits. . . . It comes from him! O so dearly longed for. . . .

(The Wife bows low over the garments in a gesture of weeping. The Chorus now explains the actions of the Monk as he takes a large, black-lacquered hat from a stage attendant at the Flute Pillar, brings it to the very front of the stage and, placing it on the floor, kneels before it facing the audience.)

And forthwith does the Monk chant countless prayers of requiem. And especially even as the dead one had entreated, does he offer up that very cloak of straw, offer up that very hat of sedge.

(The Monk rubs his rosary between his palms over the hat and intones a Buddhist Sutra.)

MONK: "Hail, O Spirit. May you be delivered from the endless round of incarnations. May you attain the instantaneous enlightenment of Buddhahood."

(Rising, the Monk goes and takes a seat near the Flute Pillar. There is an interval of music accompanied by cries of the drummers. The curtain is swept back and the Hunter appears, now in supernatural form. He wears a tragic mask of a gaunt old man, just human enough in appearance to be unearthly, and an unkempt black wig which flares wildly down over his shoulders. Over his outer kimono, dappled with white and gray, he wears a short apron made of white and brown feathers. He carries a long stick and a fan. He comes slowly down the Bridge, as though summoned by the Monk's prayers. Reaching the Shite's Pillar, he stops and chants an old poem.)

HUNTER: "At Soto no Hama of Michinoku there is the sound of birds, tenderly calling, tenderly cherishing—'Utō,' sing the parents in the sky, 'Yasukata,' the young answer from the beaches."

(The Hunter makes a gesture indicating he is drawing near the house.)

Even as the Holy Sutra says, "Behold but once the *sotoba*, and be delivered for all time from the Three Evil Paths, beset by beasts and demons and hungry ghosts." Truly then a *sotoba* is a blessed thing, a memorial tablet carved fivefold, the five elements of the Buddha Body, the mere sight of which can save. But how much more if it be a *sotoba* raised expressly for my own sake, if a requiem be said in my own name.

For even in the icy Hell of the Scarlet Lotus the Fire of Holy Wisdom is not extinguished. For even in the Hell of Raging Fire the Waters of Dharma still quench.

And, nevertheless, still the burden of sin heaps high upon this flesh. . . . When may this soul find peace? . . . When can the birds find their stolen young? . . . O the killing!

(The Hunter turns and holds out his arms beseechingly toward the Monk.)

CHORUS: In the sunlight of Buddha, the All Compassionate, the sins of man become like dew upon the grass: make the blessing-bestowing Sun to shine on me, O monk.

(The Hunter drops his arms and turns back toward the audience. The Chorus now describes the locale, while the Hunter makes a slow tour round the stage, revisiting the scenes of his earthly life.)

The place is Michinoku. The place is Michinoku. And here, in a lonely fishing village, upon an inlet of the sea, fenced round as though on the Isle of Hedges—now by the interlacing lower branches of the pine trees which follow along the strand, now by the salt reeds which grow drooping and matted in the ebb and flow of the tide—here at Soto no Hama stands the rush-mat hut. A humble dwelling, its roof so sparsely thatched. But now when the moon shines through the thatch into the room—a home for one's heart. Oh! truly a home for one's heart.

(The Hunter returns now to the Naming-Place, where he leans motionless on his stick, looking toward the Wife and Child, indicating he has reached the house. The Wife and Child raise their heads and look toward the Hunter.)

WIFE: Softly! the shape will vanish if you but say a single word.

(They rise and the Wife leads the Child a few steps toward the Hunter, describing her actions.)

The mother and child clasp hands . . . and there is nought but weeping.

(Leaving the Child standing, the Wife returns to her original position, kneels and weeps.)

HUNTER: Alas! in other days this was the wife of my bed, the child of my heart. But now we are estranged forever—like the parent bird I cry "*Utō*" and, waiting with beating heart, never hear the answering "*Yasukata.*" Why? oh, why did I kill them? For even as my child is beloved, just so must the birds and beasts yearn for their young. And now when I long to stroke the hair of my son Chiyodō and say, "Oh, how I have missed thee!"

(The Hunter extends his arms and suddenly rushes toward the Child. But at each step of the Hunter, the Child falls back a step, as though some unseen object were keeping a fixed distance between them. It is the legendary cloud-barrier of earthly lusts which obscures the Sun of Buddha and prevents sinful spirits from visiting the earth. The Child takes a seat beside the Wife, and the Hunter returns to the center of the stage and stands with his back to the Wife and Child, indicating he has been unable to enter the house and can no longer see inside.)

CHORUS: . . . the shadows of my earthly lusts do rush before my eyes—a cloud of grief now rolls between us, a grievous cloud now hangs about.

(The Hunter makes a gesture of weeping.)

I cannot see him! just now he was standing there, my child, sturdy and strong as a young pine. . . .

Fugitive and fleeting . . . whither? . . . where? . . . I cannot find the hat—lost in the forests of the country of Tsu, in the shade of the spreading pine of Wada. I cannot reach the cloak—the flood tears, falling, drench my sleeves as might the spray from the waterfall at Minō. I cannot see the blessed *sotoba.*

(The Hunter makes slow circles round the stage, indicating his efforts to see through the cloud, and then stamps his foot in frustration.)

Who is this that stands outside, unable to enter his own home, barred from his wife and child, from cloak and hat, yes even from the *sotoba?* . . . "Having returned to Matsushima, to

Ojima, I do not see the rush-mat huts on the islands—the villages are desolate, by the waves laid waste." The song is old, but now it is I, I who cannot find, cannot enter the rush-mat hut. . . .

The bird of Soto no Hama, unable to find its nest . . . raising its voice in grief . . . nought but weeping. . . .

(The Hunter circles slowly to the Shite's Pillar, where he kneels and makes a gesture of weeping.)

The vague and boundless past, dreamlike. It was from the ruin of these past pleasures, from these evil days, that I descended to the Yellow Springs, to the bitter waters of Hell. . . .

(Still kneeling, the Hunter raises his head.)

HUNTER: My path of life led from birth far out beyond the four estates of man—I was neither scholar, farmer, artisan, nor merchant.
CHORUS: Nor did I delight in life's four pleasures—music nor chess, books nor paintings.
HUNTER: There was only the coming of day, the coming of night—and the killing!
CHORUS: Thoughtless, wasting the slow spring days in hunting—days meant for the leisurely enjoyment of living. But still the lust for killing was unappeased. And so when the nights of autumn became long and long, I kept them alight, sleepless, with my fishing flares.
HUNTER: Unheedful of the ninety days of summer's heat. . . .
CHORUS: . . . of the cold of winter's mornings.

(The Chorus now begins a description of the Hunter's past life. The Hunter, still kneeling, gradually begins to look from side to side, slowly, as though seeing the scenes being described.)

"The hunter pursues the deer and does not see the mountains," says the proverb. And truly so it was with me—thinking only of bait and snares, I was like one drugged by the day lily, oblivious to every pain of the body, to every sorrow of the heart. Lashed by wind and wave, even as is the great sand dune of Sue-no-Matsuyama . . . my garments wet and dripping as are the rocks which stand offshore, forever in the ebbing and flowing of the tide . . . coursing the beaches, crossing the sea even to the shores of the farther islands . . .

my flesh burnt as though I had approached too near the salt-kilns of Chika. . . .

Still and always I pursued my evil ways, forgetful of the days of retribution, heedless of all regret.

(The Hunter touches his hands together in the conventional gesture which introduces a principal dance, bows his head and rises, grasping his stick. He begins gradually to keep rhythm with the music, but without yet moving from place.)

Now the ways of murdering birds are many, but this scheme by which these pitiful ones are taken. . . .

HUNTER: . . . can there be one more heartless than this?

(The Hunter now begins moving slowly about the stage, searching, keeping time with the music.)

CHORUS: You stupid, foolish bird! If only you had built your nest with feathers, high in the treetops of the forests, forests dense as that which lies about the Peak of Tsukuba . . . if only you had woven floating cradles upon the waves. . . . But no! here upon the beaches, as broad and sandy as those upon which wild geese settle for a moment's rest in their northward flight, you raise your young. And here, O bird of sorrow, you think to hide them. But then I, calling "Utō," come . . . they answer "Yasukata" and the nestlings are taken. It is as simple as this!

(Still searching, the Hunter has started toward the Bridge, but when the Chorus gives the cry of "Utō" he pauses at the Naming-Place and listens. And at the cry "Yasukata" he whirls back toward the stage, as though hearing the birds in the nest. He stamps his foot once and in the midst of a profound silence gives the bird call.)

HUNTER: Utō!

(The Hunter strikes the stage with his stick and begins a pantomime of the hunt which preceded his death. The dance begins slowly with the discovery and pursuit of the birds and gradually mounts in ferocity to their capture and killing. At first the Hunter raises his stick in the direction of the Waki's Pillar, as though the imaginary birds are concealed in that vicinity, and brings it down to frighten them from the nest. The young birds are then understood to run

toward the Bridge. He follows and, stopping near the Bridge, turns his body in an arc as though searching the horizon. Finally discovering the birds near the First Pine, he again flushes them with a wave of his stick. They run toward the front of the stage with the Hunter in pursuit, wildly brandishing his stick. He catches up with them near the hat, which is still at the front of the stage, and brings his stick down with two sharp blows upon the stage, indicating the killing of the birds. Then he closes the movement with two stamps of the feet.)*

CHORUS: From the sky the parent bird is weeping tears of blood.

(The emotion of the dance now suddenly changes. The Hunter falls back a few steps and looks up fearfully. Then, hurling away his stick, he runs and snatches up the hat.)

From the sky fall tears of blood. And I, covering myself with the sedge-hat, with the cloak of straw, try to escape the falling tears, dodging now this way, now that.

(Holding the hat in both hands above his head and moving it rapidly from side to side. Then sinking for a moment to his knees.)

But alas! these are not the enchanted cloak and hat which make invisible their wearer.

(Rising and moving toward the Waki's Pillar.)

Faster and faster fall the tears of blood, until my body cannot escape their mortal touch, until the world turns crimson before my eyes—crimson as the fabled Bridge of Maple Leaves, formed of magpie wings across the sky and at the dawn stained red by the tears of two parting lover-stars.

(Throws the hat violently aside and takes out fan. The Chorus now turns from a description of past events to a recital of the tortures which the Hunter is undergoing in Hell. The dance becomes quieter now, the Hunter using the fan to indicate the actions described. The fan is a large white one on which is painted a bird in flight.)

In the earthly world I thought it only an easy prey, this bird, only an easy prey. But now here in Hell it has become a gruesome phantom-bird, pursuing the sinner, honking from its beak of iron, beating its mighty wings, sharpening its claws of copper. It tears at my eyeballs, it rends my flesh. I would cry out, but choking amid the shrieking flames and smoke, can make no sound.

(The Hunter runs wildly about the stage, in agony.)

Is it not for the sin of killing the voiceless birds that I myself now have no voice? Is it not for slaughtering the moulting, earth-bound birds that I cannot now flee?

(The Hunter has started moving rapidly toward the Gazing Pillar when suddenly he seems unable to move and sinks to his knees, cowering in the center of the stage.)

HUNTER: The gentle bird has become a falcon, a hawk!
CHORUS: And I!—I have become a pheasant, vainly seeking shelter, as though in a snowstorm on the hunting fields of Gatano, fleeing in vain over the earth, fearing also the sky, harassed by falcons above and tormented by dogs below.

(The Hunter rises and, looking up toward the sky and down to the earth, moves slowly, defeatedly, toward the Shite's Pillar.)

Ah! the killing of those birds! this heavy heart which never knows a moment's peace! this body endlessly in pain!

(The Hunter stops at the Shite's Pillar and, turning, points a finger at the Monk.)

Please help me, O worthy monk. Please help me. . . .

(The Hunter drops his arms, and the Chorus chants the conventional ending of a nō play.)

And thereupon the spirit fades and is gone. . . .

(The Hunter stamps his feet, indicating he has disappeared, that the play is done. He walks slowly down the Bridge and through the curtain, followed in turn by the other actors and the musicians. The Chorus exits by the Slit Door, and again the stage is left bare.)

———————— *Questions for Consideration* ————————

Using complete sentences, provide brief answers for the following questions.

1. The *nō* play developed out of a culture very different from that of turn-of-the-millennium America. For you the reader, what aspects of *Birds of Sorrow* transcend these cultural differences and enable you to understand and appreciate the play?

    _____

    _____

    _____

    _____

    _____

2. Apply the Buddhist concepts of *karma* and transmigration of the soul to your reading of *Birds of Sorrow*. List insights that emerge in light of these concepts.

    _____

    _____

    _____

    _____

    _____

3. If you are unfamiliar with Coleridge's long narrative poem, "The Rime of the Ancient Mariner," have a look at it. Record common concerns that link *Birds of Sorrow* and Coleridge's tale of a slain albatross.

    _____

    _____

    _____

    _____

    _____

———————————— *Writing Critically* ————————————

Select one of the topics listed below and compose a 500-word essay that discusses the topic fully. Support your thesis with evidence from the text and with critical and/or historical material. Use the space below for preparing to write the essay.

1. Present an analysis of *Birds of Sorrow* focussing on the plight of the protagonist, the hunter.

2. Greek tragedy and the Japanese *nō* play obviously differ in many ways, but a number of readers have looked for and discovered common elements. Try comparing *Birds of Sorrow* with any Greek tragedy you have read, such as *Oedipus the King* or *Medea*. In each case, there is a concern with wrongdoing that has taken place in the past and must be dealt with. Compare the hunter with Oedipus, who searched for the murderer of Laius, or with Medea, who seeks revenge because of what Jason has done to her.

3. Read Kenneth Yasuda's *Martin Luther King, Jr.: A Nō Play*, which is cited in the bibliography above. Analyze the play using terms and concepts you have become familiar with through your reading and study of *Birds of Sorrow*. Be sure to include an evaluation of how well this Asian genre serves as an effective vehicle for the subject Yasuda has undertaken to deal with.

4. Think of a subject or event in contemporary life that might lend itself to dramatic representation in the form of a *nō* play. Try writing a page or more of script for a play dealing with the topic you have identified.

Prewriting Space:

_____

_____

_____

_____

_____

_____

_____

_____

_____

_____

_____

_____

_____

_____

_____

Introduction

Niccolò (di Bernardo) Machiavelli (1469–1527)

Machiavelli has been hailed by several scholars as the founder of modern political science. T. S. Eliot once remarked that "no greater man has been so completely misunderstood." Machiavelli endured favorable reactions to many of his works as well as blistering rejections by others. Today, even his name, "Machiavelli," is synonymous with ruthlessness, hypocrisy, and diabolical political cunning.

Niccolò (di Bernardo) Machiavelli was born in Florence, Italy to a somewhat modest noble family. As a child, he received a good education, quickly becoming interested in reading the ancient classics. During his young adulthood years, Machiavelli experienced the Golden Age of the Italian Renaissance under Florence's leader at the time, Lorenzo the Magnificent. Florence, along with the Kingdom of Naples, Rome and the papal states, Venice, and Milan were constantly attempting to achieve power over the lesser cities. In addition, the Italian peninsula divided into fifty to nearly one hundred power centers which made them open to political chaos, vulnerable authority, and foreign invasions. After the death of Lorenzo the Magnificent in 1492, Florence and the rest of Italy experienced the unfortunate position of being a battleground for possession by two powerful rivals, France and Spain.

Machiavelli's initial involvement in the volatile Florentine political scene began in 1498 when he offered assistance to the political fraction that deposed Savonarola, then the primary political and religious figure in Florence. As a result of his efforts, Machiavelli rose from a minor clerk in the chancery to the Secretary to the Ten of the Republic of Florence. The position was one that chiefly dealt with foreign affairs and warfare. This gave Machiavelli the opportunity to participate in domestic politics and to serve as a diplomat to foreign governments.

It was during these fourteen years that Machiavelli began to mold his political thinking. On various diplomatic duties Machiavelli met many popes and princes, including King Louis XII of France, the Emperor Maximillian, and the most influential individual, Cesare Borgia. Borgia became, for the young diplomat, the model representation of leadership and statescraft for his work, *The Prince.*

In 1512, the Republic of Florence was overthrown by the French army. In desperation, the Florentines recalled the Medici who had for centuries ruled Florence but had been exiled since 1494. Machiavelli, however, did not prosper under this new leadership. He was fired from his office, jailed, tortured, and finally banished to his country residence. The Medici government simply did not trust him! Consequently, he spent his exiled years writing a body of works that included several literary genres. In 1520, Machiavelli was commissioned to write a *History of Florence* in which he chose not merely to list events that had occurred but to see his beloved city as a "living organism" with problems. He was rewarded in monetary form for his achievement for the *History of Florence* by Pope Clement VII.

Although Machiavelli wrote a body of political works, he also was a writer of drama, essays, poetry, letters, tales, novellas, history, and a romance novel. In 1518, he wrote the comedy *Mandragola* which was received with enthusiasm for a number of years throughout Italy. His *The Discourses on the First Ten Books of Titus Livius*, the Roman historian Livy, addressed the problem of building a lasting government. In the *Discourses*, he attacked the papacy for preventing Italian unity because of its temporal interests. *The Art of War*, a military treatise published in 1521, was the only political work published during his time. Machiavelli's most enduring work that has caused considerable controversy is *The Prince*, published five years after his death in 1532.

Soon after his exile, Machiavelli wrote *The Prince* and dedicated it to Lorenzo Medici in the vain hope of regaining political favor. Lorenzo, however, dismissed Machiavelli's efforts and perhaps never read the book himself. The book, nevertheless, achieved somewhat of a cult status during Machiavelli's lifetime, though the official publication was after his death.

The Prince is, in essence, a handbook on the science of statescraft. Machiavelli included twenty-six chapters that can be grouped essentially into four parts. Part one discusses the various types of governments. Part two deals with the need for military power. A third part discusses the qualities of a prince. The final part addresses the political climate of Italy. Machiavelli believed that a strong government for Italy could be accomplished only through a ruthless leader. This individual, exemplified by Cesare Borgia, was vital for achieving effective leadership. This leader should possess what Machiavelli termed "virtu." Virtu consists of intelligence, courage, talent, and strength. A leader must adapt himself to various circumstances and the various people he meets. Often a leader must on occasion hurt, caress, forgive, punish, and suppress. Once a policy has been chosen, the politician must act without any hesitation to carry it to its completion. If one avoids executing necessary measures, regardless of how violent and cruel they may appear, then it is considered to be merely false pity. The opposites of virtu are uncertainty and hesitation.

Machiavelli expressed in *The Prince* that the ruler of the state must try to understand that the key to success in governing is the exercise of power. In other words, power is to be used with wisdom as well as ruthlessness. A favorite illustration of Machiavelli's prince is that he must be as sly as a fox and as brutal as the lion. Success is the primary goal for a leader. Furthermore, any means may be used to gain an end for this success. It was quite immaterial how the prince achieved his goals, whether in an innocent or diabolical manner. The welfare of the state justifies any course of action. This individual must not act as if the world were a paradise of righteous individuals. The ultimate good of the prince's people may require him to lie, cheat, and even murder!

Another vital issue that Machiavelli addresses in *The Prince* is his belief that ethics or morality and politics should be separate from each other. This issue has given even Americans today much to debate, especially when there is an election year for offices in local, state, and nation levels. Many citizens feel that a political candidate's public morality should coincide with his or her private morality. Machiavelli felt that moral standards in public life must be different from those assumed to exist in private life. Moreover, the state should not have anything to do with controlling morality. Machiavelli insists that this will always be the case whether we choose to see or not. Was he right?

Several themes can be seen throughout *The Prince*. One major concept is the idea that the state is the highest achievement of man. The ruler and the people cooperate in creating and preserving it. Another major idea from Machiavelli is that nothing is superior to the state. A person must love the state more than his or her soul. A third concept involves the military. According to Machiavelli, military power is the foundation and strength of the state. Only the prince who has enough military power is able to maintain his dominion. All of these themes give us some questions to ponder in our country today. For instance, is preserving our nation the primary concern of Americans today?

The Prince does not give us the whole of Machiavelli's political thinking, but it offers his views on a country that had lost its civic virtues and what he perceived it took to regain them. Only briefly was the reaction by the public favorable towards *The Prince*. The handbook soon was condemned by many for its content bordering on tyranny. Rome placed the work on the Index of Prohibited Books in 1559. The Inquisition, with support from the Council of Trent, decreed the destruction of all Machiavelli's works. Machiavellian ideas, however, did survive. *The Prince* or even Machiavelli's name was the subject of many writers, historians, and scholars throughout Europe. The writers Christopher Marlowe in *The Jew of Malta* and William Shakespeare in *The Merry Wives of Windsor* refer to Machiavelli with a sinister connotation. It has taken centuries before the distinction has been made between the subject matter of the book and the personality of the author.

Modern critics, who have separated the work from the man, disagree on Machiavelli's purpose for writing *The Prince*. Perhaps no one single motive can be given. Some scholars see it as a political guideline while others view it as a satire. The philosopher Pierre Bayle found it "strange" that there are so many people who believe that Machiavelli teaches princes dangerous politics, when really princes have taught Machiavelli what he has written. Regardless of its purpose, most critics agree on the superb composition, even when unable to support its precepts. Francesco De Sanctis has claimed "without looking for Italian prose, he found it."

Machiavelli's name is still today a symbol of wickedness, duplicity, and wily unscrupulousness. Nevertheless, he has left a tremendous contribution as a statesman, dramatist, and above all, political theorist. Machiavellian individuals exist whether we see them as real people or as a popular television character such as the love-to-hate character J. R. Ewing of *Dallas*. Machiavelli has shocked many by what is expected of a ruler in *The Prince*. Perhaps Francis Bacon noted something about Machiavelli that would leave one thinking about this fascinating individual. Bacon said that Niccolò Machiavelli dealt with men as they are and not as they ought to be. (AHF)

BIBLIOGRAPHY

Fleisher, Martin, ed. *Machiavelli and the Nature of Political Thought*. New York: Atheneum, 1972.

Gauss, Christian. *Machiavelli's The Prince: An Introduction*. New York: New American Library, 1980.

Mansfield, Henry C., Jr. *Machiavelli's New Modes and Orders: A Study of the "Discourses on Livy."* Ithaca: Cornell University Press, 1970.

Mayer, Thomas F. "Mysterious, Hellacious Machiavelli." *The Sixteenth Century Journal* 21(1990): 105–9.

Norton, Paul. "Machiavelli and the Modes of Terrorism." *Modern Age* 29, No. 4 (Fall 1985): 304–13.

Priestley, J. B. "The Italian Scene and Machiavelli." *In his Literature and Western* Man, pp. 10–17. New York: Harper and Brothers, 1960.

Whitfield, John Humphreys. *Discourses on Machiavelli*. Cambridge, England: W. Heffer and Sons, 1960.

from The Prince

Niccolò Machiavelli

Chapter 1

Of the various kinds of Princedom, and of the ways in which they are acquired

All the States and Governments by which men are or ever have been ruled, have been and are either Republics or Princedoms. Princedoms are either hereditary, in which the sovereignty is derived through an ancient line of ancestors, or they are new. New Princedoms are either wholly new, as that of Milan to Francesco Sforza; or they are like limbs joined on to the hereditary possessions of the Prince who acquires them, as the Kingdom of Naples to the dominions of the King of Spain. The States thus acquired have either been used to live under a Prince or have been free; and he who acquires them does so either by his own arms or by the arms of others, and either by good fortune or by valour.

Chapter 11

Of hereditary Princedoms

Of Republics I shall not now speak, having elsewhere spoken of them at length. Here I shall treat exclusively of Princedoms, and, interweaving the warp above laid out, shall proceed to examine how such States are to be governed and maintained.

I say, then, that hereditary States, accustomed to the family of their Prince, are maintained with far less difficulty then new States, since all that is required is that the Prince shall not depart from the usages of his ancestors, trusting for the rest to deal with events as they arise. So that if an hereditary Prince be of average address, he will always maintain himself in his Princedom, unless deprived of it by some extraordinary and irresistible force; and even if so deprived will recover it, should any mishap overtake the usurper. We have in Italy an example of this in the Duke of Ferrara, who never could have withstood the attacks of the Venetians in 1484, nor those of Pope Julius in 1510, had not his authority in that State been consolidated by time. For since a Prince by birth has fewer occasions and less need to give offence, he ought to be better loved, and, unless outrageous vices make him odious, will naturally be popular with his subjects. Moreover, the mere antiquity and continuance of his rule will efface the memories and causes which lead to innovation. For one change always leaves a rabbeting on which another can be built.

Chapter XV

Of the qualities in respect of which men, and most of all Princes, are praised or blamed

It now remains for us to consider what ought to be the conduct and bearing of a Prince in relation to his subjects and friends. And since I know that many have written on this subject, I fear it may be thought presumptuous in me to write of it also; the more so, because in my treatment of it I depart widely from the views that others have taken.

But since it is my object to write what shall be useful to whosoever understands it, it seems to me better to follow the real truth of things than an imaginary view of them. For many Republics and Princedoms have been imagined that were never seen or known to exist in reality. And the manner in which we live, and that in which we ought to live, are things so wide asunder, that he who quits the one to betake himself to the other is more likely to destroy than to save himself; since any one who would act up to a perfect standard of goodness in everything, must be ruined among so many who are not good. It is essential, therefore, for a Prince who would maintain his position, to have learned how to be other than good, and to use or not to use his goodness as necessity requires.

Laying aside, therefore, all financial notions concerning a Prince, and considering those only that are true, I say that all men when they are spoken of, and Princes more than others from their being set so high, are noted for certain of those qualities which attach either praise or blame. Thus one is accounted liberal, another miserly (which word I use, rather than *avaricious*, to denote the man who is too sparing of what is his own, *avarice* being the disposition to take wrongfully what is another's); one is generous, another greedy; one cruel, another tenderhearted; one is faithless, another true to his word; one effeminate and cowardly, another high-spirited and courageous; one is courteous, another haughty; one lewd, another chaste; one upright, another crafty; one firm, another facile; one grave, another frivolous; one devout, another unbelieving; and the like. Every one, I know, will admit that it would be most laudable for a Prince to be endowed with all of the above qualities that are reckoned good; but since it is impossible for him to posses or constantly practise them all, the conditions of human nature not allowing it, he must be discreet enough to know how to avoid the reproach of those vices that would deprive him of his government, and, if possible, be on his guard also against those which might not deprive him of it; though if he cannot wholly restrain himself, he may with less scruple indulge in the latter. But he need never hesitate to incur the reproach of those vices without which his authority can hardly be preserved; for if he well consider the whole matter, he will find that there may be a line of conduct having the appearance of virtue, to follow which would be his ruin, and that there may be another course having the appearance of vice, by following which his safety and well-being are secured.

Chapter XVII

Of Cruelty and Clemency, and whether it is better to be Loved or Feared

Passing to the other qualities above mentioned, I say that every Prince should desire to be accounted merciful and not cruel. Nevertheless, he should be careful not to abuse this quality of mercy. Cesare Borgia was reputed cruel, yet his cruelty restored Romagna, united it, and brought it to order and obedience; so that if we look at things in their true light, it will be seen that he was in reality far more merciful than the people of Florence, who, to avoid the imputation of cruelty, suffered Pistoja to be destroyed by fictions.

A Prince should therefore disregard the reproach of cruelty where it enables him to keep his subjects united and faithful. For he who quells disorder by a very few signal examples will in the end be more merciful then he who from excessive lenience suffers things to take their course and so result in rapine and bloodshed; for these hurt the entire State, whereas the severities of the Prince injure individuals only.

And for a new Prince, above all others, it is impossible to escape a name for cruelty, since new States are full of dangers. Wherefore Virgil, by the mouth of Dido:—

*"Res dura et regni novitas me talia cogunt
Moliri, et late fines custode tueri."*[1]

Nevertheless, the new Prince should not be too ready to belief, nor too easily set in motion; nor should he himself be the first to raise alarms; but should so temper prudence with kindliness that too great confidence in others shall not throw him off his guard, nor groundless distrust render him insupportable.

And here comes in the question whether it is better to be loved rather than feared, or feared rather than loved. It might be answered that we should wish to be both; but since love and fear can hardly exist together, if we must choose between them, it is far safer to be feared then loved. For of men it may generally be affirmed that they are thankless, fickle, false, studious to avoid danger, greedy of gain, devoted to you while you confer benefits upon them, and ready, as I said before, while the need is remote, to shed their blood, and sacrifice their property, their lives, and their children for you; but when it comes near they turn against you. The Prince, therefore, who without otherwise securing himself builds wholly on their professions is undone. For the friendships we buy with a price, and do not gain by greatness and nobility of character, though fairly earned are not made good, but fail us when we need them most.

Moreover, men are less careful how they offend him who makes himself loved than him who makes himself feared. For love is held by the tie of obligation, which, because men are a sorry breed, is broken on every prompting of self-interest; but fear is bound by the apprehension of punishment which never loosens its grasp.

Nevertheless, a Prince should inspire fear in suchwise that if he do not win love he may escape hate. For a man may very well be feared and yet not hated, as will always be the case so long as he does not intermeddle with the property or with the women of his citizens and subjects. And if constrained to put any one to death, he should do so only when there is manifest cause or reasonable justification. But, above all, he must abstain from the property of others. For men will sooner forget the death of their father than the loss of their patrimony. Moreover, pretexts for confiscation are never to seek, and he who has

once begun to live by rapine always finds reasons for taking what is not his; whereas reasons for shedding blood are fewer, and sooner exhausted.

But when a Prince is with his army, and has many soldiers under his command, he must entirely disregard the reproach of cruelty, for without such a reputation in its Captain, no army can be held together or kept ready for every emergency. Among other things remarkable in Hannibal this has been noted, that having a very great army, made up of men of many different nations and brought to serve in a foreign country, no dissension ever arose among the soldiers themselves, nor any mutiny against their leader, either in his good or in his evil fortunes. This we can only ascribe to the transcendent cruelty, which, joined with numberless great qualities, rendered him at once venerable and terrible in the eyes of his soldiers; for without this reputation for cruelty his other virtues would not have effected the like results.

Unreflecting writers, indeed, while praising his achievements, have condemned the chief cause of them; but that his other merits would not by themselves have been so efficacious we may see from the case of Scipio, one of the greatest Captains, not of his own time only but of all times whereof we have record, whose armies rose against him in Spain from no other cause than his excessive leniency in allowing them freedoms inconsistent with military discipline. With which weakness Fabius Maximus taxed him in the Senate House, calling him the corrupter of the Roman soldiery. Again, when the Locrians were shamefully outraged by one of his lieutenants, he neither avenged them, nor punished the insolence of his officer; and this from the natural easiness of his disposition. So that is was said in the Senate by one who sought to excuse him, that there were many who knew better to refrain from doing wrong themselves than how to correct the wrong-doing of others. This temper, however, must in time have marred the name and fame even of Scipio, had he continued in it, and retained his command. But living as he did under the control of the Senate, this hurtful quality was not merely veiled, but came to be regarded as a glory.

Returning to the question of being loved or feared, I sum up by saying, that since his being loved depends upon his subjects, while his being feared depends upon himself, a wise Prince should build on what is his own, and not on what rests with others. Only, as I have said, he must do his best to escape hatred.

Chapter XVIII

How Princes should keep faith

Every one recognizes how praiseworthy it is in a Prince to keep faith, and to act uprightly and not craftily. Nevertheless, we see from what has happened in our own days that Princes who have set little store by their word, but have known how to overreach others by their cunning, have accomplished great things, and in the end had the better of those who trusted to honest dealing.

Be it known, then, that there are two ways of contending, one in accordance with the laws, the other by force; the first of which is proper to men, the second to beasts. But since the first method is often ineffectual, it becomes necessary to resort to the second. A Prince should, therefore, understand how to use well both the man and the beast. And this lesson has been covertly taught by the ancient writers, who relate how Anchilles and many others of these old Princes were given over to be brought up and trained by Chiron the Centaur; since the only meaning of their having for teacher one who was half man and half beast is, that it is necessary for a Prince to know how to use both natures, and that the one without the other has no stability.

But since a Prince should know how to use the beast's nature wisely, he ought of beasts to choose both the lion and the fox; for the lion cannot guard himself from the toils, nor the fox from wolves. He must therefore be a fox to discern toils, and a lion to drive off wolves.

To rely wholly on the lion is unwise; and for this reason a prudent Prince neither can nor ought to keep his words when to keep it is hurtful to him and the causes which led him to pledge it are removed. If all men were good, this would not be good advice, but since they are dishonest and do not keep faith with you, you, in return, need not keep faith with them; and no Prince was ever at a loss for plausible reasons to cloak a breach of faith. Of this numberless recent instances could be given, and it might be shown how many solemn treaties and engagements have been rendered inoperative and idle through want of faith in Princes, and that he who has best known to play the fox has had the best success.

It is necessary, indeed, to put a good colour on this nature and to be skilful in feigning and dissembling. But men are so simple, and governed so absolutely by their present needs, that he who wishes to deceive will never fail in finding willing dupes. One recent example I will not omit. Pope Alexander VI had no care or thought but how to deceive, and always found material to work on. No man ever had a more effective manner of asseverating, or made promises with more solemn protestations, or observed them less. And yet, because he understood this side of human nature, his frauds always succeeded.

It is not essential, then, that a Prince should have all the good qualities I have enumerated above, but it is most essential that he should seem to have them. Nay, I will venture to affirm that if he has and invariably practises them all, they are hurtful, whereas the appearance of having them is useful. Thus, it is well to seem merciful, faithful, humane, religious, and upright, and also to be so; but the mind should remain so balanced that were it needful not to be so, you should be able and know how to change to the contrary.

And you are to understand that a Prince, and most of all a new Prince, cannot observe all those rules of conduct in respect whereof men are accounted good, being often forced, in order to preserve his Princedom, to act in opposition to good faith, charity, humanity, and religion. He must therefore keep his mind ready to shift as the winds and tides of Fortune turn, and, as I have already said, ought not to quit good courses if he can help it, but should know how to follow evil if he must.

A Prince should therefore be very careful that nothing ever escapes his lips which is not replete with the five qualities above named, so that to see and hear him, one would think him the embodiment of mercy, good faith, integrity, kindliness, and religion. And there is no virtue which it is more necessary for him to seem to possess than this last; because men in general judge rather by the eye than by the hand, for all can see but few can touch. Every one sees what you seem, but few know that you are, and these few dare not oppose themselves to the opinion of the many who have the majesty of the State to back them up.

Moreover, in the actions of all men, and most of all of Princes, where there is no tribunal to which we can appeal, we look to results. Wherefore if a Prince succeeds in establishing and maintaining his authority, the means will always be judged honourable and be approved by every one. For the vulgar are always taken by appearances and by results, and the world is made up of the vulgar, the few only finding room when the many have no longer ground to stand on.

A certain Prince of our own days, whom it is as well not to name, is always preaching peace and good faith, although the mortal enemy of both; and both, had he practised as he preaches, would, oftener than once, have lost him his kingdom and authority.

Chapter XIX

*That a Prince should seek to escape
Contempt and Hatred*

Having now spoken of the chief of the qualities above referred to, the rest I shall dispose of briefly with these general remarks, that a Prince, as has already in part been said, should consider how he may avoid such courses as would make him hated or despised; and that whenever he succeeds in keeping clear of these, he has performed his part, and runs no risk though he incur other reproaches.

A Prince, as I have said before, sooner becomes hated by being rapacious and by interfering with the property and with the women of his subjects, than in any other way. From these, therefore, he should abstain. For so long as neither their property nor their honour is touched, the mass of mankind live contentedly, and the Prince has only to cope with the ambition of a few, which can in many ways and easily be kept within bounds.

A Prince is despised when he is seen to be fickle, frivolous, effeminate, pusillanimous, or irresolute, against which defects he ought therefore to guard most carefully, striving so to bear himself that greatness, courage, wisdom, and strength may appear in all his actions. In his private dealings with his subjects his decisions should be irrevocable, and his reputation such that no one would dream of overreaching or cajoling him.

The Prince who inspires such an opinion of himself is greatly esteemed, and against one who is greatly esteemed conspiracy is difficult; nor, when he is known to be an excellent Prince and held in reverence by his subjects, will it be easy to attack him. For a Prince is exposed to two dangers, from within in respect of his subjects, from without in respect of foreign powers. Against the latter he will defend himself with good arms and good allies, and if he have good arms he will always have good allies; and when things are settled abroad, they will always be settled at home, unless disturbed by conspiracies; and even should there be hostility from without, if he has taken those measures, and has lived in the way I have recommended, and if he never despairs, he will withstand every attack; as I have said was done by Nabis the Spartan.

As regards his own subjects, when affairs are quiet abroad, a Prince has to fear they may engage in secret plots; against which he best secures himself when he escapes being hated or despised, and keeps on good terms with his people; and this, as I have already shown at length it is essential he should do. Not to be hated or despised by the body of his subjects, is one of the surest safeguards that a Prince can have against conspiracy. For he who conspires always reckons on pleasing the people by putting the Prince to death; but when he sees that instead of pleasing he will offend them, he cannot summon courage to carry out his design. For the difficulties that attend conspirators are infinite, and we know from experience that while there have been many conspiracies few of them have succeeded.

He who conspires cannot do so alone, nor can he assume as his companions any save those whom he believes to be discontented; but so soon as you impart your design to a discontented man, you supply him with the means of removing his discontent, since by betraying you he can procure for himself every advantage; so that seeing on the one hand certain gain, and on the other a doubtful and dangerous risk, he must either be a rare friend to you, or the mortal enemy of the Prince, if he keep your secret.

To put the matter shortly, I say that on the side of the conspirator there are distrust, jealousy, and dread of punishment to deter him, while on the side of the Prince there are the laws, the majesty of the throne, the protection of friends and of the government to defend him; to which if the general good-will of the people be added, it is hardly possible that any should be rash enough to conspire. For while in ordinary cases, the conspirator has ground for fear only before the execution of his villany, in this case he has also cause to fear after, since he has the people for his enemy, and is thus cut off from all hope of shelter.

Of this, endless instances might be given, but I shall content myself with one that happened within the recollection of our fathers. Messer Annibale Bentivoglio, Lord of Bologna and grandsire of the present Messer Annibale, was conspired against and slain by the Canneschi, leaving behind none belonging to him save Messer Giovanni, then an infant in arms. Immediately upon the murder, the people rose and put all the Canneschi to death. This resulted from the goodwill then generally felt towards the House of the Bentivogli and Bologna; which feeling was so strong, that when upon the death of Messer Annibale no one was left who could govern the State, there being reason to believe that a descendant of the family (who up to that time had been thought to be the son of a smith) was living in Florence, the citizens of Bologna went there to fetch him, and entrusted him with the government of their city; which he retained until Messer Giovanni was old enough to govern.

To be brief, a Prince has little to fear from conspiracies when his subjects are well affected towards him; but when they are hostile and hold him in abhorrence, he has then reason to fear everything and every one. And well ordered States and wise Princes have provided with extreme care that the nobility shall not be driven to desperation, and that the commons shall be kept satisfied and contented; for this is one of the most important matters that a Prince has to look to.

Among the well ordered and governed Kingdoms of our day is that of France, wherein we find an infinite number of wise institutions, upon which depend the freedom and security of the King, and of which the most important are the Parliament and its authority. For he who gave its constitution to this Realm, knowing the ambition and arrogance of the nobles, and judging it necessary to bridle and restrain them, and on the other hand knowing the hatred, originating in fear, entertained against them by the commons, and desiring that they should be safe, was unwilling that the responsibility for this should rest on the King; and to relieve him of the ill-will which he might incur with the nobles by favouring the commons, or with the commons by favouring the nobles, appointed a third party to arbitrate, who without committing the King, might depress the nobles and uphold the commons. Nor could there be any better or wiser remedy than this, nor any surer safeguard for the

King and Kingdom. And hence we may draw another notable lesson, namely, that Princes should devolve on others those matters which entail responsibility, and reserve to themselves those that relate to grace and favour. And again I say that a Prince should esteem the great, but must not make himself odious to the people.

To some it may perhaps appear, that if the lives and deaths of many of the Roman Emperors be examined, they offer examples opposed to the views expressed by me; since we find that several among them who had always lived good lives, and shown themselves possessed of great qualities, were nevertheless deposed and even put to death by their subjects who had conspired against them.

In answer to such objections, I shall examine the characters of several Emperors, and show that the causes of their downfall were in no way different from those which I have indicated. In doing this I shall submit for consideration such matters only as must strike every one who reads the history of those times; and it will be enough for my purpose to take those Emperors who reigned from the time of Marcus the Philosopher to the time of Maximinus, who were, inclusively, Marcus, Commodus his son, Pertinax, Julianus, Severus, Caracalla his son, Macrinus, Heliogabalus, Alexander, and Maximinus.

In the first place, then, we have to note that while in other Princedoms the Prince has only to contend with the ambition of the nobles and the insubordination of the people, the Roman Emperors had a further difficulty to encounter in the cruelty and rapacity of their soldiers, which were so distracting as to cause the ruin of many of these Princes. For it was hardly possible for them to satisfy both the soldiers and the people; the latter loving peace and therefore preferring sober Princes, while the former preferred a Prince of a warlike spirit, however harsh, haughty, or rapacious; being willing that he should exercise these qualities against the people, as the means of procuring for themselves double pay, and indulging their greed and cruelty.

Whence it followed that those Emperors who had not inherited or won for themselves such authority as enabled them to keep both people and soldiers in check, were always ruined. The most of them, and those especially who came to the Empire new and without experience, seeing the difficulty of dealing with these conflicting humours, set themselves to satisfy the soldiers, and made little account of offending the people. And for them this was a necessary course to take; for as Princes cannot escape being hated by some, they should, in the first place, endeavour not to be hated by a class; failing wherein, they must do all they can to escape the hatred of that class which is the stronger. Consequently, those Emperors who, by reason of their newness stood in need of extraordinary support, sided with the soldiery rather than with the people; a course which turned out advantageous or otherwise, according as the Prince knew, or did not know, how to maintain his authority over them.

From the causes indicated it resulted that Marcus, Pertinax, and Alexander, being Princes of a temperate disposition, lovers of justice, enemies of cruelty, gentle, and kindly, had each, save Marcus, an unhappy end. Marcus alone lived and died honoured in the highest degree; and this because he had succeeded to the Empire by right of inheritance, and not through the favour either of the soldiery or of the people; and also because, being endowed with many virtues which made him revered, he kept, while he lived, both factions within bounds, and was never either hated or despised.

But Pertinax was chosen Emperor against the will of the soldiery, who being accustomed to live licentiously under Commodus, could not tolerate the more seemly life to which his successor sought to recall them. And having thus made himself hated, and being at the same time despised by reason of his advanced age, he was ruined at the very outset of his reign.

And here it is to be noted that hatred is incurred as well on account of good actions as of bad; for which reason, as I have already said, a Prince who would maintain his authority is often compelled to be other than good. For when the class, be it the people, the soldiers, or the nobles, on whom you judge it necessary to rely for your support, is corrupt, you must needs adapt yourself to its humours, and satisfy these, in which case virtuous conduct will only prejudice you.

Let us now come to Alexander, who was so just a ruler that among the praises ascribed to him it is recorded, that, during the fourteen years he held the Empire, no man was ever put to death by him without trial. Nevertheless, being accounted effeminate, and thought to be governed by his mother, he fell into contempt, and the army conspiring against him, slew him.

When we turn to consider the characters of Commodus, Severus, Caracalla, and Maximinus, we find them all to have been most cruel and rapacious Princes, who, to satisfy the soldiery, scrupled not to inflict every kind of wrong upon the people. And all of them, except Severus, came to a bad end. But in Severus there was such strength of character, that, keeping the soldiers his friends, he was able, although he oppressed the people, to reign on prosperously to the last; because his great qualities made him so admirable in the eyes of both the people and the soldiers, that the former remained in a manner amazed and awestruck, while the latter were respectful and contented.

And because his actions, for one who was a new Prince, were thus remarkable, I will point out shortly how well he understood to play the part both of the lion and of the fox, each of which natures, as I have already said, a Prince should know how to assume.

Knowing the sluggish disposition of the Emperor Julianus, Severus persuaded the army he commanded in Sclavonia that it was their duty to go to Rome to avenge the death of Pertinax, who had been slain by the Pretorian guards. Under this pretext, and without disclosing his design on the Empire, he put his army in march, and reached Italy before it was known that he had set out. On his arrival in Rome, the Senate, through fear, elected him Emperor and put Julianus to death. After this first step, two obstacles still remained to his becoming sole master of the Empire; one in Asia, where Niger who commanded the armies of the East had caused himself to be proclaimed Emperor; the other in the West, where Albinus, who also aspired to the Empire, was in command. And judging it dangerous to declare open war against both, he resolved to proceed against Niger by arms, against Albinus by artifice. To the latter, accordingly, he wrote, that having been chosen Emperor by the Senate, he desired to share the dignity with him; that he therefore sent him the title of Caesar, and in compliance with a resolution of the Senate assumed him as his colleague. All which statements Albinus accepted as made in good faith. But so soon as Severus had defeated and slain Niger, and restored tranquility in the East, returning to Rome he complained in the Senate that Albinus, all unmindful of the favours he had received from him; had treacherously sought to destroy him; for which cause he was compelled to go and punish his ingratitude. Whereupon he set forth to seek Albinus in Gaul, where he at once deprived him of his dignities and his life.

Whosoever, therefore, shall examine carefully the actions of this Emperor, will find in him all the fierceness of the lion and all the craft of the fox, and will note how he was feared and respected by the people, yet not hated by the army, and will not be surprised that though a new man, he was able to maintain his hold of so great an

Empire. For the splendour of his reputation always shielded him from the odium which the people might otherwise have conceived against him by reason of his cruelty and rapacity.

Caracalla, his son, was likewise a man of great parts, endowed with qualities which made him admirable in the sight of the people, and endeared him to the army, being of a warlike spirit, most patient of fatigue, and contemning all luxury in food and every other effeminacy. Nevertheless, his ferocity and cruelty were so unbridled and unheard of (he having put to death a vast number of the inhabitants of Rome at different times, and the whole of those of Alexandria at a stroke), that he came to be detested by all the world, and so dreaded even by those whom he had about him, that at the last he was slain by a centurion in the midst of his army.

And here be it noted that deaths like this which are the result of a deliberate and fixed resolve, cannot be escaped by Princes, since any one who disregards his own life can effect them. A Prince, however, needs the less to fear them as they are seldom attempted. The only precaution he can take is to avoid doing grave wrong to any of those who serve him, or whom he has near him as officers of his Court, a precaution which Caracalla neglected in putting to a shameful death the brother of this centurion, and in continually threatening the man himself, whom he nevertheless retained as one of his bodyguard. This, as the event showed, was a rash and fatal course.

We come next to Commodus, who, as he took the Empire by hereditary right, ought to have held it with much ease. For being the son of Marcus, he had only to follow in his father's footsteps to content both the people and the soldiery. But being of a cruel and brutal nature, to sate his rapacity at the expense of the people, he sought support from the army, indulging it in every kind of excess. On the other hand, by an utter disregard of his dignity, in frequently descending into the arena to fight with gladiators, and by other base acts wholly unworthy of the Imperial station, he became contemptible in the eyes of the soldiery; and being on the one hand hated, on the other despised, was at last conspired against and murdered.

The character of Maximinus remains to be touched upon. He was of a very warlike disposition, and on the death of Alexander, of whom we have already spoken, was chosen Emperor by the army who had been disgusted with the mildness of that Prince. But this dignity he did not long enjoy, since two causes concurred to render him at once odious and contemptible; the one the

baseness of his origin, he having at one time herded sheep in Thrace, a fact well known to all, and which led all to look on him with disdain; the other that on being proclaimed Emperor, delaying to repair Rome and enter on possession of the Imperial throne, he incurred a reputation for excessive cruelty by reason of the many atrocities perpetrated by his prefects in Rome and other parts of the Empire. The result was that the whole world, stirred at once with scorn of his mean birth and with the hatred which the dread of his ferocity inspired, combined against him, Africa leading the way, the Senate and people of Rome and the whole of Italy following. In which conspiracy his own army joined. For they, being engaged in the siege of Aquileja and finding difficulty in reducing it, enraged by his cruelty, and less afraid of him when they saw so many against him, put him to death.

I need say nothing of Heliogabalus, Macrinus, or Julianus, all of whom being utterly despicable were speedily got rid of, but shall conclude these remarks by observing, that the Princes of our own days are less troubled with the necessity of making constant efforts to keep their soldiers in good humour. For though they must treat them with some indulgence, the need for doing so is soon over, since none of these Princes possess a standing army which, like the armies of the Roman Empire, has strengthened with the growth of his government and the administration of his State. And if it was then necessary to satisfy the soldiers rather than the people, because the soldiers were more powerful than the people, now it is more necessary for all Princes, except the Turk and the Soldan, to satisfy the people rather than the soldiery, since the former are more powerful than the latter.

I except the Turk because he has always around him some twelve thousand foot soldiers and fifteen thousand horse, on whom depend the security and strength of his kingdom, and with whom he must needs keep on good terms, all regard for the people being subordinate. The government of the Soldan is similar, so that he too being wholly in the hands of his soldiers, must keep well with them without regard to the people.

And here you are to note that the State of the Soldan, while it is unlike all other Princedoms, resembles the Christian Pontificate in this, that it can neither be classed as new, nor as hereditary. For it is not the sons of the Soldan who dies who succeed to the kingdom and become its Lords, but he who is elected to the post by those who have authority to make such elections. And this being the ancient and established order of things, the Princedom cannot be accounted new, since none of the difficulties that attend new Princedoms are found in it. For though the Prince be new, the institutions of the State are old, and are so contrived that the elected Prince is accepted as though he were hereditary.

But returning to the matter in hand, I say that whoever reflects on the above reasoning will see that either hatred or contempt was the ruin of the Emperors whom I have named; and will also understand how it happened that some taking one way and some the opposite, one only by each of these roads came to a happy, and all the rest to an unhappy end. Because for Pertinax and Alexander, they being new Princes, it was useless and hurtful to try to imitate Marcus, who was an hereditary Prince; and similarly for Caracalla, Commodus, and Maximinus it was a fatal error to imitate Severus, since they lacked the qualities that would have enabled them to tread in his footsteps.

In short, a Prince new to the Princedom cannot imitate the actions of Marcus, nor is it necessary that he should imitate all those of Severus; but he should borrow from Severus those parts of his conduct which are needed to serve as a foundation for his government, and from Marcus those suited to maintain it and render it glorious when once established.

Chapter XXIII

That Flatters should be shunned

One error into which Princes, unless very prudent or very fortunate in their choice of friends, are apt to fall, is of such importance that I must not pass it over. I mean in respect of flatters. These abound in Courts, because men take so much pleasure in their own concerns, and so deceive themselves with regard to them, that they can hardly escape this plague; while even in the effort to escape it there is risk of incurring contempt.

For there is no way to guard against flattery but by letting it be seen that you take no offence in hearing the truth: but when every one is free to tell you the truth, respect falls short. Wherefore a prudent Prince should follow a middle course, by choosing certain discreet men from among his subjects, and allowing them alone free leave to speak their minds on any matter on which he asks their opinion, and on none other. But he ought to ask their opinion on everything, and after hearing what they have to say, should reflect and judge for himself. And with these counsellors collectively, and with each of them separately, his bearing should be such, that each and all of them may know that the more freely they speak their minds the better they will be liked. Besides these, the Prince should listen to no others, but should follow the course determined on, and afterwards adhere firmly to his resolves. Whoever acts otherwise is either undone by flatterers, or, from continually vacillat-

ing as opinions vary, comes to be held in light esteem.

With reference to this matter, I shall cite a recent instance. Father Luke, who is attached to the Court of the present Emperor Maximilian, in speaking of his Majesty told me that he seeks advice from none, yet never has his own way; and this from his following a course contrary to that above recommended. For being of a secret disposition, he never discloses his intentions to any, nor asks their opinion; so that it is only when his plans are to be carried out that they begin to be discovered and known, and at the same time to be thwarted by those he has about him, when he being facile gives way. Hence it happens that what he does one day, he undoes the next; that his wishes and designs are never fully understood; and that it is impossible to build on his resolves.

A Prince, therefore, ought always to take counsel, but at such times and seasons only as he himself pleases, and not when it pleases others; nay, should discourage every one from obtruding advice on matters on which it is not sought. But he should be free in asking advice, and afterwards, as regards the matters on which he has asked it, a patient hearer of the truth, and even displeased should he perceive that any one, from whatsoever motive, keeps it back.

But those who think that every Prince who has a name for prudence owes it to the wise counsellors he has around him, and not to any merit of his own, are undoubtedly mistaken; since it is an unerring rule and of universal application that a

Prince who is not wise himself cannot be well advised by others, unless by chance he surrender himself to be wholly governed by some one adviser who happens to be supremely prudent; in which case he may, indeed, be well advised; but not for long, since such an adviser will soon oust him from his Princedom. If he listen to a multitude of advisers, the Prince who is not wise will never have consistent counsels, nor will he know of himself how to reconcile them. Each of his counsellors will study his own advantage, and the Prince will be unable to detect or correct them. Nor could it well be otherwise, for men will always grow rogues on your hands unless they find themselves under a necessity to be honest.

We may take it therefore that good counsels, whencesoever they come, have their origin in the prudence of the Prince, and not the prudence of the Prince in wise counsels.

ENDNOTES

1. "A fate unkind, and newness in my reign Compel me thus to guard a wide domain."

————————— *Questions for Consideration* —————————

Directions: Using complete sentences, provide brief answers for the following questions.

1. Describe a "Machiavellian" individual.

   _____

   _____

   _____

   _____

   _____

2. Describe the political climate of Florence, Italy during the time of Machiavelli.

   _____

   _____

   _____

   _____

   _____

3. According to Machiavellian thought, identify some of the characteristics of an ideal ruler or prince.

   _____

   _____

   _____

   _____

   _____

————————————— *Writing Critically* —————————————

Directions: Select one of the essay topics listed below and compose a 500 word essay which discusses the topic fully.

1. Discuss in an argumentative essay whether the public morality of a leader or ruler should be the same as his or her private morality.

2. Imagine you were the ruler of a kingdom of your own. Discuss in an essay what specific qualities advocated by Machiavelli you feel would or would not be endorsed as a prince or ruler.

3. Imagine you were a reporter and assigned to interview Machiavelli. Discuss in an essay some of the questions you would ask him about his life and major work *The Prince*. Give reasons why you would ask him certain questions.

Prewriting Space:

_____

_____

_____

_____

_____

_____

_____

_____

_____

_____

_____

_____

_____

_____

_____

_____

_____

_____

_____

_____

_____

Introduction

Michel de Montaigne (1533–1592 A.D.)

Michel de Montaigne was born in 1533 into a prominent family on their estate in western France near the coastal city of Bordeaux. While his father was a typical French Catholic, his mother was descended from a Spanish-Jewish family that had converted to Catholicism under pressure from the Spanish Inquisition. The tolerance Montaigne later expressed so often in his writings was probably due in part to the cultural diversity of his background. His father was neither unschooled nor highly educated, but he did all he could to insure that Michel would have the best education available during the first half of the sixteenth century in France. A private tutor taught him Latin when he was a child, and he later studied law. In 1557, he was appointed to serve in the Bordeaux Parliament, a branch of the national judicial system of France. During a period of often violent religious conflicts between Protestants and Catholics, he was actively involved in both the controversies and the ordinary administrative issues faced by the Parliament of Bordeaux. In 1570, after a long period of public life, he went into early retirement in part because of a frustrated desire to hold a higher political office. Shortly after, at the age of thirty-eight, he decided to devote the rest of his life to study, reflection, and writing. His decision led to the creation of the brilliant autobiographical essays that are a major landmark in the literature of the late Renaissance in France. A man of Montaigne's public stature and abilities could not remain in seclusion, however; from 1581 to 1585, he served as mayor of the city of Bordeaux.

Readers of Montaigne tend to fall into two camps: Some are discouraged by his fondness for long tangled sentences that play with meaning rather than present a clear statement. Many other readers, however, rise to the challenge of his complicated writing style and savor the subtlety with which he develops a distinctive, skeptical point of view. Montaigne was above all a skeptic, an individual who held only one view with certainty: that all human knowledge was uncertain. He produced his major work, the *Essays*, toward the end of the sixteenth century, an era that was also near the end of the Renaissance or Early Modern period in France. (As is well known, the Renaissance occurred in different countries at different times. In England, for instance, the spread of humanism and other Renaissance trends was slow; the English Renaissance would be completed only in the middle of the seventeenth century.)

This time-frame means that for Montaigne, the great age of Renaissance optimism had passed. Man was still the measure of all things, but this view was now held with far less enthusiasm than at an earlier point in the century. Also weakened was the view that, through learning and careful planning, human beings could create a utopia, an ideal society where happiness was maximized. On the other hand, the Renaissance continued to be an age devoted to reviving the philosophical viewpoints of classical antiquity. Thus, while Montaigne was a skeptic, he was not at all an innovator in reviving skepticism, which was a movement in ancient Greek and Roman philosophy. These philosophers of the classical era had questioned the extent to which the human intellect was capable of interpreting the input of the senses and arriving at truth and understanding. Earlier Renaissance figures such as Rabelais had rejected the dogmatism of the medieval period and had often adopted a skeptical perspective in their writings.

There is a real difference, however, between the approach of Rabelais and of Montaigne. For Rabelais, demonstrating the uncertainty of knowledge is often a way of showing off, an intellectual *tour de force* that confirms the brilliance of a human mind that has been refined through the study of difficult literary and philosophical texts. By Montaigne's time, however, the optimism of the early sixteenth century in France was long over.

Near the beginning of the century, Rabelais had experienced disillusionment over the failure of France to work out peacefully the religious disputes associated with the Reformation. Yet his skepticism was always tied to humor as he satirized the judicial system and other aspects of his culture. In Montaigne's meandering writings, the probing and doubting of every possible view or idea becomes almost an obsession, an enterprise that is alternately humorous, ironic, sardonic, or flatly opposed to the idea that there is any strength in the human intellect.

Montaigne's skepticism plays itself out in interesting ways in his *Essays*, the rambling autobiographical writings that he wrote and revised over a period of about twenty years. In "Of Cannibals," Montaigne is refreshingly unconvinced of the validity of the values of his own culture. He is thus able to appreciate and assess, with at least some impartiality, the values of the native inhabitants of the recently discovered land of Brazil. In "Of the Inconsistency of Our Actions," he is fascinated with the inability of human beings to manifest a steady, consistent, and coherent character for more than a very brief period of time. He argues that human existence is full of frequent shifts in mood, desires, and action.

So impressed is Montaigne by the interplay of conflicting qualities in society and in the individual human life that it is appropriate to classify him not simply as a skeptic, but as a *baroque* writer and thinker. In literature of the late Renaissance, the baroque style is ornate, complicated, and often obscure. The baroque spirit is also characterized by a sense that life is full of contradictions and often seems like an illusion. The distinctive values of the baroque sensibility are obvious in the *Essays* of Montaigne.

Nonetheless, despite the uncertainty and frequent shifts in his writing, Montaigne was not without a plan or a project. During the two decades he worked on the *Essays*, Montaigne wanted to leave something of himself to the world. He wrote what is probably the first major autobiography since the early Middle Ages, when Augustine composed his *Confessions*. But whereas Augustine was obsessed with the inferiority of the self, its sinfulness, and its alienation from God, Montaigne wanted his book to live on and take the place of himself. So he set about candidly observing and recording the thoughts, actions, and opinions of a particular individual—himself.

Despite his interest in preserving a unique person in his *Essays*, which have been regarded as a literary self-portrait, he was not an individualist in the Romantic or modern sense. That is to say, he did not see himself as a separate world, a private universe apart from society. Montaigne always looked at himself as a highly educated, *introspective* person who was very much a member of society—and of an intellectual community of reflective people past and present. Thus, while Montaigne set out to construct a reliable picture of himself in words, he knew that he was a part of a great literary tradition to which many classical as well as Renaissance writers belonged. And like numerous other writers of his era, he constantly borrowed fragments and phrases of other people's writings. He often quoted them, but he also modified many of these outside sources and incorporated them into his autobiography.

Montaigne touched upon almost every conceivable subject at some point in the *Essays*—love, sex, death, history, philosophy, medicine. He had an opinion on just about everything. In the process of presenting his views, he attempted to convey the impression that his mind, his inner self, was actually there on the page—and would remain there. It is also useful to remember that the work "essay" comes from "essayer," the French verb "to try or attempt." Montaigne was trying himself out to see what he really consisted of as a person. By exploring himself from every perspective, he would no doubt succeed in putting himself into words. Each essay is thus a kind of "slice-of-life," a representation of the ongoing, vital mental activity of a congenial and reflective individual.

However strange Montaigne's writing may at times seem to us, we have all met him somewhere before. Perhaps we remember Hamlet and his immortal "To be or not to be" soliloquy. In creating the wavering and uncertain Prince of Denmark, Shakespeare was very likely influenced by Montaigne. Or perhaps we remember the elegant little essays of Francis Bacon or the confident and assertive reflections of Ralph Waldo Emerson. Montaigne exerted an immense influence on the development of the personal essay as a means to articulate individual, private views on an endless variety of topics. Anyone who has taken a composition course in college and was asked to write an essay drawn from personal experience is also participating in a tradition that leads back to Montaigne. Even if Montaigne never fully succeeded in depicting his personality in words, he set a strong precedent that has influenced autobiographical writers of every description ever since. (NW)

BIBLIOGRAPHY

Frame, Donald M. *Montaigne: A Biography*. New York: Harcourt, Brace & World, 1965.

___, translator. *The Complete Essays of Montaigne*. Stanford: Stanford University Press, 1976.

Hugo, Friedrich. *Montaigne*. Ed. Philippe Desan. Trans. Dawn Eng. Berkeley: University of California Press, 1991.

Starobinski, Jean. *Montaigne in Motion*. Trans. Arthur Goldhammer. Chicago: University of Chicago Press, 1985.

Tetel, Marcel. *Montaigne*. 2nd ed. Boston: Twayne, 1990.

Wallace, Nathaniel. "Montaigne, Lucretius, and Intertextuality in *Essais* II.xii ('Apologie de Raimond Sebond')," *Spiegel der Letteren* 29.1–2 (1987): 79–85.

from Essays

Michel de Montaigne

Of Cannibals

When King Pyrrhus passed over into Italy, after he had reconnoitered the formation of the army that the Romans were sending to meet him, he said: "I do not know what barbarians these are" (for so the Greeks called all foreign nations), "but the formation of this army that I see is not at all barbarous." The Greeks said as much of the army that Flamininus brought into their country, and so did Philip, seeing from a knoll the order and distribution of the Roman camp, in his kingdom, under Publius Sulpicius Galba. Thus we should beware of clinging to vulgar opinions, and judge things by reason's way, not by popular say.

I had with me for a long time a man who had lived for ten or twelve years in that other world which has been discovered in our century, in the place where Villegaignon landed, and which he called Antarctic France.[1] This discovery of a boundless country seems worthy of consideration. I don't know if I can guarantee that some other such discovery will not be made in the future, so many personages greater than ourselves having been mistaken about this one. I am afraid we have eyes bigger than our stomachs, and more curiosity than capacity. We embrace everything, but we clasp only wind.

Plato brings in Solon, telling how he had learned from the priests of the city of Saïs in Egypt that in days of old, before the Flood, there was a great island named Atlantis, right at the mouth of the Strait of Gibraltar, which contained more land than Africa and Asia put together, and that the kings of that country, who not only possessed that island but had stretched out so far on the mainland that they held the breadth of Africa as far as Egypt and the length of Europe as far as Tuscany, undertook to step over into Asia and subjugate all the nations that border on the Mediterranean, as far as the Black Sea; and for this purpose crossed the Spains, Gaul, Italy, as far as Greece, where the Athenians checked them; but that some time after, both the Athenians and themselves and their island were swallowed up by the Flood.

It is quite likely that that extreme devastation of waters made amazing changes in the habitations of the earth, as people maintain that the sea cut off Sicily from Italy—

> *'Tis said an earthquake once asunder tore*
> *These lands with dreadful havoc, which before*
> *Formed but one land, one coast*
>
> VIRGIL

Cyprus from Syria, the island of Euboea from the mainland of Boeotia; and elsewhere joined lands that were divided, filling the channels between them with sand and mud:

> *A sterile marsh, long fit for rowing, now*
> *Feeds neighbor towns, and feels the heavy plow.*
>
> HORACE

But there is no great likelihood that that island was the new world which we have just discovered; for it almost touched Spain, and it would be an incredible result of a flood to have forced it away as far as it is, more than twelve hundred leagues; besides, the travels of the moderns have already almost revealed that it is not an island, but a mainland connected with the East Indies on one side, and elsewhere with the lands under the two poles; or, if it is separated from them, it is by so narrow a strait and interval that it does not deserve to be called an Island on that account.

It seems that there are movements, some natural, others feverish, in these great bodies, just as in our own. When I consider the inroads that my river, the Dordogne, is making in my lifetime into the right bank in its descent, and that in twenty years it has gained so much ground and stolen away the foundations of several buildings, I clearly see that this is an extraordinary disturbance; for if it had always gone at this rate, or was to do so in the future, the face of the world would be turned topsy-turvy. But rivers are subject to changes: now they overflow in one direction, now in another, now they keep to their course. I am not speaking of the sudden inundations whose causes are manifest. In Médoc, along the seashore, my brother, the sieur d'Arsac, can see an estate of his buried under the sands that the sea spews forth; the tops of some buildings are still visible; his farms and domains have changed into very thin pasturage. The inhabitants say that for some time the sea has been pushing toward them so hard that they have lost four leagues of land. These sands are its harbingers; and we see great dunes of moving sand that march half a league ahead of it and keep conquering land.

The other testimony of antiquity with which some would connect this discovery is in Aristotle, at least if that little book *Of Unheard-of Wonders* is by him. He there relates that certain Carthaginians, after setting out upon the Atlantic Ocean from the Strait of Gibraltar and sailing a long time, at last discovered a great fertile island, all clothed in woods and watered by great deep rivers, far remote from any mainland; and that they, and others since, attracted by the goodness and fertility of the soil, went there with their wives and children, and began to settle there. The lords of Carthage, seeing that their country was gradually becoming depopulated, expressly forbade anyone to go there any more, on pain of death, and drove out these new inhabitants, fearing, it is said, that in course of time they might come to multiply so greatly as to supplant their former masters and ruin their state. This story of Aristotle does not fit our new lands any better than the other.

This man I had was a simple, crude fellow[2]—a character fit to bear true witness; for clever people observe more things and more curiously, but they interpret them; and to lend weight and conviction to their interpretation, they cannot help altering history a little. They never show you things as they are, but bend and disguise them according to the way they have seen them; and to give credence to their judgment and attract you to it, they are prone to add something to their matter, to stretch it out and amplify it. We need a man either very honest, or so simple that he has not the stuff to build up false inventions and give them plausibility; and wedded to no theory. Such was my man; and besides this, he at various times brought sailors and merchants, whom he had known on that trip to see me. So I content myself with his information, without inquiring what the cosmographers say about it.

We ought to have topographers who would give us an exact account of the places where they have been. But because they have over us the advantage of having seen Palestine, they want to enjoy the privilege of telling us news about all the rest of the world. I would like everyone to write what he knows, and as much as he knows, not only in this, but in all other subjects; for a man may have some special knowledge and experience of the nature of a river or a fountain, who in other matters knows only what everybody knows. However, to circulate this little scrap of knowledge, he will undertake to write the whole of physics. From this vice spring many great abuses.

Now, to return to my subject, I think there is nothing barbarous and savage in that nation, from what I have been told, except that each man calls barbarism whatever is not his own practice; for indeed it seems we have no other test of truth and reason than the example and pattern of the opinions and customs of the country we live in. *There* is always the perfect religion, the perfect government, the perfect and accomplished manners in all things. Those people are wild, just as we call wild the fruits that Nature has produced by herself and in her normal course; whereas really it is those that we have changed artificially and led astray from the common order, that we should rather call wild. The former retain alive and vigorous their genuine, their most useful and natural, virtues and properties, which we have debased in the latter in adapting them to gratify our corrupted taste. And yet for all that, the savor and delicacy of some uncultivated fruits of those countries is quite as excellent, even to our taste, as that of our own. It is not reasonable that art should win the place of honor over our great and powerful mother Nature. We have so overloaded the beauty and richness of her works by our inventions that we have quite smothered her. Yet wherever her purity shines forth, she wonderfully puts to shame our vain and frivolous attempts:

Ivy comes readier without our care;
In lonely caves the arbutus grows more fair;
No art with artless bird song can compare.

PROPERTIUS

All our efforts cannot even succeed in reproducing the nest of the tiniest little bird, its contexture, its beauty and convenience; or even the web of the puny spider. All things, says Plato, are produced by nature, fortune, or by art; the greatest and most beautiful by one or the other of the first two, the least and most imperfect by the last.

These nations, then, seem to me barbarous in this sense, that they have been fashioned very little by the human mind, and are still very close to their original naturalness. The laws of nature still rule them, very little corrupted by ours; and they are in such a state of purity that I am sometimes vexed that they were unknown earlier, in the days when there were men able to judge them better than we. I am sorry that Lycurgus and Plato did not know of them; for it seems to me that what we actually see in these nations surpasses not only all the pictures in which poets have idealized the golden age and all their inventions in imagining a happy state of man, but also the conceptions and the very desire of philosophy. They could not imagine a naturalness so pure and simple as we see by experience; nor could they believe that our society could be maintained with so little artifice and human solder. This is a nation, I should say to Plato, in which there is no sort of traffic, no knowledge of letters, no science of numbers, no name for a magistrate or for political superiority, no custom of servitude, no riches or poverty, no contracts, no successions, no partitions, no occupations but leisure ones, no care for any but common kinship, no clothes, no agriculture, no metal, no use of wine or wheat. The very words that signify lying, treachery, dissimulation, avarice, envy, belittling, pardon—unheard of. How far from this perfection would he find the republic that he imagined: *Men fresh sprung from the gods* [Seneca].

These manners nature first ordained.

VIRGIL

For the rest, they live in a country with a very pleasant and temperate climate, so that according to my witnesses it is rare to see a sick man there; and they have assured me that they never saw one palsied, bleary-eyed, toothless, or bent with age. They are settled along the sea and shut in on the land side by great high mountains, with a stretch about a hundred leagues wide in between. They have a great abundance of fish and flesh which bear no resemblance to ours, and they eat them with no other artifice than cooking. The first man who rode a horse there, though he had had dealings with them on several other trips, so horrified them in this posture that they shot him dead with arrows before they could recognize him.

Their buildings are very long, with a capacity of two or three hundred souls; they are covered with the bark of great trees, the strips reaching to the ground at one end and supporting and leaning on one another at the top, in the manner of some of our barns, whose covering hangs down to the ground and acts as a side. They have wood so hard that they cut with it and make of it their swords and grills to cook their food. Their beds are of a cotton weave, hung from the roof like those in our ships, each man having his own; for the wives sleep apart from their husbands.

They get up with the sun, and eat immediately upon rising, to last them through the day; for they take no other meal than that one. Like some other Eastern peoples, of whom Suidas tells us, who drank apart from meals, they do not drink then; but they drink several times a day, and to capacity. Their drink is made of some root, and is of the color of our claret wines. They drink it only lukewarm. This beverage keeps only two or three days; it has a slightly sharp taste, is not at all heady, is good for the stomach, and has a laxative effect upon those who are not used to it; it is a very pleasant drink for anyone who is accustomed to it. In place of bread they use a certain white substance like preserved coriander. I have tried it; it tastes sweet and a little flat.

The whole day is spent in dancing. The younger men go to hunt animals with bows. Some of the women busy themselves meanwhile with warming their drink, which is their chief duty. Some one of the old men, in the morning before they begin to eat, preaches to the whole barnful in common, walking from one end to the other, and repeating one single sentence several times until he has completed the circuit (for the buildings are fully a hundred paces long). He recommends to them only two things: valor against the enemy and love for their wives. And they never fail to point out this obligation, as their refrain, that it is their wives who keep their drink warm and seasoned.

There may be seen in several places, including my own house, specimens of their beds, of their ropes, of their wooden swords and the bracelets with which they cover their wrists in combats, and of the big canes, open at one end, by whose sound they keep time in their dances. They are close shaven all over, and shave themselves much more cleanly than we, with nothing but a wooden or stone razor. They believe that souls are immortal, and that those who have deserved well of the gods are lodged in that part of heaven where the sun rises, and the damned the west.

They have some sort of priests and prophets but they rarely appear before the people, having their home in the mountains. On their arrival there is a great feast and solemn assembly of several villages—each barn, as I have described it, makes up a village, and they are about one French league from each other. The prophet speaks to them in public, exhorting them to virtue and their duty; but their whole ethical science contains only these two articles: resoluteness in war and affection for their wives. He prophesies to them things to come and the results they are to expect from their undertakings, and urges them to war or holds them back from it; but this is on the condition that when he fails to prophesy correctly, and if things turn out otherwise than he has predicted, he is cut into a thousand pieces if they catch him, and condemned as a false prophet. For this reason, the prophet who has once been mistaken is never seen again.

Divination is a gift of God; that is why its abuse should be punished as imposture. Among the Scythians, when the soothsayers failed to hit the mark, they were laid, chained hand and foot, on carts full of heather and drawn by oxen, on which they were burned. Those who handle matters subject to the control of human capacity are excusable if they do the best they can. But these others, who come and trick us with assurances of an extraordinary faculty that is beyond our ken, should they not be punished for not making good their promise, and for the temerity of their imposture?

They have their wars with the nations beyond the mountains, further inland, to which they go quite naked, with no other arms than bows or wooden swords ending in a sharp point, in the manner of the tongues of our boar spears. It is astonishing what firmness they show in their combats, which never end but in slaughter and bloodshed; for as to routs and terror, they know nothing of either.

Each man brings back as his trophy the head of the enemy he has killed, and sets it up at the entrance to his dwelling. After they have treated their prisoners well for a long time with all the hospitality they can think of, each man who has a prisoner calls a great assembly of his acquaintances. He ties a rope to one of the prisoner's arms, by the end of which he holds him, a few steps away, for fear of being hurt, and gives his dearest friend the other arm to hold in the same way; and these two, in the presence of the whole assembly, kill him with their swords. This done, they roast him and eat him in common and send some pieces to their absent friends. This is not, as people think, for nourishment, as of old the Scythians used to do; it is to betoken an extreme revenge. And the proof of this came when they saw the Portuguese, who had joined forces with their adversaries, inflict a different kind of death on them when they took them prisoner, which was to bury them up to the waist, shoot the rest of their body full of arrows, and afterward hang them. They thought that these people from the other world, being men who had sown the knowledge of many vices among their neighbors and were much greater masters than themselves in every sort of wickedness, did not adopt this sort of vengeance without some reason, and that it must be more painful than their own; so they began to give up their old method and to follow this one.

I am not sorry that we notice the barbarous horror of such acts, but I am heartily sorry that, judging their faults rightly, we should be so blind to our own. I think there is more barbarity in eating a man alive than in eating him dead; and in tearing by tortures and the rack a body still full of feeling, in roasting a man bit by bit, in having him bitten and mangled by dogs and swine (as we have not only read but seen within fresh memory, not among ancient enemies, but among neighbors and fellow citizens, and what is worse, on the pretext of piety and religion), than in roasting and eating him after he is dead.

Indeed, Chrysippus and Zeno, heads of the Stoic sect, thought there was nothing wrong in using our carcasses for any purpose in case of need, and getting nourishment from them; just as our ancestors, besieged by Caesar in the city of Alésia, resolved to relieve their famine by eating old men, women, and other people useless for fighting.

The Gascons once, 'tis said, their life renewed
By eating of such food.

JUVENAL

And physicians do not fear to use human flesh in all sorts of ways for our health, applying it either inwardly or outwardly. But there never was any opinion so disordered as to excuse treachery, disloyalty, tyranny, and cruelty, which are our ordinary vices.

So we may well call these people barbarians, in respect to the rules of reason, but not in respect to ourselves, who surpass them in every kind of barbarity.

Their warfare is wholly noble and generous, and as excusable and beautiful as this human disease can be; its only basis among them is their rivalry in valor. They are not fighting for the conquest of new lands, for they still enjoy that natural abundance that provides them without toil and trouble with all necessary things in such profusion that they have no wish to enlarge their boundaries. They are still in that happy state of desiring only as much as their natural needs demand; anything beyond that is superfluous to them.

They generally call those of the same age, brothers; those who are younger, children; and the old men are fathers to all the others. These leave to their heirs in common the full possession of their property, without division or any other title at all than just the one that Nature gives to her creatures in bringing them into the world.

If their neighbors cross the mountains to attack them and win a victory, the gain of the victor is glory, and the advantage of having proved the master in valor and virtue; for apart from this they have no use for the goods of the vanquished, and they return to their own country, where they lack neither anything necessary nor that great thing, the knowledge of how to enjoy their condition happily and be content with it. These men of ours do the same in their turn. They demand of their prisoners no other ransom than that they confess and acknowledge their defeat. But there is not one in a whole century who does not choose to die rather than to relax a single bit, by word or look from the grandeur of an invincible courage; not one who would not rather be killed and eaten than so much as ask not to be. They treat them very freely, so that life may be all the dearer to them, and usually entertain them with threats of their coming death, of the torments they will have to suffer, the preparations that are being made for that purpose, the cutting up of their limbs, and the feast that will be made at their expense. All this is done for the sole purpose of extorting from their lips some weak or base word, or making them want to flee, so as to gain the advantage of having terrified them and

broken down their firmness. For indeed, if you take it the right way, it is in this point alone that true victory lies:

> *It is no victory*
> *Unless the vanquished foe admits your mastery.*

CLAUDIAN

The Hungarians, very bellicose fighters, did not in olden times pursue their advantage beyond putting the enemy at their mercy. For having wrung a confession from him to this effect, they let him go unharmed and unransomed, except, at most, for exacting his promise never again to take up arms against them.

We win enough advantages over our enemies that are borrowed advantages, not really our own. It is the quality of a porter, not of valor, to have sturdier arms and legs; agility is a dead and corporeal quality; it is a stroke of luck to make our enemy stumble, or dazzle his eyes by the sunlight; it is a trick of art and technique, which may be found in a worthless coward, to be an able fencer. The worth and value of a man is in his heart and his will; there lies his real honor. Valor is the strength, not of legs and arms, but of heart and soul; it consists not in the worth of our horse or our weapons, but in our own. He who falls obstinate in his courage, *if he has fallen, he fights on his knees* [Seneca]. He who relaxes none of his assurance, no matter how great the danger of imminent death; who, giving up his soul, still looks firmly and scornfully at his enemy—he is beaten not by us, but by fortune; he is killed, not conquered.

The most valiant are sometimes the most unfortunate. Thus there are triumphant defeats that rival victories. Nor did those four sister victories, the fairest that the sun ever set eyes on—Salamis, Plataea, Mycale, and Sicily—ever dare match all their combined glory against the glory of the annihilation of King Leonidas and his men at the pass of Thermopylae.

Who ever hastened with more glorious and ambitious desire to win a battle than Captain Ischolas to lose one? Who ever secured his safety more ingeniously and painstakingly than he did his destruction? He was charged to defend a certain pass in the Peloponnesus against the Arcadians. Finding himself wholly incapable of doing this, in view of the nature of the place and the inequality of the forces, he made up his mind that all who confronted the enemy would necessarily have to remain on the field. On the other hand, deeming it unworthy both of his own virtue and magnanimity and of the Lacedaemonian name to fail in his charge, he took a middle course between these two extremes, in this way. The youngest and fittest of his band he preserved for the defense and service of their country, and sent them home; and with those whose loss was less important, he determined to hold this pass, and by their death to make the enemy buy their entry as dearly as he could. And so it turned out. For he was presently surrounded on all sides by the Arcadians, and after slaughtering a large number of them, he and his men were all put to the sword. Is there a trophy dedicated to victors that would not be more due to these vanquished? The role of true victory is in fighting, not in coming off safely; and the honor of valor consists in combating, not in beating.

To return to our story. These prisoners are so far from giving in, in spite of all that is done to them, that on the contrary, during the two or three months that they are kept, they wear a gay expression; they urge their captors to hurry and put them to the test; they defy them, insult them, reproach them with their cowardice and the number of battles they have lost to the prisoners' own people.

I have a song composed by a prisoner which contains this challenge, that they should all come boldly and gather to dine off him, for they will be eating at the same time their own fathers and grandfathers, who have served to feed and nourish his body. "These muscles," he says, "this flesh and these veins are your own, poor fools that you are. You do not recognize that the substance of your ancestors' limbs is still contained in them. Savor them well; you will find in them the taste of your own flesh." An idea that certainly does not smack of barbarity. Those that paint these people dying, and who show the execution, portray the prisoner spitting in the face of his slayers and scowling at them. Indeed, to the last gasp they never stop braving and defying their enemies by word and look. Truly here are real savages by our standards; for either they must be thoroughly so, or we must be; there is an amazing distance between their character and ours.

The men there have several wives, and the higher their reputation for valor the more wives they have. It is a remarkably beautiful thing about their marriages that the same jealousy our wives have to keep us from the affection and kindness of other women, theirs have to win this for them. Being more concerned for their husbands' honor than for anything else, they strive and scheme to have as many companions as they can, since that is a sign of their husbands' valor.

Our wives will cry "Miracle!" but it is no miracle. It is a properly matrimonial virtue, but one of the highest order. In the Bible, Leah, Rachel, Sarah, and Jacob's wives gave their beautiful handmaids to their husbands; and Livia seconded the appetites of Augustus, to her own disadvantage; and Stratonice, the wife of King Deiotarus, not only lent her husband for his use a very beautiful young chambermaid in her service, but carefully brought up her children, and backed them up to succeed to their father's estates.

And lest it be thought that all this is done through a simple and servile bondage to usage and through the pressure of the authority of their ancient customs, without reasoning or judgment, and because their minds are so stupid that they cannot take any other course, I must cite some examples of their capacity. Besides the warlike song I have just quoted, I have another, a love song, which begins in this vein: "Adder, stay; stay, adder, that from the pattern of your coloring my sister may draw the fashion and the workmanship of a rich girdle that I may give to my love; so may your beauty and your pattern be forever preferred to all other serpents." This first couplet is the refrain of the song. Now I am familiar enough with poetry to be a judge of this: not only is there nothing barbarous in this fancy, but it is altogether Anacreontic. Their language, moreover, is a soft language, with an agreeable sound, somewhat like Greek in its endings.

Three of these men, ignorant of the price they will pay some day, in loss of repose and happiness, for gaining knowledge of the corruptions of this side of the ocean; ignorant also of the fact that of this intercourse will come their ruin (which I suppose is already well advanced: Poor wretches, to let themselves be tricked by the desire for new things, and to have left the serenity of their own sky to come and see ours!) three of these men were at Rouen, at the time the late King Charles IX was there. The king talked to them for a long time; they were shown our ways, our splendor, the aspect of a fine city. After that, someone asked their opinion, and wanted to know what they had found most amazing. They mentioned three things, of which I have forgotten the third, and I am very sorry for it; but I still remember two of them. They said that in the first place they thought it very strange that so many grown men, bearded, strong, and armed, who were around the king (it is likely that they were talking about the Swiss of his guard) should submit to obey a child, and that one of them was not chosen to command instead. Second (they have a way in their language of speaking of men as halves of one another), they had noticed that there were among us men full and gorged with all sorts of good things, and that their other halves were beggars at their doors emaciated with hunger and poverty; and they thought it strange that these needy halves could endure such an injustice, and did not take the others by the throat, or set fire to their houses.

I had a very long talk with one of them; but I had an interpreter who followed my meaning so badly, and who was so hindered by his stupidity in taking in my ideas, that I could get hardly any satisfaction from the man. When I asked him what profit he gained from his superior position among his people (for he was a captain, and our sailors called him king), he told me that it was to march foremost in war. How many men followed him? He pointed to a piece of ground, to signify as many as such a space could hold; it might have been four or five thousand men. Did all his authority expire with the war? He said that this much remained, that when he visited the villages dependent on him, they made paths for him through the underbrush by which he might pass quite comfortably.

All this is not too bad—but what's the use? They don't wear breeches.

Of the Inconsistency of Our Actions

Those who make a practice of comparing human actions are never so perplexed as when they try to see them as a whole and in the same light; for they commonly contradict each other so strangely that it seems impossible that they have come from the same shop. One moment young Marius is a son of Mars, another moment a son of Venus. Pope Boniface VIII, they say, entered office like a fox, behaved in it like a lion, and died like a dog. And who would believe that it was Nero, that living image of cruelty, who said, when they brought him in customary fashion the sentence of a condemned criminal to sign: "Would to God I had never learned to write!" So much his heart was wrung at condemning a man to death!

Everything is so full of such examples—each man, in fact, can supply himself with so many—that I find it strange to see intelligent men sometimes going to great pains to match these pieces; seeing that irresolution seems to me the most common and apparent defect of our nature, as witness that famous line of Publilius, the farce writer:

Bad is the plan that never can be changed.

PUBLILIUS SYRUS

There is some justification for basing a judgment of a man on the most ordinary acts of his life; but in view of the natural instability of our conduct and opinions, it has often seemed to me that even good authors are wrong to insist on fashioning a consistent and solid fabric out of us.

They choose one general characteristic, and go and arrange and interpret all a man's actions to fit their picture; and if they cannot twist them enough, they go and set them down to dissimulation. Augustus has escaped them; for there is in this man throughout the course of his life such an obvious, abrupt, and continual variety of actions that even the boldest judges have had to let him go, intact and unsolved. Nothing is harder for me than to believe in men's consistency, nothing easier than to believe in their inconsistency. He who would judge them in detail and distinctly, bit by bit, would more often hit upon the truth.

In all antiquity it is hard to pick out a dozen men who set their lives to a certain and constant course, which is the principal goal of wisdom. For, to comprise all wisdom in a word, says an ancient [Seneca], and to embrace all the rules of our life in one, it is "always to will the same things, and always to oppose the same things." I would not deign, he says, to add "provided the will is just"; for if it is not just, it cannot always be whole.

In truth, I once learned that vice is only unruliness and lack of moderation, and that consequently consistency cannot be attributed to it. It is a maxim of Demosthenes, they say, that the beginning of all virtue is consultation and deliberation; and the end and perfection, consistency. If it were by reasoning that we settled on a particular course of action, we would choose the fairest course—but no one has thought of that:

He spurns the thing he sought, and seeks anew
What he just spurned; he seethes, his life's
askew.

HORACE

Our ordinary practice is to follow the inclinations of our appetite, to the left, to the right, uphill and down, as the wind of circumstance carries us. We think of what we want only at the moment we want it, and we change like that animal which takes the color of the place you set it on. What we have just now planned, we presently change, and presently again we retrace our steps: nothing but oscillation and inconsistency:

Like puppets we are moved by outside strings.

HORACE

We do not go; we are carried away, like floating objects, now gently, now violently, according as the water is angry or calm:

Do we not see all humans unaware
Of what they want, and always searching every-
where,
And changing place, as if to drop the load they
bear?

LUCRETIUS

Every day a new fancy, and our humors shift with the shifts in the weather:

Such are the minds of men, as is the fertile light
That Father Jove himself sends down to make
earth bright.

HOMER

We float between different states of mind; we wish nothing freely, nothing absolutely, nothing constantly. If any man could prescribe and establish definite laws and a definite organization in his head, we should see shining throughout his life an evenness of habits, an order, and an infallible relation between his principles and his practice.

Empedocles noticed this inconsistency in the Agrigentines, that they abandoned themselves to pleasures as if they were to die on the morrow, and built as if they were never to die.

This man[3] would be easy to understand, as is shown by the example of the younger Cato: he who has touched one chord of him has touched

all; he is a harmony of perfectly concordant sounds, which cannot conflict. With us, it is the opposite: for so many actions, we need so many individual judgments. The surest thing, in my opinion, would be to trace our actions to the neighboring circumstances, without getting into any further research and without drawing from them any other conclusions.

During the disorders of our poor country,[4] I was told that a girl, living near where I then was, had thrown herself out of a high window to avoid the violence of a knavish soldier quartered in her house. Not killed by the fall, she reasserted her purpose by trying to cut her throat with a knife. From this she was prevented, but only after wounding herself gravely. She herself confessed that the soldier had as yet pressed her only with requests, solicitations, and gifts; but she had been afraid, she said, that he would finally resort to force. And all this with such words, such expressions, not to mention the blood that testified to her virtue, as would have become another Lucrece. Now, I learned that as a matter of fact, both before and since, she was a wench not so hard to come to terms with. As the story says: Handsome and gentlemanly as you may be, when you have had no luck, do not promptly conclude that your mistress is inviolably chaste; for all you know, the mule driver may get his will with her.

Antigonus, having taken a liking to one of his soldiers for his virtue and valor, ordered his physicians to treat the man for a persistent internal malady that had long tormented him. After his cure, his master noticed that he was going about his business much less warmly, and asked him what had changed him so and made him such a coward. "You yourself, Sire," he answered, "by delivering me from the ills that made my life indifferent to me." A soldier of Lucullus who had been robbed of everything by the enemy made a bold attack on them to get revenge. When he had retrieved his loss, Lucullus, having formed a good opinion of him, urged him to some dangerous exploit with all the fine expostulations he could think of,

With words that might have stirred a coward's
heart.

HORACE

"Urge some poor soldier who has been robbed to do it," he replied:

Though but a rustic lout,
"That man will go who's lost his money," he
called out;

HORACE

and resolutely refused to go.

We read that Sultan Mohammed outrageously berated Hassan, leader of his Janissaries, because he saw his troops giving way to the Hungarians and Hassan himself behaving like a coward in the fight. Hassan's only reply was to go and hurl himself furiously—alone, just as he was, arms in hand—into the first body of enemies that he met, by whom he was promptly swallowed up; this was perhaps not so much self-justification as a change of mood, nor so much his natural valor as fresh spite.

That man whom you saw so adventurous yesterday, do not think it strange to find him just as cowardly today: either anger, or necessity, or company, or wine, or the sound of a trumpet, had put his heart in his belly. His was a courage formed not by reason, but by one of these circumstances; it is no wonder if he has now been made different by other, contrary circumstances.

These supple variations and contradictions that are seen in us have made some imagine that we have two souls, and others that two powers accompany us and drive us, each in its own way, one toward good, the other toward evil; for such sudden diversity cannot well be reconciled with a simple subject.

Not only does the wind of accident move me at will, but, besides, I am moved and disturbed as a result merely of my own unstable posture; and anyone who observes carefully can hardly find himself twice in the same state. I give my soul now one face, now another, according to which direction I turn it. If I speak of myself in different ways, that is because I look at myself in different ways. All contradictions may be found in me by some twist and in some fashion. Bashful, insolent; chaste, lascivious; talkative, taciturn; tough, delicate; clever, stupid; surly, affable; lying, truthful; learned, ignorant; liberal, miserly, and prodigal: all this I see in myself to some extent according to how I turn; and whoever studies himself really attentively finds in himself, yes, even in his judgment, this gyration and discord. I have nothing to say about myself absolutely, simply, and solidly, without confusion and without mixture, or in one word. *Distinguo* is the most universal member of my logic.

Although I am always minded to say good of what is good, and inclined to interpret favorably

anything that can be so interpreted, still it is true that the strangeness of our condition makes it happen that we are often driven to do good by vice itself—were it not that doing good is judged by intention alone.

Therefore one courageous deed must not be taken to prove a man valiant; a man who was really valiant would be so always and on all occasions. If valor were a habit of virtue, and not a sally, it would make a man equally resolute in any contingency, the same alone as in company, the same in single combat as in battle; for, whatever they say, there is not one valor for the pavement and another for the camp. As bravely would he bear an illness in his bed as a wound in camp, and he would fear death no more in his home than in an assault. We would not see the same man charging into the breach with brave assurance, and later tormenting himself, like a woman, over the loss of a lawsuit or a son. When, though a coward against infamy, he is firm against poverty, when, though weak against the surgeons' knives, he is steadfast against the enemy's swords, the action is praiseworthy, not the man.

Many Greeks, says Cicero, cannot look at the enemy, and are brave in sickness; the Cimbrians and Celtiberians, just the opposite; *for nothing can be uniform that does not spring from a firm principle* [Cicero].

There is no more extreme valor of its kind than Alexander's; but it is only of one kind, and not complete and universal enough. Incomparable though it is, it still has its blemishes; which is why we see him worry so frantically when he conceives the slightest suspicion that his men are plotting against his life, and why he behaves in such matters with such violent and indiscriminate injustice and with a fear that subverts his natural reason. Also superstition, with which he was so strongly tainted, bears some stamp of pusillanimity. And the excessiveness of the penance he did for the murder of Clytus is also evidence of the unevenness of his temper.

Our actions are nothing but a patchwork—*they despise pleasure, but are too cowardly in pain; they are indifferent to glory, but infamy breaks their spirit* [Cicero]—and we want to gain honor under false colors. Virtue will not be followed except for her own sake; and if we sometimes borrow her mask for some other purpose, she promptly snatches it from our face. It is a strong and vivid dye, once the soul is steeped in it, and will not go without taking the fabric with it. That is why, to judge a man, we must follow his traces long and carefully. If he does not maintain consistency for its own sake, *with a way of life that has been well considered and preconcerted* [Cicero]; if changing circumstances make him change his pace (I mean his path, for his pace may be hastened or slowed), let him go: that man goes before the wind, as the motto of our Talbot says.

It is no wonder, says an ancient [Seneca], that chance has so much power over us, since we live by chance. A man who has not directed his life as a whole toward a definite goal cannot possibly set his particular actions in order. A man who does not have a picture of the whole in his head cannot possibly arrange the pieces. What good does it do a man to lay in a supply of paints if he does not know what he is to paint? No one makes a definite plan of his life; we think about it only piecemeal. The archer must first know what he is aiming at, and then set his hand, his bow, his string, his arrow, and his movements for that goal. Our plans go astray because they have no direction and no aim. No wind works for the man who has no port of destination.

I do not agree with the judgment given in favor of Sophocles, on the strength of seeing one of his tragedies, that it proved him competent to manage his domestic affairs, against the accusation of his son. Nor do I think that the conjecture of the Parians sent to reform the Milesians was sufficient ground for the conclusion they drew. Visiting the island, they noticed the best-cultivated lands and the best-run country houses, and noted down the names of their owners. Then they assembled the citizens in the town and appointed these owners the new governors and magistrates, judging that they, who were careful of their private affairs, would be careful of those of the public.

We are all patchwork, and so shapeless and diverse in composition that each bit, each moment, plays its own game. And there is as much difference between us and ourselves as between us and others. *Consider it a great thing to play the part of one single man* [Seneca]. Ambition can teach men valor, and temperance, and liberality, and even justice. Greed can implant in the heart of a shop apprentice, brought up in obscurity and idleness, the confidence to cast himself far from hearth and home, in a frail boat at the mercy of the waves and angry Neptune; it also teaches discretion and wisdom. Venus herself supplies resolution and boldness to boys still subject to discipline and the rod, and arms the tender hearts of virgins who are still in their mothers' laps:

> *Furtively passing sleeping guards, with Love as guide,*
> *Alone by night the girl comes to the young man's side.*

> TIBULLUS

In view of this, a sound intellect will refuse to judge men simply by their outward actions; we must probe the inside and discover what springs set men in motion. But since this is an arduous and hazardous undertaking, I wish fewer people would meddle with it.

ENDNOTES

1. In Brazil, in 1557.
2. The traveler Montaigne spoke of at the beginning of the chapter.
3. The disciplined man in the sentence before last.
4. The religious civil wars between Catholics and Protestants, which lasted intermittently from 1562 to 1594.

─────────── *Questions for Consideration* ───────────

Using complete sentences, provide brief answers for the following questions.

1. List some phrases or a sentence that you have found intriguing in one of Montaigne's essays. Comment briefly on what you have found interesting or noteworthy in the material you have selected.

    _____

    _____

    _____

    _____

    _____

2. What is cultural relativism? Why is this concept especially relevant for an understanding of Montaigne's "Of Cannibals"?

    _____

    _____

    _____

    _____

    _____

3. "Introspection" is a term often used with regard to Montaigne. What does it mean? In a few sentences, explain how introspection is evident in "Of the Inconsistency of Our Actions."

    _____

    _____

    _____

    _____

    _____

$$\text{——————————— } \textit{Writing Critically} \text{ ———————————}$$

Select one of the topics listed below and compose a 500-word essay that discusses the topic fully. Support your thesis with evidence from the text and with critical and/or historical material. Use the space below for preparing to write the essay.

1. Compare an essay by Montaigne with an essay by a twentieth-century autobiographical writer such as Joan Didion. Examine similarities as well as differences of style and outlook on life.

2. An autobiography is basically the story of one's own life. This kind of writing was new in Montaigne's day, and while reading selections from the *Essays*, you may have wondered at times what the connection was with the story of Montaigne's life. What do you think should be included in an autobiography? Look at a twentieth-century work such as Richard Wright's *Black Boy, The Diary of Anne Frank*, or *The Autobiography of Malcolm X* to enhance your familiarity with the art of autobiography in general. What kinds of subjects and events would you discuss in your own autobiography?

3. Explore the parallel between Montaigne and Hamlet. How does Hamlet reveal the hazards of too much introspection and self-examination? Explain how the character of Hamlet can be viewed as a danger inherent in Montaigne's thought. In your essay, you might also want to consider whether it is a sign of emotional and moral health to be able to question oneself as Montaigne does.

4. In the introduction above, Montaigne is at one point identified as a baroque writer. Go to the library to find out more about the term "baroque," which is a term also applied to a painting style popular at the end of the Renaissance. Look at some illustrations of baroque paintings. Discuss similarities of style or world view that cut across baroque literature and visual art.

Prewriting Space:

_____

_____

_____

_____

_____

_____

_____

_____

_____

_____

_____

_____

Introduction

Miguel De Cervantes (1547–1616)

Though he was an ambitious, prolific writer who considered his work in poetry, drama, and the form of the romance to be his highest contributions to literature, it is entirely likely that Miguel de Cervantes would today be an obscure writer, cherished only by a few specialists in Renaissance Spanish literature, had he not written the two books for which he is best known, *El ingenioso hidalgo Don Quixote de la Mancha*, and *Seguna parte del ingenioso cavaliere Don Quixote*, collectively known in English as *Don Quixote of La Mancha*, or, more simply still, *Don Quixote*. For many years, this extended prose narrative had a reputation as the first European novel. Subsequent critics and historians of the development of the novel have pointed to a history of the novel that is far too complex and too deep to allow this judgment to stand. However, it is true that *Don Quixote* served as a model for many early British novelists, including Henry Fielding, who in 1742 publicly compared his comic novel *Joseph Andrews* to *Don Quixote*, and further, that its mixture of satire, realism, symbolism, and unified theme served for many years as the earliest example of the perfection that the form of the novel can achieve.

If the more than half-century of years Cervantes lived before composing his masterpiece give any indication of the talent that would emerge when he wrote *Don Quixote*, they do so mainly by virtue of the sheer variety of ways in which he lived them. As a soldier in 1571, he was wounded in battle by three gunshot wounds, as a consequence of which the use of his right hand was permanently impaired. In 1575, he was captured in battle, and held for five years before his captors received their ransom. Though he had been considered a war hero when he was captured, he found when he was released that his fame quickly fled. He turned to writing in search of money and fame. In a few short years, he wrote at least thirty plays, possibly as many as fifty; the first one was produced; the rest appear not to have been. A publication of a pastoral romance, *La Galatea*, received little recognition from the public and did nothing to improve his financial situation. An illegitimate daughter born the same year, 1585, and the need to support her as well as his sisters and, eventually, a wife, forced Cervantes to seek employment obtaining supplies for the Spanish Armada in 1587. Unfortunately, a dispute over grain resulted in Cervantes being charged with malfeasance and thrown in jail.

There is a legend that Cervantes began writing *Don Quixote* while jailed on another occasion in 1604. Whether or not this is true, it is certain that it was during a low point of his fortunes that this writer who had yet to show any promise of literary or commercial genius completed part I of *Don Quixote, the Ingenious Gentleman Don Quixote of La Mancha*, written to satirize the widely popular genre of chivalric romance, but also to make money off of it. The novel was published the following year, 1605, and was immediately popular with the public. Although the Don's hilarious adventures quickly became popular fare, the book did little to enrich the fortunes of its author, because the many reprints of the novel that appeared across Europe were mostly unauthorized editions that paid no royalties to Cervantes or his original publisher. Although his success did not make him wealthy, its success did enable him to publish a book of shorter pieces, *Noveles exemplares*, in 1613, a highly regarded collection of fiction. In 1614, while Cervantes was completing his own sequel to *Quixote*, another writer produced a false sequel, prompting Cervantes to write a denunciation of this fraudulant work into his own novel. The sequel, part II of *Don Quixote*, appeared in 1615; it was about as popular as its predecessor had been, and did about as little to enrich its author. Once again, the novel was mostly circulated through unauthorized editions, and once again, Cervantes received little in the way of royalties. Cervantes died the following year, 1616, on April 23.

His reputation did not die with him, however; it has only grown since his death. From its appearance, this story of an old man, Alonzo Quixano, who, rather than retire quietly, goes about the modern Spain of the 1600s dressed in the armor of a knight from an earlier era, has been enthusiastically devoured by the reading public. In part this is because Cervantes took care to make the novel first and foremost entertaining; the deeper literary qualities became apparent only later. From his first adventure, in which the Don falls into the company of merchants who beat him badly when he challenges them, the writer invites the reader both to laugh at the Don, but also to consider seriously his idealism, absurdly out of place in the modern, realistic world that surrounds him.

After recovering from his injuries Quixote sallies forth again, this time with a local farm boy in tow as his squire, Sancho Panza. Throughout the rest of the novel, the uncompromising (and frequently, uncomprehending) idealism of Quixote is consistently contrasted with the pragmatism of Sancho Panza. The difference between the two is nicely captured by a scene in which Don Quixote, insulted by an inn-keeper's demand for payment, rides off without making any; his squire, Sancho, is captured and tossed in a blanket in payment for the Don's debt. Though Quixote often suffers consequences, he lives in a world of ideals unshaken by reality; Sancho Panza, however, lives in a world of consequences in which his master's idealism is one more problem which must be dealt with. They obviously need each other: without Quixote, Sancho Panza is an ordinary farmer; without a squire, Quixote's fantasy is incomplete.

The word "quixotic" has entered the English language meaning a foolish or poorly planned undertaking, and no episode in the novel embodies this spirit more than the most famous portion of the novel, the Don's attack on windmills he has mistaken for giants. Spurred by the challenge, he charges full tilt, only to be knocked in the air by one of the blades of the windmill. When Sancho runs to him, the Don explains that a magician he believes to have been hounding him was responsible for this transformation.

Such an episode is clearly filled with satiric meaning, and a reader who misses this is missing half the fun. However, if half the fun is holding up romantic notions to the cold light of reality to show how deceptive literature is about the world, the other half of the fun is in finding the ways in which the novel affirms the ideals of chivalric romance. Though the narrative voice is often openly hostile to the follies of Don Quixote, Cervantes, who himself took the form of the romance quite seriously, also wrote passages which capture the cadences and ideas of a romance in the tradition of *El Cid* quite sympathetically. The result is that the novel plays a delicate balancing act; it openly mocks Quixote's idealism—then gives us reason to take his idealism just a bit seriously. For instance, we consistently see characters participating quite willingly in the old man's folly, Sancho Panza chief among them, although he suffers from it.

The theme that thus emerges, that an unrealistic idealist can change reality a little bit, surprisingly invites us to do more than laugh at the old man, even though it continues to show him in a foolish light. This theme comes increasingly to the forefront of the novel in Book II, in which characters Quixote meets have sometimes heard of him by having read Book I. The thematic point is that Quixote's "realistic" adventures have now themselves become the stuff of romance; thus we see that the reality of an idealist can subtly alter what is real. Nonetheless, the novel eventually ends with Don Quixote reclaiming his identity as Alonso Quixano, and renouncing his identity as Don Quixote. Sancho Panza, once the pragmatist, pleads with him that the greatest madness is to accept his quiet death easily without seeking for more. The old man contradicts him, claiming that he was mad for a time, but now he's sane, and now he's Alonzo Quixano; the narrator contradicts him, however, and even as the old man, on his death bed, renounces his "mad" identity, he is referred to by the narrative voice as "Don Quixote."

The complexities of the thematic puzzles embodied by the ending have made *Don Quixote* not only the popular success it immediately was, but also the critical success it eventually became. Too absurd to be entirely serious, too serious to be merely comic, Cervantes' masterpiece invites the reader to think about how ridiculous and unrealistic are ideals, and how more ridiculous and unrealistic is their absence. (TJC)

BIBLIOGRAPHY

Aylward, E. E. *Cervantes: Pioneer and Plagiarist.* 1982.

Gilman, Stephen. *The Novel According to Cervantes.* 1989.

Nabokov, Vladimir. *Lectures on "Don Quixote."* Ed. Fredson Bowers. 1983

Russell, P. E. *Cervantes.* 1985

Weoger, John G. *The Substance of Cervantes.* 1985.

from Don Quixote de la Mancha

*translated from the Spanish of
Miguel De Cervantes Saavedra*

Chapter 1

*Which treats of the condition and pursuits of the
famous Don Quixote de la Mancha.*

In a village of la Mancha, the name of which I have no desire to recollect, there lived, not long ago, one of those gentlemen who usually keep a lance upon a rack, an old buckler, a lean horse and a coursing greyhound. Soup composed of somewhat more beef than mutton, salmagundy at night, lentils on Fridays, and a pigeon, by way of addition, on Sundays, consumed three-fourths of his income; the remainder of it supplied him with a cloak of fine cloth, velvet breeches, with slippers of the same for holidays, and a suit of the best homespun, in which he adorned himself on week days. His establishment consisted of a housekeeper above forty, a niece not quite twenty, and a lad who served him both in the field and at home, who could saddle the horse or handle the pruning hook. The age of our gentleman bordered upon fifty years; he was of a strong constitution, spare-bodied, of a meagre visage, a very early riser, and a lover of the chase. Some pretend to say, that he had the surname of Quixada or Quesada, for on this point his historians differ; but from very plausible conjectures, we may conclude that his name was Quixana. This is, however, of little importance to our history: let it suffice, that in relating it, we swerve not a jot from the truth.

Be it known then, that the above-mentioned gentleman, in his leisure moments, which composed the greater part of the year, applied himself with so much ardour and relish to the perusal of books of chivalry, that he almost wholly neglected the exercise of the chase, and even the regulation of his domestic affairs; indeed, so extravagant was his zeal in this pursuit, that he sold many acres of arable land to purchase books of knight-errantry: collecting as many as he could possibly obtain. Among these, there were none he admired so much as those written by the famous Feliciano de Silva, whose brilliant prose and intricate style were, in his opinion, infinitely precious; especially those amorous speeches and challenges in which they so abound; such as: "the reason of the unreasonable treatment of my reasons so enfeebles my reason, that with reason I complain of your beauty." And again: "the high heavens, that with your divinity, divinely fortify you with the stars, rendering you meritorious of the merit, merited by your greatness." These and similar rhapsodies distracted the poor gentleman: for he laboured to comprehend and unravel their meaning, which was more than Aristotle himself could do, were he to rise from the dead expressly for that purpose. He was not quite satisfied as to the wounds which Don Belianis gave and received; for he could not help thinking, that, however skilful the professors who healed them, his face and whole body must infallibly have been covered with seams and scars. Nevertheless, he commended his author for concluding his book with the promise of that interminable adventure; and he often felt an inclination to seize the pen himself and conclude it, literally is it is there promised: this he would doubtless have done, and with success, had he not been diverted from it by meditations of greater moment, on which his mind was incessantly employed.

He often debated with the curate of the village, a man of learning, and a graduate of Siguenza, which of the two was the best knight, Palmerin of England, or Amadis de Gaul; but master Nicholas, barber of the same place, declared, that none ever equalled the knight of the sun; if, indeed, any one could be compared to him, it was

Don Galaor, brother of Amadis de Gaul, for he had a genius suited to every thing: he was no effeminate knight, no whimperer, like his brother; and in point of courage, he was by no means his inferior. In short, he became so infatuated with this kind of study, that he passed whole days and nights over these books: and thus with little sleeping and much reading, his brains were dried up and his intellects deranged. His imagination was full of all that he had read; of enchantments, contests, battles, challenges, wounds, blandishments, amours, tortures, and impossible absurdities; and so firmly was he persuaded of the truth of the whole tissue of visionary fiction, that, in his mind, no history in the world was more authentic. The Cid Ruy Diaz, he asserted, was a very good knight, but not to be compared with the knight of the flaming sword, who with a single back-stroke, cleft asunder two fierce and monstrous giants. He was better pleased with Bernardo del Carpio, because, at Roncesvalles, he slew Roland the enchanted, by availing himself of the stratagem employed by Hercules upon Anteus, whom he squeezed to death within his arms. He spoke very favourably of the giant Morganti, for, although of that monstrous brood, who are always proud and insolent, he alone was courteous and well bred. Above all, he admired Rinaldo de Montalvan, particularly when he saw him sallying forth from his castle to plunder all he encountered; and when, moreover, he seized upon that image of Mahomet, which, according to history, was of massive gold. But he would have given his house-keeper, and even his niece into the bargain, for a fair opportunity of kicking the traitor Galalon.

In fine, his judgment being completely obscured, he was seized with one of the strangest fancies that ever entered the head of a madman; this was a persuasion, that it behoved him, as well for the advancement of his glory as the service of his country, to become a knight-errant, and traverse the world, armed and mounted, in quest of adventures, and to practise all that had been performed by the knights-errant, of whom he had read; redressing every species of grievance, and exposing himself to dangers, which, being surmounted, might secure to him eternal glory and renown. The poor gentleman imagined himself at least crowned Emperor of Trapisonda, by the valour of his arm: and thus indulging in these agreeable meditations, and borne away by the extraordinary pleasure he found in them, he hastened to put his designs into execution.

The first thing he did was to scour up some rusty armour, which belonged to his great grandfather, and had lain many years neglected in a corner. These he cleaned and adjusted as well as he could, but he found one grand defect; the helmet was incomplete; having only the morrion: this deficiency, however, he ingeniously supplied, by making a kind of vizor of pasteboard, which, being fixed to the morrion, gave the appearance of an entire helmet. True it is, that in order to prove its strength, he drew his sword and gave it two strokes, the first of which instantly demolished the labour of a week; but not altogether approving of the facility with which it was destroyed, and in order to secure himself against a similar misfortune, he made another vizor, which, having fenced in the inside with small bars of iron, he felt assured of its strength, and without making any more experiments, held it to be a most excellent helmet.

In the next place, he visited his steed; and although this animal had more blemishes than Gonela's steed, which was so much skin and bone, yet, in his eyes, neither the Bucephalus of Alexander, nor the Cid's Babieca, could be compared with him. Four days was he deliberating upon what name he should give him, for, as he said to himself, it would be very improper, that a horse so excellent, appertaining to a knight so famous, should be without an appropriate name; he therefore endeavoured to find one that should express what he had been before he belonged to a knight-errant, and also what he now was: nothing could, indeed, be more reasonable than that, when the master changed his state, the horse should likewise change his name and assume one, pompous and high-sounding, as became the new order he now professed. So after having devised, altered, lengthened, curtailed, rejected, and again framed in his imagination a variety of names, he finally determined upon Rozinante, a name in his opinion, lofty, sonorous, and full of meaning; importing that he had been only a *Rozin*, a drudge-horse, *before* his present condition, and that now he was *before* all the *Rozins* in the world.

Having given his horse a name so much to his satisfaction, he resolved to fix upon one for himself. This consideration employed him eight more days, when at length he determined to call himself Don Quixote; whence, some of the historians of this most true history, have concluded that his name was certainly Quixada and not Quesada, as others would have it. Then recollecting that the valorous Amadis, not content with the simple appellation of Amadis, added thereto the name of his kingdom, and native country, in order to render it famous, styling himself Amadis de Gaul; so he, like a good knight, also added the name of his province, and called himself Don Quixote de la Mancha; whereby, in his opinion, he fully proclaimed his lineage and country, which, at the same time, he honoured, by taking its name.

His armour being now furbished, his helmet made perfect, his horse and himself provided with names, he found nothing wanting but a lady to be in love with: for a knight-errant without the tender passion, was a tree without leaves and fruit—a body without a soul. If, said he, for my sins, or rather, through my good fortune, I encounter some giant—an ordinary occurrence to knights-errant, and overthrow him at the first onset, or cleave him in twain, or in short, vanquish him and force him to surrender, must I not have some lady, to whom I may send him, as a present; that when he enters into the presence of my charming mistress, he may throw himself upon his knees before her, and in a submissive,

humble voice, say: "Madam, in me, you behold the giant Caraculiambro, lord of the island Malendrania, who, being vanquished in single combat by the never-enough-to-be-praised Don Quixote de la Mancha, am by him commanded to present myself before you, to be disposed of according to the will and pleasure of your highness." How happy was our good knight after this harangue! How much more so, when he found a mistress! It is said, that in a neighbouring village, a good looking peasant girl resided, of whom he had formerly been enamoured, although it does not appear that she ever knew or cared about it; and this was the lady whom he chose to nominate, mistress of his heart. He then sought a name for her, which, without entirely departing from her own, should incline and approach towards that of a princess, or great lady, and determined upon Dulcinea del Toboso, (for she was a native of that village) a name, he thought, harmonious, uncommon, and expressive: like all the others, which he had adopted.

Chapter II

Which treats of the first sally that Don Quixote made from his native abode.

These arrangements being made, he would no longer defer the execution of his project, which he hastened from a consideration of what the world suffered by his delay: so many were the grievances he intended to redress, the wrongs to rectify, errors to amend, abuses to reform, and debts to discharge! Therefore, without communicating his intentions to any individual, and wholly unobserved, one morning before day, being one of the most sultry in the month of July, he armed himself cap-a-pie, mounted Rozinante, placed the helmet on his head, braced on his target, took his lance, and through the private gate of his back yard, issued forth into the open plain, in a transport of joy to think he had met with no obstacles to the commencement of his honourable enterprize. But scarcely had he found himself on the plain, when he was assailed by a recollection so terrible as almost to make him abandon the undertaking: for it just then occurred to him, that he was not yet a knight; therefore, in conformity to the laws of chivalry, he neither could nor ought to enter the lists

against any of that order; and even if he had been actually dubbed, he should, as a new knight, have worn white armour, without any device on his shield, until he had gained one by force of arms. These considerations made him irresolute whether to proceed; but phrenzy prevailing over reason, he determined to get himself made a knight by the first one he should meet, like many others, of whom he had read. As to white armour, he resolved, when he had an opportunity, to scour his own, so that it should be whiter than ermine. Having now composed his mind, he proceeded, taking whatever road his horse pleased; for therein, he believed, consisted the true spirit of adventure.

Our new adventurer, thus pursuing his way, conversed within himself saying; "Who doubts but that in future times, when the true history of my famous achievements are brought to light, the sage who records them, will, in this manner, describe my first sally? 'Scarcely had ruddy Phoebus extended over the face of this wide and spacious earth, the golden filaments of his beautiful hair, and scarcely had the little painted birds, with their forked tongues, hailed in soft and mellifluous harmony, the approach of the rosy harbinger of morn, who, leaving the soft couch of her jealous consort, had just disclosed herself to mortals through the gates and balconies of the Manchegan horizon, when the renowned knight Don Quixote de la Mancha, quitting the slothful down, mounted Rozinante, his famous steed, and proceeded over the ancient memorable plain of Montiel, (which was indeed the truth), "O happy æra, happy age," he continued, "when my glorious deeds shall be revealed to the world! deeds worthy of being engraven on brass, sculptured in marble, and recorded by the pencil! And thou, O sage enchanter, whosoever thou mayest be, destined to chronicle this extraordinary history! forget not, I beseech thee, my good Rozinante, the inseparable companion of all my toils!" Then again, as if really enamoured, he exclaimed, "O Dulcinea, my princess! sovereign of this captive heart! greatly do you wrong me by a cruel adherence to your decree, forbidding me to appear in the presence of your beauty! Deign, O lady, to think on this enslaved heart, which, for love of you, endures so many pangs!"

In this wild strain he continued, imitating the style of his books as nearly as he could, and proceeding slowly on, while the sun arose with such intense heat, that it was enough to dissolve his brains, if any had been left. He travelled almost the whole of that day without encountering any thing worthy of recital, which caused him much vexation, for he was impatient for an opportunity to prove the valour of his powerful arm.

Some authors say, his first adventure was that of the straits of Lapice; others affirm it to have been that of the wind-mills; but from what I have been able to ascertain of this matter, and have found written in the annals of La Mancha, the fact is, that he travelled all that day, and as night approached, both he and his horse were wearied and dying of hunger; and in this state as he looked around him, in hopes of discovering some castle or shepherd's cot, where he might repose and find refreshment, he descried, not far from the road, an inn, which to him was a star conducting him to the portals if not the palaces of his redemption. He made all the haste he could, and reached it at night-fall. There chanced to stand at the door two young women, ladies of pleasure, (as they are called,) on their journey to Seville, in the company of some carriers, who rested there that night. Now as every thing that our adventurer saw and conceived, was, by his imagination, moulded to what he had read, so, in his eyes, the inn appeared to be a castle, with its four

turrets, and pinnacles of shining silver, together with its draw-bridge, deep moat, and all the appurtenances with which such castles are usually described. When he had advanced within a short distance of it, he checked Rozinante, expecting some dwarf would mount the battlements, to announce, by sound of trumpet, the arrival of a knight-errant at the castle; but finding them tardy, and Rozinante impatient for the stable, he approached the inn-door, and there saw the two strolling girls, who to him appeared to be beautiful damsels or lovely dames, enjoying themselves before the gate of their castle.

It happened that just at this time, a swine-herd collecting his hogs, (I make no apology, for so they are called), from an adjoining stubble field, blew the horn which assembles them together, and instantly Don Quixote was satisfied, for he imagined it was a dwarf who had given the signal of his arrival. With extraordinary satisfaction, therefore, he went up to the, inn; upon which the ladies, being startled at the sight of a man, armed in that matter, with lance and buckler, were retreating into the house; but Don Quixote, perceiving their alarm, raised his pasteboard vizor, thereby partly discovering his meagre dusty visage, and with gentle demeanour and placid voice, thus addressed them; "Fly not, ladies, nor fear any discourtesy, for it would be wholly inconsistent with the order of knighthood which I profess, to offer insult to any person, much less to virgins of that exalted rank which your appearance indicates." The girls stared at him, and were endeavouring to find out his face, which was almost concealed by the sorry vizor; but, hearing themselves called virgins, a thing so much out of the way of their profession, they could not forbear laughing, and to such a degree that Don Quixote was displeased, and said to them; "Modesty well becomes beauty, and excessive laughter, proceeding from a slight cause, is folly; but I say not this to humble or distress you, for my part is no other than to do you service." This language, so unintelligible to the ladies, added to the uncouth figure of our knight, increased their laughter; consequently he grew more indignant, and would have proceeded further, but for the timely appearance of the inn-keeper, a very corpulent, and therefore a very pacific man, who, upon seeing so ludicrous an object, armed, and with accoutrements so ill-sorted as were the bridle, lance, buckler, and corslet, felt disposed to join the damsels in demonstrations of mirth, but in truth, apprehending some danger from a form thus strongly fortified, he resolved to behave with civility, and therefore said, "If, Sir Knight, you are seeking for a lodging, you will here find, excepting a bed (for there are none in this inn) every thing in abundance." Don Quixote perceiving the humility of the governor of the fortress, for such to him appeared the inn-keeper, answered: "For me, Signior Castellano, anything will suffice: since arms are my ornaments, warfare my repose." The host thought he called him Castellano, because he took him for a sound Castilian, whereas he was an Andalusian, of the coast of St. Lucar, as great a thief as Cacus, and not less mischievous than a collegian or a page: and he replied, "If so, your worship's beds must be hard rocks, and your sleep continual watching; and that being the case, you may dismount with a certainty of finding here sufficient cause for keeping awake the whole year, much more a single night." So saying, he laid hold of Don Quixote's stirrups, who alighted with much difficulty and pain, for he had fasted the whole of the day. He then desired the host to take especial care of his steed, for it was the finest creature that ever fed; the inn-keeper examined him, but thought him not so good by half as his master had represented him. Having led the horse to the stable, he returned to receive the orders of his guest, whom the damsels, being now reconciled to him, were disarming; they had taken off the back and breast plates, but endeavoured in vain to disengage the gorget, or take off the counterfeit beaver, which he had fastened with green ribbons, in such a manner that they could not be untied, and he would upon no account allow them to be cut; therefore he remained all that night with his helmet on, making the strangest and most ridiculous figure imaginable.

While these light girls, whom he still conceived to be persons of quality and ladies of the castle, were disarming him, he said to them with infinite grace, "Never before was Knight so honoured by ladies as Don Quixote, after his departure from his native village; damsels attended upon him! princesses took charge of his steed! O Rozinante,—for that, ladies, is the name of my horse, and Don Quixote de la Mancha my own; although it was not my intention to have discovered myself, until deeds, performed in your service should have proclaimed me; but impelled to make so just an application of that ancient romance of Lanzarote, to my present situation, I have thus prematurely disclosed my name: yet the time shall come, when your ladyship may command and I obey; when the valour of my arm shall make manifest the desire I have to serve you." The girls unaccustomed to such rhetorical flourishes, made no reply, but asked him whether he would please to eat any thing. "I shall willingly take some food," answered Don Quixote, "for I apprehend it would be of much service to me." That day happened to be Friday, and there was nothing in the house but some fish, of that kind which in Castille is called, Abadexo, in Andalusia, Bacallao, in some parts Curadillo, and in others Truchuela. They asked if his worship would like some truchuela, for they had no other fish to offer him. "If there be many troutlings," replied Don Quixote, "they will supply the place of one trout; for it is the same to me, whether I receive eight single rials or one piece of eight. Moreover, these troutlings may be preferable, as veal is better than beef, and kid superior to goat; be that as it may, let it come immediately, for the toil and weight of arms cannot be sustained by the body unless the interior be supplied with aliments." For the benefit of the cool air, they placed the table at the door of the inn, and the landlord produced some of his ill-soaked, and worse cooked bacallao, with bread as foul and black as the Knight's armour: but it was a spectacle highly risible to see him eat; for his hands being engaged in holding his helmet on, and raising the beaver, he could not feed himself, therefore one of the ladies performed this office for him; but to drink would have been utterly impossible, had not the inn-keeper bored a reed, and placing one end into his mouth, at the other poured in the wine; and all this he patiently endured rather than cut the lacings of his helmet.

In the mean time there came to the inn a sow-gelder, who as soon as he arrived, blew his pipe of reeds four or five times, which finally convinced Don Quixote that he was now in some famous castle, where he was regaled with music; that the poor jack was trout, the bread of the purest white the strolling wenches, ladies of distinction, and the inn-keeper, governor of the castle; consequently he remained satisfied with his enterprize, and first sally, though it troubled him to reflect that he was not yet a knight: being persuaded that he could not lawfully engage in any adventure until he had been invested with the order of knighthood.

Chapter III

In which is described the diverting ceremony of knighting Don Quixote.

Tormented by this idea, he abruptly finished his scanty meal, called the inn-keeper, and shutting himself up with him in the stable, he fell on his knees before him, and said, "Never will I arise from this place, valorous knight, until your courtesy shall vouchsafe to grant a boon which it is my intention to request; a boon that will redound to your glory and to the benefit of all mankind." The inn-keeper, seeing his guest at his feet, and hearing such language, stood confounded, and stared at him, without knowing what to do or say; he entreated him to rise, but in vain, until he had promised to grant the boon he requested. "I expected no less, signior, from your great magnificence;" replied Don Quixote, "know, therefore, that the boon I have demanded and which your liberality has conceded, is, that on the morrow, you will confer upon me the honour of knighthood. This night I will watch my arms in the chapel of your castle, in order that in the morning, my earnest desire may be fulfilled, and I may with propriety traverse the four quarters of the world, in quest of adventures, for the relief of the distressed; conformable to the duties of chivalry and of knights-errant, who, like myself, are devoted to such pursuits."

The host, who, as we have said, was a shrewd fellow, and had already entertained some doubts respecting the wits of his guest, was now confirmed in his suspicions; and to make sport for the night, determined to follow his humour. He told him therefore that his desire was very reasonable, and that such pursuits were natural and suitable to knights so illustrious as he appeared to be, and as his gallant demeanour fully testified; that he had himself in the days of his youth followed that honourable profession, and travelled over various parts of the world in search of adventures; failing not to visit the suburbs of Malaga, the isles of Riaran, the compass of Seville, the market place of Segovia, the olive field of Valencia, the rondilla of Grenada, the coast of St. Lucar, the fountain of Cordova, the taverns of Toledo, and divers other parts, where he had exercised the agility of his heels and the dexterity of his hands committing sundry wrongs, soliciting widows, seducing damsels, cheating youths; in short, making himself known to most of the tribunals in Spain; and that finally he had retired to this castle, where he lived upon his own revenue and that of others; entertaining therein all knights-errant of every quality and degree, solely for the great affection he bore them, and that they might share their fortune with him, in return for his good will. He further told him that in his castle there was no chapel wherein he could watch his armour, for it had been pulled down, in order to be rebuilt; but that in cases of necessity, he knew it might be done wherever he pleased: therefore he might watch it that night in a court of the castle, and the following morning, if it pleased God, the requisite ceremonies should be performed, and he should be dubbed so effectually that the world would not be able to produce a more perfect knight. He then enquired if he had any money about him; Don Quixote told him that he had none: having never read in their histories that knights-errant provided themselves with money. The inn-keeper assured him he was mistaken, for admitting that it was not mentioned in their history: the authors deeming it unnecessary to specify things so obviously requisite as money and clean shirts, yet was it not, therefore, to be inferred that they had none; but on the contrary he might consider it as an established fact, that all the knights-errant of whose histories so many volumes are filled, carried their purses well provided against accidents; that they were also supplied with shirts and a small casket full of ointments, to heal the wounds they might receive; for in plains and desarts where they fought and were wounded, no aid was near, unless they had some sage enchanter for their friend, who could give them immediate assistance, by conveying in a cloud through the air, some damsel or dwarf, with a vial of water, possessed of such virtue, that upon testing a single drop of it, they should instantly become as sound as if they had received no injury. But when the knights of former times were without such a friend, they always took care that their esquires should be provided with money, and such necessary articles as lint and salves: and when they had no esquires, which very rarely happened, they carried these things themselves, upon the crupper of their horse, in wallets so small as to be scarcely visible, that they might seem to be something of more importance: for except in such cases, the custom of carrying wallets, was not tolerated among knights-errant. He therefore advised, though as his godson (which he was soon to be) he might command him, never henceforth to travel without money and the aforesaid provisions; and he would find them serviceable when he least expected it. Don Quixote promised to follow his advice with punctuality; and an order was now given for performing the watch of the armour in a large yard adjoining the inn. Don Quixote having collected it together, placed it on a cistern which was close to a well; then bracing on his target and grasping his lance, with graceful demeanor, he paced to and fro, before the pile, beginning his parade as soon as it was dark.

The inn-keeper informed all who were in the inn, of the frenzy of his guest, the watching of his armour, and of the intended knighting. They were surprised at so singular a kind of madness, and went out to observe him at a distance. They perceived him sometimes quietly pacing along, and sometimes leaning upon his lance with his eyes fixed upon his armour, for a considerable time. It was now night, but the moon shone with a splendour, which might vie even with that, whence it was borrowed; so that every motion of our new knight might be distinctly seen.

At this time, it happened that one of the carriers wanted to give his mules some water; for which purpose it was necessary to remove Don Quixote's armour from the cistern, who seeing him advance, exclaimed with a loud voice, "O thou, whosoever thou art, rash knight! who approachest the armour of the most valiant adventurer that ever girded sword, beware of what thou dost, and touch it not, unless thou wouldst yield thy life as the forfeit of thy temerity." The carrier heeded not this admonition (though better would it have been for him if he had) but seizing hold of the straps, he threw the armour some distance from him, which Don Quixote perceiving, he raised his eyes to heaven, and addressing his thoughts, apparently to his lady Dulcinea, said: "Assist me, O lady, to avenge this first insult offered to your vassal's breast; nor let your favour and protection fail me, in this my first perilous encounter!" Having uttered these and similar ejaculations, he let slip his target, and raising his lance with both hands, he gave the carrier such a stroke upon the head, that he fell to the ground in so grievous a plight, that had the stroke been repeated, there would have been no need of a surgeon. This done, he replaced his armour, and continued his parade with the same tranquillity as before.

Soon after another carrier, not knowing what had passed, for the first yet lay stunned, came out with the same intention of watering his mules; and as he approached to take away the armour from the cistern, Don Quixote, without saying a word or imploring any protection, again let slip his target, raised his lance, and with no less effect than before, smote the head of the second carrier. The noise brought out all the people in the inn, and the landlord among the rest; upon which Don Quixote braced on his target and laying his hand upon his sword, said: "O lady of beauty! strength and vigour of my enfeebled heart! Now is the time for thee to turn thine illustrious eyes upon this thy captive knight, whom so mighty an encounter awaits!" This address had, he conceived, animated him with so much courage that were all the carriers in the world to have assailed him, he would not have retreated one step.

The comrades of the wounded, upon discovering the situation of their friends, began at a distance to discharge a shower of stones upon Don Quixote, who sheltered himself as well as he could with his target, without daring to quit the cistern, because he would not abandon his armour. The inn-keeper called aloud to them, begging they would desist, for he had already told them he was insane, and that as a madman, he would be acquitted, though he were to kill them all. Don Quixote, in a voice still louder, called them infamous traitors, and the lord of the castle, a cowardly base-born knight, for allowing knights-errant to be treated in that manner; declaring that, had he received the order of knighthood he would have made him sensible of his perfidy. "But as for you, ye vile and worthless rabble, I utterly despise ye! Advance! Come on, molest me as far as ye are able, for quickly shall ye receive the reward of your folly and insolence!" This he uttered with so much spirit and intrepidity, that the assailants were struck with terror; which in addition to the landlord's persuasions, made them cease their attack; he then permitted the wounded to be carried off, and with the same gravity and composure resumed the watch of his armour.

The host not relishing these pranks of his guest, determined to put an end to them, before any further mischief ensued, by immediately investing him with the luckless order of chivalry; approaching him, therefore, he disclaimed any concurrence on his part, in the insolent conduct of those low people, who were, he observed, well chastised for their presumption. He repeated to him that there was no chapel in the castle, nor was it by any means necessary for what remained to be done; that the stroke of knighting consisted in blows on the neck and shoulders, according to the ceremonial of the order, which might be effectually performed in the middle of a field; that the duty of watching his armour he had now completely fulfilled, for he had watched more than four hours, though only two were required. All this Don Quixote believed, and said that he was there ready to obey him, requesting him at the same time, to perform the deed as soon as possible; because, should he be assaulted again when he found himself knighted, he was resolved not to leave one person alive in the castle, excepting those, whom out of respect to him, and at his particular request, he might be induced to spare.

The constable thus warned and alarmed, immediately brought forth a book in which he kept his account of the straw and oats he furnished to the carriers, and, attended by a boy, who carried an end of candle, and the two damsels aforementioned, went towards Don Quixote, whom he commanded to kneel down; he then began reading in his manual, as if it were some devout prayer, in the course of which he raised his hand and gave him a good blow on the neck, and after that, a handsome stroke over the shoulders, with his own sword, still muttering between his teeth, as if in prayer. This being done, he commanded one of the ladies to gird on his sword, an office she performed, with much alacrity, as well as discretion, no small portion of which was necessary to avoid bursting with laughter at every part of the ceremony; but indeed the prowess they had seen displayed by the new knight kept their mirth within bounds. At girding on the sword, the good lady said: "God grant you may be a fortunate knight and successful in battle." Don Quixote enquired her name, that he might thenceforward know to whom he was indebted for the favour received, as it was his intention to bestow upon her some share of the honour he should acquire by the valour of his arm. She replied, with much humility, that her name was Tolosa, and that she was daughter of a cobler at Toledo, who lived at the stalls of Sanchobienaya; and that wherever she was, she would serve and honour him as her lord. Don Quixote in reply, requested her, for his sake, to do him the favour henceforth to add to her name the title of Don, and call herself Donna Tolosa, which she promised to do. The other girl now buckled on his spur, and with her, he held nearly the same conference as with the lady of the sword; having enquired her name, she told him it was Molinera, and that she was daughter to an honest miller of Antiquera; he then requested her likewise to assume the Don, and style herself Donna Molinera, renewing his proffers of service and thanks.

These never-till-then-seen ceremonies being thus speedily performed, Don Quixote was impatient to find himself on horseback, in quest of adventures: he therefore instantly saddled Rozinante, mounted him, and embracing his host, made his acknowledgments for the favour he had conferred, by knighting him, in terms so extraordinary that it would be in vain to attempt to repeat them. The host, in order to get rid of him the sooner, replied with no less flourish but more brevity; and without making any demand for his lodging, wished him a good journey.

Chapter IV

Of what befel our knight after he had sallied out from the inn.

It was about break of day, when Don Quixote issued forth from the inn, so satisfied, so gay, so blithe, to see himself knighted, that the joy thereof almost burst his horse's girths. But recollecting the advice of his host concerning the necessary provisions for his undertaking, especially the articles of money and clean shirts, he resolved to return home, and furnish himself accordingly, and also provide himself with a Squire: purposing to take into his service a certain country fellow of the neighbourhood, who was poor, and had children, yet was very fit for the squirely office of chivalry. With this determination he turned Rozinante towards his village, and the steed, as if aware of his master's intention, began to put on with so much alacrity, that he hardly seemed to set his feet to the ground. He had not, however, gone far, when on his right hand, from a thicket hard by, he fancied he heard feeble cries, as from some person complaining. And scarcely had he heard it, when he said: "I thank heaven for the favour it does me, by offering me so early an opportunity of complying with the duty of my profession, and of reaping the fruit of my honourable desires. These are, doubtless, the cries of some distressed person, who stands in need of my protection and assistance." Then turning the reins, he guided Rozinante towards the place, whence he thought the cries proceeded, and he had entered but a few paces into the wood, when he saw a mare tied to an oak, and a lad to another, naked from the waist upwards, about fifteen years of age, who was the person that cried out; and not without cause, for a lusty country fellow was laying him on very severely with a belt, and accompanied every lash with a reprimand and a word of advice; for, said he, "The tongue slow and the eyes quick." The boy answered, "I will do so no more, dear sir; by the passion of God, I will never do so again; and I promise for the future to take more care of the flock."

Don Quixote, observing what passed, now called out in an angry tone, "Discourteous knight, it ill becomes thee to deal thus with one who is not able to defend himself. Get upon thy horse, and take the lance, (for he had also a lance leaning against the oak, to which the mare was fastened) and I will make thee sensible of thy dastardly conduct." The countryman, seeing such a figure coming towards him, armed from head to foot, and brandishing his lance at his face, gave himself up for a dead man, and therefore humbly answered: "Signor cavalier, this lad I am chastising, is a servant of mine, whom I employ to tend a flock of sheep which I have hereabouts, but he is so careless, that I lose one every day; and because I correct him for his negligence, or roguery, he says I do it out of covetousness, and for an excuse not to pay him his wages; but, before God, and on my conscience, he lies." "Dar'st thou say so, in my presence, vile rustic?" said Don Quixote; "By the sun that shines upon us, I have a good mind to run thee through with this lance! Pay him immediately without further reply; if not, by the God that rules us, I will dispatch and annihilate thee in a moment! Unbind him instantly!" The countryman hung down his head, and, without reply, untied his boy. Don Quixote then asked the lad, how much his master owed him; and he answered, nine months wages at seven reals a month. Don Quixote, on calculation, found that it amounted to sixty-three reals, and desired the countryman instantly to disburse them, unless he meant to pay it with his life. The fellow in a fright answered, that on the word of a dying man, and upon the oath he had taken, (though by the way he had taken no oath) it was not so much; for he must deduct the price of three pair of shoes he had given him on account, and a real for two bloodlettings when he was sick. "All this is very right," said Don Quixote; but "set the shoes and

the bloodlettings against the stripes thou hast given him unjustly; for if he tore the leather of thy shoes, thou hast torn his skin; and if the barber-surgeon drew blood from him when he was sick, thou hast drawn blood from him when he is well; so that upon these accounts he owes thee nothing." "The mischief is, signor cavalier," quoth the countryman, "that I have no money about me; but let Andres go home with me, and I will pay him all, real by real." "I go with him!" said the lad; "the devil a bit! No, Sir, I will do no such thing; for when he has me alone, he will flay me like any saint Bartholomew." "He will not do so," replied Don Quixote; "to keep him in awe, it is sufficient, that I lay my commands upon him; and on condition he swears to me, by the order of knighthood, which he has received, I shall let him go free, and will be bound for the payment." "Good sir, think of what you say," quoth the boy; "for my master is no knight, nor ever received any order of knighthood; he is John Aldudo the rich, of the neighbourhood of Quintanar." "That is little to the purpose," answered Quixote; "there may be knights of the family of the Aldudos: more especially as every man is the son of his own works." "That's true," quoth Andres; "but what works is my master the son of, who refuses me the wages of my sweat and labour?" "I do not refuse thee, friend Andres," replied the countryman; "have the kindness to go with me; and, I swear, by all the orders of knighthood that are in the world, I will pay thee, every real down, and perfumed into the bargain." "For the perfuming, I thank thee," said Don Quixote; "give him the reals, and I shall be satisfied: and see that thou failest not; or else, by the same oath, I swear to return and chastise thee; nor shalt thou escape me, though thou wert to conceal thyself closer than a lizard. And if thou would'st be informed who it is thus commands, that thou may'st feel the more strictly bound to perform thy promise, know, that I am the valorous Don Quixote de la Mancha, the redressor of wrongs and abuses; so farewell, and do not forget what thou hast promised and sworn, on pain of the penalty I have denounced." So saying, he clapped spurs to Rozinante, and was soon far off.

The countryman eagerly followed him with his eyes; and, when, he saw him quite out of the wood, he turned to his man Andres, and said: "Come hither, child, I wish now to pay what I owe thee, as that redressor of wrongs commanded." "So you shall, I swear," quoth Andres; "and you will do well to obey the orders of that honest gentleman, (whom God grant to live a thousand years) who is so brave a man, and so just a judge, that, egad, if you do not pay me, he will come back and do what he has threatened." "And I swear so too," quoth the Countryman; "and to shew how much I love thee, I am resolved to augment the debt, that I may add to the payment." Then, taking him by the arm, he again tied him to the tree, where he gave him so many stripes, that he left him for dead. "Now,"said he, "master Andres, call upon that redressor of wrongs; thou wilt find he will not easily redress this; though I believe I have not quite done with thee yet: for I have a good mind to flay thee alive, as thou said'st just now." At length, however, he untied him, and gave him leave to go in quest of his judge, to execute the threatened sentence. Andres went away in dudgeon, swearing he would find out the valorous Don Quixote de la Mancha, and tell him all that had passed, and that he should pay for it sevenfold. Nevertheless he departed in tears, leaving his master laughing at him.

Thus did the valorous Don Quixote redress this wrong; and elated at so fortunate and glorious a beginning to his knight-errantry, he went on toward his village, entirely satisfied with himself, and saying in a low voice: "Well mayest thou deem thyself happy above all women living on the earth O Dulcinea del Toboso, beauteous above the most beautiful! since it has been thy lot to have subject and obedient to thy whole will and pleasure so valiant and renowned a knight, as is and ever shall be, Don Quixote de la Mancha; who, as all the world knows, received but yesterday the order of knighthood, and to day has redressed the greatest injury and grievance that injustice could invent and cruelty commit; to day hath he wrested the scourge out of the hand of that pitiless enemy, by whom a tender stripling was so undeservedly lashed."

He now came to a road, which branched out in four directions; those crossways presented themselves to his imagination, where knights-errant usually stop to consider which of the roads they shall take. Here then, following their example, he paused awhile, and, after mature consideration, let go the reins: submitting his own will to that of his horse, who, following his first motion, took the direct road towards his stable. Having proceeded about two miles, Don Quixote discovered a company of people, who, as it afterwards appeared, were merchants of Toledo, going to buy silks in Murcia. There were six of them in number; they carried umbrellas, and were attended by four servants on horseback, and three muleteers on foot. Scarcely had Don Quixote espied them, when he imagined it must be some new

adventure: and to imitate as nearly as possible, what he had read in his books, as he fancied this to be cut out on purpose for him to acheive, with a graceful deportment and intrepid air, he settled himself firmly in his stirrups, grasped his lance, covered his breast with his target, and, posting himself in the midst of the highway, awaited the approach of those whom he already judged to be knights-errant: and when they were come so near as to be seen and heard, he raised his voice, and, with an arrogant tone, cried out: "Let the whole world stand, if the whole world does not confess, that there is not in the whole world a damsel more beautiful than the empress of la Mancha, the peerless Dulcinea del Toboso!" The merchants stopped at the sound of these words, and also to behold the strange figure of him who pronounced them; and both by the one and the other, they perceived the madness of the speaker; but they were disposed to stay and see what this confession meant, which he required; and therefore one of them, who was somewhat of a wag, but withal very discreet, said to him: "Signor cavalier, we do not know who this good lady you mention may be: let us but see her, and, if she be really so beautiful as you intimate, we will, with all our hearts, and without any constraint, make the confession that you demand of us." "Should I shew her to you," replied Don Quixote, "where would be the merit in confessing a truth so manifest? It is essential, that, without seeing her, you believe, confess, affirm, swear, and maintain it; and if not, I challenge you all to battle, proud and monstrous as you are: and, whether you come on, one by one (as the laws of chivalry require) or all together, as is the custom and wicked practice of those of your stamp, here I wait for you, confiding in the justice of my cause." "Signor cavalier," replied the merchant, "I beseech your worship, in the name of all the princes here present, that we may not lay a burden upon our consciences, by confessing a thing we never saw nor heard, and especially, being so much to the prejudice of the empresses and queens of Alcarria and Estremadura, that your worship would be pleased to shew us some picture of this lady, though no bigger than a barley-corn, for we shall guess at the clue by the thread; and therewith we shall rest satisfied and safe, and your worship contented and pleased. Nay, I verily believe we are already so far inclined to your side, that, although her picture should represent her squinting with one eye, and distilling vermilion and brimstone from the other, notwithstanding all this, to oblige you, we will say whatever you please in her favour." "There distils not, base scoundrels," answered Don Quixote, burning with rage, "there distils not, from her what you say, but rather ambergrease and civet among cotton; neither doth she squint nor is she hunch-backed, but as straight as a spindle of Guadarrama: but you shall pay for the horrid blasphemy you have uttered against so transcendent a beauty!" So saying, with his lance couched, he ran at him who had spoken, with so much fury and rage, that, if good fortune had not so ordered that Rozinante stumbled and fell in the midst of his career, it had gone hard with the rash merchant. Rozinante fell, and his master lay rolling abut the field for some time, endeavouring to rise, but in vain: so encumbered was he with his lance, target, spurs and helmet, added to the weight of his antiquated armour. And while he was thus struggling to get up, he continued calling out: "Fly not, ye dastardly rabble; stay, ye race of slaves; for it is through my horse's fault, and not my own that I lie here extended." A muleteer of the company, not over good-natured, hearing the arrogant language of the poor fallen gentleman, could not bear it without returning him in answer on his ribs; and, coming

to him, he took the lance, which having broken to pieces, he applied one of the splinters, with so much agility upon Don Quixote, that, in spite of his armour, he was threshed like wheat. His masters called out, desiring him to forbear! but the lad was provoked, and would not quit the game, until he had quite spent the remainder of his choler: and seizing the other pieces of the lance, he completely demolished them, upon the unfortunate knight; who, notwithstanding the tempest of blows that rained upon him, never shut his mouth, incessantly threatening heaven and earth, and those who to him appeared to be assassins. At length the fellow was tired, and the merchants departed: sufficiently furnished with matter of discourse concerning the poor belaboured knights who, when he found himself alone, again endeavoured to rise; but if he could not do it when sound and well, how should he in so bruised and battered a condition? Yet he was consoled in looking upon this as a misfortune peculiar to knights-errant; and imputing the whole blame to his horse: although to raise himself up, was impossible, his whole body was so horribly bruised.

Chapter V

Wherein is continued the narration of our knight's misfortune.

Don Quixote finding that he was really not able to stir, had recourse to his usual remedy, which was to recollect some incident in his books; and his frenzy instantly suggested to him that of Valdovinos and the marquis of Mantua, when Carloto left him wounded on the mountain: a story familiar to children, not unknown to youth, commended and even credited by old men: yet no more true than the miracles of Mahomet. Now this seemed to him exactly suited to his case, therefore with signs of great bodily pain, he began to roll himself on the ground, and to repeat in a faint voice, what they affirm was said by the wounded knight of the wood:

"Where art thou, mistress of my heart,
Unconscious of thy lover's smart?
Ah me! thou know'st not my distress;
Or thou art false and pitiless."

In this manner he went on with the romance, until he came to those verses where it is said; "O noble marquis of Mantua, my uncle and lord by blood!"—just at that instant it so happened that a peasant of his own village, a near neighbour, who had been carrying a load of wheat to the mill, passed by; and seeing a man lying stretched on the earth, he came up, and asked him, who he was, and what was the cause of his doleful lamentations? Don Quixote firmly believing him to be the marquis of Mantua his uncle, returned him no answer, but proceeded with the romance, giving an account of his misfortune, and of the amours of the emperor's son with his spouse, just as it is there recounted. The peasant was astonished at his extravagant discourse, and, taking off his vizor, now battered all to pieces, he wiped the dust from his face; upon which he instantly recognized him, and exclaimed, "Ah, signor Quixada!" (for so he was called before he had lost his senses, and was transformed from a sober gentleman to a knight-errant) "How came your worship in this condition?" But still he answered out of his romance to whatever question he was asked.

The good man, seeing this, contrived to take off the back and breast-piece of his armour, to examine if he had any wound; but he saw no blood, nor sign of any hurt. He then endeavoured to raise him from the ground, and with no little trouble placed him upon his ass, as being the beast of easier carriage. He gathered together all the arms, not excepting the broken pieces of the lance, and tied them upon Rozinante; then taking him by the bridle, and his ass by the halter, he went on towards his village, full of concern at the wild language of Don Quixote. No less thoughtful was the knight, who was so cruelly beaten and bruised, that he could scarcely keep himself upon the ass, and ever and anon he sent forth groans that seemed to pierce the skies, insomuch that the peasant was again forced to enquire what ailed him. And surely, the devil alone could have furnished his memory with stories so applicable to what had befallen him; for at that instant, forgetting Valdovinos, he recollected the Moor Abindarraez, at the time when the governor of Antequera, Roderigo of Narvaez, had taken him prisoner, and conveyed him to his castle; so that when the peasant asked again, how he was, and what he felt, he answered him in the very same terms that were used by the prisoner Abindarraez to Roderigo of Narvaez, as he had read in the *Diana* of George of Montemayor, applying it so aptly to his own case, that the peasant went on cursing himself to the devil, to hear such a monstrous head of nonsense, which convinced him that his neighbour had run mad, and he therefore made what haste he could to reach the village, and thereby escape the plague of Don Quixote's long speeches; who still continuing, said: "Be it known to your worship, Signor Don Rodrigo de Narvaez, that this beauteous Xarifa, whom I mentioned, is now the fair Dulcinea del Toboso, for whom I have done, do, and will do, the most famous exploits of chivalry, that have been, are, or shall be seen in the world." To this the peasant answered: "Look you, Sir, as I am a sinner, I am not Don Rodrigo de Narvaez, nor the Marquis of Mantua, but Pedro Alonso your neighbour: neither is your worship, Valdovinos, nor Abindarraez, but the worthy gentleman Signor Quixada." "I know who I am," answered Don Quixote; "and I know too, that I am not only capable of being those I have mentioned, but all the twelve peers of France, yea, and the nine worthies, since my exploits will far exceed all that they have, jointly or separately, achieved."

With this and similar conversation, they reached the village about sun-set: but the peasant waited until the night was a little advanced, that the poor battered gentleman might not be seen so scurvily mounted. When he thought it the proper time, he entered the village, and arrived at Don Quixote's house, which he found all in confusion. The priest and the barber of the place, who were Don Quixote's particular friends, happened to be there: and the house-keeper was saying to them aloud: "What do you think, Signor Licentiate Pero Perez," (for that was the priest's name) "of my master's misfortune? for neither he, nor his horse, nor the target, nor the lance, nor the armour, have been seen these six days past. Woe is me! I am verily persuaded, and it is as certainly true as I was born to die, that these cursed books of knight-errantry, which he is so often reading, have turned his brain; and now I think of it, I have often heard him say, talking to himself, that he would turn knight-errant, and go about the world in quest of adventures. The devil and Barabbas take all such books, that have spoiled the finest understanding in all la Mancha." The niece joined with her, adding "And you must know, master Nicholas," (for that was the barber's name) "that it has often happened, that my honoured uncle has continued poring on these wicked books of misadventures two whole days and nights; then throwing the book out of his hand, he would draw his sword and strike against the walls; and when he was heartily tired, would say, he had killed four giants, as tall as so many steeples, and that the sweat, which his labour occasioned, was the blood of the wounds he had received in the fight; then, after drinking off a large pitcher of cold water, he would be as quiet as ever, telling us, that the water was a most precious liquor, brought him by the sage Esquife, a great enchanter, and his friend. But I take the blame of all this to myself, for not informing you, gentlemen, of my dear uncle's extravagancies, that they might have been cured before they had gone so far, by burning all those cursed books, which as justly deserve to be committed to the flames, as if they were heretical," "I say the same," quoth the priest; "and in faith to-morrow shall not pass without holding a public inquisition upon them, and condemning them to the fire, that they may not occasion others to act as I fear my good friend has done."

All this was overheard by Don Quixote and the peasant; and as it confirmed the latter in the belief of his neighbour's infirmity, he began to cry aloud: "Open the doors, gentlemen, to Signor Valdovinos and the Marquis of Mantua, who comes danger-ously wounded, and to Signor Abindarraez the Moor, whom the valorous Rodrigo de Narvaez, governor of Antequera, brings as his prisoner." Hearing this they all came out; and immediately recognising their friend, they ran to embrace him, although he had not yet alighted from the ass, for indeed it was not in his power. "Forbear all of you," he cried, "for I am sorely wounded through my horse's fault: carry me to my bed; and, if it be possible, send for the sage Urganda, to search and heal my wounds." "Look ye," said the housekeeper immediately, "if my heart did not tell me truly, on which leg my master halted. Get up stairs in God's name; for, without the help of that same Urganda, we shall find a way to cure you ourselves. Cursed, say I again, and a hundred times cursed, be those books of knight-errantry, that have brought your worship to this pass!" They carried him directly to his chamber, where, on searching for his wounds, they could discover none. He then told them "he was only bruised by a great fall he got with his horse Rozinante, as he was fighting with ten of the most prodigious and audacious giants on the face of the earth. "Ho, ho!" says the priest, "what, there are giants too in the dance: by my faith, I shall set fire to them all before tomorrow night." They asked Don Quixote a thousand questions, to which he would return no answer; he only desired that they would give him some food, and allow him to sleep, that being what he most required. Having done this, the priest enquired particularly of the countryman in what condition Don Quixote had been found. The countryman gave him an account of the whole, with the extravagancies he had uttered, both at the time of finding him, and during their journey home; which made the Licentiate impatient to carry into execution what he had determined to do the following day, when, for that purpose, calling upon his friend master Nicholas the barber, they proceeded together to Don Quixote's house.

Chapter VI

Of the grand and diverting scrutiny made by the priest and the barber, in the library of our ingenious gentleman.

Whilst Don Quixote continued sleeping, the priest asked the niece for the keys of the chamber, which contained the books, those authors of the mischief; and she delivered them with a very good will. They entered, attended by the housekeeper, and found above a hundred large volumes well bound, besides a great number of smaller size. No sooner did the housekeeper see them, than she ran out of the room in great haste, and immediately returned with a pot of holy water, and a bunch of hyssop, saying: "Signor Licentiate, take this, and sprinkle the room, lest some enchanter, of the many these books abound with, should enchant us, as a punishment for our intention to banish them out of the world." The priest smiled at the housekeeper's simplicity, and ordered the barber to reach him the books, one by one, that they might see what they treated of; as they might perhaps find some that deserved not to be chastised by fire. "No," said the niece, "there is no reason why any of them should be spared, for they have all been mischief-makers: so let them all be thrown out of the window into the court-yard; and having made a pile of them, set fire to it; or else make a bonfire of them in the back-yard, where the smoke will offend nobody." The housekeeper said the same; so eagerly did they both thirst for the death of those innocents. But the priest would not consent to it without first reading the titles at least.

The first that master Nicholas put into his hands, was *Amadis de Gaul*[1] in four parts; and the priest said, "There seems to be some mystery in this for I have heard say, that this was the first book of chivalry printed in Spain, and that all the rest had their foundation and rise from it; I think, therefore, as head of so pernicious a sect, we ought to condemn him to the fire without mercy." "Not so, sir," said the barber; "for I have heard also, that it is the best of all the books of this kind; and therefore, as being unequalled in it, why, it ought to be spared." "You are right," said the priest; "and for that reason its life is granted for the present. Let us see that other next to him." "It is," said the barber, "the *Adventures of Esplandian*, the legitimate son of Amadis de Gaul." "Verily," said the priest, "the goodness of the father shall avail the son nothing; take him, mistress house-keeper; open that casement, and throw him into the yard, and let him make a beginning to the pile for the intended bonfire."

The housekeeper did so with much satisfaction, and good Esplandian was sent flying into the yard, there to wait with patience for the fire with which he was threatened. "Proceed," said the priest. "The next," said the barber, "is *Amadis of Greece*: yea, and all these on this side, I believe, are of the lineage of Amadis." "Then into the yard with them all!" quoth the priest; "for rather than not burn queen Pintiquiniestra, and the shepherd Darinel with his eclogues, and the devilish perplexities of the author, I would burn the father who begot me, were I to meet him in the shape of a knight-errant." "Of the same opinion am I," said the barber; "and I too," added the niece. "Well then," said the housekeeper, "away with them all into the yard." They handed them to her; and, as they were numerous, to save herself the trouble of the stairs, she threw them all out of the window.

"What tome is that?" said the priest. "This," answered the barber, "is *Don Olivante de Laura.*" "The author of that book," said the priest, "was the same who composed the *Garden of Flowers*; and in good truth I know not which of the two books is the truest, or rather the least lying; I can only say, that this goes to the yard for its arrogance and absurdity." "This that follows is *Florismarte of Hyrcania*," said the barber. "What! is signor Florismarte there," replied the priest; "now, by my faith, he shall soon make his appearance in the yard, notwithstanding his strange birth and chimerical adventures; for the harshness and dryness of his style will admit of no excuse. To the yard with him, and this other, mistress housekeeper." "With all my heart, dear sir," answered she; and with much joy executed what she was commanded. "Here is *The Knight Platir*," said the barber. "That," said the priest, "is an ancient book, and I find nothing in him deserving pardon: without more words, let him be sent after the rest;" which was accordingly done. They opened another book, and found it intitled the *Knight of the Cross*. "So religious a title," quoth the priest, "might, one would think, atone for the ignorance of the author; but it is a common saying, the devil lurks behind the cross: so to the fire with him." The barber, taking down another book, said, "This is the *Mirrour of Chivalry*." "Oh! I know his worship very well," quoth the priest. "Here comes signor Reynaldos de Montalvan, with his friends and companions, greater thieves than Cacus; and the Twelve Peers, with the faithful historiographer Turpin. However, I am only for condemning them to perpetual banishment, because they contain some things of the famous Mateo Boyardo; from whom

the Christian poet Ludovico Ariosto spun his web: and even to him, if I find him here uttering any other language than his own, I will shew no respect; but, if he speaks in his own tongue, I will put him upon my head." "I have him in Italian," said the barber, "but I do not understand him." "Neither is it any great matter, whether you understand him or not," answered the priest; "and we would willingly have excused the good captain from bringing him into Spain, and making him a Castilian; for he has deprived him of a great deal of his native value; which indeed is the misfortune of all those who undertake the translation of poetry into other languages; for, with all their care and skill, they can never bring them on a level with the original production. In short, I sentence this, and all other books that shall be found treating of French matters, to be thrown aside, and deposited in some dry vault, until we can deliberate more maturely what is to be done with them; excepting, however, Bernardo del Carpio, and another called Roncesvalles, which, if they fall into my hands, shall pass into those of the housekeeper, and thence into the fire, without any remission." The barber confirmed the sentence, and accounted it well and rightly determined, knowing that the priest was so good a Christian, and so much a friend to truth, that he would not utter a falshood for all the world.

Then opening another book, he saw it was Palmerin de Oliva, and next to that another called Palmerin of England; on espying which the Licentiate said: "Let this Oliva be torn to pieces and so effectually burnt, that not so much as the ashes may remain; but let Palmerin of England be preserved, and kept as a unique production; and such another case be made for it, as that which Alexander found among the spoils of Darius, and appropriated to preserve the works of the poet Homer. This book, neighbour, is estimable upon two accounts; the one, that it is very good of itself; and the other, because there is a tradition that it was written by an ingenious king of Portugal. All the adventures of the Castle of Miraguarda are excellent, and contrived with much art; the dialogue courtly and clear; and all the characters, preserved with great judgment and propriety. Therefore, Master Nicholas, saving your better judgment, let this, and *Amadis de Gaul*, be exempted from the fire, and let all the rest perish without any further enquiry." "Not so, friend," replied the barber; "for this which I have here, is the renowned *Don Belianis*." The priest replied, "This, with the second, third, and fourth parts, want a little rhubarb to purge away their excess of bile: besides, we must remove all that relates to the castle of Fame, and other absurdities of greater consequence; for which, let sentence of transportation be passed upon them, and according, as they shew signs of amendment, they shall be treated with mercy or justice. In the mean time, neighbour, give them room in your house; but let them not be read." "With all my heart," quoth the barber; and, without tiring himself any further in turning over books of chivalry, he bid the housekeeper take all the great ones, and throw them into the yard. This was not spoken to the stupid or deaf, but to one who had a greater mind to be burning them, than weaving the finest and largest web; and therefore laying hold of seven or eight at once, she tost them out at the window.

But in taking so many together, one fell at the barber's feet; who had a mind to see what it was, and found it to be, *The History of the Renowned Knight Tirante the White*. "God save me!" quoth the priest, with a loud voice, "is *Tirante the White* there? Give him to me, neighbour; for in him I shall have a treasure of delight, and a mine of entertainment. Here we have Don Kirieleison of Montalvan, a valorous knight, and his brother Thomas of Montalvan, with the knight Fonseca, and the combat which the valiant Tirante fought with the bulldog, and the witticisms of the damsel Plazerdemivida, also the amours and artifices of the widow Reposada; and madam the Empress in love with her squire Hypolito. Verily, neighbour, in its way, it is the best book in the world: here the knights eat, and sleep, and die in their beds, and make their wills before their deaths; with several things, which are not to be found in any other books of this kind. Notwithstanding this, I tell you, the author deserved, for writing so many foolish things seriously, to be sent to the gallies for the whole of his life: carry it home, and read it, and you will find all I say of him to be true." "I will do so," answered the barber: "but what shall we do with these small volumes that remain?" "Those," said the priest, "are, probably, not books of chivalry, but of poetry." Then opening one, he found it was the Diana of George de Montemayor, and concluding that all the others were of the same kind, he said, "these do not deserve to be burnt like the rest; for they cannot do the mischief that those of chivalry have done; they are works of genius and fancy, and do injury to none." "O sir," said the niece, "pray order them to be burnt with the rest; for should my uncle be cured of this distemper of chivalry, he may possibly, by reading such books, take it into his head to turn shepherd, and wander through the woods and fields, singing and playing on a

pipe; and, what would be still worse, turn poet, which, they say, is an incurable and contagious disease." "The damsel says true," quoth the priest, "and it will not be amiss to remove this stumbling-block out of our friend's way. And since we begin with the *Diana* of Montemayor, my opinion is that it should not be burnt, but that all that part should be expunged which treats of the sage Felicia, and of the enchanted fountain, and also most of the longer poems; leaving him in God's name the prose, and also the honour of being the first in that kind of writing." "The next that appears," said the barber, "is the *Diana* called *The Second Part*, by Salmantino; and another of the same name, whose author is Gil Polo." "The Salmantinian," answered the priest, "may accompany and increase the number of the condemned—to the yard with him: but let that of Gil Polo be preserved, as if it were written by Apollo himself. Proceed, friend, and let us dispatch; for it grows late."

"This," said the barber, opening another, "is *The Ten Books of the Fortune of Love*, composed by Antonio de lo Frasso, a Sardinian poet." "By the holy orders I have received!" said the priest, "since Apollo was Apollo, the muses muses, and the poets poets, so humorous and so whimsical a book as this was never written; it is the best, and most extraordinary of the kind, that ever appeared in the world; and he who has not read it, may be assured that he has never read any thing of taste: give it me here, neighbour, for I am better pleased at finding it, than if I had been presented with a cassock of Florence satin." He laid it aside, with great satisfaction, and the barber proceeded, saying: "These which follow are, *The Shepherd of Iberia, The Nymphs of Enares*, and *The Cure of Jealousy*." "Then you have only to deliver them up to the secular arm of the housekeeper," said the priest, "and ask me not why, for in that case we should never have done." "The next is *The Shepherd of Filida*." "He is no shepherd," said the priest, "but an ingenious courtier; let him be preserved, and laid up as a precious jewel." "This bulky volume here," said the barber, is intitled "*The Treasure of Divers Poems*," "Had they been fewer," replied the priest, "they would have been more esteemed: it is necessary that this book should be weeded and cleared of some low things interspersed amongst its sublimities: let it be preserved, both because the author is my friend, and out of respect to other more heroic and exalted productions of his pen." "This," pursued the barber, "is *El Cancionero of Lopez Maldonado*." "The author of that book," replied the priest, "is also a great friend of mine:

his verses, when sung by himself, excite much admiration; indeed such is the sweetness of his voice in singing them, that they are perfectly enchanting. He is a little too prolix in his eclogues; but there can never be too much of what is really good: let it be preserved with the select.

"But what book is that next to it?" "*The Galatea* of Michael de Cervantes," said the barber. "That Cervantes has been an intimate friend of mine these many years, and I know that he is more versed in misfortunes than in poetry. There is a good vein of invention in his book, which proposes something, though nothing is concluded: we must wait for the second part, which he has promised; perhaps on his amendment, he may obtain that entire pardon, which is now denied him; in the mean time, neighbour, keep him a recluse in your chamber." "With all my heart," answered the barber: "now here come three to-gether: the *Araucana* of Don Alonso de Ercilla, the *Austriada* of Juan Rufo, a magistrate of Cordova, and the *Monserrato* of Christoval de Virves, a poet of Valencia." "These three books," said the priest, "are the best that are written in heroic verse in the Castilian tongue, and may stand in competition with the most renowned works of Italy. Let them be preserved as the best productions of the Spanish muse." The priest grew tired of looking over so many books, and therefore without examination proposed that all the rest should be burnt; but the barber having already opened one called the *Tears of Angelica*. "I should have shed tears myself," said the priest, on hearing the name, "had I ordered that book to be burnt; for its author was one of the most celebrated poets, not only of Spain, but of the whole world; his translations from Ovid are admirable."

Chapter VII

Of the second sally of our good knight Don Quixote de la Mancha.

While they were thus employed, Don Quixote began to call out aloud, saying: "Here, here, valorous knights! Here you must exert the force of your powerful arms: for the courtiers begin to get the advantage in the tournament." All rushing out at once to the place whence this noisy exclamation proceeded, the scrutiny was suddenly interrupted; and therefore it is believed, that to the fire, unseen, and unheard, went the Carolea, and Leon of Spain, with the Acts of the Emperor, composed by Don Louis de Avila, which, without doubt, must have been among those that were left: and perhaps, had the priest seen them, they might not have undergone so rigorous a sentence. On entering Don Quixote's chamber, they found him already out of bed, and continuing his outcries and ravings, with his drawn sword, laying furiously about him, back-stroke and fore-stroke, and as broad awake as if he had never been asleep. They closed in with him, and by main force conveyed him again to his bed, where, after he was a little composed, he said, turning himself to the priest, "Certainly, my lord archbishop Turpin, it is a great disgrace to us, who call ourselves the twelve peers, to let the knights-courtiers carry off the palm, without more opposition, after we, the adventurers, had gained the prize on the three preceding days." "Say no more, good sir," said the priest; "it may be God's will to change our fortune, and what is lost to day may be won to-morrow; mind your health for the present; for I think you must needs be extremely fatigued, if not sorely wounded." "Wounded I am not," said Don Quixote; "but bruised and battered, most certainly: for that bastard, Don Roldan has pounded me with the trunk of an oak, and all out of mere envy, because he sees that I am the sole rival of his prowess. But let me never more be called Rinaldo of Montauban, if, as soon as I can rise from this bed, he pay not dearly for it, in spite of all his enchantments: In the mean time give me some food: for that is what I am now most in need of, and leave to me the care of avenging myself." They complied with his request, and gave him something to eat; he then fell fast asleep again: leaving them in astonishment at his madness.

That same night the housekeeper set fire to, and burnt, all the books that were in the yard, and in the house. Some must have perished that deserved to be treasured up in perpetual archives: but their destiny, or the indolence of the scrutineer, forbade it; and in them was fulfilled the saying, "that the just sometimes suffer for the unjust." One of the remedies, which the priest and barber prescribed at that time, for their friend's malady, was, to wall up the chamber which had contained his books, hoping that, when the cause was removed, the effect might cease; and that they should pretend, that an enchanter had carried room and all away. This was speedily executed; and two days after, when Don Quixote left his bed, the first thing that occurred to him was to visit his books; and, not finding the room, he went up and down looking for it; when, coming to the former situation of the door, he felt with his hands, and stared about on all sides without speaking a word for some time; at length he asked the housekeeper where the chamber was, in which he kept his books. She, who was already well tutored what to answer, said to him: "What room, or what nothing, does your worship look for? there is neither room, nor books, in this house; for the devil himself has carried all away." "It was not the devil," said the niece, "but an enchanter, who came one night upon a cloud, after the day of your departure, and alighting from a serpent on which he rode, entered the room; what he did there, I know not, but after some little time, out he came, flying through the roof, and left the house full of smoke; and when we went to see what he had been doing, we saw neither books nor room; only we very well remember, both I and mistress housekeeper here, that when the wicked old thief went away, he said with a loud voice, that from a secret enmity he bore to the owner of those books and of the room, he had done a mischief in this house, which would soon be manifest: he told us also, that he was called the sage Munniaton." "Freston he meant to say," quoth Don Quixote. "I know not," answered the housekeeper, "whether his name be Freston, or Friton; all I know is, that it ended in ton." "It doth so," replied Don Quixote. "He is a sage enchanter, a great enemy of mine, and bears me malice, because by his skill and learning he knows, that, in process of time, I shall engage in single combat with a knight whom he favours, and shall vanquish him, in spite of his protection. On this account he endeavours, as much as he can, to molest me: but let him know from me, that he cannot withstand or avoid what is decreed by heaven." "Who doubts of that?" said the niece; "but, dear uncle, what have you to do with these broils? Would it not be better to stay quietly at home, and not ramble about the world seeking for better bread than wheaten; without considering that many go out for wool and return shorn?" "O niece," answered Don Quixote, "how little dost thou know of the matter? Before they shall shear me, I will pluck and tear off the beards of all those who dare think of

touching the tip of a single hair of mine." Neither of them would make any further reply; for they saw his choler begin to rise. Fifteen days he remained at home, very tranquil, discovering no symptom of an inclination to repeat his late frolics; during which time much pleasant conversation passed between him and his two neighbours, the priest and the barber: he always affirming, that the world stood in need of nothing so much as knights-errant, and the revival of chivalry. The priest sometimes contradicted him, and at other times acquiesced: for had he not been thus cautious, there would have been no means left to bring him to reason.

In the mean time Don Quixote tampered with a labourer, a neighbour of his, and an honest man (if such an epithet may be given to one that is poor) but shallow-brained; in short he said so much, used so many arguments, and made so many promises, that the poor fellow resolved to sally out with him, and serve him in the capacity of a Squire. Among other things, Don Quixote told him, that he ought to be very glad to accompany him, for such an adventure might some time or other occur, that by one stroke an island might be won, where he might leave him governor. With this and other promises, Sancho Panza (for that was the labourer's name) left his wife and children, and engaged himself as squire to his neighbour. Don Quixote now set about raising money; and, by selling one thing, pawning another, and losing by all, he collected a tolerable sum. He fitted himself likewise with a buckler, which he borrowed of a friend, and patching up his broken helmet in the best manner he could, he acquainted his squire Sancho of the day and hour he intended to set out, that he might provide himself with what he thought would be most needful. Above all, he charged him not to forget a wallet; which Sancho assured him he would not neglect, he said also that he thought of taking an ass with him, as he had a very good one, and he was not used to travel much on foot. With regard to the ass Don Quixote paused a little: endeavouring to recollect whether any knight-errant had ever carried a squire mounted on ass-back; but no instance of the kind occurred to his memory. However he consented that he should take his ass, resolving to accommodate him more honourably, the earliest opportunity, by dismounting the first discourteous knight he should meet. He provided himself also with shirts, and other things, conformably to the advice given him by the inn-keeper.

All this being accomplished, Don Quixote and Sancho Panza, without taking leave, the one of his wife and children, or the other of his house-keeper and niece, one night sallied out of the village, unperceived; and they travelled so hard, that by break of day they believed themselves secure, even if search were made after them. Sancho Panza proceed upon his ass, like a patriarch, with his wallet and leathern bottle, and with a vehement desire to find himself governor of the island, which his master had promised him. Don Quixote happened to take the same route as on his first expedition, over the plain of Montiel, which he passed with less inconvenience than before; for it was early in the morning, and the rays of the sun, darting on them horizontally, did not annoy them. Sancho Panza now said to his master: "I beseech your worship, good sir knight-errant, not to forget your promise concerning that same island; for I shall know how to govern it, be it ever so large." To which Don Quixote answered: "Thou must know, friend Sancho Panza, that it was a custom much in use among the knights-errant of old, to make their squires governors of the islands or kingdoms they conquered and I am determined that so laudable a custom shall not be lost through my neglect; on the contrary, I resolve to outdo them in it: for they sometimes, and perhaps most times, waited till their squires were grown old; and when they were worn out in their service, and had endured many bad days and worse nights, they conferred

on them some title, such as count, or at least marquis, of some valley or province, of more or less account; but if you live, and I live, before six days have passed, I may probably win such a kingdom, as may have others depending on it, just fit for thee to be crowned king of one of them. And do not think this any extraordinary matter; for things fall out to knights, by such unforeseen and unexpected ways, that I may easily give thee more than I promise." "So then," answered Sancho Panza, "if I were a king by some of those miracles your worship mentions, Joan Gutierrez, my duck, would come to be a Queen, and my children Infantas." "Who doubts it?" answered Don Quixote. "I doubt it," replied Sancho Panza; "for I am verily persuaded, that if God were to rain down kingdoms upon the earth, none of them would sit well upon the head of Mary Gutierrez; for you must know, sir, she is not worth two farthings for a queen. The title of Countess would sit better upon her, with the help of God, and good friends." "Recommend her to God, Sancho," answered Don Quixote, "and he will do what is best for her: but do thou have a care not to debase thy mind so low, as to content thyself with being less than a Viceroy." "Sir, I will not;" answered Sancho, "especially having so great a man for my master as your worship, who will know how to give me whatever is most fitting for me, and what I am best able to bear."

Chapter VIII

Of the valorous Don Quixote's success, in the dreadful and never-before-imagined adventure of the wind-mills; with other events worthy to be recorded.

As they were thus discoursing, they came in sight of thirty or forty wind-mills, which are in that plain; and as soon as Don Quixote espied them he said to his squire: "Fortune disposes our affairs better than we ourselves could have desired: look yonder, friend Sancho Panza, where thou mayest discover somewhat more than thirty monstrous giants, whom I intend to encounter and slay; and with their spoils we will begin to enrich ourselves: for it is lawful war, and doing God good service to remove so wicked a generation from off the face of the earth." "What

giants?" said Sancho Panza. "Those thou seest yonder," answered his master, "with their long arms; for some are wont to have them almost of the length of two leagues." "Look, sir," answered Sancho, "those, which appear yonder, are not giants, but wind-mills; and what seem to be arms, are the sails, which, whirled about by the wind, make the mill-stone go." "It is very evident," answered Don Quixote, "that thou art not versed in the business of adventures: they are giants; and, if thou art afraid, get thee aside and pray, whilst I engage with them in fierce and unequal combat." So saying, he clapped spurs to his steed, notwithstanding the cries his squire sent after him, assuring him that they were certainly wind-mills, and not giants. But he was so fully possessed that they were giants, that he neither heard the outcries of his squire Sancho, nor yet discerned what they were, though he was very near them, but went on crying out aloud: "Fly not, ye cowards and vile caitifs; for it is a single knight who assaults you." The wind now rising a little, the great sails began to move: upon which Don Quixote called out: "Although ye should move more arms than the giant, Briareus, ye shall pay for it."

Then recommending himself devoutly to his lady Dulcinea, beseeching her to succour him in the present danger, being well covered with his buckler, and setting his lance in the rest, he rushed on as fast as Rozinante could gallop, and attacked the first mill before him; when, running his lance into the sail, the wind whirled it about with so much violence, that it broke the lance to shivers, dragging horse and rider after it, and tumbling them over and over, on the plain, in very evil plight. Sancho Panza hastened to his assistance as fast as the ass could carry him; and when he came up to his master, he found him unable to stir: so violent was the blow which he and Rozinante had received in their fall. "God save me!" quoth Sancho, "did not I warn you to have a care of what you did, for that they were nothing but wind-mills? And nobody could mistake them, but one that had the like, in his head." "Peace, friend Sancho," answered Don Quixote: "for matters of war are, of all others, most subject to continual change. Now I verily believe, and it is most certainly the fact, that the sage Freston, who stole away my chamber and books, has metamorphosed these giants into wind-mills, on purpose to deprive me of the glory of vanquishing them: so great is the enmity he bears me! But his wicked arts will finally avail but little against the goodness of my sword." "God grant it!" answered Sancho Panza; then, helping him to rise, he mounted him again upon his steed, which was almost disjointed.

Conversing upon the late adventures, they followed the road that led to the pass of Lapice because there, Don Quixote said, they could not fail to meet with many and various adventures, as it was much frequented.

ENDNOTE

1. *Amadis de Gaul* and the other titles mentioned in this chapter are real works, well known in Cervantes's lifetime. Notice his modest appraisal of his own *Galatea* near the chapter's end.

Questions for Consideration

Using complete sentences, provide brief answers for the following questions.

1. What does Don Quixote believe in?

_____

_____

_____

_____

_____

2. What is Sancho Panza's relationship to Don Quixote? How are the two different?

_____

_____

_____

_____

_____

3. How does Quixote explain the "giants" he attacks turning into windmills?

_____

_____

_____

_____

_____

———————————— *Writing Critically* ————————————

Select one of the essay topics listed below and compose a 500-word essay which discusses the topic fully. Support your thesis with evidence from the text and with critical and/or historical material. Use the space below for preparing to write the essay.

1. How is Don Quixote presented as admirable? How is he presented as ridiculous? Compare and contrast these aspects of his character.

2. Is Don Quixote closer to becoming a saint than a madman, or closer to being a madman than a saint? Explain your answer by references to the text.

3. To the extent that *Don Quixote* is written as a satire, what ideals does it seem to be satirizing? Are there any ideals that it takes seriously?

Prewriting Space:

_____

_____

_____

_____

_____

_____

_____

_____

_____

_____

_____

_____

_____

_____

_____

_____

_____

_____

_____

Introduction

Shakespeare's Hamlet

The reader of Shakespeare's *Hamlet* confronts a great work that conveys its major themes and ideas in a variety of ways. As reflected in the words of its chief protagonist, Hamlet, the play is a rich tapestry of vivid and expressive language that makes use of striking similes and metaphors. These images help to define Hamlet's world and evidence his keen intellect as he struggles with the moral dilemma of avenging his father's death. Hamlet is thus emblematic of the rational soul who must contend with a world that is disturbingly "out of joint." On this level, the play is an insightful exploration of the Elizabethan ideal of order in the universe. That Hamlet does not act precipitously by killing King Claudius, the uncle who has murdered his father and now lives incestuously with his mother, may be viewed in relation to this pervasive fifteenth-century concept. In addition to these dimensions, Shakespeare's *Hamlet* also deals with the unsettling discrepancy between appearance and reality, which goes to the core of its protagonist's moral universe. This introduction will further delineate these aspects of the drama.

The figurative language that Hamlet often employs in the form of similes and metaphors offers insight into how he views and understands the world. While there is no shortage of similes (direct comparisons using *like, as, than* or some other appropriate connective) in *Hamlet*, the play abounds in revealing metaphors (implied comparisons) that show how Hamlet interprets things after the shocking death of his father. As many critics have pointed out, as a student-scholar at the University of Wittenberg, he is the embodiment of reason and morality. When, as Hamlet perceives it, his mother hastily marries his murderous uncle Claudius, in incestuous lust for him, his (Hamlet's) tranquil word is shattered. And because his mother Gertrude, a woman, is at the center of this moral betrayal, he is convinced that "Frailty, thy name is woman!" (Act I, Scene II, 145–146). Human weakness becomes summed up in the feminine sex. Hamlet thus decides that, in dealing with his mother, "I will speak daggers to her, but use none" (Act III, Scene II, 395) His words, therefore, will be the piercing weapons with which he will prick the conscience of his fallen mother. This indicting metaphorical usage on Hamlet's part also extends to Denmark itself, which he now sees as an "unweeded garden" (Act I, Scene II, 135), and as a "prison" (Act II, Scene II, 244). In the midst of this fallen world, in which individual man no longer evidences the goodness that Hamlet had come to expect, he becomes disillusioned with "this quintessence of dust" (Act I, Scene II, 309). The paragon of creation, therefore, has been dethroned in his mind. These—and other—metaphorical references shed much light on Hamlet's mental state at various points in the play.

Hamlet should also be viewed in relation to the Elizabethan concept of an orderly universe. This notion was inherited from the fourteenth-century (the Middle Ages) and assumed a God-centered world that was under divine control. The Elizabethan frame of mind also espoused an orderly universe in which reason (sometimes "right reason") was extolled as the "faculty" in the soul that allowed for the preservation of order in the individual and the state or body politic. The idea of a Great Chain of Being—extending from God, angels, man, plants, etc.—also helped to solidify belief in a rational scheme of existence. In addition, Elizabethan views on body and soul underscored the supremacy of the rational, the former being identified with unruly passions ("unreason"), the latter being guided by the principle of reason that preserve man's Godlike image in the face of tempting animality. Shakespeare's Hamlet, therefore, in "thinking too precisely on th' event" (ACT IV, Scene IV, 41) represents the principle of Reason or the rational soul that the fifteenth-century championed. Thus, unlike his foil Laertes, the brother of his love interest, Ophelia, Hamlet does not act hastily in seeking revenge for his father's death. And he does not vow, as the unreflective Laertes does, to cut the perpetrator's "throat in the church" (Act IV, Scene VII, 126) Hamlet must have rational proof for his actions. Thus, even when his uncle Claudius' murderous guilt is apparent when he flees the "Murder of Gonzago" play that Hamlet has staged, he does not immediately set about to kill him. So it is when he finds the guilty King on his knees praying. Though personal vengeance would have been satisfying at this point, his rational side causes him to conclude that slaying the culprit while he is in the midst of supplication would send his soul to heaven. For Hamlet, therefore, there are no actions without consequences. The Elizabethan rational view of the universe and man reinforced this perspective.

Another significant theme that shapes developments in *Hamlet* is that of appearance versus reality. This is evident in the madness that Hamlet feigns in search of the truth regarding his father's murder. Ophelia's father, Polonius, believes that the young prince has gone insane because she now rejects his advances. Hamlet's mother, Gertrude, also believes that he is "mad" when she sees him all disheveled. The dialogue that ensues between them turns on the irony of what "seems" or appears to be the case. When Hamlet says to his mother "Seems, Madam. I know not seems" (Act I, Scene II, 76), the reader sees the skillful manner in which he contrasts the genuineness of his character with the deceitful nature of Gertrude who "seems" to be what she is not—that is, loyal, trusting, devoted. Unlike Hamlet, then, his mother knows "seems" because she is the very embodiment of the difference between appearance and reality. Moreover, because he now sees sexual sin represented in his mother—who has hastily married his uncle, King Claudius, who killed his father—Hamlet also views his beloved Ophelia in the same light. This exchange between them is illustrative:

Hamlet   Ha, ha! are you honest?
Ophelia   My lord?
Hamlet   Are you fair?
Ophelia   What means your lordship?
Hamlet   That if you be honest and fair, your honesty should admit no discourse to your beauty. (*Hamlet*, Act III, Scene I, 104–109)

Even in Ophelia, therefore, Hamlet sees what he believes to be a stunning contrast between appearance and reality, between her beauty and any claim to truth and sincerity. His berating of her continues: ". . . God hath given you one face, and you make yourselves another." Hamlet has thus come to see his mother in particular, and women in general, as embodying the unsettling contrast between appearance and reality. The treachery of his so-called friends, Rosencrantz and Guildenstern, helps to further this theme. And Hamlet's ultimate disillusionment with his heretofore high evaluation of man—triggered by his uncle's murder of his father and his mother's incestuous marriage to him—highlights the theme of appearance versus reality in a compelling fashion:

> . . . What a piece of work is a man! How noble in reason, how infinite in faculties, in form and moving how express and admirable, in action how like an angel, in apprehension how like a god! The beauty of the world, the paragon of animals! And yet, to me, what is this quintessence of dust? Man delights not me. . . . (*Hamlet*, Act II, Scene II, 304–310) (DLP)

BIBLIOGRAPHY

Bowers, Fredson T. *Elizabethan Revenge Tragedy*, 1587–1642. Princeton, 1940.

Bradley, A. C. *Shakespearean Tragedy*. London, 1904. (Hamlet, Othello, King Lear, Macbeth.)

Lovejoy, A. O. *The Great Chain of Being*. Cambridge, Mass., 1936.

Spivack, Bernard. *Shakespeare and the Allegory of Evil*. New York, 1958.

Tillyard, E. M. W. *The Elizabethan World Picture*. London, 1943, 1967.

Walker, Roy. *The Time Is out of Joint: A Study of "Hamlet."* London and New York, 1948.

Globe Theater

The Tragedy of Hamlet, Prince of Denmark

Shakespeare

[Dramatis Personae]

CLAUDIUS, *King of Denmark*
HAMLET, *son to the late King Hamlet, and nephew to the present King*
POLONIUS, *Lord Chamberlain*
HORATIO, *friend to HAMLET*
LAERTES, *son to Polonius*
VOLTEMAND
CORNELIUS
ROSENCRANTZ   } *courtiers*
GUILDENSTERN
OSRIC
GENTLEMAN
MARCELLUS   } *officers*
BARNARDO

FRANCISCO, *a Soldier*
REYNALDO, *servant to Polonius*
FORTINBRAS, *Prince of Norway*
NORWEGIAN CAPTAIN
DOCTOR OF DIVINITY
PLAYERS
Two CLOWNS, *grave-diggers*
ENGLISH AMBASSADORS
GERTRUDE, *Queen of Denmark, and mother to hamlet*
OPHELIA, *daughter to Polonius*
GHOST *of Hamlet's Father*
LORDS, LADIES, OFFICERS, SOLDIERS, SAILORS, MESSENGERS, *and* ATTENDANTS

Scene: Denmark

[ACT I, SCENE I]

Enter BARNARDO and FRANCISCO, two sentinels, [meeting].

Bar. Who's there?
Fran. Nay, answer me. Stand and unfold
  yourself.
Bar. Long live the King!
Fran. Barnardo.
Bar. He.   5
Fran. You come most carefully upon your
  hour.
Bar. 'Tis now strook twelf. Get thee to
  bed, Francisco.
Fran. For this relief much thanks. 'Tis
  bitter cold,

And I am sick at heart.
  Bar. Have you had quiet guard?
  Fran.   Not a mouse stirring. 10
  Bar. Well, good night.
If you do meet Horatio and Marcellus,
The rivals of my watch, bid them make haste.

Enter HORATIO and MARCELLUS.

Fran. I think I hear them. Stand ho! Who is
  there?
Hor. Friends to this ground.
Mar.   And liegemen to the Dane. 15
Fran. Give you good night.
Mar.   O, farewell, honest [soldier].
Who hath reliev'd you?
  Fran.   Barnardo hath my place.
Give you good night.   *Exit Francisco.*
  Mar.   Holla, Barnardo!

794

Bar.   Say—
What, is Horatio there?
     Hor.   A piece of him.   19
     Bar. Welcome, Horatio, welcome, good
          Marcellus.
     Hor. What, has this thing appear'd again
          tonight?
     Bar. I have seen nothing.
     Mar. Horatio says 'tis but our fantasy,
And will not let belief take hold of him
Touching this dreaded sight twice seen of us; 25
Therefore I have entreated him along,
With us to watch the minutes of this night,
That if again this apparition come,
He may approve our eyes and speak to it.
     Hor. Tush, tush, 'twill not appear.
     Bar.   Sit down a while,
And let us once again assail your ears,   31
That are so fortified against our story,
What we have two nights seen.
     Hor.   Well, sit we down,
And let us hear Barnardo speak of this.
     Bar. Last night of all,   35
When yond same star that's westward from the pole
Had made his course t' illume that part of heaven
Where now it burns, Marcellus and myself,
The bell then beating one—

Enter GHOST.

     Mar. Peace, break thee off! Look where it
          comes again!   40
     Bar. In the same figure like the King that's
          dead.
     Mar. Thou art a scholar, speak to it, Horatio.
     Bar. Looks 'a not like the King? Mark it,
          Horatio.
     Hor. Most like; it [harrows] me with fear and
          wonder.
     Bar. It would be spoke to.
     Mar.   Speak to it, Horatio.
     Hor. What art thou that usurp'st this time of
          night,
Together with that fair and warlike form   47
In which the majesty of buried Denmark
Did sometimes march? By heaven I charge
          thee speak!
     Mar. It is offended.
     Bar.   See, it stalks away!   50
     Hor. Stay! Speak, speak, I charge thee
          speak!
                                   Exit Ghost.
     Mar. 'Tis gone, and will not answer.,
     Bar. How now, Horatio? you tremble and
          look pale.
Is not this something more than fantasy?

What think you on't?   55
     Hor. Before my God, I might not this
          believe
Without the sensible and true avouch
Of mine own eyes.
     Mar.   Is it not like the King?
     Hor. As thou art to thyself.
Such was the very armor he had on   60
When he the ambitious Norway combated.
So frown'd he once when in an angry parle
He smote the sledded [Polacks] on the ice.
'Tis strange.
     Mar. Thus twice before and jump at this
          dead hour,   65
With martial stalk hath he gone by our
          watch.
     Hor. In what particular thought to work I
          know not,
But in the gross and scope of mine opinion,
This bodes some strange eruption to our
          state.
     Mar. Good now, sit down, and tell me, he
          that knows,   70
Why this same strict and most observant watch
So nightly toils the subject of the land,
And [why] such daily [cast] of brazen cannon,
And foreign mart for implements of war,
Why such impress of shipwrights, whose
          sore task   75
Does not divide the Sunday from the week,
What might be toward, that this sweaty haste
Doth make the night joint-laborer with the day:
Who is't that can inform me?
     Hor.   That can I,
At least the whisper goes so: our last king,   80
Whose image even but now appear'd to us,
Was, as you know, by Fortinbras of Norway,
Thereto prick'd on by a most emulate pride,
Dar'd to the combat; in which our valiant
          Hamlet   84
(For so this side of our known world
          esteem'd him)
Did slay this Fortinbras, who, by a seal'd
          compact
Well ratified by law and heraldy,
Did forfeit (with his life) all [those] his lands
Which he stood seiz'd of, to the conqueror;
Against the which a moi'ty competent   90
Was gaged by our king, which had [return'd]
To the inheritance of Fortinbras,
Had he been vanquisher; as by the same comart
And carriage of the article [design'd],
His fell to Hamlet. Now, sir, young
          Fortinbras,   95
Of unimproved mettle hot and full,
Hath in the skirts of Norway here and there

Shark'd up a list of lawless resolutes
For food and diet to some enterprise
That hath a stomach in't, which is no other, 100
As it doth well appear unto our state,
But to recover of us, by strong hand
And terms compulsatory, those foresaid lands
So by his father lost; and this, I take it,
Is the main motive of our preparations, 105
The source of this our watch, and the chief head
Of this post-haste and romage in the land.
  Bar. I think it be no other but e'en so.
Well may it sort that this portentous figure
Comes armed through our watch so like the
  King 110
That was and is the question of these wars.
  Hor. A mote it is to trouble the mind's eye.
In the most high and palmy state of Rome,
A little ere the mightiest Julius fell,
The graves stood [tenantless] and the
  sheeted dead 115
Did squeak and gibber in the Roman streets.
As stars with trains of fire, and dews of blood,
Disasters in the sun; and the moist star
Upon whose influence Neptune's empire stands
Was sick almost to doomsday with eclipse. 120
And even the like precurse of [fear'd] events,
As harbingers preceeding still the fates
And prologue to the omen coming on,
Have heaven and earth together demonstrated
Unto our climatures and countrymen. 125

  Enter GHOST.

But soft, behold! lo where it comes again!
       It spreads his arms.
I'll cross it though it blast me. Stay, illusion!
If thou hast any sound or use of voice,
Speak to me.
If there be any good thing to be done 130
That may to thee do ease, and grace to me,
Speak to me.
If thou art privy to thy country's fate,
Which happily foreknowing may avoid,
O speak! 135
Or if thou hast uphoarded in thy life
Extorted treasure in the womb of earth,
For which, they say, your spirits oft walk in
  death,
Speak of it, stay and speak! *(The cock crows.)*
  Stop it, Marcellus.
  Mar. Shall I strike it with my partisan? 140
  Hor. Do, if it will not stand.
  Bar.   'Tis here!
  Hor.   'Tis
  here!
  Mar. 'Tis gone!   *[Exit Ghost.]*

We do it wrong, being so majestical,
To offer it the show of violence,
For it is as the air, invulnerable, 145
And our vain blows malicious mockery.
  Bar. It was about to speak when the cock
  crew.
  Hor. And then it started like a guilty thing
Upon a fearful summons. I have heard
The cock, that is the trumpet to the morn, 150
Doth with his lofty and shrill-sounding throat
Awake the god of day, and at his warning,
Whether in sea or fire, in earth or air,
Th' extravagant and erring spirit hies
To his confine; and of the truth herein 155
This present object made probation.
  Mar. It faded on the crowing of the cock.
Some say that ever 'gainst that season comes
Wherein our Saviour's birth is celebrated,
This bird of dawning singeth all night long, 160
And then they say no spirit dare stir abroad,
The nights are wholesome, then no planets
  strike,
No fairy takes, nor witch hath power to charm,
So hallowed, and so gracious, is that time.
  Hor. So have I heard and do in part
  believe it. 165
But look, the morn in russet mantle clad
Walks o'er the dew of yon high eastward hill.
Break we our watch up and by my advice
Let us impart what we have seen to-night
Unto young Hamlet, for, upon my life, 170
This spirit, dumb to us, will speak to him.
Do you consent we shall acquaint him with it,
As needful in our loves, fitting our duty?
  Mar. Let's do't, I pray, and I this morning
  know
Where we shall find him most convenient. 175
          Exeunt.

[SCENE II]

Flourish. Enter CLAUDIUS, KING OF
  DENMARK, GERTRUDE THE QUEEN;
  COUNCIL: *as* POLONIUS; *and his son*
  LAERTES, HAMLET, cum aliis [*including*
  VOLTEMAND *and* CORNELIUS].

  King. Though yet of Hamlet our dear
  brother's death
The memory be green, and that it us befitted
To bear our hearts in grief, and our whole
  kingdom
To be contracted in one brow of woe,

Yet so far hath discretion fought with nature   5
That we with wisest sorrow think on him
Together with remembrance of ourselves.
Therefore our sometime sister, now our queen,
Th' imperial jointress to this warlike state,
Have we, as 'twere with a defeated joy,   10
With an auspicious, and a dropping eye,
With mirth in funeral, and with dirge in marriage,
In equal scale weighing delight and dole,
Taken to wife; nor have we herein barr'd
Your better wisdoms, which have freely gone 15
With this affair along. For all our thanks.
Now follows that you know young Fortinbras,
Holding a weak supposal of our worth,
Or thinking by our late dear brother's death
Our state to be disjoint and out of frame,   20
Co-leagued this dream of his advantage,
He hath not fail'd to pester us with message
Importing the surrender of those lands
Lost by his father, with all bands of law,
To our most valiant brother. So much for
   him.   25
Now for ourself, and for this time of meeting,
Thus much the business is: we have here writ
To Norway, uncle of young Fortinbras—
Who, impotent and bedred, scarcely hears
Of this his nephew's purpose—to suppress   30
His further gait herein, in that the levies,
The lists, and full proportions are all made
Out of his subject; and we here dispatch
You, good Cornelius, and you, Voltemand,
For bearers of this greeting to old Norway,   35
Giving to you no further personal power
To business with the King, more than the scope
Of these delated articles allow.   [*Giving a paper.*]
Farewell, and let your haste command your
   duty.
   Cor., Vol. In that, and all things, will we
      show our duty.   40
   King. We doubt it nothing; heartily
      farewell.
                  [*Exeunt Voltemand and Cornelius.*]
And now, Laertes, what's the news with you?
You told us of some suit, what is't, Laertes?
You cannot speak of reason to the Dane
And lose your voice. What wouldst thou
   beg, Laertes
That shall not be my offer, not thy asking?   46
The head is not more native to the heart,
The hand more instrumental to the mouth,
Than is the throne of Denmark to thy father.
What wouldst thou have, Laertes?
   Laer.   My dread lord, 50
Your leave and favor to return to France,
From whence though willingly I came to
   Denmark

To show my duty in your coronation,
Yet now I must confess, that duty done,
My thoughts and wishes bend again toward
   France,   55
And bow them to your gracious leave and
   pardon.
   King. Have you your father's leave? What
      says Polonius?
   Pol. H'ath, my lord, wrung from me my
      slow leave
By laborsome petition, and at last
Upon his will I seal'd my hard consent.   60
I do beseech you give him leave to go.
   King. Take thy fair hour, Laertes, time be
      thine,
And thy best graces spend it at thy will!
But now, my cousin Hamlet, and my son—
   Ham. [*Aside.*] A little more than kin, and
      less than kind.   65
   King. How is it that the clouds still hang
      on you?
   Ham. Not so, my lord, I am too much in
      the sun.
   Queen. Good Hamlet, cast thy nighted
      color off,
And let thine eye look like a friend on Denmark.
Do not for ever with thy vailed lids   70
Seek for thy noble father in the dust.
Thou know'st 'tis common, all that lives
   must die,
Passing through nature to eternity.
   Ham. Ay, madam, it is common.
   Queen.   If it be,
Why seems it so particular with thee?   75
   Ham. Seems, madam? nay, it is, I know
      not "seems."
'Tis not alone my inky cloak, [good] mother,
Nor customary suits of solemn black,
Nor windy suspiration of forc'd breath,
No, nor the fruitful river in the eye,   80
Nor the dejected havior of the visage,
Together with all forms, moods, [shapes] of grief,
That can [denote] me truly. These indeed seem,
For they are actions that a man might play,
But I have that within which passes show,   85
These but the trappings and the suits of woe.
   King. 'Tis sweet and commendable in your
      nature, Hamlet,
To give these mourning duties to your father.
But you must know your father lost a father,
That father lost, lost his, and the survivor
   bound   90
In filial obligation for some term
To do obsequious sorrow. But to persever
In obstinate condolement is a course
Of impious stubbornness, 'tis unmanly grief,

It shows a will most incorrect to heaven,   95
A heart unfortified, or mind impatient,
An understanding simple and unschool'd
For what we know must be, and is as common
As any the most vulgar thing to sense,
Why should we in our peevish opposition   100
Take it to heart? Fie, 'tis a fault to heaven,
A fault against the dead, a fault to nature,
To reason most absurd, whose common theme
Is death of fathers, and who still hath cried,
From the first corse till he that died to-day,   105
"This must be so." We pray you throw to earth
This unprevailing woe, and think of us
As of a father, for let the world take note
You are the most immediate to our throne,
And with no less nobility of love   110
Than that which dearest father bears his son
Do I impart toward you. For your intent
In going back to school in Wittenberg,
It is most retrograde to our desire,
And we beseech you bend you to remain   115
Here in the cheer and comfort of our eye,
Our chiefest courtier, cousin, and our son.
    Queen. Let not thy mother lose her
        prayers, Hamlet,
I pray thee stay with us, go not to Wittenberg.
    Ham. I shall in all my best obey you,
        madam.   120
    King. Why, 'tis a loving and a fair reply.
Be as ourself in Denmark. Madam, come.
This gentle and unforc'd accord of Hamlet
Sits smiling to my heart, in grace whereof,
No jocund health that Denmark drinks
        to-day,   125
But the great cannon to the clouds shall tell,
And the King's rouse the heaven shall bruit
        again,
Respeaking earthly thunder. Come away.
        Flourish. Exeunt all but Hamlet.
    Ham. O that this too too sallied flesh
        would melt,
Thaw, and resolve itself into a dew!   130
Or that the Everlasting had not fix'd
His canon 'gainst [self-]slaughter! O God, God,
How [weary], stale, flat, and unprofitable
Seem to me all the uses of this world!
Fie on't, ah fie! 'tis an unweeded garden   135
That grows to seed, things rank and gross in
        nature
Possess it merely. That it should come [to this]!
But two months dead, nay, not so much, not two.
So excellent a king, that was to this
Hyperion to a satyr, so loving to my mother   140
That he might not beteem the winds of heaven
Visit her face too roughly. Heaven and earth,
Must I remember? Why, she should hang on him,

As if increase of appetite had grown
By what it fed on, and yet, within a month—145
Let me not think on't! Frailty, thy name is
        woman!—
A little month, or ere those shoes were old
With which she followed my poor father's body,
Like Niobe, all tears—why, she, [even she]—
O God, a beast that wants discourse of reason   150
Would have mourn'd longer—married with
        my uncle,
My father's brother, but no more like my father
Than I to Hercules. Within a month,
Ere yet the salt of most unrighteous tears
Had left the flushing in her galled eyes,   155
She married—O most wicked speed: to post
With such dexterity to incestious sheets,
It is not, nor it cannot come to good,
But break my heart, for I must hold my tongue.

    Enter HORATIO, MARCELLUS, *and* BAR-
NARDO.

    Hor. Hail to your lordship!
    Ham.   I am glad to see you well.
Horatio—or I do forget myself.   161
    Hor. The same, my lord, and your poor
        servant ever.
    Ham. Sir, my good friend—I'll change that
        name with you.
And what make you from Wittenberg, Horatio?
Marcellus.   165
    Mar. My good lord.
    Ham. I am very glad to see you. [*To
        Barnardo.*] Good even, sir.—
But what, in faith, make you from Wittenberg?
    Hor. A truant disposition, good my lord.
    Ham. I would not hear your enemy say so,170
Nor shall you do my ear that violence
To make it truster of your own report
Against yourself. I know you are no truant.
But what is your affair in Elsinore?
We'll teach you to drink [deep] ere you
        depart.   175
    Hor. My lord, I came to see your father's
        funeral.
    Ham. I prithee do not mock me, fellow
        student,
I think it was to [see] my mother's wedding.
    Hor. Indeed, my lord, it followed hard upon.
    Ham. Thrift, thrift, Horatio, the funeral
        bak'd meats   180
Did coldly furnish forth the marriage table.
Would I had met my dearest foe in heaven
Or ever I had seen that day, Horatio!
My father—methinks I see my father.   184
    Hor. Where, my lord?

Ham.   In my mind's eye, Horatio.

Hor. I saw him once, 'a was a goodly king.

Ham. 'A was a man, take him for all in all,
I shall not look upon his like again.

Hor. My lord, I think I saw him
    yesternight.

Ham. Saw, who?   190

Hor. My lord, the King your father.

Ham.   The King my father?

Hor. Season your admiration for a while
With an attent ear, till I may deliver,
Upon the witness of these gentlemen,
This marvel to you.

Ham.   For God's love let me hear! 195

Hor. Two nights together had these
    gentlemen,
Marcellus and Barnardo, on their watch,
In the dead waste and middle of the night,
Been thus encount'red: a figure like your father,
Armed at point exactly, cap-a-pe,   200
Appears before them, and with solemn march
Goes slow and stately by them; thrice he walk'd
By their oppress'd and fear-surprised eyes
Within his truncheon's length, whilst they,
    distill'd
Almost to jelly with the act of fear,   205
Stand dumb and speak not to him. This to me
In dreadful secrecy impart they did,
And I with them the third night kept the watch,
Where, as they had delivered, both in time,
Form of the thing, each word made true and
    good,   210
The apparition comes. I knew your father,
These hands are not more like.

Ham.   But where was this?

Mar. My lord, upon the platform where
    we watch.

Ham. Did you not speak to it?

Hor.   My lord, I
    did,
But answer made it none. Yet once
    methought   215
It lifted up its head and did address
Itself to motion like as it would speak;
But even then the morning cock crew loud,
And at the sound it shrunk in haste away
And vanish'd from our sight.

Ham.   'Tis very strange. 220

Hor. As I do live, my honor'd lord, 'tis
    true,
And we did think it writ down in our duty
To let you know of it.

Ham. Indeed, [indeed,] sirs. But this
    troubles me.
Hold you the watch to-night?

[*Mar., Bar.*]   We do, my lord. 225

Ham. Arm'd, say you?

[*Mar., Bar.*] Arm'd, my lord.

Ham. From top to toe?

[*Mar., Bar.*]   My lord, from head to foot.

Ham. Then saw you not his face.

Hor. O yes, my lord, he wore his beaver
    up.   230

Ham. What, loook'd he frowningly?

Hor.   A countenance more
In sorrow than in anger.

Ham.   Pale, or red?

Hor. Nay, very pale.

Ham.   And fix'd his eyes upon you?

Hor. Most constantly.

Ham.   I would I had been there.

Hor. It would have much amaz'd you.   235

Ham. Very like, [very like]. Stay'd it long?

Hor. While one with moderate haste might
    tell a hundreth.

Both [*Mar., Bar.*]. Longer, longer.

Hor. Not when I saw't.

Ham.   His beard was grisl'd, no?

Hor. It was, as I have seen it in his life,   240
A sable silver'd.

Ham.   I will watch to-night,
Perchance 'twill walk again.

Hor.   I warr'nt it will.

Ham. If it assume my noble father's person,
I'll speak to it though hell itself should gape
And bid me hold my peace. I pray you all,   245
If you have hitherto conceal'd this sight,
Let it be tenable in your silence still,
And whatsomever else shall hap to-night,
Give it an understanding but no tongue.
I will requite your loves. So fare you well.   250
Upon the platform 'twixt aleven and twelf
I'll visit you.

All.   Our duty to your honor.

Ham. Your loves, as mine to you; farewell.

                    Exeunt [*all but Hamlet*].
My father's spirit—in arms! All is not well, 254
I doubt some foul play. Would the night
    were come!
Till then sit still, my soul. [Foul] deeds will rise,
Though all the earth o'erwhelm them, to
    men's eyes.

                            Exit.

[SCENE III]

Enter LAERTES *and* OPHELIA, *his sister.*

Laer. My necessaries are inbark'd.
    Farewell.
And, sister, as the winds give benefit
And convey [is] assistant, do not sleep,
But let me hear from you.
    Oph.   Do you doubt that?
    Laer. For Hamlet, and the trifling of his
    favor,   5
Hold it a fashion and a toy in blood,
A violet in the youth of primy nature,
Forward, not permanent, sweet, not lasting,
The perfume and suppliance of a minute—
No more.
    Oph. No more but so?
    Laer.   Think it no more: 10
For nature crescent does not grow alone
In thews and [bulk], but as this temple waxes,
The inward service of the mind and soul
Grows wide withal. Perhaps he loves you now,
And now no soil nor cautel doth besmirch   15
The virtue of his will, but you must fear,
His greatness weigh'd, his will is not his own,
[For he himself is subject to his birth:]
He may not, as unvalued persons do,,
Carve for himself, for on his choice depends   20
The safety and health of this whole state,
And therefore must his choice be circumscrib'd
Unto the voice and yielding of that body
Whereof he is the head. Then if he says he
    loves you.
It fits your wisdom so far to believe it   25
As he in his particular act and place
May give his saying deed, which is no further
Than the main voice of Denmark goes withal.
Then weigh what loss your honor may sustain
If with too credent ear you list his songs,   30
Or lose your heart, or your chaste treasure open
To his unmast'red importunity.
Fear it, Ophelia, fear it, my dear sister,
And keep you in the rear of your affection,
Out of the shot and danger of desire.   35
The chariest maid is prodigal enough
If she unmask her beauty to the moon.
Virtue itself scapes not calumnious strokes.
The canker galls the infants of the spring
Too oft before their buttons be disclos'd,   40
And in the morn and liquid dew of youth
Contagious blastments are most imminent.
Be wary then, best safety lies in fear:
Youth to itself rebels, though none else near.

    Oph. I shall the effect of this good lesson
    keep   45
As watchman to my heart. But, good my brother,
Do not, as some ungracious pastors do,
Show me the steep and thorny way to heaven,
Whiles, [like] a puff'd and reckless libertine,
Himself the primrose path of dalliance
    treads,   50
And reaks not his own rede.
    Laer.   O, fear me not.

Enter POLONIUS.

I stay too long—but here my father comes.
A double blessing is a double grace,
Occasion smiles upon a second leave.   54
    Pol. Yet here, Laertes? Aboard, aboard, for
    shame!
The wind sits in the shoulder of your sail,
And you are stay'd for. There—[*laying his
    hand on Laertes' head*] my blessing with thee!
And these few precepts in thy memory
Look thou character. Give thy thoughts no
    tongue,
Nor any unproportion'd thought his act.   60
Be thou familiar, but by no means vulgar:
Those friends thou hast, and their adoption tried,
Grapple them unto thy soul with hoops of steel,
But do not dull thy palm with entertainment
Of each new-hatch'd, unfledg'd courage.
    Beware   65
Of entrance to a quarrel, but being in,
Bear't that th' opposed may beware of thee.
Give every man thy ear, but few thy voice,
Take each man's censure, but reserve thy
    judgment.
Costly thy habit as thy purse can buy,   70
But not express'd in fancy, rich, not gaudy,
For the apparel oft proclaims the man,
And they in France of the best rank and station
[Are] of a most select and generous chief in that.
Neither a borrower nor a lender [be],   75
For [loan] oft loses both itself and friend,
And borrowing dulleth [th'] edge of husbandry.
This above all: to thine own self be true
And it must follow, as the night the day
Thou canst not then be false to any man.   80
Farewell, my blessing season this in thee!
    Laer. Most humbly do I take my leave, my
    lord.
    Pol. The time invests you, go, your
    servants tend.
    Laer. Farewell, Ophelia, and remember well
What I have said to you.
    Oph.   'Tis in my memory lock'd.
And you yourself shall keep the key of it.   86

Laer. Farewell.   *Exit Laertes.*
Pol. What is't, Ophelia, he hath said to you?
Oph. So please you, something touching
    the Lord Hamlet.
Pol. Marry, well bethought.   90
'Tis told me, he hath very oft of late
Given private time to you, and you yourself
Have of your audience been most free and
    bounteous.
If it be so—as so 'tis put on me,
And that in way of caution—I must tell you,   95
You do not understand yourself so clearly
As it behooves my daughter and your honor.
What is between you? Give me up the truth.
    Oph. He hath, my lord, of late made many
      tenders
Of his affection to me.   100
    Pol. Affection, puh! You speak like a green
      girl,
Unsifted in such perilous circumstance.
Do you believe his tenders, as you call them?
    Oph. I do not know, my lord, what I
      should think.
    Pol. Marry, I will teach you: think yourself
      a baby   105
That you have ta'en these tenders for true pay,
Which are not sterling. Tender yourself more
    dearly,
Or (not to crack the wind of the poor phrase,
[Wringing] it thus) you'll tender me a fool.
    Oph. My lord, he hath importun'd me
      with love
In honorable fashion.   111
    Pol. Ay, fashion you may call it. Go to, go to.
    Oph. And hath given countenance to his
      speech, my lord,
With almost all the holy vows of heaven.
    Pol. Ay, springes to catch woodcocks. I do
      know,
When the blood burns, how prodigal the soul 116
Lends the tongue vows. These blazes, daughter,
Giving more light than heat, extinct in both
Even in their promise, as it is a-making,
You must not take for fire. From this time   120
Be something scanter of your maiden presence,
Set your entreatments at a higher rate
Than a command to parle. For Lord Hamlet,
Believe so much in him, that he is young,
And with a larger teder may he walk   125
Than may be given you. In few, Ophelia,
Do not believe his vows, for they are brokers,
Not of that dye which their investments show,
But mere [implorators] of unholy suits,
Breathing like sanctified and pious bonds,   130
The better to [beguile]. This is in all:
I would not, in plain terms, from this time forth

Have you so slander any moment leisure
As to give words or talk with the Lord Hamlet.
Look to't, I charge you. Come your ways.   135
    Oph. I shall obey, my lord.   *Exeunt.*

[SCENE IV]

Enter HAMLET, HORATIO, *and* MARCEL-
LUS.

Ham. The air bites shrowdly, it is very cold.
Hor. It is [a] nipping and an eager air.
Ham. What hour now?
Hor.   I think it lacks of twelf.
Mar. No, it is strook.
Hor. Indeed? I heard it not. It then draws
    near the season   5
Wherein the spirit held his wont to walk.
    A flourish of trumpets, and two pieces goes off
    [within].
What does this mean, my lord?
    Ham. The King doth wake to-night and
      takes his rouse,
Keeps wassail, and the swaggering
    up-spring reels;
And as he drains his draughts of Rhenish
    down,   10
The kettledrum and trumpet thus bray out
The triumph of his pledge.
    Hor.   Is it a custom?
    Ham. Ay, marry, is't,
But to my mind, though I am native here
And to the manner born, it is a custom   15
More honor'd in the breach than the observance.
This heavy-headed revel east and west
Makes us traduc'd and tax'd of other nations.
They clip us drunkards, and with swinish phrase
Soil our addition, and indeed it takes   20
From our achievements, though perform'd
    at height,
The pith and marrow of our attribute.
So, oft it chances in particular men,
That for some vicious mole of nature in them,
As in their birth, wherein they are not guilty   25
(Since nature cannot choose his origin),
By their overgrowth of some complexion
Oft breaking down the pales and forts of reason,
Or by some habit, that too much o'er-leavens
The form of plausive manners—that these
    men,   30
Carrying, I say, the stamp of one defect,
Being nature's livery, or fortune's star,
His virtues else, be they as pure as grace,

As infinite as man may undergo,
Shall in the general censure take corruption   35
From that particular fault: the dram of (ev'l)
Doth all the noble substance of a doubt
To his own scandal.

Enter GHOST.

  Hor.   Look, my lord, it comes!
  Ham. Angels and ministers of grace
        defend us!
Be thou a spirit of health, or goblin damn'd,   40
Bring with thee airs from heaven, or blasts
        from hell,
Be thy intents wicked, or charitable,
Thou com'st in such a questionable shape
That I will speak to thee. I'll call thee Hamlet,
King, father, royal Dane. O, answer me!   45
Let me not burst in ignorance, but tell
Why thy canoniz'd bones, hearsed in death,
Have burst their cerements; why the sepulchre,
Wherein we saw thee quietly [inurn'd,]
Hath op'd his ponderous and marble jaws   50
To cast thee up again. What may this mean,
That thou, dead corse, again in complete steel
Revisits thus the glimpses of the moon,
Making night hideous, and we fools of nature
So horridly to shake our disposition   55
With thoughts beyond the reaches of our souls?
Say why is this? wherefore? what should we do?
                [Ghost] beckons [Hamlet].
  Hor. It beckons you to go away with it,
As if it some impartment did desire
To you alone.
  Mar.   Look with what courteous action   60
It waves you to a more removed ground,
But do not go with it.
  Hor.   No, by no means.
  Ham. It will not speak, then I will follow it.
  Hor. Do not, my lord.
  Ham.   Why, what should be the fear?
I do not set my life at a pin's fee,   65
And for my soul, what can it do to that,
Being a thing immortal as itself?
It waves me forth again, I'll follow it.
  Hor. What if it tempt you toward the
        flood, my lord,
Or to the dreadful summit of the cliff   70
That beetles o'er his base into the sea,
And there assume some other horrible form
Which might deprive your sovereignty of reason,
And draw you into madness? Think of it.
The very place puts toys of desperation,   75
Without more motive, into every brain
That looks so many fadoms to the sea
And hears it roar beneath.

  Ham.   It waves me still.—
Go on, I'll follow thee.
  Mar. You shall not go, my lord.
  Ham.   Hold off your hands.   80
  Hor. Be rul'd, you shall not go.
  Ham.   My fate cries out,
And makes each petty artere in this body
As hardy as the Nemean lion's nerve.
Still am I call'd. Unhand me, gentlemen.
By heaven, I'll make a ghost of him that lets
        me!   85
I say away!—Go on, I'll follow thee.
                Exeunt Ghost and Hamlet.
  Hor. He waxes desperate with [imagination].
  Mar. Let's follow. 'Tis not fit thus to obey
        him.
  Hor. Have after. To what issue will this
        come?
  Mar. Something is rotten in the state of
        Denmark.
  Hor. Heaven will direct it.
  Mar.   Nay, let's follow him. *Exeunt.*   91

[SCENE V]

Enter GHOST *and* HAMLET.

  Ham. Whither wilt thou lead me? Speak,
        I'll go no further.
  Ghost. Mark me.
  Ham.   I will.
  Ghost.   My hour is almost come
When I to sulphurous and tormenting flames
Must render up myself.
  Ham.   Alas, poor ghost!
  Ghost. Pity me not, but lend thy serious
        hearing   5
To what I shall unfold.
  Ham.   Speak, I am bound to hear.
  Ghost. So art thou to revenge, when thou
        shalt hear.
  Ham. What?
  Ghost. I am thy father's spirit,
Doom'd for a certain term to walk the night,   10
And for the day confin'd to fast in fires,
Till the foul crimes done in my days of nature
Are burnt and purg'd away. But that I am forbid
To tell the secrets of my prison-house,
I could a tale unfold whose lightest word   15
Would harrow up thy soul, freeze thy young
        blood,
Make thy two eyes like stars start from their
        spheres,

Thy knotted and combined locks to part,
And each particular hair to stand an end,
Like quills upon the fearful porpentine.   20
But this eternal blazon must not be
To ears of flesh and blood. List, list, O, list!
If thou didst ever thy dear father love—
   Ham. O God!
   Ghost. Revenge his foul and most
     unnatural murther.   25
   Ham. Murther!
   Ghost. Murther most foul, as in the best it is,
But this most foul, strange, and unnatural.
   Ham. Haste me to know't, that I with
     wings as swift
As meditation, or the thoughts of love,   30
May sweep to my revenge.
   Ghost.   I find thee apt,
And duller shouldst thou be than the fat weed
That roots itself in ease on Lethe wharf,
Wouldst thou not stir in this. Now, Hamlet, hear:
'Tis given out that sleeping in my orchard,   35
A serpent stung me, so the whole ear of Denmark
Is by a forged process of my death
Rankly abus'd; but know, thou noble youth,
The serpent that did sting thy father's life
Now wears his crown.
   Ham.   O my prophetic soul!   40
My uncle?
   Ghost. Ay, that incestuous, that adulterate
     beast,
With witchcraft of his wits, with traitorous
     gifts—
O wicked wit and gifts that have the power
So to seduce!—won to his shameful lust   45
The will of my most seeming virtuous queen.
O Hamlet what [a] falling-off was there
From me, whose love was of that dignity
That it went hand in hand even with the vow
I made to her in marriage, and to decline   50
Upon a wretch whose natural gifts were poor
To those of mine!
But virtue, as it never will be moved,
Though lewdness court it in a shape of heaven,
So [lust], though to a radiant angel link'd,   55
Will [sate] itself in a celestial bed
And prey on garbage.
But soft, methinks I scent the morning air,
Brief let me be. Sleeping within my orchard,
My custom always of the afternoon,   60
Upon my secure hour thy uncle stole,
With juice of cursed hebona in a vial,
And in the porches of my ears did pour
The leprous distillment, whose effect
Holds such an enmity with blood of man   65
That swift as quicksilver it courses through
The natural gates and alleys of the body,

And with a sudden vigor it doth [posset]
And curd, like eager droppings into milk,
The thin and wholesome blood. So did it
     mine,   70
And a most instant tetter bark'd about,
Most lazar-like, with vile and loathsome crust
All my smooth body.
Thus was I, sleeping, by a brother's hand
Of life, of crown, of queen, at once
     dispatch'd,   75
Cut off even in the blossoms of my sin,
Unhous'led, disappointed, unanel'd,
No reck'ning made, but sent to my account
With all my imperfections on my head.
O, horrible, O, horrible, most horrible!   80
If thou hast nature in thee, bear it not,
Let not the royal bed of Denmark be
A couch for luxury and damned incest.
But howsomever thou pursues this act,
Taint not thy mind, nor let thy soul contrive   85
Against thy mother aught. Leave her to heaven,
And to those thorns that in her bosom lodge
To prick and sting her. Fare thee well at once!
The glow-worm shows the matin to be near,
And gins to pale his uneffectual fire.   90
Adieu, adieu, adieu! remember me.   [*Exit.*]
   Ham. O all you host of heaven! O earth!
     What else?
And shall I couple hell? O fie, hold, hold, my
     heart,
And you my sinews, grow not instant old,
But bear me [stiffly] up. Remember thee!   95
Ay, thou poor ghost, whiles memory holds a seat
In this distracted globe. Remember thee!
Yea, from the table of my memory
I'll wipe away all trivial fond records,
All saws of books, all forms, all pressures
     past   100
That youth and observation copied there,
And thy commandement all alone shall live
Within the book and volume of my brain,
Unmix'd with baser matter. Yes, by heaven!
O most pernicious woman!   105
O villain, villain, smiling, damned villain!
My tables—meet it is I set it down
That one may smile, and smile, and be a villain!
At least I am sure it may be so in Denmark.
          [*He writes.*]
So, uncle, there you are. Now to my word: 110
It is "Adieu, adieu! remember me."
I have sworn't.
   Hor. [*Within.*] My lord, my lord!
   Mar. [*Within.*]   Lord Hamlet!

Enter HORATIO *and* MARCELLUS.

Hor.   Heavens secure him!

Ham. So be it!

Mar. Illo, ho, ho, my lord!   115

Ham. Hillo, ho, ho, boy! Come, [bird,] come.

Mar. How is't, my noble lord?

Hor.   What news, my lord?

Ham. O, wonderful!

Hor. Good my lord, tell it.

Ham.   No, you will reveal it.

Hor. Not I, my lord, by heaven.

Mar.   Nor I, my lord.

Ham. How say you then, would heart of
man once think it?—   121

But you'll be secret?

Both [*Hor., Mar.*].   Ay, by heaven, [my lord].

Ham. There's never a villain dwelling in
all Denmark

But he's an arrant knave.

Hor. There needs no ghost, my lord, come
from the grave   125

To tell us this,

Ham.   Why, right, you are in the right,

And so, without more circumstance at all,

I hold it fit that we shake hands and part,

You, as your business and desire shall point you,

For every man hath business and desire,   130

Such as it is, and for my own poor part,

I will go pray.

Hor. These are but wild and whirling
words, my lord.

Ham. I am sorry they offend you, heartily,

Yes, faith, heartily.

Hor.   There's no offense, my lord.   135

Ham. Yes, by Saint Patrick, but there is,
Horatio,

And much offense too. Touching this vision here,

It is an honest ghost, that let me tell you.

For your desire to know what is between us,

O'ermaster't as you may. And now, good friends,

As you are friends, scholars, and soldiers,   141

Give me one poor request.

Hor. What is't, my lord, we will.

Ham. Never make known what you have
seen tonight.

Both [*Hor., Mar.*]. My lord, we will not.

Ham.   Nay, but swear't.

Hor.   In faith,

My Lord, not I.

Hor.   Nor I, my lord, in faith.   146

Ham. Upon my sword.,

Mar.   We have sworn, my lord, already.

Ham. Indeed, upon my sword, indeed.

                    Ghost cries under the stage

Ghost. Swear.

Ham. Ha, ha, boy, say'st thou so? Art thou
there truepenny?   150

Come on, you hear this fellow in the cellarage,

Consent to swear.

Hor.   Propose the oath, my lord.

Ham. Never to speak of this that you have
seen

Swear by my sword.

Ghost. [*Beneath.*] Swear.   155

Ham. Hic et ubique? Then we'll shift our
ground.

Come hither, gentlemen,

And lay your, hands again upon my sword.

Swear by my sword

Never to speak of this that you have heard.   160

Ghost. [*Beneath.*] Swear by his sword.

Ham. Well said, old mole, canst work i' th'
earth so fast?

A worthy pioner! Once more remove, good
friends.

Hor. O day and night, but this is
wondrous strange!   164

Ham. And therefore as a stranger give it
welcome.

There are more things in heaven and earth,
Horatio,

Than are dreamt of in your philosophy.

But come—

Here, as before, never, so help you mercy,

How strange or odd some'er I bear myself— 170

As I perchance hereafter shall think meet

To put an antic disposition on—

That you, at such times seeing me, never shall,

With arms encumbered thus, or this headshake,

Or by pronouncing of some doubtful phrase,175

As "Well well, we know," or "We could, and
if we would,"

Or "If we list to speak," or "There be, and if
they might,"

Or such ambiguous giving out, to note

That you know aught of me—this do swear,

So grace and mercy at your most need help
you.   180

Ghost. [*Beneath.*] Swear. [*They swear.*]

Ham. Rest, rest, perturbed spirit! So,
gentlemen,

With all my love I do commend me to you,

And what so poor a man as Hamlet is

May do t' express his love and friending to
you,   185

God willing, shall not lack. Let us go in together,

And still your fingers on your lips, I pray.

The time is out of joint—O cursed spite,

That ever I was born to set it right!

Nay, come, let's go together.   *Exeunt.*   190

[ACT II, SCENE I]

*Enter old POLONIUS with his man [REY-
NALDO].*

Pol. Give him this money and these notes,
    Reynaldo.
Rey. I will, my lord.
Pol. You shall do marvell's wisely, good
    Reynaldo,
Before you visit him to make inquire
Of his behavior.
Rey.   My lord, I did intend it.   5
Pol. Marry, well said, very well said. Look
    you, sir,
Inquire me first what Danskers are in Paris,
And how, and who, what means, and where
    they keep,
What company, at what expense; and finding
By this encompassment and drift of question 10
That they do know my son, come you more
    nearer
Than your particular demands will touch it.
Take you as 'twere some distant knowledge
    of him,
As thus, "I know his father and his friends,
And in part him." Do you mark this,
    Reynaldo?   15
Rey. Ay, very well, my lord.
Pol. "And in part him—but," you may
    say, "not well.
But if't be he I mean, he's very wild,
Addicted so and so," and there put on him
What forgeries you please: marry, none so
    rank   20
As may dishonor him, take heed of that,
But, sir, such wanton, wild, and usual slips
As are companions noted and most known
To youth and liberty.
Rey.   As gaming, my lord.
Pol. Ay, or drinking, fencing, swearing,
    quarrelling,   25
Drabbing—you may go so far.
Rey. My lord, that would dishonor him.
Pol. Faith, as you may season it in the
    charge:
You must not put another scandal on him,
That he is open to incontinency—   30
That's not my meaning. But breathe his
    faults so quaintly
That they may seem the taints of liberty,
The flash and outbreak of a fiery mind,
A savageness in unreclaimed blood,
Of general assault.

Rey.   But, my good lord—   35
Pol. Wherefore should you do this?
Rey.   Ay, my lord,
I would know that.
Pol.   Marry, sir, here's my drift,
And I believe it is a fetch of wit:
You laying these slight sallies on my son,
As 'twere a thing a little soil'd [wi' th']
    working,   40
Mark you,
Your party in converse, him you would sound,
Having ever seen in the prenominate crimes
The youth you breathe of guilty, be assur'd
He closes with you in this consequence: 45
"Good sir," or so, or "friend," or "gentleman,"
According to the phrase or the addition
Of man and country.
Rey.   Very good, my lord.
Pol. And then, sir, does 'a this—'a
    does—what was I about to say?
By the mass, I was about to say something.   50
Where did I leave?
Rey.   At "closes in the consequence."
Pol. At "closes in the consequence," ay,
    marry.
He closes thus: "I know the gentleman.
I saw him yesterday, or th' other day,
Or then, or then, with such or such, and as
    you say,   55
There was 'a gaming, there o'ertook in 's rouse,
There falling out at tennis"; or, perchance,
"I saw him enter such a house of sale,"
Videlicet, a brothel, or so forth. See you now,
Your bait of falsehood take this carp of truth, 60
And thus do we of wisdom and of reach,
With windlasses and with assays of bias,
By indirections find directions out;
So by my former lecture and advice
Shall you my son. You have me, have you
    not?   65
Rey. My lord, I have.
Pol.   God buy ye, fare ye well.
Rey. Good my lord.
Pol. Observe his inclination in yourself.
Rey. I shall, my lord.
Pol. And let him ply his music.
Rey.   Well, my lord. 70
Pol. Farewell.   *Exit Reynaldo.*

Enter OPHELIA.

How now, Ophelia, what's the matter?
Oph. O my lord, my lord, I have been, so
    affrighted!
Pol. With what, i' th' name of God?
Oph. My lord, as I was sewing in my closet,

Lord Hamlet with his doublet all unbrac'd,   75
No hat upon his head is stockings fouled,
Ungart'red, and down-gyved to his ankle,
Pale as his shirt, his knees knocking each other,
And with a look so piteous in purport
As if he had been loosed out of hell   80
To speak of horrors—he comes before me.
    Pol. Mad for thy love?
    Oph.   My lord, I do not know,
But truly I do fear it.
    Pol.   What said he?
    Oph. He took me by the wrist, and held
    me hard,
Then goes he to the length of all his arm,   85
And with his other hand thus o'er his brow,
He falls to such perusal of my face
As 'a would draw it. Long stay'd he so.
At last, a little shaking of mine arm,
And thrice his head thus waving up and
    down,   90
He rais'd a sigh so piteous and profound
As it did seem to shatter all his bulk
And end his being. That done, he lets me go,
And with his head over his shoulder turn'd,
He seem'd to find his way without his eyes,   95
For out a' doors he went without their helps,
And to the last bended their light on me.
    Pol. Come, go with me. I will go seek the
    King.
This is the very ecstasy of love,
Whose violent property fordoes itself,   100
And leads the will to desperate undertakings
As oft as any passions under heaven
That does afflict our natures. I am sorry—
What, have you given him any hard words
    of late?
    Oph. No, my good lord, but as you did
    command
I did repel his letters, and denied   106
His access to me.
    Pol.   That hath made him mad.
I am sorry that with better heed and judgment
I had not coted him. I fear'd he did but trifle
And meant to wrack thee, but beshrew my
    jealousy!
By heaven, it is as proper to our age   111
To cast beyond ourselves in our opinions,
As it is common for the younger sort
To lack discretion. Come, go we to the King.
This must be known, which, being kept
    close, might move   115
More grief to hide, than hate to utter love.
Come.   *Exeunt.*

[SCENE II]

Flourish. Enter KING *and* QUEEN, ROSEN-
CRANTZ *and* GUILDENSTERN *[Cum aliis].*

    King. Welcome, dear Rosencrantz and
    Guildenstern!
Moreover that we much did long to see you,
The need we have to use you did provoke
Our hasty sending. Something have you heard
Of Hamlet's transformation; so call it,   5
Sith nor th' exterior nor the inward man
Resembles that it was. What it should be,
More than his father's death, that thus hath
    put him
So much from th' understanding of himself,
I cannot dream of. I entreat you both   10
That, being of so young days brought up
    with him,
And sith so neighbored to his youth and havior,
That you voutsafe your rest here in our court
Some little time, so by your companies
To draw him on to pleasures, and to gather   15
So much as from occasion you may glean,
Whether aught to us unknown afflicts him thus,
That, open'd, lies within our remedy.
    Queen. Good gentlemen, he hath much
    talk'd of you,
And sure I am two men there is not living   20
To whom he more adheres. If it will please you
To show us so much gentry and good will
As to expend your time with us a while
For the supply and profit of our hope,
Your visitation shall receive such thanks   25
As fits a king's remembrance.
    Ros.   Both your Majesties
Might, by the sovereign power you have of us,
Put your dread pleasures more into command
Than to entreaty.
    Guil.   But we both obey,
And here give up ourselves, in the full bent,   30
To lay our service freely at your feet,
To be commanded.
    King. Thanks, Rosencrantz and gentle
    Guildenstern.
    Queen. Thanks, Guildenstern and gentle
    Rosencrantz.
And I beseech you instantly to visit   35
My too much changed son. Go some of you
And bring these gentlemen where Hamlet is.
    Guil. Heavens make our presence and our
    practices
Pleasant and helpful to him!
    Queen.   Ay, amen!

*Exeunt Rosencrantz and Guildenstern [with
   some Attendants].*

Enter POLONIUS.

Pol. Th'embassadors from Norway, my
   good lord,
Are joyfully return'd.   41
   King. Thou still hast been the father of
      good news.
   Pol. Have I my lord? I assurc my good liege
I hold my duty as I hold my soul,
Both to my God and to my gracious king;   45
And I do think, or else this brain of mine
Hunts not the trail of policy so sure
As it hath us'd to do, that I have found
The very cause of Hamlet's lunacy.
   King. O, speak of that, that do I long to
      hear.   50
   Pol. Give first admittance to th' embassadors;
My news shall be the fruit to that great feast.
   King. Thyself do grace to them, and bring
      them in.
                                    [*Exit Polonius.*]
He tells me, my dear Gertrude, he hath found
The head and source of all your son's
   distemper.   55
   Queen. I doubt it is no other but the main,
His father's death and our [o'erhasty] marriage.
   Enter [POLONIUS *with* VOLTEMAND *and*
      CORNELIUS, *the*] *Embassadors.*
   King. Well, we shall sift him.—Welcome,
      my good friends!
Say, Voltemand, what from our brother Norway?
   Vol. Most fair return of greetings and
      desires.   60
Upon our first, he sent out to suppress
His nephew's levies which to him appear'd
To be a preparation 'gainst the Polack;
But better look'd into, he truly found
It was against your Highness. Whereat
   griev'd,   65
That so his sickness, age, and impotence
Was falsely borne in hand, sends out arrests
On Fortinbras, which he, in brief, obeys,
Receives rebuke from Norway, and in fine,
Makes vow before his uncle never more   70
To give th' assay of arms against your Majesty.
Whereon old Norway, overcome with joy,
Gives him threescore thousand crowns in
   annual fee,
And his commission to employ those soldiers,
So levied, as before, against the Polack,   75
With an entreaty, herein further shown,
                                    [*Giving a paper.*]
That it might please you to give quiet pass

Through your dominions for this enterprise,
On such regards of safety and allowance
As therein are set down.
   King.   It likes us well,   80
And at our more considered time we'll read,
Answer, and think upon this business.
Mean time, we thank you for your well-took
   labor.
Go to your rest, at night we'll feast together.
Most welcome home!
                  Exeunt Embassadors [and Attendants].
   Pol.   This business is well ended.   85
My liege, and madam, to expostulate
What majesty should be, what duty is,
Why day is day, night night, and time is time,
Were nothing but to waste night, day, and time;
Therefore, [since] brevity is the soul of wit,   90
And tediousness the limbs and outward
   flourishes,
I will be brief. Your noble son is mad:
Mad call I it, for to define true madness,
What is't but to be nothing else but mad?
But let that go.
   Queen.   More matter with less art.   95
   Pol. Madam, I swear I use no art at all.
That he's mad, 'tis true, 'tis true 'tis pity,
And pity 'tis 'tis true—a foolish figure,
But farewell it, for I will use no art.
Mad let us grant him then, and now remains 100
That we find out the cause of this effect,
Or rather say, the cause of this defect,
For this effect defective comes by cause:
Thus it remains, and the remainder thus.
Perpend.   105
I have a daughter—have while she is mine—
Who in her duty and obedience, mark,
Hath given me this. Now gather, and surmise.
                  [*Reads the salutation of the letter.*]
"To the celestial and my soul's idol, the most
   beautified Ophelia"—   110
That's an ill phrase, a vile phrase,
   "beautified" is a vile phrase. But you shall
   hear. Thus:
"In her excellent white bosom, these, etc."
   Queen. Came this from Hamlet to her?
   Pol. Good madam, stay awhile. I will be
      faithful.
                                    [*Reads the*] *letter.*
   "Doubt thou the stars are fire,   116
      Doubt that the sun doth move,
      Doubt truth to be a liar,
      But never doubt I love.
O dear Ophelia, I am ill at these numbers. I
   have not
art to reckon my groans, but that I love thee
   best, O

most best, believe it. Adieu.   122
    Thine evermore, most dear lady,
      whilst this machine is to him, Hamlet."
This in obedience hath my daughter shown
    me,   125
And more [above], hath his solicitings,
As they fell out by time, by means, and place,
All given to mine ear.
    King.   But how hath she
Receiv'd his love?
    Pol.   What do you think of me?
    King. As of a man faithful and honorable. 130
    Pol. I would fain prove so. But what might
      you think,
When I had seen this hot love on the wing—
As I perceiv'd it (I must tell you that)
Before my daughter told me—what might you,
Or my dear Majesty your queen here, think, 135
If I had play'd the desk or table-book,
Or given my heart a [winking,] mute and dumb,
Or look'd upon this love with idle sight,
What might you think? No, I went round to
    work,
And my young mistress thus I did bespeak: 140
"Lord Hamlet is a prince out of thy star;
This must not be"; and then I prescripts
    gave her,
That she should lock herself from [his] resort,
Admit no messengers, receive no tokens.
Which done, she took the fruits of my advice; 145
And he repell'd, a short tale to make,
Fell into a sadness, then into a fast,
Thence to a watch, thence into a weakness,
Thence to [a] lightness, and by this declension,
Into the madness wherein now he raves,   150
And all we mourn for.
    King.   Do you think ['tis] this?
    Queen. It may be, very like.
    Pol. Hath there been such a time—I would
      fain know that—
That I have positively said, "'Tis so,"
When it prov'd otherwise?
    King.   Not that I know. 155
    Pol. [*Points to his head and shoulder.*] Take
      this from this, if this be otherwise.
If circumstances lead me, I will find
Where truth is hid, though it were hid indeed
Within the centre.
    King.   How may we try it further?
    Pol. You know sometimes he walks for
      hours together   160
Here in the lobby.
    Queen.   So he does indeed.
    Pol. At such a time I'll loose my daughter
      to him.
Be you and I behind an arras then,

Mark the encounter: if he love her not,
And be not from his reason fall'n thereon,   165
Let me be no assistant for a state,
But keep a farm and carters.
    King.   We will try it.
    Enter HAMLET [*reading on a book*].
    Queen. But look where sadly the poor
      wretch comes reading.
    Pol. Away, I do beseech you, both away.
I'll board him presently.   *Exeunt King and Queen.*
                O, give me leave,   170
How does my good Lord Hamlet?
    Ham. Well, God-a-mercy.
    Pol. Do you know me, my lord?
    Ham. Excellent well, you are a fishmonger.
    Pol. Not I, my lord.   175
    Ham. Then I would you were so honest a
      man.
    Pol. Honest, my lord?
    Ham. Ay, sir, to be honest, as this world
      goes, is to be one man pick'd out of ten
      thousand.
    Pol. That's very true, my lord   180
    Ham. For if the sun breed maggots in a
      dead dog,
being a good kissing carrion—Have you a
daughter?
    Pol. I have, my lord.
    Ham. Let her not walk i' th' sun. Conception is
a blessing, but as your daughter may conceive,
friend, look to't.   186
    Pol. [*Aside.*] How say you by that? still harping
on my daughter. Yet he knew me not at first, 'a
said I was a fishmonger. 'A is far gone. And truly
in my youth I suff'red much extremity for love—
very near this. I'll speak to him again.—What do
you read, my lord?   191
    Ham. Words, words, words.
    Pol. What is the matter, my lord?
    Ham. Between who?
    Pol. I mean, the matter that you read, my
      lord.   195
    Ham. Slanders, sir; for the satirical rogue says
here that old men have grey beards, that their
faces are wrinkled, their eyes purging thick amber and plum-tree gum, and that they have a
plentiful lack of wit, together with most weak
hams; all which, sir, though I most powerfully
and potently believe, yet I hold it nor honesty to
have it thus set down, for yourself, sir, shall grow
old as I am, if like a crab you could go backward.
    Pol. [*Aside.*] Though this be madness, yet there
is method in't.—Will you walk out of the air, my
lord?
    Ham. Into my grave.   207

Pol. Indeed that's out of the air. [*Aside.*] How pregnant sometimes his replies are! a happiness that often madness hits on, which reason and [sanity] could not so prosperously be deliver'd of. I will leave him, [and suddenly contrive the means of meeting between him] and my daughter.—My lord, I will take my leave of you. 214

Ham. You cannot take from me any thing that I will not more willingly part withal—except my life, except my life, except my life.

Pol. Fare you well, my lord.

Ham. These tedious old fools!

Enter GUILDENSTERN *and* ROSENCRANTZ.

Pol. You go to seek the Lord Hamlet, there he is.

Ros. [*To Polonius.*] God save you, sir! 221
[*Exit Polonius.*]

Guil. My honor'd lord!

Ros. My most dear lord!

Ham. My [excellent] good friends! How dost thou, Guildenstern? Ah, Rosencrantz! Good lads, how do you both? 226

Ros. As the indifferent children of the earth.

Guil. Happy, in that we are not [over-]happy, on Fortune's [cap] we are not the very button.

Ham. Nor the soles of her shoe? 230

Ros. Neither, my lord.

Ham. Then you live about her waist, or in the middle of her favors?

Guil. Faith, her privates we.

Ham. In the secret parts of Fortune? O, most true, she is a strumpet. What news? 236

Ros. None, my lord, but the world's grown honest.

Ham. Then is doomsday near. But your news is not true. Let me question more in particular. What have you, my good friends, deserv'd at the hands of Fortune, that she sends you to prison hither?
241

Guil. Prison, my lord?

Ham. Denmark's a prison.

Ros. Then is the world one. 244

Ham. A goodly one, in which there are many confines, wards, and dungeons, Denmark being one o' th' worst.

Ros. We think not so, my lord.

Ham. Why then 'tis none to you; for there is nothing either good or bad, but thinking makes it so. To me it is a prison. 251

Ros. Why then your ambition makes it one. 'Tis too narrow for your mind.

Ham. O God, I could be bounded in a nutshell, and count myself a king of infinite space—were it not that I have bad dreams. 256

Guil. Which dreams indeed are ambition, for the very substance of the ambitious is merely the shadow of a dream.

Ham. A dream itself is but a shadow. 260

Ros. Truly, and I hold ambition of so airy and light a quality that it is but a shadow's shadow.

Ham. Then are our beggars bodies, and our monarchs and outstretch'd heroes the beggars' shadows. Shall we to th' court? for, by my fay, I cannot reason.

Both [*Ros., Guil.*]. We'll wait upon you. 266

Ham. No such matter. I will not sort you with the rest of my servants; for to speak to you like an honest man, I am most dreadfully attended. But in the beaten way of friendship, what make you at Elsinore? 270

Ros. To visit you, my lord, no other occasion.

Ham. Beggar that I am, I am [even] poor in thanks—but I thank you, and sure, dear friends, my thanks are too dear a halfpenny. Were you not sent for? is it your own inclining? is it a free visitation? Come, come, deal justly with me. Come, come—nay, speak. 276

Guil. What should we say, my lord?

Ham. Any thing but to th' purpose. You were sent for, and there is a kind of confession in your looks, which your modesties have not craft enough to color. I know the good King and Queen have sent for you.

Ros. To what end, my lord? 282

Ham. That you must teach me. But let me conjure you, by the rights of our fellowship, by the consonancy of our youth, by the obligation of our ever-preserv'd love, and by what more dear a better proposer can charge you withal, be even and direct with me, whether you were sent for or no!

Ros. [*Aside to Guildenstern*] What say you?

Ham. [*Aside.*] Nay then I have an eye of you!—If you love me, hold not off. 291

Guil. My lord, we were sent for.

Ham. I will tell you why, so shall my anticipation prevent your discovery, and your secrecy to the King and Queen moult no feather. I have of late—but wherefore I know not—lost all my mirth, forgone all custom of exercises; and indeed it goes so heavily with my disposition, that this goodly frame, the earth, seems to me a sterile promontory; this most excellent canopy, the air, look you, this brave o'erhanging firmament, this majestical roof fretted with golden fire, why, it appeareth nothing to me but a foul and pestilent congregation of vapors. What [a] piece of work is a man, how noble in reason, how infinite in faculties, in form and moving, how express and admirable in action, how like an angel in apprehension, how like a god! the beauty of the world; the paragon of animals; and yet to me what is this quintessence of dust? Man delights not me—nor women neither, though by your smiling you seem to say so.   310

Ros. My lord, there was no such stuff in my thoughts.

Ham. Why did ye laugh then, when I said, "Man delights not me"?   314

Ros. To think, my lord, if you delight not in man, what lenten entertainment the players shall receive from you. We coted them on the way, and hither are they coming to offer you service.

Ham. He that plays the king shall be welcome—his Majesty shall have tribute on me, the adventerous knight shall use his foil and target, the lover shall not sigh gratis, the humorous man shall end his part in peace, [the clown shall make those laugh whose lungs are [tickle] a' th' sere,] and the lady shall say her mind freely, or the [blank] verse shall halt for't. What players are they?   326

Ros. Even those you were wont to take such delight in, the tragedians of the city.

Ham. How chances it they travel? Their residence, both in reputation and profit, was better both ways.   331

Ros. I think their inhibition comes by the means of the late innovation.

Ham. Do they hold the same estimation they did when I was in the city? Are they so follow'd? 335

Ros. No indeed are they not.

Ham. How comes it? do they grow rusty,?

Ros. Nay, their endeavor keeps in the wonted pace; but there is, sir, an aery of children, little eyases, that cry out on the top of question, and are most tyrannically clapp'd for't. These are now the fashion, and so [berattle] the common stages—so they call them—that many wearing rapiers are afraid of goose-quills and dare scarce come thither.   344

Ham. What, are they children? Who maintains 'em? How are they escoted? Will they pursue the quality no longer than they can sing? Will they not say afterwards, if they should grow themselves to common players (as it is [most like], if their means are [no] better), their writers do them wrong, to make them exclaim against their own succession?   351

Ros. Faith, there has been much to do on both sides, and the nation holds it no sin to tarre them to controversy. There was for a while no money

bid for argument, unless the poet and the player went to cuffs in the question.   356

Ham. Is't possible?

Guil. O, there has been much throwing about of brains.

Ham. Do the boys carry it away?   360

Ros. Ay, that they do, my lord—Hercules and his load too.

Ham. It is not very strange, for my uncle is King of Denmark, and those that would make mouths at him while my father liv'd, give twenty, forty, fifty, a hundred ducats a-piece for his picture in little. 'Sblood, there is something in this more than natural, if philosophy could find it out.   *A flourish [for the Players].*

Guil. There are the players.   369

Ham. Gentlemen, you are welcome to Elsinore. Your hands, come then: th' appurtenance of welcome is fashion and ceremony. Let me comply with you in this garb, [lest my] extent to the players, which, I tell you, must show fairly outwards, should more appear like entertainment than yours. You are welcome; but my uncle-father and aunt-mother are deceiv'd.   376

Guil. In what, my dear lord?

Ham. I am but mad north-north-west. When the wind is southerly I know a hawk from a hand-saw.

Enter POLONIUS.

Pol. Well be with you, gentlemen!   380

Ham. [*Aside to them.*] Hark you, Guildenstern, and you too—at each ear a hearer—that great baby you see there is not yet out of his swaddling-clouts.

Ros. Happily he is the second time come to them, for they say an old man is twice a child.   385

Ham. I will prophesy, he comes to tell me of the players, mark it. [*Aloud.*] You say right, sir, a' Monday morning, 'twas then indeed.

Pol. My lord, I have news to tell you.

Ham. My lord, I have news to tell you. When Roscius was an actor in Rome—   391

Pol. The actors are come hither, my lord.

Ham. Buzz, buzz!

Pol. Upon my honor—

Ham. "Then came each actor on his ass"— 395

Pol. The best actors in the world, either for tragedy, comedy, history, pastoral, pastoral-comical, historical-pastoral, [tragical-historical, tragical-comical-historical-pastoral,] scene individable, or poem unlimited; Seneca cannot be too heavy, nor Plautus too light, for the law of writ and the liberty: these are the only men.

Ham. O Jephthah, judge of Israel, what a treasure hadst thou!

 Pol. What a treasure had he, my lord?   405

 Ham. Why—

   "One fair daughter, and no more,
   The which he loved passing well."

 Pol. [*Aside.*] Still on my daughter.

 Ham. Am I not i' th' right, old Jephthah?   410

 Pol. If you call me Jephthah, my lord, I have a daughter that I love passing well.

 Ham. Nay, that follows not.

 Pol. What follows then, my lord?

 Ham. Why—   415

    "As by lot, God wot,"
and then, you know,
  "It came to pass, as most like it was"
—the first row of the pious chanson will show you more, for look where my abridgment comes.   420

Enter the PLAYERS, *[four or five].*

You are welcome, masters, welcome all. I am glad to see thee well. Welcome, good friends. O, old friend! why, thy face is valanc'd since I saw thee last; com'st thou to beard me in Denmark? What, my young lady and mistress! by' lady, your ladyship is nearer to heaven than when I saw you last, by the attitude of a chopine. Pray God your voice, like a piece of uncurrent gold, be not crack'd within the ring. Masters, you are all welcome. We'll e'en to't like [French] falc'ners— fly at any thing we see; we'll have a speech straight. Come give us a taste of your quality, come, a passionate speech.   432

 [1.] Play. What speech, my good lord?

 Ham. I heard thee speak me a speech once, but it was never acted, or if it was, not above once; for the play, I remember, pleas'd not the million, 'twas caviary to the general, but it was—as I receiv'd it, and others, whose judgments in such matters cried in the top of mine—an excellent play, well digested in the scenes, set down with as much modesty as cunning. I remember one said there were no sallets in the lines to make the matter savory, nor no matter in the phrase that might indict the author of affection, but call'd it an honest method, as wholesome as sweet, and by very much more handsome than fine. One speech in't I chiefly lov'd, 'twas Aeneas' [tale] to Dido, and thereabout of it especially when he speaks of Priam's slaughter. If it live in your memory, begin at this line—let me see, let me see: "The rugged Pyrrhus like th' Hyrcanian beast—" 'Tis not so, it begins with Pyrrhus: 451 "The rugged Pyrrhus, he whose sable arms, Black as his purpose, did the night resemble

When he lay couched in th' ominous horse, Hath now this dread and black complexion smear'd
With heraldy more dismal: head to foot   456
Now is he total gules, horridly trick'd
With blood of fathers, mothers, daughters, sons,
Bak'd and impasted with the parching streets,
That lend a tyrannous and a damned light   460
To their lord's murther. Roasted in wrath and fire,
And thus o'er-sized with coagulate gore,
With eyes like carbuncles, the hellish Pyrrhus
Old grandsire Priam seeks."
So proceed you.   465

 Pol. 'Fore God, my lord, well spoken, with good accent and good discretion.

 [1.] Play.   "Anon he finds him Striking too short at Greeks. His antique sword, Rebellious to his arm, lies where it falls,   470 Repugnant to command. Unequal match'd, Pyrrhus at Priam drives, in rage strikes wide, But with the whiff and wind of his fell sword Th' unnerved father falls. [Then senseless Ilium] Seeming to feel this blow, with flaming top   475 Stoops to his base, and with a hideous crash Takes prisoner Pyrrhus' ear; for lo his sword, Which was declining on the milky head Of reverent Priam, seem'd i' th' air to stick So as a painted tyrant Pyrrhus stood   480 [And,] like a neutral to his will and matter, Did nothing.
But as we often see, against some storm, A silence in the heavens, the rack stand still, The bold winds speechless, and the orb below   485 As hush as death, anon the dreadful thunder Doth rend the region; so after Pyrrhus' pause, A roused vengeance sets him new a-work, And never did the Cyclops' hammers fall On Mars's armor forg'd for proof eterne   490 With less remorse than Pyrrhus' bleeding sword Now falls on Priam.
Out, out, thou strumpet Fortune! All you gods, In general synod take away her power! Break all the spokes and [fellies] from her wheel,   495 And bowl the round nave down the hill of heaven
As low as to the fiends!"

 Pol. This is too long.

 Ham: It shall to the barber's with your beard. Prithee say on, he's for a jig or a tale of bawdry, or he sleeps. Say on, come to Hecuba.   501

 [1.] Play. "But who, ah woe, had seen the mobled queen"—

 Ham. "The mobled queen"?

Pol. That's good, ["[mobled] queen" is
  good].
  [1.] *Play.* "Run, barefoot, up and down,
    threat'ning the flames   505
With bisson rheum, a clout upon that head
Where late the diadem stood, and for a robe,
About her lank and all o'er-teemed loins,
A blanket, in the alarm of fear caught up— 509
Who this had seen, with tongue in venom
  steep'd,
'Gainst Fortune's state would treason have
  pronounc'd.
But if the gods themselves did see her then
When she saw Pyrrhus make malicious sport
In mincing with his sword her [husband's] limbs,
The instant burst of clamor that she made,   515
Unless things mortal move them not at all,
Would have made milch the burning eyes of
  heaven,
And passion in the gods."
  Pol. Look whe'er he has not turn'd his color
and has tears in 's eyes. Prithee no more.   520
  Ham. 'Tis well, I'll have thee speak out the rest
of this soon. Good my lord, will you see the
players well bestow'd? Do you hear, let them be
well us'd, for they are the abstract and brief
chronicles of the time. After your death you were
better have a bad epitaph than their ill report
while you live.   526
  Pol. My lord I will use them, according to their
desert.
  Ham.: God's bodkin, man, much better: use
every man after his desert, and who shall escape
whipping? Use them after your own honor and
dignity—the less they deserve, the more merit is
in your bounty. Take them in.   533
  Pol. Come sirs.   [*Exit*]
  Ham. Follow him, friends, we'll hear a play
tomorrow. [*Exeunt all the Players but the First.*]536
  Dost thou hear me, old friend? Can you play
"The Murther of Gonzago"?
  [1.] *Play.* Ay, my lord   544
  Ham. We'll ha't tomorrow night. You could for
need study a speech of some dozen lines, or sixteen lines, which I would set down, and insert
in't, could you not?
  [1.] *Play.* Ay, my, lord.
  Ham. Very well. Follow that lord, and look you
mock him not. [*Exit. First Player*] My good
friends, I'll leave you [till] night. You are welcome to Elsinore.
  Ros. Good my lord!
  Ham. Ay so, God buy to you.
              Exeunt: [*Rosencrantz and Guildenstern*]
                          Now I am alone.
O, what a rogue and peasant slave am I!   550

Is it not monstrous that this player here,
But in a fiction, in a dream of passion,
Could force his soul so to his own conceit
That from her working all the visage wann'd,
Tears in his eyes, distraction in his aspect,   555
A broken voice, an' his whole function suiting,
With forms to his conceit? And all for nothing,
For Hecuba!
What's Hecuba to him or he to [Hecuba],
That he should weep for her? What would
  he do
Had he the motive and [the cue] for passion 561
That I have? He would drown the stage with
  tears,
And cleave the general ear with horrid speech,
Make mad the guilty and appall the free,
Confound the ignorant, and amaze indeed,   565
The very faculties of eyes and ears. Yet I,
A dull and muddy-mettled rascal, peak
Like John-a-dreams, unpregnant of my cause,
And can say nothing; no, not for a king,
Upon whose property and most dear life   570
A damn'd defeat was made. Am I a coward?
Who calls me villain, breaks my pate across,
Plucks off my beard and blows it in my face,
Tweaks me by the nose, gives me the lie i'
  th' throat
As deep as to the lungs? Who does me this? 575
Hah, 'swounds, I should take it; for it cannot; be
But I am pigeon-liver'd, and lack gall
To make oppression bitter, or ere this
I should a' fatted all the region kites
With this slave's offal. Bloody, bawdy
  villain!   580
Remorseless, treacherous, lecherous,
  kindless villain!
Why, what an ass am I! This is most brave,
That I, the son of a dear [father] murthered,
Prompted to my revenge by heaven and hell,
Must like a whore unpack my heart with words,
And fall a-cursing like a very drab,   586
A stallion. Fie upon't, foh!
About, my brains! Hum—I have heard
That guilty creatures sitting at a play
Have by the very cunning of the scene   590
Been strook so to the soul, that presently
They have proclaim'd their malefactions:
For murther though it have no tongue, will speak
With most miraculous organ. I'll have these
  players
Play something like the murther of my father 595
Before mine uncle. I'll observe his looks,
I'll tent him to the quick. If 'a do blench,
I know my course. The spirit that I have seen
May be a [dev'l], and the [dev'l] hath power,

T' assume a pleasing shape, yea, and
   perhaps, 600
Out of my weakness and my melancholy,
As he is very potent with such spirits,
Abuses me to damn me. I'll have grounds
More relative than this—the play's the thing 604
   Wherein I'll catch the conscience of the
   King. *Exit.*

[ACT III, SCENE I]

Enter KING, QUEEN, POLONIUS,
OPHELIA, ROSENCRANTZ, GUILD-
ENSTERN, LORDS.

King. An' can you by no drift of conference
Get from him why he puts on this confusion,
Grating so harshly all his days of quiet
With turbulent and dangerous lunacy?
   Ros. He does confess he feels himself
     distracted,
But from what cause 'a will by no means
   speak. 6
   Guil. Nor do we find him forward to be
     sounded,
But with a crafty madness keeps aloof
When we would bring him on to some confession
Of his true state.
   Queen.   Did he receive you well? 10
   Ros. Most like a gentleman.
   Guil. But with much forcing of his
     disposition.
   Ros. Niggard of question, but of our
     demands
Most free in his reply.
   Queen.   Did you assay him
To any pastime? 15
   Ros. Madam, it so fell out that certain
     players
We o'erraught on the way; of these we told him,
And there did seem in him a kind of joy
To hear of it. They are here about the court,
And as I think, they have already order 20
This night to play before him.
   Pol.   'Tis most true,
And he beseech'd me to entreat your Majesties
To hear and see the matter.
   King. With all my heart, and it doth much
     content me
To hear him so inclin'd. 25
Good gentlemen, give him a further edge,
   And drive his purpose into these delights.
   Ros. We shall, my lord.

Exeunt Rosencrantz and Guildenstern.
   King.   Sweet Gertrude, leave us two,
For we have closely sent for Hamlet hither,
That he, as 'twere by accident may here 30
Affront Ophelia. Her father and myself,
We'll so bestow ourselves that, seeing unseen,
We may of their encounter frankly judge,
And gather by him, as he is behav'd,
If't be th' affliction of his love or no 35
That thus he suffers for.
   Queen.   I shall obey you.
And for your part, Ophelia, I do wish
That your good beauties be the happy cause
Of Hamlet's wildness. So shall I hope your
   virtues
Will bring him to his wonted way again, 40
To both your honors.
   Oph.   Madam, I wish it may. [*Exit Queen.*]
   Pol. Ophelia, walk you here.—Gracious,
     so please you,
We will bestow ourselves [*To Ophelia.*] Read
   on this book,
That show of such an exercise may color
Your [loneliness]. We are oft to blame in
   this— 45
'Tis too much prov'd—that with devotion's
   visage
And pious action we do sugar o'er
The devil himself.
   King.   [*Aside.*] O, 'tis too true!
How smart a lash that speech doth give my
   conscience!
The harlot's cheek, beautied with plastering
   art, 50
Is not more ugly to the thing that helps it
Than is my deed to my most painted word.
O heavy burthen!
   Pol. I hear him coming. Withdraw, my
     lord.

          [*Exeunt King and Polonius.*]

Enter HAMLET.

   Ham. To be, or not to be, that is the
     question: 55
Whether 'tis nobler in the mind to suffer
The slings and arrows of outrageous fortune,
Or to take arms against a sea of troubles,
And by opposing, end them. To die, to sleep—
No more, and by a sleep to say we end 60
The heart-ache and the thousand natural shocks
That flesh is heir to; 'tis a consummation
Devoutly to be wish'd. To die, to sleep—
To sleep, perchance to dream—ay, there's
   the rub,

For in that sleep of death what dreams may
    come,   65
When we have shuffled off this mortal coil,
Must give us pause; there's the respect
That makes calamity of so long life:
For who would bear the whips and scorns of
    time,
Th' oppressor's wrong, the proud man's
    contumely,   70
The pangs of despis'd love, the law's delay,
The insolence of office, and the spurns
That patient merit of th' unworthy takes,
When he himself might his quietus make
With a bare bodkin; who would fardels bear, 75
To grunt and sweat under a weary life,
But that the dread of something after death,
The undiscover'd country, from whose bourn
No traveller returns, puzzles the will,
And makes us rather bear those ills we have, 80
Than fly to others that we know not of?
Thus conscience does make cowards [of us all],
And thus the native hue of resolution
Is sicklied o'er with the pale cast of thought,
And enterprises of great pitch and moment   85
With this regard their currents turn awry,
And lose the name of action.—Soft you now,
The fair Ophelia. Nymph, in thy orisons
Be all my sins rememb'red.

    Oph.   Good my lord,
How does your honor for this many a day?   90
    Ham. I humbly thank you, well, [well,
        well].
    Oph. My lord, I have remembrances of
        yours
That I have longed long to redeliver.
I pray you now receive them.
    Ham.   No, not I,
I never gave you aught.   95
    Oph. My honor'd lord, you know right
        well you did,
And with them words of so sweet breath
    compos'd
As made these things more rich. Their
    perfume lost,
Take these again, for to the noble mind
Rich gifts wax poor when givers prove
    unkind.   100
There, my lord.
    Ham. Ha, ha! are you honest?
    Oph. My lord?
    Ham. Are you fair?
    Oph. What means your lordship?   105
    Ham. That if you be honest and fair, [your
honesty] should admit no discourse to your
beauty.

    Oph. Could beauty, my lord, have better com-
merce than with honesty?   109
    Ham. Ay, truly, for the power of beauty will
sooner transform honesty from what it is to a
bawd than the force of honesty can translate
beauty into his likeness. This was sometime a
paradox, but now the time gives it proof. I did
love you once.   114
    Oph. Indeed, my lord, you made me believe so.
    Ham. You should not have believ'd me, for
virtue cannot so [inoculate] our old stock but we
shall relish of it. I lov'd you not.
    Oph. I was the more deceiv'd.   119
    Ham. Get thee [to] a nunn'ry, why wouldst
thou be a breeder of sinners? I am myself indifferent honest, but yet I could accuse me of such
things that it were better my mother had not
borne me: I am very proud, revengeful, ambitious, with more offenses at my beck than I have
thoughts to put them in; imagination to give
them shape, or time to act them in. What should
such fellows as I do crawling between earth and
heaven? We are arrant knaves, believe none of
us. Go by ways to a nunn'ry. Where's your father?
    Oph. At home, my lord.   130
    Ham. Let the doors be shut upon him, that he
may play the fool no where but in 's own house.
Farewell.
    Oph. O, help him, you sweet heavens!
    Ham. If thou dost marry, I'll give thee this
plague for thy dowry: be thou as chaste as ice,
pure as snow, thou shalt not escape calumny. Get
thee to a nunn'ry, farewell. Or if thou wilt needs
marry, marry a fool, for wise men know well
enough what monsters you make of them. To a
nunn'ry, go, and quickly too. Farewell.   140
    Oph. Heavenly powers, restore him!
    Ham. I have heard of your paintings, well
enough. God hath given you one face, and you
make yourselves another. You jig and amble, and
you [lisp,] you nickname God's creatures and
make your wantonness [your] ignorance. Go to,
I'll no more on't, it hath made me mad. I say we
will have no more marriage. Those that are married already, (all but one) shall live, the rest shall
keep as they are. To a nunn'ry, go.   149
                                                    Exit.

    Oph. O, what a noble mind is here
        o'erthrown!
The courtier's, soldier's, scholar's, eye,
    tongue, sword,
Th' expectation and rose of the fair state,
The glass of fashion and the mould of form,
Th' observ'd of all observers, quite, quite down!
And I, of ladies most deject and wretched,   155

That suck'd the honey of his [music] vows,
Now see [that] noble and most sovereign reason
Like sweet bells jangled out of time, and harsh;
That unmatch'd form and stature of blown youth
Blasted with ecstasy. O, woe is me   160
T' have seen what I have seen, see what I see!
                              [*Ophelia withdraws.*]

Enter KING *and* POLONIUS.

   King. Love? his affections do not that way
      tend,
Nor what he spake, though it lack'd form a little,
Was not like madness. There's something in
      his soul
O'er which his melancholy, sits on brood,   165
And I do doubt the hatch and the disclose
Will be some danger; which for to prevent,
I have in quick determination
Thus set it down: he shall with speed to England
For the demand of our neglected tribute.   170
Haply the seas, and countries different,
With variable objects, shall expel
This something-settled matter in his heart,
Whereon his brains still beating puts him thus
From fashion of himself. What think you
      on't?   175
   Pol. It shall do well; but yet do I believe
The origin and commencement of his grief
Sprung from neglected love. [*Ophelia comes
      forward.*]
How now, Ophelia?
You need not tell us what Lord Hamlet said,
We heard it all. My lord, do as you please,   180
But if you hold it fit, after the play
Let his queen-mother all alone entreat him
To show his grief. Let her be round with him,
And I'll be plac'd (so please you) in the ear
Of all their conference. If she find him not,   185
To England send him, or confine him where
Your wisdom best shall think.
   King.   It shall be so.
Madness in great ones must not [unwatch'd] go.
                                          Exeunt.

[SCENE II]

Enter HAMLET *and three of the* PLAYERS.

   Ham. Speak the speech, I pray you, as I pronounc'd it to you, trippingly on the tongue, but
if you mouth it, as many of our players do, I had
as live the town-crier spoke my lines. Nor do not

saw the air too much with your hand, thus, but
use all gently, for in the very torrent, tempest,
and, as I may say, whirlwind of your passion,
you must acquire and beget a temperance that
may give it smoothness. O, it offends me to the
soul to hear a robustious periwig-pated fellow
tear a passion to totters, to very rags, to spleet the
ears of the groundlings, who for the most part are
capable of nothing but inexplicable dumb shows
and noise. I would have such a fellow whipt for
o'erdoing Termagant, it out-Herods Herod, pray
you avoid it.
   [*1.*] *Play.* I warrant your honor.   15
   Ham. Be not too tame neither, but let your own
discretion be your tutor. Suit the action to the
word, the word to the action, with this special
observance, that you o'erstep not the modesty of
nature: for any thing so o'erdone is from the
purpose of playing, whose end, both at the first
and now, was and is, to hold as 'twere the mirror
up to nature: to show virtue her feature, scorn
her own image, and the very age and body of the
time his form and pressure. Now this overdone,
or come tardy off, though it makes the unskillful
laugh, cannot but make the judicious grieve; the
censure of which one must in your allowance
o'erweigh a whole theatre of others. O, there be
players that I have seen play—and heard others
[praise], and that highly—not to speak it pro-
fanely, that, neither having th' accent of Christians nor the gait of Christian, pagan, nor man,
have so strutted and bellow'd that I have thought
some of Nature's journeymen had made men,
and not made them well, they imitated humanity
so abominably.   35
   [*1.*] *Play.* I hope we have reform'd that indifferently with us, [sir].
   Ham. O, reform it altogether. And let those that
play your clowns speak no more than is set down
for them, for there be of them that will themselves laugh to set on some quantity of barren
spectators to laugh too, though in the mean time
some necessary question of the play be then to be
considered. That's villainous, and shows a most
pitiful ambition in the fool that uses it. Go make
you ready.   45
                              [*Exeunt Players.*]

Enter POLONIUS, GUILDENSTERN, *and*
ROSENCRANTZ.

How now, my lord? Will the King hear this
      piece of work?
   Pol. And the Queen too, and that
      presently.

Ham. Bid the players make haste. [*Exit Polonius.*] Will you two help to hasten them?   50
Ros. Ay, my lord.   *Exuent they two.*
Ham. What ho, Horatio!

Enter HORATIO.

Hor. Here, sweet lord, at your service.
Ham. Horatio, thou art e'en as just a man
As e'er my conversation cop'd withal.   55
Hor. O my dear lord—
Ham.   Nay, do not think I flatter,
For what advancement may I hope from thee
That no revenue hast but thy good spirits
To feed and clothe thee? Why should the
   poor be flatter'd?
No, let the candied tongue lick absurd pomp, 60
And crook the pregnant hinges of the knee
Where thrift may follow fawning. Dost thou
   hear?
Since my dear soul was mistress of her choice
And could of men distinguish her election,
Sh' hath seal'd thee for herself, for thou hast
   been   65
As one in suff'ring all that suffers nothing,
A man that Fortune's buffets and rewards
Hast ta'en with equal thanks; and blest are those
Whose blood and judgment are so well
   co-meddled,
That they are not a pipe for Fortune's finger 70
To sound what stop she please. Give me that man
That is not passion's slave, and I will wear him
In my heart's core, ay, in my heart of heart,
As I do thee. Something too much of this.
There is a play to-night before the King,   75
One scene of it comes near the circumstance
Which I have told thee of my father's death.
I prithee, when thou seest that act afoot,
Even with the very comment of thy soul
Observe my uncle. If his occulted guilt   80
Do not itself unkennel in one speech,
It is a damned ghost that we have seen,
And my imaginations are as foul
As Vulcan's stithy. Give him heedful note,
For I mine eyes will rivet to his face,   85
And after we will both our judgments join
In censure of his seeming.
Hor.   Well, my lord.
If 'a steal aught the whilst this play is playing,
And scape [detecting], I will pay the theft.   89

[*Sound a flourish. Danish march.*] *Enter Trumpets and Kettle-drums,* KING, QUEEN, POLONIUS, OPHELIA, [ROSENCRANTZ,

GUILDENSTERN, *and other* LORDS *attendant, with his* GUARD *carrying torches*].

Ham. They are coming to the play. I must be idle; Get you a place.
King. How fares our cousin Hamlet?
Ham. Excellent, i' faith, of the chameleon's dish: I eat the air, promise-cramm'd—you cannot feed capons so.   95
King. I have nothing with this answer, Hamlet, these words are not mine.
Ham. No, nor mine now. [*To Polonius.*] My lord, you play'd once i' th' university, you say?
Pol. That did I, my lord, and was accounted a good actor.   101
Ham. What did you enact?
Pol. I did enact Julius Caesar. I was kill'd i' th' Capitol; Brutus kill'd me.
Ham. It was a brute part of him to kill so capital a calf there. Be the players ready?   106
Ros. Ay, my lord, they stay upon your patience.
Queen. Come hither, my dear Hamlet, sit by me.
Ham. No, good mother, here's metal more attractive.   [*Lying down at Ophelia's feet.*]
Pol. [*To the King.*] O ho, do you mark that? 111
Ham. Lady, shall I lie in your lap?
Oph. No, my lord.
[*Ham.* I mean, my head upon your lap?
Oph. Ay, my lord.   115
Ham. Do you think I meant country matters?
Oph. I think nothing, my lord.
Ham. That's a fair thought to lie between maids' legs.
Oph. What is, my lord?   120
Ham. Nothing.
Oph. You are merry, my lord.
Ham. Who, I?
Oph. Ay, my lord.   124
Ham. O God, your only jig-maker. What should a man do but be merry, for look you how cheerfully my mother looks, and my father died within 's two hours.
Oph. Nay, 'tis twice two months, my lord.
Ham. So long? Nay then let the dev'l wear black, for I'll have a suit of sables. O heavens, die two months ago, and not forgotten yet? Then there's hope a great man's memory may outlive his life half a year, but, by'r lady, 'a must build churches then, or else shall 'a suffer not thinking on, with the hobby-horse, whose epitaph is, "For O, for O, the hobby-horse is forgot."

The trumpets sounds. Dumb show follows.

Enter a King and a Queen [very lovingly], the Queen embracing him and he her. [She kneels and makes show of protestation unto him.] He takes her up and declines his head upon her neck. He lies him down upon a bank of flowers. She, seeing him asleep, leaves him. Anon come in another man, takes off his crown, kisses it, pours poison in the sleeper's ears, and leaves him. The Queen returns, finds the King dead, makes passionate action. The pois'ner with some three or four [mutes] come in again, seem to condole with her. The dead body is carried away. The pois'ner woos the Queen with gifts; she seems harsh [and unwilling] awhile, but in the end accepts love. [Exeunt.]

Oph. What means this, my lord?   136
Ham. Marry, this' [miching] mallecho, it
    means mischief.
Oph. Belike this show imports the
    argument of the play.   140

Enter PROLOGUE.

Ham. We shall know by this fellow. The play-
ers cannot keep [counsel], they'll tell all.
Oph. Will 'a tell us what this show meant?
Ham. Ay, or any show that you will show him.
Be not you asham'd to show, he'll not shame to
tell you what it means.   146
Oph. You are naught, you are naught. I'll mark
the play.
    Pro. For us, and for our tragedy,
    Here stoopng to your clemency,   150
    We beg your hearing patiently.   [*Exit*]
Ham. Is this a prologue, or the posy of a
    ring?
Oph. 'Tis, brief, my lord.
Ham. As woman's love.

Enter [two Players,] KING and QUEEN.

    [*P.*] *King.* Full thirty times hath Phoebus'
        cart gone round   155
Neptune's salt wash and Tellus' orbed ground,
And thirty dozen moons with borrowed sheen
About the world have times twelve thirties been,
Since love our hearts and Hymen did our hands
Unite comutual in most sacred bands.   160
    [*P.*] *Queen.* So many journeys may the sun
        and moon
Make us again count o'er ere love be done!
But woe is me, you are so sick of late,
So far from cheer and from [your] former state,
That I distrust you. Yet though I distrust,   165
Discomfort you, my lord, it nothing must,
[For] women's fear and love hold quantity,

In neither aught, or in extremity.
Now what my [love] is, proof hath made
    you know,
And as my love is siz'd, my fear is so.   170
Where love is great, the littlest doubts are fear;
Where little fears grew great, great love
    grows there.
    [*P.*] *King.* Faith, I must leave thee, love,
        and shortly too;
My operant powers their functions leave to do,
And thou shalt live in this fair world behind,   175
Honor'd, belov'd, and haply one as kind
For husband shalt thou—
    [*P.*] *Queen.*   O confound the rest!
Such love must needs be treason in my breast.
In second husband let me be accurs'd!
None wed the Second but who kill'd the first.   180
    Ham. [*Aside.*] That's wormwood!
    [*P. Queen.*] The instances that second
        marriage move
Are base respects of thrift, but none of love.
A second time I kill my husband dead,
When second husband kisses me in bed.   185
    [*P.*] *King.* I do believe you think what now
        you speak,
But what we do determine, oft we break.
Purpose is but the slave to memory,
Of violent birth, but poor validity,
Which now, the fruit unripe, sticks on the
    tree,   190
But fall unshaken when they mellow be.
Most necessary 'tis that we forget
To pay ourselves what to ourselves is debt.
What to ourselves in passion we propose,
The passion ending, doth the purpose lose.   195
The violence of either grief or joy
Their own enactures with themselves destroy.
Where joy most revels, grief doth most lament;
Grief [joys], joy grieves, on slender accident.
This world is not for aye, nor 'tis not strange   200
That even our loves should with our
    fortunes change
For 'tis a question left us yet to prove,
Whether love lead fortune, or else fortune love.
The great man down, you mark his favorite flies,
The poor advanc'd makes friends of enemies.   205
And hitherto doth love on fortune tend,
For who not needs shall never lack a friend,
And who in want a hollow friend doth try,
Directly seasons him his enemy.
But orderly to end where I begun,   210
Our wills and fates do so contrary run
That our devices still are overthrown,
Our thoughts are ours, their ends none of
    our own:
So think thou wilt no second husband wed,

But die thy thoughts when thy first lord is
    dead.   215
    [*P.*] *Queen.* Nor earth to me give food, nor
    heaven light,
Sport and repose lock from me day and night,
To desperation turn my trust and hope,
[An] anchor's cheer in prison be my scope!
Each opposite that blanks the face of joy   220
Meet what I would have well and it destroy!
Both here and hence pursue me lasting strife,
If once I be a widow, ever I be a wife!
    Ham. If she should break it now!
    [*P.*] *King.* 'Tis deeply sworn. Sweet, leave
    me here a while,   225
My spirits grow dull, and fain I would beguile
The tedious day with sleep.   [*Sleeps.*]
    [*P.*] *Queen.*   Sleep rock thy brain,
And never come mischance between us
    twain!   *Exit.*
    Ham. Madam, how like you this play?
    Queen. The lady doth protest too much, me-
thinks.
    Ham. O but she'll keep her word.   231
    King. Have you heard the argument? is there
no offense in't?
    Ham. No, no, they do but jest, poison in jest—
no offense i' th' world.   235
    King. What do you call the play?
    Ham. "The Mouse-trap." Marry, how? tropi-
cally: this play is the image of a murther done in
Vienna; Gonzago is the duke's name, his wife,
Baptista. You shall see anon. 'Tis a knavish piece
of work but what of that? Your Majesty and we
that have free souls, it touches us not. Let the
gall'd jade winch, our withers are unwrung.

Enter LUCIANUS.

This is one Lucianus, nephew to the king.
    Oph. You are as good as a chorus, my lord. 245
    Ham. I could interpret between you and your
love, if I could see the puppets dallying.
    Oph. You are keen, my lord, you are keen.
    Ham. It would cost you a groaning to take off
mine edge.
250
    Oph. Still better and worse.
    Ham. So you mistake your husbands. Begin,
murtherer leave thy damnable faces and begin.
Come, the croaking raven doth bellow for revenge.
    Luc. Thoughts black, hands apt, drugs fit, and
time agreeing,
255
[Confederate] season, else no creature seeing,
Thou mixture rank, of midnight weeds collected,

With Hecat's ban thrice blasted, thrice [infected],
Thy natural magic and dire property
On wholesome life usurps immediately.   260
    [*Pours the poison in his ears.*]
    Ham. 'A poisons him i' th' garden for his es-
tate. His name's Gonzago, the story is extant, and
written in very choice Italian. You shall see anon
how the murtherer gets the love of Gonzago's
wife.
    Oph. The King rises.   265
    [*Ham.* What, frighted with false fire?]
    Queen. How fares my lord?
    Pol. Give o'er the play.
    King. Give me some light. Away!
    Pol. Lights, lights, lights!   270
    Exeunt all but Hamlet and Horatio.
    Ham. "Why, let the strooken deer go weep,
        The hart ungalled play,
    For some must watch while some
        must sleep,
        Thus runs the world away."   274
Would not this, sir, and a forest of feathers—if
the rest of my fortunes turn Turk with me—with
[two] Provincial roses on my raz'd shoes, get me
a fellowship in a cry of players?
    Hor. Half a share.
    Ham. A whole one, I.   280
    "For thou dost know, O Damon dear,
        This realm dismantled was
    Of Jove himself, and now reigns here
        A very, very"—pajock.
    Hor. You might have rhym'd.   285
    Ham. O good Horatio, I'll take the ghost's
word for a thousand pound. Didst perceive?
    Hor. Very well, my lord.
    Ham. Upon the talk of the pois'ning?
    Hor. I did very well note him.   290
    Ham. Ah, ha! Come, some music! Come, the
recorders!
    For if the King like not the comedy,
    Why then belike he likes it not, perdy.
Come, some music!   295

Enter ROSENCRANTZ *and* GUILD-
ENSTERN.

    Guil. Good my lord, voutsafe me a word with
you.
    Ham. Sir, a whole history.
    Guil. The King, sir—
    Ham. Ay, sir, what of him?   300
    Guil. Is in his retirement marvellous
distemp'red
    Ham. With drink, sir?
    Guil. No, my lord, with choler.

Ham. Your wisdom should show itself more rich to signify this to the doctor, for for me to put him to his purgation would perhaps plunge him into more choler. 307

Guil. Good my lord, put your discourse into some frame, and [start] not so wildly from my affair.

Ham. I am tame, sir. Pronounce. 310

Guil. The Queen, your mother, in most great affliction of spirit, hath sent me to you.

Ham. You are welcome.

Guil. Nay, good my lord, this courtesy is not of the right breed. If it shall please you to make me a wholesome answer, I will do your mother's commandement; if not, your pardon and my return shall be the end of [my] business.

Ham. Sir, I cannot.

Ros. What, my lord? 320

Ham. Make you a wholesome answer—my wit's diseas'd. But, sir, such answer as I can make, you shall command, or rather, as you say, my mother.
Therefore no more, but to the matter: my
mother, you say— 325

Ros. Then thus she says: your behavior hath strook her into amazement and admiration.

Ham. O wonderful son, that can so stonish a mother! But is there no sequel at the heels of this mother's admiration? Impart. 330

Ros. She desires to speak with you in her closet ere you go to bed.

Ham. We shall obey, were she ten times our mother. Have you any further trade with us?

Ros. My lord, you once did love me. 335

Ham. And do still, by these pickers and stealers.

Ros. Good my lord, what is your cause of distemper? You do surely bar the door upon your own liberty if you deny your griefs to your friend.

Ham. Sir, I lack advancement. 340

Ros. How can that be, when you have the voice of the King himself for your succession in Denmark?

Ham. Ay, sir, but "While the grass grows"— the proverb is something musty. 344

Enter the PLAYERS *with recorders.*

O, the recorders! Let me see one.—To withdraw with you—why do you go about to recover the wind of me, as if you would drive me into a toil?

Guil. O my lord, if my duty be too bold, my love is too unmannerly. 349

Ham. I do not well understand that. Will you play upon this pipe?

Guil. My lord, I cannot.

Ham. I pray you.

Guil. Believe me, I cannot.

Ham. I do beseech you. 355

Guil. I know no touch of it, my lord.

Ham. It is as easy as lying. Govern these ventages with your fingers and [thumbs], give it breath with your mouth, and it will discourse most eloquent music. Look you, these are the stops. 360

Guil. But these cannot I command to any utt'rance of harmony. I have not the skill.

Ham. Why, look you now, how unworthy a thing you make of me! You would play upon me, you would seem to know my stops, you would pluck out the heart of my mystery, you would sound me from my lowest note to [the top of] my compass; and there is much music, excellent voice, in this little organ, yet cannot you make it speak. 'Sblood, do you think I am easier to be play'd on than a pipe? Call me what instrument you will, though you fret me, [yet] you cannot play upon me.

Enter POLONIUS.

God bless you, sir.

Pol. My lord, the Queen would speak with you, and presently. 375

Ham. Do you see yonder cloud that's almost in shape of a camel?

Pol. By th' mass and 'tis, like a camel indeed.

Ham. Methinks it is like a weasel.

Pol. It is back'd like a weasel. 380

Ham. Or like a whale.

Pol. Very like a whale.

Ham. Then I will come to my mother by and by. [*Aside.*] They fool me to the top of my bent.—I will come by and by. 385

[*Pol.*] I will say so. [*Exit.*]

Ham. "By and by" is easily said. Leave me, friends. [*Exeunt all but Hamlet.*]
'Tis now the very witching time of night,
When churchyards yawn and hell itself
  [breathes] out
Contagion to this world. Now could I drink
  hot blood,
And do such [bitter business as the] day 391
Would quake to look on. Soft, now to my mother.
O heart, lose not thy nature! let not ever
The soul of Nero enter this firm bosom,
Let me be cruel, not unnatural; 395
I will speak [daggers] to her, but use none.
My tongue and soul in this be hypocrites—

How in my words somever she be shent,
To give them seals never my soul consent!   *Exit.*

[SCENE III]

Enter KING, ROSENCRANTZ, *and*
GUILDENSTERN.
King. I like him not, nor stands it safe
with us
To let his madness range. Therefore prepare
you.
I your commission will forthwith dispatch,
And he to England shall along with you.
The terms of our estate may not endure   5
Hazard so near 's as doth hourly grow
Out of his brows.
    Guil.   We will ourselves provide.
Most holy and religious fear it is
To keep those many many bodies safe
That live and feed upon your Majesty.   10
    Ros. The single and peculiar life is bound
With all the strength and armor of the mind
To keep itself from noyance, but much more
That spirit upon whose weal depends and rests
The lives of many. The cess of majesty   15
Dies not alone, but like a gulf doth draw
What's near it with it. Or it is a massy
Fix'd on the summit of the highest mount,
To whose [huge] spokes ten thousand lesser
things
Are mortis'd and adjoin'd, which when it
falls,   20
Each small annexment, petty consequence,
Attends the boisterous [ruin]. Never alone
Did the King sigh, but [with] a general groan.
    King. Arm you, I pray you, to this speedy
viage,
For we will fetters put about this fear,   25
Which now goes too free-footed.
    Ros.   We will haste us.
        *Exeunt Gentlemen [Rosencrantz and
                            Guildenstern].*

Enter POLONIUS.

Pol. My lord, he's going to his mother's
closet.
Behind the arras I'll convey myself
To hear the process. I'll warrant she'll tax
him home,
And as you said, and wisely was it said,   30
'Tis meet that some more audience than a
mother,

Since nature makes them partial, should o'erhear
The speech, of vantage. Fare you well, my liege,
I'll call upon you ere you go to bed,
And tell you what I know.
    King.   Thanks, dear my lord. 35
                        Exit [Polonius].
O, my offense is rank, it smells to heaven,
It hath the primal eldest curse upon't,
A brother's murther. Pray can I not,
Though inclination be as sharp as will.
My stronger guilt defeats my strong intent,   40
And, like a man to double business bound,
I stand in pause where I shall first begin,
And both neglect. What if this cursed hand
Were thicker than itself with brother's blood,
Is there not rain enough in the sweet heavens 45
To wash it white as snow? Whereto serves mercy
But to confront the visage of offense?
And what's in prayer but this twofold force,
To be forestalled ere we come to fall,
Or [pardon'd] being down? then I'll look up.   50
My fault is past, but, O, what form of prayer
Can serve my turn? "Forgive me my foul
murther"?
That cannot be, since I am still possess'd
Of those effects for which I did the murther:
My crown, mine own ambition, and my
queen.   55
May one be pardon'd and retain th' offense?
In the corrupted currents of this world
Offense's gilded hand may [shove] by justice,
And oft 'tis seen the wicked prize itself
Buys out the law, but 'tis not so above: 60
There is no shuffling, there the action lies
In his true nature, and we ourselves compell'd,
Even to the teeth and forehead of our faults,
To give in evidence. What then? What rests?
Try what repentance can. What can it not?   65
Yet what can it, when one can not repent?
O wretched state! O bosom black as death!
O limed soul, that struggling to be free
Art more engag'd! Help, angels! Make assay,
Bow, stubborn knees, and heart, with strings
of steel,
Be soft as sinews of the new-born babe!   71
All may be well.   [*He kneels.*]

Enter HAMLET.

Ham. Now might I do it [pat], now 'a is
a-praying;
And now I'll do't—and so 'a goes to heaven,
And so am I (reveng'd). That would be
scann'd: 75
A villain kills my father, and for that
I, his sole son, do this same villain send

To heaven.
Why, this is [hire and salary], not revenge.
'A took my father grossly, full of bread,   80
With all his crimes broad blown, as flush as May,
And how his audit stands who knows save
    heaven?
But in our circumstance and course of thought
'Tis heavy with him. And am I then revenged,
To take him in the purging of his soul,   85
When he is fit and season'd for his passage?
No!
Up, sword, and know thou a more horrid hent:
When he is drunk asleep, or in his rage,
Or in th' incestious pleasure of his bed,   90
At game a-swearing, or about some act
That has no relish of salvation in't—
Then trip him, that his heels may kick at heaven,
And that his soul may be as damn'd and black
As hell, whereto it goes. My mother stays,   95
This physic but prolongs thy sickly days.   *Exit.*
    King. [*Rising.*] My words fly up, my
        thoughts remain below:
Words without thoughts never to heaven go. *Exit.*

[SCENE IV]

Enter [QUEEN] GERTRUDE *and*
POLONIUS.
    Pol. 'A will come straight. Look you lay
        home to him.
Tell him his pranks have been too broad to
    bear with,
And that your Grace hath screen'd and
    stood between
Much heat and him. I'll silence me even here;
Pray you be round [with him].   5
    Queen. I'll [warr'nt] you, fear me not.
        Withdraw,
I hear him coming.

    [Polonius hides behind the arras.]

Enter HAMLET.

    Ham. Now, mother, what's the matter?
    Queen. Hamlet, thou hast thy father much
        offended.
    Ham. Mother, you have my father much
        offended.
    Queen. Come, come, you answer with an
        idle tongue.   11
    Ham. Go, go, you question with a wicked
        tongue.

    Queen. Why, how now, Hamlet?
    Ham.   What's the matter now?
    Queen. Have you forgot me?
    Ham.   No, by the rood, not so:
You are the Queen, your husband's brother's
    wife,
And would it were not so, you are my
    mother.   16
    Queen. Nay, then I'll set those to you that
        can speak.
    Ham. Come, come, and sit you down, you
        shall not boudge;
You go not till I set you up a glass
Where you may see the [inmost] part of you. 20
    Queen. What wilt thou do? Thou wilt not
        murther me?
Help ho!
    Pol. [*Behind.*] What ho, help!
    Ham. [*Drawing.*] How now? A rat? Dead,
        for a ducat, dead! [*Kills Polonius through
        the arras.*]
    Pol. [*Behind.*] O, I am slain.
    Queen.   O me, what hast thou done?
    Ham. Nay, I know not, is it the King?   26
    Queen. O, what a rash and bloody deed is
        this!
    Ham. A bloody deed! almost as bad, good
        mother,
As kill a king, and marry with his brother.
    Queen. As kill a king!
    Ham.   Ay, lady it was my word.
        [*Parts the arras and discovers Polonius.*]
Thou wretched, rash, intruding fool,
    farewell!   31
I took thee for thy better. Take thy fortune;
Thou find'st to be too busy is some danger.—
Leave wringing of your hands. Peace, sit you
    down,
And let me wring your heart, for so I shall   35
If it be made of penetrable stuff,
If damned custom have not brass'd it so
That it be proof and bulwark against sense.
    Queen. What have I done, that thou dar'st
        wag thy tongue
In noise so rude against me?
    Ham.   Such an act   40
That blurs the grace and blush of modesty,
Calls virtue hypocrite, takes off the rose
From the fair forehead of an innocent love
And sets a blister there, makes marriage vows
As false as dice oaths, O, such a deed   45
As from the body of contraction plucks
The very soul, and sweet religion makes
A rhapsody of words. Heaven's face does glow
O'er this solidity and compound mass
With heated visage, as against the doom;   50

Is thought-sick at the act.

Queen.   Ay me, what act,
That roars so loud and thunders in the index?

Ham. Look here upon this picture, and on
    this,
The counterfeit presentment of two brothers.
See what a grace was seated on this brow: 55
Hyperion's curls, the front of Jove himself,
An eye like Mars, to threaten and command,
A station like the herald Mercury
New lighted on a [heaven-]kissing hill,
A combination and a form indeed,   60
Where every god did seem to set his seal
To give the world assurance of a man.
This was your husband. Look you now what
    follows:
Here is your husband, like a mildewed ear,
Blasting his wholesome brother. Have you
    eyes?   65
Could you on this fair mountain leave to feed,
And batten on this moor? ha, have you eyes?
You cannot call it love, for at your age
The heyday in the blood is tame, it's humble,
And waits upon the judgment, and what
    judgment   70
Would step from this to this? Sense sure you
    have,
Else could you not have motion, but sure
    that sense
Is apoplex'd, for madness would not err,
Nor sense to ecstasy was ne'er so thrall'd
But it reserv'd some quantity of choice   75
To serve in such a difference. What devil was't
That thus hath cozen'd you at
    hoodman-blind?
Eyes without feeling, feeling without sight,
Ears without hands or eyes, smelling sans all,
Or but a sickly part of one true sense   80
Could not so mope. O shame, where is thy blush?
Rebellious hell,
If thou canst mutine in a matron's bones,
To flaming youth let virtue be as wax
And melt in her own fire. Proclaim no shame   85
When the compulsive ardure gives the charge,
Since frost itself as actively doth burn,
And reason [panders] will.

Queen.   O Hamlet, speak no more!
Thou turn'st my [eyes into my very] soul,
And there I see such black and [grained]
    spots   90
As will [not] leave their tinct.

Ham.   Nay, but to live
In the rank sweat of an enseamed bed,
Stew'd in corruption, honeying and making love
Over the nasty sty!

Queen.   O, speak to me no more!

These words like daggers enter in my ears.   95
No more, sweet Hamlet!

Ham.   A murtherer and a villain!
A slave that is not twentith part the [tithe]
Of your precedent lord, a Vice of kings,
A cutpurse of the empire and the rule,
That from a shelf the precious diadem stole, 100
And put it in his pocket—

Queen.   No more!

Enter GHOST *[in his nightgown].*

Ham. A king of shreds and patches—
Save me, and hover o'er me with your wings,
You heavenly guards! What would your
    gracious figure?

Queen. Alas, he's mad!   105

Ham. Do you not come your tardy son to
    chide,
That, laps'd in time and passion, lets go by
Th' important acting of your dread command?
O, say!

Ghost. Do not forget! This visitation   110
Is but to whet thy almost blunted purpose.
But look, amazement on thy mother sits,
O, step between her and her fighting soul.
Conceit in weakest bodies strongest works,
Speak to her, Hamlet.

Ham.   How is it with you, lady? 115

Queen. Alas, how is't with you,
That you do bend your eye on vacancy,
And with th' incorporal air do hold discourse?
Forth at your eyes your spirits wildly peep,
And as the sleeping soldiers in th' alarm,   120
Your bedded hair, like life in excrements,
Start up and stand an end. O gentle son,
Upon the heat and flame of thy distemper
Sprinkle cool patience. Whereon do you look?

Ham. On him, on him! look you how pale
    he glares!   125
His form and cause conjoined, preaching to
    stones,
Would make them capable.—Do not look
    upon me,
Lest with this piteous action you convert
My stern effects, then what I have to do
Will want true color—tears perchance for
    blood.   130

Queen. To whom do you speak this?

Ham.   Do you see nothing there?

Queen. Nothing at all, yet all that is I see.

Ham. Nor did you nothing hear?

Queen.   No, nothing but ourselves.

Ham. Why, look you there, look how it
    steals away!
My father, in his habit as he lived!   135

Look where he goes, even now, out at the portal!
                                   Exit Ghost.
  Queen. This is the very coinage of your
    brain,
This bodiless creation ecstasy
Is very cunning in.
  Ham. [Ecstasy?]
My pulse as yours doth temperately keep
    time,   140
And makes as healthful music. It is not madness
That I have utt'red. Bring me to the test,
And [I] the matter will reword, which madness
Would gambol from. Mother, for love of grace,
Lay not that flattering unction to your soul, 145
That not your trespass but my madness speaks;
It will but skin and film the ulcerous place,
Whiles rank corruption, mining all within,
Infects unseen. Confess yourself to heaven,
Repent what's past, avoid what is to come,   150
And do not spread the compost on the weeds
To make them ranker. Forgive me this my virtue,
For in the fatness of these pursy times
Virtue itself of vice must pardon beg,
Yea, curb and woo for leave to do him good. 155
  Queen. O Hamlet, thou hast cleft my heart
    in twain.
  Ham. O, throw away the worser part of it,
And [live] the purer with the other half.
Good night, but go not to my uncle's bed—
Assume a virtue, if you have it not.   160
That monster custom, who all sense doth eat,
Of habits devil, is angel yet in this,
That to the use of actions fair and good
He likewise gives a frock or livery
That aptly is put on. Refrain [to-]night,   165
And that shall lend a kind of easiness
To the next abstinence, the next more easy;
For use almost can change the stamp of nature,
And either [. . .] the devil or throw him out
With wondrous potency. Once more good night,
And when you are desirous to be blest,   171
I'll blessing beg of you. For this same lord,
                        [*Pointing to Polonius.*]
I do repent; but heaven hath pleas'd it so
To punish me with this, and this with me,
That I must be their scourge and minister.   175
I will bestow him, and will answer well
The death I gave him. So again good night.
I must be cruel only to be kind.
This bad begins and worse remains behind.
One word more, good lady.
  Queen.   What shall I do? 180
  Ham. Not this, by no means, that I bid you
    do:
Let the bloat king tempt you again to bed,
Pinch wanton on your cheek, call you his mouse,

And let him, for a pair of reechy kisses,
Or paddling in your neck with his damn'd
    fingers,   185
Make you to ravel all this matter out,
That I essentially am not in madness,
But mad in craft. 'Twere good you let him know,
For who that's but a queen, fair, sober, wise,
Would from a paddock, from a bat, a gib,   190
Such dear concernings hide? Who would do so?
No, in despite of sense and secrecy,
Unpeg the basket on the house's top,
Let the birds fly, and like the famous ape,
To try conclusions in the basket creep,   195
And break your own neck down.
  Queen. Be thou assur'd, if words be made
    of breath,
And breath of life, I have no life to breathe
What thou hast said to me.
  Ham. I must to England, you know that?
  Queen.   Alack,   200
I had forgot. 'Tis so concluded on.
  Ham. There's letters seal'd, and my two
    school-fellows,
Whom I will trust as I will adders fang'd,
They bear the mandate, they must sweep my way
And marshal me to knavery. Let it work,   205
For 'tis the sport to have the engineer
Hoist with his own petar, an't shall go hard
But I will delve one yard below their mines,
And blow them at the moon. O, 'tis most sweet
When in one line two crafts directly meet.   210
This man shall set me packing;
I'll lug the guts into the neighbor room.
Mother, good night indeed. This counsellor
Is now most still, most secret, and most grave,
Who was in life a foolish prating knave.   215
Come, sir, to draw toward an end with you.
Good night, mother.
  Exeunt [*severally, Hamlet tugging in
    Polonius*].

[ACT IV, SCENE I]

Enter KING *and* QUEEN *with* ROSEN-
CRANTZ *and* GUILDENSTERN.

  King. There's matter in these sighs, these
    profound heaves—
You must translate, 'tis fit we understand them.
Where is your son?
  Queen. Bestow this place on us a little while.
            [*Exeunt Rosencrantz and Guildenstern.*]

Ah, mine own lord, what have I seen
   to-night!   5
   King. What, Gertrude? How does Hamlet?
   Queen. Mad as the sea and wind when
     both contend
Which is the mightier. In his lawless fit,
Behind the arras hearing something stir,
Whips out his rapier, cries, "A rat, a rat!"   10
And in this brainish apprehension kills
The unseen good old man.
   King.   O heavy deed!
It had been so with us had we been there.
His liberty is full of threats to all,
To you yourself, to us, to every one.   15
Alas, how shall this bloody deed be answer'd?
It will be laid to us, whose providence
Should have kept short, restrain'd, and out
   of haunt
This mad young man; but so much was our love,
We would not understand what was most fit, 20
But like the owner of a foul disease,
To keep it from divulging, let it feed
Even on the pith of life. Where is he gone?
   Queen. To draw apart the body he hath
     kill'd,
O'er whom his very madness, like some ore   25
Among a mineral of metals base,
Shows itself pure: 'a weeps for what is done.
   King. O Gertrude, come away!
The sun no sooner shall the mountains touch,
But we will ship him hence, and this vile
   deed   30
We must with all our majesty and skill
Both countenance and excuse. Ho,
   Guildenstern!

Enter ROSENCRANTZ *and* GUILD-
ENSTERN.

Friends both, go join you with some further aid:
Hamlet in madness hath Polonius slain,
And from his mother's closet hath he
   dragg'd him.   35
Go seek him out, speak fair, and bring the body
Into the chapel. I pray you haste in this.
             [*Exeunt Rosencrantz and Guildenstern.*
Come, Gertrude, we'll call up our wisest friends
And let them know both what we mean to do
And what's untimely done, [. . .]   40
Whose whisper o'er the world's diameter,
As level as the cannon to his blank,
Transports his poisoned shot, may miss our
   name,
And hit the woundless air. O, come away!
My soul is full of discord and dismay.
   Exeunt.   45

[SCENE II]

Enter HAMLET.

   Ham. Safely stow'd.
[*Gentlemen.* (*Within.*) Hamlet! Lord Hamlet!]
[*Ham.*] But soft, what noise? Who calls on
   Hamlet? O, here they come.

Enter ROSENCRANTZ *and* [GUILD-
ENSTERN].

   Ros. What have you done, my lord, with
     the dead body?   5
   Ham. [Compounded] it with dust, whereto
   'tis kin.
   Ros. Tell us where 'tis, that we may take it
     thence,
And bear it to the chapel,
   Ham. Do not believe it.
   Ros. Believe what?   10
   Ham. That I can keep your counsel and not
mine own. Besides, to be demanded of a spunge,
what replication should be made by the son of a
king?
   Ros. Take you me for a spunge, my lord?   14
   Ham. Ay, sir, that soaks up the King's countenance, his rewards, his authorities. But such officers do the King best service in the end: he keeps
them, like [an ape] an apple, in the corner of his
jaw, first mouth'd, to be last swallow'd. When he
needs what you have glean'd, it is but squeezing
you, and, spunge, you shall be dry again.   21
   Ros. I understand you not, my lord.
   Ham. I am glad of it, a knavish speech sleeps
in a foolish ear.
   Ros. My lord, you must tell us where the body
is, and go with us to the King.   26
   Ham. The body is with the King, but the King
is not with the body. The King is a thing—
   Guil. A thing, my lord?
   Ham. Of nothing, bring me to him. [Hide fox,
and all after.]   *Exeunt.* 31

[SCENE III]

Enter KING *and two or three.*

   King. I have sent to seek him, and to find
     the body.
How dangerous is it that this man goes loose!
Yet must not we put the strong law on him.

He's lov'd of the distracted multitude,
Who like not in their judgment, but their eyes,   5
And where 'tis so, th' offender's scourge is weigh'd,
But never the offense. To bear all smooth
    and even,
This sudden sending him away must seem
Deliberate pause. Diseases desperate grown
By desperate appliance are reliev'd,   10
Or not at all.

Enter ROSENCRANTZ.

                    How now, what hath befall'n?
Ros. Where the dead body is bestow'd, my
    lord,
We cannot get from him.
King.   But where is he?
Ros. Without, my lord, guarded, to know
    your pleasure.
King. Bring him before us.
Ros.   Ho, bring in the lord.   15
They [HAMLET *and* GUILDENSTERN] *enter.*
King. Now, Hamlet where's Polonius?
Ham. At supper.
King. At supper? where?
Ham. Not where he eats, but where 'a is eaten;
a certain convocation of politic worms are e'en at
him. Your worm is your only emperor for diet:
we fat all creatures else to fat us, and we fat
ourselves for maggots; your fat king and your
lean beggar is but variable service, two dishes,
but to one table—that's the end.   25
    King. Alas, alas!
Ham. A man may fish with the worm that hath
eat of a king, and eat of the fish hath fed that
worm.
    King. What dost thou mean by this?
Ham. Nothing but to show you how a king may
go a progress through the guts of a beggar.   31
    King. Where is Polonius?
Ham. In heaven, send thither to see; if your
messenger find him not there, seek him i' th'
other place yourself. But if indeed you find him
not within this month, you shall nose him as you
go up the stairs into the lobby.
    King. [*To Attendants.*] Go seek him there.
Ham. 'A will stay till you come.
                    [*Exeunt Attendants.*]
    King. Hamlet, this deed, for thine especial
        safety—   40
Which we do tender, as we dearly grieve
For that which thou hast done—must send
    thee hence
[With fiery quickness]; therefore prepare
    thyself,

The bark is ready, and the wind at help,
Th' associates tend, and every thing is bent   45
For England.
    Ham.   For England.
    King.   Ay, Hamlet
    Ham.   Good.
    King. So is it, if thou knew'st our purposes.
Ham. I see a cherub that sees them. But come,
for England! Farewell, dear mother.
    King. Thy loving father, Hamlet.   50
    Ham. My mother: father and mother is man
and wife, man and wife is one flesh—so, my
mother. Come, for England!   *Exit.*
    King. Follow him at foot, tempt him with
        speed aboard.
Delay it not, I'll have him hence to-night.   55
Away, for every thing is seal'd and done
That else leans on th' affair. Pray you make
        haste. [*Exeunt Rosencrantz and*
        Guildenstern.] And, England, if my love
        thou hold'st at aught—
As my great power thereof may give thee sense,
Since yet thy cicatrice looks raw and red   60
After the Danish sword, and thy free awe
Pays homage to us—thou mayst not coldly set
Our sovereign process, which imports at full,
By letters congruing to that effect,
The present death of Hamlet. Do it, England, 65
For like the hectic in my blood he rages,
And thou must cure me. Till I know 'tis
        done,
How e'er my haps, my joys [were] ne'er
        [begun].   *Exit.*

[SCENE IV]

Enter FORTINBRAS *with his army over the*
stage.

Fort. Go, captain, from me greet the
        Danish king.
Tell him that by his license Fortinbras
Craves the conveyance of a promis'd march
Over his kingdom. You know the rendezvous.
If that his Majesty would aught with us,   5
We shall express our duty in his eye,
And let him know so.
    Cap.   I will do't, my lord.
Fort. Go softly on. [*Exeunt all but the Captain.*]

Enter HAMLET, ROSENCRANTZ, [GUILD-
ENSTERN,] *etc.*

Ham. Good sir, whose powers are these?

Cap. They are of Norway, sir.   10

Ham. How purpos'd, sir, I pray you?

Cap. Against some part of Poland.

Ham. Who commands them, sir?

Cap. The nephew to old Norway,
    Fortinbras.

Ham. Goes it against the main of Poland,
    sir,   15

Or for some frontier?

Cap. Truly to speak, and with no addition,

We go to gain a little patch of ground

That hath in it no profit but the name.

To pay five ducats, five, I would not farm it;   20

Nor will it yield to Norway or the Pole

A ranker rate, should it be sold in fee.

Ham. Why then the Polack never will
    defend it.

Cap. Yes, it is already garrison'd.

Ham. Two thousand souls and twenty
    thousand ducats   25

Will not debate the question of this straw.

This is th' imposthume of much wealth and
    peace,

That inward breaks, and shows no cause
    without

Why the man dies. I humbly thank you, sir.

Cap. God buy you, sir. [*Exit.*]

Ros.   Will't please you go, my lord? 30

Ham. I'll be with you straight—go a little
    before.   [*Exeunt all but Hamlet.*]

How all occasions do inform against me,

What is a man, If his chief good and market
    of his time

Be but to sleep and feed? a beast, no more.   35

Sure He that made us with such large discourse,

Looking before and after, gave us not

That capability and godlike reason

To fust in us unus'd. Now whether it be

Bestial oblivion, or some craven scruple   40

Of thinking too precisely on th' event—

A thought which quarter'd hath but one part
    wisdom

And ever three parts coward—I do not know

Why yet I live to say, "This thing's to do,"

Sith I have cause, and will, and strength, and
    means   45

To do't. Examples gross as earth exhort me:

Witness this army of such mass and charge,

Led by a delicate and tender prince,

Whose spirit with divine ambition puff'd

Makes mouths at the invisible event,   50

Exposing what is mortal and unsure

To all that fortune, death, and danger dare,

Even for an egg-shell. Rightly to be great

Is not to stir without great argument,

But greatly to find quarrel in a straw   55

When honor's at the stake. How stand I then,

That have a father kill'd, a mother stain'd,

Excitements of my reason and my blood,

And let all sleep, while to my shame I see

The imminent death of twenty thousand
    men,   60

That for a fantasy and trick of fame

Go to their graves like beds, fight for a plot

Whereon the numbers cannot try the cause,

Which is not tomb enough and continent

To hide the slain? O, from this time forth,   65

My thoughts be bloody, or be nothing
    worth!   *Exit.*

[SCENE V]

Enter HORATIO, [QUEEN] GERTRUDE *and
a* GENTLEMAN.

Queen. I will not speak with her.

Gent. She is importunate, indeed distract.

Her mood will needs be pitied.

Queen.   What would she have?

Gent. She speaks much of her father, says she
hears

There's tricks i' th' world, and hems, and
    beats her heart,   5

Spurns enviously at straws, speaks things in
    doubt

That carry but half sense. Her speech is
    nothing,

Yet the unshaped use of it doth move

The hearers to collection; they yawn at it,

And botch the words up fit to their own
    thoughts,   10

Which as her winks and nods and gestures
    yield them,

Indeed would make one think there might
    be thought,

Though nothing sure, yet much unhappily.

Hor. 'Twere good she were spoken with,
    for she may strew

Dangerous conjectures in ill-breeding minds. 15

    [*Queen.*] Let her come in.   [*Exit Gentleman.*]

[*Aside.*] To my sick soul, as sin's true nature
is,

Each toy seems prologue to some great
    amiss,

So full of artless jealousy is guilt,

It spills itself in fearing to be spilt.   20

    Enter OPHELIA [*distracted, with her hair
    down, playing on a lute*].

Oph. Where is the beauteous majesty of
    Denmark?
Queen. How now, Ophelia?
Oph. "How should I your true   *She sings.*
    love know
      From another one?
        By his cockle hat and staff,   25
        And his sandal shoon."
Queen. Alas, sweet lady, what imports this
    song?
Oph. Say you? Nay, pray you mark.
    "He is dead and gone, lady,   *Song.*
      He is dead and gone,   30
      At his head a grass-green turf,
      At his heels a stone."
O ho!
Queen. Nay, but, Ophelia—
Oph. Pray you mark.   35
[Sings.] "White his shroud as the
    mountain snow"—

Enter KING.

Queen. Alas, look here, my lord.
Oph. "Larded all with sweet flowers, *Song*
    Which bewept to the ground did not go
      With true-love showers."   40
King. How do you, pretty lady?
Oph. Well, God dild you! They say the owl was
a baker's daughter. Lord, we know what we are,
but know not what we may be. God be at your
table!
King. Conceit upon her father.   45
Oph. Pray let's have no words of this, but when
they ask you what it means, say you this:
    "To-morrow is Saint Valentine's day
Song,
      All in the morning betime,
    And I a maid at your window,   50
      To be your Valentine.

    "Then up he rose and donn'd his clo'es,
      And dupp'd the chamber-door,
    Let in the maid, that out a maid
      Never departed more."   55
King. Pretty Ophelia!
Oph. Indeed without an oath I'll make an end
on't
[Sings.] "By Gis, and by Saint Charity,
      Alack, and fie for shame!
    Young men will do't if they come to't,60
      By Cock, they are to blame.

    "Quoth she, 'Before you tumbled me,
      You promis'd me to wed.'"

(He answers.)
    "'So would I 'a done, by yonder sun, 65
      And thou hadst not come to my bed.'"
King. How long hath she been thus?
Oph. I hope all will be well. We must be pa-
tient, but I cannot choose but weep to think they
would lay him i' th' cold ground. My brother
shall know of it, and so I thank you for your good
counsel. Come, my coach! Good night, ladies,
good night. Sweet ladies, good night, good night.
          [Exit.]
King. Follow her close, give her good
    watch, pray you.   *[Exit Horatio.]*
O, this is the poison of deep grief, it springs 75
All from her father's death—and now
    behold!
O Gertrude, Gertrude,
When sorrows come, they come not single
    spies,
But in battalions: first, her father slain;
Next, your son gone, and he most violent
    author   80
Of his own just remove; the people muddied,
Thick and unwholesome in [their] thoughts
    and whispers
For good Polonius' death; and we have done
    but greenly
In hugger-mugger to inter him; poor Ophelia
Divided from herself and her fair judgment, 85
Without the which we are pictures, or mere
    beasts;
Last, and as much containing as all these,
Her brother is in secret come from France,
Feeds on this wonder, keeps himself in clouds,
And wants not buzzers to infect his ear   90
With pestilent speeches of his father's death,
Wherein necessity, of matter beggar'd,
Will nothing stick our person to arraign
In ear and ear. O my dear Gertrude, this,
Like to a murd'ring-piece, in many places 95
Gives me superfluous death.   *A noise within.*
    [*Queen.*   Alack, what noise is this?]
    King. Attend!
Where is my Swissers? Let them guard the door.

Enter a MESSENGER.

What is the matter?
    Mess.   Save yourself, my lord!
The ocean overpeering of his list,   100
Eats not the flats with more impiteous haste
Than young Lartes, in a riotous head,
O'erbears your officers. The rabble call him lord,
And as the world were now but to begin,
Antiquity forgot, custom not known,   105
The ratifiers and props of every word,

[They] cry, "Choose we, Laertes shall be king!"
Caps, hands, and tongues applaud it to the
     clouds,
"Laertes shall be king, Laertes king!"
                              A noise within.
     Queen. How cheerfully on the false trail
          they cry!
O, this is counter, you false Danish dogs!   111

Enter LAERTES *with others.*

King. The doors are broke.
Laer. Where is this king? Sirs, stand you
     all without.
All. No, let's come in.
Laer.   I pray you give me leave.
All. We will, we will.   115
Laer. I thank you, keep the door. [*Exeunt
     Laertes' followers.*] O thou vile king,
Give me my father!
     Queen.   Calmly, good Laertes
Laer. That drop of blood that's calm
     proclaims me bastard,
Cries cuckold to my father, brands the harlot
Even here between the chaste unsmirched
     brow   120
Of my true mother.
     King. What is the cause, Laertes,
That thy rebellion looks so giant-like?
Let him go, Gertrude, do not fear our person:
There's such divinity doth hedge a king
That treason can but peep to what it would, 125
Acts little of his will. Tell me, Laertes,
Why thou art thus incens'd. Let him go,
     Gertrude.
Speak, man.
     Laer. Where is my father?
     King.   Dead.
     Queen.   But not by him
King. Let him demand his fill.   130
     Laer. How came he dead? I'll not be
          juggled with.
To hell, allegiance! vows, to the blackest devil!
Conscience and grace, to the profoundest pit!
I dare damnation. To this point I stand,
That both the worlds I give to negligence,   135
Let come what comes, only I'll be reveng'd
Most throughly for my father.
     King.   Who shall stay you?
     Laer. My will not all the world's:
And for my means I'll husband them so well,
They shall go far with little.
     King.   Good Laertes, 140
If you desire to know the certainty
Of your dear father, is't writ in your revenge

That, swoopstake, you will draw both friend
     and foe,
Winner and loser?
     Laer. None but his enemies.
     King.   Will you know them then?
     Laer. To his good friends thus wide I'll
          ope my arms,   146
And like the kind life-rend'ring pelican,
Repast them with my blood.
     King.   Why, now you speak
Like a good child and a true gentleman.
That I am guiltless of your father's death,   150
And am most sensibly in grief for it,
It shall as level to your judgmnent 'pear
As day does to your eye.
                    A noise within: "Let her come in!"
     Laer. How now, what noise is that?

Enter OPHELIA.

O heat, dry up my brains! tears seven times
     salt   155
Burn out the sense and virtue of mine eye!
By heaven, thy madness shall be paid with
     weight
[Till] our scale turn the beam. O rose of May!
Dear maid, kind sister, sweet Ophelia!
O heavens, is't possible a young maid's wits 160
Should be as mortal as [an old] man's life?
[Nature is fine in love, and where 'tis fine,
It sends some precious instance of itself
After the thing it loves.]
     Oph. "They bore him barefac'd on the   *Song.*
          bier,   165
     [Hey non nonny, nonny, hey nonny,]
     And in his grave rain'd many a tear"—
Fare you well my dove!
     Laer. Hadst thou thy wits and didst
          persuade revenge,
It could not move thus.   170
     Oph. You must sing, "A-down, a-down," and
you call him a-down-a. O how the wheel becomes it! It is the false steward, that stole his
master's daughter.
     Laer. This nothing's more than matter.   174
     Oph. There's rosemary, that's for remem-
brance; pray you, love, remember. And there is
pansies, that's for thoughts.
     Laer. A document in madness, thoughts and
remembrance fitted.   179
     Oph. [*To Claudius.*] There's fennel for you, and
columbines. [*To Gertrude.*] There's rue for you,
and here's some for me; we may call it herb of
grace a' Sundays. You may wear your rue with a
difference. There's a daisy. I would give you

some violets, but they wither'd all when my fa-
ther died. They say 'a made a good end—   186
   [*Sings.*] "For bonny sweet Robin is all my joy."
   Laer. Thought and afflictions, passion, hell it-
self,
She turns to favor and to prettiness.
   Oph. "And will 'a not come again?   *Song.*
      And will 'a not come again?   191
         No, no, he is dead,
         Go to thy death-bed,
      He never will come again.
      "His beard was as white as snow,   195
      [All] flaxen was his pole,
         He is gone, he is gone,
         And we cast away moan,
      God 'a mercy on his soul!"
And of all Christians' souls, [I pray God].
   God buy you.   [*Exit*]
   Laer. Do you [see] this, O God?   202
   King. Laertes, I must commune with your
      grief,
Or you deny me right. Go but apart,
Make choice of whom your wisest friends
   you will,
And they shall hear and judge 'twixt you
   and me.   206
If by direct or by collateral hand
They find us touch'd, we will our kingdom give,
Our crown, our life, and all that we call ours,
To you in satisfaction; but if not,   210
Be you content to lend your patience to us,
And we shall jointly labor with your soul
To give it due content.
   Laer.   Let this be so.
His means of death, his obscure funeral—
No trophy, sword, nor hatchment o'er his
   bones,   215
No noble rite nor formal ostentation—
Cry to be heard, as 'twere from heaven to earth,
That I must call't in question.
   King.   So you shall,
And where th' offense is, let the great axe
   fall.   219
I pray you go with me.

[SCENE VI]

Enter HORATIO *and others.*
   Hor. What are they that would speak with
      me?
   Gentleman. Sea-faring men, sir. They say
      they have letters for you.
   Hor. Let them come in.   [*Exit Gentleman.*]

I do not know from what part of the world   5
I should be greeted, if not from Lord Hamlet.
   Enter SAILORS.
[*1.*] *Sail.* God bless you, sir.
   Hor. Let him bless thee too.
   [*1.*] *Sail.* 'A shall, sir, and ['t] please him.
There's a letter for you, sir—it came from th'
embassador that was bound for England—if
your name be Horatio, as I am let to know it is.
   Hor. [*Reads.*] "Horatio, when thou shalt have
overlooked this, give these fellows some means
to the King, they have letters for him. Ere we
were two days old at sea, a pirate of very warlike
appointment gave us chase. Finding ourselves
too slow of sail, we put on a compell'd valor, and
in the grapple I boarded them. On the instant
they got clear of our ship, so I alone became their
prisoner. They have dealt with me like thieves of
mercy, but they knew what they did: I am to do
a [good] turn for them. Let the King have the
letters I have sent, and repair thou to me with as
much speed as thou wouldest fly death. I have
words to speak in thine ear will make thee dumb,
yet are they much too light for the [bore] of the
matter. These good fellows will bring thee where
I am. Rosencrantz and Guildenstern hold their
course for England, of them I have much to tell
thee. Farewell.

             [He] that thou knowest thine,   30

   Hamlet."
Come, I will [give] you way for these your letters,
And do't the speedier that you may direct me
To him from whom you brought them.   *Exeunt.*

[SCENE VII]

Enter KING *and* LAERTES.
   King. Now must your conscience my
      acquittance seal,
And you must put me in your heart for
   friend,
Sith you have heard, and with a knowing ear,
That he which hath. your noble father slain
Pursued my life.
   Laer.   It well appears. But tell me   5
Why you [proceeded] not against these feats
So criminal and so capital in nature,
As by your safety, greatness, wisdom, all
   things else
You mainly were stirr'd up.
   King.   O, for two special reasons,

Which may to you perhaps seem much
    unsinow'd,   10
But yet to me th' are strong. The Queen his
    mother
Lives almost by his looks, and for myself—
My virtue or my plague, be it either which—
She is so [conjunctive] to my life and soul,
That, as the star moves not but in his sphere, 15
I could not but by her. The other motive,
Why to a public count I might not go,
Is the great love the general gender bear him,
Who, dipping all his faults in their affection,
Work like the spring that turneth wood to
    stone,   20
Convert his gyves to graces, so that my
    arrows,
Too slightly timber'd for so [loud a wind],
Would have reverted to my bow again,
But not where I have aim'd them.
    Laer. And so have I a noble father lost,   25
A sister driven into desp'rate terms,
Whose worth, if praises may go back again,
Stood challenger on mount of all the age
For her perfections—but my revenge will come.
    King. Break not your sleeps for that. You
    must not think   30
That we are made of stuff so flat and dull
That we can let our beard be shook with danger
And think it pastime. You shortly shall hear
    more.
I lov'd your father, and we love ourself,
And that, I hope, will teach you to imagine— 35
    Enter a MESSENGER *with* letters.
[How now? What news?
    Mess.   Letters, my lord, from Hamlet:]
These to your Majesty, this to the Queen.
    King. From Hamlet? Who brought them?
    Mess. Sailors, my lord, they say, I saw
    them not
They were given me by Claudio. He receiv'd
    them   40
Of him that brought them.
    King.   Laertes, you shall hear them.
—Leave us.   [*Exit Messenger.*]
    [*Reads.*] "High and mighty, You shall know I
am set naked on your kingdom. Tomorrow shall
I beg leave to see your kingly eyes, when I shall,
first asking you pardon thereunto, recount the
occasion of my sudden [and more strange] return.

                             [Hamlet.]
What should this mean? Are all the rest
    come back?
Or is it some abuse, and no such thing?   50
    Laer. Know you the hand?
    King.   'Tis Hamlet's character. "Naked"!

And in a postscript here he says "alone."
Can you devise me?
    Laer. I am lost in it, my lord. But let him
    come
It warms the very sickness in my heart   55
That I [shall] live and tell him to his teeth,
"Thus didst thou."
    King.   If it be so, Laertes—
As how should it be so? how otherwise?
Will you be ruled by me?
    Laer.   Ay, my lord,
So you will not o' errule me to a peace.   60
    King. To thine own peace. If he be now
    returned
As [checking] at his voyage, and that he
    means
No more to undertake it, I will work him
To an exploit, now ripe in my device,
Under the which he shall not choose but fall; 65
And for his death no wind of blame shall
    breathe,
But even his mother shall uncharge the practice,
And call it accident.
    Laer.   My lord, I will be rul'd,
The rather if you could devise it so
That I might be the organ.
    King.   It falls right.   70
You have been talk'd of since your travel much,
And that in Hamlet's hearing, for a quality
Wherein they say you shine. Your sum of parts
Did not together pluck such envy from him
As did that one, and that, in my regard,   75
Of the unworthiest siege.
    Laer.   What part is that, my lord?
    King. A very riband in the cap of youth,
Yet needful too, for youth no less becomes
The light and careless livery that it wears
Than settled age his sables and his weeds, 80
Importing health and graveness. Two
    months since
Here was a gentleman of Normandy:
I have seen myself, and serv'd against, the
    French,
And they can well on horseback, but this gallant
Had witchcraft in't, he grew unto his seat, 85
And to such wondrous doing brought his horse,
As had he been incorps'd and demi-natur'd
With the brave beast. So far he topp'd [my]
    thought,
That I in forgery of shapes and tricks
Come short of what he did.
    Laer.   A Norman was't? 90
    King. A Norman.
    Laer. Upon my life, Lamord.
    King.   The very same.

Laer. I know him well. He is the brooch
   indeed
And gem of all the nation.
   King. He made confession of you, 95
And gave you such a masterly report
For art and exercise in your defense,
And for your rapier most especial,
That he cried out 'twould be a sight indeed
If one could match you. The scrimers of their
   nation
He swore had neither motion, guard, nor eye, 101
If you oppos'd them. Sir, this report of his
Did Hamlet so envenome with his envy
That he could nothing do but wish and beg
Your sudden coming o'er to play with you. 105
Now, out of this—
   Laer.   What out of this, my lord?
   King. Laertes, was your father dear to you?
Or are you like the painting of a sorrow,
A face without a heart?
Laer.   Why ask you this? 109
   King. Not that I think you did not love
     your father,
But that I know love is begun by time,
And that I see, in passages of proof,
Time qualifies the spark and fire of it.
There lives within the very flame of love
A kind of week or snuff that will abate it, 115
And nothing is at a like goodness still,
For goodness, growing to a plurisy,
Dies in his own too much. That we would do,
We should do when we would; for this
   "would" changes,
And hath abatements and delays as many 120
As there are tongues, are hands, are
   accidents,
And then this "should" is like a spendthrift's
   sigh,
That hurts by easing. But to the quick of th' ulcer:
Hamlet comes back. What would you undertake
To show yourself indeed your father's son 125
More than in words?
   Laer.   To cut his throat i' th' church,
   King. No place indeed should murther
     sanctuarize,
Revenge should have no bounds. But, good
   Laertes,
Will you do this, keep close within your chamber.
Hamlet return'd shall know you are come
   home. 130
We'll put on those shall praise your excellence,
And set a double varnish on the fame
The Frenchman gave you, bring you in fine
   together
And wager o'er your heads. He, being remiss,
Most generous, and free from all contriving, 135

Will not peruse' the foils, so that with ease,
Or with a little shuffling, you may choose
A sword unbated, and in a [pass] of practice
Requite him for your father.
   Laer.   I will do't,
And for [that] purpose I'll anoint my sword. 140
I bought an unction of a mountebank,
So mortal that, but dip a knife in it,
Where it draws blood, no cataplasm so rare,
Collected from all simples that have virtue
Under the moon, can save the thing from
   death 145
That is but scratch'd withal. I'll touch my point
With this contagion, that if I gall him slightly,
It may be death.
   King.   Let's further think of this,
Weigh what convenience both of time and means
May fit us to our shape. If this should fail, 150
And that our drift look through our bad
   performance
'Twere better not assay'd; therefore this project
Should have a back or second, that might hold
If this did blast in proof. Soft, let me see.
We'll make a solemn wager on your
   cunnings— 155
I ha't!
When in your motion you are hot and dry—
As make your bouts more violent to that end—
And that he calls for drink, I'll have preferr'd him
A chalice for the nonce, whereon but sipping, 160
If he by chance escape your venom'd stuck,
Our purpose may hold there. But stay, what
   noise?

Enter QUEEN.

   Queen. One woe doth tread upon
     another's heel,
So fast they follow. Your sister's drown'd,
   Laertes.
   Laer. Drown'd! O, where? 165
   Queen. There is a willow grows askaunt
     the brook,
That shows his hoary leaves in the glassy stream,
Therewith fantastic garlands did she make
Of crow-flowers, nettles, daisies, and long
   purples
That liberal shepherds give a grosser name, 170
But our cull-cold maids do dead men's
   fingers call them.
There on the pendant boughs her crownet weeds
Clamb'ring to hang, an envious sliver broke,
When down her weedy trophies and herself 174
Fell in the weeping brook. Her clothes
   spread wide,
And mermaid-like awhile they bore her up,

Which time she chaunted snatches of old lauds,
As one incapable of her own distress,
Or like a creature native and indued
Unto that element. But long it could not be   180
Till that her garments, heavy with their drink,
Pull'd the poor wretch from her melodious lay
To muddy death.
    Laer. Alas, then she is drown'd?
    Queen. Drown'd, drown'd.
    Laer. Too much of water hast thou, poor
      Ophelia,
And therefore I forbid my tears; but yet   186
It is our trick, Nature her custom holds,
Let shame say what it will; when these are gone,
The woman will be out. Adieu, my lord,
I have a speech a' fire that fain would blaze, 190
But that this folly drowns it.   *Exit.*
    King.   Let's follow, Gertrude.
How much I had to do to calm his rage!
Now fear I this will give it start again,
Therefore let's follow.   *Exeunt.*

[ACT V, SCENE I]

Enter two CLOWNS [*with spades and
    mattocks*].

    1. Clo. Is she to be buried in Christian burial
when she willfully seeks her own salvation?
    2. Clo. I tell thee she is, therefore make her
grave straight. The crowner hath sate on her, and
finds it Christian burial.   5
    1. Clo. How can that be, unless she drown'd
herself in her own defense?
    2. Clo. Why, 'tis found so.
    1. Clo. It must be [*se offendendo*], it cannot be
else. For here lies the point: if I drown myself
wittingly, lo it argues an act, and all act hath
three branches—it is to act, to do, to perform;
[argal], she drown'd herself wittingly.
    2. Clo. Nay, but hear you, goodman delver—14
    1. Clo. Give me leave. Here lies the water;
good.
Here stands the man; good. If the man go to
this water and drown himself, it is, will he, nill
he, he goes, mark you that. But if the water come
to him and drown him, he drowns not himself;
argal, he that is not guilty of his own death shortens not his own life.   20
    2. Clo. But is this law?
    1. Clo. Ay, marry, is't—crowner's quest law.

    2. Clo. Will you ha' the truth an't? If this had
not been a gentlewoman, she should have been
buried out a' Christian burial.   25
    1. Clo. Why, there thou say'st, and the more
pity that great folk should have countenance in
this world to drown or hang themselves, more
than their even—Christen. Come, my spade.
There is no ancient gentleman but gard'ners,
ditchers; and grave-makers; they hold up
Adam's profession.   31
    2. Clo. Was he a gentleman?
    1. Clo. 'A was the first that ever bore arms.
    [*2. Clo.* Why, he had none.
    1. Clo. What, art a heathen? How dost thou
understand the Scripture? The Scripture says
Adam digg'd; could he dig without arms?] I'll
put another question to thee. If thou answerest
me not to the purpose, confess thyself—
    2.Clo. Go to.   40
    1. Clo. What is he that builds stronger than
either the mason, the shipwright, or the carpenter?
    2. Clo. The gallows-maker, for that outlives a
thousand tenants.   44
    1. Clo. I like thy wit well, in good faith. The
gallows does well; but how does it well? It does
well to those that do ill. Now thou dost ill to say
the gallows is built stronger than the church;
argal, the gallows may do well to thee. To't again,
come.
    2. Clo. Who builds stronger than a mason, a
shipwright, or a carpenter?   51
    1. Clo. Ay, tell me that, and unyoke.
    2. Clo. Marry, now I can tell.
    1. Clo. To't.
    2. Clo. Mass, I cannot tell.   55

Enter HAMLET *and* HORATIO [*afar off*].

    1. Clo. Cudgel thy brains no more about it, for
your dull ass will not mend his pace with beating, and when you are ask'd this question next,
say "a grave- maker": the houses he makes lasts
till doomsday. Go get thee in, and fetch me a sup
of liquor.   60
    [*Exit Second Clown. First Clown digs.*]
  "In youth when I did love, did love,   *Song.*
    Methought it was very sweet,
To contract—O—the time for—a—my behove,
    O, methought there—a—was nothing—
a—meet."
    Ham. Has this fellow no feeling of his
      business? 'a sings in grave-making.   66
    Hor. Custom hath made it in him a
      property of easiness.

Ham. 'Tis e'en so, the hand of little employment hath the daintier sense. 70

1. Clo. "But age with his stealing steps *Song.*
   Hath clawed me in his clutch,
   And hath shipped me into the land,
      As if I had never been such." 74

[*Throws up a shovelful of earth with a skull in it.*]

Ham. That skull had a tongue in it, and could
sing once. How the knave jowls it to the ground,
as if 'twere Cain's jaw-bone, that did the first
murder! This might be the pate of a politician,
which this ass now o'erreaches, one that would
circumvent God, might it not? 80

Hor. It might, my lord.

Ham. Or of a courtier, which could say, "Good
morrow, sweet lord! How dost thou, sweet
lord?" This might be my Lord Such-a-one, that
prais'd my Lord Such-a-one's horse when 'a
[meant] to beg it, might it not? 86

Hor. Ay, my lord.

Ham. Why, e'en so, and now my Lady Worm's,
chopless, and knock'd about the [mazzard) with
a sexton's spade. Here's fine revolution, and we
had the trick to see't. Did these bones cost no
more the breeding, but to play at loggats with
them? Mine ache to think on't.

1. Clo. "A pickaxe and a spade, a spade, *Song.*
      For and a shrouding sheet: 95
   O, a pit of clay for to be made
      For such a guest is meet."
                         [*Throws up another skull.*

Ham. There's another. Why may not that be the
skull of a lawyer? Where be his quiddities now,
his quillities, his cases, his tenures, and his
tricks?   _   100
Why does he suffer this mad knave now to
knock him about the sconce with a dirty shovel,
and will not tell him of his action of battery?
Hum! This fellow might be in 's time a great
buyer of land, with his statutes, his recogni-
zances, his fines, his double vouchers, his recoveries. [Is this the fine of his fines, and the recovery of his recoveries,] to have his fine pate full of
fine dirt? Will [his] vouchers vouch him no more
of his purchases, and [double ones too], than the
length and breadth of a pair of indentures? The
very conveyances of his lands will scarcely lie in
this box, and must th' inheritor himself have no
more, ha?

Hor. Not a jot more, my lord.

Ham. Is not parchment made of sheep-skins?

Hor. Ay, my lord, and of calves'-skins too.115

Ham. They are sheep and calves which seek
out assurance in that. I will speak to this fellow.
Whose grave's this, sirrah?

1. Clo. Mine, sir.

[*Sings.*] "[O], a pit of clay for to be made 120
   [For such a guest is meet].

Ham. I think it be thine indeed, for thou liest
in't.

1. Clo. You lie out on't, sit, and therefore 'tis
not yours; for my part I do not lie in't, yet it is
mine. 124

Ham. Thou dost lie in't, to be in't and say it is
thine. 'Tis for the dead, not for the quick; therefore thou liest.

1. Clo. 'Tis a quick lie, sir, 'twill away again
from me to you.

Ham. What man dost thou dig it for? 130

1. Clo. For no man, sir.

Ham. What woman then?

1. Clo. For none neither.

Ham. Who is to be buried in't? 134

1. Clo. One that was a woman, sir, but, rest her
soul, she's dead.

Ham. How absolute the knave is! we must
speak by the card, or equivocation will undo us.
By the Lord, Horatio, this three years I have took
note of it: the age is grown so pick'd that the toe
of the peasant comes so near the heel of the courtier, he galls his kibe. How long hast thou been
grave-maker?

1. Clo. Of [all] the days i' th' year, I came to't
that day that our last king Hamlet overcame
Fortinbras.

Ham. How long is that since? 145

1. Clo. Cannot you tell that? Every fool can tell
that. It was that very day that young Hamlet was
born—he that is mad, and sent into England.

Ham. Ay, marry, why was he sent into England?

1. Clo. Why, because 'a was mad. 'A shall recover his wits there, or if 'a do not, 'tis no great
matter there. 152

Ham. Why?

1. Clo. 'Twill not be seen in him there, there the
men are as mad as he. 155

Ham. How came he mad?

1. Clo. Very strangely, they say.

Ham. How strangely?

1. Clo. Faith, e'en with losing his wits.

Ham. Upon what ground? 160

1. Clo. Why, here in Denmark. I have been
sexton here, man and boy, thirty years.

Ham. How long will a man lie i' th' earth ere
he rot? 164

1. Clo. Faith, if 'a be not rotten before 'a die—as
we have many pocky corses, that will scarce hold
the laying in—'a will last you some eight year or
nine year. A tanner will last you nine year.

Ham. Why he more than another? 169

1. Clo. Why, sir, his hide is so tann'd with his trade that 'a will keep out water a great while, and your water is a sore decayer of your whoreson dead body. Here's a skull now hath lien you i' th' earth three and twenty years.

Ham. Whose was it?   175

1. Clo. A whoreson mad fellow's it was. Whose do you think it was?

Ham. Nay, I know not.

1. Clo. A pestilence on him for a mad rogue! 'a pour'd a flagon of Rhenish on my head once. This same skull, sir, was, sir, Yorick's skull, the King's 'jester.

Ham. This?   *[Takes the skull.]* 182

1. Clo. E'en that.

Ham. Alas, poor Yorick! I knew him, Horatio, a fellow of infinite jest, of most excellent fancy. He hath bore me on his back a thousand times, and now how abhorr'd in my imagination it is! my gorge rises at it. Here hung those lips that I have kissed I know not how oft. Where be your gibes now, your gambols, your songs, your flashes of merriment, that were wont to set the table on a roar? Not one now to mock your own grinning—quite chop-fall'n. Now get you to my lady's (chamber), and tell her, let her paint an inch thick, to this favor she must come; make her laugh at that. Prithee, Horatio, tell me one thing.   195

Hor. What's that, my lord?

Ham. Dost thou think Alexander look'd a' this fashion i' th' earth?

Hor. E'en so.

Ham. And smelt so? pah!

                              [Puts down the skull.]

Hor. E'en so, my lord.   201

Ham. To what base uses we may return, Horatio! Why may not imagination trace the noble dust of Alexander, till 'a find it stopping a bunghole?

Hor. 'Twere to consider too curiously, to consider so.   206

Ham. No, faith, not a jot, but to follow him thither with modesty enough and likelihood to lead it: Alexander died, Alexander was buried, Alexander returneth to dust, the dust is earth, of earth we make loam, and why of that loam whereto he was converted might they not stop a beer-barrel?
Imperious Caesar, dead and turn'd to clay,
Might stop a hole to keep the wind away.
O that that earth which kept the world in
     awe   215
Should patch a wall t' expel the [winter's] flaw!
But soft, but soft awhile, here comes the King,

Enter KING, QUEEN, LAERTES, *and [a*
   DOCTOR OF DIVINITY, *following] the*
   corse, [with LORDS *attendant].*
The Queen, the courtiers. Who is this they
     follow?
And with such maimed rites? This doth betoken
The corse they follow did with desp'rate
     hand   220
Foredo it own life. 'Twas of some estate.
Couch we a while and mark.
                              [Retiring with Horatio.]
   Laer. What ceremony else?   225
   Ham. That is Laertes, a very noble youth.
     Mark.
   Laer. What ceremony else?
   Doctor. Her obsequies have been as far
     enlarg'd
As we have warranty. Her death was doubtful,
And but that great command o'ersways the
     order,
She should in ground unsanctified been lodg'd
Till the last trumpet; for charitable prayers,   230
[Shards,] flints, and pebbles should be
     thrown on her.
Yet here she is allow'd her virgin crants,
Her maiden strewments, and the bringing home
Of bell and burial.
   Laer. Must there no more be done?
   Doctor.   No more be done:
We should profane the service of the dead   236
To sing a requiem and such rest to her
As to peace-parted souls.
   Laer.   Lay her i' th' earth,
And from her fair and unpolluted flesh
May vioiets spring! I tell thee, churlish
     priest,   240
A minist'ring angel shall my sister be
When thou liest howling.
   Ham.   What, the fair Ophelia!
   Queen. [*Scattering flowers.*] Sweets to the
     sweet, farewell!
I hop'd thou shouldst]lave been my
     Hamlet's wife.
I thought thy bride-bed to have deck'd,
     sweet maid,
And not have strew'd thy grave.
   Laer.   O, treble woe   246
Fall ten times [treble] on that cursed head
Whose wicked deed thy most ingenious sense
Depriv'd thee of! Hold off the earth a while,
Till I have caught her once more in mine
     arms.   250
[*Leaps in the grave.*]
Now pile your dust upon the quick and dead,
Till of this flat a mountain you have made
T' o'ertop old Pelion, or the skyish head

Of blue Olympus.

Ham. [*Coming foward.*] What is he whose grief
Bears such an emphasis, whose phrase of sorrow   255
Conjures the wand'ring stars and makes them stand
Like wonder-wounded hearers? This is I,
Hamlet the Dane! [*Hamlet leaps in after Laertes.*]
    Laer. The devil take thy soul!
                  [*Grappling with him.*]
    Ham.   Thou pray'st not well.
I prithee take thy fingers from my throat.   260
For though I am not splenitive [and] rash,
Yet have I in me something dangerous,
Which let thy wisdom fear. Hold off thy hand!
    King. Pluck them asunder.
    Queen.   Hamlet, Hamlet!
    All.   Gentlemen!
    Hor. Good my lord, be quiet.   265
[*The Attendants part them, and they come out of the grave.*]
    Ham. Why, I will fight with him upon this theme
Until my eyelids will no longer wag.
    Queen. O my son, what theme?
    Ham. I lov'd Ophelia. Forty thousand brothers
Could not with all their quantity of love   270
Make up my sum. What wilt thou do for her?
    King. O, he is mad, Laertes.
    Queen. For love of God, forbear him.
    Ham. 'Swounds, show me what thou't do.
Woo't weep, woo't fight, woo't fast, woo't tear thyself?   275
Woo't drink up eisel, eat a crocodile?
I'll do't. Dost [thou] come here to whine?
To outface me with leaping in her grave?
Be buried quick with her, and so will I.
And if thou prate of mountains, let them throw   280
Millions of acres on us, till our ground,
Singeing his pate against the burning zone,
Make Ossa like a wart! Nay, and thou'lt mouth,
I'll rant as well as thou.
    Queen.   This is mere madness,
And [thus] a while the fit will work on him; 285
Anon, as patient as the female dove,
When that her golden couplets are disclosed,
His silence will sit drooping.
    Ham.   Hear you, sir,
What is the reason that you use me thus?
I lov'd you ever. But it is no matter.   290
Let Hercules himself do what he may,

The cat will mew, and dog will have his day.
                      Exit Hamlet.
    King. I pray thee, good Horatio, wait upon him.
                    [*Exit*]
    Horatio.
[*To Laertes.*] Strengthen your patience in our last night's speech,
We'll put the matter to the present push.—   295
Good Gertrude, set some watch over your son.
This grave shall have a living monument.
An hour of quiet [shortly] shall we see,
Till then in patience our proceeding be. *Exeunt.*

[SCENE II]

Enter HAMLET and HORATIO.

    Ham. So much for this, sir, now shall you see the other—
You do remember all the circumstance?
    Hor. Remember it, my lord!
    Ham. Sir, in my heart there was a kind of fighting
That would not let me sleep. [Methought] I lay   5
Worse than the mutines in the [bilboes]. Rashly—
And prais'd be rashness for it—let us know
Our indiscretion sometime serves us well
When our deep plots do pall, and that should learn us
There's a divinity that shapes our ends,   10
Rough-hew them how we will—
    Hor.   That is most certain.
    Ham. Up from my cabin,
My sea-gown scarf'd about me, in the dark
Grop'd I to find out them, had my desire,
Finger'd their packet, and in fine withdrew   15
To mine own room again, making so bold,
My fears forgetting manners, to [unseal]
Their grand commission; where I found, Horatio—
Ah, royal knavery!—an exact command,
Larded with many several sorts of reasons,   20
Importing Denmark's health and England's too,
With, ho, such bugs and goblins in my life,
That, on the supervise, no leisure bated,
No, not to stay the grinding of the axe,
My head should be strook off.
    Hor.   Is't possible?   25
    Ham. Here's the commission, read it at more leisure.
But wilt thou hear now how I did proceed?

Hor. I beseech you.

Ham. Being thus benetted round with
    [villainies],
Or I could make a prologue to my brains,   30
They had begun the play. I sat me down,
Devis'd a new commission, wrote it fair.
I once did hold it, as our statists do,
A baseness to write fair, and labor'd much
How to forget that learning, but, sir, now   35
It did me yeoman's service. Wilt thou know
Th' effect of what I wrote?

Hor.   Ay, good my lord.

Ham. An earnest conjuration from the
    King,
As England was his faithful tributary,
As love between them like the palm might
    flourish,   40
As peace should still her wheaten garland wear
And stand a comma 'tween their amities,
And many such-like [as's] of great charge,
That on the view and knowing of these contents,
Without debatement further, more or less,   45
He should those bearers put to sudden death,
Not shriving time allow'd.

Hor.   How was this seal'd?

Ham. Why, even in that was heaven
    ordinant.
I had my father's signet in my purse,
Which was the model of that Danish seal;   50
Folded the writ up in the form of th' other,
[Subscrib'd] it, gave't th' impression, plac'd
    it safely,
The changeling never known. Now the next day
Was our sea-fight, and what to this was sequent
Thou knowest already.   55

Hor. So Guildenstern and Rosencrantz go
    to't.

Ham. [Why, man, they did make love to
    this employment,]
They are not near my conscience. Their defeat
Does by their own insinuation grow.
'Tis dangerous when the baser nature comes   60
Between the pass and fell incensed points
Of mighty opposites.

Hor.   Why, what a king is this!

Ham. Does it not, think thee, stand me
    now upon—
He that hath kill'd my king and whor'd my
    mother,
Popp'd in between th' election and my
    hopes,   65
Thrown out his angle for my proper life,
And with such coz'nage—is't not perfect
    conscience
[To quit him with this arm? And is't not to
    be damn'd,

To let this canker of our nature come
In further evil?   70

Hor. It must be shortly known to him
    from England
What is the issue of the business there.

Ham. It will be short; the interim's mine,
And a man's life's no more than to say "one."
But I am very sorry, good Horatio,   75
That to Laertes I forgot myself,
For by the image of my cause I see
The portraiture of his. I'll [court] his favors.
But sure the bravery of his grief did put me
Into a tow'ring passion.

Hor.   Peace, who comes here?]   80

Enter [young OSRIC,] a courtier.

Osr. Your lordship is right welcome back to
Denmark.

Ham. I humbly thank you, sir.—Dost know
this water-fly?

Hor. No, my good lord.

Ham. Thy state is the more gracious, for 'tis a
vice to know him. He hath much land, and fertile;
let a beast be lord of beasts, and his crib shall
stand at the King's mess. 'Tis a chough, but, as I
say, spacious in the possession of dirt.

Osr. Sweet lord, if your lordship were at leisure, I should impart a thing to you from his
Majesty.   90

Ham. I will receive it, sir, with all diligence of
spirit. [Put] your bonnet to his right use, 'tis for
the head.

Osr. I thank your lordship, it is very hot.   94

Ham. No, believe me, 'tis very cold, the wind
is northerly.

Osr. It is indifferent cold, my lord, indeed.

Ham. But yet methinks it is very [sultry] and
hot [for] my complexion.   99

Osr. Exceedingly, my lord, it is very sultry—as
'twere—I cannot tell how. My lord, his Majesty
bade me signify to you that 'a has laid a great
wager on your head. Sir, this is the matter—

Ham. I beseech you remember.   104
[Hamlet moves him to put on his hat.]

Osr. Nay, good my lord, for my ease, in good
faith. Sir, here is newly come to court Laertes,
believe me, an absolute [gentleman], full of most
excellent differences, of very soft society, and
great showing; indeed, to speak sellingly of him,
he is the card or calendar of gentry; for you shall
find in him the continent of what part a gentleman would see.   111

Ham. Sir, his definement suffers no perdition
in you, though I know to divide him inventori-
ally would dozy th' arithmetic of memory, and

yet but yaw neither in respect of his quick sail; but in the verity of extolment, I take him to be a soul of great article, and his infusion of such dearth and rareness as, to make true diction of him, his semblable is his mirror, and who else would trace him, his umbrage, nothing more.   120

Osr. Your lordship speaks most infallibly of him.

Ham. The concernancy, sir? Why do we wrap the gentleman in our more rawer breath?

Osr. Sir?   124

Hor. Is't not possible to understand in another tongue? You will to't, sir, really.

Ham. What imports the nomination of this gentleman?

Osr. Of Laertes?

Hor. His purse is empty already: all 's golden words are spent.   131

Ham. Of him, sir.

Osr. I know you are not ignorant—

Ham. I would you did, sir, yet, in faith; if you did, it would not much approve me. Well, sir?   135

Osr. You are not ignorant of what excellence Laertes is—

Ham. I dare not confess that, lest I should compare with him in excellence, but to know a man well were to know himself.   140

Osr. I mean, sir, for [his] weapon, but in the imputation laid on him by them, in his meed he's unfellow'd.

Ham. What's his weapon?

Osr. Rapier and dagger.   145

Ham. That's two of his weapons—but well.

Osr. The King, sir, hath wager'd with him six Barbary horses, against the which he has impawn'd, as I take it, six French rapiers and poniards, with their assigns, as girdle, [hangers], and so. Three of the carriages, in faith, are very dear to fancy, very responsive to the hilts, most delicate carriages and of very liberal conceit.

Ham. What call you the carriages?

Hor. I knew you must be edified by the margent ere you had done.   156

Osr. The [carriages], sir, are the hangers.

Ham. The phrase would be more germane to the matter if we could carry a cannon by our sides; I would it [might be] hangers till then. But on: six Barb'ry horses against six French swords, their assigns, and three liberal-conceited carriages; that's the French bet against the Danish. Why is this all [impawn'd, as] you call it?

Osr. The King, sir, hath laid, sir, that in a dozen passes between yourself and him, he shall not exceed you three hits; he hath laid on twelve for nine; and it would come to immediate trial; if your lordship would vouchsafe the answer.

Ham. How if I answer no?   170

Osr. I mean, my lord, the opposition of your person in trial.

Ham. Sir, I will walk here in the hall. If it please his Majesty, it is the breathing time of day with me. Let the foils be brought, the gentleman willing, and the King hold his purpose, I will win for him and I can; if not, I will gain nothing but my shame and the odd hits.

Osr. Shall I deliver you so?   179

Ham. To this effect, sir—after what flourish your nature will.

Osr. I commend my duty to your lordship.

Ham. Yours. *[Exit Osric.]* ['A] does well to commend it himself, there are no tongues else for 's turn.

Hor. This lapwing runs away with the shell on his head.   186

Ham. 'A did [comply], sir, with his dug before 'a suck'd it. Thus has he, and many more of the same breed that I know the drossy age dotes on, only got the tune of the time, and out of an habit of encounter, a kind of [yesty] collection, which carries them through and through the most [profound] and [winnow'd] opinions, and do but blow them to their trial, the bubbles are out.   194

Enter a LORD.

Lord. My lord, his Majesty commended him to you by young Osric, who brings back to him that you attend him in the hall. He sends to know if your pleasure hold to play with Laertes, or that you will take longer time.   199

Ham. I am constant to my purposes, they follow the King's pleasure. If his fitness speaks, mine is ready; now or whensoever, provided I be so able as now.

Lord. The King and Queen and all are coming down.

Ham. In happy time.   205

Lord. The Queen desires you to use some gentle entertainment to Laertes before you fall to play.

Ham. She well instructs me.   *[Exit Lord.]*

Hor. You will lose, my lord.   209

Ham. I do not think so; since he went into France I have been in continual practice. I shall win at the odds. Thou wouldst not think how ill all's here about my heart—but it is no matter.

Hor. Nay, good my lord—   214

Ham. It is but foolery, but it is such a kind of [gain-]giving, as would perhaps trouble a woman.

Hor. If your mind dislike any thing, obey it. I will forestall their repair hither, and say you are not fit.

Ham. Not a whit, we defy augury. There is special providence in the fall of a sparrow. If it be [now], 'tis not to come; if it be not to come, it will be now; if it be not now, yet it [will] come— the readiness is all. Since no man, of aught he leaves, knows what is't to leave betimes, let be.

A table prepar'd, [and flagons of wine on it. Enter] Trumpets, Drums, and Officers with cushions, foils, daggers; KING, QUEEN, LAERTES, [OSRIC,] *and all the State.*

King. Come, Hamlet, come, and take this hand from me.   225
        [The King puts Laertes' hand into Hamlet's.]
Ham. Give me your pardon, sir. I have done you wrong,
But pardon't as you are a gentleman.
This presence knows,
And you must needs have heard, how I am punish'd
With a sore distraction. What I have done   230
That might your nature, honor, and exception
Roughly awake, I here proclaim was madness.
Was't Hamlet wrong'd Laertes? Never Hamlet!
If Hamlet from himself be ta'en away,
And when he's not himself does wrong Laertes,   235
Then Hamlet does it not, Hamlet denies it.
Who does it then? His madness. If't be so,
Hamlet is of the faction that is wronged,
His madness is poor Hamlet's enemy.
[Sir, in this audience,]   240
Let my disclaiming from a purpos'd evil
Free me so far in your most generous thoughts,
That I have shot my arrow o'er the house
And hurt my brother.
        Laer.   I am satisfied in nature,
Whose motive in this case should stir me most   245
To my revenge, but in my terms of honor
I stand aloof, and will no reconcilement
Till by some elder masters of known honor
I have a voice and president of peace
To [keep] my name ungor'd. But [till] that time   250
I do receive your offer'd love like love,
And will not wrong it.
        Ham.   I embrace it freely,
And will this brothers' wager frankly play.
Give us the foils. [Come on.]
        Laer.   Come, one for me.

Ham. I'll be your foil, Laertes; in mine ignorance
Your skill shall like a star i' th' darkest night 256
Stick fiery off indeed.
        Laer.   You mock me, sir.
Ham. No, by this hand.
King. Give them the foils, young Osric.
        Cousin Hamlet,
You know the wager?
        Ham.   Very well, my lord.   260
Your Grace has laid the odds a' th' weaker side.
King. I do not fear it, I have seen you both;
But since he is [better'd], we have therefore odds.
        Laer. This is too heavy; let me see another.
        Ham. This likes me well. These foils have all a length?   *[Prepare to play.]*
        Osr. Ay, my good lord.   266
        King. Set me the stoups of wine upon that table.
If Hamlet give the first or second hit,
Or quit in answer of the third exchange,
Let all the battlements their ord'nance fire.   270
The King shall drink to Hamlet's better breath,
And in the cup an [union] shall he throw,
Richer than that which four successive kings
In Denmark's crown have worn. Give me the cups,
And let the kettle to the trumpet speak,   275
The trumpet to the cannoneer without,
The cannons to the heavens, the heaven to earth,
"Now the King drinks to Hamlet." Come begin;
                                Trumpets the while.
And you, the judges, bear a wary eye.
        Ham. Come on, sir.
        Laer.   Come, my lord.
                [They play and Hamlet scores a hit.]
        Ham.   One.
        Laer.   No.
        Ham.   Judgment. 280
        Osr. A hit, a very palpable hit.
        Laer.   Well, again.
        King. Stay, give me drink. Hamlet, this pearl is thine,
Here's to thy health! Give him the cup.
        Drum, trumpets [sound] flourish. A piece goes off [within].
        Ham. I'll play this bout first, set it by a while.   284
Come. *[They play again.]* Another hit; what say you?
        Laer. [A touch, a touch,] I do confess't.
        King. Our son shall win.
        Queen.   He's fat, and scant of breath.
Here, Hamlet, take my napkin, rub thy brows.

The Queen carouses to thy fortune, Hamlet.

Ham. Good madam!

King.   Gertrude, do not drink. 290

Queen. I will, my lord, I pray you pardon me.

King. [Aside.] It is the poisoned cup, it is too late.

Ham. I dare not drink yet, madam; by and by.

Queen. Come, let me wipe thy face.

Laer. My lord, I'll hit him now.

King.   I do not think't.

Laer. [Aside.] And yet it is almost against my conscience.   296

Ham. Come, for the third, Laertes, you do but dally.

I pray you pass with your best violence;
I am sure you make a wanton of me.

Laer. Say you so? Come on.   *[They play.]*

Osr. Nothing, neither way.   301

Laer. Have at you now!

  [Laertes wounds Hamlet; then, in scuffling, they change rapiers.]

King.   Part them, they are incens'd.

Ham. Nay, come again.

  [Hamlet wounds Laertes. The Queen falls.]

Osr.   Look to the Queen there ho!

Hor. They bleed on both sides. How is it, my lord?

Osr. How is't Laertes?   305

Laer. Why, as a woodcock to mine own springe, Osric:

I am justly kill'd with mine own treachery.

Ham. How does the Queen?

King.   She sounds to see them bleed.

Queen. No, no, the drink, the drink—O my dear Hamlet—   309

The drink, the drink! I am pois'ned.   *[Dies.]*

Ham. O villainy! Ho, let the door be lock'd!

Treachery! Seek it out.

Laer. It is here, Hamlet. [Hamlet,] thou art slain.

No medicine in the world can do thee good;
In thee there is not half an hour's life.   315
The treacherous instrument is in [thy] hand,
Unbated and envenom'd. The foul practice
Hath turn'd itself on me. Lo here I lie,
Never to rise again. Thy mother's poi'soned.
I can no more—the King, the King's to blame. 320

Ham. The point envenom'd too!

Then, venom, to thy work.   *[Hurts the King.]*

All. Treason! treason!,

King. O, yet defend me, friends, I am but hurt.

Ham. Here, thou incestious, [murd'rous], damned Dane,   325

Drink [off] this potion! Is [thy union] here?
Follow my mother!   *[King dies.]*

Laer.   He is justly served,

It is a poison temper'd by himself.
Exchange forgiveness with me, noble Hamlet.
Mine and my father's death come not upon thee,   330
Nor thine on me!   *[Dies.]*

Ham. Heaven make thee free of it! I follow thee.

I am dead, Horatio. Wretched queen, adieu!
You that look pale, and tremble at this chance,
That are but mutes or audience to this act,   335
Had I but time—as this fell sergeant, Death,
Is strict in his arrest—O, I could tell you—
But let it be. Horatio, I am dead,
Thou livest. Report me and my cause aright
To the unsatisfied.

Hor.   Never believe it;   340

I am more an antique Roman than a Dane.
Here's yet some liquor left.

Ham.   As th' art a man,

Give me the cup. Let go! By heaven, I'll ha't!
O God, Horatio, what a wounded name,   344
Things standing thus unknown, shall I leave behind me!

If thou didst ever hold me in thy heart,
Absent thee from felicity a while,
And in this harsh world draw thy breath in pain
To tell my story.

  A march afar off [and a shot within].

What warlike noise is this?

  [Osric goes to the door and returns.]

Osr. Young Fortinbras, with conquest come from Poland,   350

To th' ambassadors of England gives
This warlike volley.

Ham.   O, I die, Horatio,

The potent poison quite o'er-crows my spirit.
I cannot live to hear the news from England,
But I do prophesy th' election lights   355
On Fortinbras, he has my dying voice.
So tell him, with th' occurrents more and less
Which have solicited—the rest is silence. *[Dies.]*

Hor. Now cracks a noble heart. Good night, sweet prince,

And flights of angels sing thee to thy rest!   360

  [March within.]

Why does the drum come hither?

Enter FORTINBRAS *with the* [ENGLISH] EMBASSADORS, *[with Drum, Colors, and Attendants].*

Fort. Where is this sight?

Hor.   What is it you would see?

If aught of woe or wonder, cease your search.
   Fort. This quarry cries on havoc. O proud
      death,
What feast is toward in thine eternal cell,   365
That thou so many princes at a shot
So bloodily hast strook?
   [1.] *Emb.*   The sight is dismal,
And our affairs from England come too late.
The ears are senseless that should give us
      hearing,
To tell him his commandment is fulfill'd,   370
That Rosencrantz and Guildenstern are dead.
Where should we have our thanks?
   Hor.   Not from his mouth,
Had it th' ability of life to thank you.
He never gave commandement for their death.
But since so jump upon this bloody question, 375
You from the Polack wars, and you from
      England,
Are here arrived, give order that these bodies
High on a stage be placed to the view,
And let me speak to [th'] yet unknowing world
How these things came about. So shall you
      hear   380
Of carnal, bloody, and unnatural acts,
Of accidental judgments, casual slaughters,
Of deaths put on by cunning and [forc'd] cause,
And in this upshot, purposes mistook

Fall'n on th' inventors' heads: all this can I   385
Truly deliver.
   Fort.   Let us haste to hear it,
And call the noblest to the audience.
For me, with sorrow I embrace my fortune.
I have some rights, of memory in this
      kingdom,
Which now to claim my vantage doth invite
      me.   390
   Hor. Of that I shall have also cause to
      speak,
And from his mouth whose voice will draw
      [on] more.
But let this same be presently perform'd
Even while men's minds are wild, lest more
      mischance
On plots and errors happen.
   Fort.   Let four captains 395
Bear Hamlet like a soldier to the stage,
For he was likely, had he been put on,
To have prov'd most royal; and for his passage,
The soldiers' music and the rite of war
Speak loudly for him.   400
Take up the bodies. Such a sight as this
Becomes the field, but here shows much amiss.
Go bid the soldiers shoot.
   *Exeunt [marching; after the which a peal of
      ordinance are shot off].*

———————— *Questions for Consideration* ————————

Using complete sentences, provide brief answers for the following questions.

1. Comment on appearance versus reality in *Hamlet*.

   _____

   _____

   _____

   _____

   _____

2. Explain Hamlet's view of women after his father's death.

   _____

   _____

   _____

   _____

   _____

3. Why does Hamlet turn against the institution of marriage?

   _____

   _____

   _____

   _____

4. What is the significance of the "play within the play" (i.e., the "Murder of Gonzago") in *Hamlet?*

   _____

   _____

   _____

   _____

5. Explain Hamlet's view of Denmark in the play.

    _____

    _____

    _____

    _____

6. What important comparisons does Hamlet make in lamenting the death of his father?

    _____

    _____

    _____

    _____

7. State the reason(s) for Hamlet's procrastination in terms of killing King Claudius.

    _____

    _____

    _____

    _____

8. Compare the attitude of Hamlet and Laertes on the question of revenge.

    _____

    _____

    _____

    _____

Writing Critically

Select one of the essay topics listed below and compose a 500-word essay which discusses the topic fully. Support your thesis with evidence from the text and with critical and/or historical material. Use the space below for preparing to write the essay.

1. Elaborate on the moral universe of Hamlet as a character.

2. Explain how the difference between appearance and reality contributes to Hamlet's disillusionment.

3. Choose at least three (3) key soliloquies in Hamlet and show how they shed light on his dilemma.

4. Describe how the "Murder of Gonzago" (the so-called "play within the play") that is staged in *Hamlet* "holds the mirror up to nature."

Prewriting Space:

_____

_____

_____

_____

_____

_____

_____

_____

_____

_____

_____

_____

_____

_____

_____

_____

_____

_____

_____

Introduction

Maria de Zayas y Sotomayor
(1590?-1661?/1669?)

Traditionally, world literature texts have included the works of Cervantes and Lope de Vega to represent Spain's Golden Age. In recent years, however, scholars have revised the literary canon of sixteenth and seventeenth century Spain to encompass the writings of female artists of that era. Emerging as a central figure, male or female, is Maria de Zayas y Sotomayor, a writer who is believed to be the first female novelist of Spain. Scholarship about Zayas' works has spurred the translation of her most popular novel, *The Enchantments of Love: Amorous and Exemplary Novels* into other languages including English. This factor alone has motivated more study of her contribution to the world literature canon.

Despite the increased critical attention being given to Maria de Zayas' works, her personal life remains a mystery. According to critics Welles and Gossy, a baptismal record found in the parish of Saint Sebastian in Madrid could possibly be a document that definitely establishes the year of her birth as 1590. Doña Maria de Barasa and Don Fernando de Zayas y Sotomayor are listed on the certificate as parents (507). Biographers believe that the writer's father was an infantry captain who served in the "prestigious military order of Santiago"(Welles and Gossy 507). His service in the court of Pedro Fernandez de Castro, Duque de Lemos in Naples from 1610 to 1616, was advantageous for his young daughter. From her accomplished work in the genre of the courtly romance, it is conceivable that the young Maria accompanied her father to Italy, and that she was exposed to literary life at court.

As with most of her female contemporaries, Maria did not receive a formal education, however, her schooling came as a result of experiences attendant to her social position. During her youth, Maria also participated in the academies of Madrid where the verse she composed won the praise and admiration of Lope de Vega, Alonso de Castrillo Solorzano, and Perez de Montalban, three significant figures of the Golden Age. Most of her early works were published between 1621 and 1639; these include poems that prefaced the compositions of others, and a verse written upon the deaths of Lope de Vegas and Perez de Montalban. Other extant pieces include one play entitled "The Betrayal of Friendship," and two collections of courtly romances, *The Enchantments of Love* (1637) and *The Disenchantments of Love* (1647). [The themes and the artful composition of the two prose works continue to fascinate modern readers.] Based on the number of editions that have been printed, it is evident that her novels were popular during her lifetime. In fact, the two works have maintained that status two centuries after they first appeared.

Information about the author's adult life is scanty. Whether she was single, married, or widowed is not known. It is thought that she was close to the poet and playwright Ana Cars de Mallen "with whom she shared a home in Madrid for a period of time" (Wells and Gossy, 508). A contemporary male author, Fontanella, in a satirical piece, describes Zayas' physical appearance as manly, but without the necessary "equipment." According to Fontanella, there is no "sword under her skirt" (Wells and Gossy 508). Lope de Vega, in his poetic work, *Laurel de Apolo*, suggests that Zayas writes in the tradition of Sappho of Lesbos. In an effort to shed more light on Zayas' life, some biographers have attempted to use publication facts to draw conclusions about her whereabouts at various periods. For example, the idea that she moved from Madrid to Zaragoza was based on the fact that the first editions of her two collections of stories, the *Enchantments of Love* and the *Disenchantments of Love*, were published there. Obviously, this one observation cannot provide hard evidence of the author's residence. Other critics have suggested that the protagonist of the *Disenchantments*, Lysis, is the voice of the author. One reason set forth to support the idea is that at the end of the work, Lysis enters a convent; thus, the critics suggest that Zayas' absence from public view can be attributed to her entry into a convent after the publication of the work.

Although Maria de Zayas' novel *The Enchantments of Love* and its sequel, *The Disenchantments of Love*, may not be the definitive sources of information about her life, they are significant resources for studying the Spanish Golden Age. As did a number of Renaissance writers, Zayas reworked the plots of other literary compositions to create a new work. She drew elements from the chivalric, sentimental, pastoral, picaresque, Moorish, Byzantine, and Italianate fiction of her day. Furthermore, she used the popular Golden Age genre, the comedia, to enhance her works. In *The Disenchantments*, for example, the stage device of a woman's appearance as a man (disguise), assists in furthering the irony of her plots.

A number of scholars view the stories in the two novels as realistic depictions of seventeenth century life because they are marked by graphic and lavish descriptions, and precise settings in specific moments in Spanish history. These works do not portray the lives of common persons, instead they depict the lives of the courtly nobility. This factor can be attributed to the author's own experience in that environment, and her limited exposure to other socioeconomic classes.

The twenty stories that compose the two works (ten stories in each) are unified by the structure of the frame story, the use of dramatic language, the artful development of character, and the consistency of theme. The story that frames each of the novels begins with the host, Lysis, asking each of the ladies and gentlemen visiting her home to narrate a story of love and deception. Although there are diverse voices recounting the stories, the individual narratives maintain continuity through the structure of the framed tale, which has "a beginning, [a] suspenseful development, and a resolution to the love affair" (Fox-Lockert 25). Language also plays a key role in the narratives. Zayas' use of lively dialogue gives the narrative a dramatic quality and through the use of monologues, she delineates and humanizes the characters. According to critic H. Patsy Boyer, the development of character separates Zayas from other writers of the period in that most works of this kind focus on external action (XVII). In addition, Zayas populates both sets of stories with almost all of the same characters. Finally, the author unifies the work by allowing the host to provide her guests with the themes around which their narrative should be centered—love and delusion.

As stated above, the *Enchantments* contains ten stories narrated by five men and five women attending a five night Christmas soiree at the home of Lysis, a gentlewoman. The purpose of this gathering is to entertain the hostess who is ill with quartan fever. Within the frame story the character of each storyteller is developed and the reader is given commentary from the group about the stories that have been told. Also in the frame, a love plot develops. Don Juan switches his amorous attention from Lysis to her cousin, Lisarda, and don Juan's friend, don Diego, begins to show his affection for Lysis. The collection of stories ends with the omniscient narrator promising a second group of stories that frames "don Juan's ingratitude, Lisarda's change of heart, and Lysis' wedding" (Zayas 312).

In the frame of the second collection, the *Disenchantments*, the soiree planned to celebrate Lysis' and don Diego's marriage on New Year's Day is postponed for over a year. When the festivities begin, the hostess, Lysis, establishes new rules for presenting the narratives. At this gathering, all stories are to be recounted by the women in the group. The rules also stipulate that each story has to be a true account whose aim is to inform women of the deceptive nature of men, and to "be in defense of women's good name" (Boyer XVII). When the last narrative has been told the hostess, Lysis, decides not to marry don Diego; she instead retires to a convent. Four of the other women at the soiree join her. At the conclusion of the *Disenchantments*, the omniscient narrator does not view Lysis' decision as "tragic," but as "the happiest [decision] that one could have asked for, because she, wanted and desired by many, did not subject herself to anyone" (Boyer XVII). According to critic William H. Clamurro, the *Disenchantments* dramatizes "(1) the folly and impossibility of trusting men, (2) the inevitably tragic end of any marriage or love affaire, and (3) the wisdom of necessarily rejecting all men and retreating from the secular world into the safety of the female microcosm represented by the convent" (219).

The Disenchantments is a more unified work than is its predecessor because it clearly defines a feminist theme. The stories of this group, told from the point of view of five women, recount the brutal and irrational behavior of men toward women. Six of the ten stories end with the vicious murder of the wives and in the other four the female character suffers torture and persecution before finally entering a convent.

The Enchantments, on the other hand, has a variety of voices both male and female. Each narrative represents various types of literary genre: the pastoral, the Byzantine tale, the satire, the miracle story, and the honor presses with cloak and dagger elements (Boyer XVII). In these stories the reader encounters miracles, prophetic dreams, ghosts with messages from God, the devil, and women disguised as men. As the title of the entire work suggests, the author uses these literary devices to amaze and entertain the audience. Thus, the feminist themes appearing therein are deeply embedded in the stories. The ending for six of the stories is a happy marriage, protagonists of two narratives enter the convent, and the foolish male protagonists of two satiric stories meet death.

Included in this anthology are the introductory selections from *The Enchantments of Love* entitled "To the Reader," "Prologue by an Objective Reader," "Beginning," and the novella "The Power of Love." In the introductory material, the author challenges the contemporary societal norms that prevent women from obtaining a formal education, and that places limitations on their "artistic productivity" (Saffar 198). Furthermore, she raises the issue concerning the message that contemporary literature sends about male/female relationships. In one of the most moving novellas, "The Power of Love," the reader readily sees the characteristics that are identified with the enchanting narratives while simultaneously being confronted with provocative questions relevant to male/female relationships. Its theme, wife battering, becomes one of the primary focuses of the *Disenchantments*. This narrative describes the after-marriage transformation of man from an attentive suitor to an abusive husband. More importantly, the story depicts a woman's effort to ameliorate her situation. Thus, "The Power of Love" provides a linkage between Maria de Zayas' two important prose works (EEN).

BIBLIOGRAPHY

Berry, Mary Elizabeth. "Crisis and Disorder in the World of Maria de Zayas y Sotomayor." *Maria de Zayas: The Dynamics of Discourse*. Williamsen and Whitnack 23–39.

Boyer, H. Patsy. Introduction. Zayas XI–XXXI.

Clamurro, William H. "Madness and Narrative Form in 'Estragos que causa el vicio." Williamsen and Whitenace 219–233.

Ford-Lockert, Lucia. *Women Novelists in Spanish and Spanish America*. Metuchen, N.J.: The Scarecrow Press, 1979.

Garcia, Susan Paun de. "Zayas as Writer: Hell Hath No Fury." Williamsen and Whitenack 40–57.

Miller, Beth, ed. *Women in Hispanic Literature: Icons and Fallen Idols*. Berkeley: University of California Press, 1983.

Saffar, Ruth El. "Ana/Lysis and Zayas: Reflection on Courtship and Literary Women in the *Novellas amorosos y ejemplares*." Williamsen and Whitenack, 192–216.

Ward, Phillip, ed. *The Oxford Companion to Spanish Literature*. Oxford: Oxford University Press, 1978.

Welles, Marcia L. and Mary S. Gossy "Maria de Zayas y Sotomayor (1590?–1661?/1669?)" *Spanish Women Writers: A Bio-Bibliographical Source Book*. Ed. Linda Gold Levine, Ellen Engelson Marson, and Gloria Feiman-Waldman. Westport, Connecticut: Greenwood Press, 1993.

Willamsen, Amy R. and Judith A. Whitenack, eds. *The Dynamics of Discourse*. Madison: Farileigh Dickerson University Press, 1995.

Zayas, Maria de. *The Enchantments of Love: Amorous and Exemplary Novels*. Trans. H. Patsy Boyer. Berkeley: University of California Press, 1990.

from The Enchantments of Love
Amorous and Exemplary Novels

Maria de Zayas

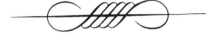

Beginning

It was one of those short December afternoons when bitter cold and terrible snowstorms make people stay indoors to enjoy a fire stoked up to produce enough heat to compete with the month of July and which even makes you thirsty. You want to please the ladies so they won't miss their walks in the Prado park or along the river or any of the other pastimes ladies enjoy in the court city of Madrid.

Lovely Lisarda, discreet Matilda, witty Nise, and wise Phyllis, all beautiful, noble, rich, and good friends, gathered together to entertain Lysis, a wonder of nature and a marvelous prodigy of this court city (her myriad charms had been attacked by a noxious ague). The ladies spent the afternoon in delightful innocent chatter to make Lysis forget her irksome illness in pleasant conversation with her good friends. (It was easy for them to get together at any time as they all lived in the same building, although in different apartments, as was the custom in Madrid.) Because it was so close to Christmas, a happy time perfect for the celebration of parties, games, and friendly joking, they decided among themselves to hold a soiree, a special entertainment for Christmas Eve and for the other days of the holiday season. In light of this agreement, they decided to invite don Juan. He was a handsome, rich, and clever young man, Nise's cousin, and the dearly beloved object of Lysis's affection. She was hoping to surrender to him in legal matrimony all the delightful charms with which heaven had endowed her.

Don Juan, however, was attracted to Lisarda, Lysis's cousin, and, since he wanted her to be the mistress of his affection, he did not return Lysis's love. The lovely lady resented having the very cause of her jealousy before her eyes and hated having to pretend to be cheerful and smile when in her heart she harbored mortal suspicions that had, in fact, occasioned her illness. Her depression was aggravated by the fact that Lisarda acted overjoyed to be the chosen one and proud that don Juan loved her. In amorous competition between the two cousins, Lisarda always won out because she was unprincipled in getting her way.

They did invite don Juan to the party and he, at the ladies' request and in appreciation of the invitation, brought don Alvaro, don Miguel, don Alonso, and don Lope, all his peers in nobility, elegance, wealth, and equally fond of passing their time in pleasant and witty conversation. They all gathered together and decided to make Lysis the president of the delightful entertainments. They asked her to organize everything and to tell each one what his or her part was to be. She tried to excuse herself from this duty because of her illness and, when they insisted, she nominated her mother to do it for her and thus she eluded the duties her friends had imposed on her.

Laura, which was the name of Lysis's mother, was a wise and noble lady whom death, life's bitter foe, had deprived of her beloved husband. The lovely widow organized the party like this: she exempted her daughter Lysis from actually participating because of her illness, but she put her in charge of organizing the music. Laura expressly commanded her daughter to give the musicians all the songs and ballads they were to perform on each of the five nights to make the entertainment more lively. She commanded her niece Lisarda and the lovely Matilda to invent a gay masque in which all the ladies and gentlemen could show off their elegance, gentility, grace, and talent. On the first night, after the masque, Lisarda and Matilda would each tell an "enchantment." In using this term she wanted to avoid the common term "novella," so trite that it was now entirely out of fashion. To keep the gentlemen from complaining about the ladies' preeminence, she would alternate their parts. On the second night, don Alvaro and don Alonso; on the third, Nise and Phyllis; on the fourth, don Miguel and don Lope; and on the fifth, don Juan and Laura herself would tell an enchantment. They would end their Christmas celebration with a sumptuous banquet, which Lysis, as hostess, wanted to offer all of her guests. They would invite the ladies' mothers and the gentlemen's fathers, for it just so happened that none of the ladies had a father and none of the gentlemen had a mother, as death does not accommodate the desires of mortals.

It was incumbent upon Lysis to inaugurate the festivities. She sent for the two ablest musicians she could find to accompany her angelic voice, for that is how she planned to contribute to the entertainment. She notified everyone that, as day took refuge and shrouded itself in night's dark mantle of mourning for the absense of the rubicund lord of Delphi, who had departed to take happy daylight to the Indies, thereby bringing dark shadows to our hemisphere, at that time they should assemble in lovely Lysis's sitting room to celebrate Christmas Eve with all the agreed upon entertainments. Her parlor was hung with heavy Flemish tapestries whose woods, groves, and flowers depicted exotic landscapes like Arcadia and the hanging gardens of Babylon. The room was crowned by a rich dais piled high with mountains of green velvet cushions ornamented with splendid silver embroidery and tassels. To one side of the dais there was a luxurious couch that was to serve as a seat, sanctuary, and throne for the lovely Lysis who, because of her illness, could enjoy this distinction. It was green brocade with gold trimming and fringe, the green symbolizing a hope she did not really feel. All around the hall were rows of green velvet chairs and numerous taborets for

the gentlemen to sit on while enjoying the warmth of a silver brazier where incense was burned to perfume the dais.

At three that afternoon, the discreet Laura and the lovely Lysis welcomed the ladies with great pleasure. Not only did the special guests come, but many others as well who had heard about the entertainment and decided to attend and occupy the numerous extra chairs. Lysis, dressed in blue, the color of jealousy, was reclining on her couch. For the sake of modesty and appearance, she had insisted upon dressing up in spite of her quartan fever. The hall looked like a landscape illuminated by the fair sun god Apollo, so many were the candles that sparkled. It delighted all eyes that beheld the scene and echoed with laughter. The musicians took their seats next to Lysis's couch and began with a *gallardia*, inviting the ladies and the gentlemen to move out onto the floor, each one bearing a flaming torch to give effect to the stately movements of the dance. The musicians had also prepared the ballad for Lysis to sing upon the conclusion of the dance.

Don Juan, as master of ceremonies and leader, started the lively dance alone. He was so handsome that the guests could not take their eyes from his elegant figure dressed in rich brown, with his golden chains and diamond buttons sparkling like stars. Lisarda and don Alvaro followed. She was wearing brown to match don Juan's colors. Don Alvaro wore Matilda's colors, as he was in her thrall. Matilda was dressed in walnut brown and silver and accompanied don Alonso, smartly dressed in black because that's the color Nise wore. Nise's dress was of soft velvet decorated with gold buttons. Don Miguel lead her by the hand. He too wore black because, although he wanted to pay court to Phyllis, he did not dare don her colors for fear of don Lope, who was wearing Phyllis's green in hope of being accepted by her.

When Lysis saw in his colors how don Juan preferred Lisarda, she understood the message stated in his dress and felt disillusioned by her love for him. She concealed her sorrow by swallowing her sighs and stifling her tears and watched the grace and dexterity with which her friends danced the spritely masque with its pirouettes so intricate, its crosses, ribbons, and labyrinths so stately that everyone wished it would last a hundred years. Then, with tears still in her eyes, Lysis prepared to display her talent by accompanying the musicians with her lovely voice. Everyone took a seat to listen while she sang the ballad:

Forests, hear my lament:
listen while I sing my plaints,
for happiness never lasts
for the unfortunate.
Long ago I testified
to your elm and ash trees,
to your crystal springs,
about Celio's faithlessness.
Tenderly you heard my plaints
and distracted me from my jealousy
with the loving music
of your gently flowing brooks.
Touched, he saw his folly,
for heaven had wrought my constancy;
briefly he sought to repay my affection
but how soon he tired!
Happy to see my love rewarded,
I hoped to enjoy my good fortune,
for even if he really didn't love me
at least he seemed responsive.
My soul judged its quarters
too small to contain my great joy,
for it mistook as favors
his discourtesy and disdain.
I adored his deception;
it served to increase my desire
to worship his charms,
what madness and folly!
Ungrateful lover, who would think
that these things I relate
would hasten and increase
your desire to forget me.

You are right to be cruel,
I complain unjustly,
because those who love least
are the most fortunate.
The village, seeing your thoughts turned
to a new mistress of your affection,
your eyes set on another love,
talks about your inconstancy,
while I, because I love you,
lament your neglect and rue your disdain.

Such an illustrious audience would not show proper gratitude if it did not praise the lovely Lysis for her beautiful voice. Don Juan's father, don Francisco, in refined and courtly language, spoke for everyone in saying how much they appreciated the great favor she had shown them. This caused the lovely lady to blush and, despite her illness, the suffusion of color that rushed to her cheeks heightened her beauty. Don Juan almost repented of his change of allegiance, but the moment he again looked at Lisarda, he became enmeshed in the bonds of her beauty as he watched her move to the special seat to tell her enchantment and thus begin this first night's entertainment.

She waited to begin until she saw everyone hushed and in suspense, hanging on each one of the well-chosen words her sweet mouth would utter. Searching her mind for just the right ones, very charmingly, she began:

Third Night

The ladies and gentlemen had their appetites whetted by the savory entertainments of the first two nights so, scarcely had the afternoon of the third soiree begun when guests started gathering in beautiful Lysis's house. She greeted them with her accustomed courtesy. On this occasion, she'd dressed in black, sprinkled with countless diamond buttons; among so many twinkling stars, she looked like the sun, so radiant was her beauty. While the guests exchanged greetings and chatted pleasantly, the afternoon passed quickly. As night began to fall, it came time to start the entertainment, so Lysis signaled the musicians who, accompanying her fine voice, sang this sonnet in honor of our King Philip IV:

Sun who draws from the heavenly sun
courage, greatness, light, and radiance;
pearl who drew his being from the love
between the sun Philip and mother-of-pearl
   Margaret;

phoenix who revives in our Spain
greater glories to make Spain greater,
garden filled with regal purple blooms
to set off your royal fleur-de-lis;

Jupiter who reigns over the holy choir,
who bathes in sweet harmony as if in light,
being the sweet musician to his nymphs;

and, if sight does not deceive truth,
a youthful cupid with his golden darts
is Philip, our sun, and King of Spain.

Disappointed in love by don Juan and grateful to don Diego, the lovely Lysis had deliberately changed the style of her song to avoid the theme of love and jealousy and so discourage the rivalry between the two men. Lysis had made don Juan promise that they'd be friends because she

loved don Diego, and they both were feigning courtesy toward each other.

It was Nise's turn to tell the fifth enchantment on this third night, so she occupied the special seat and began like this:

"No one can ignore the power of love, especially when it overwhelms noble hearts. Love is like the sun; it has a powerful effect wherever it goes. You will see this clearly in my enchantment, which starts like this":

The Power of Love

Naples, a famous city in Italy, is renowned for its wealth, noble citizens, splendid buildings, pleasant location, and great beauty. It is crowned with many gardens and adorned with crystalline fountains, lovely ladies and elegant gentlemen. Laura was born there, a rare miracle of nature, and so exquisite that, among the most beautiful and elegant ladies of the city, she was considered a heavenly wonder. Experts in the city had made a list of the eleven most beautiful women and selected from the eleven three, and Laura was one of the eleven and also one of the three. She was her parents' third child, following two brothers who were as virtuous and noble as she was beautiful. Her mother died giving birth to her, leaving her father as tutor and comfort to the three lovely children who, although motherless, had their father's wise concern to make up for this lack.

Their father, don Antonio was his name, was of the Garrafa family, closely related to the duke and duchess of Nochera. He was lord of Piedrablanca, an estate located four miles from Naples, although he maintained his house and center of activity in town.

Don Alejandro, don Carlos, and Laura were brought up with all the care and attention that their noble position required. Their father made every effort to see that they were worthy of their nobility and wealth, training the children in the manners and exercises appropriate to a lovely lady and fine gentlemen. The beautiful Laura lived with the modesty and decorum befitting such a rich and important young lady. She was the apple of her father's eye, her brothers' delight, and the splendor of the city.

The one who most doted on Laura was don Carlos, the younger of the two brothers. He loved her so dearly that he outdid himself to please her.

This was not surprising given Laura's grace, beauty, charm, discretion, and above all her modesty, which charmed not only her relatives but even those people who had only casual contact with her.

Her modesty needed no mother, for not only did her father and brothers keep vigilant watch over her beauty, her own chaste and pure thinking carefully governed her behavior. When she reached the age of discretion, she could no longer deny her company to the prominent ladies who were her relatives. For this, her great beauty would have to pay its price to misfortune.

It was the custom in Naples for maidens to attend parties and soirees given in the viceroy's palace and other private homes of the nobility. This practice isn't considered proper in other parts of Italy; indeed, in many places maidens aren't even permitted to go to mass, a custom imposed by long tradition despite the effort of ecclesiastical and lay authorities to change it.

At last, endowed with her beauty and modesty, Laura went forth to see and be seen, although, if she'd remembered the goddess Diana, she wouldn't have trusted in her modesty. Her slendid eyes were mortal basilisks to men's souls, her grace, a monster to endanger their lives, her wealth and noble condition, bait to the desires of a thousand gallant youths of the city, all of whom hoped to enjoy her great beauty in marriage.

Among the many suitors who served Laura, the most notable was don Diego Pinatelo. He was a discreet gentleman of the noble house of the dukes of Monteleon, rich and so enviable in all of his qualities that it wasn't surprising that, self-confidently, he felt sure he could win the beautiful Laura. He was certain that her family would want to have such a noble husband for their daughter because, among all the suitors for her lovely hand, don Diego was clearly superior. The moment he saw Laura, her beauty caused him to surrender his heart to her so passionately that he might have died, if it had been time for him to give up his life. (So powerful, sometimes, is the effect of beholding beauty.) He first saw her at a party given by one of the city's princes. Don Diego set eyes upon her and fell head over heels in love. His love was so intense at that moment that he felt as if he'd loved her forever, and he wanted to let her know this.

Another custom in Naples was that at parties there was a master of ceremonies who would lead the ladies out to dance and give them to a gentleman chosen by him. Don Diego took advantage of this custom; undoubtedly money was exchanged, and scarcely had he warmed the master's hands when he found in his own hands those of the beautiful Laura, just in time to dance a galliard. This arrangement did him little good, however, because his passion, inflamed by her icy aloofness, led him to blurt: "My lady, I adore you." Instantly, the beautiful lady excused herself, feigning some indisposition. She left him and returned to her seat. This made don Diego very sad, and everyone who was watching the dance wondered what had happened. Throughout the rest of the party, don Diego suffered deep remorse and despaired. He did not merit a single glance from Laura, not because the beautiful lady wasn't attracted by don Diego's appearance, but because she felt constrained to uphold her modesty as she always had.

Night came and the party ended, which was sad for don Diego because Laura went home and he likewise had to go home. He went to bed (a common recourse for the sorrowful, who consult their pillows as if pillows could offer comfort). He tossed and turned and complained bitterly about his misfortune—if indeed it was a misfortune to have seen the beauty who was driving him crazy. If Laura had heard his complaints on this occasion, she might have felt more kindly disposed toward him than she had shown herself that afternoon.

"Alas!" the wounded youth lamented. "My heavenly Laura, how cruelly you reacted to those ill-fated words I uttered! If only you could know that my soul is more yours than the one you bear within you. There can be no offense against your honor or your family for, clearly, if I intend to employ my soul in your service, I'll make you my wife and in no way will your good name suffer. Is it possible, beloved mistress mine, that one so beautiful can have a heart so cruel it won't let you

understand that now I've seen you, I'm not the same person I was before? I've lost my heart and I feel empty. Everything I am I've surrendered to your beauty. If I offend you in doing this, blame your beauty, for once human eyes behold it, they must desire it. There can be no other choice but to love you. Nothing seems more rational than for me to call myself your slave.

"Poor me! But I complain without cause. Since Laura's careful about her modesty and decorum, she was obliged to treat me harshly. It would have been improper for her to accept my love the very moment it commenced. Scarcely had my desire been born when I declared it to her. I'm rich; in nobility, my parents are in no way inferior to hers, so why should I despair? If I formally ask for her hand in marriage, why should her father refuse to give her to me? Take courage, cowardly heart, just because you love, you shouldn't fear. My misfortune can't be so great that I won't obtain what I desire so much."

Don Diego spent the night thinking these thoughts, sometimes heartened by his hopes, sometimes discouraged by his fears, as is natural in lovers. Meanwhile, the beautiful Laura had been profoundly affected by the sight of the handsome don Diego. In her memory, she kept hearing him say, "I adore you." Thoughtfully, as if loving were a crime, she pondered her freedom and the risks to her reputation. But if she rejected him, she was threatened by the same danger. Laura was the most confused woman on the face of the earth, sometimes encouraging her desires and sometimes struggling to repress them. These thoughts and worries caused her to avoid pleasurable activities. She wouldn't even talk with the people in her household. Then she began to seek occasion to see the cause of her passion.

The days slipped by and don Diego could do nothing but complain about his beloved mistress's disdain, for, even though she was in love, she granted him no favors. She only permitted him an occasional glimpse of her, and this she did so casually and nonchalantly that he never had the chance to tell her of his suffering. Although her own feelings might have led her to allow his courtship, the care with which she disguised her emotions was such that she hid the secret of her love even from her closest and most affectionate maids. Of course her sadness made her father and brothers suspicious and quite apprehensive. Don Carlos, in particular, noted her melancholy. Since he loved her most tenderly and trusted in their close relationship, he kept asking her what was causing her unhappiness. Noting that don Diego kept passing by their house, he came close to suspecting the source of her sorrow. But Laura blamed her poor health and managed to satisfy any doubts he might have had through her modesty and discretion. Even so, her family did not neglect keeping careful watch over her honor.

On one of the many night's don Diego spent outside Laura's house waiting for dawn to arrive, he brought a servant with him to play music and serve as his spokesman, since he had no other way to express his love to her. This servant had one of the sweetest voices in that city so famous for its fine voices. He was to sing a ballad that don Diego had composed for this occasion about the love and fears he felt. He was jealous of a rich, noble gentleman, a good friend of Laura's brothers, who came to their house with frequency. Don Diego feared that her inattention to him might be caused by her love for this rival—a good example of how jealousy colors even innocent situations. On that night, the musician sang the ballad:

Oh, aspiring love,
if the mistress you have chosen,
already obliged, recognizes another
more fortunate master,
why do you wander lost,
following in her footsteps,
noting all her actions,
seeking to gaze upon her?
What good does it do
for you to ask favor from heaven,
the impossible from love,
change from time?
Why do you call on jealousy
when you know that
in the impossible love
jealousy favors the beloved?
If you desire to see your beloved
far away, you are foolish,
for it makes no sense to punish yourself
simply because you wish to punish her.
If you ask discord
to wound her breast,
clearly you will see pleasure
turn into grief.
If you tell your eyes
to state their feeling,
you see that they accomplish little
no matter how tenderly they look.
If the one who could bring you
remedy for your ills,
one who is a faithful friend,
always gracious,
is also a prisoner

to that proud angel,
how can he help you
in your amorous enterprise?
If only in your love
you were to receive a reward,
if your mistress were to say
I feel sorry for you.
You look at your mistress
and see her unloving,
but even this disappointment
cannot change your desire.
You are like Tantalus
who sees the fleeting crystal
that he can never taste
reaching almost to his lips.
If only you could merit
for your great feeling
some feigned deception,
for I fear you'll die;
your sorrows must be like
the suffering of purgatory;
but I see your pain so hopeless
that it equals the torments of hell.
But you've made your choice
and death is the only remedy
for it would be a cowardly act for you
to turn your back and flee.

Sitting behind the window blind, Laura had been listening to the song from the very beginning. She decided she had to defend her reputation, because the false suspicions expressed in don Diego's verses impugned her honor. And so, what love couldn't accomplish, her fear of losing her good name did. Her shame battled with her love and finally she made up her mind to defend herself. Seeing don Diego nearby, she opened the window and softly, so no one could hear, she whispered to him:

"My lord, don Diego, it would be a miracle if, being in love, you didn't feel jealousy. There has never been a love without jealousy, or jealousy without love, but the jealousy you feel is so unfounded that I feel obliged to speak with you, something I never intended to do. I'm deeply troubled to hear my reputation sullied by the words of your song and the music of the lute, and worst of all, in the mouth of a musician who, because he's a servant, must be an enemy. I haven't scorned you for any other suitor; indeed, if anyone in the world merits my affection, it's you and you'll be the one to win me, if you're willing to take the risk. May your love pardon my daring and boldness in acting like this and in telling you that, from this day forward, you may consider yourself mine, just as I'll consider myself fortunate to think that I'm yours. Please believe that I'd never have spoken thus if the night, with her dark mantle, didn't cloak my shame and the color that rushes to my face while I voice this truth. It was born the first day I saw you and has remained locked up inside me ever since. You're the only one who knows this. It would grieve me sorely if anyone were witness to my confession, except you who obliges me to confess."

Overcome by his emotion, the enamored don Diego, the happiest man on earth, was struggling to respond and thank the beautiful Laura, when she heard the doors of her house open and saw two swordsmen assault him so suddenly that, had he not been prepared and his servant not been standing by with drawn sword, he might never have gotten to pursue his amorous desires any further.

Laura saw the attack and recognized her two brothers. Fearing they might catch her, she closed the window as quietly as she could, ran to her room, and quickly went to bed, not to seek repose but rather to dissemble for, with her beloved in such danger, she would certainly find no rest.

When don Alejandro and don Carlos heard the music, they had leapt from their beds and, as I've described, run out with their swords drawn. Although their swordsmanship was not necessarily better than that of don Diego and his servant, it was luckier. During the struggle, don Diego was wounded and had to withdraw. He complained of his misfortune, but it might be more appropriate to call it good fortune because, when his parents learned the cause of the fight, they saw how their son would profit from such a noble marriage. Knowing that this was his desire, they sought intermediaries to present their petition to Laura's father. When Laura feared that the whole episode of the duel might cause eternal discord, she suddenly found herself wed to don Diego, much to everyone's delight. Their marriage brought such joy to the two lovers that it would be foolish to try to describe it in this brief account.

Who, recalling don Diego's love, his tears, his complaints, the burning desire in his heart, can hear about the marvelously happy outcome and not consider Laura terribly fortunate? Who can doubt that everyone who has amorous hopes will say: how I wish I were so fortunate and my troubles could have such a happy conclusion as those of this noble lady? Particularly those ladies who think only of their own desires. Similarly, who can look at don Diego enjoying in Laura the epitome of beauty, lavish wealth, the culmination of

discretion, and a prodigy of love and not exclaim that heaven has never created a more fortunate man? Given their correspondence in all these fine qualities, one would think at the very least that this love would be eternal. And it might have been, if Laura hadn't been unfortunate because of her beauty; if don Diego had not been mutable like all men—if his love hadn't been a prelude to neglect, if his nobility hadn't previously restrained his appetites. Laura's wealth didn't protect her from unhappiness, nor did her beauty from scorn, her discretion from neglect, her love from thanklessness. In this day and age, all these virtues are greatly prized but little valued.

What was lacking for Laura to be happy? Nothing. She trusted in love and believed that its power could overcome the greatest impossibility; but even though she was more beautiful than Venus, don Diego began to scorn her. Is it too much to ask that a man be faithful, particularly when he enjoys possession?

It happened that before don Diego fell in love with Laura, he had fixed his attentions on Nise, an attractive woman from Naples who, while not the "crème de la crème," was certainly not from the dregs of society. Her appearance, her qualities, and her estate were not so deficient that she didn't entertain high aspirations. She wanted to be don Diego's wife, as her noble condition might warrant, and so she had already granted him all the favors he'd sought and all she had to offer. During the early days and months of his marriage he had neglected Nise. She set out to discover the cause of his neglect and it didn't take long, for there's always someone who'll tell. Since don Diego had never intended to be her husband, and the wedding had been public, he hadn't given a thought to Nise. She was terribly distressed by don Diego's marriage but, after all, she was a woman in love and always forgiving of offenses, even at the expense of her own reputation. Nise remained committed to don Diego; she thought she couldn't live without him. If she couldn't be his wife, at least she could continue to enjoy him as his mistress. To accomplish her goal, she barraged him with letters, she pressed him with tears and, finally, through her insistent pleading, she managed to get don Diego to come back to her house.

This was Laura's undoing. With all her art, Nise knew how to enamor don Diego all over again and now, because Laura was his, she seemed boring. Laura began to feel rejected because of don Diego's neglect, and she grew irksome with her jealous outbursts. Don Diego the solicitous, don Diego the persistent, don Diego the lover, don Diego who, at the beginning of their marriage, had said he was the happiest man in the world, not only denied that he'd ever been like that, he even denied to himself any acknowledgment of his obligations. Men who spurn their wives so flagrantly give wings to offence; when a man's immorality becomes flamboyant, he comes perilously close to losing his honor. Don Diego started by being inattentive, by missing bed and board. He refused to acknowledge the sorrow he was causing his wife, for it's far easier to deny one's actions than to face up to them. He disdained her favors and, in his speech, he showed contempt for her. When a man behaves so badly, what can he expect? I don't know if I ought to say that he should anticipate some offense to his honor.

Laura noted the changes in her husband's behavior, and she began to express grief, first with tears and then with words, in an effort to deal with his scorn. When a woman shows how much she's affected by her husband's errors, she's lost. When Laura felt it necessary to express her unhappiness, she gave further cause to don Diego, not just to abuse her verbally but even to lay hands upon her, heedless of the infamy of such an act. Indeed, so greatly had he come to hate and loath her that he came home only occasionally to keep up appearances. Having to face Laura was worse than death to don Diego.

Laura tried to find out the cause of these changes in behavior, and she soon learned the whole story. Servants don't have to be tortured to tell all about the failing of their masters, and they don't restrict themselves to telling only true things, they also know how to make up the most elaborate lies. Servants have been called "prose poets" because of their talent for invention, a weakness common in those who cannot help themselves. The only good it did Laura to learn the cause of her misfortunes was to make her feel her sorrows more deeply. Her situation looked hopeless to her. When the will falters there can be no hope, that's why the proverb says, "Will once twisted can never be straightened." If the remedy doesn't come from the source of the injury, no matter what the illness, there can be no cure. That's why, generally, those who are lovesick seldom want to get well.

What Laura gained from finding out the truth about don Diego's licentious behavior was to cause him to become even more shameless, pursuing his desire with greater abandon. When his vice becomes public, the vicious man knows no restraint.

One day Laura saw Nise in the church. With tears in her eyes, she begged Nise to give up her claims on don Diego. Laura told her that the only thing she was accomplishing was destroying her own honor and making Laura's life a living hell. Nise had reached the point of no longer caring about her reputation, so she didn't fear falling any lower than she already had. She replied to Laura so sharply and rudely that what Laura had thought would be the solution to her sorrow left her feeling even more hopeless, and it left Nise even more determined to pursue her love at all costs. She lost all respect for God and for the rules of society. If previously she'd pursued don Diego quietly and modestly by sending him letters, gifts, and other little things, now, shamelessly, she and her servants openly came looking for him. This license increased Laura's torment and passion, for she saw even less possibility of solution than at first. She lived the most desolate life you can imagine, absolutely without hope. No wonder! She suffered from a jealousy worse than any ravaging illness.

Laura's father and brothers noticed her unhappiness, her strained appearance, and the loss of her beauty. (Naturally she hid her sorrow from them as best she could, fearing some tragic outcome.) Finally, however, they became aware of what was going on and of the evil life don Diego was leading, and they had many arguments and ugly disagreements with him about it, which ultimately turned into open enmity.

The sad and beautiful Laura spent some time in this torment. With each day that passed, her husband's liberties increased and her patience diminished. But you can't cry over your misfortunes all the time. One night she was up late, unable to sleep because of don Diego's tardiness and her constant worries; she was sure he was in Nise's arms. She decided to ease her sorrows by singing. (Some say this eases them, but I think it makes them worse.) She took up her harp, which Italian women play very well and, sometimes singing, sometimes bursting into tears, she sang this ballad, disguising don Diego's name as Albano:

Why, tyrant Albano,
if you worship Nise
and offer all the attentions
of your love to her beauty;
why, if your heart
is prisoner to her eyes,
and to your eyes her face
is such a beautiful image;
why if you entangle your love

in the prison of her hair
and she, so responsive to you,
rewards you with her love;
why, if from her mouth,
jewelbox full of lovely pearls,
you hear love's sweet sayings,
which greatly increase your joy,
why do you repay my constancy
with disloyalty and deception
when, because I love you,
I suffer such great torment?
And if truly you give
your heart to your Nise,
why don't you give me cruel death,
since you scorn me so?
Once you feigned for me
a loving tenderness;
why didn't you at least
let me live in ignorance?
But you have used your desire,
your will, and your power,
thankless lover, all to adore her,
and never even told me.
Can't you see it isn't right,
or just, or proper
to awaken one who sleeps,
especially one who loves,
just to make her sorrow?
Woe is me, so unfortunate!
What means do I have
to make this soul of mine
come home to its body?
Tyrant, give me back my soul;
but no, don't return it to me,
it's better for the body
to die for the sake of the soul.
Alas! if in your heart
Nise's soul dwells,
even though the soul is immortal,
the body still must surely die.
Heaven, pity me, for I am dying;
jealousy torment me
like ice that burns my soul,
like fire that chills my heart.
A thousand curses,
tyrannical Albano, on the one
who lets her soul get caught
in the prison of love.
Oh my eyes, let us weep
as many tender tears
as all the waters that the ocean deep
casts upon the sands.
And to the tune of jealousy,
instrument of my complaint,
while we weep, let us sing
sad mournful songs of love.

Listen carefully,
lofty, snowy, peaks,
and let your clear echoes
serve as my response.
Listen lovely little birds,
and with melodious tongue
you shall sing my jealousy
with your sweet voices.
My Albano adores Nise
and leaves me to my sorrows;
I suffer true passion,
I suffer real pain.
He lovingly celebrates
her heavenly beauty
and praises to the skies
letters written by her hand.
Ariadne, what say you
who weep and lament
the inconstancy of your lover,
his abuse, and his absence?
And you, afflicted Prometheus,
although you feel your flesh
ravaged by the eagle
and chained to the Caucasus,
you suffer, yes, but you do not feel
as much pain as I experience,
or any fears as great.
Unhappy Ixion,
you don't feel the wracking pain
of the wheel; what you feel
are all my torments.
Tantalus reaching for the water,
always unable to touch it,
never managing to taste it,
watching it retreat as you approach,
your grief is slight,
no matter how it's described,
for there is no greater pain
than that produced by jealousy.
Ungrateful wretch, may it please heaven
for you likewise to suffer jealousy,
and rage as I am raging,
and suffer as I am suffering.
And may that enemy of mine
cause you such jealousy
that, like Midas and all his gold,
you will be rich in sorrows!

Who wouldn't be deeply touched by Laura's complaints, sung sweetly and with such great feeling? Anyone but don Diego, who was proud of his infidelity. The moment Laura reached this part of her song, her faithless husband entered and heard her words. He well understood their meaning and reacted angrily to what should have affected him differently. What he should have prized and valued filled him with rage. He began to insult Laura and said such terrible, awful things that she burst into tears. Crystal torrents poured down her heavenly cheeks (scattering pearls the dawn might have used to decorate her May flowers and lovely spring meadows). At last, Laura said to him:

"What are you doing, you thankless wretch? How can you so abuse the freedom you enjoy with all your evil ways, with no respect for heaven and no fear of hell. What you ought to praise angers you. You should be ashamed that the whole world knows and the entire city is talking about your vicious excesses. It seems as if you were deliberately stirring my passion and driving me to offend against your honor. If it troubles you that I complain about your behavior, then remove the cause of my complaints or else end my weary life. I'm fed up with your sinful wrongdoing. Is this the way you treat my love? Is this the way you appreciate my affection? Is this the way you reward my suffering? Well, it's a wonder I haven't taken the cause of all my misfortune and torn her to shreds with my bare hands!

"Poor me, to be so unfortunate! No, I'm wrong to say 'poor me.' It would be more fitting to say 'poor you' because, with your vices, you're arousing heaven's wrath, which will surely descend upon you and open wide your way to hell. God will tire of putting up with you, the world is tired of having you around; and the one you idolize will surely give you your due reward. May all women who let themselves be deceived by men's promises learn a lesson from me. May women know that if all men are like you, then women are bound to suffer instead of live. What can any husband who behaves like you expect? Only that his wife, beyond caring about honor, may destroy his honor for him. Not that I'll do that, no matter what cause you give me in your behavior, because I am who I am, and also because, to my misfortune, the great love I have for you would never let me dishonor you. But I fear that your evil ways will inspire other men, vicious like yourself, to try to take up where you leave off. I fear that the gossips and scandalmongers will imagine my dishonor and spread rumors. What man can look at a woman like me who is married to a husband like you, who wouldn't be as determined to win me as you are neglectful of me?"

These were such strong words that don Diego opened up the eyes of his heart as well as the eyes of his face, and he saw that Laura was right. But his heart was so filled with Nise that it remained empty of any sense of obligation. Overcome by an infernal rage, he rushed over to her and struck her so violently that the white pearls of her teeth, bathed in the blood shed by his angry hand, looked instead like red coral. Not satisfied with this, he drew his dagger, ready to free her from the yoke as burdensome to him as it was to her. The maids, who'd been trying to separate him from his wife, screamed even more loudly at the sight of the dagger and cried out to Laura's father and brothers.

Furiously they dashed into the room. When don Carlos saw don Diego's frenzy and Laura bathed in the blood that was still gushing from her mouth, he thought her husband had stabbed her. With a sense of dreadful grief, don Carlos attacked don Diego. He wrenched the dagger away from him and was about to thrust it through his heart, when the brazen don Diego, seeing himself in such imminent danger, embraced don Carlos. Laura threw her arms around don Carlos and begged him to come to his senses, saying:

"Oh, dear brother, with his life goes the life of your unfortunate sister!"

Don Carlo checked himself, and his father intervened between the two men and calmed things down. They all returned to their separate rooms. Don Antonio was afraid that it would be his downfall if there were scenes like that every day. He decided he couldn't bear to see with his own eyes the mistreatment of his beloved daughter Laura. The next day, he gathered up his entire household and both his sons and they went to Piedrablanca, abandoning the poor Laura to her unhappy fate. She was so sad and disconsolate to see them go that she wished she could die.

Laura had heard that there were women in the region who, through sorcery, could make the unloving love. Finding her love more despised with each passing day, she decided to remedy her problem by this means, a mistake often made by passionate people. She arranged to have a sorceress brought to her. In Naples sorceresses enjoy such freedom to exercise their superstitions and schemes that they work their spells publicly. They do strange and amazing things that appear so true you almost have to believe in their powers. The viceroy and the clergy are concerned about this problem, as there's no restriction by the Inquisition or other punishment sufficient to frighten them, for in Italy the usual penalty is a small fine.

The intermediary whom Laura had charged with bringing the sorceress to her didn't tarry. The two were probably friends, for they all know one another. The woman came, and Laura sought to curry her favor with gifts (which is what these women really want). Encouraged by the sorceress's promises, Laura told her about her misfortunes and aroused her sympathy by her many tears. She used these words to make her request:

"My friend, if you can make my husband despise his mistress Nise and love me again as he did at the beginning of our marriage when he was more faithful and I happier, you will find in my satisfaction and gratitude how much I value your services. I'll give you half of all I possess. If this isn't enough, set your fee in terms of my need, state your own price and, if what I possess isn't enough, I'll sell my body to meet it."

The woman assured Laura of her qualifications and told her of the miracles she'd performed in similar cases. She made Laura feel that her request was so feasible that Laura believed success was a sure thing. The woman said she needed certain objects that Laura should obtain and bring to her in a little pouch: hairs from the head and beard and the teeth of a hanged man. With these tokens and a fews other things, she would make don Diego change character so dramatically it would astound Laura. As for pay, she wanted only what the results were worth.

"Furthermore, my lady," the false sorceress went on, " all the beauty and all the wealth in the world aren't enough to make one happy without the help of spells such as mine. Why, if you only knew how many women enjoy peace with their husbands because of me, your fears would be allayed and you'd feel assured of your good fortune."

Laura felt very confused when she realized that the woman was asking her to obtain such difficult things. She had no idea how she could get hold of the hair and teeth of a hanged man. She gave the woman a hundred gold escudos and, since money accomplishes miracles, she told the woman to find someone to obtain them for her.

The crafty sorceress (who wanted to prolong the cure in order to bleed the lady's purse and cover up her machinations) replied that she didn't know anyone who she could trust and, besides, the power lay in the fact that Laura herself obtained those objects and gave them into her hands. Having said this, the sorceress departed, leaving Laura as sad and troubled as you can imagine.

Laura kept wondering how she could get the things the woman asked for, but every thought that occurred to her presented a thousand difficulties. Her only remedy was to shed torrents of tears from her beautiful eyes, because she couldn't think of a soul she could trust. Laura thought it was beneath the dignity of a woman like herself to stoop to such base activities. She was afraid of her servants' lack of discretion, and above all she feared that don Diego might find out. These thoughts only made her weep more and, wringing her hands, she said to herself:

"Unlucky Laura! How could you ever have expected to be lucky? Even when you were born, you cost your mother her life. Why not sacrifice your life to death! Oh Love, mortal enemy of mankind, how much evil you've brought to the world, especially to women who are weak in every way and so susceptible to deception. It seems as if you direct your full power and all your hostility against us women. I don't know why heaven made me beautiful, noble, and rich, if these qualities can't prevent misfortune. The many gifts nature and wealth have bestowed upon me have been powerless against the unlucky star under which I was born. If I am truly unlucky, what can life have in store for me?

"This wretched life is more sorrow than joy. To whom can I tell my sorrows? Who will help me? Who will listen to my complaints and be moved? Who will see my tears and dry them for me? No one. My father and my brothers abandoned me and left me helpless to avoid knowing about my plight. Even heaven, which comforts the afflicted, is deaf to my pleas. Alas, don Diego, who would ever have thought . . . ? But I should've thought, I should've known, for after all, you're a man, and men's deceptions exceed even the exploits of the devil himself. Men do greater evil than all the minions of hell. Where can a true man be found? In what man, especially when he knows he's loved, does love last more than a day? It's as if the more a man knows he is loved, the more he scorns and abuses. Cursed be the woman who believes in men! In the end, she'll find her love rewarded just as I have. Seeing so many painful examples of the way men behave, what woman can be so foolish as to want to get married. And the very woman who thinks she's the most likely to find happiness will be the one to fail most dismally.

"How can I have so little valor, such effeminate courage? How can I be such a coward that I don't strike dead the enemy of all my peace and the ingrate who treats me so harshly? But alas! I love him. I'm afraid to make him angry; I'm afraid I might lose him! Why, vain legislators of the world, do you tie our hands so that we cannot take vengeance. Because of your mistaken ideas about us, you render us powerless and deny us access to pen and sword. Isn't our soul the same as a man's soul? If the soul is what gives courage to the body, why are we so cowardly? If you men knew that we were brave and strong, I'm sure you wouldn't deceive us the way you do. By keeping us subject from the moment we're born, you weaken our strength with fears about honor and our minds with exaggerated emphasis on modesty and shame. For a sword, you give us the distaff, instead of books, a sewing cushion. Woe is me! What good do all these thoughts do? They don't solve my hopeless problem. What I must think about is how to get that sorceress the things she asked for."

As Laura said this, she set her mind to thinking about what she might do. Again she began to lament. Anyone who heard Laura's laments would say that the power of love had reached its limit, but there were greater trials ahead. Night came, and it was the darkest and the most shadowy night of the winter (to show how night felt about her plan). She didn't take into account any risk or possible consequences of her acts should don Diego come home and find her absent from the house. She instructed her servants, if her husband did by chance return, to tell him she'd gone to visit one of her many women friends in Naples.

Laura put on one of her maid's cloaks, took a little lantern and, accompanied only by her vast fears, she set out down the street with greater courage than her few years warranted. She went to get what she hoped would solve all her problems. Just thinking about where she went fills me with horror. Oh, don Diego, cause of so much evil, why doesn't God take you to account for all your wickedness? You have driven your wife beyond fear of the dreadful place where she will go, disregarding the suspicions she might arouse in her maids and risking the loss of her life if she's discovered! If only you thought about it, you'd see how much you owe her!

About a mile from the city of Naples, there's a holy image of Our Lady of Arca much venerated in the whole kingdom. The image is in a chapel just a stone's throw from the main highway that goes to Piedrablanca. The chapel is about fifty feet long and the same across; its door faces the road. In the front of the chapel, there's an altar with the holy image painted on the wall behind it. The ceiling is about nine feet high, and the floor is a pit sunk about twenty feet deep. Surrounding this great pit there's a ledge about eighteen inches wide along which you can walk around the chapel. At about the height of a man, and sometimes even lower, there are iron hooks

in the wall. After criminals sentenced to death have been publicly hanged, their corpses are brought here and hung from these hooks. As the bodies decompose, their bones fall into the pit, which, being holy ground, serves as their tomb. A few days before, six highway bandits had been hanged.

This is the dreadful place where Laura went. With the incredible courage her love inspired in her, she entered. Ignoring the great danger, she was mindful only of her terrible need. She felt less afraid of the people she was going to do business with than of falling into the abyss. If that happened, no one would ever know what had become of her. What incredible heart in such a frail, weak woman! She got to the chapel about ten and stayed until one. Who knows if it was God's will or her own limitation, but she wasn't able to accomplish her mission in spite of the fact that she could easily reach the faces of the dead men. I shall now tell you how that came about.

I've already described how Laura's father and her brothers, to keep from seeing her mistreated and to avoid the risk of open warfare with their brother-in-law, had retreated to Piedrablanca. There they lived, if not forgetful of her, at least removed from the sight of her sorry plight. The night when Laura went to the chapel, don Carlos was fast asleep in his bed. Suddenly he awoke with a start and cried out so loudly that it almost seemed as if he might die. His cry upset the whole household. Confused and worried, his father and all the servants rushed to his room. Showing their grief in tears, they asked him what had caused his outcry, but it was a mystery even to the one who'd suffered it. After don Carlos recovered his composure, he said in a loud voice, "My sister is in danger!" He jumped up, threw on his clothes, and ordered his horse to be saddled. He leapt on the horse and, without waiting for a servant to accompany him, he took the road to Naples at full gallop. He rode so fast that by one o'clock he'd gotten to the chapel. At that point the horse stopped sharply and stood stock still, as if it were a statue made of bronze or stone.

Don Carlos tried to proceed but, no matter how he tried, he couldn't make the horse budge. He couldn't get him to move either forward or backward. Each time he spurred him on, the horse would utter a frightful snort. When don Carlos couldn't solve the mystery, he remembered that the chapel was nearby. He turned to look at it and saw the light from the lantern his sister was carrying. He thought some sorceress must have detained him there. To make sure, he decided to see if the horse would move toward the chapel; the moment he turned the rein, without any other urging, the horse did his master's will. With sword in hand, he rode up to the door. (The moment whoever was inside heard him, the mysterious person snuffed out the light and huddled close to the wall.) Don Carlos called out:

"Whoever you are there, come out immediately! If you don't I swear by the king's life, that I won't leave this spot until I see who you are by the light of the sun and find out what you're doing in this place."

Laura recognized her brother's voice. Hoping he'd go away, she disguised her voice as best she could and replied:

"I'm a poor unfortunate woman come to this place for a certain purpose. It's none of your business who I am. Please, for the love of God, go away! And rest assured, kind sir, that if you insist on waiting until daylight, I shall throw myself down into the pit, even though that would cost me my life and soul."

Laura couldn't disguise her voice well enough, and her brother hadn't forgotten her as completely as she thought. He gasped and cried out loudly, saying:

"Oh, sister, how dreadful for you to be here! Not in vain did my heart warn me of your peril. Come out of there!"

Realizing that her brother had recognized her, Laura used the utmost care she could muster to keep from falling into the pit. Hugging the wall and probably also clinging to the bodies of the dead men, slowly she managed to make her way out. When she reached her grief-stricken brother she threw herself in his arms. (Who can doubt that don Carlos, loving her as much as he did, felt heartsick as he embraced her?) Together they moved away from that dread spot, and then he listened to Laura briefly relate what had brought her there. She learned how her brother had chanced to come there at that very moment. He considered the rescue miraculous, as did Laura, despite the fact that she was feeling very ashamed of what she'd done. Don Carlos decided to take her back to Piedrablanca on his horse.

Near dawn they reached Piedrablanca. After Laura's father heard the whole story, he, the two brothers, and Laura got into a coach and drove to Naples. They went straight to the palace of the viceroy, who at the time happened to be don Pedro Fernandez de Castro, count of Lemos. He was a very noble, wise, and devout prince whose rare virtues and outstanding qualities should be written on bronze plaques and on the tongue of fame rather than just on paper. Don Antonio (as I was saying) placed himself at the feet of this eminent person. He knelt down and told the viceroy that, in order to relate a most portentous event that had occurred, it was necessary for his son-in-law, don Diego Pinatelo, to be present, because the matter concerned his authority and his domestic relations.

His excellency, well aware of don Antonio's valor and nobility, immediately sent the captain of the guard to fetch don Diego. He was found in a state of despair and the entire household in turmoil. The menservants had fled, terrified of his rage, and the maids had been locked up. What caused the uproar was that he had come home late the night before and found Laura gone. Thinking that his noble wife had deserted him or run away intending to destroy his honor, he'd tried to set the house on fire. He raged like a lion.

When don Diego was informed that the viceroy required his presence, he accompanied the escort, furious and glowering. He entered the hall and was stunned to see his father-in-law, his brothers-in-law, and his wife. He was even more astonished to hear his wife, in his presence, tell the viceroy exactly what we have written here. Laura ended her story and added that she was disillusioned with the world and with men and didn't want to have to struggle any longer. When she thought about what she'd done and the awful place where she'd gone, she was horrified. For this reason, she wanted to enter a convent, the only real sanctuary for the relief of the misery to which women are subjected.

When don Diego heard Laura say this, it touched his heart to realize he'd caused so much pain. Being a well-intentioned man, he prized Laura at this moment more than ever and feared she might really do as she wished. He understood how aggrieved she was and realized he could win no concessions from her, so he tried to use the viceroy as intermediary. He begged the noble gentleman to intercede and ask Laura to come back to him. He promised to mend his way now that he knew the power of her love. To assure Laura of his own love, he would place Nise, the cause of so much misfortune, in his excellency's hands so he could put her in a convent. Separated from Nise forever and eternally grateful to Laura for the power of her love, he would adore his true wife and love her always.

The viceroy approved of don Diego's plan, as did don Antonio and his sons. But it was impossible for Laura to accept his offer. She was too afraid because of the past. Ever more resolute in her determination, she told don Diego he was wasting his time. She wanted to give to God, who was infinitely more appreciative, all the love she'd previously devoted to her thankless husband.

That very day Laura entered the rich, noble, and holy convent of the Immaculate Conception. Not even the viceroy himself could make Laura reveal the identity of the woman who'd asked for those outrageous objects in order to have her punished.

In despair, don Diego went home. He gathered up all the jewels and money he could find and, without saying good-bye to anyone, departed the city. A few months later it was learned that while serving in the army of his majesty Philip III, king of Spain, in the war with the duke of Savoy, he was blown up by a mine. Laura, now entirely free, took the habit and soon thereafter made her vows. She lives a devout life in the convent. She still regrets her daring deed and, every time she recalls that awful place where she went, she trembles. I heard this tale from her own lips, and I tell it as a true story so that everyone will know the great power of love and the marvelous enchantment of its power.

Everyone had listened with amazement to the discreet enchantment narrated by the beautiful Nise. Some praised the power of Laura's love, others her intelligence, and everyone praised her courage. They all agreed that not one among them would dare to visit such a dread place as she had. This gave Nise the opportunity to reaffirm that every word she'd spoken was true.

Lysis noted that the lovely Phyllis was preparing to tell her tale so, accompanied by the musicians, she sang this burlesque madrigal:

Let us understand one another,
sister flea: who has given you
such a tyrannical nature,
such courage and valor,
that you attack everyone?
Why are you the one who forgives no one?

And such a tiny little thing
to bite more than one poet, what a coup!
You bite people of all classes,
as a beautiful woman might confess,
that what she denied to others
the flea has thoroughly enjoyed.

When I consider your progeny
and ponder your humble lineage,
I'm amazed at your power

and so I'd call you a scandal-monger,
born, perhaps in a stable, still
you bite and martyrize the whole world.
Tailor of human flesh
who makes everyone nervous,
worrying morning, noon, and night
about where you may be wandering;
you and Love are the appellate judges
of all mortal beings.

Oh, haughty commissioner!
Oh, harsh justice!
Oh, vengeful mayor!
Oh, heartless and designing bailiff!
Oh, tricky notary,
life and death are in your hands!

Please be grateful for my friendship,
for sometimes I let you bite me;
so let's be friends, and you go bite
the judges with all your might,
and may they give the prize to me
for I've already tasted it.

The prettily sung lyrics gave much pleasure to the audience, who recognized that they'd been composed for some contest. They all thanked the heavenly Lysis, most of all don Diego. With each word the lovely lady sang, he became more passionately enamored, which made don Juan terribly jealous, although he gave a different reason for his dispute with don Diego, suggesting that it was because don Diego feared his pen more than his sword. The truth was that he loved Lisarda, still, he didn't dislike Lysis, and he didn't want to lose the affection of either woman. Such fickle men belong in solitary confinement.

While the illustrious audience was congratulating Lysis and singing her praise, Nise and Phyllis changed places. They all turned their attention to Phyllis, and she began:

"Since the lovely Nise has told all about the power of love in her enchantment, to continue in her style, I'd like to tell about the power of virtue in mine, about how a woman is disenchanted by the experiences of another woman and ultimately is rewarded. I tell this story so men will realize that there are virtuous women and that it's wrong for the name of good women to be tarnished by the deeds of bad women: all women should not be tarred by the same brush. Without departing one whit from the truth, my story goes like this":

——————————— *Questions for Consideration* ———————————

Directions: Using complete sentences, provide brief answers for the following questions.

1. Examine the Introductory segments to the *Enchantments* ("To the Reader," "Prologue By an Objective Reader," and "Beginning"). List the significant points in each selection.

   _____

   _____

   _____

   _____

   _____

2. The introductory essay about Maria de Zayas states that each story in the *Enchantments* has characteristics of one or more literary genres. Identify the genre that influenced "The Power of Love." Provide evidence of your answer with examples from the story.

   _____

   _____

   _____

   _____

   _____

3. Explain how don Diego comes to realize the power of love.

   _____

   _____

   _____

   _____

   _____

4. Discuss Laura's solution to her marital problem. Do you find it an acceptable solution?

   _____

   _____

   _____

   _____

   _____

————————— *Writing Critically* —————————

Directions: Select one of the essay topics listed below and compose a 500 word paper which discusses the topic fully. Support your thesis with evidence from the text and with critical and/or historical material. Use the space provided below for the first stages of the writing process.

1. The *Enchantments* are stories of courtly romance. Define the courtly romance and discuss the characteristics that appear in the "Power of Love."

2. Discuss what is meant by a male code of honor in Spanish society during the sixteenth and seventeenth centuries. Using stories from Maria de Zayas' *The Disenchantments*, discuss the impact that this code had on the lives of women during the Spanish Golden Age.

3. Five of the ten stories that appear in the *Enchantments* are told by women, and the other five are told by men. Examine the differences and similarities in the stories told from the male and female point of view.

4. Many scholars view Zayas' stories as realistic depictions of life in seventeenth century Spain. Select a specific idea, concept, or tradition from another story from the *Enchantments* and determine if Zayas' portrayal is true to history. For example, you may examine seventeenth century thoughts about magic, marriage, or male honor.

Prewriting Space:

_____
_____
_____
_____
_____
_____
_____
_____
_____
_____
_____
_____
_____
_____
_____

Introduction

John Milton (1608–1674)

Book I of Milton's *Paradise Lost* is pivotal to understanding many of the important themes and ideas that are raised in this epic work. It is in this book, for instance, that the reader is introduced initially to the vast scope of *Paradise Lost*, which encompasses heaven, hell, and chaos; the inevitable victory, in Miltonic terms, of good over evil as God defeats Satan and casts him into the fiery pit of hell; the spatial and imaginative distance between heaven and hell reflected in the archetypal images of height and depth, light and darkness; the nature of angels; the irony of the already defeated Satan still trying to seek revenge against God; the self-destructive pride of Satan; the heroic—albeit misleading and transparent—bravado of Satan even in the face of certain defeat. These are among the central issues in Book I of *Paradise Lost* which help to frame the whole of Milton's "great argument" as he undertakes to "justify the ways of God to men."

In Book I of *Paradise Lost*, the reader should be alert to the archetypal or universal images that Milton uses to establish difference and distance between heaven and hell. Foremost among these are repeated references to height and depth, light and darkness. In this manner heaven is linked analogously and positively to an ascending scale of values that is both Christian and Platonic. With respect to the former, the Bible exerts the greatest influence on Milton, who is firmly in the Christian tradition, in depicting a heaven that is above and a hell that is below—one fulfilling the promise of salvation, the other of damnation. Milton, of course, was also steeped in classicism, particularly the works of the great Greek writer and philosopher Plato. It was in the works of Plato that Milton read and internalized that the proper direction of the soul is upward (i.e., in a heavenly direction), and that giving in to base and wanton desires causes the soul of the would-be virtuous to sink to the animal level, thus destroying one's God-like image. By consistently employing this height (i.e., heaven) and depth (i.e., hell) contrast, Milton effectively conditions the reader to seek the former and to avoid the latter. Heaven is psychologically associated with the positive, hell with the negative. This is perhaps even more graphic in terms of the light and darkness archetypes that Milton habitually uses in describing heaven and hell, respectively. The former is always described as a radiant realm of light, the latter as a place of unrelieved darkness. In fact, Milton stresses in Book I that in casting Satan and the rebel angels out of heaven, down into the flaming gulf of hell, God had confined them to a "prison" of "utter darkness" far removed from celestial light.

Book I also establishes *Paradise Lost* as a logical epic, a facet that receives detailed treatment by Dennis H. Burden in his insightful book, *The Logical Epic: A Study of the Argument of Paradise Lost*. This symmetry is reflected as well in Isabel MacCaffrey's reference to the "architectural plan" of this work in *Paradise Lost as "Myth."* Moreover, Milton declares early in the first book that his approach to the fall of man will be basically from cause to effect in terms of rhetorical mode. He thus intends in the apostrophe to ". . . say first what cause/Moved our grand parents in that happy state,/Favored of Heaven so highly, to fall off/From their Creator, and transgress his will." (PL,I 28–31). This impressive blending of form and content, of style and substance, in which the logic of the epic itself is suggestive of an orderly world, is consistent with the view of a divinely controlled universe that Milton inherited from both the Middle Ages and the Renaissance, as well as the Christian tradition. For although science, with its attendant skepticism, had begun to take hold in the seventeenth century, Milton's Christian heritage still espoused a divinely inspired scheme.

The Miltonic cosmos, with its assumption of divine order, has its basis in several important factors in addition to the Bible itself. For Medieval man (i.e., A.D. 476–A.D. 1453) the universe is definitely God-centered and the primary aim of life is to seek salvation. The main journey, therefore, is from this world to the next. This is the theme of such morality plays as *Everyman* and Dante's seminal work, *The Divine Comedy*, with its tripartite division of Hell (Inferno), Purgatory, and Paradise. As an errant Soul who is lost in the "dark wood"—metaphorically the fallen world—Dante's task as a spiritual pilgrim is to find his way through hell to the blissful state of Paradise. In addition to this medieval dimension, Milton's God-centered universe also has affinities with the Renaissance frame of mind, which receives detailed treatment in E. M. W. Tillyard's *The Elizabethan World Picture*. This work and Rene Samuel's comparative study of *Dante and Milton: The Comedia and Paradise Lost* call attention to the Great Chain of Being, in which all the links (e.g., angels, stars, man, plants, animals, etc.), were all part of a "ladder" ascending to God. Milton's implicit and explicit references to the Great Chain of Being show that he was very familiar with this spiritually unifying concept.

Book I of *Paradise Lost* contains other significant themes that Milton details more fully in the course of the epic. Inordinate pride, for example, is established as the primary reason for Satan's unjustified revolt in heaven. In singling out this as Satan's chief deficiency, Milton is no doubt aware of the medieval account of the Seven Deadly Sins (i.e., pride, covetousness, lust, anger, gluttony, envy, and sloth). While all of these "sins" were detrimental to spiritual advancement, pride, which actually encompassed all of them, was viewed as most ruinous to the spiritual health of the individual. And even into the seventeenth century, when Milton is writing, sin is still the nemesis that works against the laws of order. For Milton, this order is essentially Divine. Milton also devotes much attention to the nature of angels in *Paradise Lost*, with the matter surfacing initially in Book I as Satan is astonished at the diminished brightness of his angelic partner in crime, Beelzebub, who, like him, has been expelled from the bright light of heaven and cast into the gloomy deep of hell. The reader should be aware of such terms as *incorporeal* (used to describe the angels or spiritual substances) and *corporeal* (used to describe man or bodily substances). A knowledge of the nine (9) orders of angels, stemming from the Medieval period, is also very important to a deeper understanding of the angelic question. The celestial hierarchy, ranked from lowest to highest, is as follows: angels, archangels, principalities, powers, virtues, dominions, thrones, cherubim, and seraphim. All angels in *Paradise Lost*, therefore, do not have the same rank, and the informed reader should be aware of this.

Satanic rhetoric or bravado occupies a conspicuous place in Book I of *Paradise Lost*, as Satan tries to boost the spirit of his comrade, Beelzebub, after God has cast them out of heaven. And though this boasting belies the shaky confidence of Satan in his futile war against God, masking the difference between his outward surliness and his inner dejection, his defiant rhetoric seems at times to approach the heroic. It is this sheer defiance, in the face of overwhelming odds, that has caused some critics to see him as the hero in *Paradise Lost*. The less than heroic in Satan, however, points up the distinction between the appearance and the reality of his character. The theme of appearance versus reality, that surrounds Satan in Book I, will be a crucial factor in the eventual fall in the Garden of Eden, as Eve is unable to detect the Satanic evil in the hypocrisy of the serpent and Adam is blind to the potentially sinful nature of Eve, seeing only her feminine beauty.

Finally, it is in Book I that we learn about Satan's *Modus operandi* as he plots revenge against God for his sound defeat in heaven. In talking to his next in command, Beelzebub, in the darkness of hell where they now find themselves, Satan articulates the strategy that will be employed to be victorious over the Almighty. The tactic basically sets up a choice between *force* and *guile,* issues that Milton knew also found ready expression in Dante. In specific terms, force has reference to open war or rebellion—which has already proved unsuccessful. Guile (i.e., trickery, cunning), on the other hand, opens up new possibilities, particularly when it can be practiced on the newly created Adam and Eve (Book IX), who know nothing of evil. In bringing about the fall, of course, Satan chooses guile or hypocrisy as his destructive vehicle, adopting the form of a wily serpent to undo an unsuspecting Eve. Satan's successful use of deceit to corrupt Eve and, through her, Adam, provides the most indirect means of retaliating against God, and to Satan's mind surpasses "common revenge" because it causes His prized creations to curse their fate and their creator.

The reader of Book I of *Paradise Lost* should be mindful of the themes and ideas discussed above, and how they help to frame other books. Such awareness will make reading this great epic an even more rewarding and enriching experience. (DLP)

BIBLIOGRAPHY

Burden, Dennis H. *The Logical Epic: A Study of the Argument of Paradise Lost.* Cambridge, Massachusetts, 1967.

Bush, Douglas. *John Milton.* New York, 1964.

___, ed. *The Portable Milton.* New York, 1977. *Critical Essays on Milton from ELH.* Baltimore, 1969.

Curry, Walter C. *Milton's Ontology, Cosmogony, and Physics.* Lexington, 1966.

Lawry, Jon S. *The Shadow of Heaven: Matter and Stance in Milton's Poetry.* New York, 1968.

MacCaffrey, Isabel G. *Paradise Lost as "Myth."* Cambridge, Massachusetts, 1967.

Samuel, Irene. *Dante and Milton: The Commedia and Paradise Lost,* Ithaca, New York, 1966.

___. *Plato and Milton.* Ithaca, New York, 1947.

Stevenson, David L. *The Elizabethan Age.* New York, 1966.

Tillyard, E. M. W. *The Elizabethan World Picture.* New York.

Willey, Basil. *The Seventeenth Century Background.* Garden City, New York, 1953.

from Paradise Lost: Book 1

John Milton

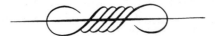

THE ARGUMENT

This First Book proposes, first, in brief, the whole subject, Man's disobedience, and the loss thereupon of Paradise, wherein he was placed: then touches the prime cause of his fall, the Serpent, or rather Satan in the serpent; who revolting from God, and drawing to his side many legions of Angels, was, by the command of God, driven out of Heaven, with all his crew, into the great deep. Which action passed over, the poem hastens into the midst of things, presenting Satan with his Angels now fallen into Hell, described here, not in the centre (for Heaven and Earth may be supposed as yet not made, certainly not yet accursed) but in a place of utter darkness, fitliest called Chaos: here Satan with his Angels lying on the burning lake, thunderstruck and astonished, after a certain space recovers, as from confusion, calls up him who next in order and dignity lay by him; they confer of their miserable fall. Satan awakens all his legions, who lay till then in the same manner confounded: they rise; their numbers, array of battle, their chief leaders named, according to the idols known afterward in Canaan and the countries adjoining. To these Satan directs his speech, comforts them with hope yet of regaining Heaven, but tells them lastly of a new world and new kind of creature to be created, according to an ancient prophecy or report in Heaven; for that Angels were long before this visible creation, was the opinion of many ancient Fathers. To find out the truth of this prophecy, and what to determine thereon he refers to a full council. What his associates thence attempt. Pandemonium, the palace of Satan, rises, suddenly built out of the deep: the infernal peers there sit in council.

INTRODUCTORY REMARKS

This Book on the whole is so perfect from beginning to end, that it would be difficult to find a single superfluous passage. The matter, the illustrations and the allusions, are historically, naturally, and philosophically true. The learning is of every extent and diversity; recondite, classical, scientific, antiquarian. But the most surprising thing is, the manner in which he vivifies every topic he touches: he gives life and picturesqueness to the driest catalogue of buried names personal or geographical. They who bring no learning, yet feel themselves charmed by sounds and epithets which give a vague pleasure, and stir up the imagination into an indistinct emotion.

Poetical imagination is the power, not only of conceiving, but of creating embodied illustrations of abstract truths, which are sublime, or pathetic, or beautiful; but those ideas, which Milton has embodied, no imagination but his own would have dared to attempt; none else would have risen "to the height of this great argument." Every one else would have fallen short of it, and degraded it.

Among the miraculous acquirements of Milton, was his deep and familiar intimacy with all classical and all chivalrous literature; the amalgamation in his mind of all the philosophy and all the sublime and ornamental literature of the ancients, and all the abstruse, the laborious, the immature learning of those who again drew off the mantle of time from the ancient treasures of genius, and mingled with them their own crude conceptions and fantastic theories. He extracted from this mine all that would aid the imagination without shocking the reason. He never rejected philosophy; but where it was fabulous, only offered it as ornament.

In Milton's language though there is internal force and splendor, there is outward plainness.

Common readers think that it sounds and looks like prose. This is one of its attractions; while all that is stilted, and decorated, and affected, soon fatigues and satiates.

Johnson says that "an inconvenience of Milton's design is, that it requires the description of what cannot be described,—the agency of spirits. He saw that immateriality supplied no images, and that he could not show angels acting but by instruments of action: he therefore invested them with form and matter. This, being necessary, was therefore defensible, and he should have secured the consistency of his system by keeping immateriality out of sight, and enticing his reader to drop it from his thoughts." Surely this was quite impossible, for the reason which Johnson himself has given. The imagination, by its natural tendencies, always embodies spirit. Poetry deals in pictures, though not exclusively in pictures.—E. B.

Upon the interesting topic here thus summarily though satisfactorily disposed of, Macaulay has furnished the following, among other admirable remarks:

The most fatal error which a poet can possibly commit in the management of his machinery, is that of attempting to philosophise too much. Milton has been often censured for ascribing to spirits many functions of which spirits must be incapable. But these objections, though sanctioned by eminent names, originate, we venture to say, in profound ignorance of the art of poetry.

What is spirit? What are our own minds, the portion of spirit with which we are best acquainted? We observe certain phenomena. We cannot explain them into material causes. We therefore infer that there exists something which is not material, but of this something we have no idea. We can define it only by negatives. We can reason about it only by symbols. We use the word but we have no image of the thing; and the business of poetry is with images, and not with words. The poet uses words indeed, but they are merely the instruments of his art, not its objects. They are the materials which he is to dispose in such a manner as to present a picture to the mental eye. And, if they are not so disposed, they are no more entitled to be called poetry than a bale of canvas and a box of colors are to be called a painting.

Logicians may reason about abstractions, but the great mass of mankind can never feel an interest in them. They must have images. The strong tendency of the multitude in all ages and nations to idolatry can be explained on no other principles. The first inhabitants of Greece, there is every reason to believe, worshipped one invisible Deity; but the necessity of having something more definite to adore produced, in a few centuries, the innumerable crowd of gods and goddesses. In like manner the ancient Persians thought it impious to exhibit the Creator under a human form. Yet even they transferred to the sun the worship which, speculatively, they considered due only to the supreme mind. The history of Jews is the record of a continual struggle between pure Theism, supported by the most terrible sanctions, and the strangely fascinating desire of having some visible and tangible object of adoration. Perhaps none of the secondary causes which Gibbon has assigned for the rapidity with which Christianity spread over the world, while Judaism scarcely ever acquired a proselyte, operated more powerfully than this feeling. God, the uncreated, the incomprehensible, the invisible, attracted but few worshippers. A philosopher might admire so noble a conception; but the crowd turned away in disgust from words which presented no image to their minds. It was before Deity embodied in a human form, walking among men, partaking of their infirmities, leaning on their bosoms, weeping over their graves, slumbering in the manger, bleeding on the cross, that the prejudices of the synagogue, and the doubts of the Academy, and the pride of the Portico, and the forces of the lictor, and the swords of thirty legions, were humbled in the dust.

Soon after Christianity had achieved its triumph, the principle which had assisted it began to corrupt it. It became a new Paganism. Patron saints assumed the offices of household gods. St. George took the place of Mars. St. Elmo consoled the mariner for the loss of Castor and Pollux. The virgin Mary and Cecilia succeed to Venus and the Muses. The fascination of sex and loveliness was again joined to that of celestial dignity; and the homage of chivalry was blended with that of religion. Reformers have often made a stand against these feelings; but never with more than apparent and partial success. The men who demolished the images in cathedrals have not always been able to demolish those which were enshrined in their minds. It would not be difficult to show that in politics the same rule holds good. Doctrines, we are afraid, must generally be *embodied* before they can excite strong public feeling. The multitude is more easily interested for the most unmeaning badge, or the most insignificant name, than for the most important principle.

From these considerations, we infer that no poet who should affect that metaphysical accuracy for the want of which Milton has been blamed, would escape a disgraceful failure, still, however, there was another extreme, which, though one less dangerous, was also to be avoided. The imaginations of men are in a great measure under the control of their opinions. The most exquisite art of a poetical coloring can produce no illusion when it is employed to represent that which is at once perceived to be incongruous and absurd. Milton wrote in an age of philosophers and theologians. It was necessary therefore for him to abstain from giving such a shock to their understandings, as might break the charm which it was his object to throw over their imaginations. This is the real explanation of the indistinctness and inconsistency with which he has often been reproached. Dr. Johnson acknowledges that it was absolutely necessary for him to clothe his spirits with material forms. "But," says he, "he should have secured the consistency of his system, by keeping immateriality out of sight, and seducing the reader to drop it from his thoughts." This is easily said; but what if he could not seduce the reader to drop it from *his* thoughts? What if the contrary opinion had taken so full a possession of the minds of men, as to leave no room even for the *quasi-belief* which poetry requires? Such we suspect to have been the case. It was impossible for the poet to adopt altogether the material or the immaterial system. He therefore took his stand on the debatable ground. He left the whole in ambiguity. He has doubtless, by so doing, laid himself open to the charge of inconsistency. But, though philosophically in the wrong, we cannot but believe that he was poetically in the right. This task, which almost any other writer would have found impracticable, was easy to him. The peculiar art which he possessed of communicating his meaning circuitously, through a long succession of associated ideas, and of intimating more than he expressed, enabled him to disguise those incongruities which he could not avoid.

The spirits of Milton are unlike those of almost all other writers. His fiends, in particular, are wonderful creations. They are not metaphysical abstractions. They are not wicked men. They are not ugly beasts. They have no horns, no tails. They have just enough in common with human nature to be intelligible to human beings. Their characters are, like their forms, marked by a certain dim resemblance to those of men, but exaggerated to gigantic dimensions and veiled in mysterious gloom.

Book 1

Of man's first disobedience, and the fruit
Of that forbidden tree, whose mortal taste
Brought death into the world, and all our woe,
With loss of Eden, till one greater man
Restore us, and regain the blissful seat,   5
Sing Heav'nly Muse, that on the secret top
Of Oreb, or of Sinai, didst inspire
That Shepherd, who first taught the chosen seed
In the beginning, how the heav'ns and earth
Rose out of Chaos. Or if Sion hill   10
Delight thee more, and Siloa's brook that flow'd
Fast by the oracle of God, I thence
Invoke thy aid to my adventurous song,
That with no middle flight intends to soar
Above the Aonian Mount, while it pursues   15
Things unattempted yet in prose or rhyme.
And chiefly Thou, O Spirit, that dost prefer
Before all temples the upright heart and pure,
Instruct me, for Thou know'st; Thou from the first
Wast present, and with mighty wings outspread   20
Dovelike sat'st brooding on the vast abyss,
And madest it pregnant: What in me is dark,

Illumine; what is low, raise and support;
That to the height of this great argument
I may assert eternal Providence, 25
And justify the ways of God to Men.
 Say first, for Heav'n hides nothing from thy view,
Nor the deep tract of Hell; say first what cause
Moved our grand parents, in that happy state,
Favor'd of Heav'n so highly, to fall off 30
From their Creator, and trangress his will
For one restraint, lords of the world besides?
Who first seduced them to that foul revolt?
Th' infernal Serpent: he it was whose guile,
Stirr'd up with envy and revenge, deceived 35
The mother of mankind, what time his pride
Had cast him out from Heav'n, with all his host
Of rebel Angels; by whose aid aspiring
To set himself in glory 'bove his peers,
He trusted to have equall'd the Most High, 40
If he opposed; and with ambitious aim
Against the throne and monarchy of God,
Raised impious war in Heav'n, and battle proud
With vain attempt. Him the Almighty Power
Hurl'd headlong flaming from th' ethereal sky, 45
With hideous ruin and combustion, down
To bottomless perdition; there to dwell
In adamantine chains and penal fire,
Who durst defy th' Omnipotent to arms.
Nine times the space that measures day and night 50
To mortal men, he with his horrid crew
Lay vanquish'd, rolling in the fiery gulf,
Confounded though immortal: But his doom
Reserved him to more wrath; for now the thought
Both of lost happiness and lasting pain 55
Torments him; round he throws his baleful eyes,
That witness'd huge affliction and dismay,
Mix'd with obdurate pride and steadfast hate:
At once, as far as angels' ken, he views
The dismal situation waste and wild: 60
A dungeon horrible on all sides round,
As one great furnace flamed; yet from those flames
No light; but rather darkness visible
Served only to discover sights of woe,
Regions of sorrow, doleful shades, where peace 65
And rest can never dwell: hope never comes,
That comes to all: but torture without end
Still urges, and a fiery deluge, fed
With ever-burning sulphur unconsumed:
Such place eternal justice had prepared 70
For those rebellious; here their pris'n ordained
In utter darkness, and their portion set
As far removed from God and light of heaven,
As from the centre thrice to th' utmost pole.
O how unlike the place from whence they fell! 75
There the companions of his fall, overwhelmed
With floods and whirlwinds of tempestuous fire,
He soon discerns, and welt'ring by his side

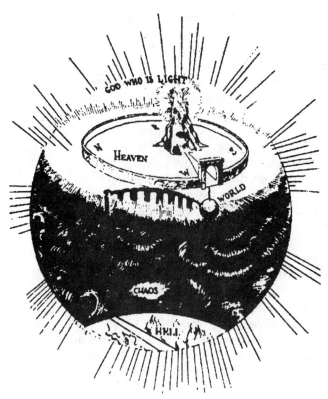

A diagram suggesting the relationship between God, who is infinite light, and total space with its content of emanated and created reality.

One next himself in power, and next in crime,
Long after known in Palestine, and named   80
Beëlzebub. To whom th' Arch-Enemy,
And thence in Heav'n call'd Satan, with bold words
Breaking the horrid silence thus began:
    If thou beest he; but O how fallen! how changed
From him who, in the happy realms of light   85
Cloth'd with transcendent brightness didst outshine
Myriads though bright! If he whom mutual league,
United thoughts and counsels, equal hope
And hazard in the glorious enterprise,
Join'd with me once, now misery hath join'd   90
In equal ruin: into what pit thou seest
From what height fall'n, so much the stronger proved
He with his thunder: and till then who knew
The force of those dire arms? yet not for those
Nor what the potent victor in his rage   95
Can else inflict, do I repent or change,
Though changed in outward lustre, that fix'd mind
And high disdain from sense of injured merit,
That with the Mightiest raised me to contend,
And to the fierce contention brought along   100
Innumerable force of Spirits arm'd,
That durst dislike his reign, and me preferring,
His utmost pow'r with adverse pow'r opposed
In dubious battle on the plains of Heav'n,
And shook his throne. What though the field be lost?   105

All is not lost; th' unconquerable will
And study of revenge, immortal hate,
And courage never to submit or yield:
And what is else not to be overcome;
That glory never shall his wrath or might   110
Extort from me. To bow and sue for grace
With suppliant knee, and deify his pow'r,
Who from the terror of this arm so late
Doubted his empire; that were low indeed!
That were an ignominy and shame beneath   115
This downfall: since by fate the strength of Gods
And this empyreal substance cannot fail,
Since through experience of this great event
In arms not worse, in foresight much advanced,
We may with more successful hope resolve   120
To wage by force or guile eternal war,
Irreconcileable to our grand foe,
Who no triumphs, and in th' excess of joy
Sole reigning holds the tyranny of heav'n.
   So spake th' apostate Angel, though in pain,   125
Vaunting aloud, but rack'd with deep despair:
And him thus answer'd soon his bold compeer.
   O Prince, O Chief of many throned powers!
That led the embattled Seraphim to war
Under thy conduct, and in dreadful deeds   130
Fearless, endangered heav'n's perpetual King,
And put to proof his high supremacy,
Whether upheld by strength, or chance, or fate;
Too well I see and rue the dire event,
That with sad overthrow and foul defeat   135
Hath lost us heav'n, and all this mighty host
In horrible destruction laid thus low,
As far as Gods and heav'nly essences
Can perish; for the mind and spirit remains
Invincible, and vigor soon returns,   140
Though all our glory extinct, and happy state
Here swallow'd up in endless misery
But what if he our conqu'ror (whom I now
Of force believe almighty, since no less
Than such could have overpowered such force as ours)   145
Have left us this our spirit and strength entire
Strongly to suffer and support our pains,
That we may so suffice his vengeful ire,
Or do him mightier service as his thralls
By right of war, whate'er his business be   150
Here in the heart of Hell to work in fire,
Or do his errands in the gloomy deep;
What can it then avail, though yet we feel
Strength undiminish'd, or eternal being
To undergo eternal punishment?   155
Whereto with speedy words th' Arch-Fiend replied:
   Fall'n Cherub, to be weak is miserable
Doing or suffering: but of this be sure,
To do aught good never will be our task,
But ever to do ill our sole delight   160
As being the contrary to his high will

Whom we resist. If then his providence
Out of our evil seek to bring forth good,
Our labor must be to pervert that end,
And out of good still to find means of evil;   165
Which oft-times may succeed, so as perhaps
Shall grieve him, if I fail not, and disturb
His inmost counsels from their destined aim.
But see, the angry victor hath recall'd
His ministers of vengeance and pursuit   170
Back to the gates of Heav'n; the sulph'rous hail
Shot after us in storm, o'erblown hath laid
The fiery surge, that from the precipice
Of Heav'n received us falling; and the thunder,
Wing'd with red lightning and impetuous rage,   175
Perhaps hath spent his shafts, and ceases now
To bellow through the vast and boundless deep,
Let us not slip th' occasion, whether scorn
Or satiate fury yield it from our foe.
Seest thou yon dreary plain, forlorn and wild,   180
The seat of desolation, void of light,
Save what the glimmering of these livid flames
Casts pale and dreadful? Thither let us tend
From off the tossing of these fiery waves,
There rest, if any rest can harbor there,   185
And reassembling our afflicted powers,
Consult how we may henceforth most offend
Our enemy, our own loss how repair,
How overcome this dire calamity,
What reinforcement we may gain from hope,   190
If not, what resolution from despair.
   Thus Satan talking to his nearest mate
With head uplift above the wave, and eyes
That sparkling blazed, his other parts besides
Prone on the flood, extended long and large,   195
Lay floating many a rood, in bulk as huge
As whom the fables name of monstrous size;
Titanian, or Earth-born, that warr'd on Jove,
Briareos, or Typhon, whom the den
By ancient Tarsus held, or that sea-beast   200
Leviathan, which God of all his works
Created hugest that swim the ocean stream;
Him haply slumbering on the Norway foam
The pilot of some small night-founder'd skiff
Deeming some island, oft, as seamen tell,   205
With fixed anchor in his scaly rind
Moors by his side under the lea, while night
Invests the sea, and wished morn delays:
So stretch'd out huge in length the Arch-Fiend lay
Chain'd on the burning lake, nor ever thence   210
Had ris'n or heaved his head, but that the will
And high permission of all-ruling Heav'n
Left him, at large to his own dark designs,
That with reiterated crimes he might
Heap on himself damnation while he sought   215
Evil to others, and enraged might see
How all his malice served but to bring forth

Infinite goodness, grace, and, mercy shewn
On Man, by him seduced; but on himself
Treble confusion, wrath, and vengeance pour'd.   220
Forthwith upright he rears from off the pool
His mighty stature; on each hand the flames
Driv'n backward slope their pointing spires, and roll'd
In billows, leave i' th' midst a horrid vale.
Then with expanded wings he steers his flight   225
Aloft, incumbent on the dusky air,
That felt unusual weight; till on dry land
He lights, as if it were land that ever burn'd
With solid, as the lake with liquid fire;
And such appear'd in hue, as when the force   230
Of subterranean wind transports a hill
Torn from Pelorus, or the shatter'd side
Of thundering Ætna, whose combustible
And fuel'd entrails thence conceiving fire,
Sublimed with min'ral fury, aid the winds,   235
And leave a singed bottom all involved
With stench and smoke; such resting found the sole
Of unblest feet. Him follow'd his next mate,
Both glorying to have 'scap'd the Stygian flood
As Gods, and by their own recover'd strength,   240
Not by the suff'rance of Supernal Power.
   Is this the region, this the soil, the clime,
Said then the lost Arch-Angel, this the seat
That we must change for heav'n, this mournful gloom
For that celestial light? Be it so, since he   245
Who now is Sovran can dispose and bid
What shall be right farthest from him is best,
Whom reason hath equall'd, force hath made supreme
Above his equals. Farewell happy fields,
Where joy forever dwells: Hail horrors, hail   250
Infernal world, and thou profoundest Hell
Receive thy new possessor; one who brings
A mind not to be changed by place or time.
The mind is its own place, and in itself
Can make a Heav'n of Hell, a Hell of Heav'n.   255
What matter where, if I be still the same,
And what I should be, all but less than he
Whom thunder hath made greater? Here at least
We shall be free; th' Almighty hath not built
Here for his envy, will not drive us hence: 260
Here we may reign secure, and in my choice
To reign is worth ambition, though in hell;
Better to reign in hell than serve in heaven.
But wherefore let we then our faithful friends,
Th' associates and copartners of our loss,   265
Lie thus astonished on th' oblivious pool,
And call them not to share with us their part
In this unhappy mansion, or once more
With rallied arms to try what may be yet
Regain'd in Heav'n, or what more lost in Hell?   270
   So Satan spake; and him Beëlzebub
Thus answer'd: Leader of those armies bright,
Which but th' Omnipotent none could have foil'd,

If once they hear that voice, their liveliest pledge
Of hope in fears and dangers, heard so oft   275
In worst extremes, and on the perilous edge
Of battle when it raged, in all assaults
Their surest signal, they will soon resume
New courage and revive, though now they be
Grov'ling and prostrate on yon lake of fire,   280
As we ere while, astounded and amazed,
No wonder, fall'n such a pernicious height.
    He scarce had ceased when the superior Fiend
Was moving tow'rd the shore; his pond'rous shield
Ethereal temper, massy, large, and round,   285
Behind him cast; the broad circumference
Hung on his shoulders like the moon, whose orb
Through optic glass the Tuscan artist views
At evening from the top of Fesolé,
Or in Valdarno, to descry new lands,   290
Rivers, or mountains, on her spotty globe.
His spear, to equal which the tallest pine
Hewn on Norwegian hills, to be the mast
Of some great ammiral, were but a wand,
He walk'd with to support uneasy steps   295
Over the burning marle; not like those steps
On Heaven's azure, and the torrid clime
Smote on him sore besides, vaulted with fire:
Nathless he so endured, till on the beach
Of that inflamed sea he stood, and call'd   300
His legions, Angel forms, who lay entranced
Thick as autumnal leaves that strow the brooks
In Vallombrosa, where the Etrurian shades
High over-arch'd imbow'r; or scatter'd sedge
Afloat, when with fierce winds Orion arm'd   305
Hath vex'd the Red Sea coast, whose waves o'erthrew
Busiris and his Memphian chivalry,
While with perfidious hatred they pursued
The sojourners of Goshen, who beheld
From the safe shore their floating carcasses   310
And broken chariot wheels, so thick bestrown,
Abject and lost lay these, covering the flood,
Under amazement of their hideous change.
He call'd so loud, that all the hollow deep
Of Hell resounded. Princes, Potentates,   315
Warriors, the flow'r of heav'n, once yours, now lost,
If such astonishment as this can seize
Eternal spirits; or have ye chos'n this place
After the toil of battle to repose
Your wearied virtue, for the ease you find   320
To slumber here, as in the vales of Heaven?
Or in this abject posture have ye sworn
T' adore the conqueror? who now beholds
Cherub and Seraph rolling in the flood
With scatter'd arms and ensigns till anon   325
His swift pursuers from heav'n gates discern
Th' advantage, and descending tread us down
Thus drooping, or with linked thunderbolts
Transfix us to the bottom of this gulf.

Awake, arise, or be for ever fall'n.   330
   They heard, and were abash'd, and up they sprung
Upon the wing, as when men wont to watch
On duty, sleeping found by whom they dread,
Rouse and bestir themselves ere well awake.
Nor did they not perceive the evil plight   335
In which they were, or the fierce pains not feel;
Yet to their gen'ral's voice they soon obey'd
Innumerable. As when the potent rod
Of Amram's son, in Egypt's evil day,
Waved round the coast, up call'd a pitchy cloud   340
Of locusts, warping on the eastern wind,
That o'er the realm of impious Pharaoh hung
Like night, and darken'd all the land of Nile:
So numberless were those bad Angels seen
Hov'ring on wing under the cope of Hell   345
'Twixt upper, nether, and surrounding fires;
Till, as a signal giv'n, th' uplifted spear
Of their great Sultan waving to direct
Their course, in even balance down they light
On the firm brimstone, and fill all the plain;   350
A multitude, like which the populous north
Pour'd never from her frozen loins, to pass
Rhene or the Danaw, when her barb'rous sons
Came like a deluge on the south, and spread
Beneath Gibraltar to the Lybian sands.   355
Forthwith from ev'ry squadron and each band
The heads and leaders thither haste where stood
Their great commander; Godlike shapes and forms
Excelling human, princely dignities,
And Pow'rs that erst in Heaven sat on thrones;   360
Though of their names in heav'nly records now
Be no memorial, blotted out and rased
By their rebellion from the books of life.
Nor had they yet among the sons of Eve
Got them new names, till wand'ring o'er the earth,   365
Thro' God's high suff'rance for the trial of man,
By falsities and lies the great part
Of mankind they corrupted, to forsake
God their Creator, and th' invisible
Glory of him that made them to transform   370
Oft to the image of a brute, adorn'd
With gay religions full of pomp and gold,
And Devils to adore for Deities:
Then were they known to men by various names,
And various idols through the Heathen world,   375
Say, Muse, their names then known, who first, who last
Roused from the slumber, on that fiery couch,
At their great emp'ror's call, as next in worth
Came singly when he stood on the bare strand,
While the promiscuous crowd stood yet aloof.   380
The chief were those who from the pit of Hell
Roaming to seek their prey on earth, durst fix
Their seats long after next the seat of God,
Their altars by his altar, Gods adored
Among the nations round, and durst abide

And black Gehenna call'd, the type of Hell.   405
Next Chemos, the óbscene dread of Moab's sons,
From Aroar to Nebo, and the wild
Of southmost Abarim; in Hesebon
And Horonaim, Seon's realm, beyond
The flowery dale of Sibma clad with vines,   410
And Eleälé to th' Asphaltic pool.
Peor his other name, when he enticed
Israel in Sittim, on their march from Nile,
To do him wanton rites, which cost them woe.
Yet thence his lustful orgies he enlarged   415
E'en to that hill of scandal, by the grove
Of Moloch homicide; lust hard by hate;
Till good Josiah drove them thence to Hell.
Their living Strength, and unfrequented left
His righteous altar, bowing lowly down
To bestial gods; for which their head as low   435
Bow'd down in battle, sunk before the spear
Of despicable foes. With these in troop
Came Astoreth, whom the Phoenicians call'd
Astarte, queen of heaven, with crescent horns
To whose bright image nightly by the moon   440
Sidonian virgins paid their vows and songs;
In Sion also not unsung, where stood
Her temple on th' offensive mountain, built
By that uxorious king, whose heart, though large,
Beguiled by fair idolatresses, fell   445
To idols foul. Thammuz came next behind,
Whose annual wound in Lebanon allured
The Syrian damsels to lament his fate
In amorous ditties all a summer's day;
While smooth Adonis from his native rock   450
Ran purple to the sea, supposed with blood
Of Thammuz yearly wounded: the love-tale
Infected Sion's daughters with like heat;
Whose wanton passions in the sacred porch
Ezekiel saw, when by the vision led,   455
His eye survey'd the dark idolatries
Of alienated Judah. Next came one
Who mourn'd in earnest when the captive ark
Maim'd his brute image, head and hands lopp'd off
In his own temple, on the grunsel edge,   460
Where he fell flat, and shamed his worshippers:
Dagon his name, sea-monster, upward man
And downward fish: yet had his temple high
Rear'd in Azotus, dreaded through the coast
Of Palestine, in Gath and Ascalon,   465
And Accaron and Gaza's frontier bounds.
Him follow'd Rimmon, whose delightful seat
Was fair Damascus, on the fertile banks
Of Abbana and Pharphar, lucid streams.
He also 'gainst the house of God was bold: 470
A leper once he lost, and gain'd a king;
Ahaz his sottish conqu'ror, whom he drew
God's altar to disparage and displace
For one of Syrian mode, whereon to burn

His odious offerings, and adore the gods   475
Whom he had vanquish'd. After these appear'd
A crew, who, under names of old renown,
Osiris, Iris, Orus, and their train,
With monstrous shapes and sorceries abused
Fanatic Egypt and her priests, to seek   480
Their wandering gods disguised in brutish forms
Rather than human. Nor did Israel 'scape
Th' infection, when their borrow'd gold composed
The calf in Oreb; and the rebel king
Doubled that sin in Bethel and in Dan,   485
Likening his Maker to the grazed ox;
Jehovah, who in one night when he pass'd
From Egypt marching, equall'd with one stroke
Both her first-born, and all her bleating gods.
Belial came last, than whom a spirit more lewd   490
Fell not from heaven, or more gross to love
Vice for itself: to whom no temple stood,
Nor altar smoke; yet who more oft than he
In temples and at altars, when the priest
Turns atheist, as did Eli's sons, who fill'd   495
With lust and violence the house of God?
In courts and palaces he also reigns,
And in luxurious cities, where the noise
Of riot ascends above their loftiest towers,
And injury and outrage: and when night   500
Darkens the streets, then wander forth the sons
Of Belial, flown with insolence and wine.
Witness the streets of Sodom, and that night
In Gibeah, when the hospitable door
Exposed a matron, to avoid worse rape.   505
These were the prime in order and in might
The rest were long to tell, though far renown'd,
Th' Ionian gods, of Javan's issue held
Gods, yet confess'd later than Heaven and Earth,
Their boasted parent Titan, Heav'n's first-born   50
With his enormous brood, and birthright seized
By younger Saturn: he from mightier Jove,
His own and Rhea's son, like measure found;
So Jove usurping reign'd: these first in Crete
And Ida known, thence on the snowy top   515
Of cold Olympus, ruled the middle air,
Their highest heav'n; or on the Delphian cliff,
Or in Dodona, and through all the bounds
Of Doric land; or who with Saturn old
Fled over Adria to th' Hesperian fields,   520
And o'er the Celtic roam'd the utmost isles.
    All these and more came flocking; but with looks
Downcast and damp; yet such wherein appear'd
Obscure some glimpse of joy, to have found their chief
Not in despair, to have found themselves not lost   525
In loss itself: which on his countenance cast
Like doubtful hue: but he, his wonted pride
Soon recollecting, with high words, that bore
Semblance of worth, not substance, gently raised
Their fainting courage and dispell'd their fears.   530

Then straight commands, that at the warlike sound
Of trumpets loud and clarions be uprear'd
His mighty standard; that proud honor claim'd
Azazel as his right, a cherub tall;
Who forthwith from the glittering staff unfurl'd   535
Th' imperial ensign; which, full high advanced,
Shone like a meteor, streaming to the wind,
With gems and golden lustre rich emblazed
Seraphic arms and trophies; all the while
Sonorous metal blowing martial sounds: 540
At which the universal host up-sent
A shout, that tore hell's concave, and beyond
Frighted the reign of Chaos and old Night.
All in a moment through the gloom were seen
Ten thousand banners rise into the air,   545
With orient colors waving: with them rose
A forest huge of spears; and thronging helms
Appear'd, and serried shields in thick array
Of depth immeasurable: anon they move
In perfect phalanx to the Dorian mood   550
Of flutes and soft recorders; such as raised
To height of noblest temper heroes old
Arming to battle; and instead of rage
Deliberate valor breath'd, firm and unmoved
With dread of deal to flight or foul retreat   555
Nor wanting power to mitigate and 'suage,
With solemn touches troubled thoughts, and chase
Anguish, and doubt, and fear, and sorrow, and pain
From mortal or immortal minds. Thus they,
Breathing united force, with fixed thought,   560
Moved on in silence, to soft pipes, that charm'd
Their painful steps o'er the burnt soil: and now
Advanced in view they stand; a horrid front
Of dreadful length and dazzling arms, in guise
Of warriors old with order'd spear and shield,   565
Awaiting what command their mighty chief
Had to impose: he through the armed files
Darts his experienced eye, and soon traverse
The whole battalion views, their order due,
Their visages and stature as of gods: 570
Their number last he sums. And now his heart
Distends with pride, and hardening in his strength
Glories; for never since created man
Met such embodied force, as, named with these,
Could merit more than that small infantry   575
Warr'd on by cranes: though all the giant brood
Of Phlegra with th' heroic race were join'd
That fought at Thebes and Ilium, on each side
Mix'd with auxiliar gods; and what resounds
In fable or romance of Uther's son   580
Begirt with British and Armoric knights;
And all who since, baptized or infidel,
Jousted in Aspramont, or Montalban,
Damasco, or Marocco, or Trebisond,
Or whom Biserta sent from Afric shore,   585
When Charlemagne with all his peerage fell

By Fontarabia. Thus far these beyond
Compare of mortal prowess, yet observed
Their dread commander: he, above the rest
In shape and gesture proudly eminent,   590
Stood like a tower; his form had not yet lost
All her original brightness, nor appear'd
Less than archangel ruin'd, and the excess
Of glory obscured; as when the sun, new risen,
Looks through the horizontal misty air   595
Shorn of his beams; or from behind the moon,
In dim eclipse, disastrous twilight sheds
On half the nations, and with fear of change
Perplexes monarchs. Darken'd so, yet shone
Above them all the Arch-angel: but his face   600
Deep scars of thunder had intrench'd, and care
Sat on his faded cheek; but under brows
Of dauntless courage, and considerate pride
Waiting revenge; cruel his eye, but cast
Signs of remorse and passion, to behold   605
The fellows of his crime, the followers rather
(Far other once beheld in bliss), condemned
For ever now to have their lot in pain:
Millions of Spirits for his fault amerced
Of heaven, and from eternal splendours flung   610
For his revolt, yet faithful how they stood,
Their glory wither'd: as when Heav'n's fire
Hath scath'd the forest oaks, or mountain pines,
With singed top their stately growth tho' bare
Stands on the blasted heath. He now prepared   615
To speak; whereat their doubled ranks they bend
From wing to wing, and half inclose him round
With all his peers. Attention held them mute.
Thrice he essay'd, and thrice, in spite of scorn,
Tears, such as angels weep, burst forth. At last   620
Words interwove with sighs found out their way.
      O myriads of immortal Spirits, O Powers
Matchless, but with th' Almighty, and that strife
Was not inglorious, though the event was dire,
As this place testifies, and this dire change,   625
Hateful to utter; but what power of mind,
Foreseeing or presaging, from the depth
Of knowledge past or present, could have fear'd
How such united force of Gods, how such
As stood like these, could ever know repulse;   630
For who can yet believe, though after loss,
That all these puissant legions, whose exile
Hath emptied Heav'n, shall fail to re-ascend
Self-raised, and repossess their native seat?
For me, be witness all the host of Heav'n,   635
If counsels different, or danger shunn'd
By me, have lost our hopes. But he who reigns
Monarch in Heav'n, till then as one secure
Sat on his throne, upheld by old repute,
Consent, or custom, and his regal state   640
Put forth at full, but still his strength conceal'd,
Which tempted our attempt, and wrought our fall.

Henceforth his might we know, and know our own,
So as not either to provoke or dread
New war, provoked; our better part remains   645
To work in close design, by fraud or guile,
What force effected not; that he no less
At length from us may find, who overcomes
By force, hath overcome but half his foe.
Space may produce new worlds; whereof so rife   650
There went a fame in Heav'n that he ere long
Intended to create, and therein plant
A generation, whom his choice regard
Should favour equal to the sons of Heav'n:
Thither, if but to pry, shall be perhaps   655
Our first eruption, thither or elsewhere:
For this infernal pit shall never hold
Celestial Spirits in bondage, nor th' abyss
Long under darkness cover. But these thoughts
Full counsel must mature Peace is despair'd,   660
For who can think submission? War then, War,
Open or understood, must be resolved.
    He spake: and, to confirm his words, out flew
Millions of flaming swords, drawn from the thighs
Of mighty Cherubim: the sudden blaze   665
Far round illumined Hell. Highly they raged
Against the Highest, and fierce with grasped arms
Clash'd on their sounding shields the din of war,
Hurling defiance tow'rd the vault of Heaven.
    There stood a hill not far, whose grisly top   670
Belch'd fire and rolling smoke; the rest entire
Shone with a glossy scurf, undoubted sign
That in his womb was hid metallic ore,
The work of sulphur. Thither wing'd with speed
A num'rous brigade hasten'd: as when bands   675
Of pioneers, with spade and pickaxe arm'd,
Forerun the royal camp to trench a field,
Or cast a rampart. Mammon led them on;
Mammon, the least erected Spirit that fell
From Heav'n: for e'en in Heav'n his looks and thoughts   680
Were always downward bent, admiring more
The riches of Heav'n's pavement, trodden gold,
Than aught divine or holy else enjoy'd
In vision beatific. By him first
Men also, and by his suggestion taught,   685
Ransack'd the centre, and with impious hands
Rifled the bowels of their mother earth
For treasures better hid. Soon had his crew
Open'd into the hill a spacious wound,
And digg'd out ribs of gold. Let none admire   690
That riches grow in Hell; that soil may best
Deserve the precious bane. And here let those
Who boast in mortal things, and wond'ring tell
Of Babel, and the works of Memphian kings,
Learn how their greatest monuments of fame,   695
And strength, and art, are easily outdone
By Spirits reprobate, and in an hour
What in an age they with incessant toil

And hands innumerable scarce perform.
Nigh on the plain in many cells prepared,   700
That underneath had veins of liquid fire
Sluiced from the lake, a second multitude
With wond'rous art founded the massy ore,
Severing each kind, and scumm'd the bullion dross;
A third as soon had form'd within the ground   705
A various mould, and from the boiling cells
By strange conveyance filled each hollow nook,
As in an organ, from one blast of wind,
To many a row of pipes, the sound-board breathes
Anon out of the earth a fabric huge   710
Rose like an exhalation, with the sound
Of dulcet symphonies and voices sweet,
Built like a temple, where pilasters round
Were set, and Doric pillars overlaid
With golden architrave; nor did there want   715
Cornice or frieze, with bossy sculptures grav'n
The roof was fretted gold. Not Babylon,
Nor great Alcairo such magnificence
Equall'd in all their glories, to inshrine
Belus of Serapis their Gods, or seat   720
Their kings, when Egypt with Assyria strove
In wealth and luxury. Th' ascending pile
Stood fix'd her stately height; and straight the doors,
Op'ning their brazen folds, discover wide
Within her ample spaces, o'er the smooth   725
And level pavement. From the arched roof,
Pendant by subtle magic, many a row
Of starry lamps and blazing cressets, fed
With naphtha and asphaltus, yielded light
As from a sky. The hasty multitude   730
Admiring enter'd; and the work some praise,
And some the architect: his hand was known
In heaven by many a tower'd structure high,
Where sceptred angels held their residence,
And sat as princes; whom the supreme King   735
Exalted to such power and gave to rule
Each in his hierarchy, the orders bright.
Nor was his name unheard or unadored
in ancient Greece; and in Ausonian land
Men call'd him Mulciber; and how he fell   740
From Heaven, they fabled, thrown by angry Jove
Sheer o'er the crystal battlements: from morn
To noon he fell, from noon to dewy eve,
A summer's day; and with the setting sun
Dropt from the zenith like a falling star,   745
On Lemnos, th' Ægean isle: thus they relate,
Erring; for he with this rebellious rout
Fell long before; nor ought avail'd him now
T' have built in heav'n high tow'rs; nor did he 'scape
By all his engines, but was headlong sent   750
With his industrious crew to build in hell.
    Meanwhile, the winged heralds, by command
Of sovereign power, with awful ceremony
And trumpet's sound, throughout the host proclaim

A solemn council, forthwith to be held   755
At Pandemonium, the high capital
Of Satan and his peers: their summons call'd
From every band and squared regiment
By place or choice the worthiest: they anon,
With hundreds and with thousands, trooping came   760
Attended: all access was throng'd: the gates
And porches wide, but chief the spacious hall
(Though like a cover'd field, where champions bold
Won't ride in arm'd, and at the soldan's chair
Defied the best of Panim chivalry   765
To mortal combat or career with lance),
Thick swarm'd both on the ground and in the air,
Brush'd with the hiss of rustling wings. As bees
In spring time, when the sun with Taurus rides,
Pour forth their populous youth about the hive   770
In clusters; they among fresh dews and flowers
Fly to and fro, or in the smoothed plank,
The suburb of their straw-built citadel,
New rubb'd with balm, expatiate and confer
Their state affairs; so thick the aëry crowd   775
Swarm'd and were straiten'd, till, the signal given,
Behold a wonder! They but now who seem'd
In bigness to surpass earth's giant sons,
Now less than smallest dwarfs, in narrow room
Throng numberless, like that pygmean race   780
Beyond the Indian mount; or fairy elves,
Whose midnight revels, by a forest-side
Or fountain, some belated peasant sees,
Or dreams he sees, while over head the moon
Sits arbitress, and nearer to the earth   785
Wheels her pale course; they, on their mirth and dance
Intent, with jocund music charm his ear;
At once with joy and fear his heart rebounds.
Thus incorporeal spirits to smallest forms
Reduced their shapes immense, and were at large,   790
Though without number still, amidst the hall
Of that infernal court. But far within,
And in their own dimensions like themselves,
The great Seraphic Lords and Cherubim,
In close recess and secret conclave sat,   795
A thousand Demi-gods on golden seats,
Frequent and full. After short silence then,
And summons read, the great consult began.

Milton, in imitation of Homer and Virgil, opens his Paradise Lost with an infernal council, plotting the fall of man, which is the *action* he proposed to celebrate; and as for those great actions, the battle of the angels and the creation of the world, which preceded, in point of time, and which would have entirely destroyed the unity of the principal action, had he related them in the same order in which they happened, he cast them into the fifth, sixth, and seventh books, by way of episode to this noble poem. It may be re- marked of all the episodes introduced by Milton, that they arise naturally from the subject. In relating the fall of man, he has (by way of episode) related the fall of those angels who were his professed enemies; and the two narratives are so conducted as not to destroy unity of action, having a close affinity for each other.

In respect to the rule of epic poetry, which requires the action to be entire or complete, in all its parts, having a beginning, a middle, and an end, the action in the Paradise Lost was contrived in Hell, executed upon Earth, and punished by Heaven. The parts are distinct yet grow out of one another in the most natural method.— A.

THE CHARACTERS IN PARADISE LOST

Addison, in his Spectator, has some learned and interesting remarks upon this topic, of which the substance is now to be presented. Homer has excelled all the heroic poets in the multitude and variety of his characters. Every god that is admitted into the Iliad, acts a part which would have been suitable to no other deity. His princes are as much distinguished by their manners as by their dominions; and even those among them, whose characters seem wholly made up of courage, differ from one another as to the particular kinds of courage in which they excel.

Homer excels, moreover, in the novelty of his characters. Some of them, also, possess a dignity which adapts them, in a peculiar manner, to the nature of an heroic poem.

If we look into the characters of Milton, we shall find that he has introduced all the variety his narrative was capable of receiving. The whole species of mankind was in two persons at the time to which the subject of his poem is confined. We have, however, four distinct characters in these two persons. We see man and woman in the highest innocence and perfection, and in the most abject state of guilt and infirmity. The last two characters are now, indeed, very common and obvious; but the first two are not only more magnificent, but more new than any characters either in Virgil or Homer, or, indeed, in the whole circle of nature.

To supply the lack of characters, Milton has brought into his poem two actors of a shadowy and fictitious nature, in the persons of Sin and Death, by which means he has wrought into the body of his fable a very beautiful and well-invented allegory.—(See Note, Book II. 649.)

Another principal actor in this poem is the great Adversary of mankind. The part of Ulysses, in Homer's Odyssey, is very much admired by Aristotle, as perplexing that fable with very agreeable plots and intricacies, not only by the many adventures in his voyage, and the subtlety of his behaviour, but by the various concealments and discoveries of his person in several parts of that poem. But the crafty being, mentioned above, makes a much longer voyage than Ulysses, puts in practice many more wiles and stratagems, and hides himself under a greater variety of shapes and appearances, all of which are severally detected, to the great delight and surprise of the reader.

It may, likewise, be observed, with how much art the poet has varied several characters of the persons that speak in his infernal assembly. On the contrary, he has represented the whole Godhead exerting itself towards man, in its full benevolence, under the threefold distinction of a Creator, Redeemer, and Comforter.

The angels are as much diversified in Milton, and distinguished by their proper parts, as the gods are in Homer or Virgil. The reader will find nothing ascribed to Uriel, Gabriel, Michael, or Raphael, which is not in a particular manner suitable to their respective characters.

The heroes of the Iliad and Æneid were nearly related to the people for whom Virgil and Homer wrote: their adventures would be read, consequently, with the deeper interest by their respective countrymen. But Milton's poem has an advantage, in this respect, above both the others, since it is impossible for any of its readers, whatever nation or country he may belong to, not to be related to the persons who are the principal actors in it; but, what is still infinitely more to its advantage, the principal actors in this poem, are not only our progenitors, but our representatives. We have an actual interest in everything they do, and no less than our utmost happiness is concerned, and lies at stake in all their behaviour.

OBJECTION TO MYTHOLOGICAL ALLUSIONS CONSIDERED

The charge is brought against Milton of blending the Pagan and Christian forms. The great realities of angels and archangels, are continually combined into the same groups with the fabulous impersonations of the Greek Mythology.

In other poets, this combination might be objected to, but not in Milton, for the following reason: Milton has himself laid an early foundation for his introduction of the pagan pantheism into Christian groups; the false gods of the heathen were, according to Milton, the fallen angels. They are not false, therefore, in the sense of being unreal, baseless, and having a merely fantastical existence, like the European fairies, but as having drawn aside mankind from a pure worship. As ruined angels, under other names, they are no less real than the faithful and loyal angels of the Christian Heaven. And in that one difference of the Miltonic creed, which the poet has brought pointedly and elaborately under his readers' notice by his matchless catalogue of the rebellious angels, and of *their pagan transformations*, in the very first book of the Paradise Lost, is laid beforehand the amplest foundation for his subsequent practice; and, at the same time, therefore, the amplest answer to the charge preferred against him by Dr. Johnson, and by so many other critics, who had not sufficiently penetrated the latent theory on which he acted.—BLACKWOOD'S MAG.

THE CHARACTER OF MILTON'S SATAN

"Satan is the most heroic subject that ever was chosen for a poem; and the execution is as perfect as the design is lofty. He was the first of created beings, who, for endeavouring to be equal with the Highest, and to divide the empire of Heaven with the Almighty, was hurled down to Hell. His aim was no less than the throne of the universe; his means, myriads of angelic armies bright, who durst defy the Omnipotent in arms. His strength of mind was matchless, as his strength of body: the vastness of his designs did not surpass the firm, inflexible determination with which he submitted to his irreversible doom, and final loss of all good. His power of action and of suffering was equal. He was the greatest power that was ever overthrown, with the strongest will left to resist or to endure. He was baffled, not confounded. The fierceness of tormenting flames is qualified and made innoxious by the greater fierceness of his pride: the loss of infinite happiness to himself, is compensated in thought by the power of inflicting infinite misery on others. Yet, Satan is not the principle of malignity, or of the abstract love of evil, but of the abstract love of power, of pride, of self-will personified, to which principle all other good and evil, and even his own, are subordinate. He expresses the sum and substance of ambition in one line, "Fallen cherub, to be weak is miserable, doing or suffering." He founds a new empire in Hell, and from it conquers this new world, whither he bends his undaunted flight, forcing his way through nether and surrounding fires. The Achilles of Homer is not more distinct; the Titans were not more vast; Prometheus, chained to his rock, was not a more terrific example of suffering and of crime. Wherever the figure of Satan is introduced, whether he walks or flies, "rising aloft incumbent on the dusky air," it is illustrated with the most striking and appropriate images: so that we see it always before us, gigantic, irregular, portentous, uneasy, and disturbed, but dazzling in its faded splendor, the clouded ruins of a god. The deformity, to excite our loathing or disgust.

"Not only the figure of Satan, but his speeches in council, his soliloquies, his address to Eve, his share in the war in heaven, show the same decided superiority of character."—HAZLITT.

Another sketch of Satan may be found at the close of Book III, from the dashing pen of Gilfillan.

Hazlitt, in the above sketch of Milton's Satan, had no authority for saying that he was not a personification of malice, but, simply, of pride and self-will: this will appear on referring to Book I. 215–17; Book V. 666; Book VI. 151, 270; Book IX. 126, 134.

ENDNOTES

Books I and II reprinted from *The Paradise Lost* by John Milton, with notes explanatory and critical; edited by Rev. James Robert Boyd. New York: Baker and Scribner, 1850.

1. As in the commencement of the Iliad, of the Odyssey, and of the Æneid, so here the subject of the poem is the first announcement that is made, and precedes the verb with which it stands connected, thus giving it due prominence. Besides the plainness and simplicity of the exordium, there is (as Newton has observed) a further beauty in the variety of the numbers, which of themselves charm every reader without any sublimity of thought or pomp of expression; and this variety of the numbers consists chiefly in the pause being so artfully

varied that it falls upon a different syllable in almost every line. Thus, in the successive lines it occurs after the words *disobedience, tree, world, Eden, us, Muse.* In Milton's verse the pause is continually varied according to the sense through all the ten syllables of which it is composed; and to this peculiarity is to be ascribed the surpassing harmony of his numbers.

4. *Eden:* Here the whole is put for a part. It was the loss of *Paradise* only, the garden, the most beautiful part of Eden; for after the expulsion of our first parents from Paradise we read of their pursuing their solitary way in Eden, which was an extensive region.

5. *Regain, etc.:* Compare XII. 463, whence it appears that in the opinion of Milton, after the general conflagration, the whole earth would be formed into another, and more beautiful, Paradise than the one that was lost.

6. *Muse:* One of those nine imaginary heathen divinities, that were thought to preside over certain arts and sciences, is here, in conformity to classical custom, addressed. *Secret* top: set apart, interdicted. The Israelites, during the delivery of the law were not allowed to ascend that mountain.

7. *Horeb* and *Sinai* were the names of two contiguous eminences of the same chain of mountains. Compare Exod. iii. 1, with Acts vii. 30.

8. *Shepherd:* Moses. Exod. iii. 1.

12. *Oracle:* God's temple; so called from the divine communications which were there granted to men.

15. *The Aonian Mount;* or Mount Helicon, the fabled residence of the Muses, in Boeotia, the earlier name of which was Aonia. Virgil's Eclog. vi. 65. Georg, iii. 11.

16. *Things unattempted:* There were but few circumstances upon which Milton could raise his poem, and in everything which he added out of his own invention he was obliged, from the nature of the subject, to proceed with the greatest caution; yet he has filled his story with a surprising number of incidents, which bear so close an analogy with what is delivered in holy writ that it is capable of pleasing the most delicate reader without giving offence to the most scrupulous.—A.

17. *Chiefly Thou, O Spirit:* Invoking the Muse is commonly a matter of mere form, wherein the (modern) poets neither mean, nor desire to be thought to mean, anything seriously. But the Holy Spirit, here invoked, is too solemn a name to be used insignificantly: and besides, our author, in the beginning of his next work, "Paradise Regained," scruples not to say to the same Divine Person—"Inspire As Thou art wont, my prompted song, else mute." This address therefore is no mere formality.—HEYLIN. It is thought by Bp. Newton that the poet is liable to the charge of enthusiasm; having expected from the Divine Spirit a kind and degree of inspiration similar to that which the writers of the sacred scriptures enjoyed. The widow of Milton was accustomed to affirm that he considered himself as inspired; and this report is confirmed by a passage in his Second Book on Church Government, already quoted in our preliminary observations.

24. The *height* of the argument is precisely what distinguishes this poem of Milton from all others. In other works of imagination the difficulty lies in giving sufficient elevation to the subject; here it lies in raising the imagination up to the grandeur of the subject, in adequate conception of its mightiness and in finding language of such majesty as will not degrade it. A genius less gigantic and less holy than Milton's would have shrunk from the attempt. Milton not only does not lower; but he illumines the bright, and enlarges the great: he expands his wings, and "sails with supreme dominion" up to the heavens, parts the clouds, and communes with angels and unembodied spirits.—E.B.

27. The poets attribute a kind of omniscience to the Muse, as it enables them to speak of things which could not otherwise be supposed to come to their knowledge. Thus Homer, Iliad ii. 485, and Virgil, Æn. vii. 645. Milton's Muse, being the Holy Spirit, must of course be omniscient.—N.

30. Greatness is in important requisite in the action or subject of an epic poem; and Milton here surpasses both Homer and Virgil. The anger of Achilles embroiled the kings of Greece, destroyed the heroes of Troy, and engaged all the gods in factions. Æneas' settlement in Italy produced the Caesars and gave birth to the Roman empire. Milton's subject does not determine the fate merely of single persons, or of a nation, but of an entire species. The united powers of Hell are joined together for the destruction of mankind, which they effected in part and would have completed, had not Omnipotence itself interposed. The principled actors are man in his greatest perfection, and woman in her highest beauty. Their enemies are the fallen angels; the Messiah their friend, and the Almighty their Protector. In short, everything that is great is the whole circle of being, whether within the range of nature or beyond it, finds a place in this admirable poem.—A. "The sublimest of all subjects (says Cowper) was reserved for Milton and, bringing to the contemplation of that subject, not only a genius equal to the best of the ancients, but a heart also deeply impregnated with the divine truths which lay before him, it is no wonder that he has produced a composition, on the whole, superior to any that we have received from former ages. But he who addresses himself to the perusal of this work with a mind entirely unaccustomed to serious and spiritual contemplation, unacquainted with the word of God, or prejudiced against it, is ill qualified to appreciate the value of a poem built upon it, or to taste its beauties.

32. *One restraint:* one subject of restraint—the tree of knowledge of good and evil.

34. *Serpent:* Compare Gen. iii. I Tim. ii. 14. John viii. 44.

38. *Aspiring:* I Tim. ii. 6.

39. *In glory:* a divine glory, such as God himself possessed. This charge is brought against him, V. 725; it is also asserted in line 40; again in VI. 88. VII. 140.

46. *Ruin* is derived from *ruo,* and includes the idea of falling with violence and precipitation: combustion is more than *flaming* in the foregoing line; it is burning in a dreadful manner.—N.

48. *Chains.* Compare with Epistle of *Jude v.* 8. Also, Æschylus Prometh. 6.

50. *Nine times the space, etc.* Propriety sometimes requires the use of circumlocution as in this case. To have said *nine days and nights* would not have been proper when talking of a period before the creation of the sun, and consequently before time was portioned out to any being in that manner.—CAMPBELL, Phil. Rhet.

52–3. The nine days' astonishment, in which the angels lay entranced after their dreadful overthrow and fall from heaven, before they could recover the use either of thought or speech, is a noble circumstance and very finely imagined. The division of hell into seas of fire, and into firm ground (227–8) impregnated with the same furious element with that particular circumstance of the exclusion of hope from those infernal regions, are instances of the same great and fruitful invention.—A.

63. *Darkness visible:* gloom. Absolute darkness is, strictly speaking, invisible; but where there is a gloom only, there is so much light remaining as serves to show that there are objects, and yet those objects cannot be distinctly seen. Compare with the Peneroso, 79, 80: "Where glowing embers through the room Teach light to counterfeit a gloom."

72. *Utter,* has the same meaning as the word *outer,* which is applied to darkness in the Scriptures. Spenser uses *utter* in this sense.

74. Thrice as far as it is from the centre of the *earth* (which is the centre of the *world,* (universe,) according to Milton's system, IX. 103, and X. 671,) to the pole of the world; for it is the pole of the *universe,* far beyond the pole of the earth, which is here called the *utmost* pole. It is observable that Homer makes the seat of hell as far beneath the deepest pit of earth as the heaven is above the earth, Iliad viii. 16; Virgil makes it twice as far, Æneid vi.

577; and Milton thrice as far: as if these three great poets had stretched their utmost genius, and vied with each other in extending his idea of Hell farthest—N.

75. The language of the inspired writings (says Dugald Stewart) is on this as on other occasions, beautifully accommodated to the irresistible impressions of nature; availing itself of such popular and familiar words as *upwards* and *downwards, above* and *below,* in condescension to the frailty of the human mind, governed so much by sense and imagination, and so little by the abstractions of philosophy. Hence the expression of *fallen* angels, which, by recalling to us the eminence from which they fell, communicates, in a single word, a character of sublimity to the bottomless abyss—WORKS, vol. iv. 288.

77. *Fire.* Compare with *Mark* ix. 45, 46.

81. *Beelzebub.* Compare with *Mat.* xii. 24. 2 Kings i. 2. The word means *god of flies.* Here he is made second to Satan.

82. *Satan.* Many other names are assigned to this arch enemy of God and man in the sacred scriptures. He is called the Devil, the Dragon, the Evil One, the Angel of the Bottomless Pit, the Prince of this World, the Prince of the power of the air, the God of this World, Apollyon, Abaddon, Belial, Beelzebub. Milton, it will be seen, applies some of the terms to other evil angels. The term Satan denotes adversary; the term Devil denotes an accuser, See Kitto's Bib. Cycl. Upon the *character of Satan* as described by Milton, Hazlitt has penned an admirable criticism, which will be found at the end of Book I.

84. The confusion of mind felt by Satan is happily shown by the abrupt and halting manner in which he commences this speech. *Fallen;* see Isaiah xiv. 12. *Changes:* See Virg. Æn ii. 274: : "Hei mihi qualis erat! Quantum mutatus ab illo!"

93. *He with his thunder.* There is an uncommon beauty in this expression. Satan disdains to utter the name of God, though he cannot but acknowledge his superiority. So again, line 257.—N.

94. *Those:* compare Æsch. Prometh. 991.

95–116. Amidst those impieties which this enraged spirit utters in various parts of the poem, the author has taken care to introduce none that is not big with absurdity, and incapable of shocking a religious reader; his words, as the poet himself describes them, bearing only a "semblance of worth, not substance." He is likewise with great art described as owning his adversary to be Almighty. Whatever perverse interpretation he puts on the justice, mercy, and other attributes of the Supreme Being, he frequently confesses his omnipotence, that being the perfection he was forced to allow, and the only consideration which could support his pride under the shame of his defeat.—A. Upon this important point Dr. Channing has made the following observations: "Some have doubted whether the moral effect of such delineations (as Milton has given) of the stormy and terrible workings of the soul is good; whether the interest felt in a spirit so transcendently evil as Satan favors our sympathies with virtue. But our interest fastens, in this and like cases, on what is not evil. We gaze on Satan with an awe not unmixed with mysterious pleasure, as on *a miraculous manifestation of the power of mind.* What chains us, as with a resistless spell, in such a character, is spiritual might (might of soul), made visible by the racking pains which it overpowers. There is something kindling and ennobling in the consciousness, however awakened, of the energy which resides in mind; and many a virtuous man has borrowed new strength from the force, constancy, and dauntless courage of evil agents."

109. *Overcome:* in some editions an interrogation point is placed after this word, but improperly; for as Pearce remarks, the line means, "and if there be anything else (besides the particulars mentioned) which is not to be overcome."

110. *That glory:* referring to the possession of an unconquerable will, and the other particulars mentioned 107–9.

114. *Doubted his empire:* that is, doubted the stability of it.

116. *Fate.* Satan supposes the angels to subsist by necessity, and represents them of an *empyreal*, that it *fiery* substance as the Scripture does, Ps. civ. 4. Heb. i. 7. Satan disdains to submit, since the angels (as he says) are necessarily immortal and cannot be destroyed, and since too they are now improved in experience.

129. *Seraphim.* Compare with *Isaiah* vi. 2–6. An order of angels near the throne of God.

157. *Cherub.* One of an order of angels next in rank to a seraph. Compare with Gen. iii. 24. *Ezek.* ch. x.

169. The account here given by Satan differs materially from that which Raphael gives, book ii. 880, but this is satisfactorily explained by referring to the circumstances of the two relators. Raphael's account may be considered as the true one; but, as Newton remarks, in the other passages Satan himself is the speaker, or some of his angels; and they were too proud and obstinate to acknowledge the Messiah for their conqueror; as their rebellion was raised on his account they would never own his superiority; they would rather ascribe their defeat to the whole host of heaven than to him alone. In book vi. 830 the rote of his chariot is compared to the *sound of a numerous host;* and perhaps their fears led them to think that they were really pursued by a numerous army. And what a sublime idea does it give us of the terrors of the Messiah, that he alone should be as formidable as if the whole host of Heaven were in pursuit of them.

192. The incidents, in the passage that follows, to which Addison calls attention, are, Satan's being the first that wakens out of the general trance, his posture on the burning lake, his rising from it, and the description of his shield and spear; also his call to the fallen angels that lay plunged and stupified in the sea of fire. (314–5.)

193. *Prone on the flood,* somewhat like those two monstrous serpents described by Virgil ii. 206: Pectora quorum inter fluctus arrecta, jubæque Sanguinæ

exsuperant undas; pars coetera pontum Pone legit.

196. *Rood, etc.:* a rood is the fourth part of an acre, so that the bulk of Satan is expressed by the same sort of measure, as that of one of the giants in Virgil, Æn. vi. 596. Per tota novem cui *jugera* corpus Porrigitur. And also that of the old dragon in Spenser's Fairy Queen, book i. "That with his largeness measured much land."—N.

198. *Titanian, or Earth-born:* Genus antiquum terræ, Titania pubes Æn. vi. 580. Here Milton commences that train of learned allusions which was among six peculiarities, and which he always makes poetical by some picturesque spithet, or simile.—E. B.

199. *Briareos,* a fabled giant (one of the Titans) possessed of a hundred hands. "Et centumgeminus Briareus." Virg. Æn. vi. 287.

201. *Leviathan,* a marine animal finely described in the book of *Job,* ch. xii. It is supposed by some to be the whale; by others, the crocodile, with less probability. See Brande's Cy.

202. *Swim the ocean-stream:* What a force of imagination is there in this last expression! What an idea it conveys of the size of that largest of created beings, as if it shrunk up the ocean to a stream and took up the sea in its nostrils as a very little thing! Force of style is one of Milton's great excellencies. Hence, perhaps, he stimulates us more in the reading, and less afterwards. The way to defend Milton against all impugners is to take down the book and read it.—HAZLITT. This line is by some found fault with as inharmonious; but good taste approves its structure, as being on this account better suited to convey a just idea of the size of this monster.

204. *Night-foundered:* overtaken by the night, and thus arrested in its course. The metaphor, as Hume observes, is taken from a foundered horse that can go no further.

207. *Under the lee:* in a place defended from the wind.

208. *Invests the sea:* an allusion to the figurative description of the Night given by Spenser. "By this the drooping daylight 'gan to fade, And

yield his room to sad succeeding *night, Who with her sable mantle 'gan to shade The face of Earth.*" Milton also, in the same taste, speaking of the moon, IV. 609: "And o'er the dark her silver mantle threw."—N.

209. There are many examples in Milton of musical expression, or of an adaptation of the sound and movement of the verse to the meaning of the passage. This line is an instance. By its great length, and peculiar structure, being composed of monosyllables, it is admirably adapted to convey the idea of immense size.

210. *Chained on the burning lake:* There seems to be an allusion here to the legend of Prometheus, one of the Titans, who was exposed to the wrath of Jupiter on account of his having taught mortals the arts, and especially the use of fire, which he was said to have stolen from heaven, concealed in a reed. According to another story he was actually the creator of men, or at least inspired them with thought and sense. His punishment was to be *chained to a rock* on Caucasus, where a vulture perpetually gnawed his liver; from which he was finally rescued by Hercules. This legend has formed the subject of the grandest of all the poetical illustrations of Greek supernatural belief, the *Prometheus Bound* of Æschylus. Many have recognized in the indomitable resolution of this suffering Titan, and his stern endurance of the evils inflicted on him by a power with which he had vainly warred for supremacy, the prototype of the arch-fiend of Milton.—BRANDE.

226-7. *That felt unusual weight:* This conceit (as Thyer remarks) is borrowed from Spenser, who thus describes the old dragon, book i. "Then with his waving wings displayed wide Himself up high he lifted from the ground, And with strong flight did forcibly divide The yielding *air,* which nigh *too feeble* found Her flitting parts, and element unsound, *To bear so great a weight.*"

229. *Liquid fire.* Virg. Ec. vi. 33. Et liquidi simul ignis.—N.

230. There are several *noble similies and allusions* in the first book of Paradise Lost. And here it must be observed that when Milton alludes either to things or persons he never quits his simile until it rises to some very great idea, which is often foreign to the occasion that gave birth to it. The simile does not perhaps occupy above a line or two, but the poet runs on with the hint until he has raised out of it some brilliant image or sentiment adapted to inflame the mind of the reader and to give it that sublime kind of entertainment which is suitable to the nature of an heroic poem. In short, if we look into the poems of Homer, Virgil, and Milton, we must observe, that as the great fable is the soul of each poem, so, to give their works the greater variety, the episodes employed by these authors may be regarded as so many short fables, their similes as so many short episodes, and their metaphors as so many short similes. If the comparisons in the first book of Milton, of the sun in an eclipse of the sleeping leviathan, of the bees swarming about their hive, of the fairy dance, be regarded in this light the great beauties existing in each of these passages will readily be discovered.—A.

231. *Wind:* this should be altered to *winds,* to agree with the reading in line 235; or that should be altered to agree with this.

232. *Pelorus:* the eastern promontory of Sicily.

234. *Thence conceiving fire:* the combustible and fuelled entrails, or interior contents, of the mountain, are here represented as *taking fire,* as the result of the action of the subterranean wind, in removing the side of the mountain. The fire thus kindled was *sublimed with mineral fury,* that is, was heightened by the rapid combustion of mineral substances of a bituminous nature. The poet seems to have in his mind the description of Ætna by Virgil (book iii 572, 578.) Sed horrificis juxta tonat Ætna ruinis, Interdumque atram prorumpit ad æthera nubem, Turbine fumantem piceo, et candente favillâ Attollitque globos flammarum, et sidera lambit: Interdum scopulos

avulsaque viscera montis Erigit eructans liquefactaque saxa sub auras Cum gemitu glomerat, fundoque exæstuat imo.

239. *Stygian flood;* an expression here of the same import with *infernal flood,* alluding to the fabulous river Styx of the lower world, which the poets represented as a broad, dull and sluggish stream.

246. *Sovran:* from the Italian word sovrano.

250. Dr. Channing, writing upon Satan's character as drawn by the poet observes: "Hell yields to the spirit which it imprisons. The intensity of its fires reveals the intense passion and more vehement will of Satan; and the ruined archangel gathers into himself the sublimity of the scene which surrounds him. This forms the tremendous interest of these wonderful books. We see mind triumphant over the most terrible powers of nature. We see unutterable agony subdued by energy of soul." Addison remarks that Milton has attributed to Satan those sentiments which are every way answerable to his character, and suited to a created being of the most exalted and most depraved nature; as in this passage, which describes him as taking possession of his place of torments, 250–263.

253–5. These are some of the extravagances of the Stoics, and could not be better ridiculed than they are here by being put into the mouth of Satan in his present situation.—THYER. Shakespeare, in Hamlet, says: There is nothing either good or bad, but Thinking makes it so.

254. This sentiment of the great foundation on which the Stoics build their whole system of ethics.—S.

263. This sentiment is an improvement of that which is put by Æschylus into the mouth of Prometheus, 965; and it was a memorable saying of Julius Cæsar that he would rather be the first man in a village, than the second in Rome. Compare Virg. Georg. i. 36.—N. The lust of power and the hatred of moral excellence are Satan's prominent characteristics.

276. *Edge of battle:* from the Latin word *acies,* which signifies both the edge of a weapon and also an army in battle array. See book VI. 108.—N.

287. Homer and Ossian describe in a like splendid manner the shields of their heroes.

288. *Galileo:* He was the first who applied the telescope to celestial observations, and was the discoverer of the satellites of Jupiter in 1610, which, in honor of his patron, Cosmo Medici, he called the *Medicean stars.* From the tower of St Mark he showed the Venetian senators not only the satellites of Jupiter but the crescent of Venus, the triple appearance of Saturn, and the inequalities on the Moon's surface. At this conference he also endeavored to convince them of the truth of the Copernican system.

289–90. *Fesolé:* a city of Tuscany. *Valdarno,* the valley of Arno, in the same district. The very sound of these names is charming.

294. *Ammiral:* the obsolete form of admiral, the principal ship in a fleet. The idea contained in this passage, may, as Dr. Johnson suggests, be drawn from the following lines of Cowley, but who does not admire the vast improvements in form? He says of Goliath, "His spear, the trunk was of a loft tree, Which nature meant some tall ship's mast should be." Compare Hom. Odys. ix. 322. Æn. iii. 659. Tasso, canto vi. 40.

299. *Nathless:* nevertheless.

302. Etc.: Here we see the impression of scenery made upon Milton's mind in his youth when he was at Florence. This is a favorite passage with all readers of descriptive poetry.—E. B.

302. *Autumnal leaves.* Compare Virgil's lines, Æn. vi.

309. Quam multa in sylvis autumni frigore primo Lapsa cadunt folia. "That as the leaves in autumn strow the woods." DRYDEN. But Milton's comparison is the more exact by far; it not only expresses a multitude but also the posture and situation of the angels. Their lying confusedly in heaps covering the lake is finely represented by this image of the leaves in the brooks.—N.

303. *Vallombrosa:* a Tuscan valley: the name is composed of *vallis* and *umbra,* and thus denotes a shady valley.

305. *Orion arm'd:* Orion is a constellation represented in the figure of an armed man, and supposed to be attended with stormy weather, *assurgens fluctu nimbosus Orion,* Virg. Æn. i. 539. The Red Sea abounds so much with sedge that in the Hebrew Scriptures it is called the *Sedgy Sea.* The wind usually drives the sedge in great quantities against the shore.—N.

306. *Busiris:* Bentley objects to Milton giving this name to Pharaoh since history does not support him in it. But Milton uses the liberty of a poet in giving Pharoah this name, because some had already attached it to him. *Chivalry,* denotes here those who use horses in fight, whether by riding on them, or riding in chariots drawn by them. See line 765. Also Paradise Regained iii. 343, compared with line 328.

308. *Perfidious:* he permitted them to have the country, but afterwards pursued them.

315. This magnificent call of Satan to his prostrate host could have been written by nobody but Milton.—E B.

325. *Anon:* Soon.

329. An allusion seems here to be made to the Æneid, book i. 44–5. Ilium, exspirantem transfixo pectore flammas, Turbine corripuit scopuloque infixit acuto.

338. *Amram's son:* Moses. See Exod. x.

341. *Warping:* Moving like waves; or, working themselves forward.—H.

345. *Cope.* Roof.

352. *Frozen loins:* In Scripture children are said to *come out of the loins,* Gen. xxxv. 11. The term *frozen* is here used only on account of the coldness of the climate. *Rhene* and *Danaw,* the one from the Latin, the other from the German, are chosen because uncommon. *Barbarous:* The Goths, Huns, and Vandals, wherever their conquests extended, destroyed the monuments of ancient learning and taste. *Beneath Gibraltar:* That is, southward of it, the northern portion of the globe being regarded as uppermost.—N. The three comparisons relate to the three different states in which these fallen angels are represented. When abject and lying supine on the lake, they are fitly compared to vast heaps of leaves which in autumn the poet himself had observed to bestrew the water-courses and bottoms of Vallombrosa. When roused by their great leader's objurgatory summons, they are compared, in number, with the countless locusts of Egypt. The object of the third comparison is to illustrate their number when assembled as soldiers on the firm brimstone, and here they are compared with the most troops which history had made mention of.—DUNSTER.

360. *Erst:* Formerly.

364–75. The subject of Paradise Lost is the origin of evil—an event, in its nature connected with everything important in the circumstances of human existence; and; amid these circumstances, Milton saw that the *Fables of Paganism* were too important and poetical to be omitted. As a Christian he was entitled wholly to neglect them, but as a poet he chose to treat them not as the dreams of the human mind, but as the delusions of infernal existences. Thus anticipating a beautiful propriety for all classical allusions; thus connecting and reconciling the co-existence of fable and of truth; and thus identifying the fallen angels with the deities of "gay religions full of pomp and gold," he yoked the heathen mythology in triumph to his subject, and clothed himself in the spoils of superstition. —EDINB. ENCYC. This subject is again presented in the last note on Book I.

369. Rom. i. 18–25.

372. *Religions:* That is, religious rites.

375. *Idols.* Heathen idols are here described as the representatives of these demons. Addison remarks that the catalogue of evil spirits has abundance of learning in it and a very agreeable turn of poetry, which rises in a great measure from its describing the places where they were worshipped, by those beautiful marks of rivers so frequent among the ancient poets. The author had doubtless in this place Homer's

catalogue of ships, and Virgil's list of warriors in his view.

376. When they apostatised, they acquired new and dishonorable names.

406. *Chemos:* The god of the Moabites. Consult 1 Kings xi. 6, 7. 2 Kings xxiii. 13. It is supposed to be same as Baal-Peor, and as Priapus. Numb. xxv. 1–9.

408. *Hesebon* (Heshbon): Twenty-one miles east of the mouth of the Jordan. Its situation is still marked by a few broken pillars, several large cisterns and wells, together with extensive ruins which overspread a high hill, commanding a wild and desolate scenery on every side. *Abarim* is a chain of mountains running north and south, east of the Dead Sea; *Pisgah* is some eminence in this chain at the northern part, and *Nebo* is supposed to be the summit of Pisgah, nearly opposite Jericho. It was here that the great leader of the Israelites was favored with a view of the land of promise, and yielded up his life at the command of the Lord, B.C. 1451. *Aroar* (Aroer) was a place situated on the river Arnon, which formed the northern boundary of the kingdom of Moab. *Seon* (Sihon) was king of the Amorites. *Sibma* was half a mile from Heshbon; *Eleälé*, two and a half miles south of it. The *Asphaltic pool* is the Dead Sea. *Sittim* is written Shittim in the Bible.

415. *Orgies:* Wild, frantic rites. The term is generally applied to the feasts of Bacchus, but is equally applicable to the obscene practices connected with the worship of Chemos, or Peor.

417. *Lust hard by hate:* The figure contained in this verse conveys a strong moral truth. Had it not been, however, that the music of the verse would have been injured, the idea would have been more correct by the transposition of the words lust and hate.—S. Our author might perhaps have in view Spenser's Mask of Cupid, where Anger, Strife, etc., are represented as immediately following Cupid in the procession.—T. 438. Jerem. vii. 18; xliv. 17, 18. 1 Kings xi. 5. 2 Kings xxiii. 13.

443. *Offensive:* So called on account of the idolatrous worship there performed; in other places called by Milton, for the same reason, the *mountain of corruption, opprobrious hill,* and *hill of scandal.*

444. *Uxorious king:* Solomon, who was too much influenced by his wives.

451. *Thammuz:* This idol is the same as the Phenician Adonis. *Ezek.* viii. 14. Adonis, in the heathen mythology, was a beautiful youth, son of Cinyrus, king of Cyprus, beloved by Venus, and killed by a wild boar, to the great regret of the goddess. It is also the name of a river of Phenicia, on the banks of which Adonis, or Thammuz as he is called in the East, was supposed to have been killed. At certain seasons of the year this river acquires a high red color by the rains washing up red earth. The ancient poets ascribed this to a sympathy in the river for the death of Adonis. This season was observed as a festival in the adjacent country. To these circumstances Milton has here beautifully alluded.—Brande's Cyc.

460. *Grunsel edge:* Groundsill edge—the threshold of the gate of the temple.

462. *Dagon:* A god of the Philistines. Consult Judges xvi. 23. 1 Sam. v. 4; vi. 17.

467. *Rimmon:* A god of the Syrians. Consult 2 Kings v. 18.

467-9. The power of Milton's mind is stamped on every line. The fervour of his imagination melts down and renders malleable, as in a furnace, the most contradictory materials. Milton's learning has all the affect of intuition. He describes objects, of which he could only have read in books, with the vividness of actual observation. His imagination has the force of nature. He makes words tell as pictures, as in these lines. The word *lucid,* here used, gives us all the sparkling effect of the most perfect landscape. There is great depth of impression in his descriptions of the objects of all the different senses, whether colours, or sounds, or smells; the same absorption of mind in whatever engaged his attention at the time. He forms the most intense conceptions of things, and then embodies them by a single stroke of his pen.—HAZLITT.

471. 2 Kings viii. xvi. 10. 2 Chron. xxviii. 23.

478. *Osiris,* one of the principal Egyptian gods, was brother to Isis, and the father of Orus (Horus). Osiris was worshipped under the form of the sacred bulls, Apis and Mnevis, and as it is usual in the Egyptian symbolical language to represent their deities with human forms, and with the heads of the animals which were their representatives, we find statues of Osiris with the horns of a bull.—ANTHON. The reason alleged for worshipping their gods under the monstrous forms of bulls, cats, etc., is the fabulous tradition that when the Giants invaded heaven, the gods were so affrighted that they fled into Egypt, and there concealed themselves in the shapes of various animals. See Ovid Met. v. 319—N.

483. *Infection:* The Israelites, by dwelling so long in Egypt, were infected with the superstitions of the Egyptians.—E.B.

484. *Oreb:* Horeb. *Rebel king:* Jeroboam. Consult 1 Kings xii. 26–33.

485. *Doubled that sin,* by making two golden calves, probably in imitation of the Egyptians among whom he had been, who worshipped two oxen; one called Apis, at Memphis, the metropolis of Upper Egypt; the other called Mnevis, at Hieropolis, the chief city of Lower Egypt. *Bethel* and *Dan* were at the southern and northern extremities of Palestine. See Psalm cvi. 20.—N.

489. *Bleating gods:* Sheep; and hence shepherds who raised sheep to kill for food were "an abomination" to the Egyptians.

495. *Eli's sons:* Consult I Sam. ii.

502. *Flown:* A better reading is *blown,* inflated. Virg. Ec. vi. 15.

504. *Gibeah:* Consult Judges xix 14–30.

506. *Prime:* Being mentioned in the oldest records, the Hebrew.

508. *Javan:* The fourth son of Japhet, from whom the Ionians and the Greeks are supposed to have descended.

509. *Heaven and Earth:* The god Uranus and the goddess Gaia.

510–21. *Titan* was their eldest son: he was the father of the Giants, and his empire was seized by his younger brother *Saturn,* as Saturn's was by *Jupiter,* the son of Saturn and Rhea. These first were known in the island of *Crete,* now Candia, in which is Mount *Ida,* where Jupiter is said to have been born; thence passed over into Greece, and resided on Mount *Olympus* in Thessaly; *the snowy top of cold Olympus,* as Homer calls it, Iliad i. 420. xviii. 615, which mountain afterwards became the name of Heaven among their worshippers; *or on the Delphian cliff,* Parnassus, on which was seated the city of Delphi, famous for the temple and oracle of Apollo; *or in Dodona,* a city and wood adjoining, sacred to Jupiter, *and through all the bounds of Doric land,* that is, of Greece, Doris being a part of Greece; *or fled over Hadria,* the Adriatic sea, *to the Hesperian fields,* to Italy; *and o'er the Celtic,* France and the other countries *overrun* by the Celts; *roamed the utmost isles,* Britain, Ireland, the Orkneys, Thule, or Iceland, *Ultima Thule,* as it is called, the utmost boundary of the world.—N.

534. *Azazel:* The name signifies *brave in retreating.*

543. *Reign,* in the sense of *regnum,* kingdom.

546. *Orient:* Brilliant

548. *Serried shields:* Locked one within another, linked and clasped together, from the French *serrer,* to lock, to shut close.—HUME.

550. There were three kinds of music among the ancients; the Lydian, the most melancholy; the Phrygian, the most lively; and the Dorian, the most majestic (exciting to cool and deliberate courage.—N.), Milton has been very exact in employing music fit for each particular purpose.—S.

551. *Recorders:* Flageolets.

560. Homer's Iliad, iii. 8.

568. *Traverse:* across.

575. All the heroes and armies that ever were assembled were no more than pigmies in comparison with these angels.—N. See note on Book I. 780.

577. *Phlegra:* The earlier name of the peninsula Pallene in Macedonia and the fabled scene of a conflict between the gods and the earth-born Titans.

580. Uther was the father of King Arthur. This and the following allusions are derived from the old romances on the subject. Charlemagne is said not to have died at Fontarabia, but some years after, and in peace.—S.

581. *Armoric:* Celtic—those on the sea-coast of Brittany in the northwest part of France.

583. *Jousted:* Engaged in mock fights on horseback. *Aspramont* and *Montalban:* Fictitious names of places mentioned in Orlando Furioso.

585. *Biserta:* Formerly called Utica. The Saracens are referred to as being sent thence to Spain. *Fontarabia:* A fortified town in Biscay, in Spain, near France.

590–99. Here, says Burke, is a very noble picture; and in what does this poetical picture consist? in images of a town, an archangel, the sun rising through the mists, or in an eclipse, the ruin of monarchs, and the revolutions of kingdoms. The mind is hurried out of itself by a crowd of great and confused images, which affect because they are crowded and confused: for separate them, and you lose much of the greatness; join them, and you infallibly lose the clearness. There are reasons in nature why the obscure idea, when properly conveyed, should be more affecting than the clear. It is our (comparative) ignorance of things that causes all our admiration, and chiefly excites our passions. Knowledge and acquaintance make the most striking causes affect but little. It is thus with the vulgar, and all men are as the vulgar in what they do not understand. 595–6. When Milton sought license to publish his poem, the licenser was strongly inclined to withhold it, on the ground that he discovered treason in this noble simile of the sun eclipsed! a striking example of the acute remark of Lord Lyttleton that "the politics of Milton at that time brought his poetry into disgrace; for it is a rule with the English to see no good in a man whose politics they dislike."—T.

597. *Eclipse:* Derived from a Greek word which signifies to fail, to faint or swoon away; since the moon, at the period of her greatest brightness, falling in the shadow of the earth, was imagined by the ancients to sicken and swoon, as if she were going to die. By some very ancient nations she was supposed, at such times, to be in pain; and, in order to relieve her fancied distress, they lifted torches high in the atmosphere, blew horns and trumpets, beat upon brazen vessels, and even, after the eclipse was over, they offered sacrifices to the moon. The opinion also extensively prevailed, that it was in the power of witches, by their spells and charms, not only to darken the moon, but to bring her down from her orbit, and to compel her to shed her baleful influences upon the earth. In solar eclipses, also, especially when total, the sun was supposed to turn away his face in abhorrence of some atrocious crime, that had either been perpetrated, or was about to be perpetrated, and to threaten mankind with everlasting night and the destruction of the world. To such superstitions Milton, in this passage alludes.—OLMSTED'S LETTERS ON ASTRON. No where is the person of Satan described with more sublimity than in this part of the poem.

600. *Intrenched:* Cut into, made trenches there.—N.

606. *Fellows.* The nice moral discrimination displayed in this line, is worthy of notice.

609. *Amerced:* Judicially deprived. See Hom. Odys. vii. 64.

611. *Yet faithful:* We must refer to line 605, and thence supply here "to behold."

619. Allusion to Ovid. Met. xi. 419: Ter conata loqui, ter fletibus ora rigavit.

620. *Tears, such as angels weep.* Like Homer's ichor of the gods, which was different from the blood of mortals. This weeping of Satan on surveying his numerous host, and the thoughts of their wretched state, put one in mind of the story of Xerxes, weeping at the sight of his immense army, and reflecting that they were mortal, at the time that he was hastening them to their fate, and to the intended destruction of the most polished people in the world, to gratify his own vain glory.—N.

633. *Emptied:* An instance of arrogant boasting and falsehood.

642. *Tempted our attempt:* Words which, though well-chosen and significant enough, yet of jingling and unpleasant sound, and, like marriages between persons too near of kin, to be avoided.

650. *Rife:* Prevalent. This *fame,* or report, serves to exalt the dignity and importance of our race.

662. *Understood:* Not declared.

664. *Drawn from the thighs:* A Homeric expression, Iliad i. 190, more dignified than "drawn from the sides."

668. *Clashed:* Alluding to a custom among Roman soldiers of striking their shields with their swords, when they applauded the speeches of their commanders.

671. *Belched:* An idea borrowed, perhaps, from an expression of Virg. (Æn. iii. 576), *eructans,* in describing Ætna.

674. *The work of sulphur:* Metals were in the time of Milton supposed to consist of two component parts, mercury, as the basis, or metallic matter and sulphur as the binder or cement, which fixes the fluid mercury into a coherent, malleable mass. So Jonson in the Alchemist, Act 2, Scene 3: "It turns to sulphur, or to quicksilver, Who are the parents of all other metals."

678. *Mammon:* The god of riches; the same as the Pluto of the Greek and Romans. The delineation of his character and agency by Milton abounds in *literary* beauties.

685. *Suggestion:* Milton here alludes to a superstitious opinion former current with the miners, that there is a sort of demons who have much to do with minerals, being frequently seen occupying themselves with the various processes of the workmen. So that Milton (as Warburton remarks) poetically supposes *Mammon* and his clan to have taught the sons of earth by example and practical instruction as well as precept and mental suggestion.

687. Compare Ovid Met. i. 138, etc.—HUME.

688. *Better hid.* Compare Hor. Od. III. iii. 49: "Aurum irrepertum et sic melius situm."

694. *Works:* The pyramids.

696. *Strength and art:* These words are in the nominative case, connected with *monuments.*

699. Diodorus Siculus says that 360,000 men were employed about twenty years on one of the pyramids.

703–4. The sense of the passage is this: The *founded,* or melted, the *ore* that was in the *mass,* by separating, or *severing,* each kind, that is, the sulphur, earth, etc., from the metal; and, after that, they *scummed* the *dross* that floated on the top of the boiling ore, or bullion. The word *bullion* does not here signify purified ore, but ore boiling.—PEARCE.

708. *Organ:* A very complete simile is here used. Milton, being fond of music, often draws fine illustrations from it.

710. *Anon:* At once.

715. *Architrave:* The part of a pillar above the capital. Above this is the *frieze,* which is surmounted by the *cornice.*

718. *Alcairo:* Cairo, a famous city in Egypt, built from the splendid ruins of Memphis, which was partially destroyed by Arabian invaders, in the seventh century. The god Serapis is by some supposed to be the same as Osiris, or Apis. The Belus of Assyria is thought to be the same as the great Bali of Hindoo mythology, and Baal mentioned in the Scriptures.

723. *Her stately height:* At her stately height.

725. *Within:* Is an adverb and not a preposition. So Virg. En. ii. 483. Apparet domus *intus,* et atria longa patescunt.

728. *Cressets:* Torches.

740. *Mulciber:* Or Vulcan, to which god was ascribed the invention of arts connected with the melting and working of metals by fire. The term Vulcan is, hence, sometimes used as synonymous with fire. *How he fell, etc.:* See Homer's Iliad, i. 590. "Once in your cause I felt his (Jove's) matchless might, Hurl'd headlong downward from the ethereal height; Tost all the day in rapid circles round; Nor till the sun descended, touched the ground; Breathless I fell, in giddy motion lost; The Sinthians raised me on the Lemnian coast." It is worth observing how Milton lengthens out the time of Vulcan's fall. He not only says with Homer, that it was all day long, but we

are led through the parts of the day *from morn to noon, from noon to evening,* and this *a summer's day.*—N.

742.   *Sheer:* Quite, or at once.

750.   *Engines:* It is said that in the old English, this word was often used for devices, wit, contrivance.

763.   *Covered:* Enclosed.

764.   *Won't ride in:* Were accustomed to ride in. *Soldan's:* Sultan's.

765.   *Panim:* Pagan, infidel.

768.   *As bees, etc.:* Iliad, ii. 87. "As from some rocky cleft the shepherd sees Clustering in heaps on heaps the driving bees, Rolling and blackening, swarms succeeding swarms, With deeper murmurs and more hoarse alarms; Dusky they spread, a close embodi'd crowd, And o'er the vale descends the living cloud. So," etc.

769.   *Taurus:* One of the signs of the Zodiac, Book X. 663.

777.   *A wonder:* consult the note on line 423.

780.   *Pygmean, etc.:* A fabulous nation of dwarfs that contended annually with cranes. They advanced against these birds mounted on the backs of rams and goats, and armed with bows and arrows.—Iliad, iii. 3.

785.   *Nearer to the earth,* etc.: Referring to the superstitious notion that witches and fairies exert great power over the moon.

789.   *Spirits, etc.:* For some further account of the nature and properties of spirits consult Book VI. 344–353.

795.   *Secret conclave:* An evident allusion to the *conclaves* of the cardinals on the death of a Pope.—E. B.

797.   *Frequent:* Crowded, as in the Latin phrase, *frequens senatus.*

798.   *Consult:* Consultation.

Name _____ Date _____ Grade _____

———————— *Questions for Consideration* ————————

Using complete sentences, provide brief answers for the following questions:

1. List several examples of *archetypal* or universal images. What makes these images effective in general? What makes the archetypal images (i.e., height and depth, darkness and light) in Book I of *Paradise Lost* effective?

_____

_____

_____

_____

_____

_____

2. Relate the concept of Order in the universe to various aspects of contemporary society, such as the state, the church, the family, etc. In your view, how important is it to believe (or not believe) in the idea of Order?

_____

_____

_____

_____

_____

_____

3. Pride is often considered by critics as the chief fault of Milton's Satan in Book I of *Paradise Lost*. In what sense is pride viewed in a negative (or positive) way today? What do you consider to be examples of prideful behavior?

_____

_____

_____

_____

_____

4. Book I of *Paradise Lost* shows Milton's curiosity about angels and their nature. To what extent is modern man concerned about the existence of ethereal beings?

    _____

    _____

    _____

    _____

    _____

    _____

5. Find a pictorial representation of Milton's Hell in *Paradise Lost* and Dante's Hell in the *Divine Comedy*. How are they similar? different?

    _____

    _____

    _____

    _____

    _____

    _____

———————— *Writing Critically* ————————

Select one of the topics listed below and compose a 500 word essay which discusses the topic fully. Support your thesis with evidence from the text and with critical and/or historical material. Use the space below for preparing to write the essay.

1. Elaborate on the qualities that Milton attributes to angels in Book I of *Paradise Lost*. Consider what is said about the angelic nature before and after the rebellion in heaven.

2. Summarize your impressions of Satan as an effective or ineffective leader. Give examples to substantiate your position.

3. In the fourteenth century, pride was often viewed as the one sin in which all of the "seven deadly sins" could be summed up. Critics of Satan argue that this is what motivates his actions. When is pride justifiable (not justifiable)?

4. Explain Milton's view of Hell in Book I of *Paradise Lost*. Cite specific references to support your position.

Prewriting Space:

_____

_____

_____

_____

_____

_____

_____

_____

_____

_____

_____

_____

_____

_____

_____

_____

_____

_____

_____

Introduction

John Milton (1608–1674)

It is useful to view Book II of *Paradise Lost* along several distinct lines: (1) the manner in which Satan parodies the Divine; (2) the rhetorical mode or style reflected in the various arguments of the fallen angels as they "debate" their position in hell; and (3) the knowledge theme as it applies to Satan and looks forward to the crucial issue of forbidden knowledge in Book IX, where the Fall in the Garden of Eden actually occurs.

Book II opens with the defeated Satan "High on a throne of royal state." This image of Satan occupying a throne in hell is in clear imitation of God who rightly holds this kingly position of power in Book III. That Satan's assumption of a throne in hell is nothing more than parody—a poor imitation of God—is seen in the fact that he has already been cast out of heaven by his rival, thus establishing his powerlessness in relation to the true God. Satan's mimicry of the divine assumes an added dimension in Book II when he puts himself in the role of a sacrificial deliverer who, in place of his loyal followers, will himself undertake the dangerous voyage to Paradise to bring about the fall of the newly created Adam and Eve. Satan's calculated selflessness, of course, calls to mind Christ who is the true deliverer and spiritual paradigm of self-abnegation. Another striking instance of parody in the above book occurs when Satan meets his daughter, Sin, as he makes his way out of hell. After their relationship has been clarified, Sin tells her father, the author or engenderer of all sin and evil, that she ". . . shall reign/At thy right hand voluptuous, as beseems/Thy daughter and thy darling, without end" (PL, II, 868–870). Sin's assertion that she will govern at the "right hand" of her sire is a clear parody of the true Son of God who rules at the right hand of the Father in heaven throughout eternity.

The "debate" in hell in Book II of *Paradise Lost* affords Milton an opportunity to explore various rhetorical styles or modes, as the fallen angels set forth their individual positions on how best to seek vengeance against God. The angels' verbal jousting has overtones of the kind of academic disputation that characterizes Milton's treatment of "L'Allegro" and "Il Penseroso," which focus on the contrast between the happy and the pensive man, respectively. As each angel states his position in the infernal debate, Milton's authorial voice or stance invariably indicates the strength or weakness of the argument, as well as the character or shallowness of the speaker. Moloch, the first of the fallen angels to speak, for example, is labeled a "fierce spirit" who is "Now fiercer by despair." His declaration of "open war" against God is thus seen as an act of desperation rather than a carefully conceived strategy. Belial, who next addresses the infernal crew, ". . . seemed/For dignity composed and high exploit:/But all was false and hollow, though his tongue/Dropped manna, and could make the worse appear/The better reason" (PL, II, 110–114). Belial is thus a clever rhetorical deceiver in the same vein as Comus and Satan, the former being the precursor to Satan in the verbal strategies he devises to tempt the Lady in the masque, *Comus*. Mammon, who follows Belial in the hellish debate, is simply dubbed a materialist who is willing to settle for his new-found home with its gems and gold which, in his distorted view, rivals the wealth of heaven. Milton, therefore, attributes no depth to Mammon's argument. The final speaker to take center stage in the infernal debate is Beelzebub, Satan's second-in-command. It is Beelzebub who articulates the plan to tempt God's new creation, man, but the author of this cunning scheme is clearly Satan. Beelzebub's strategy to seduce innocent Adam and Eve, who are unacquainted with the reality of evil, proves the most powerful argument in that the result "would surpass/ Common revenge" against God, because the Edenic couple "shall curse/Their frail original, and faded bliss,/Faded so soon" (PL, II, 374–376).

The knowledge theme in Book II also deserves careful attention. This is because the question of forbidden knowledge will be at the core of the Fall in Book IX of *Paradise Lost*. For in order for Adam and Eve to sustain their blissful existence in the Garden of Eden, it is incumbent upon them to recognize the limits of their human capacity and not to seek Godhead. That they have an assigned place in the Divine scheme is a state of awareness that is crucial to Adam and Eve. Milton had broached the cognition issue in Book I when Satan apparently was unaware that Beelzebub had lost some of his angelic brightness when he was cast out of heaven into hell.

References to "know" in various passages of *Paradise Lost* surface again in Book II when Satan meets his allegorical daughter, Sin, and his allegorical son, Death. Upon first encounter Satan does not recognize his paternal relationship to these characters. Sin, however, bridges this knowledge gap by explaining that she issued from Satan's head in heaven and was soon set upon and raped by him because of her attractiveness. The offspring produced as the result of this incestuous father-daughter involvement is Death, Satan's gruesome and ravenous son, who later rapes his mother, Sin, and begets the yelping hellhounds who constantly gnaw away at her bowels. Sin's graphic and convincing account to Satan of these developments, however repulsive, keeps the knowledge theme before the reader. (DLP)

BIBLIOGRAPHY

Bush, Douglas. *John Milton.* New York, 1964.

___. *The Portable Milton.* New York, 1977.

Moore, Olin H. "The Infernal Council." MP. 16 (1918), 169–193.

Richards, I. A. *The Philosophy of Rhetoric.* New York, 1936.

Samuel, Irene. *Dante and Milton: The Commedia and Paradise Lost.* Ithaca, New York, 1966

Willey, Basil. *The Seventeenth Century Background.* Garden City, New York, 1953.

from Paradise Lost: Book II

John Milton

THE ARGUMENT

The consultation begun, Satan debates whether another battle is to be hazarded for the recovery of Heaven; some advise it, others dissuade; a third proposal is preferred, mentioned before by Satan, to search the truth of that prophecy or tradition in Heaven concerning another world, and another kind of creature, equal or not much inferior to themselves, about this time to be created: their doubt who shall be sent on this difficult search: Satan, their chief, undertakes alone the voyage, is honoured and applauded. The council thus ended, the rest betake them several ways, and to several employments, as their inclinations lead them, to entertain the time till Satan return. He passes on his journey to Hell-gates, finds them shut, and who sat there to guard them, by whom at length they are opened, and discover to him the great gulf between Hell and Heaven; with what difficulty he passes through, directed by Chaos, the power of that place, to the sight of this new world which he sought.

INTRODUCTORY REMARKS

In tracing the progress of this poem by deliberate and minute steps, our wonder and admiration increase. The inexhaustible invention continues to grow upon us; each page, each line, is pregnant with something new, picturesque, and great; the condensity of the matter is without parallel; the imagination often contained in a single passage is more than equal to all that secondary poets have produced. The fable of the voyage through Chaos is alone a sublime poem. Milton's descriptions of materiality have always touches of the spiritual, the lofty and the empyreal.

Milton has too much condensation to be fluent: a line or two often contains a world of images and ideas. He expatiates over all time, all space, all possibilities; he unites Earth with Heaven, with Hell, with all intermediate existences, animate and inanimate; and his illustrations are drawn from all learning, historical, natural, and speculative. In him, almost always, "more is meant than meets the eye." An image, an epithet, conveys a rich picture.

What is the subject of observation, may be told without genius; but the wonder and the greatness lie in invention, if the invention be noble, and according to the principles of possibility. Who could have conceived, or, if conceived, who could have described the voyage of Satan through Chaos, but Milton? Who could have invented so many distinct and grand obstacles in his way, and all picturesque, all poetical, and all the topics of intellectual meditation and reflection, or of spiritual sentiment.

All the faculties of the mind are exercised, stretched and elevated at once by every page of Paradise Lost. That Milton could bring so much learning, as well as so much imaginative invention, to bear on every part of his infinitely-extended, yet thick-compacted story, is truly miraculous. Were the learning superficial and loosely applied, the wonder would not be great, or not nearly so great; but it is always profound, solid, conscientious; and in its combinations original.—E. B.

Book II

High on a throne of royal state, which far
Outshone the wealth of Ormus and of Ind,
Or where the gorgeous East with richest hand
Show'rs on her kings barbaric pearl and gold,
Satan exalted sat, by merit raised   5
To that bad eminence; and from despair
Thus high uplifted beyond hope, aspires
Beyond thus high, insatiate to pursue
Vain war with Heaven: and, by success untaught.
His proud imaginations thus display'd: 10
    Pow'rs and Dominions, Deities of Heaven,
For since no deep within her gulf can hold
Immortal vigour, though oppress'd and fall'n,
I give not Heav'n for lost. From this descent
Celestial virtues rising, will appear   15
More glorios and more dread than from no fall,
And trust themselves to fear no second fate.
Me, though just right, and the fix'd laws of Heav'n,
Did first create your leader, next free choice,
With what besides, in council or in fight,   20
Hath been achieved of merit; yet this loss,
Thus far at least recover'd hath much more
Establish'd in a safe unenvied throne,
Yielded with full consent. The happier state
In Heaven, which follows dignity, might draw   25
Envy from each inferior; but who here
Will envy whom the highest place exposes
Foremost to stand against the Thund'rer's aim
Your bulwark, and condemns to greatest share
Of endless pain? Where there is then no good   30
For which to strive, no strife can grow up there
From faction; for none sure will claim in Hell
Precedence; none, whose portion is so small
Of present pain, that with ambitious mind
Will covet more. With this advantage then   35
To union, and firm faith, and firm accord,
More than can be in Heav'n, we now return
To claim our just inheritance of old,
Surer to prosper than prosperity
Could have assured us; and by what best way,   40
Whether of open war or covert guile,
We now debate: who can advise, may speak.
    He ceased: and next him Moloch, Scepter'd king,
Stood up, the strongest and the fiercest Sp'rit
That fought in Heav'n, now fiercer by despair.   45
His trust was with th' Eternal to be deem'd
Equal in strength; and rather than be less,
Cared not to be at all. With that care lost
Went all his fear: of God, or hell, or worse,
He reck'd ont; and these words thereafter spake: 50
    My sentence is for open war: of wiles
More unexpert I boast not: them let those

Contrive who need, or when they need, not now.
For while they sit contriving, shall the rest,
Millions that stand in arms, and longing wait   55
The signal to ascend, sit ling'ring here
Heav'n's fugitives, and for their dwelling-place
Accept this dark opprobrious den of shame,
The prison of his tyranny who reigns
By our delay? No, let us rather choose,   60
Arm'd with Hell-flames and fury, all at once
O'er Heav'n's high tow'rs to force resistless way,
Turning our tortures, into horrid arms
Against the torturer, when to meet the noise
Of his almighty engine he shall hear,   65
Infernal thunder, and for lightning see
Black fire and horror shot with equal rage
Among his Angels, and his throne itself
Mix'd with Tartarean sulphur, and strange fire,
His own invented torments. But perhaps   70
The way seems difficult and steep, to scale
With upright wing against a higher foe.
Let such bethink them, if the sleepy drench
Of that forgetful lake benumb not still,
That in our proper motion we ascend   75
Up to our native seat; descent and fall
To us is adverse. Who but felt of late,
When the fierce foe hung on our broken rear
Insulting, and pursued us through the deep,
With what compulsion and laborious flight   80
We sunk thus low? Th' ascent is easy then;
Th' event is fear'd. Should we again provoke
Our stronger, some worse way his wrath may find
To our destruction, if there be in Hell
Fear to be worse destroy'd. What can be worse   85
Than to dwell here, driv'n out from bliss, condemn'd
In this abhorred deep to utter woe,
Where pain of unextinguishable fire
Must exercise us without hope of end,
The vassals of his anger, when the scourge   90
Inexorably, and the tort'ring hour
Calls us to penance? more destroy'd than thus,
We should be quite abolish'd, and expire.
What fear we then? what doubt we to incense
His utmost ire? which to the height enraged   95
Will either quite consume us, and reduce
To nothing this essential, happier far
Than mis'rable to have eternal being.
Or if our substance be indeed divine,
And cannot cease to be, we are at worst   100
On this side nothing; and by proof we feel
Our pow'r sufficient to disturb his Heav'n,
And with perpetual inroads to alarm,
Though inaccessible, his fatal throne:
Which, if not victory, is yet revenge.   105
    He ended frowning, and his look denounced
Desp'rate revenge, and battle dangerous
To less than Gods. On th' other side up rose

Belial, in act more graceful and humane:
A fairer person lost not Heav'n; he seem'd   110
For dignity composed and high exploit:
But all was false and hollow, though his tongue
Dropt manna, and could make the worse appear
The better reason, to perplex and dash
Maturest counsels: for his thoughts were low;   115
To vice industrious, but to nobler deeds
Tim'rous and slothful: yet he pleased the ear,
And with persuasive accent thus began:
    I should be much for open war, O Peers!
As not behind in hate, if what was urged   120
Main reason to persuade immediate war,
Did not dissuade me most, and seem to cast
Ominous conjecture on the whole success:
When he who most excels in fact of arms,
In what he counsels and in what excels   125
Mistrustful, grounds his courage on despair,
And utter dissolution, as the scope
Of all his aim, after some dire revenge.
First, what revenge? The tow'rs of Heav'n are fill'd
With armed watch, that render all access   130
Impregnable; oft on the bord'ring deep
Encamp their legions, or with obscure wing
Scout far and wide into the realms of night,
Scorning surprise. Or could we break our way
By force, and at our heels all hell should rise   135
With blackest insurrection, to confound
Heav'n's purest light, yet our Great Enemy,
All incorruptible, would on his throne
Sit unpolluted, and th' ethereal mould
Incapable of stain would soon expel   140
Her mischief, and purge off the baser fire
Victorious. Thus repulsed, our final hope
Is flat despair. We must exasperate
Th' Almighty Victor to spend all his rage,
And that must end us, that must be our cure,   145
To be no more? Sad cure; for who would lose,
Though full of pain, this intellectual being,
Those thoughts that wander through eternity,
To perish rather, swallow'd up and lost
In the wide womb of uncreated night,   150
Devoid of sense and motion? And who knows,
Let this be good, whether our angry Foe
Can give it, or will ever? How he can
Is doubtful; that he never will is sure.
Will he, so wise, let loose at once his ire   155
Belike through impotence, or unaware,
To give his enemies their wish, and end
Them in his anger, whom his anger saves
To punish endless? Wherefore cease we then?
Say they who counsel war, we are decreed,   160
Reserved, and destined, to eternal woe:
Whatever doing, what can we suffer more,
What can we suffer worse? Is this then worst,
Thus sitting, thus consulting, thus in arms?

What when we fled amain, pursued and struck   165
With Heav'n's afflicting thunder, and besought
The deep to shelter us? This Hell then seem'd
A refuge from those wounds: or when we lay
Chain'd on the burning lake? that sure was worse.
What if the breath that kindled those grim fires,   170
Awaked should blow them into sev'nfold rage,
And plunge us in the flames? Or from above
Should intermitted vengeance arm again
His red right hand to plague us? What if all
Her stores were open'd, and this firmament   175
Of Hell should spout her cataracts of fire,
Impendent horrors, threatening hideous fall
One day upon our heads; while we perhaps
Designing or exhorting glorious war,
Caught in a fiery tempest, shall be hurl'd   180
Each on his rock, transfix'd, the sport and prey
Of wracking whirlwinds, or for ever sunk
Under yon boiling ocean, wrapt in chains;
There to converse with everlasting groans,
Unrespited, unpitied, unreprieved,   185
Ages of hopeless end? This would be worse.
War therefore, open or conceal'd, alike
My voice dissuades; for what can force or guile
With him, or who deceive his mind, whose eye
Views all thing at one view? He from Heav'n's height   190
All these our motions vain, sees and derides;
Not more almighty to resist our might
Than wise to frustrate all our plots and wiles.
Shall we then live thus vile, the race of Heav'n
Thus trampled, thus expell'd, to suffer here   195
Chains and these torments? Better these than worse,
By my advice: since fate inevitable
Subdues us, and omnipotent decree,
The Victor's will. To suffer, as to do,
Our strength is equal; nor the law unjust   200
That so ordains. This was at first resolved,
If we were wise, against so great a Foe
Contending, and so doubtful what might fall.
I laugh, when those who at the spear are bold
And vent'rous, if that fail them, shrink and fear   205
What yet they know must follow, to endure
Exile or ignominy, or bonds, or pain,
The sentence of their Conqu'ror. This is now
Our doom; which if we can sustain and bear,
Our Supreme Foe in time may much remit   210
His anger, and perhaps, thus far removed,
Not mind us not offending, satisfy'd
With what is punish'd; whence these raging fires
Will slacken, if his breath stir not their flames.
Our purer essence then will overcome   215
Their noxious vapour, or inured not feel,
Or changed at length, and to the place conform'd
In temper and in nature, will receive
Familiar the fierce heat, and void of pain;
This horror will grow mild, this darkness light,   220

Besides what hope the never-ending flight
Of future days may bring, what chance, what change
Worth waiting, since our present lot appears
For happy though but ill, for ill not worst,
If we procure not to ourselves more woe.   225
    Thus Belial, with words cloth'd in reason's garb,
Counsel'd ignoble ease and peaceful sloth,
Not peace: and after him thus Mammon spake:
    Either to disenthrone the King of Heav'n
We war, if war be best, or to regain   230
Our own right lost: him to unthrone we then
May hope, when everlasting Fate shall yield
To fickle Chance, and Chaos judge the strife.
The former vain to hope, argues as vain
The latter; for what place can be for us   235
Within Heav'n's bound, unless Heav'n's Lord Supreme
We overpow'r? Suppose he should relent,
And publish grace to all, on promise made
Of new subjection; with what eyes could we
Stand in his presence humble, and receive   240
Strict laws imposed, to celebrate his throne
With warbled hymns, and to his Godhead sing
Forced hallelujahs, while he lordly sits
Our envied Sovereign, and his altar breathes
Ambrosial odours and ambrosial flow'rs,   245
Our servile offerings? This must be our task
In Heav'n, this our delight. How wearisome
Eternity so spent in worship paid
To whom we hate! Let us not then pursue
By force impossible, by leave obtain'd   250
Unacceptable, though in Heav'n, our state
Of splendid vassalage; but rather seek
Our own good from ourselves, and from our own
Live to ourselves though in this vast recess,
Free, and to none accountable, preferring   255
Hard liberty before the easy yoke
Of servile pomp. Our greatness will appear
Then most conspicuous, when great things of small,
Useful of hurtful, prosp'rous of adverse,
We can create, and in what place soe'er,   260
Thrive under evil, and work ease out of pain
Through labour and endurance. This deep world
Of darkness do we dread? How oft amidst
Thick clouds and dark doth heav'n all-ruling Sire
Choose to reside, his glory unobscured,   265
And with the majesty of darkness round
Covers his throne; from whence deep thunders roar,
Must'ring their rage, and Heav'n resembles Hell?
As he our darkness, cannot we his light
Imitate when we please? This desert soil   270
Wants not her hidden lustre, gems and gold;
Nor want we skill or art, from whence to raise
Magnificence: and what can Heav'n shew more?
Our torments also may in length of time
Become our elements; these piercing fires   275
As soft as now severe, our temper changed

Into their temper; which must needs remove
The sensible pain. All things invite
To peaceful counsels, and the settled state
Of order, how in safety best we may   280
Compose our present evils, with regard
Of what we are and where, dismissing quite
All thoughts of war. Ye have what I advise.
   He scarce had finish'd, when such murmur fill'd
Th' assembly, as when hollow rocks retain   285
The sound of blust'ring winds, which all night long
Had roused the sea, now with hoarse cadence lull
Seafaring men o'erwatch'd, whose bark by chance
Or pinnace anchors in a craggy bay
After the tempest. Such applause was heard   290
As Mammon ended, and his sentence pleased,
Advising peace; for such another field
They dreaded worse than Hell: so much the fear
Of thunder and the sword of Michaël
Wrought still within them; and no less desire   295
To found this nether empire, which might rise
By policy and long process of time,
In emulation opposite to Heav'n:
Which when Beëlzebub perceived, than whom,
Satan except, none higher sat, with grave   300
Aspect he rose, and in his rising seem'd
A pillar of state: deep on his front engraven
Deliberation sat and public care;
And princely counsel in his face yet shone,
Majestic though in ruin: sage he stood,   305
With Atlantean shoulders fit to bear
The weight of mightiest monarchies; his look
Drew audience and attention still as night
Or summer's noon-tide air, while thus he spake:
   Thrones and Imperial Powers, Offspring of Heav'n   310
Ethereal Virtues; or these titles now
Must we renounce, and changing style be call'd
Princes of Hell? for so the popular vote
Inclines here to continue, and build up here
A growing empire; doubtless, while we dream,   315
And know not that the King of Heav'n hath doom'd
This place our dungeon, not our safe retreat
Beyond his potent arm, to live exempt
From Heav'n's high jurisdiction, in new league
Banded against his throne, but to remain   320
In strictest bondage, though thus far moved,
Under th' inevitable curb, reserved
His captive multitude: for he, be sure,
In height or depth, still first and last will reign
Sole King, and of his kingdom lose no part   325
By our revolt; but over Hell extend
His empire, and with iron sceptre rule
Us here, as with his golden those in Heav'n
What sit we then projecting peace and war?
War hath determined us, and foil'd with loss   330
Irreparable: terms of peace yet none
Vouchsafed or sought: for what peace will be giv'n

To us enslaved, but custody severe,
And stripes and arbitrary punishment
Inflicted? And what peace can we return,   335
But to our power hostility and hate,
Untamed reluctance, and revenge though slow,
Yet ever plotting how the Conqu'ror least
May reap his conquest, and may least rejoice
In doing what we most in suff'ring feel?   340
Nor will occasion want, nor shall we need
With dang'rous expedition to invade
Heav'n, whose high walls fear no assault or siege,
Or ambush from the deep. What if we find
Some easier enterprise? There is a place,   345
(If ancient and prophetic fame in Heav'n
Err not) another world, the happy seat
Of some new race call'd Man, about this time
To be created like to us, though less
In pow'r and excellence, but favour'd more   350
Of Him who rules above; so was his will
Pronounced among the Gods, and by an oath,
That shook Heav'n's whole circumference, confirm'd.
Thither let us bend all our thoughts, to learn
What creatures there inhabit, of what mould   355
Or substance, how endued, and what their pow'r,
And where their weakness; how attempted best,
By force or subtlety. Though Heav'n be shut,
And Heav'n's high Arbitrator sit secure
In his own strength, this place may lie exposed   360
The utmost border of his kingdom, left
To their defence who hold it. Here perhaps
Some advantageous act may be achieved
By sudden onset, either with Hell fire
To waste his whole creation, or possess   365
All as our own, and drive as we were driv'n,
The puny habitants; or if not drive,
Seduce them to our party, that their God
May prove their Foe, and with repenting hand
Abolish his own works. This would surpass   370
Common revenge, and interrupt his joy
In our confusion, and our joy upraise
In his disturbance; when his darling sons,
Hurl'd headlong to partake with us, shall curse
Their frail original and faded bliss,   375
Faded so soon. Advise if this be worth
Attempting, or to sit in darkness here
Hatching vain empires. Thus Beëlzebub
Pleaded his dev'lish counsel, first devised
By Satan, and in part proposed: for whence,   380
But from the author of all ill, could spring
So deep a malice, to confound the race
Of mankind in one root, and Earth with Hell
To mingle and involve, done all to spite
The great Creator? But their spite still serves   385
His glory to augment. The bold design
Pleased highly those infernal States, and joy
Sparkled in all their eyes. With full assent

They vote; whereat his speech he thus renews:
   Well have ye judged, well ended long debate,   390
Synod of Gods, and like to what ye are,
Great things resolved, which from the lowest deep
Will once more lift us up, in spite of fate,
Nearer our ancient seat; perhaps in view
Of those bright confines, whence with neighb'ring arms   395
And opportune excursion, we may chance
Re-enter Heav'n; or else in some mild zone
Dwell not unvisited of Heav'n's fair light
Secure, and at the brightening orient beam
Purge off this gloom: the soft delicious air,   400
To heal the scar of these corrosive fires,
Shall breathe her balm. But first, whom shall we send
In search of this new world? whom shall we find
Sufficient? who shall 'tempt with wand'ring feet
The dark unbottom'd infinite abyss,   405
And through the palpable obscure find out
His uncouth way, or spread his aery flight,
Upborne with indefatigable wings
Over the vast abrupt, ere he arrive
The happy isle? What strength, what art, can then   410
Suffice, or what evasion bear him safe
Through the strict senteries and stations thick
Of Angels watching round? Here he had need
All circumspection, and we now no less
Choice in our suffrage; for on whom we send,   415
The weight of all and our last hope relies.
   This said, he sat; and expectation held
His look suspense, awaiting who appear'd
To second or oppose, or undertake
The perilous attempt: but all sate mute   420
Pond'ring the danger with deep thoughts; and each
In other's count'nance read his own dismay
Astonish'd. None among the choice and prime
Of those Heav'n-warring champions could be found
So hardy as to proffer or accept   425
Alone the dreadful voyage; till at last
Satan whom now transcendent glory raised
Above his fellows, with monarchal pride,
Conscious of highest worth, unmoved, thus spake:
   O Progeny of Heav'n, empyreal Thrones,   430
With reason hath deep silence and demur
Seized us, though undismayed; long is the way
And hard that out of Hell leads up to light;
Our prison strong; this huge convex of fire,
Outrageous to devour, immures us round   435
Ninefold, and gates of burning adamant
Barr'd over us prohibit all egress.
These pass'd if any pass, the void profound
Of unessential Night receives him next
Wide gaping, and with utter loss of being   440
Threatens him, plunged in that abortive gulf,
If thence he 'scape into whatever world,
Or unknown region, what remains him less
Than unknown dangers, and as hard escape?

But I should ill-become this throne, O Peers,   445
And this imperial sov'reignty, adorn'd
With splendour, arm'd with pow'r, if aught propos'd
And judged of public moment, in the shape
Of difficulty or danger, could deter
Me from attempting. Wherefore do I assume   450
These royalties, and not refuse to reign,
Refusing to accept as great a share
Of hazard as of honour; due alike
To him who reigns and so much to him due
Of hazard more, as he above the rest   455
High honour'd sits? Go, therefore, mighty Powers,
Terror of Heav'n, though fall'n; intend at home,
While here shall be our home, what best may ease
The present misery, and render Hell
More tolerable; if there be cure or charm   460
To respite, or deceive, or slack the pain
Of this ill mansion; intermit no watch
Against a wakeful foe, while I abroad
Through all the casts of dark destruction, seek,
Deliv'rance for us all. This enterprise   465
None shall partake with me. Thus saying rose
The Monarch, and prevented all reply,
Prudent, lest from his resolution raised,
Others among the chief might offer now
(Certain to be refused) what erst they fear'd: 470
And so refused might in opinion stand
His rivals, winning cheap the high repute
Which he through hazard huge must earn. But they
Dreaded not more th' adventure than his voice
Forbidding: and at once with him they rose;   475
Their rising all at once was as the sound
Of thunder heard remote. Tow'rds him they bend
With awful rev'rence prone; and as a God
Extol him equal to the High'st in Heav'n:
Nor fail'd they to express how much they praised,   480
That for the gen'ral safety he despised
His own: for neither do the Spirits damn'd
Lose all their virtue: lest bad men should boast
Their specious deeds on earth, which glory excites,
Or close ambition, varnish'd o'er with zeal.   485
Thus they their doubtful consultations dark
Ended, rejoicing in their matchless chief:
As when from mountain-tops the dusky clouds
Ascending, while the north wind sleeps, o'erspread
Heav'n's cheerful face. The low'ring element   490
Scowls o'er the darken'd landscape snow, or show'r,
If chance the radiant Sun with farewell sweet
Extend his ev'ning beam, the fields revive,
The birds their notes renew, and bleating herds
Attest their joy, that hill and valley rings.   495
O shame to men! Devil with Devil damn'd
Firm concord holds, men only disagree
Of creatures rational, though under hope
Of heav'nly grace: and God proclaiming peace,
Yet live in hatred, enmity, and strife   500

Among themselves, and levy cruel wars,
Wasting the earth, each other to destroy;
As if (which might induce us to accord)
Man had not hellish foes enough besides,
That day and night for his destruction wait.   505
   The Stygian council thus dissolved; and forth
In order came the grand infernal peers:
'Midst came their mighty Paramount, and seem'd
Alone th' antagonist of Heav'n, nor less
Than Hell's dread emperor with pomp supreme,   510
And God-like imitated state; him round
A globe of fiery Seraphim inclosed
With bright emblazonry, and horrent arms.
Then of their session ended they bid cry
With trumpets' regal sound the great result: 515
Towards the four winds four speedy Cherubim
Put to their mouths the sounding alchemy
By herald vote explain'd; the hollow abyss
Heard far and wide, and all the host of Hell
With deaf'ning shout return'd the loud acclaim.   520
Thence more at ease their minds, and somewhat raised
By false presumptuous hope, the ranged Pow'rs
Disband, and wand'ring, each his sev'ral way
Pursues, as inclination or sad choice
Leads him perplex'd, where he may likeliest find   525.
Truce to his restless thoughts, and entertain
The irksome hours till his great chief return
Part on the plain, or in the air sublime,
Upon the wing, or in swift race contend,
As at th' Olympian games or Pythian fields   530
Part curb their fiery steeds, or shun the goal
With rapid wheels, or fronted brigades form,
As when to arm proud cities war appears
Waged in the troubled sky, and armies rush
To battle in the clouds, before each van   535
Prick forth the airy knights, and couch their spears
Till thickest legions close; with feats of arms
From either end of Heav'n the welkin burns.
Others, with vast Typhoean rage more fell,
Rend up both rocks and hills, and ride the air   540
In whirlwind; Hell scarce holds the wild uproar.
As when Alcides, from Oechalia crown'd
With conquest, felt the envenom'd robe, and tore
Through pain up by the roots Thessalian pines,
And Lichas from the top of Oeta threw   545
Into th' Euboic sea. Others more mild,
Retreated in a silent valley, sing
With notes angelical to many a harp
Their own heroic deeds and hapless fall
By doom of battle; and complain that Fate   550
Free virtue should inthrall to force or chance.
Their song was partial, but the harmony
(What could it less when Spirits immortal sing?)
Suspended Hell, and took with ravishment
The thronging audience. In discourse more sweet   555
(For eloquence the soul, song charms the sense)

Others apart sat on a hill retired,
In thoughts more elevate, and reason'd high
Of providence, foreknowledge, will, and fate,
Fix'd fate, free-will, foreknowledge absolute,   560
And found no end, in wand'ring mazes lost.
Of good and evil much they argued then,
Of happiness and final misery,
Passion and apathy, glory and shame,
Vain wisdom all, and false philosophy: 565
Yet with a pleasing sorcery could charm
Pain for a while, or anguish, and excite
Fallacious hope, or arm th' obdured breast
With stubborn patience as with triple steel.
Another part in squadrons and gross bands,   570
On bold adventure to discover wide
That dismal world, if any clime perhaps
Might yield the easier habitation, bend
Four ways their flying march, along the banks
Of four infernal rivers, that disgorge   575
Into the burning lake their baleful stream
Abhorred Styx, the flood of deadly hate;
Sad Acheron of sorrow, black and deep;
Cocytus, named of lamentation loud
Heard on the rueful stream; fierce Phlegethon,   580
Whose waves of torrent fire inflame with rage.
Far off from these a slow and silent stream,
Lethe, the river of oblivion, rolls
Her wat'ry labyrinth; whereof who drinks,
Forthwith his former state and being forgets,   585
Forgets both joy and grief, pleasure and pain.
Beyond this flood a frozen continent
Lies dark and wild, beat with perpetual storms
Of whirlwind and dire hail, which on firm land
Thaws not, but gathers heap, and ruin seems   590
Of ancient pile all else deep snow and ice
A gulf profound as that Servonian bog
Betwixt Damiata and Mount Caisus old,
Where armies whole have sunk: the parching air
Burns frore, and cold performs th' effect of fire.   595
Thither, by harpy-footed furies haled,
At certain revolutions, all the damn'd
Are brought: and feel by turns the bitter change
Of fierce extremes, extremes by change more fierce,
From beds of raging fire to starve in ice   600
Their soft ethereal warmth, and there to pine
Immoveable, infix'd, and frozen round,
Periods of time, thence hurried back to fire.
They ferry over this Lethean sound
Both to and fro, their sorrow to augment,   605
And wish and struggle, as they past to reach
The tempting steam, with one small drop to lose
In sweet forgetfulness all pain and woe,
All in one moment, and so near the brink;
But fate withstands, and to oppose th' attempt   610
Medusa with Gorgonian terror guards
The ford, and of itself the water flies

All taste of living wight, as once it fled
The lip of Tantalus. Thus roving on
In confused march forlorn, th' advent'rous bands   615
With shuddering horror pale, and eyes aghast,
View'd first their lamentable lot, and found
No rest. Through many a dark and dreary vale
They pass'd, and many a region dolorous,
O'er many a frozen, many a fiery Alp,   620
Rocks, caves, lakes, fens, bogs, dens, and shades of death,
A universe of death, which God by curse
Created evil, for evil only good,
Where all life dies, death lives, and nature breeds,
Perverse, all monstrous, all prodigious things,   625
Abominable, inutterable, and worse
Than fables yet have feign'd, or fear conceived,
Gorgons and Hydras, and Chimeras dire.
      Meanwhile the adversary of God and Man,
Satan, with thoughts inflamed of high'st design,   630
Puts on swift wings, and tow'rds the gates of Hell
Explores his solitary flight. Sometimes
He scours the right hand coast, sometimes the left,
Now shaves with level wing the deep, then soars
Up to the fiery concave tow'ring high.   635
      As when far off at sea a fleet descry'd
Hangs in the clouds, by equinoctial winds
Close sailing from Bengala, or the isles
Of Ternate and Tidore, whence merchants bring
Their spicy drugs; they on the trading flood   640
Through the wide Ethiopian to the Cape
Ply stemming nightly tow'rd the pole. So seem'd
Far off the flying Fiend: at last appear
Hell bounds, high reaching to the horrid roof,
And thrice threefold the gates; three folds were brass,   645
Three iron, three of adamantine rock,
Impenetrable, impaled with circling fire,
Yet unconsumed. Before the gates there sat
On either side a formidable shape;
The one seem'd woman to the waist, and fair,   650
But ended foul in many a scaly fold
Voluminous and vast, a serpent arm'd
With mortal sting: about her middle round
A cry of Hell-hounds never ceasing, bark'd
With wide Cerberean mouths full loud, and rung   655
A hideous peal: yet, when they list, would creep,
If aught disturb'd their noise into her womb,
And kennel there, yet there still bark'd and howl'd
Within unseen. Far less abhorr'd than these
Vex'd Scylla, bathing in the sea that parts   660
Calabria from the hoarse Trinacrian shore;
Nor uglier follow the night-hag, when call'd
In secret, riding through the air she comes,
Lured with the smell of infant blood, to dance
With Lapland witches, while the laboring moon   665
Eclipses at their charms. The other shape,
If shape it might be call'd that shape had none
Distinguishable in member, joint, or limb,

Or substance might be call'd that shadow seem'd,
For each seem'd either, black it stood as Night,   670
Fierce as ten Furies, terrible as Hell,
And shook a dreadful dart. What seem'd his head
The likeness of a kingly crown had on.
Satan was now at hand, and from his seat,
The monster moving onward, came as fast   675
With horrid strides, Hell trembled as he strode.
Th' undaunted Fiend what this might be admired—
Admired, not fear'd: God and his Son except,
Created thing nought valued he nor shunn'd;
And with disdainful look thus first began: 680
    Whence and what art thou, execrable shape,
That darest, though grim and terrible, advance
Thy miscreated front athwart my way
To yonder gates? Through them I mean to pass,
That be assured, without leave ask'd of thee: 685
Retire or taste thy folly, and learn by proof,
Hell-born, not to contend with Spirits of Heav'n.
    To whom the goblin full of wrath reply'd,
Art thou that traitor Angel, art thou He,
Who first broke peace in Heav'n, and faith, till then   690
Unbroken, and in proud rebellious arms
Drew after him the third part of Heav'n's sons,
Conjured against the High'st, for which both thou
And they, outcast from God, are here condemn'd
To waste eternal days in woe and pain?   695
And reckon'st thou thyself with Spirits of Heav'n,
Hell-doom'd, and breath'st defiance here and scorn
Where I reign king, and to enrage thee more,
Thy king and lord? Back to thy punishment,
False fugitive, and to thy speed add wings,   700
Lest with a whip of scorpions I pursue
Thy ling'ring, or with one stroke of this dart
Strange horror seize thee, and pangs unfelt before.
    So spake the grisly terror, and in shape,
So speaking, and so threat'ning, grew tenfold   705
More dreadful and deform. On th' other side,
Incensed with indignation, Satan stood
Unterrify'd, and like a comet burn'd,
That fires the length of Ophiuchus huge
In th' arctic sky, and from his horrid hair   710
Shakes pestilence and war. Each at the head
Levell'd his deadly aim; their fatal hands
No second stroke intend, and such a frown
Each cast at th' other, as when two black clouds,
With Heav'n's artill'ry fraught, come rattling on   715
Over the Caspian; then stand front to hunt
Hov'ring a space, till winds the signal blow
To join their dark encounter in mid-air.
So frown'd the mighty combatants, that Hell
Grew darker at their frown, so match'd they stood: 720
For never but once more was either like
To meet so great a foe: and now great deeds
Had been achieved, whereof all Hell had rung,
Had not the snaky sorceress that sat

Fast by Hell's gate, and kept the fatal key,   725
Ris'n and with hideous outcry rush'd between.
    O Father, what intends thy hand, she cry'd,
Against thy only Son? What fury, O Son,
Possesses thee to bend that mortal dart
Against thy Father's head? and know'st for whom?   730
For Him who sits above and laughs the while
At thee ordain's his drudge, to execute
Whate'er his wrath, which he calls justice, bids:
His wrath, which one day will destroy ye both.
    She spake, and at her words the hellish pest   735
Forbore; then these to her Satan return'd.
    So strange thy outcry, and thy words so strange
Thou interposest, that my sudden hand
Prevented, spares to tell thee yet by deeds
What it intends, till first I know of thee,   740
What thing thou art, thus double-form'd, and why
In this infernal vale first met thou call'st
Me Father, and that phantasm call'st my Son;
I know thee not, nor ever saw till now
Sight more detestable than him and thee.   745
    T' whom thus the portress of Hell gate reply'd:
Hast thou forgot me then, and do I seem
Now in thine eyes so foul? once deem'd so fair
In Heav'n, when at th' assembly, and in sight
Of all the Seraphim with thee combined   750
In bold conspiracy against Heav'n's King,
All on a sudden miserable pain
Surprised thee, dim thine eyes, and dizzy swum
In darkness, while thy head flames think and fast
Threw forth, till on the left side op'ning wide,   755
Likest to thee in shape and countenance bright,
Then shining heav'nly fair, a Goddess arm'd
Out of thy head I sprung; amazement seized
All th' host of Heav'n; back they recoil'd, afraid
At first, and call'd me Sin, and for a sign   760
Portentous held me; but familiar grown
I pleased, and with attractive graces won
The most averse, thee chiefly, who full oft
Thyself in me thy perfect image viewing
Becam'st enamour'd, and such joy thou took'st   765
With me in secret, that my womb conceived
A growing burthen. Meanwhile war arose,
And fields were fought in Heav'n; wherein remain'd
(For what could else?) to our Almighty Foe
Clear victory; to our part loss and rout   770
Through all the empyrean. Down they fell,
Driv'n headlong from the pitch of Heav'n, down
Into this deep, and in the general fall
I also; at which time this powerful key
Into my hand was giv'n, with charge to keep   775
These gates for ever shut; which none can pass
Without my op'ning. Pensive here I sat
Alone; but long I sat not, till my womb
Pregnant by thee, and now excessive grown,
Prodigious motion felt and rueful throes   780

At last this odious offspring whom thou seest
Thine own begotten, breaking violent way,
Tore through my entrails, that with fear and pain
Distorted, all my nether shape thus grew
Transform'd: but he my inbred enemy   785
Forth issued, brandishing his fatal dart,
Made to destroy. I fled, and cry'd out Death;
Hell trembled at the hideous name, and sigh'd
From all her caves, and back resounded Death.
I fled, but he pursued (though more, it seems,   790
Inflamed with lust than rage), and swifter far,
Me overtook, his mother all dismay'd,
And in embraces forcible and foul
Ingend'ring with me, of that rape begot
These yelling monsters, that with ceaseless cry   795
Surround me, as thou saw'st, hourly conceived
And hourly born, with sorrow infinite
To me; for when they list, into the womb
That bred them they return, and howl and gnaw
My bowels, their repast; then bursting forth   800
Afresh with conscious terrors vex me round,
That rest or intermission none I find.
Before mine eyes in opposition sits
Grim Death, my son and foe, who sets them on,
And me, his parent, would full soon devour   805
For want of other prey, but that he knows
His end with mine involved; and knows that I
Should prove a bitter morsel, and his bane,
Whenever that shall be. So Fate pronounced.
But thou, O Father, I forewarn thee, shun   810
His deadly arrow; neither vainly hope
To be invulnerable in those bright arms,
Though temper'd heav'nly, for that mortal dint,
Save He who reigns above, none can resist.
        She finish'd and the subtle Fiend his lore   815
Soon learn'd, now milder, and thus answer'd smooth.
Dear Daughter, since thou claim'st me for thy sire,
And my fair son here show'st me, the dear pledge
Of dalliance had with thee in Heav'n, and joys
Then sweet, now sad to mention, through dire change   820
Befall'n us unforeseen, unthought of; know
I come no enemy, but to set free
From out this dark and dismal house of pain
Both him and thee, and all the heav'nly host
Of Spirits, that in our just pretences arm'd   825
Fell with us from on high: from them I go
This uncouth errand sole, and one for all
Myself expose, with lonely steps to tread
Th' unfounded deep, and through the void immense
To search with wand'ring quest a place foretold   830
Should be, and, by concurring signs, ere now
Created vast and round, a place of bliss
In the purlieus of Heav'n, and therein placed
A race of upstart creatures to supply
Perhaps our vacant room, though more removed,   835
Lest Heav'n surcharged with potent multitude

Might hap to move new broils: Be this aught
Than this more secret now design'd, I haste
To know, and this once known, shall soon return,
And bring ye to the place where thou and Death   840
Shall dwell at ease, and up and down unseen
Wing silently the buxom air, embalm'd
With odours: there ye shall be fed and fill'd
Immeasurably, all things shall be your prey.
    He ceased, for both seem'd highly pleased; and Death   845
Grinn'd horrible a ghastly smile, to hear
His famine should be fill'd, and blest his maw
Destined to that good hour: no less rejoiced
His mother bad, and thus bespake her sire:
    The key of this infernal pit by due,   850
And by command of Heav'n's all-powerful King,
I keep, by him forbidden to unlock
These adamantine gates; against all force
Death ready stands to interpose his dart,
Fearless to be o'ermatch'd by living might.   855
But what owe I to his commands above
Who hates me, and hath hither thrust me down
Into this gloom of Tartarus profound,
To sit in hateful office here confined,
Inhabitant of Heav'n, and heav'nly born,   860
Here in perpetual agony and pain,
With terrors and with clamours compass'd round
Of mine own brood, that on my bowels feed?
Thou art my father, thou my author, thou
My being gav'st me; whom should I obey   865
But thee, whom follow? thou wilt bring me soon
To that new world of light and bliss, among
The Gods who live at ease, where I shall reign
At thy right hand voluptuous, as beseems
Thy daughter and thy darling, without end.   870
    Thus saying, from her side the fatal ken
Sad instrument of all our woe, she took;
And tow'rds the gate rolling her bestial train,
Forthwith the huge portcullis high up-drew,
Which but herself, not all the Stygian pow'rs   875
Could once have moved; then in the key-hole turns
Th' intricate wards, and ev'ry bolt and bar
Of massy iron or solid rock with ease
Unfastens. On a sudden open fly
With impetuous recoil and jarring sound   880
Th' infernal doors, and on their hinges grate
Harsh thunder, that the lowest bottom shook
Of Erebus. She open'd; but to shut
Excell'd her pow'r: the gates wide open stood,
That with extended wings a banner'd host   885
Under spread ensigns marching might pass through
With horse and chariots rank'd in loose array;
So wide they stood, and like a furnace mouth
Cast forth redounding smoke and ruddy flame.
Before their eyes in sudden view appear   890
The secrets of the hoary deep, a dark
Illimitable ocean, without bound,

Without dimension, where length, breadth, and heighth,
And time, and place, are lost; where eldest Night
And Chaos, ancestors of Nature, hold   895
Eternal anarchy, amidst the noise
Of endless wars, and by confusion stand.
For hot, cold, moist, and dry, four champions fierce
Strive here for mast'ry, and to battle bring
Their embryon atoms; they around the flag   900
Of each his faction, in their sev'ral clans,
Light-arm'd or heavy, sharp, smooth, swift, or slow,
Swarm populous, unnumbered as the sands
Of Barca or Cyrene's torrid soil,
Levy'd to side with warring winds, and poise   905
Their lighter wings. To whom these most adhere,
He rules a moment; Chaos umpire sits,
And by decision more embroils the fray
By which he reigns: next him high arbiter
Chance governs all. Into this wild abyss,   910
The womb of Nature, and perhaps her grave,
Of neither sea, nor shore, nor air, nor fire,
But all these in their pregnant causes mix'd
Confus'dly, and which thus must ever fight,
Unless th' Almighty Maker them ordain   915
His dark materials to create more worlds;
Into this wild abyss the wary Fiend
Stood on the brink of Hell and look'd a while,
Pond'ring his voyage: for no narrow frith
He had to cross. Nor was his ear less peal'd   920
With noises loud and ruinous (to compare
Great things with small) than when Bellona storms
With all her batt'ring engines bent, to raze
Some capital city; or less than if this frame
Of Heav'n were falling, and these elements   925
In mutiny had from her axle torn
The steadfast earth. At last his sail-broad vans
He spreads for flight, and in the surging smoke
Uplifted spurns and ground; thence many a league,
As in a cloudy chair, ascending rides   930
Audacious; but that seat soon failing, meets
A vast vacuity: all unawares
Flutt'ring his pennons vain, plumb down he drops
Ten thousand fathom deep, and to this hour
Down had been falling, had not by ill chance,   935
The strong rebuff of some tumultuous cloud,
Instinct with fire and nitre, hurried him
As many miles aloft: that fury stay'd,
Quench'd in a boggy Syrtis, neither sea,
Nor good dry land: nigh founder'd on he fares,   940
Treading the crude consistence, half on foot,
Half flying; behoves him now both oar and sail.
As when a gryphon through the wilderness
With winged course, o'er hill or moory dale,
Pursues the Arimaspian, who by stealth   945
Had from his wakeful custody purloin'd
The guarded gold: so eagerly the Fiend
O'er bog, or steep, through strait, rough, dense or rare,

With head, hands, wings, or feet pursues his way,
And swims, or sinks, or wades, or creeps, or flies: 950
At length a universal hubbub wild
Of stunning sounds and voices all confused,
Borne through the hollow dark, assaults his ear
With loudest vehemence: thither he plies,
Undaunted to meet there whatever Pow'r   955
Or Spirit of the nethermost abyss
Might in that noise reside, of whom to ask
Which way the nearest coast of darkness lies
Bord'ring on light; when strait behold the throne
Of Chaos, and his dark pavilion spread   960
Wide on the wasteful deep; with him enthroned
Sat sable-vested Night, eldest of things,
The consort of his reign; and by them stood
Orcus and Ades, and the dreaded name
Of Demogorgon; Rumour next and Chance   965
And Tumult and Confusion, all embroil'd,
And Discord, with a thousand various mouths.
     T' whom Satan turning boldly, thus: Ye Pow'rs
And Spirits of this nethermost abyss,
Chaos and ancient Night, I come no spy,   970
With purpose to explore or to disturb
The secrets of your realm, but by constraint
Wand'ring this darksome desert, as my way
Lies through your spacious empire up to light,
Alone, and without guide, half lost, I seek   975
What readiest path leads where your gloomy bounds
Confine with Heav'n: or if some other place
From your dominion won, th' ethereal King
Possesses lately, thither to arrive
I travel this profound; direct my course;   980
Direct no mean recompense it brings
To your behoof, if I that region lost,
All usurpation thence expell'd, reduce
To her original darkness and your sway
(Which is my present journey), and once more   985
Erect the standard there of ancient Night;
Yours be th' advantage all, mine the revenge.
     Thus Satan; and him thus the Anarch old,
With fault'ring speech and visage incomposed,
Answer'd: I know thee, stranger, who thou art;   990
That mighty leading Angel, who of late
Made head against Heav'n's King, though overthrown.
I saw and heard; for such a num'rous host
Fled not in silence, through the frighted deep
With ruin upon ruin, rout on rout,   995
Confusion worse confounded; and Heav'n gates
Pour'd out by millions her victorious bands
Pursuing. I upon my frontiers here
Keep residence; if all I can will serve
That little which is left so to defend,   1000
Encroach'd on still through your intestine broils,
Weak'ning the sceptre of old Night: first Hell
Your dungeon stretching far and wide beneath,
Now lately Heav'n and Earth, another world,

Hung o'er my realm, link'd in a golden chain   1005
To that side Heav'n from whence your legions fell:
If that way be your walk, you have not far;
So much the nearer danger; go and speed;
Havock, and spoil, and ruin, are my gain.
   He ceased, and Satan stay'd not to reply;   1010
But glad that now his sea should find a shore,
With fresh alacrity and force renew'd,
Springs upward like a pyramid of fire
Into the wild expanse, and through the shock
Of fighting elements, on all sides round   1015
Environ'd, wins his way harder beset
And more endangered than when Argo pass'd
Through Bosphorus, betwixt the justling rocks;
Or when Ulysses on the larboard shunn'd
Charybdis, and by th' other whirlpool steer'd.   1020
So he with difficulty and labour hard
Moved on, with difficulty and labour he;
But he once past, soon after when man fell,
Strange alteration! Sin and Death amain
Following his track, such was the will of Heav'n,   1025
Paved after him a broad and beaten way
Over the dark abyss, whose boiling gulf
Tamely endured a bridge of wondrous length
From Hell continued reaching th' utmost orb
Of this frail world; by which the Spirits perverse   1030
With easy intercourse pass to and fro
To tempt or punish mortals, except whom
God and good Angels guard by special grace
But now at last the sacred influence
Of light appears, and from the walls of Heav'n   1035
Shoots far into the bosom of dim Night
A glimm'ring dawn. Here Nature first begins
Her farthest verge, and Chaos to retire
As from her outmost works a broken foe
With tumult less, and with less hostile din,   1040
That Satan with less toil, and now with ease,
Wafts on the calmer wave by dubious light,
And like a weather-beaten vessel holds
Gladly the port, though shrouds and tackle torn;
Or in the emptier waste, resembling air,   1045
Weighs his spread wings, at leisure to behold
Far off th' empyreal Heav'n, extended wide
In circuit, undetermined square or round,
With opal tow'rs and battlements adorn'd
Of living sapphire, once his native seat;   1050
And fast by hanging in a golden chain
This pendent world, in bigness as a star
Of smallest magnitude close by the moon.
Thither full fraught with mischievous revenge,
Accursed, and in a cursed hour he hies.   1055

POETIC DICTION OF MILTON

To some readers it will not be unprofitable or unacceptable to offer some remarks on this subject, drawn from Addison's Spectator.

Milton, in conformity with the practice of the ancient poets, has infused a great many Latinisms, as well as Græcisms, and sometimes Hebraisms, into the language of his poem. Under this head may be ranked the placing the adjective after the substantive, the transposition of words, the turning the adjective into a substantive, with several other foreign modes of speech which this poet has naturalized, to give his verse the greater sound, and throw it out of prose. Sometimes particular words are extended or contracted by the insertion or omission of certain syllables. Milton has put in practice this method of raising his language, as far as the nature of our tongue will permit, as *eremite* for hermit. For the sake of the measure of his verse, he has with great judgment suppressed a syllable in several words, and shortened those of two syllables into one, this expedient giving a greater variety to his numbers. It is chiefly observable in the names of persons and countries, as Beelzebub, Hessebon, and in many other particulars, wherein he has either changed the name, or made use of that which is not the most commonly known, that he might the further deviate from the language of common life.

The same reason recommended to him several old words, which also makes his poem appear the more venerable, and gives it a greater air of antiquity.

There are also in Milton several words of his own coining, as Cerberean, miscreate, hell-doomed, embryon, atomy, and many others. The same liberty was made use of by Homer.

Milton, by the above-mentioned helps, and by the choice of the noblest words and phrases which our tongue would afford him, has carried our language to a greater height than any of the English poets have ever done before or after him, and made the sublimity of his style equal to that of his sentiments; yet in some places his style is rendered stiff and obscure by the methods which he adopted for raising his style above the prosaic.

These forms of expression, however, with which Milton has so very much enriched, and in some places darkened the language of his poem, were the more proper for him to use, because his poem is written in blank verse. Rhyme, without any other assistance, throws the language off from prose, and often makes an indifferent phrase pass unregarded; but where the verse is not built upon rhymes, there pomp of sound and energy of expression are indispensably necessary to support the style and keep it from falling into the flatness of prose.

Upon the subject of Poetic Diction, Dugald Stewart offers some excellent observations, (Works, vol. i. 280–3). He says:

As it is one great object of the poet, in his serious productions, to elevate the imagination of his readers above the grossness of sensible objects, and the vulgarity of common life, it becomes peculiarly necessary for him to reject the use of all words and phrases which are trivial and hackneyed. Among those which are equally pure and equally perspicuous, he, in general, finds it expedient to adopt that which is the least common. Milton prefers the words Rhene and Danaw, to the more common words Rhine and Danube.

"A multitude, like which the populous Nortii
Poured never from his frozen loins, to pass
Rhene or the Danaw."—Book I. 353.

In the following line,

"Things unattempted yet in prose or rhyme,"

how much more suitable to the poetical style does the expression appear than if the author had said,

"Things unattempted yet in prose or verse."

In another passage, where, for the sake of variety, he has made use of the last phrase, he adds an epithet to remove it a little from the familiarity of ordinary discourse,

". . . in prose or numerous verse."

In consequence of this circumstance, there arises gradually in every language a poetical diction, which differs widely from the common diction of prose. It is much less subject to the vicissitudes of fashion than the polite modes of expression in familiar conversation; because, when it has once been adopted by the poet, it is avoided by good prose writers, as being too elevated for that species of composition. It may, therefore, retain its charm as long as the language exists; nay, the charm may increase, as the language grows older.

Indeed, the charm of poetical diction must increase to a certain degree, as polite literature advances. For, when once a set of words has been consecrated to poetry, the very sound of them, independently of the ideas they convey, awakens, every time we hear it, the agreeable impressions which were connected with it, when we met with them in the performances of our favourite authors. Even when strung together in sentences which convey no meaning, they produce some effect on the mind of a reader of sensibility; an effect, at least, extremely different from that of an unmeaning sentence in prose.

Nor is it merely by a difference of words that the language of poetry is distinguished from that of prose. When a poetical *arrangement* of words has once been established by authors of reputation, the most common expressions, by being presented in this consecrated order, may serve to excite poetical associations.

On the other hand, nothing more completely destroys the charm of poetry, than a string of words which the custom of ordinary discourse has arranged in so invariable an order, that the whole phrase may be anticipated from hearing its commencement. A single word frequently strikes us as flat and prosaic, in consequence of its familiarity; but two such words, coupled together in the order of conversation, can scarcely be introduced into serious poetry without approaching the ludicrous.

No poet in our language has shown so strikingly as Milton, the wonderful elevation which style may derive from an arrangement of words, which, while it is perfectly intelligible, departs widely from that to which we are in general accustomed. Many of his most sublime periods, when the order of the words is altered, are reduced nearly to the level of prose.

To copy this artifice with success, is a much more difficult attainment than is commonly imagined; and, of consequence, when it is acquired, it secures an author, to a great degree, from that crowd of imitators who spoil the effect of whatever is not beyond their reach. To the poet, who uses blank verse, it is an acquisition of still more essential consequence than to him who expresses himself in rhyme; for the more that the structure of the verse approaches to prose, the more it is necessary to give novelty and dignity to the composition. And, accordingly, among our magazine poets, ten thousand catch the structure of Pope's versification, for one who approaches to the manner of Milton or Thomson.

ENDNOTES

1. *Throne, etc.:* "The all-enduring, all-defying pride of Satan, assuming so majestically Hell's burning throne, and coveting the diadem which scorches his thunder-blasted brow, is a creation requiring in its author almost the spiritual (mental) energy with which he invests the fallen seraph."—CHANNING.

2. *Ormus:* An island in the Persian Gulf. *Ind*: India. The wealth consisted chiefly in diamonds and pearls and gold, called *barbaric,* after the manner of Greeks and Romans, who accounted all nations but their own barbarous.

4. *Showers on, etc.:* It was an Eastern custom, as we learn from a Persian life of Timur-bec, or Tamerlane, at the coronation of their kings, to powder them with *gold-dust or seed-pearl.* —WARBURTON. See Virg. Æn. ii. 504.

10. All the speeches and debates in Pandemonium are well worthy of the place and the occasion, with gods for speakers, and angels and archangels for hearers. There is a decided manly tone in the arguments and sentiments, an eloquent dogmatism, as if each person spoke from thorough conviction. The rout in heaven is like the fall of some mighty structure, nodding to its base, "with hideous ruin and combustion down." —HAZLITT.

15. *Virtues:* Powers, or spirits. Thus, in Book V., the angels are addressed under the following names: thrones, dominations, princedoms, *virtues,* powers. So in this Book, 1.315, 316.

17. *Fate:* Destruction.

18. *Me:* The position of this word at the commencement of the sentence,

indicates, in a vivid manner, the arrogance and pride of the speaker. That superior greatness and mock-majesty which is ascribed to the prince of fallen angels, is admirably preserved in the beginning of this book. His opening and closing the debate, his taking on himself that great enterprise, at the thought of which the whole infernal assembly trembled; his encountering the hideous phantom, who guarded the gates of hell, and appeared to him in all his terrors, are instances of that daring mind which could not brook submission even to Omnipotence—A.

43. *Moloch:* The put of Moloch is, in all its circumstances, full of that fire and fury which distinguish this spirit from the rest of the fallen angels. He is described in the First Book (l. 392) as besmeared with the blood of human sacrifices, and delighted with the tears of parents, and the cries of children. In this Second Book, he is marked out as the fiercest spirit that fought in heaven; and, if we consider the figure which he makes in the Sixth Book, where the battle of the angels is described, we find it every way answerable to the same furious, enraged character. All his sentiments are rash, audacious, and desperate, particularly from the sixtieth to seventieth line. His preferring annihilation to shame or misery, is also highly suitable to his character: so the comfort he draws from their disturbing the peace of heaven—that if it be not victory it is revenge—is a sentiment truly diabolical, and becoming the bitterness of this implacable fiend.—A.

69. *Mix'd:* Filled. Virg. Æn. ii. 487.

74. *Forgetful:* Causing forgetfulness. An allusion is here made to Lethe, the River of Oblivion, one of the fabled streams of the infernal regions. Its waters possessed the quality of causing those who drank them to forget the whole of their former existence. This river is finely described by Milton in this Second Book, (l. 583–586, 603–614.)

83. *Our stronger:* Our superior in strength.

89. *Exercise:* Torment. Virg. Georg. iv. 453.

92. By *calling to penance,* Milton seems to intimate, that the sufferings of the condemned spirits are not always equally severe.—S.

97. *Essential:* The adjective for the substantive, essence, or existence.

97–8. The sense is this: which (annihilation) is far happier than, in a condition of misery, to have eternal being. See Mat. xxvi. 24. Mark xiv. 21.

100. *At worst:* In the worst possible condition.

104. *Fatal:* Sustained by fate, (I. 133.)

108. *Gods,* in the proper sense. See IX. 937, where gods are distinguished from angels, who are called demi-gods.

109. *Belial,* is described in the First Book as the idol of the lewd and luxurious. He is, in this Second Book, pursuant to that description, characterized as timorous and slothful; and, if we look into the Sixth Book, we find him celebrated in the battle of the angels for nothing but that scoffing speech which he makes to Satan, on their supposed advantage over the enemy. As his appearance is uniform, and of a piece in these three several views, we find his sentiments in the infernal assembly every way conformable to his character. Such are his apprehensions of a second battle, his horror of annihilation, his preferring to be miserable rather than "not to be." The contrast of thought in this speech, and that which precedes it, gives an agreeable variety to the debate.—A.

113–14. *Could make the worse appear the better reason:* An exact translation of what the Greek sophists professed to accomplish.

124. *Fact:* Deed of arms, battle.

139. *On his throne sit unpolluted:* This is a reply to that part of Moloch's speech, where he had threatened to mix the throne itself, of God, with infernal sulphur and strange fire.—N. *Mould:* Substance, or form.

152. *Let this be good:* Grant that this is good.

156. *Belike:* Perhaps. *Impotence:* Want of self-command.

159. *Wherefore cease, etc.:* Why then should we cease to exist? What reason is there to expect annihilation?

170. Is. xxx. 33.

180. See Note, Book I. 329.

181. Virg. Æn. vi. 75, . . . "rapidis ludibria ventis."
188. *Can:* Can (accomplish).
191. Allusion to Ps. ii. 4.
199. *To suffer, as to do:* Scævola boasted that he was a Roman, and knew as well how to suffer as to act. "Et facere et pati fortia Romanum est."—LIVY ii. 12.—N.
201. *This was at first resolved:* Our minds were made up at first to this.
218–19. *Receive familiar:* Receive as a matter made easy (by habit). The same idea is uttered by Mammon, l. 274–78 of this Book.
223. *Waiting:* Waiting for.
223–5. Since our present lot appears for (as) a happy one, though it is, indeed, but an ill one, for, though ill, it is not the worst, etc.
228. *Mammon:* His character is so fully drawn in the First Book, that the poet adds nothing to it in the Second. We were before told that he was the first who taught mankind to ransack the earth for gold and silver, and, that he was the architect of Pandemoniun, or the infernal palace where the evil spirits were to meet in council. His speech, in this Book, is every way suitable to so depraved a character. How proper is that reflection of their being unable to taste the happiness of heaven, were they actually there, in the mouth of one who, while he was in heaven, is said to have had his mind dazzled with the outward pomps and glories of the place, and to have been more intent on the riches of the pavement than on the beatific vision. The sentiments uttered in lines 262–273 are admirably characteristic of the same being.—A.
233. *The Strife:* Between the King of Heaven and us, not between Fate and Chance—PEARCE.
244. *Breathes:* Throws out the smell of, etc. See IV. 265.
250. *By force, etc.:* What is impossible to attain by force, what is unacceptable is obtained by permission.
263–8. The imagery of this passage is drawn from Ps. xviii. 11, 13; xcvii. 2.
278. *The sensible of pain:* The feeling, the sensation of pain.

279. These speeches are wonderfully fine; but the question is changed in the course of the debate—N.
294. *Michael:* A holy angel, who, in the Book of Daniel, chap. x. 3–21, is represented as having charge of the Jewish nation; and, in the book of Jude, verse 9, as contending with Satan about the body of Moses. His name is introduced also in Rev. xii. 7–9.
296. *Nether:* Lower.
299. *Beelzebub:* This evil spirit, who is reckoned the second in dignity that fell, and is, in the First Book, the second that awakes out of the trance, and confers with Satan upon the situation of their affairs, maintains his rank in the Book now before us. There is a wonderful majesty exhibited in his rising up to speak. He acts as a kind of moderator between the two opposite parties, and proposes a third undertaking, which the whole assembly approves. The motion he makes to detach one of their body in search of a new mold, is grounded upon a project devised by Satan, and cursorily proposed by him, in the First Book, 650–660. It is on this project that Beelzebub grounds his proposal —"What if we find," etc. Book II. 344–353. It may be observed how just it was, not to omit in the First Book, the project upon which the whole poem turns; as, also, that the prince of the fallen angels was the only proper person to give it birth, and that the next to him in dignity was the fittest to second and support it.
306. *Atlantean:* An allusion to King Atlas, who, according to ancient mythology, was changed into a mountain on the northern coast of Africa, which, from its great height, was represented as supporting the atmosphere.
329. *What:* For what? or, why?
336. *But to:* But according to. The word *but* in this line, and in line 333, is used with a poetic freedom, somewhat as the word *except* is employed in line 678.
346. *Fame in Heaven:* There is something wonderfully beautiful, and very apt to affect the reader's imagination, in this ancient prophecy, or report in Heaven, concerning the creation of man. Nothing could better show the dignity

of the species, than this tradition respecting them before their existence. They are represented to have been the talk of Heaven before they were created.—A.

352. Heb. vi. 17. An allusion, also, to Jupiter's oath. Virg. Æn. ix. 104, Hom. Iliad, i. 528.

360. It has been objected that there is a contradiction between this part of Beelzebub's speech and what he says afterwards, speaking of the same thing; but, in reply, it may be observed, that his design is different in these different speeches. In the former, where he is encouraging the assembly to undertake an expedition against this world, he says things to *lessen* the difficulty and danger; but in the latter, when they are seeking a proper person to perform it, he says things to *magnify* the danger, in order to make them more cautious in their choice.—N.

367. *Puny:* newly-created; derived from the French expression, *puis né*, born since. The idea of feebleness is involved.

382. *Confound:* Overthrow, destroy.

393. *Fate:* The decree of God.

404. *'Tempt:* Try.

405. *Obscure:* Obscurity, an adjective being used for a substantive.

409. *Arrive:* Arrive at.

410. *Isle:* The earth is so called because surrounded by an atmospheric sea; or, perhaps, because swimming in space.

412. *Had need:* Would need, as in the phrase "You had better go." The meaning is, "You would better go"—"It would be better for you to go."

414. *All:* The greatest.

415. *Choice:* Judgment or care in choosing.

417. *Expectation* is here personified. *His looks suspense* means, His countenance in a fixed, serious position. Compare Virg. Æn. ii. 1.

429. *Unmoved:* That is by the dangers in view.

431. *Demur:* Suspense.

434. *Convex:* Vault of fire, bending down on all sides around us. The word properly denotes the exterior surface of a globe, and *concave* the interior, but the poets use them promiscuously, as here. What is here called *convex* is called *concave* in line 635.

436. Virg. Æn. vi. 439, 552.

439. *Unessential:* Unsubstantial, void of materiality.

445–466. An imitation of one of the noblest speeches in the Iliad, xii. 310, etc.; but a great improvement upon it.

457. *Intend:* Regard, deliberate upon.

470. *Erst:* At first.

482. *For neither, etc.:* This seems to have been a sarcasm on the bad men of Milton's time.—E.B.

483. *lest:* Before this word supply, or understand, "this remark is made."

485. Milton intimates above, that the fallen and degraded state of man, or his individual vice, is not at all disproved by some of his external actions not appearing totally base. The commentators should have observed, in explaining this passage, that the whole grand mystery on which the poem depends, is the first fearful spiritual alienation of Satan from God, the only fountain of truth and all real positive good; and that, when thus separated, whether the spirit be that of man or devil, it may perform actions fair in appearance, but not essentially good, because springing from no fixed principle of good.—S.

489. *While the north wind sleeps:* A simile of perfect beauty: it illustrates the delightful feeling resulting from the contrast of the stormy debate with the light that seems subsequently to break in upon the assembly.—E. B.

491. *Scowls:* Drives in a frowning manner.

496. *O shame to men:* The reflections of the poet here are of great practical wisdom and importance. They were suggested, probably, by the civil commotions and animosities of his own times.

507. *Stygian:* An epithet derived from Styx, the name of a distinguished river in the infernal regions, according to the Pagan mythology; it here means the same as the word infernal.

512. *Globe:* A body of men formed into a circle. Virgil (Æn. x. 373) uses a similar expression: "Qua globus ille virum densissimus urguet."

513. That is, with glittering ensigns, and bristled arms, or arms with points, standing outward. The word *horrent* was, probably, suggested by "horrentia Maris arma," of the Æneid,

book i., or by the "horrentibus hastis" of Æn. x. 178.

517.   *Alchemy:* An alloy or mixed metal, out of which the trumpets were made: here, by metonymy, denotes trumpets.

528.   *Part on the plain, etc.:* The diversions of the fallen angels, with the particular account of their place of habitation, are described with great pregnancy of thought and copiousness of invention. The diversions are every way suitable to beings who had nothing left them but strength and knowledge misapplied. Such are their contentions at the race, and in feats of arms, with their entertainment, described in lines 539–541, etc.—A. Compare Ovid, Met. iv. 445.

529–30. These warlike diversions of the fallen angels seem to be copied from the military exercises of the Myrmidons during the absence of their chief from the war.—Hom. Iliad, ii. 774, etc. See also Æn. vi. 64.

531.   *Rapid Wheels:* Hor. Ode i. 1:4, "Metaque fervidis evitata rotis."

536.   *Couch their spears:* Put them in a posture for attack: put them in their rests.

538.   *Welkin:* Atmosphere.

539.   *Typhoean:* Gigantic, from Typhoeus, one of the giants of Pagan mythology, that fought against Heaven.

542.   *Alcides:* A name of Hercules, from a word signifying *strength*. He was a celebrated hero, who received, after death, divine honours. Having killed the King of Oechalia, in Greece, and led away his beautiful daughter Iole, as a captive, he raised an altar to Jupiter, and sent off for a splendid robe to wear when he should offer a sacrifice. Deianira, in a fit of jealousy, before sending the robe, tinged it with a certain poisonous preparation. Hercules soon found that the robe was consuming his flesh, and adhered so closely to his skin, that it could not be separated. In the agony of the moment, he seized Lichas, the bearer of the robe, by the foot, and hurled him from the top of Mount Oeta, into the sea. This name is given to a chain of mountains in Thessaly, the eastern extremity of which, in conjunction

with the sea, formed the celebrated pass of Thermopylae.

547.   *Sing, etc.:* Their music is employed in celebrating their own criminal exploits, and their discourse in sounding the unfathomable depths of fate, free-will, and foreknowledge. —A.

552.   *Partial:* Too favourable to themselves. Or the word may express this idea. Confined to few and inferior topics—those relating to war.

554.   *Suspended Hell:* The effect of their singing is somewhat like that of Orpheous in Hell. Virg. Geor. iv. 481.—N.

556.   *Eloquence, etc.:* the preference is here given to intellect above the pleasures of the senses.—E. B.

557.   *Apart:* Hor. Ode ii 13:23, "Sedesque *discretas* piorum."

563.   *Good and evil,* and de finibus bonorum et malorum, etc., were more particularly the subjects of disputation among the philosophers and sophists of old; as *providence, free-will, etc.,* were among the school-men and divines of later times, especially upon the introduction of the free notions of Arminius upon these subjects; and our author shows herein what an opinion he had of all books and learning of this kind.—N.

566.   *Charm:* Allay, beguile.

569.   *Triple:* Hor. Ode i. 3:9 "Illi robur, et *aes* triple, Circa pectus erat."

575–91. *Four infernal rivers, etc.:* The several circumstances in the description of Hell, are finely imagined; as the four rivers which disgorge themselves into the sea of fire, the extremes of cold and heat and the river of Oblivion. The monstrous animals produced in that infernal world, are represented by a single line, which gives us a more horrid idea of them than a much longer description would have done: "Nature breeds Perverse; all monstrous, all prodigious things," etc. This episode of the fallen spirits and their place of habitation, comes in very happily to unbend the mind of the reader from its attention to the debate.—A.

577– *Abhorred Styx, etc.:* The Greeks reckon
614.   up five rivers in Hell, and call them

after the names of the noxious springs and rivers in their own county. Our poet follows the example both as to the number and the names of these infernal rivers, and excellently describes their nature and properties, with the explanation of their names. As to the situation of these rivers, Milton does not confine himself to the statements of Greek or Latin poets, but draws out a new map of these rivers. He supposes a *burning lake,* agreeably to Scripture; and into this lake he makes these four rivers to flow from different directions, which gives us a greater idea than any of the heathen poets have furnished. The river of Oblivion is rightly placed *far off* from the rivers of Hatred, Sorrow, Lamentation, and Rage; and divides the frozen continent from the region of fire, and, thereby, completes the map of Hell with its general divisions.—N.

589. *Dire had:* Compare Horace, Ode ii., *Dirae grandinis.*

590. *Gathers heap:* Accumulates.

592. *Serbonian bog:* A morass between Egypt and Palestine, near Mount Casius. The loose sand of the adjacent country sometimes covered it to such an extent as to give it the appearance of firm land.

594. *Parching:* Scorching, drying. *Burns frore:* Burns frosty, or with frost. Ecclus. xliii. 20, 21, "When the *cold* north wind bloweth, it devoureth the mountains, and *burneth* the wilderness, and consumeth the grass *as fire.*" Newton also refers us to the old English and Septuagint translations of Ps. cxxi. 6: "The sun shall not burn thee by day, nor the moon by night." The same idea is introduced in Virgil, Georg. i. 93. ". . . rapidive potentia solis Acrior, aut Boreae penctrabile frigus adurat." This passage may have been in the mind of Milton, as it ascribes a scorching, drying, or parching influence alike to the vehement sun and to the penetrating cold of the north wind.

600. *Starve:* Kill with cold; a sense common in England, but not used in this country.

603. *Thence hurried etc:* This circumstance of the damned's suffering the extremes of heat and cold by turns, is finely invented to aggravate the horror of the description, and seems to be founded on Job. xxiv. 19, in the *Latin* version, which Milton frequently used. "Ad nimium calorem transeat ab aquis nivium." So Jerome and other commentators understand it.—N.

608. This is a fine allegory, designed to show that there is *no forgetfulness in Hell.* Memory makes a part of the punishment of the damned, and the reflection but increases their misery.—N.

611. *Medusa:* A fabulous being, who had two sisters. The three were called *Gorgons,* from their terrible aspect which turned the beholder into stone. The upper part of the body and the head, according to the fable, resembled those of a woman; the lower part was like a serpent.

614. *Tantalus:* A Grecian prince, who, for cruelty to his son, was condemned to perpetual hunger and thirst in hell. The English word *tantalize* is derived from this story, which is adapted, if not designed, to show that there is no forgetfulness in hell, but that memory and reflection torture its inhabitants.

618–22. By words we have it in our power (says Burke) to make such *combinations* as we cannot possibly make otherwise. By this power of combining, we are able, by the addition of well-chosen circumstances, to give a new life and force to the simple object. The words *rocks, caves,* etc., would lose the greatest part of the effect if they were not the "Rocks, caves, lakes, dens, bogs, fens, and shades *of death,*" and the idea, caused by a word, which nothing but a word could annex to the others, raises a very great degree of the sublime; which is raised yet higher by what follows, A UNIVERSE OF DEATH.

620. *Milton's Hell* is the most fantastic piece of fancy, based on the broadest superstructure of imagination. It presents such a scene *as though Switzerland were set on fire.* Such an uneven, colossal region, full of bogs, caves, hollow valleys, broad lakes and towering Alps, has Milton's genius cut out from Chaos, and wrapped in devouring flames, leaving, indeed,

here and there a snowy mountain, or a frozen lake, for a variety in the horror. This wilderness of death is the platform which imagination raises and peoples with the fallen thrones, dominations, princedoms, virtues, and powers. On it the same poem, in its playful fanciful mood, piles up the pandemonian palace, suggests the trick by which the giant fiends reduce their stature, shrinking into imps, and seats at the gates of Hell the monstrous forms of Sin and Death. These have often been objected to, as if they were unsuccessful and abortional efforts of imagination whereas they are the curvettings and magnificent nonsense of that power after its proper work, the creation of Hell, has been performed. The great (literary) merit of Milton's Hell, especially as compared to Dante's, is the union of a general sublime indistinctness, with a clear *statuesque* marking out from, or painting on, the gloom, of individual forms. The one describes Hell like an angel passing through it in haste, and with time only to behold its leading outlines and figures; the other, like a pilgrim compelled with slow and painful steps to thread all its high-ways and by-ways of pain and punishments. GILFILLAN.

623. *Good:* Adapted.

628. *Hydra:* A fabled monster serpent in the marsh of Lemnos in the Peloponnesus, which had many heads, and those when cut off, were immediately replaced by others. *Chimera:* A fabulous monster, vomiting flames, having the head of a lion, the body of a goat, and tail of a serpent. Hence the term is now applied to anything self-contradictory or absurd—to a mere creature of the imagination.

636. *As when, etc.:* Satan, *towering high* is here compared to a fleet of Indiamen discovered at a distance as it were, *hanging in the clouds*, as a flea at a distance seems to do. Dr. Bentley asks why a *fleet* when a first-rate man-of-war would do? Dr. Pearce answers, Because a fleet gives a nobler image than a single ship; and it is a fleet of Indiamen because, coming from so long a voyage, it is the fitter to

be compared to Satan in this expedition. The *equinoctial* are the trade winds. The fleet is described as close sailing, and is therefore more proper to be compared to a single person.—N. Dr. Pearce observes that Milton in his similitudes (as is the practice of Homer and Virgil too), after he has shown the common resemblance (as here in line 637), often takes the liberty of wandering into some unresembling circumstances; which have no other relation to the comparison than that it gave him the hint, and, as it were, set fire to the train of his imagination.

638–41. *Bengala:* Bengal. *Ternate and Tidore:* Spice islands east of Borneo. *Ethiopian:* Indian Ocean. *Cape:* Of Good Hope.

642. By night they sail towards the north pole.

644. *Hell bounds.* The boundaries of Hell.

647. *Empaled:* Paled in, enclosed. The old romances frequently speak of enchanted castles being empaled with circling fire.—T

648. The allegory that follows is a poetic paraphrase upon James i. 15. "Then when lust hath conceived, it bringeth forth sin, and sin, when it is finished, bringeth forth death."

649. The picture of Sin here given, may have been suggested by a line in Horace—See Art. Poet. 4: "Desinit in piscem mulier formosa superne." Or, Milton may been indebted, in part, to Spenser's description of Error. "Half like a serpent horribly displayed, But th' other half did woman's shape retain," etc. Hesiod's Echidna is also described as half woman, and half serpent .— Theog. 298. The mention of the Hell-hounds about her middle, Milton has drawn from the fable of Scylla (660).

649. On *either side, etc.:* The allegory concerning Sin and Death is a very finished piece, of its kind, though liable to objection when considered as a part of an epic poem. The genealogy of the several persons is contrived with great delicacy. Sin is the daughter of Satan, and Death the offspring of Sin. The incestuous mixture between Sin and Death, produces those monsters and Hell-hounds which,

from time to time, enter into the mother and tear the bowels of her who gave them birth. These are the terrors of an evil conscience, and the proper fruits of sin, which naturally arise from the apprehension of death. This is clearly intimated in the speech of sin. Addison further calls our attention to the justness of thought which is observed in the generation of these several symbolical persons, that Sin was produced upon the first revolt of Satan—that Death appeared soon after he was cast into Hell, and that the terrors of conscience were conceived at the gate of this place of torment. "This," says Stebbing, "is one of the most sublime passages in the poem. Addison is generally ingenious in his criticisms, but not elevated, and when he objected to Milton's having introduced an allegory, he shows that he was incapable of entering into the magnificent conceptions of his author. Sin and Death are not allegorical beings in Paradise Lost; but real and active existences. They would have been allegorical, speaking or contending among men, but are not so in an abode of spirits, and addressing the *Prince of darkness.* See James i. 15." These remarks are a sufficient answer, also, to Dr. Johnson's objections.

655.   *Cerberean mouths:* Mouths like those of the fabled infernal god Cerberus, who possessed three heads, and guarded the entrance in Tartarus, to prevent the escape of the condemned.

660.   *Scylla:* Scylla and Charybdis are the names, the former of a rock on the Italian shore, in the strait between Sicily and the main land; and the latter of a whirlpool, or strong eddy, over against it on the Sicilian side. The ancients connected a fabulous story with each name. Scylla was originally a beautiful woman, but was changed by Circe into a monster, the parts below her waist becoming a number of dogs, incessantly barking while she had twelve feet and hands, and six heads, with three rows of teeth. Terrified at this metamorphosis, she threw herself into the sea, and was changed into the rocks which bear her name. Charybdis was a greedy

woman, who stole the oxen of Hercules, and, for that offence, was turned into the gulf, or whirlpool, above mentioned—FISKE. See Ovid. Met. xiv. 59, etc.

661.   *Trinacrian:* Sicilian. *Calabria:* Southern part of Italy.

662.   *Uglier:* Uglier (beings). *Night-hag:* Witch.

665.   *The lab'ring moon:* The ancients believed the moon to be greatly affected by magical practices; and the Latin poets call the eclipses of the moon *labores lunce.* The three foregoing lines, and the former part of this, contain a short account of what was once believed, and in Milton's time not so ridiculous as now.—R.

666.   *The other shape:* The figure of Death, the regal crown upon his head, his menace of Satan, his advancing to the combat, the outcry at his birth, are circumstances that demand admiration. This description of Death, was probably suggested by Spenser, Faery Queen, book viii. cant. 7.

671.   *Furies:* An allusion to three daughters of Pluto, whose office it was to torment the guilty in Tartarus, and often to punish the living, by producing fatal epidemics, the devastations of war, insanity, and murders. They were represented with vipers twining among their hair, usually with frightful countenances, in dark and bloody robes, and holding the torch of discord or vengeance.—FISKE'S CL. MANUAL. 675, etc. That superior greatness and mock-majesty which is ascribed to the prince of fallen angels, is admirably preserved in every Portion of this book. His opening and closing the debate; his taking on himself that great enterprise, at the thought of which the whole infernal assembly trembled; his encountering the hideous phantom who guarded the gates of Hell, and appeared to him in all its terrors, are instances of that proud and daring mind which could not brook submission even to Omnipotence. The same boldness and intrepidity of behaviour discovers itself in the several adventures which he meets with during his passage through the regions of unformed

matter, and, particularly in his address to those tremendous Powers who are described (960–970) as presiding over it.—A.

678–79.   *Except:* This passage will not bear a critical examination, for it implies that God and his Son are created things; but the poet intended to convey no such idea. If for *created,* the word *existing* be substituted, the sense would be unembarassed. The word *but* is used with similar looseness in lines 333, 336. Richardson has pointed out a similar passage in Milton's Prose Works, "No place in Heaven and Earth, except Hell."

693.   *Conjured:* Leagued together. Virg. Georg. i. 280. "Et *conjuratos* coelum rescindere fratres."

709.   *Ophiuchus,* or *Serpentarius:* One of the *northern* constellations.

710.   Pliny has this expression (ii. 22). "Cometas horrentes crine sanguineo." The ancient poets frequently compare a hero in his shining armour, to a comets. Poetry delights in omens, prodigies and such wonderful events as were supposed to follow upon the appearance of comets, eclipses, and like events.—N.

715.   *Artillery:* Thunder.

716.   The *Caspian* is said to be subject to violent storms. Hor, Ode. ii. 9:2.

721.   *Once more:* In the person of Jesus Christ (734). Heb. ii. 14.

758.   *Out of thy head I sprung:* An allusion to the heathen fable of the goddess Minerva springing out of the head of Jupiter. Her appearance is represented as producing, among the heavenly beings, at first, amazement and terror; but afterwards securing the approbation and favour of a multitude of them. This representation exhibits the horror in which the idea of sinning against God was first regarded, and the change of views among the sinning angels, upon becoming accustomed to acts of transgression. The same thing is true among men, particularly among the young when led astray from a moral course. In the seventh and eighth chapters of Paul's Epistle to the Romans, and in the first chapter of the Epistle of James, may be found, also, a vivid personification of sin.

760.   *For a sign:* As a prodigy, or phenomenon.

767.   *Growing burthen:* This symbolizes the increasing atrocity and hideousness of a course of transgression, or its tendency to propagate itself.

772.   *Pitch:* Height.

787.   *Death:* Death is represented, in the Holy Scriptures, as the product of sin. Rom. v. 12, "By one man sin entered into the world, and death by sin, and so death hath passed upon all men, for that all have sinned."

789.   An imitation of Virg. Æn. ii. 53. "Insonuere cavae, gemitumque dedere cavenae."

795.   *Yelling monsters:* These creatures symbolize the pangs of remorse which torment the sinner, and his fearful apprehensions in prospect of death. See Heb. x. 27.

802.   *Rest:* See Isaiah lviii. 20, 21.

805–7.   There is a beautiful circumstance alluded to in these lines.—A.

807.   *His end, etc.:* Death *lives* by sin.

809.   The heathen poets make Jupiter *superior* to Fate. Iliad i. 5; Æn. iii. 375; iv. 614. But Milton, with great propriety, makes the fallen angels and Sin here attribute events to Fate, without any mention of the Supreme Being.—N.

813.   *Dint:* Stroke.

817.   *Dear Daughter:* Satan had now learned his *lore* or lesson, and the reader will observe how artfully he changes his language. He had said before (745), that he had never seen sight more detestable; but now it is *dear daughter,* and *my fair son.*

824.   *Both him and thee, etc.:* The reader will observe how naturally the three persons concerned in this allegory are tempted by one common interest to enter into a confederacy together, and how properly Sin is made the portress of Hell, and the only being that can open the gates to that world of torture.

827.   *Uncouth:* Unusual. *Sole:* Alone.

833.   *Purlieus:* Neighbourhood.

840.   *Bring ye:* It was Satan's horrid design to introduce sin and death into our world.

842.   *Buxom:* Yielding, flexible, from a Saxon word, signifying "to bend." The word has this sense in a prose sentence

of Milton. "Thinking thereby to make them more tractable and *buxom* to his government."—N.

850. *Due:* Right.

854. *Death:* The penalty of disobeying God.

855. *Living might:* Except that of God, at whose command Sin and Death were appointed to guard the gates of Hell.

856. *Owe I:* Sin refuses obedience to God, casts off allegiance to Him.

860. Sin was born in Heaven when Satan committed his first offence (864–5).

866. *Whom follow:* That is, whom shall I follow? Sin yields obedience to Satan. So every act of human transgression is represented in Scripture as an act of homage to Satan. John viii. 44; Ephes. ii. 1–3.

871. It is one great part of the poet's art, to know when to describe things in general, and when to be very circumstantial and particular. Milton has, in this and the following lines, shown his judgment in this respect. The first opening of the gates of Hell by Sin, is an incident of such importance, that every reader's attention must have been greatly excited, and, consequently, as highly gratified by the minute detail of particulars our author has given us. It may, with justice, be further observed, that in no part of the poem the versification is better accommodated to the sense. The drawing up of the portcullis, the turning of the key, the sudden shooting of the bolts, and the flying open of the doors, are, in some sort, described by the very break and sound of the verse.—T.

872. *Sad instrument of all our woe:* The escape of Satan to our world was the occasion of human sin and misery.

879–83. *On a sudden, etc.:* The description just given of the gates is highly poetical, and now of the opening of the gates. There is a harshness in the sound of the words, that happily corresponds to the meaning conveyed, or to the fact described. This correspondence of the sound of the language to the sense, is a great rhetorical beauty: in this case, it also admirably serves to impress the mind with horror.

883. See Virg. Georg. in 471, "Erebi de sedibus imis." *Erebus:* According to ideas of the Homeric and Hesiodic ages, the world or universe was a hollow globe, divided into two equal portions by the flat disk of the earth. The external shell of this globe is called by the poets *brazen and iron*, probably only to express its solidity. The superior hemisphere was named Heaven: the inferior one, *Tartarus*. The length of the diameter of the hollow sphere is thus given by Hesiod. It would take, he says, nine days for an anvil to fall from Heaven to Earth; and an equal space of time would be occupied by its fall from Earth to the bottom of Tartarus. The luminaries which gave light to gods and men, shed their radiance through all the interior of the upper hemisphere; while that of the inferior one was filled with gloom and darkness, and its still air was unmoved by any wind. Tartarus was regarded, at this period, as the prison of the gods, and not as the place of torment for wicked men, being to the gods what *Erebus* was to men—the abode of those who were driven from the supernal world. Erebus lay between the Earth and Hades, beneath the latter of which was Tartarus.—ANTHON.

883–4. *But to shut, etc.:* An impressive lesson is here incidentally conveyed—that it is easy to sin, but not so easy to avoid the penal consequences.

894–5. *Night:* By the Romans, Night was personified as the daughter of *Chaos.* Both are here represented as progenitors of Nature, by which the arranged creation is meant. Dropping the allegory, the idea conveyed is that night and chaos, or darkness and a confused state of matter, preceded the existence of nature, or of the universe in its fully arranged and organized form. Night and Chaos are represented as the monarchs of a confused state of the elements of things among which hot, cold, moist, or dry, like four fierce champions, are striving for the mastery. The false Epicurean theory of Creation is here alluded to, according to which the worlds were produced by a fortuitous concourse of atoms. "Chance governs all."

898. *For hot:* Ovid i. 19, etc. "Frigida pugnabant calidis, humentia siccis Mollia cum duris, sine pondere habentia pondus." Milton has, in this description, omitted all the puerilities that disfigure Ovid's.—N.

904. *Barca:* For the most part a desert country, on the northern coast of Africa, extending from the Syrtis Major as far as Egypt. *Cyrene* was the capital of Cyrenaica (which was included in Barca), on the shore of the Mediterranean, west of Egypt.

905. The atoms, or indivisible particles of matter, are compared, in respect to number and motion, to the sands of an African desert, which are mustered to side with, or assist, contending winds in their mutual struggles. *Poise their lighter wings:* Give weight, or ballast, to the lighter wings of the winds. An allusion is here made to the birds described by Pliny, as ballasting themselves with small stones when a storm rises; or, to the bees described by Virg. Georg. iv. 194.—R.

906. *To whom these most:* The reason why any one of these champions *rules* (though but for a *moment*), is, because the atoms of his faction *adhere most* to him; or, the meaning may be, to whatever side the atoms temporarily adhere, that side rules for the moment.—E. B.

910. *Wild abyss:* Milton's system of the universe is, in short, that the Empyrean Heaven, and Chaos, and Darkness, were before the Creation—Heaven above and Chaos beneath; and then, upon the rebellion of the angels, first Hell was formed out of Chaos, stretching far and wide *beneath*; and afterwards Heaven and Earth were formed—another world hanging *over* the realm of Chaos, and won from his dominion.—N.

912. Possessing neither sea nor shore, etc.

918. *Stood . . . and looked:* These words are to be transposed to make the sense plain; which is, that the wary Fiend stood on the brink of Hell, and looked a while into this wild abyss. A similar liberty is taken by the poet, in the transposition of words, in Book V. 368.

919. *Pondering his voyage:* In Satan's voyage through the chaos, there are several imaginary persons described as residing in that immense waste of matter. This may, perhaps, be conformable to the taste of those critics who are pleased with nothing in a poet which has not life and manners ascribed to it; but, for my own part, says Addison, I am pleased most with those passages in this description, which carry in them a greater measure of probability, and are such as might possibly have happened. Of this kind is his first mounting in the smoke that rises from the infernal pit; his falling into a cloud of nitre, and the like combustible materials, which, by their explosion, still hurried him onward in his voyage; his springing up like a pyramid of fire, with his laborious passage through that confusion of elements which the poet calls "the womb of Nature, and perhaps her grave."—A.

921. *Compare, etc.:* Virg. Ec. i. 24, "Parvis componere magna."

922. *Bellona:* The goddess of war.

927. *Vans:* Wings. As the air and water are both fluids, the metaphors taken from the one are often applied to the other, and flying is compared to sailing, and sailing to flying. Says Virg. Æn. iii. 520, "Velorum pandimus alas," and in Æn. i. 300. ". . . volat ille per aera magnum Remigio alarum." Newton has furnished examples also from Spenser.

933. *Pennons:* The common meaning is banners; but it probably is used for *pinions*, and is synonymous with *vans*, used above. *Plumb:* Perpendicularly.

935. *Ill chance:* An ill chance for mankind that he was so far speeded on his journey.—P.

938. *That fury stay'd:* That fiery rebuff ceased, quenched and put out by a soft quicksand. *Syrtis* is explained by *neither sea nor land*, exactly agreeing with Lucan. "Syrtes—in dubio pelagi, terraeque reliquit."

940. *Fares:* Goes.

942. *Behoves him, etc.:* It behoveth him more to use both his oars and his sails, as galleys do, according to the proverb, Remis velisque, with might and main.—H.

943. *Gryphon:* An imaginary animal, part eagle and part lion, said to watch over mines of gold, and whatever was hidden for safe keeping. The *Arimaspians* were a people of Scythia, who, according to the legend related by Herodotus, had but one eye, and waged a continual warfare with the griffons that guarded the gold which was found in great abundance where these people resided.

948. The difficulty of Satan's voyage is very well expressed by so many monosyllables, which cannot be pronounced but slowly, and with frequent pauses.—N.

956. *Nethermost:* While the *throne of Chaos* was above Hell, and, consequently, a part of the *abyss* was so, a part of that abyss was, at the same time, far below Hell; so far below; that when Satan went from Hell on his voyage, he fell in that *abyss* ten thousand fathoms deep (934), and the poet there adds that if it had not been for an accident, he had been falling down there to this hour; nay, it was *illimitable, and where light is lost.* Of course the abyss, considered as a whole, was *nethermost* in respect to Hell.—P.

964. *Orcus and Ades:* Orcus and Hades. These terms usually denote the abodes of departed spirits; sometimes are used as names of Pluto, the fabled deity that presides over those abodes. They are here personified, and occupy a place in the court of Chaos.

965-6. *Name, etc.:* There was a notion among the ancients of a certain deity whose very name they supposed capable of producing the most terrible effect which they therefore dreaded to pronounce. He was considered as possessing great power in incantations; and to have obtained this name from the power which he had of looking with impunity upon the Gorgon, that turned all other spectators to stone. The *dreaded name* of Demogorgon here stands for "the dreaded Demogorgon," by a common figure, used especially by the sacred writers. See Rev. xi. 13, "And in the earthquake were slain *names of men* seven thousand," meaning, of course, seven thousand men.—N. *Rumor next,*

etc.: Addison seems to disapprove of these fictitious beings, thinking them, I suppose (like Sin and Death), improper for an epic poem; but I see no reason why Milton may not be allowed to place such imaginary beings in the regions of Chaos, as well as Virgil described similar beings, Grief, and Fear, and Want, and Sleep, and Death, and Discord likewise, within the confines of Hell; and why what is accounted a beauty in one should be deemed a fault in the other? See Æn. vi. 273, etc., and Dryden's translation of the passage. Other writers have introduced, with general approbation, similar fictitious beings.—N.

966. *Embroiled:* Confusedly intermixed.

972. *Secrets:* Secret places is the more probable meaning: yet it may mean, secret counsels and transactions. See Book I. 167; VII. 95.—N.

981. This passage is thus paraphrased by Newton: My course directed may bring no little recompense and advantage to you, if I reduce that *lost region,* all usurpation being thence expelled, to her original darkness and your sway, which is the purport of my present journey, etc.

982. *Behoof:* Advantage. *Lost:* That is, to those whom he addressed, having been withdrawn from a chaotic condition.

999. *Can:* Can do.

1000. *So:* In this manner; that is, by keeping my residence on the frontiers, and doing all I can.

1002. *First Hell* (was encroached on).

1004. *Another world* (was encroached on). The term Heaven is here the starry heaven, which, together with our earth, constitutes the other "world" here mentioned.

1005-6. The idea may have been suggested by the *golden chain* with which Jupiter is described in the Iliad, book viii., as drawing up the earth. *Heaven,* in these lines, denotes the residence of Deity, and the abode of righteous men and angels, called the *empyreal Heaven,* line 1047. The question arises, how the *intestine broils,* originated by the fallen angels, had produced the encroachments above referred to? To this question, the answer may be rendered, that Hell was created out of chaotic materials to serve as a prison for the apostate angels; and that our world was created out of similar materials to furnish an abode for a holy race that might serve as a compensation for the loss of the fallen angels from the services of Heaven. See Book III. 678–80. The atoms from which Hell and the Earth were formed, previously to the "intestine broils" in the angelic family, belonged to the kingdom of Chaos and Old Night. See 345–386. Night's sceptre was thus *weakened* by the withdrawment of a part of her dominions.

1011.   *Find a shore:* A metaphor, expressive of his joy that now his travel and voyage should terminate; somewhat like that of one of the ancients who, reading a tedious book, and coming near to the end, cried, *I see land,* Terram video.—N.

1013.   *Like a pyramid of fire:* To take in the full meaning of the magnificent similitude, we must imagine ourselves in chaos, and a vast luminous body rising upward near the place where we are, so swiftly as to appear a continued track of light, and lessening to the view according to the increase of distance, till it end in a point, and then disappear; and all this must be supposed to strike our eye at one instant.—BEATTIE.

1017.   *Argo:* There was an ancient fable that two small islands, called *Symplegades,* at the mouth of the Thracian Bosphorus (Straits of Constantinople), floated about, and sometimes united to crush those vessels which chanced at the time to be passing through the Straits. The ship *Argo,* on its way to Colchis, had a narrow escape in passing, having lost the extremity of the stern.

1021–2.   *With difficulty, etc.:* These lines can be pronounced only with some effort, and hence are well adapted to impress the idea which they convey. The repetition of the idea also favors the same result.

1024.   *Amain:* Violently.

1028.   *Bridge, etc.:* It has been properly objected to this passage, that the same bridge is described in Book x. for several lines together, poetically and pompously, as a thing untouched before, and an incident to surprise the reader; and therefore the poet should not have anticipated it here.—N.

1029.   *Utmost orb:* The idea here conveyed is entirely different from what to most readers will seem the obvious one. In Book X. 302, the bridge is represented as "joining to the *wall* immoveable of this now fenceless world." The same thing is described (317) as "the outside base of this round world." In Book III, 74, 75, Satan is represented as ". . . Ready now To stoop with wearied wings and willing feet On the bare outside of this world, that seem'd Firm land embosom'd, without firmament, Uncertain which, in ocean or in air." A more full description of the same locality is furnished Book III. 417–430; 497–501 526–528; 540–543. The poet, in these passages, brings up before our imagination, an immense opaque hollow sphere, separating the reign of Chaos and Old Night from the solar and sidereal system.

1046.   *Weighs:* Lifts.

1047.   *Empyreal Heaven:* The highest and purest region of heaven, or simply, the pure and brilliant heaven, from a word signifying fire.

1048.   *Undetermined square or round:* Of no definite boundaries.

1052.   *Pendent world:* From Shakespeare's Measure for Measure, Act III. Scene 1.

1052–3.   *This pendent world:* The earth alone is not meant, but the new creation, Heaven and Earth, the whole orb of fixed stars, including the planets, the earth and the sun. In line 1004, Chaos had said, "Now lately, *Heav'n and Earth,* another *world.* Hung o'er my realm, linked in a golden chain." Satan had not yet seen the earth, nor any of those other luminous bodies; he was afterwards surprised *at the sudden view of all this world at once,* III. 542, having wandered long on the *outside* of it, till at last he saw our sun, and there was informed by the archangel Uriel, where the Earth and Paradise were, III. 722. *This pendent world,* therefore, must mean the whole world, in the sense of universe, then new created, which, when observed from a distance, *afar off,* appeared, in comparison with the empyreal Heaven, no bigger than a *star of smallest magnitude,* close to the moon, appears when compared with that body. How wonderful is the imagination of prodigious distance, exhibited in these lines, that after Satan had travelled on so far, and had come in view of the whole world, it should still appear, in comparison with the empyreal Heaven, no larger than the smallest star, and that star apparently yet smaller by its proximity to the moon! How beautiful, and how poetical also, thus to open the scene by degrees! Satan at first descries the whole world at a distance, Book II.; and then, as we learn in Book III., he discovers our planetary system, and the sun, and afterwards, by the direction of Uriel, the earth and neighbouring moon.—N.

1055.   *Hies:* Hastens. This progress is described in the next Book, 418–430; 498–590; 722–743.

—————————— *Questions for Consideration* ——————————

Using complete sentences, provide brief answers for the following questions:

1. Summarize the "debate" in hell between the fallen angels that occurs in Book II of *Paradise Lost*.

   _____

   _____

   _____

   _____

   _____

2. In your judgment, which of the fallen angels makes the weakest argument during the debate? the strongest? Explain your position.

   _____

   _____

   _____

   _____

   _____

3. Look up the definition of allegory and apply it to the depiction of Sin and Death in Book II of *Paradise Lost*. Are Sin and Death effective as allegorical characters? Why, or why not?

   _____

   _____

   _____

   _____

   _____

4. Does the fact that Satan often lacks important knowledge in Book II diminish his heroic stature? Explain.

   _____

   _____

   _____

   _____

   _____

5. After you have finished reading Book II, list the qualities that you like and/or dislike about Satan's characterization. What traits would you keep or delete? Clarify your position.

_____

_____

_____

_____

_____

———————————— *Writing Critically* ————————————

Select one of the topics listed below and compose a 500 word essay which discusses the topic fully. Support your thesis with evidence from the text and with critical and/or historical material. Use the space below for preparing to write the essay.

1. How would you reconstruct the "debate" in hell?

2. Compare the rhetorical style of at least two (2) of the fallen angels.

3. What makes the use of allegory effective or ineffective? Cite other allegorical works with which you are familiar.

4. Do a detailed character analysis of Milton's Satan, indicating both strong and weak points.

Prewriting Space:

_____

_____

_____

_____

_____

_____

_____

_____

_____

_____

_____

_____

_____

_____

_____

_____

_____

_____

Introduction

Wu Ch'eng-en (ca. 1506–ca. 1582)
Journey to the West (Monkey)

The selection which follows is a key episode from one of China's most appreciated novels, *Xiyouji*, known in English as the *Journey to the West* or, in the abridged translation of Arthur Waley, as *Monkey*. This lengthy narrative, which dates from the Ming dynasty (1368–1644), runs to one hundred chapters in the original (over 1500 pages in translation). It centers on the pilgrimage of a monk, Xuan Zang, who travels to India (to the west of China) to collect Buddhist scriptures or *sutras* for dissemination in China. His journey, which actually took place, lasted for seventeen years (629–645 A.D.), but the novel completes the folkloric transformation of an historical kernel into a labyrinth of fantasy and mythical adventure, much as the prehistoric Hellenic invasion of a city in Asia Minor resulted in the fables of the *Iliad* and the *Odyssey*. Through the resources of mythological invention, the Buddhist monk, often referred to in the novel by his religious name, Tripitaka, acquires some unusual companions: a talking pig, a repentant river monster, and a monkey who possesses many supernatural powers. The latter character (Sun Wu-kong or the Monkey King) becomes the focus of narrative attention. The completed text of the *Journey to the West* dates to 1592 and is attributed to Wu Ch'eng-en, who undoubtedly utilized earlier published versions of the fictionalized travels.

The novel in its final form reveals considerable interaction between oral and written traditions. Many episodes were elaborated, perhaps over centuries, by professional storytellers. As a result, the language of the entire work is mainly colloquial Chinese *(baihua)* as opposed to the learned or classical language *(wenyan)* of central importance in literary production in China until the twentieth century. At the same time, *Journey to the West* is composed of a mixture of prose and verse, and the vividly descriptive poetic passages found throughout the novel testify to a deep familiarity with the practice of written Chinese poetry. Yet the author

has shifted the norms of traditional Chinese lyric to suit the requirements of a rapidly moving narrative.

Journey to the West is often compared to literary works of other cultures. It is likely that portions are indebted to the *Ramayana*, an ancient Indian epic that features Hanumán, a magical monkey. Also, parallels have been found in works of the European Renaissance; such comparisons are tentative because of the many cultural differences between Orient and Occident. Even classifying the *Journey to the West* as a novel, a traditional European genre, is tricky because the work lacks the cohesiveness usually associated with the novel. (At the same time, it is relevant that the prose narratives of Rabelais and Cervantes, works to which Wu's text is often likened, are not uniformly regarded as novels by European and American critics.) In addition to Cervantes' *Don Quixote* and Rabelais's tales of Gargantua and Pantagruel, the *Journey to the West* has been compared to *The Faerie Queene*, a romance in verse by Edmund Spenser, another of Wu's sixteenth-century contemporaries. All of these lengthy narratives reveal loosely connected episodes, travels and quests, satire of social and religious institutions, a blend of fantasy and reality, and a mixture of serious and frivolous meanings. In each case, the reader is at times left wondering whether mere diversion is the only effect of the text and whether instruction—typically one of the goals of literary art during this period—has been cast aside. (It is useful to contrast a work like Chaucer's *Canterbury Tales*, where the pilgrimage remains a serious concern that accompanies the storytelling of the travelers.)

Whether considered strictly as amusement, a critique of the improprieties and decadence of the late Ming dynasty, or as a testimony to the virtues of Buddhism, the *Journey to the West* has captivated generations of Chinese. Especially popular are the chapters presented here, in which the mischievous Monkey King eats a vast number of the peaches of immortality and commits other misdeeds, thereby spoiling a celestial festival. (NW)

BIBLIOGRAPHY

Dudbridge, Glen. *The Hsi-yu Chi: A Study of Antecedents to the Sixteenth-Century Chinese Novel.* Cambridge: Cambridge University Press, 1970.

Hsia, C. T. The *Classic Chinese Novel: A Critical Introduction.* Bloomington: Indiana University Press, 1968.

Liu, Xiaolian. *The Odyssey of the Buddhist Mind: The Allegory of the Later Journey to the West.* New York: University Press of America, 1994.

Plaks, Andrew H. *The Four Masterworks of the Ming Novel.* Princeton: Princeton University Press, 1987.

Wallace, Nathaniel. "Mutability East and West: The Garden of Adonis and Longevity Mountain." *American Journal of Chinese Studies* 3.1 (1996): 1–21.

Wang, Jing. *The Story of Stone: Intertextuality, Ancient Chinese Stone Lore, and the Stone Symbolism of Dream of the Red Chamber, Water Margin, and The Journey to the West.* Durham, N. C.: Duke University Press, 1992.

Yu, Anthony C., trans. *The Journey to the West.* 4 vols. Chicago: University of Chicago Press, 1977–1983.

from The Journey to the West

Wu Ch'eng-en
Translated and edited by Anthony C. Yu

Five

The Great Sage, stealing elixir, disrupts the Peach Festival;

Many gods try to catch the monster, a rebel in Heaven.

Now we must tell you that the Great Sage, after all, was a monkey monster; in truth, he had no knowledge of his title or rank, nor did he care for the size of his salary. He did nothing but place his name on the Register. At his official residence he was cared for night and day by the attending official of the two departments. His sole concern was to eat three meals a day and to sleep soundly at night. Having neither duties nor worries, he was free and content to tour the mansions and meet friends, to make new acquaintances and form new alliances at his leisure. When he met the Three Pure Ones,[1] he addressed them as "Your Reverence"; and when he ran into the Four Emperors,[2] he would say, "Your Majesty." As for the Nine Luminaries,[3] the Generals of the Five Quarters,[4] the Twenty-Eight Constellations,[5] the Four Devarājas,[6] the Twelve Horary Branches,[7] the Five Elders of the Five Regions,[8] the Star Spirits of the entire Heaven, and the numerous gods of the Milky Way, he called them all brother and treated them in a fraternal manner. Today he toured the east, and tomorrow he wandered west. Going and coming on the clouds, he had no definite itinerary.

Early one morning, when the Jade Emperor was holding court, the Taoist immortal Hsü Ching-yang stepped from the ranks and went forward to memorialize, kowtowing, "The Great Sage, Equal to Heaven, has no duties at present and merely dawdles away his time. He has become quite chummy with the various Stars and Constellations of Heaven, calling them his friends regardless of whether they are his superiors or subordinates, and I fear that his idleness may lead to roguery. It would be better to give him some assignment so that he will not grow mischievous." When the Jade Emperor heard these words, he sent for the Monkey King at once, who came amiably. "Your Majesty," he said, "what promotion or reward did you have in mind for old Monkey when you called him?" "We perceive," said the Jade Emperor, "that your life is quite indolent, since you have nothing to do, and we have decided therefore to give you an assignment. You will temporarily take care of the Garden of Immortal Peaches. Be careful and diligent, morning and evening." Delighted, the Great Sage bowed deeply and grunted his gratitude as he withdrew.

He could not restrain himself from rushing immediately into the Garden of Immortal Peaches to inspect the place. A local spirit from the garden stopped him and asked, "Where is the Great Sage going?" "I have been authorized by the Jade Emperor," said the Great Sage "to look after the Garden of Immortal Peaches. I have come to conduct an inspection." The local spirit hurriedly saluted him and then called together all the stewards in charge of hoeing, watering, tending peaches, and cleaning and sweeping. They all came to kowtow to the Great Sage and led him inside. There he saw

---

Radiantly young and lovely,
On every trunk and limb—
Radiantly young and lovely blossoms filling
the trees,
And fruits on every trunk and limb weighing
down the stems.
The fruits, weighing down the stems, hang
like balls of gilt;
The blossoms, filling the trees, form tufts of
rouge.
Ever they bloom, and ever fruit-bearing, they
ripen in a thousand years;
Not knowing winter or summer, they lengthen
out to ten thousand years.
Those that first ripen
Glow like faces reddened with wine,
While those half-grown ones
Are stalk-held and green-skinned.
Encased in smoke their flesh retains their
green,
But sunlight reverts their cinnabar grace.
Beneath the trees are rare flowers and exotic
grass
Which colors, unfading in four seasons, re-
main the same.
The towers, the terraces, and the studios left
and right
Rise so high into the air that often cloud covers
are seen.
Not planted by the vulgar or the worldly of the
Dark City,
They are grown and tended by the Queen
Mother of the Jade Pool.[9]

The Great Sage enjoyed this sight for a long time
and then asked the local spirit, "How many trees
are there?" "There are three thousand six hundred," said the local spirit. "In the front are one
thousand two hundred trees with little flowers
and small fruits. These ripen once every three
thousand years, and after one taste of them a man
will become an immortal enlightened in the way,
with healthy limbs and a lightweight body. In the
middle are one thousand two hundred trees of
layered flowers and sweet fruits. They ripen once
every six thousand years. If a man eats them, he
will ascend to Heaven with the mist and never
grow old. At the back are one thousand two
hundred trees with fruits of purple veins and
pale yellow pits. These ripen once every nine
thousand years and, if eaten, will make a man's
age equal to that of Heaven and Earth, the sun
and the moon." Highly pleased by these words,
the Great Sage that very day made thorough inspection of the trees and a listing of the arbors
and pavilions before returning to his residence.
From then on, he would go there to enjoy the
scenery once every three or four days. He no
longer consorted with his friends, nor did he take
any more trips.

One day he saw that more than half of the
peaches on the branches of the older trees had
ripened, and he wanted very much to eat one and
sample its novel taste. Closely followed, however, by the local spirit of the garden, the stewards, and the divine attendants of the Equal to
Heaven Residence, he found it inconvenient to
do so. He therefore devised a plan on the spur of
the moment and said to them, "Why don't you
all wait for me outside and let me rest a while in
this arbor?" The various immortals withdrew accordingly. That Monkey King then took off his
cap and robe and climbed up onto a big tree. He
selected the large peaches that were thoroughly
ripened and, plucking many of them, ate to his
heart's content right on the branches. Only after
he had his fill did he jump down from the tree.
Pinning back his cap and donning his robe, he
called for his train of followers to return to the
residence. After two or three days, he used the
same device to steal peaches to gratify himself
once again.

One day the Lady Queen Mother decided to
open wide her treasure chamber and to give a
banquet for the Grand Festival of Immortal
Peaches, which was to be held in the Palace of the
Jasper Pool. She ordered the various Immortal
Maidens—Red Gown, Blue Gown, White Gown,
Black Gown, Purple Gown, Yellow Gown, and
Green Gown—to go with their flower baskets to
the Garden of Immortal Peaches and pick the
fruits for the festival. The seven maidens went to
the gate of the garden and found it guarded by
the local spirit, the stewards, and the ministers
from the two departments of the Equal to Heaven
Residence. The girls approached them, saying,
"We have been ordered by the Queen Mother to
pick some peaches for our banquet." "Divine
maidens," said the local spirit, "please wait a
moment. This year is not quite the same as last
year. The Jade Emperor has put in charge here
the Great Sage, Equal to Heaven, and we must
report to him before we are allowed to open the
gate." "Where is the Great Sage?" asked the
maidens. "He is in the garden," said the local
spirit. "Because he is tired, he is sleeping alone
in the arbor." "If that's the case," said the maidens, "let us go and find him, for we cannot be
late." The local spirit went into the garden with
them; they found their way to the arbor but saw
no one. Only the cap and the robe were left in the
arbor. but there was no person to be seen. The
Great Sage, you see, had played for a while and

eaten a number of peaches. He had then changed himself into a figure only two inches high and, perching on the branch of a large tree, had fallen asleep under the cover of thick leaves. "Since we came by imperial decree," said the Seven-Gown Immortal Maidens, "how can we return empty-handed, even though we cannot locate the Great Sage?" One of the divine officials said from the side, "Since the divine maidens have come by decree, they should wait no longer. Our Great Sage has a habit of wandering off somewhere, and he must have left the garden to meet his friends. Go and pick your peaches now, and we shall report the matter for you." The Immortal Maidens followed his suggestion and went into the grove to pick their peaches.

They gathered two basketfuls from the trees in front and filled three more baskets from the trees in the middle. When they went to the trees at the back of the grove, they found that the flowers were sparse and the fruits scanty. Only a few peaches with hairy stems and green skins were left, for the fact is that the Monkey King had eaten all the ripe ones. Looking this way and that, the Seven Immortal Maidens found on a branch pointing southward one single peach that was half white and half red. The Blue Gown Maiden pulled the branch down with her hand, and the Red Gown Maiden, after plucking the fruit, let the branch snap back up into its position. This was the very branch on which the transformed Great Sage was sleeping. Startled by her, the Great Sage revealed his true form and whipped out from his ear the golden-hooped rod. One wave and it had the thickness of a rice bowl. "From what region have you come, monsters," he cried, "that you have the gall to steal my peaches?" Terrified, the Seven Immortal Maidens knelt down together and pleaded, "Let the Great Sage calm himself! We are not monsters, but the Seven-Gown Immortal Maidens sent by the Lady Queen Mother to pluck the fruits needed for the Grand Festival of Immortal Peaches, when the treasure chamber is opened wide. We just came here and first saw the local spirit of the garden, who could not find the Great Sage. Fearing that we might be delayed in fulfilling the command of the Queen Mother, we did not wait for the Great Sage but proceeded to pluck the peaches. We beg you to forgive us." When the Great Sage heard these words, his anger changed to delight. "Please arise, divine maidens," he said. "Who is invited to the banquet when the Queen Mother opens wide her treasure chamber?" "The last festival had its own set of rules," said the Immortal Maidens, "and

those invited were: the Buddha, the Bodhisattvas, the holy monks, and the arhats of the Western Heaven; Kuan-yin from the South Pole; the Holy Emperor of Great Mercy of the East, the Immortals of Ten Continents and Three Islands; the Dark Spirit of the North Pole; the Great Immortal of the Yellow Horn from the Imperial Center. These were the Elders from the Five Quarters. In addition, there were the Star Spirits of the Five Poles, the Three Pure Ones, the Four Deva Kings, the Heavenly Deva of the Great Monad, and the rest from the Upper Eight Caves. From the Middle Eight Caves there were the Jade Emperor, the Nine Heroes, the Immortals of the Seas and Mountains; and from the Lower Eight Caves, there were the Pope of Darkness and the Terrestrial Immortals. The gods and devas, both great and small, of every palace and mansion, will be attending this happy Festival of the Immortal Peaches." "Am I invited?" asked the Great Sage, laughing. "We haven't heard your name mentioned," said the Immortal Maidens. "I am the Great Sage, Equal to Heaven," said the Great Sage. "Why shouldn't I, old Monkey, be made an honored guest at the party?" "Well, we told you the rule for the last festival," said the Immortal Maidens, "but we do not know what will happen this time." "You are right," said the Great Sage, "and I don't blame you. You all just stand here and let old Monkey go and do a little detection to find out whether he's invited or not."

Dear Great Sage! He made a magic sign and recited a spell, saying to the various Immortal Maidens, "Stay! Stay! Stay!" This was the magic of immobilization, the effect of which was that the Seven Gown Immortal Maidens all stood wide-eyed and transfixed beneath the peach trees. Leaping out of the garden, the Great Sage mounted his hallowed cloud and headed straight for the Jasper Pool. As he journeyed, he saw over there

A skyful of holy mist with sparkling light,

And sacred clouds of five colors passing unendingly.

The cries of white cranes resounded in the nine Heavens;

The fine color of red blossoms spread through a thousand leaves.

Right in this midst an Immortal now appeared

With a face of natural beauty and features most distinguished.

His spirit glowed like a rainbow dancing in the air.

From his waist hung the list untouched by birth or death.

His name, the Great Joyful Immortal of Naked Feet.[10]

Going to the Peach Festival, he would add to his age.

That Great Immortal of Naked Feet ran right into the Great Sage, who, his head bowed, was just devising a plan to deceive the real Immortal. Since he wanted to go in secret to the festival, he asked, "Where is the Venerable Wisdom going?" The Great Immortal said, "On the kind Invitation of the Queen Mother, I am going to the happy Festival of Immortal Peaches." "The Venerable Wisdom has not yet learned of what I'm about to say," said the Great Sage. "Because of the speed of my cloud-somersault, the Jade Emperor has sent old Monkey out to all five thoroughfares to invite people to go first to the Hall of Perfect Light for a rehearsal of ceremonies before attending the banquet." Being a sincere and honest man, the Great Immortal took the lie for the truth, though he protested, "In years past we rehearsed right at the Jasper Pool and expressed our gratitude there. Why do we have to go to the Hall of Perfect Light for rehearsal this time before attending the banquet?" Nonetheless, he had no choice but to change the direction of his hallowed cloud and go straight to the Hall.

Treading the cloud, the Great Sage recited a spell and, with one shake of his body, changed into the form of the Great Immortal of Naked Feet. It did not take him very long before he reached the treasure chamber. He stopped his cloud and walked softly inside. There he found

Swirling waves of ambrosial fragrance,
Dense layers of holy mist,
A jade terrace decked with ornaments,
A chamber full of the life force,
Ethereal shapes of the phoenix soaring and the argus rising,
And undulant forms of gold blossoms with stems of jade.
Set upon there were the Screen of Nine Phoenixes in Twilight,
The Beacon Mound of Eight Treasures and Purple Mist,
A table inlaid with five-color gold,
And a green jade pot of a thousand flowers.
On the tables were dragon livers and phoenix marrow,
Bear paws and the lips of apes.[11]
Most tempting was every item of the hundred delicacies,
And most succulent the color of every kind of fruit and food.

Everything was laid out in an orderly fashion, but no deity had yet arrived for the feast. Our Great Sage could not make an end of staring at the scene when he suddenly felt the overpowering aroma of wine. Turning his head, he saw, in the long corridor to the right, several wine-making divine officials and grain-mashing stewards. They were giving directions to the few Taoists charged with carrying water and the boys who took care of the fire in washing out the barrels and scrubbing the jugs. For they had already finished making the wine, rich and mellow as the juices of jade. The Great Sage could not prevent the saliva from dripping out of the corner of his mouth, and he wanted to have a taste at once, except that the people were all standing there. He therefore resorted to magic. Plucking a few hairs, he threw them into his mouth and chewed them to pieces before spitting them out. He recited a spell and cried "Change!" They changed into many sleep-inducing insects, which landed on the people's faces. Look at them, how their hands grow weak, their heads droop, and their eyelids sink down. They dropped their activities, and all fell sound asleep. The Great Sage then took some of the rare delicacies and choice dainties and ran into the corridor. Standing beside the jars and leaning on the barrels, he abandoned himself to drinking. After feasting for a long time, he became thoroughly drunk, but he turned this over in his mind, "Bad! Bad! In a little while, when the invited guests arrive, won't they be indignant with me? What will happen to me once I'm caught? I'd better go back home now and sleep it off!"

Dear Great Sage! Reeling from side to side, he stumbled along solely on the strength of wine, and in a moment he lost his way. It was not the Equal to Heaven Residence that he went to, but the Tushita Palace. The moment he saw it, he realized his mistake. "The Tushita Palace is at the uppermost of the thirty-three Heavens," he said, "the Griefless Heaven which is the home of the Most High Lao Tzu. How did I get here? No matter, I've always wanted to see this old man but have never found the opportunity. Now that it's on my way, I might is well pay him a visit." He straightened out his attire and pushed his way in, but Lao Tzu was nowhere to be seen. In fact, there was not a trace of anyone. The fact of the matter is that Lao Tzu, accompanied by the

Aged Buddha Dīpaṃkara, was giving a lecture on the tall, three-storied Red Mound Elixir Platform. The various divine youths, commanders, and officials were all attending the lecture, standing on both sides of the platform. Searching around, our Great Sage went all the way to the alchemical room. He found no one but saw fire burning in an oven beside the hearth, and around the oven were five gourds in which finished elixir was stored. "This thing is the greatest treasure of immortals," said the Great Sage happily. "Since old Monkey has understood the Way and comprehended the mystery of the Internal's identity with the External, I have also wanted to produce some golden elixir on my own to benefit people. While I have been too busy at other times even to think about going home to enjoy myself, good fortune has met me at the door today and presented me with this! As long as Lao Tzu is not around, I'll take a few tablets and try the taste of something new." He poured out the contents of all the gourds and ate them like fried beans.

In a moment, the effect of the elixir had dispelled that of the wine, and he again thought to himself, "Bad! Bad! I have brought on myself calamity greater than Heaven! If the Jade Emperor has knowledge of this, it'll be difficult to preserve my life! Go! Go! Go! I'll go back to the Region Below to be a king." He ran out of the Tushita Palace and, avoiding the former way, left by the West Heavenly Gate, making himself invisible by the magic of body concealment. Lowering the direction of his cloud, he returned to the Flower-Fruit Mountain. There he was greeted by flashing banners and shining spears, for the four mighty commanders and the monster kings of seventy-two caves were engaging in a military exercise. "Little ones," the Great Sage called out loudly, "I have returned!" The monsters dropped their weapons and knelt down, saying, "Great Sage! What laxity of mind! You left us for so long, and did not even once visit us to see how we were doing." "It's not that long!" said the Great Sage. "It's not that long!" They walked as they talked, and went deep inside the cave dwelling. After sweeping the place clean and preparing a place for him to rest, and after kowtowing and doing homage, the four mighty commanders said, "The Great Sage has been living for over a century in Heaven. May we ask what appointment he actually received?" "I recall that it's been but half a year," said the Great Sage, laughing. "How can you talk of a century?" "One day in Heaven," said the commanders, "is equal to one year on Earth." The Great Sage said, "I am glad to say that the Jade Emperor this time was more favorably disposed toward me, and he did indeed appoint me Great Sage, Equal to Heaven. An official residence was built for me, and two departments—Peace and Quiet, and Serene Spirit—were established, with bodyguards and attendants in each department. Later, when it was

found that I carried no responsibility, I was asked to take care of the Garden of Immortal Peaches. Recently the Lady Queen Mother gave the Grand Festival of Immortal Peaches, but she did not invite me. Without waiting for her invitation, I went first to the Jasper Pool and secretly consumed the food and wine. Leaving that place, I staggered into the palace of Lao Tzu and finished up all the elixir stored in five gourds. I was afraid that the Jade Emperor would be offended, and so I decided to walk out of the Heavenly Gate."

The various monsters were delighted by these words, and they prepared a banquet of fruits and wine to welcome him. A stone bowl was filled with coconut wine and presented to the Great Sage, who took a mouthful and then exclaimed with a grimace, "It tastes awful! Just awful!" "The Great Sage," said Pêng and Pa, the two commanders, "has grown accustomed to tasting divine wine and food in Heaven. Small wonder that coconut wine now seems hardly delectable. But the proverb says, 'Tasty or not, it's water from home!'" "And all of you are, related or not, people from home!" said the Great Sage. "When I was enjoying myself this morning at the Jasper Pool, I saw many jars and jugs in the corridor full of the juices of jade, which you have never savored. Let me go back and steal a few bottles to bring down here. Just drink half a cup, and each one of you will live long without growing old." The various monkeys could not contain their delight. The Great Sage immediately left the cave and, with one somersault, went directly back to the Festival of Immortal Peaches, again using the magic of body concealment. As he entered the doorway of the Palace of the Jaspar Pool, he saw that the wine makers, the grain mashers, the water carriers, and the fire tenders were still asleep and snoring. He took two large bottles, one under each arm, and carried two more in his hands. Reversing the direction of his cloud, he returned to the monkeys in the cave. They held their own Festival of Immortal Wine, with each one drinking a few cups, which incident we shall relate no further.

Now we tell you about the Seven-Gown Immortal Maidens, who did not find a release from the Great Sage's magic of immobilization until a whole day had gone by. Each one of them then took her flower basket and reported to the Queen Mother, saying, "We are delayed because the Great Sage, Equal to Heaven, imprisoned us with his magic." "How many baskets of Immortal peaches have you gathered?" asked the Queen Mother. "Only two baskets of small peaches, and three of medium-sized peaches," said the Immortal Maidens, "for when we went to the back of the grove, there was not even half a large one left! We think the Great Sage must have eaten them all. As we went looking for him, he unexpectedly made his appearance and threatened us with violence and beating. He also questioned us about who had been invited to the banquet, and we gave him a thorough account of the last festival. It was then that he bound us with a spell, and we didn't know where he went. It was only a moment ago that we found release and so could come back here."

When the Queen Mother heard these words, she went immediately to the Jade Emperor and presented him with a full account of what had taken place. Before she finished speaking, the group of wine makers together with the various divine officials also came to report: "Someone unknown to us has vandalized the Festival of Immortal Peaches. The juice of jade, the eight dainties, and the hundred delicacies have all been stolen or eaten up." Four royal preceptors then came up to announce, "The Supreme Patriarch of Tao has arrived." The Jade Emperor went out with the Queen Mother to greet him. Having paid his respects to them, Lao Tzu said, "There are, in the house of this old Taoist, some finished Golden Elixir of Nine Turns,[12] which are reserved for the use of Your Majesty during the next Grand Festival of Cinnibar. Strange to say, they have been stolen by some thief, and I have come specifically to make this known to Your Majesty." This report stunned the Jade Emperor. Presently the officials from the Equal to Heaven Residence came to announce, kowtowing, "The Great Sage Sun has not been discharging his duties of late. He went out yesterday and still has not yet returned. Moreover, we do not know where he went." These words gave the Jade Emperor added anxiety. Next came the Great Immortal of Naked Feet, who prostrated himself and said, "Yesterday, in response to the Queen Mother's invitation, your subject was on his way to attend the festival when he met by chance the Great Sage, Equal to Heaven. The Sage said to your subject that Your Majesty had ordered him to send your subject first to the Hall of Perfect Light for a rehearsal of ceremonies before attending the banquet. Your subject followed his direction and duly went to the Hall. But I did not see the dragon chariot and the phoenix carriage of Your Majesty, and therefore hastened to come here to wait upon you." More astounded than ever, the Jade Emperor said, "This fellow now falsifies Imperial decrees and deceives my worthy ministers! Let the Divine Minister of Detection quickly locate his whereabouts!"

The minister received his order and left the palace to make a thorough investigation. After obtaining all the details, he returned presently to report, "The person who has so profoundly disturbed Heaven is none other than the Great Sage, Equal to Heaven." He then gave a repeated account of all the previous incidents, and the Jade Emperor was furious. He at once commanded the Four Great Devarājas to assist Devarāja Li and Prince Naṭa. Together, they called up the Twenty-Eight Constellations, the Nine Luminaries, the Twelve Horary Branches, the Fearless Guards of Five Quarters,[13] the Four Temporal Guardians,[14] the Stars of East and West, the Gods of North and South, the Deities of the Five Mountains and the Four Rivers,[15] the Star Spirits of the entire Heaven, and a hundred thousand celestial soldiers. They were ordered to set up eighteen sets of cosmic net, to journey to the Region Below, to encircle completely the Flower-Fruit Mountain, and to capture the rogue and bring him to justice. All the deities immediately alerted their troops and departed from the Heavenly Palace. As they left, this was the spectacle of the expedition:

Yellow with dust, the churning wind concealed the dark'ning sky;

Reddish with clay, the rising fog o'erlaid the dusky world.

Because an impish monkey insulted the Highest Lord,

The saints of all Heaven descended to this mortal Earth.

Those Four Great Devarājas,

Those Fearless Guards of Five Quarters—

Those Four Great Deva Kings made up the main command;

Those Fearless Guards or Five Quarters moved countless troops.

Li, the Pagoda Bearer, gave orders from the army's center.

With the fierce Naṭa as the captain of his vanward forces.

The Star of Rāhu, at the forefront, made the roll call:

The Star of Ketu, noble and tall, brought up the rear;

Sōma, the moon, displayed a spirit most eager;

Āditya, the sun, was all shining and radiant.

Heroes of special talents were the Stars of Five Phases.

The Nine Luminaries most relished a good battle.

The Horary Branches of Tzu, Wu, Mao, and Yao—

They were all celestial guardians of titanic strength.

To the east and west, the Five Plagues[16] and the Five Mountains!

To the left and right, the Six Gods of Darkness and the Six Gods of Light!

Above and below, the Dragon Gods of the Four Rivers!

And in tightest formation, the Twenty-Eight Constellations![17]

Citrā, Svātī, Viśākhā, and Anurādhā were the captains.

Revatī, Aśvinī, Apabharanī, and Kṛttikā knew combat well.

Uttara-Aṣādhā, Abhijit, Śravanā, Śraviṣṭha, Śatabhiṣā. Pūrva-Proṣṭhapada, Uttara-Proṣṭhapada,

Rohiṇī, Mūlabarhaṇī, Pūrva-Aṣādhā—every one an able star!

Punarvasu, Tiṣya, Aślesā, Maghā, Pūrva-Phalgunī, Uttara-Phagunī, and Hastā—

All brandished swords and spears to show their power.

Stopping the cloud and lowering the mist they came to this mortal world

And pitched their tents before the Mountain of Flower and Fruit.

The poem says:

Many are the forms of the changeful Heaven-born Monkey King!

Snatching wine and stealing elixir, he revels in his mountain lair,

Since he has wrecked the Grand Festival of Immortal Peaches.

A hundred thousand soldiers of Heaven now spread the net of God. Devarāja Li now gave the order for the celestial soldiers to pitch their tents, and a cordon was drawn so tightly around the Flower-Fruit Mountain that not even water could escape! Moreover, eighteen sets of cosmic net were spread out above and below the region, and the Nine luminaries were then ordered to go into battle. They led their troops and advanced to the cave, in front of which they found a troop of monkeys, both great and small, prancing about playfully. "Little monsters over there!" cried one of the Star Spirits in a severe voice, "where is your Great Sage? We are Heavenly deities sent here from the Region Above to subdue your rebellious Great Sage. Tell him to come here quickly and surrender. If he but utters half a 'No,' all of you will be executed." Hastily the little monsters reported inside, "Great Sage, dis-

aster! Disaster! Outside there are nine savage deities who claim that they are sent from the Region Above to subdue the Great Sage."

Our Great Sage was just sharing the Heavenly wine with the four mighty commanders and the monster kings of seventy-two caves. Hearing this announcement, he said in a most nonchalant manner, "'If you have wine today, get drunk today; mind not the troubles in front of your door!'" Scarcely had he uttered this proverb when another group of imps came leaping and said, "Those nine savage gods are trying to provoke battle with foul words and nasty language." "Don't listen to them," said the Great Sage, laughing. "'Let us seek today's pleasure in poetry and wine, and cease asking when we may achieve glory or fame.'" Hardly had he finished speaking when still another flock of imps arrived to report, "Father, those nine savage gods have broken down the door, and are about to fight their way in!" "The reckless, witless deities!" said the Great Sage angrily. "They really have no manners! I was not about to quarrel with them. Why are they abusing me to my face?" He gave the order for the One-Horn Demon King to lead the monster kings of seventy-two caves to battle, adding that old Monkey and the four mighty commanders would follow in the rear. The Demon King swiftly led his troops of ogres to go out to fight, but they were ambushed by the Nine Luminaries and pinned down right at the head of the sheet iron bridge.

At the height of the melee, the Great Sage arrived. "Make way!" he yelled, whipping out his iron rod. One wave of it and it was as thick as a rice bowl and about twelve feet long. The Great Sage plunged into battle, and none of the Nine Luminaries dared oppose him. In a moment, they were all beaten back. When they regrouped themselves again in battle formation, the Nine Luminaries stood still and said, "You senseless pi-ma-wên! You are guilty of the ten evils.[18] You first stole peaches and then wine, utterly disrupting the Grand Festival of Immortal Peaches. You also robbed Lao Tzu of his immortal elixir, and then you had the gall to plunder the imperial winery for your personal enjoyment. Don't you realize that you have piled up sin upon sin?" "Indeed," said the Great Sage, "these several incidents did occur! But what do you intend to do now?" The Nine Luminaries said, "We received the golden decree of the Jade Emperor to lead our troops here to subdue you. Submit at once, and spare these creatures from being slaughtered. If not, we shall level this mountain and over turn this cave!" "How great is your magical power, silly gods," retorted the Great Sage angrily, "that you dare to mouth such foolhardy words? Don't go away! Have a taste of old Monkey's rod!" The Nine Luminaries mounted a joint attack, but the Handsome Monkey King was not in the least intimidated. He wielded his golden-hooped rod, parrying left and right, and fought the Nine Luminaries until they were thoroughly exhausted. Every one of them turned around and fled, his weapons trailing behind him. Running into the tent at the center of their army, they said to the Pagoda Bearer Devarāja, "That Monkey King is indeed an intrepid warrior! We cannot withstand him, and have returned defeated." Devarāja Li then ordered the Four Great Devarājas and the Twenty-Eight Constellations to go out together to do battle. Without displaying the slightest panic, the Great Sage also ordered the One-Horn Demon King, the monster kings of seventy-two caves, and the four mighty commanders to range themselves in battle formation in front of the cave. Look at this all-out battle! It was truly terrifying with

The cold, soughing wind,
The dark, dreadful fog.
On one side, the colorful banners fluttered;
On the other, lances and halberds glimmered.
There were row upon row of shining helmets,
And coat upon coat of gleaming armor.
Row upon row of helmets shining in the sunlight
Resembled silver bells whose chimes echoed in the sky;
Coat upon coat of gleaming armor rising clifflike in layers
Seemed like glaciers crushing the earth.
The giant scimitars
Flew and flashed like lightning;
The mulberry-white spears,
Could pierce even mist and cloud!
The crosslike halberds
And tiger-eye lashes
Were arranged like thick rows of hemp;
The green swords of bronze
And four-sided shovels
Crowded together like trees in a dense forest.
Curved bows, crossbows, and stout arrows with eagle plumes,
Short staffs and snakelike lances—all could kill or maim.
That compliant rod, which the Great Sage owned,
Kept tossing and turning in this battle with gods.
They fought till the air was rid of birds flying by;

Wolves and tigers were driven from within the mount;
The planet was darkened by hurtling rocks and stones,
And the cosmos bedimmed by flying dust and dirt.
The clamor and clangor disturbed Heaven and Earth;
The scrap and scruffle alarmed both demons and gods.

Beginning with the battle formation at dawn, they fought until the sun sank down behind the western hills. The One-Horn Demon King and the monster kings of seventy-two caves were all taken captive by the forces of Heaven. Those who escaped were the four mighty commanders and the troop of monkeys, who hid themselves deep inside the Water-Curtain Cave. With his single rod, the Great Sage withstood in midair the Four Great Devarājas, Li the Pagoda Bearer, and Prince Naṭa and battled with them for a long time. When he saw that evening was approaching, the Great Sage plucked a handful of hairs, threw them into his mouth, and chewed them to pieces. He spat them out, crying, "Change!" They changed at once into many thousands of Great Sages, each employing a golden-hooped rod! They beat back Prince Naṭa and defeated the Five Devarājas.

In triumph the Great Sage collected back his hairs and hurried back to his cave. Soon, at the head of the sheet iron bridge, he was met by the four mighty commanders leading the rest of the monkeys. As they kowtowed to receive him they cried three times, sobbing aloud, and then they laughed three times, hee-heeing and ho-hoing. The Great Sage said, "Why do you all laugh and cry when you see me?" "When we fought with the Deva Kings this morning," said the four mighty commanders, "the monster kings of seventy-two caves and the One-Horn Demon King were all taken captive by the gods. We were the only ones who managed to escape alive, and that is why we cried. Now we see that the Great Sage has returned unharmed and triumphant, and so we laugh as well." "Victory and defeat," said the Great Sage, "are the common experiences of a soldier. The ancient proverb says, 'You may kill ten thousand of your enemies, but you will lose three thousand of your allies!' Moreover, those cheiftans who have been captured are tigers and leopards, wolves and insect badgers and foxes, and the like. Not a single member of our own kind has been hurt. Why then should we be disconsolate? Although our adversaries have been beaten back by my magic of body division they are still encamped at the foot of our mountain. Let us be most vigilant, therefore, in our defense. Have a good meal, rest well, and conserve your energy. When morning comes, watch me perform a great magic and capture some of these generals from Heaven, so that our comrades may be avenged." The four mighty commanders drank a few bowls of coconut wine with the host of monkeys and went to sleep peacefully. We shall speak no more of them.

When those four Devartājas retired their troops and stopped their fighting, each one of the Heavenly commanders came to report his accomplishment. There were those who had captured lions and elephants and those who had apprehended wolves, crawling creatures, and foxes.

Not a single monkey monster, however, had been seized. The camp was then secured, a great tent was pitched and those commanders with meritorious services were rewarded. The soldiers in charge of the cosmic nets were ordered to carry bells and were given passwords. They encircled the Flower-Fruit Mountain to await the great battle of the next day, and each soldier everywhere diligently kept his watch. So this is the situation:

The impish monkey in rebellion disturbs Heaven and Earth.

But the net is spread and open, ready night and day.

We do not know what took place after the next morning, and you must listen to the explanation in the next chapter.

Six

Kuan-yin, attending the banquet, inquires into the affair; The Little Sage, exerting his power, subdues the Great Sage.

For the moment we shall not tell you about the siege of the gods or the Great Sage at rest. We speak instead of the Great Compassionate Deliverer, the Efficacious Bodhisattva Kuan-yin from the Potalaka Mountain of the South Sea.[19] Invited by the Lady Queen Mother to attend the Grand Festival of Immortal Peaches, she arrived at the treasure chamber of the Jasper Pool with her senior disciple, Hui-an. There they found the whole place desolate and the banquet tables in utter disarray. Although several members of the Heavenly pantheon were present, none was seated. Instead, they were all engaged in vigorous exchanges and discussions. After the Bodhisattva had greeted the various deities, they told her what had occurred. "Since there will be no festival," said the Bodhisattva, "nor any raising of cups, all of you might as well come with this humble cleric to see the Jade Emperor." The gods followed her gladly, and they went to the entrance to the Hall of Perfect Light. There the Bodhisattva was met by the Four Heavenly Preceptors and the Immortal of Naked Feet, who recounted how the celestial soldiers, ordered by an enraged Jade Emperor to capture the monster, had not yet returned. The Bodhisattva said, "I would like to have an audience with the Jade Emperor. May I trouble one of you to announce

my arrival?" The Heavenly Preceptor Ch'iu Hung-chi went at once into the Treasure Hall of Divine Mists and, having made his report, invited Kuan-yin to enter. Lao Tzu then took the upper seat with the Emperor, while the Lady Queen Mother was in attendance behind the throne.

The Bodhisattva led the crowd inside. After paying homage to the Jade Emperor, they also saluted Lao Tzu and the Queen Mother. When each of them was seated, she asked, "How is the Grand Festival of Immortal Peaches?" "Every year when the Festival has been given," said the Jade Emperor, "we have thoroughly enjoyed ourselves. This year it has been completely ruined by a baneful monkey, leaving us with nothing but an invitation to disappointment." "Where did this baneful monkey come from?" asked the Bodhisattva. "He was born of a stone egg on top of the Flower-Fruit Mountain of the Ao-lai Country at the East Pūrvavideha Continent," said the Jade Emperor. "At the moment of his birth, two beams of golden light flashed immediately from his eyes, reaching as far as the Palace of the Polestar. We did not think much of that, but he later became a monster, subduing the Dragon and taming the Tiger as well as eradicating his name from the Register of Death. When the Dragon Kings and the Kings of the Underworld brought the matter to our attention, we wanted to capture him. The Star of Long Life, however, observed that all the beings of the three regions which possessed the nine apertures could attain immortality. We therefore decided to educate and nurture the talented monkey and summoned him to the Region Above. He was appointed to the post of pi-ma-wên at the Imperial stables, but taking offense at the lowliness of his position, he left Heaven in rebellion. We then sent Devarāja and Prince Naṭa to ask for his submission by proclaiming a decree of pacification. He was brought again to the Region Above and was appointed the Great Sage, Equal to Heaven—a rank without compensation. Since he had nothing to do but to wander east and west, we feared that he might cause further trouble. So he was asked to look after the Garden of Immortal Peaches. But he broke the Law and ate all the large peaches from the oldest trees. By then, the banquet was about to be given. As a person without salary he was, of course, not invited: nonetheless, he plotted to deceive the Immortal of Naked Feet and managed to sneak into the banquet by assuming the Immortal's appearance. He finished off all the divine wine and food, after which he also stole Lao Tzu's elixir and took away a considerable quantity of imperial wine for the enjoyment of his mountain monkeys. Our mind has been sorely vexed by this, and we therefore sent a hundred thousand celestial soldiers with cosmic nets to capture him. We haven't yet received today's report on how the battle is faring."

When the Bodhisattva heard this, she said to Disciple Hui-an, "You must leave Heaven at once, go down to the Flower-Fruit Mountain, and inquire into the military situation. If the enemy is engaged, you can lend your assistance; in any event, you must bring back a factual report." The Disciple Hui-an straightened out his attire and mounted the cloud to leave the palace, an iron rod in his hand. When he arrived at the mountain, he found layers of cosmic net drawn tightly and sentries at every gate holding bells and shouting passwords. The encirclement of the mountain was indeed watertight! Hui-an stood still and called out. "Heavenly sentinels, may I trouble you to announce my arrival? I am Prince Mokṣa, second son of Devarāja Li, and I am also Hui-an, senior disciple of Kuan-yin of South Sea. I have come to inquire about the military situation." The divine soldiers of the Five Mountains at once reported this beyond the gate. The constellations Aquarius, Pleiades, Hydra, and Scorpio then conveyed the message to the central tent. Devarāja Li issued a directorial flag, which ordered the cosmic nets to be opened and entrance permitted for the visitor. Day was just

dawning in the east as Hui-an followed the flag inside and prostrated himself before the Four Great Devarājas and Devarāja Li. After he had finished his greetings, Devarāja Li said, "My child, where have you come from?" "Your untutored son," said Hui-an, "accompanied the Bodhisattva to attend the Festival of Grand Peaches. Seeing that the festival was desolate and the Jasper Pool laid waste, the Bodhisattva led the various deities and your untutored son to have an audience with the Jade Emperor. The Jade Emperor spoke at length about Father and King's expedition to the Region Below to subdue the baneful monkey. Since no report has returned for a whole day and neither victory nor defeat has been ascertained, the Bodhisattva ordered your untutored son to come here to find out how things stand." "We came here yesterday to set up the encampment," said Devarāja Li, "and the Nine Luminaries were sent to provoke battle. But this fellow made a grand display of his magical powers, and the Nine Luminaries all returned defeated. After that, I led the troops personally to confront him, and the fellow also brought his forces into formation. Our hundred thousand celestial soldiers fought with him until evening, when he retreated from the battle by using the magic of body division. When we recalled the troops and made our investigation, we found that we had captured some wolves, crawling creatures, tigers, leopards, and the like. But we did not even catch half a monkey monster! And today we have not yet gone into battle."

As he was saying all this, someone came from the gate of the camp to report, "That Great Sage, leading his band of monkey monsters, is shouting for battle outside." The Four Devarājas, Devarāja Li, and the prince at once made plans to bring out the troops, when Mokṣa said, "Father King, your untutored son was told by the Bodhisattva to come down here to acquire information. She also told me to give you assistance should there be actual combat. Though I am not very talented, I volunteer to go out now and see what kind of a Great Sage this is!" "Child," said the Devarāja, "since you have studied with the Bodhisattva for several years, you must, I suppose, have some powers! But do be careful!"

Dear prince! Grasping the iron rod with both hands, he tightened up his embroidered garment and leaped out of the gate. "Who is the Great Sage Equal to Heaven?" he cried. Holding high his compliant rod, the Great Sage answered, "None other than old Monkey here! Who are you that you dare question me?" "I am Mokṣa, the second prince of Devarāja Li," said Mokṣa. "At present I am also the of Bodhisattva Kuan-yin, a defender of the faith before her treasure throne. And my religious name is Hui-an." "Why have you left your religious training at South Sea and come here to see me?" said the Great Sage. "I was sent by my master to inquire about the military situation," said Mokṣa. "Seeing what a nuisance you have made of yourself, I have come specifically to capture you." "You dare to talk so big?" said the Great Sage. "But don't run away! Have a taste of old Monkey's rod!" Mokṣa was not at all frightened and met his opponent squarely with his own iron rod. The two of them stood before the gate of the camp at mid-mountain, and what a magnificent battle they fought!

Though one rod is pitted against another, the iron's quite different;
Though this weapon couples with the other, the persons are not the same.
The one called the Great Sage is an apostate primordial immortal;
The other is Kuan-yin's disciple, truly heroic and proud.
The all-iron rod, pounded by a thousand hammers,
Is made by the Six Gods of Darkness and Six Gods of Light.
The compliant rod fixes the depth of Heaven's river,
A thing divine ruling the oceans with its magic might.
The two of them in meeting have found their match;
Back and forth they battle in endless rounds.
From this one the rod of stealthy hands,
Savage and fierce,
Around the waist stabs and jabs swiftly as the wind;
From the other the rod, doubling as a spear
Driving and relentless,
Lets up not a moment its parrying left and right.
On this side the banners flare and flutter;
On the other the war drums roll and rattle.
Ten thousand celestial fighters circle round and round.
The monkey monsters of a whole cave stand in rows and rows.
Weird fog and dark cloud spread throughout the earth.
The fume and smoke of battle reach even Heaven's Palace.
Yesterday's battle was something to behold.
Still more violent is the contest today.

Envy the Monkey King, for he's truly able:
Mokṣa's defeated—he's fleeing for his life!
Our Great Sage battled Hui-an for fifty or sixty rounds until the prince's arms and shoulders were sore and numb and he could fight no longer. After one final, futile swing of his weapon, he fled in defeat. The Great Sage then gathered together his monkey troops and stationed them securely outside the entrance of the cave. At the camp of the Devarāja, the celestial soldiers could be seen receiving the prince and making way for him to enter the gate. Panting and puffing, he ran in and gasped out to the Four Devarājas, Pagoda Bearer Li, and Naṭa, "That Great Sage! What an ace! Great indeed is his magical power! Your son cannot overcome him and has returned defeated." Shocked by the sight, Devarāja Li at once wrote a memorial to the Throne to request further assistance. The demon king Mahābāli and Prince Mokṣa were sent to Heaven to present the document.

The two of them dared not linger. They crashed out of the cosmic nets and mounted the holy mist and hallowed cloud. In a moment they reached the Hall of Perfect Light and met the Four Heavenly Preceptors, who led them into the Treasure Hall of Divine Mists to present their memorial. Hui-an also saluted the Bodhisattva, who asked him, "What have you found out about the situation?" "When I reached the Flower-Fruit Mountain by your order," said Hui-an, "I opened the cosmic nets by my call. Seeing my father, I told him of my master's intentions in sending me. Father King said, 'We fought a battle yesterday with that Monkey King but managed to take from him only tigers, leopards, lions, elephants, and the like. We did not catch a single one of his monkey monsters.' As we were talking, he again demanded battle. Your disciple used the iron rod to fight him for fifty or sixty rounds, but I could not prevail against him and returned to the camp defeated. Thus Father had to send the demon king Mahābāli and your pupil to come here for help." The Bodhisattva bowed her head and pondered.

We now tell you about the Jade Emperor, who opened the memorial and found a message asking for assistance. "This is rather absurd!" he said laughing. "Is this monkey monster such a wizard that not even a hundred thousand soldiers from Heaven can vanquish him? Devarāja Li is again asking for help. What division of divine warriors can we send to assist him?" Hardly he had finished speaking when Kuan-yin folded her hands and said to him, "Your Majesty, let not your mind be troubled! This humble cleric will recommend a god who can capture the monkey." "Which one would you recommend?" said the Jade Emperor. "Your Majesty's nephew," said the Bodhisattva, "the Immortal Master of Illustrious Sagacity Erh-lang,[20] who is living at the mouth of the River of Libations in the Kuan Prefecture and enjoying the incense and oblations offered to him from the Region Below. In former days he himself slew six monsters. Under his command are the Brothers of Plum Mountain and twelve hundred plant-headed deities, all possessing great magical powers. However, he will agree only to special assignments and will not obey any general summons. Your Majesty may want to send an edict transferring his troops to the scene of the battle and requesting his assistance. Our monster will surely be captured." When the Jade Emperor heard this, he immediately issued such an edict and ordered the demon king Mahābāli to present it.

Having received the edict, the demon king mounted a cloud and went straight to the mouth of the River of Libations. It took him less than half an hour to reach the temple of the Immortal Master. Immediately the demon magistrates guarding the doors made this report inside: "There is a messenger from Heaven outside who has arrived with an edict in his hand." Erh-lang and his brothers came out to receive the edict, which was read before burning incense. The edict said:

> *The Great Sage, Equal to Heaven, a monstrous monkey from the Flower-Fruit Mountain, is in revolt. At the Palace he stole peaches, wine, and elixir, and disrupted the Grand Festival of Immortal Peaches. A hundred thousand heavenly soldiers with eighteen sets of cosmic nets were dispatched to surround the mountain and capture him, but victory has not yet been secured. We therefore make this special request of our worthy nephew and his sworn brothers to go to the Flower-Fruit Mountain and assist in destroying this monster. Following your success will be lofty elevation and abundant reward.*

In great delight the Immortal Master said, "Let the messenger of heaven go back. I will go at once to offer my assistance with drawn sword." The demon king went back to report, but we shall speak no further of that.

This Immortal Master called together the Six Brothers of Plum Mountain: they were K'ang, Chang, Yao, and Li, the four grand marshals, and Kuo Shên and Chih Chien, the two generals. As they congregated before the court, he said to them, "The Jade Emperor just now sent us to the Flower-Fruit Mountain to capture a monstrous monkey. Let's get going!" Delighted and willing, the brothers at once called out the divine soldiers under their command. With falcons mounted and dogs on leashes, with arrows ready and bows drawn, they left in a violent magic wind and crossed in a moment the great Eastern Ocean. As they landed on the Flower-Fruit Mountain, they saw their way blocked by dense layers of cosmic net. "Divine commanders guarding the cosmic nets, hear us," they shouted. "We are specially assigned by the Jade Emperor to capture the monstrous monkey. Open the gate of your camp quickly and let us through." The various deities conveyed the message to the inside, level by level. The Four Devarājas and Devarāja Li then came out to the gate of the camp to receive them. After they had exchanged greetings, there were questions about the military situation, and the Devarāja gave them a thorough briefing. "Now that I, the Little Sage, have come," said the Immortal Master, laughing, "he will have to engage in a contest of transformations with his adversary. You gentlemen make sure that the cosmic nets are tightly drawn on all sides, but leave the top uncovered. Let me try my hand in this contest. If I lose, you gentlemen need not come to my assistance, for my own brothers will be there to support me. If I win, you gentlemen will not be needed in tying him up either; my own brothers will take care of that. All I need is the Pagoda Bearer Devarāja to stand in midair with his imp-reflecting mirror. If the monster should be defeated, I fear that he may try to flee to a distant locality. Make sure that his image is clearly reflected in the mirror, so that we don't lose him." The Devarājas set themselves up in the four directions, while the Heavenly soldiers all lined up according to their planned formations.

With himself as the seventh brother, the Immortal Master led the four grand marshals and the two generals out of the camp to provoke battle. The other warriors were ordered to defend their encampment with vigilance, and the plant-headed deities were ordered to have the falcons and dogs ready for battle. The Immortal Master went to the front of the Water-Curtain Cave, where he saw a troop of monkeys neatly positioned in an array that resembled a coiled dragon. At the center of the array was the banner bearing the words "The Great Sage, Equal to Heaven." "That audacious monster!" said the Immortal Master. "How dare he assume the rank 'Equal to Heaven'?" "There's no time for praise or blame," said the Six Brothers of Plum Mountain. "Let's challenge him at once!" When the little monkeys in front of the camp saw the Immortal Master, they ran quickly to make their report. Seizing his golden-hooped rod, straightening out his golden cuirass, slipping on his cloud-reading shoes, and pressing down his red-gold cap, the Monkey King leaped out of the camp. He opened his eyes wide to stare at the Immortal Master, whose features were remarkably refined and whose attire was most elegant. Truly, he was a man of

Features most comely and noble mien,

With ears reaching his shoulders and eyes alert and bright.

A cap of the Three Mountains' Phoenix flying crowned his head.

And a pale yellow robe of goose-down he wore on his frame.

His boots of gold threads matched the hoses of coiling dragons.

Eight emblems[21] like flower clusters adorned his belt of jade.

From his waist hung the pellet bow of new moon shape.

His hands held a lance with three points and two blades.

He once axed open the Peach Mountain to save his mother.

He struck with a single pellet two phoenixes of Tsung-lo.

He slew the Eight Monsters, and his fame spread wide;

He formed a chivalric alliance named the Plum Mountain's Seven Sages.

A lofty mind, he scorned being a relative of Heaven.

His proud nature led him to live near the River of Libations.

This is the Kind and Magnanimous Sage from the City of Ch'ih;[22]

Skilled in boundless transformations, his name's Erh-lang.

When the Great Sage saw him, he lifted high his golden-hooped rod with gales of laughter and called out, "What little warrior are you and where do you come from, that you dare present yourself here to provoke battle?" "You must have eyes but no pupils," shouted the Immortal Master, "if you don't recognize me! I am the maternal nephew of the Jade Emperor, Erh-lang, the King of Illustrious Grace and Spirit by imperial appointment. I have received my order from above to arrest you, the rebellious pi-ma-wên ape. Don't you know that your time has come?" "I remember," said the Great Sage, "that the sis-

ter of the Jade Emperor some years ago became enamored of the Region Below: she married a man by the name of Yang and had a son by him. Are you that boy who was reputed to have cleaved open the Peach Mountain with his ax? I would like to rebuke you roundly, but I have no grudge against you. I can hit you with this rod of mine too, but I'd like to spare your life! A little boy like you, why don't you hurry back and ask your Four Great Devarājas to come out?" When the Immortal Master heard this, he grew very angry and shouted, "Reckless ape! Don't you dare be so insolent! Take a sample of my blade!" Swerving to dodge the blow, the Great Sage quickly raised his golden-hooped rod to engage his opponent. "What a fine fight there was between the two of them:

Erh-lang, the God of Illustrious Kindness,

And the Great Sage, Equal to Heaven!

The former, haughty and high-minded, defied the Handsome Monkey King.

The latter, not knowing his man, would crush a stalwart foe.

Suddenly these two met,

And both desired a match—

They had never known which was the better man;

Today they'll learn who's strong and who's weak!

The iron rod seemed a flying dragon,

And the lance divine a dancing phoenix:

Left and right they struck,

Attacking both front and back.

The Six Brothers of Plum Mountain filled one side with their awesome presence,

While the four generals, like Ma and Liu, took command on the other side.

All worked as one to wave the flags and beat the drums;

All assisted the battle by cheering and sounding the gong.

Those two sharp weapons sought a chance to hurt,

But the thrusts and parries slacked not one whit.

The golden-hooped rod, that wonder of the sea,

Could change and fly to gain a victory.

A little lag and your life is over!

A tiny slip and your luck runs out!

The Immortal Master fought the Great Sage for more than three hundred rounds, but the result still could not be determined. The Immortal Master, therefore, summoned all his magical powers; with a shake, he made his body a hundred thousand feet tall. Holding with both hands the divine lance of three points and two blades like the peaks that cap the Hua Mountain, this green-faced, saber-toothed figure with scarlet hair aimed a violent blow at the head of the Great Sage. But the Great Sage also exerted his magical power and changed himself into a figure having the features and height of Erh-lang. He wielded a compliant golden-hooped rod that resembled the heaven-supporting pillar on top of Mount K'un-lun to oppose the god Erh-lang. This vision so terrified the marshals, Ma and Liu, that they could no longer wave the flags, and so appalled the generals, Pêng and Pa, that they could use neither scimitar nor sword. On the side of Erh-lang, the Brothers K'ang, Chang, Yao, Li, Kuo Shin, and Chih Chien gave the order to the plant-headed deities to let loose the falcons and dogs and to advance upon those monkeys in front of the Water-Curtain Cave with mounted arrows and drawn bows. The charge, alas, dispersed the four mighty commanders of monkey imps and captured two or three thousand intelligent monsters! Those monkeys dropped their spears and abandoned their armor, forsook their swords and threw away their lances. They scattered in all directions—running, screaming, scuttling up the mountain, or scrambling back to the cave. It was as if a cat at night had stolen upon resting birds: they darted up as stars to fill the sky. The Brothers thus gained a complete victory, of which we shall speak no further.

Now we were telling you about the Immortal Master and the Great Sage who had changed themselves into forms which imitated Heaven and Earth. As they were doing battle, the Great Sage suddenly perceived that the monkeys of his camp were put to rout, and his heart grew faint. He changed out of his magic form, turned around, and fled, dragging his rod behind him. When the Immortal Master saw that he was running away, he chased him with great strides saying "Where are you going? Surrender now, and your life, will be spared!" The Great Sage did not stop to fight anymore but ran as fast as he could. Near the cave's entrance, he ran right into K'ang, Chang, Yao, and Li, the four grand marshals, and Kuo Shên and Chih Chien, the two generals, who were at the head of an army blocking his way. "Lawless ape!" they cried, "where do you think you're going?" Quivering all over, the Great Sage squeezed his golden-hooped rod back into an embroidery needle and hid it in his ear. With a shake of his body, he changed himself into a small sparrow and flew to perch on top of a tree. In great agitation, the six Brothers searched all around but could not find him. "We've lost the

monkey monster! We've lost the monkey monster!" they all cried.

As they were making all that clamor, the Immortal Master arrived and asked, "Brothers, where did you lose him in the chase?" "We just had him boxed in here," said the gods, "but he simply vanished." Scanning the place with his phoenix eye wide open,[23] Erh-lang at once discovered that the Great Sage had changed into a small sparrow perched on a tree. He changed out of his magic form and took off his pellet bow. With a shake of his body, he changed into a sparrow hawk with outstretched wings, ready to attack its prey. When the Great Sage saw this, he darted up with a flutter of his wings; changing himself into a cormorant, he headed straight for the open sky. When Erh-lang saw this, he quickly shook his feathers and changed into a huge ocean crane, which could penetrate the clouds to strike with its bill. The Great Sage therefore lowered his direction, changed into a small fish, and dove into a stream with a splash. Erh-lang rushed to the edge of the water but could see no trace of him. He thought to himself, "This simian must have gone into the water and changed himself into a fish, a shrimp, or the like. I'll change again to catch him." He duly changed into a fish hawk and skimmed downstream over the waves. After a while, the fish into which the Great Sage had changed was swimming along with the current. Suddenly he saw a bird that looked like a green kite though its feathers were not entirely green, like an egret though it had small feathers, and like an old crane though its feet were not red. "That must be the transformed Erh-lang waiting for me," he thought to himself. He swiftly turned around and swam away after releasing a few bubbles. When Erh-lang saw this, he said, "The fish that released the bubbles looks like a carp though its tail is not red, like a perch though there are no patterns on its scales, like a snake fish though there are no stars on its head, like a bream though its gills have no bristles. Why does it move away the moment it sees me? It must be the transformed monkey himself!" He swooped toward the fish and snapped at it with his beak. The Great Sage shot out of the water and changed at once into a water snake; he swam toward shore and wriggled into the grass along the bank. When Erh-lang saw that he had snapped in vain and that a snake had darted away in the water with a splash, he knew that the Great Sage had changed again. Turning around quickly, he changed into a scarlet-topped gray crane, which extended its beak like sharp iron pincers to devour the snake. With a bounce, the snake changed again into a spotted bustard standing by itself rather stupidly amid the water-pepper along the bank. When Erh-lang saw that the monkey had changed into such a vulgar creature—for the spotted bustard is the basest and most promiscuous of birds, mating indiscriminately with phoenixes, hawks, or crows—he refused to approach him. Changing back into his true form, he went and stretched his bow to the fullest. With one pellet he sent the bird hurtling.

The Great Sage took advantage of this opportunity, nonetheless. Rolling down the mountain slope, he squatted there to change again—this time into a little temple for the local spirit. His wide-open mouth became the entrance, his teeth the doors, his tongue the Bodisattva, and his eyes the windows. Only his tail he found to be troublesome, so he stuck it up in the back and changed it into a flagpole. Immortal Master chased him down the slope, but instead of the bustard he had hit he found only a little temple. He opened his phoenix eye quickly and looked at it carefully. Seeing the flagpole behind it, he laughed and said, "It's the ape! Now he's trying to deceive me again! I have seen plenty of temples before but never one with a flagpole behind it. This must be another of that animal's tricks. Why should I let him lure me inside where he can bite me once I've entered? First I'll smash the windows with my fist! Then I'll kick down the doors!" The Great Sage heard this and said in dismay, "How vicious! The doors are my teeth and the windows my eyes. What am I going to do with my eyes smashed and my teeth knocked out?" Leaping up like a tiger, he disappeared again into the air. The Immortal Master was looking all around for him when the four grand marshals and the two generals arrived together. "Elder Brother," they said, "have you caught the Great Sage?" "A moment ago," said the Immortal Master laughing, "the monkey changed into a temple to trick me. I was about to smash the windows and kick down the doors when he vanished out of sight with a leap. It's all very strange! Very strange!" The Brothers were astonished, but they could find no trace of him in any direction. "Brothers," said the Immortal Master, "keep a lookout down here. Let me go up there to find him." He swiftly mounted the clouds and rose up into the sky, where he saw Devarāja Li holding high the imp-reflecting mirror and standing on top of the clouds with Naṭa. "Devarāja," said the Immortal Master, "have you seen the Monkey King?" "He hasn't come up here," said the Devarāja. "I have been watching

him in the mirror." After telling them about the duel in magic and transformations and the captivity of the rest of the monkeys, the Immortal Master said, "He finally changed into a temple. Just as I was about to attack him, he got away." When Devarāja Li heard these words, he turned the imp-reflecting mirror all the way around once more and looked into it. "Immortal Master," he said, roaring with laughter. "Go quickly! Quickly! That monkey used his magic of body concealment to escape from the cordon and he's now heading for the mouth of your River of Libations."

We now tell you about the Great Sage, who had arrived at the mouth of the River of Libations. With a shake of his body, he changed into the form of Holy Father Erh-lang. Lowering the direction of his cloud, he went straight into the temple, and the demon magistrates could not tell that he was not the real Ehr-lang. Every one of them, in fact, kowtowed to receive him. He sat down in the middle and began to examine the various offerings; the three kinds of sacrificial meat brought by Li Hu, the votive offering of Chang Lung, the petition for a son by Chao Chia, and the request for healing by Ch'ien Ping. As he was looking at these, someone made the report, "Another Holy Father has arrived!" The various demon magistrates went quickly to look and were terror-stricken, one and all. The Immortal Master asked, "Did a so-called Great Sage, Equal to Heaven, come here?" "We haven't seen any Great Sage," said the demon magistrates. "But another Holy Father is in there examining the offerings." The Immortal Master crashed through the door; seeing him, the Great Sage revealed his true form and said, "There's no need for the little boy to strive anymore! Sun is now the name of this temple!" The Immortal Master lifted his divine lance of three points and two blades and struck, but the Monkey King with agile body was quick to move out of the way. He whipped out that embroidery needle of his, and with one wave caused it to take on the thickness of a rice bowl. Rushing forward he engaged Erh-lang face to face. Starting at the door of the temple, the two combatants fought all the way to the Flower-Fruit Mountain, treading on clouds and mists and shouting insults at each other. The Four Devarājas and their followers were so startled by their appearance that they stood guard with even greater vigilance, while the grand marshals joined the Immortal Master to surround the Handsome Monkey King. But we shall speak of them no more.

We tell you instead about the demon king Mahābāli, who, having requested the Immortal Master and his Six Brothers to lead their troops to subdue the monster, returned to the Region Above to make his report. Conversing with the Bodhisattva Kuan-yin, the Queen Mother, and the various divine officials in the Hall of Divine Mists, the Jade Emperor said, "If Erh-lang has already gone into battle, why has no further report come back today?" Folding her hands, Kuan-yin said. "Permit this humble cleric to invite Your Majesty and the Patriarch of Tao to go outside the South Heavenly Gate, so that you may find out personally how things are faring." "That's a good suggestion," said the Jade Emperor. He at once sent for his imperial carriage and went with the Patriarch, Kuan-yin, the Queen Mother, and the various divine officials to the South Heavenly Gate, where the cortege was met by celestial soldiers and guardians. They opened the gate and peered into the distance; there they saw cosmic nets on every side manned by Heavenly soldiers, Devarāja Li and Naṭa in midair holding high the imp-reflecting mirror. and the Immortal Master and his Brothers encircling the Great Sage in the middle and fighting fiercely. The Bodhisattva opened her mouth and addressed Lao Tzu: "What do you think of Erh-lang, whom this humble clerk recommended? He is certainly powerful enough to have the Great Sage surrounded, if not yet captured. I shall now help him to achieve his victory and make certain that the enemy will be taken prisoner." "What weapon will the Bodhisattva use," asked Lao Tzu, "and how will you assist him?" "I shall throw down my immaculate vase which I use for holding my willow sprig," said the Bodhisattva. "When it hits that monkey, at least it will knock him over, even if it doesn't kill him. Erh-lang, the Little Sage, will then be able to capture him." "That vase of yours," said Lao Tzu "is made of porcelain. It's all right if it hits him on the head. But if it crashed on the Iron rod instead, won't it be shattered? You had better not raise your hands; let me help him win." The Bodhisattva said, "Do you have any weapon?" "I do, indeed," said Lao Tzu. He rolled up his sleeve and took down from his left arm an armlet, saying, "This is a weapon made of red steel, brought into existence during my preparation of elixir and fully charged with theurgical forces. It can be made to transform at will; indestructible by fire or water, it can entrap many things. It's called the diamond cutter or the diamond snare. The year when I crossed the Han-ku Pass, I depended on

it a great deal for the conversion of the barbarians, for it was practically my bodyguard night and day. Let me throw it down and hit him." After saying this, Lao Tzu hurled the snare down from the Heavenly Gate; it went tumbling down into the battlefield at the Flower-Fruit Mountain and landed smack on the Monkey King's head. The Monkey King was engaged in a bitter struggle with the Seven Sages and was completely unaware of this weapon which had dropped from the sky and hit him on the crown of his head. No longer able to stand on his feet, he toppled over. He managed to scramble up again and was about to flee, when the Holy Father Erh-lang's small hound dashed forward and bit him in the calf. He was pulled down for the second time and lay on the ground cursing, "You brute! Why don't you go and do your master in, instead of coming to bite old Monkey?" Rolling over quickly, he tried to get up, but the Seven Sages all pounced on him and pinned him down. They bound him with ropes and punctured his breastbone with a knife, so that he could transform no further.

Lao Tzu retrieved his diamond snare and requested the Jade Emperor to return to the Hall of Divine Mists with Kuan-yin, the Queen Mother, and the rest of the Immortals. Down below the Four Great Deva Kings and Deva King Li all retired their troops, broke camp, and went forward to congratulate Erh-lang, saying, "This is indeed a magnificent accomplishment by the Little Sage!" "This has been the great blessing of the Heavenly Devas," said the Little Sage, "and the proper exercise of their divine authority. What have I accomplished?" The Brothers K'ang, Chang, Yao, and Li said, "Elder Brother need have no further discussion. Let us take this fellow up to the Jade Emperor to see what will be done with him." "Worthy Brothers," said the Immortal Master, "you may not have a personal audience with the Jade Emperor because you have not received a divine appointment. Let the celestial guardians take him into custody. I shall go with the Devarājas to the Region Above to make our report while all of you make a thorough search of the mountain here. After you have cleaned it out, go back to the River of Libations. When I have our deeds recorded and received our rewards, I shall return to celebrate with you." The four grand marshals and the two generals followed his bidding. The Immortal Master then mounted the cloud with the rest of the deities, and they began their triumphal journey back to Heaven, singing songs of victory all the way. In a little while they reached the outer court of the Hall of Perfect Light, and the heavenly preceptor went forward to memorialize to the Throne, saying, "The Four Great Devarājas have captured the monstrous monkey, the Great Sage, Equal to Heaven. They await the commands of Your Majesty." The Jade Emperor then gave the order that the demon king Mahābāli and the heavenly guardians take the prisoner to the monster execution block, where he was to be cut to small pieces. Alas, this is what happens to

Fraud and impudence, now punished by the Law;

Heroics grand will fade in the briefest time! We do not know what will become of the Monkey King, and you must listen to the explanation in the next chapter.

Seven

From the Brazier of Eight Trigrams the Great Sage escapes; Beneath the Five Phases Mountain the Monkey of the Mind[24] is stilled.

Fame and fortune,
All predestined:
One must ever shun a guileful heart.
Rectitude and truth,
The fruits of virtue grow both long and deep.
A little presumption brings on Heaven's wrath;
Though yet unseen, it will surely come in time.
If we ask the Lord of the East[25] for reasons why
Such pains and perils now appear,
It's because pride has sought to scale the limits,
Confounding the world's order and perverting the law.

We were telling you about the Great Sage, Equal to Heaven, who was taken by the celestial guardians to the monster execution block, where he was bound to the monster-subduing pillar. They then lashed him with a scimitar, hewed him with an ax, stabbed him with a spear, and hacked him with a sword, but they could not hurt his body in any way. Next, the Star Spirit of South Pole ordered the various deities of the Fire Department to burn him with fire, but that, too, had little effect. The gods of the Thunder Department were then ordered to strike him with thunderbolts, but not a single one of his hairs was destroyed. The demon king Mahābāli and the others therefore went back to report to the Throne, saying, "Your Majesty, we don't know where this Great Sage has acquired such power to protect his body. Your subjects slashed him with a scimitar and hewed him with an ax; we also struck him with thunder and burned him with fire. Not a single one of his hairs was destroyed. What shall we do?" When the Jade Emperor heard these words,

he said, "What indeed can we do to a fellow like that, a creature of that sort?" Lao Tzu then came forward and said, "That monkey ate the immortal peaches and drank the imperial wine. Moreover, he stole the divine elixir and ate five gourdfuls of it, both raw and cooked. All this was probably refined in his stomach by the Samādhi fire[26] to form a single solid mass. The union with his constitution gave him a diamond body which cannot be quickly destroyed. It would be better, therefore, if this Taoist takes him away and places him in the Brazier of Eight Trigrams, where he will be smelted by high and low heat. When he is finally separated from my elixir, his body will certainly be reduced to ashes." When the Jade Emperor heard these words, he told the Six Guardians of Darkness and the Six Guardians of Light to release the prisoner and hand him over to Lao Tzu, who left in obedience to the divine decree. Meanwhile, the Illustrious Sage Erh-lang was rewarded with a hundred gold blossoms, a hundred bottles of imperial wine, a hundred pellets of elixir, together with rare treasures, lustrous pearls, and brocades, which he was told to share with his brothers. After expressing his gratitude, the Immortal Master returned to the mouth of the River of Libations, and for the time being we shall speak of him no further.

Arriving at the Tushita Palace, Lao Tzu loosened the ropes on the Great Sage, pulled out the weapon from his breastbone, and pushed him into the Brazier of Eight Trigrams. He then ordered the Taoist who watched over the brazier and the page boy in charge of the fire to blow up a strong flame for the smelting process. The brazier, you see, was of eight compartments corresponding to the eight trigrams of Ch'ien, K'an, Kên, Chên, Sun, Li, K'un, and Tui. The Great Sage crawled into the space beneath the compartment which corresponded to the Sun trigram. Now Sun symbolizes wind; where there is wind, there is no fire. However, wind could churn up smoke, which at that moment reddened his eyes, giving them a permanently inflamed condition. Hence they were sometimes called Fiery Eyes and Diamond Pupils.

Truly time passed by swiftly, and the forty-ninth day[27] arrived imperceptibly. The alchemical process of Lao Tzu was perfected, and on that day he come to open the brazier to take out his elixir. The Great Sage at the time was covering his eyes with both hands, rubbing his face and shedding tears. He heard noises on top of the brazier and, opening his eyes, suddenly saw light. Unable to restrain himself, he leaped out of the brazier and kicked it over with a loud crash. He began to walk straight out of the room, while a group of startled fire tenders and guardians tried desperately to grab hold of him. Every one of them was overthrown; he was as wild as a white brow tiger in a fit, a one-horn dragon with a fever. Lao Tzu rushed up to clutch at him, only to be greeted by such a violent shove that he fell head over heels while the Great Sage escaped. Whipping the compliant rod out from his ear, he waved it once in the wind and it had the thickness of a rice bowl. Holding it in his hands, without regard for good or ill, he once more careened through the Heavenly Palace, fighting so fiercely that the Nine Luminaries all shut themselves in and the Four Devarājas disappeared from sight. Dear Monkey Monster! Here is a testimonial poem for him. The poem says:

This cosmic being perfectly fused with nature's gifts
Passes with ease through ten thousand toils and tests.
Vast and motionless like the One Great Void,
Perfect and quiescent, he's named The Primal Depth.
Refined a long while in the brazier, though not of mercurial stuff,[28]
He's the very immortal, living ever above all things.
Knowing boundless transformations, he changes still;
The three refuges and five commandments[29] he all rejects.

Here is another poem:

Just as light supernal fills the boundless space,
So does that cudgel serve his master's hand.
It lengthens or shortens according to the wish of man;
Upright or recumbent, it grows or shrinks at will.

And another:

A monkey's transformed body weds the human mind.
Mind is a monkey—this, the truth profound.
The Great Sage, Equal to Heaven, is no idle thought.
For how could the post of pi-ma justly show his gifts?
The Horse works with the Monkey—this means both Mind and Will
Must firmly be harnessed and not be ruled without.
All things return to Nirvāṇa, taking this one course:
In union with Tathāgata[30] to live beneath twin trees.[31]

This time our Monkey King had no respect for persons great or small: he lashed out this way and that with his iron rod, and not a single deity could withstand him. He fought all the way into the Hall of Perfect Light and was approaching the Hall of Divine Mists, where fortunately Wang Ling-kuan, aide to the Immortal Master of Adjuvant Holiness, was on duty. He saw the Great Sage advancing recklessly and went forward to bar his way, holding high his golden whip. "Wanton monkey," he cried, "where are you going? I am here, so don't you dare be insolent!" The Great Sage did not wait for further utterance: he raised his rod and struck at once, while the Ling-kuan met him also with brandished whip. The two of them charged into each other in front of the Hall of Divine Mists. What a fight that was between

A red-blooded patriot with reputation great,
And a defier of Heaven with notorious name!
The saint and the sinner gladly do this fight,
To test the skills of two warriors brave.
Though the rod is brutal
And the whip is fleet,
How can the hero, upright and just, forbear?
This one is a supreme god of vengeance with thunderous voice;
The other, the Great Sage, Equal to Heaven, a monstrous ape.
The golden whip and the iron rod used by the two
Are both weapons divine from the House of God.
At the Treasure flail of Divine Mists this day they show their might.
Displaying each his prowess most admirably.
This one brashly seeks to take the Big Dipper Palace.
The other with all his strength defends the sacred realm.

In bitter strife relentless they show their power:

Moving back and forth, whip or rod has yet to score.

The two of them fought for some time, and neither victory nor defeat could yet be determined. The Immortal Master of Adjuvant Holiness, however, had already sent word to the Thunder Department, and thirty-six thunder deities were summoned to the scene. They surrounded the Great Sage and plunged into a fierce battle. The Great Sage was not in the least intimidated; wielding his compliant rod, he parried left and right and met his attackers to the front and to the rear. In a moment he saw that the scimitars, lances, swords, halberds, whips, maces, hammers, axes, gilt bludgeons, sickles, and spades of the thunder deities were coming thick and fast. So with one shake of his body he changed into a creature with six arms and three heads. One wave of the compliant rod and it turned into three: his six arms wielded the three rods like a spinning wheel, whirling and dancing in their midst. The various thunder deities could not approach him at all. Truly his form was

Tumbling round and round,

Bright and luminous:

A form everlasting, how imitated by men?

He cannot be burned by fire.

Can he ever be drowned in water?

A lustrous pearl of maṇi[32] he is indeed,

Immune to all the spears and the swords.

He could be good;

He could be bad;

Present good and evil he could do at will.

Immortal he'll be in goodness or a Buddha,

But working ill, he's covered by hair and horn.[33]

Endlessly changing he runs amok in Heaven,

Not to be seized by fighting lords or thunder gods.

At the time the various deities had the Great Sage surrounded, but they could not close in on him. All the hustle and bustle soon disturbed the Jade Emperor, who at once sent the Wandering Minister of Inspection and the Immortal Master of Blessed Wings to go to the Western Region and invite the aged Buddha to come and subdue the monster.

The two sages received the decree and went straight to the Spirit Mountain. After they had greeted the Four Vajra-Buddhas and the Eight Bodhisattvas in front of the Treasure Temple of thunderclap, they asked them to announce their arrival. The deities therefore went before the Treasure Lotus Platform and made their report. Tathāgata at once invited them to appear before him, and the two sages made obeisance to the Buddha three times before standing in attendance beneath the platform. Tathāgata asked, "What causes the Jade Emperor to trouble the two sages to come here?"

The two sages explained as follows: "Some time ago there was born on the Flower-Fruit Mountain a monkey who exercised his magic powers and gathered to himself a troop of monkeys to disturb the world. The Jade Emperor threw down a decree of pacification and appointed him a pi-ma-wên, but he despised the lowliness of that position and left in rebellion. Devarāja Li and Prince Naṭa were sent to capture him, but they were unsuccessful, and another proclamation of amnesty was given to him. He was then made the Great Sage, Equal to Heaven, a rank without compensation. After a while he was given the temporary job of looking after the Garden of Immortal Peaches, where almost immediately he stole the peaches. He also went to the Jasper Pool and made off with the food and wine, devastating the Grand Festival. Half-drunk, he went secretly into the Tushita Palace, stole the elixir of Lao Tzu, and then left the Celestial Palace in revolt. Again the Jade Emperor sent a hundred thousand Heavenly soldiers, but he was not to be subdued. Thereafter Kuan-yin sent for the Immortal Master Erh-lang and his sworn brothers, who fought and pursued him. Even then he knew many tricks of transformation and only after he was hit by Lao Tzu's diamond snare could Erh-lang finally capture him. Taken before the Throne, he was condemned to be executed: but, though slashed by a scimitar and hewn by an axe, burned by fire and struck by thunder, he was not hurt at all. After Lao Tzu had received royal permission to take him away, he was refined by fire, and the brazier was not opened until the forty-ninth day. Immediately he jumped out of the Brazier of Eight Trigrams and beat back the celestial guardians. He penetrated into the Hall of Perfect Light and was approaching the Hall of Divine Mists when Wang Ling-kuan, aide to the Immortal Master of Adjuvant Holiness, met and fought with him bitterly. Thirty-six thunder generals were ordered to encircle him completely, but they could never get near him. The situation is desperate, and for this reason, the Jade Emperor sent a special request for you to defend the Throne."

When Tathāgata heard this, he said to the various bodhisattvas, "All of you remain steadfast here in the chief temple, and let no one relax his meditative posture. I have to go exorcise a demon and defend the Throne."

Tathāgata then called Ānanda and Kāapa, his two venerable disciples, to follow him. They left the Thunderclap Temple and arrived at the gate of the Hall of Divine Mists, where they were met by deafening shouts and yells. There the Great Sage was being beset by the thirty-six thunder deities. The Buddhist Patriarch gave the dharma order: "Let the thunder deities lower their arms and break up their encirclement. Ask the Great Sage to come out here and let me ask him what sort of divine power he has." The various warriors retreated immediately, and the Great Sage also threw off his magical appearance. Changing back into his true form, he approached angrily and shouted with ill humor, "What region are you from, monk, that you dare stop the battle and question me?" Tathā-gata laughed and said, "I am Sākyamuni, the Venerable One from the Western Region of Ultimate Bliss. I have heard just now about your audacity, your wildness, and your repeated acts of rebellion against Heaven. Where were you born? When did you learn the Great Art? Why are you so violent and unruly?"

The Great Sage said, "I was

Born of Earth and Heaven, immortally magically fused,

An old monkey hailed from the Flower-Fruit Mount.

I made my home in the Water-Curtain Cave;

I sought friend and teacher to gain the Mystery Great.

Perfected in the many arts of ageless life,

I learned to change in ways boundless and vast.

Too narrow the space I found on that mortal earth:

I set my mind to live in the Green Jade Sky.

In Divine Mists Hall none should long reside,

For king may follow king in the reign of man.

If might is honor, let them yield to me.

Only he is hero who dares to fight and win!"

When the Buddhist Patriarch heard these words, he laughed aloud in scorn. "A fellow like you," he said, "is only a monkey who happens to become a spirit. How dare you be so presumptuous as to want to seize the honored throne of the Exalted Jade Emperor? He began practicing religion when he was very young, and he has gone through the bitter experience of one thousand, seven hundred and fifty kalpas, with each kalpa lasting a hundred and twenty-nine thousand, six hundred years. Figure out yourself how many

years it took him to rise to the enjoyment of his great and limitless position! You are merely a beast who has just attained human form in this incarnation. How dare you make such a boast? Blasphemy! This is sheer blasphemy, and it will surely shorten your allotted age. Repent while there's still time and cease your idle talk! Be wary that you don't encounter such peril that you will be cut down in an instant, and all your original gifts will be wasted."

"Even if the Jade Emperor has practiced religion from childhood," said the Great Sage, "he should not be allowed to remain here forever. The proverb says, 'Many are the turns of kingship, and next year the turn will be mine!' Tell him to move out at once and hand over the Celestial Palace to me. That'll be the end of the matter. If not, I shall continue to cause disturbances and there'll never be peace!" "Besides your immortality and your transformations," said the Buddhist Patriarch, "what other powers do you have that you dare to usurp this hallowed region of Heaven?" "I've plenty of them!" said the Great Sage, "Indeed, I know seventy-two transformations and a life that does not grow old through ten thousand kalpas. I know also how to cloud-somersault, and one leap will take me a hundred and eight thousand miles. Why can't I sit on the Heavenly throne?"

The Buddhist Patriarch said, "Let me make a wager with you. If you have the ability to somersault clear of this right palm of mine, I shall consider you the winner. You need not raise your weapon in battle then, for I shall ask the Jade Emperor to go live with me in the West and let you have the Celestial Palace. If you cannot somersault out of my hand, you can go back to the Region Below and be a monster. Work through a few more kalpas before you return to cause more trouble."

When the Great Sage heard this, he said to himself, snickering, "What a fool this Tathāgata is! A single somersault of mine can carry old Monkey a hundred and eight thousand miles, yet his palm is not even one foot across. How could I possibly not jump clear of it?" He asked quickly, "You're certain that your decision will stand?" "Certainly it will," said Tathāgata. He stretched out his right hand, which was about the size of a lotus leaf. Our Great Sage put away his compliant rod and, summoning his power, leaped up and stood right in the center of the Patiarch's hand. He said simply, "I'm off!" and he was gone—all but invisible like a streak of light in the clouds. Training the eye of wisdom on him, the Buddhist Patriarch saw that the Monkey King was hurtling along relentlessly like a whirligig.

As the Great Sage advanced, he suddenly saw five flesh-pink pillars supporting a mass of green air. "This must be the end of the road." he said. "When I go back presently, Tathāgata will be my witness and I shall certainly take up residence in the Palace of Divine Mists." But he thought to himself, "Wait a moment! I'd better leave some kind of memento if I'm going to negotiate with Tathāgata." He plucked a hair and blew a mouthful of magic breath onto it, crying, "Change!" It changed into a writing brush with extra thick hair soaked in heavy ink. On the middle pillar he then wrote in large letters the following line: "The Great Sage, Equal to Heaven has made a tour of this place." When he had finished writing, he retrieved his hair, and with a total lack of respect he left a bubbling pool of monkey urine at the base of the first pillar. He reversed his cloud-somersault and went back to where he had started. Standing on Tathāgata's palm, he said, "I left, and now I'm back. Tell the Jade Emperor to give me the Celestial Palace." "You stinking, urinous ape!" scolded Tathāgata. "Since when did you ever leave the palm of my hand?" The Great Sage said, "You are just ignorant! I went to the edge of Heaven, and I found live flesh-pink pillars supporting a mass of green air. I left a memento there. Do you dare go with me to have a look at the place?" "No need to go there," said Tathāgata. "Just lower your head and take a look." When the Great Sage stared down with his fiery eyes and diamond pupils, he found written on the middle finger of the Buddhist Patriarch's right hand the sentence "The Great Sage, Equal to Heaven, has made a tour of this place." A pungent whiff of monkey urine came from the fork between the thumb and the first finger. Astonished, the Great Sage said, "Could this really happen? Could this really happen? I wrote those words on the pillars supporting the sky. How is it that they now appear on his finger? Could it be that he is exercising the magic power of foreknowledge without divination? I won't believe it! I won't believe it! Let me go there once more!"

Dear Great Sage! Quickly he crouched and was about to jump up again, when the Buddhist Patriarch flipped his hand over, and tossed the Monkey King out of the West Heavenly Gate. The five fingers were transformed into the Five Phases of metal, wood, water, fire, and earth. They became, in fact, five connected mountains, named Five-Phases Mountain, which pinned him down with just enough pressure to keep him there. The thunder deities, Ānanda, and Kāśyapa all folded their hands and cried in acclamation:

Wonderful! Wonderful!

Taught to be manlike since hatching from an egg that year,

He set his aim to learn and walk the Way of Truth.

He lived in a lovely region by ten thousand kalpas unmoved.

But one day he changed, dissipating vigor and strength.

Craving high place, he flouted Heaven's dominion;

Mocking sages, he stole pills and upset the great relations.

Evil, full to the brim, now meets its retribution.

We know not when he may hope to find release.

After the Buddhist Patriarch Tathāgata had vanquished the monstrous monkey, he at once called Ānanda and Kāśyapa to return with him to the Western Paradise. At that moment, however, T'ien-p'êng and T'ien-yu, two heavenly messengers, came running out of Hall of Divine Mists and said, "We beg Tathāgata to wait a moment, please! Our Lord's grand carriage will arrive momentarily." When the Buddhist Patriarch heard these words, he turned around and waited with reverence. In a moment he did indeed see a chariot drawn by eight colorful phoenixes and covered by a canopy adorned with nine luminous jewels. The entire cortege was accompanied by the sound of wondrous songs and melodies, chanted by a vast celestial choir. Scattering precious blossoms and diffusing fragrant incense, it came up to the Buddha, and the Jade Emperor offered thanks, saying, "We are truly indebted to your mighty dharma for vanquishing that monster. We beseech Tathāgata to remain for one brief day, so that we may invite the immortals to join us in giving you a banquet of thanks." Not daring to refuse, Tathāgata folded his hands to thank the Jade Emperor, saying, "Your old monk came here at your command of you, Most Honorable Deva. Of what power may I boast, really? I owe my success entirely to the excellent fortune of Your Majesty and the various deities. How can I be worthy of your thanks?" The Jade Emperor then ordered the various deities from the Thunder Department to send invitations abroad to the Three Pure Ones, the Four Ministers, the Five Elders, the Six Women Officials,[34] the Seven Stars, the eight Poles, the Nine Luminaries, and the Ten Capitals. Together with a thousand immortals and ten thousand sages, they were to come to the thanksgiving banquet given for the Buddhist Patriarch. The Four Great Imperial Preceptors and the Divine Maidens of Nine Heavens were told to open wide the golden gates of the Jade Capital, the Treasure Palace of Primal Secret, and the Five Lodges of Penetrating Brightness. Tathāgata was asked to be seated high on the Spirit Platform of Seven Treasures, and the rest of the deities were then seated according to rank and age before a banquet of dragon livers, phoenix marrow, juices of jade, and immortal peaches.

In a little while, the Jade-Pure Honorable Divine of the Origin, the Exalted-Pure Honorable Divine of Spiritual Treasures, the Primal-Pure Honorable Divine of Moral Virtue, the Immortal Masters of Five Influences, the Star Spirits of Five Constellations, the Three Ministers, the Four Sages, the Nine Luminaries, the Left and Right Assistants, the Devarāja, and Prince Naṭa all marched in leading a train of flags and canopies in pairs. They were all holding rare treasures and lustrous pearls, fruits of longevity and exotic flowers to be presented to the Buddha. As they bowed before him, they said, "We are most grateful for the unfathomable power of Tathāgata, who has subdued the monstrous monkey. We are grateful, too, to the Most Honorable Deva, who is having this banquet and asked us to come here to offer our thanks. May we beseech Tathāgata to give this banquet a name?" Responding to the petition of the various deities, Tathāgata said, "If a name is desired, let this be called 'The Great Banquet for Peace in Heaven.'" "What a magnificent name!" the various Immortals cried in unison. "Indeed, it shall be the Great Banquet for Peace in Heaven." When they finished speaking, they took their seats separately, and there was the pouring of wine and exchanging of cups, pinning of corsages[35] and playing of zithers. It was indeed a magnificent banquet for which we have a testimonial poem. The poem says:

That Feast of Peaches Immortal disturbed by the ape
Is now surpassed by this Banquet for Peace in Heaven.
Dragon flags and phoenix chariots stand glowing in halos bright,
As standards and blazing banners whirl in hallowed light.
Sweet are the tunes of immortal airs and songs,
Noble the sounds of panpipes and double flutes of jade.

Incense ambrosial surrounds this assembly of saints.
The world is tranquil. May the Holy Court be praised!

As all of them were feasting happily, the Lady Queen Mother also led a host of divine maidens and immortal singing-girls to come before the Buddha, dancing with light feet. They bowed to him, and she said, "Our Festival of Immortal Peaches was ruined by that monstrous monkey. We are beholden to the mighty power of Tathāgata for the enchainment of this mischievous ape. In the celebration during this Great Banquet for Peace in Heaven, we have little to offer as a token of our thanks. Please accept, however, these few immortal peaches plucked from the large trees by our own hands." They were truly

Half red, half green, and spouting aroma sweet,
Of luscious roots immortal, and ten thousand years old.
Pity those fruits planted at the Wu-ling Spring![36]
How do they equal the marvels of Haven's home:
Those tender ones of purple veins so rare in the world,
And those of matchless sweetness with pale yellow pits?
They lengthen your age and prolong your life by changing your frame.
He who has the luck to eat them will never be the same.

After the Buddhist Patriarch had pressed together his hands to thank the Queen Mother, she ordered the immortal singing-girls and the divine maidens to sing and dance. All the immortals at the banquet applauded enthusiastically. Truly there were

Whorls of heavenly incense filling the seat,
And profuse array of divine petals and stems.
Jade capital and golden arches in what great splendor!
How priceless, too, the strange goods and rare treasures!
Every pair had the same age as Heaven.
Every set increased through ten thousand kalpas.
Mulberry fields or vast oceans, let them shift and change.
He who lives here has neither grief nor fear.

The Queen Mother commanded the immortal maidens to sing and dance, as wine cups and goblets clinked together steadily. After a little while, suddenly

A wondrous fragrance came to meet the nose,
Rousing Stars and Planets in that great hall.
The gods and the Buddha put down their cups.
Raising his head, each waited with his eyes.
There in the air appeared an aged man,
Holding a most luxuriant long-life plant.
His gourd had elixir of ten thousand years.
His book listed names twelve millennia old.
Sky and earth in his cave knew no constraint.
Sun and moon were perfected in his vase.[37]
He roamed the Four Seas in joy serene,
And made the Ten Islets[38] his tranquil home.
Getting drunk often at the Peaches Feast
He woke: the moon shone brightly as of old.
He had a long head, short frame, and large ears.

His name: Star of Long Life, from South Pole. After the Star of Long Life had arrived and had greeted the Jade Emperor, he also went up to thank Tathāgata, saying, "When I heard that the baneful monkey was being led by Lao Tzu to the Tushita Palace to be refined by alchemical fire, I thought peace was surely secured. I never suspected that he could still escape, and it was fortunate that Tathāgata in his goodness had subdued this monster. When I got word of the thanksgiving banquet, I came at once. I have no other gifts to present to you but these purple agaric, jasper plant, jade-green lotus root, and golden elixir." The poem says:

Jade-green lotus and golden drug are given to Śākya.
Like the sands of Ganges is the age of Tathāgata.
The brocade of the three wains is calm, eternal bliss.[39]
The nine-grade garland is a wholesome, endless life.[40]
In the School Mādhyamika he's the true master,[41]
Whose home is the Heaven both of form and emptiness.[42]
The great Earth and cosmos all call him Lord.
His sixteen-foot diamond body[43] abounds in blessing and life.

Tathāgata accepted the thanks cheerfully, and the Star of Long Life went to his seat. Again there was pouring of wine and exchanging of cups. The Great Immortal of Naked Feet also arrived. After prostrating himself before the Jade Emperor, he too went to thank the Buddhist Patriarch, saying, "I am profoundly grateful for your dharma which subdued the baneful monkey. I have no other things to convey my respect but two magic pears and some fire dates[44] which I now present to you." The poem says:

Fragrant are the pears and dates of the Naked-Feet Immortal.
Presented to Amitābha, whose count of years is long.
Firm as a hill is his Lotus Platform of Seven Treasures;
Brocadelike is his Flower Seat of Thousand Gold adorned.
No false speech is this—his age equals Heaven and Earth;
Nor is this a lie—his luck is great as the sea.
Blessing and long life reach in him their fullest scope,
Dwelling in that Western Region of calm, eternal bliss.

Tathāgata again thanked him and asked Ānanda and Kāyapa to put away the gifts one by one before approaching the Jade Emperor to express his gratitude for the banquet. By now, everyone was somewhat tipsy. A Spirit Minister of Inspection then arrived to make the report, "The Great Sage is sticking out his head!" "No need to worry," said the Buddhist Patriarch. He took from his sleeve a tag on which were written in gold letters the words Oṁ maṇi padme hūṁ.[45] Handing it over to Ānanda, he told him to stick it on the top of the mountain. This deva received the tag, took it out of the Heavenly Gate, and stuck it tightly on a square piece of rock at the top of the Mountain of Five Phases. The mountain immediately struck root and grew together at the seams, though there was enough space for breathing and for the prisoner's hands to crawl out and move around a bit. Ānanda then returned to report, "The tag is tightly attached."

Tathāgata then took leave of the Jade Emperor and the deities, and went with the two devas out of the Heavenly Gate. Moved by compassion, he recited a divine spell and called together a local spirit and the Fearless Guards of Five Quarters to stand watch over the Five-Phases Mountain. They were told to feed the prisoner with iron pellets when he was hungry and to give him melted copper to drink when he was thirsty. When the time of his chastisement was fulfilled, they were told, someone would be coming to deliver him. So it is that

The brash, baneful monkey in revolt against Heaven
Is brought to submission by Tathāgata.
He drinks melted copper to endure the seasons,
And feeds on iron pellets to pass the time.
Tried by this bitter misfortune sent from the Sky,

He's glad to be living, though in a piteous lot.
If this hero is allowed to struggle anew,
He'll serve Buddha in future and go to the West.
Another poem says:
Prideful of his power once the time was ripe,
He tamed dragon and tiger, exploiting wily might.
Stealing peaches and wine, he roamed the House of Heaven.
He found trust and favor in the Capital of Jade.

He's now imprisoned, for his evil's full to the brim.
By the good stock[46] unfailing his spirit will rise again.
If he's indeed to escape Tathāgata's hands,
He must await the holy monk from T'ang Court.

We do not know in what month or year hereafter the days of his penance will be fulfilled, and you must listen to the explanation in the next chapter.

ENDNOTES

1. The Three Pure Ones are the highest gods of the pantheon in popular Taoism. They are: the Jade-Pure Honorable Divine of the Origin (Yü-ch'ing yüan-shih t'ien-tsun) the Exalted-Pure Honorable Divine of Spiritual Treasures (Shang-ch'ing ling-pao t'ien-tsun) and the Primal-Pure Honorable Divine of Moral Virtue (T'ai-ch'ing tao tê t'ien-tsun, also named T'ai-ch'ing t'ai-shang lao-chün). The last one is Lao Tzu.

2. These may be the Four Heavenly Emperors in Chinese folklore. They are divided according to locations and colors: green (east), white (west), red (south), and black (north). The Yellow Emperor of the Center is often added to the group to make up the Five Emperors, and thus they may be another form of the Four (Five, if the Center is included) Deva Kings.

3. The Nine Immortals are: Āditya (the sun), Sōma (the moon). Angāraka (Mars, also in Chinese, the Planet of Fire), Budha (Mercury, the Planet of Water), Bṛhaspati (Jupiter, the planet of Wood), Sukra (Venus, the Planet of Gold), Śanaiścara (Saturn, the Planet of Earth), Rāhu (the spirit that causes eclipses), and Ketu, a comet.

4. The Generals of the Five Quarters are the five powerful Bodhisattvas who are guardians of the four quarters and the center.

5. These constellations are the twenty-eight nakṣatras, divided into four mansions (east—spring, south—summer, west—autumn, and north—winter), each of which has seven members.

6. The Four Devarājas are the external protectors of Indra, each living on a side of Mount Meru. They defend the world against the attack of evil spirits or asuras, whence the name the Four Devarājas, Guardians of the World. They are Dhṛtarāṣra, Upholder of the Kingdom; Virūḍhaka, King of Growth; Virūpākṣa, upholder of the Kingdom; Vaiśravaṇa, the God of Great Learning. Kuvera, the God of Wealth, is also a member of this group.

7. The Twelve Horary Branches are: Tzu (Rat, 11 p.m.–1 a.m.), Ch'ou (Ox, 1–3 a.m.), Yin (Tiger, 3–5 a.m.), Mao (Hare, 5–7 a.m.), Ch'ên (Dragon, 7–9 a.m.), Ssu (Serpent, 9–11. a.m.), Wu (Horse, 11 a.m.–1 p.m.), Wei (Sheep. 1–3 p.m.), Shên (Monkey, 3–5 p.m.), Yu (Cock, 5–7 p.m.), Hsü (Dog, 7–9 p.m.), Hai (Boar, 9–11 p.m.).

8. These deities of the Taoist pantheon represent the essences of the Five Phases.

9. The Queen Mother, sometimes called the Lady Queen Mother (Wang-mu niang-niang) or the Queen Mother of the West (Hsi wang-mu), is the highest goddess of popular Taoism. She lives in the Palace of the Jasper Pool located on Mount K'un-lun in Tibet.

10. A Sung document by Wang Ming-ch'ing has told the story that the crown prince, Ch'ao-ling, who later became the Emperor Jên tsung, was fond of taking off shoes and socks as a boy. He was thus nicknamed the Immortal of Naked Feet, which was explained also as another name for Lao Tzu.

11. Dragon livers, phoenix marrow, bear paws, lips of apes: these were four of the eight dainties (see the wine makers' complaint later in this chapter), the rest being rabbit embryo, carp tail, broiled osprey, and koumiss.

12. According to the fourth chapter (*Chin Tan*, "On golden elixir") of the *Pao p'u tzu nei-*

p'ien attributed to the alchemist Ko Hung (283–343), the classification of the efficacy of the elixir is as follows: "The elixir of one turn, if taken, will enable a man to become an immortal (*tê hsien*) in three years; that of two turns, if taken, will enable a man to become an immortal in two years; . . ." And so on, until one reaches the elixir of nine turns, which, if taken, "will enable a man to become an immortal in three days." The "turn" apparently refers to the process of cyclical chemical or physical manipulations of the elixir ingredients; hence the greater the number of turns, the more powerful the elixir. See Nathan Sivin, *Chinese Alchemy: Preliminary Studies* (Cambridge, Mass., 1968), pp. 36–52; Needham, 5/2, 62–71.

13. Fearless Guards: fierce custodians of the Law.

14. The Guardians of the year, the month, the day, and the hour.

15. The Five Great Mountains are: T'ai (east), Hua (west), Hêng (south), Hêng (north) Sung (central); and the four rivers are: the Yangtze, the Yellow River, the Huai, and the Chi. (Editor's note: Mt. Hêng [north] and Mt. Hêng [south] are written with two different Chinese characters.)

16. Five Plagues: possibly a reference to the five epidemics in Vaiśālī during Buddha's lifetime: eye-bleeding, nose-bleeding, pus from the ears, lockjaw, and foul taste of all food.

17. All the names in the following five lines of verse are the members of the Twenty-Eight Constellations.

18. In Buddhism, the ten evil things (daśākuśala) include killing, stealing, lying, filthy language, covetousness, anger, and perverted thoughts.

19. The Potalaka Mountain, located southeast of Malakūta, is the home of Avalokiteśvara. In the Chinese tradition of popular Buddhism, the equivalent place is the P'u-t'o Mountain, east of the port city of Ningpo in the Chê-chaing Province, where it is the center of the cult of Kuan-yin.

20. In Chinese folk religions, the immortal Master Erh-lang has been variously identified with Chao Yü of the Sui dynasty, with Li Ping of Szechuan, and with a certain Yang Ch'en, the powerful magician and warrior in the *Investiture of the Gods*, another folk novel of approximately the same period as that of the *Hsi-yu Chi*.

21. The eight emblems could refer to the eight marks of good fortune on the sole of Bud-

dha's foot—wheel, conch shell, umbrella, canopy, lotus flower, jar, pair of fishes, and mystic signs—which, in turn, were symbols of the organs in Buddha's body. On the other hand, the emblems (lit., treasures) may refer to the magic weapons of the Eight immortals of Taoism: sword, fan, flower basket, lotus flower, flute, gourd, castanet, and a stringed musical instrument.

22. The City of Ch'ih may refer to the mountain in Chê-chiang Province called the City of Red Rampart (Ch'ih-ch'êng), another name for T'ien-t'ai Mountain. Or, it can refer to the Prefecture of Kuan-chou in Szechuan Province. The second is the more likely, since the Erh-lang cult was supposed to have originated from this province.

23. In popular accounts, Erh-lang is said to have an extra eye of magic power and vision in the middle of his forehead.

24. This is the first of several instances in this chapter (e.g., the third poem on p. 966) where reference is made to the phrase "Monkey of the Mind and Horse of the Will." For the history and significance of this term in Buddhist writings, see Dudbridge, *Antecedents*, pp. 168–69; Introduction, pp. 59–61.

25. Lord of the East: possibly a reference to the Sun God.

26. Samādhi fire: the fire that is said to consume the body of Buddha when he enters Nirvāṇa. But in the Buddhism of popular fiction, this fire is possessed by many fighters or warriors who have attained immortality, and it is often used as a weapon. Cf. chapters 24 and 48 of the *Fêng-shên Yen-I* (*The Investiture of the Gods*).

27. The time is calculated according to the sacred number 7.

28. Mercury is one of the crucial elements in alchemy.

29. The "three refuges," or Triśaraṇa, refer to three kinds of surrender: to surrender to the Buddha master, to the Law (Dharma) as medicine, and to the community of monks (*Sangha*) as friends. The "five commandments" (*pañca veramaṇī*) are prohibitions against killing, stealing, adultery, lying, and intoxicating beverages.

30. Tathāgata: one of the highest titles of Buddha. It may be defined as: He who comes as do all other Buddhas; or, He who took the absolute way of cause and effect, and attained to perfect wisdom.

31. The twin Sāl trees in the grove in which Śākyamuni entered Nirvāṇa.
32. The maṇi pearl, said to give sight to the blind, is known for its luster.
33. I.e., he is reduced to an animal.
34. According to the *Sui Shu,* the Six Women Officials were established in the Han dynasty. They were in charge of palace upkeep, palatial protocol, Court attire, food and medicine, banquets, and the various artisans of the court.
35. Pinning of corsages: supposedly a custom of the Sung dynasty. After offering sacrifices at the ancestral temple of the imperial family, the emperor and the subjects would pin flowers on their clothes or on their caps.
36. Wu-ling is the prefecture in which is located the town of Ch'ang-tê, in Hunan Province. Its fame rests on the "Peach-Blossom Spring," poems written by T'ao Ch'ien (365–427) and later by Wang Wei (655–759). The spring is near the town.
37. "Sun and moon . . . vase": a metaphoric expression for the alchemical process.
38. Ten Islets: legendary home of the immortals.
39. The three wains are the three vehicles (triyāna), drawn by a goat, a deer, and an ox to convey the living across the cycles of births and deaths (saṃsāra) to the shores or Nirvāṇa.
40. "Nine-grade" refers to the nine classes or grades of rewards in the Pure Land.
41. The Mādhyamika or San-lun School advocates the doctrine of formlessness or nothingness (animitta, nirābhāsa).
42. "Form is emptiness and the very emptiness is form" is a famous statement in the *Heart Sutra.* See *Buddhist Texts through the Ages,* trans. and ed. Edward Conze, et al. (New York, 1964), p. 152.
43. Buddha's transformed body is said to be sixteen feet, the same height as his earthly body.
44. Pears and dates are the traditional fruits of *hsien*-Taoism.
45. *Om . . . hūm:* said to be a prayer to Padmapāṇi, this is a Lamaistic charm. Each syllable is supposed to have its own mystic power of salvation.
46. Good stock: the Buddhist idea of the good seeds sown by a virtuous life which will bring future rewards.

—————————— *Questions for Consideration* ——————————

Using complete sentences, provide brief answers for the following questions.

1. Focus on a passage in *Journey to the West* that held your attention. Identify the narrative techniques, such as fantasy or realism, that made this passage an interesting one.

   _____

   _____

   _____

   _____

2. Provide a verbal sketch of the Monkey King, including his magical powers, engaging characteristics, and shortcomings.

   _____

   _____

   _____

   _____

3. *Journey to the West* is usually regarded as a Buddhist allegory. Just what is an allegory? Specify any religious elements that are presented in an allegorical way in the above selection.

   _____

   _____

   _____

   _____

——————————— *Writing Critically* ———————————

Select one of the topics listed below and compose a 500-word essay that discusses the topic fully. Support your thesis with evidence from the text and with critical and/or historical material. Use the space below for preparing to write the essay.

1. *Journey to the West* is undoubtedly a masterpiece of comic writing. Its humor survives well even in translation. Discuss this selection with the intention of identifying especially amusing episodes and exploring their humor.

2. Animal fables have been popular in all cultures and in all periods of history. In several selections in this volume, animal fable is of prime importance. Examples are the *Rámáyana*, African folktales of Anansi the spider, and "The Nun's Priest's Tale" by Chaucer. Write an essay describing and analyzing the use of animal fable in *Journey to the West* and in one other text. Where relevant, draw comparisons.

3. A number of human conventions and customs are given humorous treatment in this selection. China was ruled by emperors of the Ming Dynasty when the novel was written. What is implied about the structure of Chinese society during this period? For an understanding of the historical background, look at Ray Huang's *1587, A Year of No Significance: The Ming Dynasty in Decline* (New Haven: Yale University Press, 1981).

4. *Journey to the West* contains a number of Daoist as well as Buddhist elements. A number of readers have maintained that Daoism and Buddhism are in conflict in this novel. What exactly are Daoism (alternate spelling: Taoism) and Buddhism? After consulting secondary sources on the nature of Daoism and Buddhism in China, discuss one or both movements as they appear in this section of *Journey to the West*.

Prewriting Space:

_____

_____

_____

_____

_____

_____

_____

_____

_____

_____

_____

Introduction

Oral Poetry from Africa

We must start with the recognition that poetry does exist in Africa in African languages, that it remains oral until recorded and translated, and that oral literature is not exclusively narrative forms like fables, myths, and epics. Relevant to this assertion is the African's colonial experience which forced him to face the dominant European prejudice that his language and culture could not create or produce poetry. This situation changed when Africans steeped in their traditions, languages, and societies began to study their oral literature and respond more fully to their native poetic forms. There has thus developed a strong appreciation of the existence and aesthetic qualities of African oral poetry, its genesis and place in such societies, and particularly its unique mode of existence outside the written page.

One then may want to ask what is poetic about these oral forms, or how might they be poetry, or can poetry indeed be oral. These forms are poems because they show an imaginative and creative shaping of reality, they present man's experience with different degrees of profoundness, and they show a concern for man's condition that has been universally recognized in poetry the world over. Even though oral, they do move and influence us in ways written poetry has done, for we get pleasure from them and they appeal to us rationally and emotionally. They are poetry also if we divest ourselves of the notion that only words on a page, the product of a literate culture, is poetry, and go on to accept that other oral forms of expression in their proper contexts can be poetic and are poetry.

The oral poetry represented here and which have the qualities above are (i) songs of various kinds—praise, work, dance, self-praise, hunting, funeral—whose performance context, for they may be accompanied by music, dancing and drumming, give them their formal completeness; (ii) chants as those in a prayer, an initiation rite, a funeral eulogy or public expression of sorrow, uttered aloud to a group that sees, hears and responds; (iii) other forms of vocalizations with a referential content which are euphonious due to the musical qualities they have, such as vocal and tonal elaborations and variations on words, syllables and extended texts like those so typical of Yoruba *ijala* and *ifa*, or which may accompany them like clapping and other accompaniment that is often an essential part of the context.

Since oral poetry is context bound, such poetry may also be identified by reference to the poets that create them and the circumstances and situations that engender them. This necessarily takes us into aspects of custom, tradition, social conduct, and life style not only in traditional Africa of the past and the present but also in modern African society. This is the culture which has produced these poems. In the past, rulers, chiefs, and kings had court artists, like the griot in *Sundiata*, part of whose function was to sing their praises and celebrate their achievements. Traditional society also has highly developed religious rituals whose priests (like the *babalawo* who utter the *ifa* chants of Yoruba divination poetry) either created appropriate chants or have learned them in a long period of training and therefore keep this poetry alive.

Tropical Africa has in addition produced entertainers who offer their services for reward during special seasons and at other times in places of festivity or mourning. Often uninvited and freelancing and perhaps having a drum accompaniment, they create songs and chants, using traits of the persons and features of the situations, that are appropriate to the occasion and drawing on their own skills and resources. At a funeral they may augment the solemnity of the occasion by performing traditional songs and acting like hired mourners (See Okpewho 1985). The poems presented here are examples of some of these modes of creation.

The eight poems here represent seven African languages, ethnic and sub-cultural experiences from among the many on that continent. Transmitted to us in English, they remain incomplete because, as oral poems, they have been abstracted from their original languages and contexts of delivery and performance. The loss of this irreducible element to facilitate a wider accessibility can easily lead one to think less of the poem's intrinsic merits and devalue its aesthetic and literary qualities. When written, the oral poem may appear to lack any aesthetic quality, to be simplistic, and even incomprehensible without its context. Also, much is lost in any translation though enough of the referential content often survives, but oral poetry barely exists outside of its context. And this can hardly be compensated for by editors' notes and the creative and interactive imagination of the reader. Full appreciation, enjoyment, and understanding of these poems would require a conscious effort to synaesthetically focus on and visualize the performance context where the words in the original languages were supported by voice tone modulations, movement and facial expression, audience participation, or even drumming, and where significant structural features of language like repetition contributed their fullest to meaning.

We may group these poems and highlight some of their characteristics as follows: praise poems—"Queen Gumsu," "Mwananazi" and "Ogun, God of War"; chants and prayers often associated with rituals—"Prayer," "Drum Call to the Funeral" and "Prayer for a New-Born Child"; hunters' and work songs—"Elephant" and "Pounding Song."

"Queen Gumsu," originally in Kanuri, a Nigerian language, was most likely a seventeenth century griot-style composition which uses imagery, figures of speech, genealogy and the resonance and associations of names to celebrate the character and qualities of a ruler's wife. The Swahili "Mwananazi," a husband's praise of his wife, goes back to pre-mid nineteenth century East Africa. It expresses an attitude and the quality of a relationship while also giving an impression of a way of life. Tone and voice modulation, as indicated in the notes, enhance its poetic qualities in performance. "Ogun, God of War" is a Yoruba *Oriki* (praise poem) in which man recognizes the power and terror of his God; its profundity is reflected in the paradoxical ascription of qualities and its expression of the inscrutable and enigmatic in the divinity. We may here observe a structural arrangement involving the accretion of qualities in verse paragraphs, some parallel structures, direct address, and figures of speech which are compatible with the situational features of its delivery.

The elevated poetic expressiveness which deep religious feeling and sorrow can generate permeate the Ga chant, the Acoli sacrificial ritual act, and the mournful drum message of the Batatela of Zaire. The Ga elder (Ghana) at an "out-dooring" ceremony shows the child to the world in this prayer while the group responds to the series of petitions. The simple statements expressed in parallel structures seem incantatory and consistent with evocative gestures, movement and facial expressions in a ceremonial traditional setting. Variation in the choric refrain is also consistent with an active group participation.

The Acoli prayer (Uganda) is premised on the traditional Africans' belief that their dead ancestors can intercede with spiritual forces and divinities on their behalf, hence this enactment of a ritual soliciting the ancestors' mediation. Repetition, simple and parallel structures, the chanted participatory utterances (italicized), audible vocalizations, and some performative lines are all indicative of a context where the repetitions which lend themselves to tonal modulation become more meaningful and enhance the poem's tone.

"Drum Call to the Funeral" transmits a dirge-like message and creates a heightened sense of feeling which articulates the mystery of Death and what it means for the individual and his society. Oral features include lines 1 & 2 which mimic the sounds and pitch differences from the drum, the use of "O" and exclamation marks, and the vivid diction and metaphors.

"Elephant" from the elaborate Yoruba *ijala* (hunters' song) and "Pounding Song" are both work-related. The hunter celebrates his prey for its awesome characteristics which make him a redoubtable foe. The series of appellations, the terms and vividness of the descriptions, the figures of speech rooted in the setting, the incessant resonant repetition of "elephant," vocabulary items like "Ajanaku, Laaye, Oriiribobo" which are susceptible to tonal modulation not only give the poem a distinctive rhythmic quality but also suggests the performance setting.

The pounding song from the Chilomwe in Mozambique protests an experience of Portuguese colonialism which enforced unproductive work and imposed restrictions on people. The repetition of lines is rhythmic and could be visualized as accompanying the woman's pounding movements and being uttered with tone, pitch, and voice variations. The refrain, "I suffer, my heart is weeping," and the native language items also make it not too difficult to see how an everyday activity could become a vehicle for poetic expression.

Though limited, this selection gives some insights into a vibrant literary form and yet another aspect of this culture. (ACJ)

Bibliography

Beier, U., Ed. *Yoruba Poetry*, Cambridge: Cambridge University Press, 1970.

Finnegan, R. *Oral Poetry: Its Nature, Significance, and Social Context*. Cambridge: Cambridge University Press, 1977.

Mapanje, Jack and Landeg White. *Oral Poetry from Africa: An Anthology*. London: Longman, 1983.

Ogbalu, F.C. *Igbo Poems and Songs*. Onitsha: University Publishing Co. 1974.

Okpewho, Isidore. *African Oral Literature*. Bloomington & Indianapolis: Indiana University Press, 1992.

___. *The Heritage of African Poetry*. London: Longman, 1985.

Olatunji, O. *Features of Yoruba Oral Poetry*. Ibadan: University Press, 1984.

Opland, J. *Xosa Oral Poetry*. Cambridge: Cambridge University Press, 1983.

Sunkili, L. O. and S. O. Miruka. *A Dictionary of Oral Literature*. Nairobi: East African Educational Publications, 1990.

Oral Poetry from Africa: An Anthology

Compiled by Jack Mapanje and Landeg White

Queen Gumsu[1]

Queen Gumsu, owner of Maradi town, never looks behind her:
Owner of the city of Yam and the land of Yemen,
And of N'gasargamu and Njimi town.
Your mortar is made of the scented Guinea-pepper wood,
You own a pestle of polished silver.
    Gumsu Amina, daughter of Talba,
A descendant of the great,
The great and the blessed,
Good morning, good morning!
You are like the moon at its full,
Like the morning star,
Precious as gold, daughter of a bush-cow, you are a bush-cow
    among women:
Gumsu, daughter of a lion:
She is a lion as precious as gold among all women,
Like silver, Amina, daughter Talba:
May Allah give you the long life of a frog
And the dignity of an eagle.

Elephant[2]

Elephant, opulent creature, elephant, huge as a hill even when kneeling:
Elephant, robed in honour, a demon, flapping fans of war:
Demon who splinters the tree branches, invading the forest farm:
Elephant, who disregards "I have fled to my father for refuge,"
Let alone "To my mother":
Mountainous Animal, Huge Beast, who tears a man like a garment and
    hangs him up on a tree:
At the sight of him people stampede to a hill of safety:
My chant is a salute to the elephant.
Ajanaku, who treads heavily:

Demon who swallows bunches of palm-fruits whole, including the spikes:
Elephant, praise-named Laaye, massive blackish-grey creature:
Elephant, who single-handed makes the dense forest tremble:
Elephant, who stands sturdy and upright, who strolls as if reluctantly:
Elephant, whom one sees and points at with all one's fingers.
The hunter's boast at home is not repeated when he really meets the elephant,
The hunter's boast at home is not repeated before the elephant:
Ajanaku, who looks backwards with difficulty like a man with a stiff neck:
Elephant, who has a head pad but carries no load,
Elephant, whose burden is the huge head he balances:
Elephant, praise-named Laaye, "O death, please stop following me,"
This is part and parcel of the elephant's appellation.
Learn of the elephant, the waterman elephant,
Elephant, honour's equal, elephant who constantly swings his trunk like a
     fly-whisk,
Elephant, whose eyes are like water-jars,
Elephant, the greatest of wanderers, whose molar teeth are as big as
     palm-oil pits in Ijesaland,
Elephant, lord of the forest, praise-named Oriiribobo,
Elephant, whose tusks are like shafts,
One of whose tusks is a porter's whole load, elephant, praise-named
     Otiko, with the mighty neck,
Elephant, whom the hunter sometimes sees face to face, elephant, whom
     the hunter at other times sees from the rear,
Elephant, who carries mortars, yet walks with a swaggering gait,
Primeval leper, animal treading ponderously.

Mwananazi[3]

Give me a chair that I may sit down
     And serenade my Mwananazi,
That I may serenade my wife
     Who dispels my grief and heaviness.

She stands in the doorway
     When I go out to walk,
When I go out on business:
     Then she tells her servants,

And says to them, "Sada and Rehema,
     Cook, and do not delay,
Cook and make haste,
     Cook rice and curry."

If she finds I am delayed,
     She sends her servant girl:
"Look for him in the Sultan's way,
     Or there with the sovereign prince;

Look for him on the seats at his brothers',
     Or at the home of his father's sister:
Find him, come with him quickly:
     (What are they doing at this late hour?)"

And she will tell her, "Greet your master,
   Tell him, Let's go quickly, do not delay,
   Your delay makes her weary of standing
And she suppresses the tears in her eyes.

Tell him, *Let us go, go ahead, I am following,*
   And comfort her that she may end her grief."
And she will follow him, walking elegantly,
   Smelling of musk and ambergris.

When he enters and salutes her,
   The child of Hejaz replies to him;
At once she rises and stands
   And puts her hand on his shoulder.

And he prays to God the Compeller,
   "O princess, may God supply your needs."
Then the mistress lifts up her hand
   And puts it up to the bamboo,

And takes down a handkerchief of ancient work
   With a beautiful border woven into it;
She puts it to his eyes to soothe them,
   "Son of my paternal uncle, child of my aunt."

And she says to him, "My lord, let us rest,
   Do not stand overmuch and make yourself tired.
Call Fatimi for me, let her come
   Quickly, and leave off sleeping.

Let her dish up an Indian pilau
   With raisins, without curry.
Bring a fine European chair
   And a beautiful Persian tray."

The tray-stool, beautifully engraved,
   And the plates, shining like the moon!
And she says, "Let the servants come too,
   Why are you not singing praises?"

Immediately, it is laid for him,
   And Fatimi has taken the pitcher;
The grape-juice effervesces
   And she makes him drink it like a drinker of wine.

She feeds him, putting morsels in his mouth,
   And shows him a good place for resting,
Preparing for him betel leaf from Siu
   With sweet limes from Ozi.

She folds it and puts it between his lips
   With cardamoms and almonds.
I have finished praising the lady,
   My choice one, Mwananazi.

Drum Call to the Funeral[4]

Tshe tshe tshe tshe tshe tshe
Yewu yewu yewu yewu
Isn't there a pain, O mother! O isn't there a pain!
What is it, what does it mean, O what can it be?
He has fallen to earth,
The mahogany tree has fallen,
He has laid down his foot, he has laid down his hand,
He has drawn in his leg, he has drawn in his arm;
The land is finished, the land is ruined,
The grass burned over, the little mice crouch:
O hasn't he left us trouble, O mother!
Those who wail for the dead, theirs he is.
I am dizzy with wailing, O mother!
To what land do they journey, our brothers?
What is this land where our friends go and do not return?
He has gone forever to the earth,
He has gone to the earth that devours all:
Prepare for the earth his meat.
Well, let us go,
Let us go to the resting place of our father.

Prayer[5]

The ancestors have spoken today:
Bring forth a brown billy goat,
Chicken and beer.

My father, you have asked for food;
Your food is here today,
Come to it now.
Call all your brothers,
Your food is here!

You my clansmen and clanswomen,
I have called you
Because of the food I have cooked for our fathers.
Come, let us give them food.
Today I hold a goat in my hand:
Let us give it to my father.

You, our fathers,
Accept the food we give you today:
Here is your food.
Why should we fear you?
You are our fathers.

Your billy goat is here,
Drink its blood today.
The fiends that are coming
   let them pass far away!
Your food is here today.
Let your children have good health,
Let the women have good childbirth
So that your name may not be obliterated.
Your chicken is here;
Today we give you blood.
Let us have good health,
Let there be no deaths in the homestead.
If we were not here
There would be no food for you.
Here, we give you beer;
Let us have good health,
Diseases that are coming,
   let them pass far away!

Today, I give you a goat,
Today, I give you blood,
Today, I give you beer,
I give you beer to quench your thirst:
Let us have good health.
Let there be silence, oh,
Let there be silence.
Today, we have cooked a feast for my father,
Today, I have given him food,
But, let there be silence:
Let the people have good health.
   Let the people have good health!
Let the lions be killed.
   Let them be killed, killed, killed!
Let our spears be sharp and straight.
   Let them be sharp, sharp and straight!
Let the women have good childbirth.
   Let them have good childbirth!
Let the crops germinate well,
   let the crops ripen well.
   Let the crops germinate and ripen well!
Let the children's cries be heard.
   Let them be heard, heard, heard!
The evil things that are in the homestead,
Let the setting sun take them down in the west.
   Let it take, take, take!
Let the setting sun take them.
   Let it take!
Let it take.
   Let it take!
Let the setting sun take them.
   And so it has taken them!

Ogun, God of War[6]

Ogun kills on the right and destroys on the right.
Ogun kills on the left and destroys on the left.
Ogun kills suddenly in the house and suddenly in the field.
Ogun kills the child with the iron with which it plays.
Ogun kills in silence.
Ogun kills the thief and the owner of stolen goods.
Ogun kills the owner of the house,
    and paints the hearth with his blood.

Ogun is the forest god.
He gives all his clothes to the beggars.
He gives one to the woodcock—who dyes it in indigo.
He gives one to the coucal—who dyes it in camwood.
He gives one to the cattle egret—who leaves it white.

Ogun's laughter is no joke.
His enemies scatter in all directions.
The butterflies do not have to see the leopard—
As soon as they smell his shit
They scatter in all directions!

Master of iron, chief of robbers,
You have water, but you bathe in blood.
The light shining in your face
Is not easy to behold:
Ogun, with the bloody cap,
Let me see the red of your eye.

Ogun is not like pounded yam:
Do you think you can knead him in your hand
And eat of him until you are satisfied?
Do you think Ogun is something you can throw into your cap
And walk away with it?

Ogun is a mad god
Who will ask questions after seven hundred and eighty years.
Ogun have pity on me:
Whether I can reply or whether I cannot reply:
Ogun don't ask me anything!

The lion never allows anybody to play with his cub.
Ogun will never allow his child to be punished.
Ogun, do not reject me!
Does the woman who spins ever reject a spindle?
Does the woman who dyes ever reject a cloth?
Does the eye that sees ever reject a sight?
Ogun, do not reject me.

From *Yoruba Poetry*, edited by Ulli Beier, 1970.

Prayer for a New-Born Child[7]

Hail, hail, hail, let happiness come: *yao.*
Are our voices one? *yao.*
Hail, let happiness come: *yao.*
The stranger who has come, his back is towards the darkness:
   yao
His face is towards the light: *yao.*
May he work for his father: *yao.*
May he work for his mother: *yao:*
May he not steal: *yao*
May he not be wicked: *yao*
The children of this family forgive everything
   that can be forgiven: *yao*
May he eat by the work of his five fingers: *yao*
May he come to respect the world: *yao*
Upon his mother's head, Life: *yao*
Upon his father's head, Life: *yao*
If we should join to make up a circle, may our chain be com-
   plete: *yao*
If we dig a well may we come upon water: *yao*
If we draw water to bathe our limbs may they be refreshed: *yao*
If we see white may it be white clay: *yao*
If we see black may it be our servant: *yao*
Circumspect Gā, like the blowing wind, be better than your
   word: *yao*
You see, but you have not seen: *yao*
You hear, but you have not heard: *yao*
A circumspect Gā does not lie: *yao*
If you rest, think about your work: *yao*
Today if any witch or sorcerer is passing and asks what we are
   doing and they tell him, and he says any evil word or
   wishes that the child lying here shall die, shall this blessing
   be to bless him? *Oho!*
May Wednesday and Sunday kill him: *let him die!*
Let his hoot upon his head: *ho—o—o!*
Hail, let happiness come: *yao*
Are our voices one? *yao*
Hail, let happiness come: *yao*

Pounding Song[8]

I suffer, I do,
   Oyi—ya—e—e
I suffer, I do,
   I suffer, my heart is weeping.
What's to be done?
   I suffer, my heart is weeping.
I cultivate my cotton,
   I suffer, my heart is weeping.
Picking picking a whole basketful,
   I suffer, my heart is weeping.
I've taken it to the Boma there,
   I suffer, my heart is weeping.
They've given me five escudos!
   I suffer, my heart is weeping.
When I reflect on all this,
   Oyi—ya—e—e
I suffer, I do,
   I suffer, my heart is weeping.
My husband, that man,
   I suffer, my heart is weeping.
He went there to Luabo,
   I suffer, my heart is weeping.
He went to work, work hard,
   I suffer, my heart is weeping.
He broke off some sugar cane for himself,
   I suffer, my heart is weeping.
Leaving work, he was arrested,
   I suffer, my heart is weeping.
He was taken to the police,
   I suffer, my heart is weeping.
He was beaten on the hand!
   I suffer, my heart is weeping.
When I reflect on all this
   Oyi—ya—e—e
I suffer, I do,
   I suffer, my heart is weeping.

ENDNOTES

1. *Queen Gumsu* An extract from a Kanuri Praise-Poem from the ancient kingdom of Bornu in northern Nigeria. The Gumsu was the chief wife of the king of Bornu, and the Gumsu praised in this poem was the wife of Sultan Arri Umarmi, 1645–85. The praise "never looks behind her" (l. 1) means that she never hesitates. The prayer that she should have "the long life of a frog" (l. 16) uses a common metaphor in African oral poetry that connects the frog, which survives through the dry season and croaks during the rains, with long life and prosperity. The other images all suggest wealth and great beauty.

2. *Elephant* A Yoruba poem from Nigeria, and among the noblest of all *Ijala* . Many different versions of this chant have been published, but all reveal the same admiration and wonder at this animal's qualities. The elephant is praised for its size and strength, each attribute being vividly described, and for the high value to the hunter of its tusks, hide and meat ("opulent creature," l. 1). But it is the less obvious images which make this description come alive—Elephant "who strolls as if reluctantly" (l. 13), "Whom one sees and points at with all one's fingers" (l. 14), "Who looks backwards with difficulty like a man with a stiff neck" (l. 17). We can see the animal before us at every stage of this poem.
   l. 2 "Fans of war": the elephant's ears, which are extended when it charges. l. 4–5: the implication is that there is no refuge from the elephant.
   l. 9 "Ajanaku": a praise-name for the elephant meaning "Killer of Ajana." Ajana was a hunter who, according to legend, tried to capture alive one example of every kind of animal, but was trampled to death by the elephant.
   l. 11 "Laaye": a praisename. According to legend, the elephant's size was the result of medicine given by the god Aaye.
   l. 25 "Ijesaland": the Ijesa method of producing oil from palmnuts involves the use of rectangular pits, three to four feet across.
   l. 26–28 "Oriiribobo" and "Otiko" are praise-names whose meaning is not known.

3. *Mwananazi* A Swahili poem, well known along the East Coast of Africa. The poem is a husband's praise of his wife Mwananazi, the "Coconut girl." Like *Serenade*, it is one of the many poems associated with Liyongo. Bishop Steere in 1870 described it as a *gungu* dance song, adding "It is the custom to meet about ten or eleven at night and dance on until daybreak. The men and slave women dance, the ladies sit a little retired and look on." The whole song "takes a long time to sing, as most of the syllables have several notes and flourishes or little cadences to themselves." The gungu dance is especially associated with weddings.
   Mwananazi is praised for her behaviour towards her husband, but in the course of the description we are given a fascinating glimpse of the interior of an aristocratic Swahili household, with its sophisticated tastes and its possessions drawn from all parts of the world. At the same time, there are strong hints of a religious meaning to the poem. "Sada" and "Rehema" (the servants' names in l. 9) mean "happiness" and "charity." Mwananazi's conduct is not just pleasing to her husband, but pleasing to God and therefore a pattern for womankind.

4. *Drum Call to the Funeral* A drum poem of the Batetela people of Kasai Province in Zaire. The call is played on a six-toned slit drum called Lukumbi. The drum is announcing a death and summoning people to the funeral. The metaphors express a strong sense of general disaster.

5. *Prayer* An Acoli prayer from Uganda. It is addressed to the ancestors who are offered as sacrifice: a goat, a chicken and some beer. The prayer is for good health, for protection from disease and warfare, and for good crops and many children. It is led by an elder, and the people respond in chorus at the end.

6. *Ogun, God of War* A Yoruba Praise-Poem from Nigeria. Ogun is the God of iron and metallurgy. He is pictured as a blacksmith, but presides over every activity in which iron is used—hoes for cultivating, cutlasses for reaping, guns for hunting, cars for travelling, and so on. He therefore becomes the God of creativity and of harvesting, of hunting and of warfare, of invention and exploration and destruction. He is a terrible but

necessary God, presiding over the whole cycle of birth and death. This is why, in the Praise-Poem, he is described in a series of apparent contradictions. He kills indiscriminately (l. 1–7), yet gives all his clothes to the beggars (l. 9). He is "the chief of robbers" (l. 18) yet "will never allow his child to bepunished" l. 35). If he is "a mad God" (l. 29), this is only because life itself is mad. The only suitable prayer, then, is "Ogun, do not reject me" (l. 36).

7. *Prayer for a New-Born Child* A Gā chant from Ghana. On the eighth day after a child is born, the relatives and friends gather for the "out-dooring" ceremony. Very early in the morning, the baby is brought outside for the first time. An old person takes the baby in his or her arms and raises it to the dew three times. He then chants this prayer, to which everyone present responds *Yao*, meaning "Amen."

l. 18 "White clay": clay of this colour is smeared on the victor of any dispute in the courts as a symbol of innocence and congratulation.

l. 21–23: that the child may learn to be discreet and not talkative.

8. *Pounding Song* A ChiLomwe woman's song from northern Mozambique. The first part (l. 1–16) refers to the compulsory cotton-growing scheme, enforced throughout Mozambique by the Portuguese government. Women were compelled, under threat of physical violence, to grow one half-hectare of cotton for sale to the concession-holders. These sales were at the local administrative centres (the "Bomas," l. 11). Much of Mozambique is unsuitable for cotton growing, and the profits were derisory. The singer's claim that she made 5 escudos (approximately 5p sterling) for six months' work is no exaggeration.

The second part (l. 17–36) deals with her husband's exploitation on the sugar estates of the lower Zambezi, where he has been recruited by compulsion as a migrant worker. "Luabo" (l. 21) was the headquarters of Sena Sugar Estates Ltd., where workers were forbidden to eat any of the sugar cane they were cutting. The song does not complain about work; it is a Pounding Song, sung while actually working. The complaint is about poor pay, ill-treatment, and the separation of the family under the migrant labour system.

———————— *Questions for Consideration* ————————

Using complete sentences, provide brief answers for the following questions.

1. Study the hunter's song, "Elephant," and list as many poetic devices as you can identify. Make a brief comment on what these add to your understanding and enjoyment of this poem.

    _____

    _____

    _____

    _____

    _____

    _____

2. Reread "Ogun, God of War" and the introduction to these selections. What have you learned about the qualities of this God? Pick out examples of the poetic resources used to express these qualities.

    _____

    _____

    _____

    _____

    _____

    _____

3. When you read "Prayer" or "Prayer for a New-Born Child" you get insights into some African social and religious beliefs. Briefly express some of these insights.

    _____

    _____

    _____

    _____

    _____

    _____

Writing Critically

Select one of the essay topics listed below and compose a 500 word essay which discusses the topic fully. Support your thesis with evidence from the text and with critical and/or historical material. Use the space below for preparing to write the essay.

1. Make a close study of the praise poems from the point of view of themes, language, and poetic resources, and attempt to show what they have in common.

2. What have you learned about the persona and their domestic or professional occupations in "Pounding Song" and "Elephant" respectively?

3. The poems "Prayer" and the "Prayer for a New-Born Child" reveal interesting insights on traditional ritual-like practices. Attempt to describe these and show why both poems are evocative of such situations.

4. Does the fact that these poems were all context-bound in social settings and not originally written creations make them less poetic to you?

5. Use a selection of these poems to show how they express a concern for universal human values and issues.

6. Write an interpretation of one or two poems bringing out specific poetic devices which make them successful.

7. Examine these poems and outline what they tell you of their social setting, the customs and traditions of the people who created them, and the concern for the human condition which they express.

Prewriting Space:

_____

_____

_____

_____

_____

_____

_____

_____

_____

_____

Introduction

Mirabai 1498–15??

The devotional poems to Krishna written by the sixteenth century Indian woman known as Mīrābāī (or Mīrā) are charged with a spirit of personal devotion characteristic of Indian *bhakti* poetry. The only popular female *bhakti* poet of north India, Mīrā's devotional poems to Krishna (a form of the Hindu god, Viṣṇu) are characterized by a personal, erotic devotion which is not meant as a poetic device. The voice of the lover who speaks in Mīrā's poetry is Mīrā's own voice.

Born in 1498 to one important family, and married in 1516 to another, Mīrā was childless when her husband died, and indeed, in poem 51 she calls herself a virgin "from birth to birth." Instead of being a lover of men, she presents herself as a lover of Krishna. It is possible that her passionate songs of dancing in the streets with bells on her ankles (poem #36) may strike a contemporary reader as excessive; in the context of sixteenth century India, a society which severely restricted the rights of women to appear in public, her behavior was outrageous. According to her poetry, she was imprisoned by a king (who may also have been her husband) and ordered to swallow poison, which she did without suffering any ill effect. Although the stories of Mīrā are shrouded in myth, one version of her biography holds that after the poisoning episode, she took refuge with a relative and was expelled with him in 1538. She lived as an outcast for many years afterwards One legend has it that the family which banished her later blamed the downward spiral of their city's fortunes (which was eventually occupied by Muslims in 1568) on the cruel treatment of a devoted believer, and sent Mīrā a message begging her return; she expired while praying over her response.

Bhakti poetry in general rejects social conventions. The love between god and devotee in *bhakti* poetry is often celebrated as an adulterous love; the female devotee seeks a true love with a god, instead of the lovelessness of a marriage to a man. Mīrā's poems certainly follow this tradition, but are also closely aligned to an Indian women's tradition of folk songs and traditions. In this tradition, festivals and religious occasions are marked by songs sung from one woman to another. Similarly, Mīrā's poetry is often addressed to an implied female audience. Further, some commentators have noted that her use of imagery often springs from these women's songs and traditions.

This is not to say, however, that the desire she describes in her poetry is exclusively feminine. Indeed, her poetry's greatest success is its ability to fuse the language of erotic desire and religious devotion together. Western readers might be reminded of John Donne and even Emily Dickinson in this sense. Such comparisons are apt, as might be a comparison to Joan of Arc, perhaps her nearest Western equivalent; however, though such parallels are helpful in beginning to understand such a poet, the beauty and intensity with which she boldly demands her rights to worship as she will should be appreciated on their own terms. (TJC)

Bibliography

Alston, A.J. *The Devotional Poems of Marabai.* 1980.

Hawley, John Stratton, and Mark Juergensmeyer. *Songs of the Saints of India.* 1988.

Levi, Louise Landes. *Sweet on My Lips: Love Songs of Mirabai,* 1997.

Mukta, Parita. *Upholding the Common Life: The Community of Mirabai,* 1995.

The Devotional Poems of Mirabai

1

Worship the feet of Hari, O my mind,
Beautiful to look upon, soft and cool as a lotus,
Able to remove the three kinds of pain.[1]
When Prahlād grasped those holy feet
He was elevated to the rank of Indra.[2]
When Dhruv took refuge in them
He was transported to the motionless realm.[3]
In the fair body of the holy Dwarf
They measured the universe.[4]
Their touch saved the wife of Gautam.[5]
They tamed the serpent Kāliya
When Krishna sported as a cowherd.[6]
They supported the Govardhan Mountain
When Indra was put to shame.[7]
Mirā is the servant of Lāl Giridhara,[8]
The raft on which to cross the unnavigable sea.[9]

2

I bow to Bihāri,[10]
Master of the arts of love.
His crown is a peacock's plume
And the tilak[11] gleams upon his brow.
His golden earrings and raven locks
Are waving gracefully at his ears.
He is playing the flute
That rests at His adorable lips.
Experiencing deep joy Himself,
He is charming the hearts of the women of Braj.[12]
On beholding this beautiful vision of Mohan[13] Giridhara,
Mirā swoons in ecstasy.

4

O Hari![14] Thou art the support of my life!
I have no other refuge but Thee
In all the three worlds.[15]
Though I have searched the whole universe,
Nothing pleases me but Thou.
Says Mirā, "O Lord, I am Thy slave.
Do not forget me."

11

I am utterly charmed by Mohan's beauty,
His beautiful body, His lotus-petal eyes,
His side-long glances, His gentle smiles.
He grazes His cows by the Yamunā,[16]
Playing sweetly on His flute.
I sacrifice to Giridhara
Body, mind, wealth and all.
Mirā is hugging closely those lotus feet.

My Own Path

26

Come sport with me here, my companions,
And refrain from visiting the houses of others.
False are rubies and pearls,
False all glamour and glimmer.
False is all external finery,
One's only real necklace
Is love of the Lord.
False are the silks of the south,
But the rags
Of love of the Lord are true,
For in them the body stays pure.
Eschew rich food
Cooked in the fifty-six kinds of condiments.
Flawed are all such enjoyments,
But the simple diet.
Of love of one's Lord
Is good, cooked with salt or saltless.
Do not envy the orchards of another;
Till thine own poor plot
And good things will come of it.
If someone else

Has a rich and handsome husband,
It is nothing to do with thee.
If you seek his society
No one will approve.
It is good to remain loyal
To one's own husband,
Even if he be poor and a leper,
On this all are agreed.
My Beloved is like the Indestructible Principle,
Love of Him is true love.
The Lord has revealed Himself to Mirā:
This is the path of true devotion.

Differences of Opinion among Friends

28

Do not restrain me, my companion,
I am going to visit the holy men.
Shyām's form
Has come to dwell in my heart,
And I care for no other.
All the world is sleeping happily,
But my eyes are awake.
Mad and bereft of all insight,
Is he who rejects my Shyām,
Shyām invades my heart
And I cannot sleep.
No one drinks water
From the puddles that spring up
In the rainy months;
But Hari is a perpetual fountain of nectar,
Which quenches my thirst.
Beautiful is Shyām,
I am leaving now to gaze upon His face.
Mirā is but a bewildered abandoned girl.
Come, accept her as Thine own.

36

I donned anklets and danced.
The people said "Mirā is mad."
My mother-in-law declared
That I had ruined the family's reputation.
The King sent me a cup of poison
Which I drank with a smile.
I have offered body and mind

To the feet of Hari,
And will drink the nectar of His holy sight.
Mirā's Lord is the courtly Giridhara:
My Lord, to Thee will I go for refuge.

51

What shall I say to you,
O my Shyām Giridhara?
My love is ancient
And runs from former births,
Do not abandon me, Giridhara.
I offer myself in unconditional sacrifice, my darling,
When I behold Thy beautiful face.
Come into my courtyard, Giridhara,
The women are singing auspicious hymns.
I have set aside a square for Thy welcome,
Heaped with the pearls of my tears.
I cast myself before Thee, body and mind.
Servant Mirā takes refuge at Thy feet:
For Thy sake she has remained a virgin
From birth to birth.

74

Without Krishna I cannot sleep.
Tortured by longing, I cannot sleep,
And the fire of love
Drives me to wander hither and thither.
Without the light of the Beloved
My house is dark,
And lamps do not please me.
Without the Beloved my bed is uninviting,
And I pass the nights awake.
When will my Beloved return home?
The frogs are croaking, the peacock's cry
And the cuckoo's song are heard.
Low black clouds are gathering,

Lightning flashes, stirring fear in the heart,
My eyes fill with tears.
What shall I do? Where shall I go?
Who can quench my pain?
My body has been bitten
By the snake of "absence,"
And my life is ebbing away
With every beat of the heart.
Fetch the herb quickly.

Which of my companions
Will come bringing the Beloved to meet me?
My Lord when will you come,
To meet your Mirā?
Manamohan, the Charmer of Hearts,
Fills me with delight. When, my Lord,
Will you come to laugh and talk with me?

96

Come to my house, O Lord of the Universe
My body is in pain, my breath burning.
Come and extinguish the fire of separation.
I spend the nights roving about in tears.
Appetite and sleep have left me,
But my shameless life clings on.
Grant me happiness, do not desolate me.
Delay no longer,
Thy abandoned Mirā is in sore straits.

Meeting the Beloved

144

I offer a thousand thanks
To the astrologer who predicted Shyām would come.
My joy is overflowing, my soul has access
To an incalculable storehouse of joy.
I meet with my companions
To honour and please the Beloved,
And there is joy all round.
O My dear companion,
Now that I have seen the Lord,
All my desires are fulfilled
And my sufferings forgotten.
Shyām, the Ocean of Joy, Mirā's Lord,
Has entered her home.

The Wild Woman of the Woods

186

The wild woman of the woods[17]
Found out the sweet plums by tasting them
And brought them to the Lord.
She was neither civilized nor educated
Nor possessed of physical beauty.
She was of low caste and filthy apparel,
But the Lord accepted her soiled plums,
Knowing the sincerity of her love.
She recognized no distinctions of high and low,
But sought only the pure milk of love.
Not for her the learning of the Veda,
She was transported to heaven on a chariot
At a single stroke.
Now she sports in Vaikunth,[18]
Bound to Hari by ties of love.
Says servant Mirā:
Whoso loves like this is saved.
The Lord is the Saviour of the Fallen
And I was a cowherd-maiden at Gokul
In a former birth.

ENDNOTES

1. Pain arising from the inevitable diseases of the body, pain due to the work of malignant divine or demoniac forces, and pain arising from the interplay of the elements, for example the pain arising from drought or flood.

2. Prahlāda was the son of Hiraṇyakaśipu, king of the demons. Persecuted by his father, Prahlāda remained constant in devotion to Viṣṇu. One day his father asked him, "Where is your God?" Prahlāda replied, "He is everywhere, even in this pillar." Hiraṇyakaśipu kicked the pillar with his foot, whereupon the Lord sprang out from it in the form of a "Man-Lion" and destroyed him. Eventually the Lord elevated Prahlāda to the rank of Indra, whose place as king of the gods had been usurped by the demon Hiraṇyakaśipu.

3. Dhruva performed austerities at the command of his mother while yet a child, and was eventually granted the following boon:

    "Thou shalt attain to fixity above all the worlds, planets, and constellations, and shalt exist as their support. Thy place of abode will be called Dhruva-loka." This world manifests to us as the pole-star.

4. The demon Bali threatened to conquer and tyrannize over the universe, but the Lord appeared in the form of a dwarf (Vāman) and asked to be given as much land as He could bestride in three paces. Granted the boon, He caused His body to swell in size till all heaven and earth were covered in two strides. The third stride confined Bali's powers to the infernal regions.

5. Ahalyā or Ahilyā, wife of the seer Gautama, was turned to stone by her husband's curse. But she was brought back to life by the touch of the foot of the Lord Viṣṇu in His incarnation as Rāma.

6. Kāliya was a five-headed serpent dwelling in a pool in the Jumna near Bṛndāvana, from which he would sally forth and cause great

destruction. The child Kṛṣṇa placed His foot on the middle head of the serpent and forced him to leave Bṛndāvana for the sea.

7. When Kṛṣṇa diverted the cowherds of Bṛndāvana from worship of Indra, the god threatened to deluge them with rain. But Kṛṣṇa tore up the Govardhana hill near the village and held it aloft on His little finger to serve as an umbrella.

8. The name "Giridhara" by which Mīrābāī constantly addresses Kṛṣṇa means "He who held aloft the Mountain" and refers to the incident recorded in the previous note. Lāla is an affectionate term for a child. The Sanskrit form Giridhara has been preserved in the translation, though it appears that Mīrā regularly used the form Giradhara.

9. As long as the soul remains bereft of the grace of God, it continues to act with egoism and attachment, and such action forces it to return to earth in a new body to experience the "fruits" or moral deserts of that action. Thus the soul becomes involved in continual rebirth in new bodies, exposed to the certainty of suffering, disease, and death. As this process is self-perpetuating and inevitable until the soul is rescued by the grace of the Lord, it is called an "unnavigable sea" and He the raft.

10. A name for Kṛṣṇa which means "He who enjoys the pleasures of gay company" and also "A stroller, a wanderer."

11. A small round mark of sandal-paste or other colouring matter placed between the eye-brows as an ornament or as an auspicious mark on ceremonial occasions.

12. The name of the district round Āgrā and Mathurā where Kṛṣṇa's exploits as a child took place.

13. Mohan: Krsna. This name means "The charming one."

14. An affectionate name for the Lord God Viṣṇu, explained by the Bhaktas as meaning "He who steals away the sins of His devotees."

15. From Vedic times, the Hindus have believed in three planes of existence, manifested as (1) the earth together with the nether regions, (2) the space between the earth and the "roof" of the sky, and (3) an abode of perpetual light hidden beyond the roof of the sky. The deity presiding over these three worlds is invoked in the syllables "bhūr bhuvaḥ svaḥ" pronounced before the recitation of the sacred Gāyatrī verse.

16. The old Sanskrit name "Yamunā" has been preserved to refer to the river Jumna, which flows down from Delhi past Bṛndāvana and Mathurā. But Mīrā herself uses the modern form.

17. The wild woman of the forest, Śabarī, had nothing but plums to offer the avatāra Rāma. She bit into them to pick out the ripe ones, but Rāma accepted the gift gladly and ate the soiled plums.

18. The heaven of Viṣṇu.

Questions for Consideration

Using complete sentences, provide brief answers for the following questions.

1. In poem 74, how does Mīrā contrast images of the body with images of the spirit?

_____

_____

_____

_____

_____

2. In poem 28, who do you think are the companions that are trying to restrain her? What are they trying to restrain her from? How does she advise them?

_____

_____

_____

_____

_____

3. You may have encountered other figures of faithful believers who are treated as insane, or who become outcasts. Does Mīrābāī remind you of any figures from other texts? If so, why?

_____

_____

_____

_____

_____

Writing Critically

Select one of the essay topics listed below and compose a 500-word essay which discusses the topic fully. Support your thesis with evidence from the text and with critical and/or historical material. Use the space below for preparing to write the essay.

1. Some of Mīrā's images might belong as well in more conventional love poetry. Look at poem 74, for instance. How has she used images and actions which might not be out of place in love poetry?

2. In poem 186, Mīrā tells a story about the wild woman of the forest. How does this story seem to relate to her own circumstances?

3. Pick at least two of Mīrā's poems and explore how she develops the theme of devotion to Krishna.

Prewriting Space:

_____

_____

_____

_____

_____

_____

_____

_____

_____

_____

_____

_____

_____

_____

_____

_____

_____

_____

_____

_____

Index

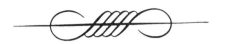